# The Cambridge Poets

*General Editor*, BLISS PERRY

---

*Edited by*

| | |
|---|---|
| BROWNING | HORACE E. SCUDDER |
| MRS. BROWNING | HARRIET WATERS PRESTON |
| BURNS | W. E. HENLEY |
| BYRON | PAUL E. MORE |
| DRYDEN | GEORGE R. NOYES |
| ENGLISH AND SCOTTISH } | HELEN CHILD SARGENT |
| POPULAR BALLADS } | GEORGE L. KITTREDGE |
| HOLMES | HORACE E. SCUDDER |
| KEATS | HORACE E. SCUDDER |
| LONGFELLOW | HORACE E. SCUDDER |
| LOWELL | HORACE E. SCUDDER |
| MILTON | WILLIAM VAUGHN MOODY |
| POPE | HENRY W. BOYNTON |
| SCOTT | HORACE E. SCUDDER |
| SHAKESPEARE | W. A. NEILSON |
| SHELLEY | GEORGE E. WOODBERRY |
| SPENSER | R. E. NEIL DODGE |
| TENNYSON | WILLIAM J. ROLFE |
| WHITTIER | HORACE E. SCUDDER |
| WORDSWORTH | A. J. GEORGE |

*In Preparation*

| | |
|---|---|
| CHAUCER | F. N. ROBINSON |

---

HOUGHTON MIFFLIN COMPANY

BOSTON AND NEW YORK

### The Cambridge Edition of the Poets

EDITED BY

HORACE E. SCUDDER

---

# TENNYSON

BY

W. J. ROLFE

# THE POETIC AND
# DRAMATIC WORKS OF ALFRED
# LORD TENNYSON
## Cambridge Edition

*Farringford, Isle of Wight*

BOSTON AND NEW YORK
HOUGHTON MIFFLIN COMPANY
The Riverside Press Cambridge

## PUBLISHERS' NOTE

IN 1842, when Tennyson published in England the two volumes which marked the beginning of his great fame, the predecessors in America of the present publishers reissued the volumes, and from that year until 1880 they and their successors continued to publish by arrangement the volumes of poetry and drama which appeared from time to time. The present Cambridge edition contains this body of verse, and other poems published later than that date, and includes moreover in the Appendix the pieces from "Poems by Two Brothers" assigned to Alfred Tennyson, together with the poems from the volumes of 1830 and 1833 and other sources, which have for the most part continued to have currency in America, though dropped from collective editions in England.

The volume has been edited by Dr. W. J. Rolfe in general conformity with the previous volumes of the series of "Cambridge" poets. The editor has brought to his task a long familiarity with the poetry, as evidenced by the several separate works of Tennyson which he has edited both for school use and for the general reader. In this comprehensive work he has given special attention to the text, which in the body of the volume has been made to follow, with most careful revision of minor details such as punctuation, the most authoritative form, and in the Earlier Poems in the Appendix has been compared as far as possible with the original issues and not with later reprints.

Lord Tennyson, as is well known, subjected his poems to frequent revision, and the editor has therefore, in addition to giving the authoritative text with scrupulous care, collated the volumes of 1830 and 1833 (in the library of the British Museum), the edition of 1842, and all others to which he has had access, and has recorded in his notes all the various readings of any importance or interest which he has detected. For most of the poems this collation has never been attempted by any other editor or commentator. The editor has also, both in his notes and in the several introductions and brief prefaces, made a thorough bibliographical study of the poetry, so that the reader is now able to trace with great exactness the history of Tennyson's work. For information concerning the origin of some of the poems, or the allusions contained in them, the editor is indebted to the "Memoir," and has made due acknowledgment in the Notes.

BOSTON, 4 PARK STREET, August 1, 1898.

# TABLE OF CONTENTS

# CONTENTS

viii                    CONTENTS

# CONTENTS

# BIOGRAPHICAL SKETCH

ALFRED TENNYSON, the fourth of eight brothers (there were also four sisters), was born on the 6th of August, 1809, at Somersby, a village in Lincolnshire containing at that time less than a hundred inhabitants. His father, Rev. George Clayton Tennyson, LL.D., was the rector of the parish, 'a man of energetic character, remarkable for his great strength and stature, and of very various talents, — something of a poet, painter, architect, and musician, and also a considerable linguist and mathematician.' Mrs. Tennyson, whose maiden name was Elizabeth Fytche, was the daughter of a clergyman, and is described as 'a sweet and gentle and most imaginative woman; so kind-hearted that it had passed into a proverb, and the wicked inhabitants of a neighboring village used to bring their dogs to her windows and beat them in order to be bribed to leave off by the gentle lady, or to make advantageous bargains by selling her the worthless curs.'[1]

In those days Somersby was quite out of the world, — so much so that the news of the battle of Waterloo did not reach it at the time, — but the Tennyson children had a world of their own with its mimic history and romance. 'The boys,' says Mrs. Ritchie, 'played great games, like Arthur's knights; they were champions and warriors defending a stone heap; or, again, they would set up opposing camps with a king in the midst of each. The king was a willow wand stuck into the ground, with an outer circle of immortals to defend him of firmer, stiffer sticks. Then each party would come with stones, hurling at each other's king, and trying to overthrow him. Perhaps as the day wore on they became romancers, leaving the jousts deserted. When dinner-time came, and they all sat round the table, each in turn put a chapter of his history underneath the potato-bowl, — long endless histories, chapter after chapter, diffuse, absorbing, unending, as are the stories of real life of which each sunrise opens on a new part. Some of these romances were in letters, like " Clarissa Harlowe." Alfred used to tell a story which lasted for months, and which was called "The Old Horse." '

Earlier even than this the boy had begun to 'lisp in numbers.' When he was only five years old, he exclaimed as the wind swept through the rectory garden, ' I hear a voice that's speaking in the wind.' Mrs. Ritchie tells how, not long afterwards, he first put his baby poetry into writing. ' Alfred's first verses were written upon a slate which his brother Charles put into his hand one Sunday at Louth, when all the elders of the party were going into church, and the child was left alone. Charles gave him a subject, — the flowers in the garden, — and when he came back from church, little Alfred brought the slate to his brother, all covered with written lines of blank verse. They were made on the model of Thomson's " Seasons," the only poetry he had ever read. One can picture it all to one's self, the flowers in the garden, the verses, the little poet with waiting eyes, and the young brother scanning the lines. " Yes, you can write," said Charles, and he gave Alfred back the slate. I have also heard another story, of his grandfather, later on,

[1] Mrs. Anne Thackeray Ritchie, in *Records of Tennyson, Ruskin, Browning* (New York, 1892), to which we are indebted for some interesting particulars of the poet's early life.

asking him to write an elegy on his grandmother, who had recently died, and, when it was written, putting ten shillings into his hands and saying, " There, that is the first money you have ever earned by your poetry, and, take my word for it, it will be the last." '

Alfred and Charles, who was a little more than a year the elder, were sent together to Louth grammar school; and there, in the latter part of 1826, we find them preparing for the press a collection of juvenile poems written from the age of fifteen upwards. It was published early in 1827 by the Messrs. Jackson, booksellers and printers in Louth, who paid the boys twenty pounds for the copyright. The book was entitled ' Poems by Two Brothers,' with the addition of the modest motto from Martial, ' Haec nos novimus esse nihil ' (We ourselves know that these are nothing). The pieces, one hundred and two in number, aside from their interest as including the first printed verses of one who has since risen to the highest position as a poet, are worthy of note for their wide range of subjects and the extensive reading in classical and modern authors which they indicate. The themes are drawn from all ages and all lands, as a few of the titles may serve to show: Antony to Cleopatra; The Gondola; Written by an Exile of Bassorah, sailing down the Euphrates; Persia; Egypt; The Druid's Prophecies; Swiss Song; The Expedition of Nadir Shah into Hindostan; Greece; The Maid of Savoy; Scotch Song; God's Denunciations against Pharaoh-Hophra; The Death of Lord Byron; The Fall of Jerusalem; Eulogium on Homer; The Scenery of South America; Babylon; Phrenology; Exhortation to the Greeks; King Charles's Vision, etc. The poems are often introduced by quotations; among others, from Addison, Byron, Cicero, Claudian, Gray, Horace, Hume, Lucretius, Milton, Moore, Ovid, Racine, Rousseau, Sallust, Scott, Tacitus, Terence, and Virgil. There are also frequent foot-notes, which are more learned than we should expect from boys of eighteen, and yet without the affectation of scholarship that we might expect in connection with such a juvenile display of erudition. The brief preface to the volume is withal very modest and manly.

Charles, who was associated with Alfred in this precocious poetical venture, afterwards took the name of Turner on inheriting certain estates from his great-uncle. He was a true poet, as his later published works amply prove. It may be mentioned incidentally here that several other of the Tennyson brothers have written poetry. Frederick, the eldest, who contributed four pieces to the ' Poems by Two Brothers,' published several volumes of verse.

Some of the critics exercised their ingenuity in trying to pick out Alfred's work from the poems in this early anonymous volume; but the most that they accomplished was to point out a few verbal resemblances between passages in the juvenile pieces and in the acknowledged productions of Tennyson. In 1893, after the poet's death, the book was reprinted by his son, with the initials of the authors (in part merely conjectural) appended to the poems.

We may see in these boyish verses of the two brothers the influence of Byron, who is quoted no less than six times, and whose recent death forms the subject of one poem while it is referred to in another. Alfred was not yet fifteen when the news of that event reached the little village in Lincolnshire. ' Byron was dead ! I thought the whole world was at an end,' he once said, recalling those early days; ' I thought everything was over and finished for every one — that nothing else mattered. I remember I walked out alone, and carved " Byron is dead " into the sandstone.'

In 1828, Charles and Alfred Tennyson went to Trinity College, Cambridge, where their elder brother Frederick had just won the prize for a Greek poem. Here Alfred made the friendship of not a few young men who were destined, like himself, to gain a name in literature, — among them Trench, Monckton Milnes, James Spedding, Henry Alford, W. H. Brookfield, J. M. Kemble, and Kinglake. More gifted than all the rest, but prevented by his early death (in his twenty-third year) from showing anything more than the budding promise of his powers, was Arthur Hallam, to whom the poet's 'In Memoriam' will be an immortal monument. 'It has pleased God that in his death, as well as in his life and nature, he should be marked beyond ordinary men.'

'The Lover's Tale,' though not published until a few years ago, was written the same year that Tennyson went to Cambridge; and the next summer he gained the Chancellor's gold medal for a poem on Timbuctoo — the first instance in which that honor had been awarded to a piece in blank verse. The 'Athenæum' of July 22, 1829, in a highly eulogistic notice, remarked: 'These productions have often been ingenious and elegant, but we have never before seen one of them which indicated really first-rate poetical genius, and which could have done honor to any man that ever wrote.'

In 1830, Tennyson brought out, under his own name, 'Poems, chiefly Lyrical,' — a volume of 154 pages, containing fifty-three pieces, thirty-two of which were suppressed in subsequent editions, though nine of these have been since restored.

This collection, published when the poet was only twenty-one, included 'Lilian,' 'Isabel,' 'The Mermaid,' 'The Merman,' 'The Owl,' 'Recollections of the Arabian Nights,' 'Ode to Memory,' 'The Poet's Mind,' and 'The Poet.' The last-named piece is of special interest as indicating the high ideal of the poet's art and vocation with which the young singer started on his career. It received just recognition and praise in a notice of the book that appeared in the 'Westminster Review,' for January, 1831. It was written, as the present Lord Tennyson informed me, by Sir John Bowring. The conclusion of the passage, which reads now like a prophecy fulfilled, was as follows:

'He has shown, in the lines from which we quote, his own just conception of the grandeur of a poet's destiny; and we look to him for its fulfilment. It is not for such men to sink into mere verse-makers for the amusement of themselves or others. They can influence the associations of unnumbered minds; they can command the sympathies of unnumbered hearts; they can disseminate principles, they can give those principles power over men's imaginations; they can excite in a good cause the sustained enthusiasm that is sure to conquer; they can blast the laurels of the tyrants, and hallow the memories of the martyrs of patriotism; they can act with a force, the extent of which it is difficult to estimate, upon national feelings and character, and consequently upon national happiness. If our estimate of Mr. Tennyson be correct, he too is a poet; and many years hence may he read his juvenile description of that character with the proud consciousness that it has become the description and history of his own work.'

Tennyson lived and wrote for more than sixty years after these eloquent and prophetic words were penned; and there could not be a more truthful description and history of his work than those inspired strains of his youth. The estimate of the critic was correct. The young singer *was* a poet, and he proved himself such a poet as he saw in that immortal vision. It was a lofty and noble ideal, but he made it a living reality.

Tennyson's book was also reviewed favorably by Leigh Hunt in 'The Tatler' for 1831, and by Arthur Hallam in 'The Englishman's Magazine' for August of the same year. In May, 1832, Christopher North (Professor Wilson) criticised the young poet's work in 'Blackwood' in a very different vein, praising it indeed, but showing up its faults and defects with merciless severity. There was justice in some of its strictures, and they may have had their influence in leading Tennyson to suppress certain of the poems in later editions. At any rate, the passages held up to ridicule by the reviewer are mostly from these suppressed pieces.

In the winter of 1832, Tennyson published another thin volume of verse, which was a great advance on that of two years previous, containing as it did some of the poems which have ever since been reckoned among his best, — as 'The Lady of Shalott,' 'The Miller's Daughter,' 'Œnone,' 'The Palace of Art,' 'The Lotos-Eaters,' and the 'Dream of Fair Women.' It is true that every one of these poems has been more or less revised since then; but a careful comparison of the earlier and later versions shows that much that we should now mark as most admirable in them is unchanged from the reading of 1832. A considerable portion of this volume, though less than of the former one, has been suppressed in the more recent editions; but a few of the omitted pieces have since been restored under the head of 'Juvenilia.' The following little hit at Christopher North has not been thus reinstated:

> 'You did late review my lays,
>   Crusty Christopher;
> You did mingle blame and praise,
>   Rusty Christopher.
> When I learnt from whom it came,
> I forgave you all the blame,
>   Musty Christopher;
> I could *not* forgive the praise,
>   Fusty Christopher.'

For the next ten years (1833–1842) Tennyson published almost nothing. 'The Lover's Tale' was printed in 1833, but withdrawn before publication and not brought out again until 1879, after a pirated edition had appeared. 'Saint Agnes' and one or two other pieces were contributed to 'Annuals' and similar collections during this period; but with these slight exceptions the silence of the poet was unbroken for the ten years.

It is probable that this long silence was mainly due to the death of his friend Hallam in 1833; perhaps also, as has been suggested by more than one critic, to his desire to perfect himself in his art before giving the world further results of it. 'In Memoriam' was elaborated during this period, though not published until 1850; and the best of the poems issued in 1830 and 1832 were carefully revised — some of them almost entirely rewritten — and sundry new poems were produced.

The fruits of this labor ('In Memoriam' excepted) appeared in 1842 in two volumes, one of which was chiefly made up of the earlier poems in their revised form, while the other was almost entirely new. Among the contents of the latter volume was the 'Morte d'Arthur,' which we know to have been written as early as 1835, and which, like 'The Lady of Shalott' in the 1832 volume, shows that the Arthurian legends had begun to interest and inspire the poet long before he planned the extended epical treatment of them in the 'Idylls of the King.'

'The Talking Oak,' 'Dora,' 'Ulysses,' 'Locksley Hall,' 'Saint Agnes,' and 'Sir Galahad' are among the other remarkable poems published in 1842.

The general recognition of Tennyson as the greatest poet of the time dates from this period. Hitherto his admirers had been the select few, and the leading critics had been divided in their estimate of his work; but now he was hailed with almost unanimous eulogies. As another has said, 'all England rang with the stirring music of "Locksley Hall,"' and 'nearly all of the choicer spirits of the age conspired to chant the praises of the poet and to do him honor.'

Up to this time Tennyson was almost unknown in this country. It is doubtful whether a dozen copies of the volumes of 1830 and 1832 ever crossed the Atlantic. Neither of them is to be found in any of our great libraries, and in private collections they are excessively rare. The only extended notice of them in any of our literary journals of that day, so far as I can learn, was in the 'Christian Examiner' in 1837, from the pen of Mr. John S. Dwight. He borrowed the books, as he told me, of Emerson, who delighted to loan them to his friends and endeavored to have them reprinted in Boston.[1]

The edition of 1842 was reprinted here; but Mr. B. H. Ticknor, the son of the publisher, informs me that 1500 copies supplied the American demand for the next three years.

By this time, his fame in England was well assured. Wordsworth, in a letter dated July 1, 1845, says: 'I saw Tennyson when I was in London several times. He is decidedly the first of our living poets, and I hope will live to give the world still better things.' It is a significant fact that, on the death of Southey in 1843, Tennyson was among the few poets who were talked of as successors to the laureateship, though the general opinion, as might have been expected, was in favor of the venerable poet on whom the honor was finally conferred.

A second edition of the 'Poems' of 1842 was called for within a year, and two more editions were issued in 1845 and 1846. In 1845 the poet was placed on the pension-list by Sir Robert Peel for an annuity of £200. The grant was the means of calling forth some ill-natured criticisms, the most notable of which was a satirical fling, in Bulwer-Lytton's 'The New Timon' (London, 1846), at the 'Theban taste' that 'pensions Tennyson while starves a Knowles.' The productions of 'school-miss Alfred' were described as 'out-babying Wordsworth and out-glittering Keats,' with much more in the same vein. The attack drew from Tennyson a rejoinder printed in 'Punch' (February 26, 1846) over the signature of 'Alcibiades,' and followed in the next number by another, less severe, entitled 'Afterthought.' In this 'sober second thought' the poet comes to the wise conclusion that *silence* is the 'noblest answer' to all such spiteful attacks. This latter poem was afterwards included in the editions of Tennyson under the title of 'Literary Squabbles.' No one would suspect any reference to Lytton in it if he did not know its history.

It is pleasant to be able to add that Bulwer struck out the sneer at Tennyson from the third edition of 'The New Timon,' and that the two poets afterwards became good friends. In a public speech in 1862, Lytton, in alluding to Prince Albert, quoted what he called 'the thought so exquisitely expressed by our Poet Laureate' — namely, that the Prince is 'The silent father of our kings to be'; and later Tennyson, in dedicating 'Harold' to the younger Lytton, gracefully acknowledged his indebtedness to the novel on the same subject by the elder Lytton. 'O strange hate-healer, Time !' as the Laureate elsewhere exclaims.

On the more recent history of the poet it is not necessary to dwell in detail. In 1847 'The Princess' appeared, and in 1850 'In Memoriam' was at last given to the world. The same year Tennyson was married, and was made Poet Laureate. In 1852 the 'Ode on the Death of Wellington' was published, and the next year the eighth edition of the complete 'Poems' was issued. 'Maud and Other Poems' appeared in 1855, and a second edition in 1856 with 'Maud' in a considerably enlarged form. In 1859 followed the 'Idylls of the King,' including 'Enid,' 'Vivien,' 'Elaine,' and 'Guinevere.' Ten thousand

[1] This I learned from Mr. Samuel Longfellow, who showed me a letter from Messrs. C. C. Little & Co. to his brother the poet, dated April 27, 1838, in which they refer to Emerson's desire for an American reprint of Tennyson and their intention of making one. Why the plan was not carried out I am unable to say.

copies of the volume were sold in a few weeks. Four more Idylls — 'The Coming of Arthur,' 'The Holy Grail,' 'Pelleas and Ettarre,' and 'The Passing of Arthur' (in which the 'Morte d'Arthur' of 1842 was incorporated) — were published ten years later, in 1869, when forty thousand copies of the book were ordered in advance. 'The Last Tournament' and 'Gareth and Lynette' were added in 1872. Meanwhile 'Enoch Arden,' etc., had appeared in 1864, and 'The Window' had been privately printed in 1867. Sundry poems had also been contributed to magazines, and were included in 'The Holy Grail and Other Poems' of 1869. In 1875 the drama of 'Queen Mary' was given to the world, and in 1877 that of 'Harold.' The former, in a condensed and altered form, was put on the stage in 1876 with moderate success, but the latter has never been acted. In 1879, as already stated, 'The Lover's Tale,' withdrawn in 1833, was published, with the addition of a third part entitled 'The Golden Supper.' Later in the same year, 'The Falcon,' a one-act play based on the well-known story of Count Federigo and Monna Giovanna from Boccaccio that had been already told in verse by Barry Cornwall and Longfellow, was produced at the St. James Theatre in London. In the 'Ballads and Other Poems' of 1880 certain pieces contributed to the 'Nineteenth Century' in 1877–1879 were gathered up, with others that had not been previously printed. Early in 1881, 'The Cup,' a tragedy in two acts, was brought out at the Lyceum Theatre, under the direction of Mr. Irving, and had a very successful run. In November, 1882, a fourth drama by Tennyson was acted in London — a prose work called 'The Promise of May.'

Late in 1883 it was announced that the Queen had offered a peerage to Tennyson, and that he had accepted it. It had been offered him twice before (in March, 1873, through Mr. Gladstone, and in December, 1874, through Mr. Disraeli) and had been declined; but he probably felt that it would be ungracious to refuse it a third time. He was gazetted Baron of Aldworth and Farringford, on the 18th of January, 1884. Among the letters he received on the occasion was one from an old woman named Susan Epton, who had been in the service of the poet's father and afterwards lady's maid to Mrs. Tennyson. 'I have received many letters of congratulation,' Tennyson remarked in a letter to a friend, 'some from great lords and ladies; but the affectionate remembrance of good old Susan Epton and her sister touched me more than all these.'

There were those, however, who found fault with the Laureate for consenting to become Lord Tennyson. 'Not only could no fame accrue to him from a title, but it was urged that, by taking one, he was scarcely true to his own ideals, — at all events, that he did not rise to the height of his own inspiration.' I know of no better answer to this than has been made by an American and a republican. Mr. Stedman ('Victorian Poets,' revised ed., 1887, p. 422) says:

'When the Laureate was raised to the peerage — a station which he twice declined in middle life — he gained some attention from the satirists, and his acceptance of rank no doubt was honestly bemoaned by many sturdy radicals. It is difficult, nevertheless, to find any violation of principle or taste in the acceptance by England's favorite and official poet of such an honor, bestowed at the climax of his years and fame. Republicans should bear in mind that the republic of letters is the only one to which Alfred Tennyson owed allegiance; that he was the "first citizen" of an ancient monarchy, which honored letters by gratefully conferring upon him its high traditional award. It would be truckling for an American, loyal to his own form of government, to receive an aristocratic title from some foreign potentate. Longfellow, for example, promptly declined an order tendered him by the King of Italy. But a sense of fitness, and even patriotism, should make it easy for an Englishman, faithful to a constitutional monarchy, to accept any well-earned dignity under that system. In every country it is thought worth while for one to be the founder of his family; and in Great Britain no able man could do more for descendants, to whom he is not sure of bequeathing his talents, than by handing down a class privilege, even though it confers no additional glory upon the original winner. Extreme British democrats, who openly or covertly wish to change the form of government, and even communists, are aware that Tennyson does not belong to their ranks. He has been a liberal conservative : liberal in humanity and progressive thought, strictly conservative in allegiance to the national system. As for that, touch but the territory, imperil the institutions of Great Britain, and Swinburne himself — the pupil of Landor, Mazzini, and Hugo — betrays the blood in his veins. Tennyson, a liberal of the Maurice group, has been cleverly styled by Whitman a " poet of feudalism ; " he is a celebrator of the past, of sovereignty and knighthood ; he is no lost leader, " just for a ribbon " leaving some gallant cause forsworn or any song unsung. In all fairness, his acceptance of rank savors less of inconsistency than does the logic of those who rail at the world for neglect of genius, and then upbraid them both for coming to an understanding.'

Early in 1885 Lord Tennyson published the drama of 'Becket,' and at the close of the same year the volume entitled 'Tiresias and Other Poems,' the larger portion of which had not previously appeared in print. 'Balin and Balan' in this volume concluded the series of Arthurian idyls. The book was dedicated to Robert Browning.

In 1886 'Locksley Hall Sixty Years After' appeared, — forty-four years after the first 'Locksley Hall' electrified the literary world. The volume also included three poems contributed to the 'Times' and other periodicals during 1885.

In 1889 'Demeter and Other Poems' came out, twenty thousand copies of which were sold within a week after publication. As the work of an octogenarian it was every way remarkable. The Laureate's eightieth birthday, August 6, 1889, called forth many tributes both in prose and verse on both sides of the Atlantic.

The romantic play of 'The Foresters,' founded on the story of Robin Hood and Maid Marian, was produced at Daly's Theatre in New York, March 17, 1892, and was published soon afterwards.

On the 6th of October of the same year Lord Tennyson died after a brief sickness, and was buried in the 'Poet's Corner' of Westminster Abbey on the 12th. The volume entitled 'The Death of Œnone, Akbar's Dream, and Other Poems,' which was in press at the time of his death, was published a few weeks later.

For fuller information concerning the poet and his works, the reader may be referred to the 'Memoir' (2 vols., London and New York, 1897) by his son, the present Lord Tennyson.

W. J. R.

CAMBRIDGE, May, 1898.

## TO THE QUEEN

This poem was prefixed to the first Laureate Edition (1851), where it included the 'Crystal-Palace' stanza (see Notes) omitted in all subsequent editions. The 4th stanza was inserted in the next edition, and a few slight changes were made elsewhere.

Revered, beloved — O you that hold
  A nobler office upon earth
  Than arms, or power of brain, or birth
Could give the warrior kings of old,

Victoria, — since your Royal grace
  To one of less desert allows
  This laurel greener from the brows
Of him that utter'd nothing base;

And should your greatness, and the care
  That yokes with empire, yield you time
  To make demand of modern rhyme
If aught of ancient worth be there;

Then — while a sweeter music wakes,
  And thro' wild March the throstle calls,
  Where all about your palace-walls
The sun-lit almond-blossom shakes —

Take, Madam, this poor book of song;
  For tho' the faults were thick as dust
  In vacant chambers, I could trust
Your kindness. May you rule us long,

And leave us rulers of your blood
  As noble till the latest day!
  May children of our children say,
'She wrought her people lasting good;

'Her court was pure; her life serene;
  God gave her peace; her land reposed;
  A thousand claims to reverence closed
In her as Mother, Wife, and Queen;

'*And statesmen at her council met*
  *Who knew the seasons when to take*
  *Occasion by the hand, and make*
*The bounds of freedom wider yet*

'*By shaping some august decree*
  *Which kept her throne unshaken still,*
  *Broad-based upon her people's will,*
*And compass'd by the inviolate sea.*'

*March*, 1851.

# JUVENILIA

Under this head, in the one-volume and seven-volume editions of 1884 and all subsequent editions, Lord Tennyson included certain poems from the volumes of 1830 and 1833 (some of which were suppressed in 1842), with others that had not appeared in any earlier authorized edition of his works. For those not printed in 1830 (or then printed, and afterwards suppressed for a time) see the prefatory notes to the poems. All those without prefatory notes (or reference in other notes) were printed in 1830 and reprinted in 1842.

## CLARIBEL

### A MELODY

In 1830 'callow' was 'fledgling'.

WHERE Claribel low-lieth
  The breezes pause and die,
    Letting the rose-leaves fall;
But the solemn oak-tree sigheth,
    Thick-leaved, ambrosial,
  With an ancient melody
  Of an inward agony,
Where Claribel low-lieth.

At eve the beetle boometh
  Athwart the thicket lone;
At noon the wild bee hummeth
  About the moss'd headstone;
At midnight the moon cometh,
  And looketh down alone.
Her song the lintwhite swelleth,
The clear-voiced mavis dwelleth,
  The callow throstle lispeth,
  The slumbrous wave outwelleth,
  The babbling runnel crispeth,
The hollow grot replieth
  Where Claribel low-lieth.

## NOTHING WILL DIE

This poem and the two next poems, first published in 1830, were omitted in 1842, but afterwards restored.

WHEN will the stream be aweary of flowing
    Under my eye?

When will the wind be aweary of blowing
    Over the sky?
When will the clouds be aweary of fleeting?
When will the heart be aweary of beating?
    And nature die?
Never, O, never, nothing will die;
    The stream flows,
    The wind blows,
    The cloud fleets,
    The heart beats,
      Nothing will die.

Nothing will die;
All things will change
Thro' eternity.
'T is the world's winter;
Autumn and summer
Are gone long ago;
Earth is dry to the centre,
But spring, a new comer,
A spring rich and strange,
Shall make the winds blow
Round and round,
Thro' and thro',
  Here and there,
  Till the air
And the ground
Shall be fill'd with life anew.

The world was never made;
It will change, but it will not fade.
So let the wind range;
For even and morn
  Ever will be
  Thro' eternity.
Nothing was born;
Nothing will die;
All things will change.

## ALL THINGS WILL DIE

CLEARLY the blue river chimes in its flowing
    Under my eye;
Warmly and broadly the south winds are
    blowing
      Over the sky.
One after another the white clouds are
    fleeting;
Every heart this May morning in joyance
    is beating
      Full merrily;
    Yet all things must die.
The stream will cease to flow;
The wind will cease to blow;
The clouds will cease to fleet;
The heart will cease to beat;
    For all things must die.
    All things must die.
Spring will come never more.
    O, vanity !
Death waits at the door.
See ! our friends are all forsaking
The wine and the merrymaking.
We are call'd — we must go.
Laid low, very low,
In the dark we must lie.
The merry glees are still;
The voice of the bird
Shall no more be heard,
Nor the wind on the hill.
    O, misery !
Hark ! death is calling
While I speak to ye,
The jaw is falling,
The red cheek paling,
The strong limbs failing;
Ice with the warm blood mixing;
The eyeballs fixing.
Nine times goes the passing bell:
Ye merry souls, farewell.
    The old earth
    Had a birth,
    As all men know,
    Long ago.
And the old earth must die.
So let the warm winds range,
And the blue wave beat the shore;
For even and morn
Ye will never see
Thro' eternity.
All things were born.
Ye will come never more,
For all things must die.

## LEONINE ELEGIACS

LOW - FLOWING breezes are roaming the
    broad valley dimm'd in the gloam-
    ing;
Thoro' the black-stemm'd pines only the
    far river shines.
Creeping thro' blossomy rushes and bowers
    of rose-blowing bushes,
Down by the poplar tall rivulets babble
    and fall.
Barketh the shepherd - dog cheerly; the
    grasshopper carolleth clearly;
Deeply the wood-dove coos ; shrilly the
    owlet halloos;
Winds creep; dews fall chilly: in her first
    sleep earth breathes stilly:
Over the pools in the burn water-gnats
    murmur and mourn.
Sadly the far kine loweth; the glimmering
    water outfloweth;
Twin peaks shadow'd with pine slope to the
    dark hyaline.
Low-throned Hesper is stayed between the
    two peaks; but the Naiad
Throbbing in mild unrest holds him be-
    neath in her breast.
The ancient poetess singeth that Hesperus
    all things bringeth,
Smoothing the wearied mind: bring me my
    love, Rosalind.
Thou comest morning or even; she cometh
    not morning or even.
False-eyed Hesper, unkind, where is my
    sweet Rosalind ?

## SUPPOSED CONFESSIONS

### OF A SECOND-RATE SENSITIVE MIND

    This poem, published in 1830, was suppressed
for more than fifty years. In 1879 the ' Christian Signal,' an English journal, announced
that its issue for September 6th would contain
' an early unpublished poem of over two hundred lines by Alfred Tennyson (P. L.), entitled
" Confessions of a Sensitive Mind ; " ' but the
publication was prevented by a legal injunc-
tion. In 1884 the poem was included in the
complete edition of the Laureate's works.

    O GOD ! my God ! have mercy now.
    I faint, I fall. Men say that Thou
    Didst die for me, for such as *me*,

Patient of ill, and death, and scorn,
And that my sin was as a thorn
Among the thorns that girt Thy brow,
Wounding Thy soul. — That even now,
In this extremest misery
Of ignorance, I should require
A sign! and if a bolt of fire           10
Would rive the slumbrous summer noon
While I do pray to Thee alone,
Think my belief would stronger grow!
Is not my human pride brought low?
The boastings of my spirit still?
The joy I had in my free-will
All cold, and dead, and corpse-like grown?
And what is left to me but Thou,
And faith in Thee?   Men pass me by;
Christians with happy countenances —     20
And children all seem full of Thee!
And women smile with saint-like glances
Like Thine own mother's when she bow'd
Above Thee, on that happy morn
When angels spake to men aloud,
And Thou and peace to earth were born.
Good-will to me as well as all —
I one of them; my brothers they;
Brothers in Christ — a world of peace
And confidence, day after day;           30
And trust and hope till things should cease,
And then one Heaven receive us all.

How sweet to have a common faith!
To hold a common scorn of death!
And at a burial to hear
The creaking cords which wound and eat
Into my human heart, whene'er
Earth goes to earth, with grief, not fear,
With hopeful grief, were passing sweet!

Thrice happy state again to be          40
The trustful infant on the knee,
Who lets his rosy fingers play
About his mother's neck, and knows
Nothing beyond his mother's eyes!
They comfort him by night and day;
They light his little life alway;
He hath no thought of coming woes;
He hath no care of life or death;
Scarce outward signs of joy arise,
Because the Spirit of happiness          50
And perfect rest so inward is;
And loveth so his innocent heart,
Her temple and her place of birth,
Where she would ever wish to dwell,
Life of the fountain there, beneath
Its salient springs, and far apart,

Hating to wander out on earth,
Or breathe into the hollow air,
Whose chillness would make visible
Her subtil, warm, and golden breath,     60
Which mixing with the infant's blood,
Fulfils him with beatitude.
O, sure it is a special care
Of God, to fortify from doubt,
To arm in proof, and guard about
With triple-mailed trust, and clear
Delight, the infant's dawning year.

Would that my gloomed fancy were
As thine, my mother, when with brows
Propt on thy knees, my hands upheld      70
In thine, I listen'd to thy vows,
For me outpour'd in holiest prayer —
For me unworthy! — and beheld
Thy mild deep eyes upraised, that knew
The beauty and repose of faith,
And the clear spirit shining thro'.
O, wherefore do we grow awry
From roots which strike so deep? why dare
Paths in the desert?   Could not I
Bow myself down, where thou hast knelt,
To the earth — until the ice would melt  81
Here, and I feel as thou hast felt?
What devil had the heart to scathe
Flowers thou hadst rear'd — to brush the
    dew
From thine own lily, when thy grave
Was deep, my mother, in the clay?
Myself?   Is it thus?   Myself?   Had I
So little love for thee?   But why
Prevail'd not thy pure prayers?   Why
    pray
To one who heeds not, who can save       90
But will not?   Great in faith, and strong
Against the grief of circumstance
Wert thou, and yet unheard.   What if
Thou pleadest still, and seest me drive
Thro' utter dark a full-sail'd skiff,
Unpiloted i' the echoing dance
Of reboant whirlwinds, stooping low
Unto the death, not sunk!   I know
At matins and at evensong,
That thou, if thou wert yet alive,       100
In deep and daily prayers wouldst strive
To reconcile me with thy God.
Albeit, my hope is gray, and cold
At heart, thou wouldest murmur still —
' Bring this lamb back into Thy fold,
My Lord, if so it be Thy will.'
Wouldst tell me I must brook the rod
And chastisement of human pride;

That pride, the sin of devils, stood
Betwixt me and the light of God;        110
That hitherto I had defied
And had rejected God — that grace
Would drop from His o'er-brimming love,
As manna on my wilderness,
If I would pray — that God would move
And strike the hard, hard rock, and thence,
Sweet in their utmost bitterness,
Would issue tears of penitence
Which would keep green hope's life.  Alas!
I think that pride hath now no place        120
Nor sojourn in me.  I am void,
Dark, formless, utterly destroyed.

Why not believe then?  Why not yet
Anchor thy frailty there, where man
Hath moor'd and rested?  Ask the sea
At midnight, when the crisp slope waves
After a tempest rib and fret
The broad-imbased beach, why he
Slumbers not like a mountain tarn?
Wherefore his ridges are not curls        130
And ripples of an inland mere?
Wherefore he moaneth thus, nor can
Draw down into his vexed pools
All that blue heaven which hues and paves
The other?  I am too forlorn,
Too shaken: my own weakness fools
My judgment, and my spirit whirls,
Moved from beneath with doubt and fear.

' Yet,' said I, in my morn of youth,
The unsunn'd freshness of my strength,        140
When I went forth in quest of truth,
' It is man's privilege to doubt,
If so be that from doubt at length
Truth may stand forth unmoved of change,
An image with profulgent brows
And perfect limbs, as from the storm
Of running fires and fluid range
Of lawless airs, at last stood out
This excellence and solid form
Of constant beauty.  For the ox        150
Feeds in the herb, and sleeps, or fills
The horned valleys all about,
And hollows of the fringed hills
In summer heats, with placid lows
Unfearing, till his own blood flows
About his hoof.  And in the flocks
The lamb rejoiceth in the year,
And raceth freely with his fere,
And answers to his mother's calls
From the flower'd furrow.  In a time        160
Of which he wots not, run short pains

Thro' his warm heart; and then, from
        whence
He knows not, on his light there falls
A shadow; and his native slope,
Where he was wont to leap and climb,
Floats from his sick and filmed eyes,
And something in the darkness draws
His forehead earthward, and he dies.
Shall man live thus, in joy and hope
As a young lamb, who cannot dream,        170
Living, but that he shall live on?
Shall we not look into the laws
Of life and death, and things that seem,
And things that be, and analyze
Our double nature, and compare
All creeds till we have found the one,
If one there be?'  Ay me!  I fear
All may not doubt, but everywhere
Some must clasp idols.  Yet, my God,
Whom call I idol?  Let Thy dove        180
Shadow me over, and my sins
Be unremember'd, and Thy love
Enlighten me.  O, teach me yet
Somewhat before the heavy clod
Weighs on me, and the busy fret
Of that sharp-headed worm begins
In the gross blackness underneath.

O weary life!  O weary death!
O spirit and heart made desolate!
O damned vacillating state!        190

## THE KRAKEN

Published in 1830, omitted in 1842, but afterwards restored, with ' fins ' changed to ' arms.'

BELOW the thunders of the upper deep,
Far, far beneath in the abysmal sea,
His ancient, dreamless, uninvaded sleep
The Kraken sleepeth: faintest sunlights
        flee
About his shadowy sides; above him swell
Huge sponges of millennial growth and
        height;
And far away into the sickly light,
From many a wondrous grot and secret
        cell
Unnumber'd and enormous polypi
Winnow with giant arms the slumbering
        green.
There hath he lain for ages, and will lie
Battening upon huge sea-worms in his
        sleep,

Until the latter fire shall heat the deep;
Then once by man and angels to be seen,
In roaring he shall rise and on the surface
    die.

## SONG

In 1830 the title was ' We are Free ' and
the two stanzas were printed as one; omitted
in 1842, but afterwards restored.

THE winds, as at their hour of birth,
    Leaning upon the ridged sea,
Breathed low around the rolling earth
    With mellow preludes, ' We are free.'

The streams, through many a lilied row
    Down-carolling to the crisped sea,
Low-tinkled with a bell-like flow
    Atween the blossoms, ' We are free.'

## LILIAN

In 1842 ' purfled ' was changed to ' gathered.'

### I

AIRY, fairy Lilian,
Flitting, fairy Lilian,
When I ask her if she love me,
Claps her tiny hands above me,
    Laughing all she can;
She 'll not tell me if she love me,
    Cruel little Lilian.

### II

When my passion seeks
Pleasance in love-sighs,
She, looking thro' and thro' me
Thoroughly to undo me,
    Smiling, never speaks:
So innocent-arch, so cunning-simple,
From beneath her gathered wimple
    Glancing with black-beaded eyes,
Till the lightning laughters dimple
    The baby-roses in her cheeks;
    Then away she flies.

### III

Prythee weep, May Lilian !
    Gaiety without eclipse
Wearieth me, May Lilian;
    Thro' my very heart it thrilleth
When from crimson-threaded lips
Silver-treble laughter trilleth:
    Prythee weep, May Lilian !

### IV

Praying all I can,
If prayers will not hush thee,
    Airy Lilian,
Like a rose-leaf I will crush thee,
    Fairy Lilian.

## ISABEL

Tennyson's mother was the basis of this
portrait.

EYES not down-dropt nor over-bright, but
        fed
    With the clear-pointed flame of chastity,
    Clear, without heat, undying, tended by
        Pure vestal thoughts in the translu-
            cent fane
Of her still spirit; locks not wide-dispread,
Madonna-wise on either side her head;
        Sweet lips whereon perpetually did
            reign
    The summer calm of golden charity,
Were fixed shadows of thy fixed mood,
        Revered Isabel, the crown and head,
The stately flower of female fortitude,
        Of perfect wifehood and pure lowli-
            head.

The intuitive decision of a bright
        And thorough-edged intellect to part
            Error from crime; a prudence to with-
                hold;
            The laws of marriage character'd in
                gold
Upon the blanched tablets of her heart;
A love still burning upward, giving light
To read those laws; an accent very low
In blandishment, but a most silver flow
        Of subtle-paced counsel in distress,
Right to the heart and brain, tho' unde-
            scried,
        Winning its way with extreme gentle-
            ness
Thro' all the outworks of suspicious pride;
A courage to endure and to obey;
A hate of gossip parlance, and of sway,
Crown'd Isabel, thro' all her placid life,
The queen of marriage, a most perfect
            wife.

The mellow'd reflex of a winter moon;
A clear stream flowing with a muddy one,

Till in its onward current it absorbs
  With swifter movement and in purer
    light
  The vexed eddies of its wayward bro-
    ther;
  A leaning and upbearing parasite,
  Clothing the stem, which else had
    fallen quite
With cluster'd flower-bells and ambrosial
    orbs
  Of rich fruit-bunches leaning on each
    other —
  Shadow forth thee: — the world hath
    not another
(Tho' all her fairest forms are types of
    thee,
And thou of God in thy great charity)
Of such a finish'd chasten'd purity.


## MARIANA

'Mariana in the moated grange.'
*Measure for Measure.*

WITH blackest moss the flower-plots
  Were thickly crusted, one and all;
The rusted nails fell from the knots
  That held the pear to the gable-wall.
The broken sheds look'd sad and strange:
  Unlifted was the clinking latch;
  Weeded and worn the ancient thatch
Upon the lonely moated grange.
    She only said, 'My life is dreary,
      He cometh not,' she said;                10
    She said, 'I am aweary, aweary,
      I would that I were dead!'

Her tears fell with the dews at even;
  Her tears fell ere the dews were dried;
She could not look on the sweet heaven,
  Either at morn or eventide.
After the flitting of the bats,
  When thickest dark did trance the sky,
  She drew her casement-curtain by,
And glanced athwart the glooming flats. 20
    She only said, 'The night is dreary,
      He cometh not,' she said;
    She said, 'I am aweary, aweary,
      I would that I were dead!'

Upon the middle of the night,
  Waking she heard the night-fowl crow;
The cock sung out an hour ere light;
  From the dark fen the oxen's low

Came to her; without hope of change,
  In sleep she seem'd to walk forlorn,   30
  Till cold winds woke the gray-eyed morn
About the lonely moated grange.
    She only said, 'The day is dreary,
      He cometh not,' she said;
    She said, 'I am aweary, aweary,
      I would that I were dead!'

About a stone-cast from the wall
  A sluice with blacken'd waters slept,
And o'er it many, round and small,
  The cluster'd marish-mosses crept.    40
Hard by a poplar shook alway,
  All silver-green with gnarled bark:
For leagues no other tree did mark
The level waste, the rounding gray.
    She only said, 'My life is dreary,
      He cometh not,' she said;
    She said, 'I am aweary, aweary,
      I would that I were dead!'

And ever when the moon was low,
  And the shrill winds were up and away,
In the white curtain, to and fro,        51
  She saw the gusty shadow sway.
But when the moon was very low,
  And wild winds bound within their cell,
  The shadow of the poplar fell
Upon her bed, across her brow.
    She only said, 'The night is dreary,
      He cometh not,' she said;
    She said, 'I am aweary, aweary,
      I would that I were dead!'       60

All day within the dreamy house,
  The doors upon their hinges creak'd;
The blue fly sung in the pane; the mouse
  Behind the mouldering wainscot shriek'd,
Or from the crevice peer'd about.
  Old faces glimmer'd thro' the doors,
  Old footsteps trod the upper floors,
Old voices called her from without.
    She only said, 'My life is dreary,
      He cometh not,' she said;          70
    She said, 'I am aweary, aweary,
      I would that I were dead!'

The sparrow's chirrup on the roof,
  The slow clock ticking, and the sound
Which to the wooing wind aloof
  The poplar made, did all confound
Her sense; but most she loathed the hour
  When the thick-moted sunbeam lay
  Athwart the chambers, and the day

Was sloping toward his western bower.    80
   Then said she, ' I am very dreary,
   He will not come,' she said;
   She wept, ' I am aweary, aweary,
     O God, that I were dead ! '

## TO ——

### I

CLEAR-HEADED friend, whose joyful scorn,
   Edged with sharp laughter, cuts atwain
   The knots that tangle human creeds,
   The wounding cords that bind and strain
   The heart until it bleeds,
Ray-fringed eyelids of the morn
   Roof not a glance so keen as thine;
   If aught of prophecy be mine,
Thou wilt not live in vain.

### II

Low-cowering shall the Sophist sit;
   Falsehood shall bare her plaited brow;
   Fair-fronted Truth shall droop not now
With shrilling shafts of subtle wit.
Nor martyr-flames, nor trenchant swords
   Can do away that ancient lie;
   A gentler death shall Falsehood die,
Shot thro' and thro' with cunning words.

### III

Weak Truth a-leaning on her crutch,
   Wan, wasted Truth in her utmost need,
   Thy kingly intellect shall feed,
Until she be an athlete bold,
And weary with a finger's touch
   Those writhed limbs of lightning speed;
Like that strange angel which of old,
   Until the breaking of the light,
Wrestled with wandering Israel,
   Past Yabbok brook the livelong night,
And heaven's mazed signs stood still
In the dim tract of Penuel.

## MADELINE

### I

THOU art not steep'd in golden languors,
   No tranced summer calm is thine,
   Ever varying Madeline.
   Thro' light and shadow thou dost range,
   Sudden glances, sweet and strange,
Delicious spites and darling angers,
   And airy forms of flitting change.

### II

Smiling, frowning, evermore,
Thou art perfect in love-lore.
Revealings deep and clear are thine
Of wealthy smiles; but who may know
Whether smile or frown be fleeter ?
Whether smile or frown be sweeter,
   Who may know ?
Frowns perfect-sweet along the brow
Light-glooming over eyes divine,
Like little clouds sun-fringed, are thine,
   Ever varying Madeline.
Thy smile and frown are not aloof
   From one another,
   Each to each is dearest brother;
Hues of the silken sheeny woof
   Momently shot into each other.
   All the mystery is thine;
Smiling, frowning, evermore,
Thou art perfect in love-lore,
   Ever varying Madeline.

### III

A subtle, sudden flame,
   By veering passion fann'd,
   About thee breaks and dances:
When I would kiss thy hand,
The flush of anger'd shame
   O'erflows thy calmer glances,
And o'er black brows drops down
A sudden-curved frown :
But when I turn away,
Thou, willing me to stay,
   Wooest not, nor vainly wranglest,
   But, looking fixedly the while,
   All my bounding heart entanglest
   In a golden-netted smile ;
Then in madness and in bliss,
If my lips should dare to kiss
Thy taper fingers amorously,
Again thou blushest angrily ;
And o'er black brows drops down
A sudden-curved frown.

## SONG — THE OWL

### I

WHEN cats run home and light is come,
   And dew is cold upon the ground,
And the far-off stream is dumb,
   And the whirring sail goes round,
   And the whirring sail goes round ;
   Alone and warming his five wits,
   The white owl in the belfry sits.

## II

When merry milkmaids click the latch,
    And rarely smells the new-mown hay,
And the cock hath sung beneath the thatch
    Twice or thrice his roundelay,
    Twice or thrice his roundelay;
    Alone and warming his five wits,
    The white owl in the belfry sits.


# SECOND SONG

### TO THE SAME

### I

THY tuwhits are lull'd, I wot,
    Thy tuwhoos of yesternight,
Which upon the dark afloat,
    So took echo with delight,
    So took echo with delight,
    That her voice, untuneful grown,
    Wears all day a fainter tone.

### II

I would mock thy chaunt anew;
    But I cannot mimic it;
Not a whit of thy tuwhoo,
    Thee to woo to thy tuwhit,
    Thee to woo to thy tuwhit,
    With a lengthen'd loud halloo,
    Tuwhoo, tuwhit, tuwhit, tuwhoo-o-o !


# RECOLLECTIONS OF THE
ARABIAN NIGHTS

WHEN the breeze of a joyful dawn blew
        free
In the silken sail of infancy,
The tide of time flow'd back with me,
    The forward-flowing tide of time;
And many a sheeny summer-morn,
Adown the Tigris I was borne,
By Bagdat's shrines of fretted gold,
High-walled gardens green and old;
True Mussulman was I and sworn,
    For it was in the golden prime          10
        Of good Haroun Alraschid.

Anight my shallop, rustling thro'
The low and bloomed foliage, drove
The fragrant, glistening deeps, and clove
The citron-shadows in the blue;

By garden porches on the brim,
The costly doors flung open wide,
Gold glittering thro' lamplight dim,
And broider'd sofas on each side.
    In sooth it was a goodly time,          20
    For it was in the golden prime
        Of good Haroun Alraschid.

Often, where clear-stemm'd platans guard
The outlet, did I turn away
The boat-head down a broad canal
From the main river sluiced, where all
The sloping of the moonlit sward
Was damask-work, and deep inlay
Of braided blooms unmown, which crept
Adown to where the water slept.           30
    A goodly place, a goodly time,
    For it was in the golden prime
        Of good Haroun Alraschid.

A motion from the river won
Ridged the smooth level, bearing on
My shallop thro' the star-strown calm,
Until another night in night
I enter'd, from the clearer light,
Imbower'd vaults of pillar'd palm,
Imprisoning sweets, which, as they clomb 40
Heavenward, were stay'd beneath the dome
    Of hollow boughs.   A goodly time,
    For it was in the golden prime
        Of good Haroun Alraschid.

Still onward; and the clear canal
Is rounded to as clear a lake.
From the green rivage many a fall
Of diamond rillets musical,
Thro' little crystal arches low
Down from the central fountain's flow      50
Fallen silver-chiming, seemed to shake
The sparkling flints beneath the prow.
    A goodly place, a goodly time,
    For it was in the golden prime
        Of good Haroun Alraschid.

Above thro' many a bowery turn
A walk with vari-colored shells
Wander'd engrain'd.   On either side
All round about the fragrant marge
From fluted vase, and brazen urn           60
In order, eastern flowers large,
Some dropping low their crimson bells
Half-closed, and others studded wide
    With disks and tiars, fed the time
    With odor in the golden prime
        Of good Haroun Alraschid.

Far off, and where the lemon grove
In closest coverture upsprung,
The living airs of middle night
Died round the bulbul as he sung; · 70
Not he, but something which possess'd
The darkness of the world, delight,
Life, anguish, death, immortal love,
Ceasing not, mingled, unrepress'd,
  Apart from place, withholding time,
  But flattering the golden prime
    Of good Haroun Alraschid.

Black the garden-bowers and grots
Slumber'd; the solemn palms were ranged
Above, unwoo'd of summer wind; 80
A sudden splendor from behind
Flush'd all the leaves with rich gold-green,
And, flowing rapidly between
Their interspaces, counterchanged
The level lake with diamond-plots
  Of dark and bright.   A lovely time,
  For it was in the golden prime
    Of good Haroun Alraschid.

Dark-blue the deep sphere overhead,
Distinct with vivid stars inlaid, 90
Grew darker from that under-flame;
So, leaping lightly from the boat,
With silver anchor left afloat,
In marvel whence that glory came
Upon me, as in sleep I sank
In cool soft turf upon the bank,
  Entranced with that place and time,
  So worthy of the golden prime
    Of good Haroun Alraschid.

Thence thro' the garden I was drawn —
A realm of pleasance, many a mound, 101
And many a shadow-chequer'd lawn
Full of the city's stilly sound,
And deep myrrh-thickets blowing round
The stately cedar, tamarisks,
Thick rosaries of scented thorn,
Tall orient shrubs, and obelisks
  Graven with emblems of the time,
  In honor of the golden prime
    Of good Haroun Alraschid. 110

With dazed vision unawares
From the long alley's latticed shade
Emerged, I came upon the great
Pavilion of the Caliphat.
Right to the carven cedarn doors,
Flung inward over spangled floors,
Broad-based flights of marble stairs

Ran up with golden balustrade,
  After the fashion of the time,
  And humor of the golden prime 120
    Of good Haroun Alraschid.

The fourscore windows all alight
As with the quintessence of flame,
A million tapers flaring bright
From twisted silvers look'd to shame
The hollow-vaulted dark, and stream'd
Upon the mooned domes aloof
In inmost Bagdat, till there seem'd
Hundreds of crescents on the roof
  Of night new-risen, that marvellous time
  To celebrate the golden prime 131
    Of good Haroun Alraschid.

Then stole I up, and trancedly
Gazed on the Persian girl alone,
Serene with argent-lidded eyes
Amorous, and lashes like to rays
Of darkness, and a brow of pearl
Tressed with redolent ebony,
In many a dark delicious curl,
Flowing beneath her rose-hued zone; 140
  The sweetest lady of the time,
  Well worthy of the golden prime
    Of good Haroun Alraschid.

Six columns, three on either side,
Pure silver, underpropt a rich
Throne of the massive ore, from which
Down-droop'd, in many a floating fold,
Engarlanded and diaper'd
With inwrought flowers, a cloth of gold.
Thereon, his deep eye laughter-stirr'd 150
With merriment of kingly pride,
  Sole star of all that place and time,
  I saw him — in his golden prime,
    THE GOOD HAROUN ALRASCHID.

## ODE TO MEMORY

### ADDRESSED TO ——

The 1830 volume, instead of ' Addressed to
——,' has ' Written very Early in Life.'

### I

THOU who stealest fire,
From the fountains of the past,
To glorify the present, O, haste,
  Visit my low desire !
Strengthen me, enlighten me !
I faint in this obscurity,
Thou dewy dawn of memory.

## II

Come not as thou camest of late,
Flinging the gloom of yesternight
On the white day, but robed in soften'd
        light                                        10
        Of orient state.
Whilome thou camest with the morning
        mist,
Even as a maid, whose stately brow
The dew-impearled winds of dawn have
        kiss'd,
        When she, as thou,
Stays on her floating locks the lovely freight
Of overflowing blooms, and earliest shoots
Of orient green, giving safe pledge of fruits,
Which in wintertide shall star
The black earth with brilliance rare.      20

## III

Whilome thou camest with the morning
        mist,
        And with the evening cloud,
Showering thy gleaned wealth into my
        open breast;
Those peerless flowers which in the rudest
        wind
        Never grow sere,
When rooted in the garden of the mind,
        Because they are the earliest of the year.
        Nor was the night thy shroud.
In sweet dreams softer than unbroken rest
Thou leddest by the hand thine infant
        Hope.                                      30
The eddying of her garments caught from
        thee
The light of thy great presence ; and the
        cope
Of the half-attain'd futurity,
        Tho' deep not fathomless,
Was cloven with the million stars which
        tremble
O'er the deep mind of dauntless infancy.
Small thought was there of life's distress;
For sure she deem'd no mist of earth could
        dull
Those spirit-thrilling eyes so keen and
        beautiful;
Sure she was nigher to heaven's spheres, 40
Listening the lordly music flowing from
        The illimitable years.
        O, strengthen me, enlighten me !
        I faint in this obscurity,
        Thou dewy dawn of memory.

## IV

Come forth, I charge thee, arise,
Thou of the many tongues, the myriad
        eyes !
Thou comest not with shows of flaunting
        vines
        Unto mine inner eye,
        Divinest Memory !                         50
Thou wert not nursed by the waterfall
Which ever sounds and shines
        A pillar of white light upon the wall
Of purple cliffs, aloof descried:
Come from the woods that belt the gray
        hillside,
The seven elms, the poplars four
That stand beside my father's door,
And chiefly from the brook that loves
To purl o'er matted cress and ribbed sand,
Or dimple in the dark of rushy coves,      60
Drawing into his narrow earthen urn,
        In every elbow and turn,
The filter'd tribute of the rough woodland;
        O, hither lead thy feet !
Pour round mine ears the livelong bleat
Of the thick-fleeced sheep from wattled
        folds,
        Upon the ridged wolds,
When the first matin-song hath waken'd
        loud
Over the dark dewy earth forlorn,
What time the amber morn                    70
Forth gushes from beneath a low-hung
        cloud.

## V

Large dowries doth the raptured eye
        To the young spirit present
        When first she is wed,
        And like a bride of old
        In triumph led,
        With music and sweet showers
        Of festal flowers,
Unto the dwelling she must sway.
Well hast thou done, great artist Memory,
In setting round thy first experiment    81
        With royal framework of wrought
        gold ;
Needs must thou dearly love thy first
        essay,
And foremost in thy various gallery
        Place it, where sweetest sunlight falls
        Upon the storied walls;
                For the discovery

And newness of thine art so pleased thee
That all which thou hast drawn of fairest
Or boldest since but lightly weighs    90
With thee unto the love thou bearest
The first-born of thy genius.  Artist-like,
Ever retiring thou dost gaze
On the prime labor of thine early days,
No matter what the sketch might be:
Whether the high field on the bushless
        pike,
Or even a sand-built ridge
Of heaped hills that mound the sea,
Overblown with murmurs harsh,
Or even a lowly cottage whence we see  100
Stretch'd wide and wild the waste enor-
        mous marsh,
Where from the frequent bridge,
Like emblems of infinity,
The trenched waters run from sky to sky;
Or a garden bower'd close
With plaited alleys of the trailing rose,
Long alleys falling down to twilight grots,
Or opening upon level plots
Of crowned lilies, standing near
Purple-spiked lavender:    110
Whither in after life retired
From brawling storms,
From weary wind,
With youthful fancy re-inspired,
We may hold converse with all forms
Of the many-sided mind,
And those whom passion hath not blinded,
Subtle-thoughted, myriad-minded.

My friend, with you to live alone
Were how much better than to own    120
A crown, a sceptre, and a throne !

O, strengthen me, enlighten me !
I faint in this obscurity,
Thou dewy dawn of memory.

## SONG

### I

A SPIRIT haunts the year's last hours
Dwelling amid these yellowing bowers.
      To himself he talks;
For at eventide, listening earnestly,
At his work you may hear him sob and
        sigh
      In the walks;
  Earthward he boweth the heavy stalks
Of the mouldering flowers.

Heavily hangs the broad sunflower
  Over its grave i' the earth so chilly;
Heavily hangs the hollyhock,
  Heavily hangs the tiger-lily.

### II

The air is damp, and hush'd, and close,
As a sick man's room when he taketh
        repose
      An hour before death;
My very heart faints and my whole soul
        grieves
At the moist rich smell of the rotting
        leaves,
      And the breath
  Of the fading edges of box beneath,
And the year's last rose.
    Heavily hangs the broad sunflower
  Over its grave i' the earth so chilly;
Heavily hangs the hollyhock,
  Heavily hangs the tiger-lily.

## A CHARACTER

WITH a half-glance upon the sky
At night he said, ' The wanderings
Of this most intricate Universe
Teach me the nothingness of things;'
Yet could not all creation pierce
Beyond the bottom of his eye.

He spake of beauty: that the dull
Saw no divinity in grass,
Life in dead stones, or spirit in air;
Then looking as 't were in a glass,
He smooth'd his chin and sleek'd his hair,
And said the earth was beautiful.

He spake of virtue: not the gods
More purely when they wish to charm
Pallas and Juno sitting by;
And with a sweeping of the arm,
And a lack-lustre dead-blue eye,
Devolved his rounded periods.

Most delicately hour by hour
He canvass'd human mysteries,
And trod on silk, as if the winds
Blew his own praises in his eyes,
And stood aloof from other minds
In impotence of fancied power.

With lips depress'd as he were meek,
Himself unto himself he sold:

Upon himself himself did feed;
Quiet, dispassionate, and cold,
And other than his form of creed,
With chisell'd features clear and sleek.


## THE POET

THE poet in a golden clime was born,
    With golden stars above;
Dower'd with the hate of hate, the scorn
    of scorn,
        The love of love.

He saw thro' life and death, thro' good and
    ill,
    He saw thro' his own soul.
The marvel of the everlasting will,
        An open scroll,

Before him lay; with echoing feet he
    threaded
    The secretest walks of fame:
The viewless arrows of his thoughts were
    headed
        And wing'd with flame,

Like Indian reeds blown from his silver
    tongue,
    And of so fierce a flight,
From Calpe unto Caucasus they sung,
        Filling with light

And vagrant melodies the winds which bore
    Them earthward till they lit;
Then, like the arrow - seeds of the field
    flower,
        The fruitful wit

Cleaving took root, and springing forth
    anew
    Where'er they fell, behold,
Like to the mother plant in semblance,
    grew
        A flower all gold,

And bravely furnish'd all abroad to fling
    The winged shafts of truth,
To throng with stately blooms the breath-
    ing spring
        Of Hope and Youth.

So many minds did gird their orbs with
    beams,
    Tho' one did fling the fire;

Heaven flow'd upon the soul in many
    dreams
        Of high desire.

Thus truth was multiplied on truth, the
    world
    Like one great garden show'd,
And thro' the wreaths of floating dark up-
    curl'd,
        Rare sunrise flow'd.

And Freedom rear'd in that august sunrise
    Her beautiful bold brow,
When rites and forms before his burning
    eyes
        Melted like snow.

There was no blood upon her maiden robes
    Sunn'd by those orient skies;
But round about the circles of the globes
        Of her keen eyes

And in her raiment's hem was traced in
    flame
    WISDOM, a name to shake
All evil dreams of power — a sacred name.
        And when she spake,

Her words did gather thunder as they ran,
    And as the lightning to the thunder
Which follows it, riving the spirit of man,
        Making earth wonder,

So was their meaning to her words.   No
    sword
    Of wrath her right arm whirl'd,
But one poor poet's scroll, and with *his*
    word
        She shook the world.


## THE POET'S MIND

### I

VEX not thou the poet's mind
    With thy shallow wit;
Vex not thou the poet's mind,
    For thou canst not fathom it.
Clear and bright it should be ever,
Flowing like a crystal river,
Bright as light, and clear as wind.

### II

Dark-brow'd sophist, come not anear;
    All the place is holy ground;

Hollow smile and frozen sneer
   Come not here.
  Holy water will I pour
  Into every spicy flower
Of the laurel-shrubs that hedge it around.
The flowers would faint at your cruel
    cheer.
  In your eye there is death,
  There is frost in your breath
  Which would blight the plants.
  Where you stand you cannot hear
    From the groves within
    The wild-bird's din.
In the heart of the garden the merry bird
    chants.
It would fall to the ground if you came in.
  In the middle leaps a fountain
    Like sheet lightning,
    Ever brightening
With a low melodious thunder;
All day and all night it is ever drawn
  From the brain of the purple mountain
Which stands in the distance yonder.
It springs on a level of bowery lawn,
And the mountain draws it from heaven
    above,
And it sings a song of undying love;
And yet, tho' its voice be so clear and full,
You never would hear it, your ears are so
    dull;
So keep where you are; you are foul with
    sin;
It would shrink to the earth if you came in.

## THE SEA–FAIRIES

First printed in 1830, but suppressed until
1853, when it appeared, with many changes, in
the 8th edition of the ' Poems.'

SLOW sail'd the weary mariners and saw,
Betwixt the green brink and the running
    foam,
Sweet faces, rounded arms, and bosoms
    prest
To little harps of gold; and while they
    mused,
Whispering to each other half in fear,
Shrill music reach'd them on the middle
    sea.

Whither away, whither away, whither
    away ? fly no more.
Whither away from the high green field,
  and the happy blossoming shore ?

Day and night to the billow the fountain
    calls;
Down shower the gambolling waterfalls   10
From wandering over the lea;
Out of the live-green heart of the dells
They freshen the silvery-crimson shells,
And thick with white bells the clover-hill
    swells
High over the full-toned sea.
O, hither, come hither and furl your sails,
Come hither to me and to me;
Hither, come hither and frolic and play;
Here it is only the mew that wails;
We will sing to you all the day.      20
Mariner, mariner, furl your sails,
For here are the blissful downs and dales,
And merrily, merrily carol the gales,
And the spangle dances in bight and bay,
And the rainbow forms and flies on the
    land
Over the islands free;
And the rainbow lives in the curve of the
    sand;
Hither, come hither and see;
And the rainbow hangs on the poising
    wave,
And sweet is the color of cove and cave,   30
And sweet shall your welcome be.
O, hither, come hither, and be our lords,
For merry brides are we.
We will kiss sweet kisses, and speak sweet
    words;
O, listen, listen, your eyes shall glisten
With pleasure and love and jubilee.
O, listen, listen, your eyes shall glisten
When the sharp clear twang of the golden
    chords
Runs up the ridged sea.
Who can light on as happy a shore     40
All the world o'er, all the world o'er ?
Whither away ? listen and stay; mariner,
    mariner, fly no more.

## THE DESERTED HOUSE

First printed in 1830, omitted in 1842, but
afterwards restored without change.

### I

LIFE and Thought have gone away
    Side by side,
  Leaving door and windows wide;
Careless tenants they !

## II

All within is dark as night:
In the windows is no light;
And no murmur at the door,
So frequent on its hinge before.

## III

Close the door, the shutters close,
　　Or thro' the windows we shall see
　　The nakedness and vacancy
Of the dark deserted house.

## IV

Come away; no more of mirth
　　Is here or merry-making sound.
The house was builded of the earth,
　　And shall fall again to ground.

## V

Come away; for Life and Thought
　　Here no longer dwell,
But in a city glorious —
A great and distant city — have bought
　　A mansion incorruptible.
Would they could have stayed with us !

## THE DYING SWAN

### I

THE plain was grassy, wild and bare,
Wide, wild, and open to the air,
Which had built up everywhere
　　An under-roof of doleful gray.
With an inner voice the river ran,
Adown it floated a dying swan,
　　And loudly did lament.
It was the middle of the day.
Ever the weary wind went on,
　　And took the reed-tops as it went.　10

### II

Some blue peaks in the distance rose,
And white against the cold-white sky
Shone out their crowning snows.
　　One willow over the river wept,
And shook the wave as the wind did sigh;
Above in the wind was the swallow,
　　Chasing itself at its own wild will,
　　And far thro' the marish green and
　　　still
The tangled water-courses slept,
Shot over with purple, and green, and
　　yellow.　20

## III

The wild swan's death-hymn took the soul
Of that waste place with joy
Hidden in sorrow.　At first to the ear
The warble was low, and full and clear;
And floating about the under-sky,
Prevailing in weakness, the coronach stole
Sometimes afar, and sometimes anear;
But anon her awful jubilant voice,
With a music strange and manifold,
Flow'd forth on a carol free and bold;　30
As when a mighty people rejoice
With shawms, and with cymbals, and harps
　　of gold,
And the tumult of their acclaim is roll'd
Thro' the open gates of the city afar,
To the shepherd who watcheth the evening
　　star.
And the creeping mosses and clambering
　　weeds,
And the willow-branches hoar and dank,
And the wavy swell of the soughing reeds,
And the wave-worn horns of the echoing
　　bank,
And the silvery marish - flowers that
　　throng　40
The desolate creeks and pools among,
Were flooded over with eddying song.

## A DIRGE

### I

Now is done thy long day's work;
Fold thy palms across thy breast,
Fold thine arms, turn to thy rest.
　　Let them rave.
Shadows of the silver birk
Sweep the green that folds thy grave.
　　Let them rave.

### II

Thee nor carketh care nor slander;
Nothing but the small cold worm
Fretteth thine enshrouded form.
　　Let them rave.
Light and shadow ever wander
O'er the green that folds thy grave.
　　Let them rave.

### III

Thou wilt not turn upon thy bed;
Chaunteth not the brooding bee
Sweeter tones than calumny ?
　　Let them rave.

Thou wilt never raise thine head
From the green that folds thy grave.
Let them rave.

### IV

Crocodiles wept tears for thee;
The woodbine and eglatere
Drip sweeter dews than traitor's tear.
Let them rave.
Rain makes music in the tree
O'er the green that folds thy grave.
Let them rave.

### V

Round thee blow, self-pleached deep,
Bramble roses, faint and pale,
And long purples of the dale.
Let them rave.
These in every shower creep
Thro' the green that folds thy grave.
Let them rave.

### VI

The gold-eyed kingcups fine,
The frail bluebell peereth over
Rare broidery of the purple clover.
Let them rave.
Kings have no such couch as thine,
As the green that folds thy grave.
Let them rave.

### VII

Wild words wander here and there;
God's great gift of speech abused
Makes thy memory confused;
But let them rave.
The balm-cricket carols clear
In the green that folds thy grave.
Let them rave.

## LOVE AND DEATH

WHAT time the mighty moon was gather-
    ing light
Love paced the thymy plots of Paradise,
And all about him roll'd his lustrous eyes;
When, turning round a cassia, full in view,
Death, walking all alone beneath a yew,
And talking to himself, first met his sight.
'You must begone,' said Death, 'these
    walks are mine.'
Love wept and spread his sheeny vans for
    flight;
Yet ere he parted said, 'This hour is thine;

Thou art the shadow of life, and as the
    tree
Stands in the sun and shadows all beneath,
So in the light of great eternity
Life eminent creates the shade of death.
The shadow passeth when the tree shall
    fall,
But I shall reign for ever over all.'

## THE BALLAD OF ORIANA

MY heart is wasted with my woe,
    Oriana.
There is no rest for me below,
    Oriana.
When the long dun wolds are ribb'd with
    snow,
And loud the Norland whirlwinds blow,
    Oriana,
Alone I wander to and fro,
    Oriana.

Ere the light on dark was growing,    10
    Oriana,
At midnight the cock was crowing,
    Oriana;
Winds were blowing, waters flowing,
We heard the steeds to battle going,
    Oriana,
Aloud the hollow bugle blowing,
    Oriana.

In the yew-wood black as night,
    Oriana,                           20
Ere I rode into the fight,
    Oriana,
While blissful tears blinded my sight
By star-shine and by moonlight,
    Oriana,
I to thee my troth did plight,
    Oriana.

She stood upon the castle wall,
    Oriana;
She watch'd my crest among them all,    30
    Oriana;
She saw me fight, she heard me call,
When forth there stept a foeman tall,
    Oriana,
Atween me and the castle wall,
    Oriana.

The bitter arrow went aside,
    Oriana;

The false, false arrow went aside,
 Oriana;                                  40
The damned arrow glanced aside,
And pierced thy heart, my love, my bride,
 Oriana !
Thy heart, my life, my love, my bride,
 Oriana !

O, narrow, narrow was the space,
 Oriana !
Loud, loud rung out the bugle's brays,
 Oriana.
O, deathful stabs were dealt apace,      50
The battle deepen'd in its place,
 Oriana;
But I was down upon my face,
 Oriana.

They should have stabb'd me where I lay,
 Oriana !
How could I rise and come away,
 Oriana ?
How could I look upon the day ?
They should have stabb'd me where I lay,
 Oriana —                                 61
They should have trod me into clay,
 Oriana.

O breaking heart that will not break,
 Oriana !
O pale, pale face so sweet and meek,
 Oriana !
Thou smilest, but thou dost not speak,
And then the tears run down my cheek,
 Oriana.                                  70
What wantest thou ? whom dost thou seek,
 Oriana ?

I cry aloud; none hear my cries,
 Oriana.
Thou comest atween me and the skies,
 Oriana.
I feel the tears of blood arise
Up from my heart unto my eyes,
 Oriana.
Within thy heart my arrow lies,          80
 Oriana.

O cursed hand !  O cursed blow !
 Oriana !
O happy thou that liest low,
 Oriana !
All night the silence seems to flow
Beside me in my utter woe,
 Oriana.

A weary, weary way I go,
 Oriana !                                 90

When Norland winds pipe down the sea,
 Oriana,
I walk, I dare not think of thee,
 Oriana.
Thou liest beneath the greenwood tree,
I dare not die and come to thee,
 Oriana.
I hear the roaring of the sea,
 Oriana.

## CIRCUMSTANCE

Two children in two neighbor villages
Playing mad pranks along the heathy leas;
Two strangers meeting at a festival;
Two lovers whispering by an orchard wall;
Two lives bound fast in one with golden
 ease;
Two graves grass - green beside a gray
 church-tower,
Wash'd with still rains and daisy - blos-
 somed;
Two children in one hamlet born and bred:
So runs the round of life from hour to
 hour.

## THE MERMAN

### I

WHO would be
A merman bold,
Sitting alone,
Singing alone
Under the sea,
With a crown of gold,
On a throne ?

### II

I would be a merman bold,
I would sit and sing the whole of the day;
I would fill the sea-halls with a voice of
 power;
But at night I would roam abroad and
 play
With the mermaids in and out of the rocks,
Dressing their hair with the white sea-
 flower;
And holding them back by their flowing
 locks
I would kiss them often under the sea,

And kiss them again till they kiss'd me
  Laughingly, laughingly;
And then we would wander away, away,
To the pale-green sea-groves straight and
  high,
  Chasing each other merrily.

### III

There would be neither moon nor star;
But the wave would make music above us
  afar —
Low thunder and light in the magic night —
  Neither moon nor star.
We would call aloud in the dreamy dells,
Call to each other and whoop and cry
  All night, merrily, merrily.
They would pelt me with starry spangles
  and shells,
Laughing and clapping their hands be-
  tween,
  All night, merrily, merrily,
But I would throw to them back in mine
Turkis and agate and almondine;
Then leaping out upon them unseen
I would kiss them often under the sea,
And kiss them again till they kiss'd me
  Laughingly, laughingly.
O, what a happy life were mine
Under the hollow-hung ocean green!
Soft are the moss-beds under the sea;
We would live merrily, merrily.

## THE MERMAID

### I

Who would be
A mermaid fair,
Singing alone,
Combing her hair
Under the sea,
In a golden curl
With a comb of pearl,
On a throne?

### II

I would be a mermaid fair;
I would sing to myself the whole of the day;
With a comb of pearl I would comb my
  hair;
And still as I comb'd I would sing and say,
'Who is it loves me? who loves not me?'
I would comb my hair till my ringlets
  would fall
    Low adown, low adown,

From under my starry sea-bud crown
    Low adown and around,
And I should look like a fountain of gold
    Springing alone
    With a shrill inner sound,
    Over the throne
    In the midst of the hall;
Till that great sea-snake under the sea
From his coiled sleeps in the central deeps
Would slowly trail himself sevenfold
Round the hall where I sate, and look in at
  the gate
With his large calm eyes for the love of
  me.
And all the mermen under the sea
Would feel their immortality
Die in their hearts for the love of me.

### III

But at night I would wander away, away,
  I would fling on each side my low-flow-
    ing locks,
And lightly vault from the throne and play
  With the mermen in and out of the
    rocks;
We would run to and fro, and hide and
  seek,
  On the broad sea-wolds in the crimson
    shells,
Whose silvery spikes are nighest the sea.
But if any came near I would call, and
  shriek,
And adown the steep like a wave I would
  leap
  From the diamond-ledges that jut from
    the dells;
For I would not be kiss'd by all who would
  list
Of the bold merry mermen under the sea.
They would sue me, and woo me, and flat-
  ter me,
In the purple twilights under the sea;
But the king of them all would carry me,
Woo me, and win me, and marry me,
In the branching jaspers under the sea.
Then all the dry pied things that be
In the hueless mosses under the sea
Would curl round my silver feet silently,
All looking up for the love of me.
And if I should carol aloud, from aloft
All things that are forked, and horned, and
  soft
Would lean out from the hollow sphere of
  the sea,
All looking down for the love of me.

## ADELINE

### I

MYSTERY of mysteries,
  Faintly smiling Adeline,
  Scarce of earth nor all divine,
Nor unhappy, nor at rest,
  But beyond expression fair
  With thy floating flaxen hair;
Thy rose-lips and full blue eyes
  Take the heart from out my breast.
Wherefore those dim looks of thine,
Shadowy, dreaming Adeline?

### II

Whence that aery bloom of thine,
  Like a lily which the sun
Looks thro' in his sad decline,
  And a rose-bush leans upon,
Thou that faintly smilest still,
  As a Naiad in a well,
  Looking at the set of day,
Or a phantom two hours old
  Of a maiden past away,
Ere the placid lips be cold?
Wherefore those faint smiles of thine,
  Spiritual Adeline?

### III

What hope or fear or joy is thine?
Who talketh with thee, Adeline?
  For sure thou art not all alone.
  Do beating hearts of salient springs
Keep measure with thine own?
  Hast thou heard the butterflies
  What they say betwixt their wings?
  Or in stillest evenings
With what voice the violet woos
To his heart the silver dews?
  Or when little airs arise,
How the merry bluebell rings
  To the mosses underneath?
Hast thou look'd upon the breath
  Of the lilies at sunrise?
Wherefore that faint smile of thine,
Shadowy, dreaming Adeline?

### IV

Some honey-converse feeds thy mind,
  Some spirit of a crimson rose
  In love with thee forgets to close
His curtains, wasting odorous sighs
All night long on darkness blind.
What aileth thee? whom waitest thou

With thy soften'd, shadow'd brow,
  And those dew-lit eyes of thine,
  Thou faint smiler, Adeline?

### V

Lovest thou the doleful wind
  When thou gazest at the skies?
Doth the low-tongued Orient
  Wander from the side of the morn,
  Dripping with Sabæan spice
On thy pillow, lowly bent
  With melodious airs lovelorn,
Breathing Light against thy face,
While his locks a-drooping twined
Round thy neck in subtle ring
Make a carcanet of rays,
  And ye talk together still,
In the language wherewith Spring
  Letters cowslips on the hill?
Hence that look and smile of thine,
  Spiritual Adeline.

## MARGARET

First printed in 1833; reprinted with slight
changes (see Notes) in 1842.

### I

O SWEET pale Margaret,
O rare pale Margaret,
What lit your eyes with tearful power,
Like moonlight on a falling shower?
Who lent you, love, your mortal dower
  Of pensive thought and aspect pale,
  Your melancholy sweet and frail
As perfume of the cuckoo flower?
From the westward-winding flood,
From the evening-lighted wood,
  From all things outward you have
    won
A tearful grace, as tho' you stood
Between the rainbow and the sun.
The very smile before you speak,
That dimples your transparent cheek,
  Encircles all the heart, and feedeth
The senses with a still delight
  Of dainty sorrow without sound,
  Like the tender amber round
  Which the moon about her spreadeth
Moving thro' a fleecy night.

### II

You love, remaining peacefully,
  To hear the murmur of the strife,

But enter not the toil of life.
Your spirit is the calmed sea,
    Laid by the tumult of the fight.
You are the evening star, alway
    Remaining betwixt dark and bright;
Lull'd echoes of laborious day
    Come to you, gleams of mellow light
    Float by you on the verge of night.

### III

What can it matter, Margaret,
    What songs below the waning stars
The lion-heart, Plantagenet,
    Sang looking thro' his prison bars ?
Exquisite Margaret, who can tell
The last wild thought of Chatelet,
    Just ere the falling axe did part
    The burning brain from the true heart,
Even in her sight he loved so well ?

### IV

A fairy shield your Genius made
    And gave you on your natal day.
Your sorrow, only sorrow's shade,
    Keeps real sorrow far away.
You move not in such solitudes,
    You are not less divine,
But more human in your moods,
    Than your twin-sister, Adeline.
Your hair is darker, and your eyes
    Touch'd with a somewhat darker hue,
    And less aërially blue,
    But ever trembling thro' the dew
Of dainty-woeful sympathies.

### V

O sweet pale Margaret,
    O rare pale Margaret,
Come down, come down, and hear me
        speak.
Tie up the ringlets on your cheek.
    The sun is just about to set,
The arching limes are tall and shady,
    And faint, rainy lights are seen,
    Moving in the leavy beech.
Rise from the feast of sorrow, lady,
    Where all day long you sit between
    Joy and woe, and whisper each.
Or only look across the lawn,
    Look out below your bower-eaves,
Look down, and let your blue eyes dawn
    Upon me thro' the jasmine-leaves.

## ROSALIND

Printed in 1833, but suppressed until 1884.
See Notes.

### I

My Rosalind, my Rosalind,
My frolic falcon, with bright eyes,
Whose free delight, from any height of
        rapid flight,
Stoops at all game that wing the skies,
My Rosalind, my Rosalind,
My bright-eyed, wild-eyed falcon, whither,
Careless both of wind and weather,
Whither fly ye, what game spy ye,
Up or down the streaming wind ?

### II

The quick lark's closest-caroll'd strains,
The shadow rushing up the sea,
The lightning flash atween the rains,
The sunlight driving down the lea,
The leaping stream, the very wind,
That will not stay, upon his way,
To stoop the cowslip to the plains,
Is not so clear and bold and free
As you, my falcon Rosalind.
You care not for another's pains,
Because you are the soul of joy,
Bright metal all without alloy.
Life shoots and glances thro' your veins,
And flashes off a thousand ways,
Thro' lips and eyes in subtle rays.
Your hawk-eyes are keen and bright,
Keen with triumph, watching still
To pierce me thro' with pointed light;
But oftentimes they flash and glitter
Like sunshine on a dancing rill,
And your words are seeming-bitter,
Sharp and few, but seeming-bitter
From excess of swift delight.

### III

Come down, come home, my Rosalind,
My gay young hawk, my Rosalind.
Too long you keep the upper skies;
Too long you roam and wheel at will;
But we must hood your random eyes,
That care not whom they kill,
And your cheek, whose brilliant hue
Is so sparkling-fresh to view,
Some red heath-flower in the dew,
Touch'd with sunrise.   We must bind
And keep you fast, my Rosalind,
Fast, fast, my wild-eyed Rosalind,

And clip your wings, and make you love.
When we have lured you from above,
And that delight of frolic flight, by day or
    night,
From North to South,
We'll bind you fast in silken cords,
And kiss away the bitter words
From off your rosy mouth.


ELEÄNORE

Reprinted in 1842 from the 1833 volume.
See Notes.

I

THY dark eyes open'd not,
    Nor first reveal'd themselves to English
    air,
For there is nothing here
Which, from the outward to the inward
    brought,
Moulded thy baby thought.
Far off from human neighborhood
    Thou wert born, on a summer morn,
A mile beneath the cedar-wood.
Thy bounteous forehead was not fann'd
    With breezes from our oaken glades, 10
But thou wert nursed in some delicious
    land
Of lavish lights, and floating shades;
And flattering thy childish thought
The oriental fairy brought,
    At the moment of thy birth,
From old well-heads of haunted rills,
And the hearts of purple hills,
And shadow'd coves on a sunny shore,
    The choicest wealth of all the earth,
Jewel or shell, or starry ore,           20
To deck thy cradle, Eleänore.


II

Or the yellow-banded bees,
Thro' half-open lattices
Coming in the scented breeze,
Fed thee, a child, lying alone,
    With whitest honey in fairy gardens
    cull'd —
A glorious child, dreaming alone,
In silk-soft folds, upon yielding down,
With the hum of swarming bees
    Into dreamful slumber lull'd.           30


III

Who may minister to thee?
Summer herself should minister

To thee, with fruitage golden-rinded
On golden salvers, or it may be,
Youngest Autumn, in a bower
Grape-thicken'd from the light, and blinded
With many a deep-hued bell-like flower
Of fragrant trailers, when the air
Sleepeth over all the heaven,
And the crag that fronts the even,        40
    All along the shadowing shore,
Crimsons over an inland mere,
        Eleänore!


IV

How may full-sail'd verse express,
    How may measured words adore
The full-flowing harmony
Of thy swan-like stateliness,
        Eleänore?
The luxuriant symmetry
Of thy floating gracefulness,             50
        Eleänore?
Every turn and glance of thine,
Every lineament divine,
        Eleänore,
    And the steady sunset glow
That stays upon thee? For in thee
Is nothing sudden, nothing single;
Like two streams of incense free
From one censer in one shrine,
Thought and motion mingle,               60
Mingle ever. Motions flow
To one another, even as tho'
They were modulated so
To an unheard melody,
Which lives about thee, and a sweep
    Of richest pauses, evermore
Drawn from each other mellow-deep;
    Who may express thee, Eleänore?


V

I stand before thee, Eleänore;
    I see thy beauty gradually unfold,    70
Daily and hourly, more and more.
I muse, as in a trance, the while
    Slowly, as from a cloud of gold,
Comes out thy deep ambrosial smile.
I muse, as in a trance, whene'er
    The languors of thy love-deep eyes
Float on to me. I would I were
    So tranced, so rapt in ecstasies,
To stand apart, and to adore,
Gazing on thee for evermore,             80
Serene, imperial Eleänore!

## VI

Sometimes, with most intensity
Gazing, I seem to see
Thought folded over thought, smiling
    asleep,
Slowly awaken'd, grow so full and deep
In thy large eyes that, overpower'd quite,
I cannot veil or droop my sight,
But am as nothing in its light.
As tho' a star, in inmost heaven set,
Even while we gaze on it,       90
Should slowly round his orb, and slowly grow
To a full face, there like a sun remain
Fix'd — then as slowly fade again,
    And draw itself to what it was before;
So full, so deep, so slow,
Thought seems to come and go
    In thy large eyes, imperial Eleänore.

## VII

As thunder-clouds that, hung on high,
Roof'd the world with doubt and fear,
Floating thro' an evening atmosphere,    100
Grow golden all about the sky;
In thee all passion becomes passionless,
Touch'd by thy spirit's mellowness,
Losing his fire and active might
    In a silent meditation,
Falling into a still delight,
    And luxury of contemplation.
As waves that up a quiet cove
    Rolling slide, and lying still
    Shadow forth the banks at will,    110
Or sometimes they swell and move,
    Pressing up against the land
    With motions of the outer sea;
And the self-same influence
Controlleth all the soul and sense
    Of Passion gazing upon thee.
His bow-string slacken'd, languid Love,
    Leaning his cheek upon his hand,
    Droops both his wings, regarding thee,
And so would languish evermore,    120
Serene, imperial Eleänore.

## VIII

But when I see thee roam, with tresses un-
    confined,
While the amorous odorous wind
Breathes low between the sunset and the
    moon;
Or, in a shadowy saloon,
On silken cushions half reclined;
    I watch thy grace, and in its place

My heart a charmed slumber keeps,
    While I muse upon thy face;
And a languid fire creeps    130
    Thro' my veins to all my frame,
Dissolvingly and slowly. Soon
    From thy rose-red lips MY name
Floweth; and then, as in a swoon,
With dinning sound my ears are rife,
    My tremulous tongue faltereth,
    I lose my color, I lose my breath,
    I drink the cup of a costly death,
Brimm'd with delirious draughts of warm-
    est life.
I die with my delight before    140
    I hear what I would hear from thee;
    Yet tell my name again to me,
I *would* be dying evermore,
    So dying ever, Eleänore.

## KATE

First printed in 1833, but suppressed until
*after the poet's death*, and not included in any
authorized edition until 1897.

I KNOW her by her angry air,
Her bright black eyes, her bright black
    hair,
    Her rapid laughters wild and shrill,
As laughters of the woodpecker
    From the bosom of a hill.
'T is Kate — she sayeth what she will;
For Kate hath an unbridled tongue,
    Clear as the twanging of a harp.
    Her heart is like a throbbing star.
Kate hath a spirit ever strung
    Like a new bow, and bright and sharp
    As edges of the scimitar.
Whence shall she take a fitting mate?
    For Kate no common love will feel;
My woman-soldier, gallant Kate,
    As pure and true as blades of steel.

Kate saith 'the world is void of might.'
Kate saith 'the men are gilded flies.'
    Kate snaps her fingers at my vows;
Kate will not hear of lovers' sighs.
I would I were an armed knight,
Far-famed for well-won enterprise,
    And wearing on my swarthy brows
The garland of new-wreathed emprise;
    For in a moment I would pierce
The blackest files of clanging fight,
And strongly strike to left and right,

In dreaming of my lady's eyes.
O, Kate loves well the bold and fierce;
But none are bold enough for Kate,
She cannot find a fitting mate.

## 'MY LIFE IS FULL OF WEARY DAYS'

First printed in 1833, with the heading, 'To
——.' The first two stanzas were not reprinted
until 1865, when they appeared in the volume of
'Selections' in their present form. The next
three stanzas were added later. See Notes.

My life is full of weary days,
  But good things have not kept aloof,
Nor wander'd into other ways;
  I have not lack'd thy mild reproof,
Nor golden largess of thy praise.

And now shake hands across the brink
  Of that deep grave to which I go,
Shake hands once more; I cannot sink
  So far — far down, but I shall know
Thy voice, and answer from below.

When in the darkness over me
  The four-handed mole shall scrape,
Plant thou no dusky cypress-tree,
  Nor wreathe thy cap with doleful crape,
But pledge me in the flowing grape.

And when the sappy field and wood
  Grow green beneath the showery gray,
And rugged barks begin to bud,
  And thro' damp holts new-flush'd with may,
Ring sudden scritches of the jay,

Then let wise Nature work her will,
  And on my clay her darnel grow;
Come only, when the days are still,
  And at my headstone whisper low,
  And tell me if the woodbines blow.

## EARLY SONNETS

### I

#### TO ——

This and the third sonnet were in the 1833
volume, but were suppressed in 1842.

As when with downcast eyes we muse and
    brood,
And ebb into a former life, or seem

To lapse far back in some confused dream
To states of mystical similitude,
If one but speaks or hems or stirs his chair,
Ever the wonder waxeth more and more,
So that we say, 'All this hath been before,
All this hath been, I know not when or
    where;'
So, friend, when first I look'd upon your
    face,
Our thought gave answer each to each, so
    true —
Opposed mirrors each reflecting each —
That, tho' I knew not in what time or place,
Methought that I had often met with you,
And either lived in either's heart and
    speech.

### II

#### TO J. M. K.

Reprinted in 1842 from the 1830 volume.
Addressed to John Mitchell Kemble (1807–
1857) who was a fellow-student of the poet at
Cambridge.

My hope and heart is with thee — thou wilt
    be
A latter Luther, and a soldier-priest
To scare church-harpies from the master's
    feast;
Our dusted velvets have much need of
    thee:
Thou art no Sabbath-drawler of old saws,
Distill'd from some worm-canker'd homily;
But spurr'd at heart with fieriest energy
To embattail and to wall about thy cause
With iron-worded proof, hating to hark
The humming of the drowsy pulpit-drone
Half God's good Sabbath, while the worn-
    out clerk
Brow-beats his desk below. Thou from a
    throne
Mounted in heaven wilt shoot into the dark
Arrows of lightnings. I will stand and
    mark.

### III

Mine be the strength of spirit, full and
    free,
Like some broad river rushing down alone,
With the selfsame impulse wherewith he
    was thrown
From his loud fount upon the echoing
    lea; —
Which with increasing might doth forward
    flee

By town, and tower, and hill, and cape, and
    isle,
And in the middle of the green salt sea
Keeps his blue waters fresh for many a
    mile.
Mine be the power which ever to its sway
Will win the wise at once, and by degrees
May into uncongenial spirits flow;
Even as the warm gulf-stream of Florida
Floats far away into the Northern seas
The lavish growths of southern Mexico.

## IV

### ALEXANDER

First published in the 'Library Edition' of
the 'Poems' in 1872.

WARRIOR of God, whose strong right arm
    debased
The throne of Persia, when her Satrap
    bled
At Issus by the Syrian gates, or fled
Beyond the Memmian naphtha-pits, dis-
    graced
For ever — thee (thy pathway sand-erased)
Gliding with equal crowns two serpents led
Joyful to that palm-planted fountain-fed
Ammonian Oasis in the waste.
There in a silent shade of laurel brown
Apart the Chamian Oracle divine
Shelter'd his unapproached mysteries:
High things were spoken there, unhanded
    down ;
Only they saw thee from the secret shrine
Returning with hot cheek and kindled eyes.

## V

### BUONAPARTE

This sonnet and the next were in the 1833
volume, but were suppressed in 1842.

HE thought to quell the stubborn hearts of
    oak,
Madman ! — to chain with chains, and bind
    with bands
That island queen who sways the floods and
    lands
From Ind to Ind, but in fair daylight woke,
When from her wooden walls, — lit by sure
    hands, —
With thunders, and with lightnings, and
    with smoke, —

Peal after peal, the British battle broke,
Lulling the brine against the Coptic sands.
We taught him lowlier moods, when Elsi-
    nore
Heard the war moan along the distant sea,
Rocking with shatter'd spars, with sudden
    fires
Flamed over; at Trafalgar yet once more
We taught him; late he learned humility
Perforce, like those whom Gideon school'd
    with briers.

## VI

### POLAND

How long, O God, shall men be ridden
    down,
And trampled under by the last and least
Of men ?  The heart of Poland hath not
    ceased
To quiver, tho' her sacred blood doth
    drown
The fields, and out of every smouldering
    town
Cries to Thee, lest brute Power be in-
    creased,
Till that o'ergrown Barbarian in the East
Transgress his ample bound to some new
    crown, —
Cries to Thee, ' Lord, how long shall these
    things be ?
How long this icy-hearted Muscovite
Oppress the region ? ' Us, O Just and
    Good,
Forgive, who smiled when she was torn in
    three ;
Us, who stand now, when we should aid the
    right —
A matter to be wept with tears of blood !

## VII

This sonnet and the two that follow were
first printed in the 'Selections' of 1865, with
the heading, 'Three Sonnets to a Coquette.'

CARESS'D or chidden by the slender hand,
And singing airy trifles this or that,
Light Hope at Beauty's call would perch
    and stand,
And run thro' every change of sharp and
    flat ;
And Fancy came and at her pillow sat,
When Sleep had bound her in his rosy
    band,

And chased away the still-recurring gnat,
And woke her with a lay from fairy land.
But now they live with Beauty less and
    less,
For Hope is other Hope and wanders far,
Nor cares to lisp in love's delicious creeds;
And Fancy watches in the wilderness,
Poor Fancy sadder than a single star,
That sets at twilight in a land of reeds.

### VIII

THE form, the form alone is eloquent !
A nobler yearning never broke her rest
Than but to dance and sing, be gaily drest,
And win all eyes with all accomplishment;
Yet in the whirling dances as we went,
My fancy made me for a moment blest
To find my heart so near the beauteous
    breast
That once had power to rob it of content.
A moment came the tenderness of tears,
The phantom of a wish that once could
    move,
A ghost of passion that no smiles re-
    store —
For ah ! the slight coquette, she cannot
    love,
And if you kiss'd her feet a thousand
    years,
She still would take the praise, and care no
    more.

### IX

WAN Sculptor, weepest thou to take the
    cast
Of those dead lineaments that near thee lie ?
O, sorrowest thou, pale Painter, for the
    past,
In painting some dead friend from mem-
    ory ?
Weep on ; beyond his object Love can
    last.
His object lives; more cause to weep
    have I :
My tears, no tears of love, are flowing fast,
No tears of love, but tears that Love can
    die.
I pledge her not in any cheerful cup,
Nor care to sit beside her where she sits —
Ah ! pity — hint it not in human tones,
But breathe it into earth and close it up
With secret death for ever, in the pits
Which some green Christmas crams with
    weary bones.

### X

Printed in 1833, but suppressed in 1842.

IF I were loved, as I desire to be,
What is there in the great sphere of the
    earth,
And range of evil between death and birth,
That I should fear, — if I were loved by
    thee ?
All the inner, all the outer world of pain
Clear Love would pierce and cleave, if thou
    wert mine,
As I have heard that, somewhere in the
    main,
Fresh-water springs come up through bitter
    brine.
'T were joy, not fear, claspt hand-in-hand
    with thee,
To wait for death — mute — careless of all
    ills,
Apart upon a mountain, tho' the surge
Of some new deluge from a thousand hills
Flung leagues of roaring foam into the
    gorge
Below us, as far on as eye could see.

### XI

### THE BRIDESMAID

First printed in 1872.

O BRIDESMAID, ere the happy knot was
    tied,
Thine eyes so wept that they could hardly
    see;
Thy sister smiled and said, ' No tears for
    me !
A happy bridesmaid makes a happy bride.'
And then, the couple standing side by side,
Love lighted down between them full of
    glee,
And over his left shoulder laugh'd at thee,
' O happy bridesmaid, make a happy bride.'
And all at once a pleasant truth I learn'd,
For while the tender service made thee
    weep,
I loved thee for the tear thou couldst not
    hide,
And prest thy hand, and knew the press
    return'd,
And thought, ' My life is sick of single
    sleep:
O happy bridesmaid, make a happy bride !'

# THE LADY OF SHALOTT

## AND OTHER POEMS

This heading does not represent a separate published volume, but is found as a division of the poems in the editions of 1884 and the more recent ones.

## THE LADY OF SHALOTT

First published in 1833, and much altered in 1842. See Notes.

### PART I

On either side the river lie
Long fields of barley and of rye,
That clothe the wold and meet the sky;
And thro' the field the road runs by
　　To many-tower'd Camelot;
And up and down the people go,
Gazing where the lilies blow
Round an island there below,
　　The island of Shalott.

Willows whiten, aspens quiver,　　　　10
Little breezes dusk and shiver
Thro' the wave that runs for ever
By the island in the river
　　Flowing down to Camelot.
Four gray walls, and four gray towers,
Overlook a space of flowers,
And the silent isle imbowers
　　The Lady of Shalott.

By the margin, willow-veil'd,
Slide the heavy barges trail'd　　　　20
By slow horses; and unhail'd
The shallop flitteth silken-sail'd
　　Skimming down to Camelot:
But who hath seen her wave her hand?
Or at the casement seen her stand?
Or is she known in all the land,
　　The Lady of Shalott?

Only reapers, reaping early
In among the bearded barley,
Hear a song that echoes cheerly　　　30
From the river winding clearly,
　　Down to tower'd Camelot;
And by the moon the reaper weary,
Piling sheaves in uplands airy,
Listening, whispers ' 'T is the fairy
　　Lady of Shalott.'

### PART II

There she weaves by night and day
A magic web with colors gay.
She has heard a whisper say,
A curse is on her if she stay　　　　40
　　To look down to Camelot.
She knows not what the curse may be,
And so she weaveth steadily,
And little other care hath she,
　　The Lady of Shalott.

And moving thro' a mirror clear
That hangs before her all the year,
Shadows of the world appear.
There she sees the highway near
　　Winding down to Camelot;　　　50
There the river eddy whirls,
And there the surly village-churls,
And the red cloaks of market girls,
　　Pass onward from Shalott.

Sometimes a troop of damsels glad,
An abbot on an ambling pad,
Sometimes a curly shepherd-lad,
Or long-hair'd page in crimson clad,
　　Goes by to tower'd Camelot;
And sometimes thro' the mirror blue　　60
The knights come riding two and two:
She hath no loyal knight and true,
　　The Lady of Shalott.

But in her web she still delights
To weave the mirror's magic sights,
For often thro' the silent nights
A funeral, with plumes and lights
　　And music, went to Camelot;
Or when the moon was overhead,
Came two young lovers lately wed:　　70
'I am half sick of shadows,' said
　　The Lady of Shalott.

### PART III

A bow-shot from her bower-eaves,
He rode between the barley-sheaves,

The sun came dazzling thro' the leaves,
And flamed upon the brazen greaves
    Of bold Sir Lancelot.
A red-cross knight for ever kneel'd
To a lady in his shield,
That sparkled on the yellow field,       80
    Beside remote Shalott.

The gemmy bridle glitter'd free,
Like to some branch of stars we see
Hung in the golden Galaxy.
The bridle bells rang merrily
    As he rode down to Camelot;
And from his blazon'd baldric slung
A mighty silver bugle hung,
And as he rode his armor rung,
    Beside remote Shalott.       90

All in the blue unclouded weather
Thick-jewell'd shone the saddle-leather,
The helmet and the helmet-feather
Burn'd like one burning flame together,
    As he rode down to Camelot;
As often thro' the purple night,
Below the starry clusters bright,
Some bearded meteor, trailing light,
    Moves over still Shalott.       99

His broad clear brow in sunlight glow'd;
On burnish'd hooves his war-horse trode;
From underneath his helmet flow'd
His coal-black curls as on he rode,
    As he rode down to Camelot.
From the bank and from the river
He flash'd into the crystal mirror,
'Tirra lirra,' by the river
    Sang Sir Lancelot.

She left the web, she left the loom,
She made three paces thro' the room,       110
She saw the water-lily bloom,
She saw the helmet and the plume,
    She look'd down to Camelot.
Out flew the web and floated wide;
The mirror crack'd from side to side;
'The curse is come upon me,' cried
    The Lady of Shalott.

PART IV

In the stormy east-wind straining,
The pale yellow woods were waning,
The broad stream in his banks complaining,
Heavily the low sky raining       121
    Over tower'd Camelot;

Down she came and found a boat
Beneath a willow left afloat,
And round about the prow she wrote
    *The Lady of Shalott.*

And down the river's dim expanse
Like some bold seër in a trance,
Seeing all his own mischance —
With a glassy countenance       130
    Did she look to Camelot.
And at the closing of the day
She loosed the chain, and down she lay;
The broad stream bore her far away,
    The Lady of Shalott.

Lying, robed in snowy white
That loosely flew to left and right —
The leaves upon her falling light —
Thro' the noises of the night
    She floated down to Camelot;       140
And as the boat-head wound along
The willowy hills and fields among,
They heard her singing her last song,
    The Lady of Shalott.

Heard a carol, mournful, holy,
Chanted loudly, chanted lowly,
Till her blood was frozen slowly,
And her eyes were darken'd wholly,
    Turn'd to tower'd Camelot.
For ere she reach'd upon the tide       150
The first house by the water-side,
Singing in her song she died,
    The Lady of Shalott.

Under tower and balcony,
By garden-wall and gallery,
A gleaming shape she floated by,
Dead-pale between the houses high,
    Silent into Camelot.
Out upon the wharfs they came,
Knight and burgher, lord and dame,       160
And round the prow they read her name,
    *The Lady of Shalott.*

Who is this? and what is here?
And in the lighted palace near
Died the sound of royal cheer;
And they cross'd themselves for fear,
    All the knights at Camelot:
But Lancelot mused a little space;
He said, 'She has a lovely face;
God in his mercy lend her grace,       170
    The Lady of Shalott.'

## MARIANA IN THE SOUTH

First printed in 1833, but changed so much
in 1842 that we give the original form in full
in the Notes.

WITH one black shadow at its feet,
  The house thro' all the level shines,
Close-latticed to the brooding heat,
  And silent in its dusty vines;
A faint-blue ridge upon the right,
  An empty river-bed before,
And shallows on a distant shore,
In glaring sand and inlets bright.
      But ' Ave Mary,' made she moan,    9
        And ' Ave Mary,' night and morn,
        And ' Ah,' she sang, ' to be all alone,
          To live forgotten, and love forlorn.'

She, as her carol sadder grew,
  From brow and bosom slowly down
Thro' rosy taper fingers drew
  Her streaming curls of deepest brown
To left and right, and made appear
  Still-lighted in a secret shrine
  Her melancholy eyes divine,
The home of woe without a tear.    20
      And ' Ave Mary,' was her moan,
        ' Madonna, sad is night and morn,'
        And ' Ah,' she sang, ' to be all alone,
          To live forgotten, and love forlorn.'

Till all the crimson changed, and past
  Into deep orange o'er the sea,
Low on her knees herself she cast,
  Before Our Lady murmur'd she;
Complaining, ' Mother, give me grace
  To help me of my weary load.'    30
And on the liquid mirror glow'd
  The clear perfection of her face.
      ' Is this the form,' she made her moan,
        ' That won his praises night and
          morn ? '
        And ' Ah,' she said, ' but I wake alone,
          I sleep forgotten, I wake forlorn.'

Nor bird would sing, nor lamb would bleat,
  Nor any cloud would cross the vault,
But day increased from heat to heat,
  On stony drought and steaming salt;    40
Till now at noon she slept again,
  And seem'd knee - deep in mountain
    grass,
  And heard her native breezes pass,
And runlets babbling down the glen.

She breathed in sleep a lower moan,
  And murmuring, as at night and
    morn,
She thought, ' My spirit is here alone,
  Walks forgotten, and is forlorn.'

Dreaming, she knew it was a dream;
  She felt he was and was not there.    50
She woke; the babble of the stream
  Fell, and, without, the steady glare
Shrank one sick willow sere and small.
  The river-bed was dusty-white;
  And all the furnace of the light
Struck up against the blinding wall.
      She whisper'd, with a stifled moan
        More inward than at night or morn,
        'Sweet Mother, let me not here alone
          Live forgotten and die forlorn.'    60

And, rising, from her bosom drew
  Old letters, breathing of her worth,
For ' Love,' they said, ' must needs be true,
  To what is loveliest upon earth.'
An image seem'd to pass the door,
  To look at her with slight, and say
  ' But now thy beauty flows away,
So be alone for evermore.'
      ' O cruel heart,' she changed her tone,
        ' And cruel love, whose end is scorn,
        Is this the end, to be left alone,    71
          To live forgotten, and die forlorn ? '

But sometimes in the falling day
  An image seem'd to pass the door,
To look into her eyes and say,
  ' But thou shalt be alone no more.'
And flaming downward over all
  From heat to heat the day decreased,
  And slowly rounded to the east
The one black shadow from the wall.    80
      ' The day to night,' she made her
        moan,
        ' The day to night, the night to
          morn,
        And day and night I am left alone
          To live forgotten, and love forlorn.'

At eve a dry cicala sung,
  There came a sound as of the sea;
Backward the lattice-blind she flung,
  And lean'd upon the balcony.
There all in spaces rosy-bright
  Large Hesper glitter'd on her tears,    90
  And deepening thro' the silent spheres
Heaven over heaven rose the night.

And weeping then she made her moan,
' The night comes on that knows not
    morn,
When I shall cease to be all alone,
    To live forgotten, and love forlorn.'


## THE TWO VOICES

Written in a period (1833) of great depression consequent upon the death of his sister.

A still small voice spake unto me,
' Thou art so full of misery,
Were it not better not to be ?'

Then to the still small voice I said:
' Let me not cast in endless shade
What is so wonderfully made.'

To which the voice did urge reply:
' To-day I saw the dragon-fly
Come from the wells where he did lie.

' An inner impulse rent the veil      10
Of his old husk; from head to tail
Came out clear plates of sapphire mail.

' He dried his wings; like gauze they grew;
Thro' crofts and pastures wet with dew
A living flash of light he flew.'

I said: ' When first the world began,
Young Nature thro' five cycles ran,
And in the sixth she moulded man.

' She gave him mind, the lordliest
Proportion, and, above the rest,      20
Dominion in the head and breast.'

Thereto the silent voice replied:
' Self-blinded are you by your pride;
Look up thro' night; the world is wide.

' This truth within thy mind rehearse,
That in a boundless universe
Is boundless better, boundless worse.

' Think you this mould of hopes and fears
Could find no statelier than his peers
In yonder hundred million spheres ?'      30

It spake, moreover, in my mind:
' Tho' thou wert scatter'd to the wind,
Yet is there plenty of the kind.'

Then did my response clearer fall:
' No compound of this earthly ball
Is like another, all in all.'

To which he answer'd scoffingly:
' Good soul ! suppose I grant it thee,
Who 'll weep for thy deficiency ?

' Or will one beam be less intense,      40
When thy peculiar difference
Is cancell'd in the world of sense ?'

I would have said, ' Thou canst not know,'
But my full heart, that work'd below,
Rain'd thro' my sight its overflow.

Again the voice spake unto me:
' Thou art so steep'd in misery,
Surely 't were better not to be.

' Thine anguish will not let thee sleep,
Nor any train of reason keep;      50
Thou canst not think, but thou wilt weep.'

I said: ' The years with change advance;
If I make dark my countenance,
I shut my life from happier chance.

' Some turn this sickness yet might take,
Even yet.'   But he: ' What drug can make
A wither'd palsy cease to shake ?'

I wept: ' Tho' I should die, I know
That all about the thorn will blow
In tufts of rosy-tinted snow;      60

' And men, thro' novel spheres of thought
Still moving after truth long sought,
Will learn new things when I am not.'

' Yet,' said the secret voice, ' some time,
Sooner or later, will gray prime
Make thy grass hoar with early rime.

' Not less swift souls that yearn for light,
Rapt after heaven's starry flight,
Would sweep the tracts of day and night.

' Not less the bee would range her cells,   70
The furzy prickle fire the dells,
The foxglove cluster dappled bells.'

I said that ' all the years invent;
Each month is various to present
The world with some development.

' Were this not well, to bide mine hour,
Tho' watching from a ruin'd tower
How grows the day of human power ?'

' The highest-mounted mind,' he said,
' Still sees the sacred morning spread   80
The silent summit overhead.

' Will thirty seasons render plain
Those lonely lights that still remain,
Just breaking over land and main ?

' Or make that morn, from his cold crown
And crystal silence creeping down,
Flood with full daylight glebe and town ?

' Forerun thy peers, thy time, and let
Thy feet, millenniums hence, be set
In midst of knowledge, dream'd not yet. 90

' Thou hast not gain'd a real height,
Nor art thou nearer to the light,
Because the scale is infinite.

' 'T were better not to breathe or speak,
Than cry for strength, remaining weak,
And seem to find, but still to seek.

' Moreover, but to seem to find
Asks what thou lackest, thought resign'd,
A healthy frame, a quiet mind.'

I said: ' When I am gone away,   100
" He dared not tarry," men will say,
Doing dishonor to my clay.'

' This is more vile,' he made reply,
' To breathe and loathe, to live and sigh,
Than once from dread of pain to die.

' Sick art thou — a divided will
Still heaping on the fear of ill
The fear of men, a coward still.

' Do men love thee ?   Art thou so bound
To men that how thy name may sound   110
Will vex thee lying underground ?

' The memory of the wither'd leaf
In endless time is scarce more brief
Than of the garner'd autumn-sheaf.

' Go, vexed spirit, sleep in trust;
The right ear that is fill'd with dust
Hears little of the false or just.'

' Hard task, to pluck resolve,' I cried,
' From emptiness and the waste wide
Of that abyss, or scornful pride !   120

' Nay — rather yet that I could raise
One hope that warm'd me in the days
While still I yearn'd for human praise.

' When, wide in soul and bold of tongue,
Among the tents I paused and sung,
The distant battle flash'd and rung.

' I sung the joyful Pæan clear,
And, sitting, burnish'd without fear
The brand, the buckler, and the spear —

' Waiting to strive a happy strife,   130
To war with falsehood to the knife,
And not to lose the good of life —

' Some hidden principle to move,
To put together, part and prove,
And mete the bounds of hate and love —

' As far as might be, to carve out
Free space for every human doubt,
That the whole mind might orb about —

' To search thro' all I felt or saw,
The springs of life, the depths of awe,   140
And reach the law within the law;

' At least, not rotting like a weed,
But, having sown some generous seed,
Fruitful of further thought and deed,

' To pass, when Life her light withdraws,
Not void of righteous self-applause,
Nor in a merely selfish cause —

' In some good cause, not in mine own,
To perish, wept for, honor'd, known,
And like a warrior overthrown;   150

' Whose eyes are dim with glorious tears,
When, soil'd with noble dust, he hears
His country's war-song thrill his ears:

' Then dying of a mortal stroke,
What time the foeman's line is broke,
And all the war is roll'd in smoke.'

' Yea !' said the voice, ' thy dream was good,
While thou abodest in the bud.
It was the stirring of the blood.

'If Nature put not forth her power    160
About the opening of the flower,
Who is it that could live an hour?

'Then comes the check, the change, the fall,
Pain rises up, old pleasures pall.
There is one remedy for all.

'Yet hadst thou, thro' enduring pain,
Link'd month to month with such a chain
Of knitted purport, all were vain.

'Thou hadst not between death and birth
Dissolved the riddle of the earth.    170
So were thy labor little worth.

'That men with knowledge merely play'd,
I told thee — hardly nigher made,
Tho' scaling slow from grade to grade;

'Much less this dreamer, deaf and blind,
Named man, may hope some truth to find,
That bears relation to the mind.

'For every worm beneath the moon
Draws different threads, and late and soon
Spins, toiling out his own cocoon.    180

'Cry, faint not: either Truth is born
Beyond the polar gleam forlorn,
Or in the gateways of the morn.

'Cry, faint not, climb: the summits slope
Beyond the furthest flights of hope,
Wrapt in dense cloud from base to cope.

'Sometimes a little corner shines,
As over rainy mist inclines
A gleaming crag with belts of pines.

'I will go forward, sayest thou,    190
I shall not fail to find her now.
Look up, the fold is on her brow.

'If straight thy track, or if oblique,
Thou know'st not.   Shadows thou dost
     strike,
Embracing cloud, Ixion-like;

'And owning but a little more
Than beasts, abidest lame and poor,
Calling thyself a little lower

'Than angels.   Cease to wail and brawl!
Why inch by inch to darkness crawl?    200
There is one remedy for all.'

'O dull, one-sided voice,' said I,
'Wilt thou make everything a lie,
To flatter me that I may die?

'I know that age to age succeeds,
Blowing a noise of tongues and deeds,
A dust of systems and of creeds.

'I cannot hide that some have striven,
Achieving calm, to whom was given
The joy that mixes man with Heaven;    210

'Who, rowing hard against the stream,
Saw distant gates of Eden gleam,
And did not dream it was a dream;

'But heard, by secret transport led,
Even in the charnels of the dead,
The murmur of the fountain-head —

'Which did accomplish their desire,
Bore and forebore, and did not tire,
Like Stephen, an unquenched fire.

'He heeded not reviling tones,    220
Nor sold his heart to idle moans,
Tho' cursed and scorn'd, and bruised with
     stones;

'But looking upward, full of grace,
He pray'd, and from a happy place
God's glory smote him on the face.'

The sullen answer slid betwixt:
'Not that the grounds of hope were fix'd,
The elements were kindlier mix'd.'

I said: 'I toil beneath the curse,
But, knowing not the universe,    230
I fear to slide from bad to worse;

'And that, in seeking to undo
One riddle, and to find the true,
I knit a hundred others new;

'Or that this anguish fleeting hence,
Unmanacled from bonds of sense,
Be fix'd and frozen to permanence:

'For I go, weak from suffering here;
Naked I go, and void of cheer:
What is it that I may not fear?'    240

'Consider well,' the voice replied,
'His face, that two hours since hath died;
Wilt thou find passion, pain or pride?

'Will he obey when one commands?
Or answer should one press his hands?
He answers not, nor understands.

'His palms are folded on his breast;
There is no other thing express'd
But long disquiet merged in rest.

'His lips are very mild and meek;          250
Tho' one should smite him on the cheek,
And on the mouth, he will not speak.

'His little daughter, whose sweet face
He kiss'd, taking his last embrace,
Becomes dishonor to her race —

'His sons grow up that bear his name,
Some grow to honor, some to shame, —
But he is chill to praise or blame.

'He will not hear the north-wind rave,
Nor, moaning, household shelter crave    260
From winter rains that beat his grave.

'High up the vapors fold and swim;
About him broods the twilight dim;
The place he knew forgetteth him.'

'If all be dark, vague voice,' I said,
'These things are wrapt in doubt and dread,
Nor canst thou show the dead are dead.

'The sap dries up: the plant declines.
A deeper tale my heart divines.
Know I not death? the outward signs? 270

'I found him when my years were few;
A shadow on the graves I knew,
And darkness in the village yew.

'From grave to grave the shadow crept;
In her still place the morning wept;
Touch'd by his feet the daisy slept.

'The simple senses crown'd his head:
"Omega! thou art Lord," they said,
"We find no motion in the dead!"

'Why, if man rot in dreamless ease,      280
Should that plain fact, as taught by these,
Not make him sure that he shall cease?

'Who forged that other influence,
That heat of inward evidence,
By which he doubts against the sense?

'He owns the fatal gift of eyes,
That read his spirit blindly wise,
Not simple as a thing that dies.

'Here sits he shaping wings to fly;
His heart forebodes a mystery;          290
He names the name Eternity.

'That type of Perfect in his mind
In Nature can he nowhere find.
He sows himself on every wind.

'He seems to hear a Heavenly Friend,
And thro' thick veils to apprehend
A labor working to an end.

'The end and the beginning vex
His reason: many things perplex,
With motions, checks, and counterchecks.

'He knows a baseness in his blood        301
At such strange war with something good,
He may not do the thing he would.

'Heaven opens inward, chasms yawn,
Vast images in glimmering dawn,
Half shown, are broken and withdrawn.

'Ah! sure within him and without,
Could his dark wisdom find it out,
There must be answer to his doubt,

'But thou canst answer not again.        310
With thine own weapon art thou slain,
Or thou wilt answer but in vain.

'The doubt would rest, I dare not solve.
In the same circle we revolve.
Assurance only breeds resolve.'

As when a billow, blown against,
Falls back, the voice with which I fenced
A little ceased, but recommenced:

'Where wert thou when thy father play'd
In his free field, and pastime made,     320
A merry boy in sun and shade?

'A merry boy they call'd him then,
He sat upon the knees of men
In days that never come again;

'Before the little ducts began
To feed thy bones with lime, and ran
Their course, till thou wert also man:

' Who took a wife, who rear'd his race,
Whose wrinkles gather'd on his face,
Whose troubles number with his days;    330

' A life of nothings, nothing worth,
From that first nothing ere his birth
To that last nothing under earth ! '

' These words,' I said, ' are like the rest;
No certain clearness, but at best
A vague suspicion of the breast:

' But if I grant, thou mightst defend
The thesis which thy words intend —
That to begin implies to end;

' Yet how should I for certain hold,    340
Because my memory is so cold,
That I first was in human mould ?

' I cannot make this matter plain,
But I would shoot, howe'er in vain,
A random arrow from the brain.

' It may be that no life is found,
Which only to one engine bound
Falls off, but cycles always round.

' As old mythologies relate,
Some draught of Lethe might await    350
The slipping thro' from state to state;

' As here we find in trances, men
Forget the dream that happens then,
Until they fall in trance again;

' So might we, if our state were such
As one before, remember much,
For those two likes might meet and touch.

' But, if I lapsed from nobler place,
Some legend of a fallen race
Alone might hint of my disgrace;    360

' Some vague emotion of delight
In gazing up an Alpine height,
Some yearning toward the lamps of night;

' Or if thro' lower lives I came—
Tho' all experience past became
Consolidate in mind and frame —

' I might forget my weaker lot;
For is not our first year forgot ?
The haunts of memory echo not.

' And men, whose reason long was blind,
From cells of madness unconfined,    371
Oft lose whole years of darker mind.

' Much more, if first I floated free,
As naked essence, must I be
Incompetent of memory;

' For memory dealing but with time,
And he with matter, could she climb
Beyond her own material prime ?

' Moreover, something is or seems,
That touches me with mystic gleams,    380
Like glimpses of forgotten dreams —

' Of something felt, like something here;
Of something done, I know not where;
Such as no language may declare.'

The still voice laugh'd.    ' I talk,' said he,
' Not with thy dreams.    Suffice it thee
Thy pain is a reality.'

' But thou,' said I, ' hast missed thy mark,
Who sought'st to wreck my mortal ark,
By making all the horizon dark.    390

' Why not set forth, if I should do
This rashness, that which might ensue
With this old soul in organs new ?

' Whatever crazy sorrow saith,
No life that breathes with human breath
Has ever truly long'd for death.

' 'T is life, whereof our nerves are scant,
O, life, not death, for which we pant;
More life, and fuller, that I want.'

I ceased, and sat as one forlorn.    400
Then said the voice, in quiet scorn,
' Behold, it is the Sabbath morn.'

And I arose, and I released
The casement, and the light increased
With freshness in the dawning east.

Like soften'd airs that blowing steal,
When meres begin to uncongeal,
The sweet church bells began to peal.

On to God's house the people prest;
Passing the place where each must rest,
Each enter'd like a welcome guest.    411

One walk'd between his wife and child,
With measured footfall firm and mild,
And now and then he gravely smiled.

The prudent partner of his blood
Lean'd on him, faithful, gentle, good,
Wearing the rose of womanhood.

And in their double love secure,
The little maiden walk'd demure,
Pacing with downward eyelids pure.          420

These three made unity so sweet,
My frozen heart began to beat,
Remembering its ancient heat.

I blest them, and they wander'd on;
I spoke, but answer came there none;
The dull and bitter voice was gone.

A second voice was at mine ear,
A little whisper silver-clear,
A murmur, ' Be of better cheer.'

As from some blissful neighborhood,        430
A notice faintly understood,
' I see the end, and know the good.'

A little hint to solace woe,
A hint, a whisper breathing low,
' I may not speak of what I know.'

Like an Æolian harp that wakes
No certain air, but overtakes
Far thought with music that it makes;

Such seem'd the whisper at my side:
' What is it thou knowest, sweet voice ? '
I cried.                                    440
' A hidden hope,' the voice replied;

So heavenly-toned, that in that hour
From out my sullen heart a power
Broke, like the rainbow from the shower,

To feel, altho' no tongue can prove,
That every cloud, that spreads above
And veileth love, itself is love.

And forth into the fields I went,
And Nature's living motion lent
The pulse of hope to discontent.            450

I wonder'd at the bounteous hours,
The slow result of winter showers;
You scarce could see the grass for flowers.

I wonder'd, while I paced along;
The woods were fill'd so full with song,
There seem'd no room for sense of wrong;

And all so variously wrought,
I marvell'd how the mind was brought
To anchor by one gloomy thought ;

And wherefore rather I made choice          460
To commune with that barren voice,
Than him that said, ' Rejoice ! Rejoice ! '


## THE MILLER'S DAUGHTER

First printed in 1833, but much changed in
1842.  See Notes.

I SEE the wealthy miller yet,
   His double chin, his portly size,
And who that knew him could forget
   The busy wrinkles round his eyes ?
The slow wise smile that, round about
   His dusty forehead drily curl'd,
Seem'd half-within and half-without,
   And full of dealings with the world ?

In yonder chair I see him sit,             9
   Three fingers round the old silver cup —
I see his gray eyes twinkle yet
   At his own jest — gray eyes lit up
With summer lightnings of a soul
   So full of summer warmth, so glad,
So healthy, sound, and clear and whole,
   His memory scarce can make me sad.

Yet fill my glass; give me one kiss:
   My own sweet Alice, we must die.
There 's somewhat in this world amiss
   Shall be unriddled by and by.            20
There 's somewhat flows to us in life,
   But more is taken quite away.
Pray, Alice, pray, my darling wife,
   That we may die the self-same day.

Have I not found a happy earth ?
   I least should breathe a thought of pain.
Would God renew me from my birth,
   I 'd almost live my life again;

So sweet it seems with thee to walk,
  And once again to woo thee mine —    30
It seems in after-dinner talk
  Across the walnuts and the wine —

To be the long and listless boy
  Late-left an orphan of the squire,
Where this old mansion mounted high
  Looks down upon the village spire;
For even here, where I and you
  Have lived and loved alone so long,
Each morn my sleep was broken thro'
  By some wild skylark's matin song.    40

And oft I heard the tender dove
  In firry woodlands making moan;
But ere I saw your eyes, my love,
  I had no motion of my own.
For scarce my life with fancy play'd
  Before I dream'd that pleasant dream —
Still hither thither idly sway'd
  Like those long mosses in the stream.

Or from the bridge I lean'd to hear
  The milldam rushing down with noise, 50
And see the minnows everywhere
  In crystal eddies glance and poise,
The tall flag-flowers when they sprung
  Below the range of stepping-stones,
Or those three chestnuts near, that hung
  In masses thick with milky cones.

But, Alice, what an hour was that,
  When after roving in the woods
('T was April then), I came and sat
  Below the chestnuts, when their buds    60
Were glistening to the breezy blue;
  And on the slope, an absent fool,
I cast me down, nor thought of you,
  But angled in the higher pool.

A love-song I had somewhere read,
  An echo from a measured strain,
Beat time to nothing in my head
  From some odd corner of the brain.
It haunted me, the morning long,
  With weary sameness in the rhymes,    70
The phantom of a silent song,
  That went and came a thousand times.

Then leapt a trout.  In lazy mood
  I watch'd the little circles die;
They past into the level flood,
  And there a vision caught my eye;

The reflex of a beauteous form,
  A glowing arm, a gleaming neck,
As when a sunbeam wavers warm
  Within the dark and dimpled beck.    80

For you remember, you had set,
  That morning, on the casement-edge
A long green box of mignonette,
  And you were leaning from the ledge;
And when I raised my eyes, above
  They met with two so full and bright —
Such eyes ! I swear to you, my love,
  That these have never lost their light.

I loved, and love dispell'd the fear
  That I should die an early death;    90
For love possess'd the atmosphere,
  And fill'd the breast with purer breath.
My mother thought, What ails the boy ?
  For I was alter'd, and began
To move about the house with joy,
  And with the certain step of man.

I loved the brimming wave that swam
  Thro' quiet meadows round the mill,
The sleepy pool above the dam,
  The pool beneath it never still,    100
The meal-sacks on the whiten'd floor,
  The dark round of the dripping wheel,
The very air about the door
  Made misty with the floating meal.

And oft in ramblings on the wold,
  When April nights began to blow,
And April's crescent glimmer'd cold,
  I saw the village lights below;
I knew your taper far away,
  And full at heart of trembling hope,    110
From off the wold I came, and lay
  Upon the freshly-flower'd slope.

The deep brook groan'd beneath the mill;
  And 'by that lamp,' I thought, 'she sits !'
The white chalk-quarry from the hill
  Gleam'd to the flying moon by fits.
'O, that I were beside her now !
  O, will she answer if I call ?
O, would she give me vow for vow,
  Sweet Alice, if I told her all ? '    120

Sometimes I saw you sit and spin;
  And, in the pauses of the wind,
Sometimes I heard you sing within;
  Sometimes your shadow cross'd the blind.

At last you rose and moved the light,
  And the long shadow of the chair
Flitted across into the night,
  And all the casement darken'd there.

But when at last I dared to speak,
  The lanes, you know, were white with
      may;                                    130
Your ripe lips moved not, but your cheek
  Flush'd like the coming of the day;
And so it was — half-sly, half-shy,
  You would, and would not, little one !
Although I pleaded tenderly,
  And you and I were all alone.

And slowly was my mother brought
  To yield consent to my desire:
She wish'd me happy, but she thought
  I might have look'd a little higher;     140
And I was young — too young to wed:
  'Yet must I love her for your sake;
Go fetch your Alice here,' she said:
  Her eyelid quiver'd as she spake.

And down I went to fetch my bride:
  But, Alice, you were ill at ease;
This dress and that by turns you tried,
  Too fearful that you should not please.
I loved you better for your fears,
  I knew you could not look but well;     150
And dews, that would have fallen in tears,
  I kiss'd away before they fell.

I watch'd the little flutterings,
  The doubt my mother would not see;
She spoke at large of many things,
  And at the last she spoke of me;
And turning look'd upon your face,
  As near this door you sat apart,
And rose, and, with a silent grace        159
  Approaching, press'd you heart to heart.

Ah, well — but sing the foolish song
  I gave you, Alice, on the day
When, arm in arm, we went along,
  A pensive pair, and you were gay
With bridal flowers — that I may seem,
  As in the nights of old, to lie
Beside the mill-wheel in the stream,
  While those full chestnuts whisper by.

  It is the miller's daughter,
    And she is grown so dear, so dear,    170
  That I would be the jewel
    That trembles in her ear;

For hid in ringlets day and night,
  I'd touch her neck so warm and white.

And I would be the girdle
  About her dainty dainty waist,
And her heart would beat against me,
  In sorrow and in rest;
And I should know if it beat right,
  I'd clasp it round so close and tight.  180

And I would be the necklace,
  And all day long to fall and rise
Upon her balmy bosom,
  With her laughter or her sighs;
And I would lie so light, so light,
  I scarce should be unclasp'd at night.

A trifle, sweet ! which true love spells —
  True love interprets — right alone.
His light upon the letter dwells,
  For all the spirit is his own.          190
So, if I waste words now, in truth
  You must blame Love.   His early rage
Had force to make me rhyme in youth,
  And makes me talk too much in age.

And now those vivid hours are gone,
  Like mine own life to me thou art,
Where Past and Present, wound in one,
  Do make a garland for the heart;
So sing that other song I made,
  Half-anger'd with my happy lot,        200
The day, when in the chestnut shade
  I found the blue forget-me-not.

    Love that hath us in the net,
      Can he pass, and we forget ?
    Many suns arise and set;
    Many a chance the years beget;
    Love the gift is Love the debt.
        Even so.
    Love is hurt with jar and fret;
    Love is made a vague regret;          210
    Eyes with idle tears are wet;
    Idle habit links us yet.
    What is love ? for we forget:
        Ah, no ! no !

Look thro' mine eyes with thine.   True
      wife,
  Round my true heart thine arms entwine;
My other dearer life in life,
  Look thro' my very soul with thine !
Untouch'd with any shade of years,
  May those kind eyes for ever dwell !    220
They have not shed a many tears,
  Dear eyes, since first I knew them well.

Yet tears they shed; they had their part
  Of sorrow; for when time was ripe,
The still affection of the heart
  Became an outward breathing type,
That into stillness past again,
  And left a want unknown before;
Although the loss had brought us pain,
  That loss but made us love the more,  230

With farther lookings on.  The kiss,
  The woven arms, seem but to be
Weak symbols of the settled bliss,
  The comfort, I have found in thee;
But that God bless thee, dear — who
      wrought
  Two spirits to one equal mind —
With blessings beyond hope or thought,
  With blessings which no words can find.

Arise, and let us wander forth
  To yon old mill across the wolds;  240
For look, the sunset, south and north,
  Winds all the vale in rosy folds,
And fires your narrow casement glass,
  Touching the sullen pool below;
On the chalk-hill the bearded grass
  Is dry and dewless.  Let us go.

## FATIMA

Reprinted in 1842 from the volume of 1833,
where, instead of the present title, it has for
heading the following quotation :

Φαινεταί μοι κῆνος ἴσος θεοῖσιν
Ἐμμεν ἀνήρ. — SAPPHO.

O Love, Love, Love !  O withering might !
O sun, that from thy noonday height
Shudderest when I strain my sight,
Throbbing thro' all thy heat and light,
  Lo, falling from my constant mind,
  Lo, parch'd and wither'd, deaf and blind,
  I whirl like leaves in roaring wind.

Last night I wasted hateful hours
Below the city's eastern towers;
I thirsted for the brooks, the showers;
I roll'd among the tender flowers;
  I crush'd them on my breast, my mouth;
  I look'd athwart the burning drouth
  Of that long desert to the south.

Last night, when some one spoke his name,
From my swift blood that went and came
A thousand little shafts of flame
Were shiver'd in my narrow frame.

O Love, O fire ! once he drew
With one long kiss my whole soul thro'
My lips, as sunlight drinketh dew.

Before he mounts the hill, I know
He cometh quickly; from below
Sweet gales, as from deep gardens, blow
Before him, striking on my brow.
  In my dry brain my spirit soon,
  Down-deepening from swoon to swoon,
  Faints like a dazzled morning moon.

The wind sounds like a silver wire,
And from beyond the noon a fire
Is pour'd upon the hills, and nigher
The skies stoop down in their desire;
  And, isled in sudden seas of light,
  My heart, pierced thro' with fierce de-
      light,
  Bursts into blossom in his sight.

My whole soul waiting silently,
All naked in a sultry sky,
Droops blinded with his shining eye;
I *will* possess him or will die.
  I will grow round him in his place,
  Grow, live, die looking on his face,
  Die, dying clasp'd in his embrace.

## ŒNONE

First printed in 1833, but materially altered
in 1842.  See Notes.

THERE lies a vale in Ida, lovelier
Than all the valleys of Ionian hills.
The swimming vapor slopes athwart the
    glen,
Puts forth an arm, and creeps from pine to
    pine,
And loiters, slowly drawn.  On either
    hand
The lawns and meadow-ledges midway
    down
Hang rich in flowers, and far below them
    roars
The long brook falling thro' the cloven
    ravine
In cataract after cataract to the sea.
Behind the valley topmost Gargarus    10
Stands up and takes the morning; but in
    front
The gorges, opening wide apart, reveal
Troas and Ilion's column'd citadel,
The crown of Troas.

Hither came at noon
Mournful Œnone, wandering forlorn
Of Paris, once her playmate on the hills.
Her cheek had lost the rose, and round her
    neck
Floated her hair or seem'd to float in rest.
She, leaning on a fragment twined with
    vine,
Sang to the stillness, till the mountain-
    shade                                    20
Sloped downward to her seat from the
    upper cliff.

' O mother Ida, many-fountain'd Ida,
Dear mother Ida, harken ere I die.
For now the noonday quiet holds the hill;
The grasshopper is silent in the grass;
The lizard, with his shadow on the stone,
Rests like a shadow, and the winds are
    dead.
The purple flower droops, the golden bee
Is lily-cradled; I alone awake
My eyes are full of tears, my heart of
    love,                                    30
My heart is breaking, and my eyes are dim,
And I am all aweary of my life

' O mother Ida, many-fountain'd Ida,
Dear mother Ida, harken ere I die.
Hear me, O earth, hear me, O hills, O caves
That house the cold crown'd snake ! O
    mountain brooks,
I am the daughter of a River-God,
Hear me, for I will speak, and build up all
My sorrow with my song, as yonder walls
Rose slowly to a music slowly breathed, 40
A cloud that gather'd shape; for it may be
That, while I speak of it, a little while
My heart may wander from its deeper woe.

' O mother Ida, many-fountain'd Ida,
Dear mother Ida, harken ere I die.
I waited underneath the dawning hills;
Aloft the mountain lawn was dewy-dark,
And dewy dark aloft the mountain pine.
Beautiful Paris, evil-hearted Paris,
Leading a jet-black goat white-horn'd,
    white-hooved,                           50
Came up from reedy Simois all alone.

' O mother Ida, harken ere I die.
Far-off the torrent call'd me from the cleft;
Far up the solitary morning smote
The streaks of virgin snow   With down-
    dropt eyes

I sat alone; white-breasted like a star
Fronting the dawn he moved; a leopard
    skin
Droop'd from his shoulder, but his sunny
    hair
Cluster'd about his temples like a God's;
And his cheek brighten'd as the foam-bow
    brightens                               60
When the wind blows the foam, and all my
    heart
Went forth to embrace him coming ere he
    came.

' Dear mother Ida, harken ere I die.
He smiled, and opening out his milk-white
    palm
Disclosed a fruit of pure Hesperian gold,
That smelt ambrosially, and while I look'd
And listen'd, the full-flowing river of
    speech
Came down upon my heart:
                            ' " My own Œnone,
Beautiful-brow'd Œnone, my own soul,
Behold this fruit, whose gleaming rind
    ingraven                                70
' For the most fair,' would seem to award
    it thine,
As lovelier than whatever Oread haunt
The knolls of Ida, loveliest in all grace
Of movement, and the charm of married
    brows."

' Dear mother Ida, harken ere I die.
He prest the blossom of his lips to mine,
And added, "This was cast upon the
    board,
When all the full-faced presence of the
    Gods
Ranged in the halls of Peleus; whereupon
Rose feud, with question unto whom 't were
    due;                                    80
But light-foot Iris brought it yester-eve,
Delivering, that to me, by common voice
Elected umpire, Herè comes to-day,
Pallas and Aphrodite, claiming each
This meed of fairest. Thou, within the
    cave
Behind yon whispering tuft of oldest pine,
Mayst well behold them unbeheld, unheard
Hear all, and see thy Paris judge of Gods."

' Dear mother Ida, harken ere I die.
It was the deep midnoon; one silvery
    cloud                                    90
Had lost his way between the piny sides

Of this long glen.   Then to the bower they
	came,
Naked they came to that smooth-swarded
	bower,
And at their feet the crocus brake like fire,
Violet, amaracus, and asphodel,
Lotos and lilies; and a wind arose,
And overhead the wandering ivy and vine,
This way and that, in many a wild fes-
	toon
Ran riot, garlanding the gnarled boughs
With bunch and berry and flower thro' and
	thro'.			100

' O mother Ida, harken ere I die.
On the tree-tops a crested peacock lit,
And o'er him flow'd a golden cloud, and
	lean'd
Upon him, slowly dropping fragrant dew.
Then first I heard the voice of her to
	whom
Coming thro' heaven, like a light that
	grows
Larger and clearer, with one mind the Gods
Rise up for reverence.   She to Paris made
Proffer of royal power, ample rule
Unquestion'd, overflowing revenue	110
Wherewith to embellish state, "from many
	a vale
And river-sunder'd champaign clothed with
	corn,
Or labor'd mine undrainable of ore.
Honor," she said, "and homage, tax and
	toll,
From many an inland town and haven
	large,
Mast-throng'd beneath her shadowing cita-
	del
In glassy bays among her tallest towers."

' O mother Ida, harken ere I die.
Still she spake on and still she spake of
	power,
"Which in all action is the end of all;	120
Power fitted to the season; wisdom-bred
And throned of wisdom — from all neigh-
	bor crowns
Alliance and allegiance, till thy hand
Fail from the sceptre-staff.   Such boon
	from me,
From me, heaven's queen, Paris, to thee
	king-born,
A shepherd all thy life but yet king-born,
Should come most welcome, seeing men, in
	power

Only, are likest Gods, who have attain'd
Rest in a happy place and quiet seats
Above the thunder, with undying bliss	130
In knowledge of their own supremacy."

' Dear mother Ida, harken ere I die.
She ceased, and Paris held the costly fruit
Out at arm's-length, so much the thought
	of power
Flatter'd his spirit ; but Pallas where she
	stood
Somewhat apart, her clear and bared limbs
O'erthwarted with the brazen-headed spear
Upon her pearly shoulder leaning cold,
The while, above, her full and earnest eye
Over her snow-cold breast and angry
	cheek			140
Kept watch, waiting decision, made reply :

'" Self-reverence, self-knowledge, self-
	control,
These three alone lead life to sovereign
	power.
Yet not for power (power of herself
Would come uncall'd for) but to live by
	law,
Acting the law we live by without fear;
And, because right is right, to follow right
Were wisdom in the scorn of consequence."

' Dear mother Ida, harken ere I die.
Again she said: " I woo thee not with
	gifts.			150
Sequel of guerdon could not alter me
To fairer.   Judge thou me by what I am,
So shalt thou find me fairest.
				Yet, indeed,
If gazing on divinity disrobed
Thy mortal eyes are frail to judge of fair,
Unbias'd by self-profit, O, rest thee sure
That I shall love thee well and cleave to
	thee,
So that my vigor, wedded to thy blood,
Shall strike within thy pulses, like a
	God's,			159
To push thee forward thro' a life of shocks,
Dangers, and deeds, until endurance grow
Sinew'd with action, and the full-grown
	will,
Circled thro' all experiences, pure law,
Commeasure perfect freedom."
				' Here she ceas'd,
And Paris ponder'd, and I cried, " O Paris,
Give it to Pallas ! " but he heard me not,
Or hearing would not hear me, woe is me !

'O mother Ida, many-fountain'd Ida,
Dear mother Ida, harken ere I die.
Idalian Aphrodite beautiful,                    170
Fresh as the foam, new-bathed in Paphian
    wells,
With rosy slender fingers backward drew
From her warm brows and bosom her deep
    hair
Ambrosial, golden round her lucid throat
And shoulder; from the violets her light
    foot
Shone rosy-white, and o'er her rounded
    form
Between the shadows of the vine-bunches
Floated the glowing sunlights, as she
    moved.

'Dear mother Ida, harken ere I die.
She with a subtle smile in her mild eyes, 180
The herald of her triumph, drawing nigh
Half-whisper'd in his ear, "I promise thee
The fairest and most loving wife in
    Greece."
She spoke and laugh'd; I shut my sight for
    fear;
But when I look'd, Paris had raised his
    arm,
And I beheld great Herè's angry eyes,
As she withdrew into the golden cloud,
And I was left alone within the bower;
And from that time to this I am alone,
And I shall be alone until I die.            190

'Yet, mother Ida, harken ere I die.
Fairest — why fairest wife? am I not fair?
My love hath told me so a thousand times.
Methinks I must be fair, for yesterday,
When I past by, a wild and wanton pard,
Eyed like the evening star, with playful
    tail
Crouch'd fawning in the weed.   Most lov-
    ing is she?
Ah me, my mountain shepherd, that my
    arms
Were wound about thee, and my hot lips
    prest
Close, close to thine in that quick-falling
    dew                                       200
Of fruitful kisses, thick as autumn rains
Flash in the pools of whirling Simois!

'O mother, hear me yet before I die.
They came, they cut away my tallest pines,
My tall dark pines, that plumed the craggy
    ledge

High over the blue gorge, and all between
The snowy peak and snow-white cataract
Foster'd the callow eaglet — from beneath
Whose thick mysterious boughs in the dark
    morn
The panther's roar came muffled, while I
    sat                                       210
Low in the valley.   Never, never more
Shall lone Œnone see the morning mist
Sweep thro' them; never see them over-
    laid
With narrow moonlit slips of silver cloud,
Between the loud stream and the trembling
    stars.

'O mother, hear me yet before I die.
I wish that somewhere in the ruin'd folds,
Among the fragments tumbled from the
    glens,
Or the dry thickets, I could meet with her
The Abominable, that uninvited came       220
Into the fair Peleïan banquet-hall,
And cast the golden fruit upon the board,
And bred this change; that I might speak
    my mind,
And tell her to her face how much I hate
Her presence, hated both of Gods and men.

'O mother, hear me yet before I die.
Hath he not sworn his love a thousand
    times,
In this green valley, under this green hill,
Even on this hand, and sitting on this
    stone?
Seal'd it with kisses? water'd it with
    tears?                                    230
O happy tears, and how unlike to these!
O happy heaven, how canst thou see my
    face?
O happy earth, how canst thou bear my
    weight?
O death, death, death, thou ever-floating
    cloud,
There are enough unhappy on this earth,
Pass by the happy souls, that love to live;
I pray thee, pass before my light of life,
And shadow all my soul, that I may die.
Thou weighest heavy on the heart within,
Weigh heavy on my eyelids; let me die. 240

'O mother, hear me yet before I die.
I will not die alone, for fiery thoughts
Do shape themselves within me, more and
    more,
Whereof I catch the issue, as I hear

Dead sounds at night come from the in-
    most hills,
Like footsteps upon wool.  I dimly see
My far-off doubtful purpose, as a mother
Conjectures of the features of her child
Ere it is born.  Her child! — a shudder
    comes
Across me: never child be born of me,   250
Unblest, to vex me with his father's eyes !

'O mother, hear me yet before I die.
Hear me, O earth.  I will not die alone,
Lest their shrill happy laughter come to
    me
Walking the cold and starless road of
    death
Uncomforted, leaving my ancient love
With the Greek woman.  I will rise and go
Down into Troy, and ere the stars come
    forth
Talk with the wild Cassandra, for she says
A fire dances before her, and a sound   260
Rings ever in her ears of armed men.
What this may be I know not, but I know
That, wheresoe'er I am by night and day,
All earth and air seem only burning fire.'

## THE SISTERS

Reprinted in 1842 from the 1833 volume,
with no change except 'and' for 'an'' in 'turret and tree.'

WE were two daughters of one race;
She was the fairest in the face.
    The wind is blowing in turret and tree.
They were together, and she fell;
Therefore revenge became me well.
    O, the earl was fair to see !

She died; she went to burning flame;
She mix'd her ancient blood with shame.
    The wind is howling in turret and tree.
Whole weeks and months, and early and
    late,
To win his love I lay in wait.
    O, the earl was fair to see !

I made a feast; I bade him come;
I won his love, I brought him home.
    The wind is roaring in turret and tree.
And after supper, on a bed,
Upon my lap he laid his head.
    O, the earl was fair to see !

I kiss'd his eyelids into rest,
His ruddy cheek upon my breast.
    The wind is raging in turret and tree.
I hated him with the hate of hell,
But I loved his beauty passing well.
    O, the earl was fair to see !

I rose up in the silent night;
I made my dagger sharp and bright.
    The wind is raving in turret and tree.
As half-asleep his breath he drew,
Three times I stabb'd him thro' and thro'.
    O, the earl was fair to see !

I curl'd and comb'd his comely head,
He look'd so grand when he was dead.
    The wind is blowing in turret and tree.
I wrapt his body in the sheet,
And laid him at his mother's feet.
    O, the earl was fair to see !

## TO ——

### WITH THE FOLLOWING POEM

'The Palace of Art' was printed, with this
introduction, in 1833, but was much altered in
1842 and somewhat in more recent editions.
See Notes.

I SEND you here a sort of allegory —
For you will understand it — of a soul,
A sinful soul possess'd of many gifts,
A spacious garden full of flowering weeds,
A glorious devil, large in heart and brain,
That did love beauty only — beauty seen
In all varieties of mould and mind —
And knowledge for its beauty; or if good,
Good only for its beauty, seeing not
That Beauty, Good, and Knowledge are
    three sisters
That doat upon each other, friends to man,
Living together under the same roof,
And never can be sunder'd without tears.
And he that shuts Love out, in turn shall
    be
Shut out from Love, and on her threshold
    lie
Howling in outer darkness.  Not for this
Was common clay ta'en from the common
    earth
Moulded by God, and temper'd with the
    tears
Of angels to the perfect shape of man.

## THE PALACE OF ART

I BUILT my soul a lordly pleasure-house,
   Wherein at ease for aye to dwell.
I said, ' O Soul, make merry and carouse,
   Dear soul, for all is well.'

A huge crag-platform, smooth as burnish'd
    brass,
   I chose.  The ranged ramparts bright
From level meadow-bases of deep grass
   Suddenly scaled the light.

Thereon I built it firm.  Of ledge or shelf
   The rock rose clear, or winding stair. 10
My soul would live alone unto herself
   In her high palace there.

And ' while the world runs round and
    round,' I said,
   ' Reign thou apart, a quiet king,
Still as, while Saturn whirls, his steadfast
    shade
   Sleeps on his luminous ring.'

To which my soul made answer readily:
   ' Trust me, in bliss I shall abide
In this great mansion, that is built for
    me,
   So royal-rich and wide.'     20

.   .   .   .   .   .   .

Four courts I made, East, West and South
    and North,
   In each a squared lawn, wherefrom
The golden gorge of dragons spouted forth
   A flood of fountain-foam.

And round the cool green courts there ran
    a row
   Of cloisters, branch'd like mighty woods,
Echoing all night to that sonorous flow
   Of spouted fountain-floods;

And round the roofs a gilded gallery
   That lent broad verge to distant lands, 30
Far as the wild swan wings, to where the
    sky
   Dipt down to sea and sands.

From those four jets four currents in one
    swell
   Across the mountain stream'd below
In misty folds, that floating as they fell
   Lit up a torrent-bow.

And high on every peak a statue seem'd
   To hang on tiptoe, tossing up
A cloud of incense of all odor steam'd
   From out a golden cup.     40

So that she thought, ' And who shall gaze
    upon
   My palace with unblinded eyes,
While this great bow will waver in the
    sun,
   And that sweet incense rise ? '

For that sweet incense rose and never
    fail'd,
   And, while day sank or mounted higher,
The light aerial gallery, golden-rail'd,
   Burnt like a fringe of fire.

Likewise the deep-set windows, stain'd and
    traced,
   Would seem slow-flaming crimson fires 50
From shadow'd grots of arches interlaced,
   And tipt with frost-like spires.

.   .   .   .   .   .

Full of long-sounding corridors it was,
   That over-vaulted grateful gloom,
Thro' which the livelong day my soul did
    pass,
   Well-pleased, from room to room.

Full of great rooms and small the palace
    stood,
   All various, each a perfect whole
From living Nature, fit for every mood
   And change of my still soul.     60

For some were hung with arras green and
    blue,
   Showing a gaudy summer-morn,
Where with puff'd cheek the belted hunter
    blew
   His wreathed bugle-horn.

One seem'd all dark and red — a tract of
    sand,
   And some one pacing there alone,
Who paced for ever in a glimmering land,
   Lit with a low large moon.

One show'd an iron coast and angry waves.
   You seem'd to hear them climb and
    fall
And roar rock-thwarted under bellowing
    caves,     71
   Beneath the windy wall.

And one, a full-fed river winding slow
  By herds upon an endless plain,
The ragged rims of thunder brooding low,
  With shadow-streaks of rain.

And one, the reapers at their sultry toil.
  In front they bound the sheaves.  Be-
    hind
Were realms of upland, prodigal in oil,
  And hoary to the wind.                    80

And one a foreground black with stones
    and slags;
  Beyond, a line of heights; and higher
All barr'd with long white cloud the scorn-
    ful crags;
  And highest, snow and fire.

And one, an English home — gray twilight
    pour'd
  On dewy pastures, dewy trees,
Softer than sleep — all things in order
    stored,
  A haunt of ancient Peace.

Nor these alone, but every landscape fair,
  As fit for every mood of mind,          90
Or gay, or grave, or sweet, or stern, was
    there,
  Not less than truth design'd.
      .    .    .    .    .    .    .    .

Or the maid-mother by a crucifix,
  In tracts of pasture sunny-warm,
Beneath branch-work of costly sardonyx
  Sat smiling, babe in arm.

Or in a clear-wall'd city on the sea,
  Near gilded organ-pipes, her hair
Wound with white roses, slept Saint Cecily;
  An angel look'd at her.                 100

Or thronging all one porch of Paradise
  A group of Houris bow'd to see
The dying Islamite, with hands and eyes
  That said, We wait for thee.

Or mythic Uther's deeply-wounded son
  In some fair space of sloping greens
Lay, dozing in the vale of Avalon,
  And watch'd by weeping queens.

Or hollowing one hand against his ear,
  To list a foot-fall, ere he saw          110

The wood-nymph, stay'd the Ausonian king
    to hear
  Of wisdom and of law.

Or over hills with peaky tops engrail'd,
  And many a tract of palm and rice,
The throne of Indian Cama slowly sail'd
  A summer fann'd with spice.

Or sweet Europa's mantle blew unclasp'd,
  From off her shoulder backward borne;
From one hand droop'd a crocus; one hand
    grasp'd
  The mild bull's golden horn.            120

Or else flush'd Ganymede, his rosy thigh
  Half-buried in the eagle's down,
Sole as a flying star shot thro' the sky
  Above the pillar'd town.

Nor these alone; but every legend fair
  Which the supreme Caucasian mind
Carved out of Nature for itself was there,
  Not less than life design'd.
      .    .    .    .    .    .    .    .

Then in the towers I placed great bells
    that swung,
  Moved of themselves, with silver sound;
And with choice paintings of wise men I
    hung                                   131
  The royal dais round.

For there was Milton like a seraph strong,
  Beside him Shakespeare bland and mild;
And there the world-worn Dante grasp'd
    his song,
  And somewhat grimly smiled.

And there the Ionian father of the rest;
  A million wrinkles carved his skin;
A hundred winters snow'd upon his breast,
  From cheek and throat and chin.         140

Above, the fair hall-ceiling stately-set
  Many an arch high up did lift,
And angels rising and descending met
  With interchange of gift.

Below was all mosaic choicely plann'd
  With cycles of the human tale
Of this wide world, the times of every
    land
  So wrought they will not fail.

The people here, a beast of burden slow,
  Toil'd onward, prick'd with goads and
    stings;                                150
Here play'd, a tiger, rolling to and fro
  The heads and crowns of kings;

Here rose, an athlete, strong to break or
    bind
  All force in bonds that might endure,
And here once more like some sick man
    declined,
  And trusted any cure.

But over these she trod; and those great
    bells
  Began to chime.  She took her throne;
She sat betwixt the shining oriels,
  To sing her songs alone.                 160

And thro' the topmost oriels' colored flame
  Two godlike faces gazed below;
Plato the wise, and large-brow'd Verulam,
  The first of those who know.

And all those names that in their motion
    were
  Full-welling fountain-heads of change,
Betwixt the slender shafts were blazon'd fair
  In diverse raiment strange;

Thro' which the lights, rose, amber, em-
    erald, blue,
  Flush'd in her temples and her eyes,     170
And from her lips, as morn from Memnon,
    drew
  Rivers of melodies.

No nightingale delighteth to prolong
  Her low preamble all alone,
More than my soul to hear her echo'd
    song
  Throb thro' the ribbed stone;

Singing and murmuring in her feastful
    mirth,
  Joying to feel herself alive,
Lord over Nature, lord of the visible earth,
  Lord of the senses five;                 180

Communing with herself: 'All these are
    mine,
  And let the world have peace or wars,
'T is one to me.'  She — when young night
    divine
  Crown'd dying day with stars,

Making sweet close of his delicious toils —
  Lit light in wreaths and anadems,
And pure quintessences of precious oils
  In hollow'd moons of gems,

To mimic heaven; and clapt her hands and
    cried,
  'I marvel if my still delight            190
In this great house so royal-rich and wide
  Be flatter'd to the height.

'O all things fair to sate my various eyes!
  O shapes and hues that please me well!
O silent faces of the Great and Wise,
  My Gods, with whom I dwell!

'O Godlike isolation which art mine,
  I can but count thee perfect gain,
What time I watch the darkening droves
    of swine
  That range on yonder plain.              200

'In filthy sloughs they roll a prurient
    skin,
  They graze and wallow, breed and sleep;
And oft some brainless devil enters in,
  And drives them to the deep.'

Then of the moral instinct would she prate
  And of the rising from the dead,
As hers by right of full-accomplish'd Fate;
  And at the last she said:

'I take possession of man's mind and deed.
  I care not what the sects may brawl.     210
I sit as God holding no form of creed,
  But contemplating all.'

  .    .    .    .    .    .    .    .

Full oft the riddle of the painful earth
  Flash'd thro' her as she sat alone,
Yet not the less held she her solemn mirth,
  And intellectual throne.

And so she throve and prosper'd; so three
    years
  She prosper'd; on the fourth she fell,
Like Herod, when the shout was in his
    ears,
  Struck thro' with pangs of hell.         220

Lest she should fail and perish utterly,
  God, before whom ever lie bare
The abysmal deeps of personality,
  Plagued her with sore despair.

When she would think, where'er she turn'd
        her sight
The airy hand confusion wrought,
Wrote, 'Mene, mene,' and divided quite
        The kingdom of her thought.

Deep dread and loathing of her solitude
Fell on her, from which mood was born
Scorn of herself; again, from out that
        mood                                    231
        Laughter at her self-scorn.

'What ! is not this my place of strength,'
        she said,
        'My spacious mansion built for me,
Whereof the strong foundation-stones were
        laid
        Since my first memory ?'

But in dark corners of her palace stood
        Uncertain shapes; and unawares
On white-eyed phantasms weeping tears of
        blood,
        And horrible nightmares,                240

And hollow shades enclosing hearts of
        flame,
        And, with dim fretted foreheads all,
On corpses three-months-old at noon she
        came,
        That stood against the wall.

A spot of dull stagnation, without light
        Or power of movement, seem'd my soul,
Mid onward-sloping motions infinite
        Making for one sure goal;

A still salt pool, lock'd in with bars of
        sand,
Left on the shore, that hears all night 250
The plunging seas draw backward from
        the land
        Their moon-led waters white;

A star that with the choral starry dance
        Join'd not, but stood, and standing saw
The hollow orb of moving Circumstance
        Roll'd round by one fix'd law.

Back on herself her serpent pride had
        curl'd.
'No voice,' she shriek'd in that lone hall,
'No voice breaks thro' the stillness of this
        world;
        One deep, deep silence all !'          260

She, mouldering with the dull earth's
        mouldering sod,
        Inwrapt tenfold in slothful shame,
Lay there exiled from eternal God,
        Lost to her place and name;

And death and life she hated equally,
        And nothing saw, for her despair,
But dreadful time, dreadful eternity,
        No comfort anywhere;

Remaining utterly confused with fears,
        And ever worse with growing time, 270
And ever unrelieved by dismal tears,
        And all alone in crime.

Shut up as in a crumbling tomb, girt round
        With blackness as a solid wall,
Far off she seem'd to hear the dully sound
        Of human footsteps fall:

As in strange lands a traveller walking
        slow,
        In doubt and great perplexity,
A little before moonrise hears the low
        Moan of an unknown sea;                 280

And knows not if it be thunder, or a sound
        Of rocks thrown down, or one deep cry
Of great wild beasts; then thinketh, 'I
        have found
        A new land, but I die.'

She howl'd aloud, 'I am on fire within.
        There comes no murmur of reply.
What is it that will take away my sin,
        And save me lest I die?'

So when four years were wholly finished,
        She threw her royal robes away.       290
'Make me a cottage in the vale,' she said,
        'Where I may mourn and pray.

'Yet pull not down my palace towers, that
        are
        So lightly, beautifully built;
Perchance I may return with others there
        When I have purged my guilt.'

## LADY CLARA VERE DE VERE

First printed in 1842, but written in 1833.

LADY Clara Vere de Vere,
        Of me you shall not win renown:

You thought to break a country heart
　For pastime, ere you went to town.
At me you smiled, but unbeguiled
　I saw the snare, and I retired;
The daughter of a hundred earls,
　You are not one to be desired.

Lady Clara Vere de Vere,
　I know you proud to bear your name,
Your pride is yet no mate for mine,
　Too proud to care from whence I came.
Nor would I break for your sweet sake
　A heart that dotes on truer charms.
A simple maiden in her flower
　Is worth a hundred coats-of-arms.

Lady Clara Vere de Vere,
　Some meeker pupil you must find,
For, were you queen of all that is,
　I could not stoop to such a mind.
You sought to prove how I could love,
　And my disdain is my reply.
The lion on your old stone gates
　Is not more cold to you than I.

Lady Clara Vere de Vere,
　You put strange memories in my head.
Not thrice your branching limes have
　　blown
Since I beheld young Laurence dead.
O, your sweet eyes, your low replies !
　A great enchantress you may be;
But there was that across his throat
　Which you had hardly cared to see.

Lady Clara Vere de Vere,
　When thus he met his mother's view,
She had the passions of her kind,
　She spake some certain truths of you.
Indeed I heard one bitter word
　That scarce is fit for you to hear;
Her manners had not that repose
　Which stamps the caste of Vere de
　　Vere.

Lady Clara Vere de Vere,
　There stands a spectre in your hall;
The guilt of blood is at your door;
　You changed a wholesome heart to
　　gall.
You held your course without remorse,
　To make him trust his modest worth,
And, last, you fix'd a vacant stare,
　And slew him with your noble birth.

Trust me, Clara Vere de Vere,
　From yon blue heavens above us bent
The gardener Adam and his wife
　Smile at the claims of long descent.
Howe'er it be, it seems to me,
　'T is only noble to be good.
Kind hearts are more than coronets,
　And simple faith than Norman blood.

I know you, Clara Vere de Vere,
　You pine among your halls and towers;
The languid light of your proud eyes
　Is wearied of the rolling hours.
In glowing health, with boundless wealth,
　But sickening of a vague disease,
You know so ill to deal with time,
　You needs must play such pranks as
　　these.

Clara, Clara Vere de Vere,
　If time be heavy on your hands,
Are there no beggars at your gate,
　Nor any poor about your lands ?
O, teach the orphan-boy to read,
　Or teach the orphan-girl to sew;
Pray Heaven for a human heart,
　And let the foolish yeoman go.

## THE MAY QUEEN

Printed in 1833, with the exception of the
' Conclusion,' which was added in 1842.

You must wake and call me early, call me
　　early, mother dear;
To-morrow 'ill be the happiest time of all
　　the glad New-year;
Of all the glad New-year, mother, the mad-
　　dest merriest day,
For I 'm to be Queen o' the May, mother,
　　I 'm to be Queen o' the May.

There 's many a black, black eye, they say,
　　but none so bright as mine;
There 's Margaret and Mary, there 's Kate
　　and Caroline;
But none so fair as little Alice in all the
　　land they say,
So I 'm to be Queen o' the May, mother,
　　I 'm to be Queen o' the May.

I sleep so sound all night, mother, that I
　　shall never wake,
If you do not call me loud when the day
　　begins to break;                    10

But I must gather knots of flowers, and
    buds and garlands gay,
For I 'm to be Queen o' the May, mother,
    I 'm to be Queen o' the May.

As I came up the valley whom think ye
    should I see
But Robin leaning on the bridge beneath
    the hazel-tree ?
He thought of that sharp look, mother, I
    gave him yesterday,
But I 'm to be Queen o' the May, mother,
    I 'm to be Queen o' the May.

He thought I was a ghost, mother, for I
    was all in white,
And I ran by him without speaking, like a
    flash of light.
They call me cruel-hearted, but I care not
    what they say,
For I 'm to be Queen o' the May, mother,
    I 'm to be Queen o' the May.    20

They say he 's dying all for love, but that
    can never be;
They say his heart is breaking, mother —
    what is that to me ?
There 's many a bolder lad 'ill woo me any
    summer day,
And I 'm to be Queen o' the May, mother,
    I'm to be Queen o' the May.

Little Effie shall go with me to-morrow to
    the green,
And you 'll be there, too, mother, to see
    me made the Queen;
For the shepherd lads on every side 'ill come
    from far away,
And I 'm to be Queen o' the May, mother,
    I 'm to be Queen o' the May.

The honeysuckle round the porch has
    woven its wavy bowers,
And by the meadow-trenches blow the faint
    sweet cuckoo-flowers;    30
And the wild marsh-marigold shines like
    fire in swamps and hollows gray,
And I 'm to be Queen o' the May, mother,
    I 'm to be Queen o' the May.

The night-winds come and go, mother, upon
    the meadow-grass,
And the happy stars above them seem to
    brighten as they pass;

There will not be a drop of rain the whole
    of the livelong day,
And I 'm to be Queen o' the May, mother,
    I 'm to be Queen o' the May.

All the valley, mother, 'ill be fresh and
    green and still,
And the cowslip and the crowfoot are over
    all the hill,
And the rivulet in the flowery dale 'ill mer-
    rily glance and play,
For I 'm to be Queen o' the May, mother,
    I 'm to be Queen o' the May.    40

So you must wake and call me early, call
    me early, mother dear,
To-morrow 'ill be the happiest time of all
    the glad New-year;
To-morrow 'ill be of all the year the mad-
    dest merriest day,
For I 'm to be Queen o' the May, mother,
    I 'm to be Queen o' the May.

NEW–YEAR'S EVE

IF you 're waking call me early, call me
    early, mother dear,
For I would see the sun rise upon the glad
    New-year.
It is the last New-year that I shall ever
    see,
Then you may lay me low i' the mould and
    think no more of me.

To-night I saw the sun set; he set and left
    behind
The good old year, the dear old time, and
    all my peace of mind;
And the New-year's coming up, mother,
    but I shall never see
The blossom on the blackthorn, the leaf
    upon the tree.

Last May we made a crown of flowers; we
    had a merry day;
Beneath the hawthorn on the green they
    made me Queen of May;    10
And we danced about the may-pole and in
    the hazel copse,
Till Charles's Wain came out above the tall
    white chimney-tops.

There 's not a flower on all the hills; the
    frost is on the pane.

I only wish to live till the snowdrops come
 again;
I wish the snow would melt and the sun
 come out on high;
I long to see a flower so before the day I die.

The building rook 'll caw from the windy
 tall elm-tree,
And the tufted plover pipe along the fallow lea,
And the swallow 'ill come back again with
 summer o'er the wave,
But I shall lie alone, mother, within the
 mouldering grave.   20

Upon the chancel-casement, and upon that
 grave of mine,
In the early early morning the summer sun
 'ill shine,
Before the red cock crows from the farm
 upon the hill,
When you are warm-asleep, mother, and
 all the world is still.

When the flowers come again, mother, beneath the waning light
You 'll never see me more in the long gray
 fields at night;
When from the dry dark wold the summer
 airs blow cool
On the oat-grass and the sword-grass, and
 the bulrush in the pool.

You 'll bury me, my mother, just beneath
 the hawthorn shade,
And you 'll come sometimes and see me
 where I am lowly laid.   30
I shall not forget you, mother, I shall hear
 you when you pass,
With your feet above my head in the long
 and pleasant grass.

I have been wild and wayward, but you 'll
 forgive me now;
You 'll kiss me, my own mother, and forgive me ere I go;
Nay, nay, you must not weep, nor let your
 grief be wild;
You should not fret for me, mother, you
 have another child.

If I can I 'll come again, mother, from out
 my resting-place;
Tho' you 'll not see me, mother, I shall look
 upon your face;

Tho' I cannot speak a word, I shall harken
 what you say,
And be often, often with you when you
 think I 'm far away.   40

Good-night, good-night, when I have said
 good-night for evermore,
And you see me carried out from the
 threshold of the door,
Don't let Effie come to see me till my grave
 be growing green.
She 'll be a better child to you than ever I
 have been.

She 'll find my garden-tools upon the gran-
 ary floor.
Let her take 'em, they are hers; I shall
 never garden more;
But tell her, when I 'm gone, to train the
 rosebush that I set
About the parlor-window and the box of
 mignonette.

Good-night, sweet mother; call me before
 the day is born.
All night I lie awake, but I fall asleep at
 morn;   50
But I would see the sun rise upon the glad
 New-year,
So, if you 're waking, call me, call me
 early, mother dear.

## CONCLUSION

I THOUGHT to pass away before, and yet
 alive I am;
And in the fields all round I hear the bleating of the lamb.
How sadly, I remember, rose the morning
 of the year !
To die before the snowdrop came, and now
 the violet 's here.

O, sweet is the new violet, that comes beneath the skies,
And sweeter is the young lamb's voice to
 me that cannot rise,
And sweet is all the land about, and all the
 flowers that blow,
And sweeter far is death than life to me
 that long to go.

It seem'd so hard at first, mother, to leave
 the blessed sun,

And now it seems as hard to stay, and yet
  His will be done !                10
But still I think it can't be long before I
  find release;
And that good man, the clergyman, has
  told me words of peace.

O, blessings on his kindly voice and on his
  silver hair !
And blessings on his whole life long, until
  he meet me there !
O, blessings on his kindly heart and on his
  silver head !
A thousand times I blest him, as he knelt
  beside my bed.

He taught me all the mercy, for he show'd
  me all the sin.
Now, tho' my lamp was lighted late, there's
  One will let me in;
Nor would I now be well, mother, again, if
  that could be,
For my desire is but to pass to Him that
  died for me.                20

I did not hear the dog howl, mother, or the
  death-watch beat,
There came a sweeter token when the night
  and morning meet;
But sit beside my bed, mother, and put
  your hand in mine,
And Effie on the other side, and I will tell
  the sign.

All in the wild March-morning I heard the
  angels call;
It was when the moon was setting, and the
  dark was over all;
The trees began to whisper, and the wind
  began to roll,
And in the wild March-morning I heard
  them call my soul.

For lying broad awake I thought of you
  and Effie dear;
I saw you sitting in the house, and I no
  longer here;                30
With all my strength I pray'd for both,
  and so I felt resign'd,
And up the valley came a swell of music
  on the wind.

I thought that it was fancy, and I listen'd
  in my bed,

And then did something speak to me — I
  know not what was said;
For great delight and shuddering took hold
  of all my mind,
And up the valley came again the music on
  the wind.

But you were sleeping; and I said, 'It's
  not for them, it's mine.'
And if it come three times, I thought, I
  take it for a sign.
And once again it came, and close beside
  the window-bars,
Then seem'd to go right up to heaven and
  die among the stars.                40

So now I think my time is near.   I trust it
  is.   I know
The blessed music went that way my soul
  will have to go.
And for myself, indeed, I care not if I go
  to-day;
But, Effie, you must comfort *her* when I
  am past away.

And say to Robin a kind word, and tell him
  not to fret;
There's many a worthier than I, would
  make him happy yet.
If I had lived — I cannot tell — I might
  have been his wife;
But all these things have ceased to be, with
  my desire of life.

O, look ! the sun begins to rise, the heavens
  are in a glow;
He shines upon a hundred fields, and all of
  them I know.                50
And there I move no longer now, and there
  his light may shine —
Wild flowers in the valley for other hands
  than mine.

O, sweet and strange it seems to me, that
  ere this day is done
The voice, that now is speaking, may be
  beyond the sun —
For ever and for ever with those just souls
  and true —
And what is life, that we should moan ?
  why make we such ado ?

For ever and for ever, all in a blessed
  home —

And there to wait a little while till you
    and Effie come —
To lie within the light of God, as I lie upon
    your breast —
And the wicked cease from troubling, and
    the weary are at rest.                60

## THE LOTOS-EATERS

First printed in 1833, but considerably altered in 1842.

'COURAGE!' he said, and pointed toward
    the land,
'This mounting wave will roll us shore-
    ward soon.'
In the afternoon they came unto a land
In which it seemed always afternoon.
All round the coast the languid air did
    swoon,
Breathing like one that hath a weary
    dream.
Full-faced above the valley stood the
    moon;
And, like a downward smoke, the slender
    stream
Along the cliff to fall and pause and fall
    did seem.

A land of streams! some, like a downward
    smoke,
Slow-dropping veils of thinnest lawn, did
    go;
And some thro' wavering lights and
    shadows broke,
Rolling a slumbrous sheet of foam below.
They saw the gleaming river seaward flow
From the inner land; far off, three moun-
    tain-tops,
Three silent pinnacles of aged snow,
Stood sunset-flush'd; and, dew'd with
    showery drops,
Up-clomb the shadowy pine above the
    woven copse.

The charmed sunset linger'd low adown
In the red West; thro' mountain clefts the
    dale
Was seen far inland, and the yellow down
Border'd with palm, and many a winding
    vale
And meadow, set with slender galingale;
A land where all things always seem'd the
    same!

And round about the keel with faces pale,
Dark faces pale against that rosy flame,
The mild-eyed melancholy Lotos-eaters
    came.

Branches they bore of that enchanted stem,
Laden with flower and fruit, whereof they
    gave
To each, but whoso did receive of them
And taste, to him the gushing of the wave
Far far away did seem to mourn and rave
On alien shores; and if his fellow spake,
His voice was thin, as voices from the
    grave;
And deep-asleep he seem'd, yet all awake,
And music in his ears his beating heart did
    make.

They sat them down upon the yellow sand,
Between the sun and moon upon the shore;
And sweet it was to dream of Fatherland,
Of child, and wife, and slave; but ever-
    more
Most weary seem'd the sea, weary the oar,
Weary the wandering fields of barren
    foam.
Then some one said, 'We will return no
    more;'
And all at once they sang, 'Our island
    home
Is far beyond the wave; we will no longer
    roam.'

### CHORIC SONG

#### I

THERE is sweet music here that softer falls
Than petals from blown roses on the grass,
Or night-dews on still waters between walls
Of shadowy granite, in a gleaming pass;
Music that gentlier on the spirit lies,
Than tired eyelids upon tired eyes;
Music that brings sweet sleep down from
    the blissful skies.
Here are cool mosses deep,
And thro' the moss the ivies creep,
And in the stream the long-leaved flowers
    weep,                                  10
And from the craggy ledge the poppy
    hangs in sleep.

#### II

Why are we weigh'd upon with heaviness,
And utterly consumed with sharp distress,

While all things else have rest from weari-
    ness ?
All things have rest: why should we toil
    alone,
We only toil, who are the first of things,
And make perpetual moan,
Still from one sorrow to another thrown;
Nor ever fold our wings,
And cease from wanderings,                    20
Nor steep our brows in slumber's holy
    balm;
Nor harken what the inner spirit sings,
'There is no joy but calm ! ' —
Why should we only toil, the roof and
    crown of things ?

### III

Lo ! in the middle of the wood,
The folded leaf is woo'd from out the bud
With winds upon the branch, and there
Grows green and broad, and takes no care,
Sun-steep'd at noon, and in the moon
Nightly dew-fed; and turning yellow      30
Falls, and floats adown the air.
Lo ! sweeten'd with the summer light,
The full-juiced apple, waxing over-mellow,
Drops in a silent autumn night.
All its allotted length of days
The flower ripens in its place,
Ripens and fades, and falls, and hath no
    toil,
Fast-rooted in the fruitful soil.

### IV

Hateful is the dark-blue sky,
Vaulted o'er the dark-blue sea.          40
Death is the end of life; ah, why
Should life all labor be ?
Let us alone.    Time driveth onward fast,
And in a little while our lips are dumb.
Let us alone.    What is it that will last ?
All things are taken from us, and become
Portions and parcels of the dreadful past.
Let us alone.    What pleasure can we have
To war with evil ?    Is there any peace
In ever climbing up the climbing wave ? 50
All things have rest, and ripen toward the
    grave
In silence — ripen, fall, and cease :
Give us long rest or death, dark death, or
    dreamful ease.

### V

How sweet it were, hearing the downward
    stream,

With half-shut eyes ever to seem
Falling asleep in a half-dream !
To dream and dream, like yonder amber
    light,
Which will not leave the myrrh-bush on
    the height;
To hear each other's whisper'd speech;
Eating the Lotos day by day,                  60
To watch the crisping ripples on the beach,
And tender curving lines of creamy spray;
To lend our hearts and spirits wholly
To the influence of mild-minded melan-
    choly;
To muse and brood and live again in mem-
    ory,
With those old faces of our infancy
Heap'd over with a mound of grass,
Two handfuls of white dust, shut in an urn
    of brass !

### VI

Dear is the memory of our wedded lives,
And dear the last embraces of our wives
And their warm tears; but all hath suffer'd
    change;                                      71
For surely now our household hearths are
    cold,
Our sons inherit us, our looks are strange,
And we should come like ghosts to trouble
    joy.
Or else the island princes over-bold
Have eat our substance, and the minstrel
    sings
Before them of the ten years' war in Troy,
And our great deeds, as half - forgotten
    things.
Is there confusion in the little isle ?
Let what is broken so remain.                  80
The Gods are hard to reconcile;
'T is hard to settle order once again.
There *is* confusion worse than death,
Trouble on trouble, pain on pain,
Long labor unto aged breath,
Sore task to hearts worn out by many wars
And eyes grown dim with gazing on the
    pilot-stars.

### VII

But, propt on beds of amaranth and moly,
How sweet — while warm airs lull us, blow-
    ing lowly —
With half-dropt eyelid still,                  90
Beneath a heaven dark and holy,
To watch the long bright river drawing
    slowly

His waters from the purple hill —
To hear the dewy echoes calling
From cave to cave thro' the thick-twined
vine —
To watch the emerald-color'd water falling
Thro' many a woven acanthus-wreath di-
vine !
Only to hear and see the far-off sparkling
brine,
Only to hear were sweet, stretch'd out be-
neath the pine.                         99

### VIII

The Lotos blooms below the barren peak,
The Lotos blows by every winding creek;
All day the wind breathes low with mel-
lower tone;
Thro' every hollow cave and alley lone
Round and round the spicy downs the yel-
low Lotos-dust is blown.
We have had enough of action, and of
motion we,
Roll'd to starboard, roll'd to larboard, when
the surge was seething free,
Where the wallowing monster spouted his
foam-fountains in the sea.
Let us swear an oath, and keep it with an
equal mind,
In the hollow Lotos-land to live and lie re-
clined
On the hills like Gods together, careless of
mankind.                                110
For they lie beside their nectar, and the
bolts are hurl'd
Far below them in the valleys, and the
clouds are lightly curl'd
Round their golden houses, girdled with
the gleaming world;
Where they smile in secret, looking over
wasted lands,
Blight and famine, plague and earthquake,
roaring deeps and fiery sands,
Clanging fights, and flaming towns, and
sinking ships, and praying hands.
But they smile, they find a music centred
in a doleful song
Steaming up, a lamentation and an ancient
tale of wrong,
Like a tale of little meaning tho' the
words are strong;
Chanted from an ill-used race of men that
cleave the soil,                        120
Sow the seed, and reap the harvest with
enduring toil,

Storing yearly little dues of wheat, and
wine and oil;
Till they perish and they suffer — some, 't is
whisper'd — down in hell
Suffer endless anguish, others in Elysian
valleys dwell,
Resting weary limbs at last on beds of
asphodel.
Surely, surely, slumber is more sweet than
toil, the shore
Than labor in the deep mid-ocean, wind and
wave and oar;
O, rest ye, brother mariners, we will not
wander more.

## A DREAM OF FAIR WOMEN

First printed in 1833, considerably altered in
1842, and again retouched in 1845, 1853, and
(in one passage) in 1884.  See Notes.

I READ, before my eyelids dropt their
shade,
' *The Legend of Good Women*,' long ago
Sung by the morning star of song, who
made
His music heard below;

Dan Chaucer, the first warbler, whose
sweet breath
Preluded those melodious bursts that fill
The spacious times of great Elizabeth
With sounds that echo still.

And, for a while, the knowledge of his art
Held me above the subject, as strong
gales                                    10
Hold swollen clouds from raining, tho' my
heart,
Brimful of those wild tales,

Charged both mine eyes with tears.   In
every land
I saw, wherever light illumineth,
Beauty and anguish walking hand in hand
The downward slope to death.

Those far-renowned brides of ancient song
Peopled the hollow dark, like burning
stars,
And I heard sounds of insult, shame, and
wrong,
And trumpets blown for wars;          20

And clattering flints batter'd with clanging
          hoofs;
    And I saw crowds in column'd sanctu-
          aries,
And forms that pass'd at windows and on
          roofs
          Of marble palaces;

Corpses across the threshold, heroes tall
    Dislodging pinnacle and parapet
Upon the tortoise creeping to the wall,
    Lances in ambush set;

And high shrine - doors burst thro' with
          heated blasts
    That run before the fluttering tongues of
          fire;                                    30
White surf wind-scatter'd over sails and
          masts,
    And ever climbing higher;

Squadrons and squares of men in brazen
          plates,
    Scaffolds, still sheets of water, divers
          woes,
Ranges of glimmering vaults with iron
          grates,
    And hush'd seraglios.

So shape chased shape as swift as, when to
          land
    Bluster the winds and tides the selfsame
          way,
Crisp foam-flakes scud along the level sand,
    Torn from the fringe of spray.          40

I started once, or seem'd to start in pain,
    Resolved on noble things, and strove to
          speak,
As when a great thought strikes along the
          brain
    And flushes all the cheek.

And once my arm was lifted to hew down
    A cavalier from off his saddle-bow,
That bore a lady from a leaguer'd town;
    And then, I know not how,

All those sharp fancies, by down-lapsing
          thought
    Stream'd onward, lost their edges, and
          did creep                               50
Roll'd on each other, rounded, smooth'd,
          and brought
    Into the gulfs of sleep.

At last methought that I had wander'd far
    In an old wood; fresh-wash'd in coolest
          dew
The maiden splendors of the morning star
    Shook in the steadfast blue.

Enormous elm-tree boles did stoop and lean
    Upon the dusky brushwood underneath
Their broad curved branches, fledged with
          clearest green,
    New from its silken sheath.               60

The dim red Morn had died, her journey
          done,
    And with dead lips smiled at the twilight
          plain,
Half-fallen across the threshold of the sun,
    Never to rise again.

There was no motion in the dumb dead air,
    Not any song of bird or sound of rill;
Gross darkness of the inner sepulchre
    Is not so deadly still

As that wide forest.  Growths of jasmine
          turn'd
    Their humid arms festooning tree to
          tree,                                   70
And at the root thro' lush green grasses
          burn'd
    The red anemone.

I knew the flowers, I knew the leaves, I
          knew
    The tearful glimmer of the languid dawn
On those long, rank, dark wood - walks
          drench'd in dew,
    Leading from lawn to lawn.

The smell of violets, hidden in the green,
    Pour'd back into my empty soul and
          frame
The times when I remember to have been
    Joyful and free from blame.               80

And from within me a clear undertone
    Thrill'd thro' mine ears in that unbliss-
          ful clime,
' Pass freely thro'; the wood is all thine
          own
    Until the end of time.'

At length I saw a lady within call,
    Stiller than chisell'd marble, standing
          there;

A daughter of the gods, divinely tall,
    And most divinely fair.

Her loveliness with shame and with sur-
        prise
    Froze my swift speech; she turning on
        my face                               90
The star-like sorrows of immortal eyes,
    Spoke slowly in her place:

'I had great beauty; ask thou not my
        name:
    No one can be more wise than destiny.
Many drew swords and died. Where'er
        I came
    I brought calamity.'

'No marvel, sovereign lady: in fair field
    Myself for such a face had boldly died,'
I answer'd free; and turning I appeal'd
    To one that stood beside.                 100

But she, with sick and scornful looks averse,
    To her full height her stately stature
        draws;
'My youth,' she said, 'was blasted with
        a curse:
    This woman was the cause.

'I was cut off from hope in that sad place
    Which men call'd Aulis in those iron
        years:
My father held his hand upon his face;
    I, blinded with my tears,

'Still strove to speak: my voice was thick
        with sighs                            109
    As in a dream.  Dimly I could descry
The stern black-bearded kings with wolf-
        ish eyes,
    Waiting to see me die.

'The high masts flicker'd as they lay afloat;
    The crowds, the temples, waver'd, and
        the shore;
The bright death quiver'd at the victim's
        throat —
    Touch'd — and I knew no more.'

Whereto the other with a downward brow:
    'I would the white cold heavy-plunging
        foam,
Whirl'd by the wind, had roll'd me deep
        below,
    Then when I left my home.'                120

Her slow full words sank thro' the silence
        drear,
    As thunder-drops fall on a sleeping sea:
Sudden I heard a voice that cried, 'Come
        here,
    That I may look on thee.'

I turning saw, throned on a flowery rise,
    One sitting on a crimson scarf unroll'd;
A queen, with swarthy cheeks and bold
        black eyes,
    Brow-bound with burning gold.

She, flashing forth a haughty smile, began:
    'I govern'd men by change, and so I
        sway'd                                130
All moods.  'T is long since I have seen
        a man.
    Once, like the moon, I made

The ever-shifting currents of the blood
    According to my humor ebb and flow.
I have no men to govern in this wood:
    That makes my only woe.

'Nay — yet it chafes me that I could not
        bend
    One will; nor tame and tutor with mine
        eye
That dull cold-blooded Cæsar. Prythee,
        friend,
    Where is Mark Antony?                     140

'The man, my lover, with whom I rode sub-
        lime
    On Fortune's neck; we sat as God by
        God:
The Nilus would have risen before his time
    And flooded at our nod.

'We drank the Libyan Sun to sleep, and
        lit
    Lamps which out-burn'd Canopus. O,
        my life
In Egypt! O, the dalliance and the wit,
    The flattery and the strife,

'And the wild kiss, when fresh from war's
        alarms,
    My Hercules, my Roman Antony,            150
My mailed Bacchus leapt into my arms,
    Contented there to die!

'And there he died: and when I heard my
        name

Sigh'd forth with life I would not brook
    my fear
Of the other; with a worm I balk'd his
    fame.
    What else was left ? look here !' —

With that she tore her robe apart, and
    half
The polish'd argent of her breast to sight
Laid bare.  Thereto she pointed with a
    laugh,
    Showing the aspick's bite. —            160

'I died a Queen.  The Roman soldier
    found
    Me lying dead, my crown about my
        brows,
A name for ever ! — lying robed and
    crown'd,
    Worthy a Roman spouse.'

Her warbling voice, a lyre of widest range
    Struck by all passion, did fall down and
        glance
From tone to tone, and glided thro' all
    change
    Of liveliest utterance.

When she made pause I knew not for de-
    light;
    Because with sudden motion from the
        ground                                170
She raised her piercing orbs, and fill'd with
    light
    The interval of sound.

Still with their fires Love tipt his keenest
    darts;
    As once they drew into two burning rings
All beams of Love, melting the mighty
    hearts
    Of captains and of kings.

Slowly my sense undazzled.  Then I heard
    A noise of some one coming thro' the
        lawn,
And singing clearer than the crested bird
    That claps his wings at dawn:            180

'The torrent brooks of hallow'd Israel
    From craggy hollows pouring, late and
        soon,
Sound all night long, in falling thro' the
    dell,
    Far-heard beneath the moon.

'The balmy moon of blessed Israel
    Floods all the deep-blue gloom with
        beams divine;
All night the splinter'd crags that wall
    the dell
    With spires of silver shine.'

As one that museth where broad sunshine
    laves
    The lawn by some cathedral, thro' the
        door                                 190
Hearing the holy organ rolling waves
    Of sound on roof and floor

Within, and anthem sung, is charm'd and
    tied
    To where he stands, — so stood I, when
        that flow
Of music left the lips of her that died
    To save her father's vow;

The daughter of the warrior Gileadite,
    A maiden pure; as when she went along
From Mizpeh's tower'd gate with welcome
    light,
    With timbrel and with song.             200

My words leapt forth: 'Heaven heads the
    count of crimes
    With that wild oath.'  She render'd
        answer high:
'Not so, nor once alone; a thousand times
    I would be born and die.

'Single I grew, like some green plant,
    whose root
    Creeps to the garden water-pipes be-
        neath,
Feeding the flower; but ere my flower to
    fruit
    Changed, I was ripe for death.

'My God, my land, my father — these did
    move
    Me from my bliss of life that Nature
        gave,                               210
Lower'd softly with a threefold cord of love
    Down to a silent grave.

'And I went mourning, "No fair Hebrew
    boy
    Shall smile away my maiden blame
        among
The Hebrew mothers" — emptied of all joy,
    Leaving the dance and song,

'Leaving the olive-gardens far below,
  Leaving the promise of my bridal bower,
The valleys of grape - loaded vines that
    glow
    Beneath the battled tower.          220

' The light white cloud swam over us.
    Anon
  We heard the lion roaring from his den;
We saw the large white stars rise one by
    one,
    Or, from the darken'd glen,

' Saw God divide the night with flying
    flame,
  And thunder on the everlasting hills.
I heard Him, for He spake, and grief be-
    came
    A solemn scorn of ills.

' When the next moon was roll'd into the
    sky,
  Strength came to me that equall'd my
    desire.          230
How beautiful a thing it was to die
    For God and for my sire !

' It comforts me in this one thought to
    dwell,
  That I subdued me to my father's will;
Because the kiss he gave me, ere I fell,
    Sweetens the spirit still.

' Moreover it is written that my race
  Hew'd Ammon, hip and thigh, from
    Aroer
On Arnon unto Minneth.'   Here her face
    Glow'd, as I look'd at her.          240

She lock'd her lips; she left me where I
    stood:
  ' Glory to God,' she sang, and past afar,
Thridding the sombre boskage of the wood,
    Toward the morning-star.

Losing her carol I stood pensively,
  As one that from a casement leans his
    head,
When midnight bells cease ringing sud-
    denly,
    And the old year is dead.

' Alas ! alas ! ' a low voice, full of care,
  Murmur'd beside me: ' Turn and look
    on me;          250

I am that Rosamond, whom men call fair,
    If what I was I be.

' Would I had been some maiden coarse
    and poor !
  O me, that I should ever see the light !
Those dragon eyes of anger'd Eleanor
    Do hunt me, day and night.'

She ceased in tears, fallen from hope and
    trust;
  To whom the Egyptian: ' O, you tamely
    died !
You should have clung to Fulvia's waist,
    and thrust
    The dagger thro' her side.'          260

With that sharp sound the white dawn's
    creeping beams,
  Stolen to my brain, dissolved the mys-
    tery
Of folded sleep.   The captain of my dreams
    Ruled in the eastern sky.

Morn broaden'd on the borders of the dark
  Ere I saw her who clasp'd in her last
    trance
Her murder'd father's head, or Joan of
    Arc,
    A light of ancient France;

Or her who knew that Love can vanquish
    Death,
  Who kneeling, with one arm about her
    king,          270
Drew forth the poison with her balmy
    breath,
    Sweet as new buds in spring.

No memory labors longer from the deep
  Gold-mines of thought to lift the hidden
    ore
That glimpses, moving up, than I from
    sleep
    To gather and tell o'er

Each little sound and sight.   With what
    dull pain
  Compass'd, how eagerly I sought to
    strike
Into that wondrous track of dreams again !
    But no two dreams are like.          280

As when a soul laments, which hath been
    blest,

Desiring what is mingled with past
    years,
In yearnings that can never be exprest
    By signs or groans or tears;

Because all words, tho' cull'd with choicest
    art,
    Failing to give the bitter of the sweet,
Wither beneath the palate, and the heart
    Faints, faded by its heat.

## THE BLACKBIRD

First published in 1842, but written in 1833.

O BLACKBIRD! sing me something well:
    While all the neighbors shoot thee round,
    I keep smooth plats of fruitful ground,
Where thou mayst warble, eat, and dwell.

The espaliers and the standards all
    Are thine; the range of lawn and park;
    The unnetted black-hearts ripen dark,
All thine, against the garden wall.

Yet, tho' I spared thee all the spring,
    Thy sole delight is, sitting still,
    With that gold dagger of thy bill
To fret the summer jenneting.

A golden bill! the silver tongue,
    Cold February loved, is dry;
    Plenty corrupts the melody
That made thee famous once when young;

And in the sultry garden-squares,
    Now thy flute - notes are changed to
        coarse,
    I hear thee not at all, or hoarse
As when a hawker hawks his wares.

Take warning! he that will not sing
    While yon sun prospers in the blue,
    Shall sing for want, ere leaves are new,
Caught in the frozen palms of Spring.

## THE DEATH OF THE OLD YEAR

Reprinted in 1842 from the volume of 1833.

FULL knee-deep lies the winter snow,
    And the winter winds are wearily sighing;

Toll ye the church-bell sad and slow,
And tread softly and speak low,
For the old year lies a-dying.
    Old year, you must not die;
    You came to us so readily,
    You lived with us so steadily,
    Old year, you shall not die.

He lieth still, he doth not move;
He will not see the dawn of day.
He hath no other life above.
He gave me a friend, and a true true-love,
And the New-year will take 'em away.
    Old year, you must not go;
    So long as you have been with us,
    Such joy as you have seen with us,
    Old year, you shall not go.

He froth'd his bumpers to the brim;
A jollier year we shall not see.
But tho' his eyes are waxing dim,
And tho' his foes speak ill of him,
He was a friend to me.
    Old year, you shall not die;
    We did so laugh and cry with you,
    I 've half a mind to die with you,
    Old year, if you must die.

He was full of joke and jest,
But all his merry quips are o'er.
To see him die, across the waste
His son and heir doth ride post-haste,
But he 'll be dead before.
    Every one for his own.
    The night is starry and cold, my
        friend,
    And the New-year blithe and bold,
        my friend,
    Comes up to take his own.

How hard he breathes! over the snow
I heard just now the crowing cock.
The shadows flicker to and fro;
The cricket chirps; the light burns low;
'T is nearly twelve o'clock.
    Shake hands, before you die.
    Old year, we 'll dearly rue for you.
    What is it we can do for you?
    Speak out before you die.

His face is growing sharp and thin.
Alack! our friend is gone.
Close up his eyes; tie up his chin;
Step from the corpse, and let him in
That standeth there alone,

And waiteth at the door.
There 's a new foot on the floor, my
    friend,
And a new face at the door, my friend,
A new face at the door.


## TO J. S.

First printed in 1833, and slightly altered in
1842.

THE wind that beats the mountain blows
    More softly round the open wold,
And gently comes the world to those
    That are cast in gentle mould.

And me this knowledge bolder made,
    Or else I had not dared to flow
In these words toward you, and invade
    Even with a verse your holy woe.

'T is strange that those we lean on most,
    Those in whose laps our limbs are
        nursed,
Fall into shadow, soonest lost;
    Those we love first are taken first.

God gives us love. Something to love
    He lends us; but, when love is grown
To ripeness, that on which it throve
    Falls off, and love is left alone.

This is the curse of time. Alas !
    In grief I am not all unlearn'd;
Once thro' mine own doors Death did pass;
    One went who never hath return'd.

He will not smile — not speak to me
    Once more. Two years his chair is
        seen
Empty before us. That was he
    Without whose life I had not been.

Your loss is rarer; for this star
    Rose with you thro' a little arc
Of heaven, nor having wander'd far
    Shot on the sudden into dark.

I knew your brother; his mute dust
    I honor and his living worth;
A man more pure and bold and just
    Was never born into the earth.

I have not look'd upon you nigh
    Since that dear soul hath fallen asleep.

Great Nature is more wise than I;
    I will not tell you not to weep.

And tho' mine own eyes fill with dew,
    Drawn from the spirit thro' the brain,
I will not even preach to you,
    'Weep, weeping dulls the inward
        pain.'

Let Grief be her own mistress still.
    She loveth her own anguish deep
More than much pleasure. Let her will
    Be done — to weep or not to weep.

I will not say, 'God's ordinance
    Of death is blown in every wind;'
For that is not a common chance
    That takes away a noble mind.

His memory long will live alone
    In all our hearts, as mournful light
That broods above the fallen sun,
    And dwells in heaven half the night.

Vain solace ! Memory standing near
    Cast down her eyes, and in her throat
Her voice seem'd distant, and a tear
    Dropt on the letters as I wrote.

I wrote I know not what. In truth,
    How *should* I soothe you any way,
Who miss the brother of your youth ?
    Yet something I did wish to say;

For he too was a friend to me.
    Both are my friends, and my true
        breast
Bleedeth for both; yet it may be
    That only silence suiteth best.

Words weaker than your grief would make
    Grief more. 'T were better I should
        cease
Although myself could almost take
    The place of him that sleeps in peace.

Sleep sweetly, tender heart, in peace;
    Sleep, holy spirit, blessed soul,
While the stars burn, the moons increase,
    And the great ages onward roll.

Sleep till the end, true soul and sweet.
    Nothing comes to thee new or strange.
Sleep full of rest from head to feet;
    Lie still, dry dust, secure of change.

## ON A MOURNER

First printed in the 'Selections' of 1865.

### I

NATURE, so far as in her lies,
    Imitates God, and turns her face
To every land beneath the skies,
    Counts nothing that she meets with base,
    But lives and loves in every place;

### II

Fills out the homely quickset-screens,
    And makes the purple lilac ripe,
Steps from her airy hill, and greens
    The swamp, where humm'd the drop-
        ping snipe,
    With moss and braided marish-pipe;

### III

And on thy heart a finger lays,
    Saying, 'Beat quicker, for the time
Is pleasant, and the woods and ways
    Are pleasant, and the beech and lime
    Put forth and feel a gladder clime.'

### IV

And murmurs of a deeper voice,
    Going before to some far shrine,
Teach that sick heart the stronger choice,
    Till all thy life one way incline
    With one wide Will that closes thine.

### V

And when the zoning eve has died
    Where yon dark valleys wind forlorn,
Come Hope and Memory, spouse and bride,
    From out the borders of the morn,
    With that fair child betwixt them born.

### VI

And when no mortal motion jars
    The blackness round the tombing sod,
Thro' silence and the trembling stars
    Comes Faith from tracts no feet have
        trod,
    And Virtue, like a household god.

### VII

Promising empire; such as those
    Once heard at dead of night to greet
Troy's wandering prince, so that he rose
    With sacrifice, while all the fleet
    Had rest by stony hills of Crete.

This and the two following poems, written
in 1833, were first printed in 1842, and have
been altered but slightly. See Notes.

YOU ask me, why, tho' ill at ease,
    Within this region I subsist,
    Whose spirits falter in the mist,
And languish for the purple seas.

It is the land that freemen till,
    That sober-suited Freedom chose,
    The land, where girt with friends or foes
A man may speak the thing he will;

A land of settled government,
    A land of just and old renown,
    Where Freedom slowly broadens down
From precedent to precedent;

Where faction seldom gathers head,
    But, by degrees to fullness wrought,
    The strength of some diffusive thought
Hath time and space to work and spread.

Should banded unions persecute
    Opinion, and induce a time
    When single thought is civil crime,
And individual freedom mute,

Tho' power should make from land to
    land
    The name of Britain trebly great —
    Tho' every channel of the State
Should fill and choke with golden sand —

Yet waft me from the harbor-mouth,
    Wild wind! I seek a warmer sky,
    And I will see before I die
The palms and temples of the South.

---

OF old sat Freedom on the heights,
    The thunders breaking at her feet;
Above her shook the starry lights;
    She heard the torrents meet.

There in her place she did rejoice,
    Self-gather'd in her prophet-mind,
But fragments of her mighty voice
    Came rolling on the wind.

Then stept she down thro' town and field
    To mingle with the human race,
And part by part to men reveal'd
    The fullness of her face —

Grave mother of majestic works,
   From her isle-altar gazing down,
Who, Godlike, grasps the triple forks,
   And, king-like, wears the crown.

Her open eyes desire the truth.
   The wisdom of a thousand years
Is in them.   May perpetual youth
   Keep dry their light from tears;

That her fair form may stand and shine,
   Make bright our days and light our
      dreams,
Turning to scorn with lips divine
   The falsehood of extremes!

Love thou thy land, with love far-brought
   From out the storied past, and used
Within the present, but transfused
   Thro' future time by power of thought;

True love turn'd round on fixed poles,
   Love, that endures not sordid ends,
For English natures, freemen, friends,
   Thy brothers and immortal souls.

But pamper not a hasty time,
   Nor feed with crude imaginings       10
The herd, wild hearts and feeble wings
   That every sophister can lime.

Deliver not the tasks of might
   To weakness, neither hide the ray
From those, not blind, who wait for
      day,
Tho' sitting girt with doubtful light.

Make knowledge circle with the winds;
   But let her herald, Reverence, fly
Before her to whatever sky
   Bear seed of men and growth of minds.   20

Watch what main-currents draw the years;
   Cut Prejudice against the grain.
But gentle words are always gain;
   Regard the weakness of thy peers.

Nor toil for title, place, or touch
   Of pension, neither count on praise —
It grows to guerdon after-days.
   Nor deal in watch-words overmuch;

Not clinging to some ancient saw,
   Not master'd by some modern term,   30

Not swift nor slow to change, but firm;
   And in its season bring the law,

That from Discussion's lip may fall
   With Life that, working strongly, binds —
Set in all lights by many minds,
   To close the interests of all.

For Nature also, cold and warm,
   And moist and dry, devising long,
Thro' many agents making strong,
   Matures the individual form.       40

Meet is it changes should control
   Our being, lest we rust in ease.
We all are changed by still degrees,
   All but the basis of the soul.

So let the change which comes be free
   To ingroove itself with that which flies,
And work, a joint of state, that plies
   Its office, moved with sympathy.

A saying hard to shape in act;
   For all the past of Time reveals       50
A bridal dawn of thunder-peals,
   Wherever Thought hath wedded Fact.

Even now we hear with inward strife
   A motion toiling in the gloom —
The Spirit of the years to come
   Yearning to mix himself with Life.

A slow-develop'd strength awaits
   Completion in a painful school;
Phantoms of other forms of rule,
   New Majesties of mighty States —       60

The warders of the growing hour,
   But vague in vapor, hard to mark;
And round them sea and air are dark
   With great contrivances of Power.

Of many changes, aptly join'd,
   Is bodied forth the second whole.
Regard gradation, lest the soul
   Of Discord race the rising wind;

A wind to puff your idol-fires,
   And heap their ashes on the head;       70
To shame the boast so often made,
   That we are wiser than our sires.

O, yet, if Nature's evil star
   Drive men in manhood, as in youth,

To follow flying steps of Truth
Across the brazen bridge of war —

If New and Old, disastrous feud,
    Must ever shock, like armed foes,
    And this be true, till Time shall close,
That Principles are rain'd in blood;    80

Not yet the wise of heart would cease
    To hold his hope thro' shame and guilt,
    But with his hand against the hilt,
Would pace the troubled land, like Peace;

Not less, tho' dogs of Faction bay,
    Would serve his kind in deed and word,
    Certain, if knowledge bring the sword,
That knowledge takes the sword away —

Would love the gleams of good that broke
    From either side, nor veil his eyes;    90
    And if some dreadful need should rise
Would strike, and firmly, and one stroke.

To-morrow yet would reap to-day,
    As we bear blossom of the dead;
    Earn well the thrifty months, nor wed
Raw Haste, half-sister to Delay.

## ENGLAND AND AMERICA IN 1782

First published in the 1874 edition of the 'Poems.' See Notes.

O THOU that sendest out the man
    To rule by land and sea,
Strong mother of a Lion-line,
    Be proud of those strong sons of thine
Who wrench'd their rights from thee !

What wonder if in noble heat
    Those men thine arms withstood,
Retaught the lesson thou hadst taught,
And in thy spirit with thee fought —
    Who sprang from English blood !

But thou rejoice with liberal joy,
    Lift up thy rocky face,
And shatter, when the storms are black,
In many a streaming torrent back,
    The seas that shock thy base !

Whatever harmonies of law
    The growing world assume,

Thy work is thine — the single note
From that deep chord which Hampden smote
    Will vibrate to the doom.

## THE GOOSE

First printed in 1842, and unchanged.

I KNEW an old wife lean and poor,
    Her rags scarce held together;
There strode a stranger to the door,
    And it was windy weather.

He held a goose upon his arm,
    He utter'd rhyme and reason:
'Here, take the goose, and keep you warm,
    It is a stormy season.'

She caught the white goose by the leg,
    A goose — 't was no great matter.
The goose let fall a golden egg
    With cackle and with clatter.

She dropt the goose, and caught the pelf,
    And ran to tell her neighbors,
And bless'd herself, and cursed herself,
    And rested from her labors;

And feeding high, and living soft,
    Grew plump and able-bodied,
Until the grave churchwarden doff'd,
    The parson smirk'd and nodded.

So sitting, served by man and maid,
    She felt her heart grow prouder;
But ah ! the more the white goose laid
    It clack'd and cackled louder.

It clutter'd here, it chuckled there,
    It stirr'd the old wife's mettle;
She shifted in her elbow-chair,
    And hurl'd the pan and kettle.

'A quinsy choke thy cursed note !'
    Then wax'd her anger stronger.
'Go, take the goose, and wring her throat,
    I will not bear it longer.'

Then yelp'd the cur, and yawl'd the cat,
    Ran Gaffer, stumbled Gammer.
The goose flew this way and flew that,
    And fill'd the house with clamor.

As head and heels upon the floor
They flounder'd all together,
There strode a stranger to the door,
And it was windy weather.

He took the goose upon his arm,
He utter'd words of scorning:
'So keep you cold, or keep you warm,
It is a stormy morning.'

The wild wind rang from park and plain,
And round the attics rumbled,

Till all the tables danced again,
And half the chimneys tumbled.

The glass blew in, the fire blew out,
The blast was hard and harder.
Her cap blew off, her gown blew up,
And a whirlwind clear'd the larder;

And while on all sides breaking loose
Her household fled the danger,
Quoth she, 'The devil take the goose,
And God forget the stranger !'

# ENGLISH IDYLS

## AND OTHER POEMS

A heading adopted in the 1884 and subsequent editions.

## THE EPIC

First published in 1842, but written as early as 1835. See Notes.

AT Francis Allen's on the Christmas-
eve, —
The game of forfeits done — the girls all
kiss'd
Beneath the sacred bush and past away —
The parson Holmes, the poet Everard
Hall,
The host, and I sat round the wassail-
bowl,
Then half-way ebb'd; and there we held
a talk,
How all the old honor had from Christmas
gone,
Or gone or dwindled down to some odd
games
In some odd nooks like this; till I, tired
out
With cutting eights that day upon the
pond,                                         10
Where, three times slipping from the outer
edge,
I bump'd the ice into three several stars,
Fell in a doze; and half-awake I heard
The parson taking wide and wider sweeps,
Now harping on the church-commissioners,
Now hawking at geology and schism;
Until I woke, and found him settled down
Upon the general decay of faith

Right thro' the world: 'at home was little
left,
And none abroad; there was no anchor,
none,                                         20
To hold by.' Francis, laughing, clapt his
hand
On Everard's shoulder, with 'I hold by
him.'
'And I,' quoth Everard, 'by the wassail-
bowl.'
'Why yes,' I said, 'we knew your gift that
way
At college; but another which you had —
I mean of verse (for so we held it then),
What came of that ?' 'You know,' said
Frank, 'he burnt
His epic, his King Arthur, some twelve
books '—
And then to me demanding why: 'O, sir,
He thought that nothing new was said, or
else                                          30
Something so said 't was nothing — that
a truth
Looks freshest in the fashion of the day;
God knows; he has a mint of reasons; ask.
It pleased me well enough.' 'Nay, nay,'
said Hall,
'Why take the style of those heroic times ?'
For nature brings not back the mastodon,
Nor we those times; and why should any
man
Remodel models ? these twelve books of
mine

Were faint Homeric echoes, nothing-worth,
Mere chaff and draff, much better burnt.'
  'But I,'                                    40
Said Francis, 'pick'd the eleventh from
    this hearth,
And have it; keep a thing, its use will
    come.
I hoard it as a sugar-plum for Holmes.'
He laugh'd, and I, tho' sleepy, like a horse
That hears the corn-bin open, prick'd my
    ears;
For I remember'd Everard's college fame
When we were Freshmen.   Then at my
    request
He brought it; and the poet, little urged,
But with some prelude of disparagement,
Read, mouthing out his hollow oes and aes,
Deep-chested music, and to this result.   51


## MORTE D'ARTHUR

So all day long the noise of battle roll'd
Among the mountains by the winter sea,
Until King Arthur's table, man by man,
Had fallen in Lyonness about their lord,
King Arthur; then, because his wound was
    deep,
The bold Sir Bedivere uplifted him,
Sir Bedivere, the last of all his knights,
And bore him to a chapel nigh the field,
A broken chancel with a broken cross,   60
That stood on a dark strait of barren land.
On one side lay the ocean, and on one
Lay a great water, and the moon was full.
  Then spake King Arthur to Sir Bedi-
    vere:
'The sequel of to-day unsolders all
The goodliest fellowship of famous knights
Whereof this world holds record.   Such a
    sleep
They sleep — the men I loved.   I think
    that we
Shall never more, at any future time,
Delight our souls with talk of knightly
    deeds,                              70
Walking about the gardens and the halls
Of Camelot, as in the days that were.
I perish by this people which I made, —
Tho' Merlin sware that I should come
    again
To rule once more — but let what will be
    be,
I am so deeply smitten thro' the helm
That without help I cannot last till morn.

Thou therefore take my brand Excalibur,
Which was my pride; for thou remember-
    est how
In those old days, one summer noon, an
    arm                                 80
Rose up from out the bosom of the lake,
Clothed in white samite, mystic, wonderful,
Holding the sword — and how I row'd
    across
And took it, and have worn it, like a king;
And, wheresoever I am sung or told
In aftertime, this also shall be known.
But now delay not; take Excalibur,
And fling him far into the middle mere;
Watch what thou seest, and lightly bring
    me word.'
  To him replied the bold Sir Bedivere: 90
'It is not meet, Sir King, to leave thee
    thus,
Aidless, alone, and smitten thro' the helm.
A little thing may harm a wounded man.
Yet I thy hest will all perform at full,
Watch what I see, and lightly bring thee
    word.'
  So saying, from the ruin'd shrine he
    stept
And in the moon athwart the place of
    tombs,
Where lay the mighty bones of ancient
    men,
Old knights, and over them the sea-wind
    sang
Shrill, chill, with flakes of foam.   He, step-
    ping down                           100
By zigzag paths and juts of pointed rock,
Came on the shining levels of the lake.
  There drew he forth the brand Excali-
    bur,
And o'er him, drawing it, the winter moon,
Brightening the skirts of a long cloud, ran
    forth
And sparkled keen with frost against the
    hilt;
For all the haft twinkled with diamond
    sparks,
Myriads of topaz-lights, and jacinth-work
Of subtlest jewellery.   He gazed so long
That both his eyes were dazzled, as he
    stood,                              110
This way and that dividing the swift mind,
In act to throw; but at the last it seem'd
Better to leave Excalibur conceal'd
There in the many-knotted water-flags,
That whistled stiff and dry about the
    marge.

So strode he back slow to the wounded
    king.
Then spake King Arthur to Sir Bedivere:
'Hast thou perform'd my mission which I
    gave?
What is it thou hast seen, or what hast
    heard?'
    And answer made the bold Sir Bedi-
    vere:                                  120
'I heard the ripple washing in the reeds,
And the wild water lapping on the crag.'
    To whom replied King Arthur, faint and
    pale:
'Thou hast betray'd thy nature and thy
    name,
Not rendering true answer, as beseem'd
Thy fealty, nor like a noble knight;
For surer sign had follow'd, either hand,
Or voice, or else a motion of the mere.
This is a shameful thing for men to lie.  129
Yet now, I charge thee, quickly go again
As thou art lief and dear, and do the thing
I bade thee, watch, and lightly bring me
    word.'
    Then went Sir Bedivere the second time
Across the ridge, and paced beside the
    mere,
Counting the dewy pebbles, fix'd in thought;
But when he saw the wonder of the hilt,
How curiously and strangely chased, he
    smote
His palms together, and he cried aloud:
'And if indeed I cast the brand away,
Surely a precious thing, one worthy note,  140
Should thus be lost forever from the earth,
Which might have pleased the eyes of
    many men.
What good should follow this, if this were
    done?
What harm, undone? deep harm to dis-
    obey,
Seeing obedience is the bond of rule.
Were it well to obey then, if a king de-
    mand
An act unprofitable, against himself?
The king is sick, and knows not what he
    does.
What record, or what relic of my lord
Should be to aftertime, but empty breath  150
And rumors of a doubt? but were this
    kept,
Stored in some treasure-house of mighty
    kings,
Some one might show it at a joust of arms,
Saying, "King Arthur's sword, Excalibur,

Wrought by the lonely maiden of the lake;
Nine years she wrought it, sitting in the
    deeps
Upon the hidden bases of the hills."
So might some old man speak in the after-
    time
To all the people, winning reverence;
But now much honor and much fame were
    lost.'                                 160
    So spake he, clouded with his own con-
    ceit,
And hid Excalibur the second time,
And so strode back slow to the wounded
    king.
    Then spoke King Arthur, breathing heav-
    ily:
'What is it thou hast seen, or what hast
    heard?'
    And answer made the bold Sir Bedivere:
'I heard the water lapping on the crag,
And the long ripple washing in the reeds.'
    To whom replied King Arthur, much in
    wrath:
'Ah, miserable and unkind, untrue,  170
Unknightly, traitor-hearted! Woe is me!
Authority forgets a dying king,
Laid widow'd of the power in his eye
That bow'd the will. I see thee what thou
    art,
For thou, the latest-left of all my knights,
In whom should meet the offices of all,
Thou wouldst betray me for the precious
    hilt;
Either from lust of gold, or like a girl
Valuing the giddy pleasure of the eyes.
Yet, for a man may fail in duty twice,  180
And the third time may prosper, get thee
    hence;
But, if thou spare to fling Excalibur,
I will arise and slay thee with my hands.'
    Then quickly rose Sir Bedivere, and ran,
And, leaping down the ridges lightly,
    plunged
Among the bulrush-beds, and clutch'd the
    sword,
And strongly wheel'd and threw it. The
    great brand
Made lightnings in the splendor of the
    moon,
And flashing round and round, and whirl'd
    in an arch,
Shot like a streamer of the northern morn,
Seen where the moving isles of winter
    shock                                  191
By night, with noises of the northern sea.

So flash'd and fell the brand Excalibur;
But ere he dipt the surface, rose an arm
Cloth'd in white samite, mystic, wonderful,
And caught him by the hilt, and brandish'd
    him
Three times, and drew him under in the
    mere.
And lightly went the other to the king.
    Then spoke King Arthur, drawing thicker
    breath:
'Now see I by thine eyes that this is
    done.                                      200
Speak out; what is it thou hast heard, or
    seen?'
    And answer made the bold Sir Bedivere:
'Sir King, I closed mine eyelids, lest the
    gems
Should blind my purpose, for I never saw,
Nor shall see, here or elsewhere, till I die,
Not tho' I live three lives of mortal men,
So great a miracle as yonder hilt.
Then with both hands I flung him, wheel-
    ing him;
But when I look'd again, behold an arm,
Clothed in white samite, mystic, wonder-
    ful,                                       210
That caught him by the hilt, and bran-
    dish'd him
Three times, and drew him under in the
    mere.'
    And answer made King Arthur, breath-
    ing hard:
'My end draws nigh; 't is time that I were
    gone.
Make broad thy shoulders to receive my
    weight,
And bear me to the margin; yet I fear
My wound hath taken cold, and I shall die.'
    So saying, from the pavement he half
    rose,
Slowly, with pain, reclining on his arm,
And looking wistfully with wide blue
    eyes                                       220
As in a picture. Him Sir Bedivere
Remorsefully regarded thro' his tears,
And would have spoken, but he found not
    words,
Then took with care, and kneeling on one
    knee,
O'er both his shoulders drew the languid
    hands,
And rising bore him thro' the place of
    tombs.
    But, as he walk'd, King Arthur panted
    hard,

Like one that feels a nightmare on his bed
When all the house is mute. So sigh'd
    the king,
Muttering and murmuring at his ear,
    'Quick, quick!'                           230
I fear it is too late, and I shall die.'
But the other swiftly strode from ridge to
    ridge,
Clothed with his breath, and looking, as he
    walk'd,
Larger than human on the frozen hills.
He heard the deep behind him, and a cry
Before. His own thought drove him like a
    goad.
Dry clash'd his harness in the icy caves
And barren chasms, and all to left and
    right
The bare black cliff clang'd round him, as
    he based
His feet on juts of slippery crag that
    rang                                       240
Sharp - smitten with the dint of armed
    heels —
And on a sudden, lo! the level lake,
And the long glories of the winter moon.
    Then saw they how there hove a dusky
    barge,
Dark as a funeral scarf from stem to stern,
Beneath them; and descending they were
    ware
That all the decks were dense with stately
    forms
Black-stoled, black-hooded, like a dream —
    by these
Three queens with crowns of gold — and
    from them rose
A cry that shiver'd to the tingling stars, 250
And, as it were one voice, an agony
Of lamentation, like a wind that shrills
All night in a waste land, where no one
    comes,
Or hath come, since the making of the
    world.
    Then murmur'd Arthur, 'Place me in the
    barge,'
And to the barge they came. There those
    three queens
Put forth their hands, and took the king,
    and wept.
But she that rose the tallest of them all
And fairest laid his head upon her lap,
And loosed the shatter'd casque, and chafed
    his hands,                               260
And call'd him by his name, complaining
    loud,

And dropping bitter tears against his brow
Striped with dark blood; for all his face
     was white
And colorless, and like the wither'd moon
Smote by the fresh beam of the springing
     east;
And all his greaves and cuisses dash'd with
     drops
Of onset; and the light and lustrous curls —
That made his forehead like a rising sun
High from the dais-throne — were parch'd
     with dust;
Or, clotted into points and hanging loose,
Mix'd with the knightly growth that fringed
     his lips.                                    271
So like a shatter'd column lay the king;
Not like that Arthur who, with lance in
     rest,
From spur to plume a star of tournament,
Shot thro' the lists at Camelot, and charged
Before the eyes of ladies and of kings.
Then loudly cried the bold Sir Bedivere:
'Ah! my Lord Arthur, whither shall I go?
Where shall I hide my forehead and my
     eyes?
For now I see the true old times are
     dead,                                        280
When every morning brought a noble
     chance,
And every chance brought out a noble
     knight.
Such times have been not since the light
     that led
The holy Elders with the gift of myrrh.
But now the whole ROUND TABLE is dis-
     solved
Which was an image of the mighty world;
And I, the last, go forth companionless,
And the days darken round me, and the
     years,
Among new men, strange faces, other
     minds.'
And slowly answer'd Arthur from the
     barge:                                       290
'The old order changeth, yielding place to
     new,
And God fulfils himself in many ways,
Lest one good custom should corrupt the
     world.
Comfort thyself: what comfort is in me?
I have lived my life, and that which I have
     done
May He within himself make pure! but
     thou,
If thou shouldst never see my face again,

Pray for my soul. More things are wrought
     by prayer
Than this world dreams of. Wherefore,
     let thy voice
Rise like a fountain for me night and
     day.                                         300
For what are men better than sheep or
     goats
That nourish a blind life within the brain,
If, knowing God, they lift not hands of
     prayer
Both for themselves and those who call
     them friend?
For so the whole round earth is every way
Bound by gold chains about the feet of God.
But now farewell. I am going a long way
With these thou seest — if indeed I go —
For all my mind is clouded with a doubt —
To the island-valley of Avilion;              310
Where falls not hail, or rain, or any snow,
Nor ever wind blows loudly, but it lies
Deep-meadow'd, happy, fair with orchard
     lawns
And bowery hollows crown'd with summer
     sea,
Where I will heal me of my grievous
     wound.'
So said he, and the barge with oar and
     sail
Moved from the brink, like some full-
     breasted swan
That, fluting a wild carol ere her death,
Ruffles her pure cold plume, and takes the
     flood
With swarthy webs. Long stood Sir Bedi-
     vere                                         320
Revolving many memories, till the hull
Look'd one black dot against the verge of
     dawn,
And on the mere the wailing died away.

    Here ended Hall, and our last light, that
     long
Had wink'd and threaten'd darkness, flared
     and fell;
At which the parson, sent to sleep with
     sound,
And waked with silence, grunted 'Good!'
     but we
Sat rapt: it was the tone with which he
     read —
Perhaps some modern touches here and
     there
Redeem'd it from the charge of nothing-
     ness —                                       330

Or else we loved the man, and prized his
       work;
I know not; but we sitting, as I said,
The cock crew loud, as at that time of
       year
The lusty bird takes every hour for dawn.
Then Francis, muttering, like a man ill-
       used,
'There now — that's nothing!' drew a lit-
       tle back,
And drove his heel into the smoulder'd log,
That sent a blast of sparkles up the flue.
And so to bed, where yet in sleep I seem'd
To sail with Arthur under looming shores,
Point after point; till on to dawn, when
       dreams                              341
Begin to feel the truth and stir of day,
To me, methought, who waited with the
       crowd,
There came a bark that, blowing forward,
       bore
King Arthur, like a modern gentleman
Of stateliest port; and all the people cried,
'Arthur is come again: he cannot die.'
Then those that stood upon the hills be-
       hind
Repeated — 'Come again, and thrice as
       fair;'
And, further inland, voices echoed —
       'Come                              350
With all good things, and war shall be no
       more.'
At this a hundred bells began to peal,
That with the sound I woke, and heard in-
       deed
The clear church-bells ring in the Christ-
       mas morn.


## THE GARDENER'S DAUGHTER

### OR, THE PICTURES

First printed in 1842.

THIS morning is the morning of the day,
When I and Eustace from the city went
To see the Gardener's daughter; I and he,
Brothers in Art; a friendship so complete
Portion'd in halves between us, that we
       grew
The fable of the city where we dwelt.
   My Eustace might have sat for Her-
       cules;
So muscular he spread, so broad of breast.

He, by some law that holds in love, and
       draws
The greater to the lesser, long desired  10
A certain miracle of symmetry,
A miniature of loveliness, all grace
Summ'd up and closed in little; — Juliet,
       she
So light of foot, so light of spirit — O, she
To me myself, for some three careless
       moons,
The summer pilot of an empty heart
Unto the shores of nothing! Know you
       not
Such touches are but embassies of Love,
To tamper with the feelings, ere he found
Empire for life? but Eustace painted her,  21
And said to me, she sitting with us then,
'When will you paint like this?' and I
       replied —
My words were half in earnest, half in jest:
''Tis not your work, but Love's. Love,
       unperceived,
A more ideal artist he than all,
Came, drew your pencil from you, made
       those eyes
Darker than darkest pansies, and that hair
More black than ashbuds in the front of
       March.'
And Juliet answer'd laughing, 'Go and see
The Gardener's daughter; trust me, after
       that,                              30
You scarce can fail to match his master-
       piece.'
And up we rose, and on the spur we went.
   Not wholly in the busy world, nor quite
Beyond it, blooms the garden that I love.
News from the humming city comes to it
In sound of funeral or of marriage bells;
And, sitting muffled in dark leaves, you
       hear
The windy clanging of the minster clock;
Altho' between it and the garden lies
A league of grass, wash'd by a slow broad
       stream,                           40
That, stirr'd with languid pulses of the oar,
Waves all its lazy lilies, and creeps on,
Barge-laden, to three arches of a bridge
Crown'd with the minster-towers.
                        The fields between
Are dewy-fresh, browsed by deep-udder'd
       kine,
And all about the large lime feathers
       low —
The lime a summer home of murmurous
       wings.

In that still place she, hoarded in herself,
Grew, seldom seen; not less among us lived
Her fame from lip to lip. Who had not
  heard                                          50
Of Rose, the Gardener's daughter? Where
  was he,
So blunt in memory, so old at heart,
At such a distance from his youth in grief,
That, having seen, forgot? The common
  mouth,
So gross to express delight, in praise of her
Grew oratory. Such a lord is Love,
And Beauty such a mistress of the world.

And if I said that Fancy, led by Love,
Would play with flying forms and images,
Yet this is also true, that, long before    60
I look'd upon her, when I heard her name
My heart was like a prophet to my heart,
And told me I should love. A crowd of
  hopes,
That sought to sow themselves like winged
  seeds,
Born out of everything I heard and saw,
Flutter'd about my senses and my soul;
And vague desires, like fitful blasts of
  balm
To one that travels quickly, made the air
Of life delicious, and all kinds of thought,
That verged upon them, sweeter than the
  dream                                        70
Dream'd by a happy man, when the dark
  East,
Unseen, is brightening to his bridal morn.
  And sure this orbit of the memory folds
For ever in itself the day we went
To see her. All the land in flowery
  squares,
Beneath a broad and equal-blowing wind,
Smelt of the coming summer, as one large
  cloud
Drew downward; but all else of heaven was
  pure
Up to the sun, and May from verge to
  verge,
And May with me from head to heel. And
  now,                                          80
As tho' 't were yesterday, as tho' it were
The hour just flown, that morn with all its
  sound —
For those old Mays had thrice the life of
  these —
Rings in mine ears. The steer forgot to
  graze,
And, where the hedge-row cuts the path-
  way, stood,

Leaning his horns into the neighbor field
And lowing to his fellows. From the
  woods
Came voices of the well-contented doves.
The lark could scarce get out his notes for
  joy,
But shook his song together as he near'd
His happy home, the ground. To left and
  right,                                        91
The cuckoo told his name to all the hills;
The mellow ouzel fluted in the elm;
The redcap whistled; and the nightingale
Sang loud, as tho' he were the bird of
  day.
  And Eustace turn'd, and smiling said to
  me:
'Hear how the bushes echo! by my life,
These birds have joyful thoughts. Think
  you they sing
Like poets, from the vanity of song?      99
Or have they any sense of why they sing?
And would they praise the heavens for
  what they have?'
And I made answer: 'Were there nothing
  else
For which to praise the heavens but only
  love,
That only love were cause enough for
  praise.'
  Lightly he laugh'd, as one that read my
  thought,
And on we went; but ere an hour had
  pass'd,
We reach'd a meadow slanting to the
  North,
Down which a well-worn pathway courted
  us
To one green wicket in a privet hedge.
This, yielding, gave into a grassy walk   110
Thro' crowded lilac-ambush trimly pruned;
And one warm gust, full-fed with perfume,
  blew
Beyond us, as we enter'd in the cool.
The garden stretches southward. In the
  midst
A cedar spread his dark-green layers of
  shade.
The garden-glasses shone, and momently
The twinkling laurel scatter'd silver lights.
'Eustace,' I said, 'this wonder keeps
  the house.'
He nodded, but a moment afterwards
He cried, 'Look! look!' Before he ceased
  I turn'd,                                     120
And, ere a star can wink, beheld her there.

For up the porch there grew an Eastern rose,
That, flowering high, the last night's gale had caught
And blown across the walk.  One arm aloft —
Gown'd in pure white that fitted to the shape —
Holding the bush, to fix it back, she stood,
A single stream of all her soft brown hair
Pour'd on one side; the shadow of the flowers
Stole all the golden gloss, and, wavering
Lovingly lower, trembled on her waist — 130
Ah, happy shade! — and still went wavering down,
But, ere it touch'd a foot, that might have danced
The greensward into greener circles, dipt,
And mix'd with shadows of the common ground.
But the full day dwelt on her brows, and sunn'd
Her violet eyes, and all her Hebe bloom,
And doubled his own warmth against her lips,
And on the bounteous wave of such a breast
As never pencil drew.  Half light, half shade,
She stood, a sight to make an old man young. 140
    So rapt, we near'd the house; but she, a Rose
In roses, mingled with her fragrant toil,
Nor heard us come, nor from her tendance turn'd
Into the world without; till close at hand,
And almost ere I knew mine own intent,
This murmur broke the stillness of that air
Which brooded round about her :
                                'Ah, one rose,
One rose, but one, by those fair fingers cull'd,
Were worth a hundred kisses press'd on lips
Less exquisite than thine.'
                            She look'd; but all
Suffused with blushes — neither self-possess'd 151
Nor startled, but betwixt this mood and that,
Divided in a graceful quiet — paused,

And dropt the branch she held, and turning wound
Her looser hair in braid, and stirr'd her lips
For some sweet answer, tho' no answer came,
Nor yet refused the rose, but granted it,
And moved away, and left me, statue-like,
In act to render thanks.
                        I, that whole day,
Saw her no more, altho' I linger'd there 160
Till every daisy slept, and Love's white star
Beam'd thro' the thicken'd cedar in the dusk.
    So home we went, and all the livelong way
With solemn gibe did Eustace banter me.
'Now,' said he, ' will you climb the top of art.
You cannot fail but work in hues to dim
The Titianic Flora.  Will you match
My Juliet ? you, not you, — the master, Love,
A more ideal artist he than all.'
    So home I went, but could not sleep for joy, 170
Reading her perfect features in the gloom,
Kissing the rose she gave me o'er and o'er,
And shaping faithful record of the glance
That graced the giving — such a noise of life
Swarm'd in the golden present, such a voice
Call'd to me from the years to come, and such
A length of bright horizon rimm'd the dark.
And all that night I heard the watchman peal
The sliding season; all that night I heard
The heavy clocks knolling the drowsy hours. 180
The drowsy hours, dispensers of all good,
O'er the mute city stole with folded wings,
Distilling odors on me as they went
To greet their fairer sisters of the East.
    Love at first sight, first-born, and heir to all,
Made this night thus.  Henceforward squall nor storm
Could keep me from that Eden where she dwelt.
Light pretexts drew me: sometimes a Dutch love

For tulips; then for roses, moss or musk,
To grace my city rooms; or fruits and
   cream                                    190
Served in the weeping elm; and more and
   more
A word could bring the color to my cheek;
A thought would fill my eyes with happy
   dew;
Love trebled life within me, and with each
The year increased.
                  The daughters of the year,
One after one, thro' that still garden
   pass'd;
Each garlanded with her peculiar flower
Danced into light, and died into the shade;
And each in passing touch'd with some
   new grace
Or seem'd to touch her, so that day by
   day,                                     200
Like one that never can be wholly known,
Her beauty grew; till Autumn brought an
   hour
For Eustace, when I heard his deep 'I
   will,'
Breathed, like the covenant of a God, to
   hold
From thence thro' all the worlds; but I
   rose up
Full of his bliss, and following her dark
   eyes
Felt earth as air beneath me, till I reach'd
The wicket-gate, and found her standing
   there.
There sat we down upon a garden
   mound,
Two mutually enfolded; Love, the third, 210
Between us, in the circle of his arms
Enwound us both; and over many a range
Of waning lime the gray cathedral towers,
Across a hazy glimmer of the west,
Reveal'd their shining windows. From them
   clash'd
The bells; we listen'd; with the time we
   play'd,
We spoke of other things; we coursed
   about
The subject most at heart, more near and
   near,
Like doves about a dovecote, wheeling
   round
The central wish, until we settled there. 220
   Then, in that time and place, I spoke to
   her,
Requiring, tho' I knew it was mine own,
Yet for the pleasure that I took to hear,

Requiring at her hand the greatest gift,
A woman's heart, the heart of her I loved;
And in that time and place she answer'd me,
And in the compass of three little words,
More musical than ever came in one,
The silver fragments of a broken voice,
Made me most happy, faltering, 'I am
   thine.'                                  230
   Shall I cease here? Is this enough to
   say
That my desire, like all strongest hopes,
By its own energy fulfill'd itself,
Merged in completion? Would you learn
   at full
How passion rose thro' circumstantial
   grades
Beyond all grades develop'd? and indeed
I had not staid so long to tell you all,
But while I mused came Memory with sad
   eyes,
Holding the folded annals of my youth;
And while I mused, Love with knit brows
   went by,                                 240
And with a flying finger swept my lips,
And spake, 'Be wise: not easily forgiven
Are those who, setting wide the doors that
   bar
The secret bridal chambers of the heart,
Let in the day.' Here, then, my words
   have end.
   Yet might I tell of meetings, of fare-
   wells —
Of that which came between, more sweet
   than each,
In whispers, like the whispers of the leaves
That tremble round a nightingale — in
   sighs
Which perfect Joy, perplex'd for utter-
   ance,                                    250
Stole from her sister Sorrow. Might I not
   tell
Of difference, reconcilement, pledges given,
And vows, where there was never need of
   vows,
And kisses, where the heart on one wild
   leap
Hung tranced from all pulsation, as above
The heavens between their fairy fleeces
   pale
Sow'd all their mystic gulfs with fleeting
   stars;
Or while the balmy glooming, crescent-lit,
Spread the light haze along the river-
   shores,
And in the hollows; or as once we met 260

Unheedful, tho' beneath a whispering rain
Night slid down one long stream of sighing
    wind,
And in her bosom bore the baby, Sleep ?
    But this whole hour your eyes have been
    intent
On that veil'd picture — veil'd, for what it
    holds
May not be dwelt on by the common day.
This prelude has prepared thee.  Raise thy
    soul,
Make thine heart ready with thine eyes;
    the time
Is come to raise the veil.
                         Behold her there,
As I beheld her ere she knew my heart, 270
My first, last love; the idol of my youth,
The darling of my manhood, and, alas !
Now the most blessed memory of mine
    age.

## DORA

This poem, first printed in 1842, and unaltered since, 'was partly suggested,' as a note
in the editions of 1842 and 1843 informs us,
'by one of Miss Mitford's pastorals,' — the
story of ' Dora Cresswell ' in ' Our Village.'

WITH farmer Allan at the farm abode
William and Dora.  William was his son,
And she his niece.  He often look'd at
    them,
And often thought, ' I 'll make them man
    and wife.'
Now Dora felt her uncle's will in all,
And yearn'd toward William; but the
    youth, because
He had been always with her in the house,
Thought not of Dora.
                      Then there came a day
When Allan call'd his son, and said: ' My
    son,
I married late, but I would wish to see    10
My grandchild on my knees before I die;
And I have set my heart upon a match.
Now therefore look to Dora; she is well
To look to; thrifty too beyond her age.
She is my brother's daughter; he and I
Had once hard words, and parted, and he
    died
In foreign lands; but for his sake I bred
His daughter Dora.  Take her for your
    wife;
For I have wish'd this marriage, night and
    day,

For many years.'  But William answer'd
    short:                                    20
' I cannot marry Dora; by my life,
I will not marry Dora!'  Then the old man
Was wroth, and doubled up his hands, and
    said:
' You will not, boy! you dare to answer
    thus !
But in my time a father's word was law,
And so it shall be now for me.  Look to it;
Consider, William, take a month to think,
And let me have an answer to my wish,
Or, by the Lord that made me, you shall
    pack,                                     29
And never more darken my doors again.'
But William answer'd madly, bit his lips,
And broke away.  The more he look'd at
    her
The less he liked her; and his ways were
    harsh;
But Dora bore them meekly.  Then be-
    fore
The month was out he left his father's
    house,
And hired himself to work within the
    fields;
And half in love, half spite, he woo'd and
    wed
A laborer's daughter, Mary Morrison.
    Then, when the bells were ringing, Allan
    call'd
His niece and said: ' My girl, I love you
    well;                                     40
But if you speak with him that was my
    son,
Or change a word with her he calls his
    wife,
My home is none of yours.  My will is
    law.'
And Dora promised, being meek.  She
    thought,
' It cannot be;  my  uncle's  mind  will
    change ! '
    And days went on, and there was born
    a boy
To William; then distresses came on him,
And day by day he pass'd his father's gate,
Heart-broken, and his father help'd him
    not.
But Dora stored what little she could
    save,                                     50
And sent it them by stealth, nor did they
    know
Who sent it; till at last a fever seized
On William, and in harvest time he died.

Then Dora went to Mary. Mary sat
And look'd with tears upon her boy, and
thought
Hard things of Dora. Dora came and said:
'I have obey'd my uncle until now,
And I have sinn'd, for it was all thro' me
This evil came on William at the first.
But, Mary, for the sake of him that 's
gone,                                        60
And for your sake, the woman that he
chose,
And for this orphan, I am come to you.
You know there has not been for these five
years
So full a harvest. Let me take the boy,
And I will set him in my uncle's eye
Among the wheat; that when his heart is
glad
Of the full harvest, he may see the boy,
And bless him for the sake of him that 's
gone.'
   And Dora took the child, and went her
way
Across the wheat, and sat upon a mound 70
That was unsown, where many poppies
grew.
Far off the farmer came into the field
And spied her not, for none of all his
men
Dare tell him Dora waited with the child;
And Dora would have risen and gone to
him,
But her heart fail'd her; and the reapers
reap'd,
And the sun fell, and all the land was
dark.
   But when the morrow came, she rose
and took
The child once more, and sat upon the
mound;                                       79
And made a little wreath of all the flowers
That grew about, and tied it round his hat
To make him pleasing in her uncle's eye.
Then when the farmer pass'd into the
field
He spied her, and he left his men at work,
And came and said: 'Where were you
yesterday?
Whose child is that? What are you doing
here?'
So Dora cast her eyes upon the ground,
And answer'd softly, 'This is William's
child!'
'And did I not,' said Allan, 'did I not
Forbid you, Dora?' Dora said again: 90

'Do with me as you will, but take the
child,
And bless him for the sake of him that 's
gone!'
And Allan said: 'I see it is a trick
Got up betwixt you and the woman there.
I must be taught my duty, and by you!
You knew my word was law, and yet you
dared
To slight it. Well — for I will take the
boy;
But go you hence, and never see me more.'
   So saying, he took the boy that cried
aloud
And struggled hard. The wreath of flowers
fell                                        100
At Dora's feet. She bow'd upon her hands,
And the boy's cry came to her from the
field
More and more distant. She bow'd down
her head,
Remembering the day when first she came,
And all the things that had been. She
bow'd down
And wept in secret; and the reapers reap'd,
And the sun fell, and all the land was dark.
   Then Dora went to Mary's house, and
stood
Upon the threshold. Mary saw the boy
Was not with Dora. She broke out in
praise                                      110
To God, that help'd her in her widowhood.
And Dora said: 'My uncle took the boy;
But, Mary, let me live and work with you:
He says that he will never see me more.'
Then answer'd Mary: 'This shall never be,
That thou shouldst take my trouble on thy-
self;
And, now I think, he shall not have the boy,
For he will teach him hardness, and to
slight
His mother. Therefore thou and I will go,
And I will have my boy, and bring him
home;                                       120
And I will beg of him to take thee back.
But if he will not take thee back again,
Then thou and I will live within one house,
And work for William's child, until he
grows
Of age to help us.'
                      So the women kiss'd
Each other, and set out, and reach'd the
farm.
The door was off the latch; they peep'd,
and saw

The boy set up betwixt his grandsire's
    knees,
Who thrust him in the hollows of his arm,
And clapt him on the hands and on the
    cheeks,           130
Like one that loved him; and the lad
    stretch'd out
And babbled for the golden seal, that hung
From Allan's watch and sparkled by the
    fire.
Then they came in; but when the boy be-
    held
His mother, he cried out to come to her;
And Allan set him down, and Mary said:
    'O father! — if you let me call you so —
I never came a-begging for myself,
Or William, or this child; but now I come
For Dora; take her back, she loves you
    well.          140
O Sir, when William died, he died at peace
With all men; for I ask'd him, and he said,
He could not ever rue his marrying me —
I had been a patient wife; but, Sir, he said
That he was wrong to cross his father thus.
"God bless him!" he said, "and may he
    never know
The troubles I have gone thro'!" Then
    he turn'd
His face and pass'd — unhappy that I am!
But now, Sir, let me have my boy, for you
Will make him hard, and he will learn to
    slight          150
His father's memory; and take Dora back,
And let all this be as it was before.'
So Mary said, and Dora hid her face
By Mary. There was silence in the room;
And all at once the old man burst in
    sobs:
    'I have been to blame — to blame. I
    have kill'd my son.
I have kill'd him — but I loved him — my
    dear son.
May God forgive me! — I have been to
    blame.
Kiss me, my children.'
               Then they clung about
The old man's neck, and kiss'd him many
    times.          160
And all the man was broken with remorse;
And all his love came back a hundred-fold;
And for three hours he sobb'd o'er William's
    child
Thinking of William.
               So those four abode
Within one house together, and as years

Went forward Mary took another mate;
But Dora lived unmarried till her death.

## AUDLEY COURT

First printed in 1842, and unaltered except
for the insertion of lines 77 ('A rolling stone,'
etc.) and 86 ('Sole star,' etc.).

'THE Bull, the Fleece are cramm'd, and not
    a room
For love or money. Let us picnic there
At Audley Court.'
             I spoke, while Audley feast
Humm'd like a hive all round the narrow
    quay,
To Francis, with a basket on his arm,
To Francis just alighted from the boat
And breathing of the sea. 'With all my
    heart,'
Said Francis. Then we shoulder'd thro'
    the swarm,
And rounded by the stillness of the beach
To where the bay runs up its latest horn. 10
    We left the dying ebb that faintly lipp'd
The flat red granite; so by many a sweep
Of meadow smooth from aftermath we
    reach'd
The griffin-guarded gates, and pass'd thro'
    all
The pillar'd dusk of sounding sycamores,
And cross'd the garden to the gardener's
    lodge,
With all its casements bedded, and its
    walls
And chimneys muffled in the leafy vine.
    There, on a slope of orchard, Francis
    laid
A damask napkin wrought with horse and
    hound,          20
Brought out a dusky loaf that smelt of
    home,
And, half-cut-down, a pasty costly-made,
Where quail and pigeon, lark and leveret
    lay,
Like fossils of the rock, with golden yolks
Imbedded and injellied; last, with these,
A flask of cider from his father's vats,
Prime, which I knew; and so we sat and
    eat
And talk'd old matters over, — who was
    dead,
Who married, who was like to be, and how
The races went, and who would rent the
    hall;         30

Then touch'd upon the game, how scarce it
  was
This season; glancing thence, discuss'd the
  farm,
The four-field system, and the price of
  grain;
And struck upon the corn-laws, where we
  split,
And came again together on the king
With heated faces; till he laugh'd aloud,
And, while the blackbird on the pippin
  hung
To hear him, clapt his hand in mine and
  sang:
   'O, who would fight and march and
    countermarch,
Be shot for sixpence in a battle-field,    40
And shovell'd up into some bloody trench
Where no one knows ? but let me live my
  life.
   'O, who would cast and balance at a
    desk,
Perch'd like a crow upon a three-legg'd
  stool,
Till all his juice is dried, and all his joints
Are full of chalk ? but let me live my life.
   'Who'd serve the state ? for if I carved
    my name
Upon the cliffs that guard my native land,
I might as well have traced it in the sands;
The sea wastes all; but let me live my life.
   'O, who would love ? I woo'd a woman
    once,           51
But she was sharper than an eastern wind,
And all my heart turn'd from her, as a
  thorn
Turns from the sea; but let me live my
  life.'
   He sang his song, and I replied with
    mine.
I found it in a volume, all of songs,
Knock'd down to me, when old Sir Robert's
  pride,
His books —the more the pity, so I said —
Came to the hammer here in March — and
  this —
I set the words, and added names I knew:
   'Sleep, Ellen Aubrey, sleep, and dream
    of me:          61
Sleep, Ellen, folded in thy sister's arm,
And sleeping, haply dream her arm is
  mine.
   'Sleep, Ellen, folded in Emilia's arm;
Emilia, fairer than all else but thou,
For thou art fairer than all else that is.

   'Sleep, breathing health and peace upon
    her breast;
Sleep, breathing love and trust against her
  lip.
I go to-night; I come to-morrow morn.
   'I go, but I return; I would I were    70
The pilot of the darkness and the dream.
Sleep, Ellen Aubrey, love, and dream of
  me.'
   So sang we each to either, Francis Hale,
The farmer's son, who lived across the bay,
My friend; and I, that having where-
  withal,
And in the fallow leisure of my life
A rolling stone of here and everywhere,
Did what I would. But ere the night we
  rose
And saunter'd home beneath a moon that,
  just
In crescent, dimly rain'd about the leaf   80
Twilights of airy silver, till we reach'd
The limit of the hills; and as we sank
From rock to rock upon the glooming quay,
The town was hush'd beneath us; lower
  down
The bay was oily calm; the harbor-buoy,
Sole star of phosphorescence in the calm,
With one green sparkle ever and anon
Dipt by itself, and we were glad at heart.

## WALKING TO THE MAIL

First printed in 1842, and afterwards slightly
changed in the opening lines. See Notes.

  *John.*   I'm glad I walk'd. How fresh
    the meadows look
Above the river, and, but a month ago,
The whole hillside was redder than a fox!
Is yon plantation where this byway joins
The turnpike ?
  *James.*         Yes.
  *John.*         And when does this come by ?
  *James.*   The mail ?   At one o'clock.
  *John.*              What is it now ?
  *James.*   A quarter to.
  *John.*           Whose house is that I see ?
No, not the County Member's with the
  vane.           8
Up higher with the yew-tree by it, and half
A score of gables.
  *James.*      That ?   Sir Edward Head's.
But he's abroad; the place is to be sold.
  *John.*   O, his !   He was not broken.

*James.* No, sir, he,
Vext with a morbid devil in his blood
That veil'd the world with jaundice, hid his
   face
From all men, and commercing with him-
   self,
He lost the sense that handles daily life —
That keeps us all in order more or less —
And sick of home went overseas for
   change.
   *John.* And whither ?
   *James.* Nay, who knows ? he 's here and
      there.
But let him go; his devil goes with him, 20
As well as with his tenant, Jocky Dawes.
   *John.* What 's that ?
   *James.* You saw the man — on Monday,
      was it ? —
There by the humpback'd willow; half
   stands up
And bristles, half has fallen and made a
   bridge;
And there he caught the younker tickling
   trout —
Caught *in flagrante* — what 's the Latin
   word ? —
*Delicto ;* but his house, for so they say,
Was haunted with a jolly ghost, that shook
The curtains, whined in lobbies, tapt at
   doors,
And rummaged like a rat; no servant
   stay'd. 30
The farmer vext packs up his beds and
   chairs,
And all his household stuff; and with his boy
Betwixt his knees, his wife upon the tilt,
Sets out, and meets a friend who hails him,
   'What !
You 're flitting !' 'Yes, we 're flitting,'
   says the ghost —
For they had pack'd the thing among the
   beds.
'O, well,' says he, 'you flitting with us
   too ! —
Jack, turn the horses' heads and home
   again.'
   *John.* He left *his* wife behind; for so I
      heard.
   *James.* He left her, yes. I met my
      lady once; 40
A woman like a butt, and harsh as crabs.
   *John.* O, yet but I remember, ten years
      back —
'T is now at least ten years — and then she
   was —

You could not light upon a sweeter thing;
A body slight and round, and like a pear
In growing, modest eyes, a hand, a foot
Lessening in perfect cadence, and a skin
As clean and white as privet when it flow-
   ers.
   *James.* Ay, ay, the blossom fades, and
      they that loved
At first like dove and dove were cat and
   dog. 50
She was the daughter of a cottager,
Out of her sphere. What betwixt shame
   and pride,
New things and old, himself and her, she
   sour'd
To what she is; a nature never kind !
Like men, like manners; like breeds like,
   they say.
Kind nature is the best; those manners next
That fit us like a nature second-hand —
Which are indeed the manners of the great.
   *John.* But I had heard it was this bill
      that past,
And fear of change at home, that drove
   him hence. 60
   *James.* That was the last drop in the
      cup of gall.
I once was near him, when his bailiff
   brought
A Chartist pike. You should have seen him
   wince
As from a venomous thing; he thought
   himself
A mark for all, and shudder'd, lest a cry
Should break his sleep by night, and his
   nice eyes
Should see the raw mechanic's bloody
   thumbs
Sweat on his blazon'd chairs. But, sir, you
   know
That these two parties still divide the
   world —
Of those that want, and those that have;
   and still 70
The same old sore breaks out from age to
   age
With much the same result. Now I my-
   self,
A Tory to the quick, was as a boy
Destructive, when I had not what I would.
I was at school, — a college in the South.
There lived a flayflint near; we stole his
   fruit,
His hens, his eggs; but there was law for
   *us ;*

We paid in person. He had a sow, sir.
 She,
With meditative grunts of much content,
Lay great with pig, wallowing in sun and
 mud.                                          80
By night we dragg'd her to the college
 tower
From her warm bed, and up the corkscrew
 stair
With hand and rope we haled the groaning
 sow,
And on the leads we kept her till she
 pigg'd.
Large range of prospect had the mother
 sow,
And but for daily loss of one she loved
As one by one we took them — but for
 this —
As never sow was higher in this world —
Might have been happy; but what lot is
 pure ?
We took them all, till she was left alone  90
Upon her tower, the Niobe of swine,
And so return'd unfarrow'd to her sty.
    *John.*   They found you out ?
    *James.*                        Not they.
    *John.*              Well — after all —
What know we of the secret of a man ?
His nerves were wrong. What ails us who
 are sound,
That we should mimic this raw fool the
 world,
Which charts us all in its coarse blacks or
 whites,
As ruthless as a baby with a worm,
As cruel as a schoolboy ere he grows   99
To pity — more from ignorance than will.
    But put your best foot forward, or I fear
That we shall miss the mail; and here it
 comes
With five at top, as quaint a four-in-hand
As you shall see, — three pyebalds and a
 roan.


### EDWIN MORRIS

#### OR, THE LAKE

Written in 1839 during a visit to the Llanberis lakes in Wales. Printed in 1851.

O ME, my pleasant rambles by the lake,
My sweet, wild, fresh three quarters of a
 year,
My one oasis in the dust and drouth

Of city life ! I was a sketcher then.
See here, my doing: curves of mountain,
 bridge,
Boat, island, ruins of a castle, built
When men knew how to build, upon a
 rock
With turrets lichen-gilded like a rock;
And here, new-comers in an ancient hold,
New-comers from the Mersey, million-
 aires,                                         10
Here lived the Hills — a Tudor-chimney'd
 bulk
Of mellow brickwork on an isle of bowers.
    O me, my pleasant rambles by the lake
With Edwin Morris and with Edward Bull
The curate — he was fatter than his cure !
    But Edwin Morris, he that knew the
 names,
Long learned names of agaric, moss, and
 fern,
Who forged a thousand theories of the
 rocks,
Who taught me how to skate, to row, to
 swim,
Who read me rhymes elaborately good,   20
His own — I call'd him Crichton, for he
 seem'd
All-perfect, finish'd to the finger-nail.
    And once I ask'd him of his early life,
And his first passion; and he answer'd me,
And well his words became him — was he
 not
A full-cell'd honeycomb of eloquence
Stored from all flowers ? Poet-like he
 spoke:
' My love for Nature is as old as I;
But thirty moons, one honeymoon to that,
And three rich sennights more, my love for
 her.                                          30
My love for Nature and my love for her,
Of different ages, like twin-sisters grew,
Twin-sisters differently beautiful.
To some full music rose and sank the sun,
And some full music seem'd to move and
 change
With all the varied changes of the dark,
And either twilight and the day between;
For daily hope fulfill'd, to rise again
Revolving toward fulfilment, made it sweet
To walk, to sit, to sleep, to wake, to
 breathe.'                                     40
    Or this or something like to this he
 spoke.
Then said the fat-faced curate Edward
 Bull:

'I take it, God made the woman for the
    man,
And for the good and increase of the world.
A pretty face is well, and this is well,
To have a dame indoors, that trims us up,
And keeps us tight; but these unreal ways
Seem but the theme of writers, and indeed
Worn threadbare.  Man is made of solid
    stuff.
I say, God made the woman for the man, 50
And for the good and increase of the
    world.'
    'Parson,' said I, 'you pitch the pipe too
    low.
But I have sudden touches, and can run
My faith beyond my practice into his;
Tho' if, in dancing after Letty Hill,
I do not hear the bells upon my cap,
I scarce have other music — yet say on.
What should one give to light on such a
    dream ?'
I ask'd him half-sardonically.
                         'Give ?   59
Give all thou art,' he answer'd, and a light
Of laughter dimpled in his swarthy cheek;
'I would have hid her needle in my heart,
To save her little finger from a scratch
No deeper than the skin; my ears could
    hear
Her lightest breath ; her least remark was
    worth
The experience of the wise.  I went and
    came;
Her voice fled always thro' the summer
    land;
I spoke her name alone.  Thrice-happy
    days !
The flower of each, those moments when
    we met,                               69
The crown of all, we met to part no more.'
    Were not his words delicious, I a beast
To take them as I did ? but something
    jarr'd;
Whether he spoke too largely, that there
    seem'd
A touch of something false, some self-con-
    ceit,
Or over-smoothness; howsoe'er it was,
He scarcely hit my humor, and I said:
    'Friend Edwin, do not think yourself
    alone
Of all men happy.  Shall not Love to me,
As in the Latin song I learnt at school,
Sneeze out a full God-bless-you right and
    left ?                                80

But you can talk, yours is a kindly vein;
I have, I think, — Heaven knows, — as
    much within;
Have, or should have, but for a thought or
    two,
That like a purple beech among the greens
Looks out of place.  'T is from no want in
    her;
It is my shyness, or my self-distrust,
Or something of a wayward modern mind
Dissecting passion.  Time will set me
    right.'
    So spoke I, knowing not the things that
    were.
Then said the fat-faced curate, Edward
    Bull:                                 90
    'God made the woman for the use of
    man,
And for the good and increase of the
    world.'
And I and Edwin laughed; and now we
    paused
About the windings of the marge to hear
The soft wind blowing over meadowy
    holms
And alders, garden-isles; and now we left
The clerk behind us, I and he, and ran
By ripply shallows of the lisping lake,
Delighted with the freshness and the sound.
    But when the bracken rusted on their
    crags,                               100
My suit had wither'd, nipt to death by him
That was a god, and is a lawyer's clerk,
The rent-roll Cupid of our rainy isles.
'T is true, we met; one hour I had, no
    more:
She sent a note, the seal an *Elle vous suit*,
The close, 'Your Letty, only yours;' and
    this
Thrice underscored.  The friendly mist of
    morn
Clung to the lake.  I boated over, ran
My craft aground, and heard with beating
    heart
The sweet-gale rustle round the shelving
    keel;                                110
And out I stept, and up I crept.  She moved,
Like Proserpine in Enna, gathering flow-
    ers.
Then low and sweet I whistled thrice; and
    she,
She turn'd, we closed, we kiss'd, swore
    faith, I breathed
In some new planet.  A silent cousin stole
Upon us and departed.  'Leave,' she cried,

'O, leave me!' 'Never, dearest, never:
       here
I brave the worst;' and while we stood like
       fools
Embracing, all at once a score of pugs
And poodles yell'd within, and out they
       came,                                          120
Trustees and aunts and uncles. 'What,
       with him!
Go,' shrill'd the cotton-spinning chorus;
       'him!'
I choked. Again they shriek'd the burthen,
       'Him!'
Again with hands of wild rejection, 'Go!—
Girl, get you in!' She went—and in one
       month
They wedded her to sixty thousand pounds,
To lands in Kent and messuages in York,
And slight Sir Robert with his watery
       smile
And educated whisker. But for me,
They set an ancient creditor to work;    130
It seems I broke a close with force and
       arms:
There came a mystic token from the king
To greet the sheriff, needless courtesy!
I read, and fled by night, and flying turn'd;
Her taper glimmer'd in the lake below;
I turn'd once more, close-button'd to the
       storm;
So left the place, left Edwin, nor have seen
Him since, nor heard of her, nor cared to
       hear.
    Nor cared to hear? perhaps; yet long
       ago
I have pardon'd little Letty; not indeed,  140
It may be, for her own dear sake, but
       this,—
She seems a part of those fresh days to me;
For in the dust and drouth of London life
She moves among my visions of the lake,
While the prime swallow dips his wing, or
       then
While the gold-lily blows, and overhead
The light cloud smoulders on the summer
       crag.


## SAINT SIMEON STYLITES

First printed in 1842. In line 201 'brother'
was originally 'mother.'

ALTHO' I be the basest of mankind,
From scalp to sole one slough and crust of
       sin,

Unfit for earth, unfit for heaven, scarce
       meet
For troops of devils, mad with blasphemy,
I will not cease to grasp the hope I hold
Of saintdom, and to clamor, mourn, and
       sob,
Battering the gates of heaven with storms
       of prayer,
Have mercy, Lord, and take away my sin!
    Let this avail, just, dreadful, mighty
       God,
This not be all in vain, that thrice ten
       years,                                         10
Thrice multiplied by superhuman pangs,
In hungers and in thirsts, fevers and cold,
In coughs, aches, stitches, ulcerous throes
       and cramps,
A sign betwixt the meadow and the cloud,
Patient on this tall pillar I have borne
Rain, wind, frost, heat, hail, damp, and
       sleet, and snow;
And I had hoped that ere this period closed
Thou wouldst have caught me up into thy
       rest,
Denying not these weather-beaten limbs
The meed of saints, the white robe and the
       palm.                                          20
    O, take the meaning, Lord! I do not
       breathe,
Not whisper, any murmur of complaint.
Pain heap'd ten-hundred-fold to this, were
       still
Less burthen, by ten-hundred-fold, to bear,
Than were those lead-like tons of sin that
       crush'd
My spirit flat before thee.
                            O Lord, Lord,
Thou knowest I bore this better at the
       first,
For I was strong and hale of body then;
And tho' my teeth, which now are dropt
       away,
Would chatter with the cold, and all my
       beard                                          30
Was tagg'd with icy fringes in the moon,
I drown'd the whoopings of the owl with
       sound
Of pious hymns and psalms, and sometimes
       saw
An angel stand and watch me, as I sang.
Now am I feeble grown; my end draws
       nigh;
I hope my end draws nigh; half deaf I am,
So that I scarce can hear the people hum
About the column's base, and almost blind,

And scarce can recognize the fields I know;
And both my thighs are rotted with the
    dew;                                          40
Yet cease I not to clamor and to cry,
While my stiff spine can hold my weary
    head,
Till all my limbs drop piecemeal from the
    stone,
Have mercy, mercy ! take away my sin !
    O Jesus, if thou wilt not save my soul,
Who may be saved ? who is it may be
    saved ?
Who may be made a saint if I fail here ?
Show me the man hath suffer'd more than I.
For did not all thy martyrs die one death ?
For either they were stoned, or crucified,  50
Or burn'd in fire, or boil'd in oil, or sawn
In twain beneath the ribs; but I die here
To-day, and whole years long, a life of
    death.
Bear witness, if I could have found a way —
And heedfully I sifted all my thought —
More slowly-painful to subdue this home
Of sin, my flesh, which I despise and hate,
I had not stinted practice, O my God !
    For not alone this pillar-punishment,
Not this alone I bore; but while I lived  60
In the white convent down the valley there,
For many weeks about my loins I wore
The rope that haled the buckets from the
    well,
Twisted as tight as I could knot the noose,
And spake not of it to a single soul,
Until the ulcer, eating thro' my skin,
Betray'd my secret penance, so that all
My brethren marvell'd greatly.  More than
    this
I bore, whereof, O God, thou knowest all.
    Three winters, that my soul might grow
    to thee,                                      70
I lived up there on yonder mountain-side.
My right leg chain'd into the crag, I lay
Pent in a roofless close of ragged stones;
Inswathed sometimes in wandering mist,
    and twice
Black'd with thy branding thunder, and
    sometimes
Sucking the damps for drink, and eating
    not,
Except the spare chance-gift of those that
    came
To touch my body and be heal'd, and live.
And they say then that I work'd miracles,
Whereof my fame is loud amongst man-
    kind,                                         80

Cured lameness, palsies, cancers.  Thou,
    O God,
Knowest alone whether this was or no.
Have mercy, mercy ! cover all my sin !
    Then, that I might be more alone with
    thee,
Three years I lived upon a pillar, high
Six cubits, and three years on one of
    twelve;
And twice three years I crouch'd on one
    that rose
Twenty by measure; last of all, I grew
Twice ten long weary, weary years to this,
That numbers forty cubits from the soil.  90
    I think that I have borne as much as
    this —
Or else I dream — and for so long a time,
If I may measure time by yon slow light,
And this high dial, which my sorrow
    crowns —
So much — even so.
                        And yet I know not well,
For that the evil ones come here, and say,
'Fall down, O Simeon; thou hast suffer'd
    long
For ages and for ages !' then they prate
Of penances I cannot have gone thro',
Perplexing me with lies; and oft I fall,  100
Maybe for months, in such blind lethargies
That Heaven, and Earth, and Time are
    choked.
                                    But yet
Bethink thee, Lord, while thou and all the
    saints
Enjoy themselves in heaven, and men on
    earth
House in the shade of comfortable roofs,
Sit with their wives by fires, eat wholesome
    food,
And wear warm clothes, and even beasts
    have stalls,
I, 'tween the spring and downfall of the
    light,
Bow down one thousand and two hundred
    times,
To Christ, the Virgin Mother, and the
    saints;                                       110
Or in the night, after a little sleep,
I wake; the chill stars sparkle; I am wet
With drenching dews, or stiff with crack-
    ling frost.
I wear an undress'd goatskin on my back;
A grazing iron collar grinds my neck;
And in my weak, lean arms I lift the
    cross,

And strive and wrestle with thee till I die.
O, mercy, mercy ! wash away my sin !  118
  O Lord, thou knowest what a man I am;
A sinful man, conceived and born in sin.
'T is their own doing; this is none of mine;
Lay it not to me.  Am I to blame for this,
That here come those that worship me ?
    Ha ! ha !
They think that I am somewhat.  What
    am I ?
The silly people take me for a saint,
And bring me offerings of fruit and flow-
    ers;
And I, in truth — thou wilt bear witness
    here —
Have all in all endured as much, and
    more
Than many just and holy men, whose
    names
Are register'd and calendar'd for saints. 130
  Good people, you do ill to kneel to me.
What is it I can have done to merit this ?
I am a sinner viler than you all.
It may be I have wrought some miracles,
And cured some halt and maim'd; but what
    of that ?
It may be no one, even among the saints,
May match his pains with mine; but what
    of that ?
Yet do not rise; for you may look on me,
And in your looking you may kneel to
    God.                              139
Speak! is there any of you halt or maim'd ?
I think you know I have some power with
    Heaven
From my long penance; let him speak his
    wish.
    Yes, I can heal him.  Power goes forth
    from me.
They say that they are heal'd.  Ah, hark !
    they shout
'Saint Simeon Stylites.'  Why, if so,
God reaps a harvest in me.  O my soul,
God reaps a harvest in thee!  If this be,
Can I work miracles and not be saved ?
This is not told of any.  They were saints.
It cannot be but that I shall be saved,  150
Yea, crown'd a saint.  They shout, ' Behold
    a saint ! '
And lower voices saint me from above.
Courage, Saint Simeon !  This dull chrysalis
Cracks into shining wings, and hope ere
    death
Spreads more and more and more, that
    God hath now

Sponged and made blank of crimeful record
    all
My mortal archives.
              O my sons, my sons,
I, Simeon of the pillar, by surname
Stylites, among men; I, Simeon,        159
The watcher on the column till the end;
I, Simeon, whose brain the sunshine bakes;
I, whose bald brows in silent hours become
Unnaturally hoar with rime, do now
From my high nest of penance here pro-
    claim
That Pontius and Iscariot by my side
Show'd like fair seraphs.  On the coals I
    lay,
A vessel full of sin; all hell beneath
Made me boil over.  Devils pluck'd my
    sleeve,
Abaddon and Asmodeus caught at me.
I smote them with the cross; they swarm'd
    again.                            170
In bed like monstrous apes they crush'd
    my chest;
They flapp'd my light out as I read; I saw
Their faces grow between me and my
    book;
With coltlike whinny and with hoggish
    whine
They burst my prayer.  Yet this way was
    left,
And by this way I 'scaped them.  Mortify
Your flesh, like me, with scourges and with
    thorns;
Smite, shrink not, spare not.  If it may
    be, fast
Whole Lents, and pray.  I hardly, with
    slow steps,
With slow, faint steps, and much exceed-
    ing pain,                         180
Have scrambled past those pits of fire,
    that still
Sing in mine ears.  But yield not me the
    praise;
God only thro' his bounty hath thought fit,
Among the powers and princes of this
    world,
To make me an example to mankind,
Which few can reach to.  Yet I do not say
But that a time may come — yea, even
    now,
Now, now, his footsteps smite the thresh-
    old stairs
Of life — I say, that time is at the doors
When you may worship me without re-
    proach;                           190

For I will leave my relics in your land,
And you may carve a shrine about my dust,
And burn a fragrant lamp before my
    bones,
When I am gather'd to the glorious saints.
    While I spake then, a sting of shrewdest
    pain
Ran shrivelling thro' me, and a cloudlike
    change,
In passing, with a grosser film made thick
These heavy, horny eyes. The end! the end!
Surely the end! What 's here ? a shape,
    a shade,
A flash of light. Is that the angel there
That holds a crown ? Come, blessed bro-
    ther, come!                          201
I know thy glittering face. I waited long;
My brows are ready. What ! deny it now ?
Nay, draw, draw, draw nigh. So I clutch
    it. Christ!
'T is gone; 't is here again; the crown !
    the crown !
So now 't is fitted on and grows to me,
And from it melt the dews of Paradise,
Sweet! sweet ! spikenard, and balm, and
    frankincense.
Ah ! let me not be fool'd, sweet saints; I
    trust
That I am whole, and clean, and meet for
    Heaven.                             210
    Speak, if there be a priest, a man of
    God,
Among you there, and let him presently
Approach, and lean a ladder on the shaft,
And climbing up into my airy home,
Deliver me the blessed sacrament;
For by the warning of the Holy Ghost,
I prophesy that I shall die to-night,
A quarter before twelve.
                        But thou, O Lord,
Aid all this foolish people; let them take
Example, pattern; lead them to thy light.

## THE TALKING OAK

'An experiment meant to test the degree in
which it is within the power of poetry to human-
ize external nature' (Tennyson to Aubrey de
Vere).

ONCE more the gate behind me falls;
    Once more before my face
I see the moulder'd Abbey-walls,
    That stand within the chace.

Beyond the lodge the city lies,
    Beneath its drift of smoke;
And ah ! with what delighted eyes
    I turn to yonder oak.

For when my passion first began,
    Ere that which in me burn'd,          10
The love that makes me thrice a man,
    Could hope itself return'd,

To yonder oak within the field
    I spoke without restraint,
And with a larger faith appeal'd
    Than Papist unto Saint.

For oft I talk'd with him apart,
    And told him of my choice,
Until he plagiarized a heart,
    And answer'd with a voice.           20

Tho' what he whisper'd under heaven
    None else could understand,
I found him garrulously given,
    A babbler in the land.

But since I heard him make reply
    Is many a weary hour;
'T were well to question him, and try
    If yet he keeps the power.

Hail, hidden to the knees in fern,
    Broad Oak of Sumner-chace,           30
Whose topmost branches can discern
    The roofs of Sumner-place!

Say thou, whereon I carved her name,
    If ever maid or spouse,
As fair as my Olivia, came
    To rest beneath thy boughs.

'O Walter, I have shelter'd here
    Whatever maiden grace
The good old summers, year by year,
    Made ripe in Sumner-chace;           40

'Old summers, when the monk was fat,
    And, issuing shorn and sleek,
Would twist his girdle tight, and pat
    The girls upon the cheek,

'Ere yet, in scorn of Peter's-pence,
    And number'd bead, and shrift,
Bluff Harry broke into the spence
    And turn'd the cowls adrift.

' And I have seen some score of those
   Fresh faces that would thrive    50
When his man-minded offset rose
   To chase the deer at five;

' And all that from the town would stroll,
   Till that wild wind made work
In which the gloomy brewer's soul
   Went by me, like a stork;

' The slight she-slips of loyal blood,
   And others, passing praise,
Strait-laced, but all-too-full in bud
   For puritanic stays.    60

' And I have shadow'd many a group
   Of beauties that were born
In teacup-times of hood and hoop,
   Or while the patch was worn;

' And, leg and arm with love-knots gay,
   About me leap'd and laugh'd
The modish Cupid of the day,
   And shrill'd his tinsel shaft.

' I swear — and else may insects prick
   Each leaf into a gall ! —    70
This girl, for whom your heart is sick,
   Is three times worth them all;

' For those and theirs, by Nature's law,
   Have faded long ago;
But in these latter springs I saw
   Your own Olivia blow,

' From when she gamboll'd on the greens
   A baby-germ, to when
The maiden blossoms of her teens
   Could number five from ten.    80

' I swear, by leaf, and wind, and rain —
   And hear me with thine ears —
That, tho' I circle in the grain
   Five hundred rings of years,

' Yet, since I first could cast a shade,
   Did never creature pass
So slightly, musically made,
   So light upon the grass;

' For as to fairies, that will flit
   To make the greensward fresh,    90
I hold them exquisitely knit,
   But far too spare of flesh.'

O, hide thy knotted knees in fern,
   And overlook the chace,
And from thy topmost branch discern
   The roofs of Sumner-place !

But thou, whereon I carved her name,
   That oft hast heard my vows,
Declare when last Olivia came
   To sport beneath thy boughs.    100

' O, yesterday, you know, the fair
   Was holden at the town;
Her father left his good arm-chair,
   And rode his hunter down.

' And with him Albert came on his.
   I look'd at him with joy;
As cowslip unto oxlip is,
   So seems she to the boy.

' An hour had past — and, sitting straight
   Within the low-wheel'd chaise,    110
Her mother trundled to the gate
   Behind the dappled grays.

' But as for her, she staid at home,
   And on the roof she went,
And down the way you used to come,
   She look'd with discontent.

' She left the novel half-uncut
   Upon the rosewood shelf;
She left the new piano shut;
   She could not please herself.    120

' Then ran she, gamesome as the colt,
   And livelier than a lark
She sent her voice thro' all the holt
   Before her, and the park.

' A light wind chased her on the wing,
   And in the chase grew wild,
As close as might be would he cling
   About the darling child;

' But light as any wind that blows
   So fleetly did she stir,    130
The flower she touch'd on dipt and rose,
   And turn'd to look at her.

' And here she came, and round me play'd,
   And sang to me the whole
Of those three stanzas that you made
   About my " giant bole; "

'And in a fit of frolic mirth
  She strove to span my waist.
Alas ! I was so broad of girth,
  I could not be embraced.    140

'I wish'd myself the fair young beech
  That here beside me stands,
That round me, clasping each in each,
  She might have lock'd her hands.

'Yet seem'd the pressure thrice as sweet
  As woodbine's fragile hold,
Or when I feel about my feet
  The berried briony fold.'

O, muffle round thy knees with fern,
  And shadow Sumner-chace !    150
Long may thy topmost branch discern
  The roofs of Sumner-place !

But tell me, did she read the name
  I carved with many vows
When last with throbbing heart I came
  To rest beneath thy boughs ?

'O, yes, she wander'd round and round
  These knotted knees of mine,
And found, and kiss'd the name she found,
  And sweetly murmur'd thine.    160

'A teardrop trembled from its source,
  And down my surface crept.
My sense of touch is something coarse,
  But I believe she wept.

'Then flush'd her cheek with rosy light,
  She glanced across the plain,
But not a creature was in sight;
  She kiss'd me once again.

'Her kisses were so close and kind
  That, trust me on my word,    170
Hard wood I am, and wrinkled rind,
  But yet my sap was stirr'd;

'And even into my inmost ring
  A pleasure I discern'd,
Like those blind motions of the spring
  That show the year is turn'd.

'Thrice-happy he that may caress
  The ringlet's waving balm —
The cushions of whose touch may press
  The maiden's tender palm.    180

'I, rooted here among the groves,
  But languidly adjust
My vapid vegetable loves
  With anthers and with dust;

'For ah ! my friend, the days were brief
  Whereof the poets talk,
When that which breathes within the leaf
  Could slip its bark and walk.

'But could I, as in times foregone,
  From spray and branch and stem    190
Have suck'd and gather'd into one
  The life that spreads in them,

'She had not found me so remiss;
  But lightly issuing thro',
I would have paid her kiss for kiss,
  With usury thereto.'

O, flourish high, with leafy towers,
  And overlook the lea !
Pursue thy loves among the bowers,
  But leave thou mine to me.    200

O, flourish, hidden deep in fern,
  Old oak, I love thee well !
A thousand thanks for what I learn
  And what remains to tell.

''T is little more: the day was warm;
  At last, tired out with play,
She sank her head upon her arm
  And at my feet she lay.

'Her eyelids dropp'd their silken eaves.
  I breathed upon her eyes    210
Thro' all the summer of my leaves
  A welcome mix'd with sighs.

'I took the swarming sound of life —
  The music from the town —
The murmurs of the drum and fife,
  And lull'd them in my own.

'Sometimes I let a sunbeam slip,
  To light her shaded eye;
A second flutter'd round her lip
  Like a golden butterfly;    220

'A third would glimmer on her neck
  To make the necklace shine;
Another slid, a sunny fleck,
  From head to ankle fine.

'Then close and dark my arms I spread,
  And shadow'd all her rest —
Dropt dews upon her golden head,
  An acorn in her breast.

'But in a pet she started up,
  And pluck'd it out, and drew      230
My little oakling from the cup,
  And flung him in the dew.

'And yet it was a graceful gift —
  I felt a pang within
As when I see the woodman lift
  His axe to slay my kin.

'I shook him down because he was
  The finest on the tree.
He lies beside thee on the grass.
  O, kiss him once for me !          240

'O, kiss him twice and thrice for me,
  That have no lips to kiss !
For never yet was oak on lea
  Shall grow so fair as this.'

Step deeper yet in herb and fern,
  Look further thro' the chace,
Spread upward till thy boughs discern
  The front of Sumner-place.

This fruit of thine by Love is blest,
  That but a moment lay            250
Where fairer fruit of Love may rest
  Some happy future day.

I kiss it twice, I kiss it thrice,
  The warmth it thence shall win
To riper life may magnetize
  The baby-oak within.

But thou, while kingdoms overset,
  Or lapse from hand to hand,
Thy leaf shall never fail, nor yet
  Thine acorn in the land.         260

May never saw dismember thee,
  Nor wielded axe disjoint,
That art the fairest-spoken tree
  From here to Lizard-point.

O, rock upon thy towery top
  All throats that gurgle sweet !
All starry culmination drop
  Balm-dews to bathe thy feet !

All grass of silky feather grow —
  And while he sinks or swells      270
The full south-breeze around thee blow
  The sound of minster bells !

The fat earth feed thy branchy root,
  That under deeply strikes !
The northern morning o'er thee shoot,
  High up, in silver spikes !

Nor ever lightning char thy grain,
  But, rolling as in sleep,
Low thunders bring the mellow rain,
  That makes thee broad and deep !   280

And hear me swear a solemn oath,
  That only by thy side
Will I to Olive plight my troth,
  And gain her for my bride.

And when my marriage morn may fall,
  She, Dryad-like, shall wear
Alternate leaf and acorn-ball
  In wreath about her hair.

And I will work in prose and rhyme,
  And praise thee more in both       290
Than bard has honor'd beech or lime,
  Or that Thessalian growth

In which the swarthy ringdove sat,
  And mystic sentence spoke;
And more than England honors that,
  Thy famous brother-oak,

Wherein the younger Charles abode
  Till all the paths were dim,
And far below the Roundhead rode,
  And humm'd a surly hymn.          300

## LOVE AND DUTY

First printed in 1842, and afterwards altered
but slightly.  See Notes.

Of love that never found his earthly close,
What sequel ?   Streaming eyes and break-
    ing hearts ?
Or all the same as if he had not been ?
    Not so.  Shall Error in the round of
    time
Still father Truth ?   O, shall the braggart
    shout

For some blind glimpse of freedom work
    itself
Thro' madness, hated by the wise, to law,
System, and empire ?   Sin itself be found
The cloudy porch oft opening on the sun ?
And only he, this wonder, dead, become   10
Mere highway dust ? or year by year alone
Sit brooding in the ruins of a life,
Nightmare of youth, the spectre of him-
    self ?
    If this were thus, if this, indeed, were
      all,
Better the narrow brain, the stony heart,
The staring eye glazed o'er with sapless
    days,
The long mechanic pacings to and fro,
The set gray life, and apathetic end.
But am I not the nobler thro' thy love ?
O, three times less unworthy! likewise
    thou                                       20
Art more thro' Love, and greater than thy
    years,
The sun will run his orbit, and the moon
Her circle.   Wait, and Love himself will
    bring
The drooping flower of knowledge changed
    to fruit
Of wisdom.   Wait; my faith is large in
    Time,
And that which shapes it to some perfect
    end.
    Will some one say, Then why not ill for
      good ?
Why took ye not your pastime ?   To that
    man
My work shall answer, since I knew the
    right
And did it; for a man is not as God,   30
But then most Godlike being most a
    man. —
So let me think 't is well for thee and
    me —
Ill-fated that I am, what lot is mine
Whose foresight preaches peace, my heart
    so slow
To feel it !   For how hard it seem'd to
    me,
When eyes, love-languid thro' half tears
    would dwell
One earnest, earnest moment upon mine,
Then not to dare to see ! when thy low
    voice,
Faltering, would break its syllables, to keep
My own full-tuned, — hold passion in a
    leash,                                       40

And not leap forth and fall about thy neck,
And on thy bosom — deep desired relief ! —
Rain out the heavy mist of tears, that
    weigh'd
Upon my brain, my senses, and my soul !
    For Love himself took part against him-
      self
To warn us off, and Duty loved of Love —
O, this world's curse — beloved but hated
    — came
Like Death betwixt thy dear embrace and
    mine,
And crying, 'Who is this ?  behold thy
    bride,'                                       49
She push'd me from thee.
               If the sense is hard
To alien ears, I did not speak to these —
No, not to thee, but to thyself in me.
Hard is my doom and thine; thou knowest
    it all.
    Could Love part thus ? was it not well to
      speak,
To have spoken once ?   It could not but
    be well.
The slow sweet hours that bring us all
    things good,
The slow sad hours that bring us all things
    ill,
And all good things from evil, brought the
    night
In which we sat together and alone,
And to the want that hollow'd all the
    heart                                       60
Gave utterance by the yearning of an eye,
That burn'd upon its object thro' such tears
As flow but once a life.
               The trance gave way
To those caresses, when a hundred times
In that last kiss, which never was the last,
Farewell, like endless welcome, lived and
    died.
Then follow'd counsel, comfort, and the
    words
That make a man feel strong in speaking
    truth;
Till now the dark was worn, and over-
    head
The lights of sunset and of sunrise mix'd
In that brief night, the summer night, that
    paused                                       71
Among her stars to hear us, stars that hung
Love-charm'd to listen; all the wheels of
    Time
Spun round in station, but the end had
    come.

O, then, like those who clench their
     nerves to rush
Upon their dissolution, we two rose,
There — closing like an individual life —
In one blind cry of passion and of pain,
Like bitter accusation even to death,
Caught up the whole of love and utter'd
     it,                                    80
And bade adieu for ever.
                    Live — yet live —
Shall sharpest pathos blight us, knowing
     all
Life needs for life is possible to will? —
Live happy; tend thy flowers; be tended by
My blessing! Should my Shadow cross
     thy thoughts
Too sadly for their peace, remand it thou
For calmer hours to Memory's darkest
     hold,
If not to be forgotten — not at once —
Not all forgotten. Should it cross thy
     dreams,
O, might it come like one that looks con-
     tent,                                  90
With quiet eyes unfaithful to the truth,
And point thee forward to a distant light,
Or seem to lift a burthen from thy heart
And leave thee freer, till thou wake re-
     fresh'd
Then when the first low matin-chirp hath
     grown
Full quire, and morning driven her plow
     of pearl
Far furrowing into light the mounded
     rack,
Beyond the fair green field and eastern sea.

## THE GOLDEN YEAR

First printed in 1846, in the fourth edition
of the 'Poems,' and unaltered except in one
passage. See Notes.

WELL, you shall have that song which
     Leonard wrote:
It was last summer on a tour in Wales.
Old James was with me; we that day had
     been
Up Snowdon; and I wish'd for Leonard
     there,
And found him in Llanberis. Then we
     crost
Between the lakes, and clamber'd half-way
     up

The counter side; and that same song of
     his
He told me, for I banter'd him and swore
They said he lived shut up within himself,
A tongue-tied poet in the feverous days   10
That, setting the *how much* before the *how*,
Cry, like the daughters of the horseleech,
     'Give,
Cram us with all,' but count not me the
     herd!
To which 'They call me what they will,'
     he said:
'But I was born too late; the fair new
     forms,
That float about the threshold of an age,
Like truths of Science waiting to be
     caught —
Catch me who can, and make the catcher
     crown'd —
Are taken by the forelock. Let it be.
But if you care indeed to listen, hear    20
These measured words, my work of yester-
     morn:
  'We sleep and wake and sleep, but all
     things move;
The sun flies forward to his brother sun;
The dark earth follows wheel'd in her
     ellipse;
And human things returning on themselves
Move onward, leading up the golden year.
  'Ah! tho' the times when some new
     thought can bud
Are but as poets' seasons when they flower,
Yet seas that daily gain upon the shore
Have ebb and flow conditioning their
     march,                                 30
And slow and sure comes up the golden
     year;
  'When wealth no more shall rest in
     mounded heaps,
But smit with freer light shall slowly melt
In many streams to fatten lower lands,
And light shall spread, and man be liker
     man
Thro' all the season of the golden year.
  'Shall eagles not be eagles? wrens be
     wrens?
If all the world were falcons, what of that?
The wonder of the eagle were the less,
But he not less the eagle. Happy days    40
Roll onward, leading up the golden year.
  'Fly, happy, happy sails, and bear the
     Press;
Fly happy with the mission of the Cross;
Knit land to land, and blowing havenward

With silks, and fruits, and spices, clear of
      toll,
Enrich the markets of the golden year.
   'But we grow old.   Ah ! when shall all
      men's good
Be each man's rule, and universal Peace
Lie like a shaft of light across the land,   49
And like a lane of beams athwart the sea,
Thro' all the circle of the golden year ?'
   Thus far he flow'd, and ended; where-
      upon
'Ah, folly !' in mimic cadence answer'd
   James —
'Ah, folly ! for it lies so far away,
Not in our time, nor in our children's time,
'T is like the second world to us that live;
'T were all as one to fix our hopes on
      heaven
As on this vision of the golden year.'
   With that he struck his staff against the
      rocks
And broke it, — James, — you know him,
      — old, but full                      60
Of force and choler, and firm upon his feet,
And like an oaken stock in winter woods,
O'erflourish'd with the hoary clematis;
Then added, all in heat:
            'What stuff is this !
Old writers push'd the happy season back,—
The more fools they, — we forward; dream-
      ers both —
You most, that, in an age when every hour
Must sweat her sixty minutes to the death,
Live on, God love us, as if the seedsman,
      rapt
Upon the teeming harvest, should not
      plunge                               70
His hand into the bag; but well I know
That unto him who works, and feels he
      works,
This same grand year is ever at the doors.'
   He spoke; and, high above, I heard them
      blast
The steep slate-quarry, and the great echo
      flap
And buffet round the hills, from bluff to
      bluff.

## ULYSSES

First printed in 1842, and unaltered.

IT little profits that an idle king,
By this still hearth, among these barren
      crags,

Match'd with an aged wife, I mete and
      dole
Unequal laws unto a savage race,
That hoard, and sleep, and feed, and know
      not me.
I cannot rest from travel; I will drink
Life to the lees.   All times I have enjoy'd
Greatly, have suffer'd greatly, both with
      those
That loved me, and alone; on shore, and
      when
Thro' scudding drifts the rainy Hyades   10
Vext the dim sea.   I am become a name;
For always roaming with a hungry heart
Much have I seen and known, — cities of
      men
And manners, climates, councils, govern-
      ments,
Myself not least, but honor'd of them
      all, —
And drunk delight of battle with my
      peers,
Far on the ringing plains of windy Troy.
I am a part of all that I have met;
Yet all experience is an arch wherethro'
Gleams that untravell'd world whose mar-
      gin fades                           20
For ever and for ever when I move.
How dull it is to pause, to make an end,
To rust unburnish'd, not to shine in use !
As tho' to breathe were life ! Life piled
      on life
Were all too little, and of one to me
Little remains; but every hour is saved
From that eternal silence, something more,
A bringer of new things; and vile it were
For some three suns to store and hoard
      myself,
And this gray spirit yearning in desire   30
To follow knowledge like a sinking star,
Beyond the utmost bound of human
      thought.
   This is my son, mine own Telemachus,
To whom I leave the sceptre and the
      isle, —
Well-loved of me, discerning to fulfil
This labor, by slow prudence to make mild
A rugged people, and thro' soft degrees
Subdue them to the useful and the good.
Most blameless is he, centred in the sphere
Of common duties, decent not to fail   40
In offices of tenderness, and pay
Meet adoration to my household gods,
When I am gone.   He works his work, I
      mine.

There lies the port; the vessel puffs her
sail;
There gloom the dark, broad seas.   My
mariners,
Souls that have toil'd, and wrought, and
thought with me, —
That ever with a frolic welcome took
The thunder and the sunshine, and op-
posed
Free hearts, free foreheads, — you and I
are old;
Old age hath yet his honor and his toil.   50
Death closes all; but something ere the
end,
Some work of noble note, may yet be done,
Not unbecoming men that strove with
Gods.
The lights begin to twinkle from the rocks;
The long day wanes; the slow moon climbs;
the deep
Moans round with many voices.   Come,
my friends.
'T is not too late to seek a' newer world.
Push off, and sitting well in order smite
The sounding furrows; for my purpose
holds
To sail beyond the sunset, and the baths  60
Of all the western stars, until I die.
It may be that the gulfs will wash us
down;
It may be we shall touch the Happy Isles,
And see the great Achilles, whom we knew.
Tho' much is taken, much abides; and
tho'
We are not now that strength which in old
days
Moved earth and heaven, that which we
are, we are, —
One equal temper of heroic hearts,
Made weak by time and fate, but strong in
will
To strive, to seek, to find, and not to
yield.                                      70

## TITHONUS

First printed in the ' Cornhill Magazine ' for
February, 1860, and afterwards included in the
' Enoch Arden ' volume in 1864.   See Notes.

THE woods decay, the woods decay and
fall,
The vapors weep their burthen to the
ground,

Man comes and tills the field and lies be-
neath,
And after many a summer dies the swan.
Me only cruel immortality
Consumes; I wither slowly in thine arms,
Here at the quiet limit of the world,
A white-hair'd shadow roaming like a
dream
The ever-silent spaces of the East,
Far-folded mists, and gleaming halls of
morn.                                       10
Alas ! for this gray shadow, once a
man —
So glorious in his beauty and thy choice,
Who madest him thy chosen, that he
seem'd
To his great heart none other than a God!
I ask'd thee, ' Give me immortality.'
Then didst thou grant mine asking with a
smile,
Like wealthy men who care not how they
give.
But thy strong Hours indignant work'd
their wills,
And beat me down and marr'd and wasted
me,
And tho' they could not end me, left me
maim'd                                      20
To dwell in presence of immortal youth,
Immortal age beside immortal youth,
And all I was in ashes.   Can thy love,
Thy beauty, make amends, tho' even now,
Close over us, the silver star, thy guide,
Shines in those tremulous eyes that fill with
tears
To hear me ?   Let me go; take back thy
gift.
Why should a man desire in any way
To vary from the kindly race of men,
Or pass beyond the goal of ordinance    30
Where all should pause, as is most meet
for all ?
A soft air fans the cloud apart; there
comes
A glimpse of that dark world where I was
born.
Once more the old mysterious glimmer
steals
From thy pure brows, and from thy shoul-
ders pure,
And bosom beating with a heart renew'd.
Thy cheek begins to redden thro' the
gloom,
Thy sweet eyes brighten slowly close to
mine,

Ere yet they blind the stars, and the wild
    team
Which love thee, yearning for thy yoke,
    arise,                    40
And shake the darkness from their loosen'd
    manes,
And beat the twilight into flakes of fire.
  Lo ! ever thus thou growest beautiful
In silence, then before thine answer given
Departest, and thy tears are on my cheek.
  Why wilt thou ever scare me with thy
    tears,
And make me tremble lest a saying learnt,
In days far-off, on that dark earth, be true ?
' The Gods themselves cannot recall their
    gifts.'
  Ay me ! ay me ! with what another
    heart                   50
In days far-off, and with what other eyes
I used to watch — if I be he that watch'd —
The lucid outline forming round thee; saw
The dim curls kindle into sunny rings;
Changed with thy mystic change, and felt
    my blood
Glow with the glow that slowly crimson'd
    all
Thy presence and thy portals, while I lay,
Mouth, forehead, eyelids, growing dewy-
    warm
With kisses balmier than half-opening buds
Of April, and could hear the lips that
    kiss'd                60
Whispering I knew not what of wild and
    sweet,
Like that strange song I heard Apollo
    sing,
While Ilion like a mist rose into towers.
  Yet hold me not for ever in thine East;
How can my nature longer mix with thine ?
Coldly thy rosy shadows bathe me, cold
Are all thy lights, and cold my wrinkled
    feet
Upon thy glimmering thresholds, when the
    steam
Floats up from those dim fields about the
    homes
Of happy men that have the power to
    die,                  70
And grassy barrows of the happier dead.
Release me, and restore me to the ground.
Thou seest all things, thou wilt see my
    grave;
Thou wilt renew thy beauty morn by morn,
I earth in earth forget these empty courts,
And thee returning on thy silver wheels.

## LOCKSLEY HALL

First printed in 1842, and slightly altered in
subsequent editions.  See Notes.

COMRADES, leave me here a little, while as
    yet 't is early morn;
Leave me here, and when you want me,
    sound upon the bugle-horn.

'T is the place, and all around it, as of old,
    the curlews call,
Dreary gleams about the moorland flying
    over Locksley Hall;

Locksley Hall, that in the distance over-
    looks the sandy tracts,
And the hollow ocean-ridges roaring into
    cataracts.

Many a night from yonder ivied casement,
    ere I went to rest,
Did I look on great Orion sloping slowly
    to the west.

Many a night I saw the Pleiads, rising
    thro' the mellow shade,
Glitter like a swarm of fireflies tangled in
    a silver braid.          10

Here about the beach I wander'd, nour-
    ishing a youth sublime
With the fairy tales of science, and the
    long result of time;

When the centuries behind me like a fruit-
    ful land reposed;
When I clung to all the present for the
    promise that it closed;

When I dipt into the future far as human
    eye could see,
Saw the vision of the world and all the
    wonder that would be. —

In the spring a fuller crimson comes upon
    the robin's breast;
In the spring the wanton lapwing gets him-
    self another crest;

In the spring a livelier iris changes on the
    burnish'd dove;
In the spring a young man's fancy lightly
    turns to thoughts of love.      20

Then her cheek was pale and thinner than
   should be for one so young,
And her eyes on all my motions with a
   mute observance hung.

And I said, 'My cousin Amy, speak, and
   speak the truth to me,
Trust me, cousin, all the current of my
   being sets to thee.'

On her pallid cheek and forehead came a
   color and a light,
As I have seen the rosy red flushing in the
   northern night.

And she turn'd — her bosom shaken with
   a sudden storm of sighs —
All the spirit deeply dawning in the dark
   of hazel eyes —

Saying, 'I have hid my feelings, fearing
   they should do me wrong;'
Saying, 'Dost thou love me, cousin?' weeping, 'I have loved thee long.'   30

Love took up the glass of Time, and turn'd
   it in his glowing hands;
Every moment, lightly shaken, ran itself
   in golden sands.

Love took up the harp of Life, and smote
   on all the chords with might;
Smote the chord of Self, that, trembling,
   past in music out of sight.

Many a morning on the moorland did we
   hear the copses ring,
And her whisper throng'd my pulses with
   the fulness of the spring.

Many an evening by the waters did we
   watch the stately ships,
And our spirits rush'd together at the
   touching of the lips.

O my cousin, shallow - hearted! O my
   Amy, mine no more!
O the dreary, dreary moorland! O the
   barren, barren shore!   40

Falser than all fancy fathoms, falser than
   all songs have sung,
Puppet to a father's threat, and servile to
   a shrewish tongue!

Is it well to wish thee happy? — having
   known me — to decline
On a range of lower feelings and a narrower heart than mine!

Yet it shall be; thou shalt lower to his level
   day by day,
What is fine within thee growing coarse to
   sympathize with clay.

As the husband is, the wife is; thou art
   mated with a clown,
And the grossness of his nature will have
   weight to drag thee down.

He will hold thee, when his passion shall
   have spent its novel force,
Something better than his dog, a little
   dearer than his horse.   50

What is this? his eyes are heavy; think
   not they are glazed with wine.
Go to him, it is thy duty; kiss him, take
   his hand in thine.

It may be my lord is weary, that his brain
   is overwrought;
Soothe him with thy finer fancies, touch
   him with thy lighter thought.

He will answer to the purpose, easy things
   to understand —
Better thou wert dead before me, tho' I
   slew thee with my hand!

Better thou and I were lying, hidden from
   the heart's disgrace,
Roll'd in one another's arms, and silent in
   a last embrace.

Cursed be the social wants that sin against
   the strength of youth!
Cursed be the social lies that warp us from
   the living truth!   60

Cursed be the sickly forms that err from
   honest Nature's rule!
Cursed be the gold that gilds the straiten'd
   forehead of the fool!

Well — 't is well that I should bluster! —
   Hadst thou less unworthy proved —
Would to God — for I had loved thee more
   than ever wife was loved.

Am I mad, that I should cherish that
    which bears but bitter fruit ?
I will pluck it from my bosom, tho' my
    heart be at the root.

Never, tho' my mortal summers to such
    length of years should come
As the many-winter'd crow that leads the
    clanging rookery home.

Where is comfort ? in division of the rec-
    ords of the mind ?
Can I part her from herself, and love her,
    as I knew her, kind ?        70

I remember one that perish'd; sweetly did
    she speak and move;
Such a one do I remember, whom to look
    at was to love.

Can I think of her as dead, and love her
    for the love she bore ?
No — she never loved me truly; love is
    love for evermore.

Comfort? comfort scorn'd of devils ! this
    is truth the poet sings,
That a sorrow's crown of sorrow is remem-
    bering happier things.

Drug thy memories, lest thou learn it, lest
    thy heart be put to proof,
In the dead unhappy night, and when the
    rain is on the roof.

Like a dog, he hunts in dreams, and thou
    art staring at the wall,
Where the dying night-lamp flickers, and
    the shadows rise and fall.        80

Then a hand shall pass before thee, pointing
    to his drunken sleep,
To thy widow'd marriage-pillows, to the
    tears that thou wilt weep.

Thou shalt hear the 'Never, never,' whis-
    per'd by the phantom years,
And a song from out the distance in the
    ringing of thine ears;

And an eye shall vex thee, looking ancient
    kindness on thy pain.
Turn thee, turn thee on thy pillow; get
    thee to thy rest again.

Nay, but Nature brings thee solace; for a
    tender voice will cry.
'T is a purer life than thine, a lip to drain
    thy trouble dry.

Baby lips will laugh me down; my latest
    rival brings thee rest.
Baby fingers, waxen touches, press me from
    the mother's breast.        90

O, the child too clothes the father with a
    dearness not his due.
Half is thine and half is his; it will be
    worthy of the two.

O, I see thee old and formal, fitted to thy
    petty part,
With a little hoard of maxims preaching
    down a daughter's heart.

'They were dangerous guides the feelings
    — she herself was not exempt —
Truly, she herself had suffer'd ' — Perish in
    thy self-contempt !

Overlive it — lower yet — be happy ! where-
    fore should I care ?
I myself must mix with action, lest I
    wither by despair.

What is that which I should turn to, light-
    ing upon days like these ?
Every door is barr'd with gold, and opens
    but to golden keys.        100

Every gate is throng'd with suitors, all the
    markets overflow.
I have but an angry fancy; what is that
    which I should do ?

I had been content to perish, falling on the
    foeman's ground,
When the ranks are roll'd in vapor, and
    the winds are laid with sound.

But the jingling of the guinea helps the
    hurt that Honor feels,
And the nations do but murmur, snarling at
    each other's heels.

Can I but relive in sadness?   I will turn
    that earlier page.
Hide me from my deep emotion, O thou
    wondrous Mother-Age !

Make me feel the wild pulsation that I felt
  before the strife,
When I heard my days before me, and the
  tumult of my life;                    110

Yearning for the large excitement that the
  coming years would yield,
Eager-hearted as a boy when first he leaves
  his father's field,

And at night along the dusky highway
  near and nearer drawn,
Sees in heaven the light of London flaring
  like a dreary dawn;

And his spirit leaps within him to be gone
  before him then,
Underneath the light he looks at, in among
  the throngs of men;

Men, my brothers, men the workers, ever
  reaping something new;
That which they have done but earnest of
  the things that they shall do.

For I dipt into the future, far as human eye
  could see,
Saw the Vision of the world, and all the
  wonder that would be;        120

Saw the heavens fill with commerce, argosies of magic sails,
Pilots of the purple twilight, dropping
  down with costly bales;

Heard the heavens fill with shouting, and
  there rain'd a ghastly dew
From the nations' airy navies grappling in
  the central blue;

Far along the world-wide whisper of the
  south-wind rushing warm,
With the standards of the peoples plunging thro' the thunder-storm;

Till the war-drum throbb'd no longer, and
  the battle-flags were furl'd
In the Parliament of man, the Federation
  of the world.

There the common sense of most shall hold
  a fretful realm in awe,
And the kindly earth shall slumber, lapt in
  universal law.              130

So I triumph'd ere my passion sweeping
  thro' me left me dry,
Left me with the palsied heart, and left me
  with the jaundiced eye;

Eye, to which all order festers, all things
  here are out of joint.
Science moves, but slowly, slowly, creeping
  on from point to point;

Slowly comes a hungry people, as a lion,
  creeping nigher,
Glares at one that nods and winks behind a
  slowly-dying fire.

Yet I doubt not thro' the ages one increasing purpose runs,
And the thoughts of men are widen'd with
  the process of the suns.

What is that to him that reaps not harvest
  of his youthful joys,
Tho' the deep heart of existence beat for
  ever like a boy's ?              140

Knowledge comes, but wisdom lingers, and
  I linger on the shore,
And the individual withers, and the world
  is more and more.

Knowledge comes, but wisdom lingers, and
  he bears a laden breast,
Full of sad experience, moving toward the
  stillness of his rest.

Hark, my merry comrades call me, sounding on the bugle-horn,
They to whom my foolish passion were a
  target for their scorn.

Shall it not be scorn to me to harp on such
  a moulder'd string ?
I am shamed thro' all my nature to have
  loved so slight a thing.

Weakness to be wroth with weakness !
  woman's pleasure, woman's pain —
Nature made them blinder motions bounded
  in a shallower brain.          150

Woman is the lesser man, and all thy
  passions, match'd with mine,
Are as moonlight unto sunlight, and as
  water unto wine —

Here at least, where nature sickens, nothing.
    Ah, for some retreat
Deep in yonder shining Orient, where my
    life began to beat,

Where in wild Mahratta-battle fell my
    father evil-starr'd; —
I was left a trampled orphan, and a selfish
    uncle's ward.

Or to burst all links of habit — there to
    wander far away,
On from island unto island at the gateways
    of the day.

Larger constellations burning, mellow
    moons and happy skies,
Breadths of tropic shade and palms in clus-
    ter, knots of Paradise.    160

Never comes the trader, never floats an
    European flag,
Slides the bird o'er lustrous woodland,
    swings the trailer from the crag;

Droops the heavy-blossom'd bower, hangs
    the heavy-fruited tree —
Summer isles of Eden lying in dark-purple
    spheres of sea.

There methinks would be enjoyment more
    than in this march of mind,
In the steamship, in the railway, in the
    thoughts that shake mankind.

There the passions cramp'd no longer shall
    have scope and breathing space;
I will take some savage woman, she shall
    rear my dusky race.

Iron-jointed, supple-sinew'd, they shall dive,
    and they shall run,
Catch the wild goat by the hair, and hurl
    their lances in the sun;    170

Whistle back the parrot's call, and leap the
    rainbows of the brooks,
Not with blinded eyesight poring over mis-
    erable books —

Fool, again the dream, the fancy ! but I
    *know* my words are wild,

But I count the gray barbarian lower than
    the Christian child.

I, to herd with narrow foreheads, vacant of
    our glorious gains,
Like a beast with lower pleasures, like a
    beast with lower pains !

Mated with a squalid savage — what to me
    were sun or clime ?
I the heir of all the ages, in the foremost
    files of time —

I that rather held it better men should per-
    ish one by one,
Than that earth should stand at gaze like
    Joshua's moon in Ajalon !    180

Not in vain the distance beacons. Forward,
    forward let us range,
Let the great world spin for ever down the
    ringing grooves of change.

Thro' the shadow of the globe we sweep
    into the younger day;
Better fifty years of Europe than a cycle
    of Cathay.

Mother-Age, — for mine I knew not, — help
    me as when life begun;
Rift the hills, and roll the waters, flash the
    lightnings, weigh the sun.

O, I see the crescent promise of my spirit
    hath not set.
Ancient founts of inspiration well thro' all
    my fancy yet.

Howsoever these things be, a long farewell
    to Locksley Hall !
Now for me the woods may wither, now for
    me the roof-tree fall.    190

Comes a vapor from the margin, blacken-
    ing over heath and holt,
Cramming all the blast before it, in its
    breast a thunderbolt.

Let it fall on Locksley Hall, with rain or
    hail, or fire or snow;
For the mighty wind arises, roaring sea-
    ward, and I go.

## GODIVA

First published in 1842, when line 64 had 'archways.'

*I WAITED for the train at Coventry;*
*I hung with grooms and porters on the bridge,*
*To watch the three tall spires; and there I shaped*
*The city's ancient legend into this : —*

Not only we, the latest seed of Time,
New men, that in the flying of a wheel
Cry down the past, not only we, that prate
Of rights and wrongs, have loved the people well,
And loathed to see them overtax'd; but she  9
Did more, and underwent, and overcame,
The woman of a thousand summers back,
Godiva, wife to that grim Earl, who ruled
In Coventry; for when he laid a tax
Upon his town, and all the mothers brought
Their children, clamoring, 'If we pay, we starve !'
She sought her lord, and found him, where he strode
About the hall, among his dogs, alone,
His beard a foot before him, and his hair
A yard behind. She told him of their tears,
And pray'd him, ' If they pay this tax, they starve.'  20
Whereat he stared, replying, half-amazed,
' You would not let your little finger ache
For such as *these ?* ' — ' But I would die,' said she.
He laugh'd, and swore by Peter and by Paul,
Then fillip'd at the diamond in her ear:
' O, ay, ay, ay, you talk !' — ' Alas !' she said,
' But prove me what it is I would not do.'
And from a heart as rough as Esau's hand,
He answer'd, ' Ride you naked thro' the town,  29
And I repeal it;' and nodding, as in scorn,
He parted, with great strides among his dogs.
So left alone, the passions of her mind,
As winds from all the compass shift and blow,
Made war upon each other for an hour,
Till pity won. She sent a herald forth,
And bade him cry, with sound of trumpet, all
The hard condition, but that she would loose
The people; therefore, as they loved her well,
From then till noon no foot should pace the street,  39
No eye look down, she passing, but that all
Should keep within, door shut, and window barr'd.
Then fled she to her inmost bower, and there
Unclasp'd the wedded eagles of her belt,
The grim Earl's gift; but ever at a breath
She linger'd, looking like a summer moon
Half-dipt in cloud. Anon she shook her head,
And shower'd the rippled ringlets to her knee;
Unclad herself in haste; adown the stair
Stole on; and like a creeping sunbeam slid
From pillar unto pillar, until she reach'd  50
The gateway; there she found her palfrey trapt
In purple blazon'd with armorial gold.
Then she rode forth, clothed on with chastity.
The deep air listen'd round her as she rode,
And all the low wind hardly breathed for fear.
The little wide-mouth'd heads upon the spout
Had cunning eyes to see; the barking cur
Made her cheek flame; her palfrey's foot-fall shot
Light horrors thro' her pulses; the blind walls
Were full of chinks and holes; and over-head  60
Fantastic gables, crowding, stared; but she
Not less thro' all bore up, till, last, she saw
The white-flower'd elder-thicket from the field
Gleam thro' the Gothic archway in the wall.
Then she rode back, clothed on with chastity.
And one low churl, compact of thankless earth,
The fatal byword of all years to come,
Boring a little auger-hole in fear,
Peep'd — but his eyes, before they had their will,

Were shrivell'd into darkness in his head,
And dropt before him.  So the Powers,
       who wait                              71
On noble deeds, cancell'd a sense misused;
And she, that knew not, pass'd; and all at
       once,
With twelve great shocks of sound, the
       shameless noon
Was clash'd and hammer'd from a hun-
       dred towers,
One after one; but even then she gain'd
Her bower, whence reissuing, robed and
       crown'd,
To meet her lord, she took the tax away
And built herself an everlasting name.


## THE DAY-DREAM

The part of this poem entitled 'The Sleeping Beauty' was printed in 1830; the rest was
added in 1842, and a few alterations have since
been made.

### PROLOGUE

O LADY FLORA, let me speak;
   A pleasant hour has passed away
While, dreaming on your damask cheek,
   The dewy sister-eyelids lay.
As by the lattice you reclined,
   I went thro' many wayward moods
To see you dreaming — and, behind,
   A summer crisp with shining woods.
And I too dream'd, until at last
   Across my fancy, brooding warm,     10
The reflex of a legend past,
   And loosely settled into form.
And would you have the thought I had,
   And see the vision that I saw,
Then take the broidery-frame, and add
   A crimson to the quaint macaw,
And I will tell it.  Turn your face,
   Nor look with that too-earnest eye —
The rhymes are dazzled from their place
   And order'd words asunder fly.       20


### THE SLEEPING PALACE

#### I

THE varying year with blade and sheaf
   Clothes and reclothes the happy plains,
Here rests the sap within the leaf,
   Here stays the blood along the veins.

Faint shadows, vapors lightly curl'd,
   Faint murmurs from the meadows come,
Like hints and echoes of the world
   To spirits folded in the womb.

#### II

Soft lustre bathes the range of urns
   On every slanting terrace-lawn.      30
The fountain to his place returns
   Deep in the garden lake withdrawn.
Here droops the banner on the tower,
   On the hall-hearths the festal fires,
The peacock in his laurel bower,
   The parrot in his gilded wires.

#### III

Roof-haunting martins warm their eggs;
   In these, in those the life is stay'd.
The mantles from the golden pegs
   Droop sleepily; no sound is made,    40
Not even of a gnat that sings.
   More like a picture seemeth all
Than those old portraits of old kings,
   That watch the sleepers from the wall.

#### IV

Here sits the butler with a flask
   Between his knees, half-drain'd; and
       there
The wrinkled steward at his task,
   The maid-of-honor blooming fair.
The page has caught her hand in his;
   Her lips are sever'd as to speak;    50
His own are pouted to a kiss;
   The blush is fix'd upon her cheek.

#### V

Till all the hundred summers pass,
   The beams that thro' the oriel shine
Make prisms in every carven glass
   And beaker brimm'd with noble wine.
Each baron at the banquet sleeps,
   Grave faces gather'd in a ring.
His state the king reposing keeps.
   He must have been a jovial king.     60

#### VI

All round a hedge upshoots, and shows
   At distance like a little wood;
Thorns, ivies, woodbine, mistletoes,
   And grapes with bunches red as blood;
All creeping plants, a wall of green
   Close-matted, bur and brake and brier,
And glimpsing over these, just seen,
   High up, the topmost palace spire.

### VII

When will the hundred summers die,
  And thought and time be born again,  70
And newer knowledge, drawing nigh,
  Bring truth that sways the soul of
    men ?
Here all things in their place remain,
  As all were order'd, ages since.
Come, Care and Pleasure, Hope and Pain,
  And bring the fated fairy Prince.

## THE SLEEPING BEAUTY

### I

YEAR after year unto her feet,
  She lying on her couch alone,
Across the purple coverlet  79
  The maiden's jet-black hair has grown,
On either side her tranced form
  Forth streaming from a braid of pearl;
The slumbrous light is rich and warm,
  And moves not on the rounded curl.

### II

The silk star-broider'd coverlid
  Unto her limbs itself doth mould
Languidly ever; and, amid
  Her full black ringlets downward roll'd,
Glows forth each softly-shadow'd arm
  With bracelets of the diamond bright. 90
Her constant beauty doth inform
  Stillness with love, and day with light.

### III

She sleeps; her breathings are not heard
  In palace chambers far apart.
The fragrant tresses are not stirr'd
  That lie upon her charmed heart.
She sleeps; on either hand upswells
  The gold-fringed pillow lightly prest;
She sleeps, nor dreams, but ever dwells
  A perfect form in perfect rest.  100

## THE ARRIVAL

### I

ALL precious things, discover'd late,
  To those that seek them issue forth;
For love in sequel works with fate,
  And draws the veil from hidden worth.
He travels far from other skies —
  His mantle glitters on the rocks —

A fairy Prince, with joyful eyes,
  And lighter-footed than the fox.

### II

The bodies and the bones of those
  That strove in other days to pass  110
Are wither'd in the thorny close,
  Or scatter'd blanching on the grass.
He gazes on the silent dead:
  ' They perish'd in their daring deeds.'
This proverb flashes thro' his head,
  ' The many fail, the one succeeds.'

### III

He comes, scarce knowing what he seeks;
  He breaks the hedge; he enters there;
The color flies into his cheeks;
  He trusts to light on something fair;  120
For all his life the charm did talk
  About his path, and hover near
With words of promise in his walk,
  And whisper'd voices at his ear.

### IV

More close and close his footsteps wind;
  The Magic Music in his heart,
Beats quick and quicker, till he find
  The quiet chamber far apart.
His spirit flutters like a lark,
  He stoops — to kiss her — on his knee.
' Love, if thy tresses be so dark,  131
  How dark those hidden eyes must be !'

## THE REVIVAL

### I

A TOUCH, a kiss ! the charm was snapt.
  There rose a noise of striking clocks,
And feet that ran, and doors that clapt,
  And barking dogs, and crowing cocks;
A fuller light illumined all,
  A breeze thro' all the garden swept,
A sudden hubbub shook the hall,
  And sixty feet the fountain leapt.  140

### II

The hedge broke in, the banner blew,
  The butler drank, the steward scrawl'd,
The fire shot up, the martin flew,
  The parrot scream'd, the peacock squall'd,
The maid and page renew'd their strife,
  The palace bang'd and buzz'd and clackt,
And all the long-pent stream of life
  Dash'd downward in a cataract.

### III

And last with these the king awoke,
  And in his chair himself uprear'd,     150
And yawn'd, and rubb'd his face, and
    spoke,
  'By holy rood, a royal beard!
How say you? we have slept, my lords.
  My beard has grown into my lap.'
The barons swore, with many words,
  'T was but an after-dinner's nap.

### IV

'Pardy,' return'd the king, 'but still
  My joints are somewhat stiff or so.
My lord, and shall we pass the bill
  I mention'd half an hour ago?'     160
The chancellor, sedate and vain,
  In courteous words return'd reply,
But dallied with his golden chain,
  And, smiling, put the question by.

### THE DEPARTURE

#### I

AND on her lover's arm she leant,
  And round her waist she felt it fold,
And far across the hills they went
  In that new world which is the old;
Across the hills, and far away
  Beyond their utmost purple rim,     170
And deep into the dying day
  The happy princess follow'd him.

#### II

'I'd sleep another hundred years,
  O love, for such another kiss;'
'O, wake for ever, love,' she hears;
  'O love, 't was such as this and this.'
And o'er them many a sliding star
  And many a merry wind was borne,
And, stream'd thro' many a golden bar,
  The twilight melted into morn.     180

#### III

'O eyes long laid in happy sleep!'
  'O happy sleep, that lightly fled!'
'O happy kiss, that woke thy sleep!'
  'O love, thy kiss would wake the dead!'
And o'er them many a flowing range
  Of vapor buoy'd the crescent-bark,
And, rapt thro' many a rosy change,
  The twilight died into the dark.

#### IV

'A hundred summers! can it be?
  And whither goest thou, tell me where?'
'O, seek my father's court with me,     191
  For there are greater wonders there.'
And o'er the hills, and far away
  Beyond their utmost purple rim,
Beyond the night, across the day,
  Thro' all the world she follow'd him.

### MORAL

#### I

So, Lady Flora, take my lay,
  And if you find no moral there,
Go, look in any glass and say,
  What moral is in being fair.     200
O, to what uses shall we put
  The wildweed-flower that simply blows?
And is there any moral shut
  Within the bosom of the rose?

#### II

But any man that walks the mead,
  In bud or blade or bloom, may find,
According as his humors lead,
  A meaning suited to his mind.
And liberal applications lie
  In Art like Nature, dearest friend;     210
So 't were to cramp its use if I
  Should hook it to some useful end.

### L'ENVOI

#### I

YOU shake your head. A random string
  Your finer female sense offends.
Well — were it not a pleasant thing
  To fall asleep with all one's friends;
To pass with all our social ties
  To silence from the paths of men,
And every hundred years to rise
  And learn the world, and sleep again;     220
To sleep thro' terms of mighty wars,
  And wake on science grown to more,
On secrets of the brain, the stars,
  As wild as aught of fairy lore;
And all that else the years will show,
  The Poet-forms of stronger hours,
The vast Republics that may grow,
  The Federations and the Powers;

Titanic forces taking birth
  In divers seasons, divers climes ?     230
For we are Ancients of the earth,
  And in the morning of the times.

### II

So sleeping, so aroused from sleep
  Thro' sunny decads new and strange,
Or gay quinquenniads, would we reap
  The flower and quintessence of change.

### III

Ah, yet would I — and would I might !
  So much your eyes my fancy take —
Be still the first to leap to light
  That I might kiss those eyes awake !    240
For, am I right, or am I wrong,
  To choose your own you did not care;
You 'd have *my* moral from the song,
  And I will take my pleasure there;
And, am I right or am I wrong,
  My fancy, ranging thro' and thro',
To search a meaning for the song,
  Perforce will still revert to you,
Nor finds a closer truth than this
  All-graceful head, so richly curl'd,    250
And evermore a costly kiss
  The prelude to some brighter world.

### IV

For since the time when Adam first
  Embraced his Eve in happy hour,
And every bird of Eden burst
  In carol, every bud to flower,
What eyes, like thine, have waken'd hopes,
  What lips, like thine, so sweetly join'd ?
Where on the double rosebud droops
  The fulness of the pensive mind;    260
Which, all too dearly self-involved,
  Yet sleeps a dreamless sleep to me, —
A sleep by kisses undissolved,
  That lets thee neither hear nor see:
But break it.   In the name of wife,
  And in the rights that name may give,
Are clasp'd the moral of thy life,
  And that for which I care to live.

### EPILOGUE

So, Lady Flora, take my lay,
  And if you find a meaning there,    270
O, whisper to your glass, and say,
  ' What wonder if he thinks me fair ? '
What wonder I was all unwise,
  To shape the song for your delight

Like long-tail'd birds of Paradise
  That float thro' heaven, and cannot light?
Or old-world trains, upheld at court
  By Cupid-boys of blooming hue —
But take it — earnest wed with sport,
  And either sacred unto you.    280

## AMPHION

First printed in 1842, and altered but
slightly.

MY father left a park to me,
  But it is wild and barren,
A garden too with scarce a tree,
  And waster than a warren;
Yet say the neighbors when they call
  It is not bad but good land,
And in it is the germ of all
  That grows within the woodland.

O, had I lived when song was great
  In days of old Amphion,    10
And ta'en my fiddle to the gate,
  Nor cared for seed or scion !
And had I lived when song was great,
  And legs of trees were limber,
And ta'en my fiddle to the gate,
  And fiddled in the timber !

'T is said he had a tuneful tongue,
  Such happy intonation,
Wherever he sat down and sung
  He left a small plantation;    20
Wherever in a lonely grove
  He set up his forlorn pipes,
The gouty oak began to move,
  And flounder into hornpipes.

The mountain stirr'd its bushy crown,
  And, as tradition teaches,
Young ashes pirouetted down
  Coquetting with young beeches;
And briony-vine and ivy-wreath
  Ran forward to his rhyming,    30
And from the valleys underneath
  Came little copses climbing.

The linden broke her ranks and rent
  The woodbine wreaths that bind her,
And down the middle, buzz ! she went
  With all her bees behind her;
The poplars, in long order due,
  With cypress promenaded,

The shock-head willows two and two
    By rivers gallopaded.    40

Came wet-shod alder from the wave,
    Came yews, a dismal coterie;
Each pluck'd his one foot from the grave,
    Poussetting with a sloe-tree;
Old elms came breaking from the vine,
    The vine stream'd out to follow,
And, sweating rosin, plump'd the pine
    From many a cloudy hollow.

And was n't it a sight to see,
    When, ere his song was ended,    50
Like some great landslip, tree by tree,
    The country-side descended;
And shepherds from the mountain-eaves
    Look'd down, half-pleased, half-fright-
        en'd,
As dash'd about the drunken leaves
    The random sunshine lighten'd ?

O, Nature first was fresh to men,
    And wanton without measure;
So youthful and so flexile then,
    You moved her at your pleasure.    60
Twang out, my fiddle ! shake the twigs !
    And make her dance attendance;
Blow, flute, and stir the stiff-set sprigs,
    And scirrhous roots and tendons !

'T is vain ! in such a brassy age
    I could not move a thistle;
The very sparrows in the hedge
    Scarce answer to my whistle;
Or at the most, when three-parts-sick
    With strumming and with scraping,    70
A jackass heehaws from the rick,
    The passive oxen gaping.

But what is that I hear ? a sound
    Like sleepy counsel pleading;
O Lord ! — 't is in my neighbor's ground,
    The modern Muses reading.
They read Botanic Treatises,
    And Works on Gardening thro' there,
And Methods of Transplanting Trees
    To look as if they grew there.    80

The wither'd Misses ! how they prose
    O'er books of travell'd seamen,
And show you slips of all that grows
    From England to Van Diemen.
They read in arbors clipt and cut,
    And alleys, faded places,

By squares of tropic summer shut
    And warm'd in crystal cases.

But these, tho' fed with careful dirt,
    Are neither green nor sappy;    90
Half-conscious of the garden-squirt,
    The spindlings look unhappy.
Better to me the meanest weed
    That blows upon its mountain,
The vilest herb that runs to seed
    Beside its native fountain.

And I must work thro' months of toil,
    And years of cultivation,
Upon my proper patch of soil
    To grow my own plantation.    100
I 'll take the showers as they fall,
    I will not vex my bosom;
Enough if at the end of all
    A little garden blossom.

## SAINT AGNES' EVE

First published in ' The Keepsake ' for 1837,
and reprinted in 1842.   Until 1855 the title
was 'Saint Agnes.'

DEEP on the convent-roof the snows
    Are sparkling to the moon;
My breath to heaven like vapor goes;
    May my soul follow soon !
The shadows of the convent-towers
    Slant down the snowy sward,
Still creeping with the creeping hours
    That lead me to my Lord.
Make Thou my spirit pure and clear
    As are the frosty skies,
Or this first snowdrop of the year
    That in my bosom lies.

As these white robes are soil'd and dark,
    To yonder shining ground;
As this pale taper's earthly spark,
    To yonder argent round;
So shows my soul before the Lamb,
    My spirit before Thee;
So in mine earthly house I am,
    To that I hope to be.
Break up the heavens, O Lord ! and far,
    Thro' all yon starlight keen,
Draw me, thy bride, a glittering star,
    In raiment white and clean.

He lifts me to the golden doors;
    The flashes come and go;

All heaven bursts her starry floors,
   And strows her lights below,
And deepens on and up ! the gates
   Roll back, and far within
For me the Heavenly Bridegroom waits,
   To make me pure of sin.
The Sabbaths of Eternity,
   One Sabbath deep and wide —
A light upon the shining sea —
   The Bridegroom with his bride !

## SIR GALAHAD

First printed in 1842.  In line 15 'till' was
originally 'to.'

MY good blade carves the casques of men,
   My tough lance thrusteth sure,
My strength is as the strength of ten,
   Because my heart is pure.
The shattering trumpet shrilleth high,
   The hard brands shiver on the steel,
The splinter'd spear-shafts crack and fly,
   The horse and rider reel;
They reel, they roll in clanging lists,
   And when the tide of combat stands,  10
Perfume and flowers fall in showers,
   That lightly rain from ladies' hands.

How sweet are looks that ladies bend
   On whom their favors fall !
For them I battle till the end,
   To save from shame and thrall;
But all my heart is drawn above,
   My knees are bow'd in crypt and shrine;
I never felt the kiss of love,
   Nor maiden's hand in mine.  20
More bounteous aspects on me beam,
   Me mightier transports move and thrill;
So keep I fair thro' faith and prayer
   A virgin heart in work and will.

When down the stormy crescent goes,
   A light before me swims,
Between dark stems the forest glows,
   I hear a noise of hymns.
Then by some secret shrine I ride;
   I hear a voice, but none are there;  30
The stalls are void, the doors are wide,
   The tapers burning fair.
Fair gleams the snowy altar-cloth,
   The silver vessels sparkle clean,
The shrill bell rings, the censer swings,
   And solemn chaunts resound between.

Sometimes on lonely mountain-meres
   I find a magic bark.
I leap on board; no helmsman steers;
   I float till all is dark.  40
A gentle sound, an awful light !
   Three angels bear the Holy Grail;
With folded feet, in stoles of white,
   On sleeping wings they sail.
Ah, blessed vision ! blood of God !
   My spirit beats her mortal bars,
As down dark tides the glory slides,
   And starlike mingles with the stars.

When on my goodly charger borne
   Thro' dreaming towns I go,  50
The cock crows ere the Christmas morn,
   The streets are dumb with snow.
The tempest crackles on the leads,
   And, ringing, springs from brand and
      mail;
But o'er the dark a glory spreads,
   And gilds the driving hail.
I leave the plain, I climb the height;
   No branchy thicket shelter yields;
But blessed forms in whistling storms
   Fly o'er waste fens and windy fields.  60

A maiden knight — to me is given
   Such hope, I know not fear;
I yearn to breathe the airs of heaven
   That often meet me here.
I muse on joy that will not cease,
   Pure spaces clothed in living beams,
Pure lilies of eternal peace,
   Whose odors haunt my dreams;
And, stricken by an angel's hand,
   This mortal armor that I wear,  70
This weight and size, this heart and eyes,
   Are touch'd, are turn'd to finest air.

The clouds are broken in the sky,
   And thro' the mountain-walls
A rolling organ-harmony
   Swells up and shakes and falls.
Then move the trees, the copses nod,
   Wings flutter, voices hover clear:
'O just and faithful knight of God !
   Ride on ! the prize is near.'  80
So pass I hostel, hall, and grange;
   By bridge and ford, by park and pale,
All-arm'd I ride, whate'er betide,
   Until I find the Holy Grail.

## EDWARD GRAY

First printed in 1842, and unaltered.

Sweet Emma Moreland of yonder town
    Met me walking on yonder way;
'And have you lost your heart?' she
        said;
    'And are you married yet, Edward
        Gray?'

Sweet Emma Moreland spoke to me;
    Bitterly weeping I turn'd away:
'Sweet Emma Moreland, love no more
    Can touch the heart of Edward Gray.

'Ellen Adair she loved me well,
    Against her father's and mother's will;
To-day I sat for an hour and wept
    By Ellen's grave, on the windy hill.

'Shy she was, and I thought her cold,
    Thought her proud, and fled over the
        sea;
Fill'd I was with folly and spite,
    When Ellen Adair was dying for me.

'Cruel, cruel the words I said!
    Cruelly came they back to-day:
"You're too slight and fickle," I said,
    "To trouble the heart of Edward Gray."

'There I put my face in the grass —
    Whisper'd, "Listen to my despair;
I repent me of all I did;
    Speak a little, Ellen Adair!"

'Then I took a pencil, and wrote
    On the mossy stone, as I lay,
"Here lies the body of Ellen Adair;
    And here the heart of Edward Gray!"

'Love may come, and love may go,
    And fly, like a bird, from tree to tree;
But I will love no more, no more,
    Till Ellen Adair come back to me.

'Bitterly wept I over the stone;
    Bitterly weeping I turn'd away.
There lies the body of Ellen Adair!
    And there the heart of Edward Gray!'

## WILL WATERPROOF'S LYRICAL MONOLOGUE

### MADE AT THE COCK

First printed in 1842, and slightly altered
since. See Notes.

O plump head-waiter at The Cock,
    To which I most resort,
How goes the time? 'T is five o'clock.
    Go fetch a pint of port;
But let it not be such as that
    You set before chance-comers,
But such whose father-grape grew fat
    On Lusitanian summers.

No vain libation to the Muse,
    But may she still be kind,            10
And whisper lovely words, and use
    Her influence on the mind,
To make me write my random rhymes,
    Ere they be half-forgotten;
Nor add and alter, many times,
    Till all be ripe and rotten.

I pledge her, and she comes and dips
    Her laurel in the wine,
And lays it thrice upon my lips,
    These favor'd lips of mine;            20
Until the charm have power to make
    New life-blood warm the bosom,
And barren commonplaces break
    In full and kindly blossom.

I pledge her silent at the board;
    Her gradual fingers steal
And touch upon the master-chord
    Of all I felt and feel.
Old wishes, ghosts of broken plans,
    And phantom hopes assemble;            30
And that child's heart within the man's
    Begins to move and tremble.

Thro' many an hour of summer suns,
    By many pleasant ways,
Against its fountain upward runs
    The current of my days.
I kiss the lips I once have kiss'd;
    The gaslight wavers dimmer;
And softly, thro' a vinous mist,
    My college friendships glimmer.        40

I grow in worth and wit and sense,
  Unboding critic-pen,
Or that eternal want of pence
  Which vexes public men,
Who hold their hands to all, and cry
  For that which all deny them —
Who sweep the crossings, wet or dry,
  And all the world go by them.

Ah ! yet, tho' all the world forsake,
  Tho' fortune clip my wings,            50
I will not cramp my heart, nor take
  Half-views of men and things.
Let Whig and Tory stir their blood;
  There must be stormy weather;
But for some true result of good
  All parties work together.

Let there be thistles, there are grapes;
  If old things, there are new;
Ten thousand broken lights and shapes,
  Yet glimpses of the true.              60
Let raffs be rife in prose and rhyme,
  We lack not rhymes and reasons,
As on this whirligig of Time
  We circle with the seasons.

This earth is rich in man and maid,
  With fair horizons bound;
This whole wide earth of light and shade
  Comes out a perfect round.
High over roaring Temple-bar,
  And set in heaven's third story,       70
I look at all things as they are,
  But thro' a kind of glory.

Head-waiter, honor'd by the guest
  Half-mused, or reeling ripe,
The pint you brought me was the best
  That ever came from pipe.
But tho' the port surpasses praise,
  My nerves have dealt with stiffer.
Is there some magic in the place ?
  Or do my peptics differ ?             80

For since I came to live and learn,
  No pint of white or red
Had ever half the power to turn
  This wheel within my head,
Which bears a season'd brain about,
  Unsubject to confusion,
Tho' soak'd and saturate, out and out,
  Thro' every convolution.

For I am of a numerous house,
  With many kinsmen gay,                 90
Where long and largely we carouse
  As who shall say me nay ?
Each month, a birthday coming on,
  We drink, defying trouble,
Or sometimes two would meet in one,
  And then we drank it double;

Whether the vintage, yet unkept,
  Had relish fiery-new,
Or elbow-deep in sawdust slept,
  As old as Waterloo,                   100
Or, stow'd when classic Canning died,
  In musty bins and chambers,
Had cast upon its crusty side
  The gloom of ten Decembers.

The Muse, the jolly Muse, it is !
  She answer'd to my call;
She changes with that mood or this,
  Is all-in-all to all;
She lit the spark within my throat,
  To make my blood run quicker,         110
Used all her fiery will, and smote
  Her life into the liquor.

And hence this halo lives about
  The waiter's hands, that reach
To each his perfect pint of stout,
  His proper chop to each.
He looks not like the common breed
  That with the napkin dally;
I think he came, like Ganymede,
  From some delightful valley.          120

The Cock was of a larger egg
  Than modern poultry drop,
Stept forward on a firmer leg,
  And cramm'd a plumper crop,
Upon an ampler dunghill trod,
  Crow'd lustier late and early,
Sipt wine from silver, praising God,
  And raked in golden barley.

A private life was all his joy,
  Till in a court he saw                130
A something-pottle-bodied boy
  That knuckled at the taw.
He stoop'd and clutch'd him, fair and
        good,
  Flew over roof and casement;
His brothers of the weather stood
  Stock-still for sheer amazement.

But he, by farmstead, thorpe, and spire,
    And follow'd with acclaims,
A sign to many a staring shire,
    Came crowing over Thames.          140
Right down by smoky Paul's they bore,
    Till, where the street grows straiter,
One fix'd for ever at the door,
    And one became head-waiter.

But whither would my fancy go?
    How out of place she makes
The violet of a legend blow
    Among the chops and steaks!
'T is but a steward of the can,
    One shade more plump than common;
As just and mere a serving-man          151
    As any born of woman.

I ranged too high: what draws me down
    Into the common day?
Is it the weight of that half-crown
    Which I shall have to pay?
For, something duller than at first,
    Nor wholly comfortable,
I sit, my empty glass reversed,
    And thrumming on the table;          160

Half fearful that, with self at strife,
    I take myself to task,
Lest of the fulness of my life
    I leave an empty flask,
For I had hope, by something rare,
    To prove myself a poet,
But, while I plan and plan, my hair
    Is gray before I know it.

So fares it since the years began,
    Till they be gather'd up;          170
The truth, that flies the flowing can,
    Will haunt the vacant cup;
And others' follies teach us not,
    Nor much their wisdom teaches;
And most, of sterling worth, is what
    Our own experience preaches.

Ah, let the rusty theme alone!
    We know not what we know.
But for my pleasant hour, 't is gone;
    'T is gone, and let it go.          180
'T is gone: a thousand such have slipt
    Away from my embraces,
And fallen into the dusty crypt
    Of darken'd forms and faces.

Go, therefore, thou! thy betters went
    Long since, and came no more;
With peals of genial clamor sent
    From many a tavern-door,
With twisted quirks and happy hits,
    From misty men of letters;          190
The tavern-hours of mighty wits, —
    Thine elders and thy betters;

Hours when the Poet's words and looks
    Had yet their native glow,
Nor yet the fear of little books
    Had made him talk for show;
But, all his vast heart sherris-warm'd,
    He flash'd his random speeches,
Ere days that deal in ana swarm'd
    His literary leeches.          200

So mix for ever with the past,
    Like all good things on earth!
For should I prize thee, couldst thou last,
    At half thy real worth?
I hold it good, good things should pass;
    With time I will not quarrel;
It is but yonder empty glass
    That makes me maudlin-moral.

Head-waiter of the chop-house here,
    To which I most resort,          210
I too must part; I hold thee dear
    For this good pint of port.
For this, thou shalt from all things suck
    Marrow of mirth and laughter;
And wheresoe'er thou move, good luck
    Shall fling her old shoe after.

But thou wilt never move from hence,
    The sphere thy fate allots;
Thy latter days increased with pence
    Go down among the pots;          220
Thou battenest by the greasy gleam
    In haunts of hungry sinners,
Old boxes, larded with the steam
    Of thirty thousand dinners.

We fret, we fume, would shift our skins,
    Would quarrel with our lot;
Thy care is, under polish'd tins,
    To serve the hot-and-hot;
To come and go, and come again,
    Returning like the pewit,          230
And watch'd by silent gentlemen,
    That trifle with the cruet.

Live long, ere from thy topmost head
  The thick-set hazel dies;
Long, ere the hateful crow shall tread
  The corners of thine eyes;
Live long, nor feel in head or chest
  Our changeful equinoxes,
Till mellow Death, like some late guest,
  Shall call thee from the boxes.    240

But when he calls, and thou shalt cease
  To pace the gritted floor,
And, laying down an unctuous lease
  Of life, shalt earn no more,
No carved cross-bones, the types of Death,
  Shall show thee past to heaven,
But carved cross-pipes, and, underneath,
  A pint-pot neatly graven.

## LADY CLARE

First printed in 1842. A note in that edition
and the next stated that the ballad was 'partly
suggested by the novel of "Inheritance"' (Miss
Ferrier's), the heroine of which is a Miss St.
Clair.

It was the time when lilies blow,
  And clouds are highest up in air,
Lord Ronald brought a lily-white doe
  To give his cousin, Lady Clare.

I trow they did not part in scorn;
  Lovers long-betroth'd were they;
They two will wed the morrow morn —
  God's blessing on the day!

'He does not love me for my birth,
  Nor for my lands so broad and fair;   10
He loves me for my own true worth,
  And that is well,' said Lady Clare.

In there came old Alice the nurse,
  Said, 'Who was this that went from thee?'
'It was my cousin,' said Lady Clare;
  'To-morrow he weds with me.'

'O, God be thank'd,' said Alice the nurse,
  'That all comes round so just and fair!
Lord Ronald is heir of all your lands,
  And you are *not* the Lady Clare.'   20

'Are ye out of your mind, my nurse, my
    nurse,'
  Said Lady Clare, 'that ye speak so wild?'

'As God's above,' said Alice the nurse,
  'I speak the truth: you are my child.

'The old earl's daughter died at my breast;
  I speak the truth, as I live by bread!
I buried her like my own sweet child,
  And put my child in her stead.'

'Falsely, falsely have ye done,
  O mother,' she said, 'if this be true,   30
To keep the best man under the sun
  So many years from his due.'

'Nay now, my child,' said Alice the nurse,
  'But keep the secret for your life,
And all you have will be Lord Ronald's,
  When you are man and wife.'

'If I'm a beggar born,' she said,
  'I will speak out, for I dare not lie.
Pull off, pull off, the brooch of gold,
  And fling the diamond necklace by.'   40

'Nay now, my child,' said Alice the nurse,
  'But keep the secret all ye can.'
She said, 'Not so; but I will know
  If there be any faith in man.'

'Nay now, what faith?' said Alice the
    nurse;
  'The man will cleave unto his right.'
'And he shall have it,' the lady replied,
  'Tho' I should die to-night.'

'Yet give one kiss to your mother dear!
  Alas, my child, I sinn'd for thee!'   50
'O mother, mother, mother,' she said,
  'So strange it seems to me.

'Yet here's a kiss for my mother dear,
  My mother dear, if this be so,
And lay your hand upon my head,
  And bless me, mother, ere I go.'

She clad herself in a russet gown,
  She was no longer Lady Clare;
She went by dale, and she went by down,
  With a single rose in her hair.   60

The lily-white doe Lord Ronald had
    brought
  Leapt up from where she lay,
Dropt her head in the maiden's hand,
  And follow'd her all the way.

Down stept Lord Ronald from his tower:
  ' O Lady Clare, you shame your worth !
Why come you drest like a village maid,
  That are the flower of the earth ? '

' If I come drest like a village maid,
  I am but as my fortunes are;    70
I am a beggar born,' she said,
  ' And not the Lady Clare.'

' Play me no tricks,' said Lord Ronald,
  ' For I am yours in word and in deed.
Play me no tricks,' said Lord Ronald,
  ' Your riddle is hard to read.'

O, and proudly stood she up !
  Her heart within her did not fail;
She look'd into Lord Ronald's eyes,
  And told him all her nurse's tale.    80

He laugh'd a laugh of merry scorn;
  He turn'd and kiss'd her where she stood;
' If you are not the heiress born,
  And I,' said he, ' the next in blood, —

' If you are not the heiress born,
  And I,' said he, ' the lawful heir,
We two will wed to-morrow morn,
  And you shall still be Lady Clare.'

## THE CAPTAIN

### A LEGEND OF THE NAVY

First printed in the ' Selections ' of 1865,
and unaltered.

HE that only rules by terror
  Doeth grievous wrong.
Deep as hell I count his error.
  Let him hear my song.
Brave the Captain was; the seamen
  Made a gallant crew,
Gallant sons of English freemen,
  Sailors bold and true.
But they hated his oppression;
  Stern he was and rash,
So for every light transgression
  Doom'd them to the lash.
Day by day more harsh and cruel
  Seem'd the Captain's mood.
Secret wrath like smother'd fuel
  Burnt in each man's blood.
Yet he hoped to purchase glory,

Hoped to make the name
  Of his vessel great in story,
  Wheresoe'er he came.
So they past by capes and islands,
  Many a harbor-mouth,
Sailing under palmy highlands
  Far within the South.
On a day when they were going
  O'er the lone expanse,
In the north, her canvas flowing,
  Rose a ship of France.
Then the Captain's color heighten'd,
  Joyful came his speech;
But a cloudy gladness lighten'd
  In the eyes of each.
' Chase,' he said; the ship flew forward,
  And the wind did blow;
Stately, lightly, went she norward,
  Till she near'd the foe.
Then they look'd at him they hated,
  Had what they desired;
Mute with folded arms they waited —
  Not a gun was fired.
But they heard the foeman's thunder
  Roaring out their doom;
All the air was torn in sunder,
  Crashing went the boom;
Spars were splinter'd, decks were shatter'd,
  Bullets fell like rain;
Over mast and deck were scatter'd
  Blood and brains of men.
Spars were splinter'd; decks were broken;
  Every mother's son —
Down they dropt — no word was spoken —
  Each beside his gun.
On the decks as they were lying,
  Were their faces grim.
In their blood, as they lay dying,
  Did they smile on him.
Those in whom he had reliance
  For his noble name
With one smile of still defiance
  Sold him unto shame.
Shame and wrath his heart confounded,
  Pale he turn'd and red,
Till himself was deadly wounded
  Falling on the dead.
Dismal error ! fearful slaughter !
  Years have wander'd by;
Side by side beneath the water
  Crew and Captain lie;
There the sunlit ocean tosses
  O'er them mouldering,
And the lonely seabird crosses
  With one waft of the wing.

# THE LORD OF BURLEIGH

First printed in 1842, and unaltered.

In her ear he whispers gaily,
  ' If my heart by signs can tell,
Maiden, I have watch'd thee daily,
  And I think thou lov'st me well.'
She replies, in accents fainter,
  ' There is none I love like thee.'
He is but a landscape-painter,
  And a village maiden she.
He to lips that fondly falter
  Presses his without reproof,          10
Leads her to the village altar,
  And they leave her father's roof.
' I can make no marriage present;
  Little can I give my wife.
Love will make our cottage pleasant,
  And I love thee more than life.'
They by parks and lodges going
  See the lordly castles stand;
Summer woods, about them blowing,
  Made a murmur in the land.            20
From deep thought himself he rouses,
  Says to her that loves him well,
' Let us see these handsome houses
  Where the wealthy nobles dwell.'
So she goes by him attended,
  Hears him lovingly converse,
Sees whatever fair and splendid
  Lay betwixt his home and hers;
Parks with oak and chestnut shady,
  Parks and order'd gardens great,      30
Ancient homes of lord and lady,
  Built for pleasure and for state.
All he shows her makes him dearer;
  Evermore she seems to gaze
On that cottage growing nearer,
  Where they twain will spend their days.
O, but she will love him truly !
  He shall have a cheerful home;
She will order all things duly,
  When beneath his roof they come.      40
Thus her heart rejoices greatly,
  Till a gateway she discerns
With armorial bearings stately,
  And beneath the gate she turns,
Sees a mansion more majestic
  Than all those she saw before.
Many a gallant gay domestic
  Bows before him at the door;

And they speak in gentle murmur,
  When they answer to his call,         50
While he treads with footstep firmer,
  Leading on from hall to hall.
And, while now she wonders blindly,
  Nor the meaning can divine,
Proudly turns he round and kindly,
  ' All of this is mine and thine.'
Here he lives in state and bounty,
  Lord of Burleigh, fair and free;
Not a lord in all the county
  Is so great a lord as he.             60
All at once the color flushes
  Her sweet face from brow to chin;
As it were with shame she blushes,
  And her spirit changed within.
Then her countenance all over
  Pale again as death did prove;
But he clasp'd her like a lover,
  And he cheer'd her soul with love.
So she strove against her weakness,
  Tho' at times her spirit sank,        70
Shaped her heart with woman's meekness
  To all duties of her rank;
And a gentle consort made he,
  And her gentle mind was such
That she grew a noble lady,
  And the people loved her much.
But a trouble weigh'd upon her,
  And perplex'd her, night and morn,
With the burthen of an honor
  Unto which she was not born.          80
Faint she grew, and ever fainter,
  And she murmur'd, ' O, that he
Were once more that landscape-painter
  Which did win my heart from me ! '
So she droop'd and droop'd before him,
  Fading slowly from his side;
Three fair children first she bore him,
  Then before her time she died.
Weeping, weeping late and early,
  Walking up and pacing down,           90
Deeply mourn'd the Lord of Burleigh,
  Burleigh-house by Stamford-town.
And he came to look upon her,
  And he look'd at her and said,
' Bring the dress and put it on her,
  That she wore when she was wed.'
Then her people, softly treading,
  Bore to earth her body, drest
In the dress that she was wed in,
  That her spirit might have rest.      100

## THE VOYAGE

First printed in the ' Enoch Arden ' volume
in 1864.
' Life as Energy, in the great ethical sense
of the word, — Life as the pursuit of the Ideal,
— is figured in this brilliantly descriptive allegory ' (Palgrave).

### I

WE left behind the painted buoy
  That tosses at the harbor-mouth;
And madly danced our hearts with joy,
  As fast we fleeted to the south.
How fresh was every sight and sound
  On open main or winding shore !
We knew the merry world was round,
  And we might sail for evermore.

### II

Warm broke the breeze against the brow,
  Dry sang the tackle, sang the sail;        10
The Lady's-head upon the prow
  Caught the shrill salt, and sheer'd the
    gale.
The broad seas swell'd to meet the keel,
  And swept behind; so quick the run,
We felt the good ship shake and reel,
  We seem'd to sail into the sun !

### III

How oft we saw the sun retire,
  And burn the threshold of the night,
Fall from his Ocean-lane of fire,
  And sleep beneath his pillar'd light !      20
How oft the purple-skirted robe
  Of twilight slowly downward drawn,
As thro' the slumber of the globe
  Again we dash'd into the dawn !

### IV

New stars all night above the brim
  Of waters lighten'd into view;
They climb'd as quickly, for the rim
  Changed every moment as we flew.
Far ran the naked moon across
  The houseless ocean's heaving field,       30
Or flying shone, the silver boss
  Of her own halo's dusky shield.

### V

The peaky islet shifted shapes,
  High towns on hills were dimly seen;
We past long lines of Northern capes
  And dewy Northern meadows green.

We came to warmer waves, and deep
  Across the boundless east we drove,
Where those long swells of breaker sweep
  The nutmeg rocks and isles of clove.      40

### VI

By peaks that flamed, or, all in shade,
  Gloom'd the low coast and quivering brine
With ashy rains, that spreading made
  Fantastic plume or sable pine;
By sands and steaming flats, and floods
  Of mighty mouth, we scudded fast,
And hills and scarlet-mingled woods
  Glow'd for a moment as we past.

### VII

O hundred shores of happy climes,
  How swiftly stream'd ye by the bark !     50
At times the whole sea burn'd, at times
  With wakes of fire we tore the dark;
At times a carven craft would shoot
  From havens hid in fairy bowers,
With naked limbs and flowers and fruit,
  But we nor paused for fruit nor flowers.

### VIII

For one fair Vision ever fled
  Down the waste waters day and night,
And still we follow'd where she led,
  In hope to gain upon her flight.          60
Her face was evermore unseen,
  And fixt upon the far sea-line;
But each man murmur'd, ' O my Queen,
  I follow till I make thee mine.'

### IX

And now we lost her, now she gleam'd
  Like Fancy made of golden air,
Now nearer to the prow she seem'd
  Like Virtue firm, like Knowledge fair,
Now high on waves that idly burst
  Like Heavenly Hope she crown'd the
    sea,                                     70
And now, the bloodless point reversed,
  She bore the blade of Liberty.

### X

And only one among us — him
  We pleased not — he was seldom pleased;
He saw not far, his eyes were dim,
  But ours he swore were all diseased.
' A ship of fools,' he shriek'd in spite,
  ' A ship of fools,' he sneer'd and wept.
And overboard one stormy night
  He cast his body, and on we swept.        80

### XI

And never sail of ours was furl'd,
  Nor anchor dropt at eve or morn;
We loved the glories of the world,
  But laws of nature were our scorn.
For blasts would rise and rave and cease,
  But whence were those that drove the
    sail
Across the whirlwind's heart of peace,
  And to and thro' the counter gale?

### XII

Again to colder climes we came,
  For still we follow'd where she led;  90
Now mate is blind and captain lame,
  And half the crew are sick or dead,
But, blind or lame or sick or sound,
  We follow that which flies before;
We know the merry world is round,
  And we may sail for evermore.

## SIR LAUNCELOT AND QUEEN GUINEVERE

#### A FRAGMENT

First printed in 1842. In the 1st stanza ' elm-
tree ' was originally ' linden '; and in the 4th
' In ' was ' On,' and ' fleeter now ' was ' still more
fleet.'

LIKE souls that balance joy and pain,
With tears and smiles from heaven again
The maiden Spring upon the plain
Came in a sunlit fall of rain.
  In crystal vapor everywhere
Blue isles of heaven laugh'd between,
And far, in forest-deeps unseen,
The topmost elm-tree gather'd green
  From draughts of balmy air.

Sometimes the linnet piped his song;
Sometimes the throstle whistled strong;
Sometimes the sparhawk, wheel'd along,
Hush'd all the groves from fear of wrong;
  By grassy capes with fuller sound
In curves the yellowing river ran,
And drooping chestnut-buds began
To spread into the perfect fan,
  Above the teeming ground.

Then, in the boyhood of the year,
Sir Launcelot and Queen Guinevere

Rode thro' the coverts of the deer,
With blissful treble ringing clear.
  She seem'd a part of joyous Spring;
A gown of grass-green silk she wore,
Buckled with golden clasps before;
A light-green tuft of plumes she bore
  Closed in a golden ring.

Now on some twisted ivy-net,
Now by some tinkling rivulet,
In mosses mixt with violet
Her cream-white mule his pastern set;
  And fleeter now she skimm'd the
    plains
Than she whose elfin prancer springs
By night to eery warblings,
When all the glimmering moorland rings
  With jingling bridle-reins.

As she fled fast thro' sun and shade,
The happy winds upon her play'd,
Blowing the ringlet from the braid.
She look'd so lovely, as she sway'd
  The rein with dainty finger-tips,
A man had given all other bliss,
And all his worldly worth for this,
To waste his whole heart in one kiss
  Upon her perfect lips.

## A FAREWELL

First printed in 1842, and unaltered except
' thousand suns ' for ' hundred suns.'

FLOW down, cold rivulet, to the sea,
  Thy tribute wave deliver;
No more by thee my steps shall be,
  For ever and for ever.

Flow, softly flow, by lawn and lea,
  A rivulet, then a river;
Nowhere by thee my steps shall be,
  For ever and for ever.

But here will sigh thine alder-tree,
  And here thine aspen shiver;
And here by thee will hum the bee,
  For ever and for ever.

A thousand suns will stream on thee,
  A thousand moons will quiver;
But not by thee my steps shall be,
  For ever and for ever.

## THE BEGGAR MAID

First printed in 1842, and unaltered. It is founded on the old ballad of 'King Cophetua and the Beggar Maid,' which was very popular in its day, and is alluded to by Shakespeare in 'Love's Labour's Lost,' 'Richard II.,' and 'Romeo and Juliet.'

HER arms across her breast she laid;
  She was more fair than words can say;
Barefooted came the beggar maid
  Before the king Cophetua.
In robe and crown the king stept down,
  To meet and greet her on her way;
'It is no wonder,' said the lords,
  'She is more beautiful than day.'

As shines the moon in clouded skies,
  She in her poor attire was seen;
One praised her ankles, one her eyes,
  One her dark hair and lovesome mien.
So sweet a face, such angel grace,
  In all that land had never been.
Cophetua sware a royal oath:
  'This beggar maid shall be my queen!'

## THE EAGLE

### FRAGMENT

First printed in the edition of 1851.

HE clasps the crag with crooked hands;
Close to the sun in lonely lands,
Ring'd with the azure world, he stands.

The wrinkled sea beneath him crawls;
He watches from his mountain walls,
And like a thunderbolt he falls.

## 'MOVE EASTWARD, HAPPY EARTH'

First printed in 1842, when the ninth line had 'lightly' instead of 'smoothly.'
The 'silver sister-world' is Venus, the morning-star, not the moon, as some have assumed.

MOVE eastward, happy earth, and leave
  Yon orange sunset waning slow;
From fringes of the faded eve,
  O happy planet, eastward go,
Till over thy dark shoulder glow
  Thy silver sister-world, and rise

To glass herself in dewy eyes
That watch me from the glen below.

Ah, bear me with thee, smoothly borne,
  Dip forward under starry light,
And move me to my marriage-morn,
  And round again to happy night.

## 'COME NOT, WHEN I AM DEAD'

First printed in 'The Keepsake' for 1851, under the title of 'Stanzas;' included in the seventh edition of the 'Poems' the same year.

COME not, when I am dead,
  To drop thy foolish tears upon my grave,
To trample round my fallen head,
  And vex the unhappy dust thou wouldst
    not save.
There let the wind sweep and the plover
    cry;
      But thou, go by.

Child, if it were thine error or thy crime
  I care no longer, being all unblest;
Wed whom thou wilt, but I am sick of
    time,
  And I desire to rest.
Pass on, weak heart, and leave me where I
    lie;
      Go by, go by.

## THE LETTERS

First published with 'Maud' in 1855, and unaltered.

### I

STILL on the tower stood the vane,
  A black yew gloom'd the stagnant air;
I peer'd athwart the chancel pane
  And saw the altar cold and bare.
A clog of lead was round my feet,
  A band of pain across my brow;
'Cold altar, heaven and earth shall meet
  Before you hear my marriage vow.'

### II

I turn'd and humm'd a bitter song
  That mock'd the wholesome human
    heart,
And then we met in wrath and wrong,
  We met, but only meant to part.
Full cold my greeting was and dry;
  She faintly smiled, she hardly moved;

I saw with half-unconscious eye
  She wore the colors I approved.

### III

She took the little ivory chest,
  With half a sigh she turn'd the key,
Then raised her head with lips comprest,
  And gave my letters back to me;
And gave the trinkets and the rings,
  My gifts, when gifts of mine could
     please.
As looks a father on the things
  Of his dead son, I look'd on these.

### IV

She told me all her friends had said;
  I raged against the public liar;
She talk'd as if her love were dead,
  But in my words were seeds of fire.
'No more of love, your sex is known;
  I never will be twice deceived.
Henceforth I trust the man alone,
  The woman cannot be believed.

### V

'Thro' slander, meanest spawn of hell, —
  And women's slander is the worst, —
And you, whom once I loved so well,
  Thro' you my life will be accurst.'
I spoke with heart and heat and force,
  I shook her breast with vague alarms —
Like torrents from a mountain source
  We rush'd into each other's arms.

### VI

We parted; sweetly gleam'd the stars,
  And sweet the vapor-braided blue;
Low breezes fann'd the belfry bars,
  As homeward by the church I drew.
The very graves appear'd to smile,
  So fresh they rose in shadow'd swells;
'Dark porch,' I said, 'and silent aisle,
  There comes a sound of marriage bells.'

## THE VISION OF SIN

First printed in 1842. Lines 97, 98, 121, 122
at first had 'minute' for 'moment'; 106, 'in'
for 'by'; 128, 'the' for 'a'; 188, 'or' for
'nor'; 208, 'Again' for 'Once more'; and
213, 'said' for 'spake.' In the 'Selections' of
1865 (but only there) the following couplet appears after line 214 : —

  Another answer'd : ' But a crime of sense ?
  Give him new nerves with old experience.'

### I

I HAD a vision when the night was late;
A youth came riding toward a palace-gate.
He rode a horse with wings, that would
    have flown,
But that his heavy rider kept him down.
And from the palace came a child of sin,
And took him by the curls, and led him
    in,
Where sat a company with heated eyes,
Expecting when a fountain should arise.
A sleepy light upon their brows and lips —
As when the sun, a crescent of eclipse,   10
Dreams over lake and lawn, and isles and
    capes —
Suffused them, sitting, lying, languid
    shapes,
By heaps of gourds, and skins of wine, and
    piles of grapes.

### II

Then methought I heard a mellow sound,
Gathering up from all the lower ground;
Narrowing in to where they sat assem-
    bled,
Low voluptuous music winding trembled,
Woven in circles. They that heard it sigh'd,
Panted hand-in-hand with faces pale,
Swung themselves, and in low tones re-
    plied;   20
Till the fountain spouted, showering wide
Sleet of diamond-drift and pearly hail.
Then the music touch'd the gates and died,
Rose again from where it seem'd to fail,
Storm'd in orbs of song, a growing gale;
Till thronging in and in, to where they
    waited,
As 't were a hundred-throated nightingale,
The strong tempestuous treble throbb'd
    and palpitated;
Ran into its giddiest whirl of sound,
Caught the sparkles, and in circles,   30
Purple gauzes, golden hazes, liquid mazes,
Flung the torrent rainbow round.
Then they started from their places,
Moved with violence, changed in hue,
Caught each other with wild grimaces,
Half-invisible to the view,
Wheeling with precipitate paces
To the melody, till they flew,
Hair and eyes and limbs and faces,
Twisted hard in fierce embraces,   40
Like to Furies, like to Graces,
Dash'd together in blinding dew;

Till, kill'd with some luxurious agony,
The nerve-dissolving melody
Flutter'd headlong from the sky.

### III

And then I look'd up toward a mountain-
    tract,
That girt the region with high cliff and
    lawn.
I saw that every morning, far withdrawn
Beyond the darkness and the cataract,
God made Himself an awful rose of dawn,
Unheeded; and detaching, fold by fold,   51
From those still heights, and, slowly draw-
    ing near,
A vapor heavy, hueless, formless, cold,
Came floating on for many a month and
    year,
Unheeded; and I thought I would have
    spoken,
And warn'd that madman ere it grew too
    late,
But, as in dreams, I could not. Mine was
    broken,
When that cold vapor touch'd the palace-
    gate,
And link'd again. I saw within my head
A gray and gap-tooth'd man as lean as
    death,   60
Who slowly rode across a wither'd heath,
And lighted at a ruin'd inn, and said:

### IV

'Wrinkled ostler, grim and thin!
    Here is custom come your way;
Take my brute, and lead him in,
    Stuff his ribs with mouldy hay.

'Bitter barmaid, waning fast!
    See that sheets are on my bed.
What! the flower of life is past;
    It is long before you wed.   70

'Slip-shod waiter, lank and sour,
    At the Dragon on the heath!
Let us have a quiet hour,
    Let us hob-and-nob with Death.

'I am old, but let me drink;
    Bring me spices, bring me wine;
I remember, when I think,
    That my youth was half divine.

'Wine is good for shrivell'd lips,
    When a blanket wraps the day,   80

When the rotten woodland drips,
    And the leaf is stamp'd in clay.

'Sit thee down, and have no shame,
    Cheek by jowl, and knee by knee;
What care I for any name?
    What for order or degree?

'Let me screw thee up a peg;
    Let me loose thy tongue with wine;
Callest thou that thing a leg?
    Which is thinnest? thine or mine?   90

'Thou shalt not be saved by works,
    Thou hast been a sinner too;
Ruin'd trunks on wither'd forks,
    Empty scarecrows, I and you!

'Fill the cup and fill the can,
    Have a rouse before the morn;
Every moment dies a man,
    Every moment one is born.

'We are men of ruin'd blood;
    Therefore comes it we are wise.   100
Fish are we that love the mud,
    Rising to no fancy-flies.

'Name and fame! to fly sublime
    Thro' the courts, the camps, the schools,
Is to be the ball of Time,
    Bandied by the hands of fools.

'Friendship! — to be two in one —
    Let the canting liar pack!
Well I know, when I am gone,
    How she mouths behind my back.   110

'Virtue! — to be good and just —
    Every heart, when sifted well,
Is a clot of warmer dust,
    Mix'd with cunning sparks of hell.

'O, we two as well can look
    Whited thought and cleanly life
As the priest, above his book
    Leering at his neighbor's wife.

'Fill the cup and fill the can,
    Have a rouse before the morn:   120
Every moment dies a man,
    Every moment one is born.

'Drink, and let the parties rave;
    They are fill'd with idle spleen,

Rising, falling, like a wave,
  For they know not what they mean.

'He that roars for liberty
  Faster binds a tyrant's power,
And the tyrant's cruel glee
  Forces on the freer hour.      130

'Fill the can and fill the cup;
  All the windy ways of men
Are but dust that rises up,
  And is lightly laid again.

'Greet her with applausive breath,
  Freedom, gaily doth she tread;
In her right a civic wreath,
  In her left a human head.

'No, I love not what is new;
  She is of an ancient house,      140
And I think we know the hue
  Of that cap upon her brows.

'Let her go ! her thirst she slakes
  Where the bloody conduit runs,
Then her sweetest meal she makes
  On the first-born of her sons.

'Drink to lofty hopes that cool, —
  Visions of a perfect State;
Drink we, last, the public fool,
  Frantic love and frantic hate.      150

'Chant me now some wicked stave,
  Till thy drooping courage rise,
And the glow-worm of the grave
  Glimmer in thy rheumy eyes.

'Fear not thou to loose thy tongue,
  Set thy hoary fancies free;
What is loathsome to the young
  Savors well to thee and me.

'Change, reverting to the years,
  When thy nerves could understand  160
What there is in loving tears,
  And the warmth of hand in hand.

'Tell me tales of thy first love —
  April hopes, the fools of chance —
Till the graves begin to move,
  And the dead begin to dance.

'Fill the can and fill the cup;
  All the windy ways of men

Are but dust that rises up,
  And is lightly laid again.      170

'Trooping from their mouldy dens
  The chap-fallen circle spreads —
Welcome, fellow-citizens,
  Hollow hearts and empty heads !

'You are bones, and what of that ?
  Every face, however full,
Padded round with flesh and fat,
  Is but modell'd on a skull.

'Death is king, and Vivat Rex !
  Tread a measure on the stones,      180
Madam — if I know your sex
  From the fashion of your bones.

'No, I cannot praise the fire
  In your eye — nor yet your lip;
All the more do I admire
  Joints of cunning workmanship.

'Lo ! God's likeness — the ground-plan —
  Neither modell'd, glazed, nor framed;
Buss me, thou rough sketch of man,
  Far too naked to be shamed !      190

'Drink to Fortune, drink to Chance,
  While we keep a little breath !
Drink to heavy Ignorance !
  Hob-and-nob with brother Death !

'Thou art mazed, the night is long,
  And the longer night is near —
What ! I am not all as wrong
  As a bitter jest is dear.

'Youthful hopes, by scores, to all,
  When the locks are crisp and curl'd;  200
Unto me my maudlin gall
  And my mockeries of the world.

'Fill the cup and fill the can;
  Mingle madness, mingle scorn !
Dregs of life, and lees of man;
  Yet we will not die forlorn.'

V

The voice grew faint; there came a further
    change;
Once more uprose the mystic mountain-
    range.
Below were men and horses pierced with
    worms,      209

And slowly quickening into lower forms;
By shards and scurf of salt, and scum of
    dross,
Old plash of rains, and refuse patch'd with
    moss.
Then some one spake: 'Behold! it was a
    crime
Of sense avenged by sense that wore with
    time.'
Another said: 'The crime of sense became
The crime of malice, and is equal blame.'
And one: 'He had not wholly quench'd his
    power;
A little grain of conscience made him sour.'
At last I heard a voice upon the slope    219
Cry to the summit, 'Is there any hope?'
To which an answer peal'd from that high
    land,
But in a tongue no man could understand;
And on the glimmering limit far with-
    drawn
God made Himself an awful rose of dawn.

## TO ——

#### AFTER READING A LIFE AND LETTERS

'Cursed be he that moves my bones.'
                    *Shakespeare's Epitaph.*

First printed in the 'Examiner' for March 24,
1849, and included in the sixth edition of the
'Poems' in 1850. The second part of the title,
'After Reading a Life and Letters,' was added
in 1853.

You might have won the Poet's name,
    If such be worth the winning now,
    And gain'd a laurel for your brow
Of sounder leaf than I can claim;

But you have made the wiser choice,
    A life that moves to gracious ends
    Thro' troops of unrecording friends,
A deedful life, a silent voice.

And you have miss'd the irreverent doom
    Of those that wear the Poet's crown;
    Hereafter, neither knave nor clown
Shall hold their orgies at your tomb.

For now the Poet cannot die,
    Nor leave his music as of old,
    But round him ere he scarce be cold
Begins the scandal and the cry:

'Proclaim the faults he would not show;
    Break lock and seal, betray the trust;
    Keep nothing sacred, 't is but just
The many-headed beast should know.'

Ah, shameless! for he did but sing
    A song that pleased us from its worth;
    No public life was his on earth,
No blazon'd statesman he, nor king.

He gave the people of his best;
    His worst he kept, his best he gave.
    My Shakespeare's curse on clown and
        knave
Who will not let his ashes rest!

Who make it seem more sweet to be
    The little life of bank and brier,
    The bird that pipes his lone desire
And dies unheard within his tree,

Than he that warbles long and loud
    And drops at Glory's temple-gates,
    For whom the carrion vulture waits
To tear his heart before the crowd!

## TO E. L., ON HIS TRAVELS IN GREECE

First printed in 1853, and unaltered. It was
addressed to Edward Lear, the painter, and
refers to his 'Landscape-Painter in Albania
and Illyria,' 1851.

Illyrian woodlands, echoing falls
    Of water, sheets of summer glass,
    The long divine Peneïan pass,
The vast Akrokeraunian walls,

Tomohrit, Athos, all things fair,
    With such a pencil, such a pen,
    You shadow forth to distant men,
I read and felt that I was there.

And trust me while I turn'd the page,
    And track'd you still on classic ground,
    I grew in gladness till I found
My spirits in the golden age.

For me the torrent ever pour'd
    And glisten'd — here and there alone
    The broad-limb'd Gods at random thrown
By fountain-urns; — and Naiads oar'd

A glimmering shoulder under gloom
  Of cavern pillars; on the swell
  The silver lily heaved and fell;
And many a slope was rich in bloom,

From him that on the mountain lea
  By dancing rivulets fed his flocks
  To him who sat upon the rocks
And fluted to the morning sea.

---

First printed in 1842, and unaltered. Various fanciful accounts of its origin have been published; but, according to the poet himself, ' it was made in a Lincolnshire lane at five o'clock in the morning between blossoming hedges.'

BREAK, break, break,
  On thy cold gray stones, O Sea!
And I would that my tongue could utter
  The thoughts that arise in me.

O, well for the fisherman's boy,
  That he shouts with his sister at play!
O, well for the sailor lad,
  That he sings in his boat on the bay!

And the stately ships go on
  To their haven under the hill;
But O for the touch of a vanish'd hand,
  And the sound of a voice that is still!

Break, break, break,
  At the foot of thy crags, O Sea!

But the tender grace of a day that is dead
  Will never come back to me.

## THE POET'S SONG

First printed in 1842, and unaltered for more than forty years, when 'fly' was substituted for 'bee' in the first line of the second stanza.

THE rain had fallen, the Poet arose,
  He pass'd by the town and out of the
    street;
A light wind blew from the gates of the
    sun,
  And waves of shadow went over the
    wheat;
And he sat him down in a lonely place,
  And chanted a melody loud and sweet,
That made the wild-swan pause in her
    cloud,
  And the lark drop down at his feet.

The swallow stopt as he hunted the fly,
  The snake slipt under a spray,
The wild hawk stood with the down on his
    beak,
  And stared, with his foot on the prey;
And the nightingale thought, 'I have sung
    many songs,
  But never a one so gay,
For he sings of what the world will be
  When the years have died away.'

# THE PRINCESS; A MEDLEY

The poem was first published in 1847, but has since undergone many changes. In the second edition, issued in 1848, the dedication to Henry Lushington was added (omitted in the recent editions), and the text was slightly revised. In the third (1850) the six intercalary songs were inserted, many additions and alterations were made in the body of the poem, and the Prologue and Conclusion were partially rewritten. The most important change in the fourth edition (1851) was the introduction of the passages relating to the 'weird seizures' of the Prince. In the fifth edition (1853) lines 35–49 of the Prologue (' O miracle of women,' etc.) first appeared, and the text was settled in the form which it has since preserved. For the various readings, etc., see the Notes.

## PROLOGUE

SIR WALTER VIVIAN all a summer's day
Gave his broad lawns until the set of sun
Up to the people; thither flock'd at noon
His tenants, wife and child, and thither
  half

The neighboring borough with their Institute,
Of which he was the patron. I was there
From college, visiting the son, — the son
A Walter too, — with others of our set,
Five others; we were seven at Vivian-
  place.

And me that morning Walter show'd the
   house,          10
Greek, set with busts.  From vases in the
   hall
Flowers of all heavens, and lovelier than
   their names,
Grew side by side; and on the pavement lay
Carved stones of the Abbey-ruin in the
   park,
Huge Ammonites, and the first bones of
   Time;
And on the tables every clime and age
Jumbled together; celts and calumets,
Claymore and snow-shoe, toys in lava, fans
Of sandal, amber, ancient rosaries,
Laborious orient ivory sphere in sphere,  20
The cursed Malayan crease, and battle-
   clubs
From the isles of palm; and higher on the
   walls,
Betwixt the monstrous horns of elk and
   deer,
His own forefathers' arms and armor hung.

And 'this,' he said, 'was Hugh's at Agin-
   court;
And that was old Sir Ralph's at Ascalon.
A good knight he! we keep a chronicle
With all about him,' — which he brought,
   and I
Dived in a hoard of tales that dealt with
   knights      29
Half-legend, half-historic, counts and kings
Who laid about them at their wills and
   died;
And mixt with these a lady, one that arm'd
Her own fair head, and sallying thro' the
   gate,
Had beat her foes with slaughter from her
   walls.

'O miracle of women,' said the book,
'O noble heart who, being strait-besieged
By this wild king to force her to his wish,
Nor bent, nor broke, nor shunn'd a soldier's
   death,
But now when all was lost or seem'd as
   lost —      39
Her stature more than mortal in the burst
Of sunrise, her arm lifted, eyes on fire —
Brake with a blast of trumpets from the
   gate,
And, falling on them like a thunderbolt,
She trampled some beneath her horses'
   heels,

And some were whelm'd with missiles of
   the wall,
And some were push'd with lances from
   the rock,
And part were drown'd within the whirling
   brook;
O miracle of noble womanhood!'

So sang the gallant glorious chronicle;
And, I all rapt in this, 'Come out,' he
   said,      50
'To the Abbey; there is Aunt Elizabeth
And sister Lilia with the rest.'  We went —
I kept the book and had my finger in
   it —
Down thro' the park.  Strange was the sight
   to me;
For all the sloping pasture murmur'd,
   sown
With happy faces and with holiday.
There moved the multitude, a thousand
   heads;
The patient leaders of their Institute
Taught them with facts.  One rear'd a font
   of stone      59
And drew, from butts of water on the slope,
The fountain of the moment, playing, now
A twisted snake, and now a rain of pearls,
Or steep-up spout whereon the gilded ball
Danced like a wisp; and somewhat lower
   down
A man with knobs and wires and vials fired
A cannon; Echo answer'd in her sleep
From hollow fields; and here were tele-
   scopes
For azure views; and there a group of girls
In circle waited, whom the electric shock
Dislink'd with shrieks and laughter; round
   the lake      70
A little clock-work steamer paddling plied
And shook the lilies; perch'd about the
   knolls
A dozen angry models jetted steam;
A petty railway ran; a fire-balloon
Rose gem-like up before the dusky groves
And dropt a fairy parachute and past;
And there thro' twenty posts of telegraph
They flash'd a saucy message to and fro
Between the mimic stations; so that sport
Went hand in hand with science; other-
   where      80
Pure sport; a herd of boys with clamor
   bowl'd
And stump'd the wicket; babies roll'd
   about

Like tumbled fruit in grass; and men and
    maids
Arranged a country dance, and flew thro'
    light
And shadow, while the twangling violin
Struck up with Soldier-laddie, and over-
    head
The broad ambrosial aisles of lofty lime
Made noise with bees and breeze from end
    to end.

  Strange was the sight and smacking of
    the time;    89
And long we gazed, but satiated at length
Came to the ruins. High-arch'd and ivy-
    claspt,
Of finest Gothic lighter than a fire,
Thro' one wide chasm of time and frost
    they gave
The park, the crowd, the house; but all
    within
The sward was trim as any garden lawn.
And here we lit on Aunt Elizabeth,
And Lilia with the rest, and lady friends
From neighbor seats; and there was Ralph
    himself,
A broken statue propt against the wall,
As gay as any. Lilia, wild with sport,   100
Half child, half woman as she was, had
    wound
A scarf of orange round the stony helm,
And robed the shoulders in a rosy silk,
That made the old warrior from his ivied
    nook
Glow like a sunbeam. Near his tomb a feast
Shone, silver-set; about it lay the guests,
And there we join'd them; then the maiden
    aunt
Took this fair day for text, and from it
    preach'd
An universal culture for the crowd,
And all things great. But we, unworthier,
    told    110
Of college: he had climb'd across the spikes,
And he had squeezed himself betwixt the
    bars,
And he had breathed the Proctor's dogs;
    and one
Discuss'd his tutor, rough to common men,
But honeying at the whisper of a lord;
And one the Master, as a rogue in grain
Veneer'd with sanctimonious theory.

  But while they talk'd, above their heads
    I saw

The feudal warrior lady - clad; which
    brought    119
My book to mind, and opening this I read
Of old Sir Ralph a page or two that rang
With tilt and tourney; then the tale of her
That drove her foes with slaughter from
    her walls,
And much I praised her nobleness, and
    'Where,'
Ask'd Walter, patting Lilia's head—she lay
Beside him — 'lives there such a woman
    now ? '

  Quick answer'd Lilia: 'There are thou-
    sands now
Such women, but convention beats them
    down;
It is but bringing up; no more than that.
You men have done it — how I hate you
    all !    130
Ah, were I something great ! I wish I were
Some mighty poetess, I would shame you
    then,
That love to keep us children ! O, I wish
That I were some great princess, I would
    build
Far off from men a college like a man's,
And I would teach them all that men are
    taught;
We are twice as quick ! ' And here she
    shook aside
The hand that play'd the patron with her
    curls.

  And one said smiling: 'Pretty were the
    sight
If our old halls could change their sex, and
    flaunt    140
With prudes for proctors, dowagers for
    deans,
And sweet girl-graduates in their golden
    hair.
I think they should not wear our rusty
    gowns,
But move as rich as Emperor-moths, or
    Ralph
Who shines so in the corner; yet I fear,
If there were many Lilias in the brood,
However deep you might embower the nest,
Some boy would spy it.'
               At this upon the sward
She tapt her tiny silken-sandall'd foot:
'That's your light way; but I would make
    it death    150
For any male thing but to peep at us.'

Petulant she spoke, and at herself she
    laugh'd;
A rosebud set with little wilful thorns,
And sweet as English air could make her,
    she!
But Walter hail'd a score of names upon
    her,
And 'petty Ogress,' and 'ungrateful Puss,'
And swore he long'd at college, only long'd,
All else was well, for she-society.
They boated and they cricketed; they talk'd
At wine, in clubs, of art, of politics;    160
They lost their weeks; they vext the souls
    of deans;
They rode; they betted; made a hundred
    friends,
And caught the blossom of the flying
    terms,
But miss'd the mignonette of Vivian-place,
The little hearth-flower Lilia. Thus he
    spoke,
Part banter, part affection.
            'True,' she said,
'We doubt not that. O, yes, you miss'd us
    much!
I'll stake my ruby ring upon it you did.'

She held it out; and as a parrot turns
Up thro' gilt wires a crafty loving eye,    170
And takes a lady's finger with all care,
And bites it for true heart and not for
    harm,
So he with Lilia's. Daintily she shriek'd
And wrung it. 'Doubt my word again!'
    he said.
'Come, listen! here is proof that you were
    miss'd:
We seven stay'd at Christmas up to read;
And there we took one tutor as to read:
The hard-grain'd Muses of the cube and
    square
Were out of season; never man, I think,
So moulder'd in a sinecure as he;    180
For while our cloisters echo'd frosty feet,
And our long walks were stript as bare as
    brooms,
We did but talk you over, pledge you all
In wassail; often, like as many girls —
Sick for the hollies and the yews of home —
As many little trifling Lilias — play'd
Charades and riddles as at Christmas here,
And *what's my thought* and *when and where
    and how*,
And often told a tale from mouth to mouth
As here at Christmas.'

She remember'd that;    190
A pleasant game, she thought. She liked it
    more
Than magic music, forfeits, all the rest.
But these — what kind of tales did men tell
    men,
She wonder'd, by themselves?
            A half-disdain
Perch'd on the pouted blossom of her lips;
And Walter nodded at me: '*He* began,
The rest would follow, each in turn; and so
We forged a sevenfold story. Kind? what
    kind?
Chimeras, crotchets, Christmas solecisms;
Seven-headed monsters only made to kill
Time by the fire in winter.'
            'Kill him now,
The tyrant! kill him in the summer too,'
Said Lilia; 'Why not now?' the maiden
    aunt.    203
'Why not a summer's as a winter's tale?
A tale for summer as befits the time,
And something it should be to suit the
    place,
Heroic, for a hero lies beneath,
Grave, solemn!'
            Walter warp'd his mouth at this
To something so mock-solemn, that I
    laugh'd,
And Lilia woke with sudden-shrilling mirth
An echo like a ghostly woodpecker    211
Hid in the ruins; till the maiden aunt —
A little sense of wrong had touch'd her
    face
With color — turn'd to me with 'As you
    will;
Heroic if you will, or what you will,
Or be yourself your hero if you will.'

'Take Lilia, then, for heroine,' clamor'd
    he,
'And make her some great princess, six
    feet high,
Grand, epic, homicidal; and be you    219
The prince to win her!'
            'Then follow me, the prince,
I answer'd, 'each be hero in his turn!
Seven and yet one, like shadows in a
    dream. —
Heroic seems our princess as required —
But something made to suit with time and
    place,
A Gothic ruin and a Grecian house,
A talk of college and of ladies' rights,
A feudal knight in silken masquerade,

And, yonder, shrieks and strange experi-
    ments
For which the good Sir Ralph had burnt
    them all —
This *were* a medley ! we should have him
    back                                               230
Who told the " Winter's Tale " to do it for
    us.
No matter; we will say whatever comes.
And let the ladies sing us, if they will,
From time to time, some ballad or a song
To give us breathing-space.'
                  So I began,
And the rest follow'd; and the women
    sang
Between the rougher voices of the men,
Like linnets in the pauses of the wind:
And here I give the story and the songs.


## I

A Prince I was, blue-eyed, and fair in face,
Of temper amorous as the first of May,
With lengths of yellow ringlet, like a girl,
For on my cradle shone the Northern star.

    There lived an ancient legend in our
    house.
Some sorcerer, whom a far-off grandsire
    burnt
Because he cast no shadow, had foretold,
Dying, that none of all our blood should
    know
The shadow from the substance, and that
    one
Should come to fight with shadows and to
    fall;                                              10
For so, my mother said, the story ran.
And, truly, waking dreams were, more or
    less,
An old and strange affection of the house.
Myself too had weird seizures, Heaven
    knows what!
On a sudden in the midst of men and day,
And while I walk'd and talk'd as hereto-
    fore,
I seem'd to move among a world of ghosts,
And feel myself the shadow of a dream.
Our great court-Galen poised his gilt-head
    cane,
And paw'd his beard, and mutter'd ' cata-
    lepsy.'                                            20
My mother pitying made a thousand
    prayers.
My mother was as mild as any saint,

Half-canonized by all that look'd on her,
So gracious was her tact and tenderness;
But my good father thought a king a king.
He cared not for the affection of the house;
He held his sceptre like a pedant's wand
To lash offence, and with long arms and
    hands
Reach'd out and pick'd offenders from the
    mass
For judgment.
            Now it chanced that I had been,
While life was yet in bud and blade, be-
    troth'd                                            31
To one, a neighboring Princess.   She to me
Was proxy-wedded with a bootless calf
At eight years old; and still from time to
    time
Came murmurs of her beauty from the
    South,
And of her brethren, youths of puissance;
And still I wore her picture by my heart,
And one dark tress; and all around them
    both
Sweet thoughts would swarm as bees about
    their queen.

    But when the days drew nigh that I
    should wed,                                        40
My father sent ambassadors with furs
And jewels, gifts, to fetch her.   These
    brought back
A present, a great labor of the loom;
And therewithal an answer vague as wind.
Besides, they saw the king; he took the
    gifts;
He said there was a compact; that was
    true;
But then she had a will; was he to blame ?
And maiden fancies; loved to live alone
Among her women; certain, would not wed.

    That morning in the presence room I
    stood                                              50
With Cyril and with Florian, my two
    friends:
The first, a gentleman of broken means —
His father's fault — but given to starts and
    bursts
Of revel; and the last, my other heart,
And almost my half-self, for still we moved
Together, twinn'd as horse's ear and eye.

    Now, while they spake, I saw my father's
    face
Grow long and troubled like a rising moon,

Inflamed with wrath.  He started on his
     feet,
Tore the king's letter, snow'd it down, and
     rent                                          60
The wonder of the loom thro' warp and
     woof
From skirt to skirt; and at the last he
     sware
That he would send a hundred thousand
     men,
And bring her in a whirlwind; then he
     chew'd
The thrice-turn'd cud of wrath, and cook'd
     his spleen,
Communing with his captains of the war.

At last I spoke: ' My father, let me go.
It cannot be but some gross error lies
In this report, this answer of a king      69
Whom all men rate as kind and hospitable;
Or, maybe, I myself, my bride once seen,
Whate'er my grief to find her less than
     fame,
May rue the bargain made.'  And Florian
     said:
' I have a sister at the foreign court,
Who moves about the Princess; she, you
     know,
Who wedded with a nobleman from thence.
He, dying lately, left her, as I hear,
The lady of three castles in that land;
Thro' her this matter might be sifted
     clean.'
And Cyril whisper'd: ' Take me with you
     too.'                                         80
Then laughing, ' What if these weird seiz-
     ures come
Upon you in those lands, and no one near
To point you out the shadow from the
     truth !
Take me; I 'll serve you better in a strait;
I grate on rusty hinges here.'  But ' No ! '
Roar'd the rough king, ' you shall not; we
     ourself
Will crush her pretty maiden fancies dead
In iron gauntlets; break the council up.'

But when the council broke, I rose and
     past
Thro' the wild woods that hung about the
     town;                                         90
Found a still place, and pluck'd her like-
     ness out;
Laid it on flowers, and watch'd it lying
     bathed

In the green gleam of dewy-tassell'd trees.
What were those fancies ? wherefore break
     her troth ?
Proud look'd the lips; but while I medi-
     tated
A wind arose and rush'd upon the South,
And shook the songs, the whispers, and the
     shrieks
Of the wild woods together, and a Voice
Went with it, ' Follow, follow, thou shalt
     win.'                                         99

Then, ere the silver sickle of that month
Became her golden shield, I stole from
     court
With Cyril and with Florian, unperceived,
Cat-footed thro' the town and half in dread
To hear my father's clamor at our backs
With ' Ho ! ' from some bay-window shake
     the night;
But all was quiet.  From the bastion'd walls
Like threaded spiders, one by one, we
     dropt,
And flying reach'd the frontier; then we
     crost
To a livelier land; and so by tilth and
     grange,
And vines, and blowing bosks of wilder-
     ness,                                         110
We gain'd the mother-city thick with
     towers,
And in the imperial palace found the king.

His name was Gama; crack'd and small
     his voice,
But bland the smile that like a wrinkling
     wind
On glassy water drove his cheek in lines;
A little dry old man, without a star,
Not like a king.  Three days he feasted us,
And on the fourth I spake of why we came,
And my betroth'd.  ' You do us, Prince,'
     he said,
Airing a snowy hand and signet gem,      120
' All honor.  We remember love ourself
In our sweet youth.  There did a compact
     pass
Long summers back, a kind of ceremony —
I think the year in which our olives fail'd.
I would you had her, Prince, with all my
     heart,
With my full heart; but there were widows
     here,
Two widows, Lady Psyche, Lady Blanche;
They fed her theories, in and out of place

Maintaining that with equal husbandry
The woman were an equal to the man.    130
They harp'd on this; with this our banquets
   rang;
Our dances broke and buzz'd in knots of
   talk;
Nothing but this; my very ears were hot
To hear them.  Knowledge, so my daughter
   held,
Was all in all; they had but been, she
   thought,
As children; they must lose the child, as-
   sume
The woman.  Then, sir, awful odes she
   wrote,
Too awful, sure, for what they treated of,
But all she is and does is awful; odes    139
About this losing of the child; and rhymes
And dismal lyrics, prophesying change
Beyond all reason.  These the women sang;
And they that know such things — I sought
   but peace;
No critic I — would call them master-
   pieces.
They master'd *me*.  At last she begg'd a
   boon,
A certain summer-palace which I have
Hard by your father's frontier.  I said no,
Yet being an easy man, gave it; and there,
All wild to found an University
For maidens, on the spur she fled; and
   more    150
We know not, — only this: they see no
   men,
Not even her brother Arac, nor the twins
Her brethren, tho' they love her, look upon
   her
As on a kind of paragon; and I —
Pardon me saying it — were much loth to
   breed
Dispute betwixt myself and mine; but
   since —
And I confess with right — you think me
   bound
In some sort, I can give you letters to her;
And yet, to speak the truth, I rate your
   chance    159
Almost at naked nothing.'
              Thus the king;
And I, tho' nettled that he seem'd to slur
With garrulous ease and oily courtesies
Our formal compact, yet, not less — all frets
But chafing me on fire to find my bride —
Went forth again with both my friends.
   We rode

Many a long league back to the North.
   At last
From hills that look'd across a land of
   hope
We dropt with evening on a rustic town
Set in a gleaming river's crescent-curve,
Close at the boundary of the liberties;    170
There, enter'd an old hostel, call'd mine
   host
To council, plied him with his richest wines,
And show'd the late-writ letters of the
   king.

   He with a long low sibilation, stared
As blank as death in marble; then ex-
   claim'd,
Averring it was clear against all rules
For any man to go; but as his brain
Began to mellow, 'If the king,' he said,
'Had given us letters, was he bound to
   speak?
The king would bear him out;' and at the
   last —    180
The summer of the vine in all his veins —
'No doubt that we might make it worth
   his while.
She once had past that way; he heard her
   speak;
She scared him; life! he never saw the
   like;
She look'd as grand as doomsday and as
   grave!
And he, he reverenced his liege-lady there;
He always made a point to post with
   mares;
His daughter and his housemaid were the
   boys;
The land, he understood, for miles about
Was till'd by women; all the swine were
   sows,    190
And all the dogs' —
            But while he jested thus,
A thought flash'd thro' me which I clothed
   in act,
Remembering how we three presented
   Maid,
Or Nymph, or Goddess, at high tide of
   feast,
In masque or pageant at my father's court.
We sent mine host to purchase female
   gear;
He brought it, and himself, a sight to shake
The midriff of despair with laughter, holp
To lace us up, till each in maiden plumes
We rustled; him we gave a costly bribe    200

To guerdon silence, mounted our good
    steeds,
And boldly ventured on the liberties.

We follow'd up the river as we rode,
And rode till midnight, when the college
    lights
Began to glitter firefly-like in copse
And linden alley; then we past an arch,
Whereon a woman-statue rose with wings
From four wing'd horses dark against the
    stars,
And some inscription ran along the front,
But deep in shadow.  Further on we gain'd
A little street half garden and half house,
But scarce could hear each other speak for
    noise                                    212
Of clocks and chimes, like silver hammers
    falling
On silver anvils, and the splash and stir
Of fountains spouted up and showering
    down
In meshes of the jasmine and the rose;
And all about us peal'd the nightingale,
Rapt in her song and careless of the snare.

There stood a bust of Pallas for a sign,
By two sphere lamps blazon'd like Heaven
    and Earth                                220
With constellation and with continent,
Above an entry.  Riding in, we call'd;
A plump-arm'd ostleress and a stable wench
Came running at the call, and help'd us
    down.
Then stept a buxom hostess forth, and sail'd,
Full - blown, before us into rooms which
    gave
Upon a pillar'd porch, the bases lost
In laurel.  Her we ask'd of that and this,
And who were tutors.  'Lady Blanche.'
    she said,
'And Lady Psyche.'  'Which was pret-
    tiest,                                   230
Best natured?'  'Lady Psyche.'  'Hers
    are we,'
One voice, we cried; and I, sat down and
    wrote
In such a hand as when a field of corn
Bows all its ears before the roaring East:

'Three ladies of the Northern empire
    pray
Your Highness would enroll them with
    your own,
As Lady Psyche's pupils.'

                This I seal'd;
The seal was Cupid bent above a scroll,
And o'er his head Uranian Venus hung,
And raised the blinding bandage from his
    eyes.                                    240
I gave the letter to be sent with dawn;
And then to bed, where half in doze I
    seem'd
To float about a glimmering night, and
    watch
A full sea glazed with muffled moonlight
    swell
On some dark shore just seen that it was
    rich.

    As thro' the land at eve we went,
      And pluck'd the ripen'd ears,
    We fell out, my wife and I,
    O, we fell out, I know not why,
      And kiss'd again with tears.            250
    And blessings on the falling out
      That all the more endears,
    When we fall out with those we love
      And kiss again with tears!
    For when we came where lies the child
      We lost in other years,
    There above the little grave,
    O, there above the little grave,
      We kiss'd again with tears.

## II

At break of day the College Portress
    came;
She brought us academic silks, in hue
The lilac, with a silken hood to each,
And zoned with gold; and now when these
    were on,
And we as rich as moths from dusk co-
    coons,
She, curtseying her obeisance, let us know
The Princess Ida waited.  Out we paced,
I first, and following thro' the porch that
    sang
All round with laurel, issued in a court
Compact of lucid marbles, boss'd with
    lengths                                   10
Of classic frieze, with ample awnings gay
Betwixt the pillars, and with great urns of
    flowers.
The Muses and the Graces, group'd in
    threes,
Enring'd a billowing fountain in the midst,
And here and there on lattice edges lay
Or book or lute; but hastily we past,
And up a flight of stairs into the hall.

There at a board by tome and paper
  sat,
With two tame leopards couch'd beside
  her throne,
All beauty compass'd in a female form,   20
The Princess; liker to the inhabitant
Of some clear planet close upon the sun,
Than our man's earth; such eyes were in
  her head,
And so much grace and power, breathing
  down
From over her arch'd brows, with every
  turn
Lived thro' her to the tips of her long
  hands,
And to her feet.   She rose her height, and
  said:

'We give you welcome; not without re-
  dound
Of use and glory to yourselves ye come,
The first-fruits of the stranger; aftertime,
And that full voice which circles round the
  grave,   31
Will rank you nobly, mingled up with me.
What! are the ladies of your land so
  tall?'
'We of the court,' said Cyril.   'From the
  court,'
She answer'd, 'then ye know the Prince?'
  and he:
'The climax of his age! as tho' there
  were
One rose in all the world, your Highness
  that,
He worships your ideal.'   She replied:
'We scarcely thought in our own hall to
  hear   39
This barren verbiage, current among men,
Light coin, the tinsel clink of compliment.
Your flight from out your bookless wilds
  would seem
As arguing love of knowledge and of
  power;
Your language proves you still the child.
  Indeed,
We dream not of him; when we set our
  hand
To this great work, we purposed with our-
  self
Never to wed.   You likewise will do well,
Ladies, in entering here, to cast and fling
The tricks which make us toys of men,
  that so
Some future time, if so indeed you will,   50

You may with those self-styled our lords
  ally
Your fortunes, justlier balanced, scale with
  scale.'

  At those high words, we, conscious of
  ourselves,
Perused the matting; then an officer
Rose up, and read the statutes, such as
  these:
Not for three years to correspond with
  home;
Not for three years to cross the liberties;
Not for three years to speak with any men;
And many more, which hastily subscribed,
We enter'd on the boards.   And 'Now,' she
  cried,   60
'Ye are green wood, see ye warp not.
  Look, our hall!
Our statues! — not of those that men de-
  sire,
Sleek Odalisques, or oracles of mode,
Nor stunted squaws of West or East; but
  she
That taught the Sabine how to rule, and
  she
The foundress of the Babylonian wall,
The Carian Artemisia strong in war,
The Rhodope that built the pyramid,
Clelia, Cornelia, with the Palmyrene
That fought Aurelian, and the Roman
  brows   70
Of Agrippina.   Dwell with these, and lose
Convention, since to look on noble forms
Makes noble thro' the sensuous organism
That which is higher.   O, lift your natures
  up;
Embrace our aims; work out your freedom.
  Girls,
Knowledge is now no more a fountain
  seal'd!
Drink deep, until the habits of the slave,
The sins of emptiness, gossip and spite
And slander, die.   Better not be at all
Than not be noble.   Leave us; you may
  go.   80
To-day the Lady Psyche will harangue
The fresh arrivals of the week before;
For they press in from all the provinces,
And fill the hive.'
                    She spoke, and bowing waved
Dismissal; back again we crost the court
To Lady Psyche's.   As we enter'd in,
There sat along the forms, like morning
  doves

That sun their milky bosoms on the thatch,
A patient range of pupils; she herself
Erect behind a desk of satin-wood,          90
A quick brunette, well-moulded, falcon-
    eyed,
And on the hither side, or so she look'd,
Of twenty summers.  At her left, a child,
In shining draperies, headed like a star,
Her maiden babe, a double April old,
Aglaïa slept.  We sat; the lady glanced;
Then Florian, but no livelier than the
    dame
That whisper'd ' Asses' ears' among the
    sedge,
' My sister.'  ' Comely, too, by all that 's
    fair,'          99
Said Cyril.  ' O, hush, hush!' and she began.

' This world was once a fluid haze of
    light,
Till toward the centre set the starry tides,
And eddied into suns, that wheeling cast
The planets; then the monster, then the
    man;
Tattoo'd or woaded, winter-clad in skins,
Raw from the prime, and crushing down
    his mate,
As yet we find in barbarous isles, and here
Among the lowest.'
                    Thereupon she took
A bird's-eye view of all the ungracious
    past;
Glanced at the legendary Amazon          110
As emblematic of a nobler age;
Appraised the Lycian custom, spoke of
    those
That lay at wine with Lar and Lucumo;
Ran down the Persian, Grecian, Roman
    lines
Of empire, and the woman's state in each,
How far from just; till warming with her
    theme
She fulmined out her scorn of laws Salique
And little-footed China, touch'd on Ma-
    homet
With much contempt, and came to chiv-
    alry,
When some respect, however slight, was
    paid          120
To woman, superstition all awry.
However, then commenced the dawn; a
    beam
Had slanted forward, falling in a land
Of promise; fruit would follow.  Deep,
    indeed,

Their debt of thanks to her who first had
    dared
To leap the rotten pales of prejudice,
Disyoke their necks from custom, and as-
    sert
None lordlier than themselves but that
    which made
Woman and man.  She had founded; they
    must build.
Here might they learn whatever men were
    taught.          130
Let them not fear, some said their heads
    were less;
Some men's were small, not they the least
    of men;
For often fineness compensated size.
Besides the brain was like the hand, and
    grew
With using; thence the man's, if more was
    more.
He took advantage of his strength to be
First in the field; some ages had been lost;
But woman ripen'd earlier, and her life
Was longer; and albeit their glorious
    names
Were fewer, scatter'd stars, yet since in
    truth          140
The highest is the measure of the man,
And not the Kaffir, Hottentot, Malay,
Nor those horn-handed breakers of the
    glebe,
But Homer, Plato, Verulam, even so
With woman; and in arts of government
Elizabeth and others, arts of war
The peasant Joan and others, arts of grace
Sappho and others vied with any man;
And, last not least, she who had left her
    place,
And bow'd her state to them, that they
    might grow          150
To use and power on this oasis, lapt
In the arms of leisure, sacred from the
    blight
Of ancient influence and scorn.
                              At last
She rose upon a wind of prophecy
Dilating on the future: ' everywhere
Two heads in council, two beside the
    hearth,
Two in the tangled business of the world,
Two in the liberal offices of life,
Two plummets dropt for one to sound the
    abyss
Of science and the secrets of the mind; 160
Musician, painter, sculptor, critic, more;

And everywhere the broad and bounteous
Earth
Should bear a double growth of those rare
souls,
Poets, whose thoughts enrich the blood of
the world.'

She ended here, and beckon'd us; the
rest
Parted; and, glowing full-faced welcome,
she
Began to address us, and was moving on
In gratulation, till as when a boat
Tacks and the slacken'd sail flaps, all her
voice
Faltering and fluttering in her throat, she
cried,                                            170
'My brother!' 'Well, my sister.' 'O,'
she said,
'What do you here? and in this dress?
and these?
Why, who are these? a wolf within the
fold!
A pack of wolves! the Lord be gracious
to me!
A plot, a plot, a plot, to ruin all!'
'No plot, no plot,' he answer'd. 'Wretched
boy,
How saw you not the inscription on the
gate,
LET NO MAN ENTER IN ON PAIN OF
DEATH?'
'And if I had,' he answer'd, 'who could
think
The softer Adams of your Academe,          180
O sister, Sirens tho' they be, were such
As chanted on the blanching bones of
men?'
'But you will find it otherwise,' she said.
'You jest; ill jesting with edge-tools! my
vow
Binds me to speak, and O that iron will,
That axelike edge unturnable, our Head,
The Princess!' 'Well then, Psyche, take
my life,
And nail me like a weasel on a grange
For warning; bury me beside the gate,
And cut this epitaph above my bones:       190
*Here lies a brother by a sister slain,*
*All for the common good of womankind.*'
'Let me die too,' said Cyril, 'having seen
And heard the Lady Psyche.'
                                    I struck in:
'Albeit so mask'd, madam, I love the
truth;

Receive it, and in me behold the Prince
Your countryman, affianced years ago
To the Lady Ida. Here, for here she was,
And thus — what other way was left? — I
came.'
'O sir, O Prince, I have no country,
none;                                          200
If any, this; but none. Whate'er I was
Disrooted, what I am is grafted here.
Affianced, sir? love-whispers may not
breathe
Within this vestal limit, and how should I,
Who am not mine, say, live? The thun-
derbolt
Hangs silent; but prepare. I speak, it
falls.'
'Yet pause,' I said: 'for that inscription
there,
I think no more of deadly lurks therein,
Than in a clapper clapping in a garth,
To scare the fowl from fruit; if more
there be,                                       210
If more and acted on, what follows? war;
Your own work marr'd; for this your
Academe,
Whichever side be victor, in the halloo
Will topple to the trumpet down, and pass
With all fair theories only made to gild
A stormless summer.' 'Let the Princess
judge
Of that,' she said: 'farewell, sir — and to
you.
I shudder at the sequel, but I go.'

'Are you that Lady Psyche,' I rejoin'd,
'The fifth in line from that old Florian,    220
Yet hangs his portrait in my father's hall —
The gaunt old baron with his beetle brow
Sun-shaded in the heat of dusty fights —
As he bestrode my grandsire, when he fell,
And all else fled? we point to it, and we
say,
The loyal warmth of Florian is not cold,
But branches current yet in kindred veins.'
'Are you that Psyche,' Florian added; 'she
With whom I sang about the morning
hills,
Flung ball, flew kite, and raced the purple
fly,                                            230
And snared the squirrel of the glen? are
you
That Psyche, wont to bind my throbbing
brow,
To smooth my pillow, mix the foaming
draught

Of fever, tell me pleasant tales, and read
My sickness down to happy dreams ? are
    you
That brother-sister Psyche, both in one ?
You were that Psyche, but what are you
    now ? '
' You are that Psyche,' Cyril said, ' for
    whom
I would be that forever which I seem,
Woman, if I might sit beside your feet, 240
And glean your scatter'd sapience.'
                    Then once more,
' Are you that Lady Psyche,' I began,
' That on her bridal morn before she past
From all her old companions, when the king
Kiss'd her pale cheek, declared that an-
    cient ties
Would still be dear beyond the southern
    hills;
That were there any of our people there
In want or peril, there was one to hear
And help them ? look ! for such are these
    and I.'
' Are you that Psyche,' Florian ask'd, ' to
    whom,                                  250
In gentler days, your arrow-wounded fawn
Came flying while you sat beside the well ?
The creature laid his muzzle on your lap
And sobb'd, and you sobb'd with it, and
    the blood
Was sprinkled on your kirtle, and you
    wept.
That was fawn's blood, not brother's, yet
    you wept.
O, by the bright head of my little niece,
You were that Psyche, and what are you
    now ? '
' You are that Psyche,' Cyril said again,
' The mother of the sweetest little maid 260
That ever crow'd for kisses.'
                    ' Out upon it ! '
She answer'd, ' peace ! and why should I
    not play
The Spartan Mother with emotion, be
The Lucius Junius Brutus of my kind ?
Him you call great; he for the common
    weal,
The fading politics of mortal Rome,
As I might slay this child, if good need
    were,
Slew both his sons; and I, shall I, on
    whom
The secular emancipation turns
Of half this world, be swerved from right
    to save                                270

A prince, a brother ? a little will I yield.
Best so, perchance, for us, and well for
    you.
O, hard when love and duty clash ! I fear
My conscience will not count me fleckless;
    yet —
Hear my conditions: promise — otherwise
You perish — as you came, to slip away
To-day, to-morrow, soon. It shall be said,
These women were too barbarous, would
    not learn;
They fled, who might have shamed us.
    Promise, all.'

    What could we else, we promised each;
        and she,                           280
Like some wild creature newly-caged, com-
    menced
A to-and-fro, so pacing till she paused
By Florian; holding out her lily arms
Took both his hands, and smiling faintly
    said:
' I knew you at the first; tho' you have
    grown
You scarce have alter'd. I am sad and
    glad
To see you, Florian. *I* give thee to death,
My brother ! it was duty spoke, not I.
My needful seeming harshness, pardon it.
Our mother, is she well ? '
                    With that she kiss'd
His forehead, then, a moment after, clung
About him, and betwixt them blossom'd
    up                                      292
From out a common vein of memory
Sweet household talk, and phrases of the
    hearth,
And far allusion, till the gracious dews
Began to glisten and to fall; and while
They stood, so rapt, we gazing, came a
    voice,
' I brought a message here from Lady
    Blanche.'
Back started she, and turning round we
    saw
The Lady Blanche's daughter where she
    stood,                                  300
Melissa, with her hand upon the lock,
A rosy blonde, and in a college gown,
That clad her like an April daffodilly —
Her mother's color — with her lips apart,
And all her thoughts as fair within her
    eyes,
As bottom agates seen to wave and float
In crystal currents of clear morning seas.

So stood that same fair creature at the door.
Then Lady Psyche, 'Ah — Melissa — you !
You heard us ?' and Melissa, 'O, pardon
me !                                            310
I heard, I could not help it, did not wish;
But, dearest lady, pray you fear me not,
Nor think I bear that heart within my
breast,
To give three gallant gentlemen to death.'
' I trust you,' said the other, ' for we two
Were always friends, none closer, elm and
vine;
But yet your mother's jealous tempera-
ment —
Let not your prudence, dearest, drowse, or
prove
The Danaïd of a leaky vase, for fear
This whole foundation ruin, and I lose    320
My honor, these their lives.' ' Ah, fear me
not,'
Replied Melissa; ' no — I would not tell,
No, not for all Aspasia's cleverness,
No, not to answer, madam, all those hard
things
That Sheba came to ask of Solomon.'
' Be it so,' the other, 'that we still may
lead
The new light up, and culminate in peace,
For Solomon may come to Sheba yet.'
Said Cyril, ' Madam, he the wisest man
Feasted the woman wisest then, in halls   330
Of Lebanonian cedar; nor should you —
Tho', madam, *you* should answer, *we* would
ask —
Less welcome find among us, if you came
Among us, debtors for our lives to you,
Myself for something more.' He said not
what,
But ' Thanks,' she answer'd, ' go; we have
been too long
Together; keep your hoods about the face;
They do so that affect abstraction here.
Speak little; mix not with the rest; and
hold
Your promise. All, I trust, may yet be
well.'                                          340

We turn'd to go, but Cyril took the
child,
And held her round the knees against his
waist,
And blew the swollen cheek of a trumpeter,
While Psyche watch'd them, smiling, and
the child

Push'd her flat hand against his face and
laugh'd;
And thus our conference closed.
                          And then we strolled
For half the day thro' stately theatres
Bench'd crescent-wise.  In each we sat, we
heard
The grave professor.  On the lecture slate
The circle rounded under female hands   350
With flawless demonstration; follow'd then
A classic lecture, rich in sentiment,
With scraps of thunderous epic lilted out
By violet-hooded Doctors, elegies
And quoted odes, and jewels five-words-
long
That on the stretch'd forefinger of all
Time
Sparkle forever.  Then we dipt in all
That treats of whatsoever is, the state,
The total chronicles of man, the mind,
The morals, something of the frame, the
rock,                                          360
The star, the bird, the fish, the shell, the
flower,
Electric, chemic laws, and all the rest,
And whatsoever can be taught and known;
Till like three horses that have broken
fence,
And glutted all night long breast-deep in
corn,
We issued gorged with knowledge, and I
spoke:
' Why, sirs, they do all this as well as we.'
' They hunt old trails,' said Cyril, ' very
well;
But when did woman ever yet invent ?'
' Ungracious !' answer'd Florian; ' have you
learnt                                          370
No more from Psyche's lecture, you that
talk'd
The trash that made me sick, and almost
sad ?'
' O, trash,' he said, ' but with a kernel in it!
Should I not call her wise who made me
wise ?
And learnt ?  I learnt more from her in a
flash
Than if my brainpan were an empty hull,
And every Muse tumbled a science in.
A thousand hearts lie fallow in these halls,
And round these halls a thousand baby
loves
Fly twanging headless arrows at the hearts,
Whence follows many a vacant pang; but O,
                                               381

With me, sir, enter'd in the bigger boy,
The head of all the golden-shafted firm,
The long-limb'd lad that had a Psyche too;
He cleft me thro' the stomacher. And now
What think you of it, Florian? do I chase
The substance or the shadow? will it
    hold?
I have no sorcerer's malison on me,
No ghostly hauntings like his Highness. I
Flatter myself that always everywhere   390
I know the substance when I see it. Well,
Are castles shadows? Three of them?
    Is she
The sweet proprietress a shadow? If not,
Shall those three castles patch my tatter'd
    coat?
For dear are those three castles to my wants,
And dear is sister Psyche to my heart,
And two dear things are one of double
    worth;
And much I might have said, but that my
    zone
Unmann'd me. Then the Doctors! O, to
    hear
The Doctors! O, to watch the thirsty
    plants   400
Imbibing! once or twice I thought to roar,
To break my chain, to shake my mane; but
    thou,
Modulate me, soul of mincing mimicry!
Make liquid treble of that bassoon, my
    throat;
Abase those eyes that ever loved to meet
Star - sisters answering under crescent
    brows;
Abate the stride which speaks of man, and
    loose
A flying charm of blushes o'er this cheek,
Where they like swallows coming out of
    time
Will wonder why they came. But hark the
    bell   410
For dinner, let us go!'
                And in we stream'd
Among the columns, pacing staid and still
By twos and threes, till all from end to end
With beauties every shade of brown and
    fair
In colors gayer than the morning mist,
The long hall glitter'd like a bed of flow-
    ers.
How might a man not wander from his
    wits
Pierced thro' with eyes, but that I kept
    mine own

Intent on her, who rapt in glorious dreams,
The second-sight of some Astræan age,   420
Sat compass'd with professors; they, the
    while,
Discuss'd a doubt and tost it to and fro.
A clamor thicken'd, mixt with inmost terms
Of art and science; Lady Blanche alone
Of faded form and haughtiest lineaments,
With all her autumn tresses falsely brown,
Shot sidelong daggers at us, a tiger-cat
In act to spring.
              At last a solemn grace
Concluded, and we sought the gardens.
    There
One walk'd reciting by herself, and one   430
In this hand held a volume as to read,
And smoothed a petted peacock down with
    that.
Some to a low song oar'd a shallop by,
Or under arches of the marble bridge
Hung, shadow'd from the heat; some hid
    and sought
In the orange thickets; others tost a ball
Above the fountain-jets, and back again
With laughter; others lay about the lawns,
Of the older sort, and murmur'd that their
    May
Was passing—what was learning unto
    them?   440
They wish'd to marry; they could rule a
    house;
Men hated learned women. But we three
Sat muffled like the Fates; and often came
Melissa hitting all we saw with shafts
Of gentle satire, kin to charity,
That harm'd not. Then day droopt; the
    chapel bells
Call'd us; we left the walks; we mixt with
    those
Six hundred maidens clad in purest white,
Before two streams of light from wall to
    wall,
While the great organ almost burst his
    pipes,   450
Groaning for power, and rolling thro' the
    court
A long melodious thunder to the sound
Of solemn psalms and silver litanies,
The work of Ida, to call down from heaven
A blessing on her labors for the world.

    Sweet and low, sweet and low,
      Wind of the western sea,
    Low, low, breathe and blow,
      Wind of the western sea!

Over the rolling waters go,
Come from the dying moon, and blow,
   Blow him again to me ;
While my little one, while my pretty one
   sleeps.

Sleep and rest, sleep and rest,
   Father will come to thee soon ;
Rest, rest, on mother's breast,
   Father will come to thee soon ;
Father will come to his babe in the nest,
Silver sails all out of the west
   Under the silver moon ;
Sleep, my little one, sleep, my pretty one, sleep.

### III

Morn in the white wake of the morning
      star
Came furrowing all the orient into gold.
We rose, and each by other drest with
      care
Descended to the court that lay three parts
In shadow, but the Muses' heads were
      touch'd
Above the darkness from their native East.

   There while we stood beside the fount,
      and watch'd
Or seem'd to watch the dancing bubble,
      approach'd
Melissa, tinged with wan from lack of
      sleep,
Or grief, and glowing round her dewy
      eyes                                        10
The circled Iris of a night of tears ;
And ' Fly,' she cried, ' O fly, while yet you
      may !
My mother knows.'  And when I ask'd her
      ' how,'
' My fault,' she wept, 'my fault ! and yet
      not mine ;
Yet mine in part.  O, hear me, pardon me !
My mother, 't is her wont from night to
      night
To rail at Lady Psyche and her side.
She says the Princess should have been the
      Head,
Herself and Lady Psyche the two arms ;  19
And so it was agreed when first they came ;
But Lady Psyche was the right hand now,
And she the left, or not or seldom used ;
Hers more than half the students, all the
      love.
And so last night she fell to canvass you,
Her countrywomen !  she did not envy her.

" Who ever saw such wild barbarians ?
Girls ? — more like men ! " and at these
      words the snake,
My secret, seem'd to stir within my breast ;
And O, sirs, could I help it, but my cheek
Began to burn and burn, and her lynx eye
To fix and make me hotter, till she laugh'd :
" O marvellously modest maiden, you !  32
Men ! girls, like men ! why, if they had
      been men
You need not set your thoughts in rubric
For wholesale comment."  Pardon, I am
      shamed
That I must needs repeat for my excuse
What looks so little graceful: " men "— for
      still
My mother went revolving on the word —
" And so they are, — very like men in-
      deed —
And with that woman closeted for hours ! "
Then came these dreadful words out one
      by one,                                     41
" Why — these — are — men; " I shud-
      der'd ; " and you know it."
" O, ask me nothing," I said.    " And she
      knows too,
And she conceals it."  So my mother
      clutch'd
The truth at once, but with no word from
      me ;
And now thus early risen she goes to in-
      form
The Princess.  Lady Psyche will be crush'd ;
But you may yet be saved, and therefore
      fly ;
But heal me with your pardon ere you go.'

   ' What pardon, sweet Melissa, for a
      blush ? '                                   50
Said Cyril : ' Pale one, blush again ; than
      wear
Those lilies, better blush our lives away.
Yet let us breathe for one hour more in
      heaven,'
He added, ' lest some classic angel speak
In scorn of us, " They mounted, Ganymedes,
To tumble, Vulcans, on the second morn."
But I will melt this marble into wax
To yield us farther furlough ; ' and he went.

   Melissa shook her doubtful curls, and
      thought
He scarce would prosper.  ' Tell us,' Flo-
      rian ask'd,                                 60

'How grew this feud betwixt the right and
    left.'
'O, long ago,' she said, 'betwixt these two
Division smoulders hidden; 't is my mother,
Too jealous, often fretful as the wind
Pent in a crevice: much I bear with her.
I never knew my father, but she says —
God help her! — she was wedded to a fool;
And still she rail'd against the state of
    things.
She had the care of Lady Ida's youth,
And from the Queen's decease she brought
    her up.                                    70
But when your sister came she won the
    heart
Of Ida; they were still together, grew —
For so they said themselves — inosculated;
Consonant chords that shiver to one note;
One mind in all things. Yet my mother still
Affirms your Psyche thieved her theories,
And angled with them for her pupil's love;
She calls her plagiarist, I know not what.
But I must go; I dare not tarry,' and light,
As flies the shadow of a bird, she fled.  80

    Then murmur'd Florian, gazing after
        her:
'An open-hearted maiden, true and pure.
If I could love, why this were she. How
    pretty
Her blushing was, and how she blush'd
    again,
As if to close with Cyril's random wish!
Not like your Princess cramm'd with err-
    ing pride,
Nor like poor Psyche whom she drags in
    tow.'

    'The crane,' I said, 'may chatter of the
        crane,
The dove may murmur of the dove, but I
An eagle clang an eagle to the sphere.   90
My princess, O my princess! true she errs,
But in her own grand way; being herself
Three times more noble than three score of
    men,
She sees herself in every woman else,
And so she wears her error like a crown
To blind the truth and me. For her, and
    her,
Hebes are they to hand ambrosia, mix
The nectar; but — ah, she — whene'er she
    moves
The Samian Herè rises, and she speaks  99
A Memnon smitten with the morning sun.'

    So saying from the court we paced, and
        gain'd
The terrace ranged along the northern
    front,
And leaning there on those balusters, high
Above the empurpled champaign, drank
    the gale
That blown about the foliage underneath,
And sated with the innumerable rose,
Beat balm upon our eyelids. Hither came
Cyril, and yawning, 'O hard task,' he cried:
'No fighting shadows here. I forced a way
Thro' solid opposition crabb'd and gnarl'd.
Better to clear prime forests, heave and
    thump                                     111
A league of street in summer solstice down,
Than hammer at this reverend gentle-
    woman.
I knock'd and, bidden, enter'd; found her
    there
At point to move, and settled in her eyes
The green malignant light of coming storm.
Sir, I was courteous, every phrase well-
    oil'd,
As man's could be; yet maiden-meek I
    pray'd
Concealment. She demanded who we were,
And why we came? I fabled nothing fair,
But, your example pilot, told her all.   121
Up went the hush'd amaze of hand and eye.
But when I dwelt upon your old affiance,
She answer'd sharply that I talk'd astray.
I urged the fierce inscription on the gate,
And our three lives. True — we had limed
    ourselves
With open eyes, and we must take the
    chance.
But such extremes, I told her, well might
    harm
The woman's cause. "Not more than
    now," she said,
"So puddled as it is with favoritism."   130
I tried the mother's heart. Shame might
    befall
Melissa, knowing, saying not she knew;
Her answer was, "Leave me to deal with
    that."
I spoke of war to come and many deaths,
And she replied, her duty was to speak,
And duty duty, clear of consequences.
I grew discouraged, sir; but since I knew
No rock so hard but that a little wave
May beat admission in a thousand years,
I recommenced: "Decide not ere you
    pause.                                    140

I find you here but in the second place,
Some say the third — the authentic foun-
    dress you.
I offer boldly; we will seat you highest.
Wink at our advent; help my prince to
    gain
His rightful bride, and here I promise you
Some palace in our land, where you shall
    reign
The head and heart of all our fair she-
    world,
And your great name flow on with broad-
    ening time
For ever." Well, she balanced this a lit-
    tle,                                          149
And told me she would answer us to-day,
Meantime be mute; thus much, nor more I
    gain'd.'

He ceasing, came a message from the
    Head.
'That afternoon the Princess rode to take
The dip of certain strata to the north.
Would we go with her? we should find the
    land
Worth seeing, and the river made a fall
Out yonder;' then she pointed on to where
A double hill ran up his furrowy forks
Beyond the thick-leaved platans of the
    vale.

Agreed to, this, the day fled on thro'
    all                                           160
Its range of duties to the appointed hour.
Then summon'd to the porch we went. She
    stood
Among her maidens, higher by the head,
Her back against a pillar, her foot on one
Of those tame leopards. Kitten-like he
    roll'd
And paw'd about her sandal. I drew near;
I gazed. On a sudden my strange seizure
    came
Upon me, the weird vision of our house.
The Princess Ida seem'd a hollow show,
Her gay-furr'd cats a painted fantasy,     170
Her college and her maidens empty masks,
And I myself the shadow of a dream,
For all things were and were not. Yet I
    felt
My heart beat thick with passion and with
    awe;
Then from my breast the involuntary sigh
Brake, as she smote me with the light of
    eyes

That lent my knee desire to kneel, and
    shook
My pulses, till to horse we got, and so
Went forth in long retinue following up
The river as it narrow'd to the hills.    180

I rode beside her and to me she said:
'O friend, we trust that you esteem'd us
    not
Too harsh to your companion yestermorn;
Unwillingly we spake.' 'No — not to her,'
I answer'd, 'but to one of whom we spake
Your Highness might have seem'd the thing
    you say.'
'Again?' she cried, 'are you ambassa-
    dresses
From him to me? we give you, being
    strange,
A license; speak, and let the topic die.'

I stammer'd that I knew him — could
    have wish'd —                                  190
'Our king expects — was there no precon-
    tract?
There is no truer-hearted — ah, you seem
All he prefigured, and he could not see
The bird of passage flying south but long'd
To follow. Surely, if your Highness keep
Your purport, you will shock him even to
    death,
Or baser courses, children of despair.'

'Poor boy,' she said, 'can he not read —
    no books?
Quoit, tennis, ball — no games? nor deals
    in that
Which men delight in, martial exercise?
To nurse a blind ideal like a girl,         201
Methinks he seems no better than a girl;
As girls were once, as we ourself have been.
We had our dreams; perhaps he mixt with
    them.
We touch on our dead self, nor shun to do
    it,
Being other — since we learnt our meaning
    here,
To lift the woman's fallen divinity
Upon an even pedestal with man.'

She paused, and added with a haughtier
    smile,
'And as to precontracts, we move, my
    friend,                                        210
At no man's beck, but know ourself and
    thee,

O Vashti, noble Vashti ! Summon'd out
She kept her state, and left the drunken
  king
To brawl at Shushan underneath the
  palms.'

  ' Alas, your Highness breathes full East,'
    I said,
' On that which leans to you ! I know the
    Prince,
I prize his truth. And then how vast a
    work
To assail this gray preëminence of man !
You grant me license; might I use it ?
    think;
Ere half be done perchance your life may
    fail;                                   220
Then comes the feebler heiress of your
    plan,
And takes and ruins all; and thus your
    pains
May only make that footprint upon sand
Which old-recurring waves of prejudice
Resmooth to nothing. Might I dread that
    you,
With only Fame for spouse and your great
    deeds
For issue, yet may live in vain, and miss
Meanwhile what every woman counts her
    due,
Love, children, happiness ? '
                    And she exclaim'd,
' Peace, you young savage of the Northern
    wild !                                  230
What ! tho' your Prince's love were like a
    god's,
Have we not made ourself the sacrifice ?
You are bold indeed; we are not talk'd to
    thus.
Yet will we say for children, would they
    grew
Like field - flowers everywhere ! we like
    them well:
But children die; and let me tell you, girl,
Howe'er you babble, great deeds cannot
    die;
They with the sun and moon renew their
    light
For ever, blessing those that look on them.
Children — that men may pluck them from
    our hearts,                             240
Kill us with pity, break us with our-
    selves —
O — children — there is nothing upon earth
More miserable than she that has a son

And sees him err. Nor would we work for
    fame;
Tho' she perhaps might reap the applause
    of Great,
Who learns the one POU STO whence after-
    hands
May move the world, tho' she herself
    effect
But little; wherefore up and act, nor
    shrink
For fear our solid aim be dissipated
By frail successors. Would, indeed, we
    had been,                              250
In lieu of many mortal flies, a race
Of giants living each a thousand years,
That we might see our own work out, and
    watch
The sandy footprint harden into stone.'

  I answer'd nothing, doubtful in myself
If that strange poet - princess with her
    grand
Imaginations might at all be won.
And she broke out interpreting my
    thoughts:

  ' No doubt we seem a kind of monster
    to you;
We are used to that; for women, up till
    this                                    260
Cramp'd under worse than South-sea-isle
    taboo,
Dwarfs of the gynæceum, fail so far
In high desire, they know not, cannot guess
How much their welfare is a passion to us.
If we could give them surer, quicker
    proof —
O, if our end were less achievable
By slow approaches than by single act
Of immolation, any phase of death,
We were as prompt to spring against the
    pikes,
Or down the fiery gulf as talk of it,     270
To compass our dear sisters' liberties.'

  She bow'd as if to veil a noble tear;
And up we came to where the river sloped
To plunge in cataract, shattering on black
    blocks
A breadth of thunder. O'er it shook the
    woods,
And danced the color, and, below, stuck
    out
The bones of some vast bulk that lived
    and roar'd

Before man was. She gazed awhile and
said,
' As these rude bones to us, are we to her
That will be.' 'Dare we dream of that,'
I ask'd,                                           280
' Which wrought us, as the workman and
his work,
That practice betters ?' 'How,' she cried,
' you love
The metaphysics ! read and earn our prize,
A golden brooch. Beneath an emerald
plane
Sits Diotima, teaching him that died
Of hemlock — our device, wrought to the
life —
She rapt upon her subject, he on her;
For there are schools for all.' 'And yet,'
I said,
' Methinks I have not found among them
all
One anatomic.' 'Nay, we thought of that,'
She answer'd, 'but it pleased us not; in
truth                                              291
We shudder but to dream our maids should
ape
Those monstrous males that carve the liv-
ing hound,
And cram him with the fragments of the
grave,
Or in the dark dissolving human heart,
And holy secrets of this microcosm,
Dabbling a shameless hand with shameful
jest,
Encarnalize their spirits. Yet we know
Knowledge is knowledge, and this matter
hangs.
Howbeit ourself, foreseeing casualty,     300
Nor willing men should come among us,
learnt,
For many weary moons before we came,
This craft of healing. Were you sick, our-
self
Would tend upon you. To your question
now,
Which touches on the workman and his
work.
Let there be light and there was light;
't is so,
For was, and is, and will be, are but is,
And all creation is one act at once,
The birth of light; but we that are not all,
As parts, can see but parts, now this, now
that,                                             310
And live, perforce, from thought to
thought, and make

One act a phantom of succession. Thus
Our weakness somehow shapes the shadow,
Time;
But in the shadow will we work, and mould
The woman to the fuller day.'
                                        She spake
With kindled eyes: we rode a league be-
yond,
And, o'er a bridge of pinewood crossing,
came
On flowery levels underneath the crag,
Full of all beauty. 'O, how sweet,' I said, —
For I was half-oblivious of my mask, —   320
' To linger here with one that loved us !'
                                        ' Yea,'
She answer'd, 'or with fair philosophies
That lift the fancy; for indeed these fields
Are lovely, lovelier not the Elysian lawns,
Where paced the demigods of old, and
saw
The soft white vapor streak the crowned
towers
Built to the Sun.' Then, turning to her
maids,
' Pitch our pavilion here upon the sward;
Lay out the viands.' At the word, they
raised
A tent of satin, elaborately wrought     330
With fair Corinna's triumph; here she
stood,
Engirt with many a florid maiden-cheek,
The woman-conqueror; woman-conquer'd
there
The bearded Victor of ten-thousand hymns,
And all the men mourn'd at his side. But
we
Set forth to climb; then, climbing, Cyril
kept
With Psyche, with Melissa Florian, I
With mine affianced. Many a little hand
Glanced like a touch of sunshine on the
rocks,
Many a light foot shone like a jewel set
In the dark crag. And then we turn'd, we
wound                                       341
About the cliffs, the copses, out and in,
Hammering and clinking, chattering stony
names
Of shale and hornblende, rag and trap and
tuff,
Amygdaloid and trachyte, till the sun
Grew broader toward his death and fell,
and all
The rosy heights came out above the
lawns.

The splendor falls on castle walls
    And snowy summits old in story;
The long light shakes across the lakes,
    And the wild cataract leaps in glory.
Blow, bugle, blow, set the wild echoes flying,
Blow, bugle; answer, echoes, dying, dying,
        dying.

O, hark, O, hear! how thin and clear,
    And thinner, clearer, farther going!
O, sweet and far from cliff and scar
    The horns of Elfland faintly blowing!
Blow, let us hear the purple glens replying,
Blow, bugle; answer, echoes, dying, dying,
        dying.

O love, they die in yon rich sky,
    They faint on hill or field or river;
Our echoes roll from soul to soul,
    And grow for ever and for ever.
Blow, bugle, blow, set the wild echoes flying,
And answer, echoes, answer, dying, dying,
        dying.

## IV

' There sinks the nebulous star we call the
        sun,
If that hypothesis of theirs be sound,'
Said Ida; 'let us down and rest;' and we
Down from the lean and wrinkled preci-
        pices,
By every coppice - feather'd chasm and
        cleft,
Dropt thro' the ambrosial gloom to where
        below
No bigger than a glowworm shone the
        tent
Lamp-lit from the inner.  Once she lean'd
        on me,
Descending; once or twice she lent her
        hand,
And blissful palpitations in the blood     10
Stirring a sudden transport rose and fell.

    But when we planted level feet, and
        dipt
Beneath the satin dome and enter'd in,
There leaning deep in broider'd down we
        sank
Our elbows; on a tripod in the midst
A fragrant flame rose, and before us glow'd
Fruit, blossom, viand, amber wine, and
        gold.

    Then she, ' Let some one sing to us;
        lightlier move

The minutes fledged with music;' and a
        maid,
Of those beside her, smote her harp and
        sang.                                      20

    ' Tears, idle tears, I know not what they
        mean,
Tears from the depth of some divine despair
Rise in the heart, and gather to the eyes,
In looking on the happy autumn-fields,
And thinking of the days that are no more.

    ' Fresh as the first beam glittering on a sail,
That brings our friends up from the underworld,
Sad as the last which reddens over one
That sinks with all we love below the verge;
So sad, so fresh, the days that are no more.   30

    ' Ah, sad and strange as in dark summer
        dawns
The earliest pipe of half-awaken'd birds
To dying ears, when unto dying eyes
The casement slowly grows a glimmering
        square;
So sad, so strange, the days that are no more.

    ' Dear as remember'd kisses after death,
And sweet as those by hopeless fancy feign'd
On lips that are for others; deep as love,
Deep as first love, and wild with all regret;
O Death in Life, the days that are no more!'   40

    She ended with such passion that the
        tear
She sang of shook and fell, an erring pearl
Lost in her bosom; but with some disdain
Answer'd the Princess: 'If indeed there
        haunt
About the moulder'd lodges of the past
So sweet a voice and vague, fatal to men,
Well needs it we should cram our ears with
        wool
And so pace by.  But thine are fancies
        hatch'd
In silken-folded idleness; nor is it
Wiser to weep a true occasion lost,           50
But trim our sails, and let old bygones be,
While down the streams that float us each
        and all
To the issue, goes, like glittering bergs of
        ice,
Throne after throne, and molten on the
        waste
Becomes a cloud; for all things serve their
        time
Toward that great year of equal mights
        and rights.

Nor would I fight with iron laws, in the end
Found golden.  Let the past be past, let be
Their cancell'd Babels; tho' the rough kex break
The starr'd mosaic, and the beard-blown goat                                    60
Hang on the shaft, and the wild fig-tree split
Their monstrous idols, care not while we hear
A trumpet in the distance pealing news
Of better, and Hope, a poising eagle, burns
Above the unrisen morrow.'  Then to me,
' Know you no song of your own land,' she said,
' Not such as moans about the retrospect,
But deals with the other distance and the hues
Of promise; not a death's - head at the wine ? '

Then I remember'd one myself had made,                                    70
What time I watch'd the swallow winging south
From mine own land, part made long since, and part
Now while I sang, and maiden-like as far
As I could ape their treble did I sing.

' O Swallow, Swallow, flying, flying south,
Fly to her, and fall upon her gilded eaves,
And tell her, tell her, what I tell to thee.

' O, tell her, Swallow, thou that knowest each,
That bright and fierce and fickle is the South,
And dark and true and tender is the North.  80

' O Swallow, Swallow, if I could follow, and light
Upon her lattice, I would pipe and trill,
And cheep and twitter twenty million loves.

' O, were I thou that she might take me in,
And lay me on her bosom, and her heart
Would rock the snowy cradle till I died !

' Why lingereth she to clothe her heart with love,
Delaying as the tender ash delays
To clothe herself, when all the woods are green ?

' O, tell her, Swallow, that thy brood is flown ;
Say to her, I do but wanton in the South,    91
But in the North long since my nest is made.

' O, tell her, brief is life but love is long,
And brief the sun of summer in the North,
And brief the moon of beauty in the South.

' O Swallow, flying from the golden woods,
Fly to her, and pipe and woo her, and make her mine,
And tell her, tell her, that I follow thee.'

I ceased, and all the ladies, each at each,
Like the Ithacensian suitors in old time,  100
Stared with great eyes, and laugh'd with alien lips,
And knew not what they meant; for still my voice
Rang false.  But smiling, ' Not for thee,' she said,
' O Bulbul, any rose of Gulistan
Shall burst her veil; marsh-divers, rather, maid,
Shall croak thee sister, or the meadow-crake
Grate her harsh kindred in the grass — and this
A mere love-poem ! O, for such, my friend,
We hold them slight; they mind us of the time
When we made bricks in Egypt.  Knaves are men,                                    110
That lute and flute fantastic tenderness,
And dress the victim to the offering up,
And paint the gates of Hell with Paradise,
And play the slave to gain the tyranny.
Poor soul ! I had a maid of honor once;
She wept her true eyes blind for such a one,
A rogue of canzonets and serenades.
I loved her.  Peace be with her.  She is dead.
So they blaspheme the muse ! But great is song
Used to great ends; ourself have often tried                                    120
Valkyrian hymns, or into rhythm have dash'd
The passion of the prophetess; for song
Is duer unto freedom, force and growth
Of spirit, than to junketing and love.
Love is it ?  Would this same mock-love, and this
Mock-Hymen were laid up like winter bats,
Till all men grew to rate us at our worth,
Not vassals to be beat, nor pretty babes
To be dandled, no, but living wills, and sphered

Whole in ourselves and owed to none.
 Enough! 130
But now to leaven play with profit, you,
Know you no song, the true growth of your
 soil,
That gives the manners of your country-
 women?'

She spoke and turn'd her sumptuous head
 with eyes
Of shining expectation fixt on mine.
Then while I dragg'd my brains for such a
 song,
Cyril, with whom the bell-mouth'd glass
 had wrought,
Or master'd by the sense of sport, began
To troll a careless, careless tavern-catch
Of Moll and Meg, and strange experi-
 ences 140
Unmeet for ladies. Florian nodded at
 him,
I frowning; Psyche flush'd and wann'd and
 shook;
The lilylike Melissa droop'd her brows.
'Forbear,' the Princess cried; 'Forbear,
 sir,' I;
And heated thro' and thro' with wrath and
 love,
I smote him on the breast. He started up;
There rose a shriek as of a city sack'd;
Melissa clamor'd, 'Flee the death;' 'To
 horse!'
Said Ida, 'home! to horse!' and fled, as
 flies
A troop of snowy doves athwart the dusk
When some one batters at the dovecote
 doors, 151
Disorderly the women. Alone I stood
With Florian, cursing Cyril, vext at heart
In the pavilion. There like parting hopes
I heard them passing from me; hoof by
 hoof,
And every hoof a knell to my desires,
Clang'd on the bridge; and then another
 shriek,
'The Head, the Head, the Princess, O the
 Head!'
For blind with rage she miss'd the plank,
 and roll'd
In the river. Out I sprang from glow to
 gloom; 160
There whirl'd her white robe like a blos-
 som'd branch
Rapt to the horrible fall. A glance I gave,
No more, but woman-vested as I was

Plunged, and the flood drew; yet I caught
 her; then
Oaring one arm, and bearing in my left
The weight of all the hopes of half the
 world,
Strove to buffet to land in vain. A tree
Was half-disrooted from his place and
 stoop'd
To drench his dark locks in the gurgling
 wave
Mid-channel. Right on this we drove and
 caught, 170
And grasping down the boughs I gain'd
 the shore.

There stood her maidens glimmeringly
 group'd
In the hollow bank. One reaching forward
 drew
My burthen from mine arms; they cried,
 'She lives.'
They bore her back into the tent: but I,
So much a kind of shame within me
 wrought,
Not yet endured to meet her opening eyes,
Nor found my friends; but push'd alone on
 foot —
For since her horse was lost I left her
 mine —
Across the woods, and less from Indian
 craft 180
Than beelike instinct hiveward, found at
 length
The garden portals. Two great statues,
 Art
And Science, Caryatids, lifted up
A weight of emblem, and betwixt were
 valves
Of open-work in which the hunter rued
His rash intrusion, manlike, but his brows
Had sprouted, and the branches thereupon
Spread out at top, and grimly spiked the
 gates.

A little space was left between the
 horns,
Thro' which I clamber'd o'er at top with
 pain, 190
Dropt on the sward, and up the linden
 walks,
And, tost on thoughts that changed from
 hue to hue,
Now poring on the glowworm, now the star,
I paced the terrace, till the Bear had
 wheel'd

Thro' a great arc his seven slow suns.
                                        A step
Of lightest echo, then a loftier form
Than female, moving thro' the uncertain
    gloom,
Disturb'd me with the doubt 'if this were
    she,'
But it was Florian. 'Hist, O, hist!' he
    said,
'They seek us; out so late is out of rules.
Moreover, "Seize the strangers" is the
    cry.                                   201
How came you here?' I told him. 'I,'
    said he,
'Last of the train, a moral leper, I,
To whom none spake, half-sick at heart,
    return'd.
Arriving all confused among the rest
With hooded brows I crept into the hall,
And, couch'd behind a Judith, underneath
The head of Holofernes peep'd and saw.
Girl after girl was call'd to trial; each
Disclaim'd all knowledge of us; last of
    all,                                   210
Melissa; trust me, sir, I pitied her.
She, question'd if she knew us men, at first
Was silent; closer prest, denied it not,
And then, demanded if her mother knew,
Or Psyche, she affirm'd not, or denied;
From whence the Royal mind, familiar
    with her,
Easily gather'd either guilt. She sent
For Psyche, but she was not there; she
    call'd
For Psyche's child to cast it from the
    doors;
She sent for Blanche to accuse her face to
    face;                                  220
And I slipt out. But whither will you now?
And where are Psyche, Cyril? both are
    fled;
What, if together? that were not so well.
Would rather we had never come! I dread
His wildness, and the chances of the dark.'

'And yet,' I said, 'you wrong him more
    than I
That struck him; this is proper to the
    clown,
Tho' smock'd, or furr'd and purpled, still
    the clown,
To harm the thing that trusts him, and to
    shame
That which he says he loves. For Cyril,
    howe'er                               230

He deal in frolic, as to-night — the song
Might have been worse and sinn'd in
    grosser lips
Beyond all pardon — as it is, I hold
These flashes on the surface are not he.
He has a solid base of temperament;
But as the water-lily starts and slides
Upon the level in little puffs of wind,
Tho' anchor'd to the bottom, such is he.'

Scarce had I ceased when from a tama-
    risk near
Two Proctors leapt upon us, crying,
    'Names!'                              240
He, standing still, was clutch'd; but I be-
    gan
To thrid the musky-circled mazes, wind
And double in and out the boles, and race
By all the fountains. Fleet I was of foot;
Before me shower'd the rose in flakes; be-
    hind
I heard the puff'd pursuer; at mine ear
Bubbled the nightingale and heeded not,
And secret laughter tickled all my soul.
At last I hook'd my ankle in a vine
That claspt the feet of a Mnemosyne,   250
And falling on my face was caught and
    known.

They haled us to the Princess where she
    sat
High in the hall; above her droop'd a lamp,
And made the single jewel on her brow
Burn like the mystic fire on a mast-head,
Prophet of storm; a handmaid on each
    side
Bow'd toward her, combing out her long
    black hair
Damp from the river; and close behind her
    stood
Eight daughters of the plough, stronger
    than men,
Huge women blowzed with health, and
    wind, and rain,                       260
And labor. Each was like a Druid rock;
Or like a spire of land that stands apart
Cleft from the main, and wail'd about with
    mews.

Then, as we came, the crowd dividing
    clove
An advent to the throne; and therebeside,
Half-naked as if caught at once from bed
And tumbled on the purple footcloth, lay
The lily-shining child; and on the left,

Bow'd on her palms and folded up from
    wrong, .
Her round white shoulder shaken with her
    sobs, 270
Melissa knelt; but Lady Blanche erect
Stood up and spake, an affluent orator:

'It was not thus, O Princess, in old days;
You prized my counsel, lived upon my lips.
I led you then to all the Castalies;
I fed you with the milk of every Muse;
I loved you like this kneeler, and you me
Your second mother, those were gracious
    times.
Then came your new friend; you began to
    change —
I saw it and grieved — to slacken and to
    cool; 280
Till taken with her seeming openness
You turn'd your warmer currents all to
    her,
To me you froze; this was my meed for
    all.
Yet I bore up in part from ancient love,
And partly that I hoped to win you back,
And partly conscious of my own deserts,
And partly that you were my civil head,
And chiefly you were born for something
    great,
In which I might your fellow-worker be,
When time should serve; and thus a noble
    scheme 290
Grew up from seed we two long since had
    sown;
In us true growth, in her a Jonah's gourd,
Up in one night and due to sudden sun.
We took this palace; but even from the
    first
You stood in your own light and darken'd
    mine.
What student came but that you planed her
    path
To Lady Psyche, younger, not so wise,
A foreigner, and I your countrywoman,
I your old friend and tried, she new in
    all ?
But still her lists were swell'd and mine
    were lean; 300
Yet I bore up in hope she would be
    known.
Then came these wolves; *they* knew her;
    *they* endured,
Long-closeted with her the yestermorn,
To tell her what they were, and she to
    hear.

And me none told. Not less to an eye like
    mine,
A lidless watcher of the public weal,
Last night, their mask was patent, and my
    foot
Was to you. But I thought again; I fear'd
To meet a cold " We thank you, we shall
    hear of it
From Lady Psyche;" you had gone to
    her, 310
She told, perforce, and winning easy grace,
No doubt, for slight delay, remain'd
    among us
In our young nursery still unknown, the
    stem
Less grain than touchwood, while my hon-
    est heat
Were all miscounted as malignant haste
To push my rival out of place and power.
But public use required she should be
    known;
And since my oath was ta'en for public
    use,
I broke the letter of it to keep the sense.
I spoke not then at first, but watch'd them
    well, 320
Saw that they kept apart, no mischief
    done;
And yet this day — tho' you should hate me
    for it —
I came to tell you; found that you had gone,
Ridden to the hills, she likewise. Now, I
    thought,
That surely she will speak; if not, then I.
Did she ? These monsters blazon'd what
    they were,
According to the coarseness of their kind,
For thus I hear; and known at last — my
    work —
And full of cowardice and guilty shame —
I grant in her some sense of shame — she
    flies; 330
And I remain on whom to wreak your rage,
I, that have lent my life to build up yours,
I, that have wasted here health, wealth, and
    time,
And talent, I — you know it — I will not
    boast;
Dismiss me, and I prophesy your plan,
Divorced from my experience, will be chaff
For every gust of chance, and men will
    say
We did not know the real light, but chased
The wisp that flickers where no foot can
    tread.'

She ceased; the Princess answer'd coldly,
'Good;                                          340
Your oath is broken; we dismiss you, go.
For this lost lamb ' — she pointed to the
     child —
' Our mind is changed; we take it to our-
     self.'

Thereat the lady stretch'd a vulture
     throat,
And shot from crooked lips a haggard
     smile.
' The plan was mine.   I built the nest,' she
     said,
' To hatch the cuckoo.   Rise ! ' and stoop'd
     to updrag
Melissa.   She, half on her mother propt,
Half-drooping from her, turn'd her face,
     and cast
A liquid look on Ida, full of prayer,      350
Which melted Florian's fancy as she hung,
A Niobeän daughter, one arm out,
Appealing to the bolts of heaven; and
     while
We gazed upon her came a little stir
About the doors, and on a sudden rush'd
Among us, out of breath, as one pursued,
A woman-post in flying raiment.   Fear
Stared in her eyes, and chalk'd her face,
     and wing'd
Her transit to the throne, whereby she fell
Delivering seal'd dispatches which the
     Head                                       360
Took half-amazed, and in her lion's mood
Tore open, silent we with blind surmise
Regarding, while she read, till over brow
And cheek and bosom brake the wrathful
     bloom
As of some fire against a stormy cloud,
When the wild peasant rights himself, the
     rick
Flames, and his anger reddens in the hea-
     vens;
For anger most it seem'd, while now her
     breast,
Beaten with some great passion at her
     heart,                                     369
Palpitated, her hand shook, and we heard
In the dead hush the papers that she held
Rustle.   At once the lost lamb at her feet
Sent out a bitter bleating for its dam.
The plaintive cry jarr'd on her ire; she
     crush'd
The scrolls together, made a sudden turn
As if to speak, but, utterance failing her,

She whirl'd them on to me, as who should
     say
' Read,' and I read — two letters — one
     her sire's:

' Fair daughter, when we sent the Prince
     your way
We knew not your ungracious laws, which
     learnt,                                    380
We, conscious of what temper you are
     built,
Came all in haste to hinder wrong, but
     fell
Into his father's hand, who has this night,
You lying close upon his territory,
Slipt round and in the dark invested you,
And here he keeps me hostage for his son.'

The second was my father's running
     thus:
' You have our son; touch not a hair of his
     head;
Render him up unscathed; give him your
     hand;
Cleave to your contract — tho' indeed we
     hear                                       390
You hold the woman is the better man;
A rampant heresy, such as if it spread
Would make all women kick against their
     lords
Thro' all the world, and which might well
     deserve
That we this night should pluck your pal-
     ace down;
And we will do it, unless you send us back
Our son, on the instant, whole.'
                              So far I read;
And then stood up and spoke impetuously:

' O, not to pry and peer on your reserve,
But led by golden wishes, and a hope    400
The child of regal compact, did I break
Your precinct; not a scorner of your sex
But venerator, zealous it should be
All that it might be.   Hear me, for I bear,
Tho' man, yet human, whatsoe'er your
     wrongs,
From the flaxen curl to the gray lock a life
Less mine than yours.   My nurse would tell
     me of you;
I babbled for you, as babies for the moon,
Vague brightness; when a boy, you stoop'd
     to me
From all high places, lived in all fair
     lights,                                    410

Came in long breezes rapt from inmost
  south
And blown to inmost north; at eve and
  dawn
With Ida, Ida, Ida, rang the woods;
The leader wild-swan in among the stars
Would clang it, and lapt in wreaths of
  glowworm light
The mellow breaker murmur'd Ida.  Now,
Because I would have reach'd you, had you
  been
Sphered up with Cassiopeia, or the en-
  throned
Persephone in Hades, now at length,    419
Those winters of abeyance all worn out,
A man I came to see you; but, indeed,
Not in this frequence can I lend full tongue,
O noble Ida, to those thoughts that wait
On you, their centre.  Let me say but this,
That many a famous man and woman, town
And landskip, have I heard of, after seen
The dwarfs of presage; tho' when known,
  there grew
Another kind of beauty in detail
Made them worth knowing; but in you I
  found
My boyish dream involved and dazzled
  down                                 430
And master'd, while that after - beauty
  makes
Such head from act to act, from hour to
  hour,
Within me, that except you slay me here,
According to your bitter statute-book,
I cannot cease to follow you, as they say
The seal does music; who desire you more
Than growing boys their manhood; dying
  lips,
With many thousand matters left to do,
The breath of life; O, more than poor men
  wealth,
Than sick men health — yours, yours, not
  mine — but half                      440
Without you; with you, whole; and of those
  halves
You worthiest; and howe'er you block and
  bar
Your heart with system out from mine, I
  hold
That it becomes no man to nurse despair,
But in the teeth of clench'd antagonisms
To follow up the worthiest till he die.
Yet that I came not all unauthorized
Behold your father's letter.'
                      On one knee

Kneeling, I gave it, which she caught, and
  dash'd
Unopen'd at her feet.  A tide of fierce    450
Invective seem'd to wait behind her lips,
As waits a river level with the dam
Ready to burst and flood the world with
  foam;
And so she would have spoken, but there
  rose
A hubbub in the court of half the maids
Gather'd together; from the illumined hall
Long lanes of splendor slanted o'er a press
Of snowy shoulders, thick as herded ewes,
And rainbow robes, and gems and gemlike
  eyes,
And gold and golden heads.  They to and
  fro                                  460
Fluctuated, as flowers in storm, some red,
  some pale,
All open-mouth'd, all gazing to the light,
Some crying there was an army in the
  land,
And some that men were in the very walls,
And some they cared not; till a clamor
  grew
As of a new-world Babel, woman-built,
And worse-confounded.  High above them
  stood
The placid marble Muses, looking peace.

  Not peace she look'd, the Head; but ris-
  ing up
Robed in the long night of her deep hair,
  so                                   470
To the open window moved, remaining
  there
Fixt like a beacon-tower above the waves
Of tempest, when the crimson-rolling eye
Glares ruin, and the wild birds on the light
Dash themselves dead.  She stretch'd her
  arms and call'd
Across the tumult, and the tumult fell.

  ' What fear ye, brawlers ? am not I your
  Head ?
On me, me, me, the storm first breaks;
  I dare
All these male thunderbolts; what is it ye
  fear ?
Peace ! there are those to avenge us and
  they come;                          480
If not, — myself were like enough, O girls,
To unfurl the maiden banner of our rights,
And clad in iron burst the ranks of war,
Or, falling, protomartyr of our cause,

Die; yet I blame you not so much for fear;
Six thousand years of fear have made you
  that
From which I would redeem you.  But for
  those
That stir this hubbub — you and you — I
  know
Your faces there in the crowd — to-morrow
  morn
We hold a great convention; then shall
  they                                        490
That love their voices more than duty,
  learn
With whom they deal, dismiss'd in shame
  to live
No wiser than their mothers, household
  stuff,
Live chattels, mincers of each other's fame,
Full of weak poison, turnspits for the
  clown,
The drunkard's football, laughing-stocks
  of Time,
Whose brains are in their hands and in
  their heels,
But fit to flaunt, to dress, to dance, to
  thrum,
To tramp, to scream, to burnish, and to
  scour,                                      499
For ever slaves at home and fools abroad.'

  She, ending, waved her hands; thereat
  the crowd
Muttering, dissolved; then with a smile,
  that look'd
A stroke of cruel sunshine on the cliff,
When all the glens are drown'd in azure
  gloom
Of thunder-shower, she floated to us and
  said:

  'You have done well and like a gentleman,
And like a prince; you have our thanks for
  all.
And you look well too in your woman's
  dress.
Well have you done and like a gentleman.
You saved our life; we owe you bitter
  thanks.                                      510
Better have died and spilt our bones in the
  flood —
Then men had said — but now — what
  hinders me
To take such bloody vengeance on you
  both ? —

Yet since our father — wasps in our good
  hive,
You would-be quenchers of the light to
  be,
Barbarians, grosser than your native
  bears —
O, would I had his sceptre for one hour !
You that have dared to break our bound,
  and gull'd
Our servants, wrong'd and lied and
  thwarted us —
I wed with thee !  I bound by precontract
Your bride, your bondslave ! not tho' all
  the gold                                     521
That veins the world were pack'd to make
  your crown,
And every spoken tongue should lord you.
  Sir,
Your falsehood and yourself are hateful to
  us;
I trample on your offers and on you.
Begone; we will not look upon you more.
Here, push them out at gates.'
                        In wrath she spake.
Then those eight mighty daughters of the
  plough
Bent their broad faces toward us and ad-
  dress'd
Their motion.  Twice I sought to plead my
  cause,                                       530
But on my shoulder hung their heavy
  hands,
The weight of destiny; so from her face
They push'd us, down the steps, and thro'
  the court,
And with grim laughter thrust us out at
  gates.

  We cross'd the street and gain'd a petty
  mound
Beyond it, whence we saw the lights and
  heard
The voices murmuring.  While I listen'd,
  came
On a sudden the weird seizure and the
  doubt.
I seem'd to move among a world of ghosts;
The Princess with her monstrous woman-
  guard,                                       540
The jest and earnest working side by side,
The cataract and the tumult and the kings
Were shadows; and the long fantastic
  night
With all its doings had and had not been,
And all things were and were not.

This went by
As strangely as it came, and on my spirits
Settled a gentle cloud of melancholy —
Not long; I shook it off; for spite of doubts
And sudden ghostly shadowings I was one
To whom the touch of all mischance but
came                                            550
As night to him that sitting on a hill
Sees the midsummer, midnight, Norway sun
Set into sunrise; then we moved away.


### INTERLUDE

Thy voice is heard thro' rolling drums
  That beat to battle where he stands;
Thy face across his fancy comes,
  And gives the battle to his hands.
A moment, while the trumpets blow,
  He sees his brood about thy knee;
The next, like fire he meets the foe,
  And strikes him dead for thine and thee.


So Lilia sang. We thought her half-pos-
      sess'd,
She struck such warbling fury thro' the
      words;                                      10
And, after, feigning pique at what she call'd
The raillery, or grotesque, or false sub-
      lime —
Like one that wishes at a dance to change
The music — clapt her hands and cried for
      war,
Or some grand fight to kill and make an
      end.
And he that next inherited the tale,
Half turning to the broken statue, said,
'Sir Ralph has got your colors; if I prove
Your knight, and fight your battle, what
      for me?'
It chanced, her empty glove upon the tomb
Lay by her like a model of her hand.      21
She took it and she flung it. 'Fight,' she
      said,
'And make us all we would be, great and
      good.'
He knightlike in his cap instead of casque,
A cap of Tyrol borrow'd from the hall,
Arranged the favor, and assumed the
      Prince.


### V

Now, scarce three paces measured from
      the mound,
We stumbled on a stationary voice,

And 'Stand, who goes?' 'Two from the
      palace,' I.
'The second two; they wait,' he said, 'pass
      on;
His Highness wakes;' and one, that clash'd
      in arms,
By glimmering lanes and walls of canvas
      led
Threading the soldier-city, till we heard
The drowsy folds of our great ensign shake
From blazon'd lions o'er the imperial tent
Whispers of war.
                      Entering, the sudden light
Dazed me half-blind. I stood and seem'd
      to hear,                                   11
As in a poplar grove when a light wind
      wakes
A lisping of the innumerous leaf and dies,
Each hissing in his neighbor's ear; and
      then
A strangled titter, out of which there brake
On all sides, clamoring etiquette to death,
Unmeasured mirth; while now the two old
      kings
Began to wag their baldness up and down,
The fresh young captains flash'd their glit-
      tering teeth,
The huge bush-bearded barons heaved and
      blew,                                       20
And slain with laughter roll'd the gilded
      squire.

  At length my sire, his rough cheek wet
      with tears,
Panted from weary sides, 'King, you are
      free!
We did but keep you surety for our son,
If this be he, — or a draggled mawkin,
      thou,
That tends her bristled grunters in the
      sludge;'
For I was drench'd with ooze, and torn
      with briers,
More crumpled than a poppy from the
      sheath,
And all one rag, disprinced from head to
      heel.
Then some one sent beneath his vaulted
      palm                                        30
A whisper'd jest to some one near him,
      'Look,
He has been among his shadows.' 'Satan
      take
The old women and their shadows!'— thus
      the king

Roar'd — 'make yourself a man to fight
with men.
Go; Cyril told us all.'
As boys that slink
From ferule and the trespass-chiding eye,
Away we stole, and transient in a trice
From what was left of faded woman-slough
To sheathing splendors and the golden scale
Of harness, issued in the sun, that now  40
Leapt from the dewy shoulders of the
earth,
And hit the Northern hills.  Here Cyril
met us,
A little shy at first, but by and by
We twain, with mutual pardon ask'd and
given
For stroke and song, resolder'd peace,
whereon
Follow'd his tale.  Amazed he fled away
Thro' the dark land, and later in the night
Had come on Psyche weeping: 'then we
fell  48
Into your father's hand, and there she lies,
But will not speak nor stir.'
He show'd a tent
A stone-shot off; we enter'd in, and there
Among piled arms and rough accoutre-
ments,
Pitiful sight, wrapp'd in a soldier's cloak,
Like some sweet sculpture draped from
head to foot,
And push'd by rude hands from its pedes-
tal,
All her fair length upon the ground she
lay;
And at her head a follower of the camp,
A charr'd and wrinkled piece of woman-
hood,
Sat watching like a watcher by the dead.

Then Florian knelt, and 'Come,' he whisper'd to her,  60
'Lift up your head, sweet sister; lie not
thus.
What have you done but right? you could
not slay
Me, nor your prince; look up, be comforted.
Sweet is it to have done the thing one
ought,
When fallen in darker ways.'  And likewise I:
'Be comforted; have I not lost her too,
In whose least act abides the nameless
charm

That none has else for me?'  She heard,
she moved,
She moan'd, a folded voice; and up she
sat,
And raised the cloak from brows as pale
and smooth  70
As those that mourn half-shrouded over
death
In deathless marble.  'Her,' she said, 'my
friend —
Parted from her — betray'd her cause and
mine —
Where shall I breathe? why kept ye not
your faith?
O base and bad! what comfort? none for
me!'
To whom remorseful Cyril, 'Yet I pray
Take comfort; live, dear lady, for your
child!'
At which she lifted up her voice and cried:

'Ah me, my babe, my blossom, ah, my
child,
My one sweet child, whom I shall see no
more!  80
For now will cruel Ida keep her back;
And either she will die from want of care,
Or sicken with ill-usage, when they say
The child is hers — for every little fault,
The child is hers; and they will beat my
girl
Remembering her mother — O my flower!
Or they will take her, they will make her
hard,
And she will pass me by in after-life
With some cold reverence worse than were
she dead.  89
Ill mother that I was to leave her there,
To lag behind, scared by the cry they made,
The horror of the shame among them all.
But I will go and sit beside the doors,
And make a wild petition night and day,
Until they hate to hear me like a wind
Wailing for ever, till they open to me,
And lay my little blossom at my feet,
My babe, my sweet Aglaïa, my one child;
And I will take her up and go my way,
And satisfy my soul with kissing her.  100
Ah! what might that man not deserve
of me
Who gave me back my child?'  'Be com-
forted,'
Said Cyril, 'you shall have it;' but again
She veil'd her brows, and prone she sank,
and so,

Like tender things that being caught feign
    death,
Spoke not, nor stirr'd.
                    By this a murmur ran
Thro' all the camp, and inward raced the
    scouts
With rumor of Prince Arac hard at hand.
We left her by the woman, and without
Found the gray kings at parle; and ' Look
    you,' cried                              110
My father, ' that our compact be fulfill'd.
You have spoilt this child; she laughs at
    you and man;
She wrongs herself, her sex, and me, and
    him.
But red-faced war has rods of steel and
    fire;
She yields, or war.'
                    Then Gama turn'd to me:
' We fear, indeed, you spent a stormy time
With our strange girl; and yet they say
    that still
You love her.  Give us, then, your mind
    at large:
How say you, war or not ? '
                    ' Not war, if possible,
O king,' I said, ' lest from the abuse of
    war,                                      120
The desecrated shrine, the trampled year,
The smouldering homestead, and the house-
    hold flower
Torn from the lintel — all the common
    wrong —
A smoke go up thro' which I loom to her
Three times a monster.  Now she lightens
    scorn
At him that mars her plan, but then would
    hate —
And every voice she talk'd with ratify it,
And every face she look'd on justify it —
The general foe.  More soluble is this knot
By gentleness than war.  I want her love. 130
What were I nigher this altho' we dash'd
Your cities into shards with catapults ? —
She would not love — or brought her
    chain'd, a slave,
The lifting of whose eyelash is my lord ?
Not ever would she love, but brooding turn
The book of scorn, till all my flitting chance
Were caught within the record of her
    wrongs
And crush'd to death; and rather, Sire,
    than this
I would the old god of war himself were
    dead,

Forgotten, rusting on his iron hills,      140
Rotting on some wild shore with ribs of
    wreck,
Or like an old-world mammoth bulk'd in
    ice,
Not to be molten out.'
                    And roughly spake
My father: ' Tut, you know them not, the
    girls.
Boy, when I hear you prate I almost think
That idiot legend credible.  Look you, sir !
Man is the hunter; woman is his game.
The sleek and shining creatures of the
    chase,
We hunt them for the beauty of their skins;
They love us for it, and we ride them
    down.                                     150
Wheedling and siding with them !  Out !
    for shame !
Boy, there 's no rose that 's half so dear to
    them
As he that does the thing they dare not do,
Breathing and sounding beauteous battle,
    comes
With the air of the trumpet round him, and
    leaps in
Among the women, snares them by the
    score
Flatter'd and fluster'd, wins, tho' dash'd
    with death
He reddens what he kisses.  Thus I won
Your mother, a good mother, a good wife,
Worth winning; but this firebrand — gen-
    tleness                                   160
To such as her ! if Cyril spake her true,
To catch a dragon in a cherry net,
To trip a tigress with a gossamer,
Were wisdom to it.'
                    ' Yea, but, Sire,' I cried,
' Wild natures need wise curbs.  The sol-
    dier ?  No !
What dares not Ida do that she should
    prize
The soldier ?  I beheld her, when she rose
The yesternight, and storming in extremes
Stood for her cause, and flung defiance
    down
Gagelike to man, and had not shunn'd the
    death,                                    170
No, not the soldier's; yet I hold her, king,
True woman; but you clash them all in one,
That have as many differences as we.
The violet varies from the lily as far
As oak from elm.  One loves the soldier,
    one

The silken priest of peace, one this, one that,
And some unworthily; their sinless faith,
A maiden moon that sparkles on a sty,
Glorifying clown and satyr; whence they
    need    179
More breadth of culture.  Is not Ida right?
They worth it? truer to the law within?
Severer in the logic of a life?
Twice as magnetic to sweet influences
Of earth and heaven? and she of whom
    you speak,
My mother, looks as whole as some serene
Creation minted in the golden moods
Of sovereign artists; not a thought, a touch,
But pure as lines of green that streak the
    white
Of the first snowdrop's inner leaves; I say,
Not like the piebald miscellany, man,  190
Bursts of great heart and slips in sensual
    mire,
But whole and one; and take them all-in-all,
Were we ourselves but half as good, as
    kind,
As truthful, much that Ida claims as right
Had ne'er been mooted, but as frankly
    theirs
As dues of Nature.  To our point; not war,
Lest I lose all.'
           ' Nay, nay, you spake but sense,'
Said Gama.  ' We remember love ourself
In our sweet youth; we did not rate him
    then    199
This red-hot iron to be shaped with blows.
You talk almost like Ida; she can talk;
And there is something in it as you say:
But you talk kindlier; we esteem you for
    it. —
He seems a gracious and a gallant Prince,
I would he had our daughter.  For the rest,
Our own detention, why, the causes weigh'd,
Fatherly fears — you used us courteously —
We would do much to gratify your Prince —
We pardon it; and for your ingress here 209
Upon the skirt and fringe of our fair land,
You did but come as goblins in the night,
Nor in the furrow broke the ploughman's
    head,
Nor burnt the grange, nor buss'd the milk-
    ing-maid,
Nor robb'd the farmer of his bowl of cream.
But let your Prince — our royal word
    upon it,
He comes back safe — ride with us to our
    lines,
And speak with Arac.  Arac's word is thrice

As ours with Ida; something may be done —
I know not what — and ours shall see us
    friends.
You, likewise, our late guests, if so you
    will,    220
Follow us.  Who knows? we four may build
    some plan
Foursquare to opposition.'
                Here he reach'd
White hands of farewell to my sire, who
    growl'd
An answer which, half-muffled in his beard,
Let so much out as gave us leave to go.

Then rode we with the old king across
    the lawns
Beneath huge trees, a thousand rings of
    Spring
In every bole, a song on every spray
Of birds that piped their Valentines, and
    woke
Desire in me to infuse my tale of love  230
In the old king's ears, who promised help,
    and oozed
All o'er with honey'd answer as we rode;
And blossom-fragrant slipt the heavy dews
Gather'd by night and peace, with each
    light air
On our mail'd heads.  But other thoughts
    than peace
Burnt in us, when we saw the embattled
    squares
And squadrons of the Prince, trampling
    the flowers
With clamor; for among them rose a cry
As if to greet the king; they made a halt;
The horses yell'd; they clash'd their arms;
    the drum    240
Beat; merrily-blowing shrill'd the martial
    fife ;
And in the blast and bray of the long horn
And serpent-throated bugle, undulated
The banner.  Anon to meet us lightly
    pranced
Three captains out; nor ever had I seen
Such thews of men.  The midmost and the
    highest
Was Arac; all about his motion clung
The shadow of his sister, as the beam
Of the East, that play'd upon them, made
    them glance
Like those three stars of the airy Giant's
    zone,    250
That glitter burnish'd by the frosty dark;
And as the fiery Sirius alters hue,

And bickers into red and emerald, shone
Their morions, wash'd with morning, as
    they came.

    And I that prated peace, when first I
      heard
War-music, felt the blind wild-beast of
    force,
Whose home is in the sinews of a man,
Stir in me as to strike.   Then took the king
His three broad sons; with now a wander-
    ing hand          259
And now a pointed finger, told them all.
A common light of smiles at our disguise
Broke from their lips, and, ere the windy
    jest
Had labor'd down within his ample lungs,
The genial giant, Arac, roll'd himself
Thrice in the saddle, then burst out in
    words:

  'Our land invaded, 'sdeath ! and he him-
    self
Your captive, yet my father wills not war!
And, 'sdeath! myself, what care I, war
    or no ?
But then this question of your troth re-
    mains;
And there 's a downright honest meaning
    in her.          270
She flies too high, she flies too high ! and
    yet
She ask'd but space and fair-play for her
    scheme;
She prest and prest it on me — I myself,
What know I of these things ? but, life
    and soul !
I thought her half - right talking of her
    wrongs;
I say she flies too high, 'sdeath ! what of
    that ?
I take her for the flower of womankind,
And so I often told her, right or wrong;
And, Prince, she can be sweet to those she
    loves,          279
And, right or wrong, I care not; this is all,
I stand upon her side; she made me swear
    it —
'Sdeath ! — and with solemn rites by can-
    dle-light —
Swear by Saint something — I forget her
    name —
Her that talk'd down the fifty wisest men;
*She* was a princess too; and so I swore.

Come, this is all; she will not; waive your
    claim.
If not, the foughten field, what else, at
    once
Decides it, 'sdeath ! against my father's
    will.'

I lagg'd in answer, loth to render up  289
My precontract, and loth by brainless war
To cleave the rift of difference deeper yet;
Till one of those two brothers, half aside
And fingering at the hair about his lip,
To prick us on to combat, ' Like to like !
The woman's garment hid the woman's
    heart.'
A taunt that clench'd his purpose like a
    blow !
For fiery-short was Cyril's counter-scoff,
And sharp I answer'd, touch'd upon the
    point
Where idle boys are cowards to their
    shame,
' Decide it here; why not ? we are three to
    three.'          300

    Then spake the third: ' But three to
      three ? no more ?
No more, and in our noble sister's cause ?
More, more, for honor ! every captain waits
Hungry for honor, angry for his king.
More, more, some fifty on a side, that each
May breathe himself, and quick ! by over-
    throw
Of these or those, the question settled die.'

    ' Yea,' answer'd I, ' for this wild wreath
      of air,
This flake of rainbow flying on the highest
Foam of men's deeds — this honor, if ye
    will.          310
It needs must be for honor if at all;
Since, what decision ? if we fail we fail,
And if we win we fail; she would not keep
Her compact.'   ' 'Sdeath ! but we will send
    to her,'
Said Arac, ' worthy reasons why she should
Bide by this issue; let our missive thro',
And you shall have her answer by the
    word.'

    ' Boys ! ' shriek'd the old king, but vain-
      lier than a hen
To her false daughters in the pool; for
    none

Regarded; neither seem'd there more to
  say.                                     320
Back rode we to my father's camp, and
  found
He thrice had sent a herald to the gates,
To learn if Ida yet would cede our claim,
Or by denial flush her babbling wells
With her own people's life; three times he
  went.
The first, he blew and blew, but none ap-
  pear'd;
He batter'd at the doors, none came; the
  next,
An awful voice within had warn'd him
  thence;
The third, and those eight daughters of the
  plough
Came sallying thro' the gates, and caught
  his hair,                               330
And so belabor'd him on rib and cheek
They made him wild.   Not less one glance
  he caught
Thro' open doors of Ida station'd there
Unshaken, clinging to her purpose, firm
Tho' compass'd by two armies and the noise
Of arms; and standing like a stately pine
Set in a cataract on an island-crag,
When storm is on the heights, and right
  and left
Suck'd from the dark heart of the long hills
  roll
The torrents, dash'd to the vale; and yet
  her will                               340
Bred will in me to overcome it or fall.

    But when I told the king that I was
      pledged
To fight in tourney for my bride, he clash'd
His iron palms together with a cry;
Himself would tilt it out among the lads;
But overborne by all his bearded lords
With reasons drawn from age and state,
  perforce
He yielded, wroth and red, with fierce de-
  mur;
And many a bold knight started up in heat,
And sware to combat for my claim till
  death.                                 350

    All on this side the palace ran the field
Flat to the garden-wall; and likewise here,
Above the garden's glowing blossom-belts,
A column'd entry shone and marble stairs,
And great bronze valves, emboss'd with
  Tomyris

And what she did to Cyrus after fight,
But now fast barr'd.   So here upon the flat
All that long morn the lists were hammer'd
  up,
And all that morn the heralds to and fro,
With message and defiance, went and came;
Last, Ida's answer, in a royal hand,      361
But shaken here and there, and rolling
  words
Oration-like.   I kiss'd it and I read:

    'O brother, you have known the pangs
      we felt,
What heats of indignation when we heard
Of those that iron-cramp'd their women's
  feet;
Of lands in which at the altar the poor
  bride
Gives her harsh groom for bridal-gift a
  scourge;
Of living hearts that crack within the fire
Where smoulder their dead despots; and of
  those, —                               370
Mothers, — that, all prophetic pity, fling
Their pretty maids in the running flood,
  and swoops
The vulture, beak and talon, at the heart
Made for all noble motion.   And I saw
That equal baseness lived in sleeker times
With smoother men; the old leaven lea-
  ven'd all;
Millions of throats would bawl for civil
  rights,
No woman named; therefore I set my face
Against all men, and lived but for mine
  own.
Far off from men I built a fold for them;
I stored it full of rich memorial;        381
I fenced it round with gallant institutes,
And biting laws to scare the beasts of prey,
And prosper'd, till a rout of saucy boys
Brake on us at our books, and marr'd our
  peace,
Mask'd like our maids, blustering I know
  not what
Of insolence and love, some pretext held
Of baby troth, invalid, since my will
Seal'd not the bond — the striplings ! —
  for their sport ! —
I tamed my leopards; shall I not tame
  these ?                                390
Or you ? or I ? for since you think me
  touch'd
In honor — what !   I would not aught of
  false —

Is not our cause pure ? and whereas I know
Your prowess, Arac, and what mother's
    blood
You draw from, fight ! You failing, I abide
What end soever; fail you will not. Still,
Take not his life, he risk'd it for my own;
His mother lives. Yet whatsoe'er you do,
Fight and fight well; strike and strike
    home. O dear
Brothers, the woman's angel guards you,
    you                                    400
The sole men to be mingled with our cause,
The sole men we shall prize in the after-
    time,
Your very armor hallow'd, and your statues
Rear'd, sung to, when, this gadfly brush'd
    aside,
We plant a solid foot into the Time,
And mould a generation strong to move
With claim on claim from right to right,
    till she
Whose name is yoked with children's
    know herself;
And Knowledge in our own land make her
    free,
And, ever following those two crowned
    twins,                                 410
Commerce and Conquest, shower the fiery
    grain
Of freedom broadcast over all that orbs
Between the Northern and the Southern
    morn.'

Then came a postscript dash'd across the
    rest:
' See that there be no traitors in your camp.
We seem a nest of traitors — none to trust
Since our arms fail'd — this Egypt-plague
    of men !
Almost our maids were better at their
    homes,
Than thus man-girdled here. Indeed I
    think
Our chiefest comfort is the little child   420
Of one unworthy mother, which she left.
She shall not have it back; the child shall
    grow
To prize the authentic mother of her mind.
I took it for an hour in mine own bed
This morning; there the tender orphan
    hands
Felt at my heart, and seem'd to charm from
    thence
The wrath I nursed against the world.
    Farewell.'

I ceased; he said, ' Stubborn, but she
    may sit
Upon a king's right hand in thunder-
    storms,
And breed up warriors ! See now, tho'
    yourself                              430
Be dazzled by the wildfire Love to sloughs
That swallow common sense, the spindling
    king,
This Gama swamp'd in lazy tolerance.
When the man wants weight, the woman
    takes it up,
And topples down the scales; but this is
    fixt
As are the roots of earth and base of all, —
Man for the field and woman for the
    hearth;
Man for the sword, and for the needle she;
Man with the head, and woman with the
    heart;
Man to command, and woman to obey;   440
All else confusion. Look you ! the gray
    mare
Is ill to live with, when her whinny shrills
From tile to scullery, and her small good-
    man
Shrinks in his arm-chair while the fires of
    hell
Mix with his hearth. But you — she 's yet
    a colt —
Take, break her; strongly groom'd and
    straitly curb'd
She might not rank with those detestable
That let the bantling scald at home, and
    brawl
Their rights or wrongs like potherbs in the
    street.
They say she 's comely; there 's the fairer
    chance.                              450
I like her none the less for rating at her !
Besides, the woman wed is not as we,
But suffers change of frame. A lusty brace
Of twins may weed her of her folly. Boy,
The bearing and the training of a child
Is woman's wisdom.'
                        Thus the hard old king.
I took my leave, for it was nearly noon;
I pored upon her letter which I held,
And on the little clause, ' take not his life;'
I mused on that wild morning in the woods,
And on the ' Follow, follow, thou shalt
    win;'                                461
I thought on all the wrathful king had said,
And how the strange betrothment was to
    end.

Then I remember'd that burnt sorcerer's
    curse
That one should fight with shadows and
    should fall;
And like a flash the weird affection came.
King, camp, and college turn'd to hollow
    shows;
I seem'd to move in old memorial tilts,
And doing battle with forgotten ghosts,
To dream myself the shadow of a dream;
And ere I woke it was the point of noon,
The lists were ready. Empanoplied and
    plumed      472
We enter'd in, and waited, fifty there
Opposed to fifty, till the trumpet blared
At the barrier like a wild horn in a land
Of echoes, and a moment, and once more
The trumpet, and again; at which the
    storm
Of galloping hoofs bare on the ridge of
    spears
And riders front to front, until they closed
In conflict with the crash of shivering
    points,      480
And thunder. Yet it seem'd a dream, I
    dream'd
Of fighting. On his haunches rose the
    steed,
And into fiery splinters leapt the lance,
And out of stricken helmets sprang the fire.
Part sat like rocks; part reel'd but kept
    their seats;
Part roll'd on the earth and rose again and
    drew;
Part stumbled mixt with floundering horses.
    Down
From those two bulks at Arac's side, and
    down
From Arac's arm, as from a giant's flail,
The large blows rain'd, as here and every-
    where      490
He rode the mellay, lord of the ringing
    lists,
And all the plain — brand, mace, and
    shaft, and shield —
Shock'd, like an iron-clanging anvil bang'd
With hammers; till I thought, can this be he
From Gama's dwarfish loins? if this be so,
The mother makes us most — and in my
    dream
I glanced aside, and saw the palace-front
Alive with fluttering scarfs and ladies' eyes,
And highest, among the statues, statue-like,
Between a cymbal'd Miriam and a Jael,
With Psyche's babe, was Ida watching us,

A single band of gold about her hair,    502
Like a saint's glory up in heaven; but she,
No saint — inexorable — no tenderness —
Too hard, too cruel. Yet she sees me fight,
Yea, let her see me fall. With that I drave
Among the thickest and bore down a
    prince,
And Cyril one. Yea, let me make my
    dream
All that I would. But that large-moulded
    man,
His visage all agrin as at a wake,    510
Made at me thro' the press, and, stagger-
    ing back
With stroke on stroke the horse and
    horseman, came
As comes a pillar of electric cloud,
Flaying the roofs and sucking up the
    drains,
And shadowing down the champaign till it
    strikes
On a wood, and takes, and breaks, and
    cracks, and splits,
And twists the grain with such a roar that
    Earth
Reels, and the herdsmen cry; for every-
    thing
Gave way before him. Only Florian, he
That loved me closer than his own right
    eye,    520
Thrust in between; but Arac rode him
    down.
And Cyril seeing it, push'd against the
    Prince,
With Psyche's color round his helmet,
    tough,
Strong, supple, sinew-corded, apt at arms;
But tougher, heavier, stronger, he that
    smote
And threw him. Last I spurr'd; I felt my
    veins
Stretch with fierce heat; a moment hand to
    hand,
And sword to sword, and horse to horse we
    hung,
Till I struck out and shouted; the blade
    glanced,
I did but shear a feather, and dream and
    truth    530
Flow'd from me; darkness closed me, and
    I fell.

> Home they brought her warrior dead;
>   She nor swoon'd nor utter'd cry.
> All her maidens, watching, said,
>   'She must weep or she will die.'

Then they praised him, soft and low,
Call'd him worthy to be loved,
Truest friend and noblest foe ;
Yet she neither spoke nor moved.

Stole a maiden from her place,
Lightly to the warrior stept,
Took the face-cloth from the face ;
Yet she neither moved nor wept.

Rose a nurse of ninety years,
Set his child upon her knee —
Like summer tempest came her tears —
'Sweet my child, I live for thee.'


## VI

My dream had never died or lived again ;
As in some mystic middle state I lay.
Seeing I saw not, hearing not I heard ;
Tho', if I saw not, yet they told me all
So often that I speak as having seen.

For so it seem'd, or so they said to me,
That all things grew more tragic and more
        strange ;
That when our side was vanquish'd and my
        cause
For ever lost, there went up a great cry,
'The Prince is slain!'   My father heard
        and ran                                            10
In on the lists, and there unlaced my
        casque
And grovell'd on my body, and after him
Came Psyche, sorrowing for Aglaïa.

But high upon the palace Ida stood
With Psyche's babe in arm ; there on the
        roofs
Like that great dame of Lapidoth she
        sang.

'Our enemies have fallen, have fallen : the
        seed,
The little seed they laugh'd at in the dark,
Has risen and cleft the soil, and grown a bulk
Of spanless girth, that lays on every side    20
A thousand arms and rushes to the sun.

'Our enemies have fallen, have fallen : they
        came ;
The leaves were wet with women's tears ; they
        heard
A noise of songs they would not understand ;
They mark'd it with the red cross to the fall,
And would have strown it, and are fallen them-
        selves.

'Our enemies have fallen, have fallen : they
        came,
The woodmen with their axes : lo the tree !
But we will make it faggots for the hearth,
And shape it plank and beam for roof and
        floor,                                            30
And boats and bridges for the use of men.

'Our enemies have fallen, have fallen ; they
        struck ;
With their own blows they hurt themselves,
        nor knew
There dwelt an iron nature in the grain ;
The glittering axe was broken in their arms,
Their arms were shatter'd to the shoulder
        blade.

'Our enemies have fallen, but this shall
        grow
A night of Summer from the heat, a breadth
Of Autumn, dropping fruits of power ; and
        roll'd
With music in the growing breeze of Time,   40
The tops shall strike from star to star, the
        fangs
Shall move the stony bases of the world.

'And now, O maids, behold our sanctu-
        ary
Is violate, our laws broken ; fear we not
To break them more in their behoof, whose
        arms
Champion'd our cause and won it with a
        day
Blanch'd in our annals, and perpetual feast,
When dames and heroines of the golden
        year
Shall strip a hundred hollows bare of
        Spring,
To rain an April of ovation round           50
Their statues, borne aloft, the three ; but
        come,
We will be liberal, since our rights are
        won.
Let them not lie in the tents with coarse
        mankind,
Ill nurses ; but descend, and proffer these
The brethren of our blood and cause, that
        there
Lie bruised and maim'd, the tender minis-
        tries
Of female hands and hospitality.'

She spoke, and with the babe yet in her
        arms,
Descending, burst the great bronze valves,
        and led                                           59
A hundred maids in train across the park.

Some cowl'd, and some bare-headed, on
    they came,
Their feet in flowers, her loveliest.    By
    them went
The enamor'd air sighing, and on their
    curls
From the high tree the blossom wavering
    fell,
And over them the tremulous isles of light
Slided, they moving under shade; but
    Blanche
At distance follow'd.    So they came: anon
Thro' open field into the lists they wound
Timorously; and as the leader of the herd
That holds a stately fretwork to the sun,  70
And follow'd up by a hundred airy does,
Steps with a tender foot, light as on air,
The lovely, lordly creature floated on
To where her wounded brethren lay; there
    stay'd,
Knelt on one knee, — the child on one, —
    and prest
Their hands, and call'd them dear deliver-
    ers,
And happy warriors, and immortal names,
And said, ' You shall not lie in the tents,
    but here,
And nursed by those for whom you fought,
    and served
With female hands and hospitality.'    80

    Then, whether moved by this, or was it
    chance,
She past my way.    Up started from my
    side
The old lion, glaring with his whelpless eye,
Silent; but when she saw me lying stark,
Dishelm'd and mute, and motionlessly pale,
Cold even to her, she sigh'd; and when she
    saw
The haggard father's face and reverend
    beard
Of grisly twine, all dabbled with the blood
Of his own son, shudder'd, a twitch of pain
Tortured her mouth, and o'er her forehead
    past                                90
A shadow, and her hue changed, and she
    said:
' He saved my life; my brother slew him
    for it.'
No more; at which the king in bitter scorn
Drew from my neck the painting and the
    tress,
And held them up.    She saw them, and a
    day

Rose from the distance on her memory,
When the good queen, her mother, shore
    the tress
With kisses, ere the days of Lady Blanche.
And then once more she look'd at my pale
    face;
Till understanding all the foolish work  100
Of Fancy, and the bitter close of all,
Her iron will was broken in her mind;
Her noble heart was molten in her breast;
She bow'd, she set the child on the earth;
    she laid
A feeling finger on my brows, and pre-
    sently
' O Sire,' she said, ' he lives; he is not
    dead!
O, let me have him with my brethren here
In our own palace; we will tend on him
Like one of these; if so, by any means,
To lighten this great clog of thanks, that
    make                                110
Our progress falter to the woman's goal.'

    She said; but at the happy word ' he
    lives! '
My father stoop'd, re-father'd o'er my
    wounds.
So those two foes above my fallen life,
With brow to brow like night and evening
    mixt
Their dark and gray, while Psyche ever
    stole
A little nearer, till the babe that by us,
Half - lapt in glowing gauze and golden
    brede,
Lay like a new-fallen meteor on the grass,
Uncared for, spied its mother and began
A blind and babbling laughter, and to
    dance                                121
Its body, and reach its fatling innocent
    arms
And lazy lingering fingers.    She the appeal
Brook'd not, but clamoring out ' Mine —
    mine — not yours!
It is not yours, but mine; give me the
    child ! '
Ceased all on tremble; piteous was the
    cry.
So stood the unhappy mother open-
    mouth'd,
And turn'd each face her way.    Wan was
    her cheek
With hollow watch, her blooming mantle
    torn,
Red grief and mother's hunger in her eye,

And down dead-heavy sank her curls, and
        half
                                            131
The sacred mother's bosom, panting, burst
The laces toward her babe; but she nor
        cared
Nor knew it, clamoring on, till Ida heard,
Look'd up, and rising slowly from me,
        stood
Erect and silent, striking with her glance
The mother, me, the child.   But he that lay
Beside us, Cyril, batter'd as he was,
Trail'd himself up on one knee; then he
        drew
Her robe to meet his lips, and down she
        look'd                                140
At the arm'd man sideways, pitying as it
        seem'd,
Or self-involved; but when she learnt his
        face,
Remembering his ill-omen'd song, arose
Once more thro' all her height, and o'er
        him grew
Tall as a figure lengthen'd on the sand
When the tide ebbs in sunshine, and he
        said:

' O fair and strong and terrible !  Lioness
That with your long locks play the lion's
        mane !
But Love and Nature, these are two more
        terrible
And stronger.    See, your foot is on our
        necks,                                150
We vanquish'd, we the victor of your will.
What would you more ? give her the child !
        remain
Orb'd in your isolation; he is dead,
Or all as dead: henceforth we let you be.
Win you the hearts of women; and beware
Lest, where you seek the common love of
        these,
The common hate with the revolving wheel
Should drag you down, and some great
        Nemesis
Break from a darken'd future, crown'd
        with fire,
And tread you out for ever.   But howso-
        e'er                                160
Fixt in yourself, never in your own arms
To hold your own, deny not hers to her,
Give her the child !   O, if, I say, you keep
One pulse that beats true woman, if you
        loved
The breast that fed or arm that dandled
        you,

Or own one port of sense not flint to
        prayer,
Give her the child! or if you scorn to lay it,
Yourself, in hands so lately claspt with
        yours,
Or speak to her, your dearest, her one
        fault
The tenderness, not yours, that could not
        kill,
Give me it; I will give it her.'        170
                                    He said.
At first her eye with slow dilation roll'd
Dry flame, she listening; after sank and
        sank
And, into mournful twilight mellowing,
        dwelt
Full on the child.    She took it: ' Pretty
        bud !
Lily of the vale ! half-open'd bell of the
        woods !
Sole comfort of my dark hour, when a
        world
Of traitorous friend and broken system
        made
No purple in the distance, mystery,    179
Pledge of a love not to be mine, farewell !
These men are hard upon us as of old,
We two must part; and yet how fain was I
To dream thy cause embraced in mine, to
        think
I might be something to thee, when I felt
Thy helpless warmth about my barren
        breast
In the dead prime; but may thy mother
        prove
As true to thee as false, false, false to me !
And, if thou needs must bear the yoke, I
        wish it
Gentle as freedom ' — here she kiss'd it;
        then —                                189
' All good go with thee! take it, sir,' and so
Laid the soft babe in his hard - mailed
        hands,
Who turn'd half-round to Psyche as she
        sprang
To meet it, with an eye that swum in
        thanks;
Then felt it sound and whole from head
        to foot,
And hugg'd and never hugg'd it close
        enough,
And in her hunger mouth'd and mumbled
        it,
And hid her bosom with it; after that
Put on more calm and added suppliantly:

'We two were friends: I go to mine
     own land
For ever.  Find some other; as for me  200
I scarce am fit for your great plans: yet
     speak to me,
Say one soft word and let me part for-
     given.'

But Ida spoke not, rapt upon the child.
Then Arac: 'Ida — 'sdeath! you blame the
     man;
You wrong yourselves — the woman is so
     hard
Upon the woman.  Come, a grace to me!
I am your warrior; I and mine have
     fought
Your battle.  Kiss her; take her hand, she
     weeps.
'Sdeath!  I would sooner fight thrice o'er
     than see it.'                            209

But Ida spoke not, gazing on the ground;
And reddening in the furrows of his chin,
And moved beyond his custom, Gama said:

'I 've heard that there is iron in the
     blood,
And I believe it.  Not one word? not
     one?
Whence drew you this steel temper? not
     from me,
Not from your mother, now a saint with
     saints.
She said you had a heart — I heard her say
     it —
"Our Ida has a heart" — just ere she
     died —
"But see that some one with authority
Be near her still;" and I — I sought for
     one —                                    220
All people said she had authority —
The Lady Blanche — much profit!  Not one
     word;
No! tho' your father sues.  See how you
     stand
Stiff as Lot's wife, and all the good knights
     maim'd,
I trust that there is no one hurt to death,
For your wild whim.  And was it then for
     this,
Was it for this we gave our palace up,
Where we withdrew from summer heats
     and state,
And had our wine and chess beneath the
     planes,

And many a pleasant hour with her that 's
     gone,                                    230
Ere you were born to vex us?  Is it kind?
Speak to her, I say; is this not she of
     whom,
When first she came, all flush'd you said to
     me,
Now had you got a friend of your own age,
Now could you share your thought, now
     should men see
Two women faster welded in one love
Than pairs of wedlock?  she you walk'd
     with, she
You talk'd with, whole nights long, up in
     the tower,
Of sine and arc, spheroid and azimuth,
And right ascension, heaven knows what;
     and now                                  240
A word, but one, one little kindly word,
Not one to spare her!  Out upon you, flint!
You love nor her, nor me, nor any; nay,
You shame your mother's judgment too.
     Not one?
You will not?  well — no heart have you,
     or such
As fancies like the vermin in a nut
Have fretted all to dust and bitterness.'
So said the small king moved beyond his
     wont.

But Ida stood nor spoke, drain'd of her
     force                                    249
By many a varying influence and so long.
Down thro' her limbs a drooping languor
     wept;
Her head a little bent; and on her mouth
A doubtful smile dwelt like a clouded
     moon
In a still water.  Then brake out my sire,
Lifting his grim head from my wounds:
'O you,
Woman, whom we thought woman even
     now,
And were half fool'd to let you tend our
     son,
Because he might have wish'd it — but we
     see
The accomplice of your madness unfor-
     given,
And think that you might mix his draught
     with death,                             260
When your skies change again; the rougher
     hand
Is safer.  On to the tents; take up the
     Prince.'

He rose, and while each ear was prick'd
  to attend
A tempest, thro' the cloud that dimm'd her
  broke
A genial warmth and light once more, and
  shone
Thro' glittering drops on her sad friend.
                              'Come hither,
O Psyche,' she cried out, 'embrace me,
  come,
Quick while I melt; make reconcilement
  sure
With one that cannot keep her mind an
  hour;                                    269
Come to the hollow heart they slander
  so!
Kiss and be friends, like children being
  chid!
*I* seem no more, *I* want forgiveness too;
I should have had to do with none but
  maids,
That have no links with men. Ah false
  but dear,
Dear traitor, too much loved, why? —
  why? — yet see
Before these kings we embrace you yet
  once more
With all forgiveness, all oblivion,
And trust, not love, you less.
                              And now, O Sire,
Grant me your son, to nurse, to wait upon
  him,
Like mine own brother. For my debt to
  him,                                     280
This nightmare weight of gratitude, I know
  it.
Taunt me no more; yourself and yours
  shall have
Free adit; we will scatter all our maids
Till happier times each to her proper
  hearth.
What use to keep them here — now? grant
  my prayer.
Help, father, brother, help; speak to the
  king;
Thaw this male nature to some touch of
  that
Which kills me with myself, and drags me
  down
From my fixt height to mob me up with
  all                                      289
The soft and milky rabble of womankind,
Poor weakling even as they are.'
                              Passionate tears
Follow'd; the king replied not; Cyril said:

'Your brother, lady, — Florian, — ask for
  him
Of your great Head — for he is wounded
  too —
That you may tend upon him with the
  Prince.'
'Ay, so,' said Ida with a bitter smile,
'Our laws are broken; let him enter too.'
Then Violet, she that sang the mournful
  song,
And had a cousin tumbled on the plain,
Petition'd too for him. 'Ay, so,' she
  said,                                    300
'I stagger in the stream; I cannot keep
My heart an eddy from the brawling hour.
We break our laws with ease, but let it
  be.'
'Ay, so?' said Blanche: 'Amazed am I to
  hear
Your Highness; but your Highness breaks
  with ease
The law your Highness did not make;
  't was I.
I had been wedded wife, I knew man-
  kind,
And block'd them out; but these men came
  to woo
Your Highness, — verily I think to win.'

So she, and turn'd askance a wintry eye;
But Ida, with a voice that, like a bell    311
Toll'd by an earthquake in a trembling
  tower,
Rang ruin, answer'd full of grief and scorn:

'Fling our doors wide! all, all, not one,
  but all,
Not only he, but by my mother's soul,
Whatever man lies wounded, friend or foe,
Shall enter, if he will! Let our girls flit,
Till the storm die! but had you stood by
  us,
The roar that breaks the Pharos from his
  base
Had left us rock. She fain would sting us
  too,                                     320
But shall not. Pass, and mingle with your
  likes.
We brook no further insult, but are gone.'

She turn'd; the very nape of her white
  neck
Was rosed with indignation; but the Prince
Her brother came; the king her father
  charm'd

Her wounded soul with words; nor did
  mine own
Refuse her proffer, lastly gave his hand.

    Then us they lifted up, dead weights,
      and bare
Straight to the doors; to them the doors
  gave way            329
Groaning, and in the vestal entry shriek'd
The virgin marble under iron heels.
And on they moved and gain'd the hall,
  and there
Rested; but great the crush was, and each
  base,
To left and right, of those tall columns
  drown'd
In silken fluctuation and the swarm
Of female whisperers.  At the further end
Was Ida by the throne, the two great cats
Close by her, like supporters on a shield,
Bow-back'd with fear; but in the centre
  stood
The common men with rolling eyes;
  amazed         340
They glared upon the women, and aghast
The women stared at these, all silent, save
When armor clash'd or jingled, while the
  day,
Descending, struck athwart the hall, and
  shot
A flying splendor out of brass and steel,
That o'er the statues leapt from head to
  head,
Now fired an angry Pallas on the helm,
Now set a wrathful Dian's moon on flame;
And now and then an echo started up,
And shuddering fled from room to room,
  and died        350
Of fright in far apartments.
               Then the voice
Of Ida sounded, issuing ordinance;
And me they bore up the broad stairs, and
  thro'
The long - laid galleries past a hundred
  doors
To one deep chamber shut from sound, and
  due
To languid limbs and sickness, left me
  in it;
And others otherwhere they laid; and all
That afternoon a sound arose of hoof
And chariot, many a maiden passing home
Till happier times; but some were left of
  those        360
Held sagest, and the great lords out and in,

From those two hosts that lay beside the
  wall,
Walk'd at their will, and everything was
  changed.

Ask me no more : the moon may draw the sea ;
  The cloud may stoop from heaven and take
    the shape,
  With fold to fold, of mountain or of cape ;
But O too fond, when have I answer'd thee ?
         Ask me no more.

Ask me no more : what answer should I give ?
  I love not hollow cheek or faded eye :
  Yet, O my friend, I will not have thee die !
Ask me no more, lest I should bid thee live ;
         Ask me no more.

Ask me no more : thy fate and mine are seal'd ;
  I strove against the stream and all in vain ;
  Let the great river take me to the main.
No more, dear love, for at a touch I yield ;
         Ask me no more.


## VII

So was their sanctuary violated,
So their fair college turn'd to hospital,
At first with all confusion; by and by
Sweet order lived again with other laws,
A kindlier influence reign'd, and every-
  where
Low voices with the ministering hand
Hung round the sick.   The maidens came,
  they talk'd,
They sang, they read; till she not fair be-
  gan
To gather light, and she that was became
Her former beauty treble; and to and
  fro        10
With books, with flowers, with angel offices,
Like creatures native unto gracious act,
And in their own clear element, they
  moved.

    But sadness on the soul of Ida fell,
And hatred of her weakness, blent with
  shame.
Old studies fail'd; seldom she spoke; but
  oft
Clomb to the roofs, and gazed alone for
  hours
On that disastrous leaguer, swarms of men
Darkening her female field.  Void was her
  use,
And she as one that climbs a peak to gaze

O'er land and main, and sees a great black
    cloud                         21
Drag inward from the deeps, a wall of
    night,
Blot out the slope of sea from verge to
    shore,
And suck the blinding splendor from the
    sand,
And quenching lake by lake and tarn by
    tarn
Expunge the world; so fared she gazing
    there,
So blacken'd all her world in secret, blank
And waste it seem'd and vain; till down
    she came,
And found fair peace once more among the
    sick.

And twilight dawn'd; and morn by morn
    the lark                    30
Shot up and shrill'd in flickering gyres,
    but I
Lay silent in the muffled cage of life.
And twilight gloom'd, and broader-grown
    the bowers
Drew the great night into themselves, and
    heaven,
Star after star, arose and fell; but I,
Deeper than those weird doubts could reach
    me, lay
Quite sunder'd from the moving Universe,
Nor knew what eye was on me, nor the
    hand
That nursed me, more than infants in their
    sleep.

But Psyche tended Florian; with her oft 40
Melissa came, for Blanche had gone, but
    left
Her child among us, willing she should
    keep
Court-favor.  Here and there the small
    bright head,
A light of healing, glanced about the couch,
Or thro' the parted silks the tender face
Peep'd, shining in upon the wounded man
With blush and smile, a medicine in them-
    selves
To wile the length from languorous hours,
    and draw
The sting from pain; nor seem'd it strange
    that soon                49
He rose up whole, and those fair charities
Join'd at her side; nor stranger seem'd that
    hearts

So gentle, so employ'd, should close in love,
Than when two dewdrops on the petal
    shake
To the same sweet air, and tremble deeper
    down,
And slip at once all-fragrant into one.

Less prosperously the second suit ob-
    tain'd
At first with Psyche.  Not tho' Blanche
    had sworn
That after that dark night among the fields
She needs must wed him for her own good
    name;                   59
Not tho' he built upon the babe restored;
Not tho' she liked him, yielded she, but
    fear'd
To incense the Head once more; till on a
    day
When Cyril pleaded, Ida came behind
Seen but of Psyche; on her foot she hung
A moment, and she heard, at which her
    face
A little flush'd, and she past on; but each
Assumed from thence a half-consent in-
    volved
In stillness, plighted troth, and were at
    peace.

Nor only these; Love in the sacred halls
Held carnival at will, and flying struck  70
With showers of random sweet on maid and
    man.
Nor did her father cease to press my claim,
Nor did mine own now reconciled; nor yet
Did those twin brothers, risen again and
    whole;
Nor Arac, satiate with his victory.

But I lay still, and with me oft she sat.
Then came a change; for sometimes I
    would catch
Her hand in wild delirium, gripe it hard,
And fling it like a viper off, and shriek,
'You are not Ida;' clasp it once again,  80
And call her Ida, tho' I knew her not,
And call her sweet, as if in irony,
And call her hard and cold, which seem'd a
    truth;
And still she fear'd that I should lose my
    mind,
And often she believed that I should die;
Till out of long frustration of her care,
And pensive tendance in the all-weary
    noons,

And watches in the dead, the dark, when
    clocks
Throbb'd thunder thro' the palace floors, or
    call'd
On flying Time from all their silver
    tongues —         90
And out of memories of her kindlier days,
And sidelong glances at my father's grief,
And at the happy lovers heart in heart —
And out of hauntings of my spoken love,
And lonely listenings to my mutter'd
    dream,
And often feeling of the helpless hands,
And wordless broodings on the wasted
    cheek —
From all a closer interest flourish'd up,
Tenderness touch by touch, and last, to
    these,
Love, like an Alpine harebell hung with
    tears         100
By some cold morning glacier; frail at first
And feeble, all unconscious of itself,
But such as gather'd color day by day.

Last I woke sane, but well-nigh close to
    death
For weakness. It was evening; silent light
Slept on the painted walls, wherein were
    wrought
Two grand designs; for on one side arose
The women up in wild revolt, and storm'd
At the Oppian law. Titanic shapes, they
    cramm'd
The forum, and half-crush'd among the
    rest         110
A dwarf-like Cato cower'd. On the other
    side
Hortensia spoke against the tax; behind,
A train of dames. By axe and eagle sat,
With all their foreheads drawn in Roman
    scowls,
And half the wolf's-milk curdled in their
    veins,
The fierce triumvirs; and before them
    paused
Hortensia, pleading; angry was her face.

I saw the forms; I knew not where I
    was.
They did but look like hollow shows; nor
    more         119
Sweet Ida. Palm to palm she sat; the dew
Dwelt in her eyes, and softer all her shape
And rounder seem'd. I moved, I sigh'd;
    a touch

Came round my wrist, and tears upon my
    hand.
Then all for languor and self-pity ran
Mine down my face, and with what life I
    had,
And like a flower that cannot all unfold,
So drench'd it is with tempest, to the sun,
Yet, as it may, turns toward him, I on
    her
Fixt my faint eyes, and utter'd whisper-
    ingly:

'If you be what I think you, some sweet
    dream,         130
I would but ask you to fulfil yourself;
But if you be that Ida whom I knew,
I ask you nothing; only, if a dream,
Sweet dream, be perfect. I shall die to-
    night.
Stoop down and seem to kiss me ere I die.'

I could no more, but lay like one in
    trance,
That hears his burial talk'd of by his friends,
And cannot speak, nor move, nor make one
    sign,
But lies and dreads his doom. She turn'd,
    she paused,         139
She stoop'd; and out of languor leapt a
    cry,
Leapt fiery Passion from the brinks of
    death,
And I believed that in the living world
My spirit closed with Ida's at the lips;
Till back I fell, and from mine arms she
    rose
Glowing all over noble shame; and all
Her falser self slipt from her like a robe,
And left her woman, lovelier in her mood
Than in her mould that other, when she
    came
From barren deeps to conquer all with love,
And down the streaming crystal dropt; and
    she         150
Far-fleeted by the purple island-sides,
Naked, a double light in air and wave,
To meet her Graces, where they deck'd her
    out
For worship without end — nor end of mine,
Stateliest, for thee! but mute she glided
    forth,
Nor glanced behind her, and I sank and
    slept,
Fill'd thro' and thro' with love, a happy
    sleep.

Deep in the night I woke: she, near me, held
A volume of the poets of her land.    159
There to herself, all in low tones, she read:

'Now sleeps the crimson petal, now the white;
Nor waves the cypress in the palace walk;
Nor winks the gold fin in the porphyry font.
The fire-fly wakens; waken thou with me.

'Now droops the milk-white peacock like a ghost,
And like a ghost she glimmers on to me.

'Now lies the Earth all Danaë to the stars,
And all thy heart lies open unto me.

'Now slides the silent meteor on, and leaves
A shining furrow, as thy thoughts in me.    170

'Now folds the lily all her sweetness up,
And slips into the bosom of the lake.
So fold thyself, my dearest, thou, and slip
Into my bosom and be lost in me.'

I heard her turn the page; she found a small
Sweet idyl, and once more, as low, she read:

'Come down, O maid, from yonder mountain height.
What pleasure lives in height (the shepherd sang),
In height and cold, the splendor of the hills?
But cease to move so near the heavens, and cease    180
To glide a sunbeam by the blasted pine,
To sit a star upon the sparkling spire;
And come, for Love is of the valley, come,
For Love is of the valley, come thou down
And find him; by the happy threshold, he,
Or hand in hand with Plenty in the maize,
Or red with spirted purple of the vats,
Or foxlike in the vine; nor cares to walk
With Death and Morning on the Silver Horns,
Nor wilt thou snare him in the white ravine,
Nor find him dropt upon the firths of ice,    191
That huddling slant in furrow-cloven falls
To roll the torrent out of dusky doors.
But follow; let the torrent dance thee down
To find him in the valley; let the wild
Lean-headed eagles yelp alone, and leave
The monstrous ledges there to slope, and spill
Their thousand wreaths of dangling water-smoke,
That like a broken purpose waste in air.    199
So waste not thou, but come; for all the vales
Await thee; azure pillars of the hearth

Arise to thee; the children call, and I
Thy shepherd pipe, and sweet is every sound,
Sweeter thy voice, but every sound is sweet;
Myriads of rivulets hurrying thro' the lawn,
The moan of doves in immemorial elms,
And murmuring of innumerable bees.'

So she low-toned, while with shut eyes I lay
Listening, then look'd.    Pale was the perfect face;
The bosom with long sighs labor'd; and meek    210
Seem'd the full lips, and mild the luminous eyes,
And the voice trembled and the hand.    She said
Brokenly, that she knew it, she had fail'd
In sweet humility, had fail'd in all;
That all her labor was but as a block
Left in the quarry; but she still were loth,
She still were loth to yield herself to one
That wholly scorn'd to help their equal rights
Against the sons of men and barbarous laws.
She pray'd me not to judge their cause from her    220
That wrong'd it, sought far less for truth than power
In knowledge.    Something wild within her breast,
A greater than all knowledge, beat her down.
And she had nursed me there from week to week;
Much had she learnt in little time.    In part
It was ill counsel had misled the girl
To vex true hearts; yet was she but a girl —
'Ah fool, and made myself a queen of farce!
When comes another such? never, I think,
Till the sun drop, dead, from the signs.'
Her voice
Choked, and her forehead sank upon her hands,    231
And her great heart thro' all the faultful past
Went sorrowing in a pause I dared not break;
Till notice of a change in the dark world
Was lispt about the acacias, and a bird,
That early woke to feed her little ones,
Sent from a dewy breast a cry for light.
She moved, and at her feet the volume fell.

'Blame not thyself too much,' I said,
'nor blame
Too much the sons of men and barbarous
laws;                                                    240
These were the rough ways of the world till
now.
Henceforth thou hast a helper, me, that
know
The woman's cause is man's; they rise or
sink
Together, dwarf'd or godlike, bond or free.
For she that out of Lethe scales with man
The shining steps of Nature, shares with
man
His nights, his days, moves with him to one
goal,
Stays all the fair young planet in her
hands —
If she be small, slight-natured, miserable,
How shall men grow ? but work no more
alone !                                                    250
Our place is much; as far as in us lies
We two will serve them both in aiding
her —
Will clear away the parasitic forms
That seem to keep her up but drag her
down —
Will leave her space to burgeon out of all
Within her — let her make herself her
own
To give or keep, to live and learn and be
All that not harms distinctive womanhood.
For woman is not undevelopt man,
But diverse.   Could we make her as the
man,                                                       260
Sweet Love were slain; his dearest bond
is this,
Not like to like, but like in difference.
Yet in the long years liker must they
grow;
The man be more of woman, she of man;
He gain in sweetness and in moral height,
Nor lose the wrestling thews that throw
the world;
She mental breadth, nor fail in childward
care,
Nor lose the childlike in the larger mind;
Till at the last she set herself to man,
Like perfect music unto noble words;      270
And so these twain, upon the skirts of
Time,
Sit side by side, full-summ'd in all their
powers,
Dispensing harvest, sowing the to-be,
Self-reverent each and reverencing each,

Distinct in individualities,
But like each other even as those who love.
Then comes the statelier Eden back to
men;
Then reign the world's great bridals, chaste
and calm;
Then springs the crowning race of human-
kind.                                                      279
May these things be !'
                              Sighing she spoke: ' I fear
They will not.'
                    ' Dear, but let us type them now
In our own lives, and this proud watch-
word rest
Of equal; seeing either sex alone
Is half itself, and in true marriage lies
Nor equal, nor unequal.   Each fulfils
Defect in each, and always thought in
thought,
Purpose in purpose, will in will, they grow,
The single pure and perfect animal,
The two-cell'd heart beating, with one full
stroke,                                                    289
Life.'
     And again sighing she spoke: ' A dream
That once was mine ! what woman taught
you this ? '

' Alone,' I said, ' from earlier than I
know,
Immersed in rich foreshadowings of the
world,
I loved the woman.   He, that doth not,
lives
A drowning life, besotted in sweet self,
Or pines in sad experience worse than
death,
Or keeps his wing'd affections clipt with
crime.
Yet was there one thro' whom I loved her,
one
Not learned, save in gracious household
ways,
Not perfect, nay, but full of tender wants,
No angel, but a dearer being, all dipt    301
In angel instincts, breathing Paradise,
Interpreter between the gods and men,
Who look'd all native to her place, and yet
On tiptoe seem'd to touch upon a sphere
Too gross to tread, and all male minds per-
force
Sway'd to her from their orbits as they
moved,
And girdled her with music.   Happy he
With such a mother ! faith in womankind

Beats with his blood, and trust in all things
   high                                            310
Comes easy to him, and tho' he trip and fall
He shall not blind his soul with clay.'
                      ' But I,'
Said Ida, tremulously, ' so all unlike —
It seems you love to cheat yourself with
   words;
This mother is your model.   I have heard
Of your strange doubts; they well might
   be; I seem
A mockery to my own self.   Never, Prince!
You cannot love me.'
            ' Nay, but thee,' I said,
' From yearlong poring on thy pictured
   eyes,
Ere seen I loved, and loved thee seen, and
   saw                                           320
Thee woman thro' the crust of iron moods
That mask'd thee from men's reverence
   up, and forced
Sweet love on pranks of saucy boyhood;
   now,
Given back to life, to life indeed, thro'
   thee,
Indeed I love.   The new day comes, the
   light
Dearer for night, as dearer thou for faults
Lived over.   Lift thine eyes; my doubts are
   dead,
My haunting sense of hollow shows; the
   change,
This truthful change in thee has kill'd it.
   Dear,
Look up, and let thy nature strike on
   mine,                                          330
Like yonder morning on the blind half-
   world.
Approach and fear not; breathe upon my
   brows;
In that fine air I tremble, all the past
Melts mist-like into this bright hour, and
   this
Is morn to more, and all the rich to-come
Reels, as the golden Autumn woodland
   reels
Athwart the smoke of burning weeds.   For-
   give me,
I waste my heart in signs; let be.   My
   bride,
My wife, my life !   O, we will walk this
   world,
Yoked in all exercise of noble end,          340
And so thro' those dark gates across the
   wild

That no man knows.   Indeed I love thee;
   come,
Yield thyself up; my hopes and thine are
   one.
Accomplish thou my manhood and thyself;
Lay thy sweet hands in mine and trust to
   me.'

## CONCLUSION

So closed our tale, of which I give you all
The random scheme as wildly as it rose.
The words are mostly mine; for when we
   ceased
There came a minute's pause, and Walter
   said,
' I wish she had not yielded ! ' then to me,
' What if you drest it up poetically ! '
So pray'd the men, the women; I gave
   assent.
Yet how to bind the scatter'd scheme of
   seven
Together in one sheaf ?   What style could
   suit ?
The men required that I should give
   throughout                                     10
The sort of mock-heroic gigantesque,
With which we banter'd little Lilia first;
The women — and perhaps they felt their
   power,
For something in the ballads which they
   sang,
Or in their silent influence as they sat,
Had ever seem'd to wrestle with bur-
   lesque,
And drove us, last, to quite a solemn
   close —
They hated banter, wish'd for something
   real,
A gallant fight, a noble princess — why   19
Not make her true-heroic — true-sublime ?
Or all, they said, as earnest as the close ?
Which yet with such a framework scarce
   could be.
Then rose a little feud betwixt the two,
Betwixt the mockers and the realists;
And I, betwixt them both, to please them
   both,
And yet to give the story as it rose,
I moved as in a strange diagonal,
And maybe neither pleased myself nor
   them.

But Lilia pleased me, for she took no part
In our dispute; the sequel of the tale   30

Had touch'd her, and she sat, she pluck'd
    the grass,
She flung it from her, thinking; last, she
    fixt
A showery glance upon her aunt, and said,
' You — tell us what we are ' — who might
    have told,
For she was cramm'd with theories out of
    books,
But that there rose a shout.  The gates were
    closed
At sunset, and the crowd were swarming
    now,
To take their leave, about the garden rails.

    So I and some went out to these; we
        climb'd                                    39
The slope to Vivian - place, and turning
    saw
The happy valleys, half in light, and half
Far-shadowing from the west, a land of
    peace;
Gray halls alone among their massive
    groves;
Trim hamlets; here and there a rustic
    tower
Half-lost in belts of hop and breadths of
    wheat;
The shimmering glimpses of a stream; the
    seas;
A red sail, or a white; and far beyond,
Imagined more than seen, the skirts of
    France.

    ' Look there, a garden ! ' said my college
        friend,
The Tory member's elder son, ' and there !
God bless the narrow sea which keeps her
    off,                                           51
And keeps our Britain, whole within her-
    self,
A nation yet, the rulers and the ruled —
Some sense of duty, something of a faith,
Some reverence for the laws ourselves have
    made,
Some patient force to change them when
    we will,
Some civic manhood firm against the
    crowd —
But yonder, whiff ! there comes a sudden
    heat,
The gravest citizen seems to lose his head,
The king is scared, the soldier will not
    fight,                                         60
The little boys begin to shoot and stab,

A kingdom topples over with a shriek
Like an old woman, and down rolls the
    world
In mock heroics stranger than our own;
Revolts, republics, revolutions, most
No graver than a schoolboys' barring out;
Too comic for the solemn things they are,
Too solemn for the comic touches in them,
Like our wild Princess with as wise a
    dream
As some of theirs — God bless the narrow
    seas !                                         70
I wish they were a whole Atlantic broad.'

    ' Have patience,' I replied, ' ourselves are
        full
Of social wrong; and maybe wildest dreams
Are but the needful preludes of the truth.
For me, the genial day, the happy crowd,
The sport half-science, fill me with a faith,
This fine old world of ours is but a child
Yet in the go - cart.  Patience !  Give it
    time
To learn its limbs; there is a hand that
    guides.'

    In such discourse we gain'd the garden
        rails,                                     80
And there we saw Sir Walter where he
    stood,
Before a tower of crimson holly-oaks,
Among six boys, head under head, and
    look'd
No little lily-handed baronet he,
A great broad-shoulder'd genial English-
    man,
A lord of fat prize-oxen and of sheep,
A raiser of huge melons and of pine,
A patron of some thirty charities,
A pamphleteer on guano and on grain,
A quarter-sessions chairman, abler none; 90
Fair-hair'd and redder than a windy morn;
Now shaking hands with him, now him, of
    those
That stood the nearest — now address'd to
    speech —
Who spoke few words and pithy, such as
    closed
Welcome, farewell, and welcome for the
    year
To follow.  A shout rose again, and made
The long line of the approaching rookery
    swerve
From the elms, and shook the branches of
    the deer

From slope to slope thro' distant ferns, and
rang         99
Beyond the bourn of sunset — O, a shout
More joyful than the city-roar that hails
Premier or king ! Why should not these
great sirs
Give up their parks some dozen times a
year
To let the people breathe ? So thrice they
cried,
I likewise, and in groups they stream'd
away.

But we went back to the Abbey, and
sat on,
So much the gathering darkness charm'd;
we sat

But spoke not, rapt in nameless reverie,
Perchance upon the future man. The walls
Blacken'd about us, bats wheel'd, and owls
whoop'd,       110
And gradually the powers of the night,
That range above the region of the wind,
Deepening the courts of twilight broke
them up
Thro' all the silent spaces of the worlds,
Beyond all thought into the heaven of hea-
vens.

Last little Lilia, rising quietly,
Disrobed the glimmering statue of Sir
Ralph
From those rich silks, and home well-
pleased we went.

# IN MEMORIAM A. H. H.

## OBIIT MDCCCXXXIII

'In Memoriam' was first published in 1850. No changes were made in the second and third editions except the correction of two misprints. In the fourth edition (1851) the present 59th section ('O Sorrow, wilt thou live with me ?') was added. The present 39th section ('Old warder of these buried bones,' etc.) was added in the 'Miniature Edition' of the 'Poems' (1871). Minor changes are recorded in the Notes.

Arthur Henry Hallam, to whose memory the poem is a tribute, was the son of Henry Hallam, the historian, and was born in London, February 1, 1811. In 1818 he spent some months with his parents in Italy and Switzerland, where he became familiar with the French language, which he had already learned to read with ease. Latin he also learned to read with facility in little more than a year. When only eight or nine years old, he began to write tragedies which showed remarkable precocity.

After a brief course in a preparatory school he was sent to Eton, where he remained till 1827. He did not distinguish himself as a classical scholar, being more interested in English literature, especially the earlier dramatists. He took an active part in the Debating Society, where he showed great power in argumentative discussion ; and during his last year in the school he began to write for the 'Eton Miscellany.' After leaving Eton he spent eight months with his parents in Italy, where he mastered the language and the works of Dante and Petrarch.

In October, 1829, he went to Trinity College, Cambridge. There he soon became acquainted with the Tennysons, and thus began the ever-memorable friendship of which 'In Memoriam' is the monument. Like his friends, he was the pupil of the Rev. William Whewell. In 1831 he obtained the first prize for an English declamation on the conduct of the Independent party during the Civil War. In consequence of this success, he was called upon to deliver an oration in the chapel before the Christmas vacation, and chose as a subject the influence of Italian upon English literature. He also gained a prize for an English essay on the philosophical writings of Cicero.

He left Cambridge on taking his degree in January, 1832. He resided from that time with his father in London in 67 Wimpole Street, referred to in 'In Memoriam,' vii. : —

Dark house, by which once more I stand
Here in the long unlovely street.

Arthur used to say to his friends, 'You know you will always find us at sixes and sevens.' At the earnest desire of his father he applied himself vigorously to the study of law in the Inner Temple, entering, in the month of October, 1832, the office of an eminent conveyancer, with whom he continued till his departure from England in the following summer.

His father tells the remainder of the sad story very briefly.  Arthur accompanied him to Germany in the beginning of August.  In returning to Vienna from Pesth, a wet day probably gave rise to an intermittent fever with very slight symptoms, which were apparently subsiding, when a sudden rush of blood to the head caused his death on the 15th of September, 1833.  It appeared on examination that the cerebral vessels were weak, and that there was a lack of energy in the heart.  In the usual chances of humanity a few more years would probably have been fatal.

His 'loved remains' were brought to England and interred on the 3d of January, 1834, in Clevedon Church, Somersetshire, belonging to his maternal grandfather, Sir Abraham Elton. The place was selected by his father not only from its connection with the family, but also from its sequestered situation on a lone hill overlooking the Bristol Channel.

STRONG Son of God, immortal Love,
  Whom we, that have not seen thy face,
  By faith, and faith alone, embrace,
Believing where we cannot prove;

Thine are these orbs of light and shade;
  Thou madest Life in man and brute;
  Thou madest Death; and lo, thy foot
Is on the skull which thou hast made.

Thou wilt not leave us in the dust:
  Thou madest man, he knows not why,
  He thinks he was not made to die;
And thou hast made him: thou art just.

Thou seemest human and divine,
  The highest, holiest manhood, thou.
  Our wills are ours, we know not how;
Our wills are ours, to make them thine.

Our little systems have their day;
  They have their day and cease to be;
  They are but broken lights of thee,
And thou, O Lord, art more than they.

We have but faith: we cannot know,
  For knowledge is of things we see;
  And yet we trust it comes from thee,
A beam in darkness: let it grow.

Let knowledge grow from more to more,
  But more of reverence in us dwell;
  That mind and soul, according well,
May make one music as before,

But vaster.  We are fools and slight;
  We mock thee when we do not fear:
  But help thy foolish ones to bear;
Help thy vain worlds to bear thy light.

Forgive what seem'd my sin in me,
  What seem'd my worth since I began;
  For merit lives from man to man,
And not from man, O Lord, to thee.

Forgive my grief for one removed,
  Thy creature, whom I found so fair.
  I trust he lives in thee, and there
I find him worthier to be loved.

Forgive these wild and wandering cries,
  Confusions of a wasted youth;
  Forgive them where they fail in truth,
And in thy wisdom make me wise.
  1849.

---

I

I held it truth, with him who sings
  To one clear harp in divers tones,
  That men may rise on stepping-stones
Of their dead selves to higher things.

But who shall so forecast the years
  And find in loss a gain to match?
  Or reach a hand thro' time to catch
The far-off interest of tears?

Let Love clasp Grief lest both be drown'd,
  Let darkness keep her raven gloss.
  Ah, sweeter to be drunk with loss,
To dance with Death, to beat the ground,

Than that the victor Hours should scorn
  The long result of love, and boast,
  ' Behold the man that loved and lost,
But all he was is overworn.'

II

Old yew, which graspest at the stones
  That name the underlying dead,
  Thy fibres net the dreamless head,
Thy roots are wrapt about the bones.

The seasons bring the flower again,
  And bring the firstling to the flock;
  And in the dusk of thee the clock
Beats out the little lives of men.

O, not for thee the glow, the bloom,
  Who changest not in any gale,
  Nor branding summer suns avail
To touch thy thousand years of gloom;

And gazing on thee, sullen tree,
  Sick for thy stubborn hardihood,
  I seem to fail from out my blood
And grow incorporate into thee.

### III

O Sorrow, cruel fellowship,
  O Priestess in the vaults of Death,
  O sweet and bitter in a breath,
What whispers from thy lying lip ?

' The stars,' she whispers, ' blindly run;
  A web is woven across the sky;
  From out waste places comes a cry,
And murmurs from the dying sun;

' And all the phantom, Nature, stands —
  With all the music in her tone,
  A hollow echo of my own, —
A hollow form with empty hands.'

And shall I take a thing so blind,
  Embrace her as my natural good;
  Or crush her, like a vice of blood,
Upon the threshold of the mind ?

### IV

To Sleep I give my powers away;
  My will is bondsman to the dark;
  I sit within a helmless bark,
And with my heart I muse and say:

O heart, how fares it with thee now,
  That thou shouldst fail from thy desire,
  Who scarcely darest to inquire,
' What is it makes me beat so low ? '

Something it is which thou hast lost,
  Some pleasure from thine early years.
  Break, thou deep vase of chilling tears,
That grief hath shaken into frost !

Such clouds of nameless trouble cross
  All night below the darken'd eyes;
  With morning wakes the will, and cries,
' Thou shalt not be the fool of loss.'

### V

I sometimes hold it half a sin
  To put in words the grief I feel;

For words, like Nature, half reveal
And half conceal the Soul within.

But, for the unquiet heart and brain,
  A use in measured language lies;
  The sad mechanic exercise,
Like dull narcotics, numbing pain.

In words, like weeds, I 'll wrap me o'er,
  Like coarsest clothes against the cold;
  But that large grief which these en-
      fold
Is given in outline and no more.

### VI

One writes, that ' other friends remain,'
  That ' loss is common to the race ' —
  And common is the commonplace,
And vacant chaff well meant for grain.

That loss is common would not make
  My own less bitter, rather more.
  Too common !  Never morning wore
To evening, but some heart did break.

O father, wheresoe'er thou be,
  Who pledgest now thy gallant son,
  A shot, ere half thy draught be done,
Hath still'd the life that beat from thee.

O mother, praying God will save
  Thy sailor, — while thy head is bow'd,
  His heavy-shotted hammock-shroud
Drops in his vast and wandering grave.

Ye know no more than I who wrought
  At that last hour to please him well;
  Who mused on all I had to tell,
And something written, something thought;

Expecting still his advent home;
  And ever met him on his way
  With wishes, thinking, ' here to-day,'
Or ' here to-morrow will he come.'

O, somewhere, meek, unconscious dove,
  That sittest ranging golden hair;
  And glad to find thyself so fair,
Poor child, that waitest for thy love !

For now her father's chimney glows
  In expectation of a guest;
  And thinking ' this will please him
      best,'
She takes a riband or a rose;

For he will see them on to-night;
And with the thought her color burns;
And, having left the glass, she turns
Once more to set a ringlet right;

And, even when she turn'd, the curse
Had fallen, and her future lord
Was drown'd in passing thro' the ford,
Or kill'd in falling from his horse.

O, what to her shall be the end?
And what to me remains of good?
To her perpetual maidenhood,
And unto me no second friend.

### VII

Dark house, by which once more I stand
Here in the long unlovely street,
Doors, where my heart was used to beat
So quickly, waiting for a hand,

A hand that can be clasp'd no more —
Behold me, for I cannot sleep,
And like a guilty thing I creep
At earliest morning to the door.

He is not here; but far away
The noise of life begins again,
And ghastly thro' the drizzling rain
On the bald street breaks the blank day.

### VIII

A happy lover who has come
To look on her that loves him well,
Who 'lights and rings the gateway bell,
And learns her gone and far from home;

He saddens, all the magic light
Dies off at once from bower and hall,
And all the place is dark, and all
The chambers emptied of delight:

So find I every pleasant spot
In which we two were wont to meet,
The field, the chamber, and the street,
For all is dark where thou art not.

Yet as that other, wandering there
In those deserted walks, may find
A flower beat with rain and wind,
Which once she foster'd up with care;

So seems it in my deep regret,
O my forsaken heart, with thee

And this poor flower of poesy
Which, little cared for, fades not yet.

But since it pleased a vanish'd eye,
I go to plant it on his tomb,
That if it can it there may bloom,
Or, dying, there at least may die.

### IX

Fair ship, that from the Italian shore
Sailest the placid ocean-plains
With my lost Arthur's loved remains,
Spread thy full wings, and waft him o'er.

So draw him home to those that mourn
In vain; a favorable speed
Ruffle thy mirror'd mast, and lead
Thro' prosperous floods his holy urn.

All night no ruder air perplex
Thy sliding keel, till Phosphor, bright
As our pure love, thro' early light
Shall glimmer on the dewy decks.

Sphere all your lights around, above;
Sleep, gentle heavens, before the prow;
Sleep, gentle winds, as he sleeps now,
My friend, the brother of my love;

My Arthur, whom I shall not see
Till all my widow'd race be run;
Dear as the mother to the son,
More than my brothers are to me.

### X

I hear the noise about thy keel;
I hear the bell struck in the night;
I see the cabin-window bright;
I see the sailor at the wheel.

Thou bring'st the sailor to his wife,
And travell'd men from foreign lands;
And letters unto trembling hands;
And, thy dark freight, a vanish'd life.

So bring him; we have idle dreams;
This look of quiet flatters thus
Our home-bred fancies. O, to us,
The fools of habit, sweeter seems

To rest beneath the clover sod,
That takes the sunshine and the rains,
Or where the kneeling hamlet drains
The chalice of the grapes of God;

Than if with thee the roaring wells
  Should gulf him fathom-deep in brine,
  And hands so often clasp'd in mine,
Should toss with tangle and with shells.

### XI

Calm is the morn without a sound,
  Calm as to suit a calmer grief,
  And only thro' the faded leaf
The chestnut pattering to the ground;

Calm and deep peace on this high wold,
  And on these dews that drench the furze,
  And all the silvery gossamers
That twinkle into green and gold;

Calm and still light on yon great plain
  That sweeps with all its autumn bow-
      ers,
  And crowded farms and lessening towers,
To mingle with the bounding main;

Calm and deep peace in this wide air,
  These leaves that redden to the fall,
  And in my heart, if calm at all,
If any calm, a calm despair;

Calm on the seas, and silver sleep,
  And waves that sway themselves in rest,
  And dead calm in that noble breast
Which heaves but with the heaving deep.

### XII

Lo, as a dove when up she springs
  To bear thro' heaven a tale of woe,
  Some dolorous message knit below
The wild pulsation of her wings;

Like her I go, I cannot stay;
  I leave this mortal ark behind,
  A weight of nerves without a mind,
And leave the cliffs, and haste away

O'er ocean-mirrors rounded large,
  And reach the glow of southern skies,
  And see the sails at distance rise,
And linger weeping on the marge,

And saying, 'Comes he thus, my friend?
  Is this the end of all my care?'
  And circle moaning in the air,
'Is this the end? Is this the end?'

And forward dart again, and play
  About the prow, and back return

To where the body sits, and learn
That I have been an hour away.

### XIII

Tears of the widower, when he sees
  A late-lost form that sleep reveals,
  And moves his doubtful arms, and feels
Her place is empty, fall like these;

Which weep a loss for ever new,
  A void where heart on heart reposed;
  And, where warm hands have prest and
      closed,
Silence, till I be silent too;

Which weep the comrade of my choice,
  An awful thought, a life removed,
  The human-hearted man I loved,
A Spirit, not a breathing voice.

Come, Time, and teach me, many years,
  I do not suffer in a dream;
  For now so strange do these things seem,
Mine eyes have leisure for their tears,

My fancies time to rise on wing,
  And glance about the approaching sails,
  As tho' they brought but merchants' bales,
And not the burthen that they bring.

### XIV

If one should bring me this report,
  That thou hadst touch'd the land to-day,
  And I went down unto the quay,
And found thee lying in the port;

And standing, muffled round with woe,
  Should see thy passengers in rank
  Come stepping lightly down the plank,
And beckoning unto those they know;

And if along with these should come
  The man I held as half-divine,
  Should strike a sudden hand in mine,
And ask a thousand things of home;

And I should tell him all my pain,
  And how my life had droop'd of late,
  And he should sorrow o'er my state
And marvel what possess'd my brain;

And I perceived no touch of change,
  No hint of death in all his frame,
  But found him all in all the same,
I should not feel it to be strange.

## XV

To-night the winds begin to rise
  And roar from yonder dropping day;
  The last red leaf is whirl'd away,
The rooks are blown about the skies;

The forest crack'd, the waters curl'd,
  The cattle huddled on the lea;
  And wildly dash'd on tower and tree
The sunbeam strikes along the world:

And but for fancies, which aver
  That all thy motions gently pass
  Athwart a plane of molten glass,
I scarce could brook the strain and stir

That makes the barren branches loud;
  And but for fear it is not so,
  The wild unrest that lives in woe
Would dote and pore on yonder cloud

That rises upward always higher,
  And onward drags a laboring breast,
  And topples round the dreary west,
A looming bastion fringed with fire.

## XVI

What words are these have fallen from
    me ?
  Can calm despair and wild unrest
  Be tenants of a single breast,
Or Sorrow such a changeling be ?

Or doth she only seem to take
  The touch of change in calm or storm,
  But knows no more of transient form
In her deep self, than some dead lake

That holds the shadow of a lark
  Hung in the shadow of a heaven ?
  Or has the shock, so harshly given,
Confused me like the unhappy bark

That strikes by night a craggy shelf,
  And staggers blindly ere she sink ?
  And stunn'd me from my power to think
And all my knowledge of myself;

And made me that delirious man
  Whose fancy fuses old and new,
  And flashes into false and true,
And mingles all without a plan ?

## XVII

Thou comest, much wept for; such a breeze
  Compell'd thy canvas, and my prayer
  Was as the whisper of an air
To breathe thee over lonely seas.

For I in spirit saw thee move
  Thro' circles of the bounding sky,
  Week after week; the days go by;
Come quick, thou bringest all I love.

Henceforth, wherever thou mayst roam,
  My blessing, like a line of light,
  Is on the waters day and night,
And like a beacon guards thee home.

So may whatever tempest mars
  Mid-ocean spare thee, sacred bark,
  And balmy drops in summer dark
Slide from the bosom of the stars;

So kind an office hath been done,
  Such precious relics brought by thee,
  The dust of him I shall not see
Till all my widow'd race be run.

## XVIII

'T is well; 't is something; we may stand
  Where he in English earth is laid,
  And from his ashes may be made
The violet of his native land.

'T is little; but it looks in truth
  As if the quiet bones were blest
  Among familiar names to rest
And in the places of his youth.

Come then, pure hands, and bear the
    head
  That sleeps or wears the mask of sleep,
  And come, whatever loves to weep,
And hear the ritual of the dead.

Ah yet, even yet, if this might be,
  I, falling on his faithful heart,
  Would breathing thro' his lips impart
The life that almost dies in me;

That dies not, but endures with pain,
  And slowly forms the firmer mind,
  Treasuring the look it cannot find,
The words that are not heard again.

### XIX

The Danube to the Severn gave
  The darken'd heart that beat no more;
  They laid him by the pleasant shore,
And in the hearing of the wave.

There twice a day the Severn fills;
  The salt sea-water passes by,
  And hushes half the babbling Wye,
And makes a silence in the hills.

The Wye is hush'd nor moved along,
  And hush'd my deepest grief of all,
  When fill'd with tears that cannot fall,
I brim with sorrow drowning song.

The tide flows down, the wave again
  Is vocal in its wooded walls;
  My deeper anguish also falls,
And I can speak a little then.

### XX

The lesser griefs that may be said,
  That breathe a thousand tender vows,
  Are but as servants in a house
Where lies the master newly dead;

Who speak their feeling as it is,
  And weep the fulness from the mind.
  'It will be hard,' they say, 'to find
Another service such as this.'

My lighter moods are like to these,
  That out of words a comfort win;
  But there are other griefs within,
And tears that at their fountain freeze;

For by the hearth the children sit
  Cold in that atmosphere of death,
  And scarce endure to draw the breath,
Or like to noiseless phantoms flit;

But open converse is there none,
  So much the vital spirits sink
  To see the vacant chair, and think,
'How good ! how kind ! and he is gone.'

### XXI

I sing to him that rests below,
  And, since the grasses round me wave,
  I take the grasses of the grave,
And make them pipes whereon to blow.

The traveller hears me now and then,
  And sometimes harshly will he speak:
'This fellow would make weakness weak,
And melt the waxen hearts of men.'

Another answers: 'Let him be,
  He loves to make parade of pain,
  That with his piping he may gain
The praise that comes to constancy.'

A third is wroth: 'Is this an hour
  For private sorrow's barren song,
  When more and more the people throng
The chairs and thrones of civil power ?

'A time to sicken and to swoon,
  When Science reaches forth her arms
  To feel from world to world, and charms
Her secret from the latest moon ? '

Behold, ye speak an idle thing;
  Ye never knew the sacred dust.
  I do but sing because I must,
And pipe but as the linnets sing;

And one is glad; her note is gay,
  For now her little ones have ranged;
  And one is sad; her note is changed,
Because her brood is stolen away.

### XXII

The path by which we twain did go,
  Which led by tracts that pleased us well,
  Thro' four sweet years arose and fell,
From flower to flower, from snow to snow;

And we with singing cheer'd the way,
  And, crown'd with all the season lent,
  From April on to April went,
And glad at heart from May to May.

But where the path we walk'd began
  To slant the fifth autumnal slope,
  As we descended following Hope,
There sat the Shadow fear'd of man;

Who broke our fair companionship,
  And spread his mantle dark and cold,
  And wrapt thee formless in the fold,
And dull'd the murmur on thy lip,

And bore thee where I could not see
  Nor follow, tho' I walk in haste,
  And think that somewhere in the waste
The Shadow sits and waits for me.

### XXIII

Now, sometimes in my sorrow shut,
    Or breaking into song by fits,
    Alone, alone, to where he sits,
The Shadow cloak'd from head to foot,

Who keeps the keys of all the creeds,
    I wander, often falling lame,
    And looking back to whence I came,
Or on to where the pathway leads;

And crying, How changed from where it
        ran
    Thro' lands where not a leaf was dumb,
    But all the lavish hills would hum
The murmur of a happy Pan;

When each by turns was guide to each,
    And Fancy light from Fancy caught,
    And Thought leapt out to wed with
        Thought
Ere Thought could wed itself with Speech;

And all we met was fair and good,
    And all was good that Time could bring,
    And all the secret of the Spring
Moved in the chambers of the blood;

And many an old philosophy
    On Argive heights divinely sang,
    And round us all the thicket rang
To many a flute of Arcady.

### XXIV

And was the day of my delight
    As pure and perfect as I say?
    The very source and fount of day
Is dash'd with wandering isles of night.

If all was good and fair we met,
    This earth had been the Paradise
    It never look'd to human eyes
Since our first sun arose and set.

And is it that the haze of grief
    Makes former gladness loom so great?
    The lowness of the present state,
That sets the past in this relief?

Or that the past will always win
    A glory from its being far,
    And orb into the perfect star
We saw not when we moved therein?

### XXV

I know that this was Life, — the track
    Whereon with equal feet we fared;
    And then, as now, the day prepared
The daily burden for the back.

But this it was that made me move
    As light as carrier-birds in air;
    I loved the weight I had to bear,
Because it needed help of Love;

Nor could I weary, heart or limb,
    When mighty Love would cleave in
        twain
    The lading of a single pain,
And part it, giving half to him.

### XXVI

Still onward winds the dreary way;
    I with it, for I long to prove
    No lapse of moons can canker Love,
Whatever fickle tongues may say.

And if that eye which watches guilt
    And goodness, and hath power to see
    Within the green the moulder'd tree,
And towers fallen as soon as built —

O, if indeed that eye foresee
    Or see — in Him is no before —
    In more of life true life no more
And Love the indifference to be,

Then might I find, ere yet the morn
    Breaks hither over Indian seas,
    That Shadow waiting with the keys,
To shroud me from my proper scorn.

### XXVII

I envy not in any moods
    The captive void of noble rage,
    The linnet born within the cage,
That never knew the summer woods;

I envy not the beast that takes
    His license in the field of time,
    Unfetter'd by the sense of crime,
To whom a conscience never wakes;

Nor, what may count itself as blest,
    The heart that never plighted troth
    But stagnates in the weeds of sloth;
Nor any want-begotten rest.

I hold it true, whate'er befall;
   I feel it, when I sorrow most;
   'T is better to have loved and lost
Than never to have loved at all.

### XXVIII

The time draws near the birth of Christ.
   The moon is hid, the night is still;
   The Christmas bells from hill to hill
Answer each other in the mist.

Four voices of four hamlets round,
   From far and near, on mead and moor,
   Swell out and fail, as if a door
Were shut between me and the sound;

Each voice four changes on the wind,
   That now dilate, and now decrease,
   Peace and goodwill, goodwill and peace,
Peace and goodwill, to all mankind.

This year I slept and woke with pain,
   I almost wish'd no more to wake,
   And that my hold on life would break
Before I heard those bells again;

But they my troubled spirit rule,
   For they controll'd me when a boy;
   They bring me sorrow touch'd with
      joy,
The merry, merry bells of Yule.

### XXIX

With such compelling cause to grieve
   As daily vexes household peace,
   And chains regret to his decease,
How dare we keep our Christmas-eve,

Which brings no more a welcome guest
   To enrich the threshold of the night
   With shower'd largess of delight
In dance and song and game and jest?

Yet go, and while the holly boughs
   Entwine the cold baptismal font,
   Make one wreath more for Use and
      Wont,
That guard the portals of the house;

Old sisters of a day gone by,
   Gray nurses, loving nothing new —
   Why should they miss their yearly
      due
Before their time? They too will die.

### XXX

With trembling fingers did we weave
   The holly round the Christmas hearth;
   A rainy cloud possess'd the earth,
And sadly fell our Christmas-eve.

At our old pastimes in the hall
   We gamboll'd, making vain pretence
   Of gladness, with an awful sense
Of one mute Shadow watching all.

We paused: the winds were in the beech;
   We heard them sweep the winter land;
   And in a circle hand-in-hand
Sat silent, looking each at each.

Then echo-like our voices rang;
   We sung, tho' every eye was dim,
   A merry song we sang with him
Last year; impetuously we sang.

We ceased; a gentler feeling crept
   Upon us: surely rest is meet.
   'They rest,' we said, 'their sleep is
      sweet,'
And silence follow'd, and we wept.

Our voices took a higher range;
   Once more we sang: 'They do not die
   Nor lose their mortal sympathy,
Nor change to us, although they change;

'Rapt from the fickle and the frail
   With gather'd power, yet the same,
   Pierces the keen seraphic flame
From orb to orb, from veil to veil.'

Rise, happy morn, rise, holy morn,
   Draw forth the cheerful day from night:
   O Father, touch the east, and light
The light that shone when Hope was born.

### XXXI

When Lazarus left his charnel-cave, .
   And home to Mary's house return'd,
   Was this demanded — if he yearn'd
To hear her weeping by his grave?

'Where wert thou, brother, those four
     days?'
   There lives no record of reply,
   Which telling what it is to die
Had surely added praise to praise.

From every house the neighbors met,
  The streets were fill'd with joyful sound,
  A solemn gladness even crown'd
The purple brows of Olivet.

Behold a man raised up by Christ!
  The rest remaineth unreveal'd;
  He told it not, or something seal'd
The lips of that Evangelist.

### XXXII

Her eyes are homes of silent prayer,
  Nor other thought her mind admits
  But, he was dead, and there he sits,
And he that brought him back is there.

Then one deep love doth supersede
  All other, when her ardent gaze
  Roves from the living brother's face,
And rests upon the Life indeed.

All subtle thought, all curious fears,
  Borne down by gladness so complete,
  She bows, she bathes the Saviour's feet
With costly spikenard and with tears.

Thrice blest whose lives are faithful
      prayers,
  Whose loves in higher love endure;
  What souls possess themselves so pure,
Or is there blessedness like theirs?

### XXXIII

O thou that after toil and storm
  Mayst seem to have reach'd a purer
      air,
  Whose faith has centre everywhere,
Nor cares to fix itself to form,

Leave thou thy sister when she prays
  Her early heaven, her happy views;
  Nor thou with shadow'd hint confuse
A life that leads melodious days.

Her faith thro' form is pure as thine,
  Her hands are quicker unto good.
  O, sacred be the flesh and blood
To which she links a truth divine!

See thou, that countest reason ripe
  In holding by the law within,
  Thou fail not in a world of sin,
And even for want of such a type.

### XXXIV

My own dim life should teach me this,
  That life shall live for evermore,
  Else earth is darkness at the core,
And dust and ashes all that is;

This round of green, this orb of flame,
  Fantastic beauty; such as lurks
  In some wild poet, when he works
Without a conscience or an aim.

What then were God to such as I?
  'T were hardly worth my while to choose
  Of things all mortal, or to use
A little patience ere I die;

'T were best at once to sink to peace,
  Like birds the charming serpent draws,
  To drop head-foremost in the jaws
Of vacant darkness and to cease.

### XXXV

Yet if some voice that man could trust
  Should murmur from the narrow house,
  'The cheeks drop in, the body bows;
Man dies, nor is there hope in dust;'

Might I not say? 'Yet even here,
  But for one hour, O Love, I strive
  To keep so sweet a thing alive.'
But I should turn mine ears and hear

The moanings of the homeless sea,
  The sound of streams that swift or slow
  Draw down Æonian hills, and sow
The dust of continents to be;

And Love would answer with a sigh,
  'The sound of that forgetful shore
  Will change my sweetness more and
      more,
Half-dead to know that I shall die.'

O me, what profits it to put
  An idle case? If Death were seen
  At first as Death, Love had not been,
Or been in narrowest working shut,

Mere fellowship of sluggish moods,
  Or in his coarsest Satyr-shape
  Had bruised the herb and crush'd the
      grape,
And bask'd and batten'd in the woods.

### XXXVI

Tho' truths in manhood darkly join,
  Deep-seated in our mystic frame,
  We yield all blessing to the name
Of Him that made them current coin;

For Wisdom dealt with mortal powers,
  Where truth in closest words shall fail,
  When truth embodied in a tale
Shall enter in at lowly doors.

And so the Word had breath, and wrought
  With human hands the creed of creeds
  In loveliness of perfect deeds,
More strong than all poetic thought;

Which he may read that binds the sheaf,
  Or builds the house, or digs the grave,
  And those wild eyes that watch the
      wave
In roarings round the coral reef.

### XXXVII

Urania speaks with darken'd brow:
  'Thou pratest here where thou art least;
  This faith has many a purer priest,
And many an abler voice than thou.

'Go down beside thy native rill,
  On thy Parnassus set thy feet,
  And hear thy laurel whisper sweet
About the ledges of the hill.'

And my Melpomene replies,
  A touch of shame upon her cheek:
  'I am not worthy even to speak
Of thy prevailing mysteries;

'For I am but an earthly Muse,
  And owning but a little art
  To lull with song an aching heart,
And render human love his dues;

'But brooding on the dear one dead,
  And all he said of things divine, —
  And dear to me as sacred wine
To dying lips is all he said, —

'I murmur'd, as I came along,
  Of comfort clasp'd in truth reveal'd,
  And loiter'd in the master's field,
And darken'd sanctities with song.'

### XXXVIII

With weary steps I loiter on,
  Tho' always under alter'd skies
  The purple from the distance dies,
My prospect and horizon gone.

No joy the blowing season gives,
  The herald melodies of spring,
  But in the songs I love to sing
A doubtful gleam of solace lives.

If any care for what is here
  Survive in spirits render'd free,
  Then are these songs I sing of thee
Not all ungrateful to thine ear.

### XXXIX

Old warder of these buried bones,
  And answering now my random stroke
  With fruitful cloud and living smoke,
Dark yew, that graspest at the stones

And dippest toward the dreamless head,
  To thee too comes the golden hour
  When flower is feeling after flower;
But Sorrow, — fixt upon the dead,

And darkening the dark graves of men, —
  What whisper'd from her lying lips?
  Thy gloom is kindled at the tips,
And passes into gloom again.

### XL

Could we forget the widow'd hour
  And look on Spirits breathed away,
  As on a maiden in the day
When first she wears her orange-flower!

When crown'd with blessing she doth rise
  To take her latest leave of home,
  And hopes and light regrets that come
Make April of her tender eyes;

And doubtful joys the father move,
  And tears are on the mother's face,
  As parting with a long embrace
She enters other realms of love;

Her office there to rear, to teach,
  Becoming as is meet and fit
  A link among the days, to knit
The generations each with each;

And, doubtless, unto thee is given
  A life that bears immortal fruit
  In those great offices that suit
The full-grown energies of heaven.

Ay me, the difference I discern !
  How often shall her old fireside
  Be cheer'd with tidings of the bride,
How often she herself return,

And tell them all they would have told,
  And bring her babe, and make her
     boast,
  Till even those that miss'd her most
Shall count new things as dear as old;

But thou and I have shaken hands,
  Till growing winters lay me low;
  My paths are in the fields I know,
And thine in undiscover'd lands.

## XLI

Thy spirit ere our fatal loss
  Did ever rise from high to higher,
  As mounts the heavenward altar-fire,
As flies the lighter thro' the gross.

But thou art turn'd to something strange,
  And I have lost the links that bound
  Thy changes; here upon the ground,
No more partaker of thy change.

Deep folly ! yet that this could be —
  That I could wing my will with might
  To leap the grades of life and light,
And flash at once, my friend, to thee!

For tho' my nature rarely yields
  To that vague fear implied in death,
  Nor shudders at the gulfs beneath,
The howlings from forgotten fields;

Yet oft when sundown skirts the moor
  An inner trouble I behold,
  A spectral doubt which makes me cold,
That I shall be thy mate no more,

Tho' following with an upward mind
  The wonders that have come to thee,
  Thro' all the secular to-be,
But evermore a life behind.

## XLII

I vex my heart with fancies dim.
  He still outstript me in the race;

  It was but unity of place
That made me dream I rank'd with him.

And so may Place retain us still,
  And he the much-beloved again,
  A lord of large experience, train
To riper growth the mind and will;

And what delights can equal those
  That stir the spirit's inner deeps,
  When one that loves, but knows not, reaps
A truth from one that loves and knows ?

## XLIII

If Sleep and Death be truly one,
  And every spirit's folded bloom
  Thro' all its intervital gloom
In some long trance should slumber on;

Unconscious of the sliding hour,
  Bare of the body, might it last,
  And silent traces of the past
Be all the color of the flower:

So then were nothing lost to man;
  So that still garden of the souls
  In many a figured leaf enrolls
The total world since life began;

And love will last as pure and whole
  As when he loved me here in Time,
  And at the spiritual prime
Rewaken with the dawning soul.

## XLIV

How fares it with the happy dead ?
  For here the man is more and more;
  But he forgets the days before
God shut the doorways of his head.

The days have vanish'd, tone and tint,
  And yet perhaps the hoarding sense
  Gives out at times — he knows not
     whence —
A little flash, a mystic hint;

And in the long harmonious years —
  If Death so taste Lethean springs —
  May some dim touch of earthly things
Surprise thee ranging with thy peers.

If such a dreamy touch should fall,
  O, turn thee round, resolve the doubt;
  My guardian angel will speak out
In that high place, and tell thee all.

### XLV

The baby new to earth and sky,
  What time his tender palm is prest
  Against the circle of the breast,
Has never thought that 'this is I;'

But as he grows he gathers much,
  And learns the use of 'I' and 'me,'
  And finds 'I am not what I see,
And other than the things I touch.'

So rounds he to a separate mind
  From whence clear memory may be-
    gin,
  As thro' the frame that binds him in
His isolation grows defined.

This use may lie in blood and breath,
  Which else were fruitless of their due,
  Had man to learn himself anew
Beyond the second birth of death.

### XLVI

We ranging down this lower track,
  The path we came by, thorn and flower,
  Is shadow'd by the growing hour,
Lest life should fail in looking back.

So be it: there no shade can last
  In that deep dawn behind the tomb,
  But clear from marge to marge shall
    bloom
The eternal landscape of the past;

A lifelong tract of time reveal'd,
  The fruitful hours of still increase;
  Days order'd in a wealthy peace,
And those five years its richest field.

O Love, thy province were not large,
  A bounded field, nor stretching far;
  Look also, Love, a brooding star,
A rosy warmth from marge to marge.

### XLVII

That each, who seems a separate whole,
  Should move his rounds, and fusing
    all
  The skirts of self again, should fall
Remerging in the general Soul,

Is faith as vague as all unsweet.
  Eternal form shall still divide
The eternal soul from all beside;
  And I shall know him when we meet;

And we shall sit at endless feast,
  Enjoying each the other's good.
  What vaster dream can hit the mood
Of Love on earth? He seeks at least

Upon the last and sharpest height,
  Before the spirits fade away,
  Some landing-place, to clasp and say,
'Farewell! We lose ourselves in light.'

### XLVIII

If these brief lays, of Sorrow born,
  Were taken to be such as closed
  Grave doubts and answers here proposed,
Then these were such as men might scorn.

Her care is not to part and prove;
  She takes, when harsher moods remit,
  What slender shade of doubt may flit,
And makes it vassal unto love;

And hence, indeed, she sports with words,
  But better serves a wholesome law,
  And holds it sin and shame to draw
The deepest measure from the chords;

Nor dare she trust a larger lay,
  But rather loosens from the lip
  Short swallow-flights of song, that dip
Their wings in tears, and skim away.

### XLIX

From art, from nature, from the schools,
  Let random influences glance,
  Like light in many a shiver'd lance
That breaks about the dappled pools.

The lightest wave of thought shall lisp,
  The fancy's tenderest eddy wreathe,
  The slightest air of song shall breathe
To make the sullen surface crisp.

And look thy look, and go thy way,
  But blame not thou the winds that make
  The seeming-wanton ripple break,
The tender-pencill'd shadow play.

Beneath all fancied hopes and fears
  Ay me, the sorrow deepens down,
  Whose muffled motions blindly drown
The bases of my life in tears.

L

Be near me when my light is low,
   When the blood creeps, and the nerves
      prick
   And tingle; and the heart is sick,
And all the wheels of being slow.

Be near me when the sensuous frame
   Is rack'd with pangs that conquer trust;
   And Time, a maniac scattering dust,
And Life, a Fury slinging flame.

Be near me when my faith is dry,
   And men the flies of latter spring,
   That lay their eggs, and sting and sing
And weave their petty cells and die.

Be near me when I fade away,
   To point the term of human strife,
   And on the low dark verge of life
The twilight of eternal day.

LI

Do we indeed desire the dead
   Should still be near us at our side ?
   Is there no baseness we would hide ?
No inner vileness that we dread ?

Shall he for whose applause I strove,
   I had such reverence for his blame,
   See with clear eye some hidden shame
And I be lessen'd in his love ?

I wrong the grave with fears untrue.
   Shall love be blamed for want of faith ?
   There must be wisdom with great Death;
The dead shall look me thro' and thro'.

Be near us when we climb or fall;
   Ye watch, like God, the rolling hours
   With larger other eyes than ours,
To make allowance for us all.

LII

I cannot love thee as I ought,
   For love reflects the thing beloved;
   My words are only words, and moved
Upon the topmost froth of thought.

' Yet blame not thou thy plaintive song,'
   The Spirit of true love replied;
   ' Thou canst not move me from thy
      side,
Nor human frailty do me wrong.

' What keeps a spirit wholly true
   To that ideal which he bears ?
   What record ? not the sinless years
That breathed beneath the Syrian blue;

' So fret not, like an idle girl,
   That life is dash'd with flecks of sin.
   Abide; thy wealth is gather'd in,
When Time hath sunder'd shell from
      pearl.'

LIII

How many a father have I seen,
   A sober man, among his boys,
   Whose youth was full of foolish noise,
Who wears his manhood hale and green;

And dare we to this fancy give,
   That had the wild oat not been sown,
   The soil, left barren, scarce had grown
The grain by which a man may live ?

Or, if we held the doctrine sound
   For life outliving heats of youth,
   Yet who would preach it as a truth
To those that eddy round and round ?

Hold thou the good, define it well;
   For fear divine Philosophy
   Should push beyond her mark, and be
Procuress to the Lords of Hell.

LIV

O, yet we trust that somehow good
   Will be the final goal of ill,
   To pangs of nature, sins of will,
Defects of doubt, and taints of blood;

That nothing walks with aimless feet;
   That not one life shall be destroy'd,
   Or cast as rubbish to the void,
When God hath made the pile complete;

That not a worm is cloven in vain;
   That not a moth with vain desire
   Is shrivell'd in a fruitless fire,
Or but subserves another's gain.

Behold, we know not anything;
   I can but trust that good shall fall
   At last — far off — at last, to all,
And every winter change to spring.

So runs my dream; but what am I ?
   An infant crying in the night;

An infant crying for the light,
And with no language but a cry.

LV

The wish, that of the living whole
  No life may fail beyond the grave,
  Derives it not from what we have
The likest God within the soul?

Are God and Nature then at strife,
  That Nature lends such evil dreams?
  So careful of the type she seems,
So careless of the single life,

That I, considering everywhere
  Her secret meaning in her deeds,
  And finding that of fifty seeds
She often brings but one to bear,

I falter where I firmly trod,
  And falling with my weight of cares
  Upon the great world's altar-stairs
That slope thro' darkness up to God,

I stretch lame hands of faith, and grope,
  And gather dust and chaff, and call
  To what I feel is Lord of all,
And faintly trust the larger hope.

LVI

'So careful of the type?' but no.
  From scarped cliff and quarried stone
  She cries, 'A thousand types are gone;
I care for nothing, all shall go.

'Thou makest thine appeal to me:
  I bring to life, I bring to death;
  The spirit does but mean the breath:
I know no more.'   And he, shall he,

Man, her last work, who seem'd so fair,
  Such splendid purpose in his eyes,
  Who roll'd the psalm to wintry skies,
Who built him fanes of fruitless prayer,

Who trusted God was love indeed
  And love Creation's final law —
  Tho' Nature, red in tooth and claw
With ravine, shriek'd against his creed —

Who loved, who suffer'd countless ills,
  Who battled for the True, the Just,
  Be blown about the desert dust,
Or seal'd within the iron hills?

No more?   A monster then, a dream,
  A discord.   Dragons of the prime,
  That tare each other in their slime,
Were mellow music match'd with him.

O life as futile, then, as frail!
  O for thy voice to soothe and bless!
  What hope of answer, or redress?
Behind the veil, behind the veil.

LVII

Peace; come away: the song of woe
  Is after all an earthly song.
  Peace; come away: we do him wrong
To sing so wildly: let us go.

Come; let us go: your cheeks are pale;
  But half my life I leave behind.
  Methinks my friend is richly shrined;
But I shall pass, my work will fail.

Yet in these ears, till hearing dies,
  One set slow bell will seem to toll
  The passing of the sweetest soul
That ever look'd with human eyes.

I hear it now, and o'er and o'er,
  Eternal greetings to the dead;
  And 'Ave, Ave, Ave,' said,
'Adieu, adieu,' for evermore.

LVIII

In those sad words I took farewell.
  Like echoes in sepulchral halls,
  As drop by drop the water falls
In vaults and catacombs, they fell;

And, falling, idly broke the peace
  Of hearts that beat from day to day,
  Half-conscious of their dying clay,
And those cold crypts where they shall
    cease.

The high Muse answer'd: 'Wherefore
    grieve
  Thy brethren with a fruitless tear?
  Abide a little longer here,
And thou shalt take a nobler leave.'

LIX

O Sorrow, wilt thou live with me
  No casual mistress, but a wife,
  My bosom-friend and half of life;
As I confess it needs must be?

O Sorrow, wilt thou rule my blood,
  Be sometimes lovely like a bride,
  And put thy harsher moods aside,
If thou wilt have me wise and good?

My centred passion cannot move,
  Nor will it lessen from to-day;
  But I 'll have leave at times to play
As with the creature of my love;

And set thee forth, for thou art mine,
  With so much hope for years to come,
  That, howsoe'er I know thee, some
Could hardly tell what name were thine.

## LX

He past, a soul of nobler tone;
  My spirit loved and loves him yet,
  Like some poor girl whose heart is set
On one whose rank exceeds her own.

He mixing with his proper sphere,
  She finds the baseness of her lot,
  Half jealous of she knows not what,
And envying all that meet him there.

The little village looks forlorn;
  She sighs amid her narrow days,
  Moving about the household ways,
In that dark house where she was born.

The foolish neighbors come and go,
  And tease her till the day draws by;
  At night she weeps, 'How vain am I !
How should he love a thing so low?'

## LXI

If, in thy second state sublime,
  Thy ransom'd reason change replied
  With all the circle of the wise,
The perfect flower of human time;

And if thou cast thine eyes below,
  How dimly character'd and slight,
  How dwarf'd a growth of cold and night,
How blanch'd with darkness must I grow !

Yet turn thee to the doubtful shore,
  Where thy first form was made a man;
  I loved thee, Spirit, and love, nor can
The soul of Shakespeare love thee more.

## LXII

Tho' if an eye that 's downward cast
  Could make thee somewhat blench or fail,

Then be my love an idle tale
And fading legend of the past;

And thou, as one that once declined,
  When he was little more than boy,
  On some unworthy heart with joy,
But lives to wed an equal mind,

And breathes a novel world, the while
  His other passion wholly dies,
  Or in the light of deeper eyes
Is matter for a flying smile.

## LXIII

Yet pity for a horse o'er-driven,
  And love in which my hound has part,
  Can hang no weight upon my heart
In its assumptions up to heaven;

And I am so much more than these,
  As thou, perchance, art more than I,
  And yet I spare them sympathy,
And I would set their pains at ease.

So mayst thou watch me where I weep,
  As, unto vaster motions bound,
  The circuits of thine orbit round
A higher height, a deeper deep.

## LXIV

Dost thou look back on what hath been,
  As some divinely gifted man,
  Whose life in low estate began
And on a simple village green;

Who breaks his birth's invidious bar,
  And grasps the skirts of happy chance,
  And breasts the blows of circumstance,
And grapples with his evil star;

Who makes by force his merit known
  And lives to clutch the golden keys,
  To mould a mighty state's decrees,
And shape the whisper of the throne;

And moving up from high to higher,
  Becomes on Fortune's crowning slope
  The pillar of a people's hope,
The centre of a world's desire;

Yet feels, as in a pensive dream,
  When all his active powers are still,
  A distant dearness in the hill,
A secret sweetness in the stream,

The limit of his narrower fate,
  While yet beside its vocal springs
  He play'd at counsellors and kings,
With one that was his earliest mate;

Who ploughs with pain his native lea
  And reaps the labor of his hands,
  Or in the furrow musing stands:
'Does my old friend remember me?'

### LXV

Sweet soul, do with me as thou wilt;
  I lull a fancy trouble-tost
  With 'Love 's too precious to be lost,
A little grain shall not be spilt.'

And in that solace can I sing,
  Till out of painful phases wrought
  There flutters up a happy thought,
Self-balanced on a lightsome wing;

Since we deserved the name of friends,
  And thine effect so lives in me,
  A part of mine may live in thee
And move thee on to noble ends.

### LXVI

You thought my heart too far diseased;
  You wonder when my fancies play
  To find me gay among the gay,
Like one with any trifle pleased.

The shade by which my life was crost,
  Which makes a desert in the mind,
  Has made me kindly with my kind,
And like to him whose sight is lost;

Whose feet are guided thro' the land,
  Whose jest among his friends is free,
  Who takes the children on his knee,
And winds their curls about his hand.

He plays with threads, he beats his chair
  For pastime, dreaming of the sky;
  His inner day can never die,
His night of loss is always there.

### LXVII

When on my bed the moonlight falls,
  I know that in thy place of rest
  By that broad water of the west
There comes a glory on the walls:

Thy marble bright in dark appears,
  As slowly steals a silver flame

Along the letters of thy name,
  And o'er the number of thy years.

The mystic glory swims away,
  From off my bed the moonlight dies;
  And closing eaves of wearied eyes
I sleep till dusk is dipt in gray;

And then I know the mist is drawn
  A lucid veil from coast to coast,
  And in the dark church like a ghost
Thy tablet glimmers in the dawn.

### LXVIII

When in the down I sink my head,
  Sleep, Death's twin-brother, times my
    breath;
  Sleep, Death's twin-brother, knows not
    Death,
Nor can I dream of thee as dead.

I walk as ere I walk'd forlorn,
  When all our path was fresh with dew,
  And all the bugle breezes blew
Reveillée to the breaking morn.

But what is this?   I turn about,
  I find a trouble in thine eye,
  Which makes me sad I know not why,
Nor can my dream resolve the doubt;

But ere the lark hath left the lea
  I wake, and I discern the truth;
  It is the trouble of my youth
That foolish sleep transfers to thee.

### LXIX

I dream'd there would be Spring no more,
  That Nature's ancient power was lost;
  The streets were black with smoke and
    frost,
They chatter'd trifles at the door;

I wander'd from the noisy town,
  I found a wood with thorny boughs;
  I took the thorns to bind my brows,
I wore them like a civic crown;

I met with scoffs, I met with scorns
  From youth and babe and hoary hairs:
  They call'd me in the public squares
The fool that wears a crown of thorns.

They call'd me fool, they call'd me child:
  I found an angel of the night;

The voice was low, the look was bright;
He look'd upon my crown and smiled.

He reach'd the glory of a hand,
  That seem'd to touch it into leaf;
  The voice was not the voice of grief,
The words were hard to understand.

### LXX

I cannot see the features right,
  When on the gloom I strive to paint
  The face I know; the hues are faint
And mix with hollow masks of night;

Cloud-towers by ghostly masons wrought,
  A gulf that ever shuts and gapes,
  A hand that points, and palled shapes
In shadowy thoroughfares of thought;

And crowds that stream from yawning
    doors,
  And shoals of pucker'd faces drive;
  Dark bulks that tumble half alive,
And lazy lengths on boundless shores;

Till all at once beyond the will
  I hear a wizard music roll,
  And thro' a lattice on the soul
Looks thy fair face and makes it still.

### LXXI

Sleep, kinsman thou to death and trance
  And madness, thou hast forged at last
  A night-long present of the past
In which we went thro' summer France.

Hadst thou such credit with the soul ?
  Then bring an opiate trebly strong,
  Drug down the blindfold sense of wrong,
That so my pleasure may be whole;

While now we talk as once we talk'd
  Of men and minds, the dust of change,
  The days that grow to something strange,
In walking as of old we walk'd

Beside the river's wooded reach,
  The fortress, and the mountain ridge,
  The cataract flashing from the bridge,
The breaker breaking on the beach.

### LXXII

Risest thou thus, dim dawn, again,
  And howlest, issuing out of night,

With blasts that blow the poplar white,
And lash with storm the streaming pane ?

Day, when my crown'd estate begun
  To pine in that reverse of doom,
  Which sicken'd every living bloom,
And blurr'd the splendor of the sun;

Who usherest in the dolorous hour
  With thy quick tears that make the rose
  Pull sideways, and the daisy close
Her crimson fringes to the shower;

Who mightst have heaved a windless flame
  Up the deep East, or, whispering, play'd
  A chequer-work of beam and shade
Along the hills, yet look'd the same,

As wan, as chill, as wild as now;
  Day, mark'd as with some hideous crime,
  When the dark hand struck down thro'
    time,
And cancell'd nature's best: but thou,

Lift as thou mayst thy burthen'd brows
  Thro' clouds that drench the morning
    star,
  And whirl the ungarner'd sheaf afar,
And sow the sky with flying boughs,

And up thy vault with roaring sound
  Climb thy thick noon, disastrous day;
  Touch thy dull goal of joyless gray,
And hide thy shame beneath the ground.

### LXXIII

So many worlds, so much to do,
  So little done, such things to be,
  How know I what had need of thee,
For thou wert strong as thou wert true ?

The fame is quench'd that I foresaw,
  The head hath miss'd an earthly wreath:
  I curse not Nature, no, nor Death;
For nothing is that errs from law.

We pass; the path that each man trod
  Is dim, or will be dim, with weeds.
  What fame is left for human deeds
In endless age ?   It rests with God.

O hollow wraith of dying fame,
  Fade wholly, while the soul exults,
  And self-infolds the large results
Of force that would have forged a name.

LXXIV

As sometimes in a dead man's face,
    To those that watch it more and more,
    A likeness, hardly seen before,
Comes out — to some one of his race;

So, dearest, now thy brows are cold,
    I see thee what thou art, and know
    Thy likeness to the wise below,
Thy kindred with the great of old.

But there is more than I can see,
    And what I see I leave unsaid,
    Nor speak it, knowing Death has made
His darkness beautiful with thee.

LXXV

I leave thy praises unexpress'd
    In verse that brings myself relief,
    And by the measure of my grief
I leave thy greatness to be guess'd.

What practice howsoe'er expert
    In fitting aptest words to things,
    Or voice the richest-toned that sings,
Hath power to give thee as thou wert ?

I care not in these fading days
    To raise a cry that lasts not long,
    And round thee with the breeze of
        song
To stir a little dust of praise.

Thy leaf has perish'd in the green,
    And, while we breathe beneath the sun,
    The world which credits what is done
Is cold to all that might have been.

So here shall silence guard thy fame;
    But somewhere, out of human view,
    Whate'er thy hands are set to do
Is wrought with tumult of acclaim.

LXXVI

Take wings of fancy, and ascend,
    And in a moment set thy face
    Where all the starry heavens of space
Are sharpen'd to a needle's end;

Take wings of foresight; lighten thro'
    The secular abyss to come,
    And lo, thy deepest lays are dumb
Before the mouldering of a yew;

And if the matin songs, that woke
    The darkness of our planet, last,
    Thine own shall wither in the vast,
Ere half the lifetime of an oak.

Ere these have clothed their branchy bow-
        ers
    With fifty Mays, thy songs are vain;
    And what are they when these remain
The ruin'd shells of hollow towers ?

LXXVII

What hope is here for modern rhyme
    To him who turns a musing eye
    On songs, and deeds, and lives, that
        lie
Foreshorten'd in the tract of time ?

These mortal lullabies of pain
    May bind a book, may line a box,
    May serve to curl a maiden's locks;
Or when a thousand moons shall wane

A man upon a stall may find,
    And, passing, turn the page that tells
    A grief, then changed to something
        else,
Sung by a long-forgotten mind.

But what of that ?   My darken'd ways
    Shall ring with music all the same;
    To breathe my loss is more than fame,
To utter love more sweet than praise.

LXXVIII

Again at Christmas did we weave
    The holly round the Christmas hearth;
    The silent snow possess'd the earth,
And calmly fell our Christmas-eve.

The yule-clog sparkled keen with frost,
    No wing of wind the region swept,
    But over all things brooding slept
The quiet sense of something lost.

As in the winters left behind,
    Again our ancient games had place,
    The mimic picture's breathing grace,
And dance and song and hoodman-blind.

Who show'd a token of distress ?
    No single tear, no mark of pain —
    O sorrow, then can sorrow wane ?
O grief, can grief be changed to less ?

O last regret, regret can die !
  No — mixt with all this mystic frame,
  Her deep relations are the same,
But with long use her tears are dry.

### LXXIX

' More than my brothers are to me,' —
  Let this not vex thee, noble heart !
  I know thee of what force thou art
To hold the costliest love in fee.

But thou and I are one in kind,
  As moulded like in Nature's mint;
  And hill and wood and field did print
The same sweet forms in either mind.

For us the same cold streamlet curl'd
  Thro' all his eddying coves, the same
  All winds that roam the twilight came
In whispers of the beauteous world.

At one dear knee we proffer'd vows,
  One lesson from one book we learn'd,
  Ere childhood's flaxen ringlet turn'd
To black and brown on kindred brows.

And so my wealth resembles thine,
  But he was rich where I was poor,
  And he supplied my want the more
As his unlikeness fitted mine.

### LXXX

If any vague desire should rise,
  That holy Death ere Arthur died
  Had moved me kindly from his side,
And dropt the dust on tearless eyes;

Then fancy shapes, as fancy can,
  The grief my loss in him had wrought,
  A grief as deep as life or thought,
But stay'd in peace with God and man.

I make a picture in the brain;
  I hear the sentence that he speaks;
  He bears the burthen of the weeks,
But turns his burthen into gain.

His credit thus shall set me free;
  And, influence-rich to soothe and save,
  Unused example from the grave
Reach out dead hands to comfort me.

### LXXXI

Could I have said while he was here,
  ' My love shall now no further range;

There cannot come a mellower change,
For now is love mature in ear ' ?

Love, then, had hope of richer store:
  What end is here to my complaint ?
  This haunting whisper makes me faint,
' More years had made me love thee
    more.'

But Death returns an answer sweet:
  ' My sudden frost was sudden gain,
  And gave all ripeness to the grain
It might have drawn from after-heat.'

### LXXXII

I wage not any feud with Death
  For changes wrought on form and face;
  No lower life that earth's embrace
May breed with him can fright my faith.

Eternal process moving on,
  From state to state the spirit walks;
  And these are but the shatter'd stalks,
Or ruin'd chrysalis of one.

Nor blame I Death, because he bare
  The use of virtue out of earth;
  I know transplanted human worth
Will bloom to profit, otherwhere.

For this alone on Death I wreak
  The wrath that garners in my heart:
  He put our lives so far apart
We cannot hear each other speak.

### LXXXIII

Dip down upon the northern shore,
  O sweet new-year delaying long;
  Thou doest expectant Nature wrong;
Delaying long, delay no more.

What stays thee from the clouded noons,
  Thy sweetness from its proper place ?
  Can trouble live with April days,
Or sadness in the summer moons ?

Bring orchis, bring the foxglove spire,
  The little speedwell's darling blue,
  Deep tulips dash'd with fiery dew,
Laburnums, dropping-wells of fire.

O thou, new-year, delaying long,
  Delayest the sorrow in my blood,
  That longs to burst a frozen bud
And flood a fresher throat with song.

## LXXXIV

When I contemplate all alone
　The life that had been thine below,
　And fix my thoughts on all the glow
To which thy crescent would have grown,

I see thee sitting crown'd with good,
　A central warmth diffusing bliss
　In glance and smile, and clasp and kiss,
On all the branches of thy blood;

Thy blood, my friend, and partly mine;
　For now the day was drawing on,
　When thou shouldst link thy life with
　　　one
Of mine own house, and boys of thine

Had babbled ' Uncle ' on my knee;
　But that remorseless iron hour
　Made cypress of her orange flower,
Despair of hope, and earth of thee.

I seem to meet their least desire,
　To clap their cheeks, to call them mine.
　I see their unborn faces shine
Beside the never-lighted fire.

I see myself an honor'd guest,
　Thy partner in the flowery walk
　Of letters, genial table-talk,
Or deep dispute, and graceful jest;

While now thy prosperous labor fills
　The lips of men with honest praise,
　And sun by sun the happy days
Descend below the golden hills

With promise of a morn as fair;
　And all the train of bounteous hours
　Conduct, by paths of growing powers,
To reverence and the silver hair;

Till slowly worn her earthly robe,
　Her lavish mission richly wrought,
　Leaving great legacies of thought,
Thy spirit should fail from off the globe;

What time mine own might also flee,
　As link'd with thine in love and fate,
　And, hovering o'er the dolorous strait
To the other shore, involved in thee,

Arrive at last the blessed goal,
　And He that died in Holy Land

Would reach us out the shining hand,
And take us as a single soul.

What reed was that on which I leant?
　Ah, backward fancy, wherefore wake
　The old bitterness again, and break
The low beginnings of content?

## LXXXV

This truth came borne with bier and pall,
　I felt it, when I sorrow'd most,
　'T is better to have loved and lost,
Than never to have loved at all —

O true in word, and tried in deed,
　Demanding, so to bring relief
　To this which is our common grief,
What kind of life is that I lead;

And whether trust in things above
　Be dimm'd of sorrow, or sustain'd;
　And whether love for him have drain'd
My capabilities of love;

Your words have virtue such as draws
　A faithful answer from the breast,
　Thro' light reproaches, half exprest,
And loyal unto kindly laws.

My blood an even tenor kept,
　Till on mine ear this message falls,
　That in Vienna's fatal walls
God's finger touch'd him, and he slept.

The great Intelligences fair
　That range above our mortal state,
　In circle round the blessed gate,
Received and gave him welcome there;

And led him thro' the blissful climes,
　And show'd him in the fountain fresh
　All knowledge that the sons of flesh
Shall gather in the cycled times.

But I remain'd, whose hopes were dim,
　Whose life, whose thoughts were little
　　　worth,
　To wander on a darken'd earth,
Where all things round me breathed of
　　　him.

O friendship, equal-poised control,
　O heart, with kindliest motion warm,
　O sacred essence, other form,
O solemn ghost, O crowned soul!

Yet none could better know than I,
How much of act at human hands
The sense of human will demands
By which we dare to live or die.

Whatever way my days decline,
I felt and feel, tho' left alone,
His being working in mine own,
The footsteps of his life in mine;

A life that all the Muses deck'd
With gifts of grace, that might express
All-comprehensive tenderness,
All-subtilizing intellect:

And so my passion hath not swerved
To works of weakness, but I find
An image comforting the mind,
And in my grief a strength reserved.

Likewise the imaginative woe,
That loved to handle spiritual strife,
Diffused the shock thro' all my life,
But in the present broke the blow.

My pulses therefore beat again
For other friends that once I met;
Nor can it suit me to forget
The mighty hopes that make us men.

I woo your love: I count it crime
To mourn for any overmuch;
I, the divided half of such
A friendship as had master'd Time;

Which masters Time indeed, and is
Eternal, separate from fears.
The all-assuming months and years
Can take no part away from this;

But Summer on the steaming floods,
And Spring that swells the narrow
brooks,
And Autumn, with a noise of rooks,
That gather in the waning woods,

And every pulse of wind and wave
Recalls, in change of light or gloom,
My old affection of the tomb,
And my prime passion in the grave.

My old affection of the tomb,
A part of stillness, yearns to speak:
' Arise, and get thee forth and seek
A friendship for the years to come.

' I watch thee from the quiet shore;
Thy spirit up to mine can reach;
But in dear words of human speech
We two communicate no more.'

And I, ' Can clouds of nature stain
The starry clearness of the free ?
How is it ?   Canst thou feel for me
Some painless sympathy with pain ? '

And lightly does the whisper fall:
' 'T is hard for thee to fathom this;
I triumph in conclusive bliss,
And that serene result of all.'

So hold I commerce with the dead;
Or so methinks the dead would say;
Or so shall grief with symbols play
And pining life be fancy-fed.

Now looking to some settled end,
That these things pass, and I shall prove
A meeting somewhere, love with love,
I crave your pardon, O my friend;

If not so fresh, with love as true,
I, clasping brother-hands, aver
I could not, if I would, transfer
The whole I felt for him to you.

For which be they that hold apart
The promise of the golden hours ?
First love, first friendship, equal powers,
That marry with the virgin heart.

Still mine, that cannot but deplore,
That beats within a lonely place,
That yet remembers his embrace,
But at his footstep leaps no more,

My heart, tho' widow'd, may not rest
Quite in the love of what is gone,
But seeks to beat in time with one
That warms another living breast.

Ah, take the imperfect gift I bring,
Knowing the primrose yet is dear,
The primrose of the later year,
As not unlike to that of Spring.

LXXXVI

Sweet after showers, ambrosial air,
That rollest from the gorgeous gloom
Of evening over brake and bloom
And meadow, slowly breathing bare

The round of space, and rapt below
  Thro' all the dewy tassell'd wood,
  And shadowing down the horned flood
In ripples, fan my brows and blow

The fever from my cheek, and sigh
  The full new life that feeds thy breath
Throughout my frame, till Doubt and
    Death,
Ill brethren, let the fancy fly

From belt to belt of crimson seas
  On leagues of odor streaming far,
  To where in yonder orient star
A hundred spirits whisper ' Peace.'

### LXXXVII

I past beside the reverend walls
  In which of old I wore the gown;
  I roved at random thro' the town,
And saw the tumult of the halls;

And heard once more in college fanes
  The storm their high-built organs make,
  And thunder-music, rolling, shake
The prophet blazon'd on the panes;

And caught once more the distant shout,
  The measured pulse of racing oars
  Among the willows; paced the shores
And many a bridge, and all about

The same gray flats again, and felt
  The same, but not the same; and last
  Up that long walk of limes I past
To see the rooms in which he dwelt.

Another name was on the door.
  I linger'd; all within was noise
  Of songs, and clapping hands, and boys
That crash'd the glass and beat the floor;

Where once we held debate, a band
  Of youthful friends, on mind and art,
  And labor, and the changing mart,
And all the framework of the land;

When one would aim an arrow fair,
  But send it slackly from the string;
  And one would pierce an outer ring,
And one an inner, here and there;

And last the master-bowman, he,
  Would cleave the mark.  A willing ear

We lent him.   Who but hung to hear
The rapt oration flowing free

From point to point, with power and grace
  And music in the bounds of law,
  To those conclusions when we saw
The God within him light his face,

And seem to lift the form, and glow
  In azure orbits heavenly-wise;
  And over those ethereal eyes
The bar of Michael Angelo ?

### LXXXVIII

Wild bird, whose warble, liquid sweet,
  Rings Eden thro' the budded quicks,
  O, tell me where the senses mix,
O, tell me where the passions meet,

Whence radiate: fierce extremes employ
  Thy spirits in the darkening leaf,
  And in the midmost heart of grief
Thy passion clasps a secret joy;

And I — my harp would prelude woe —
  I cannot all command the strings;
  The glory of the sum of things
Will flash along the chords and go.

### LXXXIX

Witch-elms that counterchange the floor
  Of this flat lawn with dusk and bright;
  And thou, with all thy breadth and
    height
Of foliage, towering sycamore;

How often, hither wandering down,
  My Arthur found your shadows fair,
  And shook to all the liberal air
The dust and din and steam of town !

He brought an eye for all he saw;
  He mixt in all our simple sports;
  They pleased him, fresh from brawling
    courts
And dusty purlieus of the law.

O joy to him in this retreat,
  Immantled in ambrosial dark,
  To drink the cooler air, and mark
The landscape winking thro' the heat !

O sound to rout the brood of cares,
  The sweep of scythe in morning dew,

The gust that round the garden flew,
And tumbled half the mellowing pears !

O bliss, when all in circle drawn
  About him, heart and ear were fed
  To hear him, as he lay and read
The Tuscan poets on the lawn!

Or in the all-golden afternoon
  A guest, or happy sister, sung,
  Or here she brought the harp and flung
A ballad to the brightening moon.

Nor less it pleased in livelier moods,
  Beyond the bounding hill to stray,
  And break the livelong summer day
With banquet in the distant woods;

Whereat we glanced from theme to theme,
  Discuss'd the books to love or hate,
  Or touch'd the changes of the state,
Or threaded some Socratic dream;

But if I praised the busy town,
  He loved to rail against it still,
  For ' ground in yonder social mill
We rub each other's angles down,

' And merge,' he said, 'in form and gloss
  The picturesque of man and man.'
  We talk'd: the stream beneath us ran,
The wine-flask lying couch'd in moss,

Or cool'd within the glooming wave;
  And last, returning from afar,
  Before the crimson-circled star
Had fallen into her father's grave,

And brushing ankle-deep in flowers,
  We heard behind the woodbine veil
  The milk that bubbled in the pail,
And buzzings of the honeyed hours.

## XC

He tasted love with half his mind,
  Nor ever drank the inviolate spring
  Where nighest heaven, who first could
      fling
This bitter seed among mankind:

That could the dead, whose dying eyes
  Were closed with wail, resume their life,
  They would but find in child and wife
An iron welcome when they rise.

'T was well, indeed, when warm with wine,
  To pledge them with a kindly tear,
  To talk them o'er, to wish them here,
To count their memories half divine;

But if they came who past away,
  Behold their brides in other hands;
  The hard heir strides about their lands,
And will not yield them for a day.

Yea, tho' their sons were none of these,
  Not less the yet-loved sire would make
  Confusion worse than death, and shake
The pillars of domestic peace.

Ah, dear, but come thou back to me!
  Whatever change the years have wrought,
  I find not yet one lonely thought
That cries against my wish for thee.

## XCI

When rosy plumelets tuft the larch,
  And rarely pipes the mounted thrush,
  Or underneath the barren bush
Flits by the sea-blue bird of March;

Come, wear the form by which I know
  Thy spirit in time among thy peers;
  The hope of unaccomplish'd years
Be large and lucid round thy brow.

When summer's hourly-mellowing change
  May breathe, with many roses sweet,
  Upon the thousand waves of wheat
That ripple round the lowly grange,

Come; not in watches of the night,
  But where the sunbeam broodeth warm,
  Come, beauteous in thine after form,
And like a finer light in light.

## XCII

If any vision should reveal
  Thy likeness, I might count it vain
  As but the canker of the brain;
Yea, tho' it spake and made appeal

To chances where our lots were cast
  Together in the days behind,
  I might but say, I hear a wind
Of memory murmuring the past.

Yea, tho' it spake and bared to view
  A fact within the coming year;

And tho' the months, revolving near,
  Should prove the phantom-warning true,

They might not seem thy prophecies,
  But spiritual presentiments,
  And such refraction of events
As often rises ere they rise.

### XCIII

I shall not see thee.  Dare I say
  No spirit ever brake the band
  That stays him from the native land
Where first he walk'd when claspt in clay?

No visual shade of some one lost,
  But he, the Spirit himself, may come
  Where all the nerve of sense is numb,
Spirit to Spirit, Ghost to Ghost.

O, therefore from thy sightless range
  With gods in unconjectured bliss,
  O, from the distance of the abyss
Of tenfold-complicated change,

Descend, and touch, and enter; hear
  The wish too strong for words to name,
  That in this blindness of the frame
My Ghost may feel that thine is near.

### XCIV

How pure at heart and sound in head,
  With what divine affections bold
  Should be the man whose thought would
     hold
An hour's communion with the dead.

In vain shalt thou, or any, call
  The spirits from their golden day,
  Except, like them, thou too canst say,
My spirit is at peace with all.

They haunt the silence of the breast,
  Imaginations calm and fair,
  The memory like a cloudless air,
The conscience as a sea at rest;

But when the heart is full of din,
  And doubt beside the portal waits,
  They can but listen at the gates,
And hear the household jar within.

### XCV

By night we linger'd on the lawn,
  For underfoot the herb was dry;

And genial warmth; and o'er the sky
  The silvery haze of summer drawn;

And calm that let the tapers burn
  Unwavering: not a cricket chirr'd;
  The brook alone far-off was heard,
And on the board the fluttering urn.

And bats went round in fragrant skies,
  And wheel'd or lit the filmy shapes
  That haunt the dusk, with ermine capes
And woolly breasts and beaded eyes;

While now we sang old songs that peal'd
  From knoll to knoll, where, couch'd at
     ease,
  The white kine glimmer'd, and the trees
Laid their dark arms about the field.

But when those others, one by one,
  Withdrew themselves from me and night,
  And in the house light after light
Went out, and I was all alone,

A hunger seized my heart; I read
  Of that glad year which once had been,
  In those fallen leaves which kept their
     green,
The noble letters of the dead.

And strangely on the silence broke
  The silent-speaking words, and strange
  Was love's dumb cry defying change
To test his worth; and strangely spoke

The faith, the vigor, bold to dwell
  On doubts that drive the coward back,
  And keen thro' wordy snares to track
Suggestion to her inmost cell.

So word by word, and line by line,
  The dead man touch'd me from the
     past,
  And all at once it seem'd at last
The living soul was flash'd on mine,

And mine in this was wound, and whirl'd
  About empyreal heights of thought,
  And came on that which is, and caught
The deep pulsations of the world,

Æonian music measuring out
  The steps of Time — the shocks of
    Chance —

The blows of Death. At length my
    trance
Was cancell'd, stricken thro' with doubt.

Vague words! but ah, how hard to frame
    In matter-moulded forms of speech,
    Or even for intellect to reach
Thro' memory that which I became;

Till now the doubtful dusk reveal'd
    The knolls once more where, couch'd at
      ease,
    The white kine glimmer'd, and the trees
Laid their dark arms about the field;

And suck'd from out the distant gloom
    A breeze began to tremble o'er
    The large leaves of the sycamore,
And fluctuate all the still perfume,

And gathering freshlier overhead,
    Rock'd the full-foliaged elms, and swung
    The heavy-folded rose, and flung
The lilies to and fro, and said,

'The dawn, the dawn,' and died away;
    And East and West, without a breath,
    Mixt their dim lights, like life and
      death,
To broaden into boundless day.

### XCVI

You say, but with no touch of scorn,
    Sweet-hearted, you, whose light-blue eyes
    Are tender over drowning flies,
You tell me, doubt is Devil-born.

I know not: one indeed I knew
    In many a subtle question versed,
    Who touch'd a jarring lyre at first,
But ever strove to make it true;

Perplext in faith, but pure in deeds,
    At last he beat his music out.
    There lives more faith in honest doubt,
Believe me, than in half the creeds.

He fought his doubts and gather'd strength,
    He would not make his judgment blind,
    He faced the spectres of the mind
And laid them; thus he came at length

To find a stronger faith his own,
    And Power was with him in the night,

Which makes the darkness and the
    light,
And dwells not in the light alone,

But in the darkness and the cloud,
    As over Sinaï's peaks of old,
    While Israel made their gods of gold,
Altho' the trumpet blew so loud.

### XCVII

My love has talk'd with rocks and trees;
    He finds on misty mountain-ground
    His own vast shadow glory-crown'd;
He sees himself in all he sees.

Two partners of a married life —
    I look'd on these and thought of thee
    In vastness and in mystery,
And of my spirit as of a wife.

These two — they dwelt with eye on eye,
    Their hearts of old have beat in tune,
    Their meetings made December June,
Their every parting was to die.

Their love has never past away;
    The days she never can forget
    Are earnest that he loves her yet,
Whate'er the faithless people say.

Her life is lone, he sits apart;
    He loves her yet, she will not weep,
    Tho' rapt in matters dark and deep
He seems to slight her simple heart.

He thrids the labyrinth of the mind,
    He reads the secret of the star,
    He seems so near and yet so far,
He looks so cold: she thinks him kind.

She keeps the gift of years before,
    A wither'd violet is her bliss;
    She knows not what his greatness is,
For that, for all, she loves him more.

For him she plays, to him she sings
    Of early faith and plighted vows;
    She knows but matters of the house,
And he, he knows a thousand things.

Her faith is fixt and cannot move,
    She darkly feels him great and wise,
    She dwells on him with faithful eyes,
'I cannot understand; I love.'

### XCVIII

You leave us: you will see the Rhine,
  And those fair hills I sail'd below,
  When I was there with him; and go
By summer belts of wheat and vine

To where he breathed his latest breath,
  That city.   All her splendor seems
  No livelier than the wisp that gleams
On Lethe in the eyes of Death.

Let her great Danube rolling fair
  Enwind her isles, unmark'd of me;
  I have not seen, I will not see
Vienna; rather dream that there,

A treble darkness, Evil haunts
  The birth, the bridal; friend from friend
  Is oftener parted, fathers bend
Above more graves, a thousand wants

Gnarr at the heels of men, and prey
  By each cold hearth, and sadness flings
  Her shadow on the blaze of kings.
And yet myself have heard him say,

That not in any mother town
  With statelier progress to and fro
  The double tides of chariots flow
By park and suburb under brown

Of lustier leaves; nor more content,
  He told me, lives in any crowd,
  When all is gay with lamps, and loud
With sport and song, in booth and tent,

Imperial halls, or open plain;
  And wheels the circled dance, and breaks
  The rocket molten into flakes
Of crimson or in emerald rain.

### XCIX

Risest thou thus, dim dawn, again,
  So loud with voices of the birds,
  So thick with lowings of the herds,
Day, when I lost the flower of men;

Who tremblest thro' thy darkling red
  On yon swollen brook that bubbles fast
  By meadows breathing of the past,
And woodlands holy to the dead;

Who murmurest in the foliaged eaves
  A song that slights the coming care,

And Autumn laying here and there
A fiery finger on the leaves;

Who wakenest with thy balmy breath
  To myriads on the genial earth,
  Memories of bridal, or of birth,
And unto myriads more, of death.

O, wheresoever those may be,
  Betwixt the slumber of the poles,
  To-day they count as kindred souls;
They know me not, but mourn with me.

### C

I climb the hill: from end to end
  Of all the landscape underneath,
  I find no place that does not breathe
Some gracious memory of my friend;

No gray old grange, or lonely fold,
  Or low morass and whispering reed,
  Or simple stile from mead to mead,
Or sheepwalk up the windy wold;

Nor hoary knoll of ash and haw
  That hears the latest linnet trill,
  Nor quarry trench'd along the hill
And haunted by the wrangling daw;

Nor runlet tinkling from the rock;
  Nor pastoral rivulet that swerves
  To left and right thro' meadowy curves,
That feed the mothers of the flock;

But each has pleased a kindred eye,
  And each reflects a kindlier day;
  And, leaving these, to pass away,
I think once more he seems to die.

### CI

Unwatch'd, the garden bough shall sway,
  The tender blossom flutter down,
  Unloved, that beech will gather brown,
This maple burn itself away;

Unloved, the sunflower, shining fair,
  Ray round with flames her disk of
    seed,
  And many a rose-carnation feed
With summer spice the humming air;

Unloved, by many a sandy bar,
  The brook shall babble down the plain,
  At noon or when the Lesser Wain
Is twisting round the polar star;

Uncared for, gird the windy grove,
  And flood the haunts of hern and crake,
  Or into silver arrows break
The sailing moon in creek and cove;

Till from the garden and the wild
  A fresh association blow,
  And year by year the landscape grow
Familiar to the stranger's child;

As year by year the laborer tills
  His wonted glebe, or lops the glades,
  And year by year our memory fades
From all the circle of the hills.

## CII

We leave the well-beloved place
  Where first we gazed upon the sky;
  The roofs that heard our earliest cry
Will shelter one of stranger race.

We go, but ere we go from home,
  As down the garden-walks I move,
  Two spirits of a diverse love
Contend for loving masterdom.

One whispers, ' Here thy boyhood sung
  Long since its matin song, and heard
  The low love-language of the bird
In native hazels tassel-hung.'

The other answers, ' Yea, but here
  Thy feet have stray'd in after hours
  With thy lost friend among the bowers,
And this hath made them trebly dear.'

These two have striven half the day,
  And each prefers his separate claim,
  Poor rivals in a losing game,
That will not yield each other way.

I turn to go; my feet are set
  To leave the pleasant fields and farms;
  They mix in one another's arms
To one pure image of regret.

## CIII

On that last night before we went
  From out the doors where I was bred,
  I dream'd a vision of the dead,
Which left my after-morn content.

Methought I dwelt within a hall,
  And maidens with me; distant hills

From hidden summits fed with rills
A river sliding by the wall.

The hall with harp and carol rang.
  They sang of what is wise and good
  And graceful.   In the centre stood
A statue veil'd, to which they sang;

And which, tho' veil'd, was known to me,
  The shape of him I loved, and love
  For ever.   Then flew in a dove
And brought a summons from the sea;

And when they learnt that I must go,
  They wept and wail'd, but led the way
  To where a little shallop lay
At anchor in the flood below;

And on by many a level mead,
  And shadowing bluff that made the banks,
  We glided winding under ranks
Of iris and the golden reed;

And still as vaster grew the shore
  And roll'd the floods in grander space,
  The maidens gather'd strength and grace
And presence, lordlier than before;

And I myself, who sat apart
  And watch'd them, wax'd in every limb;
  I felt the thews of Anakim,
The pulses of a Titan's heart;

As one would sing the death of war,
  And one would chant the history
  Of that great race which is to be,
And one the shaping of a star;

Until the forward-creeping tides
  Began to foam, and we to draw
  From deep to deep, to where we saw
A great ship lift her shining sides.

The man we loved was there on deck,
  But thrice as large as man he bent
  To greet us.   Up the side I went,
And fell in silence on his neck;

Whereat those maidens with one mind
  Bewail'd their lot; I did them wrong:
  ' We served thee here,' they said, ' so long,
And wilt thou leave us now behind ? '

So rapt I was, they could not win
    An answer from my lips, but he
    Replying, 'Enter likewise ye
And go with us:' they enter'd in.

And while the wind began to sweep
    A music out of sheet and shroud,
    We steer'd her toward a crimson cloud
That landlike slept along the deep.

### CIV

The time draws near the birth of Christ;
    The moon is hid, the night is still;
    A single church below the hill
Is pealing, folded in the mist.

A single peal of bells below,
    That wakens at this hour of rest
    A single murmur in the breast,
That these are not the bells I know.

Like strangers' voices here they sound,
    In lands where not a memory strays,
    Nor landmark breathes of other days,
But all is new unhallow'd ground.

### CV

To-night ungather'd let us leave
    This laurel, let this holly stand:
    We live within the stranger's land,
And strangely falls our Christmas-eve.

Our father's dust is left alone
    And silent under other snows:
    There in due time the woodbine blows,
The violet comes, but we are gone.

No more shall wayward grief abuse
    The genial hour with mask and mime;
    For change of place, like growth of time,
Has broke the bond of dying use.

Let cares that petty shadows cast,
    By which our lives are chiefly proved,
    A little spare the night I loved,
And hold it solemn to the past.

But let no footstep beat the floor,
    Nor bowl of wassail mantle warm;
    For who would keep an ancient form
Thro' which the spirit breathes no more?

Be neither song, nor game, nor feast;
    Nor harp be touch'd, nor flute be blown;

No dance, no motion, save alone
What lightens in the lucid East

Of rising worlds by yonder wood.
    Long sleeps the summer in the seed;
    Run out your measured arcs, and lead
The closing cycle rich in good.

### CVI

Ring out, wild bells, to the wild sky,
    The flying cloud, the frosty light:
    The year is dying in the night;
Ring out, wild bells, and let him die.

Ring out the old, ring in the new,
    Ring, happy bells, across the snow:
    The year is going, let him go;
Ring out the false, ring in the true.

Ring out the grief that saps the mind,
    For those that here we see no more;
    Ring out the feud of rich and poor,
Ring in redress to all mankind.

Ring out a slowly dying cause,
    And ancient forms of party strife;
    Ring in the nobler modes of life,
With sweeter manners, purer laws.

Ring out the want, the care, the sin,
    The faithless coldness of the times;
    Ring out, ring out my mournful rhymes,
But ring the fuller minstrel in.

Ring out false pride in place and blood,
    The civic slander and the spite;
    Ring in the love of truth and right,
Ring in the common love of good.

Ring out old shapes of foul disease;
    Ring out the narrowing lust of gold;
    Ring out the thousand wars of old,
Ring in the thousand years of peace.

Ring in the valiant man and free,
    The larger heart, the kindlier hand;
    Ring out the darkness of the land,
Ring in the Christ that is to be.

### CVII

It is the day when he was born,
    A bitter day that early sank
    Behind a purple-frosty bank
Of vapor, leaving night forlorn.

The time admits not flowers or leaves
  To deck the banquet.  Fiercely flies
  The blast of North and East, and ice
Makes daggers at the sharpen'd eaves,

And bristles all the brakes and thorns
  To yon hard crescent, as she hangs
  Above the wood which grides and clangs
Its leafless ribs and iron horns

Together, in the drifts that pass
  To darken on the rolling brine
  That breaks the coast.  But fetch the
      wine,
Arrange the board and brim the glass;

Bring in great logs and let them lie,
  To make a solid core of heat;
  Be cheerful-minded, talk and treat
Of all things even as he were by;

We keep the day.  With festal cheer,
  With books and music, surely we
  Will drink to him, whate'er he be,
And sing the songs he loved to hear.

### CVIII

I will not shut me from my kind,
  And, lest I stiffen into stone,
  I will not eat my heart alone,
Nor feed with sighs a passing wind:

What profit lies in barren faith,
  And vacant yearning, tho' with might
  To scale the heaven's highest height,
Or dive below the wells of death ?

What find I in the highest place,
  But mine own phantom chanting hymns ?
  And on the depths of death there swims
The reflex of a human face.

I 'll rather take what fruit may be
  Of sorrow under human skies:
  'T is held that sorrow makes us wise,
Whatever wisdom sleep with thee.

### CIX

Heart-affluence in discursive talk
  From household fountains never dry;
  The critic clearness of an eye
That saw thro' all the Muses' walk;

Seraphic intellect and force
  To seize and throw the doubts of man;

Impassion'd logic, which outran
The hearer in its fiery course;

High nature amorous of the good,
  But touch'd with no ascetic gloom;
  And passion pure in snowy bloom
Thro' all the years of April blood;

A love of freedom rarely felt,
  Of freedom in her regal seat
  Of England; not the schoolboy heat,
The blind hysterics of the Celt;

And manhood fused with female grace
  In such a sort, the child would twine
  A trustful hand, unask'd, in thine,
And find his comfort in thy face;

All these have been, and thee mine eyes
  Have look'd on: if they look'd in vain,
  My shame is greater who remain,
Nor let thy wisdom make me wise.

### CX

Thy converse drew us with delight,
  The men of rathe and riper years;
  The feeble soul, a haunt of fears,
Forgot his weakness in thy sight.

On thee the loyal-hearted hung,
  The proud was half disarm'd of pride,
  Nor cared the serpent at thy side
To flicker with his double tongue.

The stern were mild when thou wert by,
  The flippant put himself to school
  And heard thee, and the brazen fool
Was soften'd, and he knew not why;

While I, thy nearest, sat apart,
  And felt thy triumph was as mine;
  And loved them more, that they were
      thine,
The graceful tact, the Christian art;

Nor mine the sweetness or the skill,
  But mine the love that will not tire,
  And, born of love, the vague desire
That spurs an imitative will.

### CXI

The churl in spirit, up or down
  Along the scale of ranks, thro' all,
  To him who grasps a golden ball,
By blood a king, at heart a clown, —

The churl in spirit, howe'er he veil
  His want in forms for fashion's sake,
  Will let his coltish nature break
At seasons thro' the gilded pale;

For who can always act? but he,
  To whom a thousand memories call,
  Not being less but more than all
The gentleness he seem'd to be,

Best seem'd the thing he was, and join'd
  Each office of the social hour
  To noble manners, as the flower
And native growth of noble mind;

Nor ever narrowness or spite,
  Or villain fancy fleeting by,
  Drew in the expression of an eye
Where God and Nature met in light;

And thus he bore without abuse
  The grand old name of gentleman,
  Defamed by every charlatan,
And soil'd with all ignoble use.

### CXII

High wisdom holds my wisdom less,
  That I, who gaze with temperate eyes
  On glorious insufficiencies,
Set light by narrower perfectness.

But thou, that fillest all the room
  Of all my love, art reason why
  I seem to cast a careless eye
On souls, the lesser lords of doom.

For what wert thou? some novel power
  Sprang up for ever at a touch,
  And hope could never hope too much,
In watching thee from hour to hour,

Large elements in order brought,
  And tracts of calm from tempest made,
  And world-wide fluctuation sway'd
In vassal tides that follow'd thought.

### CXIII

'T is held that sorrow makes us wise;
  Yet how much wisdom sleeps with thee
  Which not alone had guided me,
But served the seasons that may rise;

For can I doubt, who knew thee keen
  In intellect, with force and skill

To strive, to fashion, to fulfil —
I doubt not what thou wouldst have been:

A life in civic action warm,
  A soul on highest mission sent,
  A potent voice of Parliament,
A pillar steadfast in the storm,

Should licensed boldness gather force,
  Becoming, when the time has birth,
  A lever to uplift the earth
And roll it in another course,

With thousand shocks that come and go,
  With agonies, with energies,
  With overthrowings, and with cries,
And undulations to and fro.

### CXIV

Who loves not Knowledge? Who shall
    rail
  Against her beauty? May she mix
  With men and prosper! Who shall fix
Her pillars? Let her work prevail.

But on her forehead sits a fire;
  She sets her forward countenance
  And leaps into the future chance,
Submitting all things to desire.

Half-grown as yet, a child, and vain —
  She cannot fight the fear of death.
  What is she, cut from love and faith,
But some wild Pallas from the brain

Of demons? fiery-hot to burst
  All barriers in her onward race
  For power. Let her know her place;
She is the second, not the first.

A higher hand must make her mild,
  If all be not in vain, and guide
  Her footsteps, moving side by side
With Wisdom, like the younger child;

For she is earthly of the mind,
  But Wisdom heavenly of the soul.
  O friend, who camest to thy goal
So early, leaving me behind,

I would the great world grew like thee,
  Who grewest not alone in power
  And knowledge, but by year and hour
In reverence and in charity.

### CXV

Now fades the last long streak of snow,
 Now burgeons every maze of quick
 About the flowering squares, and thick
By ashen roots the violets blow.

Now rings the woodland loud and long,
 The distance takes a lovelier hue,
 And drown'd in yonder living blue
The lark becomes a sightless song.

Now dance the lights on lawn and lea,
 The flocks are whiter down the vale,
 And milkier every milky sail
On winding stream or distant sea;

Where now the seamew pipes, or dives
 In yonder greening gleam, and fly
 The happy birds, that change their sky
To build and brood, that live their lives

From land to land; and in my breast
 Spring wakens too, and my regret
 Becomes an April violet,
And buds and blossoms like the rest.

### CXVI

Is it, then, regret for buried time
 That keenlier in sweet April wakes,
 And meets the year, and gives and takes
The colors of the crescent prime?

Not all: the songs, the stirring air,
 The life re-orient out of dust,
 Cry thro' the sense to hearten trust
In that which made the world so fair.

Not all regret: the face will shine
 Upon me, while I muse alone,
 And that dear voice, I once have known,
Still speak to me of me and mine.

Yet less of sorrow lives in me
 For days of happy commune dead,
 Less yearning for the friendship fled
Than some strong bond which is to be.

### CXVII

O days and hours, your work is this,
 To hold me from my proper place,
 A little while from his embrace,
For fuller gain of after bliss;

That out of distance might ensue
 Desire of nearness doubly sweet,
 And unto meeting, when we meet,
Delight a hundredfold accrue,

For every grain of sand that runs,
 And every span of shade that steals,
 And every kiss of toothed wheels,
And all the courses of the suns.

### CXVIII

Contemplate all this work of Time,
 The giant laboring in his youth;
 Nor dream of human love and truth,
As dying Nature's earth and lime;

But trust that those we call the dead
 Are breathers of an ampler day
 For ever nobler ends.   They say,
The solid earth whereon we tread

In tracts of fluent heat began,
 And grew to seeming-random forms,
 The seeming prey of cyclic storms,
Till at the last arose the man;

Who throve and branch'd from clime to
    clime,
 The herald of a higher race,
 And of himself in higher place,
If so he type this work of time

Within himself, from more to more;
 Or, crown'd with attributes of woe
 Like glories, move his course, and show
That life is not as idle ore,

But iron dug from central gloom,
 And heated hot with burning fears,
 And dipt in baths of hissing tears,
And batter'd with the shocks of doom

To shape and use.   Arise and fly
 The reeling Faun, the sensual feast;
 Move upward, working out the beast,
And let the ape and tiger die.

### CXIX

Doors, where my heart was used to beat
 So quickly, not as one that weeps
 I come once more; the city sleeps;
I smell the meadow in the street;

I hear a chirp of birds; I see
 Betwixt the black fronts long-withdrawn

A light-blue lane of early dawn,
And think of early days and thee,

And bless thee, for thy lips are bland,
And bright the friendship of thine eye;
And in my thoughts with scarce a sigh
I take the pressure of thine hand.

### CXX

I trust I have not wasted breath:
I think we are not wholly brain,
Magnetic mockeries; not in vain,
Like Paul with beasts, I fought with Death;

Not only cunning casts in clay:
Let Science prove we are, and then
What matters Science unto men,
At least to me? I would not stay.

Let him, the wiser man who springs
Hereafter, up from childhood shape
His action like the greater ape,
But I was *born* to other things.

### CXXI

Sad Hesper o'er the buried sun
And ready, thou, to die with him,
Thou watchest all things ever dim
And dimmer, and a glory done.

The team is loosen'd from the wain,
The boat is drawn upon the shore;
Thou listenest to the closing door,
And life is darken'd in the brain.

Bright Phosphor, fresher for the night,
By thee the world's great work is heard
Beginning, and the wakeful bird;
Behind thee comes the greater light.

The market boat is on the stream,
And voices hail it from the brink;
Thou hear'st the village hammer clink,
And see'st the moving of the team.

Sweet Hesper-Phosphor, double name
For what is one, the first, the last,
Thou, like my present and my past,
Thy place is changed; thou art the same.

### CXXII

O, wast thou with me, dearest, then,
While I rose up against my doom,
And yearn'd to burst the folded gloom,
To bare the eternal heavens again,

To feel once more, in placid awe,
The strong imagination roll
A sphere of stars about my soul,
In all her motion one with law?

If thou wert with me, and the grave
Divide us not, be with me now,
And enter in at breast and brow,
Till all my blood, a fuller wave,

Be quicken'd with a livelier breath,
And like an inconsiderate boy,
As in the former flash of joy,
I slip the thoughts of life and death;

And all the breeze of Fancy blows,
And every dewdrop paints a bow,
The wizard lightnings deeply glow,
And every thought breaks out a rose.

### CXXIII

There rolls the deep where grew the tree.
O earth, what changes hast thou seen!
There where the long street roars hath
been
The stillness of the central sea.

The hills are shadows, and they flow
From form to form, and nothing stands;
They melt like mist, the solid lands,
Like clouds they shape themselves and go.

But in my spirit will I dwell,
And dream my dream, and hold it true;
For tho' my lips may breathe adieu,
I cannot think the thing farewell.

### CXXIV

That which we dare invoke to bless;
Our dearest faith; our ghastliest doubt;
He, They, One, All; within, without;
The Power in darkness whom we guess,—

I found Him not in world or sun,
Or eagle's wing, or insect's eye,
Nor thro' the questions men may try,
The petty cobwebs we have spun.

If e'er when faith had fallen asleep,
I heard a voice, 'believe no more,'
And heard an ever-breaking shore
That tumbled in the Godless deep,

A warmth within the breast would melt
The freezing reason's colder part,

And like a man in wrath the heart
Stood up and answer'd, 'I have felt.'

No, like a child in doubt and fear:
  But that blind clamor made me wise;
  Then was I as a child that cries,
But, crying, knows his father near;

And what I am beheld again
  What is, and no man understands;
  And out of darkness came the hands
That reach thro' nature, moulding men.

## CXXV

Whatever I have said or sung,
  Some bitter notes my harp would give,
  Yea, tho' there often seem'd to live
A contradiction on the tongue,

Yet Hope had never lost her youth,
  She did but look through dimmer eyes;
  Or Love but play'd with gracious lies,
Because he felt so fix'd in truth;

And if the song were full of care,
  He breathed the spirit of the song;
  And if the words were sweet and strong
He set his royal signet there;

Abiding with me till I sail
  To seek thee on the mystic deeps,
  And this electric force, that keeps
A thousand pulses dancing, fail.

## CXXVI

Love is and was my lord and king,
  And in his presence I attend
  To hear the tidings of my friend,
Which every hour his couriers bring.

Love is and was my king and lord,
  And will be, tho' as yet I keep
  Within the court on earth, and sleep
Encompass'd by his faithful guard,

And hear at times a sentinel
  Who moves about from place to place,
  And whispers to the worlds of space,
In the deep night, that all is well.

## CXXVII

And all is well, tho' faith and form
  Be sunder'd in the night of fear;
  Well roars the storm to those that hear
A deeper voice across the storm,

Proclaiming social truth shall spread,
  And justice, even tho' thrice again
  The red fool-fury of the Seine
Should pile her barricades with dead.

But ill for him that wears a crown,
  And him, the lazar, in his rags!
  They tremble, the sustaining crags;
The spires of ice are toppled down,

And molten up, and roar in flood;
  The fortress crashes from on high,
  The brute earth lightens to the sky,
And the great Æon sinks in blood,

And compass'd by the fires of hell;
  While thou, dear spirit, happy star,
  O'erlook'st the tumult from afar,
And smilest, knowing all is well.

## CXXVIII

The love that rose on stronger wings,
  Unpalsied when he met with Death,
  Is comrade of the lesser faith
That sees the course of human things.

No doubt vast eddies in the flood
  Of onward time shall yet be made,
  And throned races may degrade;
Yet, O ye mysteries of good,

Wild Hours that fly with Hope and Fear,
  If all your office had to do
  With old results that look like new —
If this were all your mission here,

To draw, to sheathe a useless sword,
  To fool the crowd with glorious lies,
  To cleave a creed in sects and cries,
To change the bearing of a word,

To shift an arbitrary power,
  To cramp the student at his desk,
  To make old bareness picturesque
And tuft with grass a feudal tower,

Why, then my scorn might well descend
  On you and yours. I see in part
  That all, as in some piece of art,
Is toil coöperant to an end.

## CXXIX

Dear friend, far off, my lost desire,
  So far, so near in woe and weal,
  O loved the most, when most I feel
There is a lower and a higher;

Known and unknown, human, divine;
  Sweet human hand and lips and eye;
  Dear heavenly friend that canst not
      die,
Mine, mine, for ever, ever mine;

Strange friend, past, present, and to be;
  Loved deeplier, darklier understood;
  Behold, I dream a dream of good,
And mingle all the world with thee.

### CXXX

Thy voice is on the rolling air;
  I hear thee where the waters run;
  Thou standest in the rising sun,
And in the setting thou art fair.

What art thou then?  I cannot guess;
  But tho' I seem in star and flower
  To feel thee some diffusive power,
I do not therefore love thee less.

My love involves the love before;
  My love is vaster passion now;
  Tho' mix'd with God and Nature thou,
I seem to love thee more and more.

Far off thou art, but ever nigh;
  I have thee still, and I rejoice;
  I prosper, circled with thy voice;
I shall not lose thee tho' I die.

### CXXXI

O living will that shalt endure
  When all that seems shall suffer shock,
  Rise in the spiritual rock,
Flow thro' our deeds and make them
      pure,

That we may lift from out of dust
  A voice as unto him that hears,
  A cry above the conquer'd years
To one that with us works, and trust,

With faith that comes of self-control,
  The truths that never can be proved
  Until we close with all we loved,
And all we flow from, soul in soul.

_____

O true and tried, so well and long,
  Demand not thou a marriage lay;
  In that it is thy marriage day
Is music more than any song.

Nor have I felt so much of bliss
  Since first he told me that he loved
  A daughter of our house, nor proved
Since that dark day a day like this;

Tho' I since then have number'd o'er
  Some thrice three years; they went and
      came,
  Remade the blood and changed the
      frame,
And yet is love not less, but more;

No longer caring to embalm
  In dying songs a dead regret,
  But like a statue solid-set,
And moulded in colossal calm.

Regret is dead, but love is more
  Than in the summers that are flown,
  For I myself with these have grown
To something greater than before;

Which makes appear the songs I made
  As echoes out of weaker times,
  As half but idle brawling rhymes,
The sport of random sun and shade.

But where is she, the bridal flower,
  That must be made a wife ere noon?
  She enters, glowing like the moon
Of Eden on its bridal bower.

On me she bends her blissful eyes
  And then on thee; they meet thy look
  And brighten like the star that shook
Betwixt the palms of Paradise.

O, when her life was yet in bud,
  He too foretold the perfect rose.
  For thee she grew, for thee she grows
For ever, and as fair as good.

And thou art worthy, full of power;
  As gentle; liberal-minded, great,
  Consistent; wearing all that weight
Of learning lightly like a flower.

But now set out: the noon is near,
  And I must give away the bride;
  She fears not, or with thee beside
And me behind her, will not fear.

For I that danced her on my knee,
  That watch'd her on her nurse's arm,

That shielded all her life from harm,
At last must part with her to thee;

Now waiting to be made a wife,
  Her feet, my darling, on the dead;
  Their pensive tablets round her head,
And the most living words of life

Breathed in her ear.  The ring is on,
  The ' Wilt thou ? ' answer'd, and again
  The ' Wilt thou ? ' ask'd, till out of twain
Her sweet ' I will ' has made you one.

Now sign your names, which shall be read,
  Mute symbols of a joyful morn,
  By village eyes as yet unborn.
The names are sign'd, and overhead

Begins the clash and clang that tells
  The joy to every wandering breeze;
  The blind wall rocks, and on the trees
The dead leaf trembles to the bells.

O happy hour, and happier hours
  Await them.  Many a merry face
  Salutes them — maidens of the place,
That pelt us in the porch with flowers.

O happy hour, behold the bride
  With him to whom her hand I gave.
  They leave the porch, they pass the grave
That has to-day its sunny side.

To-day the grave is bright for me,
  For them the light of life increased,
  Who stay to share the morning feast,
Who rest to-night beside the sea.

Let all my genial spirits advance
  To meet and greet a whiter sun;
  My drooping memory will not shun
The foaming grape of eastern France.

It circles round, and fancy plays,
  And hearts are warm'd and faces bloom,
  As drinking health to bride and groom
We wish them store of happy days.

Nor count me all to blame if I
  Conjecture of a stiller guest,
  Perchance, perchance, among the rest,
And, tho' in silence, wishing joy.

But they must go, the time draws on,
  And those white-favor'd horses wait;

They rise, but linger; it is late;
Farewell, we kiss, and they are gone.

A shade falls on us like the dark
  From little cloudlets on the grass,
  But sweeps away as out we pass
To range the woods, to roam the park,

Discussing how their courtship grew,
  And talk of others that are wed,
  And how she look'd, and what he said,
And back we come at fall of dew.

Again the feast, the speech, the glee,
  The shade of passing thought, the
    wealth
  Of words and wit, the double health,
The crowning cup, the three-times-three,

And last the dance; — till I retire.
  Dumb is that tower which spake so
    loud,
  And high in heaven the streaming cloud,
And on the downs a rising fire:

And rise, O moon, from yonder down,
  Till over down and over dale
  All night the shining vapor sail
And pass the silent-lighted town,

The white-faced halls, the glancing rills,
  And catch at every mountain head,
  And o'er the friths that branch and
    spread
Their sleeping silver thro' the hills;

And touch with shade the bridal doors,
  With tender gloom the roof, the wall;
  And breaking let the splendor fall
To spangle all the happy shores

By which they rest, and ocean sounds,
  And, star and system rolling past,
  A soul shall draw from out the vast
And strike his being into bounds,

And, moved thro' life of lower phase,
  Result in man, be born and think,
  And act and love, a closer link
Betwixt us and the crowning race

Of those that, eye to eye, shall look
  On knowledge; under whose command
  Is Earth and Earth's, and in their hand
Is Nature like an open book;

No longer half-akin to brute,
  For all we thought and loved and did,
  And hoped, and suffer'd, is but seed
Of what in them is flower and fruit;

Whereof the man that with me trod
  This planet was a noble type

Appearing ere the times were ripe,
That friend of mine who lives in God,

That God, which ever lives and loves,
  One God, one law, one element,
  And one far-off divine event,
To which the whole creation moves.


## MAUD, AND OTHER POEMS

This volume, published in 1855, contained in addition to 'Maud' the following poems: 'The Brook,' 'The Letters,' 'The Daisy,' 'Will,' 'Lines to the Rev. F. D. Maurice' (all published for the first time); with the 'Ode on the Death of the Duke of Wellington,' already printed twice (1852, 1853) in pamphlet form, and 'The Charge of the Light Brigade,' reprinted from the 'Examiner' of December 9, 1854 (also privately reprinted in 1855). A second edition of the volume was published in 1856, when 'Maud' was considerably enlarged.


### MAUD; A MONODRAMA

This poem grew out of the lines, 'O, that 't were possible,' etc., printed in 'The Tribute' in 1837, and now forming (with some alterations) the fourth section of Part II. of the poem. Sir John Simeon, to whom Tennyson read these lines in the earlier days of their friendship, suggested that something was needed to explain the story. On this hint the poem was founded, and the greater part of it was written under a certain cedar in Sir John's grounds at Swainston. For the additions made in 1856, and minor alterations made afterwards, see the Notes.

The earlier critics of the poem failed to recognize its dramatic character. They ascribed to the author the thoughts and sentiments which he puts into the mouth of the morbid young man who is the *dramatis persona;* for, as in recent editions it has been designated, the poem is a 'monodrama,' and, in that respect, unique. Tennyson, when reading it to Mr. Knowles, said (as in substance he said when reading it to me): 'It should be called "Maud, or the Madness."' It is slightly akin to "Hamlet." No other poem (a monotone with plenty of change and no weariness) has been made into a drama where successive phases of passion in one person take the place of successive persons.' At the end of 'Maud' he declared, 'I've always said that "Maud" and "Guinevere" were the finest things I've written.'

To Dr. Van Dyke, who in the first edition of 'The Poetry of Tennyson' had called 'Maud' a 'splendid failure,' he said: 'I want to read this to you because I want you to feel what the poem means. It is dramatic; it is the story of a man who has a morbid nature, with a touch of inherited insanity, and very selfish. The poem is to show what love does for him. The war is only an episode. You must remember that it is not I myself speaking. It is this man with the strain of madness in his blood, and the memory of a great trouble and wrong that has put him out with the world.'

I felt, when I heard the poet read 'Maud,' that it was the best possible commentary on the poem. I had not misunderstood it, as Dr. Van Dyke did at first, but the reading made me see heights and depths in it of which I had had no conception before. Especially was I amazed, as my friend was, at 'the intensity with which the poet had felt, and the tenacity with which he had pursued, the moral meaning of the poem. It was love, but not love in itself alone, as an emotion, an inward experience, a selfish possession, that he was revealing. It was love as a vital force, love as a part of life, love as an influence, — nay, *the* influence which rescues the soul from the prison, or the madhouse, of self, and leads it into the larger, saner existence. This was the theme of "Maud." And the poet's voice brought it out, and rang the changes on it, so that it was unmistakable and unforgettable, — the history of a man saved from selfish despair by a pure love.' For his last reading of the poem, see the 'Memoir,' vol. i. page 395.

The motto of 'Maud' might well have been the lines from 'Locksley Hall' which the poet was fond of copying when friends asked for his autograph: —

Love took up the harp of Life, and smote on all the
    chords with might;
Smote the chord of Self, that, trembling, past in music
    out of sight.

# PART I

## I

**I**

I HATE the dreadful hollow behind the little wood;
Its lips in the field above are dabbled with blood-red heath,
The red-ribb'd ledges drip with a silent horror of blood,
And Echo there, whatever is ask'd her, answers 'Death.'

## II

For there in the ghastly pit long since a body was found,
His who had given me life — O father ! O God ! was it well ? —
Mangled, and flatten'd, and crush'd, and dinted into the ground;
There yet lies the rock that fell with him when he fell.

## III

Did he fling himself down? who knows? for a vast speculation had fail'd,
And ever he mutter'd and madden'd, and ever wann'd with despair,    10
And out he walk'd when the wind like a broken worldling wail'd,
And the flying gold of the ruin'd woodlands drove thro' the air.

## IV

I remember the time, for the roots of my hair were stirr'd
By a shuffled step, by a dead weight trail'd, by a whisper'd fright,
And my pulses closed their gates with a shock on my heart as I heard
The shrill-edged shriek of a mother divide the shuddering night.

## V

Villainy somewhere! whose? One says, we are villains all.
Not he; his honest fame should at least by me be maintained;
But that old man, now lord of the broad estate and the Hall,
Dropt off gorged from a scheme that had left us flaccid and drain'd.    20

## VI

Why do they prate of the blessings of peace? we have made them a curse,
Pickpockets, each hand lusting for all that is not its own;
And lust of gain, in the spirit of Cain, is it better or worse
Than the heart of the citizen hissing in war on his own hearthstone?

## VII

But these are the days of advance, the works of the men of mind,
When who but a fool would have faith in a tradesman's ware or his word?
Is it peace or war? Civil war, as I think, and that of a kind
The viler, as underhand, not openly bearing the sword.

## VIII

Sooner or later I too may passively take the print
Of the golden age — why not? I have neither hope nor trust;    30
May make my heart as a millstone, set my face as a flint,
Cheat and be cheated, and die — who knows? we are ashes and dust.

## IX

Peace sitting under her olive, and slurring the days gone by,
When the poor are hovell'd and hustled together, each sex, like swine,
When only the ledger lives, and when only not all men lie;
Peace in her vineyard — yes! — but a company forges the wine.

## X

And the vitriol madness flushes up in the ruffian's head,
Till the filthy by-lane rings to the yell of the trampled wife,
And chalk and alum and plaster are sold to the poor for bread,
And the spirit of murder works in the very means of life,    40

## XI

And Sleep must lie down arm'd, for the villainous centre-bits
Grind on the wakeful ear in the hush of the moonless nights,

While another is cheating the sick of a few
    last gasps, as he sits
To pestle a poison'd poison behind his crim-
    son lights.

### XII

When a Mammonite mother kills her babe
    for a burial fee,
And Timour-Mammon grins on a pile of
    children's bones,
Is it peace or war ? better, war ! loud war
    by land and by sea,
War with a thousand battles, and shaking
    a hundred thrones!

### XIII

For I trust if an enemy's fleet came yonder
    round by the hill,
And the rushing battle-bolt sang from the
    three-decker out of the foam,   50
That the smooth-faced, snub-nosed rogue
    would leap from his counter and till,
And strike, if he could, were it but with his
    cheating yardwand, home. —

### XIV

What ! am I raging alone as my father
    raged in his mood ?
Must *I* too creep to the hollow and dash
    myself down and die
Rather than hold by the law that I made,
    nevermore to brood
On a horror of shatter'd limbs and a
    wretched swindler's lie ?

### XV

Would there be sorrow for *me* ? there was
    *love* in the passionate shriek,
Love for the silent thing that had made
    false haste to the grave —
Wrapt in a cloak, as I saw him, and thought
    he would rise and speak
And rave at the lie and the liar, ah God, as
    he used to rave.   60

### XVI

I am sick of the Hall and the hill, I am
    sick of the moor and the main.
Why should I stay ? can a sweeter chance
    ever come to me here ?
O, having the nerves of motion as well as
    the nerves of pain,
Were it not wise if I fled from the place
    and the pit and the fear ?

### XVII

Workmen up at the Hall ! — they are com-
    ing back from abroad;
The dark old place will be gilt, by the touch
    of a millionaire.
I have heard, I know not whence, of the
    singular beauty of Maud;
I play'd with the girl when a child; she
    promised then to be fair.

### XVIII

Maud, with her venturous climbings and
    tumbles and childish escapes,
Maud, the delight of the village, the ring-
    ing joy of the Hall,   70
Maud, with her sweet purse-mouth when
    my father dangled the grapes,
Maud, the beloved of my mother, the
    moon-faced darling of all, —

### XIX

What is she now ? My dreams are bad.
    She may bring me a curse.
No, there is fatter game on the moor; she
    will let me alone.
Thanks; for the fiend best knows whether
    woman or man be the worse.
I will bury myself in myself, and the Devil
    may pipe to his own.

### II

Long have I sigh'd for a calm; God grant
    I may find it at last !
It will never be broken by Maud; she has
    neither savor nor salt,
But a cold and clear-cut face, as I found
    when her carriage past,
Perfectly beautiful; let it be granted her;
    where is the fault ?   80
All that I saw — for her eyes were down-
    cast, not to be seen —
Faultily faultless, icily regular, splendidly
    null,
Dead perfection, no more; nothing more,
    if it had not been
For a chance of travel, a paleness, an hour's
    defect of the rose,
Or an underlip, you may call it a little too
    ripe, too full,
Or the least little delicate aquiline curve
    in a sensitive nose,
From which I escaped heart-free, with the
    least little touch of spleen.

### III

Cold and clear-cut face, why come you so
    cruelly meek,
Breaking a slumber in which all spleenful
    folly was drown'd ?
Pale with the golden beam of an eyelash
    dead on the cheek,                    90
Passionless, pale, cold face, star-sweet on
    a gloom profound ;
Womanlike, taking revenge too deep for a
    transient wrong
Done but in thought to your beauty, and
    ever as pale as before
Growing and fading and growing upon me
    without a sound,
Luminous, gemlike, ghostlike, deathlike,
    half the night long
Growing and fading and growing, till I
    could bear it no more,
But arose, and all by myself in my own
    dark garden ground,
Listening now to the tide in its broad-flung
    shipwrecking roar,
Now to the scream of a madden'd beach
    dragg'd down by the wave,
Walk'd in a wintry wind by a ghastly
    glimmer, and found                    100
The shining daffodil dead, and Orion low
    in his grave.

### IV

#### I

A million emeralds break from the ruby-
    budded lime
In the little grove where I sit — ah, where-
    fore cannot I be
Like things of the season gay, like the
    bountiful season bland,
When the far-off sail is blown by the breeze
    of a softer clime,
Half-lost in the liquid azure bloom of a
    crescent of sea,
The silent sapphire-spangled marriage ring
    of the land ?

#### II

Below me, there, is the village, and looks
    how quiet and small !
And yet bubbles o'er like a city, with gos-
    sip, scandal, and spite ;
And Jack on his ale-house bench has as
    many lies as a Czar ;                    110

And here on the landward side, by a red
    rock, glimmers the Hall ;
And up in the high Hall-garden I see her
    pass like a light ;
But sorrow seize me if ever that light be
    my leading star !

#### III

When have I bow'd to her father, the
    wrinkled head of the race ?
I met her to-day with her brother, but not
    to her brother I bow'd ;
I bow'd to his lady-sister as she rode by on
    the moor,
But the fire of a foolish pride flash'd over
    her beautiful face.
O child, you wrong your beauty, believe it,
    in being so proud ;
Your father has wealth well-gotten, and I
    am nameless and poor.

#### IV

I keep but a man and a maid, ever ready
    to slander and steal ;                    120
I know it, and smile a hard-set smile, like
    a stoic, or like
A wiser epicurean, and let the world have
    its way.
For nature is one with rapine, a harm no
    preacher can heal ;
The Mayfly is torn by the swallow, the
    sparrow spear'd by the shrike,
And the whole little wood where I sit is a
    world of plunder and prey.

#### V

We are puppets, Man in his pride, and
    Beauty fair in her flower ;
Do we move ourselves, or are moved by an
    unseen hand at a game
That pushes us off from the board, and
    others ever succeed ?
Ah yet, we cannot be kind to each other
    here for an hour ;
We whisper, and hint, and chuckle, and
    grin at a brother's shame ;                    130
However we brave it out, we men are a
    little breed.

#### VI

A monstrous eft was of old the lord and
    master of earth,
For him did his high sun flame, and his
    river billowing ran,
And he felt himself in his force to be Na-
    ture's crowning race.

As nine months go to the shaping an infant
　　ripe for his birth,
So many a million of ages have gone to the
　　making of man:
He now is first, but is he the last? is he
　　not too base?

### VII

The man of science himself is fonder of
　　glory, and vain,
An eye well-practised in nature, a spirit
　　bounded and poor;
The passionate heart of the poet is whirl'd
　　into folly and vice.          140
I would not marvel at either, but keep a
　　temperate brain;
For not to desire or admire, if a man could
　　learn it, were more
Than to walk all day like the sultan of old
　　in a garden of spice.

### VIII

For the drift of the Maker is dark, an Isis
　　hid by the veil.
Who knows the ways of the world, how
　　God will bring them about?
Our planet is one, the suns are many, the
　　world is wide.
Shall I weep if a Poland fall? shall I shriek
　　if a Hungary fail?
Or an infant civilization be ruled with rod
　　or with knout?
*I* have not made the world, and He that
　　made it will guide.

### IX

Be mine a philosopher's life in the quiet
　　woodland ways,          150
Where if I cannot be gay let a passionless
　　peace be my lot,
Far-off from the clamor of liars belied in
　　the hubbub of lies;
From the long-neck'd geese of the world
　　that are ever hissing dispraise
Because their natures are little, and,
　　whether he heed it or not,
Where each man walks with his head in a
　　cloud of poisonous flies.

### X

And most of all would I flee from the cruel
　　madness of love
The honey of poison-flowers and all the
　　measureless ill.
Ah, Maud, you milk-white fawn, you are
　　all unmeet for a wife.

Your mother is mute in her grave as her
　　image in marble above;
Your father is ever in London, you wander
　　about at your will;          160
You have but fed on the roses and lain in
　　the lilies of life.

### V

#### I

A voice by the cedar tree
In the meadow under the Hall!
She is singing an air that is known to me,
A passionate ballad gallant and gay,
A martial song like a trumpet's call!
Singing alone in the morning of life,
In the happy morning of life and of May,
Singing of men that in battle array,
Ready in heart and ready in hand,          170
March with banner and bugle and fife
To the death, for their native land.

#### II

Maud with her exquisite face,
And wild voice pealing up to the sunny sky,
And feet like sunny gems on an English
　　green,
Maud in the light of her youth and her
　　grace,
Singing of Death, and of Honor that can-
　　not die,
Till I well could weep for a time so sordid
　　and mean,
And myself so languid and base.

#### III

Silence, beautiful voice!          180
Be still, for you only trouble the mind
With a joy in which I cannot rejoice,
A glory I shall not find.
Still! I will hear you no more,
For your sweetness hardly leaves me a
　　choice
But to move to the meadow and fall before
Her feet on the meadow grass, and adore,
Not her, who is neither courtly nor kind,
Not her, not her, but a voice.

### VI

#### I

Morning arises stormy and pale,          190
No sun, but a wannish glare
In fold upon fold of hueless cloud;

And the budded peaks of the wood are
    bow'd,
Caught, and cuff'd by the gale:
I had fancied it would be fair.

II

Whom but Maud should I meet
Last night, when the sunset burn'd
On the blossom'd gable-ends
At the head of the village street,
Whom but Maud should I meet ?    200
And she touch'd my hand with a smile so
    sweet,
She made me divine amends
For a courtesy not return'd.

III

And thus a delicate spark
Of glowing and growing light
Thro' the livelong hours of the dark
Kept itself warm in the heart of my dreams,
Ready to burst in a color'd flame;
Till at last, when the morning came
In a cloud, it faded, and seems    210
But an ashen-gray delight.

IV

What if with her sunny hair,
And smile as sunny as cold,
She meant to weave me a snare
Of some coquettish deceit,
Cleopatra-like as of old
To entangle me when we met,
To have her lion roll in a silken net
And fawn at a victor's feet.

V

Ah, what shall I be at fifty    220
Should Nature keep me alive,
If I find the world so bitter
When I am but twenty-five ?
Yet, if she were not a cheat,
If Maud were all that she seem'd,
And her smile were all that I dream'd,
Then the world were not so bitter
But a smile could make it sweet.

VI

What if, tho' her eye seem'd full
Of a kind intent to me,    230
What if that dandy-despot, he,
That jewell'd mass of millinery,
That oil'd and curl'd Assyrian bull
Smelling of musk and of insolence,
Her brother, from whom I keep aloof,

Who wants the finer politic sense
To mask, tho' but in his own behoof,
With a glassy smile his brutal scorn —
What if he had told her yestermorn
How prettily for his own sweet sake    240
A face of tenderness might be feign'd,
And a moist mirage in desert eyes,
That so, when the rotten hustings shake
In another month to his brazen lies,
A wretched vote may be gain'd ?

VII

For a raven ever croaks, at my side,
Keep watch and ward, keep watch and
    ward,
Or thou wilt prove their tool.
Yea, too, myself from myself I guard,
For often a man's own angry pride    250
Is cap and bells for a fool.

VIII

Perhaps the smile and tender tone
Came out of her pitying womanhood,
For am I not, am I not, here alone
So many a summer since she died,
My mother, who was so gentle and good ?
Living alone in an empty house,
Here half-hid in the gleaming wood,
Where I hear the dead at midday moan,
And the shrieking rush of the wainscot
    mouse,    260
And my own sad name in corners cried,
When the shiver of dancing leaves is
    thrown
About its echoing chambers wide,
Till a morbid hate and horror have grown
Of a world in which I have hardly mixt,
And a morbid eating lichen fixt
On a heart half-turn'd to stone.

IX

O heart of stone, are you flesh, and caught
By that you swore to withstand ?    269
For what was it else within me wrought
But, I fear, the new strong wine of love,
That made my tongue so stammer and
    trip
When I saw the treasured splendor, her
    hand,
Come sliding out of her sacred glove,
And the sunlight broke from her lip ?

X

I have play'd with her when a child;
She remembers it now we meet.

Ah, well, well, well, I *may* be beguiled
By some coquettish deceit.
Yet, if she were not a cheat,                    280
If Maud were all that she seem'd,
And her smile had all that I dream'd,
Then the world were not so bitter
But a smile could make it sweet.


## VII

### I

Did I hear it half in a doze
Long since, I know not where ?
Did I dream it an hour ago,
    When asleep in this arm-chair ?

### II

Men were drinking together,
    Drinking and talking of me:          290
' Well, if it prove a girl, the boy
    Will have plenty; so let it be.'

### III

Is it an echo of something
    Read with a boy's delight,
Viziers nodding together
    In some Arabian night ?

### IV

Strange, that I hear two men,
    Somewhere, talking of me:
' Well, if it prove a girl, my boy
    Will have plenty; so let it be.'      300


## VIII

She came to the village church,
And sat by a pillar alone;
An angel watching an urn
Wept over her, carved in stone;
And once, but once, she lifted her eyes,
And suddenly, sweetly, strangely blush'd
To find they were met by my own;
And suddenly, sweetly, my heart beat
    stronger
And thicker, until I heard no longer
The snowy-banded, dilettante,            310
Delicate-handed priest intone;
And thought, is it pride ? and mused and
    sigh'd,
' No surely, now it cannot be pride.'


## IX

I was walking a mile,
More than a mile from the shore,
The sun look'd out with a smile
Betwixt the cloud and the moor;
And riding at set of day
Over the dark moor land,
Rapidly riding far away,                  320
She waved to me with her hand.
There were two at her side,
Something flash'd in the sun,
Down by the hill I saw them ride,
In a moment they were gone;
Like a sudden spark
Struck vainly in the night,
Then returns the dark
With no more hope of light.


## X

### I

Sick, am I sick of a jealous dread ?     330
Was not one of the two at her side
This new-made lord, whose splendor plucks
The slavish hat from the villager's head ?
Whose old grandfather has lately died,
Gone to a blacker pit, for whom
Grimy nakedness dragging his trucks
And laying his trams in a poison'd gloom
Wrought, till he crept from a gutted mine
Master of half a servile shire,
And left his coal all turn'd into gold    340
To a grandson, first of his noble line,
Rich in the grace all women desire,
Strong in the power that all men adore,
And simper and set their voices lower,
And soften as if to a girl, and hold
Awe-stricken breaths at a work divine,
Seeing his gewgaw castle shine,
New as his title, built last year,
There amid perky larches and pine,
And over the sullen-purple moor —         350
Look at it — pricking a cockney ear.

### II

What, has he found my jewel out ?
For one of the two that rode at her side
Bound for the Hall, I am sure was he;
Bound for the Hall, and I think for a
    bride.
Blithe would her brother's acceptance be.

Maud could be gracious too, no doubt,
To a lord, a captain, a padded shape,
A bought commission, a waxen face,
A rabbit mouth that is ever agape —     360
Bought ? what is it he cannot buy ?
And therefore splenetic, personal, base,
A wounded thing with a rancorous cry,
At war with myself and a wretched race,
Sick, sick to the heart of life, am I.

### III

Last week came one to the county town,
To preach our poor little army down,
And play the game of the despot kings,
Tho' the state has done it and thrice as
    well.                                   369
This broad-brimm'd hawker of holy things,
Whose ear is cramm'd with his cotton, and
    rings
Even in dreams to the chink of his pence,
This huckster put down war ! can he tell
Whether war be a cause or a consequence ?
Put down the passions that make earth
    hell !
Down with ambition, avarice, pride,
Jealousy, down ! cut off from the mind
The bitter springs of anger and fear!
Down too, down at your own fireside,
With the evil tongue and the evil ear,    380
For each is at war with mankind !

### IV

I wish I could hear again
The chivalrous battle-song
That she warbled alone in her joy !
I might persuade myself then
She would not do herself this great wrong,
To take a wanton dissolute boy
For a man and leader of men.

### V

Ah God, for a man with heart, head,
    hand,
Like some of the simple great ones gone
For ever and ever by,                     391
One still strong man in a blatant land,
Whatever they call him — what care I ? —
Aristocrat, democrat, autocrat — one
Who can rule and dare not lie !

### VI

And ah for a man to arise in me,
That the man I am may cease to be !

### XI

#### I

O, let the solid ground
    Not fail beneath my feet
Before my life has found
    What some have found so sweet !    400
Then let come what come may,
What matter if I go mad,
I shall have had my day.

#### II

Let the sweet heavens endure,
    Not close and darken above me
Before I am quite quite sure
    That there is one to love me !
Then let come what come may
To a life that has been so sad,          410
I shall have had my day.

### XII

#### I

Birds in the high Hall-garden
    When twilight was falling,
Maud, Maud, Maud, Maud,
    They were crying and calling.

#### II

Where was Maud ? in our wood;
    And I — who else ? — was with her,
Gathering woodland lilies,
    Myriads blow together.

#### III

Birds in our wood sang                   420
    Ringing thro' the valleys,
Maud is here, here, here
    In among the lilies.

#### IV

I kiss'd her slender hand,
    She took the kiss sedately;
Maud is not seventeen,
    But she is tall and stately.

#### V

I to cry out on pride
    Who have won her favor !
O, Maud were sure of heaven            430
    If lowliness could save her !

### VI

I know the way she went
  Home with her maiden posy,
For her feet have touch'd the meadows
  And left the daisies rosy.

### VII

Birds in the high Hall-garden
  Were crying and calling to her,
Where is Maud, Maud, Maud?
  One is come to woo her.

### VIII

Look, a horse at the door,     440
  And little King Charley snarling!
Go back, my lord, across the moor,
  You are not her darling.

## XIII

### I

Scorn'd, to be scorn'd by one that I scorn,
Is that a matter to make me fret?
That a calamity hard to be borne?
Well, he may live to hate me yet.
Fool that I am to be vext with his pride!
I past him, I was crossing his lands;
He stood on the path a little aside;   450
His face, as I grant, in spite of spite,
Has a broad - blown comeliness, red and
    white,
And six feet two, as I think, he stands;
But his essences turn'd the live air sick,
And barbarous opulence jewel-thick
Sunn'd itself on his breast and his hands.

### II

Who shall call me ungentle, unfair?
I long'd so heartily then and there
To give him the grasp of fellowship;
But while I past he was humming an air, 460
Stopt, and then with a riding-whip
Leisurely tapping a glossy boot,
And curving a contumelious lip,
Gorgonized me from head to foot
With a stony British stare.

### III

Why sits he here in his father's chair?
That old man never comes to his place;
Shall I believe him ashamed to be seen?
For only once, in the village street,   469

Last year, I caught a glimpse of his face,
A gray old wolf and a lean.
Scarcely, now, would I call him a cheat;
For then, perhaps, as a child of deceit,
She might by a true descent be untrue;
And Maud is as true as Maud is sweet,
Tho' I fancy her sweetness only due
To the sweeter blood by the other side;
Her mother has been a thing complete,
However she came to be so allied.
And fair without, faithful within,   480
Maud to him is nothing akin.
Some peculiar mystic grace
Made her only the child of her mother,
And heap'd the whole inherited sin
On that huge scapegoat of the race,
All, all upon the brother.

### IV

Peace, angry spirit, and let him be!
Has not his sister smiled on me?

## XIV

### I

Maud has a garden of roses
And lilies fair on a lawn;   490
There she walks in her state
And tends upon bed and bower,
And thither I climb'd at dawn
And stood by her garden-gate.
A lion ramps at the top,
He is claspt by a passion-flower.

### II

Maud's own little oak-room —
Which Maud, like a precious stone
Set in the heart of the carven gloom,
Lights with herself, when alone   500
She sits by her music and books
And her brother lingers late
With a roystering company — looks
Upon Maud's own garden-gate;
And I thought as I stood, if a hand, as
    white
As ocean-foam in the moon, were laid
On the hasp of the window, and my De-
    light
Had a sudden desire, like a glorious ghost,
    to glide,
Like a beam of the seventh heaven, down
    to my side,
There were but a step to be made.   510

### III

The fancy flatter'd my mind,
And again seem'd overbold;
Now I thought that she cared for me,
Now I thought she was kind
Only because she was cold.

### IV

I heard no sound where I stood
But the rivulet on from the lawn
Running down to my own dark wood,
Or the voice of the long sea-wave as it
    swell'd
Now and then in the dim-gray dawn;      520
But I look'd, and round, all round the
    house I beheld
The death-white curtain drawn,
Felt a horror over me creep,
Prickle my skin and catch my breath,
Knew that the death-white curtain meant
    but sleep,
Yet I shudder'd and thought like a fool of
    the sleep of death.

## XV

So dark a mind within me dwells,
    And I make myself such evil cheer,
That if *I* be dear to some one else,
    Then some one else may have much to
        fear;
                                        530
But if *I* be dear to some one else,
    Then I should be to myself more dear.
Shall I not take care of all that I think,
Yea, even of wretched meat and drink,
If I be dear,
If I be dear to some one else ?

## XVI

### I

This lump of earth has left his estate
The lighter by the loss of his weight;
And so that he find what he went to seek,
And fulsome pleasure clog him, and
    drown
                                        540
His heart in the gross mud-honey of town,
He may stay for a year who has gone for a
    week.
But this is the day when I must speak,
And I see my Oread coming down,
O, this is the day !

O beautiful creature, what am I
That I dare to look her way ?
Think I may hold dominion sweet,
Lord of the pulse that is lord of her breast,
And dream of her beauty with tender
    dread,
                                        550
From the delicate Arab arch of her feet
To the grace that, bright and light as the
    crest
Of a peacock, sits on her shining head,
And she knows it not — O, if she knew it,
To know her beauty might half undo it !
I know it the one bright thing to save
My yet young life in the wilds of Time,
Perhaps from madness, perhaps from crime,
Perhaps from a selfish grave.

### II

What, if she be fasten'd to this fool lord,
Dare I bid her abide by her word ?      561
Should I love her so well if she
Had given her word to a thing so low ?
Shall I love her as well if she
Can break her word were it even for me ?
I trust that it is not so.

### III

Catch not my breath, O clamorous heart,
Let not my tongue be a thrall to my eye,
For I must tell her before we part,
I must tell her, or die.
                                        570

## XVII

Go not, happy day,
    From the shining fields,
Go not, happy day,
    Till the maiden yields.
Rosy is the West,
    Rosy is the South,
Roses are her cheeks,
    And a rose her mouth.
When the happy Yes
    Falters from her lips,          580
Pass and blush the news
    Over glowing ships;
Over blowing seas,
    Over seas at rest,
Pass the happy news,
    Blush it thro' the West;
Till the red man dance
    By his red cedar-tree,
And the red man's babe
    Leap, beyond the sea.
                                        599

Blush from West to East,
    Blush from East to West,
Till the West is East,
    Blush it thro' the West.
Rosy is the West,
    Rosy is the South,
Roses are her cheeks,
    And a rose her mouth.


## XVIII

### I

I have led her home, my love, my only
        friend.
There is none like her, none.          600
And never yet so warmly ran my blood
And sweetly, on and on
Calming itself to the long-wish'd-for end,
Full to the banks, close on the promised
        good.

### II

None like her, none.
Just now the dry-tongued laurels' pattering
        talk
Seem'd her light foot along the garden
        walk,
And shook my heart to think she comes
        once more.
But even then I heard her close the door;
The gates of heaven are closed, and she is
        gone.          610

### III

There is none like her, none,
Nor will be when our summers have de-
        ceased.
O, art thou sighing for Lebanon
In the long breeze that streams to thy de-
        licious East,
Sighing for Lebanon,
Dark cedar, tho' thy limbs have here in-
        creased,
Upon a pastoral slope as fair,
And looking to the South and fed
With honey'd rain and delicate air,
And haunted by the starry head          620
Of her whose gentle will has changed my
        fate,
And made my life a perfumed altar-flame;
And over whom thy darkness must have
        spread
With such delight as theirs of old, thy
        great

Forefathers of the thornless garden, there
Shadowing the snow-limb'd Eve from
        whom she came?

### IV

Here will I lie, while these long branches
        sway,
And you fair stars that crown a happy day
Go in and out as if at merry play,
Who am no more so all forlorn          630
As when it seem'd far better to be born
To labor and the mattock-harden'd hand
Than nursed at ease and brought to under-
        stand
A sad astrology, the boundless plan
That makes you tyrants in your iron skies,
Innumerable, pitiless, passionless eyes,
Cold fires, yet with power to burn and
        brand
His nothingness into man.

### V

But now shine on, and what care I,
Who in this stormy gulf have found a
        pearl          640
The countercharm of space and hollow
        sky,
And do accept my madness, and would
        die
To save from some slight shame one sim-
        ple girl? —

### VI

Would die, for sullen-seeming Death may
        give
More life to Love than is or ever was
In our low world, where yet 't is sweet to
        live.
Let no one ask me how it came to pass;
It seems that I am happy, that to me
A livelier emerald twinkles in the grass,
A purer sapphire melts into the sea.          650

### VII

Not die, but live a life of truest breath,
And teach true life to fight with mortal
        wrongs.
O, why should Love, like men in drinking-
        songs,
Spice his fair banquet with the dust of
        death?
Make answer, Maud my bliss,
Maud made my Maud by that long loving
        kiss,
Life of my life, wilt thou not answer this?

'The dusky strand of Death inwoven here
With dear Love's tie, makes Love himself
    more dear.'

### VIII

Is that enchanted moan only the swell    660
Of the long waves that roll in yonder bay ?
And hark the clock within, the silver knell
Of twelve sweet hours that past in bridal
    white,
And died to live, long as my pulses play;
But now by this my love has closed her
    sight
And given false death her hand, and stolen
    away
To dreamful wastes where footless fancies
    dwell
Among the fragments of the golden day.
May nothing there her maiden grace af-
    fright !
Dear heart, I feel with thee the drowsy
    spell.      670
My bride to be, my evermore delight,
My own heart's heart, my ownest own,
    farewell;
It is but for a little space I go.
And ye meanwhile far over moor and fell
Beat to the noiseless music of the night !
Has our whole earth gone nearer to the
    glow
Of your soft splendors that you look so
    bright ?
*I* have climb'd nearer out of lonely hell.
Beat, happy stars, timing with things be-
    low,
Beat with my heart more blest than heart
    can tell,      680
Blest, but for some dark undercurrent woe
That seems to draw — but it shall not be
    so;
Let all be well, be well.

### XIX

### I

Her brother is coming back to-night,
Breaking up my dream of delight.

### II

My dream ? do I dream of bliss ?
I have walk'd awake with Truth.
O, when did a morning shine
So rich in atonement as this
For my dark-dawning youth,      690

Darken'd watching a mother decline
And that dead man at her heart and mine;
For who was left to watch her but I ?
Yet so did I let my freshness die.

### III

I trust that I did not talk
To gentle Maud in our walk —
For often in lonely wanderings
I have cursed him even to lifeless things —
But I trust that I did not talk,
Not touch on her father's sin.      700
I am sure I did but speak
Of my mother's faded cheek
When it slowly grew so thin
That I felt she was slowly dying
Vext with lawyers and harass'd with debt;
For how often I caught her with eyes all
    wet,
Shaking her head at her son and sighing
A world of trouble within !

### IV

And Maud too, Maud was moved
To speak of the mother she loved      710
As one scarce less forlorn,
Dying abroad and it seems apart
From him who had ceased to share her
    heart,
And ever mourning over the feud,
The household Fury sprinkled with blood
By which our houses are torn.
How strange was what she said,
When only Maud and the brother
Hung over her dying bed —
That Maud's dark father and mine      720
Had bound us one to the other,
Betrothed us over their wine,
On the day when Maud was born;
Seal'd her mine from her first sweet breath!
Mine, mine by a right, from birth till death!
Mine, mine — our fathers have sworn!

### V

But the true blood spilt had in it a heat
To dissolve the precious seal on a bond,
That, if left uncancell'd, had been so sweet;
And none of us thought of a something
    beyond,      730
A desire that awoke in the heart of the
    child,
As it were a duty done to the tomb,
To be friends for her sake, to be recon-
    ciled;
And I was cursing them and my doom,

And letting a dangerous thought run
    wild
While often abroad in the fragrant gloom
Of foreign churches — I see her there,
Bright English lily, breathing a prayer
To be friends, to be reconciled !

### VI

But then what a flint is he !    740
Abroad, at Florence, at Rome,
I find whenever she touch'd on me
This brother had laugh'd her down,
And at last, when each came home,
He had darken'd into a frown,
Chid her, and forbid her to speak
To me, her friend of the years before;
And this was what had redden'd her
    cheek
When I bow'd to her on the moor.

### VII

Yet Maud, altho' not blind    750
To the faults of his heart and mind,
I see she cannot but love him,
And says he is rough but kind,
And wishes me to approve him,
And tells me, when she lay
Sick once, with a fear of worse,
That he left his wine and horses and
    play,
Sat with her, read to her, night and day,
And tended her like a nurse.

### VIII

Kind ? but the death-bed desire    760
Spurn'd by this heir of the liar —
Rough but kind ? yet I know
He has plotted against me in this,
That he plots against me still.
Kind to Maud ? that were not amiss.
Well, rough but kind; why, let it be so,
For shall not Maud have her will ?

### IX

For, Maud, so tender and true,
As long as my life endures
I feel I shall owe you a debt    770
That I never can hope to pay;
And if ever I should forget
That I owe this debt to you
And for your sweet sake to yours,
O, then, what then shall I say ? —
If ever I *should* forget,
May God make me more wretched
Than ever I have been yet !

### X

So now I have sworn to bury
All this dead body of hate,    780
I feel so free and so clear
By the loss of that dead weight,
That I should grow light-headed, I fear,
Fantastically merry,
But that her brother comes, like a blight
On my fresh hope, to the Hall to-night.

## XX

### I

Strange, that I felt so gay,
Strange, that I tried to-day
To beguile her melancholy;
The Sultan, as we name him —    790
She did not wish to blame him —
But he vext her and perplext her
With his worldly talk and folly.
Was it gentle to reprove her
For stealing out of view
From a little lazy lover
Who but claims her as his due ?
Or for chilling his caresses
By the coldness of her manners,
Nay, the plainness of her dresses ?    800
Now I know her but in two,
Nor can pronounce upon it
If one should ask me whether
The habit, hat, and feather,
Or the frock and gipsy bonnet
Be the neater and completer;
For nothing can be sweeter
Than maiden Maud in either.

### II

But to-morrow, if we live,
Our ponderous squire will give    810
A grand political dinner
To half the squirelings near;
And Maud will wear her jewels,
And the bird of prey will hover,
And the titmouse hope to win her
With his chirrup at her ear.

### III

A grand political dinner
To the men of many acres,
A gathering of the Tory,
A dinner and then a dance    820
For the maids and marriage-makers,
And every eye but mine will glance
At Maud in all her glory.

### IV

For I am not invited,
  But, with the Sultan's pardon,
I am all as well delighted,
  For I know her own rose-garden,
  And mean to linger in it
Till the dancing will be over;
And then, O, then, come out to me          830
For a minute, but for a minute,
Come out to your own true lover,
That your true lover may see
Your glory also, and render
All homage to his own darling,
Queen Maud in all her splendor.

### XXI

Rivulet crossing my ground,
  And bringing me down from the Hall
This garden-rose that I found,
  Forgetful of Maud and me,                840
And lost in trouble and moving round
Here at the head of a tinkling fall,
  And trying to pass to the sea;
O rivulet, born at the Hall,
My Maud has sent it by thee —
  If I read her sweet will right —
On a blushing mission to me,
  Saying in odor and color, 'Ah, be
Among the roses to-night.'

### XXII

#### I

Come into the garden, Maud,                850
  For the black bat, night, has flown,
Come into the garden, Maud,
  I am here at the gate alone;
And the woodbine spices are wafted abroad,
  And the musk of the rose is blown.

#### II

For a breeze of morning moves,
  And the planet of Love is on high,
Beginning to faint in the light that she
      loves
  On a bed of daffodil sky,
To faint in the light of the sun she loves,
  To faint in his light, and to die.       861

#### III

All night have the roses heard
  The flute, violin, bassoon;

All night has the casement jessamine stirr'd
  To the dancers dancing in tune;
Till a silence fell with the waking bird,
  And a hush with the setting moon.

#### IV

I said to the lily, 'There is but one,
  With whom she has heart to be gay.
When will the dancers leave her alone ?    870
  She is weary of dance and play.'
Now half to the setting moon are gone,
  And half to the rising day;
Low on the sand and loud on the stone
  The last wheel echoes away.

#### V

I said to the rose, 'The brief night goes
  In babble and revel and wine.
O young lord-lover, what sighs are those,
  For one that will never be thine ?
But mine, but mine,' so I sware to the
      rose,                                880
  'For ever and ever, mine.'

#### VI

And the soul of the rose went into my
      blood,
  As the music clash'd in the hall;
And long by the garden lake I stood,
  For I heard your rivulet fall
From the lake to the meadow and on to the
      wood,
  Our wood, that is dearer than all;

#### VII

From the meadow your walks have left so
      sweet
  That whenever a March-wind sighs
He sets the jewel-print of your feet        890
  In violets blue as your eyes,
To the woody hollows in which we meet
  And the valleys of Paradise.

#### VIII

The slender acacia would not shake
  One long milk-bloom on the tree;
The white lake - blossom fell into the
      lake
  As the pimpernel dozed on the lea;
But the rose was awake all night for your
      sake,
  Knowing your promise to me;
The lilies and roses were all awake,        900
  They sigh'd for the dawn and thee.

## IX

Queen rose of the rosebud garden of girls,
  Come hither, the dances are done,
In gloss of satin and glimmer of pearls,
  Queen lily and rose in one;
Shine out, little head, sunning over with
    curls,
  To the flowers, and be their sun.

## X

There has fallen a splendid tear
  From the passion-flower at the gate.
She is coming, my dove, my dear;    910
  She is coming, my life, my fate.
The red rose cries, ' She is near, she is
    near;'
  And the white rose weeps, ' She is late;'
The larkspur listens, ' I hear, I hear;'
  And the lily whispers, ' I wait.'

## XI

She is coming, my own, my sweet;
  Were it ever so airy a tread,
My heart would hear her and beat,
  Were it earth in an earthy bed;
My dust would hear her and beat,    920
  Had I lain for a century dead,
Would start and tremble under her feet,
  And blossom in purple and red.

# PART II

## I

### I

' The fault was mine, the fault was mine ' —
Why am I sitting here so stunn'd and still,
Plucking the harmless wild-flower on the
    hill ? —
It is this guilty hand ! —
And there rises ever a passionate cry
From underneath in the darkening land —
What is it, that has been done ?
O dawn of Eden bright over earth and sky,
The fires of hell brake out of thy rising
    sun,
The fires of hell and of hate;    10
For she, sweet soul, had hardly spoken a
    word,
When her brother ran in his rage to the
    gate,
He came with the babe-faced lord,
Heap'd on her terms of disgrace;

And while she wept, and I strove to be cool,
He fiercely gave me the lie,
Till I with as fierce an anger spoke,
And he struck me, madman, over the face,
Struck me before the languid fool,
Who was gaping and grinning by;    20
Struck for himself an evil stroke,
Wrought for his house an irredeemable
    woe.
For front to front in an hour we stood,
And a million horrible bellowing echoes
    broke
From the red-ribb'd hollow behind the
    wood,
And thunder'd up into heaven the Christless
    code
That must have life for a blow.
Ever and ever afresh they seem'd to grow.
Was it he lay there with a fading eye ?
' The fault was mine,' he whisper'd, ' fly !'
Then glided out of the joyous wood    31
The ghastly Wraith of one that I know,
And there rang on a sudden a passionate
    cry,
A cry for a brother's blood;
It will ring in my heart and my ears, till I
    die, till I die.

## II

Is it gone ? my pulses beat —
What was it ? a lying trick of the brain ?
Yet I thought I saw her stand,
A shadow there at my feet,
High over the shadowy land.    40
It is gone; and the heavens fall in a gentle
    rain,
When they should burst and drown with
    deluging storms
The feeble vassals of wine and anger and
    lust,
The little hearts that know not how to for-
    give.
Arise, my God, and strike, for we hold
    Thee just,
Strike dead the whole weak race of venom-
    ous worms,
That sting each other here in the dust;
We are not worthy to live.

## II

### I

See what a lovely shell,
  Small and pure as a pearl,    50

Lying close to my foot,
Frail, but a work divine,
Made so fairily well
With delicate spire and whorl,
How exquisitely minute,
A miracle of design !

### II

What is it ? a learned man
Could give it a clumsy name.
Let him name it who can,
The beauty would be the same.        60

### III

The tiny cell is forlorn,
Void of the little living will
That made it stir on the shore.
Did he stand at the diamond door
Of his house in a rainbow frill ?
Did he push, when he was uncurl'd,
A golden foot or a fairy horn
Thro' his dim water-world ?

### IV

Slight, to be crush'd with a tap
Of my finger-nail on the sand,        70
Small, but a work divine,
Frail, but of force to withstand,
Year upon year, the shock
Of cataract seas that snap
The three-decker's oaken spine
Athwart the ledges of rock,
Here on the Breton strand !

### V

Breton, not Briton; here
Like a shipwreck'd man on a coast
Of ancient fable and fear —        80
Plagued with a flitting to and fro,
A disease, a hard mechanic ghost
That never came from on high
Nor ever arose from below,
But only moves with the moving eye,
Flying along the land and the main —
Why should it look like Maud ?
Am I to be overawed
By what I cannot but know
Is a juggle born of the brain ?        90

### VI

Back from the Breton coast,
Sick of a nameless fear,
Back to the dark sea-line
Looking, thinking of all I have lost;

An old song vexes my ear,
But that of Lamech is mine.

### VII

For years, a measureless ill,
For years, for ever, to part —
But she, she would love me still;
And as long, O God, as she        100
Have a grain of love for me,
So long, no doubt, no doubt,
Shall I nurse in my dark heart,
However weary, a spark of will
Not to be trampled out.

### VIII

Strange, that the mind, when fraught
With a passion so intense
One would think that it well
Might drown all life in the eye, —        109
That it should, by being so overwrought,
Suddenly strike on a sharper sense
For a shell, or a flower, little things
Which else would have been past by !
And now I remember, I,
When he lay dying there,
I noticed one of his many rings —
For he had many, poor worm — and
      thought,
It is his mother's hair.

### IX

Who knows if he be dead ?
Whether I need have fled ?        120
Am I guilty of blood ?
However this may be,
Comfort her, comfort her, all things good,
While I am over the sea !
Let me and my passionate love go by,
But speak to her all things holy and high,
Whatever happen to me !
Me and my harmful love go by;
But come to her waking, find her asleep,
Powers of the height, Powers of the deep,
And comfort her tho' I die !        131

### III

Courage, poor heart of stone !
I will not ask thee why
Thou canst not understand
That thou art left for ever alone;
Courage, poor stupid heart of stone ! —
Or if I ask thee why,

Care not thou to reply:
She is but dead, and the time is at hand
When thou shalt more than die.        140

## IV

### I

O that 't were possible
After long grief and pain
To find the arms of my true love
Round me once again !

### II

When I was wont to meet her
In the silent woody places
By the home that gave me birth,
We stood tranced in long embraces
Mixt with kisses sweeter, sweeter
Than anything on earth.        150

### III

A shadow flits before me,
Not thou, but like to thee.
Ah, Christ, that it were possible
For one short hour to see
The souls we loved, that they might tell us
What and where they be !

### IV

It leads me forth at evening,
It lightly winds and steals
In a cold white robe before me,
When all my spirit reels        160
At the shouts, the leagues of lights,
And the roaring of the wheels.

### V

Half the night I waste in sighs,
Half in dreams I sorrow after
The delight of early skies;
In a wakeful doze I sorrow
For the hand, the lips, the eyes,
For the meeting of the morrow,
The delight of happy laughter,
The delight of low replies.        170

### VI

'T is a morning pure and sweet,
And a dewy splendor falls
On the little flower that clings
To the turrets and the walls;
'T is a morning pure and sweet,
And the light and shadow fleet.

She is walking in the meadow,
And the woodland echo rings;
In a moment we shall meet.
She is singing in the meadow,        180
And the rivulet at her feet
Ripples on in light and shadow
To the ballad that she sings.

### VII

Do I hear her sing as of old,
My bird with the shining head,
My own dove with the tender eye ?
But there rings on a sudden a passionate cry,
There is some one dying or dead,
And a sullen thunder is roll'd;
For a tumult shakes the city,        190
And I wake, my dream is fled.
In the shuddering dawn, behold,
Without knowledge, without pity,
By the curtains of my bed
That abiding phantom cold !

### VIII

Get thee hence, nor come again,
Mix not memory with doubt,
Pass, thou deathlike type of pain,
Pass and cease to move about !
'T is the blot upon the brain        200
That *will* show itself without.

### IX

Then I rise, the eave-drops fall,
And the yellow vapors choke
The great city sounding wide;
The day comes, a dull red ball
Wrapt in drifts of lurid smoke
On the misty river-tide.

### X

Thro' the hubbub of the market
I steal, a wasted frame;
It crosses here, it crosses there,        210
Thro' all that crowd confused and loud,
The shadow still the same;
And on my heavy eyelids
My anguish hangs like shame.

### XI

Alas for her that met me,
That heard me softly call,
Came glimmering thro' the laurels
At the quiet evenfall,
In the garden by the turrets
Of the old manorial hall !        220

## XII

Would the happy spirit descend
From the realms of light and song,
In the chamber or the street,
As she looks among the blest,
Should I fear to greet my friend
Or to say ' Forgive the wrong,'
Or to ask her, ' Take me, sweet,
To the regions of thy rest ' ?

## XIII

But the broad light glares and beats,
And the shadow flits and fleets        230
And will not let me be;
And I loathe the squares and streets,
And the faces that one meets,
Hearts with no love for me.
Always I long to creep
Into some still cavern deep,
There to weep, and weep, and weep
My whole soul out to thee.

## V

### I

Dead, long dead,
Long dead !        240
And my heart is a handful of dust,
And the wheels go over my head,
And my bones are shaken with pain,
For into a shallow grave they are thrust,
Only a yard beneath the street,
And the hoofs of the horses beat, beat,
The hoofs of the horses beat,
Beat into my scalp and my brain,
With never an end to the stream of passing
    feet,
Driving, hurrying, marrying, burying,    250
Clamor and rumble, and ringing and clat-
    ter;
And here beneath it is all as bad,
For I thought the dead had peace, but it is
    not so.
To have no peace in the grave, is that not
    sad ?
But up and down and to and fro,
Ever about me the dead men go;
And then to hear a dead man chatter
Is enough to drive one mad.

### II

Wretchedest age, since Time began,
They cannot even bury a man;        260

And tho' we paid our tithes in the days
    that are gone,
Not a bell was rung, not a prayer was read.
It is that which makes us loud in the
    world of the dead;
There is none that does his work, not one.
A touch of their office might have sufficed,
But the churchmen fain would kill their
    church,
As the churches have kill'd their Christ.

### III

See, there is one of us sobbing,
No limit to his distress;        269
And another, a lord of all things, praying
To his own great self, as I guess;
And another, a statesman there, betraying
His party-secret, fool, to the press;
And yonder a vile physician, blabbing
The case of his patient — all for what ?
To tickle the maggot born in an empty
    head,
And wheedle a world that loves him not,
For it is but a world of the dead.

### IV

Nothing but idiot gabble !
For the prophecy given of old        280
And then not understood,
Has come to pass as foretold;
Not let any man think for the public good,
But babble, merely for babble.
For I never whisper'd a private affair
Within the hearing of cat or mouse,
No, not to myself in the closet alone,
But I heard it shouted at once from the
    top of the house;
Everything came to be known.
Who told *him* we were there ?        290

### V

Not that gray old wolf, for he came not
    back
From the wilderness, full of wolves, where
    he used to lie;
He has gather'd the bones for his o'ergrown
    whelp to crack —
Crack them now for yourself, and howl, and
    die.

### VI

Prophet, curse me the blabbing lip,
And curse me the British vermin, the rat;
I know not whether he came in the Han-
    over ship,

But I know that he lies and listens mute
In an ancient mansion's crannies and holes.
Arsenic, arsenic, sure, would do it,     300
Except that now we poison our babes, poor
    souls !
It is all used up for that.

### VII

Tell him now: she is standing here at my
    head;
Not beautiful now, not even kind;
He may take her now; for she never speaks
    her mind,
But is ever the one thing silent here.
She is not *of* us, as I divine;
She comes from another stiller world of the
    dead,
Stiller, not fairer than mine.

### VIII

But I know where a garden grows,     310
Fairer than aught in the world beside,
All made up of the lily and rose
That blow by night, when the season is
    good,
To the sound of dancing music and flutes:
It is only flowers, they had no fruits,
And I almost fear they are not roses, but
    blood;
For the keeper was one, so full of pride,
He linkt a dead man there to a spectral
    bride;
For he, if he had not been a Sultan of
    brutes,
Would he have that hole in his side ?     320

### IX

But what will the old man say ?
He laid a cruel snare in a pit
To catch a friend of mine one stormy
    day;
Yet now I could even weep to think of
    it;
For what will the old man say
When he comes to the second corpse in the
    pit ?

### X

Friend, to be struck by the public foe,
Then to strike him and lay him low,
That were a public merit, far,
Whatever the Quaker holds, from sin;     330
But the red life spilt for a private blow —
I swear to you, lawful and lawless war
Are scarcely even akin.

### XI

O me, why have they not buried me deep
    enough ?
Is it kind to have made me a grave so
    rough,
Me, that was never a quiet sleeper ?
Maybe still I am but half-dead;
Then I cannot be wholly dumb.
I will cry to the steps above my head
And somebody, surely, some kind heart
    will come     340
To bury me, bury me
Deeper, ever so little deeper.

## PART III

### I

My life has crept so long on a broken wing
Thro' cells of madness, haunts of horror
    and fear,
That I come to be grateful at last for a lit-
    tle thing.
My mood is changed, for it fell at a time
    of year
When the face of night is fair on the dewy
    downs,
And the shining daffodil dies, and the
    Charioteer
And starry Gemini hang like glorious
    crowns
Over Orion's grave low down in the west,
That like a silent lightning under the stars
She seem'd to divide in a dream from a
    band of the blest,     10
And spoke of a hope for the world in the
    coming wars —
' And in that hope, dear soul, let trouble
    have rest,
Knowing I tarry for thee,' and pointed to
    Mars
As he glow'd like a ruddy shield on the
    Lion's breast.

### II

And it was but a dream, yet it yielded a
    dear delight
To have look'd, tho' but in a dream, upon
    eyes so fair,
That had been in a weary world my one
    thing bright;
And it was but a dream, yet it lighten'd
    my despair

When I thought that a war would arise in
    defence of the right,
That an iron tyranny now should bend or
    cease,        20
The glory of manhood stand on his ancient
    height,
Nor Britain's one sole God be the million-
    aire.
No more shall commerce be all in all, and
    Peace
Pipe on her pastoral hillock a languid note,
And watch her harvest ripen, her herd
    increase,
Nor the cannon-bullet rust on a slothful
    shore,
And the cobweb woven across the cannon's
    throat
Shall shake its threaded tears in the wind
    no more.

## III

And as months ran on and rumor of battle
    grew,
'It is time, it is time, O passionate heart,'
    said I, —        30
For I cleaved to a cause that I felt to be
    pure and true, —
'It is time, O passionate heart and morbid
    eye,
That old hysterical mock-disease should
    die.'
And I stood on a giant deck and mixt my
    breath
With a loyal people shouting a battle-
    cry,
Till I saw the dreary phantom arise and
    fly
Far into the North, and battle, and seas of
    death.

## IV

Let it go or stay, so I wake to the higher
    aims
Of a land that has lost for a little her lust
    of gold,
And love of a peace that was full of wrongs
    and shames,    40
Horrible, hateful, monstrous, not to be
    told;
And hail once more to the banner of battle
    unroll'd !
Tho' many a light shall darken, and many
    shall weep
For those that are crush'd in the clash of
    jarring claims,

Yet God's just wrath shall be wreak'd on a
    giant liar,
And many a darkness into the light shall
    leap,
And shine in the sudden making of splen-
    did names,
And noble thought be freer under the
    sun,
And the heart of a people beat with one
    desire;
For the peace, that I deem'd no peace, is
    over and done,    50
And now by the side of the Black and the
    Baltic deep,
And deathful-grinning mouths of the for-
    tress, flames
The blood-red blossom of war with a heart
    of fire.

## V

Let it flame or fade, and the war roll down
    like a wind,
We have proved we have hearts in a cause,
    we are noble still,
And myself have awaked, as it seems, to
    the better mind.
It is better to fight for the good than to
    rail at the ill;
I have felt with my native land, I am one
    with my kind,
I embrace the purpose of God, and the
    doom assign'd.

# THE BROOK

'HERE by this brook we parted, I to the
    East
And he for Italy — too late — too late:
One whom the strong sons of the world de-
    spise;
For lucky rhymes to him were scrip and
    share,
And mellow metres more than cent for
    cent.
Nor could he understand how money breeds,
Thought it a dead thing; yet himself could
    make
The thing that is not as the thing that is.
O, had he lived ! In our schoolbooks we
    say
Of those that held their heads above the
    crowd,    10
They flourish'd then or then; but life in
    him

Could scarce be said to flourish, only
　　touch'd
On such a time as goes before the leaf,
When all the wood stands in a mist of
　　green,
And nothing perfect.　Yet the brook he
　　loved,
For which, in branding summers of Ben-
　　gal,
Or even the sweet half-English Neilgherry
　　air,
I panted, seems, as I re-listen to it,
Prattling the primrose fancies of the boy
To me that loved him; for " O brook," he
　　says,　　　　　　　　　　　　　　20
"O babbling brook," says Edmund in his
　　rhyme,
" Whence come you ? " and the brook —
　　why not ? — replies:

　　I come from haunts of coot and hern,
　　　　I make a sudden sally,
　　And sparkle out among the fern,
　　　　To bicker down a valley.

　　By thirty hills I hurry down,
　　　　Or slip between the ridges,
　　By twenty thorps, a little town,
　　　　And half a hundred bridges.　　30

　　Till last by Philip's farm I flow
　　　　To join the brimming river,
　　For men may come and men may go,
　　　　But I go on for ever.

' Poor lad, he died at Florence, quite worn
　　out,
Travelling to Naples.　There is Darnley
　　bridge,
It has more ivy; there the river; and there
Stands Philip's farm where brook and river
　　meet.

　　I chatter over stony ways,
　　　　In little sharps and trebles,
　　I bubble into eddying bays,　　　　40
　　　　I babble on the pebbles.

　　With many a curve my banks I fret
　　　　By many a field and fallow,
　　And many a fairy foreland set
　　　　With willow-weed and mallow.

　　I chatter, chatter, as I flow
　　　　To join the brimming river,
　　For men may come and men may go,
　　　　But I go on for ever.　　　　50

' But Philip chatter'd more than brook
　　or bird,
Old Philip; all about the fields you caught
His weary daylong chirping, like the
　　dry
High-elbow'd grigs that leap in summer
　　grass.

　　I wind about, and in and out,
　　　　With here a blossom sailing,
　　And here and there a lusty trout,
　　　　And here and there a grayling,

　　And here and there a foamy flake
　　　　Upon me, as I travel　　　　60
　　With many a silvery water-break
　　　　Above the golden gravel,

　　And draw them all along, and flow
　　　　To join the brimming river,
　　For men may come and men may go,
　　　　But I go on for ever.

' O darling Katie Willows, his one child !
A maiden of our century, yet most meek;
A daughter of our meadows, yet not coarse;
Straight, but as lissome as a hazel wand;
Her eyes a bashful azure, and her hair　71
In gloss and hue the chestnut, when the
　　shell
Divides threefold to show the fruit within.

' Sweet Katie, once I did her a good
　　turn,
Her and her far-off cousin and betrothed,
James Willows, of one name and heart
　　with her.
For here I came, twenty years back — the
　　week
Before I parted with poor Edmund — crost
By that old bridge which, half in ruins
　　then,　　　　　　　　　　　　　79
Still makes a hoary eyebrow for the gleam
Beyond it, where the waters marry — crost,
Whistling a random bar of Bonny Doon,
And push'd at Philip's garden-gate.　The
　　gate,
Half-parted from a weak and scolding
　　hinge,
Stuck; and he clamor'd from a casement,
　　" Run,"
To Katie somewhere in the walks below,
" Run, Katie ! " Katie never ran; she
　　moved
To meet me, winding under woodbine bow-
　　ers,

A little flutter'd, with her eyelids down, 89
Fresh apple-blossom, blushing for a boon.

'What was it ? less of sentiment than
      sense
Had Katie; not illiterate, nor of those
Who dabbling in the fount of fictive tears,
And nursed by mealy-mouth'd philanthro-
      pies,
Divorce the Feeling from her mate the
      Deed.

'She told me. She and James had
      quarrell'd. Why ?
What cause of quarrel ? None, she said,
      no cause;
James had no cause: but when I prest the
      cause,
I learnt that James had flickering jealousies
Which anger'd her. Who anger'd James ?
      I said. 100
But Katie snatch'd her eyes at once from
      mine,
And sketching with her slender pointed
      foot
Some figure like a wizard pentagram
On garden gravel, let my query pass
Unclaim'd, in flushing silence, till I ask'd
If James were coming. " Coming every
      day,"
She answer'd, " ever longing to explain,
But evermore her father came across
With some long-winded tale, and broke
      him short;
And James departed vext with him and
      her." 110
How could I help her ? " Would I — was
      it wrong ? " —
Claspt hands and that petitionary grace
Of sweet seventeen subdued me ere she
      spoke —
" O, would I take her father for one hour,
For one half-hour, and let him talk to me!"
And even while she spoke, I saw where
      James
Made toward us, like a wader in the surf,
Beyond the brook, waist-deep in meadow-
      sweet.

'O Katie, what I suffer'd for your sake !
For in I went, and call'd old Philip out 120
To show the farm. Full willingly he rose;
He led me thro' the short sweet-smelling
      lanes
Of his wheat-suburb, babbling as he went.

He praised his land, his horses, his ma-
      chines;
He praised his ploughs, his cows, his hogs,
      his dogs;
He praised his hens, his geese, his guinea-
      hens,
His pigeons, who in session on their roofs
Approved him, bowing at their own deserts.
Then from the plaintive mother's teat he
      took
Her blind and shuddering puppies, naming
      each, 130
And naming those, his friends, for whom
      they were;
Then crost the common into Darnley chase
To show Sir Arthur's deer. In copse and
      fern
Twinkled the innumerable ear and tail.
Then, seated on a serpent-rooted beech,
He pointed out a pasturing colt, and said,
" That was the four-year-old I sold the
      Squire."
And there he told a long, long-winded tale
Of how the Squire had seen the colt at
      grass,
And how it was the thing his daughter
      wish'd, 140
And how he sent the bailiff to the farm
To learn the price, and what the price he
      ask'd,
And how the bailiff swore that he was mad,
But he stood firm, and so the matter
      hung;
He gave them line; and five days after
      that
He met the bailiff at the Golden Fleece,
Who then and there had offer'd something
      more,
But he stood firm, and so the matter hung;
He knew the man, the colt would fetch its
      price;
He gave them line; and how by chance at
      last — 150
It might be May or April, he forgot,
The last of April or the first of May —
He found the bailiff riding by the farm,
And, talking from the point, he drew him in,
And there he mellow'd all his heart with
      ale,
Until they closed a bargain, hand in hand.

'Then, while I breathed in sight of haven,
      he —
Poor fellow, could he help it ? — recom-
      menced,

And ran thro' all the coltish chronicle,  159
Wild Will, Black Bess, Tantivy, Tallyho,
Reform, White Rose, Bellerophon, the
    Jilt,
Arbaces, and Phenomenon, and the rest,
Till, not to die a listener, I arose,
And with me Philip, talking still; and so
We turn'd our foreheads from the falling
    sun,
And following our own shadows thrice as
    long
As when they follow'd us from Philip's
    door,
Arrived, and found the sun of sweet con-
    tent
Re - risen in Katie's eyes, and all things
    well.

            I steal by lawns and grassy plots,  170
              I slide by hazel covers ;
            I move the sweet forget-me-nots
              That grow for happy lovers.

            I slip, I slide, I gloom, I glance,
              Among my skimming swallows ;
            I make the netted sunbeam dance
              Against my sandy shallows.

            I murmur under moon and stars
              In brambly wildernesses ;
            I linger by my shingly bars,  180
              I loiter round my cresses ;

            And out again I curve and flow
              To join the brimming river,
            For men may come and men may go,
              But I go on for ever.

Yes, men may come and go; and these are
    gone,
All gone.  My dearest brother, Edmund,
    sleeps,
Not by the well-known stream and rustic
    spire,
But unfamiliar Arno, and the dome
Of Brunelleschi, sleeps in peace; and he,
Poor Philip, of all his lavish waste of
    words  191
Remains the lean P. W. on his tomb;
I scraped the lichen from it.  Katie walks
By the long wash of Australasian seas
Far off, and holds her head to other
    stars,
And breathes in April-autumns.  All are
    gone.'

    So Lawrence Aylmer, seated on a stile
In the long hedge, and rolling in his mind
Old waifs of rhyme, and bowing o'er the
    brook
A tonsured head in middle age forlorn,  200
Mused, and was mute.  On a sudden a low
    breath
Of tender air made tremble in the hedge
The fragile bindweed - bells and briony
    rings;
And he look'd up.  There stood a maiden
    near,
Waiting to pass.  In much amaze he stared
On eyes a bashful azure, and on hair
In gloss and hue the chestnut, when the
    shell
Divides threefold to show the fruit with-
    in ;
Then, wondering, ask'd her, 'Are you from
    the farm ?'
'Yes,' answer'd she.  'Pray stay a little;
    pardon me,  210
What do they call you ?'  'Katie.'  'That
    were strange.
What surname ?'  'Willows.'  'No !'  'That
    is my name.'
'Indeed !'  and here he look'd so self-
    perplext,
That Katie laugh'd, and laughing blush'd,
    till he
Laugh'd also, but as one before he wakes,
Who feels a glimmering strangeness in his
    dream.
Then looking at her: 'Too happy, fresh
    and fair,
Too fresh and fair in our sad world's best
    bloom,
To be the ghost of one who bore your
    name  219
About these meadows, twenty years ago.'

    'Have you not heard ?' said Katie, 'we
    came back.
We bought the farm we tenanted be-
    fore.
Am I so like her ? so they said on board.
Sir, if you knew her in her English days,
My mother, as it seems you did, the
    days
That most she loves to talk of, come with
    me.
My brother James is in the harvest-field;
But she — you will be welcome — O, come
    in !'

## THE DAISY

### WRITTEN AT EDINBURGH

'A tender dream of the poet; musing in a murky street in Edinburgh over a daisy picked on the "Snowy Splügen" gives him opportunity for many varied sketches of Southern life, full of color and spirit and movement' (Waugh, 'Alfred Lord Tennyson,' 1892). The Italian journey was made in 1851, the year after the poet's marriage.

O LOVE, what hours were thine and mine,
In lands of palm and southern pine;
　In lands of palm, or orange-blossom,
Of olive, aloe, and maize and vine!

What Roman strength Turbìa show'd
In ruin, by the mountain road;
　How like a gem, beneath, the city
Of little Monaco, basking, glow'd!

How richly down the rocky dell
The torrent vineyard streaming fell　10
　To meet the sun and sunny waters,
That only heaved with a summer swell!

What slender campanili grew
By bays, the peacock's neck in hue;
　Where, here and there, on sandy beaches
A milky-bell'd amaryllis blew!

How young Columbus seem'd to rove,
Yet present in his natal grove,
　Now watching high on mountain cornice,
And steering, now, from a purple cove,　20

Now pacing mute by ocean's rim;
Till, in a narrow street and dim,
　I stay'd the wheels at Cogoletto,
And drank, and loyally drank to him!

Nor knew we well what pleased us most;
Not the clipt palm of which they boast,
　But distant color, happy hamlet,
A moulder'd citadel on the coast,

Or tower, or high hill-convent, seen
A light amid its olives green;　30
　Or olive-hoary cape in ocean;
Or rosy blossom in hot ravine,

Where oleanders flush'd the bed
Of silent torrents, gravel-spread;
　And, crossing, oft we saw the glisten
Of ice, far up on a mountain head.

We loved that hall, tho' white and cold,
Those niched shapes of noble mould,
　A princely people's awful princes,
The grave, severe Genovese of old.　40

At Florence too what golden hours,
In those long galleries, were ours;
　What drives about the fresh Cascinè,
Or walks in Boboli's ducal bowers!

In bright vignettes, and each complete,
Of tower or duomo, sunny-sweet,
　Or palace, how the city glitter'd,
Thro' cypress avenues, at our feet!

But when we crost the Lombard plain
Remember what a plague of rain;　50
　Of rain at Reggio, rain at Parma,
At Lodi rain, Piacenza rain.

And stern and sad — so rare the smiles
Of sunlight — look'd the Lombard piles;
　Porch-pillars on the lion resting,
And sombre, old, colonnaded aisles.

O Milan, O the chanting quires,
The giant windows' blazon'd fires,
　The height, the space, the gloom, the glory!
A mount of marble, a hundred spires!　60

I climb'd the roofs at break of day;
Sun-smitten Alps before me lay.
　I stood among the silent statues,
And statued pinnacles, mute as they.

How faintly-flush'd, how phantom-fair,
Was Monte Rosa, hanging there
　A thousand shadowy-pencill'd valleys
And snowy dells in a golden air!

Remember how we came at last
To Como; shower and storm and blast　70
　Had blown the lake beyond his limit,
And all was flooded; and how we past

From Como, when the light was gray,
And in my head, for half the day,
　The rich Virgilian rustic measure
Of 'Lari Maxume,' all the way,

Like ballad-burthen music, kept,
As on the Lariano crept
    To that fair port below the castle
Of Queen Theodolind, where we slept;  80

Or hardly slept, but watch'd awake
A cypress in the moonlight shake,
    The moonlight touching o'er a terrace
One tall agavè above the lake.

What more ? we took our last adieu,
And up the snowy Splügen drew;
    But ere we reach'd the highest summit
I pluck'd a daisy, I gave it you.

It told of England then to me,
And now it tells of Italy.  90
    O love, we two shall go no longer
To lands of summer across the sea,

So dear a life your arms enfold
Whose crying is a cry for gold;
    Yet here to-night in this dark city,
When ill and weary, alone and cold,

I found, tho' crush'd to hard and dry,
This nursling of another sky
    Still in the little book you lent me,
And where you tenderly laid it by;  100

And I forgot the clouded Forth,
The gloom that saddens heaven and earth,
    The bitter east, the misty summer
And gray metropolis of the North.

Perchance to lull the throbs of pain,
Perchance to charm a vacant brain,
    Perchance to dream you still beside
      me,
My fancy fled to the South again.


## TO THE REV. F. D. MAURICE

Come, when no graver cares employ,
Godfather, come and see your boy;
    Your presence will be sun in winter,
Making the little one leap for joy.

For, being of that honest few
Who give the Fiend himself his due,
    Should eighty thousand college-councils
Thunder ' Anathema,' friend, at you,

Should all our churchmen foam in spite
At you, so careful of the right,  10
    Yet one lay-hearth would give you wel-
      come —
Take it and come — to the Isle of Wight;

Where, far from noise and smoke of
      town,
I watch the twilight falling brown
    All round a careless-order'd garden
Close to the ridge of a noble down.

You 'll have no scandal while you dine,
But honest talk and wholesome wine,
    And only hear the magpie gossip
Garrulous under a roof of pine;  20

For groves of pine on either hand,
To break the blast of winter, stand,
    And further on, the hoary Channel
Tumbles a billow on chalk and sand;

Where, if below the milky steep
Some ship of battle slowly creep,
    And on thro' zones of light and shadow
Glimmer away to the lonely deep,

We might discuss the Northern sin
Which made a selfish war begin,  30
    Dispute the claims, arrange the
      chances, —
Emperor, Ottoman, which shall win;

Or whether war's avenging rod
Shall lash all Europe into blood;
    Till you should turn to dearer matters,
Dear to the man that is dear to God, —

How best to help the slender store,
How mend the dwellings, of the poor,
    How gain in life, as life advances,
Valor and charity more and more.  40

Come, Maurice, come; the lawn as yet
Is hoar with rime or spongy-wet,
    But when the wreath of March has blos-
      som'd, —
Crocus, anemone, violet, —

Or later, pay one visit here,
For those are few we hold as dear;
    Nor pay but one, but come for many,
Many and many a happy year.

January, 1854.

## WILL

### I

O, WELL for him whose will is strong !
He suffers, but he will not suffer long;
He suffers, but he cannot suffer wrong.
For him nor moves the loud world's random
    mock,
Nor all Calamity's hugest waves confound,
Who seems a promontory of rock,
That, compass'd round with turbulent
    sound,
In middle ocean meets the surging shock,
Tempest-buffeted, citadel-crown'd.

### II

But ill for him who, bettering not with
    time,
Corrupts the strength of heaven-descended
    Will,
And ever weaker grows thro' acted crime,
Or seeming-genial venial fault,
Recurring and suggesting still !
He seems as one whose footsteps halt,
Toiling in immeasurable sand,
And o'er a weary sultry land,
Far beneath a blazing vault,
Sown in a wrinkle of the monstrous hill,
The city sparkles like a grain of salt.

## ODE ON THE DEATH OF THE DUKE OF WELLINGTON

This poem, originally published on the day of the Duke's funeral in 1852, was probably written in some haste. It underwent considerable revision before it was reprinted in 1853, and was further retouched before it appeared with 'Maud' in 1855. The variations of the present text from the first edition are given in the Notes.

Shepherd ('Tennysoniana,' 1879), in his chapter on 'Tennyson's Versification,' remarks : ' In the "Ode on the Death of the Duke of Wellington," he has soared to lyric heights to which, perhaps, even Pindar never attained. The tolling of the bell, the solemn and slow funeral march, the quick rush of battle, and the choral chant of the cathedral all succeed one another, and the verse sinks and swells, rises and falls to every alternation with equal power.'

### I

BURY the Great Duke
  With an empire's lamentation;
Let us bury the Great Duke
  To the noise of the mourning of a mighty
    nation;
Mourning when their leaders fall,
Warriors carry the warrior's pall,
And sorrow darkens hamlet and hall.

### II

Where shall we lay the man whom we de-
    plore ?
Here, in streaming London's central roar.
Let the sound of those he wrought for,   10
And the feet of those he fought for,
Echo round his bones for evermore.

### III

Lead out the pageant: sad and slow,
As fits an universal woe,
Let the long, long procession go,
And let the sorrowing crowd about it grow,
And let the mournful martial music blow;
The last great Englishman is low.

### IV

Mourn, for to us he seems the last,   19
Remembering all his greatness in the past.
No more in soldier fashion will he greet
With lifted hand the gazer in the street.
O friends, our chief state-oracle is mute !
Mourn for the man of long-enduring blood,
The statesman-warrior, moderate, resolute,
Whole in himself, a common good.
Mourn for the man of amplest influence,
Yet clearest of ambitious crime,
Our greatest yet with least pretence,
Great in council and great in war,   30
Foremost captain of his time,
Rich in saving common-sense,
And, as the greatest only are,
In his simplicity sublime.
O good gray head which all men knew,
O voice from which their omens all men
    drew,
O iron nerve to true occasion true,
O fallen at length that tower of strength
Which stood four-square to all the winds
    that blew !
Such was he whom we deplore.   40
The long self-sacrifice of life is o'er.
The great World-victor's victor will be
    seen no more.

### V

All is over and done.
Render thanks to the Giver,

England, for thy son.
Let the bell be toll'd.
Render thanks to the Giver,
And render him to the mould.
Under the cross of gold
That shines over city and river,          50
There he shall rest for ever
Among the wise and the bold.
Let the bell be toll'd,
And a reverent people behold
The towering car, the sable steeds.
Bright let it be with its blazon'd deeds,
Dark in its funeral fold.
Let the bell be toll'd,
And a deeper knell in the heart be knoll'd;
And the sound of the sorrowing anthem
        roll'd                            60
Thro' the dome of the golden cross;
And the volleying cannon thunder his loss;
He knew their voices of old.
For many a time in many a clime
His captain's-ear has heard them boom
Bellowing victory, bellowing doom.
When he with those deep voices wrought,
Guarding realms and kings from shame,
With those deep voices our dead captain
        taught
The tyrant, and asserts his claim        70
In that dread sound to the great name
Which he has worn so pure of blame,
In praise and in dispraise the same,
A man of well-attemper'd frame.
O civic muse, to such a name,
To such a name for ages long,
To such a name,
Preserve a broad approach of fame,
And ever-echoing avenues of song !

### VI

'Who is he that cometh, like an honor'd
        guest,                           80
With banner and with music, with soldier
        and with priest,
With a nation weeping, and breaking on
        my rest ? ' —
Mighty Seaman, this is he
Was great by land as thou by sea.
Thine island loves thee well, thou famous
        man,
The greatest sailor since our world began.
Now, to the roll of muffled drums,
To thee the greatest soldier comes;
For this is he
Was great by land as thou by sea.        90
His foes were thine; he kept us free;

O, give him welcome, this is he
Worthy of our gorgeous rites,
And worthy to be laid by thee;
For this is England's greatest son,
He that gain'd a hundred fights,
Nor ever lost an English gun;
This is he that far away
Against the myriads of Assaye
Clash'd with his fiery few and won;      100
And underneath another sun,
Warring on a later day,
Round affrighted Lisbon drew
The treble works, the vast designs
Of his labor'd rampart-lines,
Where he greatly stood at bay,
Whence he issued forth anew,
And ever great and greater grew,
Beating from the wasted vines
Back to France her banded swarms,        110
Back to France with countless blows,
Till o'er the hills her eagles flew
Beyond the Pyrenean pines,
Follow'd up in valley and glen
With blare of bugle, clamor of men,
Roll of cannon and clash of arms,
And England pouring on her foes.
Such a war had such a close.
Again their ravening eagle rose
In anger, wheel'd on Europe - shadowing
        wings,                           120
And barking for the thrones of kings;
Till one that sought but Duty's iron crown
On that loud Sabbath shook the spoiler
        down;
A day of onsets of despair !
Dash'd on every rocky square,
Their surging charges foam'd themselves
        away;
Last, the Prussian trumpet blew;
Thro' the long-tormented air
Heaven flash'd a sudden jubilant ray,
And down we swept and charged and over-
        threw.                           130
So great a soldier taught us there
What long-enduring hearts could do
In that world-earthquake, Waterloo !
Mighty Seaman, tender and true,
And pure as he from taint of craven guile,
O saviour of the silver-coasted isle,
O shaker of the Baltic and the Nile,
If aught of things that here befall
Touch a spirit among things divine,      139
If love of country move thee there at all,
Be glad, because his bones are laid by
        thine !

And thro' the centuries let a people's voice
In full acclaim,
A people's voice,
The proof and echo of all human fame,
A people's voice, when they rejoice
At civic revel and pomp and game,
Attest their great commander's claim
With honor, honor, honor, honor to him,
Eternal honor to his name.          150

### VII

A people's voice! we are a people yet.
Tho' all men else their nobler dreams for-
    get,
Confused by brainless mobs and lawless
    Powers,
Thank Him who isled us here, and roughly
    set
His Briton in blown seas and storming
    showers,
We have a voice with which to pay the
    debt
Of boundless love and reverence and regret
To those great men who fought, and kept
    it ours.
And keep it ours, O God, from brute con-
    trol!
O Statesmen, guard us, guard the eye, the
    soul          160
Of Europe, keep our noble England whole,
And save the one true seed of freedom
    sown
Betwixt a people and their ancient throne,
That sober freedom out of which there
    springs
Our loyal passion for our temperate kings!
For, saving that, ye help to save mankind
Till public wrong be crumbled into dust,
And drill the raw world for the march of
    mind,
Till crowds at length be sane and crowns
    be just.
But wink no more in slothful overtrust.  170
Remember him who led your hosts;
He bade you guard the sacred coasts.
Your cannons moulder on the seaward
    wall;
His voice is silent in your council-hall
For ever; and whatever tempests lour
For ever silent; even if they broke
In thunder, silent; yet remember all
He spoke among you, and the Man who
    spoke;
Who never sold the truth to serve the
    hour,          179

Nor palter'd with Eternal God for power;
Who let the turbid streams of rumor flow
Thro' either babbling world of high and
    low;
Whose life was work, whose language
    rife
With rugged maxims hewn from life;
Who never spoke against a foe;
Whose eighty winters freeze with one
    rebuke
All great self-seekers trampling on the
    right.
Truth-teller was our England's Alfred
    named;
Truth-lover was our English Duke;
Whatever record leap to light          190
He never shall be shamed.

### VIII

Lo! the leader in these glorious wars
Now to glorious burial slowly borne,
Follow'd by the brave of other lands,
He, on whom from both her open hands
Lavish Honor shower'd all her stars,
And affluent Fortune emptied all her horn.
Yea, let all good things await
Him who cares not to be great
But as he saves or serves the state.          200
Not once or twice in our rough island-
    story
The path of duty was the way to glory.
He that walks it, only thirsting
For the right, and learns to deaden
Love of self, before his journey closes,
He shall find the stubborn thistle bursting
Into glossy purples, which outredden
All voluptuous garden-roses.
Not once or twice in our fair island-story
The path of duty was the way to glory.  210
He, that ever following her commands,
On with toil of heart and knees and hands,
Thro' the long gorge to the far light has
    won
His path upward, and prevail'd,
Shall find the toppling crags of Duty
    scaled
Are close upon the shining table-lands
To which our God Himself is moon and
    sun.
Such was he: his work is done.
But while the races of mankind endure
Let his great example stand          220
Colossal, seen of every land,
And keep the soldier firm, the statesman
    pure;

Till in all lands and thro' all human story
The path of duty be the way to glory.
And let the land whose hearths he saved
    from shame
For many and many an age proclaim
At civic revel and pomp and game,
And when the long-illumined cities flame,
Their ever-loyal iron leader's fame,
With honor, honor, honor, honor to him,
Eternal honor to his name.    231

IX

Peace, his triumph will be sung
By some yet unmoulded tongue
Far on in summers that we shall not see.
Peace, it is a day of pain
For one about whose patriarchal knee
Late the little children clung.
O peace, it is a day of pain
For one upon whose hand and heart and
    brain
Once the weight and fate of Europe hung.
Ours the pain, be his the gain !    241
More than is of man's degree
Must be with us, watching here
At this, our great solemnity.
Whom we see not we revere;
We revere, and we refrain
From talk of battles loud and vain,
And brawling memories all too free
For such a wise humility
As befits a solemn fane:    250
We revere, and while we hear
The tides of Music's golden sea
Setting toward eternity,
Uplifted high in heart and hope are we,
Until we doubt not that for one so true
There must be other nobler work to do
Than when he fought at Waterloo,
And Victor he must ever be.
For tho' the Giant Ages heave the hill
And break the shore, and evermore    260
Make and break, and work their will,
Tho' world on world in myriad myriads
    roll
Round us, each with different powers,
And other forms of life than ours,
What know we greater than the soul ?
On God and Godlike men we build our
    trust.
Hush, the Dead March wails in the people's
    ears;
The dark crowd moves, and there are sobs
    and tears;

The black earth yawns; the mortal disap-
    pears;
Ashes to ashes, dust to dust;    270
He is gone who seem'd so great. —
Gone, but nothing can bereave him
Of the force he made his own
Being here, and we believe him
Something far advanced in State,
And that he wears a truer crown
Than any wreath that man can weave him.
Speak no more of his renown,
Lay your earthly fancies down,
And in the vast cathedral leave him,    280
God accept him, Christ receive him !
1852.

## THE CHARGE OF THE LIGHT BRIGADE

For the successive versions of this lyric, see
the Notes.

I

HALF a league, half a league,
Half a league onward,
All in the valley of Death
    Rode the six hundred.
'Forward, the Light Brigade !
Charge for the guns ! ' he said.
Into the valley of Death
    Rode the six hundred.

II

'Forward, the Light Brigade !'
Was there a man dismay'd ?
Not tho' the soldier knew
    Some one had blunder'd.
Theirs not to make reply,
Theirs not to reason why,
Theirs but to do and die.
Into the valley of Death
    Rode the six hundred.

III

Cannon to right of them,
Cannon to left of them,
Cannon in front of them
    Volley'd and thunder'd;
Storm'd at with shot and shell,
Boldly they rode and well,
Into the jaws of Death,
Into the mouth of hell
    Rode the six hundred.

IV

Flash'd all their sabres bare,
Flash'd as they turn'd in air
Sabring the gunners there,
Charging an army, while
    All the world wonder'd.
Plunged in the battery-smoke
Right thro' the line they broke;
Cossack and Russian
Reel'd from the sabre-stroke
Shatter'd and sunder'd.
Then they rode back, but not,
    Not the six hundred.

V

Cannon to right of them,
Cannon to left of them,

Cannon behind them
    Volley'd and thunder'd;
Storm'd at with shot and shell,
While horse and hero fell,
They that had fought so well
Came thro' the jaws of Death,
Back from the mouth of hell,
All that was left of them,
    Left of six hundred.

VI

When can their glory fade ?
O the wild charge they made !
    All the world wonder'd.
Honor the charge they made !
Honor the Light Brigade,
Noble six hundred !

# ENOCH ARDEN

## AND OTHER POEMS

This was the title of the volume, published in 1864, containing, besides 'Enoch Arden,' the following poems: 'Aylmer's Field,' 'Sea Dreams,' 'Ode sung at Opening of International Exhibition,' 'The Grandmother,' 'The Northern Farmer (Old Style),' 'Tithonus,' 'The Voyage,' 'In the Valley of Cauteretz, 'The Flower,' 'Requiescat,' 'The Sailor Boy,' 'The Islet,' 'The Ringlet' (afterwards suppressed), 'Welcome to Alexandra,' 'Dedication,' 'Attempts at Classic Metres in Quantity,' and 'Specimen of Blank Verse Translation of the Iliad.' The list given under the title of this volume in the English editions is misleading, as it includes only two of the above poems, with two ('The Brook' and 'Lucretius') published in other volumes.

### ENOCH ARDEN

'Enoch Arden' has been one of the most popular of the poet's works, not only in English-speaking countries, but also on the continent of Europe. Mr. Eugene Parsons, in his pamphlet on 'Tennyson's Life and Poetry' (2d edition, 1893), enumerates no less than twenty-four translations: nine in German, two in Dutch, one in Danish, one in Bohemian, eight in French, one in Spanish, and two in Italian. There is also a Latin version by Mr. W. Selwyn (London, 1867).

According to the 'British Quarterly Review' for October, 1880, the stories of both 'Enoch Arden' and 'Aylmer's Field' were 'told by a friend to the poet, who, struck by their aptitude for versification, requested to have them at length in writing. When they were thus supplied, the poetic versions were made as we now have them.' This is confirmed by the 'Memoir' (vol. ii. p. 7), where we learn that the 'friend' was Woolner the sculptor.

LONG lines of cliff breaking have left a
    chasm;
And in the chasm are foam and yellow
    sands;
Beyond, red roofs about a narrow wharf
In cluster; then a moulder'd church; and
    higher
A long street climbs to one tall-tower'd
    mill;
And high in heaven behind it a gray down
With Danish barrows; and a hazel-wood,
By autumn nutters haunted, flourishes
Green in a cuplike hollow of the down.
Here on this beach a hundred years ago, 10
Three children of three houses, Annie Lee,
The prettiest little damsel in the port,
And Philip Ray, the miller's only son,
And Enoch Arden, a rough sailor's lad
Made orphan by a winter shipwreck, play'd
Among the waste and lumber of the shore,
Hard coils of cordage, swarthy fishing-nets,

Anchors of rusty fluke, and boats updrawn;
And built their castles of dissolving sand
To watch them overflow'd, or following up
And flying the white breaker, daily left    21
The little footprint daily wash'd away.

A narrow cave ran in beneath the cliff;
In this the children play'd at keeping
    house.
Enoch was host one day, Philip the next,
While Annie still was mistress; but at
    times
Enoch would hold possession for a week:
'This is my house and this my little wife.'
'Mine too,' said Philip; 'turn and turn
    about;'
When, if they quarrell'd, Enoch stronger-
    made    30
Was master.    Then would Philip, his blue
    eyes
All flooded with the helpless wrath of tears,
Shriek out, 'I hate you, Enoch,' and at this
The little wife would weep for company,
And pray them not to quarrel for her sake,
And say she would be little wife to both.

But when the dawn of rosy childhood
    past,
And the new warmth of life's ascending
    sun
Was felt by either, either fixt his heart
On that one girl; and Enoch spoke his
    love,    40
But Philip loved in silence; and the girl
Seem'd kinder unto Philip than to him;
But she loved Enoch, tho' she knew it not,
And would if ask'd deny it.    Enoch set
A purpose evermore before his eyes,
To hoard all savings to the uttermost,
To purchase his own boat, and make a
    home
For Annie; and so prosper'd that at last
A luckier or a bolder fisherman,
A carefuller in peril, did not breathe    50
For leagues along that breaker-beaten
    coast
Than Enoch.    Likewise had he served a
    year
On board a merchantman, and made him-
    self
Full sailor; and he thrice had pluck'd a
    life
From the dread sweep of the down-stream-
    ing seas,
And all men look'd upon him favorably.

And ere he touch'd his one-and-twentieth
    May
He purchased his own boat, and made a
    home
For Annie, neat and nestlike, halfway up
The narrow street that clamber'd toward
    the mill.    60

Then, on a golden autumn eventide,
The younger people making holiday,
With bag and sack and basket, great and
    small,
Went nutting to the hazels.    Philip stay'd—
His father lying sick and needing him—
An hour behind; but as he climb'd the hill,
Just where the prone edge of the wood be-
    gan
To feather toward the hollow, saw the pair,
Enoch and Annie, sitting hand-in-hand,
His large gray eyes and weather-beaten
    face    70
All-kindled by a still and sacred fire,
That burn'd as on an altar.    Philip look'd,
And in their eyes and faces read his doom;
Then, as their faces drew together, groan'd,
And slipt aside, and like a wounded life
Crept down into the hollows of the wood;
There, while the rest were loud in merry-
    making,
Had his dark hour unseen, and rose and
    past
Bearing a lifelong hunger in his heart.

So these were wed, and merrily rang the
    bells,    80
And merrily ran the years, seven happy
    years,
Seven happy years of health and compe-
    tence,
And mutual love and honorable toil,
With children, first a daughter.    In him
    woke,
With his first babe's first cry, the noble
    wish
To save all earnings to the uttermost,
And give his child a better bringing-up
Than his had been, or hers; a wish re-
    new'd,
When two years after came a boy to be
The rosy idol of her solitudes,    90
While Enoch was abroad on wrathful seas,
Or often journeying landward; for in truth
Enoch's white horse, and Enoch's ocean-
    spoil
In ocean-smelling osier, and his face,

Rough - redden'd with a thousand winter
    gales,
Not only to the market-cross were known,
But in the leafy lanes behind the down,
Far as the portal-warding lion-whelp
And peacock yew-tree of the lonely Hall,
Whose Friday fare was Enoch's minister-
    ing.                                    100

    Then came a change, as all things human
        change.
Ten miles to northward of the narrow port
Open'd a larger haven.  Thither used
Enoch at times to go by land or sea;
And once when there, and clambering on a
    mast
In harbor, by mischance he slipt and fell.
A limb was broken when they lifted him;
And while he lay recovering there, his wife
Bore him another son, a sickly one.
Another hand crept too across his trade  110
Taking her bread and theirs; and on him
    fell,
Altho' a grave and staid God-fearing man,
Yet lying thus inactive, doubt and gloom.
He seem'd, as in a nightmare of the night,
To see his children leading evermore
Low miserable lives of hand-to-mouth,
And her he loved a beggar.  Then he pray'd,
' Save them from this, whatever comes
    to me.'
And while he pray'd, the master of that
    ship
Enoch had served in, hearing his mis-
    chance,                                120
Came, for he knew the man and valued
    him,
Reporting of his vessel China-bound,
And wanting yet a boatswain.  Would
    he go ?
There yet were many weeks before she
    sail'd,
Sail'd from this port.  Would Enoch have
    the place ?
And Enoch all at once assented to it,
Rejoicing at that answer to his prayer.

    So now that shadow of mischance ap-
        pear'd
No graver than as when some little cloud
Cuts off the fiery highway of the sun,    130
And isles a light in the offing.  Yet the
    wife —
When he was gone — the children — what
    to do ?

Then Enoch lay long - pondering on his
    plans:
To sell the boat — and yet he loved her
    well —
How many a rough sea had he weather'd
    in her !
He knew her, as a horseman knows his
    horse —
And yet to sell her — then with what she
    brought
Buy goods and stores — set Annie forth in
    trade
With all that seamen needed or their
    wives —
So might she keep the house while he was
    gone.                                   140
Should he not trade himself out yonder ?
    go
This voyage more than once ? yea, twice
    or thrice —
As oft as needed — last, returning rich,
Become the master of a larger craft,
With fuller profits lead an easier life,
Have all his pretty young ones educated,
And pass his days in peace among his own.

    Thus Enoch in his heart determined all;
Then moving homeward came on Annie
    pale,
Nursing the sickly babe, her latest-born. 150
Forward she started with a happy cry,
And laid the feeble infant in his arms;
Whom Enoch took, and handled all his
    limbs,
Appraised his weight and fondled father-
    like,
But had no heart to break his purposes
To Annie, till the morrow, when he spoke.

    Then first since Enoch's golden ring had
        girt
Her finger, Annie fought against his will;
Yet not with brawling opposition she,
But manifold entreaties, many a tear,     160
Many a sad kiss by day, by night, renew'd —
Sure that all evil would come out of it —
Besought him, supplicating, if he cared
For her or his dear children, not to go.
He not for his own self caring, but her,
Her and her children, let her plead in vain;
So grieving held his will, and bore it thro'.

    For Enoch parted with his old sea-friend,
Bought Annie goods and stores, and set his
    hand

To fit their little streetward sitting-room
With shelf and corner for the goods and
     stores.                                        171
So all day long till Enoch's last at home,
Shaking their pretty cabin, hammer and
     axe,
Auger and saw, while Annie seem'd to
     hear
Her own death-scaffold raising, shrill'd and
     rang,
Till this was ended, and his careful hand, —
The space was narrow, — having order'd
     all
Almost as neat and close as Nature packs
Her blossom or her seedling, paused; and
     he,
Who needs would work for Annie to the
     last,                                          180
Ascending tired, heavily slept till morn.

And Enoch faced this morning of fare-
     well
Brightly and boldly. All his Annie's fears,
Save as his Annie's, were a laughter to
     him.
Yet Enoch as a brave God-fearing man
Bow'd himself down, and in that mystery
Where God-in-man is one with man-in-
     God,
Pray'd for a blessing on his wife and babes,
Whatever came to him; and then he said:
' Annie, this voyage by the grace of God
Will bring fair weather yet to all of us. 191
Keep a clean hearth and a clear fire for me,
For I 'll be back, my girl, before you
     know it; '
Then lightly rocking baby's cradle, ' and
     he,
This pretty, puny, weakly little one, —
Nay — for I love him all the better for
     it —
God bless him, he shall sit upon my knees
And I will tell him tales of foreign parts,
And make him merry, when I come home
     again.                                        199
Come, Annie, come, cheer up before I go.'

Him running on thus hopefully she
     heard,
And almost hoped herself; but when he
     turn'd
The current of his talk to graver things
In sailor fashion roughly sermonizing
On providence and trust in heaven, she
     heard,

Heard and not heard him; as the village
     girl,
Who sets her pitcher underneath the
     spring,
Musing on him that used to fill it for her,
Hears and not hears, and lets it overflow.

At length she spoke: ' O Enoch, you are
     wise;                                          210
And yet for all your wisdom well know I
That I shall look upon your face no more.'

' Well, then,' said Enoch, ' I shall look
     on yours.
Annie, the ship I sail in passes here ' —
He named the day; — ' get you a seaman's
     glass,
Spy out my face, and laugh at all your
     fears.'

But when the last of those last moments
     came:
' Annie, my girl, cheer up, be comforted,
Look to the babes, and till I come again
Keep everything shipshape, for I must
     go.                                            220
And fear no more for me; or if you fear,
Cast all your cares on God; that anchor
     holds.
Is He not yonder in those uttermost
Parts of the morning ? if I flee to these,
Can I go from Him ? and the sea is His,
The sea is His; He made it.'

                                        Enoch rose,
Cast his strong arms about his drooping
     wife,
And kiss'd his wonder-stricken little ones;
But for the third, the sickly one, who slept
After a night of feverous wakefulness,   230
When Annie would have raised him Enoch
     said,
' Wake him not, let him sleep; how should
     the child
Remember this ? ' and kiss'd him in his
     cot.
But Annie from her baby's forehead clipt
A tiny curl, and gave it; this he kept
Thro' all his future, but now hastily caught
His bundle, waved his hand, and went his
     way.

She, when the day that Enoch mention'd
     came,
Borrow'd a glass, but all in vain. Perhaps

She could not fix the glass to suit her eye;
Perhaps her eye was dim, hand tremulous;
She saw him not, and while he stood on
    deck                                    242
Waving, the moment and the vessel past.

Even to the last dip of the vanishing sail
She watch'd it, and departed weeping for
    him;
Then, tho' she mourn'd his absence as his
    grave,
Set her sad will no less to chime with his,
But throve not in her trade, not being bred
To barter, nor compensating the want
By shrewdness, neither capable of lies,    250
Nor asking overmuch and taking less,
And still foreboding ' what would Enoch
    say ? '
For more than once, in days of difficulty
And pressure, had she sold her wares for
    less
Than what she gave in buying what she
    sold.
She fail'd and sadden'd knowing it; and
    thus,
Expectant of that news which never came,
Gain'd for her own a scanty sustenance,
And lived a life of silent melancholy.

Now the third child was sickly-born and
    grew                                    260
Yet sicklier, tho' the mother cared for it
With all a mother's care; nevertheless,
Whether her business often call'd her
    from it,
Or thro' the want of what it needed most,
Or means to pay the voice who best could
    tell
What most it needed — howsoe'er it was,
After a lingering, — ere she was aware, —
Like the caged bird escaping suddenly,
The little innocent soul flitted away.

In that same week when Annie buried
    it,                                     270
Philip's true heart, which hunger'd for her
    peace, —
Since Enoch left he had not look'd upon
    her, —
Smote him, as having kept aloof so long.
' Surely,' said Philip, ' I may see her now,
May be some little comfort;' therefore
    went,
Past thro' the solitary room in front,
Paused for a moment at an inner door,

Then struck it thrice, and, no one opening,
Enter'd, but Annie, seated with her grief,
Fresh from the burial of her little one,    280
Cared not to look on any human face,
But turn'd her own toward the wall and
    wept.
Then Philip standing up said falteringly,
' Annie, I came to ask a favor of you.'

He spoke; the passion in her moan'd re-
    ply,
' Favor from one so sad and so forlorn
As I am !' half abash'd him; yet unask'd,
His bashfulness and tenderness at war,
He set himself beside her, saying to her:

' I came to speak to you of what he
    wish'd,                                 290
Enoch, your husband.   I have ever said
You chose the best among us — a strong
    man;
For where he fixt his heart he set his hand
To do the thing he will'd, and bore it thro'.
And wherefore did he go this weary way,
And leave you lonely ? not to see the
    world —
For pleasure ? — nay, but for the where-
    withal
To give his babes a better bringing up
Than his had been, or yours; that was his
    wish.
And if he come again, vext will he be    300
To find the precious morning hours were
    lost.
And it would vex him even in his grave,
If he could know his babes were running
    wild
Like colts about the waste.   So, Annie,
    now —
Have we not known each other all our
    lives ?
I do beseech you by the love you bear
Him and his children not to say me nay —
For, if you will, when Enoch comes again
Why then he shall repay me — if you will,
Annie — for I am rich and well-to-do.    310
Now let me put the boy and girl to school;
This is the favor that I came to ask.'

Then Annie with her brows against the
    wall
Answer'd, ' I cannot look you in the face;
I seem so foolish and so broken down.
When you came in my sorrow broke me
    down;

And now I think your kindness breaks me
    down.
But Enoch lives; that is borne in on me;
He will repay you.  Money can be repaid,
Not kindness such as yours.'

                        And Philip ask'd,
'Then you will let me, Annie ? '

                        There she turn'd,
She  rose, and fixt her swimming eyes upon
    him,                                    322
And dwelt a moment on his kindly face,
Then calling down a blessing on his head
Caught at his hand, and wrung it passion-
    ately,
And past into the little garth beyond.
So lifted up in spirit he moved away.

    Then Philip put the boy and girl to
        school,
And bought them needful books, and every
    way,
Like one who does his duty by his own,   330
Made himself theirs; and tho' for Annie's
    sake,
Fearing the lazy gossip of the port,
He oft denied his heart his dearest wish,
And seldom crost her threshold, yet he
    sent
Gifts by the children, garden - herbs and
    fruit,
The late and early roses from his wall,
Or conies from the down, and now and
    then,
With some pretext of fineness in the meal
To save the offence of charitable, flour
From his tall mill that whistled on the
    waste.                                  340

    But Philip did not fathom Annie's mind;
Scarce could the woman, when he came
    upon her,
Out of full heart and boundless gratitude
Light on a broken word to thank him with.
But Philip was her children's all-in-all;
From distant corners of the street they ran
To greet his hearty welcome heartily;
Lords of his house and of his mill were
    they,
Worried his passive ear with petty wrongs
Or pleasures, hung upon him, play'd with
    him                                     350
And call'd him Father Philip.  Philip
    gain'd

As Enoch lost, for Enoch seem'd to them
Uncertain as a vision or a dream,
Faint as a figure seen in early dawn
Down at the far end of an avenue,
Going we know not where; and so ten
    years,
Since Enoch left his hearth and native land,
Fled forward, and no news of Enoch came.

    It chanced one evening Annie's children
        long'd
To go with others nutting to the wood,   360
And Annie would go with them; then they
    begg'd
For Father Philip, as they call'd him, too.
Him, like the working bee in blossom-dust,
Blanch'd with his mill, they found; and
    saying to him,
'Come with us, Father Philip,' he denied;
But when the children pluck'd at him to go,
He laugh'd, and yielded readily to their
    wish,
For was not Annie with them ? and they
    went.

    But after scaling half the weary down,
Just where the prone edge of the wood
    began                                   370
To feather toward the hollow, all her force
Fail'd her; and sighing, ' Let me rest,' she
    said.
So Philip rested with her well-content;
While all the younger ones with jubilant
    cries
Broke from their elders, and tumultuously
Down thro' the whitening hazels made a
    plunge
To the bottom, and dispersed, and bent or
    broke
The lithe reluctant boughs to tear away
Their tawny clusters, crying to each other
And calling, here and there, about the
    wood.                                   380

    But Philip sitting at her side forgot
Her presence, and remember'd one dark
    hour
Here in this wood, when like a wounded
    life
He crept into the shadow.  At last he said,
Lifting his honest forehead, ' Listen, Annie,
How merry they are down yonder in the
    wood.
Tired, Annie ? ' for she did not speak a
    word.

'Tired ?' but her face had fallen upon her
    hands;
At which, as with a kind of anger in him,
'The ship was lost,' he said, 'the ship was
    lost !                                    390
No more of that ! why should you kill
    yourself
And make them orphans quite ?'   And
    Annie said,
'I thought not of it; but — I know not
    why —
Their voices make me feel so solitary.'

Then Philip coming somewhat closer
    spoke:
'Annie, there is a thing upon my mind,
And it has been upon my mind so long
That, tho' I know not when it first came
    there,
I know that it will out at last.   O Annie,
It is beyond all hope, against all chance,
That he who left you ten long years ago
Should still be living; well, then — let me
    speak.                                    402
I grieve to see you poor and wanting help;
I cannot help you as I wish to do
Unless — they say that women are so
    quick —
Perhaps you know what I would have you
    know —
I wish you for my wife.   I fain would
    prove
A father to your children; I do think
They love me as a father; I am sure
That I love them as if they were mine
    own;                                      410
And I believe, if you were fast my wife,
That after all these sad uncertain years
We might be still as happy as God grants
To any of his creatures.   Think upon it;
For I am well-to-do — no kin, no care,
No burthen, save my care for you and
    yours,
And we have known each other all our lives,
And I have loved you longer than you
    know.'

Then answer'd Annie — tenderly she
    spoke:
'You have been as God's good angel in our
    house.                                    420
God bless you for it, God reward you for it,
Philip, with something happier than my-
    self.
Can one love twice ? can you be ever loved

As Enoch was ?  what is it that you ask ?'
'I am content,' he answer'd, ' to be loved
A little after Enoch.'   'O,' she cried,
Scared as it were, ' dear Philip, wait a
    while.
If Enoch comes — but Enoch will not
    come —
Yet wait a year, a year is not so long.
Surely I shall be wiser in a year.          430
O, wait a little !'   Philip sadly said,
'Annie, as I have waited all my life
I well may wait a little.'   'Nay,' she cried,
'I am bound: you have my promise — in a
    year.
Will you not bide your year as I bide
    mine ?'
And Philip answer'd, 'I will bide my year.'

Here both were mute, till Philip glancing
    up
Beheld the dead flame of the fallen day
Pass from the Danish barrow overhead;
Then, fearing night and chill for Annie,
    rose                                      440
And sent his voice beneath him thro' the
    wood.
Up came the children laden with their
    spoil;
Then all descended to the port, and there
At Annie's door he paused and gave his
    hand,
Saying gently, ' Annie, when I spoke to you,
That was your hour of weakness.   I was
    wrong,
I am always bound to you, but you are
    free.'
Then Annie weeping answer'd, 'I am
    bound.'

She spoke; and in one moment as it were,
While yet she went about her household
    ways,                                     450
Even as she dwelt upon his latest words,
That he had loved her longer than she
    knew,
That autumn into autumn flash'd again,
And there he stood once more before her
    face,
Claiming her promise.   'Is it a year ?'
    she ask'd.
'Yes, if the nuts,' he said, ' be ripe again;
Come out and see.'   But she — she put him
    off —
So much to look to — such a change — a
    month —

Give her a month — she knew that she was
　　bound —
A month — no more.   Then Philip with his
　　eyes　　　　　　　　　　　　　　　460
Full of that lifelong hunger, and his voice
Shaking a little like a drunkard's hand,
'Take your own time, Annie, take your own
　　time.'
And Annie could have wept for pity of him;
And yet she held him on delayingly
With many a scarce-believable excuse,
Trying his truth and his long-sufferance,
Till half another year had slipt away.

By this the lazy gossips of the port,
Abhorrent of a calculation crost,　　　470
Began to chafe as at a personal wrong.
Some thought that Philip did but trifle
　　with her;
Some that she but held off to draw him on;
And others laugh'd at her and Philip too,
As simple folk that knew not their own
　　minds;
And one, in whom all evil fancies clung
Like serpent eggs together, laughingly
Would hint at worse in either.   Her own son
Was silent, tho' he often look'd his wish;
But evermore the daughter prest upon her
To wed the man so dear to all of them　481
And lift the household out of poverty;
And Philip's rosy face contracting grew
Careworn and wan; and all these things
　　fell on her
Sharp as reproach.

　　　　　At last one night it chanced
That Annie could not sleep, but earnestly
Pray'd for a sign, 'My Enoch, is he gone?'
Then compass'd round by the blind wall of
　　night
Brook'd not the expectant terror of her
　　heart,
Started from bed, and struck herself a
　　light,　　　　　　　　　　　　　490
Then desperately seized the holy Book,
Suddenly set it wide to find a sign,
Suddenly put her finger on the text,
'Under the palm-tree.'   That was nothing
　　to her,
No meaning there; she closed the Book and
　　slept.
When lo! her Enoch sitting on a height,
Under a palm-tree, over him the sun.
'He is gone,' she thought, 'he is happy, he
　　is singing

Hosanna in the highest; yonder shines
The Sun of Righteousness, and these be
　　palms　　　　　　　　　　　　　500
Whereof the happy people strowing cried
" Hosanna in the highest!"'   Here she
　　woke,
Resolved, sent for him and said wildly to
　　him,
'There is no reason why we should not wed.'
'Then for God's sake,' he answer'd, 'both
　　our sakes,
So you will wed me, let it be at once.'

So these were wed, and merrily rang the
　　bells,
Merrily rang the bells, and they were wed.
But never merrily beat Annie's heart.　509
A footstep seem'd to fall beside her path,
She knew not whence; a whisper on her ear,
She knew not what; nor loved she to be
　　left
Alone at home, nor ventured out alone.
What ail'd her then that, ere she enter'd,
　　often
Her hand dwelt lingeringly on the latch,
Fearing to enter?   Philip thought he knew:
Such doubts and fears were common to her
　　state,
Being with child; but when her child was
　　born,
Then her new child was as herself renew'd,
Then the new mother came about her heart,
Then her good Philip was her all-in-all, 521
And that mysterious instinct wholly died.

And where was Enoch?   Prosperously
　　sail'd
The ship 'Good Fortune,' tho' at setting
　　forth
The Biscay, roughly ridging eastward,
　　shook
And almost overwhelm'd her, yet unvext
She slipt across the summer of the world,
Then after a long tumble about the Cape
And frequent interchange of foul and fair,
She passing thro' the summer world again,
The breath of heaven came continually　531
And sent her sweetly by the golden isles,
Till silent in her oriental haven.

There Enoch traded for himself, and
　　bought
Quaint monsters for the market of those
　　times,
A gilded dragon also for the babes.

Less lucky her home-voyage: at first
    indeed
Thro' many a fair sea-circle, day by day,
Scarce-rocking, her full-busted figure-head
Stared o'er the ripple feathering from her
    bows:        540
Then follow'd calms, and then winds vari-
    able,
Then baffling, a long course of them; and
    last
Storm, such as drove her under moonless
    heavens
Till hard upon the cry of 'breakers' came
The crash of ruin, and the loss of all
But Enoch and two others.  Half the
    night,
Buoy'd upon floating tackle and broken
    spars,
These drifted, stranding on an isle at morn
Rich, but the loneliest in a lonely sea.

No want was there of human suste-
    nance,        550
Soft fruitage, mighty nuts, and nourishing
    roots;
Nor save for pity was it hard to take
The helpless life so wild that it was tame.
There in a seaward-gazing mountain-gorge
They built, and thatch'd with leaves of
    palm, a hut,
Half hut, half native cavern.  So the three,
Set in this Eden of all plenteousness,
Dwelt with eternal summer, ill-content.
For one, the youngest, hardly more than
    boy,
Hurt in that night of sudden ruin and
    wreck,        560
Lay lingering out a five-years' death-in-
    life.
They could not leave him.  After he was
    gone,
The two remaining found a fallen stem;
And Enoch's comrade, careless of himself,
Fire-hollowing this in Indian fashion, fell
Sun-stricken, and that other lived alone.
In those two deaths he read God's warning
    ' wait.'

The mountain wooded to the peak, the
    lawns
And winding glades high up like ways to
    heaven,
The slender coco's drooping crown of
    plumes,        570
The lightning flash of insect and of bird,

The lustre of the long convolvuluses
That coil'd around the stately stems, and
    ran
Even to the limit of the land, the glows
And glories of the broad belt of the
    world, —
All these he saw; but what he fain had
    seen
He could not see, the kindly human face,
Nor ever hear a kindly voice, but heard
The myriad shriek of wheeling ocean-fowl,
The league-long roller thundering on the
    reef,        580
The moving whisper of huge trees that
    branch'd
And blossom'd in the zenith, or the sweep
Of some precipitous rivulet to the wave,
As down the shore he ranged, or all day
    long
Sat often in the seaward-gazing gorge,
A shipwreck'd sailor, waiting for a sail.
No sail from day to day, but every day
The sunrise broken into scarlet shafts
Among the palms and ferns and precipices;
The blaze upon the waters to the east;  590
The blaze upon his island overhead;
The blaze upon the waters to the west;
Then the great stars that globed them-
    selves in heaven,
The hollower-bellowing ocean, and again
The scarlet shafts of sunrise — but no sail.

There often as he watch'd or seem'd to
    watch,
So still the golden lizard on him paused,
A phantom made of many phantoms moved
Before him haunting him, or he himself
Moved haunting people, things, and places,
    known        600
Far in a darker isle beyond the line;
The babes, their babble, Annie, the small
    house,
The climbing street, the mill, the leafy
    lanes,
The peacock yew-tree and the lonely Hall,
The horse he drove, the boat he sold, the
    chill
November dawns and dewy-glooming
    downs,
The gentle shower, the smell of dying
    leaves,
And the low moan of leaden-color'd seas.

Once likewise, in the ringing of his ears,
Tho' faintly, merrily — far and far away —

He heard the pealing of his parish bells;  611
Then, tho' he knew not wherefore, started
    up
Shuddering, and when the beauteous hate-
    ful isle
Return'd upon him, had not his poor heart
Spoken with That which being everywhere
Lets none who speaks with Him seem all
    alone,
Surely the man had died of solitude.

    Thus over Enoch's early-silvering head
The sunny and rainy seasons came and
    went
Year after year.   His hopes to see his
    own,                                        620
And pace the sacred old familiar fields,
Not yet had perish'd, when his lonely doom
Came suddenly to an end.   Another ship —
She wanted water — blown by baffling
    winds,
Like the 'Good Fortune,' from her destined
    course,
Stay'd by this isle, not knowing where she
    lay;
For since the mate had seen at early dawn
Across a break on the mist-wreathen isle
The silent water slipping from the hills,  629
They sent a crew that landing burst away
In search of stream or fount, and fill'd the
    shores
With clamor.   Downward from his moun-
    tain gorge
Stept the long-hair'd, long-bearded soli-
    tary,
Brown, looking hardly human, strangely
    clad,
Muttering and mumbling, idiot - like it
    seem'd,
With inarticulate rage, and making signs
They knew not what; and yet he led the
    way
To where the rivulets of sweet water ran,
And ever as he mingled with the crew,
And heard them talking, his long-bounden
    tongue                                       640
Was loosen'd, till he made them under-
    stand;
Whom, when their casks were fill'd, they
    took aboard.
And there the tale he utter'd brokenly,
Scarce-credited at first but more and more,
Amazed and melted all who listen'd to it;
And clothes they gave him and free passage
    home,

But oft he work'd among the rest and
    shook
His isolation from him.   None of these
Came from his country, or could answer
    him,
If question'd, aught of what he cared to
    know.                                        650
And dull all the voyage was with long de-
    lays,
The vessel scarce sea-worthy; but ever-
    more
His fancy fled before the lazy wind
Returning, till beneath a clouded moon
He like a lover down thro' all his blood
Drew in the dewy meadowy morning-breath
Of England, blown across her ghostly wall.
And that same morning offrcers and men
Levied a kindly tax upon themselves,
Pitying the lonely man, and gave him it;
Then moving up the coast they landed
    him,                                        661
Even in that harbor whence he sail'd be-
    fore.

    There Enoch spoke no word to any one,
But homeward — home — what home ? had
    he a home ? —
His home, he walk'd.   Bright was that af-
    ternoon,
Sunny but chill; till drawn thro' either
    chasm,
Where either haven open'd on the deeps,
Roll'd a sea-haze and whelm'd the world
    in gray,
Cut off the length of highway on before,
And left but narrow breadth to left and
    right                                        670
Of wither'd holt or tilth or pasturage.
On the nigh-naked tree the robin piped
Disconsolate, and thro' the dripping haze
The dead weight of the dead leaf bore it
    down.
Thicker the drizzle grew, deeper the gloom;
Last, as it seem'd, a great mist - blotted
    light
Flared on him, and he came upon the
    place.

    Then down the long street having slowly
    stolen,
His heart foreshadowing all calamity,
His eyes upon the stones, he reach'd the
    home                                         680
Where Annie lived and loved him, and his
    babes

In those far-off seven happy years were
    born;
But finding neither light nor murmur
    there —
A bill of sale gleam'd thro' the drizzle —
    crept
Still downward thinking, ' dead or dead to
    me ! '

Down to the pool and narrow wharf he
    went,
Seeking a tavern which of old he knew,
A front of timber-crost antiquity,
So propt, worm-eaten, ruinously old,
He thought it must have gone; but he was
    gone        690
Who kept it, and his widow Miriam Lane,
With daily - dwindling profits held the
    house;
A haunt of brawling seamen once, but
    now
Stiller, with yet a bed for wandering men.
There Enoch rested silent many days.

But Miriam Lane was good and garru-
    lous,
Nor let him be, but often breaking in,
Told him, with other annals of the port,
Not knowing — Enoch was so brown, so
    bow'd,
So broken — all the story of his house:  700
His baby's death, her growing poverty,
How Philip put her little ones to school,
And kept them in it, his long wooing her,
Her slow consent and marriage, and the
    birth
Of Philip's child; and o'er his countenance
No shadow past, nor motion.   Any one,
Regarding, well had deem'd he felt the
    tale
Less than the teller; only when she closed,
' Enoch, poor man, was cast away and
    lost,'
He, shaking his gray head pathetically,  710
Repeated muttering, 'cast away and lost;'
Again in deeper inward whispers, ' lost ! '

But Enoch yearn'd to see her face again:
' If I might look on her sweet face again,
And know that she is happy.'   So the
    thought
Haunted and harass'd him, and drove him
    forth,
At evening when the dull November day
Was growing duller twilight, to the hill.

There he sat down gazing on all below;
There did a thousand memories roll upon
    him,        720
Unspeakable for sadness.   By and by
The ruddy square of comfortable light,
Far-blazing from the rear of Philip's house,
Allured him, as the beacon-blaze allures
The bird of passage, till he madly strikes
Against it and beats out his weary life.

For Philip's dwelling fronted on the
    street,
The latest house to landward; but behind,
With one small gate that open'd on the
    waste,
Flourish'd a little garden square and
    wall'd,        730
And in it throve an ancient evergreen,
A yew-tree, and all round it ran a walk
Of shingle, and a walk divided it.
But Enoch shunn'd the middle walk and
    stole
Up by the wall, behind the yew; and
    thence
That which he better might have shunn'd,
    if griefs
Like his have worse or better, Enoch saw.

For cups and silver on the burnish'd
    board
Sparkled and shone; so genial was the
    hearth;
And on the right hand of the hearth he
    saw        740
Philip, the slighted suitor of old times,
Stout, rosy, with his babe across his knees;
And o'er her second father stoopt a girl,
A later but a loftier Annie Lee,
Fair-hair'd and tall, and from her lifted
    hand
Dangled a length of ribbon and a ring
To tempt the babe, who rear'd his creasy
    arms,
Caught at and ever miss'd it, and they
    laugh'd;
And on the left hand of the hearth he
    saw
The mother glancing often toward her
    babe,        750
But turning now and then to speak with
    him,
Her son, who stood beside her tall and
    strong,
And saying that which pleased him, for he
    smiled.

Now when the dead man come to life beheld
His wife his wife no more, and saw the babe
Hers, yet not his, upon the father's knee,
And all the warmth, the peace, the happiness,
And his own children tall and beautiful,
And him, that other, reigning in his place,
Lord of his rights and of his children's
love —        760
Then he, tho' Miriam Lane had told him
all,
Because things seen are mightier than things
heard,
Stagger'd and shook, holding the branch,
and fear'd
To send abroad a shrill and terrible cry,
Which in one moment, like the blast of
doom,
Would shatter all the happiness of the
hearth.

He therefore turning softly like a thief,
Lest the harsh shingle should grate underfoot,
And feeling all along the garden-wall,
Lest he should swoon and tumble and be
found,        770
Crept to the gate, and open'd it and
closed,
As lightly as a sick man's chamber-door,
Behind him, and came out upon the waste.

And there he would have knelt, but that
his knees
Were feeble, so that falling prone he dug
His fingers into the wet earth, and pray'd:

'Too hard to bear ! why did they take
me thence ?
O God Almighty, blessed Saviour, Thou
That didst uphold me on my lonely isle,
Uphold me, Father, in my loneliness        780
A little longer ! aid me, give me strength
Not to tell her, never to let her know.
Help me not to break in upon her peace.
My children too ! must I not speak to
these ?
They know me not.  I should betray myself.
Never ! no father's kiss for me — the girl
So like her mother, and the boy, my son.'

There speech and thought and nature
fail'd a little,

And he lay tranced; but when he rose and
paced
Back toward his solitary home again,        790
All down the long and narrow street he
went
Beating it in upon his weary brain,
As tho' it were the burthen of a song,
'Not to tell her, never to let her know.'

He was not all unhappy.  His resolve
Upbore him, and firm faith, and evermore
Prayer from a living source within the
will,
And beating up thro' all the bitter world,
Like fountains of sweet water in the sea,
Kept him a living soul.  'This miller's
wife,'        800
He said to Miriam, 'that you spoke about,
Has she no fear that her first husband
lives ?'
'Ay, ay, poor soul,' said Miriam, 'fear
enow !
If you could tell her you had seen him
dead,
Why, that would be her comfort;' and he
thought,
'After the Lord has call'd me she shall
know,
I wait His time;' and Enoch set himself,
Scorning an alms, to work whereby to live.
Almost to all things could he turn his
hand.
Cooper he was and carpenter, and wrought
To make the boatmen fishing-nets, or
help'd        811
At lading and unlading the tall barks
That brought the stinted commerce of
those days,
Thus earn'd a scanty living for himself.
Yet since he did but labor for himself,
Work without hope, there was not life in
it
Whereby the man could live; and as the
year
Roll'd itself round again to meet the day
When Enoch had return'd, a languor came
Upon him, gentle sickness, gradually        820
Weakening the man, till he could do no
more,
But kept the house, his chair, and last his
bed.
And Enoch bore his weakness cheerfully.
For sure no gladlier does the stranded
wreck
See thro' the gray skirts of a lifting squall

The boat that bears the hope of life approach
To save the life despair'd of, than he saw
Death dawning on him, and the close of all.

For thro' that dawning gleam'd a kindlier hope
On Enoch thinking, 'after I am gone,   830
Then may she learn I loved her to the last.'
He call'd aloud for Miriam Lane and said:
'Woman, I have a secret — only swear,
Before I tell you — swear upon the book
Not to reveal it, till you see me dead.'
'Dead,' clamor'd the good woman, 'hear him talk!
I warrant, man, that we shall bring you round.'
'Swear,' added Enoch sternly, 'on the book;'
And on the book, half-frighted, Miriam swore.
Then Enoch rolling his gray eyes upon her,   840
'Did you know Enoch Arden of this town?'
'Know him?' she said, 'I knew him far away.
Ay, ay, I mind him coming down the street;
Held his head high, and cared for no man, he.'
Slowly and sadly Enoch answer'd her:
'His head is low, and no man cares for him.
I think I have not three days more to live;
I am the man.'   At which the woman gave
A half-incredulous, half-hysterical cry:
'You Arden, you! nay, — sure he was a foot   850
Higher than you be.'   Enoch said again:
'My God has bow'd me down to what I am;
My grief and solitude have broken me;
Nevertheless, know you that I am he
Who married — but that name has twice been changed —
I married her who married Philip Ray.
Sit, listen.'   Then he told her of his voyage,
His wreck, his lonely life, his coming back,
His gazing in on Annie, his resolve,   859
And how he kept it.   As the woman heard,
Fast flow'd the current of her easy tears,
While in her heart she yearn'd incessantly

To rush abroad all round the little haven,
Proclaiming Enoch Arden and his woes;
But awed and promise-bounden she forbore,
Saying only, 'See your bairns before you go!
Eh, let me fetch 'em, Arden,' and arose
Eager to bring them down, for Enoch hung
A moment on her words, but then replied:

'Woman, disturb me not now at the last,   870
But let me hold my purpose till I die.
Sit down again; mark me and understand,
While I have power to speak.   I charge you now,
When you shall see her, tell her that I died
Blessing her, praying for her, loving her;
Save for the bar between us, loving her
As when she laid her head beside my own.
And tell my daughter Annie, whom I saw
So like her mother, that my latest breath
Was spent in blessing her and praying for her.   880
And tell my son that I died blessing him.
And say to Philip that I blest him too;
He never meant us anything but good.
But if my children care to see me dead,
Who hardly knew me living, let them come,
I am their father; but she must not come,
For my dead face would vex her after-life.
And now there is but one of all my blood
Who will embrace me in the world-to-be.
This hair is his, she cut it off and gave it,
And I have borne it with me all these years,   891
And thought to bear it with me to my grave;
But now my mind is changed, for I shall see him,
My babe in bliss.   Wherefore when I am gone,
Take, give her this, for it may comfort her;
It will moreover be a token to her
That I am he.'

He ceased; and Miriam Lane
Made such a voluble answer promising all,
That once again he roll'd his eyes upon her
Repeating all he wish'd, and once again   900
She promised.

Then the third night after this,
While Enoch slumber'd motionless and
  pale,
And Miriam watch'd and dozed at inter-
  vals,
There came so loud a calling of the sea
That all the houses in the haven rang.
He woke, he rose, he spread his arms
  abroad,
Crying with a loud voice, ' A sail ! a sail !
I am saved; ' and so fell back and spoke
  no more.

So past the strong heroic soul away.
And when they buried him the little port
Had seldom seen a costlier funeral.     911

## AYLMER'S FIELD

### 1793

This poem, first published with ' Enoch Arden,' was less favorably received than the latter by the English critics, on account of what
' Blackwood' calls ' Tennyson's old infelicity
in dealing with the higher orders.' That reviewer also finds fault with the construction of
the story : ' The incidents are somewhat trite,
and its characters more than somewhat improbable. Its heroine is a model of every
Christian virtue ; yet she deceives her father,
and carries on a clandestine correspondence
with her lover. Her pastor is an excellent
clergyman ; yet when two of his parishioners
seek the sanctuary for the first time after their
daughter's death, he seizes the opportunity to
preach publicly against them — an act surely
unbefitting the pulpit of any period or of any
country, but simply impossible in that of a decent rector in the decorous Church of England
of the eighteenth century. . . . Averill's ser-
mon doubtless contains what a man, situated as
he was, could not help thinking ; but no less
certainly what a gentleman and a Christian
would, when the mischief was done and the
punishment had fallen, have scrupulously re-
frained from publicly expressing. Why pour
the molten lead of those fierce denunciations
into wounds yet deeper than his own ? Why
smite those afresh whom God had smitten so
terribly already ? The preacher, arising from
his own desolate hearth, like a prophet of old,
to denounce the crime which has laid it waste,
is unquestionably a grandly tragic figure. But
a deeper sense of the proprieties of character
might have enabled its possessor to attain this
fine effect without that perilous approach to
the unreal and to the theatrical, by which, as it

appears to us, it has been purchased in the present instance.'

The ' Quarterly Review ' says of the poem:
' Full of wonderful beauty in places, and written throughout as Mr. Tennyson alone can
write, we must, by the standard of his former
work, pronounce it a comparative failure. The
story does not bear the marks of such careful
thought, in its design, nor in the grouping of
its parts. After the simple and clear effect of
" Enoch Arden," " Aylmer's Field " gives an
uncertain impression, and wants a like repose.
Nor is there the same continuous unfolding of
probabilities in the action, nor the same pure
and noble feeling in the persons. . . . Sir Aylmer Aylmer is drawn with no kindly insight;
he is a stupid ruffian, and being so is no type
of an English gentleman.  His wife is a mere
shadow upon the page, and the author writes
throughout more in the spirit of a radical pamphleteer than of the poet laureate.'

Peter Bayne, on the other hand, remarks:
' " Aylmer's Field " seems to me the companion picture to " Locksley Hall."  It is one of
the most tragic of Tennyson's pieces — one of
the saddest, sternest, and I might almost add
mightiest, poems in the world.  In " Locksley
Hall " we see desecrated affection making two
persons unhappy; in " Aylmer's Field " the
blight is more deadly and more comprehensive.
I know nothing of Tennyson's in which the
moral earnestness is so prophet-like as in this
great poem.  With all the might of his genius
in its maturity, he pours a molten torrent of indignation and of scorn upon that pride which
is, perhaps, the central vice of England, that
pride which displays itself in many ways — in
pride of birth, in pride of gold, in pride of in-
sular superiority, and which is always desolating and deadly.   Pride, in this instance, trampling love under its feet, provides exquisite pain
for all the chief personages in the poem, and
obliterates two ancient families from the face
of the earth. . . .

' In this poem Tennyson has reaped the highest honor man can attain, namely, that of adding to the Scripture of his country; nor should
I think it a much less dark or pernicious error
than the pride which caused all this woe, to
hold that the Almighty could speak only
through or to Jewish seers, and that there is
no true inspiration in such writing as this.'

The fact (see page 227 above) that the story
of the poem is true is a sufficient reply to the
criticisms of ' Blackwood ' and the ' Quarterly '
upon what seems ' improbable ' in it.

The present Lord Tennyson says, in the
' Memoir ' (vol. ii. p. 9): ' The opening lines of
" Aylmer's Field " unfold the moral of that
poem.  The sequel describes the Nemesis which
fell upon Sir Aylmer Aylmer in his pride of

wealth. My father always felt a prophet's
righteous wrath against this form of selfishness; and no one can read his terrible denunciations of such pride trampling on a holy
human love, without being aware that the
poet's heart burnt within him while at work on
this tale of wrong.'

DUST are our frames; and, gilded dust,
    our pride
Looks only for a moment whole and sound,
Like that long-buried body of the king,
Found lying with his urns and ornaments,
Which at a touch of light, an air of heaven,
Slipt into ashes, and was found no more.

Here is a story which in rougher shape
Came from a grizzled cripple, whom I saw
Sunning himself in a waste field alone —
Old, and a mine of memories — who had
    served,                                    10
Long since, a bygone rector of the place,
And been himself a part of what he told.

SIR AYLMER AYLMER, that almighty
    man,
The county God — in whose capacious hall,
Hung with a hundred shields, the family
    tree
Sprang from the midriff of a prostrate
    king —
Whose blazing wyvern weathercock'd the
    spire,
Stood from his walls and wing'd his entry-
    gates,
And swang besides on many a windy sign —
Whose eyes from under a pyramidal head
Saw from his windows nothing save his
    own —                                      21
What lovelier of his own had he than her,
His only child, his Edith, whom he loved
As heiress and not heir regretfully?
But 'he that marries her marries her name.'
This fiat somewhat soothed himself and
    wife,
His wife a faded beauty of the Baths,
Insipid as the queen upon a card;
Her all of thought and bearing hardly
    more
Than his own shadow in a sickly sun.     30

A land of hops and poppy-mingled corn,
Little about it stirring save a brook!
A sleepy land, where under the same wheel
The same old rut would deepen year by
    year;

Where almost all the village had one name;
Where Aylmer followed Aylmer at the
    Hall
And Averill Averill at the Rectory
Thrice over; so that Rectory and Hall,
Bound in an immemorial intimacy,
Were open to each other; tho' to dream     40
That Love could bind them closer well had
    made
The hoar hair of the baronet bristle up
With horror, worse than had he heard his
    priest
Preach an inverted scripture, sons of men,
Daughters of God; so sleepy was the land.

And might not Averill, had he will'd it
    so,
Somewhere beneath his own low range of
    roofs,
Have also set his many-shielded tree?
There was an Aylmer - Averill marriage
    once,
When the red rose was redder than itself,
And York's white rose as red as Lancas-
    ter's,                                     51
With wounded peace which each had prick'd
    to death.
'Not proven,' Averill said, or laughingly,
'Some other race of Averills' — proven or
    no,
What cared he? what, if other or the
    same?
He lean'd not on his fathers but himself.
But Leolin, his brother, living oft
With Averill, and a year or two before
Call'd to the bar, but ever call'd away
By one low voice to one dear neighborhood,
Would often, in his walks with Edith
    claim
A distant kinship to the gracious blood
That shook the heart of Edith hearing him.

Sanguine he was; a but less vivid hue
Than of that islet in the chestnut-bloom
Flamed in his cheek; and eager eyes, that
    still
Took joyful note of all things joyful,
    beam'd,
Beneath a mane-like mass of rolling gold,
Their best and brightest when they dwelt
    on hers,
Edith, whose pensive beauty, perfect else,
But subject to the season or the mood,     71
Shone like a mystic star between the less
And greater glory varying to and fro,

We know not wherefore; bounteously made,
And yet so finely, that a troublous touch
Thinn'd, or would seem to thin her in a day,
A joyous to dilate, as toward the light.
And these had been together from the first.
Leolin's first nurse was, five years after,
   hers.
So much the boy foreran; but when his
   date					80
Doubled her own, for want of playmates,
   he —
Since Averill was a decad and a half
His elder, and their parents underground —
Had tost his ball and flown his kite, and
   roll'd
His hoop to pleasure Edith, with her dipt
Against the rush of the air in the prone
   swing,
Made blossom-ball or daisy-chain, arranged
Her garden, sow'd her name and kept it
   green
In living letters, told her fairy-tales,
Show'd her the fairy footings on the grass,
The little dells of cowslip, fairy palms,			91
The petty mare's-tail forest, fairy pines,
Or from the tiny pitted target blew
What look'd a flight of fairy arrows aim'd
All at one mark, all hitting, make-believes
For Edith and himself; or else he forged,
But that was later, boyish histories
Of battle, bold adventure, dungeon, wreck,
Flights, terrors, sudden rescues, and true
   love
Crown'd after trial; sketches rude and
   faint,					100
But where a passion yet unborn perhaps
Lay hidden as the music of the moon
Sleeps in the plain eggs of the nightingale.
And thus together, save for college-times
Or Temple-eaten terms, a couple, fair
As ever painter painted, poet sang,
Or heaven in lavish bounty moulded, grew.
And more and more, the maiden woman-
   grown,
He wasted hours with Averill; there, when
   first
The tented winter-field was broken up		110
Into that phalanx of the summer spears
That soon should wear the garland; there
   again
When burr and bine were gather'd; lastly
   there
At Christmas; ever welcome at the Hall,
On whose dull sameness his full tide of
   youth

Broke with a phosphorescence charming
   even
My lady, and the baronet yet had laid
No bar between them.  Dull and self-in-
   volved,
Tall and erect, but bending from his height
With half-allowing smiles for all the world,
And mighty courteous in the main — his
   pride					121
Lay deeper than to wear it as his ring —
He, like an Aylmer in his Aylmerism,
Would care no more for Leolin's walking
   with her
Than for his old Newfoundland's, when they
   ran
To loose him at the stables, for he rose
Two-footed at the limit of his chain,
Roaring to make a third; and how should
   Love,
Whom the cross-lightnings of four chance-
   met eyes
Flash into fiery life from nothing, follow
Such dear familiarities of dawn ?			131
Seldom, but when he does, master of all.

So these young hearts, not knowing that
   they loved,
Not she at least, nor conscious of a bar
Between them, nor by plight or broken
   ring
Bound, but an immemorial intimacy,
Wander'd at will, and oft accompanied
By Averill; his, a brother's love, that hung
With wings of brooding shelter o'er her
   peace,
Might have been other, save for Leolin's —
Who knows ? but so they wander'd, hour
   by hour					141
Gather'd the blossom that re-bloom'd, and
   drank
The magic cup that fill'd itself anew.

A whisper half reveal'd her to herself.
For out beyond her lodges, where the brook
Vocal, with here and there a silence, ran
By sallowy rims, arose the laborers' homes,
A frequent haunt of Edith, on low knolls
That dimpling died into each other, huts
At random scatter'd, each a nest in bloom.
Her art, her hand, her counsel, all had
   wrought					151
About them.  Here was one that, summer-
   blanch'd,
Was parcel-bearded with the traveller's-
   joy

In autumn, parcel ivy-clad; and here
The warm-blue breathings of a hidden
    hearth
Broke from a bower of vine and honey-
    suckle.
One look'd all rose-tree, and another wore
A close-set robe of jasmine sown with stars.
This had a rosy sea of gillyflowers
About it; this, a milky-way on earth,    160
Like visions in the Northern dreamer's
    heavens,
A lily-avenue climbing to the doors;
One, almost to the martin-haunted eaves
A summer burial deep in hollyhocks;
Each, its own charm; and Edith's every-
    where;
And Edith ever visitant with him,
He but less loved than Edith, of her poor.
For she — so lowly-lovely and so loving,
Queenly responsive when the loyal hand
Rose from the clay it work'd in as she
    past,    170
Not sowing hedgerow texts and passing by,
Nor dealing goodly counsel from a height
That makes the lowest hate it, but a voice
Of comfort and an open hand of help,
A splendid presence flattering the poor
    roofs
Revered as theirs, but kindlier than them-
    selves
To ailing wife or wailing infancy
Or old bedridden palsy, — was adored;
He, loved for her and for himself.  A grasp
Having the warmth and muscle of the
    heart,    180
A childly way with children, and a laugh
Ringing like proven golden coinage true,
Were no false passport to that easy realm,
Where once with Leolin at her side the girl,
Nursing a child, and turning to the warmth
The tender pink five-beaded baby-soles,
Heard the good mother softly whisper,
    'Bless,
God bless 'em! marriages are made in
    heaven.'

A flash of semi-jealousy clear'd it to her.
My lady's Indian kinsman unannounced    190
With half a score of swarthy faces came.
His own, tho' keen and bold and soldierly,
Sear'd by the close ecliptic, was not fair;
Fairer his talk, a tongue that ruled the
    hour,
Tho' seeming boastful.  So when first he
    dash'd

Into the chronicle of a deedful day,
Sir Aylmer half forgot his lazy smile
Of patron, 'Good! my lady's kinsman!
    good!'
My lady with her fingers interlock'd,
And rotatory thumbs on silken knees,    200
Call'd all her vital spirits into each ear
To listen; unawares they flitted off,
Busying themselves about the flowerage
That stood from out a stiff brocade in
    which,
The meteor of a splendid season, she,
Once with this kinsman, ah! so long ago,
Stept thro' the stately minuet of those
    days.
But Edith's eager fancy hurried with him
Snatch'd thro' the perilous passes of his life;
Till Leolin, ever watchful of her eye,    210
Hated him with a momentary hate.
Wife-hunting, as the rumor ran, was he.
I know not, for he spoke not, only show-
    er'd
His oriental gifts on every one
And most on Edith.  Like a storm he came,
And shook the house, and like a storm he
    went.

Among the gifts he left her — possibly
He flow'd and ebb'd uncertain, to return
When others had been tested — there was
    one,    219
A dagger, in rich sheath with jewels on it
Sprinkled about in gold that branch'd itself
Fine as ice-ferns on January panes
Made by a breath.  I know not whence at
    first,
Nor of what race, the work; but as he told
The story, storming a hill-fort of thieves
He got it; for their captain after fight,
His comrades having fought their last be-
    low,
Was climbing up the valley, at whom he
    shot.
Down from the beetling crag to which he
    clung
Tumbled the tawny rascal at his feet,    230
This dagger with him, which, when now
    admired
By Edith whom his pleasure was to please,
At once the costly Sahib yielded to her.

And Leolin, coming after he was gone,
Tost over all her presents petulantly;
And when she show'd the wealthy scabbard,
    saying,

'Look what a lovely piece of workman-
    ship!'
Slight was his answer, 'Well — I care not
    for it.'
Then playing with the blade he prick'd his
    hand,
'A gracious gift to give a lady, this!'   240
'But would it be more gracious,' ask'd the
    girl,
'Were I to give this gift of his to one
That is no lady?'   'Gracious?   No,' said
    he.
'Me? — but I cared not for it.   O, par-
    don me,
I seem to be ungraciousness itself.'
'Take it,' she added sweetly, 'tho' his gift;
For I am more ungracious even than you,
I care not for it either;' and he said,
'Why, then I love it;' but Sir Aylmer
    past,
And neither loved nor liked the thing he
    heard.   250

    The next day came a neighbor.   Blues
        and reds
They talk'd of; blues were sure of it, he
        thought;
Then of the latest fox — where started —
        kill'd
In such a bottom.   'Peter had the brush,
My Peter, first;' and did Sir Aylmer know
That great pock-pitten fellow had been
        caught?
Then made his pleasure echo, hand to hand,
And rolling as it were the substance of it
Between his palms a moment up and
        down —
'The birds were warm, the birds were
        warm upon him;   260
We have him now;' and had Sir Aylmer
        heard —
Nay, but he must — the land was ringing
        of it —
This blacksmith border - marriage — one
        they knew —
Raw from the nursery — who could trust a
        child?
That cursed France with her egalities!
And did Sir Aylmer — deferentially
With nearing chair and lower'd accent —
        think —
For people talk'd — that it was wholly wise
To let that handsome fellow Averill walk
So freely with his daughter?   people
        talk'd —   270

The boy might get a notion into him;
The girl might be entangled ere she knew.
Sir Aylmer Aylmer slowly stiffening spoke:
'The girl and boy, sir, know their differ-
        ences!'
'Good,' said his friend, 'but watch!' and
        he, 'Enough,
More than enough, sir!   I can guard my
        own.'
They parted, and Sir Aylmer Aylmer
        watch'd.

    Pale, for on her the thunders of the
        house
Had fallen first, was Edith that same night;
Pale as the Jephtha's daughter, a rough
        piece   280
Of early rigid color, under which
Withdrawing by the counter door to that
Which Leolin open'd, she cast back upon
        him
A piteous glance, and vanish'd.   He, as one
Caught in a burst of unexpected storm,
And pelted with outrageous epithets,
Turning beheld the Powers of the House
On either side the hearth, indignant; her,
Cooling her false cheek with a feather fan,
Him, glaring, by his own stale devil
        spurr'd,   290
And, like a beast hard-ridden, breathing
        hard.
'Ungenerous, dishonorable, base,
Presumptuous!   trusted as he was with her,
The sole succeeder to their wealth, their
        lands,
The last remaining pillar of their house,
The one transmitter of their ancient name,
Their child.'   'Our child!'   'Our heiress!'
        'Ours!' for still,
Like echoes from beyond a hollow, came
Her sicklier iteration.   Last he said:
'Boy, mark me!   for your fortunes are to
        make.   300
I swear you shall not make them out of
        mine.
Now inasmuch as you have practised on her,
Perplext her, made her half forget herself,
Swerve from her duty to herself and us —
Things in an Aylmer deem'd impossible,
Far as we track ourselves — I say that
        this —
Else I withdraw favor and countenance
From you and yours for ever — shall you do.
Sir, when you see her — but you shall not
        see her —

No, you shall write, and not to her, but
    me;                          310
And you shall say that having spoken with
    me,
And after look'd into yourself, you find
That you meant nothing — as indeed you
    know
That you meant nothing.  Such a match as
    this !
Impossible, prodigious !' These were
    words,
As meted by his measure of himself,
Arguing boundless forbearance: after
    which,
And Leolin's horror-stricken answer, 'I
So foul a traitor to myself and her !
Never, O, never !' for about as long   320
As the wind-hover hangs in balance,
    paused
Sir Aylmer reddening from the storm
    within,
Then broke all bonds of courtesy, and cry-
    ing,
' Boy, should I find you by my doors again,
My men shall lash you from them like a
    dog;
Hence !' with a sudden execration drove
The footstool from before him, and arose;
So, stammering ' scoundrel' out of teeth
    that ground                  328
As in a dreadful dream, while Leolin still
Retreated half-aghast, the fierce old man
Follow'd, and under his own lintel stood
Storming with lifted hands, a hoary face
Meet for the reverence of the hearth, but
    now,
Beneath a pale and unimpassion'd moon,
Vext with unworthy madness, and de-
    form'd.

Slowly and conscious of the rageful eye
That watch'd him, till he heard the pon-
    derous door
Close, crashing with long echoes thro' the
    land,
Went Leolin; then, his passions all in flood
And masters of his motion, furiously   340
Down thro' the bright lawns to his bro-
    ther's ran,
And foam'd away his heart at Averill's
    ear;
Whom Averill solaced as he might,
    amazed:
The man was his, had been his father's,
    friend;

He must have seen, himself had seen it
    long;
He must have known, himself had known;
    besides,
He never yet had set his daughter forth
Here in the woman-markets of the west,
Where our Caucasians let themselves be
    sold.
Some one, he thought, had slander'd Leo-
    lin to him.                 350
' Brother, for I have loved you more as
    son
Than brother, let me tell you: I myself —
What is their pretty saying ? jilted, is it ?
Jilted I was; I say it for your peace.
Pain'd, and, as bearing in myself the
    shame
The woman should have borne, humiliated,
I lived for years a stunted sunless life;
Till after our good parents past away
Watching your growth, I seem'd again to
    grow.
Leolin, I almost sin in envying you.   360
The very whitest lamb in all my fold
Loves you; I know her; the worst thought
    she has
Is whiter even than her pretty hand.
She must prove true; for, brother, where
    two fight
The strongest wins, and truth and love are
    strength,
And you are happy; let her parents be.'

But Leolin cried out the more upon
    them —
Insolent, brainless, heartless ! heiress,
    wealth,
Their wealth, their heiress ! wealth enough
    was theirs
For twenty matches. Were he lord of
    this,                    370
Why, twenty boys and girls should marry
    on it,
And forty blest ones bless him, and him-
    self
Be wealthy still, ay, wealthier. He be-
    lieved
This filthy marriage-hindering Mammon
    made
The harlot of the cities; Nature crost
Was mother of the foul adulteries
That saturate soul with body. Name, too !
    name,
Their ancient name ! they *might* be proud;
    its worth

Was being Edith's.  Ah, how pale she had
   look'd
Darling, to-night ! they must have rated
   her                                    380
Beyond all tolerance.  These old pheasant-
   lords,
These partridge - breeders of a thousand
   years,
Who had mildew'd in their thousands, do-
   ing nothing
Since Egbert — why, the greater their dis-
   grace !
Fall back upon a name ! rest, rot in that !
Not *keep* it noble, make it nobler ? fools,
With such a vantage - ground for noble-
   ness !
He had known a man, a quintessence of
   man,
The life of all — who madly loved — and
   he,                                    389
Thwarted by one of these old father-fools,
Had rioted his life out, and made an end.
He would not do it ! her sweet face and
   faith
Held him from that; but he had powers,
   he knew it.
Back would he to his studies, make a
   name,
Name, fortune too; the world should ring
   of him,
To shame these mouldy Aylmers in their
   graves.
Chancellor, or what is greatest would he
   be —
' O brother, I am grieved to learn your
   grief —
Give me my fling, and let me say my say.'

   At which, like one that sees his own ex-
      cess,                               400
And easily forgives it as his own,
He laugh'd, and then was mute, but pre-
   sently
Wept like a storm; and honest Averill,
   seeing
How low his brother's mood had fallen,
   fetch'd
His richest bee's-wing from a binn reserved
For banquets, praised the waning red, and
   told
The vintage — when *this* Aylmer came of
   age —
Then drank and past it; till at length the
   two,
Tho' Leolin flamed and fell again, agreed

That much allowance must be made for
   men.                                   410
After an angry dream this kindlier glow
Faded with morning, but his purpose held.

   Yet once by night again the lovers met,
A perilous meeting under the tall pines
That darken'd all the northward of her
   Hall.
Him, to her meek and modest bosom prest
In agony, she promised that no force,
Persuasion, no, nor death could alter her;
He, passionately hopefuller, would go,
Labor for his own Edith, and return   420
In such a sunlight of prosperity
He should not be rejected.  ' Write to me !
They loved me, and because I love their
   child
They hate me.  There is war between us,
   dear,
Which breaks all bonds but ours; we must
   remain
Sacred to one another.'  So they talk'd,
Poor children, for their comfort.  The wind
   blew,
The rain of heaven and their own bitter
   tears,
Tears and the careless rain of heaven,
   mixt                                   429
Upon their faces, as they kiss'd each other
In darkness, and above them roar'd the
   pine.

   So Leolin went; and as we task our-
      selves
To learn a language known but smatter-
   ingly
In phrases here and there at random, toil'd
Mastering the lawless science of our law,
That codeless myriad of precedent,
That wilderness of single instances,
Thro' which a few, by wit or fortune led,
May beat a pathway out to wealth and
   fame.
The jests, that flash'd about the pleader's
   room,                                 440
Lightning of the hour, the pun, the scurri-
   lous tale, —
Old scandals buried now seven decads deep
In other scandals that have lived and died,
And left the living scandal that shall die —
Were dead to him already; bent as he was
To make disproof of scorn, and strong in
   hopes,
And prodigal of all brain-labor he,

Charier of sleep, and wine, and exercise,
Except when for a breathing-while at eve,
Some niggard fraction of an hour, he ran
Beside the river-bank. And then indeed  451
Harder the times were, and the hands of
power
Were bloodier, and the according hearts of
men
Seem'd harder too; but the soft river-
breeze,
Which fann'd the gardens of that rival
rose
Yet fragrant in a heart remembering
His former talks with Edith, on him
breathed
Far purelier in his rushings to and fro,
After his books, to flush his blood with air,
Then to his books again. My lady's
cousin,  460
Half-sickening of his pension'd afternoon,
Drove in upon the student once or twice,
Ran a Malayan amuck against the times,
Had golden hopes for France and all man-
kind,
Answer'd all queries touching those at
home
With a heaved shoulder and a saucy smile,
And fain had haled him out into the world,
And air'd him there. His nearer friend
would say,
'Screw not the chord too sharply lest it
snap.'
Then left alone he pluck'd her dagger
forth  470
From where his worldless heart had kept
it warm,
Kissing his vows upon it like a knight.
And wrinkled benchers often talk'd of him
Approvingly, and prophesied his rise;
For heart, I think, help'd head. Her let-
ters too,
Tho' far between, and coming fitfully
Like broken music, written as she found
Or made occasion, being strictly watch'd,
Charm'd him thro' every labyrinth till he
saw
An end, a hope, a light breaking upon
him.  480

But they that cast her spirit into flesh,
Her worldly-wise begetters, plagued them-
selves
To sell her, those good parents, for her
good.
Whatever eldest-born of rank or wealth

Might lie within their compass, him they
lured
Into their net made pleasant by the baits
Of gold and beauty, wooing him to woo.
So month by month the noise about their
doors,
And distant blaze of those dull banquets,
made  489
The nightly wirer of their innocent hare
Falter before he took it. All in vain.
Sullen, defiant, pitying, wroth, return'd
Leolin's rejected rivals from their suit
So often, that the folly taking wings
Slipt o'er those lazy limits down the wind
With rumor, and became in other fields
A mockery to the yeomen over ale,
And laughter to their lords. But those at
home,
As hunters round a hunted creature draw
The cordon close and closer toward the
death,  500
Narrow'd her goings out and comings in;
Forbade her first the house of Averill,
Then closed her access to the wealthier
farms,
Last from her own home-circle of the poor
They barr'd her. Yet she bore it, yet her
cheek
Kept color — wondrous! but, O mystery!
What amulet drew her down to that old
oak,
So old, that twenty years before, a part
Falling had let appear the brand of John —
Once grove-like, each huge arm a tree, but
now  510
The broken base of a black tower, a cave
Of touchwood, with a single flourishing
spray.
There the manorial lord too curiously
Raking in that millennial touchwood-dust
Found for himself a bitter treasure-trove;
Burst his own wyvern on the seal, and read
Writhing a letter from his child, for which
Came at the moment Leolin's emissary,
A crippled lad, and coming turn'd to fly,
But scared with threats of jail and halter
gave  520
To him that fluster'd his poor parish wits
The letter which he brought, and swore
besides
To play their go-between as heretofore
Nor let them know themselves betray'd;
and then,
Soul-stricken at their kindness to him, went
Hating his own lean heart and miserable.

Thenceforward oft from out a despot
dream
The father panting woke, and oft, as dawn
Aroused the black republic on his elms,
Sweeping the froth-fly from the fescue
brush'd                                    530
Thro' the dim meadow toward his treasure-
trove,
Seized it, took home, and to my lady,—
who made
A downward crescent of her minion mouth,
Listless in all despondence,— read; and
tore,
As if the living passion symboll'd there
Were living nerves to feel the rent; and
burnt,
Now chafing at his own great self defied,
Now striking on huge stumbling-blocks of
scorn
In babyisms and dear diminutives
Scatter'd all over the vocabulary          540
Of such a love as like a chidden child,
After much wailing, hush'd itself at last
Hopeless of answer.  Then tho' Averill
wrote
And bade him with good heart sustain him-
self—
All would be well— the lover heeded not,
But passionately restless came and went,
And rustling once at night about the place,
There by a keeper shot at, slightly hurt,
Raging return'd.  Nor was it well for her
Kept to the garden now, and grove of
pines,                                     550
Watch'd even there; and one was set to
watch
The watcher, and Sir Aylmer watch'd them
all,
Yet bitterer from his readings.  Once in-
deed,
Warm'd with his wines, or taking pride in
her,
She look'd so sweet, he kiss'd her tenderly,
Not knowing what possess'd him.  That one
kiss
Was Leolin's one strong rival upon earth;
Seconded, for my lady follow'd suit,
Seem'd hope's returning rose; and then en-
sued
A Martin's summer of his faded love,     560
Or ordeal by kindness.  After this
He seldom crost his child without a sneer;
The mother flow'd in shallower acrimonies,
Never one kindly smile, one kindly word;
So that the gentle creature shut from all

Her charitable use, and face to face
With twenty months of silence, slowly lost,
Nor greatly cared to lose, her hold on life.
Last some low fever ranging round to spy
The weakness of a people or a house,     570
Like flies that haunt a wound, or deer, or
men,
Or almost all that is, hurting the hurt—
Save Christ as we believe him — found the
girl
And flung her down upon a couch of fire,
Where careless of the household faces
near,
And crying upon the name of Leolin,
She, and with her the race of Aylmer,
past.

Star to star vibrates light; may soul to
soul
Strike thro' a finer element of her own?
So,— from afar,— touch as at once? or
why                                        580
That night, that moment, when she named
his name,
Did the keen shriek, ' Yes, love, yes, Edith,
yes,'
Shrill, till the comrade of his chambers
woke,
And came upon him half-arisen from sleep,
With a weird bright eye, sweating and
trembling,
His hair as it were crackling into flames,
His body half flung forward in pursuit,
And his long arms stretch'd as to grasp a
flyer.
Nor knew he wherefore he had made the
cry;
And being much befool'd and idioted     590
By the rough amity of the other, sank
As into sleep again.  The second day,
My lady's Indian kinsman rushing in,
A breaker of the bitter news from home,
Found a dead man, a letter edged with
death
Beside him, and the dagger which himself
Gave Edith, redden'd with no bandit's
blood;
' From Edith ' was engraven on the blade.

Then Averill went and gazed upon his
death.
And when he came again, his flock be-
lieved—                                    600
Beholding how the years which are not
Time's

Had blasted him — that many thousand days
Were clipt by horror from his term of life.
Yet the sad mother, for the second death
Scarce touch'd her thro' that nearness of the first,
And being used to find her pastor texts,
Sent to the harrow'd brother, praying him
To speak before the people of her child,
And fixt the Sabbath.  Darkly that day rose.
Autumn's mock sunshine of the faded woods          610
Was all the life of it; for hard on these,
A breathless burthen of low - folded heavens
Stifled and chill'd at once; but every roof
Sent out a listener.  Many too had known
Edith among the hamlets round, and since
The parents' harshness and the hapless loves
And double death were widely murmur'd, left
Their own gray tower, or plain-faced tabernacle,
To hear him; all in mourning these, and those          619
With blots of it about them, ribbon, glove,
Or kerchief; while the church, — one night, except
For greenish glimmerings thro' the lancets, — made
Still paler the pale head of him, who tower'd
Above them, with his hopes in either grave.

Long o'er his bent brows linger'd Averill,
His face magnetic to the hand from which
Livid he pluck'd it forth, and labor'd thro'
His brief prayer-prelude, gave the verse,
'Behold,
Your house is left unto you desolate !'
But lapsed into so long a pause again          630
As half amazed, half frighted, all his flock;
Then, from his height and loneliness of grief
Bore down in flood, and dash'd his angry heart
Against the desolations of the world.

Never since our bad earth became one sea,
Which rolling o'er the palaces of the proud,

And all but those who knew the living God —
Eight that were left to make a purer world —
When since had flood, fire, earthquake, thunder, wrought
Such waste and havoc as the idolatries          640
Which from the low light of mortality
Shot up their shadows to the heaven of heavens,
And worshipt their own darkness in the Highest ?
'Gash thyself, priest, and honor thy brute Baäl,
And to thy worst self sacrifice thyself,
For with thy worst self hast thou clothed thy God.
Then came a Lord in no wise like to Baäl.
The babe shall lead the lion.  Surely now
The wilderness shall blossom as the rose.
Crown thyself, worm, and worship thine own lusts ! —          650
No coarse and blockish God of acreage
Stands at thy gate for thee to grovel to —
Thy God is far diffused in noble groves
And princely halls, and farms, and flowing lawns,
And heaps of living gold that daily grow,
And title-scrolls and gorgeous heraldries.
In such a shape dost thou behold thy God.
Thou wilt not gash thy flesh for *him;* for thine
Fares richly, in fine linen, not a hair
Ruffled upon the scarfskin, even while          660
The deathless ruler of thy dying house
Is wounded to the death that cannot die;
And tho' thou numberest with the followers
Of One who cried, "Leave all and follow me."
Thee therefore with His light about thy feet,
Thee with His message ringing in thine ears,
Thee shall thy brother man, the Lord from heaven,
Born of a village girl, carpenter's son,
Wonderful, Prince of Peace, the Mighty God,
Count the more base idolater of the two;          670
Crueller, as not passing thro' the fire
Bodies, but souls — thy children's — thro' the smoke,
The blight of low desires — darkening thine own

To thine own likeness; or if one of these,
Thy better born unhappily from thee,
Should, as by miracle, grow straight and
     fair —
Friends, I was bid to speak of such a one
By those who most have cause to sorrow
     for her —
Fairer than Rachel by the palmy well,  679
Fairer than Ruth among the fields of corn,
Fair as the Angel that said "Hail!" she
     seem'd,
Who entering fill'd the house with sudden
     light.
For so mine own was brighten'd — where
     indeed
The roof so lowly but that beam of heaven
Dawn'd sometime thro' the doorway?
     whose the babe
Too ragged to be fondled on her lap,
Warm'd at her bosom?  The poor child of
     shame,
The common care whom no one cared for,
     leapt
To greet her, wasting his forgotten heart,
As with the mother he had never known,  690
In gambols; for her fresh and innocent eyes
Had such a star of morning in their blue,
That all neglected places of the field
Broke into nature's music when they saw
     her.
Low was her voice, but won mysterious
     way
Thro' the seal'd ear to which a louder one
Was all but silence — free of alms her
     hand —
The hand that robed your cottage-walls
     with flowers
Has often toil'd to clothe your little ones;
How often placed upon the sick man's
     brow            700
Cool'd it, or laid his feverish pillow smooth!
Had you one sorrow and she shared it not?
One burthen and she would not lighten it?
One spiritual doubt she did not soothe?
Or when some heat of difference sparkled
     out,
How sweetly would she glide between your
     wraths,
And steal you from each other! for she
     walk'd
Wearing the light yoke of that Lord of love
Who still'd the rolling wave of Galilee!
And one — of him I was not bid to speak —
Was always with her, whom you also
     knew.            711

Him too you loved, for he was worthy
     love.
And these had been together from the
     first;
They might have been together till the last.
Friends, this frail bark of ours, when sorely
     tried,
May wreck itself without the pilot's guilt,
Without the captain's knowledge; hope
     with me.
Whose shame is that, if he went hence with
     shame?
Nor mine the fault, if losing both of these
I cry to vacant chairs and widow'd walls,
"My house is left unto me desolate."'  721

While thus he spoke, his hearers wept;
     but some,
Sons of the glebe, with other frowns than
     those
That knit themselves for summer shadow,
     scowl'd
At their great lord.  He, when it seem'd
     he saw
No pale sheet-lightnings from afar, but
     fork'd
Of the near storm, and aiming at his head,
Sat anger - charm'd from sorrow, soldier-
     like,
Erect; but when the preacher's cadence
     flow'd
Softening thro' all the gentle attributes  730
Of his lost child, the wife, who watch'd his
     face,
Paled at a sudden twitch of his iron mouth;
And 'O, pray God that he hold up!' she
     thought,
'Or surely I shall shame myself and him.'

'Nor yours the blame — for who beside
     your hearths
Can take her place — if echoing me you
     cry
"Our house is left unto us desolate"?
But thou, O thou that killest, hadst thou
     known,
O thou that stonest, hadst thou understood
The things belonging to thy peace and
     ours!            740
Is there no prophet but the voice that calls
Doom upon kings, or in the waste "Re-
     pent"?
Is not our own child on the narrow way,
Who down to those that saunter in the
     broad

Cries, " Come up hither," as a prophet to
    us ?
Is there no stoning save with flint and
    rock ?
Yes, as the dead we weep for testify —
No desolation but by sword and fire ?   748
Yes, as your moanings witness, and myself
Am lonelier, darker, earthlier for my loss.
Give me your prayers, for he is past your
    prayers,
Not past the living fount of pity in heaven.
But I that thought myself long-suffering,
    meek,
Exceeding " poor in spirit " — how the
    words
Have twisted back upon themselves, and
    mean
Vileness, we are grown so proud — I wish'd
    my voice
A rushing tempest of the wrath of God
To blow these sacrifices thro' the world —
Sent like the twelve-divided concubine
To inflame the tribes; but there — out
    yonder — earth   760
Lightens from her own central hell — O,
    there
The red fruit of an old idolatry —
The heads of chiefs and princes fall so fast,
They cling together in the ghastly sack —
The land all shambles — naked marriages
Flash from the bridge, and ever-murder'd
    France,
By shores that darken with the gathering
    wolf,
Runs in a river of blood to the sick sea.
Is this a time to madden madness then ?
Was this a time for these to flaunt their
    pride ?   770
May Pharaoh's darkness, folds as dense as
    those
Which hid the Holiest from the people's
    eyes
Ere the great death, shroud this great sin
    from all !
Doubtless our narrow world must canvass
    it.
O, rather pray for those and pity them,
Who, thro' their own desire accomplish'd,
    bring
Their own gray hairs with sorrow to the
    grave —
Who broke the bond which they desired to
    break,
Which else had link'd their race with times
    to come —   779

Who wove coarse webs to snare her purity,
Grossly contriving their dear daughter's
    good —
Poor souls, and knew not what they did,
    but sat
Ignorant, devising their own daughter's
    death !
May not that earthly chastisement suffice ?
Have not our love and reverence left them
    bare ?
Will not another take their heritage ?
Will there be children's laughter in their
    hall
For ever and for ever, or one stone
Left on another, or is it a li ht thing
That I, their guest, their host, their ancient
    friend,   790
I made by these the last of all my race,
Must cry to these the last of theirs, as cried
Christ ere His agony to those that swore
Not by the temple but the gold, and made
Their own traditions God, and slew the
    Lord,
And left their memories a world's curse —
    " Behold,
Your house is left unto you desolate " ? '

    Ended he had not, but she brook'd no
    more;
Long since her heart had beat remorse-
    lessly,
Her crampt-up sorrow pain'd her, and a
    sense   800
Of meanness in her unresisting life.
Then their eyes vext her; for on entering
He had cast the curtains of their seat
    aside —
Black velvet of the costliest — she herself
Had seen to that. Fain had she closed them
    now,
Yet dared not stir to do it, only near'd
Her husband inch by inch, but when she laid,
Wifelike, her hand in one of his, he veil'd
His face with the other, and at once, as
    falls
A creeper when the prop is broken, fell   810
The woman shrieking at his feet, and
    swoon'd.
Then her own people bore along the nave
Her pendent hands, and narrow meagre
    face
Seam'd with the shallow cares of fifty
    years.
And her the lord of all the landscape
    round

Even to its last horizon, and of all
Who peer'd at him so keenly, follow'd out
Tall and erect, but in the middle aisle
Reel'd, as a footsore ox in crowded ways
Stumbling across the market to his death,
Unpitied; for he groped as blind, and
    seem'd                                    821
Always about to fall, grasping the pews
And oaken finials till he touch'd the door;
Yet to the lychgate, where his chariot
    stood,
Strode from the porch, tall and erect
    again.

But nevermore did either pass the gate
Save under pall with bearers. In one
    month,
Thro' weary and yet ever wearier hours,
The childless mother went to seek her
    child;
And when he felt the silence of his house
About him, and the change and not the
    change,                                  831
And those fixt eyes of painted ancestors
Staring for ever from their gilded walls
On him their last descendant, his own head
Began to droop, to fall.  The man became
Imbecile; his one word was ' desolate.'
Dead for two years before his death was
    he;
But when the second Christmas came, es-
    caped
His keepers, and the silence which he felt,
To find a deeper in the narrow gloom    840
By wife and child; nor wanted at his end
The dark retinue reverencing death
At golden thresholds; nor from tender
    hearts,
And those who sorrow'd o'er a vanish'd
    race,
Pity, the violet on the tyrant's grave.
Then the great Hall was wholly broken
    down,
And the broad woodland parcell'd into
    farms;
And where the two contrived their daugh-
    ter's good,
Lies the hawk's cast, the mole has made his
    run,
The hedgehog underneath the plantain
    bores,                                   850
The rabbit fondles his own harmless face,
The slow-worm creeps, and the thin weasel
    there
Follows the mouse, and all is open field.

# SEA DREAMS

This poem was first printed in ' Macmillan's
Magazine ' for January, 1860, and afterwards
included in the ' Enoch Arden ' volume.
    ' The grace of the poem,' says the ' Quarterly
Review,' ' is equalled by the winning kindliness of it.'   Stedman calls it ' a poem of measureless satire and much idyllic beauty.'

A CITY clerk, but gently born and bred;
His wife, an unknown artist's orphan
    child —
One babe was theirs, a Margaret, three
    years old.
They, thinking that her clear germander
    eye
Droopt in the giant-factoried city-gloom,
Came, with a month's leave given them, to
    the sea;
For which his gains were dock'd, however
    small.
Small were his gains, and hard his work;
    besides,
Their slender household fortunes — for the
    man                                        9
Had risk'd his little — like the little thrift,
Trembled in perilous places o'er a deep.
And oft, when sitting all alone, his face
Would darken, as he cursed his credulous-
    ness,
And that one unctuous mouth which lured
    him, rogue,
To buy strange shares in some Peruvian
    mine.
Now seaward-bound for health they gain'd
    a coast,
All sand and cliff and deep-inrunning cave,
At close of day; slept, woke, and went the
    next,
The Sabbath, pious variers from the church,
To chapel; where a heated pulpiteer,     20
Not preaching simple Christ to simple
    men,
Announced the coming doom, and fulmi-
    nated
Against the Scarlet Woman and her creed.
For sideways up he swung his arms, and
    shriek'd
' Thus, thus with violence,' even as if he
    held
The Apocalyptic millstone, and himself
Were that great angel; ' Thus with vio-
    lence
Shall Babylon be cast into the sea;

Then comes the close.' The gentle-hearted
    wife
Sat shuddering at the ruin of a world,   30
He at his own; but when the wordy storm
Had ended, forth they came and paced the
    shore,
Ran in and out the long sea-framing caves,
Drank the large air, and saw, but scarce
    believed —
The soot-flake of so many a summer still
Clung to their fancies — that they saw, the
    sea.
So now on sand they walk'd, and now on
    cliff,
Lingering about the thymy promontories,
Till all the sails were darken'd in the west,
And rosed in the east, then homeward and
    to bed;   40
Where she, who kept a tender Christian
    hope,
Haunting a holy text, and still to that
Returning, as the bird returns, at night,
'Let not the sun go down upon your
    wrath,'
Said, 'Love, forgive him.' But he did not
    speak;
And silenced by that silence lay the wife,
Remembering her dear Lord who died for
    all,
And musing on the little lives of men,
And how they mar this little by their
    feuds.

  But while the two were sleeping, a full
    tide   50
Rose with ground - swell, which, on the
    foremost rocks
Touching, upjetted in spirts of wild sea-
    smoke,
And scaled in sheets of wasteful foam, and
    fell
In vast sea-cataracts — ever and anon
Dead claps of thunder from within the
    cliffs
Heard thro' the living roar. At this the
    babe,
Their Margaret cradled near them, wail'd
    and woke
The mother, and the father suddenly cried,
'A wreck, a wreck!' then turn'd and
    groaning said:

  'Forgive! How many will say, "for-
    give," and find   60
A sort of absolution in the sound

To hate a little longer! No; the sin
That neither God nor man can well for-
    give,
Hypocrisy, I saw it in him at once.
Is it so true that second thoughts are best?
Not first, and third, which are a riper
    first?
Too ripe, too late! they come too late for
    use.
Ah, love, there surely lives in man and
    beast
Something divine to warn them of their
    foes;
And such a sense, when first I fronted him,
Said, "Trust him not;" but after, when I
    came   71
To know him more, I lost it, knew him
    less,
Fought with what seem'd my own un-
    charity,
Sat at his table, drank his costly wines,
Made more and more allowance for his
    talk;
Went further, fool! and trusted him with
    all,
All my poor scrapings from a dozen years
Of dust and desk-work. There is no such
    mine,
None; but a gulf of ruin, swallowing gold,
Not making. Ruin'd! ruin'd! the sea
    roars   80
Ruin — a fearful night!'

              'Not fearful; fair,'
Said the good wife, 'if every star in heaven
Can make it fair; you do but hear the tide.
Had you ill dreams?'

          'O, yes,' he said, 'I dream'd
Of such a tide swelling toward the land,
And I from out the boundless outer deep
Swept with it to the shore, and enter'd one
Of those dark caves that run beneath the
    cliffs.
I thought the motion of the boundless deep
Bore thro' the cave, and I was heaved upon
    it   90
In darkness; then I saw one lovely star
Larger and larger. "What a world," I
    thought,
"To live in!" but in moving on I found
Only the landward exit of the cave,
Bright with the sun upon the stream be-
    yond;
And near the light a giant woman sat,

All over earthy, like a piece of earth,
A pickaxe in her hand.   Then out I slipt
Into a land all sun and blossom, trees
As high as heaven, and every bird that
      sings;                                          100
And here the night-light flickering in my
      eyes
Awoke me.'

      ' That was then your dream,' she said,
' Not sad, but sweet.'

                        ' So sweet, I lay,' said he,
' And mused upon it, drifting up the stream
In fancy, till I slept again, and pieced
The broken vision; for I dream'd that
      still
The motion of the great deep bore me
      on,
And that the woman walk'd upon the
      brink.
I wonder'd at her strength, and ask'd her
      of it.
"It came," she said, "by working in the
      mines."                                        110
O, then to ask her of my shares, I thought;
And ask'd; but not a word; she shook her
      head.
And then the motion of the current ceased,
And there was rolling thunder; and we
      reach'd
A mountain, like a wall of burs and thorns;
But she with her strong feet up the steep
      hill
Trod out a path.   I follow'd, and at top
She pointed seaward; there a fleet of glass,
That seem'd a fleet of jewels under me,
Sailing along before a gloomy cloud     120
That not one moment ceased to thunder,
      past
In sunshine.   Right across its track there
      lay,
Down in the water, a long reef of gold,
Or what seem'd gold; and I was glad at
      first
To think that in our often-ransack'd world
Still so much gold was left; and then I
      fear'd
Lest the gay navy there should splinter
      on it,
And fearing waved my arm to warn them
      off;
An idle signal, for the brittle fleet —
I thought I could have died to save it —
      near'd,                                        130

Touch'd, clink'd, and clash'd, and vanish'd,
      and I woke,
I heard the clash so clearly.   Now I see
My dream was Life, the woman honest
      Work,
And my poor venture but a fleet of glass
Wreck'd on a reef of visionary gold.'

      ' Nay,' said the kindly wife to comfort
      him,
' You raised your arm, you tumbled down
      and broke
The glass with little Margaret's medicine
      in it;
And, breaking that, you made and broke
      your dream.
A trifle makes a dream, a trifle breaks.' 140

      ' No trifle,' groan'd the husband; ' yester-
      day
I met him suddenly in the street, and ask'd
That which I ask'd the woman in my dream.
Like her, he shook his head.   " Show me
      the books ! "
He dodged me with a long and loose ac-
      count.
" The books, the books ! " but he, he could
      not wait,
Bound on a matter he of life and death;
When the great Books — see Daniel seven
      and ten —
Were open'd, I should find he meant me
      well;                                          149
And then began to bloat himself, and ooze
All over with the fat affectionate smile
That makes the widow lean.   " My dearest
      friend,
Have faith, have faith !   We live by faith,"
      said he;
" And all things work together for the
      good
Of those " — it makes me sick to quote
      him — last
Gript my hand hard, and with God-bless-
      you went.
I stood like one that had received a blow.
I found a hard friend in his loose accounts,
A loose one in the hard grip of his hand,
A curse in his God-bless-you; then my
      eyes                                           160
Pursued him down the street, and far
      away,
Among the honest shoulders of the crowd,
Read rascal in the motions of his back,
And scoundrel in the supple-sliding knee.'

'Was he so bound, poor soul ? ' said the
    good wife;
'So are we all; but do not call him, love,
Before you prove him, rogue, and proved,
    forgive.
His gain is loss; for he that wrongs his
    friend
Wrongs himself more, and ever bears
    about
A silent court of justice in his breast,    170
Himself the judge and jury, and himself
The prisoner at the bar, ever condemn'd.
And that drags down his life; then comes
    what comes
Hereafter; and he meant, he said he meant,
Perhaps he meant, or partly meant, you
    well.'

'"With all his conscience and one eye
    askew" —
Love, let me quote these lines, that you
    may learn
A man is likewise counsel for himself,
Too often, in that silent court of yours —
"With all his conscience and one eye
    askew,                                  180
So false, he partly took himself for true;
Whose pious talk, when most his heart was
    dry,
Made wet the crafty crowsfoot round his eye;
Who, never naming God except for gain,
So never took that useful name in vain,
Made Him his catspaw and the Cross his
    tool,
And Christ the bait to trap his dupe and
    fool;
Nor deeds of gift, but gifts of grace he
    forged,
And snake-like slimed his victim ere he
    gorged;
And oft at Bible meetings, o'er the rest   190
Arising, did his holy oily best,
Dropping the too rough H in Hell and
    Heaven,
To spread the Word by which himself had
    thriven."
How like you this old satire ? '

                          'Nay,' she said,
'I loathe it; he had never kindly heart,
Nor ever cared to better his own kind,
Who first wrote satire, with no pity in it.
But will you hear my dream, for I had one
That altogether went to music ?   Still
It awed me.'

                Then she told it, having dream'd   200
Of that same coast. —

                    But round the North, a light,
A belt, it seem'd, of luminous vapor, lay,
And ever in it a low musical note
Swell'd up and died; and, as it swell'd, a
    ridge
Of breaker issued from the belt, and still
Grew with the growing note, and when the
    note
Had reach'd a thunderous fulness, on those
    cliffs
Broke, mixt with awful light — the same as
    that
Living within the belt — whereby she saw
That all those lines of cliffs were cliffs no
    more,                                  210
But huge cathedral fronts of every age,
Grave, florid, stern, as far as eye could see,
One after one; and then the great ridge
    drew,
Lessening to the lessening music, back,
And past into the belt and swell'd again
Slowly to music.   Ever when it broke
The statues, king, or saint, or founder
    fell;
Then from the gaps and chasms of ruin
    left
Came men and women in dark clusters
    round,
Some crying, 'Set them up ! they shall not
    fall !'                                220
And others, 'Let them lie, for they have
    fallen.'
And still they strove and wrangled; and
    she grieved
In her strange dream, she knew not why,
    to find
Their wildest wailings never out of tune
With that sweet note; and ever as their
    shrieks
Ran highest up the gamut, that great wave
Returning, while none mark'd it, on the
    crowd
Broke, mixt with awful light, and show'd
    their eyes
Glaring, and passionate looks, and swept
    away
The men of flesh and blood, and men of
    stone,                                 230
To the waste deeps together.

                          'Then I fixt
My wistful eyes on two fair images,

Both crown'd with stars and high among
    the stars, —
The Virgin Mother standing with her child
High up on one of those dark minster-
    fronts —
Till she began to totter, and the child
Clung to the mother, and sent out a cry
Which mixt with little Margaret's, and I
    woke,
And my dream awed me; — well — but
    what are dreams?
Yours came but from the breaking of a
    glass,      240
And mine but from the crying of a child.'

    'Child? No!' said he, 'but this tide's
    roar, and his,
Our Boanerges with his threats of doom
And loud-lung'd Antibabylonianisms —
Altho' I grant but little music there —
Went both to make your dream; but if
    there were
A music harmonizing our wild cries,
Sphere-music such as that you dream'd
    about,
Why, that would make our passions far too
    like
The discords dear to the musician. No —
One shriek of hate would jar all the hymns
    of heaven.    251
True devils with no ear, they howl in tune
With nothing but the devil!'

        '"True" indeed!
One of our town, but later by an hour
Here than ourselves, spoke with me on the
    shore;
While you were running down the sands,
    and made
The dimpled flounce of the sea-furbelow
    flap,
Good man, to please the child. She brought
    strange news.
Why were you silent when I spoke to-
    night?    259
I had set my heart on your forgiving him
Before you knew. We *must* forgive the
    dead.'

    'Dead! who is dead?'

        'The man your eye pursued.
A little after you had parted with him,
He suddenly dropt dead of heart-disease.'

'Dead? he? of heart-disease? what
    heart had he
To die of? dead!'

        'Ah, dearest, if there be
A devil in man, there is an angel too,
And if he did that wrong you charge him
    with,
His angel broke his heart. But your rough
    voice —
You spoke so loud — has roused the child
    again.    270
Sleep, little birdie, sleep! will she not
    sleep
Without her "little birdie"? well, then,
    sleep,
And I will sing you "birdie."'

            Saying this,
The woman half turn'd round from him
    she loved,
Left him one hand, and reaching thro' the
    night
Her other, found — for it was close beside —
And half-embraced the basket cradle-
    head
With one soft arm, which, like the pliant
    bough
That moving moves the nest and nestling,
    sway'd    279
The cradle, while she sang this baby-song:

    What does little birdie say
    In her nest at peep of day?
    Let me fly, says little birdie,
    Mother, let me fly away.
    Birdie, rest a little longer,
    Till the little wings are stronger,
    So she rests a little longer,
    Then she flies away.

    What does little baby say,
    In her bed at peep of day?    290
    Baby says, like little birdie,
    Let me rise and fly away.
    Baby, sleep a little longer,
    Till the little limbs are stronger;
    If she sleeps a little longer,
    Baby too shall fly away.

'She sleeps; let us too, let all evil, sleep.
He also sleeps — another sleep than ours.
He can do no more wrong; forgive him,
    dear,
And I shall sleep the sounder!'

Then the man,
'His deeds yet live, the worst is yet to come.                301
Yet let your sleep for this one night be sound;
I do forgive him!'

          'Thanks, my love,' she said,
'Your own will be the sweeter,' and they slept.

## ODE SUNG AT THE OPENING OF THE INTERNATIONAL EXHIBITION

Originally entitled: 'May the First, 1862,' and first printed, incorrectly and with omissions, in the 'Times,' April 24, 1862. A correct version appeared in 'Fraser's Magazine,' for June, 1862.

A Greek translation of the Ode, signed W. G. C., appeared in the 'Times,' July 14, 1862 (when the original poem was reprinted with errors that called forth a letter from the poet to the editor); and a Latin verse translation, signed W., in the same journal, Jul 1862.

I

UPLIFT a thousand voices full and sweet,
    In this wide hall with earth's invention stored,
    And praise the invisible universal Lord,
Who lets once more in peace the nations meet,
    Where Science, Art, and Labor have outpour'd
Their myriad horns of plenty at our feet.

II

O silent father of our Kings to be,
Mourn'd in this golden hour of jubilee,
For this, for all, we weep our thanks thee!

III

The world-compelling plan was thine,—
And, lo! the long laborious miles
Of Palace; lo! the giant aisles,
Rich in model and design;
Harvest-tool and husbandry,
Loom and wheel and enginery,
Secrets of the sullen mine,
Steel and gold, and corn and wine,
Fabric rough, or fairy-fine,

Sunny tokens of the Line,
Polar marvels, and a feast
Of wonder, out of West and East,
And shapes and hues of Art divine!
All of beauty, all of use,
That one fair planet can produce,
    Brought from under every star,
Blown from over every main,
And mixt, as life is mixt with pain,
    The works of peace with works of war.

IV

    Is the goal so far away?
    Far, how far no tongue can say,
    Let us dream our dream to-day.

V

O ye, the wise who think, the wise who reign,
From growing Commerce loose her latest chain,
And let the fair white-wing'd peacemaker fly
To happy havens under all the sky,
And mix the seasons and the golden hours;
Till each man find his own in all men's good,
And all men work in noble brotherhood,
Breaking their mailed fleets and armed towers,
And ruling by obeying Nature's powers,
And gathering all the fruits of earth and crown'd with all her flowers.

## A WELCOME TO ALEXANDRA

### MARCH 7, 1863

Written on the arrival of the Princess Alexandra in England just before her marriage to the Prince of Wales on the 10th of March, 1863; published separately the same month; and afterwards included in the 'Enoch Arden' volume. Thackeray, in the 'Cornhill Magazine,' compared the poem to the waving of a flaring pine-tree torch on a windy headland.

SEA-KINGS' daughter from over the sea,
                    Alexandra!
Saxon and Norman and Dane are we,
But all of us Danes in our welcome of thee,
                    Alexandra!

Welcome her, thunders of fort and of fleet !
Welcome her, thundering cheer of the
    street !
Welcome her, all things youthful and
    sweet,
Scatter the blossom under her feet !
Break, happy land, into earlier flowers !
Make music, O bird, in the new - budded
    bowers !
Blazon your mottoes of blessing and prayer !
Welcome her, welcome her, all that is
    ours !
Warble, O bugle, and trumpet, blare !
Flags, flutter out upon turrets and towers !
Flames, on the windy headland flare !
Utter your jubilee, steeple and spire !
Clash, ye bells, in the merry March air !
Flash, ye cities, in rivers of fire !
Rush to the roof, sudden rocket, and
    higher
Melt into stars for the land's desire !
Roll and rejoice, jubilant voice,
Roll as a ground - swell dash'd on the
    strand,
Roar as the sea when he welcomes the land,
And welcome her, welcome the land's de-
    sire,
The sea-kings' daughter as happy as fair,
Blissful bride of a blissful heir,
Bride of the heir of the kings of the sea —
O joy to the people and joy to the throne,
Come to us, love us and make us your
    own;
For Saxon or Dane or Norman we,
Teuton or Celt, or whatever we be,
We are each all Dane in our welcome of
    thee,
                    Alexandra !

## THE GRANDMOTHER

First printed in ' Once a Week,' July 16,
1859, with the title, ' The Grandmother's Apology,' and an illustration by Millais.

### I

And Willy, my eldest-born, is gone, you
    say, little Anne ?
Ruddy and white, and strong on his legs,
    he looks like a man.
And Willy's wife has written; she never
    was over-wise,
Never the wife for Willy; he would n't
    take my advice.

### II

For, Annie, you see, her father was not the
    man to save,
Had n't a head to manage, and drank him-
    self into his grave.
Pretty enough, very pretty ! but I was
    against it for one.
Eh ! — but he would n't hear me — and
    Willy, you say, is gone.

### III

Willy, my beauty, my eldest - born, the
    flower of the flock;
Never a man could fling him, for Willy
    stood like a rock.          10
' Here 's a leg for a babe of a week ! ' says
    Doctor; and he would be bound
There was not his like that year in twenty
    parishes round.

### IV

Strong of his hands, and strong on his legs,
    but still of his tongue !
I ought to have gone before him; I wonder
    he went so young.
I cannot cry for him, Annie; I have not
    long to stay.
Perhaps I shall see him the sooner, for he
    lived far away.

### V

Why do you look at me, Annie ? you think
    I am hard and cold;
But all my children have gone before me,
    I am so old.
I cannot weep for Willy, nor can I weep
    for the rest;
Only at your age, Annie, I could have wept
    with the best.          20

### VI

For I remember a quarrel I had with your
    father, my dear,
All for a slanderous story, that cost me
    many a tear.
I mean your grandfather, Annie; it cost
    me a world of woe,
Seventy years ago, my darling, seventy
    years ago.

### VII

For Jenny, my cousin, had come to the
    place, and I knew right well
That Jenny had tript in her time; I knew,
    but I would not tell.

And she to be coming and slandering me,
    the base little liar !
But the tongue is a fire, as you know, my
    dear, the tongue is a fire.

### VIII

And the parson made it his text that week,
    and he said likewise
That a lie which is half a truth is ever the
    blackest of lies,                                30
That a lie which is all a lie may be met and
    fought with outright,
But a lie which is part a truth is a harder
    matter to fight.

### IX

And Willy had not been down to the farm
    for a week and a day;
And all things look'd half-dead, tho' it was
    the middle of May.
Jenny, to slander me, who knew what
    Jenny had been !
But soiling another, Annie, will never
    make oneself clean.

### X

And I cried myself well-nigh blind, and all
    of an evening late
I climb'd to the top of the garth, and stood
    by the road at the gate.
The moon like a rick on fire was rising
    over the dale,
And whit, whit, whit, in the bush beside
    me chirrupt the nightingale.             40

### XI

All of a sudden he stopt; there past by the
    gate of the farm
Willy, — he did n't see me, — and Jenny
    hung on his arm.
Out into the road I started, and spoke I
    scarce knew how;
Ah, there 's no fool like the old one — it
    makes me angry now.

### XII

Willy stood up like a man, and look'd the
    thing that he meant;
Jenny, the viper, made me a mocking curt-
    sey and went.
And I said, 'Let us part; in a hundred
    years it 'll all be the same.
You cannot love me at all, if you love not
    my good name.'

### XIII

And he turn'd, and I saw his eyes all wet,
    in the sweet moonshine:
'Sweetheart, I love you so well that your
    good name is mine.                          50
And what do I care for Jane, let her speak
    of you well or ill;
But marry me out of hand; we two shall be
    happy still.'

### XIV

'Marry you, Willy !' said I, 'but I needs
    must speak my mind,
And I fear you 'll listen to tales, be jealous
    and hard and unkind.'
But he turn'd and claspt me in his arms,
    and answer'd, 'No, love, no;'
Seventy years ago, my darling, seventy
    years ago.

### XV

So Willy and I were wedded. I wore a
    lilac gown;
And the ringers rang with a will, and he
    gave the ringers a crown.
But the first that ever I bare was dead be-
    fore he was born;
Shadow and shine is life, little Annie,
    flower and thorn.                              60

### XVI

That was the first time, too, that ever I
    thought of death.
There lay the sweet little body that never
    had drawn a breath.
I had not wept, little Anne, not since I had
    been a wife;
But I wept like a child that day, for the
    babe had fought for his life.

### XVII

His dear little face was troubled, as if with
    anger or pain;
I look'd at the still little body — his trouble
    had all been in vain.
For Willy I cannot weep, I shall see him
    another morn;
But I wept like a child for the child that
    was dead before he was born.

### XVIII

But he cheer'd me, my good man, for he
    seldom said me nay.
Kind, like a man, was he; like a man, too,
    would have his way;                          70

Never jealous — not he.   We had many a
    happy year;
And he died, and I could not weep — my
    own time seem'd so near.

### XIX

But I wish'd it had been God's will that I,
    too, then could have died;
I began to be tired a little, and fain had
    slept at his side.
And that was ten years back, or more, if I
    don't forget;
But as to the children, Annie, they 're all
    about me yet.

### XX

Pattering over the boards, my Annie who
    left me at two,
Patter she goes, my own little Annie, an
    Annie like you;
Pattering over the boards, she comes and
    goes at her will,
While Harry is in the five-acre and Charlie
    ploughing the hill.            80

### XXI

And Harry and Charlie, I hear them too
    — they sing to their team;
Often they come to the door in a pleasant
    kind of a dream.
They come and sit by my chair, they hover
    about my bed —
I am not always certain if they be alive or
    dead.

### XXII

And yet I know for a truth there 's none of
    them left alive,
For Harry went at sixty, your father at
    sixty-five,
And Willy, my eldest-born, at nigh three-
    score and ten.
I knew them all as babies, and now they 're
    elderly men.

### XXIII

For mine is a time of peace, it is not often
    I grieve;
I am oftener sitting at home in my father's
    farm at eve;                    90
And the neighbors come and laugh and
    gossip, and so do I;
I find myself often laughing at things that
    have long gone by.

### XXIV

To be sure the preacher says, our sins
    should make us sad;
But mine is a time of peace, and there is
    Grace to be had;
And God, not man, is the Judge of us all
    when life shall cease;
And in this Book, little Annie, the message
    is one of peace.

### XXV

And age is a time of peace, so it be free
    from pain,
And happy has been my life; but I would
    not live it again.
I seem to be tired a little, that 's all, and
    long for rest;
Only at your age, Annie, I could have wept
    with the best.            100

### XXVI

So Willy has gone, my beauty, my eldest-
    born, my flower;
But how can I weep for Willy, he has but
    gone for an hour, —
Gone for a minute, my son, from this room
    into the next;
I, too, shall go in a minute.   What time
    have I to be vext?

### XXVII

And Willy's wife has written, she never
    was over-wise.
Get me my glasses, Annie; thank God that
    I keep my eyes.
There is but a trifle left you, when I shall
    have past away.
But stay with the old woman now; you can-
    not have long to stay.

## NORTHERN FARMER

### OLD STYLE

The 'Northern Farmer, Old Style,' appeared
in the 'Enoch Arden' volume, 1864; the
'Northern Farmer, New Style,' in the 'Holy
Grail' volume, 1870.

Stopford Brooke ('Tennyson,' London, 1894)
says of it: 'It is a vivid piece out of the great
comedy of man, not of its mere mirth, but of
that elemental humorousness of things which
belongs to the lives of the brutes as well as to

ourselves, that steady quaintness of the ancient
earth and all who are born of her, which first
made men smile, and which has enabled us to
bear our pain better, and to love one another
more, than might appear possible in a world
where Nature generally seems to be doing her
best to hurt us first, and then to kill us. . . .
There never was a more superbly hewn piece
of rough and vital sculpture.'

### I

WHEER 'asta beän saw long and meä liggin'
 'ere aloän ?
Noorse ? thoort nowt o' a noorse; whoy,
 Doctor 's abeän an' agoän;
Says that I moänt 'a naw moor aäle, but I
 beänt a fool;
Git ma my aäle, fur I beänt a-gawin' to
 breäk my rule.

### II

Doctors, they knaws nowt, fur a says what 's
 nawways true;
Naw soort o' koind o' use to saäy the things
 that a do.
I 've 'ed my point o' aäle ivry noight sin' I
 beän 'ere.
An' I 've 'ed my quart ivry market-noight
 for foorty year.

### III

Parson 's a beän loikewoise, an' a sittin' ere
 o' my bed.
' The Amoighty 's a taäkin o' you[1] to 'issén,
 my friend,' a said,
An' a towd ma my sins, an' 's toithe were
 due, an' I gied it in hond;
I done moy duty boy 'um, as I 'a done boy
 the lond.

### IV

Larn'd a ma' beä.  I reckons I 'annot sa
 mooch to larn.
But a cast oop, thot a did, 'bout Bessy
 Marris's barne.
Thaw a knaws I hallus voäted wi' Squoire
 an' choorch an' staäte,
An' i' the woost o' toimes I wur niver agin
 the raäte.

### V

An' I hallus coom'd to 's choorch afoor moy
 Sally wur deäd,
An' 'eärd 'um a bummin' awaäy loike a
 buzzard-clock[2] ower my 'eäd,

[1] *ou* as in *hour*.   [2] Cockchafer.

An' I niver knaw'd whot a meän'd but I
 thowt a 'ad summut to saäy,
An' I thowt a said whot a owt to 'a said,
 an' I coom'd awaäy.

### VI

Bessy Marris's barne ! tha knaws she laäid
 it to meä.
Mowt a beän, mayhap, for she wur a bad
 un, sheä.
'Siver, I kep 'um, I kep 'um, my lass, tha
 mun understond;
I done moy duty boy 'um, as I 'a done boy
 the lond.

### VII

But Parson a cooms an' a goäs, an' a says
 it eäsy an' freeä:
' The Amoighty 's a taäkin o' you to 'issén,
 my friend,' says 'eä.
I weänt saäy men be loiars, thaw summun
 said it in 'aäste;
But 'e reäds wonn sarmin a weeäk, an' I 'a
 stubb'd Thurnaby waäste.

### VIII

D' ya moind the waäste, my lass ? naw,
 naw, tha was not born then;
Theer wur a boggle in it, I often 'eärd 'um
 mysén;
Moäst loike a butter-bump,[1] fur I 'eärd 'um
 about an' about,
But I stubb'd 'um oop wi' the lot, an' raäved
 an' rembled 'um out.

### IX

Keäper's it wur; fo' they fun 'um theer
 a-laäid of 'is faäce
Down i' the woild 'enemies[2] afoor I coom'd
 to the plaäce.
Noäks or Thimbleby — toäner[3] 'ed shot
 'um as deäd as a naäil.
Noäks wur 'ang'd for it oop at 'soize — but
 git ma my aäle.

### X

Dubbut looök at the waäste; theer warn't
 not feeäd for a cow;
Nowt at all but bracken an' fuzz, an' looök
 at it now —
Warn't worth nowt a haäcre, an' now
 theer 's lots o' feeäd,
Fourscoor[4] yows upon it, an' some on it
 down i' seeäd.[5]

[1] Bittern. [2] Anemones. [3] One or other.
[4] *ou* as in *hour*.  [5] Clover.

### XI

Nobbut a bit on it 's left, an' I meän'd to 'a
 stubb'd it at fall,
Done it ta-year I meän'd, an' runn'd plow
 thruff it an' all,
If Godamoighty an' parson 'ud nobbut let
 ma aloän, —
Meä, wi' haäte hoonderd haäcre o' Squoire's,
 an' lond o' my oän.

### XII

Do Godamoighty knaw what a 's doing
 a-taäkin' o' meä ?
I beänt wonn as saws 'ere a beän an' yon-
 der a peä;
An' Squoire 'ull be sa mad an' all — a' dear,
 a' dear !
And I 'a managed for Squoire coom
 Michaelmas thutty year.

### XIII

A mowt 'a taäen owd Joänes, as 'ant not a
 'aäpoth o' sense,
Or a mowt 'a taäen young Robins — a niver
 mended a fence;
But Godamoighty a moost taäke meä an'
 taäke ma now,
Wi' aäf the cows to cauve an' Thurnaby
 hoälms to plow !

### XIV

Looök 'ow quoloty smoiles when they seeäs
 ma a passin' boy,
Says to thessén, naw doubt, ' What a man
 a beä sewer-loy ! '
Fur they knaws what I beän to Squoire sin'
 fust a coom'd to the 'All;
I done moy duty by Squoire an' I done
 moy duty boy hall.

### XV

Squoire 's i' Lunnon, an' summun I reckons
 'ull 'a to wroite,
For whoä 's to howd the lond ater meä thot
 muddles ma quoit;
Sartin-sewer I beä thot a weänt niver give
 it to Joänes,
Naw, nor a moänt to Robins — a niver rem-
 bles the stoäns.

### XVI

But summun 'ull come ater meä mayhap
 wi' 'is kittle o' steäm
Huzzin' an' maäzin' the blessed feäilds wi'
 the divil's oän teäm.

Sin' I mun doy I mun doy, thaw loife they
 says is sweet,
But sin' I mun doy I mun doy, for I couldn
 abeär to see it.

### XVII

What atta stannin' theer fur, an' doesn
 bring ma the aäle ?
Doctor 's a 'toättler, lass, an a 's hallus i'
 the owd taäle;
I weänt breäk rules fur Doctor, a knaws
 naw moor nor a floy;
Git ma my aäle, I tell tha, an' if I mun doy
 I mun doy.

## NORTHERN FARMER

### NEW STYLE

### I

Dosn't thou 'ear my 'erse's legs, as they
 canters awaäy ?
Proputty, proputty, proputty — that 's what
 I 'ears 'em saäy.
Proputty, proputty, proputty — Sam, thou 's
 an ass for thy païns;
Theer 's moor sense i' one o' 'is legs, nor in
 all thy braïns.

### II

Woä — theer 's a craw to pluck wi' tha,
 Sam: yon 's parson's 'ouse —
Dosn't thou knaw that a man mun be
 eäther a man or a mouse ?
Time to think on it then; for thou 'll be
 twenty to weeäk.[1]
Proputty, proputty — woä then, woä — let
 ma 'ear mysén speäk.

### III

Me an' thy muther, Sammy, 'as beän
 a-talkin' o' thee;
Thou 's beän talkin' to muther, an' she beän
 a-tellin' it me.
Thou 'll not marry for munny — thou 's
 sweet upo' parson's lass —
Noä — thou 'll marry for luvv — an' we
 boäth on us thinks tha an ass.

### IV

Seeä'd her to-daäy goä by — Saäint's-daäy
 — they was ringing the bells.
She 's a beauty, thou thinks — an' soä is
 scoors o' gells,

[1] This week.

Them as 'as munny an' all — wot's a
 beauty ? — the flower as blaws.
But proputty, proputty sticks, an' proputty, proputty graws.

V

Do'ant be stunt;[1] taäke time.  I knaws
 what maäkes tha sa mad.
Warn't I craäzed fur the lasses mysén
 when I wur a lad ?
But I knaw'd a Quaäker feller as often 'as
 towd ma this:
'Doänt thou marry for munny, but goä
 wheer munny is !'

VI

An' I went wheer munny war; an' thy
 muther coom to 'and,
Wi' lots o' munny laaïd by, an' a nicetish
 bit o' land.
Maäybe she warn't a beauty — I niver giv
 it a thowt —
But warn't she as good to cuddle an' kiss
 as a lass as 'ant nowt ?

VII

Parson's lass 'ant nowt, an' she weänt 'a
 nowt when 'e 's deäd,
Mun be a guvness, lad, or summut, and ad-
 dle[2] her breäd.
Why ? fur 'e 's nobbut a curate, an' weänt
 niver get hissén clear,
An' 'e maäde the bed as 'e ligs on afoor 'e
 coom'd to the shere.

VIII

An' thin 'e coom'd to the parish wi' lots o'
 Varsity debt,
Stook to his taaïl they did, an' 'e 'ant got
 shut on 'em yet.
An' 'e ligs on 'is back i' the grip, wi' noän
 to lend 'im a shove,
Woorse nor a far-welter'd[3] yowe; fur,
 Sammy, 'e married fur luvv.

IX

Luvv ? what 's luvv ? thou can luvv thy
 lass an' 'er munny too,
Maäkin' 'em goä togither, as they 've good
 right to do.

[1] Obstinate.         [2] Earn.
[3] Or, fow-welter'd, — said of a sheep lying
on its back in the furrow.

Couldn I luvv thy muther by cause o' 'er
 munny laaïd by ?
Naäy — fur I luvv'd 'er a vast sight moor
 fur it; reäson why.

X

Ay, an' thy muther says thou wants to
 marry the lass,
Cooms of a gentleman burn; an' we boäth
 on us thinks tha an ass.
Woä then, proputty, wiltha ? — an ass as
 near as mays nowt[1] —
Woä then, wiltha ? dangtha ! — the bees is
 as fell as owt.[2]

XI

Breäk me a bit o' the esh for his 'eäd, lad,
 out o' the fence !
Gentleman burn ! what 's gentleman burn ?
 is it shillins an' pence ?
Proputty, proputty 's ivrything 'ere, an',
 Sammy, I 'm blest
If it is n't the saäme oop yonder, fur them
 as 'as it 's the best.

XII

Tis 'n them as 'as munny as breäks into
 'ouses an' steäls,
Them as 'as coäts to their backs an' taäkes
 their regular meäls.
Noä, but it 's them as niver knaws wheer a
 meäl 's to be 'ad.
Taäke my word for it, Sammy, the poor in
 a loomp is bad.

XIII

Them or thir feythers, tha sees, mun 'a
 beän a laäzy lot,
Fur work mun 'a gone to the gittin' whiniver munny was got.
Feyther 'ad ammost nowt; leästways 'is
 munny was 'id.
But 'e tued an' moil'd issén deäd, an' 'e died
 a good un, 'e did.

XIV

Looök thou theer wheer Wrigglesby beck
 cooms out by the 'ill !
Feyther run oop to the farm, an' I runs
 oop to the mill;

[1] Makes nothing.
[2] The flies are as fierce as anything.

An' I 'll run oop to the brig, an' that thou 'll
  live to see;
And if thou marries a good un I 'll leäve
  the land to thee.

### XV

Thim 's my noätions, Sammy, wheerby I
  meäns to stick;
But if thou marries a bad un, I 'll leäve
  the land to Dick. —
Coom oop, proputty, proputty — that 's
  what I 'ears 'im saäy —
Proputty, proputty, proputty — canter an'
  canter awaäy.

## IN THE VALLEY OF CAUTERETZ

Written in September, 1861, but not published until 1864 in the 'Enoch Arden' volume.

Cauteretz is a beautiful valley in the French
Pyrenees. The visit of Tennyson and Arthur
Hallam to the place, here commemorated, took
place in 1830. The date of the second visit
has sometimes been given as 1862, but Arthur
Hugh Clough's diary, in which he refers to
meeting Tennyson there, makes it 1861. Under date of September 1, at Mont Dore-les-
Bains, he writes: 'The Tennysons arrived at
6.30 yesterday. Tennyson was here with Arthur Hallam thirty-one years ago, and really
finds great pleasure in the place; they stayed
here and at Cauteretz. "Œnone," he said,
was written on the inspiration of the Pyrenees,
which stood for Ida.' The poet probably wrote
'two and thirty' in the verses for the sake of
euphony. 'I walk'd with *one* I loved *one* and
thirty years ago' would have offended his sensitive ear.

ALL along the valley, stream that flashest
  white,
Deepening thy voice with the deepening of
  the night,
All along the valley, where thy waters
  flow,
I walk'd with one I loved two and thirty
  years ago.
All along the valley, while I walk'd to-day,
The two and thirty years were a mist that
  rolls away;
For all along the valley, down thy rocky
  bed,
Thy living voice to me was as the voice of
  the dead,
And all along the valley, by rock and cave
  and tree,
The voice of the dead was a living voice to
  me.

## THE FLOWER

First printed in the 'Enoch Arden' volume,
and unaltered.

The poem has been supposed to have some
personal reference, but Lord Tennyson himself
assured me that it had not. According to the
'Memoir' (vol. ii. p. 10), he described it in his
manuscript notes as 'an universal apologue.'

ONCE in a golden hour
  I cast to earth a seed.
Up there came a flower,
  The people said, a weed.

To and fro they went
  Thro' my garden-bower,
And muttering discontent
  Cursed me and my flower.

Then it grew so tall
  It wore a crown of light,
But thieves from o'er the wall
  Stole the seed by night;

Sow'd it far and wide
  By every town and tower,
Till all the people cried,
  'Splendid is the flower.'

Read my little fable:
  He that runs may read.
Most can raise the flowers now
  For all have got the seed.

And some are pretty enough,
  And some are poor indeed;
And now again the people
  Call it but a weed.

## REQUIESCAT

First printed in the 'Enoch Arden' volume,
and unaltered.

FAIR is her cottage in its place,
  Where yon broad water sweetly, slowly
    glides.

It sees itself from thatch to base
  Dream in the sliding tides.

And fairer she, but ah, how soon to die !
  Her quiet dream of life this hour may
    cease.
Her peaceful being slowly passes by
  To some more perfect peace.

## THE SAILOR BOY

First printed in the ' Victoria Regia,' Christmas, 1861 (edited by Miss Emily Faithfull),
and afterwards included in the ' Enoch Arden '
volume.

HE rose at dawn and, fired with hope,
  Shot o'er the seething harbor-bar,
And reach'd the ship and caught the rope,
  And whistled to the morning star.

And while he whistled long and loud
  He heard a fierce mermaiden cry,
' O boy, tho' thou art young and proud,
  I see the place where thou wilt lie.

' The sands and yeasty surges mix
  In caves about the dreary bay,
And on thy ribs the limpet sticks,
  And in thy heart the scrawl shall play.'

' Fool,' he answer'd, ' death is sure
  To those that stay and those that roam,
But I will nevermore endure
  To sit with empty hands at home.

' My mother clings about my neck,
  My sisters crying, " Stay for shame; "
My father raves of death and wreck, —
  They are all to blame, they are all to
    blame.

'God help me ! save I take my part
  Of danger on the roaring sea,
A devil rises in my heart,
  Far worse than any death to me.'

## THE ISLET

First printed in the ' Enoch Arden ' volume,
and unaltered.

' WHITHER, O whither, love, shall we go,
For a score of sweet little summers or so ? '
The sweet little wife of the singer said,

On the day that follow'd the day she was
    wed,
' Whither, O whither, love, shall we go ? '
And the singer shaking his curly head
Turn'd as he sat, and struck the keys
There at his right with a sudden crash,
Singing, ' And shall it be over the seas
With a crew that is neither rude nor rash,
But a bevy of Eroses apple-cheek'd,
In a shallop of crystal ivory-beak'd ?
With a satin sail of a ruby glow,
To a sweet little Eden on earth that I know,
A mountain islet pointed and peak'd;
Waves on a diamond shingle dash,
Cataract brooks to the ocean run,
Fairily-delicate palaces shine
Mixt with myrtle and clad with vine,
And overstream'd and silvery-streak'd
With many a rivulet high against the sun
The facets of the glorious mountain flash
Above the valleys of palm and pine.'

' Thither, O thither, love, let us go.'

' No, no, no !
For in all that exquisite isle, my dear,
There is but one bird with a musical throat,
And his compass is but of a single note,
That it makes one weary to hear.'

' Mock me not ! mock me not ! love, let us
    go.'

' No, love, no.
For the bud ever breaks into bloom on the
    tree,
And a storm never wakes on the lonely
    sea,
And a worm is there in the lonely wood,
That pierces the liver and blackens the
    blood,
And makes it a sorrow to be.'

## A DEDICATION

Addressed to the poet's wife, and first
printed in the ' Enoch Arden ' volume. The
only alteration is in the sixth line, which originally read : ' and spite of praise and scorn.'

DEAR, near and true, — no truer Time
    himself
Can prove you, tho' he make you evermore
Dearer and nearer, as the rapid of life

Shoots to the fall, — take this and pray
    that he
Who wrote it, honoring your sweet faith in
    him,
May trust himself; and after praise and
    scorn,
As one who feels the immeasurable world,
Attain the wise indifference of the wise;
And after autumn past — if left to pass
His autumn into seeming-leafless days —
Draw toward the long frost and longest
    night,
Wearing his wisdom lightly, like the fruit
Which in our winter woodland looks a
    flower.[1]

# EXPERIMENTS

## BOÄDICÉA

First published in the 'Enoch Arden' volume. The only change since made is in the
19th line, which originally read: 'There the
hive of Roman liars worship a gluttonous em-
peror-idiot.'

WHILE about the shore of Mona those Ne-
    ronian legionaries
Burnt and broke the grove and altar of the
    Druid and Druidess,
Far in the East Boädicéa, standing loftily
    charioted,
Mad and maddening all that heard her in
    her fierce volubility,
Girt by half the tribes of Britain, near the
    colony Cámulodúne,
Yell'd and shriek'd between her daughters
    o'er a wild confederacy.

'They that scorn the tribes and call us
    Britain's barbarous populaces,
Did they hear me, would they listen, did
    they pity me supplicating?
Shall I heed them in their anguish? shall
    I brook to be supplicated?
Hear, Icenian, Catieuchlanian, hear, Cori-
    tanian, Trinobant!
Must their ever-ravening eagle's beak and
    talon annihilate us?
Tear the noble heart of Britain, leave it
    gorily quivering?

[1] The fruit of the Spindle-tree (*Euonymus
Europæus*).

Bark an answer, Britain's raven! bark and
    blacken innumerable,
Blacken round the Roman carrion, make
    the carcase a skeleton,
Kite and kestrel, wolf and wolfkin, from
    the wilderness, wallow in it,
Till the face of Bel be brighten'd, Taranis
    be propitiated.
Lo their colony half-defended! lo their
    colony, Cámulodúne!
There the horde of Roman robbers mock
    at a barbarous adversary.
There the hive of Roman liars worship an
    emperor-idiot.
Such is Rome, and this her deity; hear it,
    Spirit of Cássivëlaún!

'Hear it, Gods! the Gods have heard it,
    O Icenian, O Coritanian!
Doubt not ye the Gods have answer'd,
    Catieuchlanian, Trinobant.
These have told us all their anger in mir-
    aculous utterances,
Thunder, a flying fire in heaven, a murmur
    heard aërially,
Phantom sound of blows descending, moan
    of an enemy massacred,
Phantom wail of women and children, mul-
    titudinous agonies.
Bloodily flow'd the Tamesa rolling phan-
    tom bodies of horses and men;
Then a phantom colony smoulder'd on the
    refluent estuary;
Lastly yonder yester-even, suddenly giddily
    tottering —
There was one who watch'd and told me —
    down their statue of Victory fell.
Lo their precious Roman bantling, lo the
    colony Cámulodúne,
Shall we teach it a Roman lesson? shall
    we care to be pitiful?
Shall we deal with it as an infant? shall
    we dandle it amorously?

'Hear, Icenian, Catieuchlanian, hear,
    Coritanian, Trinobant!
While I roved about the forest, long and
    bitterly meditating,
There I heard them in the darkness, at the
    mystical ceremony;
Loosely robed in flying raiment, sang the
    terrible prophetesses:
"Fear not, isle of blowing woodland, isle
    of silvery parapets!

Tho' the Roman eagle shadow thee, tho'
    the gathering enemy narrow thee,
Thou shalt wax and he shall dwindle, thou
    shalt be the mighty one yet !
Thine the liberty, thine the glory, thine the
    deeds to be celebrated,
Thine the myriad-rolling ocean, light and
    shadow illimitable,
Thine the lands of lasting summer, many-
    blossoming Paradises,
Thine the North and thine the South and
    thine the battle-thunder of God."
So they chanted: how shall Britain light
    upon auguries happier ?
So they chanted in the darkness, and there
    cometh a victory now.

'Hear, Icenian, Catieuchlanian, hear,
    Coritanian, Trinobant !
Me the wife of rich Prasútagus, me the
    lover of liberty,
Me they seized and me they tortured, me
    they lash'd and humiliated,
Me the sport of ribald Veterans, mine of
    ruffian violators !
See, they sit, they hide their faces, miser-
    able in ignominy !
Wherefore in me burns an anger, not by
    blood to be satiated.
Lo the palaces and the temple, lo the col-
    ony Cámulodúne !
There they ruled, and thence they wasted
    all the flourishing territory,
Thither at their will they haled the yellow-
    ringlèted Britoness —
Bloodily, bloodily fall the battle-axe, unex-
    hausted, inexorable.
Shout, Icenian, Catieuchlanian, shout, Cori-
    tanian, Trinobant,
Till the victim hear within and yearn to
    hurry precipitously,
Like the leaf in a roaring whirlwind, like
    the smoke in a hurricane whirl'd.
Lo the colony, there they rioted in the city
    of Cúnobelíne !
There they drank in cups of emerald, there
    at tables of ebony lay,
Rolling on their purple couches in their
    tender effeminacy.
There they dwelt and there they rioted;
    there — there — they dwell no more.
Burst the gates, and burn the palaces, break
    the works of the statuary,
Take the hoary Roman head and shatter it,
    hold it abominable,

Cut the Roman boy to pieces in his lust
    and voluptuousness,
Lash the maiden into swooning, me they
    lash'd and humiliated,
Chop the breasts from off the mother, dash
    the brains of the little one out,
Up, my Britons ! on, my chariot ! on, my
    chargers, trample them under us !'

So the Queen Boädicéa, standing loftily
    charioted,
Brandishing in her hand a dart and rolling
    glances lioness-like,
Yell'd and shriek'd between her daughters
    in her fierce volubility.
Till her people all around the royal chariot
    agitated,
Madly dash'd the darts together, writhing
    barbarous lineaments,
Made the noise of frosty woodlands, when
    they shiver in January,
Roar'd as when the roaring breakers boom
    and blanch on the precipices,
Yell'd as when the winds of winter tear an
    oak on a promontory.
So the silent colony, hearing her tumultu-
    ous adversaries
Clash the darts and on the buckler beat
    with rapid unanimous hand,
Thought on all her evil tyrannies, all her
    pitiless avarice,
Till she felt the heart within her fall and
    flutter tremulously,
Then her pulses at the clamoring of her
    enemy fainted away.
Out of evil evil flourishes, out of tyranny
    tyranny buds.
Ran the land with Roman slaughter, mul-
    titudinous agonies.
Perish'd many a maid and matron, many a
    valorous legionary,
Fell the colony, city, and citadel, London,
    Verulam, Cámulodúne.

# IN QUANTITY

## ON TRANSLATIONS OF HOMER

### (HEXAMETERS AND PENTAMETERS)

This and the three following 'experiments
in quantity' appeared in the 'Cornhill Magazine' for December, 1863. This was not
printed with the others in the 'Enoch Arden'

volume, but was finally included in the edition
of 1884.

The 'Milton' and the 'Hendecasyllabics'
have not been altered.

The 'Specimen of a Translation of the Iliad
in Blank Verse' was prefaced in the 'Cornhill
Magazine' with the following note : —

'Some, and among these one at least of our
best and greatest, have endeavored to give us
the "Iliad" in English hexameters, and by
what appears to me their failures have gone
far to prove the impossibility of the task. I
have long held by our blank verse in this matter, and now after having spoken so disrespect-
fully here of these hexameters, I venture, or
rather feel bound, to subjoin a specimen, however brief and with whatever demerits, of a
blank verse translation.'

THESE lame hexameters the strong-wing'd
    music of Homer !
No — but a most burlesque barbarous
    experiment.
When was a harsher sound ever heard, ye
    Muses, in England ?
    When did a frog coarser croak upon our
        Helicon ?
Hexameters no worse than daring Germany
    gave us,
    Barbarous experiment, barbarous hexa-
        meters.

## MILTON

### (ALCAICS)

O MIGHTY-MOUTH'D inventor of harmonies,
O skill'd to sing of Time or Eternity,
    God-gifted organ-voice of England,
        Milton, a name to resound for ages;
Whose Titan angels, Gabriel, Abdiel,
Starr'd from Jehovah's gorgeous armories,
    Tower, as the deep-domed empyrean
        Rings to the roar of an angel onset !
Me rather all that bowery loneliness,
The brooks of Eden mazily murmuring,
    And bloom profuse and cedar arches
        Charm, as a wanderer out in ocean,
Where some refulgent sunset of India
Streams o'er a rich ambrosial ocean isle,
    And crimson-hued the stately palm-woods
        Whisper in odorous heights of even.

### (HENDECASYLLABICS)

O you chorus of indolent reviewers,
Irresponsible, indolent reviewers,
Look, I come to the test, a tiny poem

All composed in a metre of Catullus,
All in quantity, careful of my motion,
Like the skater on ice that hardly bears
    him,
Lest I fall unawares before the people,
Waking laughter in indolent reviewers.
Should I flounder awhile without a tumble
Thro' this metrification of Catullus,
They should speak to me not without a
    welcome,
All that chorus of indolent reviewers.
Hard, hard, hard is it, only not to tumble,
So fantastical is the dainty metre.
Wherefore slight me not wholly, nor be-
    lieve me
Too presumptuous, indolent reviewers.
O blatant Magazines, regard me rather —
Since I blush to belaud myself a moment —
As some rare little rose, a piece of inmost
Horticultural art, or half coquette-like
Maiden, not to be greeted unbenignly.

## SPECIMEN OF A TRANSLATION OF THE ILIAD IN BLANK VERSE

### [ILIAD, VIII. 542–561]

So Hector spake; the Trojans roar'd ap-
    plause;
Then loosed their sweating horses from the
    yoke,
And each beside his chariot bound his own;
And oxen from the city, and goodly sheep
In haste they drove, and honey-hearted
    wine
And bread from out the houses brought,
    and heap'd
Their firewood, and the winds from off the
    plain
Roll'd the rich vapor far into the heaven.
And these all night upon the bridge [1] of
    war
Sat glorying; many a fire before them
    blazed.
As when in heaven the stars about the moon
Look beautiful, when all the winds are
    laid,
And every height comes out, and jutting
    peak
And valley, and the immeasurable heavens
Break open to their highest, and all the
    stars

    [1] Or, ridge.

Shine, and the shepherd gladdens in his
    heart;
So many a fire between the ships and stream
Of Xanthus blazed before the towers of
    Troy,
A thousand on the plain; and close by each
Sat fifty in the blaze of burning fire;
And eating hoary grain and pulse the
    steeds,
Fixt by their cars, waited the golden dawn.


## THE THIRD OF FEBRUARY, 1852

This poem is one of three inspired by the
excitement in England which followed the
*coup d'état* of Louis Napoleon in December,
1851. It was 'a powerful rebuke to the House
of Lords for having deprecated the free criticism expressed in newspapers and in speeches
against the author of that crime.' It appeared
in the 'Examiner' for February 7, 1852, and
was signed 'Merlin.' The patriotic lyric, 'Hands
all round,' was printed in the same number
of the 'Examiner;' and 'Britons, guard your
own,' in the preceding number (January 31,
1852).

The poem was first acknowledged and included in the collected works in 1872.

MY Lords, we heard you speak: you told
    us all
    That England's honest censure went too
      far,
That our free press should cease to brawl,
    Not sting the fiery Frenchman into war.
It was our ancient privilege, my Lords,
To fling whate'er we felt, not fearing, into
    words.

We love not this French God, the child of
    hell,
    Wild War, who breaks the converse of
      the wise;
But though we love kind Peace so well,
    We dare not even by silence sanction lies.
It might be safe our censures to withdraw,
And yet, my Lords, not well; there is a
    higher law.

As long as we remain, we must speak free,
    Tho' all the storm of Europe on us break.
No little German state are we,
    But the one voice in Europe; we *must*
      speak,

That if to-night our greatness were struck
    dead,
There might be left some record of the
    things we said.

If you be fearful, then must we be bold.
    Our Britain cannot salve a tyrant o'er.
Better the waste Atlantic roll'd
    On her and us and ours for evermore.
What ! have we fought for Freedom from
    our prime,
At last to dodge and palter with a public
    crime ?

Shall we fear *him?* our own we never
    fear'd.
    From our first Charles by force we wrung
      our claims.
Prick'd by the Papal spur, we rear'd,
    We flung the burthen of the second
      James.
I say, we *never* fear'd ! and as for these,
We broke them on the land, we drove them
    on the seas.

And you, my Lords, you make the people
    muse
    In doubt if you be of our Barons' breed —
Were those your sires who fought at
    Lewes ?
Is this the manly strain of Runnymede ?
O fallen nobility that, overawed,
Would lisp in honey'd whispers of this
    monstrous fraud !

*We* feel, at least, that silence here were
    sin,
    Not ours the fault if we have feeble
    hosts —
If easy patrons of their kin
    Have left the last free race with naked
      coasts !
They knew the precious things they had to
    guard;
For us, we will not spare the tyrant one
    hard word.

Tho' niggard throats of Manchester may
    bawl,
    What England was, shall her true sons
    forget ?
We are not cotton-spinners all,
    But some love England and her honor
    yet.

And these in our Thermopylæ shall stand,
And hold against the world this honor of
the land.

## A WELCOME TO HER ROYAL HIGHNESS MARIE ALEXANDROVNA, DUCHESS OF EDINBURGH

### MARCH 7, 1874

Written to welcome Marie to England after
her marriage to the Duke of Edinburgh, January 23, 1874.  Printed in the 'Times,' and
afterwards included in the collected editions.

### I

THE Son of him with whom we strove for
    power —
  Whose will is lord thro' all his world-
    domain —
  Who made the serf a man, and burst his
    chain —
Has given our Prince his own imperial
    Flower,
        Alexandrovna.
And welcome, Russian flower, a people's
    pride,
  To Britain, when her flowers begin to
    blow !
From love to love, from home to home
    you go,
From mother unto mother, stately bride,
        Marie Alexandrovna !

### II

The golden news along the steppes is
    blown,
  And at thy name the Tartar tents are
    stirr'd ;
  Elburz and all the Caucasus have heard ;
And all the sultry palms of India known,
        Alexandrovna.
The voices of our universal sea
  On capes of Afric as on cliffs of Kent,
  The Maoris and that Isle of Continent,
And loyal pines of Canada murmur thee,
        Marie Alexandrovna !

### III

Fair empires branching, both, in lusty
    life ! —
  Yet Harold's England fell to Norman
    swords ;

Yet thine own land has bow'd to Tartar
    hordes
Since English Harold gave its throne a
    wife,
        Alexandrovna !
For thrones and peoples are as waifs that
    swing,
  And float or fall, in endless ebb and
    flow ;
  But who love best have best the grace to
    know
That Love by right divine is deathless
    king,
        Marie Alexandrovna !

### IV

And Love has led thee to the stranger
    land,
  Where men are bold and strongly say
    their say ; —
  See, empire upon empire smiles to-day,
As thou with thy young lover hand in hand,
        Alexandrovna !
So now thy fuller life is in the west,
  Whose hand at home was gracious to thy
    poor ;
  Thy name was blest within the narrow
    door ;
Here also, Marie, shall thy name be blest,
        Marie Alexandrovna !

### V

Shall fears and jealous hatreds flame again ?
  Or at thy coming, Princess, everywhere,
  The blue heaven break, and some diviner
    air
Breathe thro' the world and change the
    hearts of men,
        Alexandrovna ?
But hearts that change not, love that can-
    not cease,
  And peace be yours, the peace of soul in
    soul !
And howsoever this wild world may roll,
Between your peoples truth and manful
    peace,
        Alfred — Alexandrovna !

## IN THE GARDEN AT SWAINSTON

Written in 1870, and first printed in the
'Cabinet Edition,' 1874.
Swainston was the seat of the late Sir John

Simeon, in the Isle of Wight. Here the greater part of 'Maud' was written (Waugh). Sir John died at Fribourg in Switzerland in 1870. The body was brought home for burial, and this poem was written in the garden at Swainston during the week that elapsed before the funeral. See the 'Memoir,' vol. ii. p. 97.

NIGHTINGALES warbled without,
    Within was weeping for thee;
Shadows of three dead men
    Walk'd in the walks with me,
    Shadows of three dead men, and thou
        wast one of the three.

Nightingales sang in his woods,
    The Master was far away;
Nightingales warbled and sang
    Of a passion that lasts but a day;
    Still in the house in his coffin the Prince
        of courtesy lay.

Two dead men have I known
    In courtesy like to thee;
Two dead men have I loved
    With a love that ever will be;
    Three dead men have I loved, and thou
        art last of the three.

## CHILD SONGS

First printed in 'St. Nicholas' (N. Y.) for February, 1880. Set to music by Mrs. Tennyson in the same number and that for March, 1880. Reprinted in the collected edition of 1884.

### I

### THE CITY CHILD

DAINTY little maiden, whither would you
        wander?
    Whither from this pretty home, the home
        where mother dwells?
'Far and far away,' said the dainty little
        maiden,
' All among the gardens, auriculas, anemones,
    Roses and lilies and Canterbury bells.'

Dainty little maiden, whither would you
        wander?
    Whither from this pretty house, this city-
        house of ours?

' Far and far away,' said the dainty little
        maiden,
' All among the meadows, the clover and
        the clematis,
    Daisies and kingcups and honeysuckle-
        flowers.'

### II

### MINNIE AND WINNIE

MINNIE and Winnie
    Slept in a shell.
Sleep, little ladies!
    And they slept well.

Pink was the shell within,
    Silver without;
Sounds of the great sea
    Wander'd about.

Sleep, little ladies!
    Wake not soon!
Echo on echo
    Dies to the moon.

Two bright stars
    Peep'd into the shell.
' What are they dreaming of?
    Who can tell?'

Started a green linnet
    Out of the croft;
Wake, little ladies!
    The sun is aloft!

## THE SPITEFUL LETTER

Contributed to 'Once a Week' in January, 1868, and reprinted in 1884.

Attempts have been made to identify the writer of the letter; but the poet wrote to the editor of 'Once a Week': 'It is no particular letter that I meant. I have had dozens of them from one quarter and another.'

HERE, it is here, the close of the year,
    And with it a spiteful letter.
My name in song has done him much wrong,
    For himself has done much better.

O little bard, is your lot so hard,
    If men neglect your pages?
I think not much of yours or of mine,
    I hear the roll of the ages.

Rhymes and rhymes in the range of the
    times !
  Are mine for the moment stronger ?
Yet hate me not, but abide your lot;
  I last but a moment longer.

This faded leaf, our names are as brief;
  What room is left for a hater ?
Yet the yellow leaf hates the greener
    leaf,
For it hangs one moment later.

Greater than I — is that your cry ?
  And men will live to see it.
Well — if it be so — so it is, you know;
  And if it be so, so be it.

Brief, brief is a summer leaf,
  But this is the time of hollies.
O hollies and ivies and evergreens,
  How I hate the spites and the follies !

## LITERARY SQUABBLES

Originally printed in ' Punch,' March 7, 1846,
where it was entitled ' After-thought.'   It was
included, with its present title, in the ' Library
Edition ' of the ' Poems,' 1872–73.  See p. 791.

Ah God ! the petty fools of rhyme
  That shriek and sweat in pigmy wars
Before the stony face of Time,
  And look'd at by the silent stars;

Who hate each other for a song,
  And do their little best to bite
And pinch their brethren in the throng,
  And scratch the very dead for spite;

And strain to make an inch of room
  For their sweet selves, and cannot hear
The sullen Lethe rolling doom
  On them and theirs and all things here;

When one small touch of Charity
  Could lift them nearer Godlike state
Than if the crowded Orb should cry
  Like those who cried Diana great.

And I too talk, and lose the touch
  I talk of.  Surely, after all,
The noblest answer unto such
  Is perfect stillness when they brawl.

## THE VICTIM

Printed in 1867 at the private press of Sir
Ivor Bertie Guest, at Canford Manor, near
Wimborne ; contributed to ' Good Words ' for
January, 1868 ; and included in the ' Holy
Grail ' volume, 1870.

### I

A PLAGUE upon the people fell,
  A famine after laid them low;
Then thorpe and byre arose in fire,
  For on them brake the sudden foe;
So thick they died the people cried,
  ' The Gods are moved against the land.'
The Priest in horror about his altar
  To Thor and Odin lifted a hand:
    ' Help us from famine
    And plague and strife !
    What would you have of us ?
    Human life ?
    Were it our nearest,
    Were it our dearest, —
    Answer, O answer! —
    We give you his life.'

### II

But still the foeman spoil'd and burn'd,
  And cattle died, and deer in wood,
And bird in air, and fishes turn'd
  And whiten'd all the rolling flood;
And dead men lay all over the way,
  Or down in a furrow scathed with flame;
And ever and aye the Priesthood moan'd,
  Till at last it seem'd that an answer
    came:
    ' The King is happy
    In child and wife;
    Take you his dearest,
    Give us a life.'

### III

The Priest went out by heath and hill;
  The King was hunting in the wild;
They found the mother sitting still;
  She cast her arms about the child.
The child was only eight summers old,
  His beauty still with his years increased,
His face was ruddy, his hair was gold;
  He seem'd a victim due to the priest.
    The Priest beheld him,
    And cried with joy,
    ' The Gods have answer'd;
    We give them the boy.'

## IV

The King return'd from out the wild,
    He bore but little game in hand;
The mother said, 'They have taken the
        child
    To spill his blood and heal the land.
The land is sick, the people diseased,
    And blight and famine on all the lea;
The holy Gods, they must be appeased,
    So I pray you tell the truth to me.
        They have taken our son,
        They will have his life.
        Is *he* your dearest?
        Or I, the wife?'

## V

The King bent low, with hand on brow,
    He stay'd his arms upon his knee:
'O wife, what use to answer now?
    For now the Priest has judged for me.'
The King was shaken with holy fear;
    'The Gods,' he said, 'would have chosen
        well;
Yet both are near, and both are dear,
    And which the dearest I cannot tell!'
        But the Priest was happy,
        His victim won:
        'We have his dearest,
        His only son!'

## VI

The rites prepared, the victim bared,
    The knife uprising toward the blow,
To the altar-stone she sprang alone:
    'Me, not my darling, no!'
He caught her away with a sudden cry;
    Suddenly from him brake his wife,
And shrieking, '*I* am his dearest, I —
    *I* am his dearest!' rush'd on the knife.
        And the Priest was happy:
        'O Father Odin,
        We give you a life.
        Which was his nearest?
        Who was his dearest?
        The Gods have answer'd;
        We give them the wife!'

## WAGES

Contributed to 'Macmillan's Magazine' for
February, 1868; and reprinted in the 'Holy
Grail' volume.

GLORY of warrior, glory of orator, glory of
        song,
    Paid with a voice flying by to be lost
        on an endless sea —
Glory of Virtue, to fight, to struggle, to
        right the wrong —
    Nay, but she aim'd not at glory, no lover
        of glory she;
Give her the glory of going on, and still to be.

The wages of sin is death: if the wages of
        Virtue be dust,
    Would she have heart to endure for the
        life of the worm and the fly?
She desires no isles of the blest, no quiet
        seats of the just,
    To rest in a golden grove, or to bask in
        a summer sky;
Give her the wages of going on, and not to
        die.


## THE HIGHER PANTHEISM

First published in the 'Holy Grail' volume.

THE sun, the moon, the stars, the seas, the
        hills and the plains, —
Are not these, O Soul, the Vision of Him
        who reigns?

Is not the Vision He, tho' He be not that
        which He seems?
Dreams are true while they last, and do we
        not live in dreams?

Earth, these solid stars, this weight of body
        and limb,
Are they not sign and symbol of thy divi-
        sion from Him?

Dark is the world to thee; thyself art the
        reason why,
For is He not all but thou, that hast power
        to feel 'I am I'?

Glory about thee, without thee; and thou
        fulfillest thy doom,
Making Him broken gleams and a stifled
        splendor and gloom.

Speak to Him, thou, for He hears, and
        Spirit with Spirit can meet —
Closer is He than breathing, and nearer
        than hands and feet.

God is law, say the wise; O Soul, and let
　　us rejoice,
For if He thunder by law the thunder is
　　yet His voice.

Law is God, say some; no God at all, says
　　the fool,
For all we have power to see is a straight
　　staff bent in a pool;

And the ear of man cannot hear, and the
　　eye of man cannot see;
But if we could see and hear, this Vision —
　　were it not He ?

## THE VOICE AND THE PEAK

First published in the 'Cabinet Edition' of
the 'Poems,' 1874.

### I

THE voice and the Peak
　　Far over summit and lawn,
The lone glow and long roar
　　Green-rushing from the rosy thrones of
　　　dawn !

### II

All night have I heard the voice
　　Rave over the rocky bar,
But thou wert silent in heaven,
　　Above thee glided the star.

### III

Hast thou no voice, O Peak,
　　That standest high above all ?
' I am the voice of the Peak,
　　I roar and rave, for I fall.

### IV

' A thousand voices go
　　To North, South, East, and West;
They leave the heights and are troubled,
　　And moan and sink to their rest.

### V

' The fields are fair beside them,
　　The chestnut towers in his bloom;
But they — they feel the desire of the
　　deep —
　　Fall, and follow their doom.

### VI

' The deep has power on the height,
　　And the height has power on the deep;

They are raised for ever and ever,
　　And sink again into sleep.'

### VII

Not raised for ever and ever,
　　But when their cycle is o'er,
The valley, the voice, the peak, the star
　　Pass, and are found no more.

### VIII

The Peak is high and flush'd
　　At his highest with sunrise fire;
The Peak is high, and the stars are high,
　　And the thought of a man is higher.

### IX

A deep below the deep,
　　And a height beyond the height!
Our hearing is not hearing,
　　And our seeing is not sight.

### X

The voice and the Peak
　　Far into heaven withdrawn,
The lone glow and long roar
　　Green-rushing from the rosy thrones of
　　　dawn !

First published in the 'Holy Grail' volume.

FLOWER in the crannied wall,
I pluck you out of the crannies,
I hold you here, root and all, in my hand,
Little flower — but if I could understand
What you are, root and all, and all in all,
I should know what God and man is.

## LUCRETIUS

First published in 'Macmillan's Magazine'
for May, 1868, and afterwards included in the
' Holy Grail ' volume of 1869.

The story on which the poem is founded is
taken from Jerome's additions to the ' Euse-
bian Chronicle,' under the year B. C. 94 : ' Titus
Lucretius poeta nascitur ; postea amatorio po-
culo in furorem versus, cum aliquot libellos per
intervalla insaniae conscripsisset, quos postea
Cicero emendavit, propria se manu interfecit
anno aetatis xliii.'

LUCILIA, wedded to Lucretius, found
Her master cold; for when the morning
　　flush

Of passion and the first embrace had died
Between them, tho' he loved her none the
　　less,
Yet often when the woman heard his foot
Return from pacings in the field, and ran
To greet him with a kiss, the master took
Small notice, or austerely, for — his mind
Half buried in some weightier argument,
Or fancy-borne perhaps upon the rise　10
And long roll of the hexameter — he past
To turn and ponder those three hundred
　　scrolls
Left by the Teacher, whom he held divine.
She brook'd it not, but wrathful, petulant,
Dreaming some rival, sought and found a
　　witch
Who brew'd the philtre which had power,
　　they said,
To lead an errant passion home again.
And this, at times, she mingled with his
　　drink,
And this destroy'd him; for the wicked
　　broth
Confused the chemic labor of the blood,　20
And tickling the brute brain within the
　　man's
Made havoc among those tender cells, and
　　check'd
His power to shape. He loathed himself,
　　and once
After a tempest woke upon a morn
That mock'd him with returning calm, and
　　cried:

'Storm in the night! for thrice I heard
　　the rain
Rushing; and once the flash of a thunder-
　　bolt —
Methought I never saw so fierce a fork —
Struck out the streaming mountain-side,
　　and show'd
A riotous confluence of watercourses　30
Blanching and billowing in a hollow of it,
Where all but yester-eve was dusty-dry.

'Storm, and what dreams, ye holy Gods,
　　what dreams!
For thrice I waken'd after dreams. Per-
　　chance
We do but recollect the dreams that come
Just ere the waking. Terrible: for it seem'd
A void was made in Nature; all her bonds
Crack'd; and I saw the flaring atom-streams
And torrents of her myriad universe,
Ruining along the illimitable inane,　40

Fly on to clash together again, and make
Another and another frame of things
For ever. That was mine, my dream, I
　　knew it —
Of and belonging to me, as the dog
With inward yelp and restless forefoot
　　plies
His function of the woodland; but the
　　next!
I thought that all the blood by Sylla shed
Came driving rainlike down again on earth,
And where it dash'd the reddening meadow,
　　sprang　49
No dragon warriors from Cadmean teeth,
For these I thought my dream would show
　　to me,
But girls, Hetairai, curious in their art,
Hired animalisms, vile as those that made
The mulberry-faced Dictator's orgies worse
Than aught they fable f the quiet Gods.
And hands they mixt, and yell'd and round
　　me drove
In narrowing circles till I yell'd again
Half-suffocated, and sprang up, and saw —
Was it the first beam of my latest day?

'Then, then, from utter gloom stood out
　　the breasts,　60
The breasts of Helen, and hoveringly a
　　sword
Now over and now under, now direct,
Pointed itself to pierce, but sank down
　　shamed
At all that beauty; and as I stared, a
　　fire,
The fire that left a roofless Ilion,
Shot out of them, and scorch'd me that I
　　woke.

'Is this thy vengeance, holy Venus,
　　thine,
Because I would not one of thine own
　　doves,
Not even a rose, were offer'd to thee?
　　thine,
Forgetful how my rich proœmion makes　70
Thy glory fly along the Italian field,
In lays that will outlast thy deity?

'Deity? nay, thy worshippers. My
　　tongue
Trips, or I speak profanely. Which of
　　these
Angers thee most, or angers thee at all?
Not if thou be'st of those who, far aloof

From envy, hate and pity, and spite and
        scorn,
Live the great life which all our greatest fain
Would follow, centred in eternal calm.

    'Nay, if thou canst, O Goddess, like our-
        selves                              80
Touch, and be touch'd, then would I cry to
        thee
To kiss thy Mavors, roll thy tender arms
Round him, and keep him from the lust of
        blood
That makes a steaming slaughter-house of
        Rome.

    'Ay, but I meant not thee; I meant not
        her
Whom all the pines of Ida shook to see
Slide from that quiet heaven of hers, and
        tempt
The Trojan, while his neatherds were
        abroad;
Nor her that o'er her wounded hunter wept
Her deity false in human-amorous tears;  90
Nor whom her beardless apple-arbiter
Decided fairest.  Rather, O ye Gods,
Poet-like, as the great Sicilian called
Calliope to grace his golden verse —
Ay, and this Kypris also — did I take
That popular name of thine to shadow
        forth
The all-generating powers and genial heat
Of Nature, when she strikes thro' the
        thick blood
Of cattle, and light is large, and lambs are
        glad                                99
Nosing the mother's udder, and the bird
Makes his heart voice amid the blaze of
        flowers;
Which things appear the work of mighty
        Gods.

    'The Gods ! and if I go my work is left
Unfinish'd — if I go.  The Gods, who haunt
The lucid interspace of world and world,
Where never creeps a cloud, or moves a
        wind,
Nor ever falls the least white star of snow,
Nor ever lowest roll of thunder moans,
Nor sound of human sorrow mounts to mar
Their sacred everlasting calm ! and such,
Not all so fine, nor so divine a calm,    111
Not such, nor all unlike it, man may gain
Letting his own life go.  The Gods, the
        Gods !

If all be atoms, how then should the Gods
Being atomic not be dissoluble,
Not follow the great law ?  My master
        held
That Gods there are, for all men so believe.
I prest my footsteps into his, and meant
Surely to lead my Memmius in a train
Of flowery clauses onward to the proof  120
That Gods there are, and deathless.
        Meant ?   I meant ?
I have forgotten what I meant; my mind
Stumbles, and all my faculties are lamed.

    'Look where another of our Gods, the
        Sun,
Apollo, Delius, or of older use
All-seeing Hyperion — what you will —
Has mounted yonder; since he never sware,
Except his wrath were wreak'd on wretched
        man,
That he would only shine among the dead
Hereafter — tales ! for never yet on earth
Could dead flesh creep, or bits of roasting
        ox                                 131
Moan round the spit — nor knows he what
        he sees;
King of the East altho' he seem, and girt
With song and flame and fragrance, slowly
        lifts
His golden feet on those empurpled stairs
That climb into the windy halls of heaven.
And here he glances on an eye new-born,
And gets for greeting but a wail of pain;
And here he stays upon a freezing orb
That fain would gaze upon him to the last;
And here upon a yellow eyelid fallen     141
And closed by those who mourn a friend
        in vain,
Not thankful that his troubles are no more.
And me, altho' his fire is on my face
Blinding, he sees not, nor at all can tell
Whether I mean this day to end myself,
Or lend an ear to Plato where he says,
That men like soldiers may not quit the
        post
Allotted by the Gods.  But he that holds
The Gods are careless, wherefore need he
        care                               150
Greatly for them, nor rather plunge at
        once,
Being troubled, wholly out of sight, and
        sink
Past earthquake — ay, and gout and stone,
        that break
Body toward death, and palsy, death-in-life,

And wretched age — and worst disease of
    all,
These prodigies of myriad nakednesses,
And twisted shapes of lust, unspeakable,
Abominable, strangers at my hearth
Not welcome, harpies miring every dish,
The phantom husks of something foully
    done,     160
And fleeting thro' the boundless universe,
And blasting the long quiet of my breast
With animal heat and dire insanity ?

'How should the mind, except it loved
    them, clasp
These idols to herself ? or do they fly
Now thinner, and now thicker, like the
    flakes
In a fall of snow, and so press in, perforce
Of multitude, as crowds that in an hour
Of civic tumult jam the doors, and bear
The keepers down, and throng, their rags
    and they     170
The basest, far into that council-hall
Where sit the best and stateliest of the
    land ?

'Can I not fling this horror off me again,
Seeing with how great ease Nature can
    smile,
Balmier and nobler from her bath of storm,
At random ravage ? and how easily
The mountain there has cast his cloudy
    slough,
Now towering o'er him in serenest air,
A mountain o'er a mountain, — ay, and
    within     179
All hollow as the hopes and fears of men ?

'But who was he that in the garden
    snared
Picus and Faunus, rustic Gods ? a tale
To laugh at — more to laugh at in my-
    self —
For look ! what is it ? there ? yon arbutus
Totters; a noiseless riot underneath
Strikes through the wood, sets all the tops
    quivering —
The mountain quickens into Nymph and
    Faun;
And here an Oread — how the sun delights
To glance and shift about her slippery
    sides,
And rosy knees and supple roundedness, 190
And budded bosom-peaks — who this way
    runs

Before the rest! — A satyr, a satyr, see,
Follows; but him I proved impossible;
Twy-natured is no nature.   Yet he draws
Nearer and nearer, and I scan him now
Beastlier than any phantom of his kind
That ever butted his rough brother-brute
For lust or lusty blood or provender.
I hate, abhor, spit, sicken at him; and she
Loathes him as well; such a precipitate
    heel,     200
Fledged as it were with Mercury's ankle-
    wing,
Whirls her to me — but will she fling herself
Shameless upon me ?  Catch her, goat-
    foot ! nay,
Hide, hide them, million-myrtled wilder-
    ness,
And cavern-shadowing laurels, hide ! do I
    wish —
What ? — that the bush were leafless ? or
    to whelm
All of them in one massacre ?  O ye Gods,
I know you careless, yet, behold, to you
From childly wont and ancient use I call —
I thought I lived securely as yourselves —
No lewdness, narrowing envy, monkey-
    spite,     211
No madness of ambition, avarice, none;
No larger feast than under plane or pine
With neighbors laid along the grass, to
    take
Only such cups as left us friendly-warm,
Affirming each his own philosophy —
Nothing to mar the sober majesties
Of settled, sweet, Epicurean life.
But now it seems some unseen monster
    lays
His vast and filthy hands upon my will, 220
Wrenching it backward into his, and spoils
My bliss in being; and it was not great,
For save when shutting reasons up in
    rhythm,
Or Heliconian honey in living words,
To make a truth less harsh, I often grew
Tired of so much within our little life,
Or of so little in our little life —
Poor little life that toddles half an hour
Crown'd with a flower or two, and there an
    end —     229
And since the nobler pleasure seems to fade,
Why should I, beastlike as I find myself,
Not manlike end myself ? — our privi-
    lege —
What beast has heart to do it ? And what
    man,

What Roman would be dragg'd in triumph
    thus ?
Not I; not he, who bears one name with
    her
Whose death-blow struck the dateless doom
    of kings,
When, brooking not the Tarquin in her
    veins,
She made her blood in sight of Collatine
And all his peers, flushing the guiltless air,
Spout from the maiden fountain in her
    heart.                                      240
And from it sprang the Commonwealth,
    which breaks
As I am breaking now !

            ' And therefore now
Let her, that is the womb and tomb of all,
Great Nature, take, and forcing far apart
Those blind beginnings that have made me
    man,
Dash them anew together at her will
Thro' all her cycles — into man once more,
Or beast or bird or fish, or opulent flower.
But till this cosmic order everywhere
Shatter'd into one earthquake in one day
Cracks all to pieces, — and that hour per-
    haps                                      251
Is not so far when momentary man
Shall seem no more a something to himself,
But he, his hopes and hates, his homes and
    fanes,
And even his bones long laid within the
    grave,
The very sides of the grave itself shall
    pass,

Vanishing, atom and void, atom and void,
Into the unseen for ever, — till that hour,
My golden work in which I told a truth
That stays the rolling Ixionian wheel,    260
And numbs the Fury's ringlet-snake, and
    plucks
The mortal soul from out immortal hell,
Shall stand.  Ay, surely; then it fails at
    last
And perishes as I must; for O Thou,
Passionless bride, divine Tranquillity,
Yearn'd after by the wisest of the wise,
Who fail to find thee, being as thou art
Without one pleasure  and without one
    pain,
Howbeit I know thou surely must be mine
Or soon or late, yet out of season, thus   270
I woo thee roughly, for thou carest not
How roughly men may woo thee so they
    win —
Thus — thus — the soul flies out and dies in
    the air.'

   With that he drove the knife into his
    side.
She heard him raging, heard him fall, ran
    in,
Beat breast, tore hair, cried out upon her-
    self
As having fail'd in duty to him, shriek'd
That she but meant to win him back, fell
    on him,
Clasp'd, kiss'd him, wail'd.  He answer'd,
    ' Care not thou !
Thy duty?  What is duty?  Fare thee
    well !'                                     280

## THE WINDOW; OR, THE SONG OF THE WRENS

First printed in 1867 at the private press of Sir Ivor Bertie Guest, at Canford Manor, near Wimborne.  Only a few copies were printed, and one is rarely found in the market.  Reprinted, with variations in the text, and with music by Sir Arthur Sullivan, in December, 1870.  This edition had the following preface, which was retained in the edition of 1884, when the poems next appeared : —

Four years ago Mr. Sullivan requested me to write a little song-cycle, German fashion, for him to exercise his art upon.  He had been very successful in setting such old songs, as ' Orpheus with his lute,' and I drest up for him, partly in the old style, a puppet, whose almost only merit is, perhaps, that it can dance to Mr. Sullivan's instrument.  I am sorry that my four-year-old pup-pet should have to dance at all in the dark shadow of these days ; but the music is now com-pleted, and I am bound by my promise.

                                         A. TENNYSON.

December, 1870.

# THE WINDOW

## ON THE HILL

The lights and shadows fly !
Yonder it brightens and darkens down on
the plain.
A jewel, a jewel dear to a lover's eye !
O, is it the brook, or a pool, or her window-
pane,
When the winds are up in the morn-
ing ?

Clouds that are racing above,
And winds and lights and shadows that
cannot be still,
All running on one way to the home of
my love,
You are all running on, and I stand on the
slope of the hill,                          9
And the winds are up in the morning !

Follow, follow the chase !
And my thoughts are as quick and as quick,
ever on, on, on.
O lights, are you flying over her sweet
little face ?
And my heart is there before you are come,
and gone,
When the winds are up in the morning !

Follow them down the slope !
And I follow them down to the window-
pane of my dear,
And it brightens and darkens and bright-
ens like my hope,
And it darkens and brightens and darkens
like my fear,                               19
And the winds are up in the morning !

## AT THE WINDOW

Vine, vine and eglantine,
Clasp her window, trail and twine !
Rose, rose and clematis,
Trail and twine and clasp and kiss,
Kiss, kiss; and make her a bower
All of flowers, and drop me a flower,
Drop me a flower.

Vine, vine and eglantine,
Cannot a flower, a flower, be mine ?
Rose, rose and clematis,                    30

Drop me a flower, a flower, to kiss,
Kiss, kiss — and out of her bower
All of flowers, a flower, a flower,
Dropt, a flower.

## GONE

Gone !
Gone, till the end of the year,
Gone, and the light gone with her, and left
me in shadow here !
Gone — flitted away,
Taken the stars from the night and the
sun from the day !
Gone, and a cloud in my heart, and a storm
in the air !                                40
Flown to the east or the west, flitted I
know not where !
Down in the south is a flash and a groan:
she is there ! she is there !

## WINTER

The frost is here,
And fuel is dear,
And woods are sear,
And fires burn clear,
And frost . here
And has bitten the heel of the going year.

Bite, frost, bite !
You roll up away from the light         50
The blue wood-louse and the plump dor-
mouse,
And the bees are still'd, and the flies are
kill'd,
And you bite far into the heart of the
house,
But not into mine.

Bite, frost, bite !
The woods are all the searer,
The fuel is all the dearer,
The fires are all the clearer,
My spring is all the nearer,
You have bitten into the heart of the
earth,                                  60
But not into mine.

## SPRING

Birds' love and birds' song
Flying here and there,
Birds' song and birds' love,
And you with gold for hair !

Birds' song and birds' love,
  Passing with the weather,
Men's song and men's love,
  To love once and for ever.

Men's love and birds' love,                    70
  And women's love and men's !
And you my wren with a crown of gold,
  You my queen of the wrens !
You the queen of the wrens —
  We 'll be birds of a feather,
I 'll be King of the Queen of the wrens,
  And all in a nest together.


THE LETTER

Where is another sweet as my sweet,
  Fine of the fine, and shy of the shy ?
Fine little hands, fine little feet —         80
  Dewy blue eye.
Shall I write to her ? shall I go ?
  Ask her to marry me by and by ?
Somebody said that she 'd say no;
  Somebody knows that she 'll say ay !

Ay or no, if ask'd to her face ?
  Ay or no, from shy of the shy ?
Go, little letter, apace, apace,
  Fly;
Fly to the light in the valley below —        90
  Tell my wish to her dewy blue eye.
Somebody said that she 'd say no;
  Somebody knows that she 'll say ay !


NO ANSWER

The mist and the rain, the mist and the
    rain !
  Is it ay or no ? is it ay or no ?
And never a glimpse of her window-pane !
  And I may die but the grass will grow,
And the grass will grow when I am gone,
  And the wet west wind and the world will
    go on.

Ay is the song of the wedded spheres,        100
  No is trouble and cloud and storm,
Ay is life for a hundred years,
  No will push me down to the worm,
And when I am there and dead and gone,
The wet west wind and the world will go on.

The wind and the wet, the wind and the wet!
  Wet west wind, how you blow, you blow !

And never a line from my lady yet !
  Is it ay or no ? is it ay or no ?
Blow then, blow, and when I am gone,         110
The wet west wind and the world may go
    on.


NO ANSWER

Winds are loud and you are dumb,
Take my love, for love will come,
  Love will come but once a life.
Winds are loud and winds will pass !
Spring is here with leaf and grass;
  Take my love and be my wife.
After-loves of maids and men
Are but dainties drest again.
Love me now, you 'll love me then;           120
  Love can love but once a life.


THE ANSWER

Two little hands that meet,
Claspt on her seal, my sweet !
Must I take you and break you,
Two little hands that meet ?
I must take you, and break you,
And loving hands must part —
Take, take — break, break —
Break — you may break my heart.
  Faint heart never won —                     130
  Break, break, and all 's done.


AY

Be merry, all birds, to-day,
  Be merry on earth as you never were
    merry before,
Be merry in heaven, O larks, and far
    away,
  And merry for ever and ever, and one day
    more.
      Why ?
  For it 's easy to find a rhyme.
Look, look, how he flits,
  The fire-crown'd king of the wrens, from
    out of the pine !
Look how they tumble the blossom, the
    mad little tits !                         140
  'Cuck-oo ! Cuck-oo !' was ever a May
    so fine ?
      Why ?
  For it 's easy to find a rhyme.
O merry the linnet and dove,
  And swallow and sparrow and throstle,
    and have your desire !

O merry my heart, you have gotten the
    wings of love,
And flit like the king of the wrens with
    a crown of fire.
        Why ?
    For it 's ay ay, ay ay.

### WHEN

Sun comes, moon comes,      150
    Time slips away.
Sun sets, moon sets,
    Love, fix a day.

'A year hence, a year hence.'
    'We shall both be gray.'
'A month hence, a month hence.'
    'Far, far away.'

'A week hence, a week hence.'
    'Ah, the long delay !'
'Wait a little, wait a little,    160
    You shall fix a day.'

'To-morrow, love, to-morrow,
    And that 's an age away.'
Blaze upon her window, sun,
    And honor all the day.

### MARRIAGE MORNING

Light, so low upon earth,
    You send a flash to the sun.
Here is the golden close of love,
    All my wooing is done.
O, the woods and the meadows,    170
    Woods where we hid from the wet,
Stiles where we stay'd to be kind,
    Meadows in which we met !

Light, so low in the vale
    You flash and lighten afar,
For this is the golden morning of love,
    And you are his morning star.
Flash, I am coming, I come,
    By meadow and stile and wood,
O, lighten into my eyes and my heart,  180
    Into my heart and my blood !

Heart, are you great enough
    For a love that never tires ?
O heart, are you great enough for love ?
    I have heard of thorns and briers.
Over the thorns and briers,
    Over the meadows and stiles,
Over the world to the end of it
    Flash for a million miles.

# THE LOVER'S TALE

This poem (written in 1828) was printed in 1833, but withdrawn before publication for reasons which the author gives in the following preface to the reprint of 1879 : —

The original Preface to 'The Lover's Tale' states that it was composed in my nineteenth year. Two only of the three parts then written were printed, when, feeling the imperfection of the poem, I withdrew it from the press. One of my friends, however, who, boylike, admired the boy's work, distributed among our common associates of that hour some copies of these two parts, without my knowledge, without the omissions and amendments which I had in contemplation, and marred by the many misprints of the compositor. Seeing that these two parts have of late been mercilessly pirated, and that what I had deemed scarce worthy to live is not allowed to die, may I not be pardoned if I suffer the whole poem at last to come into the light — accompanied with a reprint of the sequel — a work of my mature life — 'The Golden Supper' ?

May, 1879.

### ARGUMENT

Julian, whose cousin and foster-sister, Camilla, has been wedded to his friend and rival, Lionel, endeavors to narrate the story of his own love for her, and the strange sequel. He speaks (in Parts II. and III.) of having been haunted by visions and the sound of bells, tolling for a funeral, and at last ringing for a marriage ; but he breaks away, overcome, as he approaches the Event, and a witness to it completes the tale.

### I

HERE far away, seen from the topmost
    cliff,
Filling with purple gloom the vacancies

Between the tufted hills, the sloping seas
Hung in mid-heaven, and half-way down
    rare sails,
White as white clouds, floated from sky to
    sky.

O pleasant breast of waters, quiet bay,
Like to a quiet mind in the loud world,
Where the chafed breakers of the outer
     sea
Sank powerless, as anger falls aside
And withers on the breast of peaceful
     love !                                    10
Thou didst receive the growth of pines
     that fledged
The hills that watch'd thee, as Love watch-
     eth Love,
In thine own essence, and delight thyself
To make it wholly thine on sunny days.
Keep thou thy name of ' Lover's Bay.'
     See, sirs,
Even now the Goddess of the Past, that
     takes
The heart, and sometimes touches but one
     string
That quivers and is silent, and sometimes
Sweeps suddenly all its half - moulder'd
     chords
To some old melody, begins to play      20
That air which pleased her first. I feel thy
     breath;
I come, great Mistress of the ear and
     eye;
Thy breath is of the pine-wood, and tho'
     years
Have hollow'd out a deep and stormy strait
Betwixt the native land of Love and me,
Breathe but a little on me, and the sail
Will draw me to the rising of the sun,
The lucid chambers of the morning star,
And East of Life.

               Permit me, friend, I prythee,
To pass my hand across my brows, and
     muse                                      30
On those dear hills, that nevermore will
     meet
The sight that throbs and aches beneath
     my touch,
As tho' there beat a heart in either eye;
For when the outer lights are darken'd
     thus,
The memory's vision hath a keener edge.
It grows upon me now — the semicircle
Of dark-blue waters and the narrow fringe
Of curving beach — its wreaths of drip-
     ping green —
Its pale pink shells — the summer-house
     aloft
That open'd on the pines with doors of
     glass,                                    40

A mountain nest — the pleasure-boat that
     rock'd,
Light-green with its own shadow, keel to
     keel,
Upon the dappled dimplings of the wave
That blanch'd upon its side.

               O Love, O Hope !
They come, they crowd upon me all at
     once —
Moved from the cloud of unforgotten
     things,
That sometimes on the horizon of the mind
Lies folded, often sweeps athwart in
     storm —
Flash upon flash they lighten thro' me —
     days
Of dewy dawning and the amber eves     50
When thou and I, Camilla, thou and I
Were borne about the bay or safely moor'd
Beneath a low-brow'd cavern, where the
     tide
Plash'd, sapping its worn ribs; and all
     without
The slowly-ridging rollers on the cliffs
Clash'd, calling to each other, and thro' the
     arch
Down those loud waters, like a setting star,
Mixt with the gorgeous west the lighthouse
     shone,
And silver-smiling Venus ere she fell
Would often loiter in her balmy blue,    60
To crown it with herself.

                         Here, too, my love
Waver'd at anchor with me, when day
     hung
From his mid-dome in heaven's airy halls;
Gleams of the water-circles as they broke
Flicker'd like doubtful smiles about her
     lips,
Quiver'd a flying glory on her hair,
Leapt like a passing thought across her
     eyes;
And mine with one that will not pass, till
     earth
And heaven pass too, dwelt on my heaven,
     a face
Most starry-fair, but kindled from within
As 't were with dawn. She was dark-
     hair'd, dark-eyed —                       71
O, such dark eyes ! a single glance of
     them
Will govern a whole life from birth to
     death,

Careless of all things else, led on with
    light
In trances and in visions.  Look at them,
You lose yourself in utter ignorance;
You cannot find their depth; for they go
    back,
And farther back, and still withdraw them-
    selves
Quite into the deep soul, that evermore
Fresh springing from her fountains in the
    brain,        80
Still pouring thro', floods with redundant
    life
Her narrow portals.

                Trust me, long ago
I should have died, if it were possible
To die in gazing on that perfectness
Which I do bear within me.  I had died,
But from my farthest lapse, my latest ebb,
Thine image, like a charm of light and
    strength
Upon the waters, push'd me back again
On these deserted sands of barren life.
Tho' from the deep vault where the heart
    of Hope        90
Fell into dust, and crumbled in the dark —
Forgetting how to render beautiful
Her countenance with quick and healthful
    blood —
Thou didst not sway me upward; could I
    perish
While thou, a meteor of the sepulchre,
Didst swathe thyself all round Hope's quiet
    urn
For ever ?  He that saith it hath o'er-
    stept
The slippery footing of his narrow wit,
And fallen away from judgment.  Thou
    art light,
To which my spirit leaneth all her flowers,
And length of days, and immortality   101
Of thought, and freshness ever self-re-
    new'd.
For Time and Grief abode too long with
    Life,
And, like all other friends i' the world, at
    last
They grew aweary of her fellowship.
So Time and Grief did beckon unto Death,
And Death drew nigh and beat the doors
    of Life;
But thou didst sit alone in the inner house,
A wakeful portress, and didst parle with
    Death, —

'This is a charmed dwelling which I
    hold;'        110
So Death gave back, and would no further
    come.
Yet is my life nor in the present time,
Nor in the present place.  To me alone,
Push'd from his chair of regal heritage,
The Present is the vassal of the Past:
So that, in that I *have* lived, do I live,
And cannot die, and am, in having been —
A portion of the pleasant yesterday,
Thrust forward on to-day and out of place;
A body journeying onward, sick with toil,
The weight as if of age upon my limbs,   121
The grasp of hopeless grief about my
    heart,
And all the senses weaken'd, save in that,
Which long ago they had glean'd and gar-
    ner'd up
Into the granaries of memory —
The clear brow, bulwark of the precious
    brain,
Chink'd as you see, and seam'd — and all
    the while
The light soul twines and mingles with the
    growths
Of vigorous early days, attracted, won,   129
Married, made one with, molten into all
The beautiful in Past of act or place,
And like the all-enduring camel, driven
Far from the diamond fountain by the
    palms,
Who toils across the middle moonlit nights,
Or when the white heats of the blinding
    noons
Beat from the concave sand; yet in him
    keeps
A draught of that sweet fountain that he
    loves,
To stay his feet from falling and his spirit
From bitterness of death.

                Ye ask me, friends,
When I began to love.  How should I tell
    you ?        140
Or from the after-fulness of my heart,
Flow back again unto my slender spring
And first of love, tho' every turn and depth
Between is clearer in my life than all
Its present flow.  Ye know not what ye
    ask.
How should the broad and open flower
    tell
What sort of bud it was, when, prest to-
    gether

In its green sheath, close-lapt in silken
    folds,
It seem'd to keep its sweetness to itself,
Yet was not the less sweet for that it
    seem'd ?                                    150
For young Life knows not when young
    Life was born,
But takes it all for granted: neither Love,
Warm in the heart, his cradle, can remem-
    ber
Love in the womb, but resteth satisfied,
Looking on her that brought him to the
    light;
Or as men know not when they fall asleep
Into delicious dreams, our other life,
So know I not when I began to love.
This is my sum of knowledge — that my love
Grew with myself — say rather, was my
    growth,                                     160
My inward sap, the hold I have on earth,
My outward circling air wherewith I
    breathe,
  hich yet upholds my life, and evermore
Is to me daily life and daily death.
For how should I have lived and not have
    loved ?
Can ye take off the sweetness from the
    flower,
The color and the sweetness from the rose,
And place them by themselves; or set
    apart
Their motions and their brightness from
    the stars,                                  169
And then point out the flower or the star ?
Or build a wall betwixt my life and love,
And tell me where I am ?  'T is even thus:
In that I live I love; because I love
I live.  Whate'er is fountain to the one
Is fountain to the other; and whene'er
Our God unknits the riddle of the one,
There is no shade or fold of mystery
Swathing the other.

                        Many, many years —
For they seem many and my most of life,
And well I could have linger'd in that
    porch,                                      180
So unproportion'd to the dwelling-place, —
In the May-dews of childhood, opposite
The flush and dawn of youth, we lived to-
    gether,
Apart, alone together on those hills.

Before he saw my day my father died,
And he was happy that he saw it not;

But I and the first daisy on his grave
From the same clay came into light at
    once.
As Love and I do number equal years,
So she, my love, is of an age with me.   190
How like each other was the birth of each !
On the same morning, almost the same
    hour,
Under the selfsame aspect of the stars —
O, falsehood of all star-craft ! — we were
    born.
How like each other was the birth of each !
The sister of my mother — she that bore
Camilla close beneath her beating heart,
Which to the imprison'd spirit of the child,
With its true-touched pulses in the flow
And hourly visitation of the blood,      200
Sent notes of preparation manifold,
And mellow'd echoes of the outer world —
My mother's sister, mother of my love,
Who had a twofold claim upon my heart,
One twofold mightier than the other was,
In giving so much beauty to the world,
And so much wealth as God had charged
    her with —
Loathing to put it from herself for ever,
Left her own life with it; and dying thus,
Crown'd with her highest act the placid
    face                                        210
And breathless body of her good deeds
    past.

    So were we born, so orphan'd.  She was
    motherless,
And I without a father.  So from each
Of those two pillars which from earth up-
    hold
Our childhood, one had fallen away, and all
The careful burthen of our tender years
Trembled upon the other.  He that gave
Her life, to me delightedly fulfill'd
All loving kindnesses, all offices
Of watchful care and trembling tenderness.
He waked for both, he pray'd for both, he
    slept                                       221
Dreaming of both; nor was his love the
    less
Because it was divided, and shot forth
Boughs on each side, laden with wholesome
    shade,
Wherein we nested sleeping or awake,
And sang aloud the matin-song of life.

    She was my foster-sister.  On one arm
The flaxen ringlets of our infancies

Wander'd, the while we rested; one soft lap
Pillow'd us both; a common light of eyes
Was on us as we lay; our baby lips,        231
Kissing one bosom, ever drew from thence
The stream of life, one stream, one life,
     one blood,
One sustenance, which, still as thought
     grew large,
Still larger moulding all the house of
     thought,
Made all our tastes and fancies like, per-
     haps —
All — all but one; and strange to me, and
     sweet,
Sweet thro' strange years to know that
     whatsoe'er
Our general mother meant for me alone,
Our mutual mother dealt to both of us.   240
So what was earliest mine in earliest life,
I shared with her in whom myself remains.

     As was our childhood, so our infancy,
They tell me, was a very miracle
Of fellow-feeling and communion.
They tell me that we would not be alone, —
We cried when we were parted; when I
     wept,
Her smile lit up the rainbow on my tears,
Stay'd on the cloud of sorrow; that we
     loved
The sound of one another's voices more  250
Than the gray cuckoo loves his name, and
     learn'd
To lisp in tune together; that we slept
In the same cradle always, face to face,
Heart beating time to heart, lip pressing
     lip,
Folding each other, breathing on each other,
Dreaming together — dreaming of each
     other,
They should have added, — till the morning
     light
Sloped thro' the pines, upon the dewy pane
Falling, unseal'd our eyelids, and we woke
To gaze upon each other.   If this be true,
At thought of which my whole soul lan-
     guishes                               261
And faints, and hath no pulse, no breath
     — as tho'
A man in some still garden should infuse
Rich atar in the bosom of the rose,
Till, drunk with its own wine, and overfull
Of sweetness, and in smelling of itself,
It fall on its own thorns — if this be true —
And that way my wish leads me evermore

Still to believe it, 't is so sweet a thought —
Why in the utter stillness of the soul      270
Doth question'd memory answer not, nor
     tell
Of this our earliest, our closest-drawn,
Most loveliest, earthly - heavenliest har-
     mony?

     O blossom'd portal of the lonely house,
Green prelude, April promise, glad new-
     year
Of being, which with earliest violets
And lavish carol of clear-throated larks
Fill'd all the March of life! — I will not
     speak of thee,
These have not seen thee, these can never
     know thee,
They cannot understand me.   Pass we
     then                                   280
A term of eighteen years.   Ye would but
     laugh
If I should tell you how I hoard in thought
The faded rhymes and scraps of ancient
     crones,
Gray relics of the nurseries of the world,
Which are as gems set in my memory,
Because she learnt them with me; or what
     use
To know her father left us just before
The daffodil was blown? or how we found
The dead man cast upon the shore?   All
     this
Seems to the quiet daylight of your minds
But cloud and smoke, and in the dark of
     mine                                   291
Is traced with flame.   Move with me to the
     event.

     There came a glorious morning, such a
     one
As dawns but once a season.   Mercury
On such a morning would have flung him-
     self
From cloud to cloud, and swum with bal-
     anced wings
To some tall mountain.   When I said to her,
' A day for gods to stoop,' she answered,
     ' Ay,
And men to soar;' for as that other gazed,
Shading his eyes till all the fiery cloud,  300
The prophet and the chariot and the steeds,
Suck'd into oneness like a little star
Were drunk into the inmost blue, we stood,
When first we came from out the pines at
     noon,

With hands for eaves, uplooking and al-
most
Waiting to see some blessed shape in hea-
ven,
So bathed we were in brilliance.  Never yet
Before or after have I known the spring
Pour with such sudden deluges of light
Into the middle summer; for that day    310
Love, rising, shook his wings, and charged
the winds
With spiced May - sweets from bound to
bound, and blew
Fresh fire into the sun, and from within
Burst thro' the heated buds, and sent his
soul
Into the songs of birds, and touch'd far-off
His mountain-altars, his high hills, with
flame
Milder and purer.

                  Thro' the rocks we wound;
The great pine shook with lonely sounds
of joy
That came on the sea-wind.  As mountain
streams
Our bloods ran free; the sunshine seem'd
to brood     320
More warmly on the heart than on the
brow.
We often paused, and, looking back, we saw
The clefts and openings in the mountains
fill'd
With the blue valley and the glistening
brooks,
And all the low dark groves, a land of love !
A land of promise, a land of memory,
A land of promise flowing with the milk
And honey of delicious memories !
And down to sea, and far as eye could ken,
Each way from verge to verge a Holy
Land,     330
Still growing holier as you near'd the bay,
For there the Temple stood.

                  When we had reach'd
The grassy platform on some hill, I stoop'd,
I gather'd the wild herbs, and for her brows
And mine made garlands of the selfsame
flower,
Which she took smiling, and with my work
thus
Crown'd her clear forehead.  Once or twice
she told me —
For I remember all things — to let grow
The flowers that run poison in their veins.

She said, 'The evil flourish in the world.'
Then playfully she gave herself the lie —
'Nothing in nature is unbeautiful;     342
So, brother, pluck and spare not.'  So I
wove
Even the dull-blooded poppy-stem, 'whose
flower,
Hued with the scarlet of a fierce sunrise,
Like to the wild youth of an evil prince,
Is without sweetness, but who crowns him-
self
Above the naked poisons of his heart
In his old age.'  A graceful thought of
hers
Graven on my fancy !  And O, how like a
nymph,     350
A stately mountain nymph she look'd !  how
native
Unto the hills she trod on !  While I gazed
My coronal slowly disentwined itself
And fell between us both; tho' while I
gazed
My spirit leap'd as with those thrills of bliss
That strike across the soul in prayer, and
show us
That we are surely heard.  Methought a
light
Burst from the garland I had woven, and
stood
A solid glory on her bright black hair;
A light methought broke from her dark,
dark eyes,     360
And shot itself into the singing winds;
A mystic light flash'd even from her white
robe
As from a glass in the sun, and fell about
My footsteps on the mountains.

                  Last we came
To what our people call 'The Hill of Woe.'
A bridge is there, that, look'd at from be-
neath,
Seems but a cobweb filament to link
The yawning of an earthquake - cloven
chasm.
And thence one night, when all the winds
were loud,
A woful man — for so the story went—     370
Had thrust his wife and child and dash'd
himself
Into the dizzy depth below.  Below,
Fierce in the strength of far descent, a
stream
Flies with a shatter'd foam along the
chasm.

The path was perilous, loosely strown
  with crags.
We mounted slowly; yet to both there
  came
The joy of life in steepness overcome,
And victories of ascent, and looking down
On all that had look'd down on us; and joy
In breathing nearer heaven; and joy to me,
High over all the azure-circled earth,    381
To breathe with her as if in heaven itself;
And more than joy that I to her became
Her guardian and her angel, raising her
Still higher, past all peril, until she saw
Beneath her feet the region far away,
Beyond the nearest mountain's bosky brows,
Arise in open prospect — heath and hill,
And hollow lined and wooded to the lips,
And steep - down walls of battlemented
  rock                                     390
Gilded with broom, or shatter'd into spires,
And glory of broad waters interfused,
Whence rose as it were breath and steam
  of gold,
And over all the great wood rioting
And climbing, streak'd or starr'd at inter-
  vals
With falling brook or blossom'd bush —
  and last,
Framing the mighty landscape to the west,
A purple range of mountain-cones, between
Whose interspaces gush'd in blinding bursts
The incorporate blaze of sun and sea.

                                At length
Descending from the point, and standing
  both                                     401
There on the tremulous bridge, that from
  beneath
Had seem'd a gossamer filament up in air,
We paused amid the splendor. All the
  west
And even unto the middle south was ribb'd
And barr'd with bloom on bloom. The sun
  below,
Held for a space 'twixt cloud and wave,
  shower'd down
Rays of a mighty circle, weaving over
That various wilderness a tissue of light
Unparallel'd. On the other side, the
  moon,                                    410
Half-melted into thin blue air, stood still,
And pale and fibrous as a wither'd leaf,
Nor yet endured in presence of His eyes
To indue his lustre; most unloverlike,
Since in his absence full of light and joy,

And giving light to others. But this most,
Next to her presence whom I loved so well,
Spoke loudly even into my inmost heart   418
As to my outward hearing. The loud
  stream,
Forth issuing from his portals in the crag, —
A visible link unto the home of my heart, —
Ran amber toward the west, and nigh the
  sea
Parting my own loved mountains was re-
  ceived,
Shorn of its strength, into the sympathy
Of that small bay, which out to open main
Glow'd intermingling close beneath the sun.
Spirit of Love ! that little hour was bound,
Shut in from Time, and dedicate to thee;
Thy fires from heaven had touch'd it, and
  the earth
They fell on became hallow'd evermore.   430

    We turn'd, our eyes met; hers were
      bright, and mine
Were dim with floating tears, that shot the
  sunset
In lightnings round me, and my name was
  borne
Upon her breath. Henceforth my name
  has been
A hallow'd memory like the names of old,
A centred, glory-circled memory,
And a peculiar treasure, brooking not
Exchange or currency; and in that hour
A hope flow'd round me, like a golden mist
Charm'd amid eddies of melodious airs,   440
A moment, ere the onward whirlwind
  shatter it,
Waver'd and floated — which was less than
  Hope,
Because it lack'd the power of perfect
  Hope;
But which was more and higher than all
  Hope,
Because all other Hope had lower aim;
Even that this name to which her gracious
  lips
Did lend such gentle utterance, this one
  name,
In some obscure hereafter, might in-
  wreathe —
How lovelier, nobler then ! — her life, her
  love,
With my life, love, soul, spirit, and heart
  and strength.                           450
'Brother,' she said, 'let this be call'd hence-
  forth

The Hill of Hope;' and I replied, 'O sister,
My will is one with thine; the Hill of
    Hope.'
Nevertheless, we did not change the name.

I did not speak; I could not speak my
    love.
Love lieth deep, Love dwells not in lip-
    depths.
Love wraps his wings on either side the
    heart,
Constraining it with kisses close and warm,
Absorbing all the incense of sweet thoughts
So that they pass not to the shrine of
    sound.    460
Else had the life of that delighted hour
Drunk in the largeness of the utterance
Of Love; but how should earthly measure
    mete
The heavenly - unmeasured or unlimited
    Love,
Who scarce can tune his high majestic
    sense
Unto the thunder - song that wheels the
    spheres,
Scarce living in the Æolian harmony,
And flowing odor of the spacious air,
Scarce housed within the circle of this
    earth,
Be cabin'd up in words and syllables,    470
Which pass with that which breathes them?
    Sooner earth
Might go round heaven, and the strait
    girth of Time
Inswathe the fulness of Eternity,
Than language grasp the infinite of Love.

O day which did enwomb that happy
    hour,
Thou art blessed in the years, divinest day!
O Genius of that hour which dost uphold
Thy coronal of glory like a god,
Amid thy melancholy mates far-seen,    479
Who walk before thee, ever turning round
To gaze upon thee till their eyes are dim
With dwelling on the light and depth of
    thine,
Thy name is ever worshipp'd among hours!
Had I died then, I had not seem'd to die,
For bliss stood round me like the light of
    heaven, —
Had I died then, I had not known the
    death;
Yea, had the Power from whose right hand
    the light

Of Life issueth, and from whose left hand
    floweth
The Shadow of Death, perennial effluences,
Whereof to all that draw the wholesome air,
Somewhile the one must overflow the
    other —    491
Then had he stemm'd my day with night,
    and driven
My current to the fountain whence it
    sprang, —
Even his own abiding excellence —
On me, methinks, that shock of gloom had
    fallen
Unfelt, and in this glory I had merged
The other, like the sun I gazed upon,
Which seeming for the moment due to
    death,
And dipping his head low beneath the
    verge,    499
Yet bearing round about him his own day,
In confidence of unabated strength,
Steppeth from heaven to heaven, from light
    to light,
And holdeth his undimmed forehead far
Into a clearer zenith, pure of cloud.

We trod the shadow of the downward hill;
We past from light to dark. On the other
    side
Is scoop'd a cavern and a mountain hall,
Which none have fathom'd. If you go
    far in —
The country people rumor — you may hear
The moaning of the woman and the child,
Shut in the secret chambers of the rock. 511
I too have heard a sound — perchance of
    streams
Running far on within its inmost halls,
The home of darkness; but the cavern-
    mouth,
Half overtrailed with a wanton weed,
Gives birth to a brawling brook, that pass-
    ing lightly
Adown a natural stair of tangled roots,
Is presently received in a sweet grave
Of eglantines, a place of burial
Far lovelier than its cradle; for unseen,  520
But taken with the sweetness of the place,
It makes a constant bubbling melody
That drowns the nearer echoes. Lower
    down
Spreads out a little lake, that, flooding,
    leaves
Low banks of yellow sand; and from the
    woods

That belt it rise three dark, tall cy-
    presses, —
Three cypresses, symbols of mortal woe,
That men plant over graves.

                            Hither we came,
And sitting down upon the golden moss,
Held converse sweet and low — low con-
    verse sweet,                           530
In which our voices bore least part.  The
    wind
Told a love-tale beside us, how he woo'd
The waters, and the waters answering
    lisp'd
To kisses of the wind, that, sick with love,
Fainted at intervals, and grew again
To utterance of passion.  Ye cannot shape
Fancy so fair as is this memory.
Methought all excellence that ever was
Had drawn herself from many thousand
    years,                                 539
And all the separate Edens of this earth,
To centre in this place and time.  I lis-
    ten'd,
And her words stole with most prevailing
    sweetness
Into my heart, as thronging fancies come
To boys and girls when summer days are
    new,
And soul and heart and body are all at
    ease.
What marvel my Camilla told me all ?
It was so happy an hour, so sweet a place,
And I was as the brother of her blood,
And by that name I moved upon her
    breath;
Dear name, which had too much of near-
    ness in it                            550
And heralded the distance of this time !
At first her voice was very sweet and low,
As if she were afraid of utterance;
But in the onward current of her speech, —
As echoes of the hollow-banked brooks
Are fashion'd by the channel which they
    keep, —
Her words did of their meaning borrow
    sound,
Her cheek did catch the color of her words.
I heard and trembled, yet I could but
    hear;
My heart paused — my raised eyelids would
    not fall,                             560
But still I kept my eyes upon the sky.
I seem'd the only part of Time stood still,
And saw the motion of all other things;

While her words, syllable by syllable,
Like water, drop by drop, upon my ear
Fell, and I wish'd, yet wish'd her not to
    speak;
But she spake on, for I did name no wish.
What marvel my Camilla told me all
Her maiden dignities of Hope and Love —
' Perchance,' she said, ' return'd ' ?  Even
    then the stars                        570
Did tremble in their stations as I gazed;
But she spake on, for I did name no wish,
No wish — no hope.  Hope was not wholly
    dead,
But breathing hard at the approach of
    death, —
Camilla, my Camilla, who was mine
No longer in the dearest sense of mine —
For all the secret of her inmost heart,
And all the maiden empire of her mind,
Lay like a map before me, and I saw
There, where I hoped myself to reign as
    king,                                 580
There, where that day I crown'd myself as
    king,
There in my realm and even on my throne,
*Another!*  Then it seem'd as tho' a link
Of some tight chain within my inmost
    frame
Was riven in twain; that life I heeded not
Flow'd from me, and the darkness of the
    grave,
The darkness of the grave and utter night,
Did swallow up my vision; at her feet,
Even the feet of her I loved, I fell,
Smit with exceeding sorrow unto death.   590

Then had the earth beneath me yawning
    cloven
With such a sound as when an iceberg
    splits
From cope to base — had Heaven from all
    her doors,
With all her golden thresholds clashing,
    roll'd
Her heaviest thunder — I had lain as dead,
Mute, blind, and motionless as then I lay;
Dead, for henceforth there was no life for
    me !
Mute, for henceforth what use were words
    to me ?
Blind, for the day was as the night to me !
The night to me was kinder than the day;
The night in pity took away my day,    601
Because my grief as yet was newly born
Of eyes too weak to look upon the light;

And thro' the hasty notice of the ear
Frail Life was startled from the tender
    love
Of him she brooded over.  Would I had
    lain
Until the plaited ivy-tress had wound
Round my worn limbs, and the wild brier
    had driven
Its knotted thorns thro' my unpaining
    brows,
Leaning its roses on my faded eyes.    610
The wind had blown above me, and the
    rain
Had fallen upon me, and the gilded snake
Had nestled in this bosom-throne of Love,
But I had been at rest for evermore.

    Long time entrancement held me.  All
        too soon
Life — like a wanton, too-officious friend,
Who will not *hear* denial, vain and rude
With proffer of unwish'd-for services —
Entering all the avenues of sense
Past thro' into his citadel, the brain,    620
With hated warmth of apprehensiveness.
And first the chillness of the sprinkled
    brook
Smote on my brows, and then I seem'd to
    hear
Its murmur, as the drowning seaman hears,
Who with his head below the surface dropt
Listens the muffled booming indistinct
Of the confused floods, and dimly knows
His head shall rise no more; and then came
    in
The white light of the weary moon above,
Diffused and molten into flaky cloud.    630
Was my sight drunk that it did shape to
    me
Him who should own that name ?  Were
    it not well
If so be that the echo of that name
Ringing within the fancy had updrawn
A fashion and a phantasm of the form
It should attach to ?  Phantom ! — had the
    ghastliest
That ever lusted for a body, sucking
The foul steam of the grave to thicken by
    it,
There in the shuddering moonlight brought
    its face                               639
And what it has for eyes as close to mine
As he did — better that than his, than he
The friend, the neighbor, Lionel, the be-
    loved,

The loved, the lover, the happy Lionel,
The low-voiced, tender-spirited Lionel,
All joy, to whom my agony was a joy.
O, how her choice did leap forth from his
    eyes !
O, how her love did clothe itself in smiles
About his lips ! and — not one moment's
    grace —
Then when the effect weigh'd seas upon
    my head
To come my way ! to twit me with the
    cause !                                 650

    Was not the land as free thro' all her
        ways
To him as me ?  Was not his wont to
    walk
Between the going light and growing
    night ?
Had I not learnt my loss before he came ?
Could that be more because he came my
    way ?
Why should he not come my way if he
    would ?
And yet to-night, to-night — when all my
    wealth
Flash'd from me in a moment and I fell
Beggar'd for ever — why *should* he come
    my way
Robed in those robes of light I must not
    wear,                                  660
With that great crown of beams about his
    brows —
Come like an angel to a damned soul,
To tell him of the bliss he had with God —
Come like a careless and a greedy heir
That scarce can wait the reading of the
    will
Before he takes possession ?  Was mine a
    mood
To be invaded rudely, and not rather
A sacred, secret, unapproached woe,
Unspeakable ?  I was shut up with Grief;
She took the body of my past delight,    670
Narded and swathed and balm'd it for her-
    self,
And laid it in a sepulchre of rock
Never to rise again.  I was led mute
Into her temple like a sacrifice;
I was the High Priest in her holiest place,
Not to be loudly broken in upon.

    O friend, thoughts deep and heavy as
        these well-nigh
O'erbore the limits of my brain: but he

Bent o'er me, and my neck his arm up-
　　stay'd.
I thought it was an adder's fold, and once
I strove to disengage myself, but fail'd,　681
Being so feeble.　She bent above me, too;
Wan was her cheek, for whatsoe'er of
　　blight
Lives in the dewy touch of pity had made
The red rose there a pale one — and her
　　eyes —
I saw the moonlight glitter on their tears —
And some few drops of that distressful rain
Fell on my face, and her long ringlets
　　moved,
Drooping and beaten by the breeze, and
　　brush'd
My fallen forehead in their to and fro,　690
For in the sudden anguish of her heart
Loosed from their simple thrall they had
　　flow'd abroad,
And floated on and parted round her neck,
Mantling her form halfway.　She, when I
　　woke,
Something she ask'd, I know not what, and
　　ask'd,
Unanswer'd, since I spake not; for the
　　sound
Of that dear voice so musically low,
And now first heard with any sense of pain,
As it had taken life away before,　699
Choked all the syllables that strove to rise
From my full heart.

　　　　　　The blissful lover, too,
From his great hoard of happiness dis-
　　till'd
Some drops of solace; like a vain rich
　　man,
That, having always prosper'd in the world,
Folding his hands, deals comfortable words
To hearts wounded for ever; yet, in truth,
Fair speech was his and delicate of phrase,
Falling in whispers on the sense, address'd
More to the inward than the outward ear,
As rain of the midsummer midnight soft,
Scarce-heard, recalling fragrance and the
　　green　711
Of the dead spring: but mine was wholly
　　dead,
No bud, no leaf, no flower, no fruit for me.
Yet who had done, or who had suffer'd
　　wrong?
And why was I to darken their pure love?
If, as I found, they two did love each
　　other,

Because my own was darken'd?　Why
　　was I
To cross between their happy star and
　　them?
To stand a shadow by their shining doors,
And vex them with my darkness?　Did I
　　love her?　720
Ye know that I did love her; to this pre-
　　sent
My full-orb'd love has waned not.　Did I
　　love her,
And could I look upon her tearful eyes?
What had *she* done to weep?　Why should
　　*she* weep?
O innocent of spirit — let my heart
Break rather — whom the gentlest airs of
　　heaven
Should kiss with an unwonted gentleness.
Her love did murder mine?　What then?
　　She deem'd
I wore a brother's mind; she call'd me
　　brother.
She told me all her love; she shall not
　　weep.　730

　　　The brightness of a burning thought,
　　awhile
In battle with the glooms of my dark will,
Moonlike emerged, and to itself lit up
There on the depth of an unfathom'd woe
Reflex of action.　Starting up at once,
As from a dismal dream of my own death,
I, for I loved her, lost my love in Love;
I, for I loved her, graspt the hand she
　　loved,
And laid it in her own, and sent my cry
Thro' the blank night to Him who loving
　　made　740
The happy and the unhappy love, that He
Would hold the hand of blessing over
　　them,
Lionel, the happy, and her, and her, his
　　bride!
Let them so love that men and boys may
　　say,
'Lo! how they love each other!' till their
　　love
Shall ripen to a proverb, unto all
Known, when their faces are forgot in the
　　land —
One golden dream of love, from which may
　　death
Awake them with heaven's music in a life
More living to some happier happiness,　750
Swallowing its precedent in victory.

And as for me, Camilla, as for me, —
The dew of tears is an unwholesome dew,
They will but sicken the sick plant the
      more.
Deem that I love thee but as brothers do,
So shalt thou love me still as sisters do;
Or if thou dream aught farther, dream but
      how
I could have loved thee, had there been
      none else
To love as lovers, loved again by thee.

      Or this, or somewhat like to this, I
         spake,                                760
When I beheld her weep so ruefully;
For sure my love should ne'er indue the
      front
And mask of Hate, who lives on others'
      moans.
Shall Love pledge Hatred in her bitter
      draughts,
And batten on her poisons?   Love forbid!
Love passeth not the threshold of cold
      Hate,
And Hate is strange beneath the roof of
      Love.
O Love, if thou be'st Love, dry up these
      tears
Shed for the love of Love; for tho' mine
      image,
The subject of thy power, be cold in her,
Yet, like cold snow, it melteth in the
      source                                771
Of these sad tears, and feeds their down-
      ward flow.
So Love, arraign'd to judgment and to
      death,
Received unto himself a part of blame,
Being guiltless, as an innocent prisoner,
Who, when the woful sentence hath been
      past,
And all the clearness of his fame hath
      gone
Beneath the shadow of the curse of man,
First falls asleep in swoon, wherefrom
      awaked,
And looking round upon his tearful friends,
Forthwith and in his agony conceives   781
A shameful sense as of a cleaving crime —
For whence without some guilt should such
      grief be?

      So died that hour, and fell into the
         abysm
Of forms outworn, but not to me outworn,

Who never hail'd another — was there
      one?
There might be one — one other, worth the
      life
That made it sensible.   So that hour died
Like odor rapt into the winged wind
Borne into alien lands and far away.     790

      There be some hearts so airily built, that
         they,
They — when their love is wreck'd — if
      Love can wreck —
On that sharp ridge of utmost doom ride
      highly
Above the perilous seas of Change and
      Chance,
Nay, more, hold out the lights of cheerful-
      ness;
As the tall ship, that many a dreary year
Knit to some dismal sandbank far at sea,
All thro' the livelong hours of utter dark,
Showers slanting light upon the dolorous
      wave.
For me — what light, what gleam on those
      black ways                                800
Where Love could walk with banish'd Hope
      no more?

      It was ill-done to part you, sisters fair;
Love's arms were wreath'd about the neck
      of Hope,
And Hope kiss'd Love, and Love drew in
      her breath
In that close kiss, and drank her whisper'd
      tales.
They said that Love would die when Hope
      was gone,
And Love mourn'd long, and sorrow'd after
      Hope;
At last she sought out Memory, and they
      trod
The same old paths where Love had walk'd
      with Hope,
And Memory fed the soul of Love with
      tears.                                810

## II

From that time forth I would not see her
      more;
But many weary moons I lived alone —
Alone, and in the heart of the great forest.
Sometimes upon the hills beside the sea
All day I watch'd the floating isles of
      shade,

And sometimes on the shore, upon the
    sands
Insensibly I drew her name, until
The meaning of the letters shot into
My brain; anon the wanton billow wash'd
Them over, till they faded like my love.
The hollow caverns heard me — the black
    brooks              11
Of the mid-forest heard me — the soft
    winds,
Laden with thistle-down and seeds of
    flowers,
Paused in their course to hear me, for my
    voice
Was all of thee; the merry linnet knew
    me,
The squirrel knew me, and the dragon-fly
Shot by me like a flash of purple fire.
The rough brier tore my bleeding palms;
    the hemlock,
Brow-high, did strike my forehead as I
    past;                19
Yet trod I not the wild-flower in my path,
Nor bruised the wild-bird's egg.

                  Was this the end?
Why grew we then together in one plot?
Why fed we from one fountain? drew one
    sun?
Why were our mothers branches of one
    stem?
Why were we one in all things, save in
    that
Where to have been one had been the cope
    and crown
Of all I hoped and fear'd? — if that same
    nearness
Were father to this distance, and that *one*
Vauntcourier to this *double?* if Affection
Living slew Love, and Sympathy hew'd
    out              30
The bosom-sepulchre of Sympathy?

    Chiefly I sought the cavern and the hill
Where last we roam'd together, for the
    sound
Of the loud stream was pleasant, and the
    wind
Came wooingly with woodbine smells.
    Sometimes
All day I sat within the cavern-mouth,
Fixing my eyes on those three cypress-
    cones
That spired above the wood; and with
    mad hand

Tearing the bright leaves of the ivy-screen,
I cast them in the noisy brook beneath,   40
And watch'd them till they vanish'd from
    my sight
Beneath the bower of wreathed eglantines.
And all the fragments of the living rock, —
Huge blocks, which some old trembling of
    the world
Had loosen'd from the mountain, till they
    fell
Half-digging their own graves, — these in
    my agony
Did I make bare of all the golden moss,
Wherewith the dashing runnel in the spring
Had liveried them all over.   In my brain
The spirit seem'd to flag from thought to
    thought,              50
As moonlight wandering thro' a mist; my
    blood
Crept like marsh drains thro' all my lan-
    guid limbs;
The motions of my heart seem'd far within
    me,
Unfrequent, low, as tho' it told its pulses;
And yet it shook me, that my frame would
    shudder,
As if 't were drawn asunder by the rack.
But over the deep graves of Hope and
    Fear,
And all the broken palaces of the past,
Brooded one master-passion evermore,
Like to a low-hung and a fiery sky       60
Above some fair metropolis, earth-
    shock'd, —
Hung round with ragged rims and burning
    folds, —
Embathing all with wild and woful hues,
Great hills of ruins, and collapsed masses
Of thunder-shaken columns indistinct,
And fused together in the tyrannous
    light —
Ruins, the ruin of all my life and me!

    Sometimes I thought Camilla was no
    more;
Some one had told me she was dead, and
    ask'd
If I would see her burial.   Then I seem'd
To rise, and through the forest-shadow
    borne              71
With more than mortal swiftness, I ran
    down
The steepy sea-bank, till I came upon
The rear of a procession, curving round
The silver-sheeted bay, in front of which

Six stately virgins, all in white, upbare
A broad earth-sweeping pall of whitest
      lawn,
Wreathed round the bier with garlands.  In
      the distance,
From out the yellow woods upon the hill
Look'd forth the summit and the pinnacles
Of a gray steeple — thence at intervals   81
A low bell tolling.  All the pageantry,
Save those six virgins which upheld the
      bier,
Were stoled from head to foot in flowing
      black;
One walk'd abreast with me, and veil'd his
      brow,
And he was loud in weeping and in praise
Of her we follow'd.  A strong sympathy
Shook all my soul; I flung myself upon him
In tears and cries.  I told him all my love,
How I had loved her from the first;
      whereat                            90
He shrank and howl'd, and from his brow
      drew back
His hand to push me from him, and the
      face,
The very face and form of Lionel
Flash'd thro' my eyes into my innermost
      brain,
And at his feet I seem'd to faint and fall,
To fall and die away.  I could not rise,
Albeit I strove to follow.  They past on,
T    lordly phantasms ! in their floating
      folds
They past and were no more; but I had
      fallen                            99
Prone by the dashing runnel on the grass.

    Alway the inaudible, invisible thought,
Artificer and subject, lord and slave,
Shaped by the audible and visible,
Moulded the audible and visible.
All crisped sounds of wave and leaf and
      wind
Flatter'd the fancy of my fading brain;
The cloud-pavilion'd element, the wood,
The mountain, the three cypresses, the
      cave,
Storm, sunset, glows and glories of the
      moon
Below black firs, when silent-creeping
      winds                            110
Laid the long night in silver streaks and
      bars,
Were wrought into the tissue of my dream.
The moanings in the forest, the loud brook,

Cries of the partridge like a rusty key
Turn'd in a lock, owl-whoop and dorhawk-
      whirr
Awoke me not, but were a part of sleep,
And voices in the distance calling to me
And in my vision bidding me dream on,
Like sounds without the twilight realm of
      dreams,
Which wander round the bases of the hills,
And murmur at the low-dropt eaves of
      sleep,                           121
Half-entering the portals.  Oftentimes
The vision had fair prelude, in the end
Opening on darkness, stately vestibules
To caves and shows of death — whether the
      mind,
With some revenge — even to itself un-
      known —
Made strange division of its suffering
With her, whom to have suffering view'd
      had been
Extremest pain; or that the clear-eyed
      Spirit,
Being blunted in the present, grew at
      length                           130
Prophetical and prescient of whate'er
The future had in store; or that which
      most
Enchains belief, the sorrow of my spirit
Was of so wide a compass it took in
All I had loved, and my dull agony,
Ideally to her transferr'd, became
Anguish intolerable.

                        The day waned;
Alone I sat with her.  About my brow
Her warm breath floated in the utterance
Of silver-chorded tones; her lips were
      sunder'd                         140
With smiles of tranquil bliss, which broke
      in light
Like morning from her eyes — her eloquent
      eyes —
As I have seen them many a hundred
      times —
Fill'd all with pure clear fire, thro' mine
      down rain'd
Their spirit-searching splendors.  As a
      vision
Unto a haggard prisoner, iron-stay'd
In damp and dismal dungeons underground,
Confined on points of faith, when strength
      is shock'd
With torment, and expectancy of worse
Upon the morrow, thro' the ragged walls,

All unawares before his half-shut eyes, 151
Comes in upon him in the dead of night,
And with the excess of sweetness and of
    awe,
Makes the heart tremble, and the sight run
    over
Upon his steely gyves; so those fair eyes
Shone on my darkness, forms which ever
    stood
Within the magic cirque of memory,
Invisible but deathless, waiting still
The edict of the will to reassume
The semblance of those rare realities    160
Of which they were the mirrors.  Now the
    light
Which was their life burst through the
    cloud of thought
Keen, irrepressible.

It was a room
Within the summer-house of which I spake,
Hung round with paintings of the sea, and
    one
A vessel in mid-ocean, her heaved prow
Clambering, the mast bent and the ravin
    wind
In her sail roaring.  From the outer day,
Betwixt the close-set ivies came a broad
And solid beam of isolated light,    170
Crowded with driving atomies, and fell
Slanting upon that picture, from prime
    youth
Well-known, well-loved.  She drew it long
    ago
Forthgazing on the waste and open sea,
One morning when the upblown billow
    ran
Shoreward beneath red clouds, and I had
    pour'd
Into the shadowing pencil's naked forms
Color and life.  It was a bond and seal
Of friendship, spoken of with tearful smiles;
A monument of childhood and of love;    180
The poesy of childhood, my lost love
Symboll'd in storm.  We gazed on it to-
    gether
In mute and glad remembrance, and each
    heart
Grew closer to the other, and the eye
Was riveted and charm-bound, gazing like
The Indian on a still-eyed snake, low-
    couch'd —
A beauty which is death; when all at once
That painted vessel, as with inner life,
Began to heave upon that painted sea.

An earthquake, my loud heart-beats, made
    the ground    190
Reel under us, and all at once, soul, life
And breath and motion, past and flow'd
    away
To those unreal billows.  Round and round
A whirlwind caught and bore us; mighty
    gyres
Rapid and vast, of hissing spray wind-
    driven
Far thro' the dizzy dark.  Aloud she
    shriek'd;
My heart was cloven with pain; I wound
    my arms
About her; we whirl'd giddily; the wind
Sung, but I clasp'd her without fear.  Her
    weight
Shrank in my grasp, and over my dim
    eyes,    200
And parted lips which drank her breath,
    down-hung
The jaws of Death.  I, groaning, from me
    flung
Her empty phantom; all the sway and
    whirl
Of the storm dropt to windless calm, and I
Down welter'd thro' the dark ever and
    ever.

III

I came one day and sat among the stones
Strewn in the entry of the moaning cave;
A morning air, sweet after rain, ran over
The rippling levels of the lake, and blew
Coolness and moisture and all smells of
    bud
And foliage from the dark and dripping
    woods
Upon my fever'd brows that shook and
    throbb'd
From temple unto temple.  To what height
The day had grown I know not.  Then
    came on me
The hollow tolling of the bell, and all    10
The vision of the bier.  As heretofore
I walk'd behind with one who veil'd his
    brow.
Methought by slow degrees the sullen bell
Toll'd quicker, and the breakers on the
    shore
Sloped into louder surf.  Those that went
    with me,
And those that held the bier before my
    face,

Moved with one spirit round about the bay,
Trod swifter steps; and while I walk'd
        with these
In marvel at that gradual change, I thought
Four bells instead of one began to ring,  20
Four merry bells, four merry marriage-
        bells,
In clanging cadence jangling peal on
        peal —
A long loud clash of rapid marriage-bells.
Then those who led the van, and those in
        rear,
Rush'd into dance, and like wild Baccha-
        nals
Fled onward to the steeple in the woods.
I, too, was borne along and felt the blast
Beat on my heated eyelids.  All at once
The front rank made a sudden halt; the
        bells
Lapsed into frightful stillness; the surge
        fell                                            30
From thunder into whispers; those six
        maids
With shrieks and ringing laughter on the
        sand
Threw down the bier; the woods upon the
        hill
Waved with a sudden gust that sweeping
        down
Took the edges of the pall, and blew it far
Until it hung, a little silver cloud
Over the sounding seas.  I turn'd; my
        heart
Shrank in me, like a snowflake in the hand,
Waiting to see the settled countenance  39
Of her I loved, adorn'd with fading flowers.
But she from out her death-like chrysalis,
She from her bier, as into fresher life,
My sister, and my cousin, and my love,
Leapt lightly clad in bridal white — her
        hair
Studded with one rich Provence rose — a
        light
Of smiling welcome round her lips — her
        eyes
And cheeks as bright as when she climb'd
        the hill.
One hand she reach'd to those that came
        behind,
And while I mused nor yet endured to
        take
So rich a prize, the man who stood with
        me                                              50
Stept gaily forward, throwing down his
        robes,

And claspt her hand in his.  Again the bells
Jangled and clang'd; again the stormy surf
Crash'd in the shingle; and the whirling
        rout
Led by those two rush'd into dance, and
        fled
Wind-footed to the steeple in the woods,
Till they were swallow'd in the leafy
        bowers,
And I stood sole beside the vacant bier.

There, there, my latest vision — then the
        event !

## IV

### THE GOLDEN SUPPER [1]

*(Another speaks)*

He flies the event; he leaves the event to
        me.
Poor Julian — how he rush'd away; the
        bells,
Those marriage-bells, echoing in ear and
        heart —
But cast a parting glance at me, you saw,
As who should say 'Continue.'  Well, he
        had
One golden hour — of triumph shall I say ?
Solace at least — before he left his home.

    Would you had seen him in that hour of
        his !
He moved thro' all of it majestically —
Restrain'd himself quite to the close — but
        now —                                         10
Whether they *were* his lady's marriage-
        bells,
Or prophets of them in his fantasy,
I never ask'd; but Lionel and the girl
Were wedded, and our Julian came again
Back to his mother's house among the
        pines.
But these, their gloom, the mountains and
        the Bay,
The whole land weigh'd him down as Ætna
        does
The Giant of Mythology; he would go,
Would leave the land for ever, and had
        gone

[1] This poem is founded upon a story in Boccaccio.  See Introduction, p. 281.

Surely, but for a whisper, 'Go not yet,'    20
Some  warning — sent  divinely — as  it
    seem'd
By  that  which  follow'd — but of  this  I
    deem
As of the visions that he told — the event
Glanced back upon them in his after life,
And  partly  made  them — tho' he  knew  it
    not.

And  thus  he  stay'd  and  would  not  look
    at her —
No, not for months; but, when the eleventh
    moon
After their marriage lit the lover's Bay,
Heard  yet  once  more  the  tolling  bell, and
    said,
'Would you could toll me out of life !' but
    found —                                       30
All softly as his mother broke it to him —
A  crueller  reason  than  a  crazy  ear
For  that  low  knell  tolling  his  lady  dead —
Dead — and  had  lain  three  days  without  a
    pulse;
All  that  look'd  on  her  had  pronounced  her
    dead.
And so they bore her — for in Julian's land
They  never  nail  a  dumb  head  up  in  elm —
Bore  her  free-faced  to  the  free  airs  of
    heaven,
And  laid  her  in  the  vault  of  her  own  kin.

What did he then ? not die — he is here
    and hale —                                    40
Not  plunge  headforemost  from  the  moun-
    tain there,
And  leave  the  name  of  Lover's  Leap, not
    he.
He  knew  the  meaning  of  the  whisper  now,
Thought  that  he  knew  it.  'This, I  stay'd
    for this;
O Love, I have not seen you for so long !
Now, now, will I go down into the grave,
I  will be all alone with all I love,
And  kiss  her  on  the  lips.  She  is  his  no
    more;
The dead returns to me, and I go down    49
To kiss the dead.'

                    The fancy stirr'd him so
He  rose  and  went, and, entering  the  dim
    vault
And  making  there  a  sudden  light, beheld
All  round  about  him  that  which  all  will
    be.

The light was but a flash, and went again.
Then at the far end of the vault he saw
His  lady  with  the  moonlight  on  her  face;
Her  breast  as  in  a  shadow-prison, bars
Of  black  and  bands  of  silver, which  the
    moon
Struck  from  an  open  grating  overhead
High  in  the  wall, and  all  the  rest  of  her  60
Drown'd  in  the  gloom  and  horror  of  the
    vault.

    'It  was  my  wish,' he  said, 'to  pass, to
        sleep,
To rest, to be with her — till the great day
Peal'd  on  us  with  that  music  which  rights
    all,
And  raised  us  hand  in  hand.'  And  kneel-
    ing there
Down in the dreadful dust that once was
    man,
'Dust,' as  he  said, 'that  once  was  loving
    hearts,
Hearts  that  had  beat  with  such  a  love  as
    mine —
Not such as mine, no, nor for such as her, —
He  softly  put  his  arm  about  her  neck    70
And  kiss'd  her  more  than  once, till  helpless
    death
And  silence  made  him  bold — nay, but  I
    wrong him,
He reverenced his dear lady even in death;
But, placing his true hand upon her heart,
'O  you  warm  heart,' he  moan'd, 'not  even
    death
Can  chill  you  all  at  once ' — then, starting,
    thought
His  dreams  had  come  again.  'Do I wake
    or sleep ?
Or am I made immortal, or my love
Mortal  once  more ? '  It  beat — the  heart
    — it beat;                                    79
Faint — but it beat; at which his own began
To  pulse  with  such  a  vehemence  that  it
    drown'd
The  feebler  motion  underneath  his  hand.
But when at last his doubts were satisfied
He  raised  her  softly  from  the  sepulchre,
And, wrapping  her  all  over  with  the  cloak
He  came  in, and  now  striding  fast, and
    now
Sitting  awhile  to  rest, but  evermore
Holding  his  golden  burthen  in  his  arms,
So  bore  her  thro' the  solitary  land
Back to the mother's house where she was
    born.                                         90

There the good mother's kindly minister-
    ing,
With half a night's appliances, recall'd
Her fluttering life.   She rais'd an eye that
    ask'd
'Where?' till the things familiar to her
    youth
Had made a silent answer; then she spoke
'Here! and how came I here?' and learn-
    ing it —
They told her somewhat rashly, as I
    think —
At once began to wander and to wail,
'Ay, but you know that you must give me
    back.
Send! bid him come;' but Lionel was
    away —                                          100
Stung by his loss had vanish'd, none knew
    where.
'He casts me out,' she wept, 'and goes' —
    a wail
That, seeming something, yet was nothing,
    born
Not from believing mind but shatter'd
    nerve,
Yet haunting Julian, as her own reproof
At some precipitance in her burial.
Then, when her own true spirit had return'd,
'O, yes, and you,' she said, 'and none but
    you?
For you have given me life and love again,
And none but you yourself shall tell him
    of it,                                            110
And you shall give me back when he re-
    turns.'
'Stay then a little,' answer'd Julian, 'here,
And keep yourself, none knowing, to your-
    self;
And I will do your will.   I may not stay,
No, not an hour; but send me notice of
    him
When he returns, and then will I return,
And I will make a solemn offering of you
To him you love.'   And faintly she re-
    plied,
'And I will do your will, and none shall
    know.'

    Not know? with such a secret to be
        known.                                        120
But all their house was old and loved them
    both,
And all the house had known the loves of
    both,
Had died almost to serve them any way,

And all the land was waste and solitary.
And then he rode away; but after this,
An hour or two, Camilla's travail came
Upon her, and that day a boy was born,
Heir of his face and land, to Lionel.

    And thus our lonely lover rode away,
And pausing at a hostel in a marsh,          130
There fever seized upon him.   Myself was
    then
Travelling that land, and meant to rest an
    hour;
And sitting down to such a base repast,
It makes me angry yet to speak of it —
I heard a groaning overhead, and climb'd
The moulder'd stairs — for everything was
    vile —
And in a loft, with none to wait on him,
Found, as it seem'd, a skeleton alone,
Raving of dead men's dust and beating
    hearts.

    A dismal hostel in a dismal land,        140
A flat malarian world of reed and rush!
But there from fever and my care of him
Sprang up a friendship that may help us
    yet.
For while we roam'd along the dreary
    coast,
And waited for her message, piece by
    piece
I learnt the drearier story of his life;
And, tho' he loved and honor'd Lionel,
Found that the sudden wail his lady made
Dwelt in his fancy.   Did he know her worth,
Her beauty even? should he not be taught,
Even by the price that others set upon it,   151
The value of that jewel he had to guard?

    Suddenly came her notice and we past,
I with our lover to his native Bay.

    This love is of the brain, the mind, the
        soul;
That makes the sequel pure, tho' some of
    us
Beginning at the sequel know no more.
Not such am I; and yet I say the bird
That will not hear my call, however sweet,
But if my neighbor whistle answers him —
What matter? there are others in the
    wood.                                            161
Yet when I saw her — and I thought him
    crazed,
Tho' not with such a craziness as needs

A cell and keeper — those dark eyes of
    hers —
O, such dark eyes ! and not her eyes alone,
But all from these to where she touch'd on
    earth,
For such a craziness as Julian's look'd
No less than one divine apology.

    So sweetly and so modestly she came  169
To greet us, her young hero in her arms !
' Kiss him,' she said. ' You gave me life
    again.
He, but for you, had never seen it once.
His other father you ! Kiss him, and
    then
Forgive him, if his name be Julian too.'

    Talk of lost hopes and broken heart ! his
    own
Sent such a flame into his face, I knew
Some sudden vivid pleasure hit him there.

    But he was all the more resolved to go,
And sent at once to Lionel, praying him,
By that great love they both had borne the
    dead,  180
To come and revel for one hour with him
Before he left the land for evermore;
And then to friends — they were not many
    — who lived
Scatteringly about that lonely land of his,
And bade them to a banquet of farewells.

    And Julian made a solemn feast; I never
Sat at a costlier, for all round his hall
From column on to column, as in a wood,
Not such as here — an equatorial one,
Great garlands swung and blossom'd; and
    beneath,  190
Heirlooms, and ancient miracles of art,
Chalice and salver, wines that, heaven knows
    when,
Had suck'd the fire of some forgotten sun,
And kept it thro' a hundred years of
    gloom,
Yet glowing in a heart of ruby — cups
Where nymph and god ran ever round in
    gold —
Others of glass as costly — some with gems
Movable and resettable at will,
And trebling all the rest in value — Ah
    heavens !
Why need I tell you all ? — suffice to say
That whatsoever such a house as his,  201
And his was old, has in it rare or fair

Was brought before the guest. And they,
    the guests,
Wonder'd at some strange light in Julian's
    eyes —
I told you that he had his golden hour —
And such a feast, ill-suited as it seem'd
To such a time, to Lionel's loss and his
And that resolved self-exile from a land
He never would revisit, such a feast
So rich, so strange, and stranger even than
    rich,  210
But rich as for the nuptials of a king.

    And stranger yet, at one end of the
    hall
Two great funereal curtains, looping down,
Parted a little ere they met the floor,
About a picture of his lady, taken
Some years before, and falling hid the
    frame.
And just above the parting was a lamp;
So the sweet figure folded round with night
Seem'd stepping out of darkness with a
    smile.

    Well, then — our solemn feast — we ate
    and drank,  220
And might — the wines being of such no-
    bleness —
Have jested also, but for Julian's eyes,
And something weird and wild about it
    all.
What was it ? for our lover seldom spoke,
Scarce touch'd the meats, but ever and
    anon
A priceless goblet with a priceless wine
Arising show'd he drank beyond his use;
And when the feast was near an end, he
    said:

    ' There is a custom in the Orient,
    friends —
I read of it in Persia — when a man  230
Will honor those who feast with him, he
    brings
And shows them whatsoever he accounts
Of all his treasures the most beautiful,
Gold, jewels, arms, whatever it may be.
This custom — '

                Pausing here a moment, all
The guests broke in upon him with meeting
    hands
And cries about the banquet — ' Beautiful !
Who could desire more beauty at a feast ?'

The lover answer'd: 'There is more than
        one                                        239
Here sitting who desires it.   Laud me not
Before my time, but hear me to the close.
This custom steps yet further when the
        guest
Is loved and honor'd to the uttermost.
For after he hath shown him gems or gold,
He brings and sets before him in rich
        guise
That which is thrice as beautiful as these,
The beauty that is dearest to his heart —
"O my heart's lord, would I could show
        you," he says,
"Even my heart too."   And I propose to-
        night                                      249
To show you what is dearest to my heart,
And my heart too.

                'But solve me first a doubt.
I knew a man, nor many years ago;
He had a faithful servant, one who loved
His master more than all on earth beside.
He falling sick, and seeming close on
        death,
His master would not wait until he died,
But bade his menials bear him from the
        door,
And leave him in the public way to die.
I knew another, not so long ago,
Who found the dying servant, took him
        home,                                      260
And fed, and cherish'd him, and saved his
        life.
I ask you now, should this first master
        claim
His service, whom does it belong to ? him
Who thrust him out, or him who saved his
        life ?'

   This question, so flung down before the
        guests,
And balanced either way by each, at
        length
When some were doubtful how the law
        would hold,
Was handed over by consent of all
To one who had not spoken, Lionel.

   Fair speech was his, and delicate of
        phrase.                                    270
And he, beginning languidly — his loss
Weigh'd on him yet — but warming as he
        went,
Glanced at the point of law, to pass it by,

Affirming that as long as either lived,
By all the laws of love and gratefulness,
The service of the one so saved was due
All to the saver — adding, with a smile,
The first for many weeks — a semi-smile
As at a strong conclusion — 'body and soul
And life and limbs, all his to work his
        will.'                                     280

   Then Julian made a secret sign to me
To bring Camilla down before them all.
And crossing her own picture as she came,
And looking as much lovelier than herself
Is lovelier than all others — on her head
A diamond circlet, and from under this
A veil, that seem'd no more than gilded
        air,
Flying by each fine ear, an Eastern gauze
With seeds of gold — so, with that grace of
        hers,                                      289
Slow-moving as a wave against the wind,
That flings a mist behind it in the sun —
And bearing high in arms the mighty babe,
The younger Julian, who himself was
        crown'd
With roses, none so rosy as himself —
And over all her babe and her the jewels
Of many generations of his house
Sparkled and flash'd, for he had deck'd
        them out
As for a solemn sacrifice of love —
So she came in — I am long in telling it,
I never yet beheld a thing so strange,    300
Sad, sweet, and strange together — floated
        in —
While all the guests in mute amazement
        rose —
And slowly pacing to the middle hall,
Before the board, there paused and stood,
        her breast
Hard-heaving, and her eyes upon her feet,
Not daring yet to glance at Lionel.
But him she carried, him nor lights nor
        feast
Dazed or amazed, nor eyes of men; who
        cared
Only to use his own, and staring wide
And hungering for the gilt and jewell'd
        world                                      310
About him, look'd, as he is like to prove,
When Julian goes, the lord of all he saw.

   'My guests,' said Julian, 'you are hon-
        or'd now
Even to the uttermost; in her behold

Of all my treasures the most beautiful,
Of all things upon earth the dearest to
me;'
Then waving us a sign to seat ourselves,
Led his dear lady to a chair of state.
And I, by Lionel sitting, saw his face
Fire, and dead ashes and all fire again 320
Thrice in a second, felt him tremble too,
And heard him muttering, ' So like, so
like;
She never had a sister. I knew none.
Some cousin of his and hers — O God, so
like !'
And then he suddenly ask'd her if she
were.
She shook, and cast her eyes down, and was
dumb.
And then some other question'd if she
came
From foreign lands, and still she did not
speak.
Another, if the boy were hers; but she 329
To all their queries answer'd not a word,
Which made the amazement more, till one
of them
Said, shuddering, ' Her spectre !' But his
friend
Replied, in half a whisper, ' Not at least
The spectre that will speak if spoken to.
Terrible pity, if one so beautiful
Prove, as I almost dread to find her,
dumb !'

But Julian, sitting by her, answer'd
all:
' She is but dumb, because in her you
see
That faithful servant whom we spoke
about,
Obedient to her second master now; 340
Which will not last. I have here to-night
a guest
So bound to me by common love and loss —
What ! shall I bind him more ? in his be-
half,
Shall I exceed the Persian, giving him
That which of all things is the dearest to
me,
Not only showing ? and he himself pro-
nounced
That my rich gift is wholly mine to give.

' Now all be dumb, and promise all of
you
Not to break in on what I say by word

Or whisper, while I show you all my
heart.' 350
And then began the story of his love
As here to-day, but not so wordily —
The passionate moment would not suffer
that —
Past thro' his visions to the burial; thence
Down to this last strange hour in his own
hall;
And then rose up, and with him all his
guests
Once more as by enchantment; all but
he,
Lionel, who fain had risen, but fell again,
And sat as if in chains — to whom he said:

' Take my free gift, my cousin, for your
wife; 360
And were it only for the giver's sake,
And tho' she seem so like the one you
lost,
Yet cast her not away so suddenly,
Lest there be none left here to bring her
back.
I leave this land for ever.' Here he ceased.

Then taking his dear lady by one hand,
And bearing on one arm the noble babe,
He slowly brought them both to Lionel.
And there the widower husband and dead
wife
Rush'd each at each with a cry that rather
seem'd 370
For some new death than for a life re-
new'd;
Whereat the very babe began to wail.
At once they turn'd, and caught and
brought him in
To their charm'd circle, and, half killing
him
With kisses, round him closed and claspt
again.
But Lionel, when at last he freed himself
From wife and child, and lifted up a face
All over glowing with the sun of life,
And love, and boundless thanks — the sight
of this
So frighted our good friend that, turning
to me 380
And saying, ' It is over; let us go ' —
There were our horses ready at the doors —
We bade them no farewell, but mounting
these
He past for ever from his native land;
And I with him, my Julian, back to mine.

# IDYLLS OF THE KING

## IN TWELVE BOOKS

*'Flos Regum Arthurus.'* — JOSEPH OF EXETER

The poet became interested in the Arthurian story long before the first series of the 'Idylls' was published. 'The Lady of Shalott,' which appeared in 1832, is founded upon the legend which was later made the subject of 'Lancelot and Elaine.' 'The Palace of Art' in the same volume contained an allusion to 'that deep-wounded child of Pendragon,' or 'mythic Uther's deeply wounded son,' as it now reads. 'Sir Galahad' and 'Sir Lancelot and Queen Guinevere' were printed in 1842, when the 'Morte d'Arthur' was also given to the world. This latter poem, afterwards incorporated in 'The Passing of Arthur,' must have been written as early as 1835, when Fitzgerald heard it read from manuscript ('Memoir,' vol. i. p. 194). Landor also writes under date of December 9, 1837: 'Yesterday a Mr. Moreton, a young man of rare judgment, read to me a manuscript by Mr. Tennyson, very different in style from his printed poems. The subject is the death of Arthur. It is more Homeric than any poem of our time, and rivals some of the noblest parts of the Odyssea' (Forster's 'Life of Landor,' ii. 323).

In 1857 the poet printed 'six trial-copies' of 'Enid and Nimuë: the True and the False,' containing the stories of 'Enid' and 'Vivien,' afterwards revised for the edition of 1859. The copy of this book in the library of the British Museum is believed to be the 'sole survivor' of the six.

There is a still earlier form of 'Enid' in the Forster Bequest Library of the South Kensington Museum, London, which appears to be a first proof of the poem as printed in the 1857 volume. In the same collection there is a volume of proof-sheets, the title-page of which reads: 'The True and the False. Four Idylls of the King,' with the date 1859. It contains the four Idylls which, after further revision, were published the same year with the simpler title of 'Idylls of the King.'

This first instalment of the 'Idylls' as finally published in July, 1859, included 'Enid,' 'Vivien,' 'Elaine,' and 'Guinevere,' as they were then entitled. Ten thousand copies were sold in about six weeks, and the critics were almost unanimous in their praise of the book. Among its warmest admirers was Prince Albert, who sent his copy to the poet, asking him to write his name in it. The note continued : —

'You would thus add a peculiar interest to the book containing those beautiful songs, from the perusal of which I derived the greatest enjoyment. They quite rekindle the feeling with which the legends of King Arthur must have inspired the chivalry of old, whilst the graceful form in which they are presented blends those feelings with the softer tone of our present age.'

In 1862, a new edition of the 'Idylls' appeared, with the dedication to the memory of the Prince, who died in December, 1861.

In 1869, four more Idylls were brought out, — 'The Coming of Arthur,' 'The Holy Grail,' 'Pelleas and Ettarre,' and 'The Passing of Arthur,' in which, as already mentioned, the 'Morte d'Arthur' of 1842 is incorporated.

In 1872, 'The Last Tournament' (contributed to the 'Contemporary Review' for December, 1871) and 'Gareth and Lynette' appeared ; and in 1885 'Balin and Balan,' the last of the series, was included in 'Tiresias and Other Poems.'

In 1884, 'Enid,' already entitled 'Geraint and Enid,' was divided into two parts (numbered I. and II.), and in 1888 these parts received their present titles. The poems were now described as 'twelve books,' and arranged in the order in which the author intended they should be read.

In the order of *publication* the last Idyll (or the portion of it included in the 'Morte d'Arthur' of 1842) was the first, followed successively by the third, fourth (these two, as just explained, being originally one), sixth, seventh, eleventh (as the five were arranged in 1859), first, eighth, ninth, twelfth) as arranged in 1869, the twelfth being the amplification of the 'Morte d'Arthur'), second, tenth, and fifth. 'Nave and transept, aisle after aisle, the Gothic minster has extended, until, with the addition of a cloister here and a chapel yonder, the structure stands complete.' Stedman, from whose 'Victorian Poets' we quote this, adds : —

'It has grown insensibly, under the hands of one man who has given it the best years of his life, — but somewhat as Wolf conceived the Homeric poems to have grown, chant by chant, until the time came for the whole to be welded together in heroic form. . . . It is the epic of chivalry,— the Christian ideal of chivalry which we have deduced from a barbaric source, —

our conception of what knighthood should be, rather than what it really was; but so skilfully wrought of high imaginings, faery spells, fantastic legends, and mediæval splendors, that the whole work, suffused with the Tennysonian glamor of golden mist, seems like a chronicle illuminated by saintly hands, and often blazes with light like that which flashed from the holy wizard's book when the covers were unclasped. And, indeed, if this be not the greatest narrative poem since "Paradise Lost," what other English production are you to name in its place ? Never so lofty as the grander portions of Milton's epic, it is more evenly sustained and has no long prosaic passages; while "Paradise Lost" is justly declared to be a work of superhuman genius impoverished by dreary wastes of theology.'

For the origin and development of the story of the 'Idylls,' see 'Studies in the Arthurian Legend,' by John Rhys, M. A. (Oxford, 1891), 'Tennyson's Idylls of the King and Arthurian Story from the 16th Century,' by M. W. Maccallum, M. A. (London, 1894), 'Essays on Lord Tennyson's Idylls of the King,' by Harold Littledale, M. A. (London, 1893), 'The Growth of the Idylls of the King,' by Richard Jones, Ph. D.( Philadelphia, 1895), 'King Arthur and the Table Round,' by W. W. Newell (Boston, 1897), etc. For the allegory in the poems, see 'Studies in the Idylls,' by Henry Elsdale (London, 1878), and the articles in the 'Contemporary Review' for January, 1870 (by Dean Alford), and May, 1873 (by the editor), both of which were based on the poet's own explanations. For general criticism, see particularly 'Tennyson, his Art and Relation to Modern Life,' by Rev. Stopford A. Brooke (London and New York, 1894), in which pp. 255–391 are devoted to the 'Idylls,' and 'The Poetry of Tennyson,' by Rev. Dr. Henry van Dyke (3d ed., New York, 1892, pp. 133–196). For bibliographical and miscellaneous information, see the 'Handbook to the Works of Alfred Lord Tennyson,' by Morton Luce (London, 1895), 'A Tennyson Primer,' by William M. Dixon, Litt. D. (London and New York, 1896), and Nicoll and Wise's 'Literary Anecdotes of the Nineteenth Century,' vol. ii. (London, 1896). The 'Bibliography of Tennyson,' by the author of 'Tennysoniana' (R. H. Shepherd), published by subscription (London, 1896), though the most complete up to the present time (1898), is sometimes inaccurate. Malory's 'Morte Darthur,' from which the poet drew much of his material, is accessible in the 'Globe' edition (London and New York, revised ed. 1893), and in the 'Temple Classics' edition (London, 1897).

## DEDICATION

THESE to His Memory — since he held
    them dear,
Perchance as finding there unconsciously
Some image of himself — I dedicate,
I dedicate, I consecrate with tears —
These Idylls.

        And indeed he seems to me
Scarce other than my king's ideal knight,
'Who reverenced his conscience as his
    king;
Whose glory was, redressing human wrong;
Who spake no slander, no, nor listen'd to
    it;
Who loved one only and who clave to
    her —'                                    10
Her — over all whose realms to their last
    isle,
Commingled with the gloom of imminent
    war,
The shadow of his loss drew like eclipse,
Darkening the world. We have lost him;
    he is gone.
We know him now; all narrow jealousies
Are silent, and we see him as he moved,

How modest, kindly, all-accomplish'd, wise,
With what sublime repression of himself,
And in what limits, and how tenderly;
Not swaying to this faction or to that;    20
Not making his high place the lawless
    perch
Of wing'd ambitions, nor a vantage-ground
For pleasure; but thro' all this tract of
    years
Wearing the white flower of a blameless
    life,
Before a thousand peering littlenesses,
In that fierce light which beats upon a
    throne
And blackens every blot; for where is he
Who dares foreshadow for an only son
A lovelier life, a more unstain'd, than his ?
Or how should England dreaming of his
    sons                                      30
Hope more for these than some inheritance
Of such a life, a heart, a mind as thine,
Thou noble Father of her Kings to be,
Laborious for her people and her poor —
Voice in the rich dawn of an ampler
    day —
Far-sighted summoner of War and Waste
To fruitful strifes and rivalries of peace —

Sweet nature gilded by the gracious gleam
Of letters, dear to Science, dear to Art,
Dear to thy land and ours, a Prince in-
  deed,                                    40
Beyond all titles, and a household name,
Hereafter, thro' all times, Albert the Good.

Break not, O woman's - heart, but still
  endure;
Break not, for thou art royal, but endure,
Remembering all the beauty of that star
Which shone so close beside thee that ye
  made
One light together, but has past and leaves
The Crown a lonely splendor.

                                May all love,
His love, unseen but felt, o'ershadow thee,
The love of all thy sons encompass thee,  50
The love of all thy daughters cherish thee,
The love of all thy people comfort thee,
Till God's love set thee at his side again !

## THE COMING OF ARTHUR

Leodogran, the king of Cameliard,
Had one fair daughter, and none other
  child;
And she was fairest of all flesh on earth,
Guinevere, and in her his one delight.

For many a petty king ere Arthur came
Ruled in this isle and, ever waging war
Each upon other, wasted all the land;
And still from time to time the heathen
  host
Swarm'd over-seas, and harried what was
  left.
And so there grew great tracts of wilder-
  ness,                                    10
Wherein the beast was ever more and
  more,
But man was less and less, till Arthur came.
For first Aurelius lived and fought and
  died,
And after him King Uther fought and died,
But either fail'd to make the kingdom
  one.
And after these King Arthur for a space,
And thro' the puissance of his Table
  Round,
Drew all their petty princedoms under him,
Their king and head, and made a realm and
  reign'd.

And thus the land of Cameliard was
  waste,                                   20
Thick with wet woods, and many a beast
  therein,
And none or few to scare or chase the
  beast;
So that wild dog and wolf and boar and
  bear
Came night and day, and rooted in the
  fields,
And wallow'd in the gardens of the King.
And ever and anon the wolf would steal
The children and devour, but now and then,
Her own brood lost or dead, lent her fierce
  teat
To human sucklings; and the children,
  housed
In her foul den, there at their meat would
  growl,                                   30
And mock their foster-mother on four feet,
Till, straighten'd, they grew up to wolf-like
  men,
Worse than the wolves. And King Leo-
  dogran
Groan'd for the Roman legions here again
And Cæsar's eagle. Then his brother king,
Urien, assail'd him; last a heathen horde,
Reddening the sun with smoke and earth
  with blood,
And on the spike that split the mother's
  heart
Spitting the child, brake on him, till,
  amazed,                                  39
He knew not whither he should turn for aid.

But — for he heard of Arthur newly
  crown'd,
Tho' not without an uproar made by those
Who cried, 'He is not Uther's son ' — the
  King
Sent to him, saying, 'Arise, and help us
  thou !
For here between the man and beast we
  die.'

And Arthur yet had done no deed of
  arms,
But heard the call and came; and Guine-
  vere
Stood by the castle walls to watch him pass;
But since he neither wore on helm or shield
The golden symbol of his kinglihood,      50
But rode a simple knight among his knights,
And many of these in richer arms than he,
She saw him not, or mark'd not, if she saw,

One among many, tho' his face was bare.
But Arthur, looking downward as he past,
Felt the light of her eyes into his life
Smite on the sudden, yet rode on, and
  pitch'd
His tents beside the forest.  Then he drave
The heathen; after, slew the beast, and
  fell'd
The forest, letting in the sun, and made  60
Broad pathways for the hunter and the
  knight,
And so return'd.

            For while he linger'd there,
A doubt that ever smoulder'd in the hearts
Of those great lords and barons of his realm
Flash'd forth and into war; for most of
  these,
Colleaguing with a score of petty kings,
Made head against him, crying: 'Who is
  he
That he should rule us ?  who hath proven
  him
King Uther's son ?  for lo !  we look at him,
And find nor face nor bearing, limbs nor
  voice,                                      70
Are like to those of Uther whom we knew.
This is the son of Gorloïs, not the King;
This is the son of Anton, not the King.'

  And Arthur, passing thence to battle, felt
Travail, and throes and agonies of the life,
Desiring to be join'd with Guinevere;
And thinking as he rode: 'Her father said
That there between the man and beast they
  die.
Shall I not lift her from this land of beasts
Up to my throne and side by side with me ?
What happiness to reign a lonely king,  81
Vext — O ye stars that shudder over me,
O earth that soundest hollow under me,
Vext with waste dreams ?  for saving I be
  join'd
To her that is the fairest under heaven,
I seem as nothing in the mighty world,
And cannot will my will nor work my work
Wholly, nor make myself in mine own
  realm
Victor and lord.  But were I join'd with
  her,
Then might we live together as one life,  90
And reigning with one will in everything
Have power on this dark land to lighten it,
And power on this dead world to make it
  live.'

Thereafter — as he speaks who tells the
  tale —
When Arthur reach'd a field of battle
  bright
With pitch'd pavilions of his foe, the world
Was all so clear about him that he saw
The smallest rock far on the faintest hill,
And even in high day the morning star.  99
So when the King had set his banner broad,
At once from either side, with trumpet-
  blast,
And shouts, and clarions shrilling unto
  blood,
The long-lanced battle let their horses run.
And now the barons and the kings pre-
  vail'd,
And now the King, as here and there that
  war
Went swaying; but the Powers who walk
  the world
Made lightnings and great thunders over
  him,
And dazed all eyes, till Arthur by main
  might,
And mightier of his hands with every blow,
And leading all his knighthood threw the
  kings,                                      110
Carádos, Urien, Cradlemont of Wales,
Claudius, and Clariance of Northumber-
  land,
The King Brandagoras of Latangor,
With Anguisant of Erin, Morganore,
And Lot of Orkney.  Then, before a voice
As dreadful as the shout of one who sees
To one who sins, and deems himself alone
And all the world asleep, they swerved and
  brake
Flying, and Arthur call'd to stay the
  brands
That hack'd among the flyers, 'Ho !  they
  yield !'                                     120
So like a painted battle the war stood
Silenced, the living quiet as the dead,
And in the heart of Arthur joy was lord.
He laugh'd upon his warrior whom he loved
And honor'd most.  'Thou dost not doubt
  me King,
So well thine arm hath wrought for me to-
  day.'
'Sir and my liege,' he cried, 'the fire of
  God
Descends upon thee in the battle-field.
I know thee for my King !'  Whereat the
  two,
For each had warded either in the fight,

Sware on the field of death a deathless
　　love.　　　　　　　　　　　　　131
And Arthur said, 'Man's word is God in
　　man;
Let chance what will, I trust thee to the
　　death.'

Then quickly from the foughten field he
　　sent
Ulfius, and Brastias, and Bedivere,
His new-made knights, to King Leodogran,
Saying, 'If I in aught have served thee
　　well,
Give me thy daughter Guinevere to wife.'

Whom when he heard, Leodogran in
　　heart
Debating — 'How should I that am a king,
However much he holp me at my need,　141
Give my one daughter saving to a king,
And a king's son ? ' — lifted his voice, and
　　call'd
A hoary man, his chamberlain, to whom
He trusted all things, and of him required
His counsel: 'Knowest thou aught of Ar-
　　thur's birth ? '

Then spake the hoary chamberlain and
　　said:
'Sir King, there be but two old men that
　　know;
And each is twice as old as I; and one　149
Is Merlin, the wise man that ever served
King Uther thro' his magic art, and one
Is Merlin's master — so they call him —
　　Bleys,
Who taught him magic; but the scholar
　　ran
Before the master, and so far that Bleys
Laid magic by, and sat him down, and
　　wrote
All things and whatsoever Merlin did
In one great annal-book, where after-years
Will learn the secret of our Arthur's birth.'

To whom the King Leodogran replied:
'O friend, had I been holpen half as well
By this King Arthur as by thee to-day,　161
Then beast and man had had their share of
　　me;
But summon here before us yet once more
Ulfius, and Brastias, and Bedivere.'

Then, when they came before him, the
　　king said:

'I have seen the cuckoo chased by lesser
　　fowl,
And reason in the chase; but wherefore
　　now
Do these your lords stir up the heat of war,
Some calling Arthur born of Gorloïs,
Others of Anton ?  Tell me, ye yourselves,
Hold ye this Arthur for King Uther's
　　son ? '　　　　　　　　　　　　　171

And Ulfius and Brastias answer'd, ' Ay.'
Then Bedivere, the first of all his knights
Knighted by Arthur at his crowning,
　　spake —
For bold in heart and act and word was he,
Whenever slander breathed against the
　　King —

'Sir, there be many rumors on this head;
For there be those who hate him in their
　　hearts,
Call him baseborn, and since his ways are
　　sweet,
And theirs are bestial, hold him less than
　　man;　　　　　　　　　　　　　180
And there be those who deem him more
　　than man,
And dream he dropt from heaven.  But my
　　belief
In all this matter — so ye care to learn —
Sir, for ye know that in King Uther's time
The prince and warrior Gorloïs, he that
　　held
Tintagil castle by the Cornish sea,
Was wedded with a winsome wife, Ygerne;
And daughters had she borne him, — one
　　whereof,
Lot's wife, the Queen of Orkney, Bellicent,
Hath ever like a loyal sister cleaved　190
To Arthur, — but a son she had not borne.
And Uther cast upon her eyes of love;
But she, a stainless wife to Gorloïs,
So loathed the bright dishonor of his love
That Gorloïs and King Uther went to war,
And overthrown was Gorloïs and slain.
Then Uther in his wrath and heat besieged
Ygerne within Tintagil, where her men,
Seeing the mighty swarm about their walls,
Left her and fled, and Uther enter'd in,　200
And there was none to call to but himself.
So, compass'd by the power of the king,
Enforced she was to wed him in her tears,
And with a shameful swiftness; afterward,
Not many moons, King Uther died him-
　　self,

Moaning and wailing for an heir to rule
After him, lest the realm should go to wrack.
And that same night, the night of the new year,
By reason of the bitterness and grief     209
That vext his mother, all before his time
Was Arthur born, and all as soon as born
Deliver'd at a secret postern-gate
To Merlin, to be holden far apart
Until his hour should come, because the lords
Of that fierce day were as the lords of this,
Wild beasts, and surely would have torn the child
Piecemeal among them, had they known; for each
But sought to rule for his own self and hand,
And many hated Uther for the sake
Of Gorloïs. Wherefore Merlin took the child,     220
And gave him to Sir Anton, an old knight
And ancient friend of Uther; and his wife
Nursed the young prince, and rear'd him with her own;
And no man knew. And ever since the lords
Have foughten like wild beasts among themselves,
So that the realm has gone to wrack; but now,
This year, when Merlin — for his hour had come —
Brought Arthur forth, and set him in the hall,
Proclaiming, "Here is Uther's heir, your king,"
A hundred voices cried: "Away with him!     230
No king of ours! a son of Gorloïs he,
Or else the child of Anton, and no king,
Or else baseborn." Yet Merlin thro' his craft,
And while the people clamor'd for a king,
Had Arthur crown'd; but after, the great lords
Banded, and so brake out in open war.'

    Then while the king debated with himself
If Arthur were the child of shamefulness,
Or born the son of Gorloïs after death,     239
Or Uther's son and born before his time,
Or whether there were truth in anything
Said by these three, there came to Cameliard,
With Gawain and young Modred, her two sons,
Lot's wife, the Queen of Orkney, Bellicent;
Whom as he could, not as he would, the king
Made feast for, saying, as they sat at meat:
'A doubtful throne is ice on summer seas.
Ye come from Arthur's court. Victor his men
Report him! Yea, but ye — think ye this king —
So many those that hate him, and so strong,     250
So few his knights, however brave they be —
Hath body enow to hold his foemen down?'

    'O King,' she cried, 'and I will tell thee: few,
Few, but all brave, all of one mind with him;
For I was near him when the savage yells
Of Uther's peerage died, and Arthur sat
Crowned on the daïs, and his warriors cried,
"Be thou the king, and we will work thy will
Who love thee." Then the King in low deep tones,
And simple words of great authority,     260
Bound them by so strait vows to his own self
That when they rose, knighted from kneeling, some
Were pale as at the passing of a ghost,
Some flush'd, and others dazed, as one who wakes
Half-blinded at the coming of a light.

    'But when he spake, and cheer'd his Table Round
With large, divine, and comfortable words,
Beyond my tongue to tell thee — I beheld
From eye to eye thro' all their Order flash
A momentary likeness of the King;     270
And ere it left their faces, thro' the cross
And those around it and the Crucified,
Down from the casement over Arthur, smote

Flame-color, vert, and azure, in three rays,
One falling upon each of three fair queens
Who stood in silence near his throne, the
    friends
Of Arthur, gazing on him, tall, with bright
Sweet faces, who will help him at his need.

'And there I saw mage Merlin, whose
    vast wit                                        279
And hundred winters are but as the hands
Of loyal vassals toiling for their liege.

'And near him stood the Lady of the
    Lake,
Who knows a subtler magic than his
    own —
Clothed in white samite, mystic, wonderful.
She gave the King his huge cross-hilted
    sword,
Whereby to drive the heathen out. A mist
Of incense curl'd about her, and her face
Wellnigh was hidden in the minster gloom;
But there was heard among the holy hymns
A voice as of the waters, for she dwells      290
Down in a deep — calm, whatsoever storms
May shake the world — and when the sur-
    face rolls,
Hath power to walk the waters like our
    Lord.

'There likewise I beheld Excalibur
Before him at his crowning borne, the
    sword
That rose from out the bosom of the lake,
And Arthur row'd across and took it —
    rich
With jewels, elfin Urim, on the hilt,
Bewildering heart and eye — the blade so
    bright                                        299
That men are blinded by it — on one side,
Graven in the oldest tongue of all this
    world,
"Take me," but turn the blade and ye
    shall see,
And written in the speech ye speak your-
    self,
"Cast me away!" And sad was Arthur's
    face
Taking it, but old Merlin counsell'd him,
"Take thou and strike! the time to cast
    away
Is yet far-off." So this great brand the
    king
Took, and by this will beat his foemen
    down.'

Thereat Leodogran rejoiced, but thought
To sift his doubtings to the last, and ask'd,
Fixing full eyes of question on her face,   311
'The swallow and the swift are near akin,
But thou art closer to this noble prince,
Being his own dear sister;' and she said,
'Daughter of Gorloïs and Ygerne am I;'
'And therefore Arthur's sister?' ask'd the
    king.
She answer'd, 'These be secret things,'
    and sign'd
To those two sons to pass, and let them be.
And Gawain went, and breaking into song
Sprang out, and follow'd by his flying hair
Ran like a colt, and leapt at all he saw;   321
But Modred laid his ear beside the doors,
And there half-heard — the same that after-
    ward
Struck for the throne, and striking found
    his doom.

And then the Queen made answer:
    'What know I?
For dark my mother was in eyes and hair,
And dark in hair and eyes am I; and dark
Was Gorloïs; yea, and dark was Uther
    too,
Wellnigh to blackness; but this king is
    fair
Beyond the race of Britons and of men.  330
Moreover, always in my mind I hear
A cry from out the dawning of my life,
A mother weeping, and I hear her say,
"O that ye had some brother, pretty one,
To guard thee on the rough ways of the
    world."'

'Ay,' said the king, 'and hear ye such
    a cry?
But when did Arthur chance upon thee
    first?'

'O King!' she cried, 'and I will tell
    thee true.
He found me first when yet a little maid.
Beaten I had been for a little fault        340
Whereof I was not guilty; and out I ran
And flung myself down on a bank of heath,
And hated this fair world and all therein,
And wept, and wish'd that I were dead;
    and he —
I know not whether of himself he came,
Or brought by Merlin, who, they say, can
    walk
Unseen at pleasure — he was at my side,

And spake sweet words, and comforted my
    heart,                                          348
And dried my tears, being a child with me.
And many a time he came, and evermore
As I grew greater grew with me; and sad
At times he seem'd, and sad with him was I,
Stern too at times, and then I loved him
    not,
But sweet again, and then I loved him well.
And now of late I see him less and less,
But those first days had golden hours for
    me,
For then I surely thought he would be
    king.

'But let me tell thee now another tale:
For Bleys, our Merlin's master, as they
    say,
Died but of late, and sent his cry to me,   360
To hear him speak before he left his life.
Shrunk like a fairy changeling lay the
    mage;
And when I enter'd told me that himself
And Merlin ever served about the king,
Uther, before he died; and on the night
When Uther in Tintagil past away
Moaning and wailing for an heir, the two
Left the still king, and passing forth to
    breathe,
Then from the castle gateway by the chasm
Descending thro' the dismal night — a
    night                                           370
In which the bounds of heaven and earth
    were lost —
Beheld, so high upon the dreary deeps
It seem'd in heaven, a ship, the shape
    thereof
A dragon wing'd, and all from stem to
    stern
Bright with a shining people on the decks,
And gone as soon as seen. And then the
    two
Dropt to the cove, and watch'd the great
    sea fall,
Wave after wave, each mightier than the
    last,
Till last, a ninth one, gathering half the
    deep                                            379
And full of voices, slowly rose and plunged
Roaring, and all the wave was in a flame;
And down the wave and in the flame was
    borne
A naked babe, and rode to Merlin's feet,
Who stoopt and caught the babe, and cried,
    "The King!

Here is an heir for Uther!" And the
    fringe
Of that great breaker, sweeping up the
    strand,
Lash'd at the wizard as he spake the word,
And all at once all round him rose in fire,
So that the child and he were clothed in
    fire.
And presently thereafter follow'd calm,   390
Free sky and stars. "And this same child,"
    he said,
"Is he who reigns; nor could I part in
    peace
Till this were told." And saying this the
    seer
Went thro' the strait and dreadful pass of
    death,
Not ever to be question'd any more
Save on the further side; but when I met
Merlin, and ask'd him if these things were
    truth —
The shining dragon and the naked child
Descending in the glory of the seas —
He laugh'd as is his wont, and answer'd
    me                                             400
In riddling triplets of old time, and said: —

'"Rain, rain, and sun! a rainbow in the
    sky!
A young man will be wiser by and by;
An old man's wit may wander ere he die.

'"Rain, rain, and sun! a rainbow on the
    lea!
And truth is this to me, and that to thee;
And truth or clothed or naked let it be.

'"Rain, sun, and rain! and the free blossom
    blows;
Sun, rain, and sun! and where is he who
    knows?
From the great deep to the great deep he
    goes."                                          410

'So Merlin riddling anger'd me; but
    thou
Fear not to give this King thine only
    child,
Guinevere; so great bards of him will sing
Hereafter; and dark sayings from of old
Ranging and ringing thro' the minds of
    men,
And echo'd by old folk beside their fires
For comfort after their wage-work is done,
Speak of the King; and Merlin in our time
Hath spoken also, not in jest, and sworn

Tho' men may wound him that he will not
die,                                        420
But pass, again to come, and then or now
Utterly smite the heathen underfoot,
Till these and all men hail him for their
king.'

She spake and King Leodogran rejoiced,
But musing 'Shall I answer yea or nay?'
Doubted, and drowsed, nodded and slept,
and saw,
Dreaming, a slope of land that ever grew,
Field after field, up to a height, the peak
Haze-hidden, and thereon a phantom king,
Now looming, and now lost; and on the
slope                                       430
The sword rose, the hind fell, the herd was
driven,
Fire glimpsed; and all the land from roof
and rick,
In drifts of smoke before a rolling wind,
Stream'd to the peak, and mingled with
the haze
And made it thicker; while the phantom
king
Sent out at times a voice; and here or there
Stood one who pointed toward the voice,
the rest
Slew on and burnt, crying, 'No king of
ours,
No son of Uther, and no king of ours;'
Till with a wink his dream was changed,
the haze                                    440
Descended, and the solid earth became
As nothing, but the King stood out in hea-
ven,
Crown'd.   And Leodogran awoke, and sent
Ulfius, and Brastias, and Bedivere,
Back to the court of Arthur answering
yea.

Then Arthur charged his warrior whom
he loved
And honor'd most, Sir Lancelot, to ride
forth
And bring the Queen, and watch'd him
from the gates;
And Lancelot past away among the flowers —                                       449
For then was latter April — and return'd
Among the flowers, in May, with Guinevere.
To whom arrived, by Dubric the high
saint,

Chief of the church in Britain, and before
The stateliest of her altar-shrines, the
King
That morn was married, while in stainless
white,
The fair beginners of a nobler time,
And glorying in their vows and him, his
knights
Stood round him, and rejoicing in his joy.
Far shone the fields of May thro' open
door,
The sacred altar blossom'd white with
May,                                        460
The sun of May descended on their King,
They gazed on all earth's beauty in their
Queen,
Roll'd incense, and there past along the
hymns
A voice as of the waters, while the two
Sware at the shrine of Christ a deathless
love.
And Arthur said, 'Behold, thy doom is
mine.
Let chance what will, I love thee to the
death!'
To whom the Queen replied with drooping
eyes,
'King and my lord, I love thee to the
death!'
And holy Dubric spread his hands and
spake:                                      470
'Reign ye, and live and love, and make the
world
Other, and may thy Queen be one with
thee,
And all this Order of thy Table Round
Fulfil the boundless purpose of their King!'

So Dubric said; but when they left the
shrine
Great lords from Rome before the portal
stood,
In scornful stillness gazing as they past;
Then while they paced a city all on fire
With sun and cloth of gold, the trumpets
blew,
And Arthur's knighthood sang before the
King: —                                     480

'Blow trumpet, for the world is white with
May!
Blow trumpet, the long night hath roll'd away!
Blow thro' the living world — "Let the King
reign!"

'Shall Rome or Heathen rule in Arthur's
  realm?
Flash brand and lance, fall battle-axe upon
  helm,
Fall battle-axe, and flash brand! Let the
  King reign!

'Strike for the King and live! his knights
  have heard
That God hath told the King a secret word.
Fall battle-axe, and flash brand! Let the
  King reign!

'Blow trumpet! he will lift us from the
  dust.
Blow trumpet! live the strength, and die the  490
  lust!
Clang battle-axe, and clash brand! Let the
  King reign!

'Strike for the King and die! and if thou
  diest,
The King is king, and ever wills the high-
  est.
Clang battle-axe, and clash brand! Let the
  King reign!

'Blow, for our Sun is mighty in his May!
Blow, for our Sun is mightier day by day!
Clang battle-axe, and clash brand! Let the
  King reign!

'The King will follow Christ, and we the
  King,
In whom high God hath breathed a secret
  thing.  500

Fall battle-axe, and clash brand! Let the
  King reign!'

So sang the knighthood, moving to their
  hall.
There at the banquet those great lords from
  Rome,
The slowly-fading mistress of the world,
Strode in and claim'd their tribute as of
  yore.
But Arthur spake: 'Behold, for these have
  sworn
To wage my wars, and worship me their
  King;
The old order changeth, yielding place to
  new,
And we that fight for our fair father
  Christ,  509
Seeing that ye be grown too weak and old
To drive the heathen from your Roman wall,
No tribute will we pay.' So those great
  lords
Drew back in wrath, and Arthur strove
  with Rome.

And Arthur and his knighthood for a
  space
Were all one will, and thro' that strength
  the King
Drew in the petty princedoms under him,
Fought, and in twelve great battles overcame
The heathen hordes, and made a realm and
  reign'd.

## THE ROUND TABLE

## GARETH AND LYNETTE

THE last tall son of Lot and Bellicent,
And tallest, Gareth, in a showerful spring
Stared at the spate. A slender-shafted
  pine
Lost footing, fell, and so was whirl'd away.
'How he went down,' said Gareth, 'as a
  false knight
Or evil king before my lance, if lance

Were mine to use — O senseless cataract,
Bearing all down in thy precipitancy —
And yet thou art but swollen with cold
  snows
And mine is living blood. Thou dost His
  will,  10
The Maker's, and not knowest, and I that
  know,
Have strength and wit, in my good mother's
  hall

Linger with vacillating obedience,
Prison'd, and kept and coax'd and whistled
    to —
Since the good mother holds me still a
    child !
Good mother is bad mother unto me !
A worse were better; yet no worse would I.
Heaven yield her for it, but in me put force
To weary her ears with one continuous
    prayer,
Until she let me fly discaged to sweep     20
In ever-highering eagle-circles up
To the great Sun of Glory, and thence
    swoop
Down upon all things base, and dash them
    dead,
A knight of Arthur, working out his will,
To cleanse the world.  Why, Gawain, when
    he came
With Modred hither in the summer-time,
Ask'd me to tilt with him, the proven
    knight.
Modred for want of worthier was the judge.
Then I so shook him in the saddle, he said,
" Thou hast half prevail'd against me," said
    so — he —                               30
Tho' Modred biting his thin lips was mute,
For he is alway sullen — what care I ? '

    And Gareth went, and hovering round
        her chair
Ask'd, ' Mother, tho' ye count me still the
    child,
Sweet mother, do ye love the child ? '  She
    laugh'd,
' Thou art but a wild-goose to question it.'
' Then, mother, an ye love the child,' he
    said,
' Being a goose and rather tame than wild,
Hear the child's story.'  ' Yea, my well-
    beloved,
An 't were but of the goose and golden
    eggs.'                                    40

    And Gareth answer'd her with kindling
        eyes:
' Nay, nay, good mother, but this egg of
    mine
Was finer gold than any goose can lay;
For this an eagle, a royal eagle, laid
Almost beyond eye-reach, on such a palm
As glitters gilded in thy Book of Hours.
And there was ever haunting round the
    palm
A lusty youth, but poor, who often saw

The splendor sparkling from aloft, and
    thought,
" An I could climb and lay my hand upon
    it,                                       50
Then were I wealthier than a leash of
    kings."
But ever when he reach'd a hand to climb,
One that had loved him from his childhood
    caught
And stay'd him, " Climb not lest thou break
    thy neck,
I charge thee by my love," and so the boy,
Sweet mother, neither clomb nor brake his
    neck,
But brake his very heart in pining for it,
And past away.'

                        To whom the mother said,
' True love, sweet son, had risk'd himself
    and climb'd,
And handed down the golden treasure to
    him.'                                     60

    And Gareth answer'd her with kindling
        eyes:
' Gold ? said I gold ? — ay then, why he, or
    she,
Or whosoe'er it was, or half the world
Had ventured — had the thing I spake of
    been
Mere gold — but this was all of that true
    steel
Whereof they forged the brand Excalibur,
And lightnings play'd about it in the storm,
And all the little fowl were flurried at it,
And there were cries and clashings in the
    nest,
That sent him from his senses.  Let me
    go.'                                      70

    Then Bellicent bemoan'd herself and
        said:
' Hast thou no pity upon my loneliness ?
Lo, where thy father Lot beside the hearth
Lies like a log, and all but smoulder'd out!
For ever since when traitor to the King
He fought against him in the barons' war,
And Arthur gave him back his territory,
His age hath slowly droopt, and now lies
    there
A yet-warm corpse, and yet unburiable,
No more; nor sees, nor hears, nor speaks,
    nor knows.                               80
And both thy brethren are in Arthur's hall,
Albeit neither loved with that full love

I feel for thee, nor worthy such a love.
Stay therefore thou; red berries charm the
    bird,
And thee, mine innocent, the jousts, the
    wars,
Who never knewest finger-ache, nor pang
Of wrench'd or broken limb — an often
    chance
In those brain-stunning shocks, and tour-
    ney-falls,
Frights to my heart.    But stay; follow the
    deer                                    89
By these tall firs and our fast-falling burns;
So make thy manhood mightier day by
    day.
Sweet is the chase; and I will seek thee out
Some comfortable bride and fair, to grace
Thy climbing life, and cherish my prone
    year,
Till falling into Lot's forgetfulness
I know not thee, myself, nor anything.
Stay, my best son! ye are yet more boy
    than man.'

   Then Gareth: 'An ye hold me yet for
    child,
Hear yet once more the story of the child.
For, mother, there was once a king, like
    ours.                                   100
The prince his heir, when tall and mar-
    riageable,
Ask'd for a bride; and thereupon the king
Set two before him.    One was fair, strong,
    arm'd —
But to be won by force — and many men
Desired her; one, good lack, no man de-
    sired.
And these were the conditions of the king:
That save he won the first by force, he
    needs
Must wed that other, whom no man de-
    sired,
A red-faced bride who knew herself so
    vile                                     109
That evermore she long'd to hide herself,
Nor fronted man or woman, eye to eye —
Yea — some she cleaved to, but they died
    of her.
And one — they call'd her Fame; and one
    — O mother,'
How can ye keep me tether'd to you ? —
    Shame.
Man am I grown, a man's work must I do.
Follow the deer ? follow the Christ, the
    King,

Live pure, speak true, right wrong, follow
    the King —
Else, wherefore born ? '

                    To whom the mother said:
' Sweet son, for there be many who deem
    him not,
Or will not deem him, wholly proven
    king —                                  120
Albeit in mine own heart I knew him King
When I was frequent with him in my youth,
And heard him kingly speak, and doubted
    him
No more than he, himself; but felt him
    mine,
Of closest kin to me.    Yet — wilt thou leave
Thine easeful biding here, and risk thine
    all,
Life, limbs, for one that is not proven king ?
Stay, till the cloud that settles round his
    birth
Hath lifted but a little.    Stay, sweet son.'

   And Gareth answer'd quickly: ' Not an
    hour,                                   130
So that ye yield me — I will walk thro'
    fire,
Mother, to gain it — your full leave to go.
Not proven, who swept the dust of ruin'd
    Rome
From off the threshold of the realm, and
    crush'd
The idolaters, and made the people free ?
Who should be king save him who makes
    us free ? '

   So when the Queen, who long had sought
    in vain
To break him from the intent to which he
    grew,
Found her son's will unwaveringly one,
She answer'd craftily: ' Will ye walk thro'
    fire ?                                  140
Who walks thro' fire will hardly heed the
    smoke.
Ay, go then, an ye must; only one proof,
Before thou ask the King to make thee
    knight,
Of thine obedience and thy love to me,
Thy mother, — I demand.'

                    And Gareth cried:
' A hard one, or a hundred, so I go.
Nay — quick ! the proof to prove me to the
    quick ! '

But slowly spake the mother looking at
        him:
'Prince, thou shalt go disguised to Arthur's
        hall,
And hire thyself to serve for meats and
        drinks                                    150
Among the scullions and the kitchen-
        knaves,
And those that hand the dish across the
        bar.
Nor shalt thou tell thy name to any one.
And thou shalt serve a twelvemonth and a
        day.'

For so the Queen believed that when her
        son
Beheld his only way to glory lead
Low down thro' villain kitchen-vassalage,
Her own true Gareth was too princely-
        proud
To pass thereby; so should he rest with her,
Closed in her castle from the sound of
        arms.                                     160

Silent awhile was Gareth, then replied:
'The thrall in person may be free in soul,
And I shall see the jousts.  Thy son am I,
And, since thou art my mother, must obey.
I therefore yield me freely to thy will;
For hence will I, disguised, and hire myself
To serve with scullions and with kitchen-
        knaves;
Nor tell my name to any — no, not the
        King.'

Gareth awhile linger'd.  The mother's
        eye
Full of the wistful fear that he would go,
And turning toward him wheresoe'er he
        turn'd,                                   171
Perplext his outward purpose, till an hour
When, waken'd by the wind which with
        full voice
Swept bellowing thro' the darkness on to
        dawn,
He rose, and out of slumber calling two
That still had tended on him from his
        birth,
Before the wakeful mother heard him,
        went.

The three were clad like tillers of the
        soil.
Southward they set their faces.  The birds
        made

Melody on branch and melody in mid air.
The damp hill-slopes were quicken'd into
        green,                                    181
And the live green had kindled into flow-
        ers,
For it was past the time of Easter-day.

So, when their feet were planted on the
        plain
That broaden'd toward the base of Came-
        lot,
Far off they saw the silver-misty morn
Rolling her smoke about the royal mount,
That rose between the forest and the field.
At times the summit of the high city
        flash'd;
At times the spires and turrets half-way
        down                                      190
Prick'd thro' the mist; at times the great
        gate shone
Only, that open'd on the field below;
Anon, the whole fair city had disappear'd.

Then those who went with Gareth were
        amazed,
One crying, ' Let us go no further, lord;
Here is a city of enchanters, built
By fairy kings.'  The second echo'd him,
' Lord, we have heard from our wise man
        at home
To northward, that this king is not the
        King,
But only changeling out of Fairyland,    200
Who drave the heathen hence by sorcery
And Merlin's glamour.'  Then the first
        again,
' Lord, there is no such city anywhere,
But all a vision.'

                Gareth answer'd them
With laughter, swearing he had glamour
        enow
In his own blood, his princedom, youth,
        and hopes,
To plunge old Merlin in the Arabian sea;
So push'd them all unwilling toward the
        gate.
And there was no gate like it under
        heaven.
For barefoot on the keystone, which was
        lined                                     210
And rippled like an ever-fleeting wave,
The Lady of the Lake stood; all her dress
Wept from her sides as water flowing
        away;

But like the cross her great and goodly
    arms
Stretch'd under all the cornice and up-
    held.
And drops of water fell from either hand;
And down from one a sword was hung,
    from one
A censer, either worn with wind and storm;
And o'er her breast floated the sacred
    fish;
And in the space to left of her, and
    right, 220
Were Arthur's wars in weird devices done,
New things and old co-twisted, as if Time
Were nothing, so inveterately that men
Were giddy gazing there; and over all
High on the top were those three queens,
    the friends
Of Arthur, who should help him at his
    need.

Then those with Gareth for so long a
    space
Stared at the figures that at last it seem'd
The dragon-boughts and elvish emblem-
    ings
Began to move, seethe, twine, and curl.
    They call'd 230
To Gareth, 'Lord, the gateway is alive.'

And Gareth likewise on them fixt his
    eyes
So long that even to him they seem'd to
    move.
Out of the city a blast of music peal'd.
Back from the gate started the three, to
    whom
From out thereunder came an ancient man,
Long-bearded, saying, 'Who be ye, my
    sons?'

Then Gareth: 'We be tillers of the soil,
Who leaving share in furrow come to
    see
The glories of our King; but these, my
    men,— 240
Your city moved so weirdly in the mist—
Doubt if the King be king at all, or come
From Fairyland; and whether this be built
By magic, and by fairy kings and queens;
Or whether there be any city at all,
Or all a vision; and this music now
Hath scared them both, but tell thou these
    the truth.'

Then that old Seer made answer, playing
    on him
And saying: 'Son, I have seen the good
    ship sail
Keel upward, and mast downward, in the
    heavens, 250
And solid turrets topsy-turvy in air;
And here is truth, but an it please thee
    not,
Take thou the truth as thou hast told it me.
For truly, as thou sayest, a fairy king
And fairy queens have built the city, son;
They came from out a sacred mountain-
    cleft
Toward the sunrise, each with harp in
    hand,
And built it to the music of their harps.
And, as thou sayest, it is enchanted, son,
For there is nothing in it as it seems 260
Saving the King; tho' some there be that
    hold
The King a shadow, and the city real.
Yet take thou heed of him, for, so thou
    pass
Beneath this archway, then wilt thou be-
    come
A thrall to his enchantments, for the King
Will bind thee by such vows as is a shame
A man should not be bound by, yet the
    which
No man can keep; but, so thou dread to
    swear,
Pass not beneath this gateway, but abide
Without, among the cattle of the field. 270
For an ye heard a music, like enow
They are building still, seeing the city is
    built
To music, therefore never built at all,
And therefore built for ever.'

                  Gareth spake
Anger'd: 'Old master, reverence thine own
    beard
That looks as white as utter truth, and
    seems
Wellnigh as long as thou art statured tall!
Why mockest thou the stranger that hath
    been
To thee fair-spoken?'

             But the Seer replied:
'Know ye not then the Riddling of the
    Bards: 280
"Confusion, and illusion, and relation,

Elusion, and occasion, and evasion " ?
I mock thee not but as thou mockest me,
And all that see thee, for thou art not who
Thou seemest, but I know thee who thou
    art.
And now thou goest up to mock the King,
Who cannot brook the shadow of any lie.'

Unmockingly the mocker ending here
Turn'd to the right, and past along the
    plain;
Whom Gareth looking after said: ' My
    men,          290
Our one white lie sits like a little ghost
Here on the threshold of our enterprise.
Let love be blamed for it, not she, nor I.
Well, we will make amends.'

             With all good cheer
He spake and laugh'd, then enter'd with his
    twain
Camelot, a city of shadowy palaces
And stately, rich in emblem and the work
Of ancient kings who did their days in
    stone;
Which Merlin's hand, the Mage at Arthur's
    court,
Knowing all arts, had touch'd, and every-
    where,         300
At Arthur's ordinance, tipt with lessening
    peak
And pinnacle, and had made it spire to
    heaven.
And ever and anon a knight would pass
Outward, or inward to the hall; his arms
Clash'd, and the sound was good to Gar-
    eth's ear.
And out of bower and casement shyly
    glanced
Eyes of pure women, wholesome stars of
    love;
And all about a healthful people stept
As in the presence of a gracious king.

Then into hall Gareth ascending heard
A voice, the voice of Arthur, and beheld  311
Far over heads in that long-vaulted hall
The splendor of the presence of the King
Throned, and delivering doom — and
    look'd no more —
But felt his young heart hammering in his
    ears,
And thought, ' For this half-shadow of a lie
The truthful King will doom me when I
    speak.'

Yet pressing on, tho' all in fear to find
Sir Gawain or Sir Modred, saw nor one
Nor other, but in all the listening eyes  320
Of those tall knights that ranged about
    the throne
Clear honor shining like the dewy star
Of dawn, and faith in their great King,
    with pure
Affection, and the light of victory,
And glory gain'd, and evermore to gain.

Then came a widow crying to the King:
' A boon, Sir King ! Thy father, Uther,
    reft
From my dead lord a field with violence;
For howsoe'er at first he proffer'd gold,  329
Yet, for the field was pleasant in our eyes,
We yielded not; and then he reft us of it
Perforce and left us neither gold nor field.'

    Said Arthur, ' Whether would ye ? gold
    or field ?'
To whom the woman weeping, ' Nay, my
    lord,
The field was pleasant in my husband's
    eye.'

    And Arthur: ' Have thy pleasant field
    again,
And thrice the gold for Uther's use thereof,
According to the years. No boon is here,
But justice, so thy say be proven true.
Accursed, who from the wrongs his father
    did       340
Would shape himself a right !'

             And while she past,
Came yet another widow crying to him:
' A boon, Sir King ! Thine enemy, King,
    am I.
With thine own hand thou slewest my dear
    lord,
A knight of Uther in the barons' war,
When Lot and many another rose and
    fought
Against thee, saying thou wert basely born.
I held with these, and loathe to ask thee
    aught.
Yet lo ! my husband's brother had my son
Thrall'd in his castle, and hath starved him
    dead,       350
And standeth seized of that inheritance
Which thou that slewest the sire hast left
    the son.
So, tho' I scarce can ask it thee for hate,

Grant me some knight to do the battle for
me,
Kill the foul thief, and wreak me for my
son.'

Then strode a good knight forward, crying to him,
' A boon, Sir King ! I am her kinsman, I.
Give me to right her wrong, and slay the
man.'

Then came Sir Kay, the seneschal, and
cried,
' A boon, Sir King ! even that thou grant
her none,                                              360
This railer, that hath mock'd thee in full
hall —
None; or the wholesome boon of gyve and
gag.'

But Arthur: ' We sit King, to help the
wrong'd
Thro' all our realm. The woman loves her
lord.
Peace to thee, woman, with thy loves and
hates !
The kings of old had doom'd thee to the
flames;
Aurelius Emrys would have scourged thee
dead,
And Uther slit thy tongue; but get thee
hence —                                              368
Lest that rough humor of the kings of old
Return upon me ! Thou that art her kin,
Go likewise; lay him low and slay him not,
But bring him here, that I may judge the
right,
According to the justice of the King.
Then, be he guilty, by that deathless King
Who lived and died for men, the man shall
die.'

Then came in hall the messenger of
Mark,
A name of evil savor in the land,
The Cornish king. In either hand he bore
What dazzled all, and shone far - off as
shines
A field of charlock in the sudden sun      380
Between two showers, a cloth of palest gold,
Which down he laid before the throne, and
knelt,
Delivering that his lord, the vassal king,
Was even upon his way to Camelot;
For having heard that Arthur of his grace

Had made his goodly cousin Tristram
knight,
And, for himself was of the greater state,
Being a king, he trusted his liege-lord
Would yield him this large honor all the
more;
So pray'd him well to accept this cloth of
gold,                                              390
In token of true heart and fealty.

Then Arthur cried to rend the cloth, to
rend
In pieces, and so cast it on the hearth.
An oak - tree smoulder'd there. ' The
goodly knight !
What ! shall the shield of Mark stand
among these ? '
For, midway down the side of that long
hall,
A stately pile, — whereof along the front,
Some blazon'd, some but carven, and some
blank,
There ran a treble range of stony shields, —
Rose, and high-arching overbrow'd the
hearth.                                              400
And under every shield a knight was
named.
For this was Arthur's custom in his hall:
When some good knight had done one
noble deed,
His arms were carven only; but if twain,
His arms were blazon'd also; but if none,
The shield was blank and bare, without a
sign
Saving the name beneath. And Gareth saw
The shield of Gawain blazon'd rich and
bright,
And Modred's blank as death; and Arthur
cried                                              409
To rend the cloth and cast it on the hearth.

' More like are we to reave him of his
crown
Than make him knight because men call
him king.
The kings we found, ye know we stay'd
their hands
From war among themselves, but left them
kings;
Of whom were any bounteous, merciful,
Truth-speaking, brave, good livers, them
we enroll'd
Among us, and they sit within our hall.
But Mark hath tarnish'd the great name of
king,

As Mark would sully the low state of churl;
And, seeing he hath sent us cloth of gold,
Return, and meet, and hold him from our
      eyes,                                        421
Lest we should lap him up in cloth of
      lead,
Silenced for ever — craven — a man of
      plots,
Craft, poisonous counsels, wayside ambush-
      ings —
No fault of thine; let Kay the seneschal
Look to thy wants, and send thee satis-
      fied —
Accursed, who strikes nor lets the hand be
      seen ! '

And many another suppliant crying came
With noise of ravage wrought by beast and
      man,                                         429
And evermore a knight would ride away.

Last, Gareth leaning both hands heavily
Down on the shoulders of the twain, his
      men,
Approach'd between them toward the King,
      and ask'd,
' A boon, Sir King,' — his voice was all
      ashamed, —
' For see ye not how weak and hunger-
      worn
I seem — leaning on these ? grant me to
      serve
For meat and drink among thy kitchen-
      knaves
A twelvemonth and a day, nor seek my
      name.
Hereafter I will fight.'

                        To him the King:
' A goodly youth and worth a goodlier
      boon !                                       440
But so thou wilt no goodlier, then must
      Kay,
The master of the meats and drinks, be
      thine.'

He rose and past; then Kay, a man of
      mien
Wan-sallow as the plant that feels itself
Root-bitten by white lichen:

                              ' Lo ye now !
This fellow hath broken from some abbey,
      where,
God wot, he had not beef and brewis enow,

However that might chance ! but an he
      work,
Like any pigeon will I cram his crop,      449
And sleeker shall he shine than any hog.'

Then Lancelot standing near: ' Sir Senes-
      chal,
Sleuth-hound thou knowest, and gray, and
      all the hounds;
A horse thou knowest, a man thou dost not
      know.
Broad brows and fair, a fluent hair and
      fine,
High nose, a nostril large and fine, and
      hands
Large, fair, and fine ! — Some young lad's
      mystery —
But, or from sheepcot or king's hall, the
      boy
Is noble-natured.  Treat him with all grace,
Lest he should come to shame thy judging
      of him.'

Then Kay: ' What murmurest thou of
      mystery ?                                    460
Think ye this fellow will poison the King's
      dish ?
Nay, for he spake too fool-like — mystery !
Tut, an the lad were noble, he had ask'd
For horse and armor.  Fair and fine, for-
      sooth !
Sir Fine-face, Sir Fair-hands ? but see thou
      to it
That thine own fineness, Lancelot, some
      fine day
Undo thee not — and leave my man to
      me.'

So Gareth all for glory underwent
The sooty yoke of kitchen-vassalage,
Ate with young lads his portion by the
      door,                                        470
And couch'd at night with grimy kitchen-
      knaves.
And Lancelot ever spake him pleasantly,
But Kay the seneschal, who loved him not,
Would hustle and harry him, and labor
      him
Beyond his comrade of the hearth, and set
To turn the broach, draw water, or hew
      wood,
Or grosser tasks; and Gareth bow'd him-
      self
With all obedience to the King, and
      wrought

All kind of service with a noble ease
That graced the lowliest act in doing it. 480
And when the thralls had talk among
    themselves,
And one would praise the love that linkt
    the King
And Lancelot — how the King had saved
    his life
In battle twice, and Lancelot once the
    King's —
For Lancelot was first in the tournament,
But Arthur mightiest on the battle-field —
Gareth was glad.  Or if some other told
How once the wandering forester at dawn,
Far over the blue tarns and hazy seas, 489
On Caer-Eryri's highest found the King,
A naked babe, of whom the Prophet spake,
' He passes to the Isle Avilion,
He passes and is heal'd and cannot die ' —
Gareth was glad.  But if their talk were
    foul,
Then would he whistle rapid as any lark,
Or carol some old roundelay, and so loud
That first they mock'd, but, after, rever-
    enced him.
Or Gareth, telling some prodigious tale
Of knights who sliced a red life-bubbling
    way 499
Thro' twenty folds of twisted dragon, held
All in a gap-mouth'd circle his good mates
Lying or sitting round him, idle hands,
Charm'd; till Sir Kay, the seneschal, would
    come
Blustering upon them, like a sudden wind
Among dead leaves, and drive them all
    apart.
Or when the thralls had sport among them-
    selves,
So there were any trial of mastery,
He, by two yards in casting bar or stone,
Was counted best; and if there chanced a
    joust, 509
So that Sir Kay nodded him leave to go,
Would hurry thither, and when he saw the
    knights
Clash like the coming and retiring wave,
And the spear spring, and good horse reel,
    the boy
Was half beyond himself for ecstasy.

  So for a month he wrought among the
    thralls;
But in the weeks that follow'd, the good
    Queen,

Repentant of the word she made him
    swear,
And saddening in her childless castle, sent,
Between the in-crescent and de-crescent
    moon,
Arms for her son, and loosed him from his
    vow. 520

  This, Gareth hearing from a squire of
    Lot
With whom he used to play at tourney
    once,
When both were children, and in lonely
    haunts
Would scratch a ragged oval on the sand,
And each at either dash from either end —
Shame never made girl redder than Gareth
    joy.
He laugh'd, he sprang.  ' Out of the smoke,
    at once
I leap from Satan's foot to Peter's knee —
These news be mine, none other's — nay,
    the King's —
Descend into the city; ' whereon he sought
The King alone, and found, and told him
    all. 531

  ' I have stagger'd thy strong Gawain in
    a tilt
For pastime; yea, he said it; joust can I.
Make me thy knight — in secret ! let my
    name
Be hidden, and give me the first quest, I
    spring
Like flame from ashes.'

                    Here the King's calm eye
Fell on, and check'd, and made him flush,
    and bow
Lowly, to kiss his hand, who answer'd him:
' Son, the good mother let me know thee
    here,
And sent her wish that I would yield thee
    thine. 540
Make thee my knight ? my knights are
    sworn to vows
Of utter hardihood, utter gentleness,
And, loving, utter faithfulness in love,
And uttermost obedience to the King.'

  Then Gareth, lightly springing from his
    knees:
' My King, for hardihood I can promise
    thee.
For uttermost obedience make demand

Of whom ye gave me to, the Seneschal,
No mellow master of the meats and drinks !
And as for love, God wot, I love not yet,
But love I shall, God willing.'

                         And the King:
' Make thee my knight in secret ? yea, but
      he,                                    552
Our noblest brother, and our truest man,
And one with me in all, he needs must
      know.'

   ' Let Lancelot know, my King, let Lance-
      lot know,
Thy noblest and thy truest ! '

                         And the King:
' But wherefore would ye men should won-
      der at you ?
Nay, rather for the sake of me, their King,
And the deed's sake my knighthood do the
      deed,                                  559
Than to be noised of.'

                    Merrily Gareth ask'd:
' Have I not earn'd my cake in baking of it ?
Let be my name until I make my name !
My deeds will speak; it is but for a day.'
So with a kindly hand on Gareth's arm
Smiled the great King, and half-unwill-
      ingly
Loving his lusty youthhood yielded to him.
Then, after summoning Lancelot privily:
' I have given him the first quest; he is not
      proven.
Look therefore, when he calls for this in
      hall,
Thou get to horse and follow him far
      away.                                  570
Cover the lions on thy shield, and see,
Far as thou mayest, he be nor ta'en nor
      slain.'

   Then that same day there past into the
      hall
A damsel of high lineage, and a brow
May-blossom, and a cheek of apple-blossom,
Hawk-eyes; and lightly was her slender
      nose
Tip-tilted like the petal of a flower.
She into hall past with her page and cried:

   ' O King, for thou hast driven the foe
      without,                               579
See to the foe within ! bridge, ford, beset

By bandits, every one that owns a tower
The lord for half a league.  Why sit ye
      there ?
Rest would I not, Sir King, an I were
      king,
Till even the lonest hold were all as free
From cursed bloodshed as thine altar-cloth
From that best blood it is a sin to spill.'

   ' Comfort thyself,' said Arthur, ' I nor
      mine
Rest; so my knighthood keep the vows
      they swore,
The wastest moorland of our realm shall
      be
Safe, damsel, as the centre of this hall.  590
What is thy name ? thy need ? '

                    ' My name ? ' she said —
' Lynette, my name; noble; my need, a
      knight
To combat for my sister, Lyonors,
A lady of high lineage, of great lands,
And comely, yea, and comelier than my-
      self.
She lives in Castle Perilous.  A river
Runs in three loops about her living-place;
And o'er it are three passings, and three
      knights
Defend the passings, brethren, and a fourth,
And of that four the mightiest, holds her
      stay'd                                 600
In her own castle, and so besieges her
To break her will, and make her wed with
      him;
And but delays his purport till thou send
To do the battle with him thy chief man
Sir Lancelot, whom he trusts to overthrow,
Then wed, with glory; but she will not
      wed
Save whom she loveth, or a holy life.
Now therefore have I come for Lancelot.'

   Then Arthur mindful of Sir Gareth
      ask'd:                                 609
' Damsel, ye know this Order lives to crush
All wrongers of the realm.  But say, these
      four,
Who be they ?  What the fashion of the
      men ? '

   ' They be of foolish fashion, O Sir King,
The fashion of that old knight-errantry
Who ride abroad, and do but what they
      will;

Courteous or bestial from the moment,
    such
As have nor law nor king; and three of
    these
Proud in their fantasy call themselves the
    Day,
Morning-Star, and Noon-Sun, and Evening-
    Star,
Being strong fools; and never a whit more
    wise                                        620
The fourth, who alway rideth arm'd in
    black,
A huge man-beast of boundless savagery.
He names himself the Night and oftener
    Death,
And wears a helmet mounted with a skull,
And bears a skeleton figured on his arms,
To show that who may slay or scape the
    three,
Slain by himself, shall enter endless night.
And all these four be fools, but mighty
    men,
And therefore am I come for Lancelot.'

Hereat Sir Gareth call'd from where he
    rose,                                       630
A head with kindling eyes above the
    throng,
'A boon, Sir King — this quest!' then —
    for he mark'd
Kay near him groaning like a wounded
    bull —
'Yea, King, thou knowest thy kitchen-
    knave am I,
And mighty thro' thy meats and drinks
    am I,
And I can topple over a hundred such.
Thy promise, King,' and Arthur glancing
    at him,
Brought down a momentary brow. 'Rough,
    sudden,
And pardonable, worthy to be knight — 639
Go therefore,' and all hearers were amazed.

But on the damsel's forehead shame,
    pride, wrath
Slew the may - white. She lifted either
    arm,
'Fie on thee, King! I ask'd for thy chief
    knight,
And thou hast given me but a kitchen-
    knave.'
Then ere a man in hall could stay her,
    turn'd,

Fled down the lane of access to the King,
Took horse, descended the slope street, and
    past
The weird white gate, and paused without,
    beside
The field of tourney, murmuring 'kitchen-
    knave!'

Now two great entries open'd from the
    hall,                                       650
At one end one that gave upon a range
Of level pavement where the King would
    pace
At sunrise, gazing over plain and wood;
And down from this a lordly stairway
    sloped
Till lost in blowing trees and tops of
    towers;
And out by this main doorway past the
    King.
But one was counter to the hearth, and
    rose
High that the highest-crested helm could
    ride
Therethro' nor graze; and by this entry
    fled
The damsel in her wrath, and on to this   660
Sir Gareth strode, and saw without the door
King Arthur's gift, the worth of half a
    town,
A war-horse of the best, and near it stood
The two that out of north had follow'd
    him.
This bare a maiden shield, a casque; that
    held
The horse, the spear; whereat Sir Gareth
    loosed
A cloak that dropt from collar-bone to
    heel,
A cloth of roughest web, and cast it down,
And from it, like a fuel-smother'd fire
That lookt half-dead, brake bright, and
    flash'd as those                           670
Dull-coated things, that making slide apart
Their dusk wing-cases, all beneath there
    burns
A jewell'd harness, ere they pass and fly.
So Gareth ere he parted flash'd in arms.
Then as he donn'd the helm, and took the
    shield
And mounted horse and graspt a spear, of
    grain
Storm-strengthen'd on a windy site, and
    tipt

With trenchant steel, around him slowly
    prest
The people, while from out of kitchen
    came
The thralls in throng, and seeing who had
    work'd                                        680
Lustier than any, and whom they could but
    love,
Mounted in arms, threw up their caps and
    cried,
'God bless the King, and all his fellow-
    ship!'
And on thro' lanes of shouting Gareth rode
Down the slope street, and past without the
    gate.

So Gareth past with joy; but as the cur
Pluckt from the cur he fights with, ere his
    cause
Be cool'd by fighting, follows, being
    named,                                        688
His owner, but remembers all, and growls
Remembering, so Sir Kay beside the door
Mutter'd in scorn of Gareth whom he used
To harry and hustle.

                        'Bound upon a quest
With horse and arms — the King hath past
    his time —
My scullion knave! Thralls, to your work
    again,
For an your fire be low ye kindle mine!
Will there be dawn in West and eve in
    East?
Begone! — my knave! — belike and like
    enow
Some old head-blow not heeded in his
    youth
So shook his wits they wander in his
    prime —
Crazed! How the villain lifted up his
    voice,                                         700
Nor shamed to bawl himself a kitchen-
    knave!
Tut, he was tame and meek enow with me,
Till peacock'd up with Lancelot's noticing.
Well — I will after my loud knave, and
    learn
Whether he know me for his master yet.
Out of the smoke he came, and so my
    lance
Hold, by God's grace, he shall into the
    mire —
Thence, if the King awaken from his craze,
Into the smoke again.'

                        But Lancelot said:
'Kay, wherefore wilt thou go against the
    King,                                         710
For that did never he whereon ye rail,
But ever meekly served the King in thee?
Abide; take counsel, for this lad is great
And lusty, and knowing both of lance and
    sword.'
'Tut, tell not me,' said Kay, 'ye are over-
    fine
To mar stout knaves with foolish courte-
    sies;'
Then mounted, on thro' silent faces rode
Down the slope city, and out beyond the
    gate.

But by the field of tourney lingering yet
Mutter'd the damsel: 'Wherefore did the
    King                                          720
Scorn me? for, were Sir Lancelot lackt, at
    least
He might have yielded to me one of those
Who tilt for lady's love and glory here,
Rather than — O sweet heaven! O, fie
    upon him! —
His kitchen-knave.'

                        To whom Sir Gareth drew —
And there were none but few goodlier
    than he —
Shining in arms, 'Damsel, the quest is
    mine.
Lead, and I follow.' She thereat, as one
That smells a foul-flesh'd agaric in the
    holt,
And deems it carrion of some woodland
    thing,                                        730
Or shrew or weasel, nipt her slender nose
With petulant thumb and finger, shrilling,
    'Hence!
Avoid, thou smellest all of kitchen-grease.
And look who comes behind;' for there
    was Kay.
'Knowest thou not me? thy master? I
    am Kay.
We lack thee by the hearth.'

                        And Gareth to him,
'Master no more! too well I know thee,
    ay —
The most ungentle knight in Arthur's hall.'
'Have at thee then,' said Kay; they shock'd,
    and Kay                                       739
Fell shoulder-slipt, and Gareth cried again,
'Lead, and I follow,' and fast away she fled.

But after sod and shingle ceased to fly
Behind her, and the heart of her good
    horse
Was nigh to burst with violence of the
    beat,
Perforce she stay'd, and overtaken spoke:

'What doest thou, scullion, in my fellow-
    ship?
Deem'st thou that I accept thee aught the
    more
Or love thee better, that by some device
Full cowardly, or by mere unhappiness,
Thou hast overthrown and slain thy master
    — thou! —                              750
Dish-washer and broach-turner, loon! — to
    me
Thou smellest all of kitchen as before.'

'Damsel,' Sir Gareth answer'd gently,
    'say
Whate'er ye will, but whatsoe'er ye say,
I leave not till I finish this fair quest,
Or die therefore.'

                'Ay, wilt thou finish it?
Sweet lord, how like a noble knight he
    talks!
The listening rogue hath caught the man-
    ner of it.
But, knave, anon thou shalt be met with,
    knave,
And then by such a one that thou for all
The kitchen brewis that was ever supt   761
Shalt not once dare to look him in the face.'

'I shall assay,' said Gareth with a smile
That madden'd her, and away she flash'd
    again
Down the long avenues of a boundless
    wood;
And Gareth following was again beknaved:

'Sir Kitchen-knave, I have miss'd the
    only way
Where Arthur's men are set along the
    wood;
The wood is nigh as full of thieves as
    leaves.                               769
If both be slain, I am rid of thee; but
    yet,
Sir Scullion, canst thou use that spit of
    thine?
Fight, an thou canst; I have miss'd the only
    way.'

So till the dusk that follow'd evensong
Rode on the two, reviler and reviled;
Then after one long slope was mounted,
    saw,
Bowl-shaped, thro' tops of many thousand
    pines
A gloomy-gladed hollow slowly sink
To westward — in the deeps whereof a
    mere,
Round as the red eye of an eagle-owl,
Under the half-dead sunset glared; and
    shouts                               780
Ascended, and there brake a servingman
Flying from out of the black wood, and
    crying,
'They have bound my lord to cast him in
    the mere.'
Then Gareth, 'Bound am I to right the
    wrong'd,
But straitlier bound am I to bide with
    thee.'
And when the damsel spake contemptu-
    ously,
'Lead, and I follow,' Gareth cried again,
'Follow, I lead!' so down among the
    pines
He plunged; and there, black-shadow'd
    nigh the mere,                       789
And mid-thigh-deep in bulrushes and reed,
Saw six tall men haling a seventh along,
A stone about his neck to drown him in it.
Three with good blows he quieted, but
    three
Fled thro' the pines; and Gareth loosed the
    stone
From off his neck, then in the mere beside
Tumbled it; oilily bubbled up the mere.
Last, Gareth loosed his bonds and on free
    feet
Set him, a stalwart baron, Arthur's friend.

'Well that ye came, or else these caitiff
    rogues
Had wreak'd themselves on me; good cause
    is theirs                           800
To hate me, for my wont hath ever been
To catch my thief, and then like vermin
    here
Drown him, and with a stone about his
    neck;
And under this wan water many of them
Lie rotting, but at night let go the stone,
And rise, and flickering in a grimly light
Dance on the mere. Good now, ye have
    saved a life

Worth somewhat as the cleanser of this
    wood.
And fain would I reward thee worshipfully.
What guerdon will ye ?'

                 Gareth sharply spake:
'None ! for the deed's sake have I done the
    deed,                     811
In uttermost obedience to the King.
But wilt thou yield this damsel harbor-
    age ?'

   Whereat the baron saying, 'I well be-
    lieve
You be of Arthur's Table,' a light laugh
Broke from Lynette: 'Ay, truly of a truth,
And in a sort, being Arthur's kitchen-
    knave ! —
But deem not I accept thee aught the more,
Scullion, for running sharply with thy spit
Down on a rout of craven foresters.    820
A thresher with his flail had scatter'd them.
Nay — for thou smellest of the kitchen
    still.
But an this lord will yield us harborage;
Well.'

   So she spake.   A league beyond the
    wood,
All in a full-fair manor and a rich,
His towers, where that day a feast had
    been
Held in high hall, and many a viand left,
And many a costly cate, received the three.
And there they placed a peacock in his
    pride
Before the damsel, and the baron set   830
Gareth beside her, but at once she rose.

   'Meseems, that here is much discourtesy,
Setting this knave, Lord Baron, at my side.
Hear me — this morn I stood in Arthur's
    hall,
And pray'd the King would grant me
    Lancelot
To fight the brotherhood of Day and
    Night —
The last a monster unsubduable
Of any save of him for whom I call'd —
Suddenly bawls this frontless kitchen-
    knave,
"The quest is mine; thy kitchen-knave
    am I,                840
And mighty thro' thy meats and drinks
    am I."

Then Arthur all at once gone mad replies,
"Go therefore," and so gives the quest to
    him —
Him — here — a villain fitter to stick swine
Than ride abroad redressing women's
    wrong,
Or sit beside a noble gentlewoman.'

   Then half-ashamed and part-amazed, the
    lord
Now look'd at one and now at other, left
The damsel by the peacock in his pride,
And, seating Gareth at another board,   850
Sat down beside him, ate and then began:

   'Friend, whether thou be kitchen-knave,
    or not,
Or whether it be the maiden's fantasy,
And whether she be mad, or else the King,
Or both or neither, or thyself be mad,
I ask not; but thou strikest a strong stroke,
For strong thou art and goodly therewithal,
And saver of my life; and therefore now,
For here be mighty men to joust with,
    weigh
Whether thou wilt not with thy damsel
    back               860
To crave again Sir Lancelot of the King.
Thy pardon; I but speak for thine avail,
The saver of my life.'

                   And Gareth said,
'Full pardon, but I follow up the quest,
Despite of Day and Night and Death and
    Hell.'

   So when, next morn, the lord whose life
    he saved
Had, some brief space, convey'd them on
    their way
And left them with God-speed, Sir Gareth
    spake,
'Lead, and I follow.'  Haughtily she re-
    plied:

   'I fly no more; I allow thee for an hour.
Lion and stoat have isled together, knave,
In time of flood.  Nay, furthermore, me-
    thinks              872
Some ruth is mine for thee.  Back wilt
    thou, fool ?
For hard by here is one will overthrow
And slay thee; then will I to court again,
And shame the King for only yielding me
My champion from the ashes of his hearth.'

To whom Sir Gareth answer'd courte-
ously:
'Say thou thy say, and I will do my deed.
Allow me for mine hour, and thou wilt
   find              880
My fortunes all as fair as hers who lay
Among the ashes and wedded the King's
   son.'

  Then to the shore of one of those long
   loops
Wherethro' the serpent river coil'd, they
   came.
Rough-thicketed were the banks and steep;
   the stream
Full, narrow; this a bridge of single arc
Took at a leap; and on the further side
Arose a silk pavilion, gay with gold
In streaks and rays, and all Lent-lily in hue,
Save that the dome was purple, and above,
Crimson, a slender banneret fluttering.  891
And therebefore the lawless warrior paced
Unarm'd, and calling, 'Damsel, is this he,
The champion thou hast brought from Ar-
   thur's hall,
For whom we let thee pass?' 'Nay, nay,'
   she said,
'Sir Morning-Star. The King in utter
   scorn
Of thee and thy much folly hath sent thee
   here
His kitchen-knave; and look thou to thy-
   self.
See that he fall not on thee suddenly,
And slay thee unarm'd; he is not knight
   but knave.'       900

  Then at his call, 'O daughters of the
   Dawn,
And servants of the Morning-Star, ap-
   proach,
Arm me,' from out the silken curtain-folds
Bare-footed and bare-headed three fair
   girls
In gilt and rosy raiment came. Their feet
In dewy grasses glisten'd; and the hair
All over glanced with dewdrop or with
   gem
Like sparkles in the stone Avanturine.
These arm'd him in blue arms, and gave a
   shield      909
Blue also, and thereon the morning star.
And Gareth silent gazed upon the knight,
Who stood a moment, ere his horse was
   brought,

Glorying; and in the stream beneath him
   shone,
Immingled with heaven's azure waveringly,
The gay pavilion and the naked feet,
His arms, the rosy raiment, and the star.

  Then she that watch'd him: 'Wherefore
   stare ye so?
Thou shakest in thy fear. There yet is
   time;
Flee down the valley before he get to horse.
Who will cry shame? Thou art not knight
   but knave.'      920

  Said Gareth: 'Damsel, whether knave or
   knight,
Far liefer had I fight a score of times
Than hear thee so missay me and revile.
Fair words were best for him who fights
   for thee;
But truly foul are better, for they send
That strength of anger thro' mine arms, I
   know
That I shall overthrow him.'

               And he that bore
The star, when mounted, cried from o'er
   the bridge:
'A kitchen-knave, and sent in scorn of
   me!
Such fight not I, but answer scorn with
   scorn.      930
For this were shame to do him further
   wrong
Than set him on his feet, and take his
   horse
And arms, and so return him to the King.
Come, therefore, leave thy lady lightly,
   knave.
Avoid; for it beseemeth not a knave
To ride with such a lady.'

             'Dog, thou liest!
I spring from loftier lineage than thine
   own.'
He spake; and all at fiery speed the two
Shock'd on the central bridge, and either
   spear
Bent but not brake, and either knight at
   once,      940
Hurl'd as a stone from out of a catapult
Beyond his horse's crupper and the bridge,
Fell, as if dead; but quickly rose and drew,
And Gareth lash'd so fiercely with his
   brand

He drave his enemy backward down the
    bridge,
The damsel crying, 'Well-stricken, kitch-
    en-knave!'
Till Gareth's shield was cloven; but one
    stroke
Laid him that clove it grovelling on the
    ground.

    Then cried the fallen, 'Take not my life;
    I yield.'
And Gareth, 'So this damsel ask it of me
Good — I accord it easily as a grace.'   951
She reddening, 'Insolent scullion! I of
    thee?
I bound to thee for any favor ask'd!'
'Then shall he die.' And Gareth there
    unlaced
His helmet as to slay him, but she shriek'd,
'Be not so hardy, scullion, as to slay
One nobler than thyself.' 'Damsel, thy
    charge
Is an abounding pleasure to me. Knight,
Thy life is thine at her command. Arise
And quickly pass to Arthur's hall, and say
His kitchen-knave hath sent thee. See thou
    crave   961
His pardon for thy breaking of his laws.
Myself when I return will plead for thee.
Thy shield is mine — farewell; and, dam-
    sel, thou,
Lead, and I follow.'

            And fast away she fled;
Then when he came upon her, spake:
    'Methought,
Knave, when I watch'd thee striking on the
    bridge,
The savor of thy kitchen came upon me
A little faintlier; but the wind hath
    changed,
I scent it twenty-fold.' And then she sang,
'"O morning star" — not that tall felon
    there   971
Whom thou, by sorcery or unhappiness
Or some device, hast foully overthrown, —

"O morning star that smilest in the blue,
O star, my morning dream hath proven true,
Smile sweetly, thou! my love hath smiled on
    me."

    'But thou begone, take counsel, and
    away,
For hard by here is one that guards a
    ford —

The second brother in their fool's para-
    ble —
Will pay thee all thy wages, and to boot.
Care not for shame; thou art not knight
    but knave.'   981

    To whom Sir Gareth answer'd, laugh-
    ingly:
'Parables? Hear a parable of the knave.
When I was kitchen-knave among the
    rest,
Fierce was the hearth, and one of my co-
    mates
Own'd a rough dog, to whom he cast his
    coat,
"Guard it," and there was none to meddle
    with it.
And such a coat art thou, and thee the
    King
Gave me to guard, and such a dog am I,
To worry, and not to flee — and — knight
    or knave   990
The knave that doth thee service as full
    knight
Is all as good, meseems, as any knight
Toward thy sister's freeing.'

                 'Ay, Sir Knave!
Ay, knave, because thou strikest as a
    knight,
Being but knave, I hate thee all the more.'

    'Fair damsel, you should worship me the
    more,
That, being but knave, I throw thine ene-
    mies.'

    'Ay, ay,' she said, 'but thou shalt meet
    thy match.'

    So when they touch'd the second river-
    loop,   999
Huge on a huge red horse, and all in mail
Burnish'd to blinding, shone the Noonday
    Sun
Beyond a raging shallow. As if the flower
That blows a globe of after arrowlets
Ten-thousand-fold had grown, flash'd the
    fierce shield,
All sun; and Gareth's eyes had flying blots
Before them when he turn'd from watch-
    ing him.
He from beyond the roaring shallow roar'd,
'What doest thou, brother, in my marches
    here?'

And she athwart the shallow shrill'd again,
'Here is a kitchen-knave from Arthur's
    hall                                       1010
Hath overthrown thy brother, and hath his
    arms.'
'Ugh!' cried the Sun, and, vizoring up a
    red
And cipher face of rounded foolishness,
Push'd horse across the foamings of the
    ford,
Whom Gareth met mid-stream; no room
    was there
For lance or tourney-skill.  Four strokes
    they struck
With sword, and these were mighty; the
    new knight
Had fear he might be shamed; but as the
    Sun
Heaved up a ponderous arm to strike the
    fifth,
The hoof of his horse slipt in the stream,
    the stream                                 1020
Descended, and the Sun was wash'd away.

Then Gareth laid his lance athwart the
    ford;
So drew him home; but he that fought no
    more,
As being all bone-batter'd on the rock,
Yielded, and Gareth sent him to the King.
'Myself when I return will plead for thee.
Lead, and I follow.'  Quietly she led.
'Hath not the good wind, damsel, changed
    again?'
'Nay, not a point; nor art thou victor
    here.                                      1029
There lies a ridge of slate across the ford;
His horse thereon stumbled — ay, for I
    saw it.

'"O sun"— not this strong fool whom
    thou, Sir Knave,
Hast overthrown thro' mere unhappiness —

"O sun, that wakenest all to bliss or pain,
O moon, that layest all to sleep again,
Shine sweetly; twice my love hath smiled on
    me."

'What knowest thou of love-song or of
    love?
Nay, nay, God wot, so thou wert nobly
    born,
Thou hast a pleasant presence.  Yea, per-
    chance,—

'"O dewy flowers that open to the sun,
O dewy flowers that close when day is
    done,                                      1041
Blow sweetly; twice my love hath smiled
    on me."

'What knowest thou of flowers, except,
    belike,
To garnish meats with?  hath not our good
    King
Who lent me thee, the flower of kitchendom,
A foolish love for flowers? what stick ye
    round
The pasty? wherewithal deck the boar's
    head?
Flowers? nay, the boar hath rosemaries
    and bay.

'"O birds that warble to the morning
    sky,                                       1049
O birds that warble as the day goes by,
Sing sweetly; twice my love hath smiled on
    me."

'What knowest thou of birds, lark, mavis,
    merle,
Linnet? what dream ye when they utter
    forth
May-music growing with the growing light,
Their sweet sun-worship? these be for the
    snare —
So runs thy fancy — these be for the spit,
Larding and basting.  See thou have not
    now
Larded thy last, except thou turn and fly.
There stands the third fool of their alle-
    gory.'

For there beyond a bridge of treble
    bow,                                       1060
All in a rose-red from the west, and all
Naked it seem'd, and glowing in the broad
Deep - dimpled current underneath, the
    knight
That named himself the Star of Evening
    stood.

And Gareth, 'Wherefore waits the mad-
    man there
Naked in open dayshine?'  'Nay,' she
    cried,
'Not naked, only wrapt in harden'd skins
That fit him like his own; and so ye cleave
His armor off him, these will turn the
    blade.'

Then the third brother shouted o'er the
    bridge,                                    1070
'O brother-star, why shine ye here so low?
Thy ward is higher up; but have ye slain
The damsel's champion?' and the damsel
    cried:

    'No star of thine, but shot from Arthur's
        heaven
With all disaster unto thine and thee!
For both thy younger brethren have gone
    down
Before this youth; and so wilt thou, Sir
    Star.
Art thou not old?'

                        'Old, damsel, old and hard,
Old, with the might and breath of twenty
    boys.'
Said Gareth, 'Old, and over-bold in brag!
But that same strength which threw the
    Morning Star                              1081
Can throw the Evening.'

                        Then that other blew
A hard and deadly note upon the horn.
'Approach and arm me!' With slow
    steps from out
An old storm-beaten, russet, many-stain'd
Pavilion, forth a grizzled damsel came,
And arm'd him in old arms, and brought a
    helm
With but a drying evergreen for crest,
And gave a shield whereon the star of
    even
Half-tarnish'd and half-bright, his emblem,
    shone.                                     1090
But when it glitter'd o'er the saddle-bow,
They madly hurl'd together on the bridge;
And Gareth overthrew him, lighted, drew,
There met him drawn, and overthrew him
    again,
But up like fire he started; and as oft
As Gareth brought him grovelling on his
    knees,
So many a time he vaulted up again;
Till Gareth panted hard, and his great
    heart,
Foredooming all his trouble was in vain,
Labor'd within him, for he seem'd as one
That all in later, sadder age begins         1101
To war against ill uses of a life,
But these from all his life arise, and cry,
'Thou hast made us lords, and canst not
    put us down!'

He half despairs; so Gareth seem'd to
    strike
Vainly, the damsel clamoring all the while,
'Well done, knave-knight, well stricken, O
    good knight-knave —
O knave, as noble as any of all the
    knights —
Shame me not, shame me not. I have
    prophesied —
Strike, thou art worthy of the Table
    Round —                                    1110
His arms are old, he trusts the harden'd
    skin —
Strike — strike — the wind will never
    change again.'
And Gareth hearing ever stronglier smote,
And hew'd great pieces of his armor off
    him,
But lash'd in vain against the harden'd
    skin,
And could not wholly bring him under,
    more
Than loud Southwesterns, rolling ridge on
    ridge,
The buoy that rides at sea, and dips and
    springs
For ever; till at length Sir Gareth's brand
Clash'd his, and brake it utterly to the
    hilt.                                      1120
'I have thee now;' but forth that other
    sprang,
And, all unknightlike, writhed his wiry
    arms
Around him, till he felt, despite his mail,
Strangled, but straining even his utter-
    most
Cast, and so hurl'd him headlong o'er the
    bridge
Down to the river, sink or swim, and cried,
'Lead, and I follow.'

                        But the damsel said:
'I lead no longer; ride thou at my side;
Thou art the kingliest of all kitchen-
    knaves.

    '"O trefoil, sparkling on the rainy
        plain,                                 1130
O rainbow with three colors after rain,
Shine sweetly; thrice my love hath smiled on
    me."

'Sir, — and, good faith, I fain had added
    — Knight,
But that I heard thee call thyself a knave, —

Shamed am I that I so rebuked, reviled,
Missaid thee.  Noble I am, and thought the
    King
Scorn'd me and mine; and now thy pardon,
    friend,
For thou hast ever answer'd courteously,
And wholly bold thou art, and meek withal
As any of Arthur's best, but, being knave,
Hast maz'd my wit.  I marvel what thou
    art.'                                          1141

  'Damsel,' he said, 'you be not all to
    blame,
Saving that you mistrusted our good King
Would handle scorn, or yield you, asking,
    one
Not fit to cope your quest.  You said your
    say;
Mine answer was my deed.  Good sooth!
    I hold
He scarce is knight, yea but half-man, nor
    meet
To fight for gentle damsel, he, who lets
His heart be stirr'd with any foolish heat
At any gentle damsel's waywardness.   1150
Shamed? care not! thy foul sayings fought
    for me;
And seeing now thy words are fair, me-
    thinks
There rides no knight, not Lancelot, his
    great self,
Hath force to quell me.'

                    Nigh upon that hour
When the lone hern forgets his melan-
    choly,
Lets down his other leg, and stretching
    dreams
Of goodly supper in the distant pool,
Then turn'd the noble damsel smiling at
    him,
And told him of a cavern hard at hand,
Where bread and baken meats and good
    red wine                                      1160
Of Southland, which the Lady Lyonors
Had sent her coming champion, waited
    him.

  Anon they past a narrow comb wherein
Were slabs of rock with figures, knights on
    horse
Sculptured, and deckt in slowly-waning
    hues.
'Sir Knave, my knight, a hermit once was
    here,

Whose holy hand hath fashion'd on the
    rock
The war of Time against the soul of man.
And yon four fools have suck'd their alle-
    gory
From these damp walls, and taken but the
    form.                                          1170
Know ye not these?' and Gareth lookt
    and read —
In letters like to those the vexillary
Hath left crag-carven o'er the streaming
    Gelt —
'PHOSPHORUS,' then 'MERIDIES,' — 'HES-
    PERUS' —
'NOX' — 'MORS,' beneath five figures,
    armed men,
Slab after slab, their faces forward all,
And running down the Soul, a shape that
    fled
With broken wings, torn raiment, and loose
    hair,
For help and shelter to the hermit's cave.
'Follow the faces, and we find it.  Look,
Who comes behind?'

                    For one — delay'd at first
Thro' helping back the dislocated Kay   1182
To Camelot, then by what thereafter
    chanced,
The damsel's headlong error thro' the
    wood —
Sir Lancelot, having swum the river-
    loops —
His blue shield-lions cover'd — softly drew
Behind the twain, and when he saw the star
Gleam, on Sir Gareth's turning to him,
    cried,
'Stay, felon knight, I avenge me for my
    friend.'
And Gareth crying prick'd against the
    cry;                                           1190
But when they closed — in a moment — at
    one touch
Of that skill'd spear, the wonder of the
    world —
Went sliding down so easily, and fell,
That when he found the grass within his
    hands
He laugh'd.  The laughter jarr'd upon Ly-
    nette.
Harshly she ask'd him, 'Shamed and over-
    thrown,
And tumbled back into the kitchen-knave,
Why laugh ye? that ye blew your boast in
    vain?'

'Nay, noble damsel, but that I, the son
Of old King Lot and good Queen Belli-
    cent,    1200
And victor of the bridges and the ford,
And knight of Arthur, here lie thrown by
    whom
I know not, all thro' mere unhappiness —
Device and sorcery and unhappiness —
Out, sword; we are thrown!' And Lance-
    lot answer'd: 'Prince,
O Gareth — thro' the mere unhappiness
Of one who came to help thee, not to harm,
Lancelot, and all as glad to find thee whole
As on the day when Arthur knighted him.'

Then Gareth: 'Thou — Lancelot! —
    thine the hand    1210
That threw me? An some chance to mar
    the boast
Thy brethren of thee make — which could
    not chance —
Had sent thee down before a lesser spear,
Shamed had I been, and sad — O Lance-
    lot — thou!'

Whereat the maiden, petulant: 'Lance-
    lot,
Why came ye not, when call'd? and where-
    fore now
Come ye, not call'd? I gloried in my
    knave,
Who being still rebuked would answer still
Courteous as any knight — but now, if
    knight,
The marvel dies, and leaves me fool'd and
    trick'd,    1220
And only wondering wherefore play'd
    upon;
And doubtful whether I and mine be
    scorn'd.
Where should be truth if not in Arthur's
    hall,
In Arthur's presence? Knight, knave,
    prince and fool,
I hate thee and forever.'

            And Lancelot said:
'Blessed be thou, Sir Gareth! knight art
    thou
To the King's best wish. O damsel, be
    you wise,
To call him shamed who is but over-
    thrown?
Thrown have I been, nor once, but many a
    time.    1229

Victor from vanquish'd issues at the last,
And overthrower from being overthrown.
With sword we have not striven, and thy
    good horse
And thou are weary; yet not less I felt
Thy manhood thro' that wearied lance of
    thine.
Well hast thou done; for all the stream is
    freed,
And thou hast wreak'd his justice on his
    foes,
And when reviled hast answer'd graciously,
And makest merry when overthrown.
    Prince, knight,
Hail, knight and prince, and of our Table
    Round!'

    And then when turning to Lynette he
    told    1240
The tale of Gareth, petulantly she said:
'Ay, well — ay, well — for worse than be-
    ing fool'd
Of others, is to fool one's self. A cave,
Sir Lancelot, is hard by, with meats and
    drinks
And forage for the horse, and flint for fire.
But all about it flies a honeysuckle.
Seek, till we find.' And when they sought
    and found,
Sir Gareth drank and ate, and all his life
Past into sleep; on whom the maiden
    gazed:
'Sound sleep be thine! sound cause to
    sleep hast thou.    1250
Wake lusty! Seem I not as tender to him
As any mother? Ay, but such a one
As all day long hath rated at her child,
And vext his day, but blesses him asleep —
Good lord, how sweetly smells the honey-
    suckle
In the hush'd night, as if the world were one
Of utter peace, and love, and gentleness!
O Lancelot, Lancelot,' — and she clapt her
    hands —
'Full merry am I to find my goodly knave
Is knight and noble. See now, sworn
    have I,    1260
Else yon black felon had not let me pass,
To bring thee back to do the battle with
    him.
Thus an thou goest, he will fight thee first;
Who doubts thee victor? so will my knight-
    knave
Miss the full flower of this accomplish-
    ment.'

Said Lancelot: 'Peradventure he you name
May know my shield.   Let Gareth, an he will,
Change his for mine, and take my charger, fresh,
Not to be spurr'd, loving the battle as well
As he that rides him.'   'Lancelot-like,' she said,                                          1270
'Courteous in this, Lord Lancelot, as in all.'

And Gareth, wakening, fiercely clutch'd the shield:
'Ramp, ye lance-splintering lions, on whom all spears
Are rotten sticks ! ye seem agape to roar !
Yea, ramp and roar at leaving of your lord ! —
Care not, good beasts, so well I care for you.
O noble Lancelot, from my hold on these
Streams virtue — fire — thro' one that will not shame
Even the shadow of Lancelot under shield.
Hence;  let us go.'

                        Silent the silent field
They traversed.   Arthur's Harp tho' sum-
        mer-wan,                              1281
In counter motion to the clouds, allured
The glance of Gareth dreaming on his liege.
A star shot: 'Lo,' said Gareth, 'the foe falls !'
An owl whoopt: 'Hark the victor pealing there !'
Suddenly she that rode upon his left
Clung to the shield that Lancelot lent him, crying:
'Yield, yield him this again; 't is he must fight:
I curse the tongue that all thro' yesterday
Reviled thee, and hath wrought on Lance-
        lot now                              1290
To lend thee horse and shield.   Wonders ye have done,
Miracles ye cannot.   Here is glory enow
In having flung the three.   I see thee maim'd,
Mangled; I swear thou canst not fling the fourth.'

    'And wherefore, damsel ? tell me all ye know.
You cannot scare me; nor rough face, or voice,

Brute bulk of limb, or boundless savagery
Appal me from the quest.'

                        'Nay, prince,' she cried,
'God wot, I never look'd upon the face,
Seeing he never rides abroad by day,       1300
But watch'd him have I like a phantom pass
Chilling the night; nor have I heard the voice.
Always he made his mouthpiece of a page
Who came and went, and still reported him
As closing in himself the strength of ten,
And when his anger tare him, massacring
Man, woman, lad, and girl — yea, the soft babe !
Some hold that he hath swallow'd infant flesh,
Monster !   O prince, I went for Lancelot first,
The quest is Lancelot's; give him back the shield.'                                         1310

    Said Gareth laughing, 'An he fight for this,
Belike he wins it as the better man;
Thus — and not else !'

                        But Lancelot on him urged
All the devisings of their chivalry
When one might meet a mightier than him-
        self;
How best to manage horse, lance, sword, and shield,
And so fill up the gap where force might fail
With skill and fineness.   Instant were his words.

    Then Gareth: 'Here be rules.   I know but one —
To dash against mine enemy and to win. 1320
Yet have I watch'd thee victor in the joust,
And seen thy way.'   'Heaven help thee !' sigh'd Lynette.

    Then for a space, and under cloud that grew
To thunder-gloom palling all stars, they rode
In converse till she made her palfrey halt,
Lifted an arm, and softly whisper'd, 'There.'

And all the three were silent seeing, pitch'd
Beside the Castle Perilous on flat field,
A huge pavilion like a mountain peak   1329
Sunder the glooming crimson on the marge,
Black, with black banner, and a long black
    horn
Beside it hanging; which Sir Gareth graspt,
And so, before the two could hinder him,
Sent all his heart and breath thro' all the
    horn.
Echo'd the walls; a light twinkled; anon
Came lights and lights, and once again he
    blew;
Whereon were hollow tramplings up and
    down
And muffled voices heard, and shadows
    past;
Till high above him, circled with her maids,
The Lady Lyonors at a window stood,   1340
Beautiful among lights, and waving to
    him
White hands and courtesy.   But when the
    prince
Three times had blown — after long hush
    — at last —
The huge pavilion slowly yielded up,
Thro' those black foldings, that which
    housed therein.
High on a night-black horse, in night-black
    arms,
With white breast-bone, and barren ribs of
    Death,
And crown'd with fleshless laughter —
    some ten steps —
In the half-light — thro' the dim dawn —
    advanced
The monster, and then paused, and spake
    no word.   1350

But Gareth spake and all indignantly:
'Fool, for thou hast, men say, the strength
    of ten,
Canst thou not trust the limbs thy God
    hath given,
But must, to make the terror of thee more,
Trick thyself out in ghastly imageries
Of that which Life hath done with, and the
    clod,
Less dull than thou, will hide with man-
    tling flowers
As if for pity?'   But he spake no word;
Which set the horror higher.   A maiden
    swoon'd;
The Lady Lyonors wrung her hands and
    wept,   1360

As doom'd to be the bride of Night and
    Death;
Sir Gareth's head prickled beneath his
    helm;
And even Sir Lancelot thro' his warm
    blood felt
Ice strike, and all that mark'd him were
    aghast.

At once Sir Lancelot's charger fiercely
    neigh'd,
And Death's dark war-horse bounded for-
    ward with him.
Then those that did not blink the terror
    saw
That Death was cast to ground, and slowly
    rose.
But with one stroke Sir Gareth split the
    skull.   1369
Half fell to right and half to left and
    lay.
Then with a stronger buffet he clove the
    helm
As throughly as the skull; and out from
    this
Issued the bright face of a blooming boy
Fresh as a flower new-born, and crying,
    'Knight,
Slay me not; my three brethren bade me
    do it,
To make a horror all about the house,
And stay the world from Lady Lyonors.
They never dream'd the passes would be
    past.'
Answer'd Sir Gareth graciously to one
Not many a moon his younger, 'My fair
    child,   1380
What madness made thee challenge the
    chief knight
Of Arthur's hall?'   'Fair Sir, they bade
    me do it.
They hate the King and Lancelot, the
    King's friend;
They hoped to slay him somewhere on the
    stream,
They never dream'd the passes could be
    past.'

Then sprang the happier day from under-
    ground;
And Lady Lyonors and her house, with
    dance
And revel and song, made merry over
    Death,
As being after all their foolish fears   1389

And horrors only proven a blooming boy.
So large mirth lived, and Gareth won the
    quest.

And he that told the tale in older times
Says that Sir Gareth wedded Lyonors,
But he that told it later says Lynette.


## THE MARRIAGE OF GERAINT

THE brave Geraint, a knight of Arthur's
    court,
A tributary prince of Devon, one
Of that great Order of the Table Round,
Had married Enid, Yniol's only child,
And loved her as he loved the light of
    heaven.
And as the light of heaven varies, now
At sunrise, now at sunset, now by night
With moon and trembling stars, so loved
    Geraint
To make her beauty vary day by day,
In crimsons and in purples and in gems.   10
And Enid, but to please her husband's eye,
Who first had found and loved her in a
    state
Of broken fortunes, daily fronted him
In some fresh splendor; and the Queen
    herself,
Grateful to Prince Geraint for service
    done,
Loved her, and often with her own white
    hands
Array'd and deck'd her, as the loveliest,
Next after her own self, in all the court.
And Enid loved the Queen, and with true
    heart
Adored her, as the stateliest and the best   20
And loveliest of all women upon earth.
And seeing them so tender and so close,
Long in their common love rejoiced Ge-
    raint.
But when a rumor rose about the Queen,
Touching her guilty love for Lancelot,
Tho' yet there lived no proof, nor yet was
    heard
The world's loud whisper breaking into
    storm,
Not less Geraint believed it; and there
    fell
A horror on him lest his gentle wife,   29
Thro' that great tenderness for Guinevere,
Had suffer'd or should suffer any taint
In nature.   Wherefore, going to the King,

He made this pretext, that his princedom lay
Close on the borders of a territory
Wherein were bandit earls, and caitiff
    knights,
Assassins, and all flyers from the hand
Of Justice, and whatever loathes a law;
And therefore, till the King himself should
    please
To cleanse this common sewer of all his
    realm,
He craved a fair permission to depart,   40
And there defend his marches.   And the
    King
Mused for a little on his plea, but, last,
Allowing it, the prince and Enid rode,
And fifty knights rode with them, to the
    shores
Of Severn, and they past to their own
    land;
Where, thinking that, if ever yet was wife
True to her lord, mine shall be so to me,
He compass'd her with sweet observances
And worship, never leaving her, and grew
Forgetful of his promise to the King,   50
Forgetful of the falcon and the hunt,
Forgetful of the tilt and tournament,
Forgetful of his glory and his name,
Forgetful of his princedom and its cares.
And this forgetfulness was hateful to her.
And by and by the people, when they met
In twos and threes, or fuller companies,
Began to scoff and jeer and babble of him
As of a prince whose manhood was all
    gone,
And molten down in mere uxoriousness.   60
And this she gather'd from the people's
    eyes;
This too the women who attired her head,
To please her, dwelling on his boundless
    love,
Told Enid, and they sadden'd her the more;
And day by day she thought to tell Geraint,
But could not out of bashful delicacy,
While he, that watch'd her sadden, was
    the more
Suspicious that her nature had a taint.

At last, it chanced that on a summer
    morn —
They sleeping each by either — the new
    sun   70
Beat thro' the blindless casement of the
    room,
And heated the strong warrior in his
    dreams;

Who, moving, cast the coverlet aside,
And bared the knotted column of his throat,
The massive square of his heroic breast,
And arms on which the standing muscle
      sloped,
As slopes a wild brook o'er a little stone,
Running too vehemently to break upon it.
And Enid woke and sat beside the couch,
Admiring him, and thought within herself,
Was ever man so grandly made as he ?   81
Then, like a shadow, past the people's talk
And accusation of uxoriousness
Across her mind, and, bowing over him,
Low to her own heart piteously she said:

'O noble breast and all-puissant arms,
Am I the cause, I the poor cause that men
Reproach you, saying all your force is
      gone ?
I *am* the cause, because I dare not speak
And tell him what I think and what they
      say.                                  90
And yet I hate that he should linger here;
I cannot love my lord and not his name.
Far liefer had I gird his harness on him,
And ride with him to battle and stand
      by,
And watch his mightful hand striking
      great blows
At caitiffs and at wrongers of the world.
Far better were I laid in the dark earth,
Not hearing any more his noble voice,
Not to be folded more in these dear arms,
And darken'd from the high light in his
      eyes,                                100
Than that my lord thro' me should suffer
      shame.
Am I so bold, and could I so stand by,
And see my dear lord wounded in the strife,
Or maybe pierced to death before mine
      eyes,
And yet not dare to tell him what I think,
And how men slur him, saying all his force
Is melted into mere effeminacy ?
O me, I fear that I am no true wife !'

Half inwardly, half audibly she spoke,
And the strong passion in her made her
      weep                                 110
True tears upon his broad and naked
      breast,
And these awoke him, and by great mis-
      chance
He heard but fragments of her later words,
And that she fear'd she was not a true wife.

And then he thought, 'In spite of all my
      care,
For all my pains, poor man, for all my
      pains,
She is not faithful to me, and I see her
Weeping for some gay knight in Arthur's
      hall.'
Then, tho' he loved and reverenced her too
      much
To dream she could be guilty of foul act,
Right thro' his manful breast darted the
      pang                                 121
That makes a man, in the sweet face of her
Whom he loves most, lonely and miserable.
At this he hurl'd his huge limbs out of bed,
And shook his drowsy squire awake and
      cried,
'My charger and her palfrey;' then to her,
'I will ride forth into the wilderness,
For, tho' it seems my spurs are yet to win,
I have not fallen so low as some would
      wish.
And thou, put on thy worst and meanest
      dress                                130
And ride with me.'   And Enid ask'd,
      amazed,
'If Enid errs, let Enid learn her fault.'
But he, 'I charge thee, ask not, but obey.'
Then she bethought her of a faded silk,
A faded mantle and a faded veil,
And moving toward a cedarn cabinet,
Wherein she kept them folded reverently
With sprigs of summer laid between the
      folds,
She took them, and array'd herself therein,
Remembering when first he came on her
Drest in that dress, and how he loved her
      in it,                               141
And all her foolish fears about the dress,
And all his journey to her, as himself
Had told her, and their coming to the
      court.

For Arthur on the Whitsuntide before
Held court at old Caerleon upon Usk.
There on a day, he sitting high in hall,
Before him came a forester of Dean,
Wet from the woods, with notice of a hart
Taller than all his fellows, milky-white,
First seen that day; these things he told the
      King.                               151
Then the good King gave order to let blow
His horns for hunting on the morrow morn,
And when the Queen petition'd for his leave
To see the hunt, allow'd it easily.

So with the morning all the court were
    gone.
But Guinevere lay late into the morn,
Lost in sweet dreams, and dreaming of her
    love
For Lancelot, and forgetful of the hunt,
But rose at last, a single maiden with her,
Took horse, and forded Usk, and gain'd the
    wood;         161
There, on a little knoll beside it, stay'd
Waiting to hear the hounds, but heard in-
    stead
A sudden sound of hoofs, for Prince Ge-
    raint,
Late also, wearing neither hunting-dress
Nor weapon save a golden-hilted brand,
Came quickly flashing thro' the shallow
    ford
Behind them, and so gallop'd up the knoll.
A purple scarf, at either end whereof
There swung an apple of the purest gold,
Sway'd round about him, as he gallop'd
    up         171
To join them, glancing like a dragon-fly
In summer suit and silks of holiday.
Low bow'd the tributary prince, and she,
Sweetly and statelily, and with all grace
Of womanhood and queenhood, answer'd
    him:
'Late, late, Sir Prince,' she said, 'later
    than we !'
'Yea, noble Queen,' he answer'd, 'and so
    late
That I but come like you to see the hunt,
Not join it.' 'Therefore wait with me,'
    she said;       180
'For on this little knoll, if anywhere,
There is good chance that we shall hear the
    hounds:
Here often they break covert at our feet.'

And while they listen'd for the distant
    hunt,
And chiefly for the baying of Cavall,
King Arthur's hound of deepest mouth,
    there rode
Full slowly by a knight, lady, and dwarf;
Whereof the dwarf lagg'd latest, and the
    knight
Had vizor up, and show'd a youthful face,
Imperious, and of haughtiest lineaments.
And Guinevere, not mindful of his face  191
In the King's hall, desired his name, and
    sent
Her maiden to demand it of the dwarf,

Who being vicious, old, and irritable,
And doubling all his master's vice of pride,
Made answer sharply that she should not
    know.
'Then will I ask it of himself,' she said.
'Nay, by my faith, thou shalt not,' cried
    the dwarf;
'Thou art not worthy even to speak of
    him;'
And when she put her horse toward the
    knight,       200
Struck at her with his whip, and she re-
    turn'd
Indignant to the Queen; whereat Geraint
Exclaiming, 'Surely I will learn the name,'
Made sharply to the dwarf, and ask'd it of
    him,
Who answer'd as before; and when the
    prince
Had put his horse in motion toward the
    knight,
Struck at him with his whip, and cut his
    cheek.
The prince's blood spirted upon the scarf,
Dyeing it; and his quick, instinctive hand
Caught at the hilt, as to abolish him:  210
But he, from his exceeding manfulness
And pure nobility of temperament,
Wroth to be wroth at such a worm, re-
    frain'd
From even a word, and so returning said:

'I will avenge this insult, noble Queen,
Done in your maiden's person to yourself,
And I will track this vermin to their earths;
For tho' I ride unarm'd, I do not doubt
To find, at some place I shall come at,
    arms
On loan, or else for pledge; and, being
    found,       220
Then will I fight him, and will break his
    pride,
And on the third day will again be here,
So that I be not fallen in fight.  Farewell.'

'Farewell, fair prince,' answer'd the
    stately Queen.
'Be prosperous in this journey, as in all;
And may you light on all things that you
    love,
And live to wed with her whom first you
    love.
But ere you wed with any, bring your
    bride,
And I, were she the daughter of a king,

Yea, tho' she were a beggar from the
    hedge,                                    230
Will clothe her for her bridals like the
    sun.'

    And Prince Geraint, now thinking that
    he heard
The noble hart at bay, now the far horn,
A little vext at losing of the hunt,
A little at the vile occasion, rode,
By ups and downs, thro' many a grassy
    glade
And valley, with fixt eye following the
    three.
At last they issued from the world of
    wood,
And climb'd upon a fair and even ridge,
And show'd themselves against the sky,
    and sank.                                 240
And thither came Geraint, and underneath
Beheld the long street of a little town
In a long valley, on one side whereof,
White from the mason's hand, a fortress
    rose;
And on one side a castle in decay,
Beyond a bridge that spann'd a dry ra-
    vine.
And out of town and valley came a noise
As of a broad brook o'er a shingly bed
Brawling, or like a clamor of the rooks
At distance, ere they settle for the night.

    And onward to the fortress rode the
    three,                                     251
And enter'd, and were lost behind the
    walls.
'So,' thought Geraint, 'I have track'd him
    to his earth.'
And down the long street riding wearily,
Found every hostel full, and everywhere
Was hammer laid to hoof, and the hot hiss
And bustling whistle of the youth who
    scour'd
His master's armor; and of such a one
He ask'd, 'What means the tumult in the
    town?'
Who told him, scouring still, 'The spar-
    row-hawk!'                                260
Then riding close behind an ancient churl,
Who, smitten by the dusty sloping beam,
Went sweating underneath a sack of corn,
Ask'd yet once more what meant the hub-
    bub here?
Who answer'd gruffly, 'Ugh! the sparrow-
    hawk!'

Then riding further past an armorer's,
Who, with back turn'd, and bow'd above
    his work,
Sat riveting a helmet on his knee,
He put the selfsame query, but the man
Not turning round, nor looking at him,
    said:                                     270
'Friend, he that labors for the sparrow-
    hawk
Has little time for idle questioners.'
Whereat Geraint flash'd into sudden spleen:
'A thousand pips eat up your sparrow-
    hawk!
Tits, wrens, and all wing'd nothings peck
    him dead!
Ye think the rustic cackle of your bourg
The murmur of the world! What is it to
    me?
O wretched set of sparrows, one and all,
Who pipe of nothing but of sparrow-hawks!
Speak, if ye be not like the rest, hawk-
    mad,                                      280
Where can I get me harborage for the
    night?
And arms, arms, arms to fight my enemy?
    Speak!'
Whereat the armorer turning all amazed
And seeing one so gay in purple silks,
Came forward with the helmet yet in hand
And answer'd: 'Pardon me, O stranger
    knight;
We hold a tourney here to-morrow morn,
And there is scantly time for half the
    work.
Arms? truth! I know not; all are wanted
    here.
Harborage? truth, good truth, I know not,
    save,                                     290
It may be, at Earl Yniol's, o'er the bridge
Yonder.' He spoke and fell to work again.

    Then rode Geraint, a little spleenful
    yet,
Across the bridge that spann'd the dry ra-
    vine.
There musing sat the hoary-headed earl —
His dress a suit of fray'd magnificence,
Once fit for feasts of ceremony — and said:
'Whither, fair son?' to whom Geraint re-
    plied,
'O friend, I seek a harborage for the
    night.'
Then Yniol, 'Enter therefore and partake
The slender entertainment of a house      301
Once rich, now poor, but ever open-door'd.'

'Thanks, venerable friend,' replied Geraint;
'So that ye do not serve me sparrow-hawks
For supper, I will enter, I will eat
With all the passion of a twelve hours'
    fast.'
Then sigh'd and smiled the hoary-headed
    earl,
And answer'd, 'Graver cause than yours is
    mine
To curse this hedgerow thief, the sparrow-
    hawk.
But in, go in; for save yourself desire it, 310
We will not touch upon him even in jest.'

Then rode Geraint into the castle court,
His charger trampling many a prickly
    star
Of sprouted thistle on the broken stones.
He look'd and saw that all was ruinous.
Here stood a shatter'd archway plumed
    with fern;
And here had fallen a great part of a
    tower,
Whole, like a crag that tumbles from the
    cliff,
And like a crag was gay with wilding flow-
    ers;
And high above a piece of turret stair, 320
Worn by the feet that now were silent,
    wound
Bare to the sun, and monstrous ivy-stems
Claspt the gray walls with hairy-fibred
    arms,
And suck'd the joining of the stones, and
    look'd
A knot, beneath, of snakes, aloft, a grove.

And while he waited in the castle court,
The voice of Enid, Yniol's daughter, rang
Clear thro' the open casement of the hall,
Singing; and as the sweet voice of a bird,
Heard by the lander in a lonely isle, 330
Moves him to think what kind of bird it
    is
That sings so delicately clear, and make
Conjecture of the plumage and the form,
So the sweet voice of Enid moved Ge-
    raint,
And made him like a man abroad at morn
When first the liquid note beloved of men
Comes flying over many a windy wave
To Britain, and in April suddenly
Breaks from a coppice gemm'd with green
    and red, 339
And he suspends his converse with a friend,

Or it may be the labor of his hands,
To think or say, 'There is the nightin-
    gale:'
So fared it with Geraint, who thought and
    said,
'Here, by God's grace, is the one voice for
    me.'

It chanced the song that Enid sang was
    one
Of Fortune and her wheel, and Enid sang:

'Turn, Fortune, turn thy wheel, and lower
    the proud;
Turn thy wild wheel thro' sunshine, storm, and
    cloud;
Thy wheel and thee we neither love nor hate.

'Turn, Fortune, turn thy wheel with smile or
    frown; 350
With that wild wheel we go not up or down;
Our hoard is little, but our hearts are great.

'Smile and we smile, the lords of many
    lands;
Frown and we smile, the lords of our own
    hands;
For man is man and master of his fate.

'Turn, turn thy wheel above the staring
    crowd;
Thy wheel and thou are shadows in the cloud;
Thy wheel and thee we neither love nor hate.'

'Hark, by the bird's song ye may learn
    the nest,'
Said Yniol; 'enter quickly.' Entering
    then, 360
Right o'er a mount of newly-fallen stones,
The dusky-rafter'd many-cobweb'd hall,
He found an ancient dame in dim bro-
    cade;
And near her, like a blossom vermeil-white
That lightly breaks a faded flower-sheath,
Moved the fair Enid, all in faded silk,
Her daughter. In a moment thought Ge-
    raint,
'Here, by God's rood, is the one maid for
    me.'
But none spake word except the hoary
    earl:
'Enid, the good knight's horse stands in the
    court; 370
Take him to stall, and give him corn, and
    then
Go to the town and buy us flesh and wine;

And we will make us merry as we may.
Our hoard is little, but our hearts are
    great.'

    He spake; the prince, as Enid past him,
        fain
To follow, strode a stride, but Yniol caught
His purple scarf, and held, and said, 'For-
    bear !
Rest ! the good house, tho' ruin'd, O my
    son,
Endures not that her guest should serve
    himself.'                                379
And reverencing the custom of the house
Geraint, from utter courtesy, forebore.

    So Enid took his charger to the stall,
And after went her way across the bridge,
And reach'd the town, and while the prince
    and earl
Yet spoke together, came again with one,
A youth that, following with a costrel,
    bore
The means of goodly welcome, flesh and
    wine.
And Enid brought sweet cakes to make
    them cheer,
And, in her veil enfolded, manchet bread.
And then, because their hall must also
    serve                                   390
For kitchen, boil'd the flesh, and spread
    the board,
And stood behind, and waited on the three.
And, seeing her so sweet and serviceable,
Geraint had longing in him evermore
To stoop and kiss the tender little thumb
That crost the trencher as she laid it
    down.
But after all had eaten, then Geraint,
For now the wine made summer in his
    veins,
Let his eye rove in following, or rest
On Enid at her lowly handmaid-work,    400
Now here, now there, about the dusky
    hall;
Then suddenly addrest the hoary earl:

    'Fair host and earl, I pray your cour-
        tesy;
This sparrow-hawk, what is he ? tell me of
    him.
His name ? but no, good faith, I will not
    have it;
For if he be the knight whom late I saw
Ride into that new fortress by your town,

White from the mason's hand, then have I
    sworn
From his own lips to have it — I am Ge-
    raint
Of Devon — for this morning when the
    Queen                                   410
Sent her own maiden to demand the name,
His dwarf, a vicious under-shapen thing,
Struck at her with his whip, and she re-
    turn'd
Indignant to the Queen; and then I swore
That I would track this caitiff to his hold,
And fight and break his pride, and have it
    of him.
And all unarm'd I rode, and thought to
    find
Arms in your town, where all the men are
    mad;
They take the rustic murmur of their
    bourg
For the great wave that echoes round the
    world.                                  420
They would not hear me speak; but if ye
    know
Where I can light on arms, or if yourself
Should have them, tell me, seeing I have
    sworn
That I will break his pride and learn his
    name,
Avenging this great insult done the Queen.'

    Then cried Earl Yniol: 'Art thou he in-
        deed,
Geraint, a name far-sounded among men
For noble deeds ? and truly I, when first
I saw you moving by me on the bridge,
Felt ye were somewhat, yea, and by your
    state                                   430
And presence might have guess'd you one
    of those
That eat in Arthur's hall at Camelot.
Nor speak I now from foolish flattery;
For this dear child hath often heard me
    praise
Your feats of arms, and often when I
    paused
Hath ask'd again, and ever loved to hear;
So grateful is the noise of noble deeds
To noble hearts who see but acts of wrong.
O, never yet had woman such a pair    439
Of suitors as this maiden; first Limours,
A creature wholly given to brawls and
    wine,
Drunk even when he woo'd; and be he
    dead

I know not, but he past to the wild land.
The second was your foe, the sparrow-
hawk,
My curse, my nephew — I will not let his
name
Slip from my lips if I can help it — he,
When I that knew him fierce and turbu-
lent
Refused her to him, then his pride awoke;
And since the proud man often is the
mean,                                          449
He sow'd a slander in the common ear,
Affirming that his father left him gold,
And in my charge, which was not render'd
to him;
Bribed with large promises the men who
served
About my person, the more easily
Because my means were somewhat broken
into
Thro' open doors and hospitality;
Raised my own town against me in the
night
Before my Enid's birthday, sack'd my
house;
From mine own earldom foully ousted me;
Built that new fort to overawe my friends,
For truly there are those who love me yet; 461
And keeps me in this ruinous castle here,
Where doubtless he would put me soon to
death
But that his pride too much despises me.
And I myself sometimes despise myself;
For I have let men be and have their way,
Am much too gentle, have not used my
power;
Nor know I whether I be very base
Or very manful, whether very wise
Or very foolish; only this I know,           470
That whatsoever evil happen to me,
I seem to suffer nothing heart or limb,
But can endure it all most patiently.'

'Well said, true heart,' replied Geraint,
    'but arms,
That if the sparrow-hawk, this nephew,
fight
In next day's tourney I may break his
pride.'

And Yniol answer'd: 'Arms, indeed, but
old
And rusty, old and rusty, Prince Geraint,
Are mine, and therefore, at thine asking,
thine.                                         479

But in this tournament can no man tilt,
Except the lady he loves best be there.
Two forks are fixt into the meadow ground,
And over these is placed a silver wand,
And over that a golden sparrow-hawk,
The prize of beauty for the fairest there.
And this, what knight soever be in field
Lays claim to for the lady at his side,
And tilts with my good nephew thereupon,
Who being apt at arms and big of bone
Has ever won it for the lady with him,       490
And toppling over all antagonism
Has earn'd himself the name of sparrow-
hawk.
But thou, that hast no lady, canst not
fight.'

To whom Geraint with eyes all bright
    replied,
Leaning a little toward him: 'Thy leave !
Let me lay lance in rest, O noble host,
For this dear child, because I never saw,
Tho' having seen all beauties of our time,
Nor can see elsewhere, anything so fair.
And if I fall her name will yet remain       500
Untarnish'd as before; but if I live,
So aid me heaven when at mine utter-
most
As I will make her truly my true wife !'

Then, howsoever patient, Yniol's heart
Danced in his bosom, seeing better days.
And looking round he saw not Enid there —
Who hearing her own name had stolen
away —
But that old dame, to whom full tenderly
And fondling all her hand in his he said:
'Mother, a maiden is a tender thing,         510
And best by her that bore her under-
stood.
Go thou to rest, but ere thou go to rest
Tell her, and prove her heart toward the
prince.'

So spake the kindly-hearted earl, and
    she
With frequent smile and nod departing
found,
Half disarray'd as to her rest, the girl;
Whom first she kiss'd on either cheek, and
then
On either shining shoulder laid a hand,
And kept her off and gazed upon her face,
And told her all their converse in the
hall,                                          520

Proving her heart.    But never light and
    shade
Coursed one another more on open ground
Beneath a troubled heaven than red and
    pale
Across the face of Enid hearing her;
While slowly falling as a scale that falls,
When weight is added only grain by grain,
Sank her sweet head upon her gentle
    breast;
Nor did she lift an eye nor speak a word,
Rapt in the fear and in the wonder of it.
So moving without answer to her rest    530
She found no rest, and ever fail'd to draw
The quiet night into her blood, but lay
Contemplating her own unworthiness;
And when the pale and bloodless east be-
    gan
To quicken to the sun, arose, and raised
Her mother too, and hand in hand they
    moved
Down to the meadow where the jousts
    were held,
And waited there for Yniol and Geraint.

    And thither came the twain, and when
    Geraint
Beheld her first in field, awaiting him,    540
He felt, were she the prize of bodily force,
Himself beyond the rest pushing could
    move
The Chair of Idris.    Yniol's rusted arms
Were on his princely person, but thro'
    these
Prince-like his bearing shone; and errant
    knights
And ladies came, and by and by the town
Flow'd in and settling circled all the lists.
And there they fixt the forks into the
    ground,
And over these they placed the silver
    wand,
And over that the golden sparrow-hawk. 550
Then Yniol's nephew, after trumpet blown,
Spake to the lady with him and proclaim'd,
' Advance and take, the fairest of the fair,
What I these two years past have won for
    thee,
The prize of beauty.'    Loudly spake the
    prince,
' Forbear; there is a worthier,' and the
    knight
With some surprise and thrice as much
    disdain

Turn'd, and beheld the four, and all his
    face
Glow'd like the heart of a great fire at
    Yule,
So burnt he was with passion, crying out,
' Do battle for it then,' no more; and
    thrice                                        561
They clash'd together, and thrice they
    brake their spears.
Then each, dishorsed and drawing, lash'd
    at each
So often and with such blows that all the
    crowd
Wonder'd, and now and then from distant
    walls
There came a clapping as of phantom
    hands.
So twice they fought, and twice they
    breathed, and still
The dew of their great labor and the blood
Of their strong bodies, flowing, drain'd
    their force.
But either's force was match'd till Yniol's
    cry,                                          570
' Remember that great insult done the
    Queen,'
Increased Geraint's, who heaved his blade
    aloft,
And crack'd the helmet thro', and bit the
    bone,
And fell'd him, and set foot upon his
    breast,
And said, ' Thy name ? '    To whom the
    fallen man
Made answer, groaning: ' Edyrn, son of
    Nudd !
Ashamed am I that I should tell it thee.
My pride is broken; men have seen my
    fall.'
' Then, Edyrn, son of Nudd,' replied Ge-
    raint,
' These two things shalt thou do, or else
    thou diest.                                   580
First, thou thyself, with damsel and with
    dwarf,
Shalt ride to Arthur's court and, coming
    there,
Crave pardon for that insult done the
    Queen,
And shalt abide her judgment on it; next,
Thou shalt give back their earldom to thy
    kin.
These two things shalt thou do, or thou
    shalt die.'

And Edyrn answer'd, 'These things will I
    do,
For I have never yet been overthrown,
And thou hast overthrown me, and my
    pride                                    589
Is broken down, for Enid sees my fall!'
And rising up he rode to Arthur's court,
And there the Queen forgave him easily.
And, being young, he changed and came to
    loathe
His crime of traitor, slowly drew himself
Bright from his old dark life, and fell at
    last
In the great battle fighting for the King.

But when the third day from the hunt-
    ing-morn
Made a low splendor in the world, and
    wings
Moved in her ivy, Enid, for she lay
With her fair head in the dim-yellow
    light,                                   600
Among the dancing shadows of the birds,
Woke and bethought her of her promise
    given
No later than last eve to Prince Geraint —
So bent he seem'd on going the third day,
He would not leave her till her promise
    given —
To ride with him this morning to the court,
And there be made known to the stately
    Queen,
And there be wedded with all ceremony.
At this she cast her eyes upon her dress,
And thought it never yet had look'd so
    mean.                                    610
For as a leaf in mid-November is
To what it was in mid-October, seem'd
The dress that now she look'd on to the
    dress
She look'd on ere the coming of Geraint.
And still she look'd, and still the terror
    grew
Of that strange bright and dreadful thing,
    a court,
All staring at her in her faded silk;
And softly to her own sweet heart she
    said:

'This noble prince who won our earldom
    back,
So splendid in his acts and his attire,   620
Sweet heaven, how much I shall discredit
    him!
Would he could tarry with us here awhile,

But being so beholden to the prince,
It were but little grace in any of us,
Bent as he seem'd on going this third day,
To seek a second favor at his hands.
Yet if he could but tarry a day or two,
Myself would work eye dim and finger
    lame
Far liefer than so much discredit him.'

And Enid fell in longing for a dress    630
All branch'd and flower'd with gold, a
    costly gift
Of her good mother, given her on the night
Before her birthday, three sad years ago,
That night of fire, when Edyrn sack'd their
    house
And scatter'd all they had to all the winds;
For while the mother show'd it, and the
    two
Were turning and admiring it, the work
To both appear'd so costly, rose a cry
That Edyrn's men were on them, and they
    fled
With little save the jewels they had on,  640
Which being sold and sold had bought
    them bread.
And Edyrn's men had caught them in their
    flight,
And placed them in this ruin; and she
    wish'd
The prince had found her in her ancient
    home;
Then let her fancy flit across the past,
And roam the goodly places that she knew,
And last bethought her how she used to
    watch,
Near that old home, a pool of golden carp;
And one was patch'd and blurr'd and lustre-
    less
Among his burnish'd brethren of the pool;
And half asleep she made comparison    651
Of that and these to her own faded self
And the gay court, and fell asleep again,
And dreamt herself was such a faded form
Among her burnish'd sisters of the pool.
But this was in the garden of a king,
And tho' she lay dark in the pool she knew
That all was bright; that all about were
    birds
Of sunny plume in gilded trellis-work;
That all the turf was rich in plots that
    look'd                                  660
Each like a garnet or a turkis in it;
And lords and ladies of the high court
    went

In silver tissue talking things of state;
And children of the King in cloth of gold
Glanced at the doors or gambol'd down the
    walks.
And while she thought, 'They will not see
    me,' came
A stately queen whose name was Guin-
    evere,
And all the children in their cloth of gold
Ran to her, crying, 'If we have fish at all
Let them be gold; and charge the garden-
    ers now                                          670
To pick the faded creature from the pool,
And cast it on the mixen that it die.'
And therewithal one came and seized on
    her,
And Enid started waking, with her heart
All overshadowed by the foolish dream,
And lo! it was her mother grasping her
To get her well awake; and in her hand
A suit of bright apparel, which she laid
Flat on the couch, and spoke exultingly:

'See here, my child, how fresh the colors
    look,                                            680
How fast they hold, like colors of a shell
That keeps the wear and polish of the
    wave.
Why not? It never yet was worn, I trow:
Look on it, child, and tell me if ye know
    it.'

    And Enid look'd, but, all confused at
    first,
Could scarce divide it from her foolish
    dream.
Then suddenly she knew it and rejoiced,
And answer'd, 'Yea, I know it; your good
    gift,
So sadly lost on that unhappy night;
Your own good gift!' 'Yea, surely,'
    said the dame,                                  690
'And gladly given again this happy morn.
For when the jousts were ended yesterday,
Went Yniol thro' the town, and every-
    where
He found the sack and plunder of our
    house
All scatter'd thro' the houses of the town,
And gave command that all which once was
    ours
Should now be ours again; and yester-eve,
While ye were talking sweetly with your
    prince,
Came one with this and laid it in my hand,

For love or fear, or seeking favor of us,    700
Because we have our earldom back again.
And yester-eve I would not tell you of it,
But kept it for a sweet surprise at morn.
Yea, truly is it not a sweet surprise?
For I myself unwillingly have worn
My faded suit, as you, my child, have yours,
And, howsoever patient, Yniol his.
Ah, dear, he took me from a goodly house,
With store of rich apparel, sumptuous fare,
And page, and maid, and squire, and senes-
    chal,                                           710
And pastime both of hawk and hound, and
    all
That appertains to noble maintenance.
Yea, and he brought me to a goodly house;
But since our fortune swerved from sun to
    shade,
And all thro' that young traitor, cruel need
Constrain'd us, but a better time has come.
So clothe yourself in this, that better fits
Our mended fortunes and a prince's bride;
For tho' ye won the prize of fairest fair,
And tho' I heard him call you fairest fair,
Let never maiden think, however fair,       721
She is not fairer in new clothes than old.
And should some great court-lady say, the
    prince
Hath pick'd a ragged-robin from the hedge,
And like a madman brought her to the
    court,
Then were ye shamed, and, worse, might
    shame the prince
To whom we are beholden; but I know,
When my dear child is set forth at her best,
That neither court nor country, tho' they
    sought
Thro' all the provinces like those of old    730
That lighted on Queen Esther, has her
    match.'

    Here ceased the kindly mother out of
    breath,
And Enid listen'd brightening as she lay;
Then, as the white and glittering star of
    morn
Parts from a bank of snow, and by and by
Slips into golden cloud, the maiden rose,
And left her maiden couch, and robed her-
    self,
Help'd by the mother's careful hand and
    eye,
Without a mirror, in the gorgeous gown;
Who, after, turn'd her daughter round, and
    said                                            740

She never yet had seen her half so fair;
And call'd her like that maiden in the tale,
Whom Gwydion made by glamour out of
    flowers,
And sweeter than the bride of Cassivelaun,
Flur, for whose love the Roman Cæsar first
Invaded Britain: ' But we beat him back,
As this great prince invaded us, and we,
Not beat him back, but welcomed him with
    joy.
And I can scarcely ride with you to court,
For old am I, and rough the ways and
    wild;                                    750
But Yniol goes, and I full oft shall dream
I see my princess as I see her now,
Clothed with my gift and gay among the
    gay.'

But while the women thus rejoiced, Ge-
    raint
Woke where he slept in the high hall, and
    call'd
For Enid, and when Yniol made report
Of that good mother making Enid gay
In such apparel as might well beseem
His princess, or indeed the stately Queen,
He answer'd: ' Earl, entreat her by my
    love,                                    760
Albeit I give no reason but my wish,
That she ride with me in her faded silk.'
Yniol with that hard message went; it fell
Like flaws in summer laying lusty corn;
For Enid, all abash'd she knew not why,
Dared not to glance at her good mother's
    face,
But silently, in all obedience,
Her mother silent too, nor helping her,
Laid from her limbs the costly-broider'd
    gift,                                    769
And robed them in her ancient suit again,
And so descended.   Never man rejoiced
More than Geraint to greet her thus at-
    tired;
And glancing all at once as keenly at her
As careful robins eye the delver's toil,
Made her cheek burn and either eyelid fall,
But rested with her sweet face satisfied;
Then seeing cloud upon the mother's brow,
Her by both hands he caught, and sweetly
    said:

' O my new mother, be not wroth or
    grieved
At thy new son, for my petition to her.  780
When late I left Caerleon, our great Queen,

In words whose echo lasts, they were so
    sweet,
Made promise that, whatever bride I
    brought,
Herself would clothe her like the sun in
    heaven.
Thereafter, when I reach'd this ruin'd hall,
Beholding one so bright in dark estate,
I vow'd that, could I gain her, our fair
    Queen,
No hand but hers, should make your Enid
    burst
Sunlike from cloud — and likewise thought
    perhaps,                               789
That service done so graciously would bind
The two together; fain I would the two
Should love each other.   How can Enid find
A nobler friend ?   Another thought was
    mine:
I came among you here so suddenly
That tho' her gentle presence at the lists
Might well have served for proof that I
    was loved,
I doubted whether daughter's tenderness,
Or easy nature, might not let itself
Be moulded by your wishes for her weal;
Or whether some false sense in her own
    self                                    800
Of my contrasting brightness overbore
Her fancy dwelling in this dusky hall,
And such a sense might make her long for
    court
And all its perilous glories; and I thought,
That could I someway prove such force in
    her
Link'd with such love for me that at a
    word,
No reason given her, she could cast aside
A splendor dear to women, new to her,
And therefore dearer; or if not so new,
Yet therefore tenfold dearer by the power
Of intermitted usage; then I felt        811
That I could rest, a rock in ebbs and flows,
Fixt on her faith.   Now, therefore, I do
    rest,
A prophet certain of my prophecy,
That never shadow of mistrust can cross
Between us.   Grant me pardon for my
    thoughts;
And for my strange petition I will make
Amends hereafter by some gaudy-day,
When your fair child shall wear your costly
    gift
Beside your own warm hearth, with, on her
    knees,                                  820

Who knows? another gift of the high God,
Which, maybe, shall have learn'd to lisp
  you thanks.'

He spoke; the mother smiled, but half
  in tears,
Then brought a mantle down and wrapt her
  in it,
And claspt and kiss'd her, and they rode
  away.

Now thrice that morning Guinevere had
  climb'd
The giant tower, from whose high crest,
  they say,
Men saw the goodly hills of Somerset,
And white sails flying on the yellow sea;
But not to goodly hill or yellow sea     830
Look'd the fair Queen, but up the vale of
  Usk,
By the flat meadow, till she saw them
  come;
And then descending met them at the gates,
Embraced her with all welcome as a friend,
And did her honor as the prince's bride,
And clothed her for her bridals like the
  sun;
And all that week was old Caerleon gay,
For by the hands of Dubric, the high saint,
They twain were wedded with all ceremony.

And this was on the last year's Whitsun-
  tide.                                   840
But Enid ever kept the faded silk,
Remembering how first he came on her
Drest in that dress, and how he loved her
  in it,
And all her foolish fears about the dress,
And all his journey toward her, as himself
Had told her, and their coming to the
  court.

And now this morning when he said to
  her,
'Put on your worst and meanest dress,' she
  found
And took it, and array'd herself therein.

## GERAINT AND ENID

O PURBLIND race of miserable men,
How many among us at this very hour
Do forge a lifelong trouble for ourselves,
By taking true for false, or false for true;

Here, thro' the feeble twilight of this
  world
Groping, how many, until we pass and
  reach
That other where we see as we are seen!

So fared it with Geraint, who issuing
  forth
That morning, when they both had got to
  horse,                                    9
Perhaps because he loved her passionately,
And felt that tempest brooding round his
  heart
Which, if he spoke at all, would break per-
  force
Upon a head so dear in thunder, said:
'Not at my side. I charge thee ride before
Ever a good way on before; and this
I charge thee, on thy duty as a wife,
Whatever happens, not to speak to me,
No, not a word!' and Enid was aghast;
And forth they rode, but scarce three paces
  on,
When crying out, 'Effeminate as I am,    20
I will not fight my way with gilded arms,
All shall be iron;' he loosed a mighty
  purse,
Hung at his belt, and hurl'd it toward the
  squire.
So the last sight that Enid had of home
Was all the marble threshold flashing,
  strown
With gold and scatter'd coinage, and the
  squire
Chafing his shoulder. Then he cried again,
'To the wilds!' and Enid leading down the
  tracks
Thro' which he bade her lead him on, they
  past                                      29
The marches, and by bandit-haunted holds,
Gray swamps and pools, waste places of
  the hern,
And wildernesses, perilous paths, they rode.
Round was their pace at first, but slacken'd
  soon.
A stranger meeting them had surely
  thought,
They rode so slowly and they look'd so pale,
That each had suffer'd some exceeding
  wrong.
For he was ever saying to himself,
'O, I that wasted time to tend upon her,
To compass her with sweet observances,
To dress her beautifully and keep her
  true'—                                   40

And there he broke the sentence in his
    heart
Abruptly, as a man upon his tongue
May break it when his passion masters
    him.
And she was ever praying the sweet hea-
    vens
To save her dear lord whole from any
    wound.
And ever in her mind she cast about
For that unnoticed failing in herself
Which made him look so cloudy and so
    cold;
Till the great plover's human whistle
    amazed
Her heart, and glancing round the waste
    she fear'd                                      50
In every wavering brake an ambuscade;
Then thought again, 'If there be such in
    me,
I might amend it by the grace of Heaven,
If he would only speak and tell me of it.'

But when the fourth part of the day was
    gone,
Then Enid was aware of three tall knights
On horseback, wholly arm'd, behind a rock
In shadow, waiting for them, caitiffs all;
And heard one crying to his fellow, 'Look,
Here comes a laggard hanging down his
    head,                                          60
Who seems no bolder than a beaten hound;
Come, we will slay him and will have his
    horse
And armor, and his damsel shall be ours.'

Then Enid ponder'd in her heart, and
    said:
'I will go back a little to my lord,
And I will tell him all their caitiff talk;
For, be he wroth even to slaying me,
Far liefer by his dear hand had I die
Than that my lord should suffer loss or
    shame.'

Then she went back some paces of re-
    turn,                                          70
Met his full frown timidly firm, and said:
'My lord, I saw three bandits by the rock
Waiting to fall on you, and heard them
    boast
That they would slay you, and possess your
    horse
And armor, and your damsel should be
    theirs.'

He made a wrathful answer: 'Did I
    wish
Your warning or your silence? one com-
    mand
I laid upon you, not to speak to me,
And thus ye keep it! Well then, look —
    for now,
Whether ye wish me victory or defeat,     80
Long for my life or hunger for my death,
Yourself shall see my vigor is not lost.'

Then Enid waited pale and sorrowful,
And down upon him bare the bandit three.
And at the midmost charging, Prince Ge-
    raint
Drave the long spear a cubit thro' his
    breast
And out beyond; and then against his
    brace
Of comrades, each of whom had broken on
    him
A lance that splinter'd like an icicle,
Swung from his brand a windy buffet out   90
Once, twice, to right, to left, and stunn'd
    the twain
Or slew them, and dismounting, like a
    man
That skins the wild beast after slaying
    him,
Stript from the three dead wolves of woman
    born
The three gay suits of armor which they
    wore,
And let the bodies lie, but bound the suits
Of armor on their horses, each on each,
And tied the bridle-reins of all the three
Together, and said to her, 'Drive them on
Before you;' and she drove them thro' the
    waste.                                         100

He follow'd nearer; ruth began to work
Against his anger in him, while he watch'd
The being he loved best in all the world,
With difficulty in mild obedience
Driving them on. He fain had spoken to
    her,
And loosed in words of sudden fire the
    wrath
And smoulder'd wrong that burnt him all
    within;
But evermore it seem'd an easier thing
At once without remorse to strike her dead
Than to cry 'Halt,' and to her own bright
    face                                           110
Accuse her of the least immodesty:

And thus tongue-tied, it made him wroth
    the more
That she *could* speak whom his own ear
    had heard
Call herself false, and suffering thus he
    made
Minutes an age; but in scarce longer time
Than at Caerleon the full-tided Usk,
Before he turn to fall seaward again,
Pauses, did Enid, keeping watch, behold
In the first shallow shade of a deep wood,
Before a gloom of stubborn-shafted oaks,
Three other horsemen waiting, wholly
    arm'd,                                       121
Whereof one seem'd far larger than her
    lord,
And shook her pulses, crying, 'Look, a
    prize !
Three horses and three goodly suits of
    arms,
And all in charge of whom ? a girl! set
    on.'
'Nay,' said the second, 'yonder comes a
    knight.'
The third, 'A craven; how he hangs his
    head !'
The giant answer'd merrily, 'Yea, but
    one ?
Wait here, and when he passes fall upon
    him !'

And Enid ponder'd in her heart and said:
'I will abide the coming of my lord,     131
And I will tell him all their villainy.
My lord is weary with the fight before,
And they will fall upon him unawares.
I needs must disobey him for his good;
How should I dare obey him to his harm ?
Needs must I speak, and tho' he kill me
    for it,
I save a life dearer to me than mine.'

And she abode his coming, and said to
    him
With timid firmness, 'Have I leave to
    speak ?'                                   140
He said, 'Ye take it, speaking,' and she
    spoke:

'There lurk three villains yonder in the
    wood,
And each of them is wholly arm'd, and one
Is larger-limb'd than you are, and they say
That they will fall upon you while ye
    pass.'

To which he flung a wrathful answer
    back:
'And if there were an hundred in the
    wood,
And every man were larger-limb'd than I,
And all at once should sally out upon me,
I swear it would not ruffle me so much   150
As you that not obey me.   Stand aside,
And if I fall, cleave to the better man.'

And Enid stood aside to wait the event,
Not dare to watch the combat, only breathe
Short fits of prayer, at every stroke a
    breath.
And he she dreaded most bare down upon
    him.
Aim'd at the helm, his lance err'd; but
    Geraint's,
A little in the late encounter strain'd,
Struck thro' the bulky bandit's corselet
    home,
And then brake short, and down his enemy
    roll'd,                                     160
And there lay still; as he that tells the
    tale
Saw once a great piece of a promontory,
That had a sapling growing on it, slide
From the long shore-cliff's windy walls to
    the beach,
And there lie still, and yet the sapling
    grew;
So lay the man transfixt.   His craven pair
Of comrades making slowlier at the prince,
When now they saw their bulwark fallen,
    stood;
On whom the victor, to confound them
    more,
Spurr'd with his terrible war-cry; for as
    one,                                       170
That listens near a torrent mountain-brook,
All thro' the crash of the near cataract
    hears
The drumming thunder of the huger fall
At distance, were the soldiers wont to hear
His voice in battle, and be kindled by it,
And foemen scared, like that false pair
    who turn'd
Flying, but, overtaken, died the death
Themselves had wrought on many an in-
    nocent.

Thereon Geraint, dismounting, pick'd the
    lance
That pleased him best, and drew from
    those dead wolves                           180

Their three gay suits of armor, each from
    each,
And bound them on their horses, each on
    each,
And tied the bridle-reins of all the three
Together, and said to her, 'Drive them on
Before you,' and she drove them thro' the
    wood.

    He follow'd nearer still.   The pain she
        had
To keep them in the wild ways of the
    wood,
Two sets of three laden with jingling arms,
Together, served a little to disedge      189
The sharpness of that pain about her heart;
And they themselves, like creatures gently
    born
But into bad hands fallen, and now so
    long
By bandits groom'd, prick'd their light
    ears, and felt
Her low firm voice and tender government.

    So thro' the green gloom of the wood
        they past,
And issuing under open heavens beheld
A little town with towers, upon a rock,
And close beneath, a meadow gemlike
    chased
In the brown wild, and mowers mowing
    in it;                                    199
And down a rocky pathway from the place
There came a fair-hair'd youth, that in his
    hand
Bare victual for the mowers; and Geraint
Had ruth again on Enid looking pale.
Then, moving downward to the meadow
    ground,
He, when the fair-hair'd youth came by
    him, said,
'Friend, let her eat; the damsel is so faint.'
'Yea, willingly,' replied the youth; 'and
    thou,
My lord, eat also, tho' the fare is coarse,
And only meet for mowers;' then set down
His basket, and dismounting on the sward
They let the horses graze, and ate them-
    selves.                                    211
And Enid took a little delicately,
Less having stomach for it than desire
To close with her lord's pleasure, but Ge-
    raint
Ate all the mowers' victual unawares,
And when he found all empty was amazed;

And 'Boy,' said he, 'I have eaten all, but
    take
A horse and arms for guerdon; choose the
    best.'
He, reddening in extremity of delight,
'My lord, you overpay me fifty-fold.'     220
'Ye will be all the wealthier,' cried the
    prince.
'I take it as free gift, then,' said the boy,
'Not guerdon; for myself can easily,
While your good damsel rests, return and
    fetch
Fresh victual for these mowers of our earl;
For these are his, and all the field is his,
And I myself am his; and I will tell him
How great a man thou art.   He loves to
    know
When men of mark are in his territory;
And he will have thee to his palace here, 230
And serve thee costlier than with mowers'
    fare.'

    Then said Geraint: 'I wish no better fare;
I never ate with angrier appetite
Than when I left your mowers dinnerless.
And into no earl's palace will I go.
I know, God knows, too much of palaces!
And if he want me, let him come to me.
But hire us some fair chamber for the
    night,
And stalling for the horses, and return
With victual for these men, and let us
    know.'                                    240

    'Yea, my kind lord,' said the glad youth,
        and went,
Held his head high, and thought himself a
    knight,
And up the rocky pathway disappear'd,
Leading the horse, and they were left alone.

    But when the prince had brought his
        errant eyes
Home from the rock, sideways he let them
    glance
At Enid, where she droopt.   His own false
    doom,
That shadow of mistrust should never cross
Betwixt them, came upon him, and he
    sigh'd;
Then with another humorous ruth remark'd
The lusty mowers laboring dinnerless,     251
And watch'd the sun blaze on the turning
    scythe,
And after nodded sleepily in the heat.

But she, remembering her old ruin'd hall,
And all the windy clamor of the daws
About her hollow turret, pluck'd the grass
There growing longest by the meadow's
      edge,
And into many a listless annulet,
Now over, now beneath her marriage ring,
Wove and unwove it, till the boy return'd
And told them of a chamber, and they
      went;                                    261
Where, after saying to her, ' If ye will,
Call for the woman of the house,' to which
She answer'd, ' Thanks, my lord; ' the two
      remain'd
Apart by all the chamber's width, and mute
As creatures voiceless thro' the fault of
      birth,
Or two wild men supporters of a shield,
Painted, who stare at open space, nor
      glance
The one at other, parted by the shield.

On a sudden, many a voice along the
      street,                                   270
And heel against the pavement echoing,
      burst
Their drowse; and either started while the
      door,
Push'd from without, drave backward to
      the wall,
And midmost of a rout of roisterers,
Femininely fair and dissolutely pale,
Her suitor in old years before Geraint
Enter'd, the wild lord of the place, Li-
      mours.
He moving up with pliant courtliness
Greeted Geraint full face, but stealthily,
In the mid-warmth of welcome and graspt
      hand,                                     280
Found Enid with the corner of his eye,
And knew her sitting sad and solitary.
Then cried Geraint for wine and goodly
      cheer
To feed the sudden guest, and sumptu-
      ously,
According to his fashion, bade the host
Call in what men soever were his friends,
And feast with these in honor of their
      earl;
' And care not for the cost; the cost is
      mine.'

And wine and food were brought, and Earl
      Limours
Drank till he jested with all ease, and told

Free tales, and took the word and play'd
      upon it,                                  291
And made it of two colors; for his talk,
When wine and free companions kindled
      him,
Was wont to glance and sparkle like a
      gem
Of fifty facets; thus he moved the prince
To laughter and his comrades to applause.
Then, when the prince was merry, ask'd
      Limours,
' Your leave, my lord, to cross the room,
      and speak
To your good damsel there who sits apart,
And seems so lonely ? '  ' My free leave,'
      he said;                                  300
' Get her to speak; she doth not speak to
      me.'
Then rose Limours, and looking at his feet,
Like him who tries the bridge he fears may
      fail,
Crost and came near, lifted adoring eyes,
Bow'd at her side and utter'd whisper-
      ingly :

' Enid, the pilot star of my lone life,
Enid, my early and my only love,
Enid, the loss of whom hath turn'd me
      wild —
What chance is this ? how is it I see you
      here ?
Ye are in my power at last, are in my
      power.                                     310
Yet fear me not; I call mine own self wild,
But keep a touch of sweet civility
Here in the heart of waste and wilderness.
I thought, but that your father came be-
      tween,
In former days you saw me favorably.
And if it were so do not keep it back.
Make me a little happier; let me know it.
Owe you me nothing for a life half-lost ?
Yea, yea, the whole dear debt of all you
      are.
And, Enid, you and he, I see with joy,    320
Ye sit apart, you do not speak to him,
You come with no attendance, page or
      maid,
To serve you — doth he love you as of
      old ?
For, call it lovers' quarrels, yet I know
Tho' men may bicker with the things they
      love,
They would not make them laughable in
      all eyes,

Not while they loved them; and your
    wretched dress,
A wretched insult on you, dumbly speaks
Your story, that this man loves you no
    more.
Your beauty is no beauty to him now.   330
A common chance — right well I know it
    — pall'd —
For I know men; nor will ye win him back,
For the man's love once gone never re-
    turns.
But here is one who loves you as of old;
With more exceeding passion than of old.
Good, speak the word; my followers ring
    him round.
He sits unarm'd; I hold a finger up;
They understand.  Nay, I do not mean
    blood;
Nor need ye look so scared at what I say.
My malice is no deeper than a moat,   340
No stronger than a wall.  There is the
    keep;
He shall not cross us more; speak but the
    word.
Or speak it not; but then by Him that
    made me
The one true lover whom you ever own'd,
I will make use of all the power I have.
O, pardon me ! the madness of that hour
When first I parted from thee moves me
    yet.'

    At this the tender sound of his own voice
And sweet self-pity, or the fancy of it,
Made his eye moist; but Enid fear'd his
    eyes,   350
Moist as they were, wine-heated from the
    feast,
And answer'd with such craft as women
    use,
Guilty or guiltless, to stave off a chance
That breaks upon them perilously, and
    said:

    ' Earl, if you love me as in former years,
And do not practise on me, come with
    morn,
And snatch me from him as by violence.
Leave me to-night; I am weary to the
    death.'

    Low at leave-taking, with his brandish'd
    plume
Brushing his instep, bow'd the all-amorous
    earl,   360

And the stout prince bade him a loud good-
    night.
He moving homeward babbled to his men,
How Enid never loved a man but him,
Nor cared a broken egg-shell for her lord.

    But Enid left alone with Prince Geraint,
Debating his command of silence given,
And that she now perforce must violate it,
Held commune with herself, and while she
    held
He fell asleep, and Enid had no heart
To wake him, but hung o'er him, wholly
    pleased   370
To find him yet unwounded after fight,
And hear him breathing low and equally.
Anon she rose and, stepping lightly, heap'd
The pieces of his armor in one place,
All to be there against a sudden need;
Then dozed awhile herself, but, overtoil'd
By that day's grief and travel, evermore
Seem'd catching at a rootless thorn, and
    then
Went slipping down horrible precipices,
And strongly striking out her limbs awoke;
Then thought she heard the wild earl at
    the door,   381
With all his rout of random followers,
Sound on a dreadful trumpet, summoning
    her;
Which was the red cock shouting to the
    light,
As the gray dawn stole o'er the dewy world
And glimmer'd on his armor in the room.
And once again she rose to look at it,
But touch'd it unawares; jangling, the
    casque
Fell, and he started up and stared at her.
Then breaking his command of silence
    given,   390
She told him all that Earl Limours had
    said,
Except the passage that he loved her not;
Nor left untold the craft herself had used,
But ended with apology so sweet,
Low - spoken, and of so few words, and
    seem'd
So justified by that necessity,
That tho' he thought, ' Was it for him she
    wept
In Devon ?' he but gave a wrathful groan,
Saying, ' Your sweet faces make good fel-
    lows fools
And traitors.  Call the host and bid him
    bring   400

Charger and palfrey.'   So she glided out
Among the heavy breathings of the house,
And like a household spirit at the walls
Beat, till she woke the sleepers, and re-
    turn'd;
Then tending her rough lord, tho' all un-
    ask'd,
In silence, did him service as a squire;
Till issuing arm'd he found the host and
    cried,
'Thy reckoning, friend?' and ere he learnt
    it, 'Take
Five horses and their armors;' and the
    host,
Suddenly honest, answer'd in amaze,     410
'My lord, I scarce have spent the worth of
    one!'
'Ye will be all the wealthier,' said the
    prince,
And then to Enid, 'Forward! and to-day
I charge you, Enid, more especially,
What thing soever ye may hear, or see,
Or fancy — tho' I count it of small use
To charge you — that ye speak not but
    obey.'

     And Enid answer'd: 'Yea, my lord, I
         know
Your wish and would obey; but, riding
    first,
I hear the violent threats you do not hear,
I see the danger which you cannot see.     421
Then not to give you warning, that seems
    hard,
Almost beyond me; yet I would obey.'

     'Yea so,' said he, 'do it; be not too wise,
Seeing that ye are wedded to a man,
Not all mismated with a yawning clown,
But one with arms to guard his head and
    yours,
With eyes to find you out however far,
And ears to hear you even in his dreams.'

     With that he turn'd and look'd as keenly
         at her     430
As careful robins eye the delver's toil;
And that within her which a wanton fool
Or hasty judger would have call'd her guilt
Made her cheek burn and either eyelid fall.
And Geraint look'd and was not satisfied.

     Then forward by a way which, beaten
         broad,
Led from the territory of false Limours

To the waste earldom of another earl,
Doorm, whom his shaking vassals call'd the
    Bull,
Went Enid with her sullen follower on.   440
Once she look'd back, and when she saw
    him ride
More near by many a rood than yester-
    morn,
It wellnigh made her cheerful; till Geraint,
Waving an angry hand as who should say,
'Ye watch me,' sadden'd all her heart
    again.
But while the sun yet beat a dewy blade,
The sound of many a heavily - galloping
    hoof
Smote on her ear, and turning round she
    saw
Dust, and the points of lances bicker in it.
Then, not to disobey her lord's behest,   450
And yet to give him warning, for he rode
As if he heard not, moving back she held
Her finger up, and pointed to the dust.
At which the warrior in his obstinacy,
Because she kept the letter of his word,
Was in a manner pleased, and turning
    stood.
And in the moment after, wild Limours,
Borne on a black horse, like a thunder-
    cloud
Whose skirts are loosen'd by the breaking
    storm,                                459
Half ridden off with by the thing he rode,
And all in passion uttering a dry shriek,
Dash'd on Geraint, who closed with him,
    and bore
Down by the length of lance and arm be-
    yond
The crupper, and so left him stunn'd or
    dead,
And overthrew the next that follow'd him,
And blindly rush'd on all the rout behind.
But at the flash and motion of the man
They vanish'd panic-stricken, like a shoal
Of darting fish, that on a summer morn
Adown the crystal dykes at Camelot        470
Come slipping o'er their shadows on the
    sand,
But if a man who stands upon the brink
But lift a shining hand against the sun,
There is not left the twinkle of a fin
Betwixt the cressy islets white in flower;
So, scared but at the motion of the man,
Fled all the boon companions of the earl,
And left him lying in the public way;
So vanish friendships only made in wine.

Then like a stormy sunlight smiled Ge-
    raint,                                      480
Who saw the chargers of the two that fell
Start from their fallen lords and wildly fly,
Mixt with the flyers.  'Horse and man,' he
    said,
' All of one mind and all right - honest
    friends !
Not a hoof left ! and I methinks till now
Was honest — paid with horses and with
    arms;
I cannot steal or plunder, no, nor beg.
And so what say ye, shall we strip him
    there,
Your lover ? has your palfrey heart enough
To bear his armor ? shall we fast or dine ?
No ? — then do thou, being right honest,
    pray                                        491
That we may meet the horsemen of Earl
    Doorm;
I too would still be honest.'  Thus he said;
And sadly gazing on her bridle-reins,
And answering not one word, she led the
    way.

But as a man to whom a dreadful loss
Falls in a far land and he knows it not,
But coming back he learns it, and the loss
So pains him that he sickens nigh to death;
So fared it with Geraint, who, being
    prick'd                                     500
In combat with the follower of Limours,
Bled underneath his armor secretly,
And so rode on, nor told his gentle wife
What ail'd him, hardly knowing it him-
    self,
Till his eye darken'd and his helmet
    wagg'd;
And at a sudden swerving of the road,
Tho' happily down on a bank of grass,
The prince, without a word, from his horse
    fell.

And Enid heard the clashing of his fall,
Suddenly came, and at his side all pale   510
Dismounting loosed the fastenings of his
    arms,
Nor let her true hand falter, nor blue eye
Moisten, till she had lighted on his wound,
And tearing off her veil of faded silk
Had bared her forehead to the blistering
    sun,
And swathed the hurt that drain'd her dear
    lord's life.
Then, after all was done that hand could do,

She rested, and her desolation came
Upon her, and she wept beside the way.

And many past, but none regarded her,
For in that realm of lawless turbulence   521
A woman weeping for her murder'd mate
Was cared as much for as a summer
    shower.
One took him for a victim of Earl Doorm,
Nor dared to waste a perilous pity on him.
Another hurrying past, a man-at-arms,
Rode on a mission to the bandit earl;
Half whistling and half singing a coarse
    song,
He drove the dust against her veilless
    eyes.                                       529
Another, flying from the wrath of Doorm
Before an ever-fancied arrow, made
The long way smoke beneath him in his
    fear;
At which her palfrey whinnying lifted heel,
And scour'd into the coppices and was lost,
While the great charger stood, grieved like
    a man.

But at the point of noon the huge Earl
    Doorm,
Broad - faced with under - fringe of russet
    beard,
Bound on a foray, rolliug eyes of prey,
Came riding with a hundred lances up;
But ere he came, like one that hails a
    ship,                                       540
Cried out with a big voice, ' What, is he
    ' dead ? '
' No, no, not dead ! ' she answer'd in all
    haste.
' Would some of your kind people take
    him up,
And bear him hence out of this cruel sun ?
Most sure am I, quite sure, he is not dead.'

Then said Earl Doorm: ' Well, if he be
    not dead,
Why wail ye for him thus ? ye seem a
    child.
And be he dead, I count you for a fool;
Your wailing will not quicken him; dead
    or not,
Ye mar a comely face with idiot tears.   550
Yet, since the face is comely — some of you,
Here, take him up, and bear him to our
    hall.
An if he live, we will have him of our
    band;

And if he die, why earth has earth enough
To hide him.    See ye take the charger too,
A noble one.'
   He spake and past away,
But left two brawny spearmen, who ad-
 vanced,
Each growling like a dog, when his good
 bone                                    558
Seems to be pluck'd at by the village boys
Who love to vex him eating, and he fears
To lose his bone, and lays his foot upon it,
Gnawing and growling; so the ruffians
 growl'd,
Fearing to lose, and all for a dead man,
Their chance of booty from the morning's
 raid,
Yet raised and laid him on a litter-bier,
Such as they brought upon their forays out
For those that might be wounded; laid
 him on it
All in the hollow of his shield, and took
And bore him to the naked hall of Doorm —
His gentle charger following him unled —
And cast him and the bier in which he
 lay
Down on an oaken settle in the hall,     572
And then departed, hot in haste to join
Their luckier mates, but growling as be-
 fore,
And cursing their lost time, and the dead
 man,
And their own earl, and their own souls,
 and her.
They might as well have blest her; she
 was deaf
To blessing or to cursing save from one.

 So for long hours sat Enid by her lord
There in the naked hall, propping his
 head,                                   580
And chafing his pale hands, and calling to
 him,
Till at the last he waken'd from his swoon,
And found his own dear bride propping his
 head,
And chafing his faint hands, and calling to
 him;
And felt the warm tears falling on his face,
And said to his own heart, 'She weeps for
 me;'
And yet lay still, and feign'd himself as
 dead,
That he might prove her to the uttermost,
And say to his own heart, 'She weeps for
 me.'

But in the falling afternoon return'd    590
The huge Earl Doorm with plunder to the
 hall.
His lusty spearmen follow'd him with
 noise:
Each hurling down a heap of things that
 rang
Against the pavement, cast his lance aside,
And doff'd his helm; and then there flut-
 ter'd in,
Half-bold, half-frighted, with dilated eyes,
A tribe of women, dress'd in many hues,
And mingled with the spearmen; and Earl
 Doorm
Struck with a knife's haft hard against the
 board,
And call'd for flesh and wine to feed his
 spears.                                  600
And men brought in whole hogs and quar-
 ter beeves,
And all the hall was dim with steam of
 flesh.
And none spake word, but all sat down at
 once,
And ate with tumult in the naked hall,
Feeding like horses when you hear them
 feed;
Till Enid shrank far back into herself,
To shun the wild ways of the lawless tribe.
But when Earl Doorm had eaten all he
 would,
He roll'd his eyes about the hall, and found
A damsel drooping in a corner of it.     610
Then he remember'd her and how she
 wept,
And out of her there came a power upon
 him;
And rising on the sudden he said: 'Eat !
I never yet beheld a thing so pale.
God's curse, it makes me mad to see you
 weep.
Eat !   Look yourself.   Good luck had your
 good man,
For were I dead who is it would weep for
 me ?
Sweet lady, never since I first drew breath
Have I beheld a lily like yourself.
And so there lived some color in your
 cheek,                                  620
There is not one among my gentlewomen
Were fit to wear your slipper for a glove.
But listen to me, and by me be ruled,
And I will do the thing I have not done,
For ye shall share my earldom with me,
 girl,

And we will live like two birds in one nest,
And I will fetch you forage from all fields,
For I compel all creatures to my will.'

He spoke; the brawny spearman let his
    cheek
Bulge with the unswallow'd piece, and
    turning stared;                          630
While some, whose souls the old serpent
    long had drawn
Down, as the worm draws in the wither'd
    leaf
And makes it earth, hiss'd each at other's
    ear
What shall not be recorded — women they,
Women, or what had been those gracious
    things,
But now desired the humbling of their best,
Yea, would have help'd him to it; and all
    at once
They hated her, who took no thought of
    them,
But answer'd in low voice, her meek head
    yet
Drooping, 'I pray you of your courtesy,   640
He being as he is, to let me be.'

She spake so low he hardly heard her
    speak,
But like a mighty patron, satisfied
With what himself had done so graciously,
Assumed that she had thank'd him, add-
    ing, ' Yea,
Eat and be glad, for I account you mine.'

She answer'd meekly, 'How should I be
    glad
Henceforth in all the world at anything,
Until my lord arise and look upon me ? '

Here the huge earl cried out upon her
    talk,                                   650
As all but empty heart and weariness
And sickly nothing; suddenly seized on her,
And bare her by main violence to the
    board,
And thrust the dish before her, crying,
    ' Eat.'

' No, no,' said Enid, vext, ' I will not eat
Till yonder man upon the bier arise,
And eat with me.'   ' Drink, then,' he an-
    swer'd.   ' Here ! ' —
And fill'd a horn with wine and held it to
    her, —

' Lo !   I, myself, when flush'd with fight or
    hot,                                    659
God's curse, with anger — often I myself,
Before I well have drunken, scarce can
    eat;
Drink therefore, and the wine will change
    your will.'

' Not so,' she cried, ' by Heaven, I will
    not drink
Till my dear lord arise and bid me do it,
And drink with me; and if he rise no more,
I will not look at wine until I die.'

At this he turn'd all red and paced his
    hall,
Now gnaw'd his under, now his upper lip,
And coming up close to her, said at last:
' Girl, for I see ye scorn my courtesies,  670
Take warning; yonder man is surely dead,
And I compel all creatures to my will.
Not eat nor drink ?   And wherefore wail
    for one
Who put your beauty to this flout and
    scorn
By dressing it in rags ?   Amazed am I,
Beholding how ye butt against my wish,
That I forbear you thus; cross me no
    more.
At least put off to please me this poor
    gown,
This silken rag, this beggar-woman's weed.
I love that beauty should go beautifully;
For see ye not my gentlewomen here,      681
How gay, how suited to the house of one
Who loves that beauty should go beauti-
    fully ?
Rise therefore; robe yourself in this; obey.'

He spoke, and one among his gentle-
    women
Display'd a splendid silk of foreign loom,
Where like a shoaling sea the lovely blue
Play'd into green, and thicker down the
    front
With jewels than the sward with drops of
    dew,
When all night long a cloud clings to the
    hill,                                   690
And with the dawn ascending lets the day
Strike where it clung; so thickly shone the
    gems.

But Enid answer'd, harder to be moved
Than hardest tyrants in their day of power,

With lifelong injuries burning unavenged,
And now their hour has come; and Enid
said:

'In this poor gown my dear lord found
    me first,
And loved me serving in my father's hall;
In this poor gown I rode with him to
    court,
And there the Queen array'd me like the
    sun;                                    700
In this poor gown he bade me clothe my-
    self,
When now we rode upon this fatal quest
Of honor, where no honor can be gain'd;
And this poor gown I will not cast aside
Until himself arise a living man,
And bid me cast it.   I have griefs enough;
Pray you be gentle, pray you let me be.
I never loved, can never love but him.
Yea, God, I pray you of your gentleness,
He being as he is, to let me be.'          710

Then strode the brute earl up and down
    his hall,
And took his russet beard between his
    teeth;
Last, coming up quite close, and in his
    mood
Crying, 'I count it of no more avail,
Dame, to be gentle than ungentle with
    you;
Take my salute,' unknightly with flat hand,
However lightly, smote her on the cheek.

Then Enid, in her utter helplessness,
And since she thought, 'He had not dared
    to do it,                              719
Except he surely knew my lord was dead,'
Sent forth a sudden sharp and bitter cry,
As of a wild thing taken in the trap,
Which sees the trapper coming thro' the
    wood.

This heard Geraint, and grasping at his
    sword, —
It lay beside him in the hollow shield, —
Made but a single bound, and with a sweep
    of it
Shore thro' the swarthy neck, and like a
    ball
The russet-bearded head roll'd on the floor.
So died Earl Doorm by him he counted
    dead.
And all the men and women in the hall    730

Rose when they saw the dead man rise, and
    fled
Yelling as from a spectre, and the two
Were left alone together, and he said:

'Enid, I have used you worse than that
    dead man,
Done you more wrong; we both have un-
    dergone
That trouble which has left me thrice your
    own.
Henceforward I will rather die than doubt.
And here I lay this penance on myself,
Not, tho' mine own ears heard you yester-
    morn —
You thought me sleeping, but I heard you
    say,                                   740
I heard you say, that you were no true
    wife,
I swear I will not ask your meaning in it.
I do believe yourself against yourself,
And will henceforward rather die than
    doubt.'

And Enid could not say one tender
    word,
She felt so blunt and stupid at the heart.
She only pray'd him, 'Fly, they will return
And slay you; fly, your charger is without,
My palfrey lost.'   'Then, Enid, shall you
    ride                                   749
Behind me.'   'Yea,' said Enid, 'let us go.'
And moving out they found the stately
    horse,
Who now no more a vassal to the thief,
But free to stretch his limbs in lawful fight,
Neigh'd with all gladness as they came, and
    stoop'd
With a low whinny toward the pair; and
    she
Kiss'd the white star upon his noble front,
Glad also; then Geraint upon the horse
Mounted, and reach'd a hand, and on his
    foot
She set her own and climb'd; he turn'd his
    face
And kiss'd her climbing, and she cast her
    arms                                   760
About him, and at once they rode away.

And never yet, since high in Paradise
O'er the four rivers the first roses blew,
Came purer pleasure unto mortal kind
Than lived thro' her who in that perilous
    hour

Put hand to hand beneath her husband's
    heart,
And felt him hers again.  She did not weep,
But o'er her meek eyes came a happy
    mist
Like that which kept the heart of Eden
    green
Before the useful trouble of the rain.   770
Yet not so misty were her meek blue eyes
As not to see before them on the path,
Right in the gateway of the bandit hold,
A knight of Arthur's court, who laid his
    lance
In rest and made as if to fall upon him.
Then, fearing for his hurt and loss of
    blood,
She, with her mind all full of what had
    chanced,
Shriek'd to the stranger, 'Slay not a dead
    man ! '
'The voice of Enid,' said the knight; but
    she,
Beholding it was Edyrn, son of Nudd,   780
Was moved so much the more, and shriek'd
    again,
'O cousin, slay not him who gave you life.'
And Edyrn moving frankly forward spake:
'My lord Geraint, I greet you with all
    love;
I took you for a bandit knight of Doorm;
And fear not, Enid, I should fall upon
    him,
Who love you, prince, with something of
    the love
Wherewith we love the Heaven that chas-
    tens us.                              788
For once, when I was up so high in pride
That I was halfway down the slope to hell,
By overthrowing me you threw me higher.
Now, made a knight of Arthur's Table
    Round,
And since I knew this earl when I myself
Was half a bandit in my lawless hour,
I come the mouthpiece of our King to
    Doorm —
The King is close behind me — bidding
    him
Disband himself, and scatter all his powers,
Submit, and hear the judgment of the
    King.'

'He hears the judgment of the King of
    kings,'
Cried the wan prince; 'and lo, the powers
    of Doorm                            800

Are scatter'd ! ' and he pointed to the field,
Where, huddled here and there on mound
    and knoll,
Were men and women staring and aghast,
While some yet fled; and then he plainlier
    told
How the huge earl lay slain within his
    hall.
But when the knight besought him, 'Fol-
    low me,
Prince, to the camp, and in the King's own
    ear
Speak what has chanced; ye surely have
    endured
Strange chances here alone;' that other
    flush'd,
And hung his head, and halted in reply,  810
Fearing the mild face of the blameless
    King,
And after madness acted question ask'd;
Till Edyrn crying, 'If ye will not go
To Arthur, then will Arthur come to you,'
'Enough,' he said, 'I follow,' and they
    went.
But Enid in their going had two fears,
One from the bandit scatter'd in the field,
And one from Edyrn.  Every now and
    then,
When Edyrn rein'd his charger at her
    side,
She shrank a little.  In a hollow land,  820
From which old fires have broken, men
    may fear
Fresh fire and ruin.  He, perceiving, said:

'Fair and dear cousin, you that most
    had cause
To fear me, fear no longer, I am changed.
Yourself were first the blameless cause to
    make
My nature's prideful sparkle in the blood
Break into furious flame; being repulsed
By Yniol and yourself, I schemed and
    wrought
Until I overturn'd him; then set up —  829
With one main purpose ever at my heart —
My haughty jousts, and took a paramour;
Did her mock-honor as the fairest fair,
And, toppling over all antagonism,
So wax'd in pride that I believed myself
Unconquerable, for I was wellnigh mad;
And, but for my main purpose in these
    jousts,
I should have slain your father, seized
    yourself.

I lived in hope that sometime you would
    come
To these my lists with him whom best you
    loved,
And there, poor cousin, with your meek
    blue eyes,            840
The truest eyes that ever answer'd heaven,
Behold me overturn and trample on him.
Then, had you cried, or knelt, or pray'd to
    me,
I should not less have kill'd him.  And
    you came, —
But once you came, — and with your own
    true eyes
Beheld the man you loved — I speak as one
Speaks of a service done him — overthrow
My proud self, and my purpose three years
    old,
And set his foot upon me, and give me life.
There was I broken down, there was I
    saved;            850
Tho' thence I rode all-shamed, hating the
    life
He gave me, meaning to be rid of it.
And all the penance the Queen laid upon
    me
Was but to rest awhile within her court;
Where first as sullen as a beast new-caged,
And waiting to be treated like a wolf,
Because I knew my deeds were known, I
    found,
Instead of scornful pity or pure scorn,
Such fine reserve and noble reticence,
Manners so kind, yet stately, such a grace
Of tenderest courtesy, that I began    861
To glance behind me at my former life,
And find that it had been the wolf's in-
    deed.
And oft I talk'd with Dubric, the high
    saint,
Who, with mild heat of holy oratory,
Subdued me somewhat to that gentleness
Which, when it weds with manhood, makes
    a man.
And you were often there about the Queen,
But saw me not, or mark'd not if you saw;
Nor did I care or dare to speak with you,  870
But kept myself aloof till I was changed;
And fear not, cousin, I am changed in-
    deed.'

He spoke, and Enid easily believed,
Like simple noble natures, credulous
Of what they long for, good in friend or
    foe,

There most in those who most have done
    them ill.
And when they reach'd the camp the King
    himself
Advanced to greet them, and beholding her
Tho' pale, yet happy, ask'd her not a word,
But went apart with Edyrn, whom he held
In converse for a little, and return'd,    881
And, gravely smiling, lifted her from horse,
And kiss'd her with all pureness, brother-
    like,
And show'd an empty tent allotted her,
And glancing for a minute, till he saw
    her
Pass into it, turn'd to the prince, and said:

'Prince, when of late ye pray'd me for
    my leave
To move to your own land and there defend
Your marches, I was prick'd with some
    reproof,          889
As one that let foul wrong stagnate and be,
By having look'd too much thro' alien eyes,
And wrought too long with delegated hands,
Not used mine own; but now behold me
    come
To cleanse this common sewer of all my
    realm,
With Edyrn and with others.  Have ye
    look'd
At Edyrn?  have ye seen how nobly
    changed?
This work of his is great and wonderful.
His very face with change of heart is
    changed.
The world will not believe a man repents;
And this wise world of ours is mainly right.
Full seldom doth a man repent, or use  901
Both grace and will to pick the vicious
    quitch
Of blood and custom wholly out of him,
And make all clean, and plant himself
    afresh.
Edyrn has done it, weeding all his heart
As I will weed this land before I go.
I, therefore, made him of our Table Round,
Not rashly, but have proved him every way
One of our noblest, our most valorous,
Sanest and most obedient; and indeed  910
This work of Edyrn, wrought upon himself
After a life of violence, seems to me
A thousand-fold more great and wonderful
Than if some knight of mine, risking his
    life,
My subject with my subjects under him,

Should make an onslaught single on a
    realm
Of robbers, tho' he slew them one by one,
And were himself nigh wounded to the
    death.'

  So spake the King; low bow'd the
    prince, and felt                            919
His work was neither great nor wonderful,
And past to Enid's tent; and thither came
The King's own leech to look into his hurt;
And Enid tended on him there; and there
Her constant motion round him, and the
    breath
Of her sweet tendance hovering over him,
Fill'd all the genial courses of his blood
With deeper and with ever deeper love,
As the Southwest that blowing Bala lake
Fills all the sacred Dee.  So past the days.

  But while Geraint lay healing of his hurt,
The blameless King went forth and cast his
    eyes                                          931
On each of all whom Uther left in charge
Long since, to guard the justice of the
    King.
He look'd and found them wanting; and as
    now
Men weed the White Horse on the Berk-
    shire hills,
To keep him bright and clean as hereto-
    fore,
He rooted out the slothful officer
Or guilty, which for bribe had wink'd at
    wrong,
And in their chairs set up a stronger race
With hearts and hands, and sent a thou-
    sand men                                      940
To till the wastes, and moving everywhere
Clear'd the dark places and let in the law,
And broke the bandit holds and cleansed
    the land.

  Then, when Geraint was whole again, they
    past
With Arthur to Caerleon upon Usk.
There the great Queen once more embraced
    her friend,
And clothed her in apparel like the day.
And tho' Geraint could never take again
That comfort from their converse which he
    took
Before the Queen's fair name was breathed
    upon,                                         950
He rested well content that all was well.

Thence after tarrying for a space they rode,
And fifty knights rode with them to the
    shores
Of Severn, and they past to their own land.
And there he kept the justice of the King
So vigorously yet mildly that all hearts
Applauded, and the spiteful whisper died;
And being ever foremost in the chase,
And victor at the tilt and tournament,
They call'd him the great prince and man
    of men.                                        960
But Enid, whom her ladies loved to call
Enid the Fair, a grateful people named
Enid the Good; and in their halls arose
The cry of children, Enids and Geraints
Of times to be; nor did he doubt her more,
But rested in her fealty till he crown'd
A happy life with a fair death, and fell
Against the heathen of the Northern Sea
In battle, fighting for the blameless King.


## BALIN AND BALAN

PELLAM the king, who held and lost with
    Lot
In that first war, and had his realm restored
But render'd tributary, fail'd of late
To send his tribute; wherefore Arthur
    call'd
His treasurer, one of many years, and
    spake:
'Go thou with him and him and bring it to
    us,
Lest we should set one truer on his throne.
Man's word is God in man.'

                          His baron said:
'We go, but harken: there be two strange
    knights
Who sit near Camelot at a fountain side   10
A mile beneath the forest, challenging
And overthrowing every knight who comes.
Wilt thou I undertake them as we pass,
And send them to thee?'

                    Arthur laugh'd upon him:
'Old friend, too old to be so young, de-
    part,
Delay not thou for aught, but let them sit,
Until they find a lustier than themselves.'

  So these departed.  Early, one fair dawn,
The light-wing'd spirit of his youth re-
    turn'd

On Arthur's heart; he arm'd himself and
went,                                          20
So coming to the fountain-side beheld
Balin and Balan sitting statue-like,
Brethren, to right and left the spring, that
down,
From underneath a plume of lady-fern,
Sang, and the sand danced at the bottom
of it.
And on the right of Balin Balin's horse
Was fast beside an alder, on the left
Of Balan Balan's near a poplar-tree.
'Fair sirs,' said Arthur, 'wherefore sit ye
here?'
Balin and Balan answer'd: 'For the sake
Of glory; we be mightier men than all   31
In Arthur's court; that also have we
proved,
For whatsoever knight against us came
Or I or he have easily overthrown.'
'I too,' said Arthur, 'am of Arthur's hall,
But rather proven in his Paynim wars
Than famous jousts; but see, or proven or
not,
Whether me likewise ye can overthrow.'
And Arthur lightly smote the brethren
down,                                          39
And lightly so return'd, and no man knew.

Then Balin rose, and Balan, and beside
The carolling water set themselves again,
And spake no word until the shadow
turn'd;
When from the fringe of coppice round
them burst
A spangled pursuivant, and crying, 'Sirs,
Rise, follow! ye be sent for by the King,'
They follow'd; whom when Arthur seeing
ask'd,
'Tell me your names; why sat ye by the
well?'
Balin the stillness of a minute broke
Saying, 'An unmelodious name to thee,  50
Balin, "the Savage" — that addition
thine —
My brother and my better, this man here,
Balan. I smote upon the naked skull
A thrall of thine in open hall; my hand
Was gauntleted, half slew him, for I heard
He had spoken evil of me; thy just wrath
Sent me a three-years' exile from thine
eyes.
I have not lived my life delightsomely;
For I that did that violence to thy thrall,
Had often wrought some fury on myself,

Saving for Balan. Those three kingless
years                                          61
Have past — were wormwood-bitter to me.
King,
Methought that if we sat beside the well,
And hurl'd to ground what knight soever
spurr'd
Against us, thou would'st take me gladlier
back,
And make, as ten times worthier to be
thine
Than twenty Balins, Balan knight. I have
said.
Not so — not all. A man of thine to-day
Abash'd us both, and brake my boast. Thy
will?'
Said Arthur: 'Thou hast ever spoken
truth;                                         70
Thy too fierce manhood would not let thee
lie.
Rise, my true knight. As children learn,
be thou
Wiser for falling! walk with me, and
move
To music with thine Order and the King.
Thy chair, a grief to all the brethren,
stands
Vacant, but thou retake it, mine again!'

Thereafter, when Sir Balin enter'd hall,
The lost one found was greeted as in
heaven
With joy that blazed itself in woodland
wealth                                         79
Of leaf, and gayest garlandage of flowers,
Along the walls and down the board; they
sat,
And cup clash'd cup; they drank, and some
one sang,
Sweet-voiced, a song of welcome, where-
upon
Their common shout in chorus, mounting,
made
Those banners of twelve battles overhead
Stir as they stirr'd of old, when Arthur's
host
Proclaim'd him victor and the day was won.

Then Balan added to their Order lived
A wealthier life than heretofore with these
And Balin, till their embassage return'd.  90

'Sir King,' they brought report, 'we
hardly found,
So bush'd about it is with gloom, the hall

Of him to whom ye sent us, Pellam, once
A Christless foe of thine as ever dash'd
Horse against horse; but seeing that thy realm
Hath prosper'd in the name of Christ, the King
Took, as in rival heat, to holy things,
And finds himself descended from the Saint
Arimathæan Joseph, him who first
Brought the great faith to Britain over seas.                                    100
He boasts his life as purer than thine own;
Eats scarce enow to keep his pulse a-beat;
Hath push'd aside his faithful wife, nor lets
Or dame or damsel enter at his gates
Lest he should be polluted. This gray king
Show'd us a shrine wherein were wonders — yea,
Rich arks with priceless bones of martyr-dom,
Thorns of the crown and shivers of the cross,
And therewithal, — for thus he told us, — brought                            109
By holy Joseph hither, that same spear
Wherewith the Roman pierced the side of Christ.
He much amazed us; after, when we sought
The tribute, answer'd, "I have quite fore-gone
All matters of this world. Garlon, mine heir,
Of him demand it," which this Garlon gave
With much ado, railing at thine and thee.

'But when we left, in those deep woods we found
A knight of thine spear-stricken from be-hind,
Dead, whom we buried; more than one of us                                     119
Cried out on Garlon, but a woodman there
Reported of some demon in the woods
Was once a man, who, driven by evil tongues
From all his fellows, lived alone, and came
To learn black magic, and to hate his kind
With such a hate that when he died his soul
Became a fiend, which, as the man in life
Was wounded by blind tongues he saw not whence,
Strikes from behind. This woodman show'd the cave
From which he sallies and wherein he dwelt.
We saw the hoof-print of a horse, no more.'                                    130

Then Arthur, 'Let who goes before me see
He do not fall behind me. Foully slain
And villainously! who will hunt for me
This demon of the woods?' Said Balan, 'I!'
So claim'd the quest and rode away, but first,
Embracing Balin: 'Good my brother, hear!
Let not thy moods prevail when I am gone
Who used to lay them! hold them outer fiends,
Who leap at thee to tear thee; shake them aside,
Dreams ruling when wit sleeps! yea, but to dream                              140
That any of these would wrong thee wrongs thyself.
Witness their flowery welcome. Bound are they
To speak no evil. Truly, save for fears,
My fears for thee, so rich a fellowship
Would make me wholly blest; thou one of them,
Be one indeed. Consider them, and all
Their bearing in their common bond of love,
No more of hatred than in heaven itself,
No more of jealousy than in Paradise.'

So Balan warn'd, and went; Balin re-main'd,                                   150
Who — for but three brief moons had glanced away
From being knighted till he smote the thrall,
And faded from the presence into years
Of exile — now would strictlier set him-self
To learn what Arthur meant by courtesy,
Manhood, and knighthood; wherefore hov-er'd round
Lancelot, but when he mark'd his high sweet smile
In passing, and a transitory word

Make knight or churl or child or damsel
    seem
From being smiled at happier in them-
    selves —                                    160
Sigh'd, as a boy, lame - born beneath a
    height
That glooms his valley, sighs to see the
    peak
Sun-flush'd or touch at night the northern
    star;
For one from out his village lately climb'd
And brought report of azure lands and
    fair,
Far seen to left and right; and he himself
Hath hardly scaled with help a hundred
    feet
Up from the base.  So Balin, marvelling
    oft
How far beyond him Lancelot seem'd to
    move,
Groan'd, and at times would mutter :
    'These be gifts,                            170
Born with the blood, not learnable, divine,
Beyond *my* reach.  Well had I foughten
    — well —
In those fierce wars, struck hard — and
    had I crown'd
With my slain self the heaps of whom I
    slew —
So — better ! — But this worship of the
    Queen,
That honor too wherein she holds him —
    this,
This was the sunshine that hath given the
    man
A growth, a name that branches o'er the
    rest,
And strength against all odds, and what
    the King
So prizes — overprizes — gentleness.     180
Her likewise would I worship an I might.
I never can be close with her, as he
That brought her hither.  Shall I pray the
    King
To let me bear some token of his Queen
Whereon to gaze, remembering her — for-
    get
My heats and violences ? live afresh ?
What if the Queen disdain'd to grant it !
    nay,
Being so stately-gentle, would she make
My darkness blackness ? and with how
    sweet grace                                 189
She greeted my return !  Bold will I be —
Some goodly cognizance of Guinevere,

In lieu of this rough beast upon my shield,
Langued gules, and tooth'd with grinning
    savagery.'

    And Arthur, when Sir Balin sought him,
    said,
' What wilt thou bear ? '  Balin was bold,
    and ask'd
To bear her own crown-royal upon shield,
Whereat she smiled and turn'd her to the
    King,
Who answer'd: ' Thou shalt put the crown
    to use.
The crown is but the shadow of the king,
And this a shadow's shadow, let him have
    it,                                         200
So this will help him of his violences ! '
' No shadow,' said Sir Balin, ' O my Queen,
But light to me ! no shadow, O my King,
But golden earnest of a gentler life ! '

    So Balin bare the crown, and all the
    knights
Approved him, and the Queen; and all the
    world
Made music, and he felt his being move
In music with his Order and the King.

    The nightingale, full-toned in middle
    May,
Hath ever and anon a note so thin          210
It seems another voice in other groves;
Thus, after some quick burst of sudden
    wrath,
The music in him seem'd to change and
    grow
Faint and far-off.
            And once he saw the thrall
His passion half had gauntleted to death,
That causer of his banishment and shame,
Smile at him, as he deem'd, presumptu-
    ously.
His arm half rose to strike again, but fell;
The memory of that cognizance on shield
Weighted it down, but in himself he
    moan'd:                                     220

    ' Too high this mount of Camelot for
    me;
These high-set courtesies are not for me.
Shall I not rather prove the worse for
    these ?
Fierier and stormier from restraining, break
Into some madness even before the
    Queen ? '

Thus, as a hearth lit in a mountain home,
And glancing on the window, when the gloom
Of twilight deepens round it, seems a flame
That rages in the woodland far below,
So when his moods were darken'd, court and king      230
And all the kindly warmth of Arthur's hall
Shadow'd an angry distance; yet he strove
To learn the graces of their Table, fought
Hard with himself, and seem'd at length in peace.

Then chanced, one morning, that Sir Balin sat
Close-bower'd in that garden nigh the hall.
A walk of roses ran from door to door,
A walk of lilies crost it to the bower;
And down that range of roses the great Queen
Came with slow steps, the morning on her face;      240
And all in shadow from the counter door
Sir Lancelot as to meet her, then at once,
As if he saw not, glanced aside, and paced
The long white walk of lilies toward the bower.
Follow'd the Queen; Sir Balin heard her ' Prince,
Art thou so little loyal to thy Queen
As pass without good morrow to thy Queen ? '
To whom Sir Lancelot with his eyes on earth,
' Fain would I still be loyal to the Queen.'
' Yea, so,' she said; ' but so to pass me by —      250
So loyal scarce is loyal to thyself,
Whom all men rate the king of courtesy.
Let be; ye stand, fair lord, as in a dream.'

Then Lancelot with his hand among the flowers:
' Yea — for a dream. Last night methought I saw
That maiden Saint who stands with lily in hand
In yonder shrine. All round her prest the dark,
And all the light upon her silver face
Flow'd from the spiritual lily that she held.
Lo ! these her emblems drew mine eyes — away;      260

For see, how perfect-pure ! As light a flush
As hardly tints the blossom of the quince
Would mar their charm of stainless maiden-hood.'

' Sweeter to me,' she said, ' this garden rose
Deep-hued and many-folded ! sweeter still
The wild-wood hyacinth and the bloom of May !
Prince, we have ridden before among the flowers
In those fair days — not all as cool as these,
Tho' season-earlier. Art thou sad ? or sick ?
Our noble King will send thee his own leech —      270
Sick ? or for any matter anger'd at me ? '

Then Lancelot lifted his large eyes; they dwelt
Deep-tranced on hers, and could not fall. Her hue
Changed at his gaze; so turning side by side
They past, and Balin started from his bower.

' Queen ? subject ? but I see not what I see.
Damsel and lover ? hear not what I hear.
My father hath begotten me in his wrath.
I suffer from the things before me, know,
Learn nothing; am not worthy to be knight —      280
A churl, a clown ! ' and in him gloom on gloom
Deepen'd; he sharply caught his lance and shield,
Nor stay'd to crave permission of the King,
But mad for strange adventure, dash'd away.

He took the selfsame track as Balan, saw
The fountain where they sat together, sigh'd,
' Was I not better there with him ? ' and rode
The skyless woods, but under open blue
Came on the hoar - head woodman at a bough
Wearily hewing. ' Churl, thine axe ! ' he cried,      290

Descended, and disjointed it at a blow;
To whom the woodman utter'd wonder-
    ingly,
'Lord, thou couldst lay the devil of these
    woods
If arm of flesh could lay him!' Balin cried,
'Him, or the viler devil who plays his part;
To lay that devil would lay the devil in me.'
'Nay,' said the churl, 'our devil is a truth,
I saw the flash of him but yester-even.
And some *do* say that our Sir Garlon too
Hath learn'd black magic, and to ride un-
    seen.                                            300
Look to the cave.' But Balin answer'd
    him,
'Old fabler, these be fancies of the churl;
Look to thy woodcraft,' and so leaving him,
Now with slack rein and careless of him-
    self,
Now with dug spur and raving at himself,
Now with droopt brow down the long glades
    he rode;
So mark'd not on his right a cavern-chasm
Yawn over darkness, where, nor far within,
The whole day died, but, dying, gleam'd on
    rocks
Roof-pendent, sharp; and others from the
    floor,                                          310
Tusklike, arising, made that mouth of night
Whereout the demon issued up from hell.
He mark'd not this, but, blind and deaf to all
Save that chain'd rage which ever yelpt
    within,
Past eastward from the falling sun. At
    once
He felt the hollow-beaten mosses thud
And tremble, and then the shadow of a
    spear,
Shot from behind him, ran along the
    ground.
Sideways he started from the path, and
    saw,                                            319
With pointed lance as if to pierce, a shape,
A light of armor by him flash, and pass
And vanish in the woods; and follow'd this,
But all so blind in rage that unawares
He burst his lance against a forest bough,
Dishorsed himself, and rose again, and fled
Far, till the castle of a king, the hall
Of Pellam, lichen-bearded, grayly draped
With streaming grass, appear'd, low-built
    but strong;
The ruinous donjon as a knoll of moss,
The battlement overtopt with ivy-tods,   330
A home of bats, in every tower an owl.

Then spake the men of Pellam crying,
    'Lord,
Why wear ye this crown-royal upon
    shield?'
Said Balin, 'For the fairest and the best
Of ladies living gave me this to bear.'
So stall'd his horse, and strode across the
    court,
But found the greetings both of knight and
    king
Faint in the low dark hall of banquet.
    Leaves
Laid their green faces flat against the
    panes,
Sprays grated, and the canker'd boughs
    without                                          340
Whined in the wood; for all was hush'd
    within,
Till when at feast Sir Garlon likewise
    ask'd,
'Why wear ye that crown-royal?' Balin
    said,
'The Queen we worship, Lancelot, I, and
    all,
As fairest, best, and purest, granted me
To bear it!' Such a sound — for Arthur's
    knights
Were hated strangers in the hall — as
    makes
The white swan-mother, sitting, when she
    hears
A strange knee rustle thro' her secret
    reeds,
Made Garlon, hissing; then he sourly
    smiled:                                          350
'Fairest I grant her — I have seen; but
    best,
Best, purest? *thou* from Arthur's hall, and
    yet
So simple! hast thou eyes, or if, are these
So far besotted that they fail to see
This fair wife-worship cloaks a secret
    shame?
Truly, ye men of Arthur be but babes.'

A goblet on the board by Balin, boss'd
With holy Joseph's legend, on his right
Stood, all of massiest bronze. One side had
    sea
And ship and sail and angels blowing on
    it;                                              360
And one was rough with wattling, and the
    walls
Of that low church he built at Glastonbury.
This Balin graspt, but while in act to hurl,

Thro' memory of that token on the shield
Relax'd his hold. 'I will be gentle,' he
          thought,
'And passing gentle;' caught his hand
          away,
Then fiercely to Sir Garlon: 'Eyes have I
That saw to-day the shadow of a spear,
Shot from behind me, run along the ground;
Eyes too that long have watch'd how Lance-
          lot draws            370
From homage to the best and purest,
          might,
Name, manhood, and a grace, but scantly
          thine
Who, sitting in thine own hall, canst en-
          dure
To mouth so huge a foulness — to thy guest,
Me, me of Arthur's Table. Felon talk !
Let be ! no more ! '

                    But not the less by night
The scorn of Garlon, poisoning all his rest,
Stung him in dreams. At length, and dim
          thro' leaves
Blinkt the white morn, sprays grated, and
          old boughs
Whined in the wood. He rose, descended,
          met            380
The scorner in the castle court, and fain,
For hate and loathing, would have past
          him by;
But when Sir Garlon utter'd mocking-wise,
'What, wear ye still that same crown-
          scandalous ?'
His countenance blacken'd, and his fore-
          head veins
Bloated and branch'd; and tearing out of
          sheath
The brand, Sir Balin with a fiery, 'Ha !
So thou be shadow, here I make thee
          ghost,'
Hard upon helm smote him, and the blade
          flew
Splintering in six, and clinkt upon the
          stones.            390
Then Garlon, reeling slowly backward, fell,
And Balin by the banneret of his helm
Dragg'd him, and struck, but from the
          castle a cry
Sounded across the court, and — men-at-
          arms,
A score with pointed lances, making at
          him —
He dash'd the pummel at the foremost
          face,

Beneath a low door dipt, and made his feet
Wings thro' a glimmering gallery, till he
          mark'd
The portal of King Pellam's chapel wide
And inward to the wall; he stept behind;
Thence in a moment heard them pass like
          wolves            401
Howling; but while he stared about the
          shrine,
In which he scarce could spy the Christ
          for Saints,
Beheld before a golden altar lie
The longest lance his eyes had ever seen,
Point-painted red; and seizing thereupon
Push'd thro' an open casement down, lean'd
          on it,
Leapt in a semicircle, and lit on earth;
Then hand at ear, and harkening from
          what side
The blindfold rummage buried in the walls
Might echo, ran the counter path, and
          found            411
His charger, mounted on him and away.
An arrow whizz'd to the right, one to the
          left,
One overhead; and Pellam's feeble cry,
'Stay, stay him ! he defileth heavenly
          things
With earthly uses !' made him quickly
          dive
Beneath the boughs, and race thro' many a
          mile
Of dense and open, till his goodly horse,
Arising wearily at a fallen oak,
Stumbled headlong, and cast him face to
          ground.            420

     Half-wroth he had not ended, but all
          glad,
Knightlike, to find his charger yet un-
          lamed,
Sir Balin drew the shield from off his neck,
Stared at the priceless cognizance, and
          thought,
'I have shamed thee so that now thou
          shamest me,
Thee will I bear no more,' high on a branch
Hung it, and turn'd aside into the woods,
And there in gloom cast himself all along,
Moaning, 'My violences, my violences !'

     But now the wholesome music of the
          wood            430
Was dumb'd by one from out the hall of
          Mark,

A damsel-errant, warbling, as she rode
The woodland alleys, Vivien, with her
    squire.

'The fire of heaven has kill'd the barren
    cold,
And kindled all the plain and all the wold.
The new leaf ever pushes off the old.
The fire of heaven is not the flame of hell.

'Old priest, who mumble worship in your
    quire —
Old monk and nun, ye scorn the world's desire,
Yet in your frosty cells ye feel the fire!    440
The fire of heaven is not the flame of hell.

'The fire of heaven is on the dusty ways.
The wayside blossoms open to the blaze.
The whole wood-world is one full peal of
    praise.
The fire of heaven is not the flame of hell.

'The fire of heaven is lord of all things
    good,
And starve not thou this fire within thy blood,
But follow Vivien thro' the fiery flood!
The fire of heaven is not the flame of hell!'

Then turning to her squire, 'This fire of
    heaven,    450
This old sun-worship, boy, will rise again,
And beat the Cross to earth, and break the
    King
And all his Table.'

                Then they reach'd a glade,
Where under one long lane of cloudless air
Before another wood, the royal crown
Sparkled, and swaying upon a restless elm
Drew the vague glance of Vivien and her
    squire.
Amazed were these; 'Lo there,' she cried —
    'a crown —
Borne by some high lord-prince of Arthur's
    hall,
And there a horse! the rider? where is
    he?    460
See, yonder lies one dead within the wood.
Not dead; he stirs! — but sleeping. I will
    speak.
Hail, royal knight, we break on thy sweet
    rest,
Not, doubtless, all unearn'd by noble deeds.
But bounden art thou, if from Arthur's
    hall,
To help the weak. Behold, I fly from
    shame,

A lustful king, who sought to win my love
Thro' evil ways. The knight with whom I
    rode
Hath suffer'd misadventure, and my squire
Hath in him small defence; but thou, Sir
    Prince,    470
Wilt surely guide me to the warrior King,
Arthur the blameless, pure as any maid,
To get me shelter for my maidenhood.
I charge thee by that crown upon thy
    shield,
And by the great Queen's name, arise and
    hence.'

And Balin rose: 'Thither no more! nor
    prince
Nor knight am I, but one that hath de-
    famed
The cognizance she gave me. Here I dwell
Savage among the savage woods, here
    die —
Die — let the wolves' black maws ensepul-
    chre    480
Their brother beast, whose anger was his
    lord!
O me, that such a name as Guinevere's,
Which our high Lancelot hath so lifted up,
And been thereby uplifted, should thro' me,
My violence, and my villainy, come to
    shame!'

Thereat she suddenly laugh'd and shrill,
    anon
Sigh'd all as suddenly. Said Balin to her:
'Is this thy courtesy — to mock me, ha?
Hence, for I will not with thee.' Again
    she sigh'd:
'Pardon, sweet lord! we maidens often
    laugh    490
When sick at heart, when rather we should
    weep.
I knew thee wrong'd. I brake upon thy
    rest,
And now full loth am I to break thy dream,
But thou art man, and canst abide a truth,
Tho' bitter. Hither, boy — and mark me
    well.
Dost thou remember at Caerleon once —
A year ago — nay, then I love thee not —
Ay, thou rememberest well — one summer
    dawn —
By the great tower — Caerleon upon Usk —
Nay, truly we were hidden — this fair lord,
The flower of all their vestal knighthood,
    knelt    501

In amorous homage — knelt — what else ?
— O, ay,
Knelt, and drew down from out his night-
black hair
And mumbled that white hand whose ring'd
caress
Had wander'd from her own King's golden
head,
And lost itself in darkness, till she cried —
I thought the great tower would crash down
on both —
" Rise, my sweet King, and kiss me on the
lips,
Thou art my King." This lad, whose
lightest word
Is mere white truth in simple nakedness,
Saw them embrace; he reddens, cannot
speak,                                                  511
So bashful, he ! but all the maiden Saints,
The deathless mother-maidenhood of hea-
ven,
Cry out upon her. Up then, ride with me !
Talk not of shame ! thou canst not, an
thou wouldst,
Do these more shame than these have done
themselves.'

She lied with ease; but horror-stricken
he,
Remembering that dark bower at Camelot,
Breathed in a dismal whisper, 'It is truth.'

Sunnily she smiled: ' And even in this
lone wood,                                            520
Sweet lord, ye do right well to whisper this.
Fools prate, and perish traitors. Woods
have tongues,
As walls have ears; but thou shalt go with
me,
And we will speak at first exceeding low.
Meet is it the good King be not deceived.
See now, I set thee high on vantage ground,
From whence to watch the time, and eagle-
like
Stoop at thy will on Lancelot and the
Queen.'

She ceased; his evil spirit upon him
leapt,
He ground his teeth together, sprang with
a yell,                                                   530
Tore from the branch and cast on earth the
shield,
Drove his mail'd heel athwart the royal
crown,

Stampt all into defacement, hurl'd it from
him
Among the forest weeds, and cursed the
tale,
The told-of, and the teller.

                                    That weird yell,
Unearthlier than all shriek of bird or beast,
Thrill'd thro' the woods; and Balan lurk-
ing there —
His quest was unaccomplish'd — heard and
thought
' The scream of that wood-devil I came to
quell ! '
Then nearing: 'Lo ! he hath slain some
brother-knight,                                        540
And tramples on th  goodly shield to show
His loathing of our  rder and the Queen.
My quest, meseems,    here. Or devil or
man,
Guard thou thine he   ' Sir Balin spake
not word,
But snatch'd a sudde  buckler from the
squire,
And vaulted on his h rse, and so they
crash'd
In onset, and King Pella n's holy spear,
Reputed to be red with sinless blood,
Redden'd at once with sinful, for the point
Across the maiden shield of Balan prick'd
The hauberk to the flesh; and Balin's
horse                                                      551
Was wearied to the death, and, when they
clash'd,
Rolling back upon Balin, crush'd the man
Inward, and either fell and swoon'd away.

Then to her squire mutter'd the damsel:
' Fools !
This fellow hath wrought some foulness
with his Queen;
Else never had he borne her crown, nor
raved
And thus foam'd over at a rival name.
But thou, Sir Chick, that scarce hast
broken shell,
Art yet half-yolk, not even come to
down —                                                  560
Who never sawest Caerleon upon Usk —
And yet hast often pleaded for my love —
See what I see, be thou where I have been,
Or else, Sir Chick — dismount and loose
their casques;
I fain would know what manner of men
they be.'

And when the squire had loosed them,
    'Goodly ! — look !
They might have cropt the myriad flower
    of May,
And butt each other here, like brainless
    bulls,
Dead for one heifer !'

              Then the gentle squire:
'I hold them happy, so they died for love;
And, Vivien, tho' ye beat me like your
    dog,                   571
I too could die, as now I live, for thee.'

   'Live on, Sir Boy,' she cried; 'I better
    prize
The living dog than the dead lion. Away !
I cannot brook to gaze upon the dead.'
Then leapt her palfrey o'er the fallen
    oak,
And bounding forward, 'Leave them to the
    wolves.'

   But when their foreheads felt the cooling
    air,
Balin first woke, and seeing that true face,
Familiar up from cradle-time, so wan,   580
Crawl'd slowly with low moans to where he
    lay,
And on his dying brother cast himself
Dying; and *he* lifted faint eyes; he felt
One near him; all at once they found the
    world,
Staring wild-wide; then with a childlike
    wail,
And drawing down the dim disastrous brow
That o'er him hung, he kiss'd it, moan'd,
    and spake:

   'O Balin, Balin, I that fain had died
To save thy life, have brought thee to thy
    death.
Why had ye not the shield I knew ? and
    why                 590
Trampled ye thus on that which bare the
    crown ?'

   Then Balin told him brokenly and in
    gasps
All that had chanced, and Balan moan'd
    again:

   'Brother, I dwelt a day in Pellam's hall;
This Garlon mock'd me, but I heeded not.
And one said, "Eat in peace ! a liar is he,

And hates thee for the tribute !" This
    good knight
Told me that twice a wanton damsel came,
And sought for Garlon at the castle-gates,
Whom Pellam drove away with holy heat.
I well believe this damsel, and the one   601
Who stood beside thee even now, the same.
"She dwells among the woods," he said,
    "and meets
And dallies with him in the Mouth of
    Hell."
Foul are their lives, foul are their lips;
    they lied.
Pure as our own true mother is our Queen.'

   'O brother,' answer'd Balin, 'woe is me !
My madness all thy life has been thy doom,
Thy curse, and darken'd all thy day; and
    now
The night has come. I scarce can see thee
    now.                  610
Good night ! for we shall never bid again
Good morrow — Dark my doom was here,
    and dark
It will be there. I see thee now no more.
I would not mine again should darken
    thine;
Good night, true brother.'

                 Balan answer'd low,
'Good night, true brother, here ! good mor-
    row there !
We two were born together, and we die
Together by one doom:' and while he spoke
Closed his death-drowsing eyes, and slept
    the sleep              619
With Balin, either lock'd in either's arm.

## MERLIN AND VIVIEN

A STORM was coming, but the winds were
    still,
And in the wild woods of Broceliande,
Before an oak, so hollow, huge, and old
It look'd a tower of ivied masonwork,
At Merlin's feet the wily Vivien lay.

   For he that always bare in bitter grudge
The slights of Arthur and his Table, Mark
The Cornish King, had heard a wandering
    voice,
A minstrel of Caerleon by strong storm
Blown into shelter at Tintagil, say     10
That out of naked knight-like purity

Sir Lancelot worshipt no unmarried girl,
But the great Queen herself, fought in her
  name,
Sware by her — vows like theirs that high
  in heaven
Love most, but neither marry nor are given
In marriage, angels of our Lord's report.

He ceased, and then — for Vivien
  sweetly said —
She sat beside the banquet nearest Mark, —
'And is the fair example follow'd, sir,
In Arthur's household?' — answer'd inno-
  cently:                                    20

'Ay, by some few — ay, truly — youths
  that hold
It more beseems the perfect virgin knight
To worship woman as true wife beyond
All hopes of gaining, than as maiden girl.
They place their pride in Lancelot and the
  Queen.
So passionate for an utter purity
Beyond the limit of their bond are these,
For Arthur bound them not to singleness.
Brave hearts and clean! and yet — God
  guide them! — young.'

Then Mark was half in heart to hurl his
  cup                                        30
Straight at the speaker, but forbore. He
  rose
To leave the hall, and, Vivien following him,
Turn'd to her: 'Here are snakes within the
  grass;
And you methinks, O Vivien, save ye fear
The monkish manhood, and the mask of
  pure
Worn by this court, can stir them till they
  sting.'

And Vivien answer'd, smiling scornfully:
'Why fear? because that foster'd at *thy*
  court
I savor of thy — virtues? fear them? no,
As love, if love be perfect, casts out
  fear,                                      40
So hate, if hate be perfect, casts out fear.
My father died in battle against the King,
My mother on his corpse in open field;
She bore me there, for born from death
  was I
Among the dead and sown upon the wind —
And then on thee! and shown the truth
  betimes,

That old true filth, and bottom of the well,
Where Truth is hidden. Gracious lessons
  thine,
And maxims of the mud! "This Arthur
  pure!
Great Nature thro' the flesh herself hath
  made                                       50
Gives him the lie! There is no being pure,
My cherub; saith not Holy Writ the
  same?" —
If I were Arthur, I would have thy blood.
Thy blessing, stainless King! I bring thee
  back,
When I have ferreted out their burrow-
  ings,
The hearts of all this Order in mine
  hand —
Ay — so that fate and craft and folly
  close,
Perchance, one curl of Arthur's golden
  beard.
To me this narrow grizzled fork of thine
Is cleaner-fashion'd — Well, I loved thee
  first;                                     60
That warps the wit.'

        Loud laugh'd the graceless Mark.
But Vivien, into Camelot stealing, lodged
Low in the city, and on a festal day
When Guinevere was crossing the great
  hall
Cast herself down, knelt to the Queen, and
  wail'd.

'Why kneel ye there? What evil have
  ye wrought?
Rise!' and the damsel bidden rise arose
And stood with folded hands and down-
  ward eyes
Of glancing corner and all meekly said:
'None wrought, but suffer'd much, an or-
  phan maid!                                 70
My father died in battle for thy King,
My mother on his corpse — in open field,
The sad sea-sounding wastes of Lyon-
  nesse —
Poor wretch — no friend! — and now by
  Mark the king,
For that small charm of feature mine, pur-
  sued —
If any such be mine — I fly to thee.
Save, save me thou! Woman of women
  — thine
The wreath of beauty, thine the crown of
  power,

Be thine the balm of pity, O heaven's own
    white
Earth - angel, stainless bride of stainless
    King —                                    80
Help, for he follows ! take me to thyself !
O yield me shelter for mine innocency
Among thy maidens ! '

             Here her slow sweet eyes
Fear-tremulous, but humbly hopeful, rose
Fixt on her hearer's, while the Queen who
    stood
All glittering like May sunshine on May
    leaves
In green and gold, and plumed with green
    replied:
'Peace, child ! of over-praise and over-
    blame
We choose the last.  Our noble Arthur,
    him
Ye scarce can overpraise, will hear and
    know.                                    90
Nay — we believe all evil of thy Mark —
Well, we shall test thee farther; but this
    hour
We ride a-hawking with Sir Lancelot.
He hath given us a fair falcon which he
    train'd;
We go to prove it.  Bide ye here the
    while.'

    She past; and Vivien murmur'd after,
    'Go !
I bide the while.'  Then thro' the portal-
    arch
Peering askance, and muttering broken-
    wise,
As one that labors with an evil dream,
Beheld the Queen and Lancelot get to
    horse.                                    100

    'Is that the Lancelot ? goodly — ay, but
    gaunt;
Courteous — amends for gauntness — takes
    her hand —
That glance of theirs, but for the street,
    had been
A clinging kiss — how hand lingers in
    hand !
Let go at last ! — they ride away — to
    hawk
For waterfowl.  Royaller game is mine.
For such a supersensual sensual bond
As that gray cricket chirpt of at our
    hearth —

Touch flax with flame — a glance will serve
    — the liars !
Ah little rat that borest in the dyke      110
Thy hole by night to let the boundless deep
Down upon far-off cities while they dance —
Or dream — of thee they dream'd not —
    nor of me
These — ay, but each of either; ride, and
    dream
The mortal dream that never yet was
    mine —
Ride, ride and dream until ye wake — to
    me !
Then, narrow court and lubber King, fare-
    well !
For Lancelot will be gracious to the rat,
And our wise Queen, if knowing that I
    know,
Will hate, loathe, fear — but honor me the
    more.'                                   120

    Yet while they rode together down the
    plain,
Their talk was all of training, terms of art,
Diet and seeling, jesses, leash and lure.
'She is too noble,' he said, 'to check at
    pies,
Nor will she rake: there is no baseness in
    her.'
Here when the Queen demanded as by
    chance,
'Know ye the stranger woman ?' 'Let her
    be,'
Said Lancelot, and unhooded casting off
The goodly falcon free; she tower'd; her
    bells,
Tone under tone, shrill'd; and they lifted
    up                                        130
Their eager faces, wondering at the
    strength,
Boldness, and royal knighthood of the bird,
Who pounced her quarry and slew it.
    Many a time
As once — of old — among the flowers —
    they rode.

    But Vivien half-forgotten of the Queen
Among her damsels broidering sat, heard,
    watch'd,
And whisper'd.  Thro' the peaceful court
    she crept
And whisper'd; then, as Arthur in the
    highest
Leaven'd the world, so Vivien in the low-
    est,

Arriving at a time of golden rest, 140
And sowing one ill hint from ear to ear,
While all the heathen lay at Arthur's
    feet,
And no quest came, but all was joust and
    play,
Leaven'd his hall. They heard and let her
    be.

Thereafter, as an enemy that has left
Death in the living waters and withdrawn,
The wily Vivien stole from Arthur's court.

She hated all the knights, and heard in
    thought
Their lavish comment when her name was
    named. 149
For once, when Arthur walking all alone,
Vext at a rumor issued from herself
Of some corruption crept among his
    knights,
Had met her, Vivien, being greeted fair,
Would fain have wrought upon his cloudy
    mood
With reverent eyes mock-loyal, shaken
    voice,
And flutter'd adoration, and at last
With dark sweet hints of some who prized
    him more
Than who should prize him most; at which
    the King
Had gazed upon her blankly and gone by.
But one had watch'd, and had not held his
    peace; 160
It made the laughter of an afternoon
That Vivien should attempt the blameless
    King.
And after that, she set herself to gain
Him, the most famous man of all those
    times,
Merlin, who knew the range of all their
    arts,
Had built the King his havens, ships, and
    halls,
Was also bard, and knew the starry hea-
    vens;
The people call'd him wizard; whom at
    first
She play'd about with slight and sprightly
    talk,
And vivid smiles, and faintly-venom'd
    points 170
Of slander, glancing here and grazing there;
And yielding to his kindlier moods, the
    seer

Would watch her at her petulance and
    play,
Even when they seem'd unlovable, and
    laugh
As those that watch a kitten. Thus he
    grew
Tolerant of what he half disdain'd, and she,
Perceiving that she was but half disdain'd,
Began to break her sports with graver fits,
Turn red or pale, would often when they
    met
Sigh fully, or all-silent gaze upon him 180
With such a fixt devotion that the old
    man,
Tho' doubtful, felt the flattery, and at
    times
Would flatter his own wish in age for love,
And half believe her true; for thus at
    times
He waver'd, but that other clung to him,
Fixt in her will, and so the seasons went.

Then fell on Merlin a great melancholy;
He walk'd with dreams and darkness, and
    he found
A doom that ever poised itself to fall,
An ever-moaning battle in the mist, 190
World-war of dying flesh against the life,
Death in all life and lying in all love,
The meanest having power upon the high-
    est,
And the high purpose broken by the worm.

So leaving Arthur's court he gain'd the
    beach,
There found a little boat and stept into it;
And Vivien follow'd, but he mark'd her
    not.
She took the helm and he the sail; the
    boat
Drave with a sudden wind across the deeps,
And, touching Breton sands, they disem-
    bark'd. 200
And then she follow'd Merlin all the way,
Even to the wild woods of Broceliande.
For Merlin once had told her of a charm,
The which if any wrought on any one
With woven paces and with waving arms,
The man so wrought on ever seem'd to lie
Closed in the four walls of a hollow tower,
From which was no escape for evermore;
And none could find that man for ever-
    more,
Nor could he see but him who wrought
    the charm 210

Coming and going, and he lay as dead
And lost to life and use and name and
  fame.
And Vivien ever sought to work the charm
Upon the great enchanter of the time,
As fancying that her glory would be great
According to his greatness whom she
  quench'd.

There lay she all her length and kiss'd his
  feet,
As if in deepest reverence and in love.
A twist of gold was round her hair; a robe
Of samite without price, that more ex-
  prest                                   220
Than hid her, clung about her lissome
  limbs,
In color like the satin-shining palm
On sallows in the windy gleams of March.
And while she kiss'd them, crying, 'Tram-
  ple me,
Dear feet, that I have follow'd thro' the
  world,
And I will pay you worship; tread me
  down
And I will kiss you for it;' he was mute.
So dark a forethought roll'd about his
  brain,
As on a dull day in an ocean cave
The blind wave feeling round his long sea-
  hall                                    230
In silence; wherefore, when she lifted up
A face of sad appeal, and spake and said,
'O Merlin, do ye love me?' and again,
'O Merlin, do ye love me?' and once
  more,
'Great Master, do ye love me?' he was
  mute.
And lissome Vivien, holding by his heel,
Writhed toward him, slided up his knee
  and sat,
Behind his ankle twined her hollow feet
Together, curved an arm about his neck,
Clung like a snake; and letting her left
  hand                                    240
Droop from his mighty shoulder, as a leaf,
Made with her right a comb of pearl to
  part
The lists of such a beard as youth gone out
Had left in ashes.  Then he spoke and said,
Not looking at her, 'Who are wise in love
Love most, say least,' and Vivien answer'd
  quick:
'I saw the little elf-god eyeless once
In Arthur's arras hall at Camelot;

But neither eyes nor tongue — O stupid
  child!
Yet you are wise who say it; let me think
Silence is wisdom.  I am silent then,   251
And ask no kiss;' then adding all at once,
'And lo, I clothe myself with wisdom,'
  drew
The vast and shaggy mantle of his beard
Across her neck and bosom to her knee,
And call'd herself a gilded summer fly
Caught in a great old tyrant spider's web,
Who meant to eat her up in that wild
  wood
Without one word.  So Vivien call'd her-
  self,
But rather seem'd a lovely baleful star  260
Veil'd in gray vapor; till he sadly smiled:
'To what request for what strange boon,'
  he said,
'Are these your pretty tricks and fooleries,
O Vivien, the preamble? yet my thanks,
For these have broken up my melancholy.'

And Vivien answer'd smiling saucily:
'What, O my Master, have ye found your
  voice?
I bid the stranger welcome.  Thanks at
  last!
But yesterday you never open'd lip,     269
Except indeed to drink.  No cup had we;
In mine own lady palms I cull'd the spring
That gather'd trickling dropwise from the
  cleft,
And made a pretty cup of both my hands
And offer'd you it kneeling.  Then you
  drank
And knew no more, nor gave me one poor
  word;
O, no more thanks than might a goat have
  given
With no more sign of reverence than a
  beard.
And when we halted at that other well,
And I was faint to swooning, and you
  lay
Foot-gilt with all the blossom-dust of those
Deep meadows we had traversed, did you
  know                                    281
That Vivien bathed your feet before her
  own?
And yet no thanks; and all thro' this wild
  wood
And all this morning when I fondled you.
Boon, ay, there was a boon, one not so
  strange —

How had I wrong'd you ? surely ye are
    wise,
But such a silence is more wise than kind.'

And Merlin lock'd his hand in hers and
    said:
'O, did ye never lie upon the shore,
And watch the curl'd white of the coming
    wave                                    290
Glass'd in the slippery sand before it
    breaks ?
Even such a wave, but not so pleasurable,
Dark in the glass of some presageful mood,
Had I for three days seen, ready to fall.
And then I rose and fled from Arthur's
    court
To break the mood.  You follow'd me un-
    ask'd;
And when I look'd, and saw you following
    still,
My mind involved yourself the nearest
    thing
In that mind-mist — for shall I tell you
    truth ?
You seem'd that wave about to break upon
    me                                      300
And sweep me from my hold upon the
    world,
My use and name and fame.  Your pardon,
    child.
Your pretty sports have brighten'd all
    again.
And ask your boon, for boon I owe you
    thrice,
Once for wrong done you by confusion,
    next
For thanks it seems till now neglected, last
For these your dainty gambols; wherefore
    ask,
And take this boon so strange and not so
    strange.'

And Vivien answer'd smiling mourn-
    fully:
'O, not so strange as my long asking it, 310
Not yet so strange as you yourself are
    strange,
Nor half so strange as that dark mood of
    yours.
I ever fear'd ye were not wholly mine;
And see, yourself have own'd ye did me
    wrong.
The people call you prophet; let it be;
But not of those that can expound them-
    selves.

Take Vivien for expounder; she will call
That three-days-long presageful gloom of
    yours
No presage, but the same mistrustful mood
That makes you seem less noble than your-
    self,                                   320
Whenever I have ask'd this very boon,
Now ask'd again; for see you not, dear
    love,
That such a mood as that which lately
    gloom'd
Your fancy when ye saw me following
    you
Must make me fear still more you are not
    mine,
Must make me yearn still more to prove
    you mine,
And make me wish still more to learn this
    charm
Of woven paces and of waving hands,
As proof of trust.  O Merlin, teach it me !
The charm so taught will charm us both to
    rest.                                   330
For, grant me some slight power upon your
    fate,
I, feeling that you felt me worthy trust,
Should rest and let you rest, knowing you
    mine.
And therefore be as great as ye are named,
Not muffled round with selfish reticence.
How hard you look and how denyingly !
O, if you think this wickedness in me,
That I should prove it on you unawares,
That makes me passing wrathful; then our
    bond
Had best be loosed for ever; but think or
    not,                                    340
By Heaven that hears, I tell you the clean
    truth,
As clean as blood of babes, as white as
    milk !
O Merlin, may this earth, if ever I,
If these unwitty wandering wits of mine,
Even in the jumbled rubbish of a dream,
Have tript on such conjectural treachery —
May this hard earth cleave to the nadir
    hell
Down, down, and close again and nip me
    flat,
If I be such a traitress !  Yield my boon,
Till which I scarce can yield you all I am;
And grant my re-reiterated wish,          351
The great proof of your love; because I
    think,
However wise, ye hardly know me yet.'

And Merlin loosed his hand from hers
    and said:
'I never was less wise, however wise,
Too curious Vivien, tho' you talk of trust,
Than when I told you first of such a charm.
Yea, if ye talk of trust I tell you this,
Too much I trusted when I told you that,
And stirr'd this vice in you which ruin'd
    man                                            360
Thro' woman the first hour; for howsoe'er
In children a great curiousness be well,
Who have to learn themselves and all the
    world,
In you, that are no child, for still I find
Your face is practised when I spell the
    lines,
I call it, — well, I will not call it vice;
But since you name yourself the summer
    fly,
I well could wish a cobweb for the gnat
That settles beaten back, and beaten back
Settles, till one could yield for weariness.  370
But since I will not yield to give you power
Upon my life and use and name and fame,
Why will ye never ask some other boon?
Yea, by God's rood, I trusted you too
    much!'

    And Vivien, like the tenderest-hearted
    maid
That ever bided tryst at village stile,
Made answer, either eyelid wet with tears:
'Nay, Master, be not wrathful with your
    maid;
Caress her, let her feel herself forgiven
Who feels no heart to ask another boon.   380
I think ye hardly know the tender rhyme
Of " trust me not at all or all in all."
I heard the great Sir Lancelot sing it once,
And it shall answer for me.  Listen to it.

    ' " In love, if love be love, if love be ours,
Faith and unfaith can ne'er be equal powers:
Unfaith in aught is want of faith in all.

    ' " It is the little rift within the lute,
That by and by will make the music mute,
And ever widening slowly silence all.        390

    ' " The little rift within the lover's lute,
Or little pitted speck in garner'd fruit,
That rotting inward slowly moulders all.

    ' " It is not worth the keeping; let it go:
But shall it? answer, darling, answer, no.
And trust me not at all or all in all."

'O master, do ye love my tender rhyme?'

    And Merlin look'd and half believed her
    true,
So tender was her voice, so fair her face,
So sweetly gleam'd her eyes behind her
    tears                                           400
Like sunlight on the plain behind a shower;
And yet he answer'd half indignantly:

    'Far other was the song that once I heard
By this huge oak, sung nearly where we
    sit;
For here we met, some ten or twelve of us,
To chase a creature that was current then
In these wild woods, the hart with golden
    horns.
It was the time when first the question
    rose
About the founding of a Table Round,
That was to be, for love of God and men   410
And noble deeds, the flower of all the
    world;
And each incited each to noble deeds.
And while we waited, one, the youngest
    of us,
We could not keep him silent, out he
    flash'd,
And into such a song, such fire for fame,
Such trumpet-blowings in it, coming down
To such a stern and iron-clashing close,
That when he stopt we long'd to hurl to-
    gether,
And should have done it, but the beauteous
    beast                                           419
Scared by the noise upstarted at our feet,
And like a silver shadow slipt away
Thro' the dim land.    And all day long we
    rode
Thro' the dim land against a rushing wind,
That glorious roundel echoing in our ears,
And chased the flashes of his golden horns
Until they vanish'd by the fairy well
That laughs at iron — as our warriors
    did —
Where children cast their pins and nails,
    and cry,
" Laugh, little well!" but touch it with a
    sword,
It buzzes fiercely round the point; and
    there                                           430
We lost him — such a noble song was that.
But, Vivien, when you sang me that sweet
    rhyme,
I felt as tho' you knew this cursed charm,

Were proving it on me, and that I lay
And felt them slowly ebbing, name and
    fame.'

    And Vivien answer'd smiling mournfully:
'O, mine have ebb'd away for evermore,
And all thro' following you to this wild
    wood,
Because I saw you sad, to comfort you.
Lo now, what hearts have men ! they never
    mount                                    440
As high as woman in her selfless mood.
And touching fame, howe'er ye scorn my
    song,
Take one verse more — the lady speaks it
    — this:

    ' " My name, once mine, now thine, is close-
    lier mine,
For fame, could fame be mine, that fame were
    thine,
And shame, could shame be thine, that shame
    were mine.
So trust me not at all or all in all."

    'Says she not well ? and there is more
    — this rhyme
Is like the fair pearl-necklace of the Queen,
That burst in dancing and the pearls were
    spilt;                                    450
Some lost, some stolen, some as relics
    kept;
But nevermore the same two sister pearls
Ran down the silken thread to kiss each
    other
On her white neck — so is it with this
    rhyme.
It lives dispersedly in many hands,
And every minstrel sings it differently;
Yet is there one true line, the pearl of
    pearls:
" Man dreams of fame while woman wakes
    to love."
Yea ! love, tho' love were of the grossest,
    carves
A portion from the solid present, eats    460
And uses, careless of the rest; but fame,
The fame that follows death is nothing to
    us;
And what is fame in life but half-disfame
And counterchanged with darkness ? ye
    yourself
Know well that envy calls you devil's son,
And since ye seem the master of all art,
They fain would make you master of all
    vice.'

And Merlin lock'd his hand in hers and
    said:
' I once was looking for a magic weed,
And found a fair young squire who sat
    alone,                                   470
Had carved himself a knightly shield of
    wood,
And then was painting on it fancied arms,
Azure, an eagle rising or, the sun
In dexter chief; the scroll, " I follow
    fame."
And speaking not, but leaning over him,
I took his brush and blotted out the bird,
And made a gardener putting in a graff,
With this for motto, " Rather use than
    fame."
You should have seen him blush; but after-
    wards
He made a stalwart knight. O Vivien, 480
For you, methinks you think you love me
    well;
For me, I love you somewhat. Rest; and
    Love
Should have some rest and pleasure in him-
    self,
Not ever be too curious for a boon,
Too prurient for a proof against the grain
Of him ye say ye love. But Fame with
    men,
Being but ampler means to serve mankind,
Should have small rest or pleasure in her-
    self,
But work as vassal to the larger love 489
That dwarfs the petty love of one to one.
Use gave me fame at first, and fame again
Increasing gave me use. Lo, there my
    boon !
What other ? for men sought to prove me
    vile,
Because I fain had given them greater wits;
And then did envy call me devil's son.
The sick weak beast, seeking to help herself
By striking at her better, miss'd, and
    brought
Her own claw back, and wounded her own
    heart.
Sweet were the days when I was all un-
    known,                                    499
But when my name was lifted up the storm
Brake on the mountain and I cared not
    for it.
Right well know I that fame is half-dis-
    fame,
Yet needs must work my work. That
    other fame,

To one at least who hath not children
    vague,
The cackle of the unborn about the grave,
I cared not for it.   A single misty star,
Which is the second in a line of stars
That seem a sword beneath a belt of three,
I never gazed upon it but I dreamt
Of some vast charm concluded in that star
To make fame nothing.  Wherefore, if I
    fear,                                      511
Giving you power upon me thro' this charm,
That you might play me falsely, having
    power,
However well ye think ye love me now —
As sons of kings loving in pupilage
Have turn'd to tyrants when they came to
    power —
I rather dread the loss of use than fame;
If you — and not so much from wicked-
    ness,
As some wild turn of anger, or a mood
Of overstrain'd affection, it may be,        520
To keep me all to your own self, — or else
A sudden spurt of woman's jealousy, —
Should try this charm on whom ye say ye
    love.'

And Vivien answer'd smiling as in wrath:
'Have I not sworn?   I am not trusted.
    Good !
Well, hide it, hide it; I shall find it out,
And being found take heed of Vivien.
A woman and not trusted, doubtless I
Might feel some sudden turn of anger
    born
Of your misfaith; and your fine epithet 530
Is accurate too, for this full love of mine
Without the full heart back may merit
    well
Your term of overstrain'd.  So used as I,
My daily wonder is, I love at all.
And as to woman's jealousy, O, why not ?
O, to what end, except a jealous one,
And one to make me jealous if I love,
Was this fair charm invented by yourself ?
I well believe that all about this world  539
Ye cage a buxom captive here and there,
Closed in the four walls of a hollow tower
From which is no escape for evermore.'

Then the great master merrily answer'd
    her:
'Full many a love in loving youth was
    mine;
I needed then no charm to keep them mine

But youth and love; and that full heart of
    yours
Whereof ye prattle, may now assure you
    mine;
So live uncharm'd.  For those who wrought
    it first,
The wrist is parted from the hand that
    waved,
The feet unmortised from their ankle-
    bones                                      550
Who paced it, ages back — but will ye hear
The legend as in guerdon for your rhyme ?

'There lived a king in the most eastern
    East,
Less old than I, yet older, for my blood
Hath earnest in it of far springs to be.
A tawny pirate anchor'd in his port,
Whose bark had plunder'd twenty name-
    less isles;
And passing one, at the high peep of dawn,
He saw two cities in a thousand boats
All fighting for a woman on the sea.      560
And pushing his black craft among them
    all,
He lightly scatter'd theirs and brought her
    off,
With loss of half his people arrow-slain;
A maid so smooth, so white, so wonderful,
They said a light came from her when she
    moved.
And since the pirate would not yield her
    up,
The king impaled him for his piracy,
Then made her queen.  But those isle-nur-
    tured eyes
Waged such unwilling tho' successful war
On all the youth, they sicken'd; councils
    thinn'd,                                  570
And armies waned, for magnet-like she
    drew
The rustiest iron of old fighters' hearts;
And beasts themselves would worship;
    camels knelt
Unbidden, and the brutes of mountain
    back
That carry kings in castles bow'd black
    knees
Of homage, ringing with their serpent
    hands,
To make her smile, her golden ankle-bells.
What wonder, being jealous, that he sent
His horns of proclamation out thro' all
The hundred under - kingdoms that he
    sway'd                                     580

To find a wizard who might teach the
king
Some charm which, being wrought upon
the queen,
Might keep her all his own.   To such a
one
He promised more than ever king has
given,
A league of mountain full of golden mines,
A province with a hundred miles of coast,
A palace and a princess, all for him;
But on all those who tried and fail'd the
king
Pronounced a dismal sentence, meaning by
it                                          589
To keep the list low and pretenders back,
Or, like a king, not to be trifled with —
Their heads should moulder on the city
gates.
And many tried and fail'd, because the
charm
Of nature in her overbore their own;
And many a wizard brow bleach'd on the
walls,
And many weeks a troop of carrion crows
Hung like a cloud above the gateway
towers.'

And Vivien breaking in upon him, said:
'I sit and gather honey; yet, methinks,
Thy tongue has tript a little; ask thy-
self.                                       600
The lady never made *unwilling* war
With those fine eyes; she had her pleasure
in it,
And made her good man jealous with good
cause.
And lived there neither dame nor damsel
then
Wroth at a lover's loss ? were all as tame,
I mean, as noble, as their queen was fair ?
Not one to flirt a venom at her eyes,
Or pinch a murderous dust into her drink,
Or make her paler with a poison'd rose ?
Well, those were not our days — but did
they find                                   610
A wizard ?  Tell me, was he like to thee ?'

She ceased, and made her lithe arm
round his neck
Tighten, and then drew back, and let her
eyes
Speak for her, glowing on him, like a
bride's
On her new lord, her own, the first of men.

He answer'd laughing: 'Nay, not like to
me.
At last they found — his foragers for
charms —
A little glassy-headed hairless man,
Who lived alone in a great wild on grass,
Read but one book, and ever reading
grew                                        620
So grated down and filed away with thought,
So lean his eyes were monstrous; while the
skin
Clung but to crate and basket, ribs and
spine.
And since he kept his mind on one sole
aim,
Nor ever touch'd fierce wine, nor tasted
flesh,
Nor own'd a sensual wish, to him the wall
That sunders ghosts and shadow-casting
men
Became a crystal, and he saw them thro'
it,
And heard their voices talk behind the
wall,                                       629
And learnt their elemental secrets, powers
And forces; often o'er the sun's bright eye
Drew the vast eyelid of an inky cloud,
And lash'd it at the base with slanting
storm;
Or in the noon of mist and driving rain,
When the lake whiten'd and the pinewood
roar'd,
And the cairn'd mountain was a shadow,
sunn'd
The world to peace again.   Here was the
man;
And so by force they dragg'd him to the
king.
And then he taught the king to charm the
queen
In such-wise that no man could see her
more,                                       640
Nor saw she save the king, who wrought
the charm,
Coming and going, and she lay as dead,
And lost all use of life.   But when the
king
Made proffer of the league of golden mines,
The province with a hundred miles of coast,
The palace and the princess, that old
man
Went back to his old wild, and lived on
grass,
And vanish'd, and his book came down to
me.'

And Vivien answer'd smiling saucily:
'Ye have the book; the charm is written
  in it.          650
Good! take my counsel, let me know it at
  once;
For keep it like a puzzle chest in chest,
With each chest lock'd and padlock'd thir-
  ty-fold,
And whelm all this beneath as vast a
  mound
As after furious battle turfs the slain
On some wild down above the windy deep,
I yet should strike upon a sudden means
To dig, pick, open, find and read the charm;
Then, if I tried it, who should blame me
  then?'

And smiling as a master smiles at one 660
T..s not of his school, nor any school
.t that where blind and naked Igno-
  rance
Delivers brawling judgments, unashamed,
On all things all day long, he answer'd her:

'Thou read the book, my pretty Vivien!
O, ay, it is but twenty pages long,
But every page having an ample marge,
And every marge enclosing in the midst
A square of text that looks a little blot, 669
The text no larger than the limbs of fleas;
And every square of text an awful charm,
Writ in a language that has long gone
  by,
So long that mountains have arisen since
With cities on their flanks — thou read the
  book!
And every margin scribbled, crost, and
  cramm'd
With comment, densest condensation, hard
To mind and eye; but the long sleepless
  nights
Of my long life have made it easy to me.
And none can read the text, not even I;
And none can read the comment but my-
  self;          680
And in the comment did I find the charm.
O, the results are simple; a mere child
Might use it to the harm of any one,
And never could undo it. Ask no more;
For tho' you should not prove it upon me,
But keep that oath ye sware, ye might,
  perchance,
Assay it on some one of the Table Round,
And all because ye dream they babble of
  you.'

And Vivien, frowning in true anger, said:
'What dare the full-fed liars say of me?
*They* ride abroad redressing human
  wrongs!        691
They sit with knife in meat and wine in
  horn.
*They* bound to holy vows of chastity!
Were I not woman, I could tell a tale.
But you are man, you well can understand
The shame that cannot be explain'd for
  shame.
Not one of all the drove should touch me
  — swine!'

Then answer'd Merlin careless of her
  words:
'You breathe but accusation vast and vague,
Spleen-born, I think, and proofless. If ye
  know,         700
Set up the charge ye know, to stand or
  fall!'

And Vivien answer'd frowning wrath-
  fully:
'O, ay, what say ye to Sir Valence, him
Whose kinsman left him watcher o'er his
  wife
And two fair babes, and went to distant
  lands,
Was one year gone, and on returning found
Not two but three? there lay the reckling,
  one
But one hour old! What said the happy
  sire?
A seven-months' babe had been a truer
  gift.
Those twelve sweet moons confused his
  fatherhood.'      710

Then answer'd Merlin: 'Nay, I know
  the tale.
Sir Valence wedded with an outland dame;
Some cause had kept him sunder'd from
  his wife.
One child they had; it lived with her; she
  died.
His kinsman travelling on his own affair
Was charged by Valence to bring home the
  child.
He brought, not found it therefore; take
  the truth.'

'O, ay,' said Vivien, 'over-true a tale!
What say ye then to sweet Sir Sagra-
  more,

That ardent man ?  " To pluck the flower
    in season,"        720
So says the song, " I trow it is no treason."
O Master, shall we call him over-quick
To crop his own sweet rose before the
    hour ? '

    And Merlin answer'd: ' Over-quick art
    thou
To catch a loathly plume fallen from the
    wing
Of that foul bird of rapine whose whole
    prey
Is man's good name.  He never wrong'd
    his bride.
I know the tale.  An angry gust of wind
Puff'd out his torch among the myriad-
    room'd
And many-corridor'd complexities    730
Of Arthur's palace.  Then he found a door,
And darkling felt the sculptured ornament
That wreathen round it made it seem his
    own,
And wearied out made for the couch and
    slept,
A stainless man beside a stainless maid ;
And either slept, nor knew of other there,
Till the high dawn piercing the royal rose
In Arthur's casement glimmer'd chastely
    down,
Blushing upon them blushing, and at once
He rose without a word and parted from
    her.    740
But when the thing was blazed about the
    court,
The brute world howling forced them into
    bonds,
And as it chanced they are happy, being
    pure.'

    ' O, ay,' said Vivien, ' that were likely
    too !
What say ye then to fair Sir Percivale
And of the horrid foulness that he wrought,
The saintly youth, the spotless lamb of
    Christ,
Or some black wether of Saint Satan's
    fold ?    748
What, in the precincts of the chapel-yard,
Among the knightly brasses of the graves,
And by the cold Hic Jacets of the dead ! '

    And Merlin answer'd careless of her
    charge:
' A sober man is Percivale and pure,

But once in life was fluster'd with new wine,
Then paced for coolness in the chapel-yard,
Where one of Satan's shepherdesses caught
And meant to stamp him with her master's
    mark.
And that he sinn'd is not believable;
For, look upon his face ! — but if he sinn'd,
The sin that practice burns into the blood,
And not the one dark hour which brings
    remorse,    761
Will brand us, after, of whose fold we be;
Or else were he, the holy king whose hymns
Are chanted in the minster, worse than all.
But is your spleen froth'd out, or have ye
    more ? '

    And Vivien answer'd frowning yet in
    wrath:
' O, ay; what say ye to Sir Lancelot, friend,
Traitor or true ? that commerce with the
    Queen,
I ask you, is it clamor'd by the child,
Or whisper'd in the corner ? do ye know
    it ? '    770

    To which he answer'd sadly: ' Yea, I
    know it.
Sir Lancelot went ambassador, at first,
To fetch her, and she watch'd him from her
    walls.
A rumor runs, she took him for the King,
So fixt her fancy on him; let them be.
But have ye no one word of loyal praise
For Arthur, blameless king and stainless
    man ? '

    She answer'd with a low and chuckling
    laugh:
' Man ! is he man at all, who knows and
    winks ?
Sees what his fair bride is and does, and
    winks ?    780
By which the good King means to blind
    himself,
And blinds himself and all the Table
    Round
To all the foulness that they work.  Myself
Could call him — were it not for woman-
    hood —
The pretty, popular name such manhood
    earns,
Could call him the main cause of all their
    crime,
Yea, were he not crown'd king, coward and
    fool.'

Then Merlin to his own heart, loathing,
    said:
'O true and tender! O my liege and
    King!
O selfless man and stainless gentleman, 790
Who wouldst against thine own eye-witness
    fain
Have all men true and leal, all women
    pure!
How, in the mouths of base interpreters,
From over-fineness not intelligible
To things with every sense as false and
    foul
As the poach'd filth that floods the middle
    street,
Is thy white blamelessness accounted
    blame!'

But Vivien, deeming Merlin overborne
By instance, recommenced, and let her
    tongue
Rage like a fire among the noblest names,
Polluting, and imputing her whole self, 801
Defaming and defacing, till she left
Not even Lancelot brave nor Galahad
    clean.

Her words had issue other than she
    will'd.
He dragg'd his eyebrow bushes down, and
    made
A snowy pent-house for his hollow eyes,
And mutter'd in himself: 'Tell *her* the
    charm!
So, if she had it, would she rail on me
To snare the next, and if she have it not
So will she rail. What did the wanton
    say? 810
"Not mount as high!" we scarce can sink
    as low;
For men at most differ as heaven and earth,
But women, worst and best, as heaven and
    hell.
I know the Table Round, my friends of
    old;
All brave, and many generous, and some
    chaste.
She cloaks the scar of some repulse with
    lies.
I well believe she tempted them and fail'd,
Being so bitter; for fine plots may fail,
Tho' harlots paint their talk as well as
    face
With colors of the heart that are not
    theirs. 820

I will not let her know; nine tithes of
    times
Face-flatterer and backbiter are the same.
And they, sweet soul, that most impute a
    crime
Are pronest to it, and impute themselves,
Wanting the mental range, or low desire
Not to feel lowest makes them level all;
Yea, they would pare the mountain to the
    plain,
To leave an equal baseness; and in this
Are harlots like the crowd that if they find
Some stain or blemish in a name of note,
Not grieving that their greatest are so
    small, 831
Inflate themselves with some insane de-
    light,
And judge all nature from her feet of
    clay,
Without the will to lift their eyes, and see
Her godlike head crown'd with spiritual fire,
And touching other worlds. I am weary
    of her.'

He spoke in words part heard, in whis-
    pers part,
Half-suffocated in the hoary fell
And many-winter'd fleece of throat and
    chin.
But Vivien, gathering somewhat of his
    mood, 840
And hearing 'harlot' mutter'd twice or
    thrice,
Leapt from her session on his lap, and
    stood
Stiff as a viper frozen; loathsome sight,
How from the rosy lips of life and love
Flash'd the bare-grinning skeleton of
    death!
White was her cheek; sharp breaths of
    anger puff'd
Her fairy nostril out; her hand half-
    clench'd
Went faltering sideways downward to her
    belt,
And feeling. Had she found a dagger
    there —
For in a wink the false love turns to hate —
She would have stabb'd him; but she found
    it not. 851
His eye was calm, and suddenly she took
To bitter weeping like a beaten child,
A long, long weeping, not consolable.
Then her false voice made way, broken
    with sobs:

'O crueller than was ever told in tale
Or sung in song! O vainly lavish'd love!
O cruel, there was nothing wild or strange,
Or seeming shameful — for what shame in
　　love,
So love be true, and not as yours is? —
　　nothing                                    860
Poor Vivien had not done to win his trust
Who call'd her what he call'd her — all her
　　crime,
All — all — the wish to prove him wholly
　　hers.'

　　She mused a little, and then clapt her
　　　　hands
Together with a wailing shriek, and said:
'Stabb'd through the heart's affections to
　　the heart!
Seethed like the kid in its own mother's
　　milk!
Kill'd with a word worse than a life of
　　blows!
I thought that he was gentle, being great;
O God, that I had loved a smaller man!
I should have found in him a greater
　　heart.                                     871
O, I, that flattering my true passion, saw
The knights, the court, the King, dark in
　　your light,
Who loved to make men darker than they
　　are,
Because of that high pleasure which I had
To seat you sole upon my pedestal
Of worship — I am answer'd, and hence-
　　forth
The course of life that seem'd so flowery
　　to me
With you for guide and master, only you,
Becomes the sea-cliff pathway broken
　　short,                                     880
And ending in a ruin — nothing left
But into some low cave to crawl, and
　　there,
If the wolf spare me, weep my life away,
Kill'd with inutterable unkindliness.'

　　She paused, she turn'd away, she hung
　　　　her head,
The snake of gold slid from her hair, the
　　braid
Slipt and uncoil'd itself, she wept afresh,
And the dark wood grew darker toward
　　the storm
In silence, while his anger slowly died
Within him, till he let his wisdom go    890

For ease of heart, and half believed her
　　true;
Call'd her to shelter in the hollow oak,
'Come from the storm,' and having no
　　reply,
Gazed at the heaving shoulder and the
　　face
Hand-hidden, as for utmost grief or shame;
Then thrice essay'd, by tenderest-touching
　　terms,
To sleek her ruffled peace of mind, in vain.
At last she let herself be conquer'd by him,
And as the cageling newly flown returns,
The seeming-injured simple-hearted thing
Came to her old perch back, and settled
　　there.                                     901
There while she sat, half-falling from his
　　knees,
Half-nestled at his heart, and since he saw
The slow tear creep from her closed eyelid
　　yet,
About her, more in kindness than in love,
The gentle wizard cast a shielding arm.
But she dislink'd herself at once and rose,
Her arms upon her breast across, and
　　stood,
A virtuous gentlewoman deeply wrong'd,
Upright and flush'd before him; then she
　　said:                                      910

　　'There must be now no passages of love
Betwixt us twain henceforward evermore;
Since, if I be what I am grossly call'd,
What should be granted which your own
　　gross heart
Would reckon worth the taking? I will
　　go.
In truth, but one thing now — better have
　　died
Thrice than have ask'd it once — could
　　make me stay —
That proof of trust — so often ask'd in
　　vain!
How justly, after that vile term of yours,
I find with grief! I might believe you
　　then,                                      920
Who knows? once more. Lo! what was
　　once to me
Mere matter of the fancy, now hath grown
The vast necessity of heart and life.
Farewell; think gently of me, for I fear
My fate or folly, passing gayer youth
For one so old, must be to love thee still.
But ere I leave thee let me swear once
　　more

That if I schemed against thy peace in
    this,
May yon just heaven, that darkens o'er me,
    send
One flash that, missing all things else, may
    make                930
My scheming brain a cinder, if I lie.'

  Scarce had she ceased, when out of heaven
    a bolt —
For now the storm was close above them —
    struck,
Furrowing a giant oak, and javelining
With darted spikes and splinters of the
    wood
The dark earth round.   He raised his eyes
    and saw
The tree that shone white-listed thro' the
    gloom.
But Vivien, fearing heaven had heard her
    oath,
And dazzled by the livid-flickering fork,
And deafen'd with the stammering cracks
    and claps             940
That follow'd, flying back and crying out,
'O Merlin, tho' you do not love me, save,
Yet save me !' clung to him and hugg'd
    him close;
And call'd him dear protector in her fright,
Nor yet forgot her practice in her fright,
_.. wrought upon his mood and hugg'd
    him close.
The pale blood of the wizard at her touch
Took gayer colors, like an opal warm'd.
She blamed herself for telling hearsay
    tales;
She shook from fear, and for her fault she
    wept                950
Of petulancy; she call'd him lord and liege,
Her seer, her bard, her silver star of
    eve,
Her God, her Merlin, the one passionate
    love
Of her whole life; and ever overhead
Bellow'd the tempest, and the rotten branch
Snapt in the rushing of the river-rain
Above them; and in change of glare and
    gloom
Her eyes and neck glittering went and
    came;
Till now the storm, its burst of passion
    spent,
Moaning and calling out of other lands,  960
Had left the ravaged woodland yet once
    more

To peace; and what should not have been
    had been,
For Merlin, overtalk'd and overworn,
Had yielded, told her all the charm, and
    slept.

  Then, in one moment, she put forth the
    charm
Of woven paces and of waving hands,
And in the hollow oak he lay as dead,
And lost to life and use and name and
    fame.

  Then crying, 'I have made his glory
    mine,'
And shrieking out, 'O fool !' the harlot
    leapt            970
Adown the forest, and the thicket closed
Behind her, and the forest echo'd 'fool.'

## LANCELOT AND ELAINE

ELAINE the fair, Elaine the lovable,
Elaine, the lily maid of Astolat,
High in her chamber up a tower to the
    east
Guarded the sacred shield of Lancelot;
Which first she placed where morning's
    earliest ray
Might strike it, and awake her with the
    gleam;
Then fearing rust or soilure fashion'd for
    it
A case of silk, and braided thereupon
All the devices blazon'd on the shield
In their own tinct, and added, of her wit,
A border fantasy of branch and flower,  11
And yellow-throated nestling in the nest.
Nor rested thus content, but day by day,
Leaving her household and good father,
    climb'd
That eastern tower, and entering barr'd her
    door,
Stript off the case, and read the naked
    shield,
Now guess'd a hidden meaning in his arms,
Now made a pretty history to herself
Of every dint a sword had beaten in it,
And every scratch a lance had made upon
    it,         20
Conjecturing when and where: this cut is
    fresh,
That ten years back; this dealt him at
    Caerlyle,

That at Caerleon — this at Camelot —
And ah, God's mercy, what a stroke was
  there !
And here a thrust that might have kill'd,
  but God
Broke the strong lance, and roll'd his enemy
  down,
And saved him: so she lived in fantasy.

How came the lily maid by that good
  shield
Of Lancelot, she that knew not even his
  name ?
He left it with her, when he rode to tilt  30
For the great diamond in the diamond
  jousts,
Which Arthur had ordain'd, and by that
  name
Had named them, since a diamond was the
  prize.

For Arthur, long before they crown'd
  him king,
Roving the trackless realms of Lyonnesse,
Had found a glen, gray boulder and black
  tarn.
A horror lived about the tarn, and clave
Like its own mists to all the mountain
  side;
For here two brothers, one a king, had
  met
And fought together, but their names were
  lost;                                    40
And each had slain his brother at a blow;
And down they fell and made the glen ab-
  horr'd.
And there they lay till all their bones were
  bleach'd,
And lichen'd into color with the crags.
And he that once was king had on a crown
Of diamonds, one in front and four aside.
And Arthur came, and laboring up the
  pass,
All in a misty moonshine, unawares
Had trodden that crown'd skeleton, and
  the skull
Brake from the nape, and from the skull
  the crown                                50
Roll'd into light, and turning on its rims
Fled like a glittering rivulet to the tarn.
And down the shingly scaur he plunged,
  and caught,
And set it on his head, and in his heart
Heard murmurs, 'Lo, thou likewise shalt
  be king.'

Thereafter, when a king, he had the
  gems
Pluck'd from the crown, and show'd them
  to his knights
Saying: 'These jewels, whereupon I
  chanced
Divinely, are the kingdom's, not the
  King's —                                 59
For public use. Henceforward let there be,
Once every year, a joust for one of these;
For so by nine years' proof we needs must
  learn
Which is our mightiest, and ourselves shall
  grow
In use of arms and manhood, till we driv/
The heathen, who, some say, shall rule ᵗ ᵢe
  land
Hereafter, which God hinder !' Th ᵢ he
  spoke.
And eight years past, eight jousts b  ᵢ been,
  and still
Had Lancelot won the diamo .d of the
  year,
With purpose to present them ᵢo the Queen
When all were won; but, meaning all at
  once                                     70
To snare her royal fancy with a boon
Worth half her realm, had never spoken
  word.

Now for the central diamond and the
  last
And largest, Arthur, holding then his court
Hard on the river nigh the place which
  now
Is this world's hugest, let proclaim a joust
At Camelot, and when the time drew nigh
Spake — for she had been sick — to Guine-
  vere:
'Are you so sick, my Queen, you cannot
  move
To these fair jousts ? '  'Yea, lord,' she
  said, ' ye know it.'                     80
'Then will ye miss,' he answer'd, 'the
  great deeds
Of Lancelot, and his prowess in the lists,
A sight ye love to look on.' And the
  Queen
Lifted her eyes, and they dwelt languidly
On Lancelot, where he stood beside the
  King.
He, thinking that he read her meaning
  there,
'Stay with me, I am sick; my love is more
Than many diamonds,' yielded; and a heart

Love-loyal to the least wish of the Queen —
However much he yearn'd to make com-
    plete         90
The tale of diamonds for his destined
    boon —
Urged him to speak against the truth, and
    say,
'Sir King, mine ancient wound is hardly
    whole,
And lets me from the saddle;' and the
    King
Glanced first at him, then her, and went his
    way.
No sooner gone than suddenly she began:

'To blame, my lord Sir Lancelot, much
    to blame !
Why go ye not to these fair jousts ? the
    knights
Are half of them our enemies, and the
    crowd
Will murmur, "Lo the shameless ones,
    who take        100
Their pastime now the trustful King is
    gone !"'
Then Lancelot, vext at having lied in vain:
'Are ye so wise ? ye were not once so wise,
My Queen, that summer when ye loved me
    first.
Then of the crowd ye took no more account
Than of the myriad cricket of the mead,
When its own voice clings to each blade of
    grass,
And every voice is nothing. As to knights,
Them surely can I silence with all ease.
But now my loyal worship is allow'd    110
Of all men; many a bard, without offence,
Has link'd our names together in his lay,
Lancelot, the flower of bravery, Guinevere,
The pearl of beauty; and our knights at
    feast
Have pledged us in this union, while the
    King
Would listen smiling. How then ? is there
    more ?
Has Arthur spoken aught ? or would your-
    self,
Now weary of my service and devoir,
Henceforth be truer to your faultless lord ?'

She broke into a little scornful laugh:    120
'Arthur, my lord, Arthur, the faultless
    King,
That passionate perfection, my good lord —
But who can gaze upon the sun in heaven ?

He never spake word of reproach to me,
He never had a glimpse of mine untruth,
He cares not for me. Only here to-day
There gleamed a vague suspicion in his
    eyes;
Some meddling rogue has tamper'd with
    him — else
Rapt in this fancy of his Table Round,
And swearing men to vows impossible,    130
To make them like himself; but, friend, to
    me
He is all fault who hath no fault at all.
For who loves me must have a touch of
    earth;
The low sun makes the color. I am yours,
Not Arthur's, as ye know, save by the
    bond.
And therefore hear my words: go to the
    jousts;
The tiny-trumpeting gnat can break our
    dream
When sweetest; and the vermin voices
    here
May buzz so loud — we scorn them, but
    they sting.'

Then answer'd Lancelot, the chief of
    knights:    140
'... with what face, after my pretext
    made,
Shall I appear, O Queen, at Camelot, I
Before a king who honors his own word
As if it were his God's ?'

                    'Yea,' said the Queen,
'A moral child without the craft to rule,
Else had he not lost me; but listen to me,
If I must find you wit. We hear it said
That men go down before your spear at a
    touch,
But knowing you are Lancelot; your great
    name,
This conquers. Hide it therefore; go un-
    known.    150
Win ! by this kiss you will; and our true
    King
Will then allow your pretext, O my knight,
As all for glory; for to speak him true,
Ye know right well, how meek soe'er he
    seem,
No keener hunter after glory breathes.
He loves it in his knights more than him-
    self;
They prove to him his work. Win and re-
    turn.'

Then got Sir Lancelot suddenly to horse,
Wroth at himself. Not willing to be
    known,                              159
He left the barren-beaten thoroughfare,
Chose the green path that show'd the rarer
    foot,
And there among the solitary downs,
Full often lost in fancy, lost his way;
Till as he traced a faintly-shadow'd track,
That all in loops and links among the dales
Ran to the Castle of Astolat, he saw
Fired from the west, far on a hill, the tow-
    ers.
Thither he made, and blew the gateway
    horn.
Then came an old, dumb, myriad-wrinkled
    man,
Who let him into lodging and disarm'd.  170
And Lancelot marvell'd at the wordless
    man;
And issuing found the Lord of Astolat
With two strong sons, Sir Torre and Sir
    Lavaine,
Moving to meet him in the castle court;
And close behind them stept the lily maid
Elaine, his daughter; mother of the house
There was not.   Some light jest among
    them rose
With laughter dying down as the great
    knight
Approach'd them; then the Lord of Astolat:
' Whence comest thou, my guest, and by
    what name               180
Livest between the lips ? for by thy state
And presence I might guess thee chief of
    those,
After the King, who eat in Arthur's halls.
Him have I seen; the rest, his Table
    Round,
Known as they are, to me they are un-
    known.'

Then answer'd Lancelot, the chief of
    knights:
' Known am I, and of Arthur's hall, and
    known,
What I by mere mischance have brought,
    my shield.
But since I go to joust as one unknown
At Camelot for the diamond, ask me not;
Hereafter ye shall know me — and the
    shield —                191
I pray you lend me one, if such you have,
Blank, or at least with some device not
    mine.'

Then said the Lord of Astolat: ' Here is
    Torre's:
Hurt in his first tilt was my son, Sir Torre,
And so, God wot, his shield is blank enough.
His ye can have.'   Then added plain Sir
    Torre,
' Yea, since I cannot use it, ye may have it.'
Here laugh'd the father saying: ' Fie, Sir
    Churl,
Is that an answer for a noble knight ?    200
Allow him ! but Lavaine, my younger he e,
He is so full of lustihood, he will ride,
Joust for it, and win, and bring it in  1
    hour,
And set it in this damsel's golden hair,
To make her thrice as wilful as before.'

' Nay, father, nay, good father, shame m
    not
Before this noble knight,' said young La
    vaine,
' For nothing.   Surely I but play'd on
    Torre,
He seem'd so sullen, vext he could not go;
A jest, no more ! for, knight, the maiden
    dreamt                  210
That some one put this diamond in her
    hand,
And that it was too slippery to be held,
And slipt and fell into some pool or stream,
The castle-well, belike; and then I said
That if I went and if I fought and won
    it —
But all was jest and joke among our-
    selves —
Then must she keep it safelier.  All was
    jest.
But, father, give me leave, an if he will,
To ride to Camelot with this noble knight.
Win shall I not, but do my best to win;  220
Young as I am, yet would I do my best.'

' So ye will grace me,' answer'd Lance-
    lot,
Smiling a moment, ' with your fellowship
O'er these waste downs whereon I lost my-
    self,
Then were I glad of you as guide and
    friend;
And you shall win this diamond, — as I
    hear,
It is a fair large diamond, — if ye may,
And yield it to this maiden, if ye will.'
' A fair large diamond,' added plain Sir
    Torre,

' Such be for queens, and not for simple
    maids.'                    230
Then she, who held her eyes upon the
    ground,
Elaine, and heard her name so tost about,
Flush'd slightly at the slight disparage-
    ment
Before the stranger knight, who, looking at
    her,
Full courtly, yet not falsely, thus return'd:
' If what is fair be but for what is fair,
And only queens are to be counted so,
Rash were my judgment then, who deem
    this maid
Might wear as fair a jewel as is on earth,
Not violating the bond of like to like.'    240

    He spoke and ceased; the lily maid
    Elaine,
Won by the mellow voice before she look'd,
Lifted her eyes and read his lineaments.
The great and guilty love he bare the
    Queen,
In battle with the love he bare his lord,
Had marr'd his face, and mark'd it ere his
    time.
Another sinning on such heights with one,
The flower of all the west and all the world,
Had been the sleeker for it; but in him   249
His mood was often like a fiend, and rose
And drove him into wastes and solitudes
For agony, who was yet a living soul.
Marr'd as he was, he seem'd the goodliest
    man
That ever among ladies ate in hall,
And noblest, when she lifted up her eyes.
However marr'd, of more than twice her
    years,
Seam'd with an ancient sword-cut on the
    cheek,
And bruised and bronzed, she lifted up her
    eyes
And loved him, with that love which was
    her doom.

    Then the great knight, the darling of the
    court,                    260
Loved of the loveliest, into that rude hall
Stept with all grace, and not with half dis-
    dain
Hid under grace, as in a smaller time,
But kindly man moving among his kind;
Whom they with meats and vintage of their
    best
And talk and minstrel melody entertain'd.

And much they ask'd of court and Table
    Round,
And ever well and readily answer'd he;
But Lancelot, when they glanced at Guine-
    vere,
Suddenly speaking of the wordless man,   270
Heard from the baron that, ten years be-
    fore,
The heathen caught and reft him of his
    tongue.
' He learnt and warn'd me of their fierce
    design
Against my house, and him they caught
    and maim'd;
But I, my sons, and little daughter fled
From bonds or death, and dwelt among the
    woods
By the great river in a boatman's hut.
Dull days were those, till our good Arthur
    broke
The Pagan yet once more on Badon hill.'

    ' O, there, great lord, doubtless,' Lavaine
    said, rapt                    280
By all the sweet and sudden passion of
    youth
Toward greatness in its elder, ' you have
    fought.
O, tell us — for we live apart — you know
Of Arthur's glorious wars.'   And Lancelot
    spoke
And answer'd him at full, as having been
With Arthur in the fight which all day
    long
Rang by the white mouth of the violent
    Glem;
And in the four loud battles by the shore
Of Duglas; that on Bassa; then the war
That thunder'd in and out the gloomy
    skirts                    290
Of Celidon the forest; and again
By Castle Gurnion, where the glorious
    King
Had on his cuirass worn our Lady's Head,
Carved of one emerald centred in a sun
Of silver rays, that lighten'd as he breathed;
And at Caerleon had he help'd his lord,
When the strong neighings of the wild
    White Horse
Set every gilded parapet shuddering;
And up in Agned-Cathregonion too,
And down the waste sand-shores of Trath
    Treroit,                    300
Where many a heathen fell; ' and on the
    mount

Of Badon I myself beheld the King
Charge at the head of all his Table Round,
And all his legions crying Christ and him,
And break them; and I saw him, after,
    stand
High on a heap of slain, from spur to
    plume
Red as the rising sun with heathen blood,
And seeing me, with a great voice he cried,
"They are broken, they are broken!" for
    the King,                                    309
However mild he seems at home, nor cares
For triumph in our mimic wars, the jousts —
For if his own knight casts him down, he
    laughs,
Saying his knights are better men than
    he —
Yet in this heathen war the fire of God
Fills him.  I never saw his like; there lives
No greater leader.'

                    While he utter'd this,
Low to her own heart said the lily maid,
'Save your great self, fair lord;' and when
    he fell                                      318
From talk of war to traits of pleasantry —
Being mirthful he, but in a stately kind —
She still took note that when the living
    smile
Died from his lips, across him came a
    cloud
Of melancholy severe, from which again,
Whenever in her hovering to and fro
The lily maid had striven to make him
    cheer,
There brake a sudden-beaming tenderness
Of manners and of nature; and she thought
That all was nature, all, perchance, for
    her.
And all night long his face before her
    lived,
As when a painter, poring on a face,       330
Divinely thro' all hindrance finds the man
Behind it, and so paints him that his face,
The shape and color of a mind and life,
Lives for his children, ever at its best
And fullest; so the face before her lived,
Dark-splendid, speaking in the silence, full
Of noble things, and held her from her
    sleep,
Till rathe she rose, half-cheated in the
    thought
She needs must bid farewell to sweet
    Lavaine.
First as in fear, step after step, she stole

Down the long tower-stairs, hesitating.   341
Anon, she heard Sir Lancelot cry in the
    court,
'This shield, my friend, where is it?' and
    Lavaine
Past inward, as she came from out the
    tower.
There to his proud horse Lancelot turn'd,
    and smooth'd
The glossy shoulder, humming to himself.
Half-envious of the flattering hand, she
    drew
Nearer and stood.  He look'd, and, more
    amazed
Than if seven men had set upon him, saw
The maiden standing in the dewy light.    350
He had not dream'd she was so beautiful.
Then came on him a sort of sacred fear,
For silent, tho' he greeted her, she stood
Rapt on his face as if it were a god's.
Suddenly flash'd on her a wild desire
That he should wear her favor at the tilt.
She braved a riotous heart in asking for it.
'Fair lord, whose name I know not —
    noble it is,
I well believe, the noblest — will you wear
My favor at this tourney?'  'Nay,' said
    he,                                          360
'Fair lady, since I never yet have worn
Favor of any lady in the lists.
Such is my wont, as those who know me
    know.'
'Yea, so,' she answer'd; 'then in wearing
    mine
Needs must be lesser likelihood, noble lord,
That those who know should know you.'
    And he turn'd
Her counsel up and down within his mind,
And found it true, and answer'd: 'True,
    my child.
Well, I will wear it; fetch it out to me.
What is it?' and she told him, 'A red
    sleeve                                       370
Broider'd with pearls,' and brought it.
    Then he bound
Her token on his helmet, with a smile
Saying, 'I never yet have done so much
For any maiden living,' and the blood
Sprang to her face and fill'd her with
    delight;
But left her all the paler when Lavaine
Returning brought the yet-unblazon'd
    shield,
His brother's, which he gave to Lancelot,
Who parted with his own to fair Elaine:

'Do me this grace, my child, to have my
     shield                                    380
In keeping till I come.'   'A grace to me,'
She answer'd, 'twice to-day.   I am your
     squire!'
Whereat Lavaine said laughing: 'Lily
     maid,
For fear our people call you lily maid
In earnest, let me bring your color back;
Once, twice, and thrice.   Now get you hence
     to bed;'
So kiss'd her, and Sir Lancelot his own
     hand,
And thus they moved away.   She staid a
     minute,
Then made a sudden step to the gate, and
     there —
Her bright hair blown about the serious
     face                                       390
Yet rosy-kindled with her brother's kiss —
Paused by the gateway, standing near the
     shield
In silence, while she watch'd their arms
     far-off
Sparkle, until they dipt below the downs.
Then to her tower she climb'd, and took
     the shield,
There kept it, and so lived in fantasy.

    Meanwhile the new companions past
     away
Far o'er the long backs of the bushless
     downs,
To where Sir Lancelot knew there lived a
     knight                                     399
Not far from Camelot, now for forty years
A hermit, who had pray'd, labor'd and
     pray'd,
And ever laboring had scoop'd himself
In the white rock a chapel and a hall
On massive columns, like a shore-cliff cave,
And cells and chambers.   All were fair
     and dry;
The green light from the meadows under-
     neath
Struck up and lived along the milky roofs;
And in the meadows tremulous aspen-trees
And poplars made a noise of falling showers.
And thither wending there that night they
     bode.                                      410

    But when the next day broke from under-
     ground,
And shot red fire and shadows thro' the
     cave,

They rose, heard mass, broke fast, and rode
     away.
Then Lancelot saying, 'Hear, but hold my
     name
Hidden, you ride with Lancelot of the
     Lake,'
Abash'd Lavaine, whose instant reverence,
Dearer to true young hearts than their own
     praise,
But left him leave to stammer, 'Is it in-
     deed?'
And after mutte   g, 'The great Lancelot,'
At last he got   s breath and answer'd:
     'One,                                      420
One have I se   — that other, our liege
     lord,
The dread    dragon, Britain's King of
     kings,
Of whom th  eople talk mysteriously,
He will be   ere — then were I stricken
     blind
That minute I might say that I had seen.'

    So spake Lavaine, and when they reach'd
     the  ists
By Camel  t in the meadow, let his eyes
Run thro  the peopled gallery which half
     round
Lay like a rainbow fallen upon the grass,
Until they found the clear-faced King, who
     sat                                        430
Robed in red samite, easily to be known,
Since to his crown the golden dragon clung,
And down his robe the dragon writhed in
     gold,
And from the carven-work behind him
     crept
Two dragons gilded, sloping down to make
Arms for his chair, while all the rest of
     them
Thro' knots and loops and folds innumera-
     ble
Fled ever thro' the woodwork, till they
     found
The new design wherein they lost them-
     selves,                                    439
Yet with all ease, so tender was the work;
And, in the costly canopy o'er him set,
Blazed the last diamond of the nameless
     king.

    Then Lancelot answer'd young Lavaine
     and said:
'Me you call great; mine is the firmer seat,
The truer lance; but there is many a youth

Now crescent, who will come to all I am
And overcome it; and in me there dwells
No greatness, save it be some far-off touch
Of greatness to know well I am not great.
There is the man.' And Lavaine gaped
  upon him                               450
As on a thing miraculous, and anon
The trumpets blew; and then did either
  side,
They that assail'd, and they that held the
  lists,
Set lance in rest, strike spur, suddenly
  move,
Meet in the midst, and there so furiously
Shock that a man far-off might well per-
  ceive,
If any man that day were left afield,
The hard earth shake, and a low thunder
  of arms.
And Lancelot bode a little, till he saw
Which were the weaker; then he hurl'd
  into it                                460
Against the stronger. Little need to speak
Of Lancelot in his glory ! King, duke, earl,
Count, baron — whom he smote, he over-
  threw.

  But in the field were Lancelot's kith and
    kin,
Ranged with the Table Round that held
  the lists,
Strong men, and wrathful that a stranger
  knight
Should do and almost overdo the deeds
Of Lancelot; and one said to the other,
  'Lo !
What is he ?  I do not mean the force
  alone —
The grace and versatility of the man !  470
Is it not Lancelot ?'  'When has Lancelot
  worn
Favor of any lady in the lists ?
Not such his wont, as we that know him
  know.'
'How then ?  who then ?' a fury seized
  them all,
A fiery family passion for the name
Of Lancelot, and a glory one with theirs.
They couch'd their spears and prick'd their
  steeds, and thus,
Their plumes driven backward by the wind
  they made
In moving, all together down upon him
Bare, as a wild wave in the wide North
  Sea,                                   480

Green - glimmering toward the summit,
  bears, with all
Its stormy crests that smoke against the
  skies,
Down on a bark, and overbears the bark
And him that helms it; so they overbore
Sir Lancelot and his charger, and a spear
Down-glancing lamed the charger, and a
  spear
Prick'd sharply his own cuirass, and the
  head
Pierced thro' his side, and there snapt and
  remain'd.

  Then Sir Lavaine did well and worship-
    fully.
He bore a knight of old repute to the
  earth,                                 490
And brought his horse to Lancelot where
  he lay.
He up the side, sweating with agony,
  got,
But thought to do while he might yet en-
  dure,
And being lustily holpen by the rest,
His party, — tho' it seem'd half-miracle
To those he fought with, — drave his kith
  and kin,
And all the Table Round that held the lists,
Back to the barrier; then the trumpets
  blew
Proclaiming his the prize who wore the
  sleeve
Of scarlet and the pearls; and all the
  knights,                              500
His party, cried, 'Advance and take thy
  prize
The diamond; ' but he answer'd: ' Diamond
  me
No diamonds ! for God's love, a little air !
Prize me no prizes, for my prize is death !
Hence will I, and I charge you, follow me
  not.'

  He spoke, and vanish'd suddenly from
    the field
With young Lavaine into the poplar grove.
There from his charger down he slid, and
  sat,
Gasping to Sir Lavaine, ' Draw the lance-
  head.'
' Ah, my sweet lord Sir Lancelot,' said La-
  vaine,                                510
' I dread me, if I draw it, you will die.'
But he, ' I die already with it; draw —

Draw,' — and Lavaine drew, and Sir
  Lancelot gave
A marvellous great shriek and ghastly
  groan,
And half his blood burst forth, and down
  he sank
For the pure pain, and wholly swoon'd
  away.
Then came the hermit out and bare him
  in,
There stanch'd his wound; and there, in
  daily doubt
Whether to live or die, for many a week
Hid from the wild world's rumor by the
  grove                                    520
Of poplars with their noise of falling show-
  ers,
And ever-tremulous aspen-trees, he lay.

But on that day when Lancelot fled the
  lists,
His party, knights of utmost North and
  West,
Lords of waste marshes, kings of desolate
  isles,
Came round their great Pendragon, saying
  to him,
' Lo, Sire, our knight, thro' whom we won
  the day,
Hath gone sore wounded, and hath left his
  prize
Untaken, crying that his prize is death.'
' Heaven hinder,' said the King, ' that such
  an one,                                  530
So great a knight as we have seen to-day —
He seem'd to me another Lancelot —
Yea, twenty times I thought him Lance-
  lot —
He must not pass uncared for. Wherefore
  rise,
O Gawain, and ride forth and find the
  knight.
Wounded and wearied, needs must he be
  near.
I charge you that you get at once to horse.
And, knights and kings, there breathes not
  one of you
Will deem this prize of ours is rashly given;
His prowess was too wondrous. We will
  do him                                   540
No customary honor; since the knight
Came not to us, of us to claim the prize,
Ourselves will send it after. Rise and
  take
This diamond, and deliver it, and return,

And bring us where he is, and how he fares,
And cease not from your quest until ye
  find.'

So saying, from the carven flower above,
To which it made a restless heart, he took
And gave the diamond. Then from where
  he sat
At Arthur's right, with smiling face arose,
With smiling face and frowning heart, a
  prince                                   551
In the mid might and flourish of his May,
Gawain, surnamed the Courteous, fair and
  strong,
And after Lancelot, Tristram, and Geraint,
And Gareth, a good knight, but there-
  withal
Sir Modred's brother, and the child of Lot,
Nor often loy' 'o his word, and now
Wroth that the  'ng's command to sally
  forth
In quest of whom he k ʒw not, made him
  leave
The banquet and concourse of knights and
  kings.                                   560

So all in wrath he got to horse and went;
While Arthur to the banquet, dark in mood,
Past, thinking, ' Is it Lancelot who hath
  come
Despite the wound he spake of, all for gain
Of glory, and hath added wound to wound,
And ridden away to die ? ' So fear'd the
  King,
And, after two days' tarriance there, re-
  turn'd.
Then when he saw the Queen, embracing
  ask'd,
' Love, are you yet so sick ? ' ' Nay, lord,'
  she said.
' And where is Lancelot ? ' Then the Queen
  amazed,                                  570
' Was he not with you ? won he not your
  prize ? '
' Nay, but one like him.' ' Why, that like
  was he.'
And when the King demanded how she
  knew,
Said: ' Lord, no sooner had ye parted from
  us
Than Lancelot told me of a common talk
That men went down before his spear at a
  touch,
But knowing he was Lancelot; his great
  name

Conquer'd; and therefore would he hide
    his name
From all men, even the King, and to this
    end
Had made the pretext of a hindering
    wound,          580
That he might joust unknown of all, and
    learn
If his old prowess were in aught decay'd;
And added, " Our true Arthur, when he
    learns,
Will well allow my pretext, as for gain
Of purer glory." '

              Then replied the King:
' Far lovelier in our Lancelot had it been,
In lieu of idly dallying with the truth,
To have trusted me as he hath trusted
    thee.
Surely his King and most familiar friend
Might well have kept his secret.  True,
    indeed,          590
Albeit I know my knights fantastical,
So fine a fear in our large Lancelot
Must needs have moved my laughter; now
    remains
But little cause for laughter.  His own
    kin —
Ill news, my Queen, for all who love him,
    this ! —
His kith and kin, not knowing, set upon
    him;
So that he went sore wounded from the
    field.
Yet good news too; for goodly hopes are
    mine
That Lancelot is no more a lonely heart.
He wore, against his wont, upon his helm
A sleeve of scarlet, broider'd with great
    pearls,          601
Some gentle maiden's gift.'

           ' Yea, lord,' she said,
' Thy hopes are mine,' and saying that, she
    choked,
And sharply turn'd about to hide her
    face,
Past to her chamber, and there flung her-
    self
Down on the great King's couch, and
    writhed upon it,
And clench'd her fingers till they bit the
    palm,
And shriek'd out ' Traitor ! ' to the unhear-
    ing wall,

Then flash'd into wild tears, and rose
    again,
And moved about her palace, proud and
    pale.          610

    Gawain the while thro' all the region
    round
Rode with his diamond, wearied of the
    quest,
Touch'd at all points except the poplar
    grove,
And came at last, tho' late, to Astolat;
Whom glittering in enamell'd arms the
    maid
Glanced at, and cried, ' What news from
    Camelot, lord ?
What of the knight with the red sleeve ? '
    ' He won.'
' I knew it,' she said.  ' But parted from
    the jousts
Hurt in the side;' whereat she caught her
    breath.
Thro' her own side she felt the sharp lance
    go.          620
Thereon she smote her hand; wellnigh she
    swoon'd.
And, while he gazed wonderingly at her,
    came
The Lord of Astolat out, to whom the
    prince
Reported who he was, and on what quest
Sent, that he bore the prize and could not
    find
The victor, but had ridden a random round
To seek him, and had wearied of the
    search.
To whom the Lord of Astolat: ' Bide with
    us,
And ride no more at random, noble prince !
Here was the knight, and here he left a
    shield;         630
This will he send or come for.  Further-
    more
Our son is with him; we shall hear anon,
Needs must we hear.'  To this the courte-
    ous prince
Accorded with his wonted courtesy,
Courtesy with a touch of traitor in it,
And staid; and cast his eyes on fair
    Elaine;
Where could be found face daintier ? then
    her shape
From forehead down to foot, perfect —
    again
From foot to forehead exquisitely turn'd.

'Well — if I bide, lo ! this wild flower for
   me !'                    640
And oft they met among the garden yews,
And there he set himself to play upon her
With sallying wit, free flashes from a
   height
Above her, graces of the court, and songs,
Sighs, and low smiles, and golden elo-
   quence
And amorous adulation, till the maid
Rebell'd against it, saying to him: ' Prince,
O loyal nephew of our noble King,
Why ask you not to see the shield he left,
Whence you might learn his name ?  Why
   slight your King,          650
And lose the quest he sent you on, and
   prove
No surer than our falcon yesterday,
Who lost the hern we slipt her at, and
   went
To all the winds ?'  ' Nay, by mine head,'
   said he,
' I lose it, as we lose the lark in heaven,
O damsel, in the light of your blue eyes;
But an ye will it let me see the shield.'
And when the shield was brought, and Ga-
   wain saw
Sir Lancelot's azure lions, crown'd with
   gold,
        the field, he smote his thigh, and
   mock'd:              660
' Right was the King ! our Lancelot ! that
   true man !'
' And right was I,' she answer'd merrily,
   ' I,
Who dream'd my knight the greatest
   knight of all.'
' And if I dream'd,' said Gawain, ' that you
   love
This greatest knight, your pardon ! lo, ye
   know it !
Speak therefore; shall I waste myself in
   vain ?'
Full simple was her answer: ' What know
   I ?
My brethren have been all my fellowship;
And I, when often they have talk'd of
   love,
Wish'd it had been my mother, for they
   talk'd,             670
Meseem'd, of what they knew not; so my-
   self —
I know not if I know what true love is,
But if I know, then, if I love not him,
I know there is none other I can love.'

' Yea, by God's death,' said he, ' ye love
   him well,
But would not, knew ye what all others
   know,
And whom he loves.' ' So be it,' cried
   Elaine,
And lifted her fair face and moved away;
But he pursued her, calling, ' Stay a little !
One golden minute's grace ! he wore your
   sleeve.           680
Would he break faith with one I may not
   name ?
Must our true man change like a leaf at
   last ?
Nay — like enow.  Why then, far be it
   from me
To cross our mighty Lancelot in his loves !
And, damsel, for I deem you know full
   well
Where your great knight is hidden, let me
   leave
My quest with you; the diamond also —
   here !
For if you love, it will be sweet to give it;
And if he love, it will be sweet to have it
From your own hand; and whether he love
   or not,          690
A diamond is a diamond.  Fare you well
A thousand times ! — a thousand times
   farewell !
Yet, if he love, and his love hold, we two
May meet at court hereafter ! there, I
   think,
So ye will learn the courtesies of the court,
We two shall know each other.'

                      Then he gave,
And slightly kiss'd the hand to which he
   gave,
The diamond, and all wearied of the quest
Leapt on his horse, and carolling as he
   went
A true-love ballad, lightly rode away.  700

    Thence to the court he past; there told
   the King
What the King knew, ' Sir Lancelot is the
   knight.'
And added, ' Sire, my liege, so much I
   learnt,
But fail'd to find him, tho' I rode all round
The region; but I lighted on the maid
Whose sleeve he wore.  She loves him;
   and to her,
Deeming our courtesy is the truest law,

I gave the diamond. She will render it;
For by mine head she knows his hiding-
    place.'

The seldom-frowning King frown'd, and
    replied,                                    710
'Too courteous truly ! ye shall go no more
On quest of mine, seeing that ye forget
Obedience is the courtesy due to kings.'

He spake and parted. Wroth, but all in
    awe,
For twenty strokes of the blood, without a
    word,
Linger'd that other, staring after him;
Then shook his hair, strode off, and buzz'd
    abroad
About the maid of Astolat, and her love.
All ears were prick'd at once, all tongues
    were loosed:
'The maid of Astolat loves Sir Lancelot,
Sir Lancelot loves the maid of Astolat.' 721
Some read the King's face, some the
    Queen's, and all
Had marvel what the maid might be, but
    most
Predoom'd her as unworthy. One old
    dame
Came suddenly on the Queen with the
    sharp news.
She, that had heard the noise of it before,
But sorrowing Lancelot should have stoop'd
    so low,
Marr'd her friend's aim with pale tran-
    quillity.
So ran the tale like fire about the court,
Fire in dry stubble a nine-days' wonder
    flared;                                      730
Till even the knights at banquet twice or
    thrice
Forgot to drink to Lancelot and the Queen,
And pledging Lancelot and the lily maid
Smiled at each other, while the Queen, who
    sat
With lips severely placid, felt the knot
Climb in her throat, and with her feet un-
    seen
Crush'd the wild passion out against the floor
Beneath the banquet, where the meats be-
    came
As wormwood and she hated all who
    pledged.

But far away the maid in Astolat,      740
Her guiltless rival, she that ever kept

The one-day-seen Sir Lancelot in her heart,
Crept to her father, while he mused alone,
Sat on his knee, stroked his gray face and
    said:
'Father, you call me wilful, and the fault
Is yours who let me have my will, and
    now,
Sweet father, will you let me lose my
    wits ?'
'Nay,' said he, 'surely.' 'Wherefore, let
    me hence,'
She answer'd, 'and find out our dear La-
    vaine.'
'Ye will not lose your wits for dear La-
    vaine.                                       750
Bide,' answer'd he: 'we needs must hear
    anon
Of him, and of that o     '  'Ay,' she said,
'And of that other, for  ʌ   ᴅs must hence
And find that other, wheresoe ʊ  ᷣᵃ be,
And with mine own hand give his diamond
    to him,
Lest I be found as faithless in the quest
As yon proud prince who left the quest to
    me.
Sweet father, I behold him in my dreams
Gaunt as it were the skeleton of himself,
Death-pale, for the lack of gentle maiden's
    aid.                                         760
The gentler-born the maiden, the more
    bound,
My father, to be sweet and serviceable
To noble knights in sickness, as ye know,
When these have worn their tokens. Let
    me hence,
I pray you.' Then her father nodding
    said:
'Ay, ay, the diamond. Wit ye well, my
    child,
Right fain were I to learn this knight were
    whole,
Being our greatest. Yea, and you must
    give it —
And sure I think this fruit is hung too
    high
For any mouth to gape for save a
    queen's —                                    770
Nay, I mean nothing; so then, get you
    gone,
Being so very wilful you must go.'

Lightly, her suit allow'd, she slipt away,
And while she made her ready for her ride
Her father's latest word humm'd in her
    ear,

'Being so very wilful you must go,'
And changed itself and echo'd in her heart,
'Being so very wilful you must die.'
But she was happy enough and shook it
    off,                                          779
As we shake off the bee that buzzes at us;
And in her heart she answer'd it and said,
'What matter, so I help him back to life?'
Then far away with good Sir Torre for
    guide
Rode o'er the long backs of the bushless
    downs
To Camelot, and before the city-gates
Came on her brother with a happy face
Making a roan horse caper and curvet
For pleasure all about a field of flowers;
Whom when she saw, 'Lavaine,' she cried,
    'Lavaine,
How fares my lord Sir Lancelot?'    He
    amazed,                                       790
'Torre and Elaine! why here?    Sir Lance-
    lot!
How know ye my lord's name is Lancelot?'
But when the maid had told him all her
    tale,
Then turn'd Sir Torre, and being in his
    moods
Left them, and under the strange-statued
    gate,
Where Arthur's wars were render'd mysti-
    cally,
Past up the still rich city to his kin,
His own far blood, which dwelt at Came-
    lot;
And her, Lavaine across the poplar grove
Led to the caves.    There first she saw the
    casque                                        800
Of Lancelot on the wall; her scarlet sleeve,
Tho' carved and cut, and half the pearls
    away,
Stream'd from it still; and in her heart she
    laugh'd,
Because he had not loosed it from his
    helm,
But meant once more perchance to tourney
    in it.
And when they gain'd the cell wherein he
    slept,
His battle-writhen arms and mighty hands
Lay naked on the wolf-skin, and a dream
Of dragging down his enemy made them
    move.
Then she that saw him lying unsleek, un-
    shorn,                                         810
Gaunt as it were the skeleton of himself,

Utter'd a little tender dolorous cry.
The sound not wonted in a place so still
Woke the sick knight, and while he roll'd
    his eyes
Yet blank from sleep, she started to him,
    saying,
'Your prize the diamond sent you by the
    King.'
His eyes glisten'd; she fancied, 'Is it for
    me?'
And when the maid had told him all the
    tale
Of king and prince, the diamond sent, the
    quest
Assign'd to her not worthy of it, she knelt
Full lowly by the corners of his bed,       821
And laid the diamond in his open hand.
Her face was near, and as we kiss the child
That does the task assign'd, he kiss'd her
    face.
At once she slipt like water to the floor.
'Alas,' he said, 'your ride hath wearied
    you.
Rest must you have.'    'No rest for me,'
    she said;
'Nay, for near you, fair lord, I am at rest.'
What might she mean by that? his large
    black eyes,
Yet larger thro' his leanness, dwelt upon
    her,                                          830
Till all her heart's sad secret blazed itself
In the heart's colors on her simple face;
And Lancelot look'd and was perplext in
    mind,
And being weak in body said no more,
But did not love the color; woman's love,
Save one, he not regarded, and so turn'd
Sighing, and feign'd a sleep until he slept.

Then rose Elaine and glided thro' the
    fields,
And past beneath the weirdly-sculptured
    gates
Far up the dim rich city to her kin;       840
There bode the night, but woke with dawn,
    and past
Down thro' the dim rich city to the fields,
Thence to the cave.    So day by day she past
In either twilight ghost-like to and fro
Gliding, and every day she tended him,
And likewise many a night; and Lancelot
Would, tho' he call'd his wound a little
    hurt
Whereof he should be quickly whole, at
    times

Brain-feverous in his heat and agony, seem
Uncourteous, even he.  But the meek maid
Sweetly forbore him ever, being to him  851
Meeker than any child to a rough nurse,
Milder than any mother to a sick child,
And never woman yet, since man's first
    fall,
Did kindlier unto man, but her deep love
Upbore her; till the hermit, skill'd in all
The simples and the science of that time,
Told him that her fine care had saved his
    life.
And the sick man forgot her simple blush,
Would call her friend and sister, sweet
    Elaine,  860
Would listen for her coming and regret
Her parting step, and held her tenderly,
And loved her with all love except the
    love
Of man and woman when they love their
    best,
Closest and sweetest, and had died the
    death
In any knightly fashion for her sake.
And peradventure had he seen her first
She might have made this and that other
    world
Another world for the sick man; but now
The shackles of an old love straiten'd him,
His honor rooted in dishonor stood,  871
And faith unfaithful kept him falsely true.

Yet the great knight in his mid-sickness
    made
Full many a holy vow and pure resolve.
These, as but born of sickness, could not
    live;
For when the blood ran lustier in him
    again,
Full often the bright image of one face,
Making a treacherous quiet in his heart,
Dispersed his resolution like a cloud.
Then if the maiden, while that ghostly
    grace  880
Beam'd on his fancy, spoke, he answer'd
    not,
Or short and coldly, and she knew right
    well
What the rough sickness meant, but what
    this meant
She knew not, and the sorrow dimm'd her
    sight,
And drave her ere her time across the
    fields
Far into the rich city, where alone

She murmur'd, 'Vain, in vain! it cannot be.
He will not love me.  How then ? must I
    die ? '
Then as a little helpless innocent bird,  889
That has but one plain passage of few notes,
Will sing the simple passage o'er and o'er
For all an April morning, till the ear
Wearies to hear it, so the simple maid
Went half the night repeating, 'Must I
    die ? '
And now to right she turn'd, and now to
    left,
And found no ease in turning or in rest;
And 'Him or death,' she mutter'd, 'death
    or him,'
Again and like a burthen, 'Him or death.'

But when Sir Lancelot's deadly hurt was
    whole,
To Astolat returning rode the three.  900
There morn by morn, arraying her sweet
    self
In that wherein she deem'd she look'd her
    best,
She came before Sir Lancelot, for she
    thought,
'If I be loved, these are my festal robes,
If not, the victim's flowers before he fall.'
And Lancelot ever prest upon the maid
That she should ask some goodly gift of
    him
For her own self or hers: 'and do not
    shun
To speak the wish most near to your true
    heart;  909
Such service have ye done me that I make
My will of yours, and prince and lord am I
In mine own land, and what I will I can.'
Then like a ghost she lifted up her face,
But like a ghost without the power to
    speak.
And Lancelot saw that she withheld her
    wish,
And bode among them yet a little space
Till he should learn it; and one morn it
    chanced
He found her in among the garden yews,
And said, 'Delay no longer, speak your
    wish,  919
Seeing I go to-day.'  Then out she brake:
'Going ? and we shall never see you more.
And I must die for want of one bold word.'
'Speak; that I live to hear,' he said, 'is
    yours.'
Then suddenly and passionately she spoke:

'I have gone mad. I love you; let me die.'
'Ah, sister,' answer'd Lancelot, 'what is
    this ?'
And innocently extending her white arms,
'Your love,' she said, 'your love — to be
    your wife.'
And Lancelot answer'd, 'Had I chosen to
    wed,                                            929
I had been wedded earlier, sweet Elaine;
But now there never will be wife of mine.'
'No, no,' she cried, 'I care not to be wife,
But to be with you still, to see your face,
To serve you, and to follow you thro' the
    world.'
And Lancelot answer'd: 'Nay, the world,
    the world,
All ear and eye, with such a stupid heart
To interpret ear and eye, and such a tongue
To blare its own interpretation — nay,
Full ill then should I quit your brother's
    love,
And your good father's kindness.' And
    she said,                                       940
Not to be with you, not to see your face —
A. is for me then, my good days are done !'
'N.y, noble maid,' he answer'd, 'ten times
    nay !
This is not love, but love's first flash in
    youth,
Most common; yea, I know it of mine own
    self,
And you yourself will smile at your own self
Hereafter, when you yield your flower of
    life
To one more fitly yours, not thrice your
    ~g~.
And then will I, for true you are and sweet
Beyond mine old belief in womanhood,  950
More specially should your good knight
    be poor,
Endow you with broad land and territory
Even to the half my realm beyond the seas,
So that would make you happy; further-
    more,
Even to the death, as tho' ye were my
    blood,
In all your quarrels will I be your knight.
This will I do, dear damsel, for your sake,
And more than this I cannot.'

                              While he spoke
She neither blush'd nor shook, but deathly-
    pale
Stood grasping what was nearest, then re-
    plied,                                          960

'Of all this will I nothing;' and so fell,
And thus they bore her swooning to her
    tower.

    Then spake, to whom thro' those black
        walls of yew
Their talk had pierced, her father: 'Ay, a
    flash,
I fear me, that will strike my blossom dead.
Too courteous are ye, fair Lord Lancelot.
I pray you, use some rough discourtesy
To blunt or break her passion.'

                              Lancelot said,
'That were against me; what I can I will;'
And there that day remain'd, and toward
    even                                            970
Sent for his shield.  Full meekly rose the
    maid,
Stript off the case, and gave the naked
    shield;
Then, when she heard his horse upon the
    stones,
Unclasping flung the casement back, and
    look'd
Down on his helm, from which her sleeve
    had gone.
And Lancelot knew the little clinking
    sound;
And she by tact of love was well aware
That Lancelot knew that she was looking
    at him.
And yet he glanced not up, nor waved his
    hand,
Nor bade farewell, but sadly rode away.  980
This was the one discourtesy that he used.

    So in her tower alone the maiden sat.
His very shield was gone; only the case,
Her own poor work, her empty labor, left.
But still she heard him, still his picture
    form'd
And grew between her and the pictured
    wall.
Then came her father, saying in low tones,
'Have comfort,' whom she greeted quietly.
Then came her brethren saying, 'Peace to
    thee,
Sweet sister,' whom she answer'd with all
    calm.                                           990
But when they left her to herself again,
Death, like a friend's voice from a distant
    field
Approaching thro' the darkness, call'd; the
    owls

Wailing had power upon her, and she mixt
Her fancies with the sallow-rifted glooms
Of evening and the moanings of the wind.

And in those days she made a little song,
And call'd her song 'The Song of Love
    and Death,'
And sang it; sweetly could she make and
    sing.

'Sweet is true love tho' given in vain, in
    vain;                                    1000
And sweet is death who puts an end to pain.
I know not which is sweeter, no, not I.

'Love, art thou sweet? then bitter death
    must be.
Love, thou art bitter; sweet is death to me.
O Love, if death be sweeter, let me die.

'Sweet love, that seems not made to fade
    away;
Sweet death, that seems to make us loveless
    clay;
I know not which is sweeter, no, not I.

'I fain would follow love, if that could be;
I needs must follow death, who calls for me;
Call and I follow, I follow! let me die.'    1011

High with the last line scaled her voice,
    and this,
All in a fiery dawning wild with wind
That shook her tower, the brothers heard,
    and thought
With shuddering, 'Hark the Phantom of
    the house
That ever shrieks before a death,' and
    call'd
The father, and all three in hurry and fear
Ran to her, and lo! the blood-red light of
    dawn
Flared on her face, she shrilling, 'Let me
    die!'

As when we dwell upon a word we
    know,                                    1020
Repeating, till the word we know so well
Becomes a wonder, and we know not why,
So dwelt the father on her face, and thought,
'Is this Elaine?' till back the maiden fell,
Then gave a languid hand to each, and lay,
Speaking a still good - morrow with her
    eyes.
At last she said: 'Sweet brothers, yester-
    night
I seem'd a curious little maid again,

As happy as when we dwelt among the
    woods,
And when ye used to take me with the
    flood                                     1030
Up the great river in the boatman's boat.
Only ye would not pass beyond the cape
That has the poplar on it; there ye fixt
Your limit, oft returning with the tide.
And yet I cried because ye would not pass
Beyond it, and far up the shining flood
Until we found the palace of the King.
And yet ye would not; but this night I
    dream'd
That I was all alone upon the flood,
And then I said, "Now shall I have my
    will;"                                   1040
And there I woke, but still the wish re-
    main'd.
So let me hence that I may pass at last
Beyond the poplar and far up the flood,
Until I find the palace of the King.
There will I enter in among them all,
And no man there will dare to mock at me;
But there the fine Gawain will wonder at
    me,
And there the great Sir Lancelot muse at
    me;
Gawain, who bade a thousand farewells to
    me,
Lancelot, who coldly went, nor bade me
    one.                                     1050
And there the King will know me and my
    love,
And there the Queen herself will pity me,
And all the gentle court will welcome me,
And after my long voyage I shall rest!'

'Peace,' said her father, 'O my child, ye
    seem
Light-headed, for what force is yours to go
So far, being sick? and wherefore would
    ye look
On this proud fellow again, who scorns us
    all?'

Then the rough Torre began to heave
    and move,
And bluster into stormy sobs and say:  1060
'I never loved him; an I meet with him,
I care not howsoever great he be,
Then will I strike at him and strike him
    down.
Give me good fortune, I will strike him
    dead,
For this discomfort he hath done the house.'

To whom the gentle sister made reply:
'Fret not yourself, dear brother, nor be
        wroth,
Seeing it is no more Sir Lancelot's fault
Not to love me than it is mine to love
Him of all men who seems to me the high-
        est.'                                    1070

   'Highest?' the father answer'd, echoing
        'highest?'—
He meant to break the passion in her—
        'nay,
Daughter, I know not what you call the
        highest;
But this I know, for all the people know it,
He loves the Queen, and in an open shame,
And she returns his love in open shame;
If this be high, what is it to be low?'

   Then spake the lily maid of Astolat:
'Sweet father, all too faint and sick am I
For anger. These are slanders; never yet
Was noble man but made ignoble talk.    1081
He makes no friend who never made a foe.
But now it is my glory to have loved
One peerless, without stain; so let me pass,
My father, howsoe'er I seem to you,
Not all unhappy, having loved God's best
And greatest, tho' my love had no return.
Yet, seeing you desire your child to live,
Thanks, but you work against your own
        desire,
For if I could believe the things you say
I should but die the sooner; wherefore
        cease,                                   1091
Sweet father, and bid call the ghostly man
Hither, and let me shrive me clean and
        die.'

   So when the ghostly man had come and
        gone,
She, with a face bright as for sin forgiven,
Besought Lavaine to write as she devised
A letter, word for word; and when he
        ask'd,
'Is it for Lancelot, is it for my dear lord?
Then will I bear it gladly;' she replied,
'For Lancelot and the Queen and all the
        world,                                   1100
But I myself must bear it.' Then he wrote
The letter she devised; which being writ
And folded, 'O sweet father, tender and
        true,
Deny me not,' she said—'ye never yet
Denied my fancies—this, however strange,

My latest. Lay the letter in my hand
A little ere I die, and close the hand
Upon it; I shall guard it even in death.
And when the heat has gone from out my
        heart,                                   1109
Then take the little bed on which I died
For Lancelot's love, and deck it like the
        Queen's
For richness, and me also like the Queen
In all I have of rich, and lay me on it.
And let there be prepared a chariot-bier
To take me to the river, and a barge
Be ready on the river, clothed in black.
I go in state to court, to meet the Queen.
There surely I shall speak for mine own
        self,
And none of you can speak for me so well.
And therefore let our dumb old man alone
Go with me; he can steer and row, and
        he                                       1121
Will guide me to that palace, to the doors.'

   She ceased. Her father promised; where-
        upon
She grew so cheerful that they deem'd her
        death
Was rather in the fantasy than the blood.
But ten slow mornings past, and on the
        eleventh
Her father laid the letter in her hand,
And closed the hand upon it, and she died.
So that day there was dole in Astolat.

   But when the next sun brake from un-
        derground,                              1130
Then, those two brethren slowly with bent
        brows
Accompanying, the sad chariot-bier
Past like a shadow thro' the field, that
        shone
Full-summer, to that stream whereon the
        barge,
Pall'd all its length in blackest samite, lay.
There sat the lifelong creature of the
        house,
Loyal, the dumb old servitor, on deck,
Winking his eyes, and twisted all his face.
So those two brethren from the chariot
        took
And on the black decks laid her in her
        bed,                                     1140
Set in her hand a lily, o'er her hung
The silken case with braided blazonings,
And kiss'd her quiet brows, and saying to
        her,

Besought me to be plain and blunt, and use,
To break her passion, some discourtesy
Against my nature; what I could, I did.
I left her and I bade her no farewell;
Tho', had I dreamt the damsel would have
    died,
I might have put my wits to some rough
    use,
And help'd her from herself.'

                    Then said the Queen —
Sea was her wrath, yet working after
    storm:
'Ye might at least have done her so much
    grace,                                1300
Fair lord, as would have help'd her from
    her death.'
He raised his head, their eyes met and hers
    fell,
He adding: 'Queen, she would not be con-
    tent
Save that I wedded her, which could not
    be.
Then might she follow me thro' the world,
    she ask'd;
It could not be.   I told her that her love
Was but the flash of youth, would darken
    down,
To rise hereafter in a stiller flame
Toward one more worthy of her — then
    would I,                              1309
More specially were he she wedded poor,
Estate them with large land and territory
In mine own realm beyond the narrow
    seas,
To keep them in all joyance.   More than
    this
I could not; this she would not, and she
    died.'

    He pausing, Arthur answer'd: 'O my
        knight,
It will be to thy worship, as my knight,
And mine, as head of all our Table Round,
To see that she be buried worshipfully.'

    So toward that shrine which then in all
        the realm
Was richest, Arthur leading, slowly went
The   marshall'd Order of their Table
    Round,                               1321
And Lancelot sad beyond his wont, to see
The maiden buried, not as one unknown,
Nor meanly, but with gorgeous obsequies,
And mass, and rolling music, like a queen.

And when the knights had laid her comely
    head
Low in the dust of half-forgotten kings,
Then Arthur spake among them: 'Let her
    tomb
Be costly, and her image thereupon,    1329
And let the shield of Lancelot at her feet
Be carven, and her lily in her hand.
And let the story of her dolorous voyage
For all true hearts be blazon'd on her tomb
In letters gold and azure !' which was
    wrought
Thereafter; but when now the lords and
    dames
And people, from the high door streaming,
    brake
Disorderly, as homeward each, the Queen,
Who mark'd Sir Lancelot where he moved
    apart,
Drew near, and sigh'd                'Lance-
    lot,
Forgive me; mine was jealousy in love.' 134
He answer'd with his eyes upon the
    ground,
'That is love's curse; pass on, my Queen,
    forgiven.'
But Arthur, who beheld his cloudy brows,
Approach'd him, and with full affection
    said:

    'Lancelot, my Lancelot, thou in whom I
        have
Most joy and most affiance, for I know
What thou hast been in battle by my side,
And many a time have watch'd thee at the
    tilt
Strike down the lusty and long practised
    knight                               1349
And let the younger and unskill'd go by
To win his honor and to make his name,
And loved thy courtesies and thee, a man
Made to be loved; but now I would to
    God,
Seeing the homeless trouble in thine eyes,
Thou couldst have loved this maiden,
    shaped, it seems,
By God for thee alone, and from her face,
If one may judge the living by the dead,
Delicately pure and marvellously fair,
Who might have brought thee, now a lonely
    man                                  1359
Wifeless and heirless, noble issue, sons
Born to the glory of thy name and fame,
My knight, the great Sir Lancelot of the
    Lake.'

Then answer'd Lancelot: ' Fair she was,
  my King,
Pure, as you ever wish your knights to be.
To doubt her fairness were to want an eye,
To doubt her pureness were to want a
  heart —
Yea, to be loved, if what is worthy love
Could bind him, but free love will not be
  bound.'

' Free love, so bound, were freest,' said
  the King.                                1369
' Let love be free; free love is for the best.
And, after heaven, on our dull side of
  death,
What should be best, if not so pure a love
Clothed in so pure a loveliness ? yet thee
She fail'd to bind, tho' being, as I think,
Unbound as yet, and gentle, as I know.'

And Lancelot answer'd nothing, but he
  went,
And at the inrunning of a little brook
Sat by the river in a cove, and watch'd
The high reed wave, and lifted up his eyes
And saw the barge that brought her mov-
  ing down,                               1380
Far-off, a blot upon the stream, and said
Low in himself: ' Ah, simple heart and
  sweet,
Ye loved me, damsel, surely with a love
Far tenderer than my Queen's.  Pray for
  thy soul ?
Ay, that will I.  Farewell too — now at
  last —
Farewell, fair lily.  " Jealousy in love ? "
Not rather dead love's harsh heir, jealous
  pride ?
Queen, if I grant the jealousy as of love,
May not your crescent fear for name and
  fame
Speak, as it waxes, of a love that wanes ?
Why did the King dwell on my name to
  me ?                                     1391
Mine own name shames me, seeming a re-
  proach,
Lancelot, whom the Lady of the Lake
Caught from his mother's arms — the won-
  drous one
Who passes thro' the vision of the night —
She chanted snatches of mysterious hymns
Heard on the winding waters, eve and
  morn
She kiss'd me saying, " Thou art fair, my
  child,

As a king's son," and often in her arms
She bare me, pacing on the dusky mere.
Would she had drown'd me in it, where'er
  it be !                                 1401
For what am I ?  what profits me my name
Of greatest knight ?  I fought for it, and
  have it.
Pleasure to have it, none; to lose it, pain;
Now grown a part of me; but what use in
  it ?
To make men worse by making my sin
  known ?
Or sin seem less, the sinner seeming great ?
Alas for Arthur's greatest knight, a man
Not after Arthur's heart !  I needs must
  break
These bonds that so defame me.   Not with-
  out                                     1410
She wills it — would I, if she will'd it ?
  nay,
Who knows ?  but if I would not, then may
  God,
I pray him, send a sudden angel down
To seize me by the hair and bear me far,
And fling me deep in that forgotten mere,
Among the tumbled fragments of the
  hills.'

So groan'd Sir Lancelot in remorseful
  pain,
Not knowing he should die a holy man.

## THE HOLY GRAIL

FROM noiseful arms, and acts of prowess
  done
In tournament or tilt, Sir Percivale
Whom Arthur and his knighthood call'd
  the Pure,
Had past into the silent life of prayer,
Praise, fast, and alms; and leaving for the
  cowl
The helmet in an abbey far away
From Camelot, there, and not long after,
  died.

And one, a fellow-monk among the rest,
Ambrosius, loved him much beyond the
  rest,
And honor'd him, and wrought into his
  heart                                     10
A way by love that waken'd love within,
To answer that which came; and as they
  sat

A strong sword-belt, and wove with silver
    thread
And crimson in the belt a strange device,
A crimson grail within a silver beam;
And saw the bright boy-knight, and bound
    it on him,
Saying: " My knight, my love, my knight
    of heaven,
O thou, my love, whose love is one with
    mine,
I, maiden, round thee, maiden, bind my
    belt.
Go forth, for thou shalt see what I have
    seen,    160
And break thro' all, till one will crown thee
    king
Far in the spiritual city;" and as she spake
She sent the deathless passion in her eyes
Thro' him, and made him hers, and laid
    her mind
On him, and he believed in her belief.

   ' Then came a year of miracle. O bro-
    ther,
In our great hall there stood a vacant
    chair,
Fashion'd by Merlin ere he past away,
And carven with strange figures; and in
    and out
The figures, like a serpent, ran a scroll  170
Of letters in a tongue no man could read.
And Merlin call'd it " the Siege Peril-
    ous,"
Perilous for good and ill; " for there," he
    said,
" No man could sit but he should lose him-
    self."
And once by misadvertence Merlin sat
In his own chair, and so was lost; but
    he,
Galahad, when he heard of Merlin's doom,
Cried, " If I lose myself, I save myself ! "

   ' Then on a summer night it came to
    pass,
While the great banquet lay along the
    hall,    180
That Galahad would sit down in Merlin's
    chair.

   ' And all at once, as there we sat, we
    heard
A cracking and a riving of the roofs,
And rending, and a blast, and overhead
Thunder, and in the thunder was a cry.

And in the blast there smote along the hall
A beam of light seven times more clear
    than day;
And down the long beam stole the Holy
    Grail
All over cover'd with a luminous cloud,
And none might see who bare it, and it
    past.    190
But every knight beheld his fellow's face
As in a glory, and all the knights arose,
And staring each at other like dumb men
Stood, till I found a voice and sware a
    vow.

   ' I sware a vow before them all, that I,
Because I had not seen the Grail, would
    ride
A twelvemonth and a day in quest of it,
Until I found and saw it, as the nun
My sister saw it; and Galahad sware the
    vow,
And good Sir Bors, our Lancelot's cousin,
    sware,    200
And Lancelot sware, and many among the
    knights,
And Gawain sware, and louder than the
    rest.'

   Then spake the monk Ambrosius, asking
    him,
' What said the King ? Did Arthur take
    the vow ?

   ' Nay, for my lord,' said Percivale, ' the
    King,
Was not in hall; for early that same day,
Scaped thro' a cavern from a bandit bold,
An outraged maiden sprang into the hall
Crying on help; for all her shining hair
Was smear'd with earth, and either milky
    arm    210
Red-rent with hooks of bramble, and all
    she wore
Torn as a sail that leaves the rope is torn
In tempest. So the King arose and went
To smoke the scandalous hive of those
    wild bees
That made such honey in his realm. How-
    beit
Some little of this marvel he too saw,
Returning o'er the plain that then began
To darken under Camelot; whence the
    King
Look'd up, calling aloud, " Lo, there ! the
    roofs

Of our great hall are roll'd in thunder-
   smoke !                                    220
Pray heaven, they be not smitten by the
   bolt ! "
For dear to Arthur was that hall of ours,
As having there so oft with all his knights
Feasted, and as the stateliest under heaven.

'O brother, had you known our mighty
   hall,
Which Merlin built for Arthur long ago !
For all the sacred mount of Camelot,
And all the dim rich city, roof by roof,
Tower after tower, spire beyond spire,
By grove, and garden - lawn, and rushing
   brook,                                    230
Climbs to the mighty hall that Merlin
   built.
And four great zones of sculpture, set be-
   twixt
With many a mystic symbol, gird the hall;
And in the lowest beasts are slaying men,
And in the second men are slaying beasts,
And on the third are warriors, perfect
   men,
And on the fourth are men with growing
   wings,
And over all one statue in the mould
Of Arthur, made by Merlin, with a crown,
And peak'd wings pointed to the Northern
   Star.                                      240
And eastward fronts the statue, and the
   crown
And both the wings are made of gold, and
   flame
At sunrise till the people in far fields,
Wasted so often by the heathen hordes,
Behold it, crying, "We have still a king."

'And, brother, had you known our hall
   within,
Broader and higher than any in all the
   lands !
Where twelve great windows blazon Ar-
   thur's wars,
And all the light that falls upon the board
Streams thro' the twelve great battles of
   our King.                                  250
Nay, one there is, and at the eastern end,
Wealthy with wandering lines of mount
   and mere,
Where Arthur finds the brand Excalibur.
And also one to the west, and counter to it,
And blank; and who shall blazon it ? when
   and how ? —

O, there, perchance, when all our wars are
   done,
The brand Excalibur will be cast away !

'So to this hall full quickly rode the
   King,
In horror lest the work by Merlin wrought,
Dreamlike, should on the sudden vanish,
   wrapt                                      260
In unremorseful folds of rolling fire.
And in he rode, and up I glanced, and
   saw
The golden dragon sparkling over all;
And many of those who burnt the hold,
   their arms
Hack'd, and their foreheads grimed with
   smoke and sear'd,
Follow'd, and in among bright faces, ours,
Full of the vision, prest; and then the King
Spake to me, being nearest, "Percivale,"—
Because the hall was all in tumult — some
Vowing, and some protesting, — "what is
   this ? "                                  270

'O brother, when I told him what had
   chanced,
My sister's vision and the rest, his face
Darken'd, as I have seen it more than once,
When some brave deed seem'd to be done
   in vain,
Darken; and "Woe is me, my knights,"
   he cried,
"Had I been here, ye had not sworn the
   vow."
Bold was mine answer, "Had thyself been
   here,
My King, thou wouldst have sworn." "Yea,
   yea," said he,
"Art thou so bold and hast not seen the
   Grail ? "

'"Nay, lord, I heard the sound, I saw
   the light,                                 280
But since I did not see the holy thing,
I sware a vow to follow it till I saw."

'Then when he ask'd us, knight by
   knight, if any
Had seen it, all their answers were as one:
"Nay, lord, and therefore have we sworn
   our vows."

'"Lo, now," said Arthur, "have ye seen
   a cloud ?
What go ye into the wilderness to see ? "

' Then Galahad on the sudden, and in a
    voice
Shrilling along the hall to Arthur, call'd,
" But I, Sir Arthur, saw the Holy Grail,   290
I saw the Holy Grail and heard a cry —
' O Galahad, and O Galahad, follow me ! ' " '

' " Ah, Galahad, Galahad," said the King,
    " for such
As thou art is the vision, not for these.
Thy holy nun and thou have seen a sign — ˙
Holier is none, my Percivale, than she —
A sign to maim this Order which I made.
But ye that follow but the leader's bell,"—
Brother, the King was hard upon his
    knights, —
" Taliessin is our fullest throat of song,   300
And one hath sung and all the dumb will
    sing.
Lancelot is Lancelot, and hath overborne
Five knights at once, and every younger
    knight,
Unproven, holds himself as Lancelot,
Till overborne by one, he learns — and ye,
What are ye ?   Galahads ? — no, nor Per-
    civales " —
For thus it pleased the King to range me
    close
After Sir Galahad; — " nay," said he, " but
    men
With strength and will to right the wrong'd,
    of power
To lay the sudden heads of violence flat,   310
Knights that in twelve great battles
    splash'd and dyed
The strong White Horse in his own heathen
    blood —
But one hath seen, and all the blind will
    see.
Go, since your vows are sacred, being made.
Yet — for ye know the cries of all my
    realm
Pass thro' this hall — how often, O my
    knights,
Your places being vacant at my side,
This chance of noble deeds will come and
    go
Unchallenged, while ye follow wandering
    fires
Lost in the quagmire !   Many of you, yea
    most,   320
Return no more.   Ye think I show myself
Too dark a prophet.   Come now, let us meet
The morrow morn once more in one full
    field

Of gracious pastime, that once more the
    King,
Before ye leave him for this quest, may
    count
The yet - unbroken strength of all his
    knights,
Rejoicing in that Order which he made."

' So when the sun broke next from under-
    ground,
All the great Table of our Arthur closed
And clash'd in such a tourney and so full,
So many lances broken — never yet   331
Had Camelot seen the like since Arthur
    came;
And I myself and Galahad, for a strength
Was in us from the vision, overthrew
So many knights that all the people cried,
And almost burst the barriers in their heat,
Shouting, " Sir Galahad and Sir Perci-
    vale ! "

' But when the next day brake from un-
    derground —
O brother, had you known our Camelot,
Built by old kings, age after age, so old
The King himself had fears that it would
    fall,   341
So strange, and rich, and dim; for where
    the roofs
Totter'd toward each other in the sky,
Met foreheads all along the street of those
Who watch'd us pass; and lower, and where
    the long
Rich galleries, lady - laden, weigh'd the
    necks
Of dragons clinging to the crazy walls,
Thicker than drops from thunder, showers
    of flowers
Fell as we past; and men and boys astride
On wyvern, lion, dragon, griffin, swan,   350
At all the corners, named us each by name,
Calling " God speed ! " but in the ways be-
    low
The knights and ladies wept, and rich and
    poor
Wept, and the King himself could hardly
    speak
For grief, and all in middle street the
    Queen,
Who rode by Lancelot, wail'd and shriek'd
    aloud,
" This madness has come on us for our sins."
So to the Gate of the Three Queens we
    came,

Where Arthur's wars are render'd mystically,
And thence departed every one his way. 360

'And I was lifted up in heart, and
thought
Of all my late-shown prowess in the lists,
How my strong lance had beaten down the
knights,
So many and famous names; and never yet
Had heaven appear'd so blue, nor earth so
green,
For all my blood danced in me, and I knew
That I should light upon the Holy Grail.

'Thereafter, the dark warning of our
King,
That most of us would follow wandering
fires,
Came like a driving gloom across my
mind. 370
Then every evil word I had spoken once,
And every evil thought I had thought of
old,
And every evil deed I ever did,
Awoke and cried, "This quest is not for
thee."
And lifting up mine eyes, I found myself
Alone, and in a land of sand and thorns,
And I was thirsty even unto death;
And I, too, cried, "This quest is not for
thee."

'And on I rode, and when I thought my
thirst
Would slay me, saw deep lawns, and then
a brook, 380
With one sharp rapid, where the crisping
white
Play'd ever back upon the sloping wave
And took both ear and eye; and o'er the
brook
Were apple-trees, and apples by the brook
Fallen, and on the lawns. "I will rest
here,"
I said, "I am not worthy of the quest;"
But even while I drank the brook, and
ate
The goodly apples, all these things at once
Fell into dust, and I was left alone 389
And thirsting in a land of sand and thorns.

'And then behold a woman at a door
Spinning; and fair the house whereby she
sat,

And kind the woman's eyes and innocent,
And all her bearing gracious; and she rose
Opening her arms to meet me, as who should
say,
"Rest here;" but when I touch'd her, lo!
she, too,
Fell into dust and nothing, and the house
Became no better than a broken shed,
And in it a dead babe; and also this
Fell into dust, and I was left alone. 400

'And on I rode, and greater was my
thirst.
Then flash'd a yellow gleam across the
world,
And where it smote the plowshare in the
field
The plowman left his plowing and fell
down
Before it; where it glitter'd on her pail
The milkmaid left her milking and fell
down
Before it, and I knew not why, but thought
"The sun is rising," tho' the sun had risen.
Then was I ware of one that on me moved
In golden armor with a crown of gold 410
About a casque all jewels, and his horse
In golden armor jewelled everywhere;
And on the splendor came, flashing me
blind,
And seem'd to me the lord of all the
world,
Being so huge. But when I thought he
meant
To crush me, moving on me, lo! he, too,
Open'd his arms to embrace me as he
came,
And up I went and touch'd him, and he,
too,
Fell into dust, and I was left alone 419
And wearying in a land of sand and thorns.

'And I rode on and found a mighty hill,
And on the top a city wall'd; the spires
Prick'd with incredible pinnacles into
heaven.
And by the gateway stirr'd a crowd; and
these
Cried to me climbing, "Welcome, Perci-
vale!
Thou mightiest and thou purest among
men!"
And glad was I and clomb, but found at top
No man, nor any voice. And thence I
past

Far thro' a ruinous city, and I saw
That man had once dwelt there; but there
   I found           430
Only one man of an exceeding age.
"Where is that goodly company," said I,
"That so cried out upon me?" and he
   had
Scarce any voice to answer, and yet gasp'd,
"Whence and what art thou?" and even
   as he spoke
Fell into dust and disappear'd, and I
Was left alone once more and cried in
   grief,
"Lo, if I find the Holy Grail itself
And touch it, it will crumble into dust!"

   ' And thence I dropt into a lowly vale,
Low as the hill was high, and where the
   vale           441
Was lowest found a chapel, and thereby
A holy hermit in a hermitage,
To whom I told my phantoms, and '
   said:

   '" O son, thou hast not true humility,
The highest virtue, mother of them all;
For when the Lord of all things made
   Himself
Naked of glory for His mortal change,
'Take thou my robe,' she said, 'for all is
   thine,'
And all her form shone forth with sudden
   light           450
So that the angels were amazed, and she
Follow'd Him down, and like a flying star
Led on the gray-hair'd wisdom of the east.
But her thou hast not known; for what is
   this
Thou thoughtest of thy prowess and thy
   sins?
Thou hast not lost thyself to save thyself
As Galahad." When the hermit made an
   end,
In silver armor suddenly Galahad shone
Before us, and against the chapel door
Laid lance and enter'd, and we knelt in
   prayer.          460
And there the hermit slaked my burning
   thirst,
And at the sacring of the mass I saw
The holy elements alone; but he,
"Saw ye no more? I, Galahad, saw the
   Grail,
The Holy Grail, descend upon the shrine.
I saw the fiery face as of a child

That smote itself into the bread and went;
And hither am I come; and never yet
Hath what thy sister taught me first to
   see,
This holy thing, fail'd from my side, nor
   come          470
Cover'd, but moving with me night and
   day,
Fainter by day, but always in the night
Blood-red, and sliding dow the blacken'd
   marsh
Blood-red, and on the d mountain top
Blood-red, and in t' eping mere below
Blood-red. And ne strength of this I
   rode,
Shattering vil customs every here,
And pas ' Pagan realms, d made
    m mine,
An sh'd with Pagan horde nd bore
   them down,
nd broke thro' all, and in th ength of
   this          480
Come victor. But my hard at
   hand,
And hence I go, will crown me
   king
Far in the spiritual city; and come thou,
   too,
For thou shalt see the vision when I go."

   ' While thus he spake, his eye, dwelling
   on mine,
Drew me, with power upon me, till I grew
One with him, to believe as he believed.
Then, when the day began to wane, we
   went.

   ' There rose a hill that none but man
   could climb,
Scarr'd with a hundred wintry water-
   courses —         490
Storm at the top, and when we gain'd it,
   storm
Round us and death; for every moment
   glanced
His silver arms and gloom'd, so quick and
   thick
The lightnings here and there to left and
   right
Struck, till the dry old trunks about us,
   dead,
Yea, rotten with a hundred years of death,
Sprang into fire. And at the base we found
On either hand, as far as eye could see,
A great black swamp and of an evil smell,

Part black, part whiten'd with the bones of
    men,                                        500
Not to be crost, save that some ancient
    king
Had built a way, where, link'd with many
    a bridge,
A thousand piers ran into the great Sea.
And Galahad fled along them bridge by
    bridge,
And every bridge as quickly as he crost
Sprang into fire and vanish'd, tho' I
    yearn'd
To follow; and thrice above him all the
    heavens
Open'd and blazed with thunder such as
    seem'd
Shoutings of all the sons of God.  And first
At once I saw him far on the great Sea,
In silver-shining armor starry-clear;   511
And o'er his head the Holy Vessel hung
Clothed in white samite or a luminous
    cloud.
And with exceeding swiftness ran the boat,
If boat it were — I saw not whence it
    came.
And when the heavens open'd and blazed
    again
Roaring, I saw him like a silver star —
And had he set the sail, or had the boat
Become a living creature clad with wings?
And o'er his head the Holy Vessel hung
Redder than any rose, a joy to me,      521
For now I knew the veil had been with-
    drawn.
Then in a moment when they blazed again
Opening, I saw the least of little stars
Down on the waste, and straight beyond
    the star
I saw the spiritual city and all her spires
And gateways in a glory like one pearl —
No larger, tho' the goal of all the saints —
Strike from the sea; and from the star
    there shot                              529
A rose-red sparkle to the city, and there
Dwelt, and I knew it was the Holy Grail,
Which never eyes on earth again shall
    see.
Then fell the floods of heaven drowning
    the deep,
And how my feet recrost the deathful
    ridge
No memory in me lives; but that I touch'd
The chapel-doors at dawn I know, and
    thence
Taking my war-horse from the holy man,

Glad that no phantom vext me more, re-
    turn'd
To whence I came, the gate of Arthur's
    wars.'

    'O brother,' ask'd Ambrosius, — 'for in
    sooth                                  540
These ancient books — and they would win
    thee — teem,
Only I find not there this Holy Grail,
With miracles and marvels like to these,
Not all unlike; which oftentime I read,
Who read but on my breviary with ease,
Till my head swims, and then go forth and
    pass
Down to the little thorpe that lies so close,
And almost plaster'd like a martin's nest
To these old walls — and mingle with our
    folk;                                  549
And knowing every honest face of theirs
As well as ever shepherd knew his sheep,
And every homely secret in their hearts,
Delight myself with gossip and old wives,
And ills and aches, and teethings, lyings-
    in,
And mirthful sayings, children of the place,
That have no meaning half a league away;
Or lulling random squabbles when they
    rise,
Chafferings and chatterings at the market-
    cross,
Rejoice, small man, in this small world of
    mine,
Yea, even in their hens and in their eggs —
O brother, saving this Sir Galahad,      561
Came ye on none but phantoms in your
    quest,
No man, no woman?'

                Then Sir Percivale:
'All men, to one so bound by such a vow,
And women were as phantoms.  O, my
    brother,
Why wilt thou shame me to confess to
    thee
How far I falter'd from my quest and
    vow?
For after I had lain so many nights,
A bed-mate of the snail and eft and snake,
In grass and burdock, I was changed to
    wan                                    570
And meagre, and the vision had not come;
And then I chanced upon a goodly town
With one great dwelling in the middle of
    it.

Thither I made, and there was I disarm'd
By maidens each as fair as any flower;
But when they led me into hall, behold,
The princess of that castle was the one,
Brother, and that one only, who had ever
Made my heart leap; for when I moved of
    old
A slender page about her father's hall,   580
And she a slender maiden, all my heart
Went after her with longing, yet we twain
Had never kiss'd a kiss or vow'd a vow.
And now I came upon her once again,
And one had wedded her, and he was dead,
And all his land and wealth and state were
    hers.
And while I tarried, every day she set
A banquet richer than the day before
By me, for all her longing and her will
Was toward me as of old; till one fair
    morn,   590
I walking to and fro beside a stream
That flash'd across her orchard underneath
Her castle-walls, she stole upon my walk,
And calling me the greatest of all knights,
Embraced me, and so kiss'd me the first
    time,
And gave herself and all her wealth to
    me.
Then I remember'd Arthur's warning word,
That most of us would follow wandering
    fires,
And the quest faded in my heart. Anon,
The heads of all her people drew to me,
With supplication both of knees and
    tongue:   601
" We have heard of thee; thou art our
    greatest knight,
Our Lady says it, and we well believe.
Wed thou our Lady, and rule over us,
And thou shalt be as Arthur in our land."
O me, my brother ! but one night my vow
Burnt me within, so that I rose and fled,
But wail'd and wept, and hated mine own
    self,
And even the holy quest, and all but her;
Then after I was join'd with Galahad   610
Cared not for her nor anything upon earth.'

Then said the monk: ' Poor men, when
    yule is cold,
Must be content to sit by little fires.
And this am I, so that ye care for me
Ever so little; yea, and blest be heaven
That brought thee here to this poor house
    of ours

Where all the brethren are so hard, to
    warm
My cold heart with a friend; but O the
    pity
To find thine own first love once more — to
    hold,
Hold her a wealthy bride within thine
    arms,   620
Or all but hold, and then — cast her aside,
Foregoing all her sweetness, like a weed !
For we that want the warmth of double
    life,
We that are plagued with dreams of some-
    thing sweet
Beyond all sweetness in a life so rich,
Ah, blessed Lord, I speak too earthly wise,
Seeing I never stray'd beyond the cell,
But live like an old badger in his earth,
With earth about him everywhere, despite
All fast and penance. Saw ye none be-
    side,   630
None of your knights ? '

                  ' Yea, so,' said Percivale:
' One night my pathway swerving east, I
    saw
The pelican on the casque of our Sir Bors
All in the middle of the rising moon,
And toward him spurr'd, and hail'd him,
    and he me,
And each made joy of either. Then he
    ask'd:
" Where is he ? hast thou seen him —
    Lancelot ? — Once,"
Said good Sir Bors, " he dash'd across me
    — mad,
And maddening what he rode; and when
    I cried,
' Ridest thou then so hotly on a quest   640
So holy ? ' Lancelot shouted, ' Stay me
    not !
I have been the sluggard, and I ride apace,
For now there is a lion in the way ! '
So vanish'd."

          ' Then Sir Bors had ridden on
Softly, and sorrowing for our Lancelot,
Because his former madness, once the talk
And scandal of our table, had return'd;
For Lancelot's kith and kin so worship him
That ill to him is ill to them, to Bors
Beyond the rest. He well had been content
Not to have seen, so Lancelot might have
    seen,   651
The Holy Cup of healing; and, indeed,

Being so clouded with his grief and love,
Small heart was his after the holy quest.
If God would send the vision, well; if not,
The quest and he were in the hands of
    Heaven.

    'And then, with small adventure met,
        Sir Bors
Rode to the lonest tract of all the realm,
And ⸮und a people there among their
        crags,
C⸮race and blood, a remnant that were
        left                                    660
Paynim amid their circles, and the stones
They pitch up straight to heaven; and their
    wise men
Were strong in that old magic which can
    trace
The wandering of the stars, and scoff'd at
    him
And this high quest as at a simple thing,
Told him he follow'd — almost Arthur's
    words —
A mocking fire: " what other fire than he
Whereby the blood beats, and the blossom
    blows,
And the sea rolls, and all the world is
    warm'd ? "
And when his answer chafed them, the
    rough crowd,                               670
Hearing he had a difference with their
    priests,
Seized him, and bound and plunged him
    into a cell
Of great piled stones; and lying bounden
    there
In darkness thro' innumerable hours
He heard the hollow-ringing heavens sweep
Over him till by miracle — what else ? —
Heavy as it was, a great stone slipt and
    fell,
Such as no wind could move; and thro' the
    gap
Glimmer'd the streaming scud.  Then came
    a night
Still as the day was loud, and thro' the
    gap                                        680
The seven clear stars of Arthur's Table
    Round —
For, brother, so one night, because they roll
Thro' such a round in heaven, we named
    the stars,
Rejoicing in ourselves and in our King —
And these, like bright eyes of familiar
    friends,

In on him shone: " And then to me, to
    me,"
Said good Sir Bors, " beyond all hopes of
    mine,
Who scarce had pray'd or ask'd it for my-
    self —
Across the seven clear stars — O grace to
    me ! —
In color like the fingers of a hand      690
Before a burning taper, the sweet Grail
Glided and past, and close upon it peal'd
A sharp quick thunder."  Afterwards, a
    maid,
Who kept our holy faith among her kin
In secret, entering, loosed and let him go.'

    To whom the monk: 'And I remember
        now
That pelican on the casque.  Sir Bors it was
Who spake so low and sadly at our board,
And mighty reverent at our grace was he;
A square-set man and honest, and his eyes,
An outdoor sign of all the warmth within,
Smiled with his lips — a smile beneath a
    cloud,                                     702
But heaven had meant it for a sunny one.
Ay, ay, Sir Bors, who else ?  But when ye
    reach'd
The city, found ye all your knights re-
    turn'd,
Or was there sooth in Arthur's prophecy,
Tell me, and what said each, and what the
    King ? '

    Then answer'd Percivale: 'And that
        can I,                                 708
Brother, and truly; since the living words
Of so great men as Lancelot and our King
Pass not from door to door and out again,
But sit within the house.  O, when we
    reach'd
The city, our horses stumbling as they
    trode
On heaps of ruin, hornless unicorns,
Crack'd basilisks, and splinter'd cocka-
    trices,
And shatter'd talbots, which had left the
    stones
Raw that they fell from, brought us to the
    hall.

    'And there sat Arthur on the dais-throne,
And those that had gone out upon the
    quest,
Wasted and worn, and but a tithe of them,

And those that had not, stood before the
    King,     721
Who, when he saw me, rose and bade me
    hail,
Saying: " A welfare in thine eyes reproves
Our fear of some disastrous chance for
    thee
On hill or plain, at sea or flooding ford.
So fierce a gale made havoc here of late
Among the strange devices of our kings,
Yea, shook this newer, stronger hall of ours,
And from the statue Merlin moulded for
    us
Half-wrench'd a golden wing; but now —
    the quest,     730
This vision — hast thou seen the Holy Cup
That Joseph brought of old to Glaston-
    bury ? "

    ' So when I told him all thyself hast
    heard,
Ambrosius, and my fresh but fixt resolve
To pass away into the quiet life,
He answer'd not, but, sharply turning,
    ask'd
Of Gawain, " Gawain, was this quest for
    thee ? "

    ' " Nay, lord," said Gawain, " not for
    such as I.
Therefore I communed with a saintly man,
Who made me sure the quest was not for
    me;     740
For I was much a-wearied of the quest,
But found a silk pavilion in a field,
And merry maidens in it; and then this
    gale
Tore my pavilion from the tenting-pin,
And blew my merry maidens all about
With all discomfort; yea, and but for this,
My twelvemonth and a day were pleasant
    to me."

    ' He ceased; and Arthur turn'd to whom
    at first
He saw not, for Sir Bors, on entering,
    push'd
Athwart the throng to Lancelot, caught his
    hand,     750
Held it, and there, half-hidden by him,
    stood,
Until the King espied him, saying to him,
" Hail, Bors ! if ever loyal man and true
Could see it, thou hast seen the Grail; "
    and Bors,

" Ask me not, for I may not speak of it;
I saw it; " and the tears were in his eyes.

    ' Then there remain'd but Lancelot, for
    the rest
Spake but of sundry perils in the storm.
Perhaps, like him of Cana in Holy Writ,
Our Arthur kept his best until the last;   760
" Thou, too, my Lancelot," ask'd the King,
    " my friend,
Our mightiest, hath this quest avail'd for
    thee ? "

    ' " Our mightiest ! " answer'd Lancelot,
    with a groan;
" O King ! " — and when he paused me-
    thought I spied
A dying fire of madness in his eyes —
" O King, my friend, if friend of thine I be,
Happier are those that welter in their sin,
Swine in the mud, that cannot see for
    slime,     768
Slime of the ditch; but in me lived a sin
So strange, of such a kind, that all of pure,
Noble, and knightly in me twined and clung
Round that one sin, until the wholesome
    flower
And poisonous grew together, each as each,
Not to be pluck'd asunder; and when thy
    knights
Sware, I sware with them only in the hope
That could I touch or see the Holy Grail
They might be pluck'd asunder. Then I
    spake
To one most holy saint, who wept and said
That, save they could be pluck'd asunder,
    all
My quest were but in vain; to whom I
    vow'd     780
That I would work according as he will'd.
And forth I went, and while I yearn'd and
    strove
To tear the twain asunder in my heart,
My madness came upon me as of old,
And whipt me into waste fields far away.
There was I beaten down by little men,
Mean knights, to whom the moving of my
    sword
And shadow of my spear had been enow
To scare them from me once; and then I
    came
All in my folly to the naked shore,     790
Wide flats, where nothing but coarse
    grasses grew;
But such a blast, my King, began to blow,

So loud a blast along the shore and sea,
Ye could not hear the waters for the blast,
Tho' heapt in mounds and ridges all the sea
Drove like a cataract, and all the sand
Swept like a river, and the clouded heavens
Were shaken with the motion and the sound.
And blackening in the sea-foam sway'd a
    boat,                                   799
Half-swallow'd in it, anchor'd with a chain;
And in my madness to myself I said,
'I will embark and I will lose myself,
A    in the great sea wash away my sin.'
I  urst the chain, I sprang into the boat.
  ven days I drove along the dreary deep,
  nd with me drove the moon and all the
    stars;
And the wind fell, and on the seventh night
I heard the shingle grinding in the surge,
And felt the boat shock earth, and looking
    up,
Behold, the enchanted towers of Carbonek,
A castle like a rock upon a rock,         811
With chasm-like portals open to the sea,
And steps that met the breaker! There
    was none
Stood near it but a lión on each side
That kept the entry, and the moon was full.
Then from the boat I leapt, and up the
    stairs,
There drew my sword. With sudden-
    flaring manes
Those two great beasts rose upright like a
    man,
Each gript a shoulder, and I stood between,
And, when I would have smitten them,
    heard a voice,                         820
'Doubt not, go forward; if thou doubt, the
    beasts
Will tear thee piecemeal.' Then with vio-
    lence
The sword was dash'd from out my hand,
    and fell.
And up into the sounding hall I past;
But nothing in the sounding hall I saw,
No bench nor table, painting on the wall
Or shield of knight, only the rounded moon
Thro' the tall oriel on the rolling sea.
But always in the quiet house I heard,
Clear as a lark, high o'er me as a lark, 830
A sweet voice singing in the topmost
    tower
To the eastward. Up I climb'd a thousand
    steps
With pain; as in a dream I seem'd to
    climb

For ever; at the last I reach'd a door,
A light was in the crannies, and I heard,
'Glory and joy and honor to our Lord
And to the Holy Vessel of the Grail!'
Then in my madness I essay'd the door;
It gave, and thro' a stormy glare, a heat
As from a seven-times-heated furnace, I,
Blasted and burnt, and blinded as I was,
With such a fierceness that I swoon'd
    away —                                 842
O, yet methought I saw the Holy Grail,
All pall'd in crimson samite, and around
Great angels, awful shapes, and wings and
    eyes!
And but for all my madness and my sin,
And then my swooning, I had sworn I saw
That which I saw; but what I saw was
    veil'd
And cover'd, and this quest was not for me.''

'So speaking, and here ceasing, Lancelot
    left                                   850
The hall long silent, till Sir Gawain — nay,
Brother, I need not tell thee foolish
    words, —
A reckless and irreverent knight was he,
Now bolden'd by the silence of his King, —
Well, I will tell thee: "O King, my liege,"
    he said,
"Hath Gawain fail'd in any quest of thine?
When have I stinted stroke in foughten
    field?
But as for thine, my good friend Percivale,
Thy holy nun and thou have driven men
    mad,
Yea, made our mightiest madder than our
    least.                                 860
But by mine eyes and by mine ears I
    swear,
I will be deafer than the blue-eyed cat,
And thrice as blind as any noonday owl,
To holy virgins in their ecstasies,
Henceforward."

    '"Deafer," said the blameless King,
"Gawain, and blinder unto holy things,
Hope not to make thyself by idle vows,
Being too blind to have desire to see.
But if indeed there came a sign from
    heaven,
Blessed are Bors, Lancelot, and Perci-
    vale,                                  870
For these have seen according to their
    sight.
For every fiery prophet in old times,

And all the sacred madness of the bard,
When God made music thro' them, could
    but speak
His music by the framework and the chord;
And as ye saw it ye have spoken truth.

'"Nay — but thou errest, Lancelot;
    never yet
Could all of true and noble in knight and
    man
Twine round one sin, whatever it might be,
With such a closeness but apart there
    grew,                                   880
Save that he were the swine thou spakest
    of,
Some root of knighthood and pure noble-
    ness;
Whereto see thou, that it may bear its
    flower.

'"And spake I not too truly, O my
    knights?
Was I too dark a prophet when I said
To those who went upon the Holy Quest,
That most of them would follow wander-
    ing fires,
Lost in the quagmire? — lost to me and
    gone,
And left me gazing at a barren board,
And a lean Order — scarce return'd a
    tithe —                                 890
And out of those to whom the vision came
My greatest hardly will believe he saw.
Another hath beheld it afar off,
And, leaving human wrongs to right them-
    selves,
Cares but to pass into the silent life.
And one hath had the vision face to face,
And now his chair desires him here in vain,
However they may crown him otherwhere.

'"And some among you held that if the
    King
Had seen the sight he would have sworn
    the vow.                               900
Not easily, seeing that the King must
    guard
That which he rules, and is but as the hind
To whom a space of land is given to plow,
Who may not wander from the allotted
    field
Before his work be done, but, being done,
Let visions of the night or of the day
Come as they will; and many a time they
    come,

Until this earth he walks on seems not
    earth,
This light that strikes his eyeball is not
    light,
This air that smites his forehead is not
    air                                     910
But vision — yea, his very hand and foot —
In moments when he feels he cannot die,
And knows himself no vision to himself,
Nor the high God a vision, nor that One
Who rose again.  Ye have seen what ye
    have seen."

'So spake the King; I knew not all he
    meant.'

## PELLEAS AND ETTARRE

KING ARTHUR made new knights to fill
    the gap
Left by the Holy Quest; and as he sat
In hall at old Caerleon, the high doors
Were softly sunder'd, and thro' these a
    youth,
Pelleas, and the sweet smell of the fields
Past, and the sunshine came along with
    him.

'Make me thy knight, because I know,
    Sir King,
All that belongs to knighthood, and I love.'
Such was his cry; for having heard the
    King
Had let proclaim a tournament — the
    prize                                   10
A golden circlet and a knightly sword,
Full fain had Pelleas for his lady won
The golden circlet, for himself the sword.
And there were those who knew him near
    the King,
And promised for him; and Arthur made
    him knight.

And this new knight, Sir Pelleas of the
    Isles —
But lately come to his inheritance,
And lord of many a barren isle was he —
Riding at noon, a day or twain before,
Across the forest call'd of Dean, to find   20
Caerleon and the King, had felt the sun
Beat like a strong knight on his helm and
    reel'd
Almost to falling from his horse, but saw
Near him a mound of even-sloping side

Whereon a hundred stately beeches grew,
And here and there great hollies under
  them;
But for a mile all round was open space
And fern and heath.  And slowly Pelleas
  drew
To that dim day, then, binding his good
  horse
To a tree, cast himself down; and as he
  lay                                        30
At random looking over the brown earth
Thro' that green-glooming twilight of the
  grove,
It seem'd to Pelleas that the fern without
Burnt as a living fire of emeralds,
So that his eyes were dazzled looking at
  it.
Then o'er it crost the dimness of a cloud
Floating, and once the shadow of a bird
Flying, and then a fawn; and his eyes
  closed.
And since he loved all maidens, but no
  maid
In special, half - awake he whisper'd:
  ' Where ?                                   40
O, where ?  I love thee, tho' I know thee
  not.
For fair thou art and pure as Guinevere,
And I will make thee with my spear and
  sword
As famous — O my Queen, my Guinevere,
For I will be thine Arthur when we meet.'

Suddenly waken'd with a sound of talk
And laughter at the limit of the wood,
And glancing thro' the hoary boles, he saw,
Strange as to some old prophet might have
  seem'd
A vision hovering on a sea of fire,          50
Damsels in divers colors like the cloud
Of sunset and sunrise, and all of them
On horses, and the horses richly trapt
Breast-high in that bright line of bracken
  stood;
And all the damsels talk'd confusedly,
And one was pointing this way and one
  that,
Because the way was lost.

              And Pelleas rose,
And loosed his horse, and led him to the
  light.
There she that seem'd the chief among
  them said:
' In happy time behold our pilot-star !     60

Youth, we are damsels-errant, and we ride,
Arm'd as ye see, to tilt against the knights
There at Caerleon, but have lost our way.
To right ? to left ? straight forward ? back
  again ?
Which ?  tell us quickly.'

               Pelleas gazing thought,
' Is Guinevere herself so beautiful ? '
For large her violet eyes look'd, and her
  bloom
A rosy dawn kindled in ⁓nless heavens,
And round her limbs ⁓ature in woman-
  hood;
And slender was h⁓ hand and small her
  shape;                                      70
And but for thos⁓ large eyes, the haunts of
  scorn,
She might h⁓ seem'd a toy to trifle with,
And pass ⁓ care no more.  But while he
  ga⁓
The bea⁓y of her flesh abash'd the boy,
As tho'⁓t were the beauty of her soul;
For a⁓ the base man, judging of the good,
Put⁓ his own baseness in him by default
Of will and nature, so did Pelleas lend
All the young beauty of his own soul to
  hers,                                       79
Believing her, and when she spake to him
Stammer'd, and could not make her a re-
  ply.
For out of the waste islands had he come,
Where saving his own sisters he had
  known
Scarce any but the women of his isles,
Rough wives, that laugh'd and scream'd
  against the gulls,
Makers of nets, and living from the sea.

  Then with a slow smile turn'd the lady
  round
And look'd upon her people; and, as when
A stone is flung into some sleeping tarn
The circle widens till it lip the marge,      90
Spread the slow smile thro' all her com-
  pany.
Three knights were thereamong, and they
  too smiled,
Scorning him; for the lady was Ettarre,
And she was a great lady in her land.

  Again she said: ' O wild and of the
  woods,
Knowest thou not the fashion of our
  speech ?

Or have the Heavens but given thee a fair
   face,
Lacking a tongue ? '

           ' O damsel,' answer'd he,
' I woke from dreams, and coming out of
   gloom
Was dazzled by the sudden light, and
   crave                100
Pardon; but will ye to Caerleon ?  I
Go likewise; shall I lead you to the King ? '

   ' Lead then,' she said; and thro' the
   woods they went.
And while they rode, the meaning in his
   eyes,
His tenderness of manner, and chaste awe,
His broken utterances and bashfulness,
Were all a burthen to her, and in her heart
She mutter'd, ' I have lighted on a fool,
Raw, yet so stale ! '  But since her mind
   was bent             109
On hearing, after trumpet blown, her name
And title, ' Queen of Beauty,' in the lists
Cried — and beholding him so strong she
   thought
That peradventure he will fight for me,
And win the circlet — therefore flatter'd
   him,
Being so gracious that he wellnigh deem'd
His wish by hers was echo'd; and her
   knights
And all her damsels too were gracious to
   him,
For she was a great lady.

           And when they reach'd
Caerleon, ere they past to lodging, she,
Taking his hand, ' O the strong hand,' she
   said,              120
' See ! look at mine ! but wilt thou fight for
   me,
And win me this fine circlet, Pelleas,
That I may love thee ? '

           Then his helpless heart
Leapt, and he cried, ' Ay ! wilt thou if I
   win ? '
' Ay, that will I,' she answer'd, and she
   laugh'd,
And straitly nipt the hand, and flung it
   from her;
Then glanced askew at those three knights
   of hers,
Till all her ladies laugh'd along with her.

' O happy world,' thought Pelleas, ' all,
   meseems,
Are happy; I the happiest of them all ! '  130
Nor slept that night for pleasure in his
   blood,
And green wood-ways, and eyes among the
   leaves;
Then being on the morrow knighted, sware
To love one only.  And as he came away,
The men who met him rounded on their
   heels
And wonder'd after him, because his face
Shone like the countenance of a priest of
   old
Against the flame about a sacrifice
Kindled by fire from heaven; so glad was he.

Then Arthur made vast banquets, and
   strange knights        140
From the four winds came in; and each
   one sat,
Tho' served with choice from air, land,
   stream, and sea,
Oft in mid-banquet measuring with his
   eyes
His neighbor's make and might; and Pel-
   leas look'd
Noble among the noble, for he dream'd
His lady loved him, and he knew himself
Loved of the King; and him his new-made
   knight
Worshipt, whose lightest whisper moved
   him more
Than all the ranged reasons of the world.

Then blush'd and brake the morning of
   the jousts,        150
And this was call'd ' The Tournament of
   Youth;'
For Arthur, loving his young knight, with-
   held
His older and his mightier from the lists,
That Pelleas might obtain his lady's love,
According to her promise, and remain
Lord of the tourney.  And Arthur had the
   jousts
Down in the flat field by the shore of Usk
Holden; the gilded parapets were crown'd
With faces, and the great tower fill'd with
   eyes        159
Up to the summit, and the trumpets blew.
There all day long Sir Pelleas kept the
   field
With honor; so by that strong hand of his
The sword and golden circlet were achieved.

Then rang the shout his lady loved; the
    heat
Of pride and glory fired her face, her eye
Sparkled; she caught the circlet from his
    lance,
And there before the people crown'd her-
    self.
So for the last time she was gracious to
    him.

Then at Caerleon for a space — her look
Bright for all others, cloudier on her
    knight —                                   170
Linger'd Ettarre; and, seeing Pelleas droop,
Said Guinevere, ' We marvel at thee much,
O damsel, wearing this unsunny face
To him who won thee glory!'   And she
    said,
' Had ye not held your Lancelot in your
    bower,
My Queen, he had not won.'   Whereat the
    Queen,
As one whose foot is bitten by an ant,
Glanced down upon her, turn'd and went
    her way.

But after, when her damsels, and her-
    self,
And those three knights all set their faces
    home,                                       180
Sir Pelleas follow'd.   She that saw him
    cried:
' Damsels — and yet I should be shamed to
    say it —
I cannot bide Sir Baby.   Keep him back
Among yourselves.   Would rather that we
    had
Some rough old knight who knew the
    worldly way,
Albeit grizzlier than a bear, to ride
And jest with!   Take him to you, keep
    him off,
And pamper him with papmeat, if ye will,
Old milky fables of the wolf and sheep,
Such as the wholesome mothers tell their
    boys.                                       190
Nay, should ye try him with a merry one
To find his mettle, good; and if he fly us,
Small matter! let him.'   This her damsels
    heard,
And, mindful of her small and cruel hand,
They, closing round him thro' the journey
    home,
Acted her hest, and always from her side
Restrain'd him with all manner of device,

So that he could not come to speech with
    her.
And when she gain'd her castle, upsprang
    the bridge,
Down rang the grate of iron thro' the
    groove,                                     200
And he was left alone in open field.

' These be the ways of ladies,' Pelleas
    thought,
' To those who love them, trials of our
    faith.
Yea, let her prove me to the uttermost,
For loyal to the uttermost am I.'
So made his moan, and, darkness falling,
    sought
A priory not far off, there lodged, but rose
With morning every day, and, moist or
    dry,
Full-arm'd upon his charger all day long
Sat by the walls, and no one open'd to
    him.                                        210

And this persistence turn'd her scorn to
    wrath.
Then, calling her three knights, she charged
    them, ' Out!
And drive him from the walls.'   And out
    they came,
But Pelleas overthrew them as they dash'd
Against him one by one; and these return'd,
But still he kept his watch beneath the
    wall.

Thereon her wrath became a hate; and
    once,
A week beyond, while walking on the walls
With her three knights, she pointed down-
    ward, ' Look,
He haunts me — I cannot breathe — be-
    sieges me!                                  220
Down! strike him! put my hate into your
    strokes,
And drive him from my walls.'   And down
    they went,
And Pelleas overthrew them one by one;
And from the tower above him cried Et-
    tarre,
' Bind him, and bring him in.'
                    He heard her voice;
Then let the strong hand, which had over-
    thrown
Her minion-knights, by those he overthrew
Be bounden straight, and so they brought
    him in.

Then when he came before Ettarre, the
sight                                                        229
Of her rich beauty made him at one glance
More bondsman in his heart than in his
bonds.
Yet with good cheer he spake: 'Behold
me, lady,
A prisoner, and the vassal of thy will;
And if thou keep me in thy donjon here,
Content am I so that I see thy face
But once a day; for I have sworn my vows,
And thou hast given thy promise, and I
know
That all these pains are trials of my faith,
And that thyself, when thou hast seen me
strain'd
And sifted to the utmost, wilt at length   240
Yield me thy love and know me for thy
knight.'

Then she began to rail so bitterly,
With all her damsels, he was stricken
mute,
But, when she mock'd his vows and the
great King,
Lighted on words: 'For pity of thine own
self,
Peace, lady, peace; is he not thine and
mine?'
'Thou fool,' she said, 'I never heard his
voice
But long'd to break away. Unbind him
now,
And thrust him out of doors; for save he
be
Fool to the midmost marrow of his bones,
He will return no more.' And those, her
three,                                                      251
Laugh'd, and unbound, and thrust him
from the gate.

And after this, a week beyond, again
She call'd them, saying: 'There he watches
yet,
There like a dog before his master's door!
Kick'd, he returns; do ye not hate him,
ye?
Ye know yourselves; how can ye bide at
peace,
Affronted with his fulsome innocence?
Are ye but creatures of the board and bed,
No men to strike? Fall on him all at
once,                                                        260
And if ye slay him I reck not; if ye fail,
Give ye the slave mine order to be bound,

Bind him as heretofore, and bring him
in.
It may be ye shall slay him in his bonds.'

She spake, and at her will they couch'd
their spears,
Three against one; and Gawain passing by,
Bound upon solitary adventure, saw
Low down beneath the shadow of those
towers
A villainy, three to one; and thro' his
heart
The fire of honor and all noble deeds     270
Flash'd, and he call'd, 'I strike upon thy
side —
The caitiffs!'  'Nay,' said Pelleas, 'but
forbear;
He needs no aid who doth his lady's will.'

So Gawain, looking at the villainy done,
Forbore, but in his heat and eagerness
Trembled and quiver'd, as the dog, with-
held
A moment from the vermin that he sees
Before him, shivers ere he springs and
kills.

And Pelleas overthrew them, one to
three;
And they rose up, and bound, and brought
him in.                                                      280
Then first her anger, leaving Pelleas,
burn'd
Full on her knights in many an evil name
Of craven, weakling, and thrice - beaten
hound:
'Yet, take him, ye that scarce are fit to
touch,
Far less to bind, your victor, and thrust
him out,
And let who will release him from his
bonds.
And if he comes again' — there she brake
short;
And Pelleas answer'd: 'Lady, for indeed
I loved you and I deem'd you beautiful,
I cannot brook to see your beauty marr'd
Thro' evil spite; and if ye love me not,   291
I cannot bear to dream you so forsworn.
I had liefer ye were worthy of my love
Than to be loved again of you — fare-
well.
And tho' ye kill my hope, not yet my
love,
Vex not yourself; ye will not see me more.'

While thus he spake, she gazed upon the
man
Of princely bearing, tho' in bonds, and
thought:
'Why have I push'd him from me? this
man loves,
If love there be; yet him I loved not.
Why?                                        300
I deem'd him fool? yea, so? or that in
him
A something — was it nobler than my-
self? —
Seem'd my reproach? He is not of my
kind.
He could not love me, did he know me
well.
Nay, let him go — and quickly.' And her
knights
Laugh'd not, but thrust him bounden out
of door.

Forth sprang Gawain, and loosed him
from his bonds,
And flung them o'er the walls; and after-
ward,
Shaking his hands, as from a lazar's rag,
'Faith of my body,' he said, 'and art thou
not —                                        310
Yea thou art he, whom late our Arthur
made
Knight of his table; yea, and he that won
The circlet? wherefore hast thou so de-
famed
Thy brotherhood in me and all the rest
As let these caitiffs on thee work their
will?'

And Pelleas answer'd: 'O, their wills are
hers
For whom I won the circlet; and mine,
hers,
Thus to be bounden, so to see her face,
Marr'd tho' it be with spite and mockery
now,                                         319
Other than when I found her in the woods;
And tho' she hath me bounden but in spite,
And all to flout me, when they bring me in,
Let me be bounden, I shall see her face;
Else must I die thro' mine unhappiness.'

And Gawain answer'd kindly tho' in
scorn:
'Why, let my lady bind me if she will,
And let my lady beat me if she will;
But an she send her delegate to thrall

These fighting hands of mine — Christ kill
me then                                      329
But I will slice him handless by the wrist,
And let my lady sear the stump for him,
Howl as he may! But hold me for your
friend.
Come, ye know nothing; here I pledge my
troth,
Yea, by the honor of the Table Round,
I will be leal to thee and work thy work,
And tame thy jailing princess to thine
hand.
Lend me thine horse and arms, and I will say
That I have slain thee. She will let me in
To hear the manner of thy fight and fall;
Then, when I come within her counsels,
then                                         340
From prime to vespers will I chant thy
praise
As prowest knight and truest lover, more
Than any have sung thee living, till she
long
To have thee back in lusty life again,
Not to be bound, save by white bonds and
warm,
Dearer than freedom. Wherefore now thy
horse
And armor; let me go; be comforted.
Give me three days to melt her fancy, and
hope
The third night hence will bring thee news
of gold.'

Then Pelleas lent his horse and all his
arms,                                        350
Saving the goodly sword, his prize, and
took
Gawain's, and said, 'Betray me not, but
help —
Art thou not he whom men call light-of-
love?'

'Ay,' said Gawain, 'for women be so
light;'
Then bounded forward to the castle walls,
And raised a bugle hanging from his neck,
And winded it, and that so musically
That all the old echoes hidden in the wall
Rang out like hollow woods at hunting-
tide.                                        359

Up ran a score of damsels to the tower;
'Avaunt,' they cried, 'our lady loves thee
not!'
But Gawain lifting up his vizor said:

'Gawain am I, Gawain of Arthur's court,
And I have slain this Pelleas whom ye hate.
Behold his horse and armor.   Open gates,
And I will make you merry.'

               And down they ran,
Her damsels, crying to their lady, ' Lo !
Pelleas is dead — he told us — he that hath
His horse and armor; will ye let him in ?
He slew him !  Gawain, Gawain of the court,        370
Sir Gawain — there he waits below the wall,
Blowing his bugle as who should say him nay.'

    And so, leave given, straight on thro' open door
Rode Gawain, whom she greeted courteously.
' Dead, is it so ? ' she ask'd.   ' Ay, ay,' said he,
' And oft in dying cried upon your name.'
' Pity on him,' she answer'd, ' a good knight,
But never let me bide one hour at peace.'
' Ay,' thought Gawain, ' and you be fair enow;
But I to your dead man have given my troth,        380
That whom ye loathe, him will I make you love.'

    So those three days, aimless about the land,
Lost in a doubt, Pelleas wandering
Waited, until the third night brought a moon
With promise of large light on woods and ways.

    Hot was the night and silent; but a sound
Of Gawain ever coming, and this lay —
Which Pelleas had heard sung before the Queen,
And seen her sadden listening — vext his heart,
And marr'd his rest — ' A worm within the rose.'        390

    ' A rose, but one, none other rose had I,
A rose, one rose, and this was wondrous fair,
One rose, a rose that gladden'd earth and sky,
One rose, my rose, that sweeten'd all mine air —
I cared not for the thorns ; the thorns were there.

    ' One rose, a rose to gather by and by,
One rose, a rose, to gather and to wear,
No rose but one — what other rose had I ?
One rose, my rose ; a rose that will not die, —
He dies who loves it, — if the worm be there.'

    This tender rhyme, and evermore the doubt,        401
' Why lingers Gawain with his golden news ? '
So shook him that he could not rest, but rode
Ere midnight to her walls, and bound his horse
Hard by the gates.   Wide open were the gates,
And no watch kept; and in thro' these he past,
And heard but his own steps, and his own heart
Beating, for nothing moved but his own self
And his own shadow.   Then he crost the court,
And spied not any light in hall or bower,
But saw the postern portal also wide        411
Yawning; and up a slope of garden, all
Of roses white and red, and brambles mixt
And overgrowing them, went on, and found,
Here too, all hush'd below the mellow moon,
Save that one rivulet from a tiny cave
Came lightening downward, and so spilt itself
Among the roses and was lost again.

    Then was he ware of three pavilions rear'd
Above the bushes, gilden-peakt.   In one,
Red after revel, droned her lurdane knights        421
Slumbering, and their three squires across their feet;
In one, their malice on the placid lip
Frozen by sweet sleep, four of her damsels lay;
And in the third, the circlet of the jousts
Bound on her brow, were Gawain and Ettarre.

    Back, as a hand that pushes thro' the leaf
To find a nest and feels a snake, he drew;

Back, as a coward slinks from what he
　　fears
To cope with, or a traitor proven, or hound
Beaten, did Pelleas in an utter shame　431
Creep with his shadow thro' the court again,
Fingering at his sword - handle until he
　　stood
There on the castle-bridge once more, and
　　thought,
'I will go back, and slay them where they
　　lie.'

　　And he went back, and seeing them yet
　　in sleep
Said, 'Ye, that so dishallow the holy sleep,
Your sleep is death,' and drew the sword,
　　and thought,
'What! slay a sleeping knight? the King
　　hath bound　　　　　　　　　　　439
And sworn me to this brotherhood;' again,
'Alas that ever a knight should be so
　　false!'
Then turn'd, and so return'd, and groaning
　　laid
The naked sword athwart their naked
　　throats,
There left it, and them sleeping; and she
　　· lay,
The circlet of the tourney round her brows,
And the sword of the tourney across her
　　throat.

　　And forth he past, and mounting on his
　　horse
Stared at her towers that, larger than
　　themselves
In their own darkness, throng'd into the
　　moon;
Then crush'd the saddle with his thighs,
　　and clench'd　　　　　　　　　　450
His hands, and madden'd with himself and
　　moan'd:

　　'Would they have risen against me in
　　their blood
At the last day? I might have answer'd
　　them
Even before high God. O towers so strong,
Huge, solid, would that even while I gaze
The crack of earthquake shivering to your
　　base
Split you, and hell burst up your harlot
　　roofs
Bellowing, and charr'd you thro' and thro'
　　within,

Black as the harlot's heart — hollow as a
　　skull!
Let the fierce east scream thro' your eye-
　　let-holes,　　　　　　　　　　　460
And whirl the dust of harlots round and
　　round
In dung and nettles! hiss, snake — I saw
　　him there —
Let the fox bark, let the wolf yell! Who
　　yells
Here in the still sweet summer night but
　　I —
I, the poor Pelleas whom she call'd her
　　fool?
Fool, beast — he, she, or I? myself most
　　fool;
Beast too, as lacking human wit — dis-
　　graced,
Dishonor'd all for trial of true love —
Love? — we be all alike; only the King
Hath made us fools and liars. O noble
　　vows!　　　　　　　　　　　　470
O great and sane and simple race of brutes
That own no lust because they have no law!
For why should I have loved her to my
　　shame?
I loathe her, as I loved her to my shame.
I never loved her, I but lusted for her —
Away!' —

　　　　He dash'd the rowel into his horse,
And bounded forth and vanish'd thro' the
　　night.

　　Then she, that felt the cold touch on her
　　throat,
Awaking knew the sword, and turn'd her-
　　self
To Gawain: 'Liar, for thou hast not slain
This Pelleas! here he stood, and might
　　have slain　　　　　　　　　　　481
Me and thyself.' And he that tells the tale
Says that her ever-veering fancy turn'd
To Pelleas, as the one true knight on earth
And only lover; and thro' her love her life
Wasted and pined, desiring him in vain.

　　But he by wild and way, for half the
　　night,
And over hard and soft, striking the sod
From out the soft, the spark from off the
　　hard,
Rode till the star above the wakening sun,
Beside that tower where Percivale was
　　cowl'd,　　　　　　　　　　　　491

Glanced from the rosy forehead of the
    dawn.
For so the words were flash'd into his
    heart
He knew not whence or wherefore: 'O
    sweet star,
Pure on the virgin forehead of the dawn !'
And there he would have wept, but felt his
    eyes
Harder and drier than a fountain bed
In summer.  Thither came the village girls
And linger'd talking, and they come no
    more
Till the sweet heavens have fill'd it from
    the heights                    500
Again with living waters in the change
Of seasons.  Hard his eyes, harder his heart
Seem'd; but so weary were his limbs that
    he,
Gasping, 'Of Arthur's hall am I, but here,
Here let me rest and die,' cast himself
    down,
And gulf'd his griefs in inmost sleep; so
    lay,
Till shaken by a dream, that Gawain fired
The hall of Merlin, and the morning star
Reel'd in the smoke, brake into flame, and
    fell.

He woke, and being ware of some one
    nigh,                    510
Sent hands upon him, as to tear him, crying,
'False ! and I held thee pure as Guine-
    vere.'

But Percivale stood near him and replied,
'Am I but false as Guinevere is pure ?
Or art thou mazed with dreams ? or being
    one
Of our free-spoken Table hast not heard
That Lancelot ' — there he check'd himself
    and paused.

Then fared it with Sir Pelleas as with one
Who gets a wound in battle, and the sword
That made it plunges thro' the wound again,
And pricks it deeper; and he shrank and
    wail'd,                    521
'Is the Queen false ? ' and Percivale was
    mute.
'Have any of our Round Table held their
    vows ? '
And Percivale made answer not a word.
'Is the King true ? '  'The King !' said
    Percivale.

'Why, then let men couple at once with
    wolves.
What ! art thou mad ?'

              But Pelleas, leaping up,
Ran thro' the doors and vaulted on his horse
And fled.  Small pity upon his horse had he,  530
Or on himself, or any, and when he met
A cripple, one that held a hand for alms —
Hunch'd as he was, and like an old dwarf-
    elm
That turns its back on the salt blast, the boy
Paused not, but overrode him, shouting,
    ' False,
And false with Gawain !' and so left him
    bruised
And batter'd, and fled on, and hill and
    wood
Went ever streaming by him till the gloom
That follows on the turning of the world
Darken'd the common path.  He twitch'd
    the reins,
And made his beast, that better knew it,
    swerve                    540
Now off it and now on; but when he saw
High up in heaven the hall that Merlin
    built,
Blackening against the dead-green stripes
    of even,
' Black nest of rats,' he groan'd, ' ye build
    too high.'

Not long thereafter from the city gates
Issued Sir Lancelot riding airily,
Warm with a gracious parting from the
    Queen,
Peace at his heart, and gazing at a star
And marvelling what it was; on whom the
    boy,
Across the silent seeded meadow-grass
Borne, clash'd; and Lancelot, saying,
    ' What name hast thou               551
That ridest here so blindly and so hard ? '
' No name, no name,' he shouted, ' a scourge
    am I
To lash the treasons of the Table Round.'
' Yea, but thy name ? '   ' I have many
    names,' he cried:
' I am wrath and shame and hate and evil
    fame,
And like a poisonous wind I pass to blast
And blaze the crime of Lancelot and the
    Queen.'
' First over me,' said Lancelot, ' shalt thou
    pass.'

'Fight therefore,' yell'd the youth, and
    either knight                         560
Drew back a space, and when they closed,
    at once
The weary steed of Pelleas floundering
    flung
His rider, who call'd out from the dark
    field,
'Thou art false as hell; slay me, I have no
    sword.'
Then Lancelot, 'Yea, between thy lips —
    and sharp;
But here will I disedge it by thy death.'
'Slay then,' he shriek'd, 'my will is to be
    slain,'
And Lancelot, with his heel upon the
    fallen,
Rolling his eyes, a moment stood, then
    spake:
'Rise, weakling; I am Lancelot; say thy
    say.'                                570

And Lancelot slowly rode his war-horse
    back
To Camelot, and Sir Pelleas in brief while
Caught his unbroken limbs from the dark
    field,
And follow'd to the city. It chanced that
    both
Brake into hall together, worn and pale.
There with her knights and dames was
    Guinevere.
Full wonderingly she gazed on Lancelot
So soon return'd, and then on Pelleas, him
Who had not greeted her, but cast himself
Down on a bench, hard-breathing. 'Have
    ye fought?'                          580
She ask'd of Lancelot. 'Ay, my Queen,'
    he said.
'And thou hast overthrown him?' 'Ay,
    my Queen.'
Then she, turning to Pelleas, 'O young
    knight,
Hath the great heart of knighthood in thee
    fail'd
So far thou canst not bide, unfrowardly,
A fall from *him?*' Then, for he answer'd
    not,
'Or hast thou other griefs? If I, the
    Queen,
May help them, loose thy tongue, and let
    me know.'
But Pelleas lifted up an eye so fierce
She quail'd; and he, hissing 'I have no
    sword,'                              590

Sprang from the door into the dark. The
    Queen
Look'd hard upon her lover, he on her,
And each foresaw the dolorous day to be;
And all talk died, as in a grove all song
Beneath the shadow of some bird of prey.
Then a long silence came upon the hall,
And Modred thought, 'The time is hard at
    hand.'


## THE LAST TOURNAMENT

DAGONET, the fool, whom Gawain in his
    mood
Had made mock-knight of Arthur's Table
    Round
At Camelot, high above the yellowing
    wood,
Danced like a wither'd leaf before the hall.
And toward him from the hall, with harp
    in hand,
And from the crown thereof a carcanet
Of ruby swaying to and fro, the prize
Of Tristram in the jousts of yesterday,
Came Tristram, saying, 'Why skip ye so,
    Sir Fool?'

For Arthur and Sir Lancelot riding once
Far down beneath a winding wall of rock  11
Heard a child wail. A stump of oak half-
    dead,
From roots like some black coil of carven
    snakes,
Clutch'd at the crag, and started thro' mid
    air
Bearing an eagle's nest; and thro' the tree
Rush'd ever a rainy wind, and thro' the
    wind
Pierced ever a child's cry; and crag and tree
Scaling, Sir Lancelot from the perilous
    nest,
This ruby necklace thrice around her neck,
And all unscarr'd from beak or talon,
    brought                             20
A maiden babe, which Arthur pitying took,
Then gave it to his Queen to rear. The
    Queen,
But coldly acquiescing, in her white arms
Received, and after loved it tenderly,
And named it Nestling; so forgot herself
A moment, and her cares; till that young
    life
Being smitten in mid heaven with mortal
    cold

Past from her, and in time the carcanet
Vext her with plaintive memories of the
  child.
So she, delivering it to Arthur, said,      30
'Take thou the jewels of this dead inno-
  cence,
And make them, an thou wilt, a tourney-
  prize.'

To whom the King: 'Peace to thine eagle-
  borne
Dead nestling, and this honor after death,
Following thy will! but, O my Queen, I
  muse
Why ye not wear on arm, or neck, or zone
Those diamonds that I rescued from the
  tarn,
And Lancelot won, methought, for thee to
  wear.'

'Would rather you had let them fall,'
  she cried,
'Plunge and be lost — ill-fated as they
  were,                                      40
A bitterness to me! — ye look amazed,
Not knowing they were lost as soon as
  given —
Slid from my hands when I was leaning
  out
Above the river — that unhappy child
Past in her barge; but rosier luck will go
With these rich jewels, seeing that they
  came
Not from the skeleton of a brother-slayer,
But the sweet body of a maiden babe.
Perchance — who knows? — the purest of
  thy knights                               49
May win them for the purest of my maids.'

She ended, and the cry of a great jousts
With trumpet-blowings ran on all the ways
From Camelot in among the faded fields
To furthest towers; and everywhere the
  knights
Arm'd for a day of glory before the King.

But on the hither side of that loud morn
Into the hall stagger'd, his visage ribb'd
From ear to ear with dogwhip-weals, his
  nose
Bridge-broken, one eye out, and one hand
  off,
And one with shatter'd fingers dangling
  lame,                                      60
A churl, to whom indignantly the King:

'My churl, for whom Christ died, what
  evil beast
Hath drawn his claws athwart thy face?
  or fiend?
Man was it who marr'd heaven's image in
  thee thus?'

Then, sputtering thro' the hedge of
  splinter'd teeth,
Yet strangers to the tongue, and with blunt
  stump
Pitch-blacken'd sawing the air, said the
  maim'd churl:

'He took them and he drave them to his
  tower —
Some hold he was a table-knight of thine —
A hundred goodly ones — the Red Knight,
  he —                                      70
Lord, I was tending swine, and the Red
  Knight
Brake in upon me and drave them to his
  tower;
And when I call'd upon thy name as one
That doest right by gentle and by churl,
Maim'd me and maul'd, and would out-
  right have slain,
Save that he sware me to a message, say-
  ing:
"Tell thou the King and all his liars that I
Have founded my Round Table in the
  North,
And whatsoever his own knights have sworn
My knights have sworn the counter to it —
  and say                                   80
My tower is full of harlots, like his court,
But mine are worthier, seeing they profess
To be none other than themselves — and
  say
My knights are all adulterers like his own,
But mine are truer, seeing they profess
To be none other; and say his hour is come,
The heathen are upon him, his long lance
Broken, and his Excalibur a straw."'

Then Arthur turn'd to Kay the senes-
  chal:
'Take thou my churl, and tend him curi-
  ously                                     90
Like a king's heir, till all his hurts be
  whole.
The heathen — but that ever-climbing wave,
Hurl'd back again so often in empty foam,
Hath lain for years at rest — and rene-
  gades,

Thieves, bandits, leavings of confusion,
    whom
The wholesome realm is purged of other-
    where,
Friends, thro' your manhood and your
    fealty, — now
Make their last head like Satan in the
    North.
My younger knights, new-made, in whom
    your flower
Waits to be solid fruit of golden deeds, 100
Move with me toward their quelling, which
    achieved,
The loneliest ways are safe from shore to
    shore.
But thou, Sir Lancelot, sitting in my place
Enchair'd to-morrow, arbitrate the field;
For wherefore shouldst thou care to mingle
    with it,
Only to yield my Queen her own again?
Speak, Lancelot, thou art silent; is it
    well?'

Thereto Sir Lancelot answer'd: 'It is
    well;
Yet better if the King abide, and leave  109
The leading of his younger knights to me.
Else, for the King has will'd it, it is well.'

Then Arthur rose and Lancelot follow'd
    him,
And while they stood without the doors,
    the King
Turn'd to him saying: 'Is it then so well?
Or mine the blame that oft I seem as he
Of whom was written, " A sound is in his
    ears " ?
The foot that loiters, bidden go, — the
    glance
That only seems half-loyal to command, —
A manner somewhat fallen from rever-
    ence —
Or have I dream'd the bearing of our
    knights                              120
Tells of a manhood ever less and lower?
Or whence the fear lest this my realm, up-
    rear'd,
By noble deeds at one with noble vows,
From flat confusion and brute violences,
Reel back into the beast, and be no more?'

He spoke, and taking all his younger
    knights,
Down the slope city rode, and sharply
    turn'd

North by the gate.  In her high bower the
    Queen,
Working a tapestry, lifted up her head,
Watch'd her lord pass, and knew not that
    she sigh'd.                          130
Then ran across her memory the strange
    rhyme
Of bygone Merlin, ' Where is he who
    knows?
From the great deep to the great deep he
    goes.'

But when the morning of a tournament,
By these in earnest those in mockery call'd
The Tournament of the Dead Innocence,
Brake with a wet wind blowing, Lancelot,
Round whose sick head all night, like birds
    of prey,
The words of Arthur flying shriek'd, arose,
And down a streetway hung with folds of
    pure                                140
White samite, and by fountains running
    wine,
Where children sat in white with cups of
    gold,
Moved to the lists, and there, with slow sad
    steps
Ascending, fill'd his double-dragon'd chair.

He glanced and saw the stately galleries,
Dame, damsel, each thro' worship of their
    Queen
White-robed in honor of the stainless child,
And some with scatter'd jewels, like a bank
Of maiden snow mingled with sparks of
    fire.
He look'd but once, and vail'd his eyes
    again.                              150

The sudden trumpet sounded as in a
    dream
To ears but half-awaked, then one low roll
Of autumn thunder, and the jousts began;
And ever the wind blew, and yellowing leaf,
And gloom and gleam, and shower and
    shorn plume
Went down it.  Sighing weariedly, as one
Who sits and gazes on a faded fire,
When all the goodlier guests are past
    away,
Sat their great umpire looking o'er the
    lists.
He saw the laws that ruled the tournament
Broken, but spake not; once, a knight cast
    down                               161

Before his throne of arbitration cursed
The dead babe and the follies of the King;
And once the laces of a helmet crack'd,
And show'd him, like a vermin in its hole,
Modred, a narrow face.  Anon he heard
The voice that billow'd round the barriers
　　roar
An ocean-sounding welcome to one knight,
But newly-enter'd, taller than the rest,　169
And armor'd all in forest green, whereon
There tript a hundred tiny silver deer,
And wearing but a holly-spray for crest,
With ever-scattering berries, and on shield
A spear, a harp, a bugle — Tristram — late
From over-seas in Brittany return'd,
And marriage with a princess of that
　　realm,
Isolt the White — Sir Tristram of the
　　Woods —
Whom Lancelot knew, had held sometime
　　with pain
His own against him, and now yearn'd to
　　shake
The burthen off his heart in one full shock
With Tristram even to death.  His strong
　　hands gript　　　　　　　　　　181
And dinted the gilt dragons right and
　　left,
Until he groan'd for wrath — so many of
　　those
That ware their ladies' colors on the casque
Drew from before Sir Tristram to the
　　bounds,
And there with gibes and flickering mock-
　　eries
Stood, while he mutter'd, 'Craven crests !
　　O shame !
What faith have these in whom they sware
　　to love ?
The glory of our Round Table is no more.'

So Tristram won, and Lancelot gave, the
　　gems,　　　　　　　　　　　　190
Not speaking other word than, ' Hast thou
　　won ?
Art thou the purest, brother ?  See, the
　　hand
Wherewith thou takest this is red ! ' to
　　whom
Tristram, half plagued by Lancelot's lan-
　　guorous mood,
Made answer: ' Ay, but wherefore toss me
　　this
Like a dry bone cast to some hungry
　　hound ?

Let be thy fair Queen's fantasy.  Strength
　　of heart
And might of limb, but mainly use and
　　skill,
Are winners in this pastime of our King.
My hand — belike the lance hath dript
　　upon it —　　　　　　　　　　　200
No blood of mine, I trow; but O chief
　　knight,
Right arm of Arthur in the battle-field,
Great brother, thou nor I have made the
　　world;
Be happy in thy fair Queen as I in mine.'

And Tristram round the gallery made
　　his horse
Caracole; then bow'd his homage, bluntly
　　saying,
' Fair damsels, each to him who worships
　　each
Sole Queen of Beauty and of love, behold
This day my Queen of Beauty is not here.'
And most of these were mute, some an-
　　ger'd, one　　　　　　　　　　210
Murmuring, ' All courtesy is dead,' and
　　one,
' The glory of our Round Table is no more.'

Then fell thick rain, plume droopt and
　　mantle clung,
And pettish cries awoke, and the wan day
Went glooming down in wet and weari-
　　ness;
But under her black brows a swarthy one
Laugh'd shrilly, crying: ' Praise the patient
　　saints,
Our one white day of Innocence hath past,
Tho' somewhat draggled at the skirt.  So
　　be it.
The snowdrop only, flowering thro' the
　　year,　　　　　　　　　　　　220
Would make the world as blank as winter-
　　tide.
Come — let us gladden their sad eyes, our
　　Queen's
And Lancelot's, at this night's solemnity
With all the kindlier colors of the field.'

So dame and damsel glitter'd at the
　　feast
Variously gay; for he that tells the tale
Liken'd them, saying, as when an hour of
　　cold
Falls on the mountain in midsummer
　　snows,

And all the purple slopes of mountain
flowers
Pass under white, till the warm hour re-
turns                                      230
With veer of wind and all are flowers
again,
So dame and damsel cast the simple white,
And glowing in all colors, the live grass,
Rose-campion, bluebell, kingcup, poppy,
glanced
About the revels, and with mirth so loud
Beyond all use, that, half - amazed, the
Queen,
And wroth at Tristram and the lawless
jousts,
Brake up their sports, then slowly to her
bower                                      238
Parted, and in her bosom pain was lord.

And little Dagonet on the morrow morn,
High over all the yellowing autumn-tide,
Danced like a wither'd leaf before the hall.
Then Tristram saying, 'Why skip ye so,
Sir Fool?'
Wheel'd round on either heel, Dagonet re-
plied,
'Belike for lack of wiser company;
Or being fool, and seeing too much wit
Makes the world rotten, why, belike I skip
To know myself the wisest knight of all.'
'Ay, fool,' said Tristram, 'but 't is eating
dry
To dance without a catch, a roundelay   250
To dance to.'  Then he twangled on his
harp,
And while he twangled little Dagonet
stood
Quiet as any water-sodden log
Stay'd in the wandering warble of a brook,
But when the twangling ended, skipt again;
And being ask'd, 'Why skipt ye not, Sir
Fool?'
Made answer, 'I had liefer twenty years
Skip to the broken music of my brains
Than any broken music thou canst make.'
Then Tristram, waiting for the quip to
come,                                      260
'Good now, what music have I broken,
fool?'
And little Dagonet, skipping, 'Arthur, the
King's;
For when thou playest that air with Queen
Isolt,
Thou makest broken music with thy bride,
Her daintier namesake down in Brittany —

And so thou breakest Arthur's music too.'
'Save for that broken music in thy brains,
Sir Fool,' said Tristram, 'I would break
thy head.
Fool, I came late, the heathen wars were
o'er,
The life had flown, we sware but by the
shell —                                    270
I am but a fool to reason with a fool —
Come, thou art crabb'd and sour; but lean
me down,
Sir Dagonet, one of thy long asses' ears,
And harken if my music be not true.

'"Free love — free field — we love but while
we may.
The woods are hush'd, their music is no more ;
The leaf is dead, the yearning past away.
New leaf, new life — the days of frost are
o'er;
New life, new love, to suit the newer day;
New loves are sweet as those that went be-
fore.                                      280
Free love — free field — we love but while we
may."

'Ye might have moved slow-measure to
my tune,
Not stood stock-still.  I made it in the
woods,
And heard it ring as true as tested gold.'

But Dagonet with one foot poised in his
hand:
'Friend, did ye mark that fountain yester-
day,
Made to run wine? — but this had run
itself
All out like a long life to a sour end —
And them that round it sat with golden
cups                                       289
To hand the wine to whosoever came —
The twelve small damosels white as Inno-
cence,
In honor of poor Innocence the babe,
Who left the gems which Innocence the
Queen
Lent to the King, and Innocence the King
Gave for a prize — and one of those white
slips
Handed her cup and piped, the pretty
one,
"Drink, drink, Sir Fool," and thereupon I
drank,
Spat — pish — the cup was gold, the draught
was mud.'

And Tristram: 'Was it muddier than
thy gibes?
Is all the laughter gone dead out of
thee? — 300
Not marking how the knighthood mock
thee, fool —
"Fear God: honor the King — his one
true knight —
Sole follower of the vows" — for here be
they
Who knew thee swine enow before I came,
Smuttier than blasted grain. But when the
King
Had made thee fool, thy vanity so shot
up
It frighted all free fool from out thy
heart;
Which left thee less than fool, and less
than swine,
A naked aught — yet swine I hold thee
still,
For I have flung thee pearls and find thee
swine.' 310

And little Dagonet mincing with his
feet:
'Knight, an ye fling those rubies round my
neck
In lieu of hers, I'll hold thou hast some
touch
Of music, since I care not for thy pearls.
Swine? I have wallow'd, I have wash'd —
the world
Is flesh and shadow — I have had my
day.
The dirty nurse, Experience, in her kind
Hath foul'd me — an I wallow'd, then I
wash'd —
I have had my day and my philosophies —
And thank the Lord I am King Arthur's
fool. 320
Swine, say ye? swine, goats, asses, rams,
and geese
Troop'd round a Paynim harper once, who
thrumm'd
On such a wire as musically as thou
Some such fine song — but never a king's
fool.'

And Tristram, 'Then were swine, goats,
asses, geese
The wiser fools, seeing thy Paynim bard
Had such a mastery of his mystery
That he could harp his wife up out of
hell.'

Then Dagonet, turning on the ball of his
foot,
'And whither harp'st thou thine? down!
and thyself 330
Down! and two more; a helpful harper
thou,
That harpest downward! Dost thou know
the star
We call the Harp of Arthur up in heaven?'

And Tristram, 'Ay, Sir Fool, for when
our King
Was victor wellnigh day by day, the
knights,
Glorying in each new glory, set his name
High on all hills and in the signs of
heaven.'

And Dagonet answer'd: 'Ay, and when
the land
Was freed, and the Queen false, ye set
yourself
To babble about him, all to show your
wit — 340
And whether he were king by courtesy,
Or king by right — and so went harping
down
The black king's highway, got so far and
grew
So witty that ye play'd at ducks and
drakes
With Arthur's vows on the great lake of fire.
Tuwhoo! do ye see it? do ye see the
star?'

'Nay, fool,' said Tristram, 'not in open
day.'
And Dagonet: 'Nay, nor will; I see it and
hear.
It makes a silent music up in heaven,
And I and Arthur and the angels hear, 350
And then we skip.' 'Lo, fool,' he said,
'ye talk
Fool's treason; is the King thy brother
fool?'
Then little Dagonet clapt his hands and
shrill'd:
'Ay, ay, my brother fool, the king of
fools!
Conceits himself as God that he can make
Figs out of thistles, silk from bristles, milk
From burning spurge, honey from hornet-
combs,
And men from beasts — Long live the king
of fools!'

And down the city Dagonet danced
    away;
But thro' the slowly-mellowing avenues  360
And solitary passes of the wood
Rode Tristram toward Lyonnesse and the
    west.
Before him fled the face of Queen Isolt
With ruby-circled neck, but evermore
Past, as a rustle or twitter in the wood
Made dull his inner, keen his outer eye
For all that walk'd, or crept, or perch'd, or
    flew.
Anon the face, as, when a gust hath blown,
Unruffling waters re-collect the shape
Of one that in them sees himself, re-
    turn'd;                                 370
But at the slot or fewmets of a deer,
Or even a fallen feather, vanish'd again.

So on for all that day from lawn to lawn
Thro' many a league-long bower he rode.
    At length
A lodge of intertwisted beechen-boughs,
Furze - cramm'd and bracken - rooft, the
    which himself
Built for a summer day with Queen Isolt
Against a shower, dark in the golden grove
Appearing, sent his fancy back to where
She lived a moon in that low lodge with
    him;                                    380
Till Mark her lord had past, the Cornish
    King,
With six or seven, when Tristram was
    away,
And snatch'd her thence, yet, dreading
    worse than shame
Her warrior Tristram, spake not any word,
But bode his hour, devising wretchedness.

And now that desert lodge to Tristram
    lookt
So sweet that, halting, in he past and sank
Down on a drift of foliage random-blown;
But could not rest for musing how to
    smooth                                  389
And sleek his marriage over to the queen.
Perchance in lone Tintagil far from all
The tonguesters of the court she had not
    heard.
But then what folly had sent him over-seas
After she left him lonely here ? a name ?
Was it the name of one in Brittany,
Isolt, the daughter of the king ?  ' Isolt
Of the White Hands ' they call'd her: the
    sweet name

Allured him first, and then the maid her-
    self,
Who served him well with those white
    hands of hers,
And loved him well, until himself had
    thought                                 400
He loved her also, wedded easily,
But left her all as easily, and return'd.
The black-blue Irish hair and Irish eyes
Had drawn him home — what marvel ?
    then he laid
His brows upon the drifted leaf and
    dream'd.

He seem'd to pace the strand of Brittany
Between Isolt of Britain and his bride,
And show'd them both the ruby-chain, and
    both
Began to struggle for it, till his queen
Graspt it so hard that all her hand was
    red.                                    410
Then cried the Breton, ' Look, her hand is
    red !
These be no rubies, this is frozen blood,
And melts within her hand — her hand is hot
With ill desires, but this I gave thee, look,
Is all as cool and white as any flower.'
Follow'd a rush of eagle's wings, and then
A whimpering of the spirit of the child,
Because the twain had spoil'd her carcanet.

He dream'd; but Arthur with a hundred
    spears
Rode far, till o'er the illimitable reed,  420
And many a glancing plash and sallowy
    isle,
The wide-wing'd sunset of the misty marsh
Glared on a huge machicolated tower
That stood with open doors, whereout was
    roll'd
A roar of riot, as from men secure
Amid their marshes, ruffians at their ease
Among their harlot-brides, an evil song.
' Lo there,' said one of Arthur's youth, for
    there,
High on a grim dead tree before the tower,
A goodly brother of the Table Round   430
Swung by the neck; and on the boughs a
    shield
Showing a shower of blood in a field noir,
And therebeside a horn, inflamed the
    knights
At that dishonor done the gilded spur,
Till each would clash the shield and blow
    the horn.

But Arthur waved them back.  Alone he
    rode.
Then at the dry harsh roar of the great
    horn,
That sent the face of all the marsh aloft
An ever upward-rushing storm and cloud
Of shriek and plume, the Red Knight
    heard, and all,                      440
Even to tipmost lance and topmost helm,
In blood-red armor sallying, howl'd to the
    King:

  'The teeth of Hell flay bare and gnash
      thee flat ! —
Lo ! art thou not that eunuch-hearted king
Who fain had clipt free manhood from the
    world —
The woman-worshipper ?  Yea, God's curse,
    and I !
Slain was the brother of my paramour
By a knight of thine, and I that heard her
    whine
And snivel, being eunuch-hearted too,
Sware by the scorpion-worm that twists in
    hell                               450
And stings itself to everlasting death,
To hang whatever knight of thine I fought
And tumbled.  Art thou king ? — Look to
    thy life !'

  He ended.  Arthur knew the voice; the
      face
Wellnigh was helmet-hidden, and the name
Went wandering somewhere darkling in
    his mind.
And Arthur deign'd not use of word or
    sword,
But let the drunkard, as he stretch'd from
    horse
To strike him, overbalancing his bulk,
Down from the causeway heavily to the
    swamp                             460
Fall, as the crest of some slow - arching
    wave,
Heard in dead night along that table-shore,
Drops flat, and after the great waters break
Whitening for half a league, and thin
    themselves,
Far over sands marbled with moon and
    cloud,
From less and less to nothing; thus he fell
Head - heavy.   Then the   knights, who
    watch'd him, roar'd
And shouted and leapt down upon the
    fallen,

There trampled out his face from being
    known,
And sank his head in mire, and slimed
    themselves;                        470
Nor heard the King for their own cries,
    but sprang
Thro' open doors, and swording right and
    left
Men, women, on their sodden faces, hurl'd
The tables over and the wines, and slew
Till all the rafters rang with woman-yells,
And all the pavement stream'd with massa-
    cre.
Then, echoing yell with yell, they fired the
    tower,
Which half that autumn night, like the live
    North,
Red-pulsing up thro' Alioth and Alcor,
Made all above it, and a hundred meres
About it, as the water Moab saw         481
Come round by the east, and out beyond
    them flush'd
The long low dune and lazy-plunging sea.

  So all the ways were safe from shore to
      shore,
But in the heart of Arthur pain was lord.

  Then, out of Tristram waking, the red
      dream
Fled with a shout, and that low lodge re-
    turn'd,
Mid-forest, and the wind among the boughs.
He whistled his good war - horse left to
    graze                              489
Among the forest greens, vaulted upon him,
And rode beneath an ever-showering leaf,
Till one lone woman, weeping near a cross,
Stay'd him.  'Why weep ye ? '  'Lord,'
    she said, 'my man
Hath left me or is dead;' whereon he
    thought —
' What, if she hate me now ?   I would not
    this.
What, if she love me still ?  I would not
    that.
I know not what I would ' — but said to her,
' Yet weep not thou, lest, if thy mate re-
    turn,
He find thy favor changed and love thee
    not ' —
Then pressing day by day thro' Lyonnesse
Last in a roky hollow, belling, heard    501
The hounds of Mark, and felt the goodly
    hounds

Yelp at his heart, but, turning, past and
    gain'd
Tintagil, half in sea and high on land,
A crown of towers.

                Down in a casement sat,
A low sea-sunset glorying round her hair
And glossy-throated grace, Isolt the queen.
And when she heard the feet of Tristram
    grind            *
The spiring stone that scaled about her
    tower,
Flush'd, started, met him at the doors, and
    there                                    510
Belted his body with her white embrace,
Crying aloud: 'Not Mark — not Mark, my
    soul !
The footstep flutter'd me at first — not he !
Catlike thro' his own castle steals my Mark,
But warrior - wise thou stridest thro' his
    halls
Who hates thee, as I him — even to the
    death.
My soul, I felt my hatred for my Mark
Quicken within me, and knew that thou
    wert nigh.'
To whom Sir Tristram smiling, 'I am here;
Let be thy Mark, seeing he is not thine.'

And drawing somewhat backward she
    replied:                                521
'Can he be wrong'd who is not even his
    own,
But save for dread of thee had beaten me,
Scratch'd, bitten, blinded, marr'd me some-
    how — Mark ?
What rights are his that dare not strike for
    them ?
Not lift a hand — not, tho' he found me
    thus !
But harken ! have ye met him ? hence he
    went
To-day for three days' hunting — as he
    said —
And so returns belike within an hour.
Mark's way, my soul ! — but eat not thou
    with Mark,                               530
Because he hates thee even more than fears,
Nor drink; and when thou passest any
    wood
Close vizor, lest an arrow from the bush
Should leave me all alone with Mark and
    hell.
My God, the measure of my hate for Mark
Is as the measure of my love for thee !'

So, pluck'd one way by hate and one by
    love,
Drain'd of her force, again she sat, and
    spake
To Tristram, as he knelt before her, say-
    ing:
'O hunter, and O blower of the horn,    540
Harper, and thou hast been a rover too,
For, ere I mated with my shambling king,
Ye twain had fallen out about the bride
Of one — his name is out of me — the prize,
If prize she were — what marvel ? — she
    could see —
Thine, friend; and ever since my craven
    seeks
To wreck thee villainously — but, O Sir
    Knight,
What dame or damsel have ye kneel'd to
    last ?'

    And Tristram, 'Last to my Queen Para-
        mount,                              549
Here now to my queen paramount of love
And loveliness — ay, lovelier than when
    first
Her light feet fell on our rough Lyonnesse,
Sailing from Ireland.'

                Softly laugh'd Isolt:
'Flatter me not, for hath not our great
    Queen
My dole of beauty trebled ?' and he said:
'Her beauty is her beauty, and thine thine,
And thine is more to me — soft, gracious,
    kind —
Save when thy Mark is kindled on thy lips
Most gracious; but she, haughty, even to
    him,                                     559
Lancelot; for I have seen him wan enow
To make one doubt if ever the great Queen
Have yielded him her love.'

                To whom Isolt:
'Ah, then, false hunter and false harper,
    thou
Who brakest thro' the scruple of my bond,
Calling me thy white hind, and saying to me
That Guinevere had sinn'd against the
    highest,
And I — misyoked with such a want of
    man —
That I could hardly sin against the lowest.'

He answer'd: 'O my soul, be comforted !
If this be sweet, to sin in leading-strings,

If here be comfort, and if ours be sin,    571
Crown'd warrant had we for the crowning
    sin
That made us happy; but how ye greet me
    — fear
And fault and doubt — no word of that
    fond tale —
Thy deep heart-yearnings, thy sweet mem-
    ories
Of Tristram in that year he was away.'

And, saddening on the sudden, spake
    Isolt:
' I had forgotten all in my strong joy
To see thee — yearnings ? — ay ! for, hour
    by hour,
Here in the never-ended afternoon,    580
O, sweeter than all memories of thee,
Deeper than any yearnings after thee
Seem'd those far-rolling, westward-smiling
    seas,
Watch'd from this tower.   Isolt of Britain
    dash'd
Before Isolt of Brittany on the strand,
Would that have chill'd her bride-kiss ?
    Wedded her ?
Fought in her father's battles ? wounded
    there ?
The King was all fulfill'd with grateful-
    ness,
And she, my namesake of the hands, that
    heal'd
Thy hurt and heart with unguent and ca-
    ress —    590
Well — can I wish her any huger wrong
Than having known thee ? her too hast
    thou left
To pine and waste in those sweet memories.
O, were I not my Mark's, by whom all
    men
Are noble, I should hate thee more than
    love.'

And Tristram, fondling her light hands,
    replied:
' Grace, queen, for being loved; she loved
    me well.
Did I love her ? the name at least I loved.
Isolt ? — I fought his battles, for Isolt !
The night was dark; the true star set.
    Isolt !    600
The name was ruler of the dark — Isolt ?
Care not for her ! patient, and prayerful,
    meek,
Pale-blooded, she will yield herself to God.'

And Isolt answer'd: ' Yea, and why not
    I ?
Mine is the larger need, who am not meek,
Pale-blooded, prayerful.   Let me tell thee
    now.
Here one black, mute midsummer night I
    sat,
Lonely, but musing on thee, wondering
    where,
Murmuring a light song I had heard thee
    sing,
And once or twice I spake thy name aloud.
Then flash'd a levin-brand; and near me
    stood,    611
In fuming sulphur blue and green, a fiend —
Mark's way to steal behind one in the
    dark —
For there was Mark: " He has wedded
    her," he said,
Not said, but hiss'd it; then this crown of
    towers
So shook to such a roar of all the sky,
That here in utter dark I swoon'd away,
And woke again in utter dark, and cried,
" I will flee hence and give myself to
    God " —
And thou wert lying in thy new leman's
    arms.'    620

Then Tristram, ever dallying with her
    hand,
' May God be with thee, sweet, when old
    and gray,
And past desire ! ' a saying that anger'd
    her.
' " May God be with thee, sweet, when
    thou art old,
And sweet no more to me ! "   I need Him
    now.
For when had Lancelot utter'd aught so
    gross
Even to the swineherd's malkin in the
    mast ?
The greater man the greater courtesy.
Far other was the Tristram, Arthur's
    knight !
But thou, thro' ever harrying thy wild
    beasts —    630
Save that to touch a harp, tilt with a
    lance
Becomes thee well — art grown wild beast
    thyself.
How darest thou, if lover, push me even
In fancy from thy side, and set me far
In the gray distance, half a life away,

Her to be loved no more ?   Unsay it, un-
      swear !
Flatter me rather, seeing me so weak,
Broken with Mark and hate and solitude,
Thy marriage and mine own, that I should
      suck                                         639
Lies like sweet wines.   Lie to me; I believe.
Will ye not lie ? not swear, as there ye
      kneel,
And solemnly as when ye sware to him,
The man of men, our King — My God, the
      power
Was once in vows when men believed the
      King !
They lied not then who sware, and thro'
      their vows
The King prevailing made his realm — I
      say,
Swear to me thou wilt love me even when
      old,
Gray - hair'd, and past desire, and in de-
      spair.'

    Then Tristram, pacing moodily up and
      down:
' Vows ! did you keep the vow you made
      to Mark                                      650
More than I mine ?   Lied, say ye ?   Nay,
      but learnt,
The vow that binds too strictly snaps it-
      self —
My knighthood taught me this — ay, being
      snapt —
We run more counter to the soul thereof
Than had we never sworn.   I swear no
      more.
I swore to the great King, and am for-
      sworn.
For once — even to the height — I honor'd
      him.
" Man, is he man at all ? " methought,
      when first
I rode from our rough Lyonnesse, and be-
      held
That victor of the Pagan throned in
      hall —                                       660
His hair, a sun that ray'd from off a brow
Like hill-snow high in heaven, the steel-
      blue eyes,
The golden beard that clothed his lips with
      light —
Moreover, that weird legend of his birth,
With Merlin's mystic babble about his
      end
Amazed me; then, his foot was on a stool

Shaped as a dragon; he seem'd to me no
      man,
But Michael trampling Satan; so I sware,
Being amazed.   But this went by — The
      vows !
O, ay — the wholesome madness of an
      hour —                                       670
They served their use, their time; for every
      knight
Believed himself a greater than himself,
And every follower eyed him as a God;
Till he, being lifted up beyond himself,
Did mightier deeds than elsewise he had
      done,
And so the realm was made.   But then
      their vows —
First mainly thro' that sullying of our
      Queen —
Began to gall the knighthood, asking
      whence
Had Arthur right to bind them to himself ?
Dropt down from heaven ? wash'd up from
      out the deep ?                              680
They fail'd to trace him thro' the flesh and
      blood
Of our old kings.   Whence then ? a doubt-
      ful lord
To bind them by inviolable vows,
Which flesh and blood perforce would vio-
      late;
For feel this arm of mine — the tide
      within
Red with free chase and heather-scented
      air,
Pulsing full man.   Can Arthur make me
      pure
As any maiden child ? lock up my tongue
From uttering freely what I freely hear ?
Bind me to one ?   The wide world laughs
      at it.                                       690
And worldling of the world am I, and
      know
The ptarmigan that whitens ere his hour
Woos his own end; we are not angels here
Nor shall be.   Vows — I am woodman of
      the woods,
And hear the garnet-headed yaffingale
Mock them — my soul, we love but while
      we may;
And therefore is my love so large for thee,
Seeing it is not bounded save by love.'

    Here ending, he moved toward her, and
      she said:
' Good; an I turn'd away my love for thee

To some one thrice as courteous as thy-
   self —                                        701
For courtesy wins woman all as well
As valor may, but he that closes both
Is perfect, he is Lancelot — taller indeed,
Rosier and comelier, thou — but say I loved
This knightliest of all knights, and cast
   thee back
Thine own small saw, " We love but while
   we may,"
Well then, what answer ? '

               He that while she spake,
Mindful of what he brought to adorn her
   with,
The jewels, had let one finger lightly touch
The warm white apple of her throat, re-
   plied,                                         711
' Press this a little closer, sweet, until —
Come, I am hunger'd and half-anger'd —
   meat,
Wine, wine — and I will love thee to the
   death,
And out beyond into the dream to come.'

  So then, when both were brought to full
   accord,
She rose, and set before him all he will'd;
And after these had comforted the blood
With meats and wines, and satiated their
   hearts —
Now talking of their woodland paradise,  720
The deer, the dews, the fern, the founts,
   the lawns;
Now mocking at the much ungainliness,
And craven shifts, and long crane legs of
   Mark —
Then Tristram laughing caught the harp
   and sang:

' Ay, ay, O, ay — the winds that bend the
   brier !
A star in heaven, a star within the mere !
Ay, ay, O, ay — a star was my desire,
And one was far apart and one was near.
Ay, ay, O, ay — the winds that bow the grass !
And one was water and one star was fire,   730
And one will ever shine and one will pass.
Ay, ay, O, ay — the winds that move the
   mere ! '

  Then in the light's last glimmer Tris-
   tram show'd
And swung the ruby carcanet.  She cried,
' The collar of some Order, which our
   King

Hath newly founded, all for thee, my soul,
For thee, to yield thee grace beyond thy
   peers.'

  ' Not so, my queen,' he said, ' but the
   red fruit
Grown on a magic oak-tree in mid-heaven,
And won by Tristram as a tourney-prize,
And hither brought by Tristram for his
   last                                            741
Love-offering and peace-offering unto thee.'

  He spoke, he turn'd, then, flinging round
   her neck,
Claspt it, and cried, ' Thine Order, O my
   queen ! '
But, while he bow'd to kiss the jewell'd
   throat,
Out of the dark, just as the lips had
   touch'd,
Behind him rose a shadow and a shriek —
' Mark's way,' said Mark, and clove him
   thro' the brain.

  That night came Arthur home, and while
   he climb'd,
All in a death - dumb autumn - dripping
   gloom,                                          750
The stairway to the hall, and look'd and
   saw
The great Queen's bower was dark, — about
   his feet
A voice clung sobbing till he question'd
   it,
' What art thou ? ' and the voice about his
   feet
Sent up an answer, sobbing, ' I am thy
   fool,
And I shall never make thee smile again.'


## GUINEVERE

QUEEN GUINEVERE had fled the court, and
   sat
There in the holy house at Almesbury
Weeping, none with her save a little maid,
A novice.  One low light betwixt them
   burn'd
Blurr'd by the creeping mist, for all abroad,
Beneath a moon unseen albeit at full,
The white mist; like a face-cloth to the
   face,
Clung to the dead earth, and the land was
   still.

For hither had she fled, her cause of flight
Sir Modred; he that like a subtle beast    10
Lay couchant with his eyes upon the throne,
Ready to spring, waiting a chance.  For this
He chill'd the popular praises of the King
With silent smiles of slow disparagement;
And tamper'd with the Lords of the White Horse,
Heathen, the brood by Hengist left; and sought
To make disruption in the Table Round
Of Arthur, and to splinter it into feuds
Serving his traitorous end; and all his aims
Were sharpen'd by strong hate for Lancelot.    20

For thus it chanced one morn when all the court,
Green-suited, but with plumes that mock'd the may,
Had been — their wont — a-maying and return'd,
That Modred still in green, all ear and eye,
Climb'd to the high top of the garden-wall
To spy some secret scandal if he might,
And saw the Queen who sat betwixt her best
Enid and lissome Vivien, of her court
The wiliest and the worst; and more than this
He saw not, for Sir Lancelot passing by    30
Spied where he couch'd, and as the gardener's hand
Picks from the colewort a green caterpillar,
So from the high wall and the flowering grove
Of grasses Lancelot pluck'd him by the heel,
And cast him as a worm upon the way;
But when he knew the prince tho' marr'd with dust,
He, reverencing king's blood in a bad man,
Made such excuses as he might, and these
Full knightly without scorn.  For in those days
No knight of Arthur's noblest dealt in scorn;    40
But, if a man were halt, or hunch'd, in him
By those whom God had made full-limb'd and tall,
Scorn was allow'd as part of his defect,

And he was answer'd softly by the King
And all his Table.  So Sir Lancelot holp
To raise the prince, who rising twice or thrice
Full sharply smote his knees, and smiled, and went;
But, ever after, the small violence done
Rankled in him and ruffled all his heart,
As the sharp wind that ruffles all day long
A little bitter pool about a stone    51
On the bare coast.

But when Sir Lancelot told
This matter to the Queen, at first she laugh'd
Lightly, to think of Modred's dusty fall,
Then shudder'd, as the village wife who cries,
' I shudder, some one steps across my grave; '
Then laugh'd again, but faintlier, for indeed
She half-foresaw that he, the subtle beast,
Would track her guilt until he found, and hers
Would be for evermore a name of scorn.    60
Henceforward rarely could she front in hall,
Or elsewhere, Modred's narrow foxy face,
Heart - hiding smile, and gray persistent eye.
Henceforward too, the Powers that tend the soul,
To help it from the death that cannot die,
And save it even in extremes, began
To vex and plague her.  Many a time for hours,
Beside the placid breathings of the King,
In the dead night, grim faces came and went
Before her, or a vague spiritual fear —    70
Like to some doubtful noise of creaking doors,
Heard by the watcher in a haunted house,
That keeps the rust of murder on the walls —
Held her awake; or if she slept she dream'd
An awful dream, for then she seem'd to stand
On some vast plain before a setting sun,
And from the sun there swiftly made at her
A ghastly something, and its shadow flew
Before it till it touch'd her, and she turn'd —

When lo ! her own, that broadening from
her feet,     80
And blackening, swallow'd all the land,
and in it
Far cities burnt, and with a cry she woke.
And all this trouble did not pass but grew,
Till even the clear face of the guileless
King,
And trustful courtesies of household life,
Became her bane ; and at the last she
said:
'O Lancelot, get thee hence to thine own
land,
For if thou tarry we shall meet again,
And if we meet again some evil chance
Will make the smouldering scandal break
and blaze     90
Before the people and our lord the King.'
And Lancelot ever promised, but remain'd,
And still they met and met.  Again she
said,
'O Lancelot, if thou love me get thee
hence.'
And then they were agreed upon a night —
When the good King should not be there
— to meet
And part for ever.  Vivien, lurking, heard.
She told Sir Modred.  Passion-pale they
met
And greeted.  Hands in hands, and eye to
eye,
Low on the border of her couch they sat   100
Stammering and staring.  It was their last
hour,
A madness of farewells.  And Modred
brought
His creatures to the basement of the tower
For testimony; and crying with full voice,
'Traitor, come out, ye are trapt at last,'
aroused
Lancelot, who rushing outward lionlike
Leapt on him, and hurl'd him headlong,
and he fell
Stunn'd, and his creatures took and bare
him off,
And all was still.  Then she, ' The end is
come,     109
And I am shamed for ever;' and he said:
'Mine be the shame, mine was the sin;
but rise,
And fly to my strong castle over-seas.
There will I hide thee till my life shall
end,
There hold thee with my life against the
world.'

She answer'd: ' Lancelot, wilt thou hold me
so ?
Nay, friend, for we have taken our fare-
wells.
Would God that thou couldst hide me from
myself !
Mine is the shame, for I was wife, and thou
Unwedded; yet rise now, and let us fly,
For I will draw me into sanctuary,   120
And bide my doom.'  So Lancelot got her
horse,
Set her thereon, and mounted on his own,
And then they rode to the divided way,
There kiss'd, and parted weeping; for he
past,
Love-loyal to the least wish of the Queen,
Back to his land; but she to Almesbury
Fled all night long by glimmering waste
and weald,
And heard the spirits of the waste and
weald
Moan as she fled, or thought she heard
them moan.
And in herself she moan'd, ' Too late, too
late ! '   130
Till in the cold wind that foreruns the
morn,
A blot in heaven, the raven, flying high,
Croak'd, and she thought, ' He spies a field
of death;
For now the heathen of the Northern Sea,
Lured by the crimes and frailties of the
court,
Begin to slay the folk and spoil the land.'

And when she came to Almesbury she
spake
There to the nuns, and said, ' Mine ene-
mies
Pursue me, but, O peaceful Sisterhood,
Receive and yield me sanctuary, nor ask   140
Her name to whom ye yield it till her time
To tell you;' and her beauty, grace, and
power
Wrought as a charm upon them, and they
spared
To ask it.

    So the stately Queen abode
For many a week, unknown, among the
nuns,
Nor with them mix'd, nor told her name,
nor sought,
Wrapt in her grief, for housel or for shrift,
But commuued only with the little maid,

Who pleased her with a babbling heedless-
    ness
Which often lured her from herself; but
    now,                                       150
This night, a rumor wildly blown about
Came that Sir Modred had usurp'd the
    realm
And leagued him with the heathen, while
    the King
Was waging war on Lancelot.  Then she
    thought,
'With what a hate the people and the
    King
Must hate me,' and bow'd down upon her
    hands
Silent, until the little maid, who brook'd
No silence, brake it, uttering ' Late ! so
    late !
What hour, I wonder now ? ' and when she
    drew
No answer, by and by began to hum    160
An air the nuns had taught her: ' Late, so
    late !'
Which when she heard, the Queen look'd
    up, and said,
' O maiden, if indeed ye list to sing,
Sing, and unbind my heart that I may
    weep.'
Whereat full willingly sang the little maid.

' Late, late, so late ! and dark the night and
    chill !
Late, late, so late ! but we can enter still.
Too late, too late ! ye cannot enter now.

' No light had we ; for that we do repent,
And learning this, the bridegroom will relent.
Too late, too late ! ye cannot enter now.    171

' No light ! so late ! and dark and chill the
    night !
O, let us in, that we may find the light !
Too late, too late ! ye cannot enter now.

' Have we not heard the bridegroom is so
    sweet ?
O, let us in, tho' late, to kiss his feet !
No, no, too late ! ye cannot enter now.'

So sang the novice, while full passion-
    ately,
Her head upon her hands, remembering
Her thought when first she came, wept the
    sad Queen.                              180
Then said the little novice prattling to
    her:

' O pray you, noble lady, weep no more;
But let my words — the words of one so
    small,
Who knowing nothing knows but to obey,
And if I do not there is penance given —
Comfort your sorrows, for they do not
    flow
From evil done; right sure am I of that,
Who see your tender grace and stateli-
    ness.
But weigh your sorrows with our lord the
    King's,
And weighing find them less; for gone is
    he                                        190
To wage grim war against Sir Lancelot
    there,
Round that strong castle where he holds
    the Queen;
And Modred whom he left in charge of
    all,
The traitor — Ah, sweet lady, the King's
    grief
For his own self, and his own Queen, and
    realm,
Must needs be thrice as great as any of
    ours !
For me, I thank the saints, I am not great;
For if there ever come a grief to me
I cry my cry in silence, and have done;
None knows it, and my tears have brought
    me good.                                  200
But even were the griefs of little ones
As great as those of great ones, yet this
    grief
Is added to the griefs the great must bear,
That, howsoever much they may desire
Silence, they cannot weep behind a cloud;
As even here they talk at Almesbury
About the good King and his wicked Queen,
And were I such a King with such a Queen,
Well might I wish to veil her wickedness,
But were I such a King it could not be.'    210

Then to her own sad heart mutter'd the
    Queen,
' Will the child kill me with her innocent
    talk ? '
But openly she answer'd, ' Must not I,
If this false traitor have displaced his lord,
Grieve with the common grief of all the
    realm ? '

' Yea,' said the maid, ' this all is woman's
    grief,
That she is woman, whose disloyal life

Hath wrought confusion in the Table
   Round
Which good King Arthur founded, years
   ago,
With signs and miracles and wonders,
   there               220
At Camelot, ere the coming of the Queen.'

Then thought the Queen within herself
   again,
' Will the child kill me with her foolish
   prate ? '
But openly she spake and said to her,
' O little maid, shut in by nunnery walls,
What canst thou know of Kings and Tables
   Round,
Or what of signs and wonders, but the signs
And simple miracles of thy nunnery ? '

To whom the little novice garrulously:
' Yea, but I know; the land was full of
   signs               230
And wonders ere the coming of the Queen.
So said my father, and himself was knight
Of the great Table — at the founding of
   it,
And rode thereto from Lyonnesse; and he
   said
That as he rode, an hour or maybe twain
After the sunset, down the coast, he heard
Strange music, and he paused, and turning
   — there,
All down the lonely coast of Lyonnesse,
Each with a beacon-star upon his head,
And with a wild sea-light about his feet, 240
He saw them — headland after headland
   flame
Far on into the rich heart of the west.
And in the light the white mermaiden
   swam,
And strong man-breasted things stood from
   the sea,
And sent a deep sea-voice thro' all the
   land,
To which the little elves of chasm and
   cleft
Made answer, sounding like a distant horn.
So said my father — yea, and furthermore,
Next morning, while he past the dim-lit
   woods             249
Himself beheld three spirits mad with joy
Come dashing down on a tall wayside
   flower,
That shook beneath them as the thistle
   shakes

When three gray linnets wrangle for the
   seed.
And still at evenings on before his horse
The flickering fairy - circle wheel'd and
   broke
Flying, and link'd again, and wheel'd and
   broke
Flying, for all the land was full of life.
And when at last he came to Camelot,
A wreath of airy dancers hand-in-hand
Swung round the lighted lantern of the
   hall;            260
And in the hall itself was such a feast
As never man had dream'd; for every
   knight
Had whatsoever meat he long'd for served
By hands unseen; and even as he said
Down in the cellars merry bloated things
Shoulder'd the spigot, straddling on the
   butts
While the wine ran; so glad were spirits
   and men
Before the coming of the sinful Queen.'

Then spake the Queen and somewhat
   bitterly,
' Were they so glad ? ill prophets were
   they all,           270
Spirits and men.   Could none of them foresee,
Not even thy wise father with his signs
And wonders, what has fallen upon the
   realm ? '

To whom the novice garrulously again:
' Yea, one, a bard, of whom my father
   said,
Full many a noble war-song had he sung,
Even in the presence of an enemy's fleet,
Between the steep cliff and the coming
   wave;
And many a mystic lay of life and death
Had chanted on the smoky mountain-
   tops,           280
When round him bent the spirits of the
   hills
With all their dewy hair blown back like
   flame.
So said my father — and that night the
   bard
Sang Arthur's glorious wars, and sang the
   King
As wellnigh more than man, and rail'd at
   those
Who call'd him the false son of Gorloïs.

For there was no man knew from whence
    he came;
But after tempest, when the long wave
    broke
All down the thundering shores of Bude
    and Bos,
There came a day as still as heaven, and
    then           290
They found a naked child upon the sands
Of dark Tintagil by the Cornish sea,
And that was Arthur, and they foster'd
    him
Till he by miracle was approven King;
And that his grave should be a mystery
From all men, like his birth; and could he
    find
A woman in her womanhood as great
As he was in his manhood, then, he sang,
The twain together well might change the
    world.
But even in the middle of his song    300
He falter'd, and his hand fell from the
    harp,
And pale he turn'd, and reel'd, and would
    have fallen,
But that they stay'd him up; nor would he
    tell
His vision; but what doubt that he fore-
    saw
This evil work of Lancelot and the Queen?'

Then thought the Queen, 'Lo! they have
    set her on,
Our simple-seeming abbess and her nuns,
To play upon me,' and bow'd her head nor
    spake.
Whereat the novice crying, with clasp'd
    hands,          309
Shame on her own garrulity garrulously,
Said the good nuns would check her gad-
    ding tongue
Full often, 'and, sweet lady, if I seem
To vex an ear too sad to listen to me,
Unmannerly, with prattling and the tales
Which my good father told me, check me
    too
Nor let me shame my father's memory,
    one
Of noblest manners, tho' himself would
    say
Sir Lancelot had the noblest; and he died,
Kill'd in a tilt, come next, five summers
    back,          319
And left me; but of others who remain,
And of the two first-famed for courtesy —

And pray you check me if I ask amiss —
But pray you, which had noblest, while
    you moved
Among them, Lancelot or our lord the
    King?'

Then the pale Queen look'd up and an-
    swer'd her:
'Sir Lancelot, as became a noble knight,
Was gracious to all ladies, and the same
In open battle or the tilting-field
Forbore his own advantage, and the King
In open battle or the tilting-field    330
Forbore his own advantage, and these
    two
Were the most nobly-manner'd men of
    all;
For manners are not idle, but the fruit
Of loyal nature and of noble mind.'

'Yea,' said the maid, 'be manners such
    fair fruit?
Then Lancelot's needs must be a thousand-
    fold
Less noble, being, as all rumor runs,
The most disloyal friend in all the world.'

To which a mournful answer made the
    Queen:
'O, closed about by narrowing nunnery-
    walls,          340
What knowest thou of the world and all its
    lights
And shadows, all the wealth and all the
    woe?
If ever Lancelot, that most noble knight,
Were for one hour less noble than himself,
Pray for him that he scape the doom of
    fire,
And weep for her who drew him to his
    doom.'

'Yea,' said the little novice, 'I pray for
    both;
But I should all as soon believe that his,
Sir Lancelot's, were as noble as the King's,
As I could think, sweet lady, yours would
    be          350
Such as they are, were you the sinful
    Queen.'

So she, like many another babbler, hurt
Whom she would soothe, and harm'd where
    she would heal;
For here a sudden flush of wrathful heat

Fired all the pale face of the Queen, who
  cried:
' Such as thou art be never maiden more
For ever ! thou their tool, set on to plague
And play upon and harry me, petty spy
And traitress !'  When that storm of an-
  ger brake
From Guinevere, aghast the maiden rose,
White as her veil, and stood before the
  Queen     361
As tremulously as foam upon the beach
Stands in a wind, ready to break and fly,
And when the Queen had added, ' Get
  thee hence !'
Fled frighted.  Then that other left alone
Sigh'd, and began to gather heart again,
Saying in herself: ' The simple, fearful
  child
Meant nothing, but my own too-fearful
  guilt,
Simpler than any child, betrays itself.
But help me, Heaven, for surely I re-
  pent !     370
For what is true repentance but in
  thought —
Not even in inmost thought to think again
The sins that made the past so pleasant to
  us ?
And I have sworn never to see him more,
To see him more.'

          And even in saying this,
Her memory from old habit of the mind
Went slipping back upon the golden days
In which she saw him first, when Lancelot
  came,
Reputed the best knight and goodliest
  man,
Ambassador, to yield her to his lord     380
Arthur, and led her forth, and far ahead
Of his and her retinue moving, they,
Rapt in sweet talk or lively, all on love
And sport and tilts and pleasure, — for
  the time
Was may - time, and as yet no sin was
  dream'd, —
Rode under groves that look'd a paradise
Of blossom, over sheets of hyacinth
That seem'd the heavens upbreaking thro'
  the earth,
And on from hill to hill, and every day
Beheld at noon in some delicious dale   390
The silk pavilions of King Arthur raised
For brief repast or afternoon repose
By couriers gone before; and on again,

Till yet once more ere set of sun they saw
The Dragon of the great Pendragonship,
That crown'd the state pavilion of the
  King,
Blaze by the rushing brook or silent well.

    But when the Queen immersed in such a
  trance,
And moving thro' the past unconsciously,
Came to that point where first she saw the
  King     400
Ride toward her from the city, sigh'd to
  find
Her journey done, glanced at him, thought
  him cold,
High, self - contain'd, and passionless, not
  like him,
' Not like my Lancelot ' — while she
  brooded thus
And grew half - guilty in her thoughts
  again,
There rode an armed warrior to the doors.
A murmuring whisper thro' the nunnery
  ran,
Then on a sudden a cry, ' The King !'  She
  sat
Stiff-stricken, listening; but when armed
  feet
Thro' the long gallery from the outer doors
Rang coming, prone from off her seat she
  fell,     411
And grovell'd with her face against the
  floor.
There with her milk-white arms and shad-
  owy hair
She made her face a darkness from the
  King,
And in the darkness heard his armed feet
Pause by her; then came silence, then a
  voice,
Monotonous and hollow like a ghost's
Denouncing judgment, but, tho' changed,
  the King's:

' Liest thou here so low, the child of one
I honor'd, happy, dead before thy shame ?
Well is it that no child is born of thee.   421
The children born of thee are sword and
  fire,
Red ruin, and the breaking up of laws,
The craft of kindred and the godless hosts
Of heathen swarming o'er the Northern
  Sea;
Whom I, while yet Sir Lancelot, my right
  arm,

The mightiest of my knights, abode with
    me,
Have everywhere about this land of Christ
In twelve great battles ruining overthrown.
And knowest thou now from whence I come
    — from him,                        430
From waging bitter war with him; and he,
That did not shun to smite me in worse
    way,
Had yet that grace of courtesy in him left,
He spared to lift his hand against the King
Who made him knight.  But many a knight
    was slain;
And many more and all his kith and kin
Clave to him, and abode in his own land.
And many more when Modred raised revolt,
Forgetful of their troth and fealty, clave
To Modred, and a remnant stays with me.
And of this remnant will I leave a part,  441
True men who love me still, for whom I
    live,
To guard thee in the wild hour coming on,
Lest but a hair of this low head be harm'd.
Fear not; thou shalt be guarded till my
    death.
Howbeit I know, if ancient prophecies
Have err'd not, that I march to meet my
    doom.
Thou hast not made my life so sweet to me,
That I the King should greatly care to
    live;                               449
For thou hast spoilt the purpose of my life.
Bear with me for the last time while I
    show,
Even for thy sake, the sin which thou hast
    sinn'd.
For when the Roman left us, and their law
Relax'd its hold upon us, and the ways
Were fill'd with rapine, here and there a
    deed
Of prowess done redress'd a random wrong.
But I was first of all the kings who drew
The knighthood-errant of this realm and all
The realms together under me, their Head,
In that fair Order of my Table Round,  460
A glorious company, the flower of men,
To serve as model for the mighty world,
And be the fair beginning of a time.
I made them lay their hands in mine and
    swear
To reverence the King, as if he were
Their conscience, and their conscience as
    their King,
To break the heathen and uphold the
    Christ,

To ride abroad redressing human wrongs,
To speak no slander, no, nor listen to it,
To honor his own word as if his God's,  470
To lead sweet lives in purest chastity,
To love one maiden only, cleave to her,
And worship her by years of noble deeds,
Until they won her; for indeed I knew
Of no more subtle master under heaven
Than is the maiden passion for a maid,
Not only to keep down the base in man,
But teach high thought, and amiable words
And courtliness, and the desire of fame,
And love of truth, and all that makes a
    man.                               480
And all this throve before I wedded thee,
Believing, "Lo, mine helpmate, one to feel
My purpose and rejoicing in my joy!"
Then came thy shameful sin with Lance-
    lot;
Then came the sin of Tristram and Isolt;
Then others, following these my mightiest
    knights,
And drawing foul ensample from fair
    names,
Sinn'd also, till the loathsome opposite
Of all my heart had destined did obtain,
And all thro' thee! so that this life of
    mine                               490
I guard as God's high gift from scathe and
    wrong,
Not greatly care to lose; but rather think
How sad it were for Arthur, should he
    live,
To sit once more within his lonely hall,
And miss the wonted number of my knights,
And miss to hear high talk of noble deeds
As in the golden days before thy sin.
For which of us who might be left could
    speak
Of the pure heart, nor seem to glance at
    thee?
And in thy bowers of Camelot or of Usk
Thy shadow still would glide from room to
    room,                             501
And I should evermore be vext with thee
In hanging robe or vacant ornament,
Or ghostly footfall echoing on the stair.
For think not, tho' thou wouldst not love
    thy lord,
Thy lord has wholly lost his love for thee.
I am not made of so slight elements.
Yet must I leave thee, woman, to thy
    shame.
I hold that man the worst of public foes
Who either for his own or children's sake,

To save his blood from scandal, lets the
   wife     511
Whom he knows false abide and rule the
   house:
For being thro' his cowardice allow'd
Her station, taken everywhere for pure,
She like a new disease, unknown to men,
Creeps, no precaution used, among the
   crowd,
Makes wicked lightnings of her eyes, and
   saps
The fealty of our friends, and stirs the
   pulse
With devil's leaps, and poisons half the
   young.
Worst of the worst were that man he that
   reigns !     520
Better the King's waste hearth and aching
   heart
Than thou reseated in thy place of light,
The mockery of my people and their
   bane !'

He paused, and in the pause she crept an
   inch
Nearer, and laid her hands about his feet.
Far off a solitary trumpet blew.
Then waiting by the doors the war-horse
   neigh'd
As at a friend's voice, and he spake again:

'Yet think not that I come to urge thy
   crimes;     529
I did not come to curse thee, Guinevere,
I, whose vast pity almost makes me die
To see thee, laying there thy golden head,
My pride in happier summers, at my feet.
The wrath which forced my thoughts on
   that fierce law,
The doom of treason and the flaming
   death, —
When first I learnt thee hidden here, — is
   past.
The pang — which, while I weigh'd thy
   heart with one
Too wholly true to dream untruth in thee,
Made my tears burn — is also past — in
   part.
And all is past, the sin is sinn'd, and I,   540
Lo, I forgive thee, as Eternal God
Forgives ! do thou for thine own soul the
   rest.
But how to take last leave of all I loved ?
O golden hair, with which I used to play
Not knowing ! O imperial-moulded form,

And beauty such as never woman wore,
Until it came a kingdom's curse with
   thee —
I cannot touch thy lips, they are not mine,
But Lancelot's; nay, they never were the
   King's.
I cannot take thy hand; that too is flesh,
And in the flesh thou hast sinn'd; and mine
   own flesh,     551
Here looking down on thine polluted, cries,
"I loathe thee;" yet not less, O Guinevere,
For I was ever virgin save for thee,
My love thro' flesh hath wrought into my
   life
So far that my doom is, I love thee still.
Let no man dream but that I love thee
   still.
Perchance, and so thou purify thy soul,
And so thou lean on our fair father Christ,
Hereafter in that world where all are pure
We two may meet before high God, and
   thou     561
Wilt spring to me, and claim me thine, and
   know
I am thine husband — not a smaller soul,
Nor Lancelot, nor another. Leave me that,
I charge thee, my last hope. Now must I
   hence.
Thro' the thick night I hear the trumpet
   blow.
They summon me their King to lead mine
   hosts
Far down to that great battle in the west,
Where I must strike against the man they
   call
My sister's son — no kin of mine, who
   leagues     570
With Lords of the White Horse, heathen,
   and knights,
Traitors — and strike him dead, and meet
   myself
Death, or I know not what mysterious
   doom.
And thou remaining here wilt learn the
   event;
But hither shall I never come again,
Never lie by thy side, see thee no more —
Farewell !'

          And while she grovell'd at his feet,
She felt the King's breath wander o'er her
   neck,
And in the darkness o'er her fallen head
Perceived the waving of his hands that
   blest.     580

Then, listening till those armed steps
      were gone,
Rose the pale Queen, and in her anguish
      found
The casement: 'peradventure,' so she
      thought,
' If I might see his face, and not be seen.'
And lo, he sat on horseback at the door !
And near him the sad nuns with each a
      light
Stood, and he gave them charge about the
      Queen,
To guard and foster her for evermore.
And while he spake to these his helm was
      lower'd,
To which for crest the golden dragon
      clung                                       590
Of Britain; so she did not see the face,
Which then was as an angel's, but she saw,
Wet with the mists and smitten by the
      lights,
The Dragon of the great Pendragonship
Blaze, making all the night a steam of fire.
And even then he turn'd; and more and
      more
The moony vapor rolling round the King,
Who seem'd the phantom of a giant in it,
Enwound him fold by fold, and made him
      gray
And grayer, till himself became as mist 600
Before her, moving ghostlike to his doom.

Then she stretch'd out her arms and
      cried aloud,
' O Arthur ! ' there her voice brake sud-
      denly,
Then — as a stream that spouting from a
      cliff
Fails in mid air, but gathering at the base
Re - makes itself, and flashes down the
      vale —
Went on in passionate utterance:

                              ' Gone — my lord !
Gone thro' my sin to slay and to be slain !
And he forgave me, and I could not speak.
Farewell ?   I should have answer'd his
      farewell.                                    610
His mercy choked me.   Gone, my lord the
      King,
My own true lord ! how dare I call him
      mine ?
The shadow of another cleaves to me,
And makes me one pollution. He, the King,
Call'd me polluted.   Shall I kill myself ?

What help in that ?   I cannot kill my sin,
If soul be soul, nor can I kill my shame;
No, nor by living can I live it down.
The days will grow to weeks, the weeks to
      months,
The months will add themselves and make
      the years,                                   620
The years will roll into the centuries,
And mine will ever be a name of scorn.
I must not dwell on that defeat of fame.
Let the world be; that is but of the
      world —
What else ? what hope ? I think there was
      a hope,
Except he mock'd me when he spake of
      hope;
His hope he call'd it; but he never mocks,
For mockery is the fume of little hearts.
And blessed be the King, who hath for-
      given
My wickedness to him, and left me hope 630
That in mine own heart I can live down
      sin
And be his mate hereafter in the heavens
Before high God !   Ah great and gentle
      lord,
Who wast, as is the conscience of a saint
Among his warring senses, to thy knights —
To whom my false voluptuous pride, that
      took
Full easily all impressions from below,
Would not look up, or half-despised the
      height
To which I would not or I could not
      climb —
I thought I could not breathe in that fine
      air,                                         640
That pure severity of perfect light —
I yearn'd for warmth and color which I
      found
In Lancelot — now I see thee what thou
      art,
Thou art the highest and most human too,
Not Lancelot, nor another.   Is there none
Will tell the King I love him tho' so late ?
Now — ere he goes to the great battle ?
      none !
Myself must tell him in that purer life,
But now it were too daring.   Ah my God,
What might I not have made of thy fair
      world,                                       650
Had I but loved thy highest creature
      here ?
It was my duty to have loved the highest;
It surely was my profit had I known;

It would have been my pleasure had I
    seen.
We needs must love the highest when we
    see it,
Not Lancelot, nor another.'

                   Here her hand
Grasp'd made her vail her eyes.  She look'd
    and saw
The novice, weeping, suppliant, and said to
    her,
' Yea, little maid, for am *I* not forgiven ? '
Then glancing up beheld the holy nuns  660
All round her, weeping; and her heart was
    loosed
Within her, and she wept with these and
    said:

    ' Ye know me then, that wicked one, who
    broke
The vast design and purpose of the King.
O, shut me round with narrowing nunnery-
    walls,
Meek maidens, from the voices crying,
    " Shame ! "
I must not scorn myself; he loves me still.
Let no one dream but that he loves me
    still.
So let me, if you do not shudder at me,
Nor shun to call me sister, dwell with you;
Wear black and white, and be a nun like
    you,                                   671
Fast with your fasts, not feasting with
    your feasts;
Grieve with your griefs, not grieving at
    your joys,
But not rejoicing; mingle with your rites;
Pray and be pray'd for; lie before your
    shrines;
Do each low office of your holy house;
Walk your dim cloister, and distribute
    dole
To poor sick people, richer in His eyes
Who ransom'd us, and haler too than I;
And treat their loathsome hurts and heal
    mine own;                               680
And so wear out in alms - deed and in
    prayer
The sombre close of that voluptuous day
Which wrought the ruin of my lord the
    King.'

    She said.  They took her to themselves;
    and she
Still hoping, fearing ' Is it yet too late ? '

Dwelt with them, till in time their abbess
    died.
Then she, for her good deeds and her pure
    life,
And for the power of ministration in her,
And likewise for the high rank she had
    borne,
Was chosen abbess, there, an abbess, lived
For three brief years, and there, an abbess,
    past                                    691
To where beyond these voices there is
    peace.

## THE PASSING OF ARTHUR

THAT story which the bold Sir Bedivere,
First made and latest left of all the knights,
Told, when the man was no more than a
    voice
In the white winter of his age, to those
With whom he dwelt, new faces, other
    minds.

    For on their march to westward, Bedi-
    vere,
Who slowly paced among the slumbering
    host,
Heard in his tent the moanings of the
    King:

    ' I found Him in the shining of the stars,
I mark'd Him in the flowering of His
    fields,                                  10
But in His ways with men I find Him not.
I waged His wars, and now I pass and
    die.
O me ! for why is all around us here
As if some lesser god had made the world,
But had not force to shape it as he would,
Till the High God behold it from beyond,
And enter it, and make it beautiful ?
Or else as if the world were wholly fair,
But that these eyes of men are dense and
    dim,
And have not power to see it as it is —  20
Perchance, because we see not to the
    close; —
For I, being simple, thought to work His
    will,
And have but stricken with the sword in
    vain,
And all whereon I lean'd in wife and friend
Is traitor to my peace, and all my realm
Reels back into the beast, and is no more.

My God, thou hast forgotten me in my
    death !
Nay — God my Christ — I pass but shall
    not die.'

Then, ere that last weird battle in the
    west,
There came on Arthur sleeping, Gawain
    kill'd                                    30
In Lancelot's war, the ghost of Gawain
    blown
Along a wandering wind, and past his ear
Went shrilling: 'Hollow, hollow all de-
    light !
Hail, King ! to-morrow thou shalt pass
    away.
Farewell ! there is an isle of rest for thee.
And I am blown along a wandering wind,
And hollow, hollow, hollow all delight !'
And fainter onward, like wild birds that
    change
Their season in the night and wail their
    way
From cloud to cloud, down the long wind
    the dream                                40
Shrill'd; but in going mingled with dim
    cries
Far in the moonlit haze among the hills,
As of some lonely city sack'd by night,
When all is lost, and wife and child with
    wail
Pass to new lords; and Arthur woke and
    call'd:
'Who spake ?  A dream.  O, light upon
    the wind,
Thine, Gawain, was the voice — are these
    dim cries
Thine ? or doth all that haunts the waste
    and wild
Mourn, knowing it will go along with me ?'

This heard the bold Sir Bedivere and
    spake:                                    50
'O me, my King, let pass whatever will,
Elves, and the harmless glamour of the
    field;
But in their stead thy name and glory
    cling
To all high places like a golden cloud
For ever; but as yet thou shalt not pass.
Light was Gawain in life, and light in death
Is Gawain, for the ghost is as the man;
And care not thou for dreams from him,
    but rise —
I hear the steps of Modred in the west,

And with him many of thy people, and
    knights                                  60
Once thine, whom thou hast loved, but
    grosser grown
Than heathen, spitting at their vows and
    thee.
Right well in heart they know thee for the
    King.
Arise, go forth and conquer as of old.'

Then spake King Arthur to Sir Bedivere:
'Far other is this battle in the west
Whereto we move than when we strove in
    youth,
And brake the petty kings, and fought with
    Rome,
Or thrust the heathen from the Roman
    wall,
And shook him thro' the north.  Ill doom
    is mine                                   70
To war against my people and my knights.
The king who fights his people fights him-
    self.
And they my knights, who loved me once,
    the stroke
That strikes them dead is as my death to
    me.
Yet let us hence, and find or feel a way
Thro' this blind haze which, ever since I
    saw
One lying in the dust at Almesbury,
Hath folded in the passes of the world.'

Then rose the King and moved his host
    by night,
And ever push'd Sir Modred, league by
    league,                                   80
Back to the sunset bound of Lyonnesse —
A land of old upheaven from the abyss
By fire, to sink into the abyss again;
Where fragments of forgotten peoples
    dwelt,
And the long mountains ended in a coast
Of ever-shifting sand, and far away
The phantom circle of a moaning sea.
There the pursuer could pursue no more,
And he that fled no further fly the King;
And there, that day when the great light
    of heaven                                90
Burn'd at his lowest in the rolling year,
On the waste sand by the waste sea they
    closed.
Nor ever yet had Arthur fought a fight
Like this last, dim, weird battle of the west.
A death-white mist slept over sand and sea,

Whereof the chill, to him who breathed it,
　drew
Down with his blood, till all his heart was
　cold
With formless fear; and even on Arthur
　fell
Confusion, since he saw not whom he
　fought.
For friend and foe were shadows in the
　mist,　　　　　　　　　　　　　　　100
And friend slew friend not knowing whom
　he slew;
And some had visions out of golden youth,
And some beheld the faces of old ghosts
Look in upon the battle; and in the mist
Was many a noble deed, many a base,
And chance and craft and strength in single
　fights,
And ever and anon with host to host
Shocks, and the splintering spear, the hard
　mail hewn,
Shield-breakings, and the clash of brands,
　the crash
Of battle - axes on shatter'd helms, and
　shrieks　　　　　　　　　　　　　110
After the Christ, of those who falling down
Look'd up for heaven, and only saw the
　mist;
And shouts of heathen and the traitor
　knights,
Oaths, insult, filth, and monstrous blasphe-
　mies,
Sweat, writhings, anguish, laboring of the
　lungs
In that close mist, and cryings for the
　light,
Moans of the dying, and voices of the dead.

Last, as by some one death-bed after wail
Of suffering, silence follows, or thro' death
Or death-like swoon, thus over all that
　shore,　　　　　　　　　　　　　120
Save for some whisper of the seething seas,
A dead hush fell; but when the dolorous
　day
Grew drearier toward twilight falling,
　came
A bitter wind, clear from the north, and
　blew
The mist aside, and with that wind the tide
Rose, and the pale King glanced across the
　field
Of battle. But no man was moving there;
Nor any cry of Christian heard thereon,
Nor yet of heathen; only the wan wave

Brake in among dead faces, to and fro　130
Swaying the helpless hands, and up and
　down
Tumbling the hollow helmets of the fallen,
And shiver'd brands that once had fought
　with Rome,
And rolling far along the gloomy shores
The voice of days of old and days to be.

Then spake King Arthur to Sir Bedivere,
And whiter than the mist that all day long
Had held the field of battle was the King:

'Hearest thou this great voice that
　shakes the world,
And wastes the narrow realm whereon we
　move,　　　　　　　　　　　　　140
And beats upon the faces of the dead,
My dead, as tho' they had not died for
　me ? —
O Bedivere, for on my heart hath fallen
Confusion, till I know not what I am,
Nor whence I am, nor whether I be king;
Behold, I seem but king among the dead.'

Then spake the bold Sir Bedivere: 'My
　King !
King everywhere ! and so the dead have
　kings,
There also will I worship thee as king.
Yet still thy life is whole, and still I live
Who love thee; but who hates thee, he that
　brought　　　　　　　　　　　　151
The heathen back among us, yonder stands,
Modred, unharm'd, the traitor of thine
　house.'

Then spake the King: 'My house hath
　been my doom.
But call not thou this traitor of my house
Who hath but dwelt beneath one roof with
　me.
My house are rather they who sware my
　vows,
Yea, even while they brake them, own'd
　me king.
And well for thee, saying in my dark hour,
When all the purport of my throne hath
　fail'd,　　　　　　　　　　　　　160
That quick or dead thou holdest me for
　king.
King am I, whatsoever be their cry;
And one last act of kinghood shalt thou see
Yet, ere I pass.' And uttering this the
　King

Made at the man.  Then Modred smote his
    liege
Hard on that helm which many a heathen
    sword
Had beaten thin; while Arthur at one blow,
Striking the last stroke with Excalibur,
Slew him, and, all but slain himself, he
    fell.           169

So all day long the noise of battle roll'd
Among the mountains by the winter sea,
Until King Arthur's Table, man by man,
Had fallen in Lyonnesse about their lord,
King Arthur; then, because his wound was
    deep,
The bold Sir Bedivere uplifted him,
And bore him to a chapel nigh the field,
A broken chancel with a broken cross,
That stood on a dark strait of barren land.
On one side lay the Ocean, and on one  179
Lay a great water, and the moon was full.

Then spake King Arthur to Sir Bedivere:
' The sequel of to-day unsolders all
The goodliest fellowship of famous knights
Whereof this world holds record.  Such a
    sleep
They sleep — the men I loved.  I think
    that we
Shall never more, at any future time,
Delight our souls with talk of knightly
    deeds,
Walking about the gardens and the halls
Of Camelot, as in the days that were.  189
I perish by this people which I made, —
Tho' Merlin sware that I should come
    again
To rule once more — but let what will be
    be,
I am so deeply smitten thro' the helm
That without help I cannot last till morn.
Thou therefore take my brand Excalibur,
Which was my pride; for thou remember-
    est how
In those old days, one summer noon, an
    arm
Rose up from out the bosom of the lake,
Clothed in white samite, mystic, wonder-
    ful,
Holding the sword — and how I row'd
    across       200
And took it, and have worn it, like a king;
And, wheresoever I am sung or told
In aftertime, this also shall be known.
But now delay not; take Excalibur,

And fling him far into the middle mere;
Watch what thou seest, and lightly bring
    me word.'

To him replied the bold Sir Bedivere:
' It is not meet, Sir King, to leave thee
    thus,
Aidless, alone, and smitten thro' the
    helm —
A little thing may harm a wounded man;
Yet I thy hest will all perform at full,  211
Watch what I see, and lightly bring thee
    word.'

So saying, from the ruin'd shrine he
    stept,
And in the moon athwart the place of
    tombs,
Where lay the mighty bones of ancient
    men,
Old knights, and over them the sea-wind
    sang
Shrill, chill, with flakes of foam.  He, step-
    ping down
By zigzag paths and juts of pointed rock,
Came on the shining levels of the lake.

There drew he forth the brand Excali-
    bur,      220
And o'er him, drawing it, the winter moon,
Brightening the skirts of a long cloud, ran
    forth
And sparkled keen with frost against the
    hilt;
For all the haft twinkled with diamond
    sparks,
Myriads of topaz-lights, and jacinth-work
Of subtlest jewellery.  He gazed so long
That both his eyes were dazzled as he
    stood,
This way and that dividing the swift mind,
In act to throw; but at the last it seem'd
Better to leave Excalibur conceal'd  230
There in the many-knotted water-flags,
That whistled stiff and dry about the
    marge.
So strode he back slow to the wounded
    King.

Then spake King Arthur to Sir Bedi-
    vere:
' Hast thou perform'd my mission which I
    gave ?
What is it thou hast seen ? or what hast
    heard ? '

And answer made the bold Sir Bedivere:
' I heard the ripple washing in the reeds,
And the wild water lapping on the crag.'

To whom replied King Arthur, faint and pale:                    240
' Thou hast betray'd thy nature and thy name,
Not rendering true answer, as beseem'd
Thy fealty, nor like a noble knight;
For surer sign had follow'd, either hand,
Or voice, or else a motion of the mere.
This is a shameful thing for men to lie.
Yet now, I charge thee, quickly go again,
As thou art lief and dear, and do the thing
I bade thee, watch, and lightly bring me word.'

Then went Sir Bedivere the second time
Across the ridge, and paced beside the mere,                    251
Counting the dewy pebbles, fixt in thought;
But when he saw the wonder of the hilt,
How curiously and strangely chased, he smote
His palms together, and he cried aloud:

' And if indeed I cast the brand away,
Surely a precious thing, one worthy note,
Should thus be lost for ever from the earth,
Which might have pleased the eyes of many men.
What good should follow this, if this were done ?                    260
What harm, undone ?   Deep harm to disobey,
Seeing obedience is the bond of rule.
Were it well to obey then, if a king demand
An act unprofitable, against himself ?
The King is sick, and knows not what he does.
What record or what relic of my lord
Should be to aftertime, but empty breath
And rumors of a doubt ?  But were this kept,
Stored in some treasure-house of mighty kings,
Some one might show it at a joust of arms,                    270
Saying: " King Arthur's sword, Excalibur,
Wrought by the lonely Maiden of the Lake.

Nine years she wrought it, sitting in the deeps
Upon the hidden bases of the hills."
So might some old man speak in the aftertime
To all the people, winning reverence.
But now much honor and much fame were lost.'

So spake he, clouded with his own conceit,
And hid Excalibur the second time,
And so strode back slow to the wounded King.                    280

Then spoke King Arthur, breathing heavily:
' What is it thou hast seen ? or what hast heard ?'

And answer made the bold Sir Bedivere:
' I heard the water lapping on the crag,
And the long ripple washing in the reeds.'

To whom replied King Arthur, much in wrath:
' Ah miserable, and unkind, untrue,
Unknightly, traitor-hearted !  Woe is me !
Authority forgets a dying king,
Laid widow'd of the power in his eye                    290
That bow'd the will.   I see thee what thou art,
For thou, the latest-left of all my knights,
In whom should meet the offices of all,
Thou wouldst betray me for the precious hilt;
Either from lust of gold, or like a girl
Valuing the giddy pleasure of the eyes.
Yet, for a man may fail in duty twice,
And the third time may prosper, get thee hence;
But, if thou spare to fling Excalibur,                    299
I will arise and slay thee with my hands.'

Then quickly rose Sir Bedivere, and ran,
And, leaping down the ridges lightly, plunged
Among the bulrush beds, and clutch'd the sword,
And strongly wheel'd and threw it.   The great brand
Made lightnings in the splendor of the moon,

And flashing round and round, and whirl'd
    in an arch,
Shot like a streamer of the northern morn,
Seen where the moving isles of winter
    shock
By night, with noises of the Northern
    Sea.                                    309
So flash'd and fell the brand Excalibur;
But ere he dipt the surface, rose an arm
Clothed in white samite, mystic, wonderful,
And caught him by the hilt, and bran-
    dish'd him
Three times, and drew him under in the
    mere.
And lightly went the other to the King.

    Then spoke King Arthur, drawing thicker
        breath:
' Now see I by thine eyes that this is done.
Speak out; what is it thou hast heard, or
    seen ? '

    And answer made the bold Sir Bedi-
        vere:
' Sir King, I closed mine eyelids, lest the
    gems                                    320
Should blind my purpose, for I never saw,
Nor shall see, here or elsewhere, till I die,
Not tho' I live three lives of mortal men,
So great a miracle as yonder hilt.
Then with both hands I flung him, wheel-
    ing him;
But when I look'd again, behold an arm,
Clothed in white samite, mystic, wonderful,
That caught him by the hilt, and bran-
    dish'd him
Three times, and drew him under in the
    mere.'

    And answer made King Arthur, breath-
        ing hard:                          330
' My end draws nigh; 't is time that I were
    gone.
Make broad thy shoulders to receive my
    weight,
And bear me to the margin; yet I fear
My wound hath taken cold, and I shall
    die.'

    So saying, from the pavement he half
        rose,
Slowly, with pain, reclining on his arm,
And looking wistfully with wide blue eyes
As in a picture.  Him Sir Bedivere
Remorsefully regarded thro' his tears,

And would have spoken, but he found not
    words;                                 340
Then took with care, and kneeling on one
    knee,
O'er both his shoulders drew the languid
    hands,
And rising bore him thro' the place of
    tombs.

    But, as he walk'd, King Arthur panted
        hard,
Like one that feels a nightmare on his
    bed
When all the house is mute.  So sigh'd the
    King,
Muttering and murmuring at his ear,
    ' Quick, quick !
I fear it is too late, and I shall die.'
But the other swiftly strode from ridge to
    ridge,
Clothed with his breath, and looking, as he
    walk'd,                               350
Larger than human on the frozen hills.
He heard the deep behind him, and a cry
Before.  His own thought drove him like
    a goad.
Dry clash'd his harness in the icy caves
And barren chasms, and all to left and
    right
The bare black cliff clang'd round him, as
    he based
His feet on juts of slippery crag that rang
Sharp - smitten with the dint of armed
    heels —
And on a sudden, lo, the level lake,     359
And the long glories of the winter moon !

    Then saw they how there hove a dusky
        barge,
Dark as a funeral scarf from stem to stern,
Beneath them; and descending they were
    ware
That all the decks were dense with stately
    forms,
Black-stoled, black-hooded, like a dream —
    by these
Three queens with crowns of gold — and
    from them rose
A cry that shiver'd to the tingling stars,
And, as it were one voice, an agony
Of lamentation, like a wind that shrills
All night in a waste land, where no one
    comes,                                370
Or hath come, since the making of the
    world.

Then murmur'd Arthur, 'Place me in
the barge.'
So to the barge they came. There those
three queens
Put forth their hands, and took the King,
and wept.
But she that rose the tallest of them all
And fairest laid his head upon her lap,
And loosed the shatter'd casque, and chafed
his hands,
And call'd him by his name, complaining
loud,
And dropping bitter tears against a brow
Striped with dark blood; for all his face
was white                                                  380
And colorless, and like the wither'd moon
Smote by the fresh beam of the springing
east;
And all his greaves and cuisses dash'd with
drops
Of onset; and the light and lustrous curls —
That made his forehead like a rising sun
High from the dais-throne — were parch'd
with dust,
Or, clotted into points and hanging loose,
Mixt with the knightly growth that fringed
his lips.
So like a shatter'd column lay the King;
Not like that Arthur who, with lance in
rest,                                                          390
From spur to plume a star of tournament,
Shot thro' the lists at Camelot, and charged
Before the eyes of ladies and of kings.

Then loudly cried the bold Sir Bedivere:
'Ah! my Lord Arthur, whither shall I
go?
Where shall I hide my forehead and my
eyes?
For now I see the true old times are dead,
When every morning brought a noble
chance,
And every chance brought out a noble
knight.
Such times have been not since the light
that led                                                      400
The holy Elders with the gift of myrrh.
But now the whole Round Table is dis-
solved
Which was an image of the mighty world;
And I, the last, go forth companionless,
And the days darken round me, and the
years,
Among new men, strange faces, other
minds.'

And slowly answer'd Arthur from the
barge:
'The old order changeth, yielding place to
new,
And God fulfils himself in many ways,
Lest one good custom should corrupt the
world.                                                        410
Comfort thyself; what comfort is in me?
I have lived my life, and that which I have
done
May He within himself make pure! but
thou,
If thou shouldst never see my face again,
Pray for my soul. More things are wrought
by prayer
Than this world dreams of. Wherefore,
let thy voice
Rise like a fountain for me night and
day.
For what are men better than sheep or
goats
That nourish a blind life within the brain,
If, knowing God, they lift not hands of
prayer                                                        420
Both for themselves and those who call
them friend?
For so the whole round earth is every way
Bound by gold chains about the feet of
God.
But now farewell. I am going a long way
With these thou seest — if indeed I go —
For all my mind is clouded with a doubt —
To the island-valley of Avilion;
Where falls not hail, or rain, or any snow,
Nor ever wind blows loudly; but it lies
Deep-meadow'd, happy, fair with orchard
lawns                                                         430
And bowery hollows crown'd with summer
sea,
Where I will heal me of my grievous
wound.'

So said he, and the barge with oar and
sail
Moved from the brink, like some full-
breasted swan
That, fluting a wild carol ere her death,
Ruffles her pure cold plume, and takes the
flood
With swarthy webs. Long stood Sir Bedi-
vere
Revolving many memories, till the hull
Look'd one black dot against the verge of
dawn,
And on the mere the wailing died away.   440

But when that moan had past for evermore,
The stillness of the dead world's winter
dawn
Amazed him, and he groan'd, ' The King
is gone.'
And therewithal came on him the weird
rhyme,
' From the great deep to the great deep he
goes.'

Whereat he slowly turn'd and slowly
clomb
The last hard footstep of that iron crag,
Thence mark'd the black hull moving yet,
and cried:
' He passes to be king among the dead,    449
And after healing of his grievous wound
He comes again; but — if he come no
more —
O me, be yon dark queens in yon black boat,
Who shriek'd and wail'd, the three whereat
we gazed
On that high day, when, clothed with living
light,
They stood before his throne in silence,
friends
Of Arthur, who should help him at his
need ? '

Then from the dawn it seem'd there
came, but faint
As from beyond the limit of the world,
Like the last echo born of a great cry,
Sounds, as if some fair city were one voice
Around a king returning from his wars.    461

Thereat once more he moved about, and
clomb
Even to the highest he could climb, and saw,
Straining his eyes beneath an arch of hand,
Or thought he saw, the speck that bare the
King,
Down that long water opening on the deep
Somewhere far off, pass on and on, and go
From less to less and vanish into light.
And the new sun rose bringing the new
year.

## TO THE QUEEN

O LOYAL to the royal in thyself,
And loyal to thy land, as this to thee —
Bear witness, that rememberable day,

When, pale as yet and fever-worn, the
Prince
Who scarce had pluck'd his flickering life
again
From halfway down the shadow of the
grave
Past with thee thro' thy people and their
love,
And London roll'd one tide of joy thro'
all
Her trebled millions, and loud leagues of
man
And welcome ! witness, too, the silent cry,
The prayer of many a race and creed, and
clime —    11
Thunderless lightnings striking under sea
From sunset and sunrise of all thy realm,
And that true North, whereof we lately
heard
A strain to shame us, ' Keep you to your-
selves;
So loyal is too costly ! friends — your love
Is but a burthen; loose the bond, and go.'
Is this the tone of empire ? here the faith
That made us rulers ?  this, indeed, her
voice
And meaning whom the roar of Hougou-
mont    20
Left mightiest of all peoples under heaven ?
What shock has fool'd her since, that she
should speak
So feebly ? wealthier — wealthier — hour
by hour !
The voice of Britain, or a sinking land,
Some third-rate isle half-lost among her
seas ?
*There* rang her voice, when the full city
peal'd
Thee and thy Prince !  The loyal to their
crown
Are loyal to their own far sons, who love
Our ocean-empire with her boundless homes
For ever - broadening England, and her
throne    30
In our vast Orient, and one isle, one isle,
That knows not her own greatness; if she
knows
And dreads it we are fallen. — But thou,
my Queen,
Not for itself, but thro' thy living love
For one to whom I made it o'er his grave
Sacred, accept this old imperfect tale,
New-old, and shadowing Sense at war with
Soul,
Ideal manhood closed in real man,

Rather than that gray king whose name, a
    ghost,
Streams like a cloud, man-shaped, from
    mountain peak,                                    40
And cleaves to cairn and cromlech still; or
    him
Of Geoffrey's book, or him of Malleor's,
    one
Touch'd by the adulterous finger of a time
That hover'd between war and wantonness,
And crownings and dethronements. Take
    withal
Thy poet's blessing, and his trust that
    Heaven
Will blow the tempest in the distance back
From thine and ours; for some are scared,
    who mark,
Or wisely or unwisely, signs of storm,
Waverings of every vane with every wind,
And wordy trucklings to the transient
    hour,                                             51
And fierce or careless looseners of the
    faith,

And Softness breeding scorn of simple life,
Or Cowardice, the child of lust for gold,
Or Labor, with a groan and not a voice,
Or Art with poisonous honey stolen from
    France,
And that which knows, but careful for it-
    self,
And that which knows not, ruling that
    which knows
To its own harm. The goal of this great
    world
Lies beyond sight; yet — if our slowly-
    grown                                             60
And crown'd Republic's crowning common-
    sense,
That saved her many times, not fail —
    their fears
Are morning shadows huger than the
    shapes
That cast them, not those gloomier which
    forego
The darkness of that battle in the west
Where all of high and holy dies away.

# BALLADS

## AND OTHER POEMS

The volume with this title appeared in 1880, and contained the poems that follow, as far as the lines ' To Dante ' inclusive. It was dedicated to the eldest son (Alfred Browning Stanley Tennyson, born in 1878) of Lionel Tennyson, the second son of the poet.

Mr. Stedman (' Victorian Poets,' revised ed., 1887, p. 419 fol.) pays a fitting tribute to the ' Ballads ' when, after commenting with qualified praise on the dramas, he goes on to say : ' In striking contrast, Tennyson's recent lyrical poetry is the afterglow of a still radiant genius. Here we see undimmed the fire and beauty of his natural gift, and wisdom increased with age. What a collection, short as it is, forms the volume of " Ballads " issued in his seventy-first year ! It opens with the thoroughly English story of " The First Quarrel," with its tragic culmination, — " And the boat went down that night, — the boat went down that night ! " Country life is what he has observed, and he reflects it with truth of action and dialect. " The Northern Cobbler " and " The Village Wife " could be written only by the idyllist whose Yorkshire ballads delighted us in 1866. But here are greater things, two or three at his highest mark. The passion and lyrical might of " Rizpah " never have been exceeded by the author, nor, I think, by any other poet of his day. " The Revenge " and " Lucknow " are magnificent ballads. . . . " The Voyage of Maeldune " is a weird and vocal fantasy, unequally poetic, with the well-known touch in every number.'

## TO ALFRED TENNYSON

### MY GRANDSON

GOLDEN-HAIR'D Ally whose name is one
    with mine,
Crazy with laughter and babble and earth's
    new wine,
Now that the flower of a year and a half is
    thine,

O little blossom, O mine, and mine of
    mine,
Glorious poet who never hast written a
    line,
Laugh, for the name at the head of my
    verse is thine.
Mayst thou never be wrong'd by the name
    that is mine !

## THE FIRST QUARREL

### (IN THE ISLE OF WIGHT)

This poem, founded on fact ('Memoir,' vol. ii. p. 249), was first published in the 'Ballads,' 1880; as were the poems that follow, unless otherwise stated in the prefatory notes.

### I

'WAIT a little,' you say, 'you are sure it 'll
    all come right,'
But the boy was born i' trouble, an' looks
    so wan an' so white;
Wait! an' once I ha' waited — I had n't
    to wait for long.
Now I wait, wait, wait for Harry. — No,
    no, you are doing me wrong!
Harry and I were married; the boy can
    hold up his head,
The boy was born in wedlock, but after my
    man was dead;
I ha' work'd for him fifteen years, an' I
    work an' I wait to the end.
I am all alone in the world, an' you are my
    only friend.

### II

Doctor, if you can wait, I 'll tell you the
    tale o' my life.
When Harry an' I were children, he call'd
    me his own little wife;    10
I was happy when I was with him, an' sorry
    when he was away,
An' when we play'd together, I loved him
    better than play;
He workt me the daisy chain — he made
    me the cowslip ball,
He fought the boys that were rude, an' I
    loved him better than all.
Passionate girl tho' I was, an' often at
    home in disgrace,
I never could quarrel with Harry — I had
    but to look in his face.

### III

There was a farmer in Dorset of Harry's
    kin, that had need
Of a good stout lad at his farm; he sent,
    an' the father agreed;
So Harry was bound to the Dorsetshire
    farm for years an' for years;
I walk'd with him down to the quay, poor
    lad, an' we parted in tears.    20

The boat was beginning to move, we heard
    them a-ringing the bell,
'I 'll never love any but you, God bless you,
    my own little Nell.'

### IV

I was a child, an' he was a child, an' he
    came to harm;
There was a girl, a hussy, that workt with
    him up at the farm,
One had deceived her an' left her alone
    with her sin an' her shame,
And so she was wicked with Harry; the
    girl was the most to blame.

### V

And years wént over till I that was little
    had grown so tall
The men would say of the maids, 'Our
    Nelly 's the flower of 'em all.'
I did n't take heed o' them, but I taught
    myself all I could
To make a good wife for Harry, when
    Harry came home for good.    30

### VI

Often I seem'd unhappy, and often as happy
    too,
For I heard it abroad in the fields, 'I 'll
    never love any but you;'
'I 'll never love any but you,' the morning
    song of the lark;
'I 'll never love any but you,' the nightin-
    gale's hymn in the dark.

### VII

And Harry came home at last, but he
    look'd at me sidelong and shy,
Vext me a bit, till he told me that so many
    years had gone by,
I had grown so handsome and tall — that I
    might ha' forgot him somehow —
For he thought — there were other lads —
    he was fear'd to look at me now.

### VIII

Hard was the frost in the field, we were
    married o' Christmas day,
Married among the red berries, an' all as
    merry as May —    40
Those were the pleasant times, my house
    an' my man were my pride,
We seem'd like ships i' the Channel a-sail-
    ing with wind an' tide.

## IX

But work was scant in the Isle, tho' he tried
    the villages round,
So Harry went over the Solent to see if
    work could be found;
An' he wrote: 'I ha' six weeks' work, little
    wife, so far as I know;
I 'll come for an hour to-morrow, an' kiss
    you before I go.'

## X

So I set to righting the house, for was n't
    he coming that day?
An' I hit on an old deal-box that was
    push'd in a corner away,
It was full of old odds an' ends, an' a letter
    along wi' the rest,
I had better ha' put my naked hand in a
    hornets' nest.     50

## XI

'Sweetheart,' — this was the letter — this
    was the letter I read —
'You promised to find me work near you,
    an' I wish I was dead —
Did n't you kiss me an' promise? you
    have n't done it, my lad,
An' I almost died o' your going away, an' I
    wish that I had.'

## XII

I too wish that I had — in the pleasant
    times that had past,
Before I quarrell'd with Harry — *my* quar-
    rel — the first an' the last.

## XIII

For Harry came in, an' I flung him the
    letter that drove me wild,
An' he told it me all at once, as simple as
    any child,
'What can it matter, my lass, what I did
    wi' my single life?
I ha' been as true to you as ever a man to
    his wife;     60
An' *she* was n't one o' the worst.' 'Then,'
    I said, ' I 'm none o' the best.'
An' he smiled at me, 'Ain't you, my love?
    Come, come, little wife, let it rest!
The man is n't like the woman, no need to
    make such a stir.'
But he anger'd me all the more, an' I said,
    'You were keeping with her,

When I was a-loving you all along an'
    the same as before.'
An' he did n't speak for a while, an' he
    anger'd me more and more.
Then he patted my hand in his gentle way,
    'Let bygones be!'
'Bygones! you kept yours hush'd,' I said,
    'when you married me!
By-gones ma' be come-agains; an' *she* — in
    her shame an' her sin —
You 'll have her to nurse my child, if I die
    o' my lying in!     70
You 'll make her its second mother! I
    hate her — an' I hate you!'
Ah, Harry, my man, you had better ha'
    beaten me black an' blue
Than ha' spoken as kind as you did, when
    I were so crazy wi' spite,
'Wait a little, my lass, I am sure it 'ill all
    come right.'

## XIV

An' he took three turns in the rain, an' I
    watch'd him, an' when he came in
I felt that my heart was hard; he was all
    wet thro' to the skin,
An' I never said, 'off wi' the wet,' I never
    said, 'on wi' the dry,'
So I knew my heart was hard, when he
    came to bid me good-bye.
'You said that you hated me, Ellen, but
    that is n't true, you know;
I am going to leave you a bit — you 'll kiss
    me before I go?'     80

## XV

'Going! you 're going to her — kiss her —
    if you will,' I said —
I was near my time wi' the boy, I must ha'
    been light i' my head —
'I had sooner be cursed than kiss'd!' — I
    did n't know well what I meant,
But I turn'd my face from *him*, an' he
    turn'd *his* face an' he went.

## XVI

And then he sent me a letter, 'I 've gotten
    my work to do;
You would n't kiss me, my lass, an' I never
    loved any but you;
I am sorry for all the quarrel an' sorry for
    what she wrote,
I ha' six weeks' work in Jersey an' go to-
    night by the boat.'

## XVII

An' the wind began to rise, an' I thought
    of him out at sea,
An' I felt I had been to blame; he was al-
    ways kind to me.                              90
'Wait a little, my lass, I am sure it 'ill all
    come right' —
An' the boat went down that night — the
    boat went down that night.


## RIZPAH

### 17—

Founded on an incident related in a penny
magazine called 'Old Brighton.' See the
'Memoir' (vol. ii. pp. 249–251) for interesting
particulars.  For the suggestion of the title of
the poem, see 2 Samuel, xxi. 1–14.

### I

WAILING, wailing, wailing, the wind over
    land and sea —
And Willy's voice in the wind, 'O mother,
    come out to me!'
Why should he call me to-night, when he
    knows that I cannot go?
For the downs are as bright as day, and the
    full moon stares at the snow.

### II

We should be seen, my dear; they would
    spy us out of the town.
The loud black nights for us, and the storm
    rushing over the down,
When I cannot see my own hand, but am
    led by the creak of the chain,
And grovel and grope for my son till I find
    myself drenched with the rain.

### III

Anything fallen again?  nay — what was
    there left to fall?
I have taken them home, I have number'd
    the bones, I have hidden them all.   10
What am I saying?  and what are *you?*
    do you come as a spy?
Falls?  what falls?  who knows?   As the
    tree falls so must it lie.

### IV

Who let her in?  how long has she been?
    you — what have you heard?
Why did you sit so quiet?  you never have
    spoken a word.

O — to pray with me — yes — a lady —
    none of their spies —
But the night has crept into my heart, and
    begun to darken my eyes.

### V

Ah — you, that have lived so soft, what
    should *you* know of the night,
The blast and the burning shame and the
    bitter frost and the fright?
I have done it, while you were asleep —
    you were only made for the day.
I have gather'd my baby together — and
    now you may go your way.            20

### VI

Nay — for it 's kind of you, madam, to sit
    by an old dying wife.
But say nothing hard of my boy, I have
    only an hour of life.
I kiss'd my boy in the prison, before he
    went out to die.
'They dared me to do it,' he said, and he
    never has told me a lie.
I whipt him for robbing an orchard once
    when he was but a child —
'The farmer dared me to do it,' he said; he
    was always so wild —
And idle — and  could n't  be  idle — my
    Willy — he never could rest.
The King should have made him a soldier,
    he would have been one of his best.

### VII

But he lived with a lot of wild mates, and
    they never would let him be good;
They swore that he dare not rob the mail,
    and he swore that he would;       30
And he took no life, but he took one purse,
    and when all was done
He flung it among his fellows — 'I 'll none
    of it,' said my son.

### VIII

I came into court to the judge and the
    lawyers.   I told them my tale,
God's own truth — but they kill'd him, they
    kill'd him for robbing the mail.
They hang'd him in chains for a show — we
    had always borne a good name —
To be hang'd for a thief — and then put
    away — is n't that enough shame?
Dust to dust — low down — let us hide!
    but they set him so high

That all the ships of the world could stare
at him, passing by.
God 'ill pardon the hell-black raven and
horrible fowls of the air,
But not the black heart of the lawyer who
kill'd him and hang'd him there.   40

### IX

And the jailer forced me away.  I had bid
him my last good-bye;
They had fasten'd the door of his cell.  ' O
mother !' I heard him cry.
I could n't get back tho' I tried, he had
something further to say,
And now I never shall know it.  The jailer
forced me away.

### X

Then since I could n't but hear that cry of
my boy that was dead,
They seized me and shut me up: they fasten'd me down on my bed.
'Mother, O mother !' — he call'd in the
dark to me year after year —
They beat me for that, they beat me —
you know that I could n't but hear;
And then at the last they found I had
grown so stupid and still
They let me abroad again — but the creatures had worked their will.   50

### XI

Flesh of my flesh was gone, but bone of
my bone was left —
I stole them all from the lawyers — and
you, will you call it a theft ? —
My baby, the bones that had suck'd me,
the bones that had laughed and had
cried —
Theirs ?  O, no ! they are mine — not theirs
— they had moved in my side.

### XII

Do you think I was scared by the bones ?
I kiss'd 'em, I buried 'em all —
I can't dig deep, I am old — in the night
by the churchyard wall.
My Willy 'ill rise up whole when the trum-
pet of judgment 'ill sound,
But I charge you never to say that I laid
him in holy ground.

### XIII

They would scratch him up — they would
hang him again on the cursed tree.

Sin ?  O, yes, we are sinners, I know — let
all that be,   60
And read me a Bible verse of the Lord's
goodwill toward men —
' Full of compassion and mercy, the Lord '
— let me hear it again;
' Full of compassion and mercy — long-suffering.'  Yes, O, yes !
For the lawyer is born but to murder —
the Saviour lives but to bless.
*He* 'll never put on the black cap except
for the worst of the worst,
And the first may be last — I have heard
it in church — and the last may be
first.
Suffering — O, long-suffering — yes, as the
Lord must know,
Year after year in the mist and the wind
and the shower and the snow.

### XIV

Heard, have you ? what ? they have told
you he never repented his sin.
How do they know it ? are *they* his mother ?
are *you* of his kin ?   70
Heard ! have you ever heard, when the
storm on the downs began,
The wind that 'ill wail like a child and the
sea that 'ill moan like a man ?

### XV

Election, Election, and Reprobation — it 's
all very well.
But I go to-night to my boy, and I shall
not find him in hell.
For I cared so much for my boy that the
Lord has look'd into my care,
And He means me I 'm sure to be happy
with Willy, I know not where.

### XVI

And if *he* be lost — but to save *my* soul,
that is all your desire —
Do you think that I care for *my* soul if my
boy be gone to the fire ?
I have been with God in the dark — go, go,
you may leave me alone —
You never have borne a child — you are
just as hard as a stone.   80

### XVII

Madam, I beg your pardon !  I think that
you mean to be kind,
But I cannot hear what you say for my
Willy's voice in the wind —

The snow and the sky so bright — he used
    but to call in the dark,
And he calls to me now from the church
    and not from the gibbet — for hark !
Nay — you can hear it yourself — it is
    coming — shaking the walls —
Willy — the moon's in a cloud —— Good-
    night. I am going. He calls.


## THE NORTHERN COBBLER

Founded on a fact which the poet heard in
early youth. The footnotes are his own.

### I

Waäit till our Sally cooms in, fur thou
    mun a' sights [1] to tell.
Eh, but I be maäin glad to seeä tha sa 'arty
    an' well.
'Cast awaäy on a disolut land wi' a vartical
    soon [2] !'
Strange fur to goä fur to think what saäilors
    a' seëan an' a' doon;
'Summat to drink — sa 'ot ?' I 'a nowt
    but Adam's wine:
What 's the 'eät o' this little 'ill-side to the
    'eät o' the line ?

### II

'What 's i' tha bottle a-stanning theer ?'
    I 'll tell tha. Gin.
But if thou wants thy grog, tha mun goä
    fur it down to the inn.
Naäy — fur I be maäin-glad, but thaw tha
    was iver sa dry,
Thou gits naw gin fro' the bottle theer, an'
    I 'll tell tha why.          10

### III

Meä an' thy sister was married, when wur
    it ? back-end o' June,
Ten year sin', and wa 'greed as well as a
    fiddle i' tune.
I could fettle and clump owd booöts and
    shoes wi' the best on 'em all,

[1] The vowels *aï*, pronounced separately
though in the closest conjunction, best render
the sound of the long *i* and *y* in this dialect.
But since such words as *craïin'*, *daïin'*, *whaï*,
*aï* (I), etc., look awkward except in a page of
express phonetics, I have thought it better to
leave the simple *i* and *y*, and to trust that my
readers will give them the broader pronunciation.
[2] The *oo* short, as in ' wood.'

As fer as fro' Thursby thurn hup to
    Harmsby and Hutterby Hall.
We was busy as beeäs i' the bloom an' as
    'appy as 'art could think,
An' then the babby wur burn, and then I
    taäkes to the drink.

### IV

An' I weänt gaäinsaäy it, my lad, thaw I
    be hafe shaämed on it now,
We could sing a good song at the Plow, we
    could sing a good song at the Plow;
Thaw once of a frosty night I slither'd an'
    hurted my huck,[1]
An' I coom'd neck-an-crop soomtimes slaäpe
    down i' the squad an' the muck:          20
An' once I fowt wi' the taäilor — not hafe
    ov a man, my lad —
Fur he scrawm'd an' scratted my faäce like
    a cat, an' it maäde 'er sa mad
That Sally she turn'd a tongue-banger,[2] an'
    raäted ma, ' Sottin' thy braäins
Guzzlin' an' soäkin' an' smoäkin' an' hawm-
    in' [3] about i' the laänes,
Soä sow-droonk that tha doesn not touch
    thy 'at to the Squire;'
An' I looök'd cock-eyed at my noäse an' I
    seeäd 'im a-gittin' o' fire;
But sin' I wur hallus i' liquor an' hallus as
    droonk as a king,
Foälks' coostom flitted awaäy like a kite
    wi' a brokken string.

### V

An' Sally she wesh'd foälks' cloäths to keep
    the wolf fro' the door,
Eh, but the moor she riled me, she druv
    me to drink the moor,          30
Fur I fun', when 'er back wur turn'd,
    wheer Sally's owd stockin' wur 'id,
An' I grabb'd the munny she maäde, and I
    weär'd it o' liquor, I did.

### VI

An' one night I cooms 'oäm like a bull
    gotten loose at a faäir,
An' she wur a-waäitin' fo'mma, an' cryin'
    and teärin' 'er aäir,
An' I tummled athurt the craädle an'
    sweär'd as I 'd breäk ivry stick
O' furnitur 'ere i' the 'ouse, an' I gied our
    Sally a kick,

[1] Hip.                    [2] Scold.
[3] Lounging.

An' I mash'd the taäbles an' chairs, an' she
    an' the babby beäl'd,[1]
Fur I knaw'd naw moor what I did nor a
    mortal beäst o' the feäld.

## VII

An' when I waäked i' the murnin' I seeäd
    that our Sally went laämed
Cos' o' the kick as I gied 'er, an' I wur
    dreädful ashaämed;                        40
An' Sally wur sloomy [2] an' draggle-taäil'd
    in an owd turn gown,
An' the babby's faäce wurn't wesh'd, an'
    the 'ole 'ouse hupside down.

## VIII

An' then I minded our Sally sa pratty an'
    neät an' sweeät,
Straät as a pole an' cleän as a flower fro'
    'eäd to feeät:
An' then I minded the fust kiss I gied 'er
    by Thursby thurn;
Theer wur a lark a-singin' 'is best of a
    Sunday at murn,
Could n't see 'im, we 'eärd 'im a-mountin'
    oop 'igher an' 'igher,
An' the... 'e turn'd to the sun, an' 'e shined
    like a sparkle o' fire.
'Does n't tha see 'im?' she axes, 'fur I can
    see 'im;' an' I
Seeäd nobbut the smile o' the sun as danced
    in 'er pratty blue eye;                   50
An' I says, 'I mun gie tha a kiss,' an'
    Sally says, 'Noä, thou moänt,'
But I gied 'er a kiss, an' then anoother, an'
    Sally says, 'doänt!'

## IX

An' when we coom'd into meeätin', at fust
    she wur all in a tew,
But, arter, we sing'd the 'ymn togither like
    birds on a beugh;
An' Muggins 'e preäch'd o' hell-fire an' the
    loov o' God fur men,
An' then upo' coomin' awaäy Sally gied me
    a kiss ov 'ersen.

## X

Heer wur a fall fro' a kiss to a kick like
    Saätan as fell
Down out o' heaven i' hell - fire — thaw
    theer 's naw drinkin' i' hell;

[1] Bellowed, cried out.
[2] Sluggish, out of spirits.

Meä fur to kick our Sally as kep the wolf
    fro' the door,
All along o' the drink, fur I loov'd 'er as
    well as afoor.                            60

## XI

Sa like a graät num-cumpus I blubber'd
    awaäy o' the bed —
'Weänt niver do it naw moor;' an' Sally
    looökt up an' she said,
'I 'll upowd it [1] tha weänt; thou 'rt like the
    rest o' the men,
Thou 'll goä sniffin' about the tap till tha
    does it ageän.
Theer 's thy hennemy, man, an' I knaws,
    as knaws tha sa well,
That, if tha seeäs 'im an' smells 'im tha 'll
    foller 'im slick into hell.'

## XII

'Naäy,' says I, 'fur I weänt goä sniffin'
    about the tap.'
'Weänt tha?' she says, an' mysen I thowt
    i' mysen 'mayhap.'
'Noä:' an' I started awaäy like a shot, an'
    down to the hinn,
An' I browt what tha seeäs stannin' theer,
    yon big black bottle o' gin.              70

## XIII

'That caps owt,'[2] says Sally, an' saw she
    begins to cry,
But I puts it inter 'er 'ands an' I says to
    'er, 'Sally,' says I,
'Stan' 'im theer i' the naäme o' the Lord
    an' the power ov 'is graäce,
Stan' 'im theer, fur I 'll looök my hennemy
    straäit i' the faäce,
Stan' 'im theer i' the winder, an' let ma
    looök at 'im then,
'E seeäms naw moor nor watter, an' 'e 's the
    divil's oän sen.'

## XIV

An' I wur down i' tha mouth, could n't do
    naw work an' all,
Nasty an' snaggy an' shaäky, an' poonch'd
    my 'and wi' the hawl,
But she wur a power o' coomfut, an' sat-
    tled 'ersen o' my knee,
An' coäxd an' coodled me oop till ageän I
    feel'd mysen free.                        80

[1] I 'll uphold it.
[2] That 's beyond everything.

### XV

An' Sally she tell'd it about, an' foälk stood
    a-gawmin' [1] in,
As thaw it wur summat bewitch'd istead
    of a quart o' gin;
An' some on 'em said it wur watter — an'
    I wur chousin' the wife,
Fur I could n't 'owd 'ands off gin, wur it
    nobbut to saäve my life;
An' blacksmith 'e strips me the thick ov 'is
    airm, an' 'e shaws it to me,
'Feëal thou this! thou can't graw this upo'
    watter!' says he.
An' Doctor 'e calls o' Sunday an' just as
    candles was lit,
'Thou moänt do it,' he says, 'tha mun
    breäk 'im off bit by bit.'
'Thou 'rt but a Methody-man,' says Par-
    son, and laäys down 'is 'at,
An' 'e points to the bottle o' gin, 'but I re-
    specks tha fur that;'     90
An Squire, his oän very sen, walks down
    fro' the 'All to see,
An' 'e spanks 'is 'and into mine, 'fur I re-
    specks tha,' says 'e;
An' coostom ageän draw'd in like a wind
    fro' far an' wide,
And browt me the booöts to be cobbled fro'
    hafe the coontryside.

### XVI

An' theer 'e stans an' theer 'e shall stan' to
    my dying daäy;
I 'a gotten to loov 'im ageän in anoother
    kind of a waäy,
Proud on 'im, like, my lad, an' I keeäps
    'im cleän an' bright,
Loovs 'im, an' roobs 'im, an' doosts 'im, an'
    puts 'im back i' the light.

### XVII

Would n't a pint a' sarved as well as a
    quart? Naw doubt;
But I liked a bigger feller to fight wi' an'
    fowt it out.     100
Fine an' meller 'e mun be by this, if I cared
    to taäste,
But I moänt, my lad, and I weänt, fur I 'd
    feäl mysen cleän disgraäced.

### XVIII

An' once I said to the Missis, 'My lass,
    when I cooms to die,

[1] Staring vacantly.

Smash the bottle to smithers, the divil's
    in 'im,' said I.
But arter I chaänged my mind, an' if Sally
    be left aloän,
I 'll hev 'im a-buried wi'mma an' taäke 'im
    afoor the Throän.

### XIX

Coom thou 'eer — yon laädy a-steppin'
    along the streeät,
Does n't tha knaw 'er — sa pratty, an' feät,
    an' neät, an' sweeät?
Look at the cloäths on 'er back, thebbe
    ammost spick-span-new,
An' Tommy's faäce be as fresh as a codlin
    wesh'd i' the dew.     110

### XX

'Ere be our Sally an' Tommy, an' we be
    a-goin to dine,
Baäcon an' taätes, an' a beslings-puddin' [1]
    an' Adam's wine;
But if tha wants ony grog tha mun goä fur
    it down to the Hinn,
Fur I weänt shed a drop on 'is blood, noä,
    not fur Sally's oän kin.

## THE REVENGE

### A BALLAD OF THE FLEET

First published in 'The Nineteenth Century'
for March, 1878, with the title, 'Sir Richard
Grenville, a Ballad of the Fleet;' afterwards
included in the 'Ballads,' 1880, with the present title.

According to Sir Walter Raleigh, who wrote
a 'Report of the truth of the fight about the
Iles of Açores this last Sommer,' the engagement began at 3 P. M. on the 31st of August,
Old Style, or the 10th of September, New
Style, in the year 1591. Gervase Markham,
who commemorated the event in a poem entitled 'The Most Honorable Tragedie of Sir
Richard Grinuile, Knight' (1595), gives the
main facts in his 'Argument,' or introduction,
as follows: —

'Sir Richard *Grinuile*, lying at anchor neere
vnto *Flores*, one of the westerlie Ilands of the
*Azores*, the last of August in the after noone,
had intelligence by one Captayne *Midleton* of
the aproch of the Spanish *Armada*, beeing in
number fiftie three saile of great ships, and
fifteene thousand men to man them. Sir *Rich-*

[1] A pudding made with the first milk of the
cow after calving.

*ard*, staying to recouer his men which were vpon the Iland, and disdayning to flie from his Countries enemy, not beeing able to recouer the winde, was instantlie inuironed with that hudge Nauie, betweene whom began a dreadfull fight, continuing the space of fifteene howers, in which conflict, Sir *Richard* sunck the great *San Phillip* of *Spaine*, the *Ascention* of *Siuel*, the Admirall of the *Hulks*, and two other great *Armados;* about midnight Sir *Richard* receiued a wound through the bodie, and as he was dressing, was shot againe into the head, and his Surgion slaine. Sir *Richard* mayntained the fight, till he had not one corne of powder left, nor one whole pike, nor fortie lyuing men ; which seeing, hee would haue sunke his owne ship, but that was gaine-stood by the Maister thereof, who contrarie to his will came to composition with the *Spanyards*, and so saued those which were left aliue. Sir *Richard* dyed aboard the Admyrall of *Spayne*, about the fourth day after the battaile, and was mightlie bewaild of all men.'

A Dutch writer, Jan Huygen van Linschoten, whose book was translated into English in 1598, gives the following account of Sir Richard's death : —

' All the rest of the Captaines and Gentlemen went to visite hym, and to comfort him in his hard fortune, wondring at his courage, and stout hart, for that he shewed not any signe of faintnes nor changing of colour. But feeling the hower of death to approch, hee spake these wordes in Spanish and said : Heere die I, *Richard Greenfield*, with a ioyfull and quiet mind, for that I haue ended my life as a true soldier ought to do, yat hath fought for his countrey, Queene, religion, and honor, whereby my soule most ioyfull departeth out of this bodie, and shall alwaies leaue behinde it an euerlasting fame of a valiant and true soldier that hath done his dutie, as he was bound to doe. When he had finished these or such other like words, hee gaue vp the ghost, with great and stout courage, and no man could perceiue any true signe of heauinesse in him.'

### I

At Flores in the Azores Sir Richard Grenville lay,
And a pinnace, like a flutter'd bird, came flying from far away:
' Spanish ships of war at sea ! we have sighted fifty-three ! '
Then sware Lord Thomas Howard: ' 'Fore God I am no coward;
But I cannot meet them here, for my ships are out of gear,

And the half my men are sick.  I must fly, but follow quick.
We are six ships of the line; can we fight with fifty-three ? '

### II

Then spake Sir Richard Grenville: ' I know you are no coward;
You fly them for a moment to fight with them again.
But I 've ninety men and more that are lying sick ashore.                          10
I should count myself the coward if I left them, my Lord Howard,
To these Inquisition dogs and the devildoms of Spain.'

### III

So Lord Howard past away with five ships of war that day,
Till he melted like a cloud in the silent summer heaven;
But Sir Richard bore in hand all his sick men from the land
Very carefully and slow,
Men of Bideford in Devon,
And we laid them on the ballast down below;
For we brought them all aboard,
And they blest him in their pain, that they were not left to Spain,           20
To the thumb-screw and the stake, for the glory of the Lord.

### IV

He had only a hundred seamen to work the ship and to fight,
And he sailed away from Flores till the Spaniard came in sight,
With his huge sea-castles heaving upon the weather bow.
' Shall we fight or shall we fly ?
Good Sir Richard, tell us now,
For to fight is but to die !
There 'll be little of us left by the time this sun be set.'
And Sir Richard said again: ' We be all good English men.
Let us bang these dogs of Seville, the children of the devil,                 30
For I never turn'd my back upon Don or devil yet.'

### V

Sir Richard spoke and he laugh'd, and we
    roar'd a hurrah, and so
The little Revenge ran on sheer into the
    heart of the foe,
With her hundred fighters on deck, and her
    ninety sick below;
For half of their fleet to the right and half
    to the left were seen,
And the little Revenge ran on thro' the long
    sea-lane between.

### VI

Thousands of their soldiers look'd down
    from their decks and laugh'd,
Thousands of their seamen made mock at
    the mad little craft
Running on and on, till delay'd
By their mountain-like San Philip that, of
    fifteen hundred tons,          40
And up-shadowing high above us with her
    yawning tiers of guns,
Took the breath from our sails, and we
    stay'd.

### VII

And while now the great San Philip hung
    above us like a cloud
Whence the thunderbolt will fall
Long and loud,
Four galleons drew away
From the Spanish fleet that day,
And two upon the larboard and two upon
    the starboard lay,
And the battle-thunder broke from them
    all.

### VIII

But anon the great San Philip, she be-
    thought herself and went,          50
Having that within her womb that had left
    her ill content;
And the rest they came aboard us, and they
    fought us hand to hand,
For a dozen times they came with their
    pikes and musqueteers,
And a dozen times we shook 'em off as a
    dog that shakes his ears
When he leaps from the water to the land.

### IX

And the sun went down, and the stars came
    out far over the summer sea,
But never a moment ceased the fight of the
    one and the fifty-three.

Ship after ship, the whole night long, their
    high-built galleons came,
Ship after ship, the whole night long, with
    her battle-thunder and flame;          59
Ship after ship, the whole night long, drew
    back with her dead and her shame.
For some were sunk and many were shat-
    ter'd, and so could fight us no more —
God of battles, was ever a battle like this
    in the world before ?

### X

For he said, ' Fight on ! fight on !'
Tho' his vessel was all but a wreck;
And it chanced that, when half of the short
    summer night was gone,
With a grisly wound to be drest he had
    left the deck,
But a bullet struck him that was dressing
    it suddenly dead,
And himself he was wounded again in the
    side and the head,
And he said, ' Fight on ! fight on !'

### XI

And the night went down, and the sun
    smiled out far over the summer sea,
And the Spanish fleet with broken sides lay
    round us all in a ring;          71
But they dared not touch us again, for they
    fear'd that we still could sting,
So they watch'd what the end would
    be.
And we had not fought them in vain,
But in perilous plight were we,
Seeing forty of our poor hundred were
    slain,
And half of the rest of us maim'd for
    life
In the crash of the cannonades and the
    desperate strife;
And the sick men down in the hold were
    most of them stark and cold,
And the pikes were all broken or bent, and
    the powder was all of it spent;          80
And the masts and the rigging were lying
    over the side;
But Sir Richard cried in his English pride:
' We have fought such a fight for a day
    and a night
As may never be fought again !
We have won great glory, my men !
And a day less or more
At sea or ashore,
We die — does it matter when ?

Sink me the ship, Master Gunner — sink
  her, split her in twain !
Fall into the hands of God, not into the
  hands of Spain ! '          90

## XII

And the gunner said, 'Ay, ay,' but the sea-
  men made reply:
' We have children, we have wives,
And the Lord hath spared our lives.
We will make the Spaniard promise, if we
  yield, to let us go;
We shall live to fight again and to strike
  another blow.'
And the lion there lay dying, and they
  yielded to the foe.

## XIII

And the stately Spanish men to their flag-
  ship bore him then,
Where they laid him by the mast, old Sir
  Richard caught at last,
And they praised him to his face with their
  courtly foreign grace;          99
But he rose upon their decks, and he cried:
' I have fought for Queen and Faith like
  a valiant man and true;
I have only done my duty as a man is
  bound to do.
With a joyful spirit I Sir Richard Gren-
  ville die ! '
And he fell upon their decks, and he died.

## XIV

And they stared at the dead that had been
  so valiant and true,
And had holden the power and glory of
  Spain so cheap
That he dared her with one little ship and
  his English few;
Was he devil or man ? He was devil for
  aught they knew,
But they sank his body with honor down
  into the deep,
And they mann'd the Revenge with a
  swarthier alien crew,          110
And away she sail'd with her loss and
  long'd for her own;
When a wind from the lands they had
  ruin'd awoke from sleep,
And the water began to heave and the
  weather to moan,
And or ever that evening ended a great
  gale blew,

And a wave like the wave that is raised by
  an earthquake grew,
Till it smote on their hulls and their sails
  and their masts and their flags,
And the whole sea plunged and fell on the
  shot-shatter'd navy of Spain,
And the little Revenge herself went down
  by the island crags
To be lost evermore in the main.

# THE SISTERS

According to the ' Memoir ' (vol. ii. p. 253),
the poem was ' partly founded on the story
known to him [Tennyson] of a girl who con-
sented to be bridesmaid to her sister, although
she secretly loved the bridegroom.'

THEY have left the doors ajar; and by
  their clash,
And prelude on the keys, I know the song,
Their favorite — which I call ' The Tables
  Turn'd.'
Evelyn begins it, ' O diviner Air.'

### EVELYN

O diviner Air,
Thro' the heat, the drowth, the dust, the
  glare,
Far from out the west in shadowing showers,
Over all the meadow baked and bare,
Making fresh and fair
All the bowers and the flowers,          10
Fainting flowers, faded bowers,
Over all this weary world of ours,
Breathe, diviner Air !

A sweet voice that — you scarce could better that !
Now follows Edith echoing Evelyn.

### EDITH

O diviner light,
Thro' the cloud that roofs our noon with
  night,
Thro' the blotting mist, the blinding showers,
Far from out a sky for ever bright,
Over all the woodland's flooded bowers,          20
Over all the meadow's drowning flowers,
Over all this ruin'd world of ours,
Break, diviner light !

Marvellously like, their voices — and themselves !
Tho' one is somewhat deeper than the
  other,

As one is somewhat graver than the
  other —
Edith than Evelyn.   Your good uncle,
  whom
You count the father of your fortune,
  longs
For this alliance.   Let me ask you then,
Which voice most takes you ? for I do not
  doubt,                              30
Being a watchful parent, you are taken
With one or other; tho' sometimes I fear
You may be flickering, fluttering in a
  doubt
Between the two — which must not be —
  which might
Be death to one.  They both are beautiful;
Evelyn is gayer, wittier, prettier, says
The common voice, if one may trust it,
  she ?
No ! but the paler and the graver, Edith.
Woo her and gain her then; no wavering,
  boy !
The graver is perhaps the one for you    40
Who jest and laugh so easily and so well.
For love will go by contrast, as by likes.

No sisters ever prized each other more.
Not so; their mother and her sister loved
More passionately still.
                      But that my best
And oldest friend, your uncle, wishes it,
And that I know you worthy every way
To be my son, I might, perchance, be
  loath
To part them, or part from them; and yet
  one
Should marry, or all the broad lands in
  your view                           50
From this bay-window — which our house
  has held
Three hundred years — will pass collater-
  ally.

My father with a child on either knee,
A hand upon the head of either child,
Smoothing their locks, as golden as his
  own
Were silver, 'get them wedded' would he
  say.
And once my prattling Edith ask'd him
  'why ?'
'Ay, why ?' said he, 'for why should I go
  lame ?'
Then told them of his wars, and of his
  wound.

For see — this wine — the grape from
  whence it flow'd                    60
Was blackening on the slopes of Portugal,
When that brave soldier, down the terrible
  ridge
Plunged in the last fierce charge at Water-
  loo,
And caught the laming bullet.  He left me
  this,
Which yet retains a memory of its youth,
As I of mine, and my first passion.  Come !
Here 's to your happy union with my
  child !

Yet must you change your name — no
  fault of mine !
You say that you can do it as willingly   69
As birds make ready for their bridal-time
By change of feather; for all that, my boy,
Some birds are sick and sullen when they
  moult.
An old and worthy name ! but mine that
  stirr'd
Among our civil wars and earlier too
Among the Roses, the more venerable.
*I* care not for a name — no fault of mine.
Once more — a happier marriage than my
  own !

You see yon Lombard poplar on the
  plain.
The highway running by it leaves a breadth
Of sward to left and right, where, long
  ago,                                80
One bright May morning in a world of
  song,
I lay at leisure, watching overhead
The aerial poplar wave, an amber spire.

I dozed; I woke.   An open landaulet
Whirl'd by, which, after it had past me,
  show'd
Turning my way, the loveliest face on
  earth.
The face of one there sitting opposite,
On whom I brought a strange unhappiness,
That time I did not see.

                          Love at first sight
May seem — with goodly rhyme and rea-
  son for it —                        90
Possible — at first glimpse, and for a face
Gone in a moment — strange.  Yet once,
  when first
I came on lake Llanberris in the dark,

A moonless night with storm — one light-
    ning-fork
Flash'd out the lake; and tho' I loiter'd
    there
The full day after, yet in retrospect
That less than momentary thunder-sketch
Of lake and mountain conquers all the day.

The sun himself has limn'd the face for
    me.
Not quite so quickly, no, nor half as well.
For look you here — the shadows are too
    deep,                                      101
And like the critic's blurring comment
    make
The veriest beauties of the work appear
The darkest faults; the sweet eyes frown,
    the lips
Seem but a gash.  My sole memorial
Of Edith — no, the other, — both indeed.

So that bright face was flash'd thro'
    sense and soul
And by the poplar vanish'd — to be found
Long after, as it seem'd, beneath the tall
Tree-bowers, and those long-sweeping
    beechen boughs                             110
Of our New Forest.  I was there alone.
The phantom of the whirling landaulet
For ever past me by; when one quick peal
Of laughter drew me thro' the glimmering
    glades
Down to the snowlike sparkle of a cloth
On fern and foxglove.  Lo, the face again,
My Rosalind in this Arden — Edith — all
One bloom of youth, health, beauty, happi-
    ness,
And moved to merriment at a passing jest.

There one of those about her knowing
    me                                         120
Call'd me to join them; so with these I
    spent
What seem'd my crowning hour, my day
    of days.

I woo'd her then, nor unsuccessfully,
The worse for her, for me !  Was I con-
    tent ?
Ay — no, not quite; for now and then I
    thought
Laziness, vague love-longings, the bright
    May,
Had made a heated haze to magnify
The charm of Edith — that a man's ideal

Is high in heaven, and lodged with Plato's
    God,
Not findable here — content, and not con-
    tent,                                      130
In some such fashion as a man may be
That having had the portrait of his friend
Drawn by an artist, looks at it, and says,
' Good !  very like !  not altogether he.'

As yet I had not bound myself by words,
Only, believing I loved Edith, made
Edith love me.  Then came the day when I,
Flattering myself that all my doubts were
    fools
Born of the fool this Age that doubts of
    all —                                      139
Not I that day of Edith's love or mine —
Had braced my purpose to declare my-
    self.
I stood upon the stairs of Paradise.
The golden gates would open at a word.
I spoke it — told her of my passion, seen
And lost and found again, had got so far,
Had caught her hand, her eyelids fell — I
    heard
Wheels, and a noise of welcome at the
    doors —
On a sudden after two Italian years
Had set the blossom of her health again,
The younger sister, Evelyn, enter'd —
    there,                                     150
There was the face, and altogether she.
The mother fell about the daughter's
    neck,
The sisters closed in one another's arms,
Their people throng'd about them from the
    hall,
And in the thick of question and reply
I fled the house, driven by one angel face,
And all the Furies.

                    I was bound to her;
I could not free myself in honor — bound
Not by the sounded letter of the word,   159
But counter-pressures of the yielded hand
That timorously and faintly echoed mine,
Quick blushes, the sweet dwelling of her
    eyes
Upon me when she thought I did not see —
Were these not bonds ?  nay, nay, but could
    I wed her
Loving the other ?  do her that great
    wrong ?
Had I not dream'd I loved her yester-
    morn ?

Had I not known where Love, at first a fear,
Grew after marriage to full height and
　form ?
Yet after marriage, that mock - sister
　there —
Brother-in-law — the fiery nearness of it —
Unlawful and disloyal brotherhood —　171
What end but darkness could ensue from
　this
For all the three ? So Love and Honor
　jarr'd,
Tho' Love and Honor join'd to raise the full
High-tide of doubt that sway'd me up and
　down
Advancing nor retreating.

　　　　　　　　　　　　Edith wrote:
' My mother bids me ask ' — I did not tell
　you —
A widow with less guile than many a child.
God help the wrinkled children that are
　Christ's
As well as the plump cheek — she wrought
　us harm,　　　　　　　　　　180
Poor soul, not knowing ! — ' Are you ill ? '
　— so ran
The letter — ' you have not been here of
　late.
You will not find me here. At last I go
On that long-promised visit to the North.
I told your wayside story to my mother
And Evelyn. She remembers you. Fare-
　well.
Pray come and see my mother. Almost
　blind
With ever-growing cataract, yet she thinks
She sees you when she hears. Again fare-
　well.'

　Cold words from one I had hoped to
　warm so far　　　　　　　　　190
That I could stamp my image on her
　heart !
' Pray come and see my mother, and fare-
　well.'
Cold, but as welcome as free airs of heaven
After a dungeon's closeness. Selfish,
　strange !
What dwarfs are men ! my strangled van-
　ity
Utter'd a stifled cry — to have vext myself
And all in vain for her — cold heart or
　none —
No bride for me. Yet so my path was clear
To win the sister.

　　　　　　　　　Whom I woo'd and won.
For Evelyn knew not of my former suit,
Because the simple mother work'd upon　201
By Edith pray'd me not to whisper of it.
And Edith would be bridesmaid on the day.

　But on that day, not being all at ease,
I from the altar glancing back upon her,
Before the first ' I will ' was utter'd, saw
The bridesmaid pale, statue-like, passion-
　less —
' No harm, no harm ' — I turn'd again, and
　placed
My ring upon the finger of my bride.

　So, when we parted, Edith spoke no
　word,　　　　　　　　　　210
She wept no tear, but round my Evelyn
　clung
In utter silence for so long, I thought,
' What, will she never set her sister free ? '

　We left her, happy each in each, and
　then,
As tho' the happiness of each in each
Were not enough, must fain have torrents,
　lakes,
Hills, the great things of Nature and the
　fair,
To lift us as it were from commonplace,
And help us to our joy. Better have sent
Our Edith thro' the glories of the earth,　220
To change with her horizon, if true Love
Were not his own imperial all-in-all.

　Far off we went. My God, I would not
　live
Save that I think this gross hard-seeming
　world
Is our misshaping vision of the Powers
Behind the world, that make our griefs our
　gains.

　For on the dark night of our marriage-
　day
The great tragedian, that had quench'd
　herself
In that assumption of the bridesmaid —
　she
That loved me — our true Edith — her
　brain broke　　　　　　　　230
With over-acting, till she rose and fled
Beneath a pitiless rush of autumn rain
To the deaf church — to be let in — to
　pray
Before *that* altar — so I think; and there

They found her beating the hard Protestant doors.
She died and she was buried ere we knew.

I learnt it first. I had to speak. At
    once
The bright quick smile of Evelyn, that had
    sunn'd
The morning of our marriage, past away.
And on our home-return the daily want 240
Of Edith in the house, the garden, still
Haunted us like her ghost; and by and by,
Either from that necessity for talk
Which lives with blindness, or plain inno-
    cence
Of nature, or desire that her lost child
Should earn from both the praise of hero-
    ism,
The mother broke her promise to the dead,
And told the living daughter with what
    love
Edith had welcomed my brief wooing of
    her,                                   249
And all her sweet self-sacrifice and death.

Henceforth that mystic bond betwixt the
    twins —
Did I not tell you they were twins? — pre-
    vail'd
So far that no caress could win my wife
Back to that passionate answer of full
    heart
I had from her at first. Not that her
    love,
Tho' scarce as great as Edith's power of
    love,
Had lessen'd, but the mother's garrulous
    wail
For ever woke the unhappy Past again,
Till that dead bridesmaid, meant to be my
    bride,
Put forth cold hands between us, and I
    fear'd                                 260
The very fountains of her life were chill'd;
So took her thence, and brought her here,
    and here
She bore a child, whom reverently we
    call'd
Edith; and in the second year was born
A second — this I named from her own
    self,
Evelyn; then two weeks — no more — she
    join'd,
In and beyond the grave, that one she
    loved.

Now in this quiet of declining life,
Thro' dreams by night and trances of the
    day,                                   269
The sisters glide about me hand in hand,
Both beautiful alike, nor can I tell
One from the other, no, nor care to tell
One from the other, only know they come,
They smile upon me, till, remembering all
The love they both have borne me, and the
    love
I bore them both — divided as I am
From either by the stillness of the grave —
I know not which of these I love the best.

But *you* love Edith; and her own true
    eyes                                   279
Are traitors to her; our quick Evelyn —
The merrier, prettier, wittier, as they talk,
And not without good reason, my good
    son —
Is yet untouch'd. And I that hold them
    both
Dearest of all things — well, I am not
    sure —
But if there lie a preference either way,
And in the rich vocabulary of Love
' Most dearest ' be a true superlative —
I think *I* likewise love your Edith most.


## THE VILLAGE WIFE; OR, THE ENTAIL [1]

The footnotes are the poet's own.

I

'OUSE-KEEPER sent tha, my lass, fur new
    Squire coom'd last night.
Butter an' heggs — yis — yis. I 'll goä wi'
    tha back; all right;
Butter I warrants be prime, an' I warrants
    the heggs be as well,
Hafe a pint o' milk runs out when ya breäks
    the shell.

II

Sit thysen down fur a bit; hev a glass o'
    cowslip wine !
I liked the owd Squire an' 'is gells as thaw
    they was gells o' mine,
Fur then we was all es one, the Squire an'
    'is darters an' me,
Hall but Miss Annie, the heldest, I niver
    not took to she.

[1] See note on pronunciation, p. 456.

But Nelly, the last of the cletch,[1] I liked
    'er the fust on 'em all,
Fur hoffens we talkt o' my darter es died
    o' the fever at fall;                       10
An' I thowt 't wur the will o' the Lord,
    but Miss Annie she said it wur
    draäins,
Fur she hed n't naw coomfut in 'er, an'
    arn'd naw thanks fur 'er paäins.
Eh! thebbe all wi' the Lord, my childer, I
    han't gotten none!
Sa new Squire's coom'd wi' 'is taäil in 'is
    'and, an' owd Squire's gone.

### III

Fur 'staäte be i' taäil, my lass — tha dosn'
    knaw what that be?
But I knaws the law, I does, for the lawyer
    ha towd it me.
'When theer's naw 'eäd to a 'Ouse by
    the fault o' that ere maäle —
The gells they counts fur nowt, and the
    next un he taäkes the taäil.'

### IV

What be the next un like? can tha tell
    ony harm on 'im, lass? —
Naäy sit down — naw 'urry — sa cowd! —
    hev another glass!                          20
Straänge an' cowd fur the time! we may
    happen a fall o' snaw —
Not es I cares fur to hear ony harm, but
    I likes to knaw.
An' I oäps es 'e beänt booöklarn'd; but 'e
    dosn' not coom fro' the shere;
We'd anew o' that wi' the Squire, an' we
    haätes booöklarnin' ere.

### V

Fur Squire wur a Varsity scholard, an
    niver lookt arter the land —
Whoäts or turmuts or taätes — 'e'd hallus
    a booök i' 'is 'and,
Hallus aloän wi' 'is booöks, thaw nigh upo'
    seventy year.
An' booöks, what's booöks? thou knaws
    thebbe neyther 'ere nor theer.

### VI

An' the gells, they hed n't naw taäils, an'
    the lawyer he towd it me
That 'is taäil were soä tied up es he
    could n't cut down a tree!                   30

[1] A brood of chickens.

"Drat the trees," says I, to be sewer I
    haätes 'em, my lass,
Fur we puts the muck o' the land, an' they
    sucks the muck fro' the grass.

### VII

An' Squire wur hallus a-smilin', an' gied
    to the tramps goin' by —
An' all o' the wust i' the parish — wi' hof-
    fens a drop in 'is eye.
An' ivry darter o' Squire's hed her awn
    ridin-erse to 'ersen,
An' they rampaged about wi' their grooms,
    an' wus 'untin' arter the men,
An' hallus a-dallackt[1] an' dizen'd out, an'
    a-buyin' new cloäthes,
While 'e sit like a greät glimmer-gowk[2]
    wi' 'is glasses athurt 'is noäse,
An' 'is noäse sa grufted wi' snuff as it
    could n't be scroob'd awaäy,
Fur 'atween 'is readin' an' writin' 'e snifft
    up a box in a daäy,                          40
An' 'e niver runn'd arter the fox, nor arter
    the birds wi' 'is gun,
An' 'e niver not shot one 'are, but 'e leäved
    it to Charlie 'is son,
An 'e niver not fish'd 'is awn ponds, but
    Charlie 'e cotch'd the pike,
Fur 'e warn't not burn to the land, an' 'e
    did n't take kind to it like;
But I eärs es 'e'd gie for a howry[3] owd
    book thutty pound an' moor,
An' 'e'd wrote an' owd book, his awn sen,
    sa I knaw'd es 'e'd coom to be poor;
An' 'e gied — I be fear'd fur to tell tha 'ow
    much — fur an owd scratted stoän,
An' 'e digg'd up a loomp i' the land an' 'e
    got a brown pot an' a boän,
An' 'e bowt owd money, es would n't goä,
    wi' good gowd o' the Queen,
An' 'e bowt little statutes all-naäkt an'
    which was a shaäme to be seen;               50
But 'e niver looökt ower a bill, nor 'e niver
    not seed to owt,
An' 'e niver knawd nowt but booöks, an'
    booöks, as thou knaws, beänt nowt.

### VIII

But owd Squire's laädy es long es she lived
    she kep' 'em all clear,
Thaw es long es she lived I niver hed none
    of 'er darters 'ere;

[1] Overdrest in gay colors.
[2] Owl.
[3] Filthy.

But arter she died we was all es one, the
 childer an' me,
An' sarvints runn'd in an' out, an' offens we
 hed 'em to tea.
Lawk! 'ow I laugh'd when the lasses 'ud
 talk o' their Missis's waäys,
An' the Missisis talk'd o' the lasses. — I 'll
 tell tha some o' these daäys.
Hoänly Miss Annie were saw stuck oop,
 like 'er mother afoor —
'Er an' 'er blessed darter — they niver
 derken'd my door.    60

### IX

An' Squire 'e smiled an' 'e smiled till 'e 'd
 gotten a fright at last,
An' 'e calls fur 'is son, fur the 'turney's letters they foller'd sa fast;
But Squire wur afear'd o' 'is son, an' 'e
 says to 'im, meek as a mouse,
' Lad, thou mun cut off thy taäil, or the
 gells 'ull goä to the 'Ouse,
Fur I finds es I be that i' debt, es I 'oäps es
 thou 'll 'elp me a bit,
An' if thou 'll 'gree to cut off thy taäil I
 may saäve mysen yit.'

### X

But Charlie 'e sets back 'is ears, an' 'e
 sweärs, an' 'e says to 'im, ' Noä.
I 've gotten the 'staäte by the taäil an' be
 dang'd if I iver let goä!
Coom! coom! feyther,' 'e says, ' why
 should n't thy booöks be sowd!
I hears es soom o' thy booöks mebbe worth
 their weight i' gowd.'    70

### XI

Heäps an' heäps o' booäks, I ha' seed 'em,
 belong'd to the Squire,
But the lasses 'ed teärd out leäves i' the
 middle to kindle the fire;
Sa moäst on 'is owd big booöks fetch'd nigh
 to nowt at the saäle,
And Squire were at Charlie ageän to git
 'im to cut off 'is taäil.

### XII

Ya would n't find Charlie's likes — 'e were
 that outdacious at 'oäm,
Not thaw ya went fur to raäke out hell wi'
 a small-tooth coämb —
Droonk wi' the Quoloty's wine, an' droonk
 wi' the farmer's aäle,
Mad wi' the lasses an' all — an' 'e would n't
 cut off the taäil.

### XIII

Thou 's coom'd oop by the beck; and a
 thurn be a-grawin' theer,
I niver ha seed it sa white wi' the maäy es
 I seed it to-year —    80
Theerabouts Charlie joompt — and it gied
 me a scare tother night,
Fur I thowt it wur Charlie's ghoäst i' the
 derk, fur it looökt sa white.
' Billy,' says 'e, ' hev a joomp!' — thaw the
 banks o' the beck be sa high,
Fur he ca'd 'is 'erse Billy-rough-un, thaw
 niver a hair wur awry;
But Billy fell bakkuds o' Charlie, an'
 Charlie 'e brok 'is neck,
Sa theer wur a hend o' the taäil, fur 'e lost
 'is taäil i' the beck.

### XIV

Sa 'is taäil wur lost an' 'is booöks wur gone
 an' 'is boy wur deäd,
An' Squire 'e smiled an' 'e smiled, but 'e
 niver not lift oop 'is 'eäd.
Hallus a soft un, Squire! an' 'e smiled, fur
 'e hed n't naw friend,
Sa feyther an' son was buried togither, an'
 this wur the hend.    90

### XV

An' Parson as hes n't the call, nor the
 mooney, but hes the pride,
'E reäds of a sewer an' sartan 'oäp o' the
 tother side;
But I beänt that sewer es the Lord, how-
 siver they praäy'd an' praäy'd,
Lets them inter 'eaven eäsy es leäves their
 debts to be paäid.
Siver the mou'ds rattled down upo' poor
 owd Squire i' the wood,
An' I cried along wi' the gells, fur they
 weänt niver coom to naw good.

### XVI

Fur Molly the long un she walkt awaäy wi'
 a hofficer lad,
An' nawbody 'eärd on 'er sin', sa o' coorse
 she be gone to the bad!
An' Lucy wur laäme o' one leg, sweet'arts
 she niver 'ed none —
Straänge an' unheppen [1] Miss Lucy! we
 naämed her ' Dot an' gaw one!'   100
An' Hetty wur weak i' the hattics, wi'out
 ony harm i' the legs,

[1] Ungainly, awkward.

An' the fever 'ed baäked Jinny's 'eäd as
    bald as one o' them heggs,
An' Nelly wur up fro' the craädle as big i'
    the mouth as a cow,
An' saw she mun hammergrate,[1] lass, or
    she weänt git a maäte onyhow !
An' es for Miss Annie es call'd me afoor
    my awn foälks to my faäce,
' A hignorant village wife es 'ud hev to be
    larn'd her awn plaäce,'
Hes fur Miss Hannie the heldest hes now
    be a-grawin' sa howd,
I knaws that mooch o' sheä, es it beänt not
    fit to be towd !

### XVII

Sa I did n't not taäke it kindly ov owd
    Miss Annie to saäy
Es I should be talkin' ageän 'em, es soon
    es they went awaäy,       110
Fur lawks ! 'ow I cried when they went,
    an' our Nelly she gied me 'er 'and,
Fur I 'd ha done owt for the Squire an' 'is
    gells es belong'd to the land;
Boooks, es I said afoor, thebbe neyther
    'ere nor theer !
But I sarved 'em wi' butter an' heggs fur
    huppuds o' twenty year.

### XVIII

An' they hallus paäid what I hax'd, sa I
    hallus deal'd wi' the Hall,
An' they knaw'd what butter wur, an' they
    knaw'd what a hegg wur an' all;
Hugger-mugger they lived, but they was n't
    that eäsy to pleäse,
Till I gied 'em Hinjian curn, an' they
    laäid big heggs es tha seeäs;
An' I niver puts saäme [2] i' *my* butter —
    they does it at Willis's farm;
Taäste another drop o' the wine — tweänt
    do tha naw harm.      120

### XIX

Sa new Squire 's coom'd wi' 'is taäil in 'is
    'and, an' owd Squire 's gone;
I heard 'im a roomlin' by, but arter my
    night-cap wur on;
Sa I han't clapt eyes on 'im yit, fur he
    coom'd last night sa laäte —
Pluksh ! ! ! [3] the hens i' the peäs ! why
    did n't tha hesp the gaäte ?

[1] Emigrate.        [2] Lard.
[3] A cry accompanied by a clapping of hands
to scare trespassing fowl.

# IN THE CHILDREN'S HOSPITAL

### EMMIE

This poem has been criticised as ' marred a
little by the needlessly harsh attack on the
practice of modern surgery, as exhibited by
one of the hospital staff;' but Mr. Palgrave
(' Lyrical Poems of Tennyson,' London, 1885)
says : ' It should be remembered that this is a
little drama, in which the Hospital Nurse, not
the Poet, is supposed to be speaking throughout. The two children, whose story was published in a Parish Magazine, are the only characters here described from actual life.' He
adds that ' this is the most absolutely pathetic
poem ' known to him. See also the ' Memoir,'
vol. ii. p. 253.

### I

OUR doctor had call'd in another, I never
    had seen him before,
But he sent a chill to my heart when I saw
    him come in at the door,
Fresh from the surgery-schools of France
    and of other lands —
Harsh red hair, big voice, big chest, big
    merciless hands !
Wonderful cures he had done, O, yes, but
    they said too of him
He was happier using the knife than in try-
    ing to save the limb,
And that I can well believe, for he look'd
    so coarse and so red,
I could think he was one of those who would
    break their jests on the dead,
And mangle the living dog that had loved
    him and fawn'd at his knee —
Drench'd with the hellish oorali — that
    ever such things should be !

### II

Here was a boy — I am sure that some of
    our children would die
But for the voice of love, and the smile,
    and the comforting eye —
Here was a boy in the ward, every bone
    seem'd out of its place —
Caught in a mill and crush'd — it was all
    but a hopeless case:
And he handled him gently enough; but his
    voice and his face were not kind,
And it was but a hopeless case, he had seen
    it and made up his mind,
And he said to me roughly, ' The lad will
    need little more of your care.'

'All the more need,' I told him, 'to seek
   the Lord Jesus in prayer;
They are all His children here, and I pray
   for them all as my own.'
But he turn'd to me, 'Ay, good woman,
   can prayer set a broken bone?'
Then he mutter'd half to himself, but I
   know that I heard him say,
'All very well — but the good Lord Jesus
   has had his day.'

### III

Had? has it come? It has only dawn'd.
   It will come by and by.
O, how could I serve in the wards if the
   hope of the world were a lie?
How could I bear with the sights and the
   loathsome smells of disease
But that He said, 'Ye do it to me, when ye
   do it to these'?

### IV

So he went. And we past to this ward
   where the younger children are laid.
Here is the cot of our orphan, our darling,
   our meek little maid;
Empty, you see, just now! We have lost
   her who loved her so much —
Patient of pain tho' as quick as a sensitive
   plant to the touch.
Hers was the prettiest prattle, it often
   moved me to tears,
Hers was the gratefullest heart I have
   found in a child of her years —
Nay you remember our Emmie; you used
   to send her the flowers.
How she would smile at 'em, play with 'em,
   talk to 'em hours after hours!
They that can wander at will where the
   works of the Lord are reveal'd
Little guess what joy can be got from a
   cowslip out of the field;
Flowers to these 'spirits in prison' are all
   they can know of the spring,
They freshen and sweeten the wards like
   the waft of an angel's wing.
And she lay with a flower in one hand and
   her thin hands crost on her breast —
Wan, but as pretty as heart can desire, and
   we thought her at rest,
Quietly sleeping — so quiet, our doctor said,
   'Poor little dear,
Nurse, I must do it to-morrow; she 'll
   never live thro' it, I fear.'

### V

I walk'd with our kindly old doctor as far
   as the head of the stair,
Then I return'd to the ward; the child
   did n't see I was there.

### VI

Never since I was nurse had I been so
   grieved and so vext!
Emmie had heard him. Softly she call'd
   from her cot to the next,
'He says I shall never live thro' it; O An-
   nie, what shall I do?'
Annie consider'd. 'If I,' said the wise
   little Annie, 'was you,
I should cry to the dear Lord Jesus to help
   me, for, Emmie, you see,
It 's all in the picture there: "Little chil-
   dren should come to me"' —
Meaning the print that you gave us, I
   find that it always can please
Our children, the dear Lord Jesus with
   children about his knees.
'Yes, and I will,' said Emmie, 'but then if
   I call to the Lord,
How should he know that it 's me? such a
   lot of beds in the ward!'
That was a puzzle for Annie. Again she
   consider'd and said:
'Emmie, you put out your arms, and you
   leave 'em outside on the bed —
The Lord has so *much* to see to! but, Em-
   mie, you tell it him plain,
It 's the little girl with her arms lying out
   on the counterpane.'

### VII

I had sat three nights by the child — I
   could not watch her for four —
My brain had begun to reel — I felt I
   could do it no more.
That was my sleeping-night, but I thought
   that it never would pass.
There was a thunderclap once, and a clatter
   of hail on the glass,
And there was a phantom cry that I heard
   as I tost about,
The motherless bleat of a lamb in the
   storm and the darkness without;
My sleep was broken besides with dreams
   of the dreadful knife
And fears for our delicate Emmie who
   scarce would escape with her life;

Then in the gray of the morning it seem'd
     she stood by me and smiled,
And the doctor came at his hour, and we
     went to see to the child.

### VIII

He had brought his ghastly tools; we be-
     lieved her asleep again —
Her dear, long, lean, little arms lying out
     on the counterpane —
Say that His day is done ! Ah, why should
     we care what they say ?
The Lord of the children had heard her,
     and Emmie had past away.

## DEDICATORY POEM TO THE PRINCESS ALICE

Contributed to ' The Nineteenth Century ' for
April, 1879, and afterwards included in the
' Ballads and Other Poems.' It is a dedication of the poem that follows, ' The Defence
of Lucknow.'

The Princess Alice, Grand Duchess of Hesse-
Darmstadt, died on the 14th of December,
1878, aged thirty-five years.

DEAD PRINCESS, living Power, if that
     which lived
True life live on — and if the fatal kiss,
Born of true life and love, divorce thee not
From earthly love and life — if what we
     call
The spirit flash not all at once from out
This shadow into Substance — then per-
     haps
The mellow'd murmur of the people's
     praise
From thine own State, and all our breadth
     of realm,
Where Love and Longing dress thy deeds
     in light,
Ascends to thee; and this March morn that
     sees
Thy Soldier-brother's bridal orange-bloom
Break thro' the yews and cypress of thy
     grave,
And thine Imperial mother smile again,
May send one ray to thee ! and who can
     tell —
Thou — England's England-loving daugh-
     ter — thou
Dying so English thou wouldst have her
     flag

Borne on thy coffin — where is he can
     swear
But that some broken gleam from our poor
     earth
May touch thee, while, remembering thee,
     I lay
At thy pale feet this ballad of the deeds
Of England, and her banner in the East ?

## THE DEFENCE OF LUCKNOW

First printed in ' The Nineteenth Century '
for April, 1879, and included in the ' Ballads,'
1880.

The events recorded in the poem occurred
during the Sepoy Rebellion in British India,
in 1857. ' Sir Henry Lawrence took charge of
Lucknow as Resident in March of that year.
The spread of rebellion in June confined him
to the defence of the city, where he died of
wounds on July 4. Brigadier Inglis, in succession, then defended Lucknow for twelve
weeks until it was relieved on September 25
by General Havelock, to whom Sir James Outram (who accompanied as volunteer) had gen-
erously ceded the exploit ' (Palgrave).

### I

BANNER of England, not for a season, O
     banner of Britain, hast thou
Floated in conquering battle or flapt to the
     battle-cry !
Never with mightier glory than when we
     had rear'd thee on high
Flying at top of the roofs in the ghastly
     siege of Lucknow —
Shot thro' the staff or the halyard, but ever
     we raised thee anew,
And ever upon the topmost roof our banner
     of England blew.

### II

Frail were the works that defended the
     hold that we held with our lives —
Women and children among us, God help
     them, our children and wives !
Hold it we might — and for fifteen days or
     for twenty at most.
' Never surrender, I charge you, but every
     man die at his post ! '                    10
Voice of the dead whom we loved, our
     Lawrence the best of the brave;
Cold were his brows when we kiss'd him —
     we laid him that night in his grave.

'Every man die at his post!' and there
  hail'd on our houses and halls
Death from their rifle-bullets, and death
  from their cannon-balls,
Death in our innermost chamber, and death
  at our slight barricade,
Death while we stood with the musket, and
  death while we stoopt to the spade,
Death to the dying, and wounds to the
  wounded, for often there fell,
Striking the hospital wall, crashing thro'
  it, their shot and their shell,
Death — for their spies were among us,
  their marksmen were told of our
  best,
So that the brute bullet broke thro' the
  brain that could think for the rest; 20
Bullets would sing by our foreheads, and
  bullets would rain at our feet —
Fire from ten thousand at once of the rebels
  that girdled us round —
Death at the glimpse of a finger from over
  the breadth of a street,
Death from the heights of the mosque and
  the palace, and death in the ground!
Mine? yes, a mine! Countermine! down,
  down! and creep thro' the hole!
Keep the revolver in hand! you can hear
  him — the murderous mole!
Quiet, ah! quiet — wait till the point of the
  pickaxe be thro'!
Click with the pick, coming nearer and
  nearer again than before —
Now let it speak, and you fire, and the
  dark pioneer is no more;
And ever upon the topmost roof our banner
  of England blew!                    30

### III

Ay, but the foe sprung his mine many
  times, and it chanced on a day
Soon as the blast of that underground
  thunder-clap echo'd away,
Dark thro' the smoke and the sulphur like
  so many fiends in their hell —
Cannot-shot, musket-shot, volley on volley,
  and yell upon yell —
Fiercely on all the defences our myriad
  enemy fell.
What have they done? where is it? Out
  yonder. Guard the Redan!
Storm at the Water-gate! storm at the
  Bailey-gate! storm, and it ran
Surging and swaying all round us, as ocean
  on every side

Plunges and heaves at a bank that is daily
  drown'd by the tide —
So many thousands that, if they be bold
  enough, who shall escape?          40
Kill or be kill'd, live or die, they shall
  know we are soldiers and men!
Ready! take aim at their leaders — their
  masses are gapp'd with our grape —
Backward they reel like the wave, like the
  wave flinging forward again,
Flying and foil'd at the last by the handful
  they could not subdue;
And ever upon the topmost roof our banner
  of England blew.

### IV

Handful of men as we were, we were English in heart and in limb,
Strong with the strength of the race to
  command, to obey, to endure,
Each of us fought as if hope for the garrison hung but on him;
Still — could we watch at all points? we
  were every day fewer and fewer.
There was a whisper among us, but only a
  whisper that past:                  50
'Children and wives — if the tigers leap
  into the fold unawares —
Every man die at his post — and the foe
  may outlive us at last —
Better to fall by the hands that they love,
  than to fall into theirs!'
Roar upon roar in a moment two mines by
  the enemy sprung
Clove into perilous chasms our walls and
  our poor palisades.
Rifleman, true is your heart, but be sure
  that your hand be as true!
Sharp is the fire of assault, better aimed
  are your flank fusillades —
Twice do we hurl them to earth from the
  ladders to which they had clung,
Twice from the ditch where they shelter
  we drive them with hand-grenades;
And ever upon the topmost roof our banner
  of England blew.                    60

### V

Then on another wild morning another wild
  earthquake out-tore
Clean from our lines of defence ten or
  twelve good paces or more.
Rifleman, high on the roof, hidden there
  from the light of the sun —

One has leapt up on the breach, crying out:
  'Follow me, follow me!' —
Mark him — he falls! then another, and
  *him* too, and down goes he.
Had they been bold enough then, who can
  tell but the traitors had won?
Boardings and rafters and doors — an em-
  brasure! make way for the gun!
Now double-charge it with grape! It is
  charged and we fire, and they run.
Praise to our Indian brothers, and let the
  dark face have his due!
Thanks to the kindly dark faces who
  fought with us, faithful and few, 70
Fought with the bravest among us, and
  drove them, and smote them, and
  slew,
That ever upon the topmost roof our banner
  in India blew.

### VI

Men will forget what we suffer and not
  what we do. We can fight!
But to be soldier all day, and be sentinel
  all thro' the night —
Ever the mine and assault, our sallies, their
  lying alarms,
Bugles and drums in the darkness, and
  shoutings and soundings to arms,
Ever the labor of fifty that had to be done
  by five,
Ever the marvel among us that one should
  be left alive,
Ever the day with its traitorous death from
  the loopholes around,
Ever the night with its coffinless corpse to
  be laid in the ground, 80
Heat like the mouth of a hell, or a deluge
  of cataract skies,
Stench of old offal decaying, and infinite
  torment of flies,
Thoughts of the breezes of May blowing
  over an English field,
Cholera, scurvy, and fever, the wound that
  *would* not be heal'd,
Lopping away of the limb by the pitiful-
  pitiless knife, —
Torture and trouble in vain, — for it never
  could save us a life.
Valor of delicate women who tended the
  hospital bed,
Horror of women in travail among the
  dying and dead,
Grief for our perishing children, and never
  a moment for grief,

Toil and ineffable weariness, faltering hopes
  of relief, 90
Havelock baffled, or beaten, or butcher'd
  for all that we knew —
Then day and night, day and night, coming
  down on the still-shatter'd walls
Millions of musket-bullets, and thousands
  of cannon-balls —
But ever upon the topmost roof our banner
  of England blew.

### VII

Hark cannonade, fusillade! is it true what
  was told by the scout,
Outram and Havelock breaking their way
  through the fell mutineers?
Surely the pibroch of Europe is ringing
  again in our ears!
All on a sudden the garrison utter a jubi-
  lant shout,
Havelock's glorious Highlanders answer
  with conquering cheers,
Sick from the hospital echo them, women
  and children come out, 100
Blessing the wholesome white faces of
  Havelock's good fusileers,
Kissing the war-harden'd hand of the High-
  lander wet with their tears!
Dance to the pibroch! — saved! we are
  saved! — is it you? is it you?
Saved by the valor of Havelock, saved by
  the blessing of heaven!
'Hold it for fifteen days!' we have held it
  for eighty-seven!
And ever aloft on the palace roof the old
  banner of England blew.

## SIR JOHN OLDCASTLE, LORD COBHAM

### (IN WALES)

Sir John Oldcastle, known in his time as 'the
good Lord Cobham,' was born in the reign of
Edward III., but in what year is unknown.
He was an ardent Wiclifite, and took part in
the presentation of a remonstrance to Parliament on the corruption of the church. In the
reign of Henry V., he was accused of heresy
and imprisoned in the Tower, whence he escaped and hid himself in Wales. A bill of
attainder was passed against him, and a reward
of a thousand marks offered for his capture.
Four years later he was taken, and, being
reckoned a traitor as well as a heretic, was

hung up alive in chains, and burned to death by a fire kindled under the gallows.

My friend should meet me somewhere hereabout
To take me to that hiding in the hills.

I have broke their cage, no gilded one, I trow —
I read no more the prisoner's mute wail
Scribbled or carved upon the pitiless stone;
I find hard rocks, hard life, hard cheer, or none,
For I am emptier than a friar's brains;
But God is with me in this wilderness,
These wet black passes and foam-churning chasms —
And God's free air, and hope of better things.          10

I would I knew their speech; not now to glean,
Not now — I hope to do it — some scatter'd ears,
Some ears for Christ in this wild field of Wales —
But, bread, merely for bread. This tongue that wagg'd
They said with such heretical arrogance
Against the proud archbishop Arundel —
So much God's cause was fluent in it — is here
But as a Latin Bible to the crowd;
' Bara ! ' — what use ? The shepherd, when I speak,
Vailing a sudden eyelid with his hard          20
' Dim Saesneg,' passes, wroth at things of old —
No fault of mine. Had he God's word in Welsh
He might be kindlier; happily come the day !

Not least art thou, thou little Bethlehem
In Judah, for in thee the Lord was born;
Nor thou in Britain, little Lutterworth,
Least, for in thee the word was born again.

Heaven-sweet Evangel, ever-living word,
Who whilome spakest to the South in Greek
About the soft Mediterranean shores,          30
And then in Latin to the Latin crowd,
As good need was — thou hast come to talk our isle.

Hereafter thou, fulfilling Pentecost,
Must learn to use the tongues of all the world.
Yet art thou thine own witness that thou bringest
Not peace, a sword, a fire.          What did he say,
My frighted Wiclif - preacher whom I crost
In flying hither ? that one night a crowd
Throng'd the waste field about the city gates;
The king was on them suddenly with a host.          40
Why there ? they came to hear their preacher.   Then
Some cried on Cobham, on the good Lord Cobham;
Ay, for they love me ! but the king — nor voice
Nor finger raised against him — took and hang'd,
Took, hang'd and burnt — how many — thirty-nine —
Call'd it rebellion — hang'd, poor friends, as rebels
And burn'd alive as heretics ! for your priest
Labels — to take the king along with him —
All heresy, treason; but to call men traitors
May make men traitors.          Rose of Lancaster,
Red in thy birth, redder with household war,          51
Now reddest with the blood of holy men,
Redder to be, red rose of Lancaster —
If somewhere in the North, as Rumor sang
Fluttering the hawks of this crown-lusting line —
By firth and loch thy silver sister grow,[1]
That were my rose, there my allegiance due.
Self - starved, they say — nay, murder'd, doubtless dead.
So to this king I cleaved.   My friend was he,
Once my fast friend; I would have given my life          60
To help his own from scathe, a thousand lives

---

[1] Richard II.

To save his soul.   He might have come to
learn
Our Wiclif's learning; but the worldly
priests,
Who fear the king's hard common-sense
should find
What rotten piles uphold their mason-
work,
Urge him to foreign war.   O, had he
will'd
I might have stricken a lusty stroke for
him,
But he would not; far liever led my friend
Back to the pure and universal church,
But he would not — whether that heirless
flaw                                                    70
In his throne's title make him feel so frail,
He leans on Antichrist; or that his mind,
So quick, so capable in soldiership,
In matters of the faith, alas the while !
More worth than all the kingdoms of this
world,
Runs in the rut, a coward to the priest.

Burnt — good Sir Roger Acton, my dear
friend !
Burnt too, my faithful preacher, Bever-
ley !
Lord, give thou power to thy two wit-
nesses,
Lest the false faith make merry over
them !                                                    80
Two — nay, but thirty-nine have risen and
stand,
Dark with the smoke of human sacrifice,
Before thy light, and cry continually —
Cry — against whom ?
            Him, who should bear the sword
Of Justice — what ! the kingly, kindly
boy;
Who took the world so easily heretofore,
My boon companion, tavern-fellow — him
Who jibed and japed — in many a merry
tale
That shook our sides — at pardoners, sum-
moners,
Friars, absolution-sellers, monkeries       90
And nunneries, when the wild hour and the
wine
Had set the wits aflame.
                        Harry of Monmouth,
Or Amurath of the East ?
                        Better to sink
Thy fleurs-de-lys in slime again, and fling
Thy royalty back into the riotous fits

Of wine and harlotry — thy shame, and
mine,
Thy comrade — than to persecute the
Lord,
And play the Saul that never will be Paul.

Burnt, burnt ! and while this mitred
Arundel
Dooms our unlicensed preacher to the
flame,                                                    100
The mitre - sanction'd harlot draws his
clerks
Into the suburb — their hard celibacy,
Sworn to be veriest ice of pureness, molten
Into adulterous living, or such crimes
As holy Paul — a shame to speak of
them —
Among the heathen —
                        Sanctuary granted
To bandit, thief, assassin — yea, to him
Who hacks his mother's throat — denied to
him
Who finds the Saviour in his mother
tongue.
The Gospel, the priest's pearl, flung down
to swine —                                             110
The swine, lay-men, lay-women, who will
come,
God willing, to outlearn the filthy friar.
Ah, rather, Lord, than that thy Gospel,
meant
To course and range thro' all the world,
should be
Tether'd to these dead pillars of the
Church —
Rather than so, if thou wilt have it so,
Burst vein, snap sinew, and crack heart,
and life
Pass in the fire of Babylon ! but how long,
O Lord, how long !
                        My friend should meet me here.
Here is the copse, the fountain and — a
cross !                                                    120
To thee, dead wood, I bow not head nor
knees.
Rather to thee, green boscage, work of
God,
Black holly, and white-flower'd wayfaring-
tree !
Rather to thee, thou living water, drawn
By this good Wiclif mountain down from
heaven,
And speaking clearly in thy native tongue—
No Latin — He that thirsteth, come and
drink !

Eh ! how I anger'd Arundel asking me
To worship Holy Cross !  I spread mine
    arms,
God's work, I said, a cross of flesh and
    blood                                      130
And holier.  That was heresy. — My good
    friend
By this time should be with me. — 'Im-
    ages ? '
' Bury them as God's truer images
Are daily buried.'  ' Heresy. — Penance ? '
    ' Fast,
Hair-shirt and scourge — nay, let a man
    repent,
Do penance in his heart, God hears him.'
    ' Heresy —
Not shriven, not saved ? '  ' What profits
    an ill priest
Between me and my God ?  I would not
    spurn
Good counsel of good friends, but shrive
    myself —
No, not to an Apostle.'  ' Heresy.' —     140
My friend is long in coming. — ' Pilgrim-
    ages ? '
' Drink, bagpipes, revelling, devil's-dances,
    vice.
The poor man's money gone to fat the
    friar.
Who reads of begging saints in Scripture ? '
    — ' Heresy ' —
Hath he been here — not found me — gone
    again ?
Have I mislearnt our place of meeting ? —
    ' Bread —
Bread left after the blessing ? ' how they
    stared,
That was their main test-question — glared
    at me !
' He veil'd Himself in flesh, and now He
    veils
His flesh in bread, body and bread to-
    gether.'                                   150
Then rose the howl of all the cassock'd
    wolves,
' No bread, no bread.  God's body ! ' Arch-
    bishop, bishop,
Priors, canons, friars, bell-ringers, parish-
    clerks —
' No bread, no bread ! ' — ' Authority of
    the Church,
Power of the keys ! ' — Then I, God help
    me, I
So mock'd, so spurn'd, so baited two whole
    days —

I lost myself and fell from evenness,
And rail'd at all the Popes that, ever since
Sylvester shed the venom of world-wealth
Into the church, had only proven them-
    selves                                     160
Poisoners, murderers.  Well — God pardon
    all —
Me, them, and all the world — yea, that
    proud priest,
That mock-meek mouth of utter Antichrist,
That traitor to King Richard and the
    truth,
Who rose and doom'd me to the fire.
                                Amen !
Nay, I can burn, so that the Lord of life
Be by me in my death.
                    Those three ! the fourth
Was like the Son of God !  Not burnt
    were they.
On *them* the smell of burning had not
    past.
That was a miracle to convert the king.  170
These Pharisees, this Caiaphas-Arundel
What miracle could turn ?  *He* here again,
*He* thwarting their traditions of Himself,
*He* would be found a heretic to Himself,
And doom'd to burn alive.
                        So, caught, I burn.
Burn ? heathen men have borne as much
    as this,
For freedom, or the sake of those they
    loved,
Or some less cause, some cause far less
    than mine ;
For every other cause is less than mine.
The moth will singe her wings, and singed
    return,                                    180
Her love of light quenching her fear of
    pain —
How now, my soul, we do not heed the
    fire ?
Faint - hearted ? tut ! — faint - stomach'd !
    faint as I am,
God willing, I will burn for Him.
                            Who comes ?
A thousand marks are set upon my head.
Friend ? — foe perhaps — a tussle for it
    then !
Nay, but my friend.  Thou art so well dis-
    guised,
I knew thee not.  Hast thou brought bread
    with thee ?
I have not broken bread for fifty hours.
None ?  I am damn'd already by the
    priest                                     190

For holding there was bread where bread
    was none —
No bread.  My friends await me yonder ?
    Yes.
Lead on then.  *Up* the mountain ?  Is it
    far ?
Not far.  Climb first and reach me down
    thy hand.
I am not like to die for lack of bread,
For I must live to testify by fire.[1]

## COLUMBUS

Founded on a passage in Irving's 'Life of
Columbus.'  'It was written after repeated
entreaties from certain prominent Americans
that he would commemorate the discovery of
America in verse' ('Memoir,' vol. ii. p. 255).

CHAINS, my good lord !  In your raised
    brows I read
Some wonder at our chamber ornaments.
We brought this iron from our isles of
    gold.

Does the King know you deign to visit him
Whom once he rose from off his throne to
    greet
Before his people, like his brother king ?
I saw your face that morning in the crowd.

At Barcelona — tho' you were not then
So bearded.  Yes.  The city deck'd herself
To meet me, roar'd my name; the King,
    the Queen,      10
Bade me be seated, speak, and tell them all
The story of my voyage, and while I spoke
The crowd's roar fell as at the 'Peace, be
    still !'
And when I ceased to speak, the King, the
    Queen,
Sank from their thrones, and melted into
    tears,
And knelt, and lifted hand and heart and
    voice
In praise to God who led me thro' the
    waste.
And then the great 'Laudamus' rose to
    heaven.

Chains for the Admiral of the Ocean !
    chains
For him who gave a new heaven, a new
    earth,      20

[1] He was burnt on Christmas Day, 1417.

As holy John had prophesied of me,
Gave glory and more empire to the kings
Of Spain than all their battles ! chains for
    him
Who push'd his prows into the setting sun,
And made West East, and sail'd the
    Dragon's Mouth,
And came upon the Mountain of the World,
And saw the rivers roll from Paradise !

Chains ! we are Admirals of the Ocean,
    we,
We and our sons for ever.  Ferdinand
Hath sign'd it and our Holy Catholic
    Queen —      30
Of the Ocean — of the Indies — Admirals
    we —
Our title, which we never mean to yield,
Our guerdon not alone for what we did,
But our amends for all we might have
    done —
The vast occasion of our stronger life —
Eighteen long years of waste, seven in
    your Spain,
Lost, showing courts and kings a truth the
    babe
Will suck in with his milk hereafter —
    earth
A sphere.

          Were *you* at Salamanca ?  No.
We fronted there the learning of all Spain,
All their cosmogonies, their astronomies. 41
Guess-work *they* guess'd it, but the golden
    guess
Is morning-star to the full round of truth.
No guess-work !  I was certain of my
    goal;
Some thought it heresy, but that would not
    hold.
King David call'd the heavens a hide, a
    tent
Spread over earth, and so this earth was flat.
Some cited old Lactantius; could it be
That trees grew downward, rain fell up-
    ward, men
Walk'd like the fly on ceilings ? and be-
    sides,      50
The great Augustine wrote that none could
    breathe
Within the zone of heat; so might there be
Two Adams, two mankinds, and that was
    clean
Against God's word.  Thus was I beaten
    back,

And chiefly to my sorrow by the Church,
And thought to turn my face from Spain,
appeal
Once more to France or England; but our
Queen
Recall'd me, for at last their Highnesses
Were half-assured this earth might be a
sphere.

All glory to the all-blessed Trinity, 60
All glory to the mother of our Lord,
And Holy Church, from whom I never
swerved
Not even by one hair's-breadth of heresy,
I have accomplish'd what I came to do.

Not yet — not all — last night a dream
— I sail'd
On my first voyage, harass'd by the frights
Of my first crew, their curses and their
groans.
The great flame-banner borne by Teneriffe,
The compass, like an old friend false at
last
In our most need, appall'd them, and the
wind 70
Still westward, and the weedy seas — at
length
The land-bird, and the branch with berries
on it,
The carven staff — and last the light, the
light
On Guanahani ! but I changed the name;
San Salvador I call'd it; and the light
Grew as I gazed, and brought out a broad
sky
Of dawning over — not those alien palms,
The marvel of that fair new nature — not
That Indian isle, but our most ancient East,
Moriah with Jerusalem; and I saw 80
The glory of the Lord flash up, and beat
Thro' all the homely town from jasper,
sapphire,
Chalcedony, emerald, sardonyx, sardius,
Chrysolite, beryl, topaz, chrysoprase,
Jacynth, and amethyst — and those twelve
gates,
Pearl — and I woke, and thought — death
— I shall die —
I am written in the Lamb's own Book of
Life
To walk within the glory of the Lord
Sunless and moonless, utter light — but no !
The Lord had sent this bright, strange
dream to me 90

To mind me of the secret vow I made
When Spain was waging war against the
Moor —
I strove myself with Spain against the
Moor.
There came two voices from the Sepulchre,
Two friars crying that, if Spain should oust
The Moslem from her limit, he, the fierce
Soldan of Egypt, would break down and
raze
The blessed tomb of Christ; whereon I
vow'd
That, if our princes harken'd to my prayer,
Whatever wealth I brought from that new
world 100
Should, in this old, be consecrate to lead
A new crusade against the Saracen,
And free the Holy Sepulchre from thrall.

Gold ?   I had brought your princes gold
enough
If left alone !   Being but a Genovese,
I am handled worse than had I been a
Moor,
And breach'd the belting wall of Cambalu,
And given the Great Khan's palaces to the
Moor,
Or clutch'd the sacred crown of Prester
John, 109
And cast it to the Moor.  But had I brought
From Solomon's now-recover'd Ophir all
The gold that Solomon's navies carried
home,
Would that have gilded me ?   Blue blood
of Spain,
Tho' quartering your own royal arms of
Spain,
I have not; blue blood and black blood of
Spain,
The noble and the convict of Castile,
Howl'd me from Hispaniola.  For you know
The flies at home, that ever swarm about
And cloud the highest heads, and murmur
down
Truth in the distance — these outbuzz'd
me so 120
That even our prudent King, our righteous
Queen —
I pray'd them being so calumniated
They would commission one of weight and
worth
To judge between my slander'd self and
me —
Fonseca my main enemy at their court,
They sent me out his tool, Bovadilla, one

As ignorant and impolitic as a beast —
Blockish irreverence, brainless greed — who
    sack'd
My dwelling, seized upon my papers, loosed
My captives, feed the rebels of the crown,
Sold the crown-farms for all but nothing,
    gave             131
All but free leave for all to work the mines,
Drove me and my good brothers home in
    chains,
And gathering ruthless gold — a single
    piece
Weigh'd nigh four thousand Castillanos —
    so
They tell me — weigh'd him down into the
    abysm —
The hurricane of the latitude on him fell,
The seas of our discovering over-roll
Him and his gold; the frailer caravel,
With what was mine, came happily to the
    shore.          140
*There* was a glimmering of God's hand.

                  And God
Hath more than glimmer'd on me.  O my
    lord,
I swear to you I heard His voice between
The thunders in the black Veragua nights,
' O soul of little faith, slow to believe !
Have I not been about thee from thy birth ?
Given thee the keys of the great Ocean-
    sea ?
Set thee in light till time shall be no more ?
Is it I who have deceived thee or the
    world ?
Endure ! thou hast done so well for men,
    that men           150
Cry out against thee.   Was it otherwise
With mine own Son ? '

           And more than once in days
Of doubt and cloud and storm, when
    drowning hope
Sank all but out of sight, I heard His
    voice,
' Be not cast down.  I lead thee by the
    hand,
Fear not.'  And I shall hear His voice
    again —
I know that He has led me all my life,
I am not yet too old to work His will —
His voice again.

          Still for all that, my lord,
I lying here bedridden and alone,    160

Cast off, put by, scouted by court and
    king —
The first discoverer starves — his followers,
    all
Flower into fortune — our world's way —
    and I,
Without a roof that I can call mine own,
With scarce a coin to buy a meal withal,
And seeing what a door for scoundrel scum
I open'd to the West, thro' which the lust,
Villainy, violence, avarice, of your Spain
Pour'd in on all those happy naked isles —
Their kindly native princes slain or slaved,
Their wives and children Spanish concu-
    bines,          171
Their innocent hospitalities quench'd in
    blood,
Some dead of hunger, some beneath the
    scourge,
Some over-labor'd, some by their own
    hands, —
Yea, the dear mothers, crazing Nature, kill
Their babies at the breast for hate of
    Spain —
Ah God, the harmless people whom we
    found
In Hispaniola's island-Paradise !
Who took us for the very gods from hea-
    ven,
And we have sent them very fiends from
    hell;          180
And I myself, myself not blameless, I
Could sometimes wish I had never led the
    way.

    Only the ghost of our great Catholic
        Queen
Smiles on me, saying, ' Be thou com-
    forted !
This creedless people will be brought to
    Christ
And own the holy governance of Rome.'

    But who could dream that we, who bore
        the Cross,
Thither, were excommunicated there,
For curbing crimes that scandalized the
    Cross,
By him, the Catalonian Minorite,    190
Rome's Vicar in our Indies ? who believe
These hard memorials of our truth to Spain
Clung closer to us for a longer term
Than any friend of ours at Court ? and yet
Pardon — too harsh, unjust.  I am rack'd
    with pains.

You see that I have hung them by my
bed,
And I will have them buried in my grave.

Sir, in that flight of ages which are God's
Own voice to justify the dead — perchance
Spain, once the most chivalric race on earth,
Spain, then the mightiest, wealthiest realm
on earth,                                                     201
So made by me, may seek to unbury me,
To lay me in some shrine of this old Spain,
Or in that vaster Spain I leave to Spain.
Then some one standing by my grave will
say,
'Behold the bones of Christopher Co-
lòn' —
'Ay, but the chains, what do *they* mean —
the chains ? ' —
I sorrow for that kindly child of Spain
Who then will have to answer, 'These
same chains
Bound these same bones back thro' the
Atlantic sea,                                                 210
Which he unchain'd for all the world to
come.'

O Queen of Heaven who seest the souls
in hell
And purgatory, I suffer all as much
As they do — for the moment. Stay, my
son
Is here anon; my son will speak for me
Ablier than I can in these spasms that
grind
Bone against bone. You will not. One
last word.

You move about the Court; I pray you
tell
King Ferdinand who plays with me, that
one
Whose life has been no play with him and
his                                                            220
Hidalgos — shipwrecks, famines, fevers,
fights,
Mutinies, treacheries — wink'd at, and con-
doned —
That I am loyal to him till the death,
And ready — tho' our Holy Catholic Queen,
Who fain had pledged her jewels on my
first voyage,
Whose hope was mine to spread the Catho-
lic faith,
Who wept with me when I return'd in
chains,

Who sits beside the blessed Virgin now,
To whom I send my prayer by night and
day —
She is gone — but you will tell the King,
that I,                                                        230
Rack'd as I am with gout, and wrench'd
with pains
Gain'd in the service of His Highness, yet
Am ready to sail forth on one last voyage,
And readier, if the King would hear, to
lead
One last crusade against the Saracen,
And save the Holy Sepulchre from thrall.

Going ? I am old and slighted; you
have dared
Somewhat perhaps in coming ? my poor
thanks !
I am but an alien and a Genovese.


## THE VOYAGE OF MAELDUNE

### (FOUNDED ON AN IRISH LEGEND.
### A. D. 700)

The original story may be found in P. W.
Joyce's ' Old Celtic Romances ' (London, 1879).
According to the tale, Maildun (*Mail Duin*,
chief of the fort) sets forth with sixty chosen
men, to seek the murderer of his father. They
come, as in the poem, to an island where the
man lives, but are driven away by a tempest.
After three days they arrive at ' the island of
the monstrous ants,' each ' as large as a foal ; '
but, not liking the ' eager and hungry look ' of
the insects, they do not land. Three days later
they reach ' the terraced island of birds,' of
which they take great numbers, and then sail
away to a large sandy island, from whose shores
they are frightened by a monster ' somewhat
like a horse in shape,' but with legs like a dog
and like claws. On the next island they see a
' demon horse-race,' and continue their voyage
to another, whereon is a magnificent palace.
Here they find ' abundance of food and ale,'
but see no inhabitants ; so after eating and
drinking their fill, they thank God and put to
sea again. The ' island of the wonderful apple-
tree,' a single apple from which serves to supply the travellers with food and drink for
forty days, and successive islands infested with
' blood-thirsty quadrupeds,' strange monsters,
and ' red-hot animals,' are visited in turn ; also
an island where a ' little cat,' living in a splendid palace, kills one of Maildun's brothers ;
another island that ' dyed white and black '
— everything on one side of a wall across it

becoming black, and on the other side white; the island 'of the burning river,' and that ' of the miller of hell,' who grinds up all the good things that men complain of, and all that they ' try to conceal from God;' with the isles of ' weeping,' of ' the four precious walls,' of ' the crystal bridge,' of ' speaking birds,' of ' the aged hermit,' and of ' the big blacksmiths,' who remind one of the Cyclops of old. The voyagers also sail over ' the crystal sea,' and another transparent sea beneath whose waters they see a country beautiful indeed, but infested with strange and monstrous animals. Later they come to another island, about which the sea rose up, forming, ' as it were, a wall all round it;' and to another spanned by a stream of water in the form of a rainbow, ' and they hooked down from it many large salmon.' A mighty ' silver pillar standing in the sea ' and an ' island standing on one pillar ' are other wonders they encounter before arriving at a lovely island, the queen of which detains them long by her magic arts. Escaping at last, they visit ' the isle of intoxicating wine-fruits ' and that of ' the mystic lake,' whose waters renewed the youth of the bather, and a third where the people were ' all continually laughing.' They pass ' the isle of the blest ' without venturing to land, and soon see a lonely rock whereon a holy hermit dwelt, who, after telling the wonderful story of his life, said to them : ' You shall all reach your own country in safety ; and you, Maildun, you shall find in an island on your way the very man that slew your father ; but you are neither to kill him nor take revenge on him in any way. As God has delivered you from the many dangers you have passed through, though you were very guilty and well deserved death at His hands, so do you forgive your enemy the crime he committed against you.' Sailing away, the voyagers come again to the island where this enemy dwelt. It is evening, and the man is at supper with his friends. Maildun and his companions stand outside the house and listen to the conversation going on within. The people happen to be talking of Maildun, and one asks, ' Supposing he came now, what should we do ?' ' I can easily answer that,' said the man of the house ; ' Maildun has been for a long time suffering great afflictions and hardships; and if he were to come now, though we were enemies once, I should certainly give him a welcome and a kind reception.' Maildun at once knocked at the door and made himself known. The wanderers were invited to enter, and ' were joyfully welcomed by the whole household ; new garments were given to them ; and they feasted and rested, till they forgot their weariness and their hardships.'

It will be seen that while the old Celtic tale has suggested to Tennyson a few of the main incidents in the poem, the details are almost entirely of his own invention. The date which he assigns to the legend (A. D. 700) is that which Joyce and others, from internal evidence, accept for the events on which it is founded.

### I

I was the chief of the race — he had
    stricken my father dead —
But I gather'd my fellows together, I swore
    I would strike off his head.
Each of them look'd like a king, and was
    noble in birth as in worth,
And each of them boasted he sprang from
    the oldest race upon earth.
Each was as brave in the fight as the bravest hero of song,
And each of them liefer had died than
    have done one another a wrong.
*He* lived on an isle in the ocean — we sail'd
    on a Friday morn —
He that had slain my father the day before
    I was born.

### II

And we came to the isle in the ocean, and
    there on the shore was he.
But a sudden blast blew us out and away
    thro' a boundless sea.    10

### III

And we came to the Silent Isle that we
    never had touch'd at before,
Where a silent ocean always broke on a
    silent shore,
And the brooks glitter'd on in the light
    without sound, and the long waterfalls
Pour'd in a thunderless plunge to the base
    of the mountain walls,
And the poplar and cypress unshaken by
    storm flourish'd up beyond sight,
And the pine shot aloft from the crag to an
    unbelievable height,
And high in the heaven above it there
    flicker'd a songless lark,
And the cock could n't crow, and the bull
    could n't low, and the dog could n't
    bark.
And round it we went, and thro' it, but
    never a murmur, a breath —
It was all of it fair as life, it was all of it
    quiet as death,    20
And we hated the beautiful isle, for whenever we strove to speak

Our voices were thinner and fainter than
    any flittermouse-shriek;
And the men that were mighty of tongue
    and could raise such a battle-cry
That a hundred who heard it would rush
    on a thousand lances and die —
O, they to be dumb'd by the charm ! —
    so fluster'd with anger were they
They almost fell on each other; but after
    we sail'd away.

### IV

And we came to the Isle of Shouting; we
    landed, a score of wild birds
Cried from the topmost summit with hu-
    man voices and words.
Once in an hour they cried, and whenever
    their voices peal'd
The steer fell down at the plow and the
    harvest died from the field,    30
And the men dropt dead in the valleys and
    half of the cattle went lame,
And the roof sank in on the hearth, and the
    dwelling broke into flame;
And the shouting of these wild birds ran
    into the hearts of my crew,
Till they shouted along with the shouting
    and seized one another and slew.
But I drew them the one from the other;
    I saw that we could not stay,
And we left the dead to the birds, and we
    sail'd with our wounded away.

### V

And we came to the Isle of Flowers; their
    breath met us out on the seas,
For the Spring and the middle Summer sat
    each on the lap of the breeze;
And the red passion-flower to the cliffs, and
    the dark-blue clematis, clung,
And starr'd with a myriad blossom the
    long convolvulus hung;    40
And the topmost spire of the mountain was
    lilies in lieu of snow,
And the lilies like glaciers winded down,
    running out below
Thro' the fire of the tulip and poppy, the
    blaze of gorse, and the blush
Of millions of roses that sprang without
    leaf or a thorn from the bush;
And the whole isle-side flashing down from
    the peak without ever a tree
Swept like a torrent of gems from the sky
    to the blue of the sea.

And we roll'd upon capes of crocus and
    vaunted our kith and our kin,
And we wallow'd in beds of lilies, and
    chanted the triumph of Finn,
Till each like a golden image was pollen'd
    from head to feet
And each was as dry as a cricket, with
    thirst in the middle-day heat.    50
Blossom and blossom, and promise of blos-
    som, but never a fruit !
And we hated the Flowering Isle, as we
    hated the isle that was mute,
And we tore up the flowers by the million
    and flung them in bight and bay,
And we left but a naked rock, and in anger
    we sail'd away.

### VI

And we came to the Isle of Fruits; all
    round from the cliffs and the capes,
Purple or amber, dangled a hundred
    fathom of grapes,
And the warm melon lay like a little sun
    on the tawny sand,
And the fig ran up from the beach and
    rioted over the land,
And the mountain arose like a jewell'd
    throne thro' the fragrant air,
Glowing with all-color'd plums and with
    golden masses of pear,    60
And the crimson and scarlet of berries that
    flamed upon bine and vine,
But in every berry and fruit was the poison-
    ous pleasure of wine;
And the peak of the mountain was apples,
    the hugest that ever were seen,
And they prest, as they grew, on each
    other, with hardly a leaflet between,
And all of them redder than rosiest health
    or than utterest shame,
And setting, when Even descended, the
    very sunset aflame.
And we stay'd three days, and we gorged
    and we madden'd, till every one
    drew
His sword on his fellow to slay him, and
    ever they struck and they slew;
And myself, I had eaten but sparely, and
    fought till I sunder'd the fray,
Then I bade them remember my father's
    death, and we sail'd away.    70

### VII

And we came to the Isle of Fire; we were
    lured by the light from afar,

For the peak sent up one league of fire to
    the Northern Star;
Lured by the glare and the blare, but
    scarcely could stand upright,
For the whole isle shudder'd and shook like
    a man in a mortal affright.
We were giddy besides with the fruits we
    had gorged, and so crazed that at last
There were some leap'd into the fire; and
    away we sail'd, and we past
Over that undersea isle, where the water is
    clearer than air.
Down we look'd — what a garden! O bliss,
    what a Paradise there!
Towers of a happier time, low down in a
    rainbow deep        79
Silent palaces, quiet fields of eternal sleep!
And three of the gentlest and best of my
    people, whate'er I could say,
Plunged head - down in the sea, and the
    Paradise trembled away.

### VIII

And we came to the Bounteous Isle, where
    the heavens lean low on the land,
And ever at dawn from the cloud glitter'd
    o'er us a sun-bright hand,
Then it open'd and dropt at the side of
    each man, as he rose from his rest,
Bread enough for his need till the laborless
    day dipt under the west;
And we wander'd about it and thro' it. O,
    never was time so good!
And we sang of the triumphs of Finn, and
    the boast of our ancient blood,
And we gazed at the wandering wave as we
    sat by the gurgle of springs,
And we chanted the songs of the Bards and
    the glories of fairy kings.        90
But at length we began to be weary, to
    sigh, and to stretch and yawn,
Till we hated the Bounteous Isle and the
    sun-bright hand of the dawn,
For there was not an enemy near, but the
    whole green isle was our own,
And we took to playing at ball, and we took
    to throwing the stone,
And we took to playing at battle, but that
    was a perilous play,
For the passion of battle was in us, we slew
    and we sail'd away.

### IX

And we came to the Isle of Witches and
    heard their musical cry —

'Come to us, O, come, come!' in the
    stormy red of a sky
Dashing the fires and the shadows of dawn
    on the beautiful shapes,
For a wild witch naked as heaven stood on
    each of the loftiest capes,        100
And a hundred ranged on the rock like
    white sea-birds in a row,
And a hundred gamboll'd and pranced on
    the wrecks in the sand below,
And a hundred splash'd from the ledges,
    and bosom'd the burst of the spray;
But I knew we should fall on each other,
    and hastily sail'd away.

### X

And we came in an evil time to the Isle of
    the Double Towers,
One was of smooth-cut stone, one carved
    all over with flowers,
But an earthquake always moved in the
    hollows under the dells,
And they shock'd on each other and butted
    each other with clashing of bells,
And the daws flew out of the towers and
    jangled and wrangled in vain,
And the clash and boom of the bells rang
    into the heart and the brain,        110
Till the passion of battle was on us, and all
    took sides with the towers,
There were some for the clean-cut stone,
    there were more for the carven
    flowers,
And the wrathful thunder of God peal'd
    over us all the day,
For the one half slew the other, and after
    we sail'd away.

### XI

And we came to the Isle of a Saint who
    had sail'd with Saint Brendan of
    yore,
He had lived ever since on the isle and his
    winters were fifteen score,
And his voice was low as from other worlds,
    and his eyes were sweet,
And his white hair sank to his heels, and
    his white beard fell to his feet,
And he spake to me: 'O Maeldune, let be
    this purpose of thine!
Remember the words of the Lord when he
    told us, "Vengeance is mine!"        120
His fathers have slain thy fathers in war or
    in single strife,

Thy fathers have slain his fathers, each
    taken a life for a life,
Thy father had slain his father, how long
    shall the murder last ?
Go back to the Isle of Finn and suffer the
    Past to be Past.'
And we kiss'd the fringe of his beard, and
    we pray'd as we heard him pray,
And the holy man he assoil'd us, and sadly
    we sail'd away.

### XII

And we came to the isle we were blown
    from, and there on the shore was he,
The man that had slain my father.  I saw
    him and let him be.
O, weary was I of the travel, the trouble,
    the strife, and the sin,
When I landed again with a tithe of my
    men, on the Isle of Finn !   130

## DE PROFUNDIS:

### THE TWO GREETINGS

First published in the 'Ballads' volume of
1880; but, according to Stopford Brooke
('Tennyson,' London, 1894), it was written on
the birth of the poet's eldest son, Hallam
(August 11, 1852), and is 'far the finest of his
speculative poems. Its stately and majestic
sublimity is warmed by the profound emotion
of his fatherhood.'

### I

OUT of the deep, my child, out of the
    deep,
Where all that was to be, in all that was,
Whirl'd for a million æons thro' the vast
Waste dawn of multitudinous - eddying
    light —
Out of the deep, my child, out of the
    deep,
Thro' all this changing world of changeless
    law,
And every phase of ever-heightening life,
And nine long months of antenatal gloom,
With this last moon, this crescent — her
    dark orb
Touch'd with earth's light — thou comest,
    darling boy;
Our own; a babe in lineament and limb
Perfect, and prophet of the perfect man;
Whose face and form are hers and mine in
    one,

Indissolubly married like our love.
Live, and be happy in thyself, and serve
This mortal race thy kin so well that men
May bless thee as we bless thee, O young
    life
Breaking with laughter from the dark; and
    may
The fated channel where thy motion lives
Be prosperously shaped, and sway thy
    course
Along the years of haste and random youth
Unshatter'd; then full - current thro' full
    man;
And last in kindly curves, with gentlest fall,
By quiet fields, a slowly-dying power,
To that last deep where we and thou are
    still.

### II

#### I

Out of the deep, my child, out of the
    deep,
From that great deep, before our world be-
    gins,
Whereon the Spirit of God moves as he
    will —
Out of the deep, my child, out of the
    deep,
From that true world within the world we
    see,
Whereof our world is but the bounding
    shore —
Out of the deep, Spirit, out of the deep,
With this ninth moon, that sends the hid-
    den sun
Down yon dark sea, thou comest, darling
    boy.

#### II

For in the world which is not ours They
    said,
'Let us make man,' and that which should
    be man,
From that one light no man can look upon,
Drew to this shore lit by the suns and
    moons
And all the shadows.  O dear Spirit, half-
    lost
In thine own shadow and this fleshly sign
That thou art thou — who wailest being
    born
And banish'd into mystery, and the pain
Of this divisible-indivisible world

Among the numerable-innumerable
Sun, sun, and sun, thro' finite-infinite space
In finite-infinite Time — our mortal veil
And shatter'd phantom of that infinite One,
Who made thee unconceivably Thyself
Out of His whole World-self and all in
    all —
Live thou ! and of the grain and husk, the
    grape
And ivy-berry, choose; and still depart
From death to death thro' life and life, and
    find
Nearer and ever nearer Him, who wrought
Not matter, nor the finite-infinite,
But this main-miracle, that thou art thou,
With power on thine own act and on the
    world.

### THE HUMAN CRY

#### I

HALLOWED be Thy name — Halleluiah ! —
    Infinite Ideality !
    Immeasurable Reality !
    Infinite Personality !
Hallowed be Thy name — Halleluiah !

#### II

We feel we are nothing — for all is Thou
    and in Thee;
We feel we are something — *that* also has
    come from Thee;
We know we are nothing — but Thou wilt
    help us to be.
Hallowed be Thy name — Halleluiah !

## SONNETS

### PREFATORY SONNET

#### TO 'THE NINETEENTH CENTURY'

Contributed to the first number of 'The
Nineteenth Century,' March, 1877, and afterwards included in the 'Ballads' volume.

THOSE that of late had fleeted far and fast
To touch all shores, now leaving to the
    skill
Of others their old craft seaworthy still,
Have charter'd this; where, mindful of the
    past,
Our true co-mates regather round the mast;
Of diverse tongue, but with a common will

Here, in this roaring moon of daffodil
And crocus, to put forth and brave the
    blast.
For some, descending from the sacred
    peak
Of hoar high-templed Faith, have leagued
    again
Their lot with ours to rove the world
    about;
And some are wilder comrades, sworn to
    seek
If any golden harbor be for men
In seas of Death and sunless gulfs of
    Doubt.

### TO THE REV. W. H. BROOK-FIELD

First printed in Lord Lyttleton's Memoir
(1869) prefixed to Brookfield's 'Sermons,' and
afterwards in the 'Ballads' volume. Brookfield was one of the poet's college friends.

BROOKS, for they call'd you so that knew
    you best,
Old Brooks, who loved so well to mouth
    my rhymes,
How oft we two have heard Saint Mary's
    chimes !
How oft the Cantab supper, host and guest,
Would echo helpless laughter to your jest !
How oft with him we paced that walk of
    limes,
Him, the lost light of those dawn-golden
    times,
Who loved you well !   Now both are gone
    to rest.
You man of humorous-melancholy mark,
Dead of some inward agony — is it so ?
Our kindlier, trustier Jaques, past away !
I cannot laud this life, it looks so dark.
Σκιᾶς ὄναρ — dream of a shadow, go —
God bless you !   I shall join you in a day.

### MONTENEGRO

First printed in 'The Nineteenth Century,'
March, 1877.

THEY rose to where their sovran eagle
    sails,
They kept their faith, their freedom, on
    the height,

Chaste, frugal, savage, arm'd by day and
    night
Against the Turk; whose inroad nowhere
    scales
Their headlong passes, but his footstep
    fails,
And red with blood the Crescent reels
    from fight
Before their dauntless hundreds, in prone
    flight
By thousands down the crags and thro' the
    vales.
O smallest among peoples! rough rock-
    throne
Of Freedom! warriors beating back the
    swarm
Of Turkish Islam for five hundred years,
Great Tsernogora! never since thine own
Black ridges drew the cloud and brake the
    storm
Has breathed a race of mightier mountain-
    eers.

## TO VICTOR HUGO

Contributed to 'The Nineteenth Century'
for June, 1877. It was written after a visit of
Lionel Tennyson to the French poet, who afterwards thanked the author for the sonnet in a
letter printed in the 'Memoir' (vol. ii. p. 218).

VICTOR in Drama, Victor in Romance,
Cloud - weaver of phantasmal hopes and
    fears,
French of the French, and Lord of human
    tears;
Child-lover; Bard whose fame-lit laurels
    glance
Darkening the wreaths of all that would
    advance,
Beyond our strait, their claim to be thy
    peers;
Weird Titan by thy winter weight of years
As yet unbroken, stormy voice of France!
Who dost not love our England — so they
    say;
I know not — England, France, all man to
    be
Will make one people ere man's race be
    run:
And I, desiring that diviner day,
Yield thee full thanks for thy full cour-
    tesy
To younger England in the boy my son.

## TRANSLATIONS, ETC.

## BATTLE OF BRUNANBURH

A translation from the Anglo-Saxon, first
printed in the 'Ballads' volume, with the following prefatory note : —
    'Constantinus, King of the Scots, after hav-
ing sworn allegiance to Athelstan, allied himself with the Danes of Ireland under Anlaf,
and invading England, was defeated by Athelstan and his brother Edmund with great
slaughter at Brunanburh in the year 937.'

I

[1] ATHELSTAN King,
Lord among Earls,
Bracelet-bestower and
Baron of Barons,
He with his brother,
Edmund Atheling,
Gaining a lifelong
Glory in battle,
Slew with the sword-edge
There by Brunanburh,
Brake the shield-wall,
Hew'd the linden-wood,[2]
Hack'd the battle-shield,
Sons of Edward with hammer'd brands.

II

Theirs was a greatness
Got from their grandsires —
Theirs that so often in
Strife with their enemies
Struck for their hoards and their hearths
    and their homes.

III

Bow'd the spoiler,
Bent the Scotsman,
Fell the ship-crews
Doom'd to the death.
All the field with blood of the fighters
    Flow'd, from when first the great
Sun-star of morning-tide,
Lamp of the Lord God
Lord everlasting,
Glode over earth till the glorious creature
Sank to his setting.

[1] I have more or less availed myself of my
son's prose translation of this poem in the
'Contemporary Review' (November, 1876).
[2] Shields of lindenwood.

#### IV

There lay many a man
Marr'd by the javelin,
Men of the Northland
Shot over shield.
There was the Scotsman
Weary of war.

#### V

We the West-Saxons,
Long as the daylight
Lasted, in companies
Troubled the track of the host that we
        hated;
Grimly with swords that were sharp from
        the grindstone,
Fiercely we hack'd at the flyers before us.

#### VI

Mighty the Mercian,
Hard was his hand-play,
Sparing not any of
Those that with Anlaf,
Warriors over the
Weltering waters
Borne in the bark's-bosom,
Drew to this island —
Doom'd to the death.

#### VII

Five young kings put asleep by the sword-
        stroke,
Seven strong earls of the army of Anlaf
Fell on the war-field, numberless numbers,
Shipmen and Scotsmen.

#### VIII

Then the Norse leader —
Dire was his need of it,
Few were his following —
Fled to his war-ship;
Fleeted his vessel to sea with the king in
        it,
Saving his life on the fallow flood.

#### IX

Also the crafty one,
Constantinus,
Crept to his North again,
Hoar-headed hero !

#### X

Slender warrant had
*He* to be proud of

The welcome of war-knives —
He that was reft of his
Folk and his friends that had
Fallen in conflict,
Leaving his son too
Lost in the carnage,
Mangled to morsels,
A youngster in war !

#### XI

Slender reason had
*He* to be glad of
The clash of the war-glaive —
Traitor and trickster
And spurner of treaties —
He nor had Anlaf
With armies so broken
A reason for bragging
That they had the better
In perils of battle
On places of slaughter —
The struggle of standards,
The rush of the javelins,
The crash of the charges,[1]
The wielding of weapons —
The play that they play'd with
The children of Edward.

#### XII

Then with their nail'd prows
Parted the Norsemen, a
Blood-redden'd relic of
Javelins over
The jarring breaker, the deep-sea billow,
Shaping their way toward Dyflen[2] again,
Shamed in their souls.

#### XIII

Also the brethren,
King and Atheling,
Each in his glory,
Went to his own in his own West-Saxon-
        land,
Glad of the war.

#### XIV

Many a carcase they left to be carrion,
Many a livid one, many a sallow-skin —
Left for the white-tail'd eagle to tear it,
        and
Left for the horny-nibb'd raven to rend it,
        and

---

[1] Lit. ' the gathering of men.'
[2] Dublin.

Gave to the garbaging war-hawk to gorge
  it, and
That gray beast, the wolf of the weald.

### XV

Never had huger
Slaughter of heroes
Slain by the sword-edge —
Such as old writers
Have writ of in histories —
Hapt in this isle, since
Up from the East hither
Saxon and Angle from
Over the broad billow
Broke into Britain with
Haughty war-workers who
Harried the Welshman, when
Earls that were lured by the
Hunger of glory gat
Hold of the land.


## ACHILLES OVER THE TRENCH

### [ILIAD, XVIII. 202]

First printed in 'The Nineteenth Century'
for August, 1877.

So saying, light-foot Iris pass'd away.
Then rose Achilles dear to Zeus; and
  round
The warrior's puissant shoulders Pallas
  flung
Her fringed ægis, and around his head
The glorious goddess wreath'd a golden
  cloud,
And from it lighted an all-shining flame.
As when a smoke from a city goes to heaven
Far off from out an island girt by foes,
All day the men contend in grievous war
From their own city, but with set of sun
Their fires flame thickly, and aloft the glare
Flies streaming, if perchance the neighbors
  round
May see, and sail to help them in the war;
So from his head the splendor went to hea-
  ven.
From wall to dyke he stept, he stood, nor
  join'd
The Achæans — honoring his wise mother's
  word —
There standing, shouted, and Pallas far
  away
Call'd; and a boundless panic shook the foe.

For like the clear voice when a trumpet
  shrills,
Blown by the fierce beleaguerers of a town,
So rang the clear voice of Æakidês;
And when the brazen cry of Æakidês
Was heard among the Trojans, all their
  hearts
Were troubled, and the full-maned horses
  whirl'd
The chariots backward, knowing griefs at
  hand;
And sheer-astounded were the charioteers
To see the dread, unweariable fire
That always o'er the great Peleion's head
Burn'd, for the bright-eyed goddess made
  it burn.
Thrice from the dyke he sent his mighty
  shout,
Thrice backward reel'd the Trojans and
  allies;
And there and then twelve of their noblest
  died
Among their spears and chariots.


## TO PRINCESS FREDERICA ON
## HER MARRIAGE

Written on the marriage of Princess Freder-
ica of Hanover to Baron Alphonse de Pawel-
Rammingen at Windsor, April 24, 1880; and
included in the 'Ballads' volume.
  The Princess was the daughter of George V.
of Hanover, who died June 12, 1878.

O YOU that were eyes and light to the
    King till he past away
  From the darkness of life —
He saw not his daughter — he blest her:
    the blind King sees you to-day,
  He blesses the wife.


## SIR JOHN FRANKLIN

### ON THE CENOTAPH IN WESTMINSTER
### ABBEY

Written in 1877, and included in the 'Ballads' volume.

NOT here ! the white North has thy bones;
    and thou,
  Heroic sailor-soul,
Art passing on thine happier voyage now
  Toward no earthly pole.

## TO DANTE

(WRITTEN AT REQUEST OF THE FLOREN-
TINES)

Written for the festival in honor of Dante, opened by the King of Italy on the 14th of May, 1865, the six hundredth anniversary of the birth of the poet; and printed in the 'Ballads' volume. Tennyson did not go to Florence at the time, but sent the lines by Lord Houghton. For some curious facts concerning them, see the 'Memoir,' vol. ii. p. 255.

KING, that hast reign'd six hundred years, and grown
In power, and ever growest, since thine own
Fair Florence honoring thy nativity,
Thy Florence now the crown of Italy,
Hath sought the tribute of a verse from me,
I, wearing but the garland of a day,
Cast at thy feet one flower that fades away.

## TIRESIAS

### AND OTHER POEMS

This volume was published in 1885, with the following dedication:—

TO MY GOOD FRIEND
ROBERT BROWNING
WHOSE GENIUS AND GENIALITY
WILL BEST APPRECIATE WHAT MAY BE BEST
AND MAKE MOST ALLOWANCE FOR WHAT MAY BE WORST
THIS VOLUME
IS
AFFECTIONATELY DEDICATED

Mr. Arthur Waugh ('Alfred Lord Tennyson,' 2d ed., London, 1893), remarks: 'It is characteristic of a certain shyness in Tennyson that he never told Browning of the dedication, and it was not until the book was in the hands of the public that the latter learned the circumstance from a friend.'

The poems that follow, as far as the lines 'To H. R. H. Princess Beatrice,' were included in the 'Tiresias' volume. The Idyll, 'Balin and Balan,' also appeared in this volume for the first time.

## TO E. FITZGERALD

This introduction to the poem that follows was apparently written on or about March 31, 1883, when Fitzgerald was seventy-five years of age. He was rather more than a year older than Tennyson, who was born August 6, 1809. He died June 14, 1883, before the volume containing the poem was published.

OLD FITZ, who from your suburb grange,
Where once I tarried for a while,
Glance at the wheeling orb of change,
And greet it with a kindly smile;
Whom yet I see as there you sit
Beneath your sheltering garden-tree,
And watch your doves about you flit,
And plant on shoulder, hand, and knee,

Or on your head their rosy feet,
As if they knew your diet spares
Whatever moved in that full sheet
Let down to Peter at his prayers;
Who live on milk and meal and grass;
And once for ten long weeks I tried
Your table of Pythagoras,
And seem'd at first 'a thing enskied,'
As Shakespeare has it, airy-light
To float above the ways of men,
Then fell from that half-spiritual height
Chill'd, till I tasted flesh again
One night when earth was winter-black,
And all the heavens flash'd in frost;
And on me, half-asleep, came back
That wholesome heat the blood had lost,
And set me climbing icy capes
And glaciers, over which there roll'd

To meet me long-arm'd vines with grapes
　Of Eshcol hugeness; for the cold
Without, and warmth within me, wrought
　To mould the dream; but none can say
That Lenten fare makes Lenten thought
　Who reads your golden Eastern lay,
Than which I know no version done
　In English more divinely well;
A planet equal to the sun
　Which cast it, that large infidel
Your Omar; and your Omar drew
　Full-handed plaudits from our best
In modern letters, and from two,
　Old friends outvaluing all the rest,
Two voices heard on earth no more;
　But we old friends are still alive,
And I am nearing seventy-four,
　While you have touch'd at seventy-five,
And so I send a birthday line
　Of greeting; and my son, who dipt
In some forgotten book of mine
　With sallow scraps of manuscript,
And dating many a year ago,
　Has hit on this, which you will take,
My Fitz, and welcome, as I know,
　Less for its own than for the sake
Of one recalling gracious times,
　When, in our younger London days,
You found some merit in my rhymes,
　And I more pleasure in your praise.


## TIRESIAS

First published in 1885, though written
much earlier, as we learn from the dedicatory
poem.

I wish I were as in the years of old,
While yet the blessed daylight made itself
Ruddy thro' both the roofs of sight, and
　　woke
These eyes, now dull, but then so keen to
　　seek
The meanings ambush'd under all they
　　saw,
The flight of birds, the flame of sacrifice,
What omens may foreshadow fate to man
And woman, and the secret of the Gods.
　My son, the Gods, despite of human
　　prayer,
Are slower to forgive than human kings. 10
The great God Arês burns in anger still
Against the guiltless heirs of him from
　　Tyre,

Our Cadmus, out of whom thou art, who
　　found
Beside the springs of Dircê, smote, and
　　still'd
Thro' all its folds the multitudinous beast,
The dragon, which our trembling fathers
　　call'd
The God's own son.
　　　　　　　　A tale, that told to me,
When but thine age, by age as winter-
　　white
As mine is now, amazed, but made me
　　yearn
For larger glimpses of that more than
　　man　　　　　　　　　　　　　　　20
Which rolls the heavens, and lifts and lays
　　the deep,
Yet loves and hates with mortal hates and
　　loves,
And moves unseen among the ways of
　　men.
　Then, in my wanderings all the lands
　　that lie
Subjected to the Heliconian ridge
Have heard this footstep fall, altho' my
　　wont
Was more to scale the highest of the
　　heights
With some strange hope to see the nearer
　　God.
One naked peak — the sister of the Sun
Would climb from out the dark, and linger
　　there　　　　　　　　　　　　　　30
To silver all the valleys with her shafts —
There once, but long ago, five - fold thy
　　term
Of years, I lay; the winds were dead for
　　heat;
The noonday crag made the hand burn;
　　and sick
For shadow — not one bush was near — I
　　rose,
Following a torrent till its myriad falls
Found silence in the hollows underneath.
　There in a secret olive-glade I saw
Pallas Athene climbing from the bath　39
In anger; yet one glittering foot disturb'd
The lucid well; one snowy knee was prest
Against the margin flowers; a dreadful
　　light
Came from her golden hair, her golden
　　helm
And all her golden armor on the grass,
And from her virgin breast, and virgin
　　eyes

Remaining fixt on mine, till mine grew
    dark
For ever, and I heard a voice that said,
'Henceforth be blind, for thou hast seen
    too much,
And speak the truth that no man may be-
    lieve.'
  Son, in the hidden world of sight that
    lives                                    50
Behind this darkness, I behold her still,
Beyond all work of those who carve the
    stone,
Beyond all dreams of Godlike womanhood,
Ineffable beauty, out of whom, at a glance,
And as it were, perforce, upon me flash'd
The power of prophesying — but to me
No power — so chain'd and coupled with
    the curse
Of blindness and their unbelief who heard
And heard not, when I spake of famine,
    plague,
Shrine - shattering earthquake, fire, flood,
    thunderbolt,                            60
And angers of the Gods for evil done
And expiation lack'd — no power on Fate
Theirs, or mine own ! for when the crowd
    would roar
For blood, for war, whose issue was their
    doom,
To cast wise words among the multitude
Was flinging fruit to lions; nor, in hours
Of civil outbreak, when I knew the twain
Would each waste each, and bring on both
    the yoke
Of stronger states, was mine the voice to
    curb                                     69
The madness of our cities and their kings.
  Who ever turn'd upon his heel to hear
My warning that the tyranny of one
Was prelude to the tyranny of all ?
My counsel that the tyranny of all
Led backward to the tyranny of one ?
  This power hath work'd no good to aught
    that lives,
And these blind hands were useless in their
    wars.
O, therefore, that the unfulfill'd desire,
The grief for ever born from griefs to be,
The boundless yearning of the prophet's
    heart —                                 80
Could *that* stand forth, and like a statue,
    rear'd
To some great citizen, win all praise from
    all
Who past it, saying, 'That was he !'

                                    In vain !
Virtue must shape itself in deed, and those
Whom weakness or necessity have cramp'd
Within themselves, immerging, each, his
    urn
In his own well, draws solace as he may.
  Menœceus, thou hast eyes, and I can hear
Too plainly what full tides of onset sap
Our seven high gates, and what a weight
    of war                                  90
Rides on those ringing axles ! jingle of
    bits,
Shouts, arrows, tramp of the horn-footed
    horse
That grind the glebe to powder ! Stony
    showers
Of that ear-stunning hail of Arês crash
Along the sounding walls. Above, below,
Shock after shock, the song-built towers
    and gates
Reel, bruised and butted with the shudder-
    ing
War-thunder of iron rams; and from within
The city comes a murmur void of joy,
Lest she be taken captive — maidens,
    wives,                                 100
And mothers with their babblers of the
    dawn,
And oldest age in shadow from the night,
Falling about their shrines before their
    Gods,
And wailing, 'Save us.'
                        And they wail to thee !
These eyeless eyes, that cannot see thine
    own,
See this, that only in thy virtue lies
The saving of our Thebes; for, yesternight,
To me, the great God Arês, whose one
    bliss
Is war and human sacrifice — himself
Blood-red from battle, spear and helmet
    tipt                                    110
With stormy light as on a mast at sea,
Stood out before a darkness, crying,
    'Thebes,
Thy Thebes shall fall and perish, for I
    loathe
The seed of Cadmus — yet if one of these
By his own hand — if one of these —'
                                    My son,
No sound is breathed so potent to coerce,
And to conciliate, as their names who dare
For that sweet mother land which gave
    them birth
Nobly to do, nobly to die. Their names,

Graven on memorial columns, are a song  120
Heard in the future; few, but more than
    wall
And rampart, their examples reach a hand
Far thro' all years, and everywhere they
    meet
And kindle generous purpose, and the
    strength
To mould it into action pure as theirs.
    Fairer thy fate than mine, if life's best
        end
Be to end well! and thou refusing this,
Unvenerable will thy memory be
While men shall move the lips; but if thou
    dare —
Thou, one of these, the race of Cadmus —
    then                                        130
No stone is fitted in yon marble girth
Whose echo shall not tongue thy glorious
    doom,
Nor in this pavement but shall ring thy
    name
To every hoof that clangs it, and the
    springs
Of Dircè laving yonder battle-plain,
Heard from the roofs by night, will mur-
    mur thee
To thine own Thebes, while Thebes thro'
    thee shall stand
Firm-based with all her Gods.
                    The Dragon's cave
Half hid, they tell me, now in flowing
    vines —
Where once he dwelt and whence he roll'd
    himself                                     140
At dead of night — thou knowest, and that
    smooth rock
Before it, altar-fashion'd, where of late
The woman-breasted Sphinx, with wings
    drawn back,
Folded her lion paws, and look'd to Thebes.
There blanch the bones of whom she slew,
    and these
Mixt with her own, because the fierce beast
    found
A wiser than herself, and dash'd herself
Dead in her rage; but thou art wise
    enough,
Tho' young, to love thy wiser, blunt the
    curse                                       149
Of Pallas, hear, and tho' I speak the truth
Believe I speak it, let thine own hand
    strike
Thy youthful pulses into rest and quench
The red God's anger, fearing not to plunge

Thy torch of life in darkness, rather — thou
Rejoicing that the sun, the moon, the stars
Send no such light upon the ways of men
As one great deed.
                    Thither, my son, and there
Thou, that hast never known the embrace
    of love,                                    158
Offer thy maiden life.
                    This useless hand!
I felt one warm tear fall upon it.   Gone!
He will achieve his greatness.
                                But for me,
I would that I were gather'd to my rest,
And mingled with the famous kings of old,
On whom about their ocean-islets flash
The faces of the Gods — the wise man's
    word,
Here trampled by the populace underfoot,
There crown'd with worship — and these
    eyes will find
The men I knew, and watch the chariot
    whirl
About the goal again, and hunters race  169
The shadowy lion, and the warrior-kings,
In height and prowess more than human,
    strive
Again for glory, while the golden lyre
Is ever sounding in heroic ears
Heroic hymns, and every way the vales
Wind, clouded with the grateful incense-
    fume
Of those who mix all odor to the Gods
On one far height in one far-shining fire.

---

'One height and one far-shining fire!'
    And while I fancied that my friend
For this brief idyll would require          180
    A less diffuse and opulent end,
And would defend his judgment well,
    If I should deem it over nice —
The tolling of his funeral bell
    Broke on my Pagan Paradise,
And mixt the dream of classic times,
    And all the phantoms of the dream,
With present grief, and made the rhymes,
    That miss'd his living welcome, seem
Like would-be guests an hour too late,   190
    Who down the highway moving on
With easy laughter find the gate
    Is bolted, and the master gone.
Gone into darkness, that full light
    Of friendship! past, in sleep, away
By night, into the deeper night!
    The deeper night?   A clearer day

Than our poor twilight dawn on earth —
  If night, what barren toil to be !
What life, so maim'd by night, were
    worth                                     200
  Our living out ?  Not mine to me
Remembering all the golden hours
  Now silent, and so many dead,
And him the last; and laying flowers,
  This wreath, above his honor'd head,
And praying that, when I from hence
  Shall fade with him into the unknown,
My close of earth's experience
  May prove as peaceful as his own.


## THE WRECK

This and the poems that follow were printed
for the first time in the ' Tiresias ' volume,
unless otherwise explained in the prefatory
notes.
' The Wreck,' as the ' Memoir ' (vol. ii. p. 318)
informs us, was ' suggested by a catastrophe
which happened to an Italian vessel, named the
Rosina, bound from Catania for New York.'

I

Hide me, mother ! my fathers belong'd to
    the church of old,
I am driven by storm and sin and death to
    the ancient fold,
I cling to the Catholic Cross once more, to
    the Faith that saves.
My brain is full of the crash of wrecks,
    and the roar of waves,
My life itself is a wreck, I have sullied a
    noble name,
I am flung from the rushing tide of the
    world as a waif of shame,
I am roused by the wail of a child, and
    awake to a livid light,
And a ghastlier face than ever has haunted
    a grave by night.
I would hide from the storm without, I
    would flee from the storm within,
I would make my life one prayer for a soul
    that died in his sin,                     10
I was the tempter, mother, and mine was
    the deeper fall;
I will sit at your feet, I will hide my face,
    I will tell you all.

II

He that they gave me to, mother, a heed-
    less and innocent bride —

I never have wrong'd his heart, I have only
    wounded his pride —
Spain in his blood and the Jew — dark-vis-
    aged, stately and tall —
A princelier-looking man never stept thro'
    a prince's hall.
And who, when his anger was kindled,
    would venture to give him the nay ?
And a man men fear is a man to be loved
    by the women, they say.
And I could have loved him too, if the
    blossom can dote on the blight,
Or the young green leaf rejoice in the frost
    that sears it at night;                   20
He would open the books that I prized, and
    toss them away with a yawn,
Repell'd by the magnet of Art to the which
    my nature was drawn,
The word of the Poet by whom the deeps
    of the world are stirr'd,
The music that robes it in language be-
    neath and beyond the word !
My Shelley would fall from my hands when
    he cast a contemptuous glance
From where he was poring over his Tables
    of Trade and Finance;
My hands, when I heard him coming, would
    drop from the chords or the keys,
But ever I fail'd to please him, however I
    strove to please —
All day long far-off in the cloud of the city,
    and there
Lost, head and heart, in the chances of
    dividend, consol, and share —            30
And at home if I sought for a kindly ca-
    ress, being woman and weak,
His formal kiss fell chill as a flake of snow
    on the cheek.
And so, when I bore him a girl, when I
    held it aloft in my joy,
He look'd at it coldly, and said to me,
    ' Pity it is n't a boy.'
The one thing given me, to love and to live
    for, glanced at in scorn !
The child that I felt I could die for — as
    if she were basely born !
I had lived a wild-flower life, I was planted
    now in a tomb;
The daisy will shut to the shadow, I closed
    my heart to the gloom;
I threw myself all abroad — I would play
    my part with the young                    39
By the low foot-lights of the world — and
    I caught the wreath that was flung.

## III

Mother, I have not — however their tongues
   may have babbled of me —
Sinn'd thro' an animal vileness, for all but
   a dwarf was he,
And all but a hunchback too; and I look'd
   at him, first, askance,
With pity — not he the knight for an am-
   orous girl's romance !
Tho' wealthy enough to have bask'd in the
   light of a dowerless smile,
Having lands at home and abroad in a rich
   West-Indian isle;
But I came on him once at a ball, the heart
   of a listening crowd —
Why, what a brow was there ! he was
   seated — speaking aloud
To women, the flower of the time, and men
   at the helm of state —
Flowing with easy greatness and touching
   on all things great,    50
Science, philosophy, song — till I felt myself ready to weep
For I knew not what, when I heard that
   voice, — as mellow and deep
As a psalm by a mighty master and peal'd
   from an organ, — roll
Rising and falling — for, mother, the voice
   was the voice of the soul;
And the sun of the soul made day in the
   dark of his wonderful eyes.
Here was the hand that would help me,
   would heal me — the heart that was
   wise !
And he, poor man, when he learnt that I
   hated the ring I wore,
He helpt me with death, and he heal'd me
   with sorrow for evermore.

## IV

For I broke the bond. That day my nurse
   had brought me the child.
The small sweet face was flush'd, but it
   coo'd to the mother and smiled.    60
' Anything ailing,' I ask'd her, ' with baby ? '
   She shook her head,
And the motherless mother kiss'd it, and
   turn'd in her haste and fled.

## V

Low warm winds had gently breathed us
   away from the land —
Ten long sweet summer days upon deck,
   sitting hand in hand —

When he clothed a naked mind with the
   wisdom and wealth of his own,
And I bow'd myself down as a slave to his
   intellectual throne,
When he coin'd into English gold some
   treasure of classical song,
When he flouted a statesman's error, or
   flamed at a public wrong,
When he rose as it were on the wings of an
   eagle beyond me, and past
Over the range and the change of the
   world from the first to the last,    70
When he spoke of his tropical home in the
   canes by the purple tide,
And the high star-crowns of his palms on
   the deep-wooded mountain-side,
And cliffs all robed in lianas that dropt to
   the brink of his bay,
And trees like the towers of a minster, the
   sons of a winterless day.
' Paradise there ! ' so he said, but I seem'd
   in Paradise then
With the first great love I had felt for the
   first and greatest of men;
Ten long days of summer and sin — if it
   must be so —
But days of a larger light than I ever again
   shall know —
Days that will glimmer, I fear, thro' life to
   my latest breath;
' No frost there,' so he said, ' as in truest
   love no death.'    80

## VI

Mother, one morning a bird with a warble
   plaintively sweet
Perch'd on the shrouds, and then fell flut-
   tering down at my feet;
I took it, he made it a cage, we fondled it,
   Stephen and I,
But it died, and I thought of the child for
   a moment, I scarce know why.

## VII

But if sin be sin, not inherited fate, as
   many will say,
My sin to my desolate little one found me
   at sea on a day,
When her orphan wail came borne in the
   shriek of a growing wind,
And a voice rang out in the thunders of
   ocean and heaven, ' Thou hast sinn'd.'
And down in the cabin were we, for the
   towering crest of the tides

Plunged on the vessel and swept in a cata-
    ract off from her sides,                90
And ever the great storm grew with a howl
    and a hoot of the blast
In the rigging, voices of hell — then came
    the crash of the mast.
'The wages of sin is death,' and there I
    began to weep,
'I am the Jonah, the crew should cast me
    into the deep,
For, ah, God! what a heart was mine to
    forsake her even for you!'
'Never the heart among women,' he said,
    'more tender and true.'
'The heart! not a mother's heart, when I
    left my darling alone.'
'Comfort yourself, for the heart of the
    father will care for his own.'
'The heart of the father will spurn her,' I
    cried, 'for the sin of the wife,
The cloud of the mother's shame will enfold
    her and darken her life.'            100
Then his pale face twitch'd. 'O Stephen,
    I love you, I love you, and yet' —
As I lean'd away from his arms — 'would
    God, we had never met!'
And he spoke not — only the storm; till
    after a little, I yearn'd
For his voice again, and he call'd to me,
    'Kiss me!' and there — as I
    turn'd —
'The heart, the heart!' I kiss'd him, I
    clung to the sinking form,
And the storm went roaring above us, and
    he — was out of the storm.

### VIII

And then, then, mother, the ship stagger'd
    under a thunderous shock,
That shook us asunder, as if she had struck
    and crash'd on a rock;
For a huge sea smote every soul from the
    decks of the Falcon but one;
All of them, all but the man that was
    lash'd to the helm had gone;    110
And I fell — and the storm and the days
    went by, but I knew no more —
Lost myself — lay like the dead by the
    dead on the cabin floor,
Dead to the death beside me, and lost to
    the loss that was mine,
With a dim dream, now and then, of a
    hand giving bread and wine,

Till I woke from the trance, and the ship
    stood still, and the skies were blue,
But the face I had known, O mother, was
    not the face that I knew.

### IX

The strange misfeaturing mask that I saw
    so amazed me that I
Stumbled on deck, half mad. I would fling
    myself over and die!
But one — he was waving a flag — the one
    man left on the wreck —
'Woman,' — he graspt at my arm, — 'stay
    there!' — I crouch'd upon deck —
'We are sinking, and yet there's hope:
    look yonder,' he cried, 'a sail!'    121
In a tone so rough that I broke into pas-
    sionate tears, and the wail
Of a beaten babe, till I saw that a boat was
    nearing us — then
All on a sudden I thought, I shall look on
    the child again.

### X

They lower'd me down the side, and there
    in the boat I lay
With sad eyes fixt on the lost sea-home, as
    we glided away,
And I sigh'd as the low dark hull dipt
    under the smiling main,
'Had I stay'd with *him*, I had now — with
    *him* — been out of my pain.'

### XI

They took us aboard. The crew were gentle,
    the captain kind,
But *I* was the lonely slave of an often-
    wandering mind;                    130
For whenever a rougher gust might tumble
    a stormier wave,
'O Stephen,' I moan'd, 'I am coming to
    thee in thine ocean-grave.'
And again, when a balmier breeze curl'd
    over a peacefuller sea,
I found myself moaning again, 'O child, I
    am coming to thee.'

### XII

The broad white brow of the isle — that
    bay with the color'd sand —
Rich was the rose of sunset there, as we
    drew to the land;
All so quiet the ripple would hardly blanch
    into spray

At the feet of the cliff; and I pray'd —
    'My child,'—for I still could pray,—
'May her life be as blissfully calm, be
    never gloom'd by the curse    139
Of a sin, not hers!'
        Was it well with the child?
          I wrote to the nurse
Who had borne my flower on her hireling
    heart; and an answer came
Not from the nurse — nor yet to the wife
    — to her maiden name!
I shook as I open'd the letter — I knew
    that hand too well —
And from it a scrap, clipt out of the
    'deaths' in a paper, fell.
'Ten long sweet summer days' of fever,
    and want of care!
And gone — that day of the storm — O
    mother, she came to me there!

## DESPAIR

First printed in 'The Nineteenth Century'
for November, 1881, with the following preface: 'A man and his wife having lost faith in
a God, and hope of a life to come, and being
utterly miserable in this, resolve to end themselves by drowning. The woman is drowned,
but the man rescued by a minister of the sect
he had abandoned.'

I

Is it you, that preach'd in the chapel there
    looking over the sand?
Follow'd us too that night, and dogg'd us,
    and drew me to land?

II

What did I feel that night? You are
    curious. How should I tell?
Does it matter so much what I felt? You
    rescued me — yet — was it well
That you came unwish'd for, uncall'd, be-
    tween me and the deep and my
    doom,
Three days since, three more dark days of
    the Godless gloom
Of a life without sun, without health, with-
    out hope, without any delight
In anything here upon earth? but, ah,
    God! that night, that night
When the rolling eyes of the lighthouse
    there on the fatal neck    9

Of land running out into rock — they had
    saved many hundreds from wreck —
Glared on our way toward death, I remem-
    ber I thought, as we past,
Does it matter how many they saved? we
    are all of us wreck'd at last —
'Do you fear?' and there came thro' the
    roar of the breaker a whisper, a
    breath,
'Fear? am I not with you? I am frighted
    at life, not death.'

III

And the suns of the limitless universe
    sparkled and shone in the sky,
Flashing with fires as of God, but we knew
    that their light was a lie —
Bright as with deathless hope — but, how-
    ever they sparkled and shone,
The dark little worlds running round them
    were worlds of woe like our own —
No soul in the heaven above, no soul on
    the earth below,
A fiery scroll written over with lamentation
    and woe.    20

IV

See, we were nursed in the drear nightfold
    of your fatalist creed,
And we turn'd to the growing dawn, we had
    hoped for a dawn indeed,
When the light of a sun that was coming
    would scatter the ghosts of the past,
And the cramping creeds that had mad-
    den'd the peoples would vanish at
    last,
And we broke away from the Christ, our
    human brother and friend,
For He spoke, or it seem'd that He spoke,
    of a hell without help, without end.

V

Hoped for a dawn, and it came, but the
    promise had faded away;
We had past from a cheerless night to the
    glare of a drearier day;
He is only a cloud and a smoke who was
    once a pillar of fire,
The guess of a worm in the dust and the
    shadow of its desire —    30
Of a worm as it writhes in a world of the
    weak trodden down by the strong,
Of a dying worm in a world, all massacre,
    murder, and wrong.

VI

O, we poor orphans of nothing — alone on
    that lonely shore —
Born of the brainless Nature who knew not
    that which she bore !
Trusting no longer that earthly flower
    would be heavenly fruit —
Come from the brute, poor souls — no souls
    — and to die with the brute —

VII

Nay, but I am not claiming your pity; I
    know you of old —
Small pity for those that have ranged
    from the narrow warmth of your
    fold,
Where you bawl'd the dark side of your
    faith and a God of eternal rage,
Till you flung us back on ourselves, and the
    human heart, and the Age.    40

VIII

But pity — the Pagan held it a vice — was
    in her and in me,
Helpless, taking the place of the pitying
    God that should be !
Pity for all that aches in the grasp of an
    idiot power,
And pity for our own selves on an earth
    that bore not a flower;
Pity for all that suffers on land or in air or
    the deep,
And pity for our own selves till we long'd
    for eternal sleep.

IX

'Lightly step over the sands ! the waters
    — you hear them call !
Life with its anguish, and horrors, and
    errors — away with it all !'
And she laid her hand in my own — she
    was always loyal and sweet —
Till the points of the foam in the dusk
    came playing about our feet.    50
There was a strong sea-current would sweep
    us out to the main.
'Ah, God !' tho' I felt as I spoke I was
    taking the name in vain —
'Ah, God !' and we turn'd to each other,
    we kiss'd, we embraced, she and I,
Knowing the love we were used to believe
    everlasting would die.
We had read their know-nothing books, and
    we lean'd to the darker side —

Ah, God, should we find Him, perhaps, per-
    haps, if we died, if we died;
We never had found Him on earth, this
    earth is a fatherless hell —
'Dear love, for ever and ever, for ever
    and ever farewell !'
Never a cry so desolate, not since the world
    began,
Never a kiss so sad, no, not since the com-
    ing of man !    60

X

But the blind wave cast me ashore, and
    you saved me, a valueless life.
Not a grain of gratitude mine ! You have
    parted the man from the wife.
I am left alone on the land, she is all alone
    in the sea;
If a curse meant aught, I would curse you
    for not having let me be.

XI

Visions of youth — for my brain was drunk
    with the water, it seems;
I had past into perfect quiet at length out
    of pleasant dreams,
And the transient trouble of drowning —
    what was it when match'd with the
    pains
Of the hellish heat of a wretched life rush-
    ing back thro' the veins ?

XII

Why should I live ? one son had forged on
    his father and fled,
And if I believed in a God, I would thank
    Him, the other is dead,    70
And there was a baby-girl, that had never
    look'd on the light;
Happiest she of us all, for she past from
    the night to the night.

XIII

But the crime, if a crime, of her eldest-
    born, her glory, her boast,
Struck hard at the tender heart of the
    mother, and broke it almost;
Tho', glory and shame dying out for ever in
    endless time,
Does it matter so much whether crown'd
    for a virtue, or hang'd for a crime ?

XIV

And ruin'd by him, by him, I stood there,
    naked, amazed

In a world of arrogant opulence, fear'd myself turning crazed,
And I would not be mock'd in a madhouse ! and she, the delicate wife,
With a grief that could only be cured, if
cured, by the surgeon's knife, —  80

### XV

Why should we bear with an hour of torture, a moment of pain,
If every man die for ever, if all his griefs
are in vain,
And the homeless planet at length will be
wheel'd thro' the silence of space,
Motherless evermore of an ever-vanishing
race,
When the worm shall have writhed its last,
and its last brother-worm will have
fled
From the dead fossil skull that is left in
the rocks of an earth that is dead ?

### XVI

Have I crazed myself over their horrible
infidel writings ?  O, yes,
For these are the new dark ages, you see,
of the popular press,
When the bat comes out of his cave, and
the owls are whooping at noon,
And Doubt is the lord of this dunghill and
crows to the sun and the moon,  90
Till the sun and the moon of our science
are both of them turn'd into blood,
And Hope will have broken her heart, running after a shadow of good;
For their knowing and know-nothing books
are scatter'd from hand to hand —
We have knelt in your know-all chapel too,
looking over the sand.

### XVII

What ! I should call on that Infinite Love
that has served us so well ?
Infinite cruelty rather that made everlasting hell,
Made us, foreknew us, foredoom'd us, and
does what he will with his own;
Better our dead brute mother who never
has heard us groan !

### XVIII

Hell ? if the souls of men were immortal,
as men have been told,  99
The lecher would cleave to his lusts, and
the miser would yearn for his gold,

And so there were hell for ever ! but were
there a God, as you say,
His love would have power over hell till it
utterly vanish'd away.

### XIX

Ah, yet — I have had some glimmer, at
times, in my gloomiest woe,
Of a God behind all — after all — the great
God, for aught that I know;
But the God of love and of hell together —
they cannot be thought,
If there be such a God, may the Great God
curse him and bring him to nought !

### XX

Blasphemy ! whose is the fault ? is it
mine ? for why would you save
A madman to vex you with wretched words,
who is best in his grave ?
Blasphemy ! ay, why not, being damn'd beyond hope of grace ?  109
O, would I were yonder with her, and
away from your faith and your face !
Blasphemy ! true ! I have scared you pale
with my scandalous talk,
But the blasphemy to *my* mind lies all in
the way that you walk.

### XXI

Hence ! she is gone ! can I stay ? can I
breathe divorced from the past ?
You needs must have good lynx-eyes if I
do not escape you at last.
Our orthodox coroner doubtless will find it
a felo-de-se,
And the stake and the cross-road, fool, if
you will, does it matter to me ?

## THE ANCIENT SAGE

The 'Memoir' (vol. ii. p. 319) quotes from
the poet's MS.: 'The whole poem is very personal. The passages about "Faith" and the
"Passion of the Past" were more especially
my own personal feelings. This "Passion of
the Past" I used to feel when a boy.'

A THOUSAND summers ere the time of
Christ,
From out his ancient city came a Seer
Whom one that loved and honor'd him, and
yet
Was no disciple, richly garb'd, but worn

From wasteful living, follow'd — in his hand
A scroll of verse — till that old man before
A cavern whence an affluent fountain pour'd
From darkness into daylight, turn'd and spoke:

'This wealth of waters might but seem to draw
From yon dark cave, but, son, the source is higher,                                   10
Yon summit half - a - league in air — and higher
The cloud that hides it — higher still the heavens
Whereby the cloud was moulded, and whereout
The cloud descended. Force is from the heights.
I am wearied of our city, son, and go
To spend my one last year among the hills.
What hast thou there? Some death-song for the Ghouls
To make their banquet relish? let me read.

'" How far thro' all the bloom and brake
    That nightingale is heard!                20
  What power but the bird's could make
    This music in the bird?
  How summer-bright are yonder skies,
    And earth as fair in hue!
  And yet what sign of aught that lies
    Behind the green and blue?
  But man to-day is fancy's fool
    As man hath ever been.
  The nameless Power, or Powers, that rule
    Were never heard or seen."                30

If thou wouldst hear the Nameless, and wilt dive
Into the temple-cave of thine own self,
There, brooding by the central altar, thou
Mayst haply learn the Nameless hath a voice,
By which thou wilt abide, if thou be wise,
As if thou knewest, tho' thou canst not know;
For Knowledge is the swallow on the lake
That sees and stirs the surface-shadow there
But never yet hath dipt into the abysm,     39
The abysm of all abysms, beneath, within
The blue of sky and sea, the green of earth,
And in the million-millionth of a grain
Which cleft and cleft again for evermore,
And ever vanishing, never vanishes,

To me, my son, more mystic than myself,
Or even than the Nameless is to me.
  'And when thou sendest thy free soul thro' heaven,
Nor understandest bound nor boundlessness,
Thou seest the Nameless of the hundred names.
  'And if the Nameless should withdraw from all                                        50
Thy frailty counts most real, all thy world
Might vanish like thy shadow in the dark.

  ' " And since — from when this earth began —
    The Nameless never came
  Among us, never spake with man,
    And never named the Name " —

Thou canst not prove the Nameless, O my son,
Nor canst thou prove the world thou movest in,
Thou canst not prove that thou art body alone,
Nor canst thou prove that thou art spirit alone,                                      60
Nor canst thou prove that thou art both in one.
Thou canst not prove thou art immortal, no,
Nor yet that thou art mortal — nay, my son,
Thou canst not prove that I, who speak with thee,
Am not thyself in converse with thyself,
For nothing worthy proving can be proven,
Nor yet disproven. Wherefore thou be wise,
Cleave ever to the sunnier side of doubt,
And cling to Faith beyond the forms of Faith!
She reels not in the storm of warring words,                                          70
She brightens at the clash of "Yes" and "No,"
She sees the best that glimmers thro' the worst,
She feels the sun is hid but for a night,
She spies the summer thro' the winter bud,
She tastes the fruit before the blossom falls,
She hears the lark within the songless egg,
She finds the fountain where they wail'd "Mirage!"

' " What Power ?  aught akin to Mind,
 The mind in me and you ?
Or power as of the Gods gone blind 80
 Who see not what they do ? "

But some in yonder city hold, my son,
That none but gods could build this house
 of ours,
So beautiful, vast, various, so beyond
All work of man, yet, like all work of man,
A beauty with defect — till That which
 knows,
And is not known, but felt thro' what we
 feel
Within ourselves is highest, shall descend
On this half-deed, and shape it at the last
According to the Highest in the High-
 est. 90

' " What Power but the Years that make
 And break the vase of clay,
And stir the sleeping earth, and wake
 The bloom that fades away ?
What rulers but the Days and Hours
 That cancel weal with woe,
And wind the front of youth with flowers,
 And cap our age with snow ? "

The days and hours are ever glancing by,
And seem to flicker past thro' sun and
 shade, 100
Or short, or long, as Pleasure leads, or
 Pain,
But with the Nameless is nor day nor hour;
Tho' we, thin minds, who creep from
 thought to thought,
Break into " Thens " and " Whens " the
 Eternal Now —
This double seeming of the single world! —
My words are like the babblings in a
 dream
Of nightmare, when the babblings break
 the dream.
But thou be wise in this dream-world of
 ours,
Nor take thy dial for thy deity,
But make the passing shadow serve thy
 will. 110

' " The years that made the stripling wise
 Undo their work again,
And leave him, blind of heart and eyes,
 The last and least of men ;
Who clings to earth, and once would dare
 Hell-heat or Arctic cold,
And now one breath of cooler air
 Would loose him from his hold.

His winter chills him to the root,
 He withers marrow and mind ; 120
The kernel of the shrivell'd fruit
 Is jutting thro' the rind ;
The tiger spasms tear his chest,
 The palsy wags his head ;
The wife, the sons, who love him best
 Would fain that he were dead ;
The griefs by which he once was wrung
 Were never worth the while " —

Who knows ? or whether this earth-narrow
 life 129
Be yet but yolk, and forming in the shell ?

' " The shaft of scorn that once had stung
 But wakes a dotard smile."

The placid gleam of sunset after storm !

' " The statesman's brain that sway'd the past
 Is feebler than his knees ;
The passive sailor wrecks at last
 In ever-silent seas ;
The warrior hath forgot his arms,
 The learned all his lore ;
The changing market frets or charms 140
 The merchant's hope no more :
The prophet's beacon burn'd in vain,
 And now is lost in cloud ;
The plowman passes, bent with pain,
 To mix with what he plow'd ;
The poet whom his age would quote
 As heir of endless fame —
He knows not even the book he wrote,
 Not even his own name.
For man has overlived his day, 150
 And, darkening in the light,
Scarce feels the senses break away
 To mix with ancient Night."

The shell must break before the bird can
 fly.

' " The years that when my youth began
 Had set the lily and rose
By all my ways where'er they ran,
 Have ended mortal foes ;
My rose of love for ever gone,
 My lily of truth and trust — 16c
They made her lily and rose in one,
 And changed her into dust.
O rose-tree planted in my grief,
 And growing on her tomb,
Her dust is greening in your leaf,
 Her blood is in your bloom.
O slender lily waving there,
 And laughing back the light,
In vain you tell me ' Earth is fair '
 When all is dark as night," 170

My son, the world is dark with griefs and
    graves,
So dark that men cry out against the hea-
    vens.
Who knows but that the darkness is in
    man?
The doors of Night may be the gates of
    Light;
For wert thou born or blind or deaf, and
    then
Suddenly heal'd, how wouldst thou glory
    in all
The splendors and the voices of the world!
And we, the poor earth's dying race, and
    yet
No phantoms, watching from a phantom
    shore                                    179
Await the last and largest sense to make
The phantom walls of this illusion fade,
And show us that the world is wholly fair.

   '" But vain the tears for darken'd years
      As laughter over wine,
    And vain the laughter as the tears,
      O brother, mine or thine,
    For all that laugh, and all that weep
      And all that breathe are one
    Slight ripple on the boundless deep
      That moves, and all is gone."      190

But that one ripple on the boundless deep
Feels that the deep is boundless, and it-
    self
For ever changing form, but evermore
One with the boundless motion of the deep.

   '" Yet wine and laughter, friends! and set
      The lamps alight, and call
      For golden music, and forget
      The darkness of the pall."

If utter darkness closed the day, my
    son —
But earth's dark forehead flings athwart
    the heavens                              200
Her shadow crown'd with stars — and yon-
    der — out
To northward — some that never set, but
    pass
From sight and night to lose themselves in
    day.
I hate the black negation of the bier,
And wish the dead, as happier than our-
    selves
And higher, having climb'd one step be-
    yond

Our village miseries, might be borne in
    white
To burial or to burning, hymn'd from
    hence
With songs in praise of death, and crown'd
    with flowers!

   '" O worms and maggots of to-day     210
     Without their hope of wings!"

But louder than thy rhyme the silent Word
Of that world-prophet in the heart of man.

   '" Tho' some have gleams, or so they say,
     Of more than mortal things."

To-day? but what of yesterday? for oft
On me, when boy, there came what then I
    call'd,
Who knew no books and no philosophies,
In my boy-phrase, "The Passion of the
    Past."
The first gray streak of earliest summer-
    dawn,                                    220
The last long strife of waning crimson
    gloom,
As if the late and early were but one —
A height, a broken grange, a grove, a
    flower
Had murmurs, "Lost and gone, and lost
    and gone!"
A breath, a whisper — some divine fare-
    well —
Desolate sweetness — far and far away —
What had he loved, what had he lost, the
    boy?
I know not, and I speak of what has been.
   ' And more, my son! for more than once
    when I
Sat all alone, revolving in myself            230
The word that is the symbol of myself,
The mortal limit of the Self was loosed,
And past into the Nameless, as a cloud
Melts into heaven. I touch'd my limbs,
    the limbs
Were strange, not mine — and yet no shade
    of doubt,
But utter clearness, and thro' loss of self
The gain of such large life as match'd with
    ours
Were sun to spark — unshadowable in
    words,
Themselves but shadows of a shadow-
    world.

   '" And idle gleams will come and go,   240
     But still the clouds remain;"

The clouds themselves are children of the
  Sun.

' " And Night and Shadow rule below
    When only Day should reign."

And Day and Night are children of the
  Sun,
And idle gleams to thee are light to me.
Some say, the Light was father of the
  Night,
And some, the Night was father of the
  Light,
No night, no day ! — I touch thy world
  again —
No ill, no good ! such counter-terms, my
  son,                                        250
Are border-races, holding each its own
By endless war.  But night enough is there
In yon dark city.  Get thee back; and since
The key to that weird casket, which for
  thee
But holds a skull, is neither thine nor mine,
But in the hand of what is more than man,
Or in man's hand when man is more than
  man,
Let be thy wail, and help thy fellow-men,
And make thy gold thy vassal, not thy
  king,                                       259
And fling free alms into the beggar's bowl,
And send the day into the darken'd heart;
Nor list for guerdon in the voice of men,
A dying echo from a falling wall;
Nor care — for Hunger hath the evil eye —
To vex the noon with fiery gems, or fold
Thy presence in the silk of sumptuous
  looms;
Nor roll thy viands on a luscious tongue,
Nor drown thyself with flies in honeyed
  wine;
Nor thou be rageful, like a handled bee,
And lose thy life by usage of thy sting; 270
Nor harm an adder thro' the lust for harm,
Nor make a snail's horn shrink for wanton-
  ness.
And more — think well !  Do-well will fol-
  low thought,
And in the fatal sequence of this world
An evil thought may soil thy children's
  blood;
But curb the beast would cast thee in the
  mire,
And leave the hot swamp of voluptuous-
  ness,
A cloud between the Nameless and thyself,

And lay thine uphill shoulder to the wheel,
And climb the Mount of Blessing, whence,
  if thou                                     280
Look higher, then — perchance — thou may-
  est — beyond
A hundred ever-rising mountain lines,
And past the range of Night and Shadow
  — see
The high-heaven dawn of more than mortal
  day
Strike on the Mount of Vision !
                          So, farewell.'

## THE FLIGHT

A very early poem, as we learn from the
' Memoir,' though not printed until 1885.

### I

ARE you sleeping ? have you forgotten ?
  do not sleep, my sister dear !
How *can* you sleep ? the morning brings
  the day I hate and fear;
The cock has crow'd already once, he crows
  before his time;
Awake ! the creeping glimmer steals, the
  hills are white with rime.

### II

Ah, clasp me in your arms, sister, ah, fold
  me to your breast !
Ah, let me weep my fill once more, and cry
  myself to rest !
To rest ? to rest and wake no more were
  better rest for me,
Than to waken every morning to that face
  I loathe to see.

### III

I envied your sweet slumber, all night so
  calm you lay;
The night was calm, the morn is calm, and
  like another day;                          10
But I could wish yon moaning sea would
  rise and burst the shore,
And such a whirlwind blow these woods as
  never blew before.

### IV

For, one by one, the stars went down across
  the gleaming pane,
And project after project rose, and all of
  them were vain;

The blackthorn-blossom fades and falls and
   leaves the bitter sloe,
The hope I catch at vanishes, and youth is
   turn'd to woe.

### V

Come, speak a little comfort ! all night I
   pray'd with tears,
And yet no comfort came to me, and now
   the morn appears,
When he will tear me from your side, who
   bought me for his slave;
This father pays his debt with me, and
   weds me to my grave.    20

### VI

What father, this or mine, was he, who, on
   that summer day
When I had fallen from off the crag we
   clamber'd up in play,
Found, fear'd me dead, and groan'd, and
   took and kiss'd me, and again
He kiss'd me; and I loved him then; he
   *was* my father then.

### VII

No father now, the tyrant vassal of a tyrant vice !
The godless Jephtha vows his child . . .
   to one cast of the dice.
These ancient woods, this Hall at last will
   go — perhaps have gone,
Except his own meek daughter yield her
   life, heart, soul to one —

### VIII

To one who knows I scorn him.  O, the
   formal mocking bow,
The cruel smile, the courtly phrase that
   masks his malice now —    30
But often in the sidelong eyes a gleam of all
   things ill —
It is not Love but Hate that weds a bride
   against her will;

### IX

Hate, that would pluck from this true
   breast the locket that I wear,
The precious crystal into which I braided
   Edwin's hair !
The love that keeps this heart alive beats
   on it night and day —
One golden curl, his golden gift, before he
   past away.

### X

He left us weeping in the woods; his boat
   was on the sand;
How slowly down the rocks he went, how
   loth to quit the land !
And all my life was darken'd, as I saw the
   white sail run,
And darken, up that lane of light into the
   setting sun.    40

### XI

How often have we watch'd the sun fade
   from us thro' the West,
And follow Edwin to those isles, those
   Islands of the Blest !
Is *he* not there ? would I were there, the
   friend, the bride, the wife,
With him, where summer never dies, with
   Love, the sun of life !

### XII

O, would I were in Edwin's arms — once
   more — to feel his breath
Upon my cheek — on Edwin's ship, with
   Edwin, even in death,
Tho' all about the shuddering wreck the
   death-white sea should rave,
Or if lip were laid to lip on the pillows of
   the wave !

### XIII

Shall I take *him?*  I kneel with *him?*  I
   swear and swear forsworn
To love him most whom most I loathe, to
   honor whom I scorn ?    50
The Fiend would yell, the grave would
   yawn, my mother's ghost would
   rise —
To lie, to lie — in God's own house — the
   blackest of all lies !

### XIV

Why — rather than that hand in mine, tho'
   every pulse would freeze,
I 'd sooner fold an icy corpse dead of some
   foul disease.
Wed him ?  I will not wed him, let them
   spurn me from the doors,
And I will wander till I die about the barren moors.

### XV

The dear, mad bride who stabb'd her bridegroom on her bridal night —

If mad, then I am mad, but sane if she
   were in the right.
My father's madness makes me mad — but
   words are only words !
I am not mad, not yet, not quite — There !
   listen how the birds       60

### XVI

Begin to warble yonder in the budding
   orchard trees !
The lark has past from earth to heaven
   upon the morning breeze !
How gladly, were I one of those, how early
   would I wake !
And yet the sorrow that I bear is sorrow
   for *his* sake.

### XVII

They love their mates, to whom they sing;
   or else their songs, that meet
The morning with such music, would never
   be so sweet !
And tho' these fathers will not hear, the
   blessed Heavens are just,
And Love is fire, and burns the feet would
   trample it to dust.

### XVIII

A door was open'd in the house — who ?
   who ? my father sleeps !
A stealthy foot upon the stair ! he — some
   one — this way creeps !       70
If he ? yes, he — lurks, listens, fears his
   victim may have fled —
He ! where is some sharp-pointed thing ?
   he comes, and finds me dead.

### XIX

Not he, not yet ! and time to act — but how
   my temples burn !
And idle fancies flutter me, I know not
   where to turn;
Speak to me, sister, counsel me; this marriage must not be.
You only know the love that makes the
   world a world to me !

### XX

Our gentle mother, had *she* lived — but we
   were left alone.
That other left us to ourselves, he cared
   not for his own;
So all the summer long we roam'd in these
   wild woods of ours,
My Edwin loved to call us then ' his two
   wild woodland flowers.'    .  80

### XXI

Wild flowers blowing side by side in God's
   free light and air,
Wild flowers of the secret woods, when
   Edwin found us there,
Wild woods in which we roved with him,
   and heard his passionate vow,
Wild woods in which we rove no more, if
   we be parted now !

### XXII

You will not leave me thus in grief to wander forth forlorn;
We never changed a bitter word, not once
   since we were born;
Our dying mother join'd our hands; she
   knew this father well;
She bade us love, like souls in heaven, and
   now I fly from hell,

### XXIII

And you with me; and we shall light upon
   some lonely shore,
Some lodge within the waste sea-dunes, and
   hear the waters roar,     90
And see the ships from out the West go
   dipping thro' the foam,
And sunshine on that sail at last which
   brings our Edwin home.

### XXIV

But look, the morning grows apace, and
   lights the old church-tower,
And lights the clock ! the hand points five
   — O, me ! — it strikes the hour —
I bide no more, I meet my fate, whatever
   ills betide !
Arise, my own true sister, come forth ! the
   world is wide.

### XXV

And yet my heart is ill at ease, my eyes are
   dim with dew,
I seem to see a new-dug grave up yonder
   by the yew !
If we should never more return, but wander hand in hand
With breaking hearts, without a friend,
   and in a distant land !    100

### XXVI

O sweet, they tell me that the world is
   hard, and harsh of mind,
But can it be so hard, so harsh, as those
   that should be kind ?

That matters not.  Let come what will; at
    last the end is sure,
And every heart that loves with truth is
    equal to endure.


## TO-MORROW

Tennyson's one poem in Irish brogue;
founded on a story told him by Aubrey de
Vere.

### I

Her, that yer Honor was spakin' to?
    Whin, yer Honor? last year —
Standin' here be the bridge, when last yer
    Honor was here?
An' yer Honor ye gev her the top of the
    mornin', 'To-morra,' says she.
What did they call her, yer Honor?  They
    call'd her Molly Magee.
An' yer Honor's the thrue ould blood that
    always manes to be kind,
But there's rason in all things, yer Honor,
    for Molly was out of her mind.

### II

Shure, an' meself remimbers wan night
    comin' down be the sthrame,
An' it seems to me now like a bit of yisther-
    day in a dhrame —
Here where yer Honor seen her — there
    was but a slip of a moon,
But I hard thim — Molly Magee wid her
    bachelor, Danny O'Roon —            10
'You've been takin' a dhrop o' the crathur,'
    an' Danny says, 'Troth, an' I been
Dhrinkin' yer health wid Shamus O'Shea
    at Katty's shebeen;[1]
But I must be lavin' ye soon.'  'Ochone,
    are ye goin' away?'
'Goin' to cut the Sassenach whate,' he says,
    'over the say' —
'An' whin will ye meet me agin?' an' I
    hard him, 'Molly asthore,
I'll meet you agin to-morra,' says he, 'be
    the chapel-door.'
'An' whin are ye goin' to lave me?'  'O'
    Monday mornin',' says he;
'An' shure thin ye'll meet me to-morra?'
    'To-morra, to-morra, machree!'
Thin Molly's ould mother, yer Honor, that
    had no likin' for Dan,

[1] Grog-shop.

Call'd from her cabin an' tould her to
    come away from the man,            20
An' Molly Magee kem flyin' acrass me, as
    light as a lark,
An' Dan stood there for a minute, an' thin
    wint into the dark.
But wirrah! the storm that night — the
    tundher, an' rain that fell,
An' the sthrames runnin' down at the back
    o' the glin 'ud 'a dhrownded hell.

### III

But airth was at pace nixt mornin', an'
    hiven in its glory smiled,
As the Holy Mother o' Glory that smiles
    at her sleepin' child —
Ethen — she stept an the chapel-green, an'
    she turn'd herself roun'
Wid a diamond dhrop in her eye, for Danny
    was not to be foun',
An' many's the time that I watch'd her at
    mass lettin' down the tear,
For the divil a Danny was there, yer
    Honor, for forty year.            30

### IV

Och, Molly Magee, wid the red o' the rose
    an' the white o' the may,
An' yer hair as black as the night, an' yer
    eyes as bright as the day!
Achora, yer laste little whishper was sweet
    as the lilt of a bird!
Acushla, ye set me heart batin' to music
    wid ivery word!
An' sorra the Queen wid her sceptre in
    sich an illigant han',
An' the fall of yer foot in the dance was as
    light as snow an the lan',
An' the sun kem out of a cloud whiniver
    ye walkt in the shtreet,
An' Shamus O'Shea was yer shadda, an' laid
    himself undher yer feet,
An' I loved ye meself wid a heart an' a
    half, me darlin', and he
'Ud 'a shot his own sowl dead for a kiss of
    ye, Molly Magee.            40

### V

But shure we wor betther frinds whin I
    crack'd his skull for her sake,
An' he ped me back wid the best he could
    give at ould Donovan's wake —
For the boys wor about her agin whin Dan
    did n't come to the fore,

An' Shamus along wid the rest, but she put
thim all to the door.
An', afther, I thried her meself av the bird
'ud come to me call,
But Molly, begorrah, 'ud listhen to naither
at all, at all:

VI

An' her nabors an' frinds 'ud consowl an'
condowl wid her, airly an' late,
'Your Danny,' they says, 'niver crasst over
say to the Sassenach whate;
He's gone to the States, aroon, an' he's
married another wife,
An' ye'll niver set eyes an the face of the
thraithur agin in life!                         50
An' to dhrame of a married man, death
alive, is a mortial sin.'
But Molly says, 'I'd his hand-promise, an'
shure he'll meet me agin.'

VII

An' afther her paärints had inter'd glory,
an' both in wan day,
She began to spake to herself, the crathur,
an' whishper, an' say,
'To-morra, to-morra!' an' Father Mo-
lowny he tuk her in han',
'Molly, you're manin',' he says, 'me dear,
av I undherstan',
That ye'll meet your paärints agin an' yer
Danny O'Roon afore God
Wid his blessed Marthyrs an' Saints;' an'
she gev him a frindly nod,
'To-morra, to-morra,' she says, an' she
did n't intind to desave,
But her wits wor dead, an' her hair was as
white as the snow an a grave.          60

VIII

Arrah now, here last month they wor dig-
gin' the bog, an' they foun'
Dhrownded in black bog-wather a corp
lyin' undher groun'.

IX

Yer Honor's own agint, he says to me
wanst, at Katty's shebeen,
'The divil take all the black lan', for a
blessin' 'ud come wid the green!'
An' where 'ud the poor man, thin, cut his
bit o' turf for the fire?
But och! bad scran to the bogs whin they
swallies the man intire!

An' sorra the bog that's in hiven wid all
the light an' the glow,
An' there's hate enough, shure, widout
*thim* in the divil's kitchen below.

X

Thim ould blind nagers in Agypt, I hard
his Riverence say,
Could keep their haithen kings in the flesh
for the Jidgmint day,                          70
An', faix, be the piper o' Moses, they kep'
the cat an' the dog,
But it 'ud 'a been aisier work av they lived
be an Irish bog.

XI

How-an-iver they laid this body they foun'
an the grass,
Be the chapel-door, an' the people 'ud see
it that wint in to mass —
But a frish gineration had riz, an' most of
the ould was few,
An' I did n't know him meself, an' nōne of
the parish knew.

XII

But Molly kem limpin' up wid her stick, —
she was lamed iv a knee, —
Thin a slip of a gossoon call'd, 'Div ye
know him, Molly Magee?'
An' she stood up strait as the queen of the
world — she lifted her head —
'He said he would meet me to-morra!'
an' dhropt down dead an the dead.       80

XIII

Och, Molly, we thought, machree, ye would
start back agin into life,
Whin we laid yez, aich be aich, at yer wake
like husban' an' wife.
Sorra the dhry eye thin but was wet for the
frinds that was gone!
Sorra the silent throat but we hard it
cryin', 'Ochone!'
An' Shamus O'Shea that has now ten
childer, hansome an' tall,
Him an' his childer wor keenin' as if he
had lost thim all.

XIV

Thin his Riverence buried thim both in
wan grave be the dead boor-tree,[1]
The young man Danny O'Roon wid his ould
woman, Molly Magee.

[1] Elder-tree.

### XV

May all the flowers o' Jeroosilim blossom
    an' spring from the grass,
Imbrashin' an' kissin' aich other — as ye
    did — over yer Crass !    90
An' the lark fly out o' the flowers wid his
    song to the sun an' the moon,
An' tell thim in hiven about Molly Magee
    an' her Danny O'Roon,
Till Holy Saint Pether gets up wid his kays
    an' opens the gate !
An' shure, be the Crass, that 's betther nor
    cuttin' the Sassenach whate,
To be there wid the Blessed Mother an'
    Saints an' Marthyrs galore,
An' singin' yer ' Aves ' an' ' Pathers ' for
    iver an' ivermore.

### XVI

An' now that I tould yer Honor whativer
    I hard an' seen,
Yer Honor 'ill give me a thrifle to dhrink
    yer health in potheen.

## THE SPINSTER'S SWEET-ARTS

### I

MILK for my sweet-arts, Bess ! fur it mun
    be the time about now
When Molly cooms in fro' the far-end close
    wi' her paäils fro' the cow.
Eh ! tha be new to the plaäce — thou 'rt
    gaäpin' — does n't tha see
I calls 'em arter the fellers es once was
    sweet upo' me ?

### II

Naäy, to be sewer, it be past 'er time.
    What maäkes 'er sa laäte ?
Goä to the laäne at the back, an' looök thruf
    Maddison's gaäte !

### III

Sweet-arts ! Molly belike may 'a lighted
    to-night upo' one.
Sweet-arts ! thanks to the Lord that I niver
    not listen'd to noän !
So I sits i' my oän armchair wi' my oän
    kettle theere o' the hob,
An' Tommy the fust, an' Tommy the sec-
    ond, an' Steevie an' Rob.    10

### IV

Rob, coom oop 'ere o' my knee. Thou sees
    that i' spite o' the men
I 'a kep' thruf thick an' thin my two
    'oonderd a-year to mysen;
Yis ! thaw tha call'd me es pretty es ony
    lass i' the Shere;
An' thou be es pretty a tabby, but Robby
    I seed thruf ya theere.

### V

Feyther 'ud saäy I wur ugly es sin, an' I
    beänt not vaäin,
But I niver wur downright hugly, thaw
    soom 'ud 'a thowt ma plaäin,
An' I was n't sa plaäin i' pink ribbons — ye
    said I wur pretty i' pinks,
An' I liked to 'ear it I did, but I beänt
    sich a fool as ye thinks;
Ye was stroäkin' ma down wi' the 'air, as I
    be a-stroäkin' o' you,
But whiniver I loooked i' the glass I wur
    sewer that it could n't be true;    20
Niver wur pretty, not I, but ye knaw'd it
    wur pleasant to 'ear,
Thaw it warn't not me es wur pretty, but
    my two 'oonderd a-year.

### VI

D' ya mind the murnin' when we was
    a-walkin' togither, an' stood
By the claäy'd-oop pond, that the foälk be
    sa scared at, i' Gigglesby wood,
Wheer the poor wench drowndid hersen,
    black Sal, es 'ed been disgraäced ?
An' I feel'd thy arm es I stood wur
    a-creeäpin' about my waäist;
An' me es wur allus afear'd of a man's git-
    tin' ower fond,
I sidled awaäy an' awaäy till I plumpt foot
    fust i' the pond;
And, Robby, I niver 'a liked tha sa well, as
    I did that daäy,
Fur tha joompt in thysen, an' tha hoickt
    my feet wi' a flop fro' the claäy.    30
Ay, stick oop thy back, an' set oop thy
    taäil, tha may gie ma a kiss,
Fur I walk'd wi' tha all the way hoäm an'
    wur niver sa nigh saäyin' Yis.
But wa boäth was i' sich a clat we was
    shaämed to cross Gigglesby Greeän,
Fur a cat may loook at a king, thou knaws,
    but the cat mun be cleän.

Sa we boäth on us kep' out o' sight o' the
    winders o' Gigglesby Hinn —
Naäy, but the claws o' tha! quiet! they
    pricks cleän thruf to the skin —
An' wa boäth slinkt 'oäm by the brokken
    shed i' the laäne at the back,
Wheer the poodle runn'd at tha once, an'
    thou runn'd oop o' the thack;
An' tha squeedg'd my 'and i' the shed, fur
    theere we was forced to 'ide,
Fur I seed that Steevie wur coomin', and
    one o' the Tommies beside.    40

### VII

Theere now, what art 'a mewin' at, Stee-
    vie? for owt I can tell —
Robby wur fust, to be sewer, or I mowt 'a
    liked tha as well.

### VIII

But, Robby, I thowt o' tha all the while I
    wur chaängin' my gown,
An' I thowt, shall I chaänge my staäte?
    but, O Lord, upo' coomin' down —
My bran-new carpet es fresh es a midder
    o' flowers i' Maäy —
Why 'ed n't tha wiped thy shoes? it wur
    clatted all ower wi' claäy.
An' I could 'a cried ammost, fur I seed that
    it could n't be,
An', Robby, I gied tha a raätin' that sat-
    tled thy coortin' o' me.
An' Molly an' me was agreed, as we was
    a-cleänin' the floor,
That a man be a durty thing an' a trouble
    an' plague wi' indoor.    50
But I rued it arter a bit, fur I stuck to tha
    moor na the rest,
But I could n't 'a lived wi' a man, an' I
    knaws it be all fur the best.

### IX

Naäy — let ma stroäk tha down till I
    maäkes tha es smooth es silk,
But if I 'ed married tha, Robby, thou 'd
    not 'a been worth thy milk,
Thou 'd niver 'a cotch'd ony mice but 'a
    left me the work to do,
And 'a taäen to the bottle beside, so es all
    that I 'ears be true;
But I loovs tha to maäke thysen 'appy, an'
    soä purr awaäy, my dear,
Thou 'ed wellnigh purr'd ma awaäy fro' my
    oän two 'oonderd a-year.

### X

Sweärin' ageän, you Toms, as ye used to do
    twelve year sin'!
Ye niver eärd Steevie sweär 'cep' it wur at
    a dog coomin' in,    60
An' boäth o' ye mun be fools to be hallus
    a-shawin' your claws,
Fur I niver cared nothink for neither — an'
    one o' ye deäd, ye knaws!
Coom, give hoäver then, weänt ye? I war-
    rant ye soom fine daäy —
Theere, lig down — I shall hev to gie one
    or tother awaäy.
Can't ye taäke pattern by Steevie? ye
    shan't hev a drop fro' the paäil.
Steevie be right good manners bang thruf
    to the tip o' the taäil.

### XI

Robby, git down wi' tha, wilt tha? let
    Steevie coom oop o' my knee.
Steevie, my lad, thou 'ed very nigh been
    the Steevie fur me!
Robby wur fust, to be sewer, 'e wur burn
    an' bröd i' the 'ouse,
But thou be es 'ansom a tabby es iver patted
    a mouse.    70

### XII

An' I beänt not vaäin, but I knaws I 'ed
    led tha a quieter life
Nor her wi' the hepitaph yonder! 'A
    faäithful an' loovin' wife!'
An' 'cos o' thy farm by the beck, an' thy
    windmill oop o' the croft,
Tha thowt tha would marry ma, did tha?
    but that wur a bit ower soft,
Thaw thou was es soäber es daäy, wi' a
    niced red faäce, an' es cleän
Es a shillin' fresh fro' the mint wi' a bran-
    new 'eäd o' the Queeän,
An' thy farmin' es cleän es thysen, fur,
    Steevie, tha kep' it sa neät
That I niver not spied sa much es a poppy
    along wi' the wheät,
An' the wool of a thistle a-flyin' an' seeädin'
    tha haäted to see;
'T wur es bad es a battle-twig[1] 'ere i' my
    oän blue chaumber to me.    80
Ay, roob thy whiskers ageän ma, fur I
    could 'a taäen to tha well,
But fur thy bairns, poor Steevie, a **bouncin'**
    boy an' a gell.

[1] Earwig.

### XIII

An' thou was es fond o' thy bairns es I be
    mysen o' my cats,
But I niver not wish'd fur childer, I hev n't
    naw likin' fur brats;
Pretty anew when ya dresses 'em oop, an'
    they goäs fur a walk,
Or sits wi' their 'ands afoor 'em, an' does n't
    not 'inder the talk !
But their bottles o' pap, an' their mucky
    bibs, an' the clats an' the clouts,
An' their mashin' their toys to pieäces an'
    maäkin' ma deäf wi' their shouts,
An' hallus a-joompin' about ma as if they
    was set upo' springs,
An' a haxin' ma hawkard questions, an'
    saäyin' ondecent things,    90
An' a-callin' ma ' hugly ' mayhap to my
    faäce, or a-teärin' my gown —
Dear ! dear ! dear ! I mun part them
    Tommies — Steevie, git down.

### XIV

Ye be wuss nor the men-tommies, you. I
    tell'd ya, na moor o' that !
Tom, lig theere o' the cushion, an' tother
    Tom 'ere o' the mat.

### XV

Theere ! I ha' master'd *them !*  Hed I mar-
    ried the Tommies — O Lord,
To loove an' obaäy the Tommies ! I could n't
    'a stuck by my word.
To be horder'd about, an' waäked, when
    Molly 'd put out the light,
By a man coomin' in wi' a hiccup at ony
    hour o' the night !
An' the taäble staäin'd wi' 'is aäle, an' the
    mud o' 'is boots o' the stairs,
An' the stink o' 'is pipe i' the 'ouse, an' the
    mark o' 'is 'eäd o' the chairs !    100
An' noän o' my four sweet-arts 'ud 'a let
    me 'a hed my oän waäy,
Sa I likes 'em best wi' taäils when they
    'ev n't a word to saäy.

### XVI

An' I sits i' my oän little parlor, an' sarved
    by my oän little lass,
Wi' my oän little garden outside, an' my
    oän bed o' sparrow-grass,
An' my oän door-poorch wi' the woodbine
    an' jessmine a-dressin' it greeän,
An' my oän fine Jackman i' purple a
    roäbin' the 'ouse like a queeän.

### XVII

An' the little gells bobs to ma hoffens es I
    be abroad i' the laänes,
When I goäs fur to coomfut the poor es be
    down wi' their haäches an' their
    paäins:
An' a haäf-pot o' jam, or a mossel o' meät
    when it beänt too dear,
They maäkes ma a graäter lady nor 'er i'
    the mansion theer,    110
Hes 'es hallus to hax of a man how much
    to spare or to spend;
An' a spinster I be an' I will be, if soä
    pleäse God, to the hend.

### XVIII

Mew ! mew ! — Bess wi' the milk ! what
    ha maäde our Molly sa laäte ?
It should 'a been 'ere by seven, an' theere
    — it be strikin' height —
' Cushie wur craäzed fur 'er cauf,' well —
    I 'eärd 'er a-maäkin' 'er moän,
An' I thowt to mysen, ' thank God that I
    hev n't naw cauf o' my oän.'
Theere !
      Set it down !
            Now, Robby !
    You Tommies shall waäit to-night
Till Robby an' Steevie 'es 'ed their lap —
    an' it sarves ye right.

## PROLOGUE

### TO GENERAL HAMLEY

The poem introduced by this Prologue was
printed in ' Macmillan's Magazine ' for March,
1882. The Prologue and Epilogue were added
when it appeared in the ' Tiresias ' volume,
1885.

Sir Edward Bruce Hamley was born at Bod-
win in Cornwall, April 27, 1824. He entered
the army in 1843 ; served in the Crimean War ;
was successively professor of military history
and commandant at the Staff College, Sand-
hurst (1858-77) ; was chief of the commission
for the delimitation of the Balkan and Arme-
nian frontiers (1879-80) ; and commanded a
division in the Egyptian war of 1882. He was
also the author of several works on military
subjects. He died August 12, 1893.

Our birches yellowing and from each
    The light leaf falling fast,

While squirrels from our fiery beech
  Were bearing off the mast,
You came, and look'd and loved the view
  Long-known and loved by me,
Green Sussex fading into blue
  With one gray glimpse of sea;
And, gazing from this height alone,
  We spoke of what had been
Most marvellous in the wars your own
  Crimean eyes had seen;
And now — like old-world inns that take
  Some warrior for a sign
That therewithin a guest may make
  True cheer with honest wine —
Because you heard the lines I read
  Nor utter'd word of blame,
I dare without your leave to head
  These rhymings with your name,
Who know you but as one of those
  I fain would meet again,
Yet know you, as your England knows
  That you and all your men
Were soldiers to her heart's desire,
  When, in the vanish'd year,
You saw the league-long rampart-fire
  Flare from Tel-el-Kebir
Thro' darkness, and the foe was driven,
  And Wolseley overthrew
Arâbi, and the stars in heaven
  Paled, and the glory grew.


## THE CHARGE OF THE HEAVY BRIGADE AT BALACLAVA

### OCTOBER 25, 1854

#### I

THE charge of the gallant three hundred,
  the Heavy Brigade !
Down the hill, down the hill, thousands of
  Russians,
Thousands of horsemen, drew to the valley
  — and stay'd;
For Scarlett and Scarlett's three hundred
  were riding by
When the points of the Russian lances
  arose in the sky;
And he call'd, ' Left wheel into line ! ' and
  they wheel'd and obey'd.
Then he look'd at the host that had halted
  he knew not why,
And he turn'd half round, and he bade his
  trumpeter sound
To the charge, and he rode on ahead, as he
  waved his blade

To the gallant three hundred whose glory
  will never die —
' Follow,' and up the hill, up the hill, up
  the hill,
Follow'd the Heavy Brigade.

#### II

The trumpet, the gallop, the charge, and
  the might of the fight !
Thousands of horsemen had gather'd there
  on the height,
With a wing push'd out to the left and a
  wing to the right,
And who shall escape if they close ? but he
  dash'd up alone
Thro' the great gray slope of men,
Sway'd his sabre, and held his own
Like an Englishman there and then.
All in a moment follow'd with force
Three that were next in their fiery course,
Wedged themselves in between horse and
  horse,
Fought for their lives in the narrow gap
  they had made —
Four amid thousands ! and up the hill, up
  the hill,
Gallopt the gallant three hundred, the
  Heavy Brigade.

#### III

Fell like a cannon-shot,
Burst like a thunderbolt,
Crash'd like a hurricane,
Broke thro' the mass from below,
Drove thro' the midst of the foe,
Plunged up and down, to and fro,
Rode flashing blow upon blow,
Brave Inniskillens and Greys
Whirling their sabres in circles of light !
And some of us, all in amaze,
Who were held for a while from the fight,
And were only standing at gaze,
When the dark-muffled Russian crowd
Folded its wings from the left and the
  right,
And roll'd them around like a cloud, —
O, mad for the charge and the battle were
  we,
When our own good redcoats sank from
  sight,
Like drops of blood in a dark-gray sea,
And we turn'd to each other, whispering,
  all dismay'd,
' Lost are the gallant three hundred of
  Scarlett's Brigade ! '

IV

' Lost one and all ' were the words
Mutter'd in our dismay;
But they rode like victors and lords
Thro' the forest of lances and swords
In the heart of the Russian hordes,
They rode, or they stood at bay —
Struck with the sword-hand and slew,
Down with the bridle-hand drew
The foe from the saddle and threw
Underfoot there in the fray —
Ranged like a storm or stood like a rock
In the wave of a stormy day;
Till suddenly shock upon shock
Stagger'd the mass from without,
Drove it in wild disarray,
For our men gallopt up with a cheer and
     a shout,
And the foeman surged, and waver'd, and
     reel'd
Up the hill, up the hill, up the hill, out of
     the field,
And over the brow and away.

V

Glory to each and to all, and the charge
     that they made !
Glory to all the three hundred, and all the
     Brigade !

NOTE. — The ' three hundred ' of the ' Heavy
Brigade ' who made this famous charge were
the Scots Greys and the 2d squadron of Inniskillens; the remainder of the ' Heavy Brigade ' subsequently dashing up to their support.
    The ' three ' were Scarlett's aide-de-camp,
Elliot, and the trumpeter, and Shegog the
orderly, who had been close behind him.


EPILOGUE

IRENE.

NOT this way will you set your name
    A star among the stars.

POET.

What way ?

IRENE.

    You praise when you should blame
The barbarism of wars.
A juster epoch has begun.

POET.

    Yet tho' this cheek be gray,
And that bright hair the modern sun,
    Those eyes the blue to-day,
You wrong me, passionate little friend.
    I would that wars should cease,
I would the globe from end to end
    Might sow and reap in peace,
And some new Spirit o'erbear the old,
    Or Trade re-frain the Powers
From war with kindly links of gold,
    Or Love with wreaths of flowers.
Slav, Teuton, Kelt, I count them all
    My friends and brother souls,
With all the peoples, great and small,
    That wheel between the poles.
But since our mortal shadow, Ill,
    To waste this earth began —
Perchance from some abuse of Will
    In worlds before the man
Involving ours — he needs must fight
    To make true peace his own,
He needs must combat might with might,
    Or Might would rule alone;
And who loves war for war's own sake
    Is fool, or crazed, or worse;
But let the patriot-soldier take
    His meed of fame in verse;
Nay — tho' that realm were in the wrong
    For which her warriors bleed,
It still were right to crown with song
    The warrior's noble deed —
A crown the Singer hopes may last,
    For so the deed endures;
But Song will vanish in the Vast;
    And that large phrase of yours
' A star among the stars,' my dear,
    Is girlish talk at best;
For dare we dally with the sphere
    As he did half in jest,
Old Horace ?  ' I will strike,' said he,
    ' The stars with head sublime,'
But scarce could see, as now we see,
    The man in space and time,
So drew perchance a happier lot
    Than ours, who rhyme to-day.
The fires that arch this dusky dot —
    Yon myriad-worlded way —
The vast sun-clusters' gather'd blaze,
    World-isles in lonely skies,
Whole heavens within themselves, amaze
    Our brief humanities.
And so does Earth; for Homer's fame,
    Tho' carved in harder stone —

The falling drop will make his name
    As mortal as my own.

IRENE.

No!

POET.

        Let it live then — ay, till when ?
    Earth passes, all is lost
In what they prophesy, our wise men,
    Sun-flame or sunless frost,
And deed and song alike are swept
    Away, and all in vain
As far as man can see, except
    The man himself remain;
And tho', in this lean age forlorn,
    Too many a voice may cry
That man can have no after-morn,
    Not yet of those am I.
The man remains, and whatsoe'er
    He wrought of good or brave
Will mould him thro' the cycle-year
    That dawns behind the grave.

And here the Singer for his art
    Not all in vain may plead
' The song that nerves a nation's heart
    Is in itself a deed.'


## TO VIRGIL

WRITTEN AT THE REQUEST OF THE
MANTUANS FOR THE NINETEENTH
CENTENARY OF VIRGIL'S DEATH

First printed in ' The Nineteenth Century '
for November, 1882.

I

ROMAN VIRGIL, thou that singest
    Ilion's lofty temples robed in fire,
Ilion falling, Rome arising,
        wars, and filial faith, and Dido's
            pyre;

II

Landscape-lover, lord of language
        more than he that sang the ' Works
            and Days,'
All the chosen coin of fancy
        flashing out from many a golden
            phrase;

III

Thou that singest wheat and woodland,
        tilth and vineyard, hive and horse
            and herd;
All the charm of all the Muses
        often flowering in a lonely word;

IV

Poet of the happy Tityrus
        piping underneath his beechen bow-
            ers;
Poet of the poet-satyr
        whom the laughing shepherd bound
            with flowers;

V

Chanter of the Pollio, glorying
        in the blissful years again to be,
Summers of the snakeless meadow,
        unlaborious earth and oarless sea;

VI

Thou that seest Universal
        Nature moved by Universal Mind;
Thou majestic in thy sadness
        at the doubtful doom of human
            kind;

VII

Light among the vanish'd ages;
        star that gildest yet this phantom
            shore;
Golden branch amid the shadows,
        kings and realms that pass to rise no
            more;

VIII

Now thy Forum roars no longer,
        fallen every purple Cæsar's dome —
Tho' thine ocean-roll of rhythm
        sound forever of Imperial Rome —

IX

Now the Rome of slaves hath perish'd,
        and the Rome of freemen holds her
            place,
I, from out the Northern Island
        sunder'd once from all the human
            race,

X

I salute thee, Mantovano,
        I that loved thee since my day began,
Wielder of the stateliest measure
        ever moulded by the lips of man.

## THE DEAD PROPHET

### 182–

Not referring to any particular prophet, or poet, as Tennyson himself declared.

### I

DEAD !
  And the Muses cried with a stormy cry,
'Send them no more, for evermore.
  Let the people die.'

### II

Dead !
  'Is it *he* then brought so low ?'
And a careless people flock'd from the fields
  With a purse to pay for the show.

### III

Dead, who had served his time,
  Was one of the people's kings,
Had labor'd in lifting them out of slime,
  And showing them, souls have wings !

### IV

Dumb on the winter heath he lay.
  His friends had stript him bare,
And roll'd his nakedness everyway
  That all the crowd might stare.

### V

A storm-worn signpost not to be read,
  And a tree with a moulder'd nest
On its barkless bones, stood stark by the dead;
  And behind him, low in the West,

### VI

With shifting ladders of shadow and light,
  And blurr'd in color and form,
The sun hung over the gates of night,
  And glared at a coming storm.

### VII

Then glided a vulturous beldam forth,
  That on dumb death had thriven;
They call'd her 'Reverence' here upon earth,
  And 'The Curse of the Prophet' in heaven.

### VIII

She knelt — 'We worship him' — all but wept —
  'So great, so noble, was he !'
She clear'd her sight, she arose, she swept
  The dust of earth from her knee.

### IX

'Great ! for he spoke and the people heard,
  And his eloquence caught like a flame
From zone to zone of the world, till his word
  Had won him a noble name.

### X

'Noble ! he sung, and the sweet sound ran
  Thro' palace and cottage door,
For he touch'd on the whole sad planet of man,
  The kings and the rich and the poor;

### XI

'And he sung not alone of an old sun set,
  But a sun coming up in his youth !
Great and noble — O, yes — but yet —
  For man is a lover of truth,

### XII

'And bound to follow, wherever she go
  Stark-naked, and up or down,
Thro' her high hill - passes of stainless snow,
  Or the foulest sewer of the town —

### XIII

'Noble and great — O, ay — but then,
  Tho' a prophet should have his due,
Was he noblier-fashion'd than other men ?
  Shall we see to it, I and you ?

### XIV

'For since he would sit on a prophet's seat,
  As a lord of the human soul,
We needs must scan him from head to feet,
  Were it but for a wart or a mole ?'

### XV

His wife and his child stood by him in tears,
  But she — she push'd them aside.

'Tho' a name may last for a thousand
    years,
  Yet a truth is a truth,' she cried.

### XVI

And she that had haunted his pathway
    still,
  Had often truckled and cower'd
When he rose in his wrath, and had yielded
    her will
  To the master, as overpower'd,

### XVII

She tumbled his helpless corpse about.
  ' Small blemish upon the skin !
But I think we know what is fair with-
    out
  Is often as foul within.'

### XVIII

She crouch'd, she tore him part from part,
  And out of his body she drew
The red 'blood-eagle' [1] of liver and heart;
  She held them up to the view;

### XIX

She gabbled, as she groped in the dead,
  And all the people were pleased;
' See, what a little heart,' she said,
  ' And the liver is half-diseased !'

### XX

She tore the prophet after death,
  And the people paid her well.
Lightnings flicker'd along the heath;
  One shriek'd, ' The fires of hell !'


## EARLY SPRING

Contributed to 'The Youth's Companion'
(Boston) for December 13, 1883.

### I

ONCE more the Heavenly Power
  Makes all things new,
And domes the red-plow'd hills
  With loving blue;
The blackbirds have their wills,
  The throstles too.

---

[1] Old Viking term for lungs, liver, etc., when
torn by the conqueror out of the body of the
conquered.

### II

Opens a door in heaven;
  From skies of glass
A Jacob's ladder falls
  On greening grass,
And o'er the mountain-walls
  Young angels pass.

### III

Before them fleets the shower,
  And burst the buds,
And shine the level lands,
  And flash the floods;
The stars are from their hands
  Flung thro' the woods,

### IV

The woods with living airs
  How softly fann'd,
Light airs from where the deep,
  All down the sand,
Is breathing in his sleep,
  Heard by the land.

### V

O, follow, leaping blood,
  The season's lure !
O heart, look down and up
  Serene, secure,
Warm as the crocus cup,
  Like snowdrops, pure !

### VI

Past, Future glimpse and fade
  Thro' some slight spell,
A gleam from yonder vale,
  Some far blue fell,
And sympathies, how frail,
  In sound and smell !

### VII

Till at thy chuckled note,
  Thou twinkling bird,
The fairy fancies range,
  And, lightly stirr'd,
Ring little bells of change
  From word to word.

### VIII

For now the Heavenly Power
  Makes all things new,
And thaws the cold, and fills
  The flower with dew;
The blackbirds have their wills,
  The poets too.

## PREFATORY POEM TO MY BROTHER'S SONNETS

### MIDNIGHT, JUNE 30, 1879

The collected edition of Charles Tennyson Turner's 'Sonnets,' for which this poem was written, was published in 1880.

#### I

MIDNIGHT — in no midsummer tune
The breakers lash the shores;
The cuckoo of a joyless June
Is calling out of doors.

And thou hast vanish'd from thine own
To that which looks like rest,
True brother, only to be known
By those who love thee best.

#### II

Midnight — and joyless June gone by,
And from the deluged park
The cuckoo of a worse July
Is calling thro' the dark;

But thou art silent underground,
And o'er thee streams the rain,
True poet, surely to be found
When Truth is found again.

#### III

And, now to these unsummer'd skies
The summer bird is still,
Far off a phantom cuckoo cries
From out a phantom hill;

And thro' this midnight breaks the sun
Of sixty years away,
The light of days when life begun,
The days that seem to-day,

When all my griefs were shared with
thee,
As all my hopes were thine —
As all thou wert was one with me,
May all thou art be mine !

## 'FRATER AVE ATQUE VALE'

First printed in 'The Nineteenth Century'
for March, 1883.
Desenzano is a town at the southern end of
Lake Garda, in Italy. The narrow peninsula
of Sermione (the Latin *Sirmio*), where Catullus had his country house, is about three miles and a half to the east of Desenzano. There are some slight remains of an ancient building on the edge of the lake, said to belong to the poet's villa; and on a hill near by are fragments of Roman baths.

Row us out from Desenzano, to your Sir-
mione row !
So they row'd, and there we landed — 'O
venusta Sirmio !'
There to me thro' all the groves of olive in
the summer glow,
There beneath the Roman ruin where the
purple flowers grow,
Came that 'Ave atque Vale' of the Poet's
hopeless woe,
Tenderest of Roman poets nineteen hun-
dred years ago,
'Frater Ave atque Vale'— as we wander'd
to and fro
Gazing at the Lydian laughter of the Garda
Lake below
Sweet Catullus's all-but-island, olive-sil-
very Sirmio !

## HELEN'S TOWER

[Written at the request of my friend, Lord Dufferin.]

Inscribed on the walls of a tower erected in 1860 by the Earl of Dufferin on his estate near Belfast, as a tribute to his mother, the late Countess of Gifford, and named after her. The fourth line refers to a poetical inscription on the tower, written by Lady Gifford to her son.
Later, in 1861, 'Helen's Tower' was privately printed by Lord Dufferin. It was also printed in 'Good Words' for January, 1884, before it appeared in the 'Tiresias' volume.

HELEN'S TOWER, here I stand,
Dominant over sea and land.
Son's love built me, and I hold
Mother's love in letter'd gold.
Love is in and out of time,
I am mortal stone and lime.
Would my granite girth were strong
As either love, to last as long !
I should wear my crown entire
To and thro' the Doomsday fire,
And be found of angel eyes
In earth's recurring Paradise.

## EPITAPH ON LORD STRATFORD DE REDCLIFFE

### IN WESTMINSTER ABBEY

This and the two following epitaphs were published in the 'Tiresias' volume.

THOU third great Canning, stand among
    our best
    And noblest, now thy long day's work
        hath ceased,
Here silent in our Minster of the West
    Who wert the voice of England in the
        East.

## EPITAPH ON GENERAL GORDON

### IN THE GORDON BOYS' NATIONAL MEMORIAL HOME NEAR WOKING

WARRIOR of God, man's friend, and ty-
    rant's foe,
    Now somewhere dead far in the waste
        Soudan,
Thou livest in all hearts, for all men know
    This earth has never borne a nobler
        man.

## EPITAPH ON CAXTON

### IN ST. MARGARET'S, WESTMINSTER

*Fiat Lux* (his motto)

THY prayer was 'Light — more Light —
    while Time shall last!'
    Thou sawest a glory growing on the
        night,
But not the shadows which that light would
    cast,
    Till shadows vanish in the Light of
        Light.

## TO THE DUKE OF ARGYLL

The Duke was an intimate friend of Tennyson, and visited him occasionally at Aldworth. This poem was probably suggested by the course of the Duke in resigning the Privy Seal in 1881, on account of his disagreement with Gladstone (who had appointed him to the office in 1880) on the Irish Bill. Tennyson himself said, in 1892: 'I love Mr. Gladstone, but hate his present Irish policy.'

O PATRIOT Statesman, be thou wise to
    know
The limits of resistance, and the bounds
Determining concession; still be bold
Not only to slight praise but suffer scorn;
And be thy heart a fortress to maintain
The day against the moment, and the year
Against the day; thy voice, a music heard
Thro' all the yells and counter-yells of
    feud
And faction, and thy will, a power to make
This ever-changing world of circumstance,
In changing, chime with never-changing
    Law.

## HANDS ALL ROUND

For the first version of this song, which appeared in the London 'Examiner' for February 7, 1852, see the Notes.

FIRST pledge our Queen this solemn night,
    Then drink to England, every guest;
That man's the best Cosmopolite
    Who loves his native country best.
May freedom's oak for ever live
    With stronger life from day to day;
That man's the true Conservative
    Who lops the moulder'd branch away.
        Hands all round!
God the traitor's hope confound!
To this great cause of Freedom drink, my
    friends,
    And the great name of England, round
    and round.

To all the loyal hearts who long
    To keep our English Empire whole!
To all our noble sons, the strong
    New England of the Southern Pole!
To England under Indian skies,
    To those dark millions of her realm!
To Canada whom we love and prize,
    Whatever statesman hold the helm.
        Hands all round!
God the traitor's hope confound!
To this great name of England drink, my
    friends,
    And all her glorious empire, round and
    round.

To all our statesmen so they be
  True leaders of the land's desire !
To both our Houses, may they see
  Beyond the borough and the shire !
We sail'd wherever ship could sail,
  We founded many a mighty state;
Pray God our greatness may not fail
  Thro' craven fears of being great !
    Hands all round !
  God the traitor's hope confound !
To this great cause of Freedom drink, my
    friends,
  And the great name of England, round
    and round.


## FREEDOM

First printed in this country in 1884, in the
New York ' Independent,' and in England in
' Macmillan's Magazine ' for December, 1884 ;
afterwards included in the ' Tiresias ' volume.


### I

O THOU so fair in summers gone,
  While yet thy fresh and virgin soul
Inform'd the pillar'd Parthenon,
  The glittering Capitol;


### II

So fair in southern sunshine bathed,
  But scarce of such majestic mien
As here with forehead vapor-swathed
  In meadows ever green;


### III

For thou — when Athens reign'd and
    Rome,
  Thy glorious eyes were dimm'd with
    pain
To mark in many a freeman's home
  The slave, the scourge, the chain;


### IV

O follower of the Vision, still
  In motion to the distant gleam
Howe'er blind force and brainless will
  May jar thy golden dream


### V

Of Knowledge fusing class with class,
  Of civic Hate no more to be,
Of Love to leaven all the mass,
  Till every soul be free;


### VI

Who yet, like Nature, wouldst not mar
  By changes all too fierce and fast
This order of her Human Star,
  This heritage of the past;


### VII

O scorner of the party cry
  That wanders from the public good,
Thou — when the nations rear on high
  Their idol smear'd with blood,


### VIII

And when they roll their idol down —
  Of saner worship sanely proud;
Thou loather of the lawless crown
  As of the lawless crowd;


### IX

How long thine ever-growing mind
  Hath still'd the blast and strown the
    wave,
Tho' some of late would raise a wind
  To sing thee to thy grave,


### X

Men loud against all forms of power —
  Unfurnish'd brows, tempestuous tongues,
Expecting all things in an hour —
  Brass mouths and iron lungs !


## POETS AND THEIR BIBLIOGRA-
PHIES

First published in the ' Tiresias ' volume, but
without the present title, which was added in
1889.

OLD poets foster'd under friendlier skies,
  Old Virgil who would write ten lines,
    they say,
    At dawn, and lavish all the golden day
  To make them wealthier in his readers'
    eyes;
And you, old popular Horace, you the wise
  Adviser of the nine-years-ponder'd lay,
  And you, that wear a wreath of sweeter
    bay,
Catullus, whose dead songster never dies;
If, glancing downward on the kindly
    sphere
  That once had roll'd you round and
    round the sun,

You see your Art still shrined in human
    shelves,
You should be jubilant that you flourish'd
    here
    Before the Love of Letters, overdone,
Had swampt the sacred poets with them-
    selves.


## TO H. R. H. PRINCESS BEATRICE

First printed in the London 'Times,' July
23, 1885.
The Princess was married to Prince Henry
of Battenberg, on that day.

Two Suns of Love make day of human life,
Which else with all its pains, and griefs,
    and deaths,
Were utter darkness — one, the Sun of
    dawn
That brightens thro' the Mother's tender
    eyes,
And warms the child's awakening world —
    and one
The later-rising Sun of spousal Love,

Which from her household orbit draws the
    child
To move in other spheres.   The Mother
    weeps
At that white funeral of the single life,
Her maiden daughter's marriage; and her
    tears
Are half of pleasure, half of pain — the
    child
Is happy — even in leaving *her!* but thou,
True daughter, whose all-faithful, filial eyes
Have seen the loneliness of earthly thrones,
Wilt neither quit the widow'd Crown, nor
    let
This later light of Love have risen in vain,
But moving thro' the Mother's home, be-
    tween
The two that love thee, lead a summer life,
Sway'd by each Love, and swaying to each
    Love,
Like some conjectured planet in mid heaven
Between two suns, and drawing down from
    both
The light and genial warmth of double
    day.


# LOCKSLEY HALL SIXTY YEARS AFTER, ETC.

This was the title of the volume published late in 1886, containing the 'Locksley Hall,' 'The
Fleet,' 'Opening of the Indian and Colonial Exhibition,' and 'The Promise of May.'  The book
had the following dedication:

TO MY WIFE
I DEDICATE
THIS DRAMATIC MONOLOGUE
AND
THE POEMS WHICH FOLLOW


## LOCKSLEY HALL SIXTY YEARS AFTER

LATE, my grandson! half the morning
    have I paced these sandy tracts,
Watch'd again the hollow ridges roaring
    into cataracts,

Wander'd back to living boyhood while I
    heard the curlews call,
I myself so close on death, and death itself
    in Locksley Hall.

So — your happy suit was blasted — she
    the faultless, the divine;

And you liken — boyish babble — this boy-
    love of yours with mine.

I myself have often babbled doubtless of a
    foolish past;
Babble, babble; our old England may go
    down in babble at last.

'Curse him!' curse your fellow-victim?
    call him dotard in your rage?
Eyes that lured a doting boyhood well
    might fool a dotard's age.    10

Jilted for a wealthier! wealthier? yet per-
    haps she was not wise;

I remember how you kiss'd the miniature
with those sweet eyes.

In the hall there hangs a painting — Amy's
arms about my neck —
Happy children in a sunbeam sitting on the
ribs of wreck.

In my life there was a picture, she that
clasp'd my neck had flown;
I was left within the shadow sitting on the
wreck alone.

Yours has been a slighter ailment, will you
sicken for her sake ?
You, not you ! your modern amorist is of
easier, earthlier make.

Amy loved me, Amy fail'd me, Amy was a
timid child;
But your Judith — but your worldling —
*she* had never driven me wild.    20

She that holds the diamond necklace dearer
than the golden ring,
She that finds a winter sunset fairer than a
morn of spring.

She that in her heart is brooding on his
briefer lease of life,
While she vows 'till death shall part us,'
she the would-be-widow wife.

She the worldling born of worldlings — father, mother — be content,
Even the homely farm can teach us there
is something in descent.

Yonder in that chapel, slowly sinking now
into the ground,
Lies the warrior, my forefather, with his
feet upon the hound.

Cross'd ! for once he sail'd the sea to crush
the Moslem in his pride;
Dead the warrior, dead his glory, dead the
cause in which he died.    30

Yet how often I and Amy in the mouldering aisle have stood,
Gazing for one pensive moment on that
founder of our blood.

There again I stood to-day, and where of
old we knelt in prayer,

Close beneath the casement crimson with
the shield of Locksley — there,

All in white Italian marble, looking still as
if she smiled,
Lies my Amy dead in childbirth, dead the
mother, dead the child.

Dead — and sixty years ago, and dead her
aged husband now —
I, this old white-headed dreamer, stoopt
and kiss'd her marble brow.

Gone the fires of youth, the follies, furies,
curses, passionate tears,
Gone like fires and floods and earthquakes
of the planet's dawning years.    40

Fires that shook me once, but now to silent
ashes fallen away.
Cold upon the dead volcano sleeps the
gleam of dying day.

Gone the tyrant of my youth, and mute below the chancel stones,
All his virtues — I forgive them — black in
white above his bones.

Gone the comrades of my bivouac, some in
fight against the foe,
Some thro' age and slow diseases, gone as
all on earth will go.

Gone with whom for forty years my life in
golden sequence ran,
She with all the charm of woman, she with
all the breadth of man,

Strong in will and rich in wisdom, Edith,
yet so lowly-sweet,
Woman to her inmost heart, and woman to
her tender feet,    50

Very woman of very woman, nurse of ailing body and mind,
She that link'd again the broken chain that
bound me to my kind.

Here to-day was Amy with me, while I
wander'd down the coast,
Near us Edith's holy shadow, smiling at the
slighter ghost.

Gone our sailor son thy father, Leonard
early lost at sea;

Thou alone, my boy, of Amy's kin and
    mine art left to me.

Gone thy tender-natured mother, wearying
        to be left alone,
Pining for the stronger heart that once had
    beat beside her own.

Truth, for truth is truth, he worshipt, being
    true as he was brave;
Good, for good is good, he follow'd, yet he
    look'd beyond the grave,          60

Wiser there than you, that crowning barren
    Death as lord of all,
Deem this over-tragic drama's closing cur-
    tain is the pall !

Beautiful was death in him, who saw the
    death, but kept the deck,
Saving women and their babes, and sinking
    with the sinking wreck,

Gone for ever !   Ever ?  no — for since our
    dying race began,
Ever, ever, and for ever was the leading
    light of man.

Those that in barbarian burials kill'd the
    slave, and slew the wife
Felt within themselves the sacred passion
    of the second life.

Indian warriors dream of ampler hunting
    grounds beyond the night;
Even the black Australian dying hopes he
    shall return, a white.          70

Truth for truth, and good for good !   The
    good, the true, the pure, the just —
Take the charm ' For ever ' from them, and
    they crumble into dust.

Gone the cry of ' Forward, Forward,' lost
    within a growing gloom;
Lost, or only heard in silence from the
    silence of a tomb.

Half the marvels of my morning, triumphs
    over time and space,
Staled by frequence, shrunk by usage into
    commonest commonplace !

' Forward ' rang the voices then, and of the
    many mine was one.

Let us hush this cry of ' Forward ' till ten
    thousand years have gone.

Far among the vanish'd races, old Assyrian
    kings would flay
Captives whom they caught in battle —
    iron-hearted victors they.          80

Ages after, while in Asia, he that led the
    wild Moguls,
Timur built his ghastly tower of eighty
    thousand human skulls;

Then, and here in Edward's time, an age
    of noblest English names,
Christian conquerors took and flung the
    conquer'd Christian into flames.

Love your enemy, bless your haters, said
    the Greatest of the great;
Christian love among the Churches look'd
    the twin of heathen hate.

From the golden alms of Blessing man had
    coin'd himself a curse:
Rome of Cæsar, Rome of Peter, which was
    crueller ?  which was worse ?

France had shown a light to all men,
    preach'd a Gospel, all men's good;
Celtic Demos rose a Demon, shriek'd and
    slaked the light with blood.          90

Hope was ever on her mountain, watching
    till the day begun —
Crown'd with sunlight — over darkness —
    from the still unrisen sun.

Have we grown at last beyond the passions
    of the primal clan ?
' Kill your enemy, for you hate him,' still,
    ' your enemy ' was a man.

Have we sunk below them ? peasants maim
    the helpless horse, and drive
Innocent cattle under thatch, and burn the
    kindlier brutes alive.

Brutes, the brutes are not your wrongers
    — burnt at midnight, found at morn,
Twisted hard in mortal agony with their
    offspring, born-unborn,

Clinging to the silent mother !   Are we
    devils ?  are we men ?

Sweet Saint Francis of Assisi, would that
  he were here again,                100

He that in his Catholic wholeness used to
  call the very flowers
Sisters, brothers — and the beasts — whose
  pains are hardly less than ours !

Chaos, Cosmos ! Cosmos, Chaos ! who can
  tell how all will end ?
Read the wide world's annals, you, and take
  their wisdom for your friend.

Hope the best, but hold the Present fatal
  daughter of the Past,
Shape your heart to front the hour, but
  dream not that the hour will last.

Ay, if dynamite and revolver leave you
  courage to be wise —
When was age so cramm'd with menace ?
  madness ? written, spoken lies ?

Envy wears the mask of Love, and, laughing sober fact to scorn,
Cries to weakest as to strongest, ' Ye are
  equals, equal-born.'          110

Equal-born ?  O, yes, if yonder hill be
  level with the flat.
Charm us, orator, till the lion look no larger
  than the cat,

Till the cat thro' that mirage of overheated
  language loom
Larger than the lion, — Demos end in
  working its own doom.

Russia bursts our Indian barrier, shall we
  fight her ? shall we yield ?
Pause ! before you sound the trumpet, hear
  the voices from the field.

Those three hundred millions under one
  Imperial sceptre now,
Shall we hold them ? shall we loose them ?
  take the suffrage of the plow.

Nay, but these would feel and follow
  Truth if only you and you,
Rivals of realm-ruining party, when you
  speak were wholly true.       120

Plowmen, shepherds, have I found, and
  more than once, and still could find,

Sons of God, and kings of men in utter nobleness of mind,

Truthful, trustful, looking upward to the
  practised hustings-liar;
So the higher wields the lower, while the
  lower is the higher.

Here and there a cotter's babe is royal-born
  by right divine;
Here and there my lord is lower than his
  oxen or his swine.

Chaos, Cosmos ! Cosmos, Chaos ! once
  again the sickening game;
Freedom, free to slay herself, and dying
  while they shout her name.

Step by step we gain'd a freedom known
  to Europe, known to all;
Step by step we rose to greatness, — thro'
  the tonguesters we may fall.   130

You that woo the Voices — tell them ' old
  experience is a fool,'
Teach your flatter'd kings that only those
  who cannot read can rule.

Pluck the mighty from their seat, but set
  no meek ones in their place;
Pillory Wisdom in your markets, pelt your
  offal at her face.

Tumble Nature heel o'er head, and, yelling
  with the yelling street,
Set the feet above the brain and swear the
  brain is in the feet.

Bring the old dark ages back without the
  faith, without the hope,
Break the State, the Church, the Throne,
  and roll their ruins down the slope.

Authors — essayist, atheist, novelist, real-
  ist, rhymester, play your part,
Paint the mortal shame of nature with the
  living hues of art.           140

Rip your brothers' vices open, strip your
  own foul passions bare;
Down with Reticence, down with Reverence
  — forward — naked — let them stare.

Feed the budding rose of boyhood with the
  drainage of your sewer;

Send the drain into the fountain, lest the
   stream should issue pure.

Set the maiden fancies wallowing in the
   troughs of Zolaism, —
Forward, forward, ay, and backward, downward too into the abysm !

Do your best to charm the worst, to lower
   the rising race of men;
Have we risen from out the beast, then
   back into the beast again ?

Only ' dust to dust ' for me that sicken at
   your lawless din,
Dust in wholesome old-world dust before
   the newer world begin.          150

Heated am I ? you — you wonder — well,
   it scarce becomes mine age —
Patience ! let the dying actor mouth his
   last upon the stage.

Cries of unprogressive dotage ere the dotard fall asleep ?
Noises of a current narrowing, not the
   music of a deep ?

Ay, for doubtless I am old, and think
   gray thoughts, for I am gray;
After all the stormy changes shall we find
   a changeless May ?

After madness, after massacre, Jacobinism
   and Jacquerie,
Some diviner force to guide us thro' the
   days I shall not see ?

When the schemes and all the systems,
   kingdoms and republics fall,
Something kindlier, higher, holier — all for
   each and each for all ?          160

All the full-brain, half-brain races, led by
   Justice, Love, and Truth;
All the millions one at length with all the
   visions of my youth ?

All diseases quench'd by Science, no man
   halt, or deaf, or blind;
Stronger ever born of weaker, lustier body,
   larger mind ?

Earth at last a warless world, a single race,
   a single tongue —

I have seen her far away — for is not Earth
   as yet so young ? —

Every tiger madness muzzled, every serpent passion kill'd,
Every grim ravine a garden, every blazing
   desert till'd,

Robed in universal harvest up to either
   pole she smiles,
Universal ocean softly washing all her
   warless isles.          170

Warless ? when her tens are thousands, and
   her thousands millions, then —
All her harvest all too narrow — who can
   fancy warless men ?

Warless ? war will die out late then. Will
   it ever ? late or soon ?
Can it, till this outworn earth be dead as
   yon dead world the moon ?

Dead the new astronomy calls her. — On
   this day and at this hour,
In this gap between the sandhills, whence
   you see the Locksley tower,

Here we met, our latest meeting — Amy —
   sixty years ago —
She and I — the moon was falling greenish
   thro' a rosy glow,

Just above the gateway tower, and even
   where you see her now —
Here we stood and claspt each other,
   swore the seeming-deathless vow. —

Dead, but how her living glory lights the
   hall, the dune, the grass !          181
Yet the moonlight is the sunlight, and the
   sun himself will pass.

Venus near her ! smiling downward at this
   earthlier earth of ours,
Closer on the sun, perhaps a world of never
   fading flowers.

Hesper, whom the poet call'd the Bringer
   home of all good things —
All good things may move in Hesper, perfect peoples, perfect kings.

Hesper — Venus — were we native to that
   splendor or in Mars,

We should see the globe we groan in,
    fairest of their evening stars.

Could we dream of wars and carnage, craft
    and madness, lust and spite,
Roaring London, raving Paris, in that point
    of peaceful light?                    190

Might we not in glancing heavenward on a
    star so silver-fair,
Yearn, and clasp the hands and murmur,
    'Would to God that we were there'?

Forward, backward, backward, forward,
    in the immeasurable sea,
Sway'd by vaster ebbs and flows than can
    be known to you or me.

All the suns — are these but symbols of in-
    numerable man,
Man or Mind that sees a shadow of the
    planner or the plan?

Is there evil but on earth? or pain in every
    peopled sphere?
Well, be grateful for the sounding watch-
    word 'Evolution' here,

Evolution ever climbing after some ideal
    good,
And Reversion ever dragging Evolution in
    the mud.                             200

What are men that He should heed us?
    cried the king of sacred song;
Insects of an hour, that hourly work their
    brother insect wrong,

While the silent heavens roll, and suns
    along their fiery way,
All their planets whirling round them, flash
    a million miles a day.

Many an æon moulded earth before her
    highest, man, was born,
Many an æon too may pass when earth is
    manless and forlorn,

Earth so huge, and yet so bounded — pools
    of salt, and plots of land —
Shallow skin of green and azure — chains
    of mountain, grains of sand!

Only That which made us meant us to be
    mightier by and by,

Set the sphere of all the boundless heavens
    within the human eye,           210

Sent the shadow of Himself, the boundless,
    thro' the human soul;
Boundless inward in the atom, boundless
    outward in the Whole.

.    .    .    .    .    .    .    .    .

Here is Locksley Hall, my grandson, here
    the lion-guarded gate.
Not to-night in Locksley Hall — to-morrow
    — you, you come so late.

Wreck'd — your   train — or   all   but
    wreck'd? a shatter'd wheel? a vi-
    cious boy!
Good, this forward, you that preach it, is it
    well to wish you joy?

Is it well that while we range with Science,
    glorying in the Time,
City children soak and blacken soul and
    sense in city slime?

There among the glooming alleys Progress
    halts on palsied feet,
Crime and hunger cast our maidens by the
    thousand on the street.            220

There the master scrimps his haggard
    sempstress of her daily bread,
There a single sordid attic holds the living
    and the dead.

There the smouldering fire of fever creeps
    across the rotted floor,
And the crowded couch of incest in the
    warrens of the poor.

Nay, your pardon, cry your 'Forward,'
    yours are hope and youth, but I —
Eighty winters leave the dog too lame to
    follow with the cry,

Lame and old, and past his time, and pass-
    ing now into the night;
Yet I would the rising race were half as
    eager for the light.

Light the fading gleam of even? light the
    glimmer of the dawn?
Aged eyes may take the growing glimmer
    for the gleam withdrawn.           230

Far away beyond her myriad coming
  changes earth will be
Something other than the wildest modern
  guess of you and me.

Earth may reach her earthly-worst, or if
  she gain her earthly-best,
Would she find her human offspring this
  ideal man at rest ?

Forward then, but still remember how the
  course of Time will swerve,
Crook and turn upon itself in many a backward streaming curve.

Not the Hall to-night, my grandson ! Death
  and Silence hold their own.
Leave the master in the first dark hour of
  his last sleep alone.

Worthier soul was he than I am, sound and
  honest, rustic Squire,
Kindly landlord, boon companion — youthful jealousy is a liar.          240

Cast the poison from your bosom, oust the
  madness from your brain.
Let the trampled serpent show you that you
  have not lived in vain.

Youthful ! youth and age are scholars yet
  but in the lower school,
Nor is he the wisest man who never proved
  himself a fool.

Yonder lies our young sea-village — Art
  and Grace are less and less:
Science grows and Beauty dwindles — roofs
  of slated hideousness !

There is one old hostel left us where they
  swing the Locksley shield,
Till the peasant cow shall butt the ' lion
  passant ' from his field.

Poor old Heraldry, poor old History, poor
  old Poetry, passing hence,
In the common deluge drowning old political common-sense !          250

Poor old voice of eighty crying after voices
  that have fled !
All I loved are vanish'd voices, all my steps
  are on the dead.

All the world is ghost to me, and as the
  phantom disappears,
Forward far and far from here is all the
  hope of eighty years.

. . . . . . . .

In this hostel — I remember — I repent it
  o'er his grave —
Like a clown — by chance he met me — I
  refused the hand he gave.

From that casement where the trailer mantles all the mouldering bricks —
I was then in early boyhood, Edith but a
  child of six —

While I shelter'd in this archway from a
  day of driving showers —
Peept the winsome face of Edith like a
  flower among the flowers.          260

Here to-night ! the Hall to-morrow, when
  they toll the chapel bell !
Shall I hear in one dark room a wailing,
  ' I have loved thee well ' ?

Then a peal that shakes the portal — one
  has come to claim his bride,
Her that shrank, and put me from her,
  shriek'd, and started from my side —

Silent echoes !  You, my Leonard, use and
  not abuse your day,
Move among your people, know them, follow him who led the way,

Strove for sixty widow'd years to help his
  homelier brother men,
Served the poor, and built the cottage,
  raised the school, and drain'd the
  fen.

Hears he now the voice that wrong'd him ?
  who shall swear it cannot be ?
Earth would never touch her worst, were
  one in fifty such as he.          270

Ere she gain her heavenly-best, a God must
  mingle with the game.
Nay, there may be those about us whom we
  neither see nor name,

Felt within us as ourselves, the Powers of
  Good, the Powers of Ill,

Strowing balm, or shedding poison in the
fountains of the will.

Follow you the star that lights a desert
pathway, yours or mine.
Forward, till you see the Highest Human
Nature is divine.

Follow Light, and do the Right — for man
can half-control his doom —
Till you find the deathless Angel seated in
the vacant tomb.

Forward, let the stormy moment fly and
mingle with the past.
I that loathed have come to love him.
Love will conquer at the last.     280

Gone at eighty, mine own age, and I and
you will bear the pall;
Then I leave thee lord and master, latest
lord of Locksley Hall.


THE FLEET [1]

Contributed to the 'Times,' April 23, 1885.
The quotation from Sir Graham Berry's speech
was added in 1886, when the poem was reprinted in the 'Locksley Hall' volume. Waugh
('Alfred Lord Tennyson,' 2d ed., London,
1893) says that the poem was 'suggested by
the speech,' which was not delivered until
more than a year after the poem was first
printed; and others have made the same mistake.

I

You, you, *if* you shall fail to understand
What England is, and what her all-in-all,
On you will come the curse of all the land,
Should this old England fall
Which Nelson left so great.

[1] The speaker said that 'he should like to
be assured that other outlying portions of the
Empire, the Crown colonies, and important
coaling stations were being as promptly and as
thoroughly fortified as the various capitals of
the self-governing colonies. He was credibly
informed this was not so. It was impossible,
also, not to feel some degree of anxiety about
the efficacy of present provision to defend and
protect, by means of swift well-armed cruisers,
the immense mercantile fleet of the Empire.
A third source of anxiety, so far as the colonies
were concerned, was the apparently insufficient
provision for the rapid manufacture of arma-

II

His isle, the mightiest Ocean-power on
earth,
Our own fair isle, the lord of every
sea —
Her fuller franchise — what would that be
worth —
Her ancient fame of Free —
Were she . . . a fallen state?

III

Her dauntless army scatter'd, and so small,
Her island - myriads fed from alien
lands —
The fleet of England is her all-in-all;
Her fleet is in your hands,
And in her fleet her fate.

IV

You, you, that have the ordering of her
fleet,
*If* you should only compass her disgrace,
When all men starve, the wild mob's mil-
lion feet
Will kick you from your place,
But then too late, too late.

ments and their prompt despatch when ordered
to their colonial destination. Hence the necessity for manufacturing appliances equal to the
requirements, not of Great Britain alone, but
of the whole Empire. But the keystone of the
whole was the necessity for an overwhelmingly
powerful fleet and efficient defence for all
necessary coaling stations. This was as essential for the colonies as for Great Britain. It
was the one condition for the continuance of
the Empire. All that Continental Powers did
with respect to armies England should effect
with her navy. It was essentially a defensive
force, and could be moved rapidly from point
to point, but it should be equal to all that was
expected from it. It was to strengthen the
fleet that colonists would first readily tax themselves, because they realized how essential a
powerful fleet was to the safety, not only of
that extensive commerce sailing in every sea,
but ultimately to the security of the distant
portions of the Empire. Who could estimate
the loss involved in even a brief period of disaster to the Imperial Navy? Any amount of
money timely expended in preparation would
be quite insignificant when compared with the
possible calamity he had referred to.' — *Extract from Sir Graham Berry's Speech at the
Colonial Institute, 9th November, 1886.*

## OPENING OF THE INDIAN AND COLONIAL EXHIBITION BY THE QUEEN

### WRITTEN AT THE REQUEST OF THE PRINCE OF WALES

The exhibition was opened on the 4th of May, 1886, and the poem was printed in the newspapers of the time.

I

WELCOME, welcome with one voice !
In your welfare we rejoice,
Sons and brothers that have sent,
From isle and cape and continent,
Produce of your field and flood,
Mount and mine, and primal wood;
Works of subtle brain and hand,
And splendors of the morning land,
Gifts from every British zone;
    Britons, hold your own !

II

May we find, as ages run,
The mother featured in the son;
And may yours for ever be
That old strength and constancy
Which has made your fathers great
In our ancient island State,
And wherever her flag fly,
Glorying between sea and sky,
Makes the might of Britain known;
    Britons, hold your own !

III

Britain fought her sons of yore —
Britain fail'd; and never more,
Careless of our growing kin,
Shall we sin our fathers' sin,
Men that in a narrower day —
Unprophetic rulers they —
Drove from out the mother's nest
That young eagle of the West
To forage for herself alone;
    Britons, hold your own !

IV

Sharers of our glorious past,
Brothers, must we part at last ?
Shall we not thro' good and ill
Cleave to one another still ?
Britain's myriad voices call,
' Sons, be welded each and all
Into one imperial whole,
One with Britain, heart and soul !
One life, one flag, one fleet, one throne ! '
    Britons, hold your own !

## TO W. C. MACREADY

### 1851

Written to be read at a dinner given to the actor, March 1, 1851, on his retirement from the stage; but not included in the poet's collected works until 1891.

FAREWELL, Macready, since to-night we part;
    Full-handed thunders often have confessed
    Thy power, well-used to move the public breast.
We thank thee with our voice, and from the heart.
Farewell, Macready, since this night we part,
    Go, take thine honors home; rank with the best,
    Garrick and statelier Kemble, and the rest
Who made a nation purer through their art.
Thine is it that our drama did not die,
    Nor flicker down to brainless pantomime,
    And those gilt gauds men-children swarm to see.
    Farewell, Macready, moral, grave, sublime;
Our Shakespeare's bland and universal eye
    Dwells pleased, through twice a hundred years, on thee.

# DEMETER

## AND OTHER POEMS

The volume with this title was published in December, 1889, when Tennyson was eighty years old, and included the poems that follow, as far as 'In Memoriam: W. G. Ward,' and also 'Crossing the Bar,' which the poet afterwards requested to have printed at the end of all collected editions of his works. Twenty thousand copies of the book were sold during the week after it appeared.

## TO THE MARQUIS OF DUFFERIN AND AVA

This dedication commemorates the death of the poet's son Lionel, which occurred on the voyage home from India, April 20, 1886. It was first printed in the 'Demeter' volume; as were the poems that follow, unless otherwise stated.

### I

At times our Britain cannot rest,
  At times her steps are swift and rash;
  She moving, at her girdle clash
The golden keys of East and West.

### II

Not swift or rash, when late she lent
  The sceptres of her West, her East,
  To one that ruling has increased
Her greatness and her self-content.

### III

Your rule has made the people love
  Their ruler. Your viceregal days
  Have added fulness to the phrase
Of 'Gauntlet in the velvet glove.'

### IV

But since your name will grow with time,
  Not all, as honoring your fair fame
  Of Statesman, have I made the name
A golden portal to my rhyme;

### V

But more, that you and yours may know
  From me and mine, how dear a debt
  We owed you, and are owing yet
To you and yours, and still would owe.

### VI

For he — your India was his Fate,
  And drew him over sea to you —

He fain had ranged her thro' and thro',
  To serve her myriads and the State, —

### VII

A soul that, watch'd from earliest youth,
  And on thro' many a brightening year,
  Had never swerved for craft or fear,
By one side-path, from simple truth;

### VIII

Who might have chased and claspt Renown
  And caught her chaplet here — and there
  In haunts of jungle-poison'd air
The flame of life went wavering down;

### IX

But ere he left your fatal shore,
  And lay on that funereal boat,
  Dying, 'Unspeakable,' he wrote,
'Their kindness,' and he wrote no more;

### X

And sacred is the latest word;
  And now the Was, the Might-have-been,
  And those lone rites I have not seen,
And one drear sound I have not heard,

### XI

Are dreams that scarce will let me be,
  Not there to bid my boy farewell,
  When That within the coffin fell,
Fell — and flash'd into the Red Sea,

### XII

Beneath a hard Arabian moon
  And alien stars. To question why
  The sons before the fathers die,
Not mine! and I may meet him soon;

### XIII

But while my life's late eve endures,
  Nor settles into hueless gray,
  My memories of his briefer day
Will mix with love for you and yours.

## ON THE JUBILEE OF QUEEN VICTORIA

Written in commemoration of the fiftieth anniversary of the Queen's accession, 1887, and printed in 'Macmillan's Magazine' for April.

### I

FIFTY times the rose has flower'd and faded,
Fifty times the golden harvest fallen,
Since our Queen assumed the globe, the sceptre.

### II

She beloved for a kindliness
Rare in fable or history,
Queen, and Empress of India,
Crown'd so long with a diadem
Never worn by a worthier,
Now with prosperous auguries
Comes at last to the bounteous
Crowning year of her Jubilee.

### III

Nothing of the lawless, of the despot,
Nothing of the vulgar, or vainglorious,
All is gracious, gentle, great and queenly.

### IV

You then joyfully, all of you,
Set the mountain aflame to-night,
Shoot your stars to the firmament,
Deck your houses, illuminate
All your towns for a festival,
And in each let a multitude
Loyal, each, to the heart of it,
One full voice of allegiance,
Hail the fair Ceremonial
Of this year of her Jubilee.

### V

Queen, as true to womanhood as Queen-hood,
Glorying in the glories of her people,
Sorrowing with the sorrows of the lowest!

### VI

You, that wanton in affluence,
Spare not now to be bountiful,
Call your poor to regale with you,
All the lowly, the destitute,
Make their neighborhood healthfuller,
Give your gold to the hospital,
Let the weary be comforted,
Let the needy be banqueted,
Let the maim'd in his heart rejoice
At this glad Ceremonial,
And this year of her Jubilee.

### VII

Henry's fifty years are all in shadow,
Gray with distance Edward's fifty summers,
Even her Grandsire's fifty half forgotten.

### VIII

You, the Patriot Architect,
You that shape for eternity,
Raise a stately memorial,
Make it regally gorgeous,
Some Imperial Institute,
Rich in symbol, in ornament,
Which may speak to the centuries,
All the centuries after us,
Of this great Ceremonial,
And this year of her Jubilee.

### IX

Fifty years of ever-broadening Commerce!
Fifty years of ever-brightening Science!
Fifty years of ever-widening Empire!

### X

You, the Mighty, the Fortunate,
You, the Lord-territorial,
You, the Lord-manufacturer,
You, the hardy, laborious,
Patient children of Albion,
You, Canadian, Indian,
Australasian, African,
All your hearts be in harmony,
All your voices in unison,
Singing, 'Hail to the glorious
Golden year of her Jubilee!'

### XI

Are there thunders moaning in the distance?
Are there spectres moving in the darkness?
Trust the Hand of Light will lead her people,
Till the thunders pass, the spectres vanish,
And the Light is Victor, and the darkness
Dawns into the Jubilee of the Ages.

## TO PROFESSOR JEBB

### WITH THE FOLLOWING POEM

Addressed to Richard Claverhouse Jebb, Professor of Greek at St. Andrews, Scotland, and afterwards at Cambridge, England, one of the most eminent Hellenists of our day. The footnotes are the poet's own.

FAIR things are slow to fade away,
Bear witness you, that yesterday [1]
   From out the Ghost of Pindar in you
Roll'd an Olympian; and they say [2]

That here the torpid mummy wheat
Of Egypt bore a grain as sweet
   As that which gilds the glebe of England,
Sunn'd with a summer of milder heat.

So may this legend for awhile,
If greeted by your classic smile,
   Tho' dead in its Trinacrian Enna,
Blossom again on a colder isle.

## DEMETER AND PERSEPHONE

### (IN ENNA)

The present Lord Tennyson says in the 'Memoir,' (vol. ii. p. 364): 'The poem was written at my request, because I knew that he considered Demeter one of the most beautiful types of womanhood.'

FAINT as a climate-changing bird that flies
All night across the darkness, and at dawn
Falls on the threshold of her native land,
And can no more, thou camest, O my child,
Led upward by the God of ghosts and dreams,
Who laid thee at Eleusis, dazed and dumb
With passing thro' at once from state to state,
Until I brought thee hither, that the day,
When here thy hands let fall the gather'd flower,
Might break thro' clouded memories once again     10
On thy lost self.  A sudden nightingale

[1] In Bologna.
[2] They say, for the fact is doubtful.

Saw thee, and flash'd into a frolic of song
And welcome; and a gleam as of the moon,
When first she peers along the tremulous deep,
Fled wavering o'er thy face, and chased away
That shadow of a likeness to the king
Of shadows, thy dark mate.  Persephone!
Queen of the dead no more — my child!
   Thine eyes
Again were human-godlike, and the Sun
Burst from a swimming fleece of winter gray,     20
And robed thee in his day from head to feet —
'Mother!' and I was folded in thine arms.

Child, those imperial, disimpassion'd eyes
Awed even me at first, thy mother — eyes
That oft had seen the serpent-wanded power
Draw downward into Hades with his drift
Of flickering spectres, lighted from below
By the red race of fiery Phlegethon;
But when before have Gods or men beheld
The Life that had descended re-arise,     30
And lighted from above him by the Sun?
So mighty was the mother's childless cry,
A cry that rang thro' Hades, Earth, and Heaven!

So in this pleasant vale we stand again,
The field of Enna, now once more ablaze
With flowers that brighten as thy footstep falls,
All flowers — but for one black blur of earth
Left by that closing chasm, thro' which the car
Of dark Aïdoneus rising rapt thee hence.
And here, my child, tho' folded in thine arms,     40
I feel the deathless heart of motherhood
Within me shudder, lest the naked glebe
Should yawn once more into the gulf, and thence
The shrilly whinnyings of the team of Hell,
Ascending, pierce the glad and songful air,
And all at once their arch'd necks, midnight-maned,
Jet upward thro' the midday blossom.  No!
For, see, thy foot has touch'd it; all the space

Of blank earth - baldness clothes itself
afresh,
And breaks into the crocus-purple hour    50
That saw thee vanish.

           Child, when thou wert gone,
I envied human wives, and nested birds,
Yea, the cubb'd lioness; went in search of
thee
Thro' many a palace, many a cot, and gave
Thy breast to ailing infants in the night,
And set the mother waking in amaze
To find her sick one whole; and forth again
Among the wail of midnight winds, and
cried,
'Where is my loved one?   Wherefore do
ye wail?'
And out from all the night an answer
shrill'd,                                            60
'We know not, and we know not why we
wail.'
I climb'd on all the cliffs of all the seas,
And ask'd the waves that moan about the
world,
'Where?  do ye make your moaning for
my child?'
And round from all the world the voices
came,
'We know not, and we know not why we
moan.'
'Where?' and I stared from every eagle-
peak,
I thridded the black heart of all the woods,
I peer'd thro' tomb and cave, and in the
storms   .                                          69
Of autumn swept across the city, and heard
The murmur of their temples chanting
me, ·
Me, me, the desolate mother!  'Where?'
—and turn'd,
And fled by many a waste, forlorn of
man,
And grieved for man thro' all my grief for
thee, —
The jungle rooted in his shatter'd hearth,
The serpent coil'd about his broken shaft,
The scorpion crawling over naked skulls;—
I saw the tiger in the ruin'd fane
Spring from his fallen God, but trace of
thee
I saw not; and far on, and, following
out                                                80
A league of labyrinthine darkness, came
On three gray heads beneath a gleaming
rift.

'Where?' and I heard one voice from all
the three,
'We know not, for we spin the lives of men,
And not of Gods, and know not why we
spin!
There is a Fate beyond us.' Nothing knew.

Last as the likeness of a dying man,
Without his knowledge, from him flits to
warn
A far-off friendship that he comes no more,
So he, the God of dreams, who heard my
cry,                                                90
Drew from thyself the likeness of thyself
Without thy knowledge, and thy shadow
past
Before me, crying, 'The Bright one in the
highest
Is brother of the Dark one in the lowest,
And Bright and Dark have sworn that I,
the child
Of thee, the great Earth-Mother, thee, the
Power
That lifts her buried life from gloom to
bloom,
Should be for ever and for evermore
The Bride of Darkness.'

           So the Shadow wail'd.
Then I, Earth-Goddess, cursed the Gods of
heaven.                                            100
I would not mingle with their feasts; to me
Their nectar smack'd of hemlock on the
lips,
Their rich ambrosia tasted aconite.
The man, that only lives and loves an hour,
Seem'd nobler than their hard eternities.
My quick tears kill'd the flower, my rav-
ings hush'd
The bird, and lost in utter grief I fail'd
To send my life thro' olive-yard and vine
And golden-grain, my gift to helpless man.
Rain-rotten died the wheat, the barley-
spears                                            110
Were hollow-husk'd, the leaf fell, and the
Sun,
Pale at my grief, drew down before his
time
Sickening, and Ætna kept her winter snow.

Then He, the brother of this Darkness,
He
Who still is highest, glancing from his
height
On earth a fruitless fallow, when he miss'd

The wonted steam of sacrifice, the praise
And prayer of men, decreed that thou
   shouldst dwell
For nine white moons of each whole year
   with me,
Three dark ones in the shadow with thy
   king.      120

Once more the reaper in the gleam of
   dawn
Will see me by the landmark far away,
Blessing his field, or seated in the dusk
Of even, by the lonely threshing-floor,
Rejoicing in the harvest and the grange.

Yet I, Earth-Goddess, am but ill-content
With them who still are highest.  Those
   gray heads,
What meant they by their 'Fate beyond
   the Fates'
But younger kindlier Gods to bear us down,
As we bore down the Gods before us?
   Gods,      130
To quench, not hurl the thunderbolt, to
   stay,
Not spread the plague, the famine; Gods
   indeed,
To send the noon into the night and break
The sunless halls of Hades into Heaven?
Till thy dark lord accept and love the Sun,
And all the Shadow die into the Light,
When thou shalt dwell the whole bright
   year with me,
And souls of men, who grew beyond their
   race,
And made themselves as Gods against the
   fear
Of Death and Hell; and thou that hast
   from men,      140
As Queen of Death, that worship which is
   Fear,
Henceforth, as having risen from out the
   dead,
Shalt ever send thy life along with mine
From buried grain thro' springing blade,
   and bless
Their garner'd autumn also, reap with me,
Earth-mother, in the harvest hymns of
   Earth
The worship which is Love, and see no more
The Stone, the Wheel, the dimly-glimmer-
   ing lawns
Of that Elysium, all the hateful fires
Of torment, and the shadowy warrior glide
Along the silent field of Asphodel.   151

# OWD ROÄ [1]

The footnotes are the poet's.

NAÄY, noä mander [2] o' use to be callin' 'im
   Roä, Roä, Roä,
Fur the dog 's stoän-deäf, an' 'e 's blind, 'e
   can naither stan' nor goä.

But I meäns fur to maäke 'is owd aäge as
   'appy as iver I can,
Fur I owäs owd Roäver moor nor I iver
   owäd mottal man.

Thou 's rode of 'is back when a babby,
   afoor thou was gotten too owd,
Fur 'e 'd fetch an' carry like owt, 'e was
   allus as good as gowd.

Eh, but 'e 'd fight wi' a will *when* 'e fowt;
   'e could howd [3] 'is oän,
An' Roä was the dog as knaw'd when an'
   wheere to bury his boäne.

An' 'e kep his heäd hoop like a king, an'
   'e 'd niver not down wi' 'is taäil,   9
Fur 'e 'd niver done nowt to be shaämed
   on, when we was i' Howlaby Daäle.

An' 'e sarved me sa well when 'e lived,
   that, Dick, when 'e cooms to be
   deäd,
I thinks as I 'd like fur to hev soom soort
   of a sarvice reäd.

Fur 'e 's moor good sense na the Parliament man 'at stans fur us 'ere,
An' I 'd voät fur 'im, my oän sen, if 'e
   could but stan' for the Shere.

'Faäithful an' True' — them words be i'
   Scriptur — an' Faäithful an' True
Ull be fun' [4] upo' four short legs ten times
   fur one upo' two.

An' maäybe they 'll walk upo' two, but I
   knaws they runs upo' four,[5] —
Bedtime, Dicky! but waäit till tha 'eärs it
   be strikin' the hour.

Fur I wants to tell tha o' Roä when we
   lived i' Howlaby Daäle,

[1] Old Rover.      [2] Manner.
[3] Hold.      [4] Found.
[5] *ou* as in 'house.'

Ten year sin' — Naäy — naäy ! tha mun
   nobbut hev' one glass of aäle.   20

Straänge an' owd-farran'd [1] the 'ouse, an'
   belt [2] long afoor my daäy,
Wi' haäfe o' the chimleys a-twizzen'd [3] an'
   twined like a band o' haäy.

The fellers as maäkes them picturs, 'ud
   coom at the fall o' the year,
An' sattle their ends upo' stools to pictur
   the door-poorch theere,

An' the Heagle 'as hed two heäds stannin'
   theere o' the brokken stick; [4]
An' they niver 'ed seed sich ivin' [5] as
   graw'd hall ower the brick;

An' theere i' the 'ouse one night — but it's
   down, an' all on it now
Goän into mangles an' tonups,[6] an' raäved
   slick thruf by the plow —

Theere, when the 'ouse wur a house, one
   night I wur sittin' aloän,
Wi' Roäver athurt my feeät, an' sleeäpin'
   still as a stoän,   30

Of a Christmas Eäve, an' as cowd as this,
   an' the midders [7] as white,
An' the fences all on 'em bolster'd oop wi'
   the windle [8] that night;

An' the cat wur a - sleeäpin' alongside
   Roäver, but I wur awaäke,
An' smoäkin' an' thinkin' o' things — Doänt
   maäke thysen sick wi' the caäke.

Fur the men ater supper 'ed sung their
   songs an' 'ed 'ed their beer,
An' 'ed goän their waäys; ther was nobbut
   three, an' noän on 'em theere.

They was all on 'em fear'd o' the Ghoäst
   an' duss n't not sleeäp i' the 'ouse,
But, Dicky, the Ghoäst moästlins [9] was
   nobbut a rat or a mouse.

1 ' Owd-farran'd,' old-fashioned.
2 Built.
3 ' Twizzen'd,' twisted.
4 On a staff *ragulé*.     5 Ivy.
6 Mangolds and turnips.
7 Meadows.
8 Drifted snow.
9 ' Moästlins,' for the most part, generally.

An' I looökt out wonst [1] at the night, an'
   the daäle was all of a thaw,
Fur I seed the beck coomin' down like a
   long black snaäke i' the snaw,   40

An' I heärd greät heäps o' the snaw slush-
   in' down fro' the bank to the beck,
An' then as I stood i' the doorwaäy, I
   feeäld it drip o' my neck.

Saw I turn'd in ageän, an' I thowt o' the
   good owd times 'at was goan,
An' the munney they maäde by the war,
   an' the times 'at was coomin' on;

Fur I thowt if the Staäte was a-gawin' to
   let in furriners' wheät,
Howiver was British farmers to stan' ageän
   o' their feeät ?

Howiver was I fur to find my rent an' to
   paäy my men ?
An' all along o' the feller [2] as turn'd 'is
   back of hissen.

Thou slep i' the chaumber above us, we
   could n't ha' 'eärd tha call,
Sa moother 'ed tell'd ma to bring tha down,
   an' thy craädle an' all;   50

Fur the gell o' the farm 'at slep wi' tha
   then 'ed gotten wer leäve,
Fur to goä that night to 'er foälk by cause
   o' the Christmas Eäve;

But I cleän forgot tha, my lad, when
   moother 'ed gotten to bed,
An' I slep i' my chair hup-on-end, an' the
   Freeä Traäde runn'd i' my 'ead,

Till I dreäm'd 'at Squire walkt in, an' I
   says to him, ' Squire, ya 're laäte,'
Then I seed 'at 'is faäce wur as red as the
   Yule-block theere i' the graäte.

An' 'e says, ' Can ya paäy me the rent to-
   night ? ' an' I says to 'im, ' Noä,'
An' 'e cotch'd howd hard o' my hairm,[3]
   ' Then hout to-night tha shall goä.'

' Tha 'll niver,' says I, ' be a-turnin' ma
   hout upo' Christmas Eäve ? '
Then I waäked an' I fun it was Roäver
   a-tuggin' an' teärin' my sleäve.   60

1 Once.     2 Peel.     3 Arm.

An' I thowt as 'e 'd goän cleän-wud,[1] fur I
    noäwaäys knaw'd 'is intent;
An' I says, 'Git awaäy, ya beast,' an' I
    fetcht 'im a kick, an' 'e went.

Then 'e tummled up stairs, fur I 'eärd 'im,
    as if 'e 'd 'a brokken 'is neck,
An' I 'd cleär forgot, little Dicky, thy
    chaumber door would n't sneck;[2]

An' I slep i' my chair ageän wi' my hairm
    hingin' down to the floor,
An' I thowt it was Roäver a-tuggin' an'
    teärin' me wuss nor afoor,

An' I thowt 'at I kick'd 'im ageän, but I
    kick'd thy moother istead.
'What arta snorin' theere fur? the house
    is afire,' she said.

Thy moother 'ed beän a-naggin' about the
    gell o' the farm,
She offens 'ud spy summut wrong when
    there warn't not a mossel o' harm; 70

An' she did n't not solidly meän I wur
    gawin' that waäy to the bad,
Fur the gell[3] was as howry a trollope as
    iver traäpes'd i' the squad.

But moother was free of 'er tongue, as I
    offens 'ev tell'd 'er mysen,
Sa I kep i' my chair, fur I thowt she was
    nobbut a-rilin' ma then.

An' I says, 'I 'd be good to tha, Bess, if
    tha'd onywaäys let ma be good,'
But she skelpt ma haäfe ower i' the chair,
    an' screeäd like a howl gone wud[4]—

'Ya mun run fur the lether.[5] Git oop, if
    ya 're onywaäys good for owt.'
And I says, 'If I beänt noäwaäys—not
    nowadaäys—good fur nowt—

'Yit I beänt sich a nowt[1] of all nowts as
    'ull hallus do as 'e 's bid.'
'But the stairs is afire,' she said; then I
    seed 'er a-cryin', I did. 80

An' she beäld, 'Ya mun saäve little Dick,
    an' be sharp about it an' all,'
Sa I runs to the yard fur a lether, an' sets
    'im ageän the wall,

An' I claums an' I mashes the winder hin,
    when I gits to the top,
But the heät druv hout i' my heyes till I
    feäld mysen ready to drop.

Thy moother was howdin' the lether, an'
    tellin' me not to be skeärd,
An' I was n't afeärd, or I thinks leästwaäys
    as I was n't afeärd;

But I could n't see fur the smoäke wheere
    thou was a-liggin, my lad,
An' Roäver was theere i' the chaumber
    a-yowlin' an' yaupin' like mad;

An' thou was a-beälin' likewise, an'
    a-squeälin', as if tha was bit,
An' it was n't a bite but a burn, fur the
    merk 's[2] o' thy shou'der yit; 90

Then I call'd out, 'Roä, Roä, Roä,' thaw I
    did n't haäfe think as 'e 'd 'ear,
*But 'e coom'd thruf the fire wi' my bairn i' 'is*
    *mouth to the winder theere!*

He coom'd like a hangel o' marcy as soon
    as 'e 'eärd 'is naäme,
Or like tother hangel i' Scriptur 'at sum-
    mun seed i' the flaäme,

When summun 'ed hax'd fur a son, an' 'e
    promised a son to she,
An' Roä was as good as the hangel i'
    saävin' a son fur me.

Sa I browt tha down, an' I says, 'I mun
    gaw up ageän fur Roä.'
'Gaw up ageän fur the varmint?' I tell'd
    'er, 'Yeäs, I mun goä.'

An' I claumb'd up ageän to the winder, an'
    clemm'd[3] owd Roä by the 'eäd,

---

[1] Mad.

[2] Latch.

[3] 'The girl was as dirty a slut as ever trudged in the mud,' but there is a sense of slatternliness in 'traäpes'd' which is not expressed in 'trudged.'

[4] 'She half overturned me and shrieked like an owl gone mad.'

[5] Ladder.

---

[1] A thoroughly insignificant or worthless person.   [2] Mark.   [3] Clutched.

An' 'is 'air coom'd off i' my 'ands an' I
   taäked 'im at fust fur deäd;    100

Fur 'e smell'd like a herse a-singein', an'
   seeäm'd as blind as a poop,
An' haäfe on 'im bare as a bublin'.[1] I
   could n't wakken 'im oop,

But I browt 'im down, an' we got to the
   barn, fur the barn would n't burn
Wi' the wind blawin' hard tother waäy, an'
   the wind was n't like to turn.

An' *I* kep a-callin' o' Roä till 'e waggled 'is
   taäil fur a bit,
But the cocks kep a-crawin' an' crawin' all
   night, an' I 'ears 'em yit;

An' the dogs was a-yowlin' all round, and
   thou was a-squeälin' thysen,
An' moother was naggin' an' groänin' an'
   moänin' an' naggin' ageän;

An' I 'eärd the bricks an' the baulks[2]
   rummle down when the roof gev
   waäy,
Fur the fire was a-raägin' an' raävin' an'
   roarin' like judgment daäy.    110

Warm enew theere sewer-ly, but the barn
   was as cowd as owt,
An' we cuddled and huddled togither, an'
   happt[3] wersens oop as we mowt.

An' I browt Roä round, but moother 'ed
   beän sa soäk'd wi' the thaw
'At she cotch'd 'er death o' cowd that night,
   poor soul, i' the straw.

Haäfe o' the parish runn'd oop when the
   rig-tree[4] was tummlin' in —
Too laäte — but it 's all ower now — hall
   hower — an' ten year sin';

Too laäte, tha mun git tha to bed, but I 'll
   coom an' I 'll squench the light,
Fur we moänt 'ev naw moor fires — and soä,
   little Dick, good-night.

---

[1] 'Bubbling,' a young unfledged bird.
[2] Beams.
[3] Wrapt ourselves.
[4] The beam that runs along the roof of the house just beneath the ridge.

# VASTNESS

First printed in ' The Nineteenth Century '
for November, 1885.

### I

Many a hearth upon our dark globe sighs
   after many a vanish'd face,
Many a planet by many a sun may roll
   with the dust of a vanish'd race.

### II

Raving politics, never at rest — as this poor
   earth's pale history runs, —
What is it all but a trouble of ants in the
   gleam of a million million of suns ?

### III

Lies upon this side, lies upon that side,
   truthless violence mourn'd by the
   wise,
Thousands of voices drowning his own in a
   popular torrent of lies upon lies;

### IV

Stately purposes, valor in battle, glorious
   annals of army and fleet,
Death for the right cause, death for the
   wrong cause, trumpets of victory,
   groans of defeat;

### V

Innocence seethed in her mother's milk,
   and Charity setting the martyr
   aflame;
Thraldom who walks with the banner of
   Freedom, and recks not to ruin a
   realm in her name.

### VI

Faith at her zenith, or all but lost in the
   gloom of doubts that darken the
   schools;
Craft with a bunch of all-heal in her hand,
   follow'd up by her vassal legion of
   fools;

### VII

Trade flying over a thousand seas with her
   spice and her vintage, her silk and
   her corn;
Desolate offing, sailorless harbors, famishing populace, wharves forlorn;

VIII

Star of the morning, Hope in the sunrise;
  gloom of the evening, Life at a
  close;
Pleasure who flaunts on her wide downway
  with her flying robe and her poison'd
  rose;

IX

Pain, that has crawl'd from the corpse of
  Pleasure, a worm which writhes all
  day, and at night
Stirs up again in the heart of the sleeper,
  and stings him back to the curse of
  the light;

X

Wealth with his wines and his wedded harlots; honest Poverty, bare to the
  bone;
Opulent Avarice, lean as Poverty; Flattery
  gilding the rift in a throne;

XI

Fame blowing out from her golden trumpet a jubilant challenge to Time and
  to Fate;
Slander, her shadow, sowing the nettle on
  all the laurell'd graves of the great;

XII

Love for the maiden, crown'd with marriage, no regrets for aught that has
  been,
Household happiness, gracious children,
  debtless competence, golden mean;

XIII

National hatreds of whole generations, and
  pigmy spites of the village spire;
Vows that will last to the last death-ruckle,
  and vows that are snapt in a moment of fire;

XIV

He that has lived for the lust of the minute, and died in the doing it, flesh
  without mind;
He that has nail'd all flesh to the Cross, till
  Self died out in the love of his kind;

XV

Spring and Summer and Autumn and Winter, and all these old revolutions of
  earth;

All new-old revolutions of Empire—
  change of the tide—what is all of
  it worth?

XVI

What the philosophies, all the sciences,
  poesy, varying voices of prayer,
All that is noblest, all that is basest, all
  that is filthy with all that is fair?

XVII

What is it all, if we all of us end but in
  being our own corpse-coffins at
  last?
Swallow'd in Vastness, lost in Silence,
  drown'd in the deeps of a meaningless Past?

XVIII

What but a murmur of gnats in the gloom,
  or a moment's anger of bees in their
  hive?—

. . . . . . . . . . . . . . . .
Peace, let it be! for I loved him, and love
  him for ever: the dead are not dead
  but alive.


# THE RING

Dedicated to the Hon. J. Russell Lowell

Mr. Lowell told Tennyson the story, ' or
something like it, of a house near where he had
once lived ' ('Memoir,' vol. ii. p. 365).

MIRIAM AND HER FATHER

MIRIAM (singing).

MELLOW moon of heaven,
    Bright in blue,
Moon of married hearts,
    Hear me, you!

Twelve times in the year
    Bring me bliss,
Globing honey moons
    Bright as this.

Moon, you fade at times
    From the night.                    10
Young again you grow
    Out of sight.

Silver crescent-curve,
    Coming soon,

Globe again, and make
  Honey moon.

Shall not *my* love last,
  Moon, with you,
  For ten thousand years
  Old and new?                                      20

FATHER.

And who was he with such love-drunken
      eyes
They made a thousand honey moons of one?

MIRIAM.

The prophet of his own, my Hubert — his
The words, and mine the setting. ' Air and
      words,'
Said Hubert, when I sang the song, ' are
      bride
And bridegroom.'  Does it please you?

FATHER.

                            Mainly, child,
Because I hear your mother's voice in
      yours.
She —, why, you shiver tho' the wind is
      west
With all the warmth of summer.

MIRIAM.

                            Well, I felt
On a sudden I know not what, a breath
      that past                                     30
With all the cold of winter.

FATHER (*muttering to himself*).

                            Even so.
The Ghost in Man, the Ghost that once was
      Man,
But cannot wholly free itself from Man,
Are calling to each other thro' a dawn
Stranger than earth has ever seen; the veil
Is rending, and the Voices of the day
Are heard across the Voices of the dark.
No sudden heaven, nor sudden hell, for
      man,
But thro' the Will of One who knows and
      rules —
And utter knowledge is but utter love —
Æonian Evolution, swift or slow,                    41
Thro' all the spheres — an ever opening
      height,
An ever lessening earth — and she per-
      haps,
My Miriam, breaks her latest earthly link
With me to-day.

MIRIAM.

You speak so low; what is it?
Your ' Miriam breaks ' — is making a new
      link
Breaking an old one?

FATHER.

                  No, for we, my child,
Have been till now each other's all-in-all.

MIRIAM.

And you the lifelong guardian of the child.

FATHER.

I, and one other whom you have not
      known.                                        50

MIRIAM.

And who? what other?

FATHER.

                  Whither are you bound?
For Naples which we only left in May?

MIRIAM.

No, father, Spain, but Hubert brings me
      home
With April and the swallow.  Wish me joy!

FATHER.

What need to wish when Hubert weds in
      you
The heart of love, and you the soul of
      truth
In Hubert?

MIRIAM.

                  Tho' you used to call me once
The lonely maiden princess of the wood,
Who meant to sleep her hundred summers
      out                                           59
Before a kiss should wake her.

FATHER.

                            Ay, but now
Your fairy prince has found you, take this
      ring.

MIRIAM.

' Io t' amo ' — and these diamonds — beau-
      tiful!
' From Walter,' and for me from you then?

FATHER.

                                  Well,
One way for Miriam.

MIRIAM.

Miriam am I not?

FATHER.

This ring bequeath'd you by your mother,
    child,
Was to be given you — such her dying
    wish —
Given on the morning when you came of
    age
Or on the day you married. Both the
    days
Now close in one. The ring is doubly
    yours.    69
Why do you look so gravely at the tower?

MIRIAM.

I never saw it yet so all ablaze
With creepers crimsoning to the pinnacles,
As if perpetual sunset linger'd there,
And all ablaze too in the lake below!
And how the birds that circle round the
    tower
Are cheeping to each other of their flight
To summer lands!

FATHER.

And that has made you grave?
Fly — care not. Birds and brides must
    leave the nest.
Child, I am happier in your happiness    79
Than in mine own.

MIRIAM.

It is not that!

FATHER.

What else?

MIRIAM.

That chamber in the tower.

FATHER.

What chamber, child?
Your nurse is here?

MIRIAM.

My mother's nurse and mine.
She comes to dress me in my bridal veil.

FATHER.

What did she say?

MIRIAM.

She said that you and I

Had been abroad for my poor health so
    long
She fear'd I had forgotten her, and I ask'd
About my mother, and she said, ' Thy hair
Is golden like thy mother's, not so fine.'

FATHER.

What then? what more?

MIRIAM.

She said — perhaps indeed
She wander'd, having wander'd now so far
Beyond the common date of death — that
    you,    91
When I was smaller than the statuette
Of my dear mother on your bracket
    here —
You took me to that chamber in the tower,
The topmost — a chest there, by which you
    knelt —
And there were books and dresses — left
    to me,
A ring too which you kiss'd, and I, she
    said,
I babbled, ' Mother, mother ' — as I used
To prattle to her picture — stretch'd my
    hands
As if I saw her; then a woman came    100
And caught me from my nurse. I hear her
    yet —
A sound of anger like a distant storm.

FATHER.

Garrulous old crone!

MIRIAM.

Poor nurse!

FATHER.

I bade her keep,
Like a seal'd book, all mention of the ring,
For I myself would tell you all to-day.

MIRIAM.

' She too might speak to-day,' she mumbled.
    Still,
I scarce have learnt the title of your book,
But you will turn the pages.

FATHER.

Ay, to-day!
I brought you to that chamber on your
    third
September birthday with your nurse, and
    felt    110

An icy breath play on me, while I stoopt
To take and kiss the ring.

### MIRIAM.

This very ring,
' Io t' amo ' ?

### FATHER.

Yes, for some wild hope was mine
That, in the misery of my married life,
Miriam your mother might appear to me.
She came to you, not me. The storm you
hear
Far-off is Muriel — your stepmother's voice.

### MIRIAM.

Vext, that you thought my mother came to
me ?
Or at my crying, ' Mother ' ? or to find
My mother's diamonds hidden from her
there,                                    120
Like worldly beauties in the cell, not shown
To dazzle all that see them ?

### FATHER.

Wait a while.
Your mother and stepmother — Miriam
Erne
And Muriel Erne — the two were cousins
— lived
With Muriel's mother on the down, that
sees
A thousand squares of corn and meadow,
far
As the gray deep, a landscape which your
eyes
Have many a time ranged over when a
babe.

### MIRIAM.

I climb'd the hill with Hubert, yesterday,
And from the thousand squares, one silent
voice                                     130
Came on the wind, and seem'd to say,
' Again.'
We saw far off an old forsaken house,
Then home, and past the ruin'd mill.

### FATHER.

And there
I found these cousins often by the brook,
For Miriam sketch'd and Muriel threw the
fly;
The girls of equal age, but one was fair,
And one was dark, and both were beautiful.
No voice for either spoke within my heart

Then, for the surface eye, that only dotes
On outward beauty, glancing from the one
To the other, knew not that which pleased
it most,                                  141
The raven ringlet or the gold; but both
Were dowerless, and myself, I used to
walk
This terrace — morbid, melancholy; mine
And yet not mine the hall, the farm, the
field;
For all that ample woodland whisper'd,
' Debt,'
The brook that feeds this lakelet mur-
mur'd, ' Debt,'
And in yon arching avenue of old elms,
Tho' mine, not mine, I heard the sober rook
And carrion crow cry, ' Mortgage.'

### MIRIAM.

Father's fault
Visited on the children !

### FATHER.

Ay, but then
A kinsman, dying, summon'd me to
Rome —                                    152
He left me wealth — and while I jour-
ney'd hence,
And saw the world fly by me like a dream,
And while I communed with my truest self,
I woke to all of truest in myself,
Till, in the gleam of those midsummer
dawns,
The form of Muriel faded, and the face
Of Miriam grew upon me, till I knew;
And past and future mixt in heaven and
made                                      160
The rosy twilight of a perfect day.

### MIRIAM.

So glad ? no tear for him who left you
wealth,
Your kinsman ?

### FATHER.

I had seen the man but once;
He loved my name, not me; and then I
pass'd
Home, and thro' Venice, where a jeweller,
So far gone down, or so far up in life,
That he was nearing his own hundred, sold
This ring to me, then laugh'd, ' The ring is
weird.'
And weird and worn and wizard-like was
he.

'Why weird?' I ask'd him; and he said,
        'The souls                          170
Of two repentant lovers guard the ring;'
Then with a ribald twinkle in his bleak
        eyes —
'And if you give the ring to any maid,
They still remember what it cost them
        here,
And bind the maid to love you by the ring;
And if the ring were stolen from the maid,
The theft were death or madness to the
        thief,
So sacred those ghost lovers hold the gift.'
And then he told their legend:
                        'Long ago
Two lovers parted by a scurrilous tale   180
Had quarrell'd, till the man repenting sent
This ring, "Io t' amo," to his best beloved,
And sent it on her birthday.  She in wrath
Return'd it on her birthday, and that day
His death-day, when, half-frenzied by the
        ring,
He wildly fought a rival suitor, him
The causer of that scandal, fought and fell;
And she that came to part them all too late,
And found a corpse and silence, drew the
        ring
From his dead finger, wore it till her death,
Shrined him within the temple of her
        heart,                               191
Made every moment of her after life
A virgin victim to his memory,
And dying rose, and rear'd her arms, and
        cried,
"I see him, Io t' amo, Io t' amo."'

MIRIAM.

Legend or true?  so tender should be true!
Did *he* believe it?  did you ask him?

FATHER.

                        Ay!
But that half skeleton, like a barren ghost
From out the fleshless world of spirits,
        laugh'd —
A hollow laughter!

MIRIAM.

                Vile, so near the ghost
Himself, to laugh at love in death!  But
        you?                                201

FATHER.

Well, as the bygone lover thro' this ring
Had sent his cry for her forgiveness, I

Would call thro' this 'Io t' amo' to the
        heart
Of Miriam; then I bade the man engrave
'From Walter' on the ring, and sent it —
        wrote
Name, surname, all as clear as noon, but
        he —
Some younger hand must have engraven
        the ring —
His fingers were so stiffen'd by the frost
Of seven and ninety winters, that he
        scrawl'd                            210
A 'Miriam' that might seem a 'Muriel;'
And Muriel claim'd and open'd what I
        meant
For Miriam, took the ring, and flaunted it
Before that other whom I loved and love.

A mountain stay'd me here, a minster
        there,
A galleried palace, or a battle-field,
Where stood the sheaf of Peace: but —
        coming home —
And on your mother's birthday — all but
        yours —
A week betwixt — and when the tower as
        now
Was all ablaze with crimson to the roof, 220
And all ablaze too plunging in the lake
Head - foremost — who were those that
        stood between
The tower and that rich phantom of the
        tower?
Muriel and Miriam, each in white, and
        like
May - blossoms in mid - autumn — was it
        they?
A light shot upward on them from the lake.
What sparkled there?  whose hand was
        that?  they stood
So close together.  I am not keen of sight,
But coming nearer — Muriel had the
        ring —
'O Miriam!  have you given your ring to
        her?                                230
O Miriam!'  Miriam redden'd, Muriel
        clench'd
The hand that wore it, till I cried again:
'O Miriam, if you love me take the ring!'
She glanced at me, at Muriel, and was
        mute.
'Nay, if you cannot love me, let it be.'
Then — Muriel standing ever statue-like —
She turn'd, and in her soft imperial way
And saying gently, 'Muriel, by your leave,'

Unclosed the hand and from it drew the
 ring,
And gave it me, who pass'd it down her
 own, 240
'Io t' amo, all is well then.' Muriel fled.

#### MIRIAM.

Poor Muriel !

#### FATHER.

        Ay, poor Muriel, when you hear
What follows ! Miriam loved me from the
 first,
Not thro' the ring; but on her marriage-
 morn
This birthday, death-day, and betrothal
 ring,
Laid on her table overnight, was gone;
And after hours of search and doubt and
 threats,
And hubbub, Muriel enter'd with it,
 'See ! —
Found in a chink of that old moulder'd
 floor !' 249
My Miriam nodded with a pitying smile,
As who should say that 'those who lose
 can find.'
    Then I and she were married for a year,
One year without a storm, or even a cloud;
And you, my Miriam, born within the
 year;
And she, my Miriam, dead within the
 year.
    I sat beside her dying, and she gaspt:
'The books, the miniature, the lace are
 hers,
My ring too when she comes of age, or
 when
She marries; you — you loved me, kept
 your word.
You love me still, " Io t' amo." — Muriel
 — no — 260
She cannot love; she loves her own hard
 self,
Her firm will, her fix'd purpose. Promise
 me,
Miriam, not Muriel — she shall have the
 ring.'
And there the light of other life, which
 lives
Beyond our burial and our buried eyes,
Gleam'd for a moment in her own on earth.
I swore the vow, then with my latest kiss
Upon them, closed her eyes, which would
 not close,

But kept their watch upon the ring and
 you.
Your birthday was her death-day. 269

#### MIRIAM.

        O poor mother !
And you, poor desolate father, and poor
 me,
The little senseless, worthless, wordless
 babe,
Saved when your life was wreck'd !

#### FATHER

        Desolate ? yes !
Desolate as that sailor whom the storm
Had parted from his comrade in the boat,
And dash'd half dead on barren sands,
 was I.
Nay, you were my one solace; only — you
Were always ailing. Muriel's mother,
 sent,
And sure am I, by Muriel, one day came
And saw you, shook her head, and patted
 yours, 280
And smiled, and making with a kindly
 pinch
Each poor pale cheek a momentary rose —
'That should be fix'd,' she said; your pretty
 bud,
So blighted here, would flower into full
 health
Among our heath and bracken. Let her
 come !
And we will feed her with our mountain
 air,
And send her home to you rejoicing.'
 No —
We could not part. And once, when you,
 my girl,
Rode on my shoulder home — the tiny fist
Had graspt a daisy from your mother's
 grave — 290
By the lych-gate was Muriel. 'Ay,' she
 said,
'Among the tombs in this damp vale of
 yours !
You scorn my mother's warning, but the
 child
Is paler than before. We often walk
In open sun, and see beneath our feet
The mist of autumn gather from your lake,
And shroud the tower; and once we only
 saw
Your gilded vane, a light above the
 mist' —

Our old bright bird that still is veering
    there                                   299
Above his four gold letters — 'and the light,'
She said, ' was like that light ' — and there
    she paused,
And long; till I, believing that the girl's
Lean fancy, groping for it, could not find
One likeness, laugh'd a little and found her
    two —
' A warrior's crest above the cloud of
    war ' —
' A fiery phœnix rising from the smoke,
The pyre he burnt in.' — ' Nay,' she said,
    ' the light
That glimmers on the marsh and on the
    grave.'
And spoke no more, but turn'd and past
    away.
    Miriam, I am not surely one of those   310
Caught by the flower that closes on the
    fly,
But after ten slow weeks her fix'd intent,
In aiming at an all but hopeless mark
To strike it, struck. I took, I left you
    there;
I came, I went, was happier day by day;
For Muriel nursed you with a mother's
    care;
Till on that clear and heather - scented
    height
The rounder cheek had brighten'd into
    bloom.
She always came to meet me carrying you,
And all her talk was of the babe she
    loved;                                  320
So, following her old pastime of the brook,
She threw the fly for me; but oftener left
That angling to the mother. ' Muriel's
    health
Had weaken'd, nursing little Miriam.
    Strange !
She used to shun the wailing babe, and
    dotes
On this of yours.' But when the matron
    saw
That hinted love was only wasted bait,
Not risen to, she was bolder. ' Ever since
You sent the fatal ring ' — I told her ' sent
To Miriam,' ' Doubtless — ay, but ever
    since                                   330
In all the world my dear one sees but
    you —
In your sweet babe she finds but you — she
    makes
Her heart a mirror that reflects but you.'

And then the tear fell, the voice broke.
    Her heart !
I gazed into the mirror, as a man
Who sees his face in water, and a stone,
That glances from the bottom of the pool,
Strike upward thro' the shadow; yet at
    last,
Gratitude — loneliness — desire to keep
So skilled a nurse about you always —
    nay !                                   340
Some half remorseful kind of pity too —
Well ! well, you know I married Muriel
    Erne.
    ' I take thee Muriel for my wedded
    wife ' —
I had forgotten it was your birthday,
    child —
When all at once with some electric thrill
A cold air pass'd between us, and the
    hands
Fell from each other, and were join'd
    again.
    No second cloudless honeymoon was
    mine.
For by and by she sicken'd of the farce,
She dropt the gracious mask of mother-
    hood,                                   350
She came no more to meet me, carrying
    you,
Nor ever cared to set you on her knee,
Nor ever let you gambol in her sight,
Nor ever cheer'd you with a kindly smile,
Nor ever ceased to clamor for the ring;
Why had I sent the ring at first to her ?
Why had I made her love me thro' the
    ring,
And then had changed ? so fickle are men
    — the best !
Not she — but now my love was hers
    again,
The ring by right, she said, was hers
    again.                                  360
At times too shrilling in her angrier moods,
' That weak and watery nature love you ?
    No !
" Io t' amo, Io t' amo " ! ' flung herself
Against my heart, but often while her lips
Were warm upon my cheek, an icy breath,
As from the grating of a sepulchre,
Past over both. I told her of my vow,
No pliable idiot I to break my vow;
But still she made her outcry for the ring;
For one monotonous fancy madden'd her,
Till I myself was madden'd with her
    cry,                                    371

And even that 'Io t' amo,' those three
    sweet
Italian words, became a weariness.
  My people too were scared with eerie
    sounds,
A footstep, a low throbbing in the walls,
A noise of falling weights that never fell,
Weird whispers, bells that rang without a
    hand,
Door-handles turn'd when none was at the
    door,
And bolted doors that open'd of themselves;
And one betwixt the dark and light had seen
*Her*, bending by the cradle of her babe. 381

#### MIRIAM.

And I remember once that being waked
By noises in the house — and no one
    near —
I cried for nurse, and felt a gentle hand
Fall on my forehead, and a sudden face
Look'd in upon me like a gleam and pass'd,
And I was quieted, and slept again.
Or is it some half memory of a dream ?

#### FATHER.

Your fifth September birthday.

#### MIRIAM.

              And the face,
The hand, — my mother.

#### FATHER.

          Miriam, on that day
Two lovers parted by no scurrilous tale —
Mere want of gold — and still for twenty
    years 392
Bound by the golden cord of their first
    love —
Had ask'd us to their marriage, and to share
Their marriage - banquet. Muriel, paler
    then
Than ever you were in your cradle, moan'd,
'I am fitter for my bed, or for my grave,
I cannot go, go you.' And then she rose,
She clung to me with such a hard embrace,
So lingeringly long, that half-amazed 400
I parted from her, and I went alone.
And when the bridegroom murmur'd,
    'With this ring,'
I felt for what I could not find, the key,
The guardian of her relics, of *her* ring.
I kept it as a sacred amulet
About me, — gone ! and gone in that em-
    brace !

Then, hurrying home, I found her not in
    house
Or garden — up the tower — an icy air
Fled by me. — There, the chest was open
    — all 409
The sacred relics tost about the floor —
Among them Muriel lying on her face —
I raised her, call'd her, 'Muriel, Muriel,
    wake ! '
The fatal ring lay near her; the glazed
    eye
Glared at me as in horror. Dead ! I took
And chafed the freezing hand. A red
    mark ran
All round one finger pointed straight, the
    rest
Were crumpled inwards. Dead ! — and
    maybe stung
With some remorse, had stolen, worn the
    ring —
Then torn it from her finger, or as if — 419
For never had I seen her show remorse —
As if —

#### MIRIAM.

    — those two ghost lovers —

#### FATHER.

              Lovers yet —

#### MIRIAM.

Yes, yes !

#### FATHER.

    — but dead so long, gone up so far,
That now their ever-rising life has dwarf'd
Or lost the moment of their past on earth,
As we forget our wail at being born —
As if —

#### MIRIAM.

    — a dearer ghost had —

#### FATHER.

            — wrench'd it away.

#### MIRIAM.

Had floated in with sad reproachful eyes,
Till from her own hand she had torn the
    ring 428
In fright, and fallen dead. And I myself
Am half afraid to wear it.

#### FATHER.

          Well, no more !
No bridal music this ! but fear not you !
You have the ring she guarded; that poor
    link

With earth is broken, and has left her
    free,
Except that, still drawn downward for an
    hour,
Her spirit hovering by the church, where
    she
Was married too, may linger, till she sees
Her maiden coming like a queen, who
    leaves
Some colder province in the North to gain
Her capital city, where the loyal bells
Clash welcome — linger, till her own, the
    babe                                    440
She lean'd to from her spiritual sphere,
Her lonely maiden princess, crowned with
    flowers,
Has enter'd on the larger woman-world
Of wives and mothers.
                    But the bridal veil —
Your nurse is waiting. Kiss me, child, and
    go.


## FORLORN

### I

'HE is fled — I wish him dead —
    He that wrought my ruin —
O, the flattery and the craft
    Which were my undoing —
    In the night, in the night,
    When the storms are blowing.

### II

'Who was witness of the crime ?
    Who shall now reveal it ?
He is fled, or he is dead,
    Marriage will conceal it —
    In the night, in the night,
    While the gloom is growing.'

### III

Catherine, Catherine, in the night,
    What is this you 're dreaming ?
There is laughter down in hell
    At your simple scheming —
    In the night, in the night,
    When the ghosts are fleeting.

### IV

You to place a hand in his
    Like an honest woman's,
You that lie with wasted lungs
    Waiting for your summons —
    In the night, O, the night !
    O, the deathwatch beating !

### V

There will come a witness soon
    Hard to be confuted,
All the world will hear a voice
    Scream you are polluted —
    In the night ! O, the night,
    When the owls are wailing !

### VI

Shame and marriage, shame and marriage,
    Fright and foul dissembling,
Bantering bridesman, reddening priest,
    Tower and altar trembling —
    In the night, O, the night,
    When the mind is failing !

### VII

Mother, dare you kill your child ?
    How your hand is shaking !
Daughter of the seed of Cain,
    What is this you 're taking ? —
    In the night, O, the night,
    While the house is sleeping.

### VIII

Dreadful ! has it come to this,
    O unhappy creature ?
You that would not tread on a worm
    For your gentle nature —
    In the night, O, the night,
    O, the night of weeping !

### IX

Murder would not veil your sin,
    Marriage will not hide it,
Earth and Hell will brand your name,
    Wretch, you must abide it —
    In the night, O, the night,
    Long before the dawning.

### X

Up, get up, and tell him all,
    Tell him you were lying !
Do not die with a lie in your mouth,
    You that know you 're dying —
    In the night, O, the night,
    While the grave is yawning.

### XI

No — you will not die before,
    Tho' you 'll ne'er be stronger;

You will live till *that* is born,
   Then a little longer —
In the night, O, the night,
   While the Fiend is prowling.

XII

Death and marriage, death and marriage !
   Funeral hearses rolling !
Black with bridal favors mixt !
   Bridal bells with tolling ! —
In the night, O, the night,
   When the wolves are howling.

XIII

Up, get up, the time is short,
   Tell him now or never !
Tell him all before you die,
   Lest you die for ever —
In the night, O, the night,
   Where there 's no forgetting.

XIV

Up she got, and wrote him all,
   All her tale of sadness,
Blister'd every word with tears,
   And eased her heart of madness —
In the night, and nigh the dawn,
   And while the moon was setting.

## HAPPY

### THE LEPER'S BRIDE

Suggested by the quotation from an archæological letter by Rev. Bourchier James, appended to the poem by Tennyson.

I

WHY wail you, pretty plover ? and what is
   it that you fear ?
   Is he sick, your mate, like mine ? have
      you lost him, is he fled ?
And there — the heron rises from his watch
   beside the mere,
   And flies above the leper's hut, where
      lives the living-dead.

II

Come back, nor let me know it ! would he
   live and die alone ?
   And has he not forgiven me yet, his over-
      jealous bride,

Who am, and was, and will be his, his own
   and only own,
   To share his living death with him, die
      with him side by side ?

III

Is that the leper's hut on the solitary moor,
   Where noble Ulric dwells forlorn, and
      wears the leper's weed ?          10
The door is open. He ! is he standing at
   the door,
   My soldier of the Cross ? it is he, and
      he indeed !

IV

My roses — will he take them *now* — mine,
   his — from off the tree
   We planted both together, happy in our
      marriage morn ?
O God, I could blaspheme, for he fought
   Thy fight for Thee,
   And Thou hast made him leper to com-
      pass him with scorn —

V

Hast spared the flesh of thousands, the
   coward and the base,
   And set a crueller mark than Cain's on
      him, the good and brave !
He sees me, waves me from him. I will
   front him face to face.
   You need not wave me from you. I
      would leap into your grave.          20
. . . . . . . . . . .

VI

My warrior of the Holy Cross and of the
   conquering sword,
   The roses that you cast aside — once
      more I bring you these.
No nearer ? do you scorn me when you tell
   me, O my lord,
   You would not mar the beauty of your
      bride with your disease.

VII

You say your body is so foul — then here
   I stand apart,
   Who yearn to lay my loving head upon
      your leprous breast.
The leper plague may scale my skin, but
   never taint my heart;
   Your body is not foul to me, and body is
      foul at best.

### VIII

I loved you first when young and fair, but
　　now I love you most;
　　The fairest flesh at last is filth on which
　　　　the worm will feast;　　30
This poor rib-grated dungeon of the holy
　　human ghost,
　　This house with all its hateful needs no
　　　　cleaner than the beast,

### IX

This coarse diseaseful creature which in
　　Eden was divine,
　　This Satan-haunted ruin, this little city
　　　　of sewers,
This wall of solid flesh that comes between
　　your soul and mine,
　　Will vanish and give place to the beauty
　　　　that endures,

### X

The beauty that endures on the Spiritual
　　height,
　　When we shall stand transfigured, like
　　　　Christ on Hermon hill,
And moving each to music, soul in soul and
　　light in light,
　　Shall flash thro' one another in a moment
　　　　as we will.　　40

### XI

Foul ! foul ! the word was yours not mine,
　　I worship that right hand
　　Which fell'd the foes before you as the
　　　　woodman fells the wood,
And sway'd the sword that lighten'd back
　　the sun of Holy Land,
　　And clove the Moslem crescent moon,
　　　　and changed it into blood.

### XII

And once I worshipt all too well this crea-
　　ture of decay,
　　For age will chink the face, and death
　　　　will freeze the supplest limbs —
Yet you in your mid manhood — O, the
　　grief when yesterday
　　They bore the Cross before you to the
　　　　chant of funeral hymns !

### XIII

' Libera me, Domine ! ' you sang the Psalm,
　　and when
　　The priest pronounced you dead, and
　　　　flung the mould upon your feet,　　50

A beauty came upon your face, not that of
　　living men,
　　But seen upon the silent brow when life
　　　　has ceased to beat.

### XIV

' Libera nos, Domine ' — you knew not one
　　was there
　　Who saw you kneel beside your bier, and
　　　　weeping scarce could see;
May I come a little nearer, I that heard,
　　and changed the prayer
　　And sang the married ' nos ' for the soli-
　　　　tary ' me ' ?

### XV

My beauty marred by you ? by you ! so be
　　it. All is well
　　If I lose it and myself in the higher
　　　　beauty, yours.
My beauty lured that falcon from his eyry
　　on the fell,
　　Who never caught one gleam of the
　　　　beauty which endures —　　60

### XVI

The Count who sought to snap the bond
　　that link'd us life to life,
　　Who whisper'd me, ' Your Ulric loves '
　　　　— a little nearer still —
He hiss'd, ' Let us revenge ourselves, your
　　Ulric woos my wife ' —
　　A lie by which he thought he could sub-
　　　　due me to his will.

### XVII

I knew that you were near me when I let
　　him kiss my brow;
　　Did he touch me on the lips ? I was
　　　　jealous, anger'd, vain,
And I meant to make you jealous. Are
　　you jealous of me now ?
　　Your pardon, O my love, if I ever gave
　　　　you pain !

### XVIII

You never once accused me, but I wept
　　alone, and sigh'd
　　In the winter of the present for the sum-
　　　　mer of the past;　　70
That icy winter silence — how it froze you
　　from your bride,
　　Tho' I made one barren effort to break it
　　　　at the last !

### XIX

I brought you, you remember, these roses,
  when I knew
  You were parting for the war, and you
  took them tho' you frown'd;
You frown'd and yet you kiss'd them. All
  at once the trumpet blew,
And you spurr'd your fiery horse, and
  you hurl'd them to the ground.

### XX

You parted for the Holy War without a
  word to me,
  And clear myself unask'd — not I. My
  nature was too proud.
And him I saw but once again, and far
  away was he,
  When I was praying in a storm — the
  crash was long and loud —      80

### XXI

That God would ever slant His bolt from
  falling on your head —
  Then I lifted up my eyes, he was coming
  down the fell —
I clapt my hands. The sudden fire from
  heaven had dash'd him dead,
  And sent him charr'd and blasted to the
  deathless fire of hell.

### XXII

See, I sinn'd but for a moment. I repented
  and repent,
  And trust myself forgiven by the God to
  whom I kneel.
A little nearer? Yes. I shall hardly be
  content
  Till I be leper like yourself, my love,
  from head to heel.

### XXIII

O foolish dreams, that you, that I, would
  slight our marriage oath!
  I held you at that moment even dearer
  than before;      90
Now God has made you leper in His loving
  care for both,
  That we might cling together, never
  doubt each other more.

### XXIV

The priest, who join'd you to the dead, has
  join'd our hands of old;
  If man and wife be but one flesh, let
  mine be leprous too,

As dead from all the human race as if beneath the mould;
  If you be dead, then I am dead, who
  only live for you.

### XXV

Would Earth tho' hid in cloud not be follow'd by the Moon?
  The leech forsake the dying bed for terror of his life?
The shadow leave the Substance in the
  brooding light of noon?
  Or if I had been the leper would you
  have left the wife?      100

### XXVI

Not take them? Still you wave me off —
  poor roses — must I go —
  I have worn them year by year — from
  the bush we both had set —
What? fling them to you? — well — that
  were hardly gracious. No!
  Your plague but passes by the touch. A
  little nearer yet!

### XXVII

There, there! he buried you, the priest;
  the priest is not to blame,
  He joins us once again, to his either
  office true.
I thank him. I am happy, happy. Kiss
  me. In the name
  Of the everlasting God, I will live and die
  with you!

[Dean Milman has remarked that the pro-
tection and care afforded by the Church to this
blighted race of lepers was among the most
beautiful of its offices during the Middle Ages.
The leprosy of the thirteenth and fourteenth
centuries was supposed to be a legacy of the
Crusades, but was in all probability the offspring of meagre and unwholesome diet, miserable lodging and clothing, physical and moral
degradation. The services of the Church in
the seclusion of these unhappy sufferers were
most affecting. The stern duty of looking
to the public welfare is tempered with exquisite compassion for the victims of this loathsome disease. The ritual for the sequestration
of the leprous differed little from the burial
service. After the leper had been sprinkled
with holy water, the priest conducted him into
the church, the leper singing the psalm 'Libera
me, Domine,' and the crucifix and bearer going
before. In the church a black cloth was
stretched over two trestles in front of the altar,

and the leper leaning at its side devoutly heard mass. The priest, taking up a little earth in his cloak, threw it on one of the leper's feet, and put him out of the church, if it did not rain too heavily ; took him to his hut in the midst of the fields, and then uttered the prohibitions : ' I forbid you entering the church . . . or entering the company of others. I forbid you quitting your home without your leper's dress.' He concluded : ' Take this dress, and wear it in token of humility ; take these gloves, take this clapper, as a sign that you are forbidden to speak to any one. You are not to be indignant at being thus separated from others, and as to your little wants, good people will provide for you, and God will not desert you.' Then in this old ritual follow these sad words : ' When it shall come to pass that the leper shall pass out of this world, he shall be buried in his hut, and not in the churchyard.' At first there was a doubt whether wives should follow their husbands who had been leprous, or remain in the world and marry again. The Church decided that the marriage-tie was indissoluble, and so bestowed on these unhappy beings this immense source of consolation. With a love stronger than this living death, lepers were followed into banishment from the haunts of men by their faithful wives. Readers of Sir J. Stephen's ' Essays on Ecclesiastical Biography ' will recollect the description of the founder of the Franciscan order, how, controlling his involuntary disgust, Saint Francis of Assisi washed the feet and dressed the sores of the lepers, once at least reverently applying his lips to their wounds. — BOURCHIER-JAMES.]

This ceremony of *quasi*-burial varied considerably at different times and in different places. In some cases a grave was dug, and the leper's face was often covered during the service.

## TO ULYSSES [1]

Mr. W. G. Palgrave, to whom the poem was addressed, was a brother of Professor F. T. Palgrave. Tennyson once said to the latter, ' I think your brother is the cleverest man I ever saw.' Waugh, who records this, adds : ' He had, indeed, earned the title [of Ulysses], having been consul in 1866 at Sonkhoum Kale, in 1867 at Trebizond, in 1873 at St. Thomas, in 1876 at Manilla, and in 1878 consul-general in Bulgaria. To these he added, in 1879, the consulship at Bangkok, and in 1884 he was

[1] ' Ulysses,' the title of a number of essays by W. G. Palgrave. He died at Montevideo before seeing my poem.

consul-general of the Republic of Uruguay, a position which he still held at his death.'

### I

ULYSSES, much-experienced man,
   Whose eyes have known this globe of ours,
   Her tribes of men, and trees, and flowers,
From Corrientes to Japan,

### II

To you that bask below the Line,
   I soaking here in winter wet —
   The century's three strong eights have met
To drag me down to seventy-nine

### III

In summer if I reach my day —
   To you, yet young, who breathe the balm
   Of summer-winters by the palm
And orange grove of Paraguay,

### IV

I, tolerant of the colder time,
   Who love the winter woods, to trace
   On paler heavens the branching grace
Of leafless elm, or naked lime,

### V

And see my cedar green, and there
   My giant ilex keeping leaf
   When frost is keen and days are brief —
Or marvel how in English air

### VI

My yucca, which no winter quells,
   Altho' the months have scarce begun,
   Has push'd toward our faintest sun
A spike of half-accomplish'd bells —

### VII

Or watch the waving pine which here
   The warrior of Caprera set,[1]
   A name that earth will not forget
Till earth has roll'd her latest year —

### VIII

I, once half-crazed for larger light
   On broader zones beyond the foam,

[1] Garibaldi said to me, alluding to his barren island, ' I wish I had your trees.'

But chaining fancy now at home
Among the quarried downs of Wight,

IX

Not less would yield full thanks to you
  For your rich gift, your tale of lands
  I know not,[1] your Arabian sands;
Your cane, your palm, tree-fern, bamboo,

X

The wealth of tropic bower and brake;
  Your Oriental Eden-isles,[2]
  Where man, nor only Nature smiles;
Your wonder of the boiling lake;[3]

XI

Phra-Chai, the Shadow of the Best,[4]
  Phra-bat [5] the step; your Pontic coast;
  Crag-cloister; [6] Anatolian Ghost; [7]
Hong-Kong,[8] Karnac,[9] and all the rest;

XII

Thro' which I follow'd line by line
  Your leading hand, and came, my friend,
  To prize your various book, and send
A gift of slenderer value, mine.


TO MARY BOYLE

WITH THE FOLLOWING POEM

For the poet's acquaintance with Mary Boyle,
see the 'Memoir,' vol. ii. p. 294.

I

'SPRING-FLOWERS' ! While you still delay
  to take
    Your leave of town,
Our elm-tree's ruddy-hearted blossom-flake
  Is fluttering down.

  [1] The tale of Nejd.
  [2] The Philippines.
  [3] In Dominica.
  [4] The Shadow of the Lord. Certain obscure markings on a rock in Siam, which express the image of Buddha to the Buddhist
more or less distinctly according to his faith
and his moral worth.
  [5] The footstep of the Lord on another rock.
  [6] The monastery of Sumelas.
  [7] Anatolian spectre stories.
  [8] The three cities.
  [9] Travels in Egypt.

II

Be truer to your promise.   There ! I heard
    Our cuckoo call.
Be needle to the magnet of your word,
    Nor wait, till all

III

Our vernal bloom from every vale and
  plain
    And garden pass,
And all the gold from each laburnum chain
    Drop to the grass.

IV

Is memory with your Marian gone to rest,
    Dead with the dead ?
For ere she left us, when we met, you prest
    My hand, and said

V

'I come with your spring-flowers.' You
  came not, friend;
    My birds would sing,
You heard not. Take then this spring-
  flower I send,
    This song of spring,

VI

Found yesterday — forgotten mine own
  rhyme
    By mine old self,
As I shall be forgotten by old Time,
    Laid on the shelf —

VII

A rhyme that flower'd betwixt the whitening sloe
    And kingcup blaze,
And more than half a hundred years ago,
    In rick-fire days,

VIII

When Dives loathed the times, and paced
  his land
    In fear of worse,
And sanguine Lazarus felt a vacant hand
    Fill with *his* purse.

IX

For lowly minds were madden'd to the
  height
    By tonguester tricks,
And once — I well remember that red night
    When thirty ricks,

X

All flaming, made an English homestead
    hell —
    These hands of mine
Have helpt to pass a bucket from the well
    Along the line,

XI

When this bare dome had not begun to
    gleam
    Thro' youthful curls,
And you were then a lover's fairy dream,
    His girl of girls;

XII

And you, that now are lonely, and with
    Grief
    Sit face to face,
Might find a flickering glimmer of relief
    In change of place.

XIII

What use to brood ?   This life of mingled
    pains
    And joys to me,
Despite of every Faith and Creed, remains
    The Mystery.

XIV

Let golden youth bewail the friend, the
    wife,
    For ever gone.
He dreams of that long walk thro' desert
    life
    Without the one.

XV

The silver year should cease to mourn and
    sigh —
    Not long to wait —
So close are we, dear Mary, you and I
    To that dim gate.

XVI

Take, read ! and be the faults your Poet
    makes
    Or many or few,
He rests content, if his young music wakes
    A wish in you

XVII

To change our dark Queen-city, all her
    realm
    Of sound and smoke,

For his clear heaven, and these few lanes
    of elm
    And whispering oak.


## THE PROGRESS OF SPRING

Written more than fifty years before it was
printed in the ' Demeter ' volume.  See stanza
vii. of the preceding poem.

I

THE ground-flame of the crocus breaks the
    mould,
    Fair Spring slides hither o'er the South-
        ern sea,
Wavers on her thin stem the snowdrop
    cold
    That trembles not to kisses of the bee.
Come, Spring, for now from all the drip-
    ping eaves
    The spear of ice has wept itself away,
And  hour  by  hour  unfolding woodbine
    leaves
    O'er his uncertain shadow droops the
        day.
She comes !   The loosen'd rivulets run;
    The frost-bead melts upon her golden
        hair;
Her mantle, slowly greening in the Sun,
    Now wraps her close, now arching leaves
        her bare
    To breaths of balmier air;

II

Up leaps the lark, gone wild to welcome
    her,
    About her glance the tits, and shriek the
        jays,
Before her skims the jubilant woodpecker
    The linnet's bosom blushes at her gaze,
While round her brows a woodland culver
    flits,
    Watching her large light eyes and gra-
        cious looks,
And in her open palm a halcyon sits
    Patient — the secret splendor of the
        brooks.
Come, Spring !   She comes on waste and
    wood,
    On farm and field; but enter also here,
Diffuse thyself at will thro' all my blood,
    And, tho' thy violet sicken into sere,
    Lodge with me all the year !

### III

Once more a downy drift against the brakes,
  Self - darken'd in the sky, descending
    slow !
But gladly see I thro' the wavering flakes
  Yon blanching apricot like snow in snow.
These will thine eyes not brook in forest-
    paths,
  On their perpetual pine, nor round the
    beech;
They fuse themselves to little spicy baths,
  Solved in the tender blushes of the
    peach;
They lose themselves and die
  On that new life that gems the hawthorn
    line;
Thy gay lent-lilies wave and put them by,
  And out once more in varnish'd glory
    shine
    Thy stars of celandine.

### IV

She floats across the hamlet. Heaven
    lours,
  But in the tearful splendor of her smiles
I see the slowly-thickening chestnut towers
  Fill out the spaces by the barren tiles.
Now past her feet the swallow circling
    flies,
  A clamorous cuckoo stoops to meet her
    hand;
Her light makes rainbows in my closing
    eyes,
  I hear a charm of song thro' all the land.
Come, Spring ! She comes, and Earth is
    glad
  To roll her North below thy deepening
    dome,
But ere thy maiden birk be wholly clad,
  And these low bushes dip their twigs in
    foam,
    Make all true hearths thy home.

### V

Across my garden ! and the thicket stirs,
  The fountain pulses high in sunnier jets,
The blackcap warbles, and the turtle purrs,
  The starling claps his tiny castanets.
Still round her forehead wheels the wood-
    land dove,
  And scatters on her throat the sparks of
    dew,
The kingcup fills her footprint, and above
  Broaden the glowing isles of vernal blue.

Hail, ample presence of a Queen,
  Bountiful, beautiful, apparell'd gay,
Whose mantle, every shade of glancing
    green,
  Flies back in fragrant breezes to display
  A tunic white as May !

### VI

She whispers, 'From the South I bring
    you balm,
  For on a tropic mountain was I born,
While some dark dweller by the coco-palm
  Watch'd my far meadow zoned with airy
    morn;
From under rose a muffled moan of floods;
  I sat beneath a solitude of snow;
There no one came, the turf was fresh, the
    woods
  Plunged gulf on gulf thro' all their vales
    below.
I saw beyond their silent tops
  The steaming marshes of the scarlet
    cranes,
The slant seas leaning on the mangrove
    copse,
  And summer basking in the sultry plains
  About a land of canes.

### VII

' Then from my vapor-girdle soaring forth
  I scaled the buoyant highway of the
    birds,
And drank the dews and drizzle of the
    North,
  That I might mix with men, and hear
    their words
On pathway'd plains; for — while my hand
    exults
  Within the bloodless heart of lowly flow-
    ers
To work old laws of Love to fresh results,
  Thro' manifold effect of simple pow-
    ers —
I too would teach the man
  Beyond the darker hour to see the
    bright,
That his fresh life may close as it began,
  The still-fulfilling promise of a light
  Narrowing the bounds of night.'

### VIII

So wed thee with my soul, that I may
    mark
  The coming year's great good and varied
    ills,

And new developments, whatever spark
   Be struck from out the clash of warring
     wills;
Or whether, since our nature cannot rest,
   The smoke of war's volcano burst again
From hoary deeps that belt the changeful
    West,
   Old Empires, dwellings of the kings of
    men;
Or should those fail that hold the helm,
   While the long day of knowledge grows
    and warms,
And in the heart of this most ancient realm
   A hateful voice be utter'd, and alarms
   Sounding ' To arms ! to arms ! '

### IX

A simpler, saner lesson might he learn
   Who reads thy gradual process, Holy
    Spring.
Thy leaves possess the season in their turn,
   And in their time thy warblers rise on
    wing.
How surely glidest thou from March to
    May,
   And changest, breathing it, the sullen
    wind,
Thy scope of operation, day by day,
   Larger and fuller, like the human mind!
Thy warmths from bud to bud
Accomplish that blind model in the seed,
And men have hopes, which race the rest-
    less blood,
   That after many changes may succeed
   Life which is Life indeed.

## MERLIN AND THE GLEAM

Compare ' The Voyage ; ' and see also ' Freedom ' (1884) :

> ' O follower of the Vision, still
>    In motion to the distant gleam,' etc.

Stopford Brooke says of this poem : ' It is as
lovely in form and rhythm and imagination, as
it is noble in thought and emotion.  It speaks
to all poetic hearts in England ; it tells them of
his coming death.  It then recalls his past, his
youth, his manhood ; his early poems, his critics, his central labor on Arthur's tale ; and we
see through its verse clear into the inmost
chamber of his heart.  What sits there upon
the throne, what has always sat thereon ?  It is
the undying longing and search after the ideal
light, the mother - passion of all the supreme
artists of the world.  "I am Merlin, who follow the Gleam." I know of no poem of Tennyson's which more takes my heart with magic
and beauty.'

### I

O YOUNG Mariner,
You from the haven
Under the sea-cliff,
You that are watching
The gray Magician
With eyes of wonder,
*I* am Merlin,
And *I* am dying,
*I* am Merlin
Who follow the Gleam.

### II

Mighty the Wizard
Who found me at sunrise
Sleeping, and woke me
And learn'd me Magic !
Great the Master,
And sweet the Magic,
When over the valley,
In early summers,
Over the mountain,
On human faces,
And all around me,
Moving to melody,
Floated the Gleam.

### III

Once at the croak of a Raven who crost it,
A barbarous people,
Blind to the magic
And deaf to the melody,
Snarl'd at and cursed me.
A demon vext me,
The light retreated,
The landskip darken'd,
The melody deaden'd,
The Master whisper'd,
' Follow the Gleam.'

### IV

Then to the melody,
Over a wilderness
Gliding, and glancing at
Elf of the woodland,
Gnome of the cavern,
Griffin and Giant,
And dancing of Fairies
In desolate hollows,
And wraiths of the mountain,
And rolling of dragons
By warble of water,

Or cataract music
Of falling torrents,
Flitted the Gleam.

V

Down from the mountain
And over the level,
And streaming and shining on
Silent river,
Silvery willow,
Pasture and plowland,
Innocent maidens,
Garrulous children,
Homestead and harvest,
Reaper and gleaner,
And rough-ruddy faces
Of lowly labor,
Slided the Gleam —

VI

Then, with a melody
Stronger and statelier,
Led me at length
To the city and palace
Of Arthur the King;
Touch'd at the golden
Cross of the churches,
Flash'd on the tournament,
Flicker'd and bicker'd
From helmet to helmet,
And last on the forehead
Of Arthur the blameless
Rested the Gleam.

VII

Clouds and darkness
Closed upon Camelot;
Arthur had vanish'd
I knew not whither,
The king who loved me,
And cannot die;
For out of the darkness
Silent and slowly
The Gleam, that had waned to a wintry
        glimmer
On icy fallow
And faded forest,
Drew to the valley
Named of the shadow,
And slowly brightening
Out of the glimmer,
And slowly moving again to a melody
Yearningly tender,
Fell on the shadow,

No longer a shadow,
But clothed with the Gleam.

VIII

And broader and brighter
The Gleam flying onward,
Wed to the melody,
Sang thro' the world;
And slower and fainter,
Old and weary,
But eager to follow,
I saw, whenever
In passing it glanced upon
Hamlet or city,
That under the Crosses
The dead man's garden,
The mortal hillock,
Would break into blossom;
And so to the land's
Last limit I came —
And can no longer,
But die rejoicing,
For thro' the Magic
Of Him the Mighty,
Who taught me in childhood,
There on the border
Of boundless Ocean,
And all but in Heaven
Hovers the Gleam.

IX

Not of the sunlight,
Not of the moonlight,
Not of the starlight!
O young Mariner,
Down to the haven,
Call your companions,
Launch your vessel
And crowd your canvas,
And, ere it vanishes
Over the margin,
After it, follow it,
Follow the Gleam.

## ROMNEY'S REMORSE

[I read Hayley's Life of Romney the other
day — Romney wanted but education and reading to make him a very fine painter: but his
ideal was not high nor fixed.  How touching
is the close of his life!  He married at nineteen, and because Sir Joshua and others had
said that 'marriage spoilt an artist' almost
immediately left his wife in the North and

scarce saw her till the end of his life ; when
old, nearly mad, and quite desolate, he went
back to her and she received him and nursed
him till he died.  This quiet act of hers is
worth all Romney's pictures ! even as a matter
of Art, I am sure. — EDWARD FITZGERALD,
' Letters and Literary Remains,' vol. i.]

'BEAT, little heart — I give you this and
   this.'
   Who are you ?   What ! the Lady Ham-
      ilton ?
Good, I am never weary painting you.
To sit once more ?  Cassandra, Hebe, Joan,
Or spinning at your wheel beside the
   vine —
Bacchante, what you will; and if I fail
To conjure and concentrate into form
And color all you are, the fault is less
In me than Art.   What artist ever yet
Could make pure light live on the canvas ?
   Art !
Why should I so disrelish that short word ?
   Where am I ? snow on all the hills ! so
      hot,
So fever'd ! never colt would more delight
To roll himself in meadow grass than I
To wallow in that winter of the hills.
   Nurse, were you hired ?  or came of your
      own will
To wait on one so broken, so forlorn ?
Have I not met you somewhere long ago ?
I am all but sure I have — in Kendal
   church —
O, yes !  I hired you for a season there,
And then we parted; but you look so kind
That you will not deny my sultry throat
One draught of icy water.  There — you
   spill
The drops upon my forehead.  Your hand
   shakes.
I am ashamed.   I am a trouble to you,
Could kneel for your forgiveness.  Are
   they tears ?
For me — they do me too much grace —
   for me ?
O Mary, Mary !
              Vexing you with words !
Words only, born of fever, or the fumes
Of that dark opiate dose you gave me, —
   words,
Wild babble.   I have stumbled back again
Into the common day, the sounder self.
God stay me there, if only for your sake,
The truest, kindliest, noblest-hearted wife
That ever wore a Christian marriage-ring.

My curse upon the Master's apothegm,
That wife and children drag an artist
   down !
This seem'd my lodestar in the heaven of
   Art,
And lured me from the household fire on
   earth.
To you my days have been a lifelong lie,
Grafted on half a truth; and tho' you say,
' Take comfort you have won the painter's
   fame,'
The best in me that sees the worst in me,
And groans to see it, finds no comfort
   there.
   What fame ?   I am not Raphael, Titian,
      — no,
Nor even a Sir Joshua, some will cry.
Wrong there !   The painter's fame ?  but
   mine, that grew
Blown into glittering by the popular breath,
May float awhile beneath the sun, may roll
The rainbow hues of heaven about it —
                                There !
The color'd bubble bursts above the abyss
Of Darkness, utter Lethe.

                   Is it so ?
Her sad eyes plead for my own fame with
   me
To make it dearer.

              Look, the sun has risen
To flame along another dreary day.
Your hand.  How bright you keep your
   marriage-ring !
Raise me.   I thank you.

              Has your opiate then
Bred this black mood ?  or am I conscious,
   more
Than other Masters, of the chasm between
Work and Ideal ?   Or does the gloom of
   age
And suffering cloud the height I stand
   upon
Even from myself ? stand ?  stood — no
   more.
            And yet
The world would lose, if such a wife as you
Should vanish unrecorded.   Might I crave
One favor ?   I am bankrupt of all claim
On your obedience, and my strongest wish
Falls flat before your least unwillingness.
Still, would you — if it please you — sit to
   me ?

I dream'd last night of that clear sum-
  mer noon,
When seated on a rock, and foot to foot
With your own shadow in the placid lake,
You claspt our infant daughter, heart to
  heart.
I had been among the hills, and brought
  you down
A length of staghorn-moss, and this you
  twined
About her cap.  I see the picture yet,
Mother and child.  A sound from far away,
No louder than a bee among the flowers,
A fall of water lull'd the noon asleep.
You still'd it for the moment with a song
Which often echo'd in me, while I stood
Before the great Madonna-masterpieces
Of ancient Art in Paris, or in Rome.

Mary, my crayons ! if I can, I will.
You should have been — I might have
  made you once,
Had I but known you as I know you now —
The true Alcestis of the time.  Your song —
Sit, listen !  I remember it, a proof
That I — even I — at times remember'd
  *you.*

' Beat upon mine, little heart ! beat, beat !
Beat upon mine ! you are mine, my sweet !
All mine from your pretty blue eyes to your feet,
            My sweet.'

Less profile ! turn to me — three-quarter
  face.

' Sleep, little blossom, my honey, my bliss !
For I give you this, and I give you this !
And I blind your pretty blue eyes with a kiss !
            Sleep ! '

Too early blinded by the kiss of death —

' Father and Mother will watch you grow ' —

You watch'd, not I ; she did not grow, she
  died.

' Father and Mother will watch you grow,
And gather the roses whenever they blow,
And find the white heather wherever you go,
            My sweet.'

Ah, my white heather only blooms in heaven
With Milton's amaranth.  There, there,
  there ! a child
Had shamed me at it — Down, you idle
  tools,

Stampt into dust — tremulous, all awry,
Blurr'd like a landskip in a ruffled pool, —
Not one stroke firm.  This Art, that harlot-
  like
Seduced me from you, leaves me harlot-
  like,
Who love her still, and whimper, impotent
To win her back before I die — and then —
Then, in the loud world's bastard judg-
  ment-day,
One truth will damn me with the mindless
  mob,
Who feel no touch of my temptation, more
Than all the myriad lies that blacken round
The corpse of every man that gains a name;
' This model husband, this fine artist ! '
Fool,
What matters ?  Six foot deep of burial
  mould
Will dull their comments !  Ay, but when
  the shout
Of His descending peals from heaven, and
  throbs
Thro' earth and all her graves, if *He* should
  ask,
' Why left you wife and children ? for my
  sake,
According to my word ? ' and I replied,
' Nay, Lord, for *Art*,' why, that would
  sound so mean
That all the dead, who wait the doom of
  hell
For bolder sins than mine, adulteries,
Wife-murders, — nay, the ruthless Mussul-
  man
Who flings his bowstrung harem in the
  sea,
Would turn, and glare at me, and point
  and jeer,
And gibber at the worm who, living, made
The wife of wives a widow-bride, and lost
Salvation for a sketch.
            I am wild again !
The coals of fire you heap upon my head
Have crazed me.  Some one knocking there
  without ?
No !  Will my Indian brother come ? to
  find
Me or my coffin ?  Should I know the
  man ?
This worn-out Reason dying in her house
May leave the windows blinded, and if so,
Bid him farewell for me, and tell him —
            Hope !
I hear a death-bed angel whisper, ' Hope.'

'The miserable have no medicine —
But only hope !' He said it — in the play.
His crime was of the senses; of the mind
Mine — worse, cold, calculated.
                    Tell my son —
O, let me lean my head upon your breast.
'Beat, little heart' on this fool brain of
    mine.
I once had friends — and many — none
    like you.
I love you more than when we married.
    Hope !
O, yes, I hope, or fancy that, perhaps,
Human forgiveness touches heaven, and
    thence —
For you forgive me, you are sure of that —
Reflected, sends a light on the forgiven.

## PARNASSUS

Exegi monumentum . . .
Quod non . . .
Possit diruere . . .
                  . . . innumerabilis
Annorum series et fuga temporum.
                    HORACE.

### I

WHAT be those crown'd forms high over
    the sacred fountain ?
Bards, that the mighty Muses have raised
    to the heights of the mountain,
And over the flight of the Ages ! O God-
    desses, help me up thither !
Lightning may shrivel the laurel of Cæsar,
    but mine would not wither.
Steep is the mountain, but you, you will
    help me to overcome it,
And stand with my head in the zenith, and
    roll my voice from the summit,
Sounding for ever and ever thro' Earth
    and her listening nations,
And mixt with the great sphere-music of
    stars and of constellations.

### II

What be those two shapes high over the
    sacred fountain,
Taller than all the Muses, and huger than
    all the mountain ?
On those two known peaks they stand ever
    spreading and heightening;
Poet, that evergreen laurel is blasted by
    more than lightning !

Look, in their deep double shadow the
    crown'd ones all disappearing !
Sing like a bird and be happy, nor hope for
    a deathless hearing !
'Sounding for ever and ever ?' pass on !
    the sight confuses —
These are Astronomy and Geology, terrible
    Muses !

### III

If the lips were touch'd with fire from off
    a pure Pierian altar,
Tho' their music here be mortal need the
    singer greatly care ?
Other songs for other worlds ! the fire
    within him would not falter;
Let the golden Iliad vanish, Homer here is
    Homer there.

## BY AN EVOLUTIONIST

THE Lord let the house of a brute to the
    soul of a man,
    And the man said, ' Am I your debtor ?'
And the Lord — ' Not yet; but make it as
    clean as you can,
    And then I will let you a better.'

### I

If my body come from brutes, my soul un-
    certain or a fable,
    Why not bask amid the senses while the
        sun of morning shines,
I, the finer brute rejoicing in my hounds,
    and in my stable,
    Youth and health, and birth and wealth,
        and choice of women and of wines ?

### II

What hast thou done for me, grim Old
    Age, save breaking my bones on the
    rack ?
    Would I had past in the morning that
    looks so bright from afar !

### OLD AGE

Done for thee ? starved the wild beast that
    was linkt with thee eighty years
    back.
    Less weight now for the ladder-of-heaven
    that hangs on a star.

### I

If my body come from brutes, tho' some-
        what finer than their own,
    I am heir, and this my kingdom.   Shall
        the royal voice be mute ?
No, but if the rebel subject seek to drag
        me from the throne,
    Hold the sceptre, Human Soul, and rule
        thy province of the brute.

### II

I have climb'd to the snows of Age, and I
        gaze at a field in the Past,
    Where I sank with the body at times in
        the sloughs of a low desire,
But I hear no yelp of the beast, and the
        Man is quiet at last,
    As he stands on the heights of his life
        with a glimpse of a height that is
        higher.


## FAR — FAR — AWAY

### (FOR MUSIC)

WHAT sight so lured him thro' the fields
        he knew
As where earth's green stole into heaven's
        own hue,
            Far — far — away ?

What sound was dearest in his native
        dells ?
The mellow lin-lan-lone of evening bells
            Far — far — away.

What vague world-whisper, mystic pain or
        joy,
Thro' those three words would haunt him
        when a boy,
            Far — far — away ?

A whisper from his dawn of life ? a
        breath
From some fair dawn beyond the doors of
        death
            Far — far — away ?

Far, far, how far ? from o'er the gates of
        birth,
The faint horizons, all the bounds of earth,
            Far — far — away ?

What charm in words, a charm no words
        could give ?
O dying words, can Music make you live
            Far — far — away ?


## POLITICS

WE move, the wheel must always move,
    Nor always on the plain,
And if we move to such a goal
    As Wisdom hopes to gain,
Then you that drive, and know your craft,
    Will firmly hold the rein,
Nor lend an ear to random cries,
    Or you may drive in vain;
For some cry 'Quick' and some cry 'Slow,'
    But, while the hills remain,
Up hill 'Too-slow' will need the whip,
    Down hill 'Too-quick' the chain.


## BEAUTIFUL CITY

BEAUTIFUL city, the centre and crater of
        European confusion,
O you with your passionate shriek for the
        rights of an equal humanity,
How often your Re-volution has proven but
        E-volution
Roll'd again back on itself in the tides of a
        civic insanity !


## THE ROSES ON THE TERRACE

ROSE, on this terrace fifty years ago,
    When I was in my June, you in your May,
Two words, ' *My* Rose,' set all your face
        aglow,
    And now that I am white and you are gray,
That blush of fifty years ago, my dear,
    Blooms in the past, but close to me to-day,
As this red rose, which on our terrace here
    Glows in the blue of fifty miles away.


## THE PLAY

ACT first, this Earth, a stage so gloom'd
        with woe
    You all but sicken at the shifting scenes.
And yet be patient.   Our Playwright may
        show
    In some fifth act what this wild Drama
        means.

## ON ONE WHO AFFECTED AN EFFEMINATE MANNER

WHILE man and woman still are incomplete,
I prize that soul where man and woman meet,
Which types all Nature's male and female plan,
But, friend, man - woman is not woman-man.

## TO ONE WHO RAN DOWN THE ENGLISH

YOU make our faults too gross, and thence maintain
Our darker future.  May your fears be vain !
At times the small black fly upon the pane
May seem the black ox of the distant plain.

## THE SNOWDROP

MANY, many welcomes,
February fair-maid,
Ever as of old time,
Solitary firstling,
Coming in the cold time,
Prophet of the gay time,
Prophet of the May time,
Prophet of the roses,
Many, many welcomes,
February fair-maid !

## THE THROSTLE

This poem, which had been printed in this country in the New York 'World,' was first published in England, 'to secure copyright, in an edition ultimately reduced to two copies, . . . a mere leaflet, consisting of a title and one page of text' (Waugh).  It was subsequently printed in the 'New Review' for October, 1889, and was included in the 'Demeter' volume, published in December of the same year.

'SUMMER is coming, summer is coming.
     I know it, I know it, I know it.
Light again, leaf again, life again, love again !'
     Yes, my wild little Poet.

Sing the new year in under the blue.
     Last year you sang it as gladly.
'New, new, new, new !'  Is it then so new
     That you should carol so madly ?

'Love again, song again, nest again, young again,'
     Never a prophet so crazy !
And hardly a daisy as yet, little friend,
     See, there is hardly a daisy.

'Here again, here, here, here, happy year !'
     O warble unchidden, unbidden !
Summer is coming, is coming, my dear,
     And all the winters are hidden.

## THE OAK

This poem, as the 'Memoir' (vol. ii. p. 366) informs us, was one which, like 'Far — far — away,' the author liked, thinking it 'clean cut like a Greek epigram.'

LIVE thy Life,
     Young and old,
Like yon oak,
     Bright in spring,
     Living gold;

Summer-rich
     Then; and then
Autumn-changed,
Soberer-hued
     Gold again.

All his leaves
     Fallen at length,
Look, he stands,
Trunk and bough,
     Naked strength.

## IN MEMORIAM

### W. G. WARD

William George Ward (1812–82) was prominent in the 'Tractarian' movement in the English Church during the second quarter of the present century.  The London 'Times' of June 21, 1887, in its jubilee retrospect of the events of Queen Victoria's reign, referring to the ecclesiastical aspect of the period, says: 'The Catholic — or, as it is named from the accident of its method, the Tractarian — movement in the Church of England, is the first to arrest the attention of the observer;' and, after discussing its influence on the religion of England, adds that its originators 'found themselves stranded in an eddy of the stream they had set in motion, and while the Catholic revival vivified and transformed the English Church, itself being modified and transformed in the process, its distinguished pioneers, with Newman and Ward at their head, joined the Church of Rome.' The life of Ward, with special reference to his connection with this religious movement, has been written by his son, Mr. Wilfrid Ward, in the two volumes entitled ' William George Ward and the Oxford Movement' (London, 1889), which was reviewed by the present Lord Tennyson in the 'Nineteenth Century,' (vol. xxvi. p. 343), and 'William George Ward and the Catholic Revival in England' (London, 1893).

FAREWELL, whose like on earth I shall not find,
　Whose Faith and Work were bells of full accord,
My friend, the most unworldly of mankind,
　Most generous of all Ultramontanes, Ward,
How subtle at tierce and quart of mind with mind,
　How loyal in the following of thy Lord !

# QUEEN MARY

## A DRAMA

This play, though the last in the chronological order of the 'historical trilogy' ('Harold,' 'Becket,' and 'Queen Mary'), was the first in the order of composition. It was published in 1875. The next year it was produced, with some necessary abridgment (it is much the longest of the three plays) at the Lyceum Theatre in London, Mr. Irving taking the part of Philip II.
'This trilogy of plays,' as the poet notes ('Memoir,' vol. ii. p. 173), 'portrays the making of England.' In 'Harold' we have 'the great conflict between Danes, Saxons, and Normans for supremacy, the awakening of the English people and clergy from the slumber into which they had for the most part fallen, and the forecast of the greatness of our composite race. In " Becket " the struggle is between the Crown and the Church for predominance, a struggle which continued for many centuries. In " Mary " are described the final downfall of Roman Catholicism in England, and the dawning of a new age ; for after the era of priestly domination comes the era of the freedom of the individual.' See also the 'Memoir,' vol. ii. pp. 176–185.

### DRAMATIS PERSONÆ

QUEEN MARY.
PHILIP, *King of Naples and Sicily, afterwards King of Spain.*
THE PRINCESS ELIZABETH.
REGINALD POLE, *Cardinal and Papal Legate.*
SIMON RENARD, *Spanish Ambassador.*
LE SIEUR DE NOAILLES, *French Ambassador.*
THOMAS CRANMER, *Archbishop of Canterbury.*
SIR NICHOLAS HEATH, *Archbishop of York ; Lord Chancellor after Gardiner.*
EDWARD COURTENAY, *Earl of Devon.*
LORD WILLIAM HOWARD, *afterwards Lord Howard, and Lord High Admiral.*
LORD WILLIAMS OF THAME.
LORD PAGET.
LORD PETRE.
STEPHEN GARDINER, *Bishop of Winchester and Lord Chancellor.*
EDMUND BONNER, *Bishop of London.*
THOMAS THIRLBY, *Bishop of Ely.*
SIR THOMAS WYATT ⎫ *Insurrectionary Leaders.*
SIR THOMAS STAFFORD ⎰
SIR RALPH BAGENHALL.
SIR ROBERT SOUTHWELL.
SIR HENRY BEDINGFIELD.
SIR WILLIAM CECIL.
SIR THOMAS WHITE, *Lord Mayor of London.*
THE DUKE OF ALVA ⎫ *attending on Philip.*
THE COUNT DE FERIA ⎰
PETER MARTYR.
FATHER COLE.
FATHER BOURNE.

VILLA GARCIA.
SOTO.
CAPTAIN BRETT }
ANTHONY KNYVETT } *Adherents of Wyatt.*
PETERS, *Gentleman of Lord Howard.*
ROGER, *Servant to Noailles.*
WILLIAM, *Servant to Wyatt.*
STEWARD OF HOUSEHOLD *to the Princess Elizabeth.*
OLD NOKES *and* NOKES.
MARCHIONESS OF EXETER, *Mother of Courtenay.*
LADY CLARENCE }
LADY MAGDALEN DACRES. } *Ladies in Waiting to the Queen.*
ALICE. }
MAID OF HONOR *to the Princess Elizabeth.*
JOAN } *two Country Wives.*
TIB }

Lords and other Attendants, Members of the Privy Council, Members of Parliament, Two Gentlemen, Aldermen, Citizens, Peasants, Ushers, Messengers, Guards, Pages, Gospellers, Marshalmen, etc.

## QUEEN MARY

### ACT I

SCENE I.—ALDGATE RICHLY DECORATED

#### CROWD. MARSHALMEN

*Marshalman.* Stand back, keep a clear lane ! When will her Majesty pass, say'st thou ? why now, even now; wherefore draw back your heads and your horns before I break them, and make what noise you will with your tongues, so it be not treason. Long live Queen Mary, the lawful and legitimate daughter of Harry the Eighth ! Shout, knaves !

*Citizens.* Long live Queen Mary !        10

*First Citizen.* That 's a hard word, legitimate; what does it mean ?

*Second Citizen.* It means a bastard.

*Third Citizen.* Nay, it means true-born.

*First Citizen.* Why, did n't the Parliament make her a bastard ?

*Second Citizen.* No; it was the Lady Elizabeth.

*Third Citizen.* That was after, man; that was after.        20

*First Citizen.* Then which is the bastard ?

*Second Citizen.* Troth, they be both bastards by Act of Parliament and Council.

*Third Citizen.* Ay, the Parliament can make every true-born man of us a bastard. Old Nokes, can't it make thee a bastard ? thou shouldst know, for thou art as white as three Christmases.

*Old Nokes (dreamily).* Who 's a-passing ? King Edward or King Richard ?        31

*Third Citizen.* No, old Nokes.

*Old Nokes.* It 's Harry !

*Third Citizen.* It 's Queen Mary.

*Old Nokes.* The blessed Mary 's a-passing !        [*Falls on his knees.*

*Nokes.* Let father alone, my masters ! he 's past your questioning.

*Third Citizen.* Answer thou for him, then ! thou 'rt no such cockerel thyself, for thou was born i' the tail end of old Harry the Seventh.        42

*Nokes.* Eh ! that was afore bastard-making began. I was born true man at five in the forenoon, i' the tail of old Harry, and so they can't make me a bastard.

*Third Citizen.* But if Parliament can make the Queen a bastard, why, it follows all the more that they can make thee one, who art fray'd i' the knees, and out at elbow, and bald o' the back, and bursten at the toes, and down at heels.        52

*Nokes.* I was born of a true man and a ring'd wife, and I can't argue upon it; but I and my old woman 'ud burn upon it, that would we.

*Marshalman.* What are you cackling of bastardy under the Queen's own nose ? I 'll have you flogg'd and burnt too, by the rood I will.        60

*First Citizen.* He swears by the rood. Whew !

*Second Citizen.* Hark ! the trumpets.

[*The Procession passes,* Mary *and* Elizabeth *riding side by side, and disappears under the gate.*

*Citizens.* Long live Queen Mary ! down with all traitors ! God save her Grace; and death to Northumberland !        [*Exeunt.*

*Manent* TWO GENTLEMEN.

*First Gentleman.* By God's light a noble creature, right royal !

*Second Gentleman.* She looks comelier than ordinary to-day; but to my mind the Lady Elizabeth is the more noble and royal.                          72

*First Gentleman.* I mean the Lady Elizabeth. Did you hear (I have a daughter in her service who reported it) that she met the Queen at Wanstead with five hundred horse, and the Queen (tho' some say they be much divided) took her hand, call'd her sweet sister, and kiss'd not her alone, but all the ladies of her following. 80

*Second Gentleman.* Ay, that was in her hour of joy. There will be plenty to sunder and unsister them again; this Gardiner for one, who is to be made Lord Chancellor, and will pounce like a wild beast out of his cage to worry Cranmer.

*First Gentleman.* And, furthermore, my daughter said that when there rose a talk of the late rebellion, she spoke even of Northumberland pitifully, and of the good Lady Jane as a poor innocent child who had but obeyed her father; and, furthermore, she said that no one in her time should be burnt for heresy.           94

*Second Gentleman.* Well, sir, I look for happy times.

*First Gentleman.* There is but one thing against them. I know not if you know.

*Second Gentleman.* I suppose you touch upon the rumor that Charles, the master of the world, has offer'd her his son Philip, the Pope and the devil. I trust it is but a rumor.                           103

*First Gentleman.* She is going now to the Tower to loose the prisoners there, and among them Courtenay, to be made Earl of Devon, of royal blood, of splendid feature, whom the council and all her people wish her to marry. May it be so, for we are many of us Catholics, but few Papists, and the Hot Gospellers will go mad upon it.                            112

*Second Gentleman.* Was she not betroth'd in her babyhood to the Great Emperor himself?

*First Gentleman.* Ay, but he's too old.

*Second Gentleman.* And again to her cousin Reginald Pole, now Cardinal; but I hear that he too is full of aches and broken before his day.           120

*First Gentleman.* Oh, the Pope could dispense with his cardinalate, and his achage, and his breakage, if that were all. Will you not follow the procession?

*Second Gentleman.* No; I have seen enough for this day.

*First Gentleman.* Well, I shall follow; if I can get near enough I shall judge with my own eyes whether her Grace incline to this splendid scion of Plantagenet.

[*Exeunt.*

## SCENE II

### A ROOM IN LAMBETH PALACE

*Cranmer.* To Strasburg, Antwerp, Frankfort, Zurich, Worms,
Geneva, Basle — our bishops from their sees
Or fled, they say, or flying — Poinet, Barlow,
Bale, Scory, Coverdale ; besides the deans
Of Christchurch, Durham, Exeter, and Wells —
Ailmer and Bullingham, and hundreds more;
So they report. I shall be left alone.
No; Hooper, Ridley, Latimer, will not fly.

*Enter* PETER MARTYR.

*Peter Martyr.* Fly, Cranmer! were there nothing else, your name
Stands first of those who sign'd the letters patent                          10
That gave her royal crown to Lady Jane.
*Cranmer.* Stand first it may, but it was written last.
Those that are now her privy council sign'd
Before me; nay, the judges had pronounced
That our young Edward might bequeath the crown
Of England, putting by his father's will.
Yet I stood out, till Edward sent for me.
The wan boy - king, with his fast - fading eyes
Fixt hard on mine, his frail transparent hand,
Damp with the sweat of death, and griping mine,                         20
Whisper'd me, if I loved him, not to yield
His Church of England to the Papal wolf
And Mary; then I could no more — I sign'd.
Nay, for bare shame of inconsistency,

She cannot pass her traitor council by,
To make me headless.
　　*Peter Martyr.* That might be forgiven.
I tell you, fly, my lord. You do not own
The bodily presence in the Eucharist,
Their wafer and perpetual sacrifice:　　29
Your creed will be your death.
　　*Cranmer.*　　　　　Step after step,
Thro' many voices crying right and left,
Have I climb'd back into the primal
　　church,
And stand within the porch, and Christ
　　with me.
My flight were such a scandal to the faith,
The downfall of so many simple souls,
I dare not leave my post.
　　*Peter Martyr.*　　　But you divorced
Queen Catharine and her father; hence, her
　　hate
Will burn till you are burn'd.
　　*Cranmer.*　　　　I cannot help it.
The Canonists and Schoolmen were with me.
'Thou shalt not wed thy brother's wife.' —
　　'T is written,　　　　　40
'They shall be childless.' True, Mary
　　was born,
But France would not accept her for a
　　bride
As being born from incest; and this
　　wrought
Upon the King; and child by child, you
　　know,
Were momentary sparkles, out as quick
Almost as kindled; and he brought his
　　doubts
And fears to me. Peter, I 'll swear for
　　him
He *did* believe the bond incestuous.
But wherefore am I trenching on the time
That should already have seen your steps a
　　mile　　　　　50
From me and Lambeth? God be with
　　you! Go.
　　*Peter Martyr.* Ah, but how fierce a letter
　　you wrote against
Their superstition when they slander'd you
For setting up a mass at Canterbury
To please the Queen!
　　*Cranmer.*　　　It was a wheedling monk
Set up the mass.
　　*Peter Martyr.* I know it, my good lord.
But you so bubbled over with hot terms
Of Satan, liars, blasphemy, Antichrist,
She never will forgive you. Fly, my lord,
　　fly!

*Cranmer.* I wrote it, and God grant me
　　power to burn!　　　60
*Peter Martyr.* They have given me a
　　safe conduct; for all that
I dare not stay. I fear, I fear, I see you,
Dear friend, for the last time; farewell,
　　and fly.
　　*Cranmer.* Fly and farewell, and let me
　　die the death.
　　　　　　　　　　[*Exit* Peter Martyr.

　　　　*Enter* OLD SERVANT.

O, kind and gentle master, the Queen's
　　Officers
Are here in force to take you to the Tower.
　　*Cranmer.* Ay, gentle friend, admit them.
　　I will go.
I thank my God it is too late to fly.
　　　　　　　　　　　　　　[*Exeunt.*


　　　　　　SCENE III

　　　ST. PAUL'S CROSS

FATHER BOURNE *in the pulpit. A crowd.*
　MARCHIONESS OF EXETER, COURTENAY.
　*The* SIEUR DE NOAILLES *and his man*
　ROGER *in front of the stage. Hubbub.*

　*Noailles.* Hast thou let fall those papers
　　in the palace?
　*Roger.* Ay, sir.
　*Noailles.* 'There will be no peace for
Mary till Elizabeth lose her head.'
　*Roger.* Ay, sir.
　*Noailles.* And the other, 'Long live
Elizabeth the Queen!'
　*Roger.* Ay, sir; she needs must tread
　　upon them.
　*Noailles.*　　　　　Well.
These beastly swine make such a grunting
　　here,
I cannot catch what Father Bourne is say-
　　ing.
　*Roger.* Quiet a moment, my masters;
hear what the shaveling has to say for him-
self.　　　　　　　　　11
　*Crowd.* Hush — hear!
　*Bourne.* — and so this unhappy land,
long divided in itself, and sever'd from the
faith, will return into the one true fold,
seeing that our gracious Virgin Queen
hath —
　*Crowd.* No pope! no pope!

*Roger* (*to those about him, mimicking* Bourne). — hath sent for the holy legate of the holy father the Pope, Cardinal Pole, to give us all that holy absolution which — 22

*First Citizen.* Old Bourne to the life!

*Second Citizen.* Holy absolution! holy Inquisition!

*Third Citizen.* Down with the Papist!
                          [*Hubbub.*

*Bourne.* — and now that your good bishop, Bonner, who hath lain so long under bonds for the faith —      [*Hubbub.*

*Noailles.* Friend Roger, steal thou in among the crowd,
And get the swine to shout 'Elizabeth.' 30
Yon gray old Gospeller, sour as midwinter,
Begin with him.

*Roger* (*goes*). By the mass, old friend, we'll have no pope here while the Lady Elizabeth lives.

*Gospeller.* Art thou of the true faith, fellow, that swearest by the mass?

*Roger.* Ay, that am I, new converted, but the old leaven sticks to my tongue yet.

*First Citizen.* He says right; by the mass, we'll have no mass here. 41

*Voices of the Crowd.* Peace! hear him; let his own words damn the Papist. From thine own mouth I judge thee — tear him down!

*Bourne.* — and since our gracious Queen, let me call her our second Virgin Mary, hath begun to re-edify the true temple — 49

*First Citizen.* Virgin Mary! we'll have no virgins here — we'll have the Lady Elizabeth!

    [*Swords are drawn, a knife is hurled and sticks in the pulpit. The mob throng to the pulpit stairs.*

*Marchioness of Exeter.* Son Courtenay, wilt thou see the holy father
Murdered before thy face? up, son, and save him!
They love thee, and thou canst not come to harm.

*Courtenay* (*in the pulpit*). Shame, shame, my masters! are you English-born,
And set yourselves by hundreds against one?

*Crowd.* A Courtenay! a Courtenay!
    [*A train of Spanish servants crosses at the back of the stage.*

*Noailles.* These birds of passage come before their time.
Stave off the crowd upon the Spaniard there. 60

*Roger.* My masters, yonder's fatter game for you
Than this old gaping gurgoyle; look you there —
The Prince of Spain coming to wed our Queen!
After him, boys! and pelt him from the city.
    [*They seize stones and follow the Spaniards. Exeunt on the other side* Marchioness of Exeter *and* Attendants.

*Noailles* (*to Roger*). Stand from me.
If Elizabeth lose her head —
That makes for France.
And if her people, anger'd thereupon,
Arise against her and dethrone the Queen —
That makes for France.
And if I breed confusion any way — 70
That makes for France.
            Good-day, my Lord of Devon;
A bold heart yours to beard that raging mob!

*Courtenay.* My mother said, Go up; and up I went,
I knew they would not do me any wrong,
For I am mighty popular with them, Noailles.

*Noailles.* You look'd a king.

*Courtenay.* Why not? I am king's blood.

*Noailles.* And in the whirl of change may come to be one.

*Courtenay.* Ah!

*Noailles.* But does your gracious Queen entreat you kinglike?

*Courtenay.* 'Fore God, I think she entreats me like a child. 80

*Noailles.* You've but a dull life in this maiden court,
I fear, my lord?

*Courtenay.*     A life of nods and yawns.

*Noailles.* So you would honor my poor house to-night,
We might enliven you. Divers honest fellows,
The Duke of Suffolk lately freed from prison,
Sir Peter Carew and Sir Thomas Wyatt,
Sir Thomas Stafford, and some more — we play.

*Courtenay.* At what?

*Noailles.*     The game of chess.

*Courtenay.*          The game of chess !
I can play well, and I shall beat you there.
  *Noailles.* Ay, but we play with Henry,
     King of France,                                90
And certain of his court.
His Highness makes his moves across the
     Channel,
We answer him with ours, and there are
     messengers
That go between us.
  *Courtenay.* Why, such a game, sir, were
     whole years a-playing.
  *Noailles.* Nay; not so long I trust.
     That all depends
Upon the skill and swiftness of the play-
     ers.
  *Courtenay.* The King is skilful at it ?
  *Noailles.*          Very, my Lord.
  *Courtenay.* And the stakes high ?
  *Noailles.*          But not beyond your means.
  *Courtenay.* Well, I 'm the first of play-
     ers.  I shall win.                            100
  *Noailles.* With our advice and in our
     company,
And so you well attend to the King's
     moves,
I think you may.
  *Courtenay.*          When do you meet ?
  *Noailles.*                    To-night.
  *Courtenay (aside).* I will be there; the
     fellow 's at his tricks —
Deep — I shall fathom him.     (*Aloud.*)
     Good morning, Noailles.
                         [*Exit* Courtenay.
  *Noailles.* Good-day, my Lord.  Strange
     game of chess ! a king
That with her own pawns plays against a
     queen,
Whose play is all to find herself a king.
Ay; but this fine blue-blooded Courtenay
     seems
Too princely for a pawn.  Call him a
     knight,                                       110
That, with an ass's, not a horse's head,
Skips every way, from levity or from
     fear.
Well, we shall use him somehow, so that
     Gardiner
And Simon Renard spy not out our game
Too early.  Roger, thinkest thou that any
     one
Suspected thee to be my man ?
  *Roger.*          Not one, sir.
  *Noailles.* No ! the disguise was perfect.
     Let 's away.                       [*Exeunt.*

SCENE IV

LONDON.  A ROOM IN THE PALACE

ELIZABETH.  *Enter* COURTENAY.

  *Courtenay.* So yet am I,
Unless my friends and mirrors lie to me,
A goodlier-looking fellow than this Philip.
Pah !
The Queen is ill advised.  Shall I turn
     traitor ?
They 've almost talked me into it; yet the
     word
Affrights me somewhat; to be such a one
As Harry Bolingbroke hath a lure in it.
Good now, my Lady Queen, tho' by your
     age
And by your looks you are not worth the
     having,                                        10
Yet by your crown you are.
                    [*Seeing* Elizabeth.
                    The Princess there ?
If I tried her, and la — she 's amorous.
Have we not heard of her in Edward's
     time,
Her freaks and frolics with the late Lord
     Admiral ?
I do believe she 'd yield.  I should be still
A party in the State; and then, who
     knows —
  *Elizabeth.* What are you musing on, my
     Lord of Devon ?
  *Courtenay.* Has not the Queen —
  *Elizabeth.*          Done what, Sir ?
  *Courtenay.*          — made you follow
The Lady Suffolk and the Lady Lennox ? —
     you,
The heir presumptive.
  *Elizabeth.* Why do you ask ? you know
     it.                                            20
  *Courtenay.* You needs must bear it
     hardly.
  *Elizabeth.*          No, indeed !
I am utterly submissive to the Queen.
  *Courtenay.* Well, I was musing upon
     that; the Queen
Is both my foe and yours; we should be
     friends.
  *Elizabeth.* My Lord, the hatred of an-
     other to us
Is no true bond of friendship.
  *Courtenay.*                    Might it not
Be the rough preface of some closer bond ?

*Elizabeth.* My lord, you late were loosed
    from out the Tower,
Where, like a butterfly in a chrysalis,
You spent your life; that broken, out you
    flutter                                           30
Thro' the new world, go zigzag, now would
    settle
Upon this flower, now that.  But all things
    here
At court are known; you have solicited
The Queen, and been rejected.
*Courtenay.*                    Flower, she !
Half faded ! but you, cousin, are fresh and
    sweet
As the first flower no bee has ever tried.
    *Elizabeth.* Are you the bee to try me ?
    why, but now
I called you butterfly.
    *Courtenay.*              You did me wrong,
I love not to be called a butterfly.
Why do you call me butterfly ?              40
    *Elizabeth.* Why do you go so gay then ?
    *Courtenay.*              Velvet and gold.
This dress was made me as the Earl of
    Devon
To take my seat in; looks it not right
    royal ?
    *Elizabeth.* So royal that the Queen for-
    bade you wearing it.
    *Courtenay.* I wear it then to spite her.
    *Elizabeth.*              My lord, my lord;
I see you in the Tower again.  Her Ma-
    jesty
Hears you affect the Prince — prelates
    kneel to you. —
    *Courtenay.* I am the noblest blood in
    Europe, Madam,
A Courtenay of Devon, and her cousin.
    *Elizabeth.* She hears you make your
    boast that after all              50
She means to wed you.  Folly, my good
    lord.
    *Courtenay.* How folly ? a great party in
    the state
Wills me to wed her.
    *Elizabeth.*              Failing her, my lord,
Doth not as great a party in the State
Will you to wed me ?
    *Courtenay.*              Even so, fair lady.
    *Elizabeth.* You know to flatter ladies.
    *Courtenay.*              Nay, I meant
True matters of the heart.
    *Elizabeth.*              My heart, my lord,
Is no great party in the State as yet.

*Courtenay.* Great, said you ? nay, you
    shall be great.  I love you,
Lay my life in your hands.  Can you be
    close ?                                        60
    *Elizabeth.* Can you, my lord ?
    *Courtenay.*       Close as a miser's casket.
Listen:
The King of France, Noailles the Ambas-
    sador,
The Duke of Suffolk and Sir Peter Carew,
Sir Thomas Wyatt, I myself, some others,
Have sworn this Spanish marriage shall
    not be.
If Mary will not hear us — well — conjec-
    ture —
Were I in Devon with my wedded bride,
The people there so worship me — your
    ear;                                           69
You shall be Queen.
    *Elizabeth.* You speak too low, my lord;
I cannot hear you.
    *Courtenay.*              I 'll repeat it.
    *Elizabeth.*                                   No !
Stand further off, or you may lose your
    head.
    *Courtenay.* I have a head to lose for
    your sweet sake.
    *Elizabeth.* Have you, my lord ?  Best
    keep it for your own.
Nay, pout not, cousin.
Not many friends are mine, except indeed
Among the many.  I believe you mine:
And so you may continue mine, farewell,
And that at once.

*Enter* MARY, *behind.*

*Mary.* Whispering — leagued together
To bar me from my Philip.
    *Courtenay.*              Pray — consider —
    *Elizabeth* (*seeing the* Queen).  Well,
    that 's a noble horse of yours, my
    lord.                                          81
I trust that he will carry you well to-day,
And heal your headache.
    *Courtenay.* You are wild; what head-
    ache ?
Heartache, perchance; not headache.
    *Elizabeth* (*aside to* Courtenay).  Are you
    blind ?
    [*Courtenay sees the* Queen *and exit.*
    *Exit* Mary.

*Enter* LORD WILLIAM HOWARD.

*Howard.* Was that my Lord of Devon ?
    do not you

Be seen in corners with my Lord of Devon.
He hath fallen out of favor with the Queen.
She fears the lords may side with you and
   him
Against her marriage; therefore is he dan-
   gerous. 89
And if this Prince of fluff and feather come
To woo you, niece, he is dangerous every-
   way.
   *Elizabeth.* Not very dangerous that way,
   my good uncle.
   *Howard.* But your own state is full of
   danger here.
The disaffected, heretics, reformers,
Look to you as the one to crown their ends.
Mix not yourself with any plot I pray you;
Nay, if by chance you hear of any such,
Speak not thereof — no, not to your best
   friend,
Lest you should be confounded with it.
   Still —
Perinde ac cadaver — as the priest says,
You know your Latin — quiet as a dead
   body. 101
What was my Lord of Devon telling you ?
   *Elizabeth.* Whether he told me anything
   or not,
I follow your good counsel, gracious uncle.
Quiet as a dead body.
   *Howard.* You do right well.
I do not care to know; but this I charge
   you,
Tell Courtenay nothing. The Lord Chan-
   cellor —
I count it as a kind of virtue in him,
He hath not many — as a mastiff dog
May love a puppy cur for no more reason
Than that the twain have been tied up to-
   gether, 111
Thus Gardiner — for the two were fellow-
   prisoners
So many years in yon accursed Tower —
Hath taken to this Courtenay. Look to it,
   niece,
He hath no fence when Gardiner ques-
   tions him;
All oozes out; yet him — because they
   know him
The last White Rose, the last Plantagenet —
Nay, there is Cardinal Pole, too — the peo-
   ple
Claim as their natural leader — ay, some
   say
That you shall marry him, make him king
   belike. 120

   *Elizabeth.* Do they say so, good uncle ?
   *Howard.* Ay, good niece !
You should be plain and open with me,
   niece.
You should not play upon me.
   *Elizabeth.* No, good uncle.

*Enter* GARDINER.

   *Gardiner.* The Queen would see your
   Grace upon the moment.
   *Elizabeth.* Why, my lord bishop ?
   *Gardiner.* I think she means to counsel
   your withdrawing
To Ashridge, or some other country house.
   *Elizabeth.* Why, my lord bishop ?
   *Gardiner.* I do but bring the message,
   know no more.
Your Grace will hear her reasons from her-
   self. 130
   *Elizabeth.* 'T is mine own wish fulfill'd
   before the word
Was spoken, for in truth I had meant to
   crave
Permission of her Highness to retire
To Ashridge, and pursue my studies there.
   *Gardiner.* Madam, to have the wish be-
   fore the word
Is man's good fairy — and the Queen is
   yours.
I left her with rich jewels in her hand,
Whereof 't is like enough she means to
   make
A farewell present to your Grace.
   *Elizabeth.* My lord,
I have the jewel of a loyal heart.
   *Gardiner.* I doubt it not, madam, most
   loyal. [*Bows low and exit.*
   *Howard.* See,
This comes of parleying with my Lord of
   Devon. 142
Well, well, you must obey; and I myself
Believe it will be better for your welfare.
Your time will come.
   *Elizabeth.* I think my time will come.
Uncle,
I am of sovereign nature, that I know,
Not to be quell'd; and I have felt within
   me
Stirrings of some great doom when God's
   just hour
Peals — but this fierce old Gardiner — his
   big baldness, 150
That irritable forelock which he rubs,
His buzzard beak and deep-incavern'd eyes
Half fright me.

*Howard.* You 've a bold heart; keep it so.

He cannot touch you save that you turn traitor;

And so take heed I pray you — you are one

Who love that men should smile upon you, niece.

They 'd smile you into treason — some of them.

*Elizabeth.* I spy the rock beneath the smiling sea.

But if this Philip, the proud Catholic prince,

And this bald priest, and she that hates me, seek        160

In that lone house to practise on my life,

By poison, fire, shot, stab —

*Howard.*                They will not, niece.

Mine is the fleet and all the power at sea —

Or will be in a moment. If they dared

To harm you, I would blow this Philip and all

Your trouble to the dog-star and the devil.

*Elizabeth.* To the Pleiads, uncle; they have lost a sister.

*Howard.* But why say that ? what have you done to lose her ?

Come, come, I will go with you to the Queen.        [*Exeunt.*


SCENE V

A ROOM IN THE PALACE

MARY *with* PHILIP'S *miniature.* ALICE.

*Mary* (*kissing the miniature*).    Most goodly, kinglike, and an emperor's son, —

A king to be, — is he not noble, girl ?

*Alice.* Goodly enough, your Grace, and yet, methinks,

I have seen goodlier.

*Mary.*            Ay; some waxen doll

Thy baby eyes have rested on, belike;

All red and white, the fashion of our land.

But my good mother came — God rest her soul ! —

Of Spain, and I am Spanish in myself,

And in my likings.

*Alice.*            By your Grace's leave,

Your royal mother came of Spain, but took

To the English red and white. Your royal father —        11

For so they say — was all pure lily and rose

In his youth, and like a lady.

*Mary.*                O just God !

Sweet mother, you had time and cause enough

To sicken of his lilies and his roses.

Cast off, betray'd, defamed, divorced, forlorn !

And then the King — that traitor past forgiveness,

The false archbishop fawning on him, married

The mother of Elizabeth — a heretic

Even as *she* is; but God hath sent me here

To take such order with all heretics        21

That it shall be, before I die, as tho'

My father and my brother had not lived.

What wast thou saying of this Lady Jane, Now in the Tower ?

*Alice.*        Why madam, she was passing

Some chapel down in Essex, and with her

Lady Anne Wharton, and the Lady Anne

Bow'd to the pyx; but Lady Jane stood up

Stiff as the very backbone of heresy.

And wherefore bow ye not, says Lady Anne,        30

To him within there who made heaven and earth ?

I cannot, and I dare not, tell your Grace

What Lady Jane replied.

*Mary.*                But I will have it.

*Alice.* She said — pray pardon me, and pity her —

She hath hearken'd evil counsel — ah ! she said

The baker made him.

*Mary.*            Monstrous ! blasphemous !

She ought to burn. Hence, thou

                [*Exit* Alice.

        No — being traitor

Her head will fall. Shall it ? she is but a child.

We do not kill the child for doing that

His father whipt him into doing — a head

So full of grace and beauty ! would that mine        40

Were half as gracious ! O, my lord to be,

My love, for thy sake only !

I am eleven years older than he is.

But will he care for that ?

No, by the holy Virgin, being noble,

But love me only. Then the bastard sprout,

My sister, is far fairer than myself.

Will he be drawn to her ?

No, being of the true faith with myself.
Paget is for him — for to wed with Spain 50
Would treble England — Gardiner is
    against him;
The Council, people, Parliament against
    him;
But I will have him! My hard father
    hated me;
My brother rather hated me than loved;
My sister cowers and hates me. Holy
    Virgin,
Plead with thy blessed Son; grant me my
    prayer.
Give me my Philip; and we two will lead
The living waters of the Faith again
Back thro' their widow'd channel here, and
    watch
The parch'd banks rolling incense, as of
    old,                                         60
To heaven, and kindled with the palms of
    Christ!

                *Enter* USHER.

Who waits, sir?
    *Usher.*    Madam, the Lord Chancellor.
    *Mary.* Bid him come in. (*Enter* GAR-
    DINER.)   Good morning, my good
    lord.               [*Exit* Usher.
    *Gardiner.* That every morning of your
    Majesty
May be most good, is every morning's
    prayer
Of your most loyal subject, Stephen Gardi-
    ner.
    *Mary.* Come you to tell me this, my
    lord?
    *Gardiner.*    And more.
Your people have begun to learn your
    worth.
Your pious wish to pay King Edward's
    debts,
Your lavish household curb'd, and the re-
    mission                                      70
Of half that subsidy levied on the peo-
    ple,
Make all tongues praise and all hearts beat
    for you.
I 'd have you yet more loved. The realm
    is poor,
The exchequer at neap-tide; we might
    withdraw
Part of our garrison at Calais.
    *Mary.*                          Calais!
Our one point on the main, the gate of
    France!

I am Queen of England; take mine eyes,
    mine heart,
But do not lose me Calais.
    *Gardiner.*                Do not fear it.
Of that hereafter. I say your Grace is
    loved.
That I may keep you thus, who am your
    friend                                       80
And ever faithful counsellor, might I
    speak?
    *Mary.* I can forespeak your speaking.
    Would I marry
Prince Philip, if all England hate him?
    That is
Your question, and I front it with another:
Is it England, or a party? Now, your
    answer.
    *Gardiner.* My answer is, I wear beneath
    my dress
A shirt of mail; my house hath been as-
    saulted,
And when I walk abroad the populace,
With fingers pointed like so many daggers,
Stab me in fancy, hissing Spain and Philip;
And when I sleep a hundred men-at-arms
Guard my poor dreams for England. Men
    would murder me,                             92
Because they think me favorer of this
    marriage.
    *Mary.* And that were hard upon you,
    my Lord Chancellor.
    *Gardiner.* But our young Earl of De-
    von —
    *Mary.*         Earl of Devon?
I freed him from the Tower, placed him
    at Court;
I made him Earl of Devon, and — the
    fool —
He wrecks his health and wealth on cour-
    tesans,
And rolls himself in carrion like a dog.
    *Gardiner.* More like a school-boy that
    hath broken bounds              100
Sickening himself with sweets.
    *Mary.*              I will not hear of him.
Good, then, they will revolt; but I am
    Tudor,
And shall control them.
    *Gardiner.*         I will help you, madam,
Even to the utmost. All the church is
    grateful.
You have ousted the mock priest, re-pul-
    pited
The shepherd of Saint Peter, raised the
    rood again,

And brought us back the mass. I am all
    thanks
To God and to your Grace; yet I know
    well,
Your people, and I go with them so far,
Will brook nor Pope nor Spaniard here to
    play                                    110
The tyrant, or in commonwealth or church.
    *Mary* (*showing the picture*). Is this the
    face of one who plays the tyrant?
Peruse it; is it not goodly, ay, and gentle?
    *Gardiner.* Madam, methinks a cold face
    and a haughty.
And when your Highness talks of Courte-
    nay —
Ay, true — a goodly one. I would his life
Were half as goodly (*aside*).
    *Mary.*      What is that you mutter?
    *Gardiner.* O, madam, take it bluntly;
    marry Philip,
And be stepmother of a score of sons!
The prince is known in Spain, in Flanders,
    ha!                                      120
For Philip —
    *Mary.* You offend us; you may leave
    us.
You see thro' warping glasses.
    *Gardiner.*        If your Majesty —
    *Mary.* I have sworn upon the body and
    blood of Christ
I 'll none but Philip.
    *Gardiner.*     Hath your Grace so sworn?
    *Mary.* Ay, Simon Renard knows it.
    *Gardiner.*                News to me!
It then remains for your poor Gardiner,
So you still care to trust him somewhat
    less
Than Simon Renard, to compose the event
In some such form as least may harm your
    Grace.
    *Mary.* I 'll have the scandal sounded to
    the mud.                                 130
I know it a scandal.
    *Gardiner.*        All my hope is now
It may be found a scandal.
    *Mary.*            You offend us.
    *Gardiner* (*aside*). These princes are like
    children, must be physick'd,
The bitter in the sweet. I have lost mine
    office,
It may be, thro' mine honesty, like a fool.
                                  [*Exit.*

       *Enter* USHER.

    *Mary.* Who waits?

    *Usher.* The ambassador from France,
    your Grace.
    *Mary* (*sits down*). Bid him come in.
    Good morning, Sir de Noailles.
                        [*Exit* Usher.
    *Noailles* (*entering*). A happy morning to
    your Majesty.
    *Mary.* And I should some time have a
    happy morning;
I have had none yet. What says the King
    your master?                             140
    *Noailles.* Madam, my master hears with
    much alarm
That you may marry Philip, Prince of
    Spain —
Foreseeing, with whate'er unwillingness,
That if this Philip be the titular King
Of England, and at war with him, your
    Grace
And kingdom will be suck'd into the war,
Ay, tho' you long for peace; wherefore, my
    master,
If but to prove your Majesty's goodwill,
Would fain have some fresh treaty drawn
    between you.
    *Mary.* Why some fresh treaty? where-
    fore should I do it?                     150
Sir, if we marry, we shall still maintain
All former treaties with his Majesty.
Our royal word for that! and your good
    master,
Pray God he do not be the first to break
    them,
Must be content with that; and so, fare-
    well.
    *Noailles* (*going, returns*). I would your
    answer had been other, madam,
For I foresee dark days.
    *Mary.*            And so do I, sir;
Your master works against me in the dark.
I do believe he holp Northumberland   159
Against me.
    *Noailles.*    Nay, pure phantasy, your
    Grace.
Why should he move against you?
    *Mary.*            Will you hear why?
Mary of Scotland, — for I have not own'd
My sister, and I will not, — after me
Is heir of England; and my royal father,
To make the crown of Scotland one with
    ours,
Had mark'd her for my brother Edward's
    bride;
Ay, but your king stole her a babe from
    Scotland

In order to betroth her to your Dauphin.
See then:
Mary of Scotland, married to your Dauphin,
Would make our England, France;    171
Mary of England, joining hands with
    Spain,
Would be too strong for France.
Yea, were there issue born to her, Spain
    and we,
One crown, might rule the world.   There
    lies your fear.
That is your drift.   You play at hide and
    seek.
Show me your faces !
    *Noailles.*              Madam, I am amazed.
French, I must needs wish all good things
    for France.
That must be pardon'd me; but I protest
Your Grace's policy hath a farther flight
Than mine into the future.   We but seek
Some settled ground for peace to stand
    upon.                                      182
    *Mary.* Well, we will leave all this, sir,
    to our council.
Have you seen Philip ever ?
    *Noailles.*                    Only once.
    *Mary.* Is this like Philip ?
    *Noailles.*          Ay, but nobler-looking.
    *Mary.* Hath he the large ability of the
    Emperor ?
    *Noailles.* No, surely.
    *Mary.*       I can make allowance for thee,
Thou speakest of the enemy of thy king.
    *Noailles.* Make no allowance for the
    naked truth.                               189
He is every way a lesser man than Charles;
Stone-hard, ice-cold — no dash of daring in
    him.
    *Mary.* If cold, his life is pure.
    *Noailles.*       Why (*smiling*), no, indeed.
    *Mary.* Say'st thou ?
    *Noailles.* A very wanton life indeed
    (*smiling*).
    *Mary.* Your audience is concluded, sir.
    (*Exit* Noailles.)   You cannot
Learn a man's nature from his natural foe.

#### Enter USHER.

Who waits ?
    *Usher.* The ambassador of Spain, your
    Grace.                          [*Exit.*

#### Enter SIMON RENARD.

    *Mary* (*rising to meet him*). Thou art
    ever welcome, Simon Renard.   Hast
    thou

Brought me the letter which thine Em-
    peror promised
Long since, a formal offer of the hand    199
Of Philip ?
    *Renard.* Nay, your Grace, it hath not
    reach'd me.
I know not wherefore — some mischance
    of flood,
And broken bridge, or spavin'd horse, or
    wave
And wind at their old battle; he must have
    written.
    *Mary.* But Philip never writes me one
    poor word,
Which in his absence had been all my
    wealth.
Strange in a wooer !
    *Renard.*          Yet I know the Prince,
So your king - parliament suffer him to
    land,
Yearns to set foot upon your island shore.
    *Mary.* God change the pebble which his
    kingly foot                                209
First presses into some more costly stone
Than ever blinded eye !   I 'll have one
    mark it
And bring it me.   I 'll have it burnish'd
    firelike;
I 'll set it round with gold, with pearl, with
    diamond.
Let the great angel of the Church come
    with him,
Stand on the deck and spread his wings
    for sail !
God lay the waves and strow the storms at
    sea,
And here at land among the people !   O
    Renard,
I am much beset, I am almost in despair.
Paget is ours.   Gardiner perchance is ours;
But for our heretic Parliament —
    *Renard.*                    O madam,
You fly your thoughts like kites.   My mas-
    ter, Charles,                             221
Bade you go softly with your heretics here,
Until your throne had ceased to tremble.
    Then
Spit them like larks for aught I care.
    Besides,
When Henry broke the carcase of your
    church
To pieces, there were many wolves among
    you
Who dragg'd the scatter'd limbs into their
    den.

The Pope would have you make them ren-
    der these;
So would your cousin, Cardinal Pole — ill
    counsel !
These let them keep at present; stir not
    yet                   230
This matter of the Church lands. At his
    coming
Your star will rise.
    *Mary.*         My star ! a baleful one.
I see but the black night, and hear the
    wolf.
What star ?
    *Renard.* Your star will be your princely
    son,
Heir of this England and the Nether-
    lands !
And if your wolf the while should howl for
    more,
We 'll dust him from a bag of Spanish
    gold.
I do believe — I have dusted some al-
    ready —
That, soon or late, your Parliament is ours.
    *Mary.* Why do they talk so foully of
    your Prince,           240
Renard ?
    *Renard.* The lot of princes. To sit high
Is to be lied about.
    *Mary.*         They call him cold,
Haughty, ay, worse.
    *Renard.*   Why, doubtless, Philip shows
Some of the bearing of your blue blood —
    still
All within measure — nay, it well becomes
    him.
    *Mary.* Hath he the large ability of his
    father ?
    *Renard.* Nay, some believe that he will
go beyond him.
    *Mary.* Is this like him ?
    *Renard.* Ay, somewhat; but your Philip
Is the most princelike prince beneath the
    sun.                    249
This is a daub to Philip.
    *Mary.*         Of a pure life ?
    *Renard.* As an angel among angels.
    Yea, by Heaven,
The text — Your Highness knows it, 'Who-
    soever
Looketh after a woman,' would not graze
The Prince of Spain. You are happy in
    him there,
Chaste as your Grace !
    *Mary.*      I am happy in him there.

    *Renard.* And would be altogether happy,
    madam,
So that your sister were but look'd to
    closer.
You have sent her from the court, but then
    she goes,
I warrant, not to hear the nightingales,
But hatch you some new treason in the
    woods.                 260
    *Mary.* We have our spies abroad to
    catch her tripping,
And then, if caught, to the Tower.
    *Renard.*        The Tower ! the block !
The word has turn'd your Highness pale;
    the thing
Was no such scarecrow in your father's time.
I have heard, the tongue yet quiver'd with
    the jest
When the head leapt — so common ! I do
    think,
To save your crown, that it must come to
    this.
    *Mary.* No, Renard; it must never come
    to this.
    *Renard.* Not yet; but your old traitors
    of the Tower —
Why, when you put Northumberland to
    death,                270
The sentence having passed upon them
    all,
Spared you the Duke of Suffolk, Guildford
    Dudley,
Even that young girl who dared to wear
    your crown ?
    *Mary.* Dared ? nay, not so; the child
    obey'd her father.
Spite of her tears her father forced it on
    her.
    *Renard.* Good madam, when the Roman
    wish'd to reign,
He slew not him alone who wore the purple,
But his assessor in the throne, perchance
A child more innocent than Lady Jane.
    *Mary.* I am English Queen, not Roman
    Emperor.            280
    *Renard.* Yet too much mercy is a want
    of mercy,
And wastes more life. Stamp out the fire,
    or this
Will smoulder and re-flame, and burn the
    throne
Where you should sit with Philip. He will
    not come
Till she be gone.
    *Mary.*      Indeed, if that were true —

For Philip comes, one hand in mine, and one
Steadying the tremulous pillars of the
    Church —
But no, no, no! Farewell. I am some-
    what faint
With our long talk. Tho' Queen, I am not
    Queen
Of mine own heart, which every now and
    then
Beats me half dead. Yet stay, this golden
    chain —
My father on a birthday gave it me,
And I have broken with my father — take
And wear it as memorial of a morning
Which found me full of foolish doubts, and
    leaves me
As hopeful.
    *Renard (aside).* Whew — the folly of
        all follies
Is to be lovesick for a shadow. (*Aloud.*)
    Madam,
This chains me to your service, not with
    gold,
But dearest links of love. Farewell, and
    trust me,                    299
Philip is yours.                [*Exit.*
    *Mary.*     Mine — but not yet all mine.

            *Enter* USHER.

*Usher.* Your Council is in session, please
    your Majesty.
*Mary.* Sir, let them sit. I must have
    time to breathe.
No, say I come. (*Exit* Usher.) I won by
    boldness once.
The Emperor counsell'd me to fly to Flan-
    ders.
I would not; but a hundred miles I rode,
Sent out my letters, call'd my friends to-
    gether,
Struck home and won.
And when the Council would not crown
    me — thought
To bind me first by oaths I could not keep,
And keep with Christ and conscience — was
    it boldness                  310
Or weakness that won there? when I, their
    Queen,
Cast myself down upon my knees before
    them,
And those hard men brake into woman-
    tears,
Even Gardiner, all amazed, and in that pas-
    sion
Gave me my Crown.

            *Enter* ALICE.

                Girl, hast thou ever heard
Slanders against Prince Philip in our
    Court?
    *Alice.* What slanders? I, your Grace?
        no, never.
    *Mary.*          Nothing?
    *Alice.* Never, your Grace.
    *Mary.* See that you neither hear them
        nor repeat!
    *Alice (aside).* Good Lord! but I have
        heard a thousand such —        320
Ay, and repeated them as often — mum!
Why comes that old fox - Fleming back
    again?

            *Enter* RENARD.

*Renard.* Madam, I scarce had left your
    Grace's presence
Before I chanced upon the messenger
Who brings that letter which we waited
    for —
The formal offer of Prince Philip's hand.
It craves an instant answer, Ay or No.
    *Mary.* An instant Ay or No! the Coun-
        cil sits.
Give it me quick.
    *Alice (stepping before her).* Your High-
        ness is all trembling.
    *Mary.* Make way.
            [*Exit into the Council Chamber.*
    *Alice.* O Master Renard, Master Re-
        nard,                       330
If you have falsely painted your fine Prince,
Praised where you should have blamed
    him, I pray God
No woman ever love you, Master Renard!
It breaks my heart to hear her moan at
    night
As tho' the nightmare never left her bed.
    *Renard.* My pretty maiden, tell me, did
        you ever
Sigh for a beard?
    *Alice.*          That's not a pretty question.
    *Renard.* Not prettily put? I mean, my
        pretty maiden,
A pretty man for such a pretty maiden.
    *Alice.* My Lord of Devon is a pretty
        man.                       340
I hate him. Well, but if I have, what
    then?
    *Renard.* Then, pretty maiden, you
        should know that whether
A wind be warm or cold, it serves to fan
A kindled fire.

*Alice.* According to the song.

His friends would praise him, I believed 'em,
  His foes would blame him, and I scorn'd 'em,
His friends — as angels I received 'em,
  His foes — the devil had suborn'd 'em.

*Renard.* Peace, pretty maiden.
I hear them stirring in the Council Chamber.         350
Lord Paget's 'Ay' is sure — who else?
  and yet,
They are all too much at odds to close at
  once
In one full-throated No! Her Highness
  comes.

*Enter* MARY.

*Alice.* How deathly pale! — a chair,
  your Highness.
        [*Bringing one to the* Queen.
*Renard.*        Madam,
The Council?
*Mary.*      Ay! My Philip is all mine.
        [*Sinks into chair, half fainting.*


## ACT II

### SCENE I. — ALINGTON CASTLE

*Sir Thomas Wyatt.* I do not hear from
  Carew or the Duke
Of Suffolk, and till then I should not move.
The Duke hath gone to Leicester; Carew
  stirs
In Devon; that fine porcelain Courtenay,
Save that he fears he might be crack'd in
  using —
I have known a semi-madman in my time
So fancy-ridden — should be in Devon too.

*Enter* WILLIAM.

News abroad, William?        8
*William.* None so new, Sir Thomas, and
none so old, Sir Thomas. No new news
that Philip comes to wed Mary, no old news
that all men hate it. Old Sir Thomas
would have hated it. The bells are ringing at Maidstone. Does n't your worship
hear?
*Wyatt.* Ay, for the Saints are come to
  reign again.
Most like it is a Saint's-day. There 's no
  call
As yet for me; so in this pause, before

The mine be fired, it were a pious work
To string my father's sonnets, left about  20
Like loosely-scatter'd jewels, in fair order,
And head them with a lamer rhyme of
  mine,
To grace his memory.
*William.* Ay, why not, Sir Thomas?
He was a fine courtier, he; Queen Anne
loved him. All the women loved him. I
loved him, I was in Spain with him. I
could n't eat in Spain, I could n't sleep in
Spain. I hate Spain, Sir Thomas.
*Wyatt.* But thou couldst drink in Spain
  if I remember.        30
*William.* Sir Thomas, we may grant
the wine. Old Sir Thomas always granted
the wine.
*Wyatt.* Hand me the casket with my
  father's sonnets.
*William.* Ay — sonnets — a fine courtier of the old Court, old Sir Thomas.
        [*Exit.*
*Wyatt.* Courtier of many courts, he
  loved the more
His own gray towers, plain life, and letter'd peace,
To read and rhyme in solitary fields,
The lark above, the nightingale below,  40
And answer them in song. The sire begets
Not half his likeness in the son. I fail
Where he was fullest. Yet — to write it
  down.        [*He writes.*

*Re-enter* WILLIAM.

*William.* There *is* news, there *is* news,
and no call for sonnet-sorting now, nor for
sonnet-making either, but ten thousand
men on Penenden Heath all calling after
your worship, and your worship's name
heard into Maidstone market, and your
worship the first man in Kent and Christendom, for the Queen 's down, and the
world 's up, and your worship a-top of it.
*Wyatt.* Inverted Æsop — mountain out
  of mouse.        53
Say for ten thousand ten — and pot-house
  knaves,
Brain-dizzied with a draught of morning
  ale.

*Enter* ANTONY KNYVETT.

*William.* Here 's Antony Knyvett.
*Knyvett.*     Look you, Master Wyatt,
Tear up that woman's work there.

*Wyatt.*                    No; not these,
Dumb children of my father, that will
      speak
When I and thou and all rebellions lie
Dead bodies without voice.  Song flies,
      you know,                               60
For ages.
      *Knyvett.*  Tut, your sonnet's a flying
            ant,
Wing'd for a moment.
      *Wyatt.*      Well, for mine own work,
                  [*Tearing the paper.*
It lies there in six pieces at your feet:
For all that, I can carry it in my head.
      *Knyvett.*  If you can carry your head
            upon your shoulders.
      *Wyatt.*  I fear you come to carry it off
            my shoulders,
And sonnet-making 's safer.
      *Knyvett.*            Why, good lord,
Write you as many sonnets as you will.
Ay, but not now; what, have you eyes, ears,
      brains ?
This Philip and the black-faced swarms of
      Spain,                                  70
The hardest, cruellest people in the world,
Come locusting upon us, eat us up,
Confiscate lands, goods, money — Wyatt,
      Wyatt,
Wake, or the stout old island will be-
      come
A rotten limb of Spain.  They roar for
      you
On Penenden Heath, a thousand of them
      — more —
All arm'd, waiting a leader; there 's no
      glory
Like his who saves his country.  And you
      sit
Sing-songing here; but, if I 'm any judge,
By God, you are as poor a poet, Wyatt,   80
As a good soldier.
      *Wyatt.*            You as poor a critic
As an honest friend; you stroke me on one
      cheek,
Buffet the other.  Come, you bluster, An-
      tony !
You know I know all this.  I must not
      move
Until I hear from Carew and the Duke.
I fear the mine is fired before the time.
      *Knyvett* (*showing a paper*).  But here 's
            some Hebrew.  Faith, I half forgot it.
Look — can you make it English?  A
      strange youth

Suddenly thrust it on me, whisper'd, ' Wy-
      att,'
And whisking round a corner, show'd his
      back                                    90
Before I read his face.
      *Wyatt.*            Ha ! Courtenay's cipher.
                        [*Reads.*
' Sir Peter Carew fled to France; it is
thought the Duke will be taken.  I am
with you still; but, for appearance sake,
stay with the Queen.  Gardiner knows, but
the Council are all at odds, and the Queen
hath no force for resistance.  Move, if you
move, at once.'

Is Peter Carew fled ?  Is the Duke taken ?
Down scabbard, and out sword ! and let
      Rebellion                              100
Roar till throne rock, and crown fall !  No,
      not that;
But we will teach Queen Mary how to
      reign.
Who are those that shout below there ?
      *Knyvett.*            Why, some fifty
That follow'd me from Penenden Heath in
      hope
To hear you speak.
      *Wyatt.*      Open the window, Knyvett;
The mine is fired, and I will speak to them.

      Men of Kent, England of England, you
that have kept your old customs upright,
while all the rest of England bowed theirs
to the Norman, the cause that hath brought
us together is not the cause of a county or
a shire, but of this England, in whose crown
our Kent is the fairest jewel.  Philip shall
not wed Mary; and ye have called me to be
your leader.  I know Spain.  I have been
there with my father; I have seen them
in their own land, have marked the haugh-
tiness of their nobles, the cruelty of their
priests.  If this man marry our Queen,
however the Council and the Commons
may fence round his power with restriction,
he will be King, King of England, my
masters; and the Queen, and the laws, and
the people, his slaves.  What ? shall we
have Spain on the throne and in the parliament; Spain in the pulpit and on the
law-bench; Spain in all the great offices of
state; Spain in our ships, in our forts, in
our houses, in our beds ?                    129
      *Crowd.*  No ! no ! no Spain !
      *William.*  No Spain in our beds — that

were worse than all. I have been there
with old Sir Thomas, and the beds I know.
I hate Spain.

*A Peasant.* But, Sir Thomas, must we
levy war against the Queen's Grace ?

*Wyatt.* No, my friend; war *for* the
Queen's Grace — to save her from herself
and Philip — war against Spain. And
think not we shall be alone — thousands
will flock to us. The Council, the Court
itself, is on our side. The Lord Chancellor
himself is on our side. The King of France
is with us; the King of Denmark is with
us; the world is with us — war against
Spain ! And if we move not now, yet it
will be known that we have moved; and if
Philip come to be King, O my God ! The
rope, the rack, the thumbscrew, the stake,
the fire. If we move not now, Spain moves,
bribes our nobles with her gold, and creeps,
creeps snake-like about our legs till we
cannot move at all; and ye know, my masters, that wherever Spain hath ruled she
hath wither'd all beneath her. Look at
the New World — a paradise made hell;
the red man, that good helpless creature,
starved, maim'd, flogg'd, flay'd, burn'd,
boil'd, buried alive, worried by dogs; and
here, nearer home, the Netherlands, Sicily,
Naples, Lombardy. I say no more — only
this, their lot is yours. Forward to London with me ! forward to London ! If ye
love your liberties or your skins, forward
to London !                                    165

*Crowd.* Forward to London ! A Wyatt !
  a Wyatt !

*Wyatt.* But first to Rochester, to take
  the guns
From out the vessels lying in the river.
Then on.

*A Peasant.* Ay, but I fear we be too
few, Sir Thomas.

*Wyatt.* Not many yet. The world as
  yet, my friend,                              171
Is not half-waked; but every parish tower
Shall clang and clash alarum as we pass,
And pour along the land, and, swollen and
  fed
With indraughts and side-currents, in full
  force
Roll upon London.

*Crowd.* A Wyatt ! a Wyatt ! Forward !

*Knyvett.* Wyatt, shall we proclaim
  Elizabeth ?

*Wyatt.* I 'll think upon it, Knyvett.

*Knyvett.*                      Or Lady Jane ?

*Wyatt.* No, poor soul, no.
Ah, gray old castle of Alington, green
  field                                        180
Beside the brimming Medway, it may
  chance
That I shall never look upon you more.

*Knyvett.* Come, now, you 're sonnetting
  again.

*Wyatt.*              Not I.
I 'll have my head set higher in the State;
Or — if the Lord God will it — on the
  stake.                              [*Exeunt.*

### SCENE II

#### GUILDHALL

SIR THOMAS WHITE (*The Lord Mayor*),
LORD WILLIAM HOWARD, SIR RALPH
BAGENHALL, ALDERMEN *and* CITIZENS.

*White.* I trust the Queen comes hither
  with her guards.

*Howard.* Ay, all in arms.
  [*Several of the citizens move hastily out
  of the hall.*
              Why do they hurry out there ?

*White.* My lord, cut out the rotten from
  your apple,
Your apple eats the better. Let them go.
They go like those old Pharisees in John
Convicted by their conscience, arrant cow-
  ards,
Or tamperers with that treason out of
  Kent.
When will her Grace be here ?

*Howard.*              In some few minutes.
She will address your guilds and compa-
  nies.
I have striven in vain to raise a man for
  her.                                          10
But help her in this exigency, make
Your city loyal, and be the mightiest man
This day in England.

*White.*              I am Thomas White.
Few things have fail'd to which I set my
  will.
I do my most and best.

*Howard.*              You know that after
The Captain Brett, who went with your
  train bands
To fight with Wyatt, had gone over to
  him
With all his men, the Queen in that distress

Sent Cornwallis and Hastings to the traitor,
Feigning to treat with him about her mar-
riage — 20
Know too what Wyatt said.
*White.* He'd sooner be,
While this same marriage question was
being argued,
Trusted than trust — the scoundrel — and
demanded
Possession of her person and the Tower.
*Howard.* And four of her poor Council
too, my Lord,
As hostages.
*White.* I know it. What do and say
Your Council at this hour?
*Howard.* I will trust you.
We fling ourselves on you, my lord. The
Council,
The Parliament as well, are troubled wa-
ters;
And yet like waters of the fen they know
not 30
Which way to flow. All hands on her ad-
dress,
And upon you, Lord Mayor.
*White.* How look'd the city
When now you past it? Quiet?
*Howard.* Like our Council,
Your city is divided. As we past,
Some hail'd, some hiss'd us. There were
citizens
Stood each before his shut-up booth, and
look'd
As grim and grave as from a funeral.
And here a knot of ruffians all in rags,
With execrating execrable eyes,
Glared at the citizen. Here was a young
mother, 40
Her face on flame, her red hair all blown
back,
She shrilling 'Wyatt,' while the boy she
held
Mimick'd and piped her 'Wyatt,' as red as
she
In hair and cheek; and almost elbowing her,
So close they stood, another, mute as death,
And white as her own milk; her babe in
arms
Had felt the faltering of his mother's heart,
And look'd as bloodless. Here a pious
Catholic,
Mumbling and mixing up in his scared
prayers
Heaven and earth's Maries; over his
bow'd shoulder 50

Scowl'd that world-hated and world-hating
beast,
A haggard Anabaptist. Many such groups.
The names of Wyatt, Elizabeth, Courtenay,
Nay, the Queen's right to reign — 'fore
God, the rogues! —
Were freely buzz'd among them. So I say
Your city is divided, and I fear
One scruple, this or that way, of success
Would turn it thither. Wherefore now the
Queen,
In this low pulse and palsy of the state,
Bade me to tell you that she counts on
you 60
And on myself as her two hands; on you,
In your own city, as her right, my lord,
For you are loyal.
*White.* Am I Thomas White?
One word before she comes. Elizabeth —
Her name is much abused among these
traitors.
Where is she? She is loved by all of us.
I scarce have heart to mingle in this matter,
If she should be mishandled.
*Howard.* No, she shall not.
The Queen had written her word to come
to court: 69
Methought I smelt out Renard in the letter,
And fearing for her, sent a secret missive,
Which told her to be sick. Happily or not,
It found her sick indeed.
*White.* God send her well!
Here comes her Royal Grace.

*Enter* GUARDS, MARY, *and* GARDINER.
SIR THOMAS WHITE *leads her to a raised
seat on the dais.*

*White.* I, the Lord Mayor, and these
our companies
And guilds of London, gathered here, be-
seech
Your Highness to accept our lowliest
thanks
For your most princely presence; and we
pray
That we, your true and loyal citizens,
From your own royal lips, at once may
know 80
The wherefore of this coming, and so learn
Your royal will, and do it. — I, Lord
Mayor
Of London, and our guilds and companies.
*Mary.* In mine own person am I come
to you,
To tell you what indeed ye see and know,

How traitorously these rebels out of Kent
Have made strong head against ourselves
    and you.
They would not have me wed the Prince of
    Spain;
That was their pretext — so they spake at
    first —                   89
But we sent divers of our Council to them,
And by their answers to the question ask'd,
It doth appear this marriage is the least
Of all their quarrel.
They have betrayed the treason of their
    hearts,
Seek to possess our person, hold our Tower,
Place and displace our councillors, and use
Both us and them according as they will.
Now what I am ye know right well — your
    Queen;
To whom, when I was wedded to the realm
And the realm's laws — the spousal ring
    whereof,                 100
Not ever to be laid aside, I wear
Upon this finger — ye did promise full
Allegiance and obedience to the death.
Ye know my father was the rightful heir
Of England, and his right came down to me,
Corroborate by your acts of Parliament.
And as ye were most loving unto him,
So doubtless will ye show yourselves to
    me.                     108
Wherefore, ye will not brook that any one
Should seize our person, occupy our state,
More specially a traitor so presumptuous
As this same Wyatt, who hath tamper'd
    with
A public ignorance, and, under color
Of such a cause as hath no color, seeks
To bend the laws to his own will, and yield
Full scope to persons rascal and forlorn,
To make free spoil and havoc of your
    goods.
Now, as your Prince, I say,
I, that was never mother, cannot tell
How mothers love their children; yet, me-
    thinks,                 120
A prince as naturally may love his people
As these their children; and be sure your
    Queen
So loves you, and so loving, needs must
    deem
This love by you return'd as heartily;
And thro' this common knot and bond of
    love,
Doubt not they will be speedily over-
    thrown.

As to this marriage, ye shall understand
We made thereto no treaty of ourselves,
And set no foot theretoward unadvised
Of all our Privy Council; furthermore,  130
This marriage had the assent of those to
    whom
The King, my father, did commit his trust;
Who not alone esteem'd it honorable,
But for the wealth and glory of our realm,
And all our loving subjects, most expedi-
    ent.
As to myself,
I am not so set on wedlock as to choose
But where I list, nor yet so amorous
That I must needs be husbanded; I thank
    God,
I have lived a virgin, and I noway doubt
But that, with God's grace, I can live so
    still.                 141
Yet if it might please God that I should
    leave
Some fruit of mine own body after me,
To be your king, ye would rejoice thereat,
And it would be your comfort, as I trust;
And truly, if I either thought or knew
This marriage should bring loss or danger
    to you,
My subjects, or impair in any way
This royal state of England, I would never
Consent thereto, nor marry while I live.
Moreover, if this marriage should not
    seem,               151
Before our own High Court of Parliament,
To be of rich advantage to our realm,
We will refrain, and not alone from this,
Likewise from any other, out of which
Looms the least chance of peril to our
    realm.
Wherefore be bold, and with your lawful
    Prince
Stand fast against our enemies and yours,
And fear them not.  I fear them not.  My
    lord,
I leave Lord William Howard in your city,
To guard and keep you whole and safe
    from all              161
The spoil and sackage aim'd at by these
    rebels,
Who mouth and foam against the Prince of
    Spain.
    *Voices.*  Long live Queen Mary !
                  Down with Wyatt !
                      The Queen !
    *White.*  Three voices from our guilds
    and companies !

You are shy and proud like Englishmen,
  my masters,
And will not trust your voices. Under-
  stand,
Your lawful Prince hath come to cast her-
  self
On loyal hearts and bosoms, hoped to
  fall
Into the wide-spread arms of fealty,   170
And finds you statues. Speak at once —
  and all !
For whom ?
Our Sovereign Lady by King Harry's
  will,
The Queen of England — or the Kentish
  Squire ?
I know you loyal. Speak ! in the name
  of God !
The Queen of England or the rabble of
  Kent ?
The reeking dungfork master of the mace !
Your havings wasted by the scythe and
  spade —
Your rights and charters hobnail'd into
  slush —
Your houses fired — your gutters bubbling
  blood —                                    180
    *Acclamation.* No ! No ! The Queen !
      the Queen !
    *White.*                 Your Highness hears
This burst and bass of loyal harmony,
And how we each and all of us abhor
The venomous, bestial, devilish revolt
Of Thomas Wyatt. Hear us now make
  oath
To raise your Highness thirty thousand
  men,
And arm and strike as with one hand, and
  brush
This Wyatt from our shoulders, like a
  flea                                       188
That might have leapt upon us unawares.
Swear with me, noble fellow-citizens, all,
With all your trades, and guilds, and com-
  panies.
    *Citizens.* We swear !
    *Mary.* We thank your lordship and your
      loyal city.
                    [*Exit* Mary, *attended.*
    *White.* I trust this day, thro' God, I have
      saved the crown.
    *First Alderman.* Ay, so my Lord of Pem-
      broke in command
Of all her force be safe; but there are
  doubts.

    *Second Alderman.* I hear that Gardiner,
      coming with the Queen,
And meeting Pembroke, bent to his saddle-
  bow,
As if to win the man by flattering him.
*Is* he so safe to fight upon her side ?    200
    *First Alderman.* If not, there's no man
      safe.
    *White.*            Yes, Thomas White.
I am safe enough; no man need flatter me.
    *Second Alderman.* Nay, no man need; but
      did you mark our Queen ?
The color freely play'd into her face,
And the half sight which makes her look so
  stern
Seem'd thro' that dim dilated world of
  hers
To read our faces; I have never seen her
So queenly or so goodly.
    *White.*             Courage, sir,
*That* makes or man or woman look their
  goodliest.
Die like the torn fox dumb, but never
  whine                                      210
Like that poor heart, Northumberland, at
  the block.
    *Bagenhall.* The man had children, and he
      whined for those.
Methinks most men are but poor-hearted,
  else
Should we so dote on courage, were it com-
  moner ?
The Queen stands up, and speaks for her
  own self;
And all men cry, She is queenly, she is
  goodly.
Yet she 's no goodlier; tho' my Lord Mayor
  here,
By his own rule, he hath been so bold to-
  day,
Should look more goodly than the rest of
  us.
    *White.* Goodly ? I feel most goodly,
      heart and hand,                        220
And strong to throw ten Wyatts and all
  Kent.
Ha ! ha ! sir; but you jest; I love it. A
  jest
In time of danger shows the pulses even.
Be merry ! yet, Sir Ralph, you look but
  sad.
I dare avouch you 'd stand up for your-
  self,
Tho' all the world should bay like winter
  wolves.

*Bagenhall.* Who knows? the man is
    proven by the hour.
*White.* The man should make the hour,
    not this the man;
And Thomas White will prove this Thomas
    Wyatt,
And he will prove an Iden to this Cade,
And he will play the Walworth to this
    Wat.                                    231
Come, sirs, we prate; hence all — gather
    your men —
Myself must bustle. Wyatt comes to South-
    wark;
I 'll have the drawbridge hewn into the
    Thames,
And see the citizens arm'd. Good day;
    good day.                    [*Exit* White.
*Bagenhall.* One of much outdoor blus-
    ter.
*Howard.*            For all that,
Most honest, brave, and skilful; and his
    wealth
A fountain of perennial alms — his fault
So thoroughly to believe in his own self.
*Bagenhall.* Yet thoroughly to believe in
    one's own self,                          240
So one's own self be thorough, were to do
Great things, my lord.
*Howard.*          *      It may be.
*Bagenhall.*                I have heard
One of your Council fleer and jeer at him.
*Howard.* The nursery - cocker'd child
    will jeer at aught
That may seem strange beyond his nursery.
The statesman that shall jeer and fleer at
    men,
Makes enemies for himself and for his king;
And if he jeer, not seeing the true man
Behind his folly, he is thrice the fool;
And if he see the man and still will jeer,
He is child and fool, and traitor to the
    State.                                   251
Who is he? let me shun him.
*Bagenhall.*                Nay, my lord,
He is damn'd enough already.
*Howard.*                I must set
The guard at Ludgate. Fare you well, Sir
    Ralph.
*Bagenhall.* 'Who knows?' I am for
    England. But who knows,
That knows the Queen, the Spaniard, and
    the Pope,
Whether I be for Wyatt, or the Queen?
                                    [*Exeunt.*

## SCENE III

### LONDON BRIDGE

*Enter* SIR THOMAS WYATT *and* BRETT.

*Wyatt.* Brett, when the Duke of Nor-
    folk moved against us
Thou criedst 'A Wyatt!' and flying to our
    side
Left his all bare, for which I love thee,
    Brett.
Have for thine asking aught that I can
    give,
For thro' thine help we are come to Lon-
    don Bridge;
But how to cross it balks me. I fear we
    cannot.
*Brett.* Nay, hardly, save by boat, swim-
    ming, or wings.
*Wyatt.* Last night I climb'd into the
    gate-house, Brett,
And scared the gray old porter and his
    wife.                                     9
And then I crept along the gloom and saw
They had hewn the drawbridge down into
    the river.
It roll'd as black as death; and that same
    tide
Which, coming with our coming, seem'd to
    smile
And sparkle like our fortune as thou said-
    est,
Ran sunless down, and moan'd against the
    piers.
But o'er the chasm I saw Lord William
    Howard
By torchlight, and his guard; four guns
    gaped at me,
Black, silent mouths. Had Howard spied
    me there
And made them speak, as well he might
    have done,
Their voice had left me none to tell you
    this.                                    20
What shall we do?
*Brett.*            On somehow. To go back
Were to lose all.
*Wyatt.*            On over London Bridge
We cannot; stay we cannot; there is ord-
    nance
On the White Tower and on the Devil's
    Tower,

And  pointed  full  at  Southwark.   We  must
 round
By  Kingston  Bridge.
 *Brett.*      Ten  miles  about.
 *Wyatt.*      Even  so.
But  I  have  notice  from  our  partisans
Within  the  city  that  they  will  stand  by
 us
If  Ludgate  can  be  reach'd  by  dawn  to-
 morrow.          29

   *Enter one of* WYATT'S *men.*

 *Man.*  Sir  Thomas,  I 've  found  this  paper;
pray  your  worship  read  it;  I  know  not
my  letters;  the  old  priests  taught  me  nothing.
 *Wyatt (reads).*  ' Whosoever  will  apprehend  the  traitor  Thomas  Wyatt  shall  have
a  hundred  pounds  for  reward.'
 *Man.*  Is  that  it ?   That 's  a  big  lot  of
money.
 *Wyatt.*  Ay,  ay,  my  friend;  not  read  it ?
't  is  not  written
Half  plain  enough.   Give  me  a  piece  of
 paper !
    [*Writes* ' THOMAS WYATT ' *large.*
There,  any  man  can  read  that.
      [*Sticks it in his cap.*
 *Brett.*      But  that 's  foolhardy.
 *Wyatt.*  No !  boldness,  which  will  give
my  followers  boldness.     41

   *Enter* MAN *with a prisoner.*

 *Man.*   We  found  him,  your  worship,
a-plundering  o'  Bishop  Winchester's  house;
he  says  he 's  a  poor  gentleman.
 *Wyatt.*  Gentleman !  a  thief !   Go  hang
 him.   Shall  we  make
Those  that  we  come  to  serve  our  sharpest
 foes ?
 *Brett.*  Sir  Thomas —
 *Wyatt.*  Hang  him,  I  say.
 *Brett.*  Wyatt,  but  now  you  promised  me
 a  boon.
 *Wyatt.*  Ay,  and  I  warrant  this  fine  fel-
 low's  life.         50
 *Brett.*  Even  so;  he  was  my  neighbor
 once  in  Kent.
He 's  poor  enough,  has  drunk  and  gambled
 out
All  that  he  had,  and  gentleman  he  was.
We  have  been  glad  together;  let  him  live.
 *Wyatt.*  He  has  gambled  for  his  life  and
 lost,  he  hangs.

No,  no,  my  word 's  my  word.   Take  thy
 poor  gentleman !
Gamble  thyself  at  once  out  of  my  sight,
Or  I  will  dig  thee  with  my  dagger.   Away !
Women  and  children !     59

 *Enter a* CROWD *of* WOMEN *and* CHILDREN.

 *First Woman.*  O Sir Thomas, Sir Thomas,
pray  you  go  away,  Sir  Thomas,  or  you 'll
make  the  White  Tower  a  black  'un  for  us
this  blessed  day.   He 'll  be  the  death  on
us;  and  you 'll  set  the  Divil's  Tower  a-spit-
ting,  and  he 'll  smash  all  our  bits  o'  things
worse  than  Philip  o'  Spain.
 *Second Woman.*  Don't  ye  now  go  to
think  that  we  be  for  Philip  o'  Spain. 68
 *Third Woman.*  No,  we  know  that  ye  be
come  to  kill  the  Queen,  and  we 'll  pray
for  you  all  on  our  bended  knees.   But  o'
God's  mercy  don't  ye  kill  the  Queen  here,
Sir  Thomas;  look  ye,  here 's  little  Dickon,
and  little  Robin,  and  little  Jenny — though
she 's  but  a  side-cousin — and  all  on  our
knees,  we  pray  you  to  kill  the  Queen  further  off,  Sir  Thomas.
 *Wyatt.*  My  friends,  I  have  not  come  to
 kill  the  Queen
Or  here  or  there;  I  come  to  save  you  all,
And  I 'll  go  further  off.     80
 *Crowd.*  Thanks,  Sir  Thomas,  we  be  be-
holden  to  you,  and  we 'll  pray  for  you  on
our  bended  knees  till  our  lives'  end.
 *Wyatt.*  Be  happy,  I  am  your  friend.
 To  Kingston,  forward !  [*Exeunt.*


     SCENE  IV

ROOM  IN  THE  GATE–HOUSE  OF  WEST-
    MINSTER  PALACE

MARY,  ALICE,  GARDINER,  RENARD,
    LADIES.

 *Gardiner.*  Their  cry  is,  Philip  never  shall
 be  king.
 *Mary.*  Lord  Pembroke  in  command  of
 all  our  force
Will  front  their  cry  and  shatter  them  into
 dust.
 *Alice.*  Was  not  Lord  Pembroke  with
 Northumberland ?
O  madam,  if  this  Pembroke  should  be
 false !

*Mary.* No, girl; most brave and loyal,
    brave and loyal.
His breaking with Northumberland broke
    Northumberland.
At the park gate he hovers with our
    guards.
These Kentish plowmen cannot break the
    guards.

*Enter* MESSENGER.

*Messenger.* Wyatt, your Grace, hath bro-
    ken thro' the guards          10
And gone to Ludgate.
*Gardiner.*          Madam, I much fear
That all is lost; but we can save your
    Grace.
The river still is free.  I do beseech you,
There yet is time, take boat and pass to
    Windsor.
*Mary.* I pass to Windsor and I lose my
    crown.
*Gardiner.* Pass, then, I pray your High-
    ness, to the Tower.
*Mary.* I shall but be their prisoner in
    the Tower.
*Cries without.*    The traitor ! treason !
    Pembroke !
*Ladies.*          Treason ! treason !
*Mary.* Peace.                19
False to Northumberland, is he false to me ?
Bear witness, Renard, that I live and die
The true and faithful bride of Philip — A
    sound
Of feet and voices thickening hither —
    blows —
Hark, there is battle at the palace gates,
And I will out upon the gallery.
*Ladies.* No, no, your Grace; see there
    the arrows flying.
*Mary.* I am Harry's daughter, Tudor,
    and not Fear.
                [*Goes out on the gallery.*
The guards are all driven in, skulk into
    corners
Like rabbits to their holes.  A gracious
    guard
Truly; shame on them ! they have shut the
    gates !                    30

*Enter* SIR ROBERT SOUTHWELL.

*Southwell.* The porter, please your Grace,
    hath shut the gates
On friend and foe.  Your gentlemen-at-
    arms,
If this be not your Grace's order, cry

To have the gates set wide again, and they
With their good battle-axes will do you
    right
Against all traitors.
*Mary.* They are the flower of England;
    set the gates wide.
                  [*Exit* Southwell.

*Enter* COURTENAY.

*Courtenay.* All lost, all lost, all yielded !
    A barge, a barge !
The Queen must to the Tower.
*Mary.*          Whence come you, sir ?
*Courtenay.* From Charing Cross; the
    rebels broke us there,          40
And I sped hither with what haste I might
To save my royal cousin.
*Mary.*          Where is Pembroke ?
*Courtenay.* I left him somewhere in the
    thick of it.
*Mary.* Left him and fled; and thou that
    wouldst be King,
And hast nor heart nor honor !  I myself
Will down into the battle and there bide
The upshot of my quarrel, or die with those
That are no cowards and no Courtenays.
*Courtenay.* I do not love your Grace
    should call me coward.

*Enter another* MESSENGER.

*Messenger.* Over, your Grace, all crush'd;
    the brave Lord William         50
Thrust him from Ludgate, and the traitor
    flying
To Temple Bar, there by Sir Maurice
    Berkeley
Was taken prisoner.
*Mary.*          To the Tower with *him* !
*Messenger.* 'T is said he told Sir Maurice
    there was one
Cognizant of this, and party thereunto,
My Lord of Devon.
*Mary.*          To the Tower with *him* !
*Courtenay.* O la, the Tower, the Tower,
    always the Tower,
I shall grow into it — I shall be the Tower.
*Mary.* Your lordship may not have so
    long to wait.               59
Remove him !
*Courtenay.*      La, to whistle out my life,
And carve my coat upon the walls again !
             [*Exit* Courtenay, *guarded.*
*Messenger.* Also this Wyatt did confess
    the Princess
Cognizant thereof, and party thereunto.

*Mary.* What ? whom — whom did you say ?

*Messenger.* Elizabeth,
Your royal sister.

*Mary.*                    To the Tower with *her !*
My foes are at my feet, and I am Queen.

[*Gardiner and her* Ladies *kneel to her.*

*Gardiner* (*rising*). There let them lie,
    your footstool ! (*Aside.*) Can I strike
Elizabeth ? — not now and save the life
Of Devon. If I save him, he and his
Are bound to me — may strike hereafter.
    (*Aloud.*) Madam,                    70
What Wyatt said, or what they said he
    said,
Cries of the moment and the street —

*Mary.*                    He said it.

*Gardiner.* Your courts of justice will determine that.

*Renard* (*advancing*). I trust by this
    your Highness will allow
Some spice of wisdom in my telling you,
When last we talk'd, that Philip would not
    come
Till Guildford Dudley and the Duke of
    Suffolk
And Lady Jane had left us.

*Mary.*                    They shall die.

*Renard.* And your so loving sister ?

*Mary.*                    She shall die.
My foes are at my feet, and Philip King. 80

[*Exeunt.*


## ACT III

SCENE I. — THE CONDUIT IN GRACE-
CHURCH

*Painted with the Nine Worthies, among them
King Henry VIII. holding a book, on it
inscribed ' Verbum Dei.'*

*Enter* SIR RALPH BAGENHALL *and* SIR
THOMAS STAFFORD.

*Bagenhall.* A hundred here and hundreds hang'd in Kent.
The tigress had unsheath'd her nails at
    last,
And Renard and the Chancellor sharpen'd
    them.
In every London street a gibbet stood.
They are down to-day. Here by this house
    was one;
The traitor husband dangled at the door,

And when the traitor wife came out for
    bread
To still the petty treason therewithin,
Her cap would brush his heels.

*Stafford.*                    It is Sir Ralph,
And muttering to himself as heretofore. 10
Sir, see you aught up yonder ?

*Bagenhall.*                    I miss something.
The tree that only bears dead fruit is gone.

*Stafford.* What tree, sir ?

*Bagenhall.* Well, the tree in Virgil, sir,
That bears not its own apples.

*Stafford.*                    What ! the gallows ?

*Bagenhall.* Sir, this dead fruit was ripening overmuch,
And had to be removed lest living Spain
Should sicken at dead England.

*Stafford.*                    Not so dead
But that a shock may rouse her.

*Bagenhall.*                    I believe
Sir Thomas Stafford ?

*Stafford.*                    I am ill disguised.

*Bagenhall.* Well, are you not in peril
    here ?

*Stafford.* I think so.                    20
I came to feel the pulse of England,
    whether
It beats hard at this marriage. Did you
    see it ?

*Bagenhall.* Stafford, I am a sad man
    and a serious.
Far liefer had I in my country hall
Been reading some old book, with mine old
    hound
Couch'd at my hearth, and mine old flask
    of wine
Beside me, than have seen it; yet I saw it.

*Stafford.* Good, was it splendid ?

*Bagenhall.*                    Ay, if dukes, and earls,
And counts, and sixty Spanish cavaliers,
Some six or seven bishops, diamonds,
    pearls,                    30
That royal commonplace too, cloth of gold,
Could make it so.

*Stafford.* And what was Mary's dress ?

*Bagenhall.* Good faith, I was too sorry
    for the woman
To mark the dress. She wore red shoes !

*Stafford.*                    Red shoes !

*Bagenhall.* Scarlet, as if her feet were
    wash'd in blood,
As if she had waded in it.

*Stafford.*                    Were your eyes
So bashful that you look'd no higher ?

*Bagenhall.*                    A diamond,

And Philip's gift, as proof of Philip's love,
Who hath not any for any, — tho' a true
     one,                                        39
Blazed false upon her heart.
     *Stafford.*          But this proud Prince —
     *Bagenhall.* Nay, he is King, you know,
     the King of Naples.
The father ceded Naples that the son,
Being a King, might wed a Queen — O, he
Flamed in brocade — white satin his trunk-
     hose,
Inwrought with•silver, — on his neck a col-
     lar,
Gold, thick with diamonds; hanging down
     from this
The Golden Fleece — and round his knee,
     misplaced,
Our English Garter, studded with great
     emeralds,
Rubies, I know not what. Have you had
     enough
Of all this gear ?
     *Stafford.* Ay, since you hate the telling
     it.                                          50
How look'd the Queen ?
     *Bagenhall.*          No fairer for her jewels.
And I could see that as the new-made
     couple
Came from the Minster, moving side by
     side
Beneath one canopy, ever and anon
She cast on him a vassal smile of love,
Which Philip with a glance of some dis-
     taste,
Or so methought, return'd. I may be
     wrong, sir.
This marriage will not hold.
     *Stafford.*          I think with you.
The King of France will help to break it.
     *Bagenhall.*                     France !
We once had half of France, and hurl'd
     our battles                                 60
Into the heart of Spain; but England now
Is but a ball chuck'd between France and
     Spain,
His in whose hand she drops. Harry of
     Bolingbroke
Had holpen Richard's tottering throne to
     stand,
Could Harry have foreseen that all our
     nobles
Would perish on the civil slaughter-field,
And leave the people naked to the Crown,
And the Crown naked to the people; the
     Crown

Female, too ! Sir, no woman's regimen
Can save us. We are fallen, and, as I
     think,                                       70
Never to rise again.
     *Stafford.*     You are too black-blooded.
I 'd make a move myself to hinder that;
I know some lusty fellows there in France.
     *Bagenhall.* You would but make us
     weaker, Thomas Stafford.
Wyatt was a good soldier, yet he fail'd,
And strengthen'd Philip.
     *Stafford.*          Did not his last breath
Clear Courtenay and the Princess from the
     charge
Of being his co-rebels ?
     *Bagenhall.*          Ay, but then
What such a one as Wyatt says is nothing;
We have no men among us. The new
     lords                                        80
Are quieted with their sop of Abbey-lands,
And even before the Queen's face Gardi-
     ner buys them
With Philip's gold. All greed, no faith,
     no courage !
Why, even the haughty prince, Northum-
     berland,
The leader of our Reformation, knelt
And blubber'd like a lad, and on the scaf-
     fold
Recanted, and resold himself to Rome.
     *Stafford.* I swear you do your country
     wrong, Sir Ralph,
I know a set of exiles over there,
Dare-devils, that would eat fire and spit it
     out                                          90
At Philip's beard; they pillage Spain al-
     ready.
The French King winks at it. An hour
     will come
When they will sweep her from the seas.
     No men ?
Did not Lord Suffolk die like a true man ?
Is not Lord William Howard a true man ?
Yea, you yourself, altho' you are black-
     blooded;
And I, by God, believe myself a man.
Ay, even in the church there is a man —
Cranmer.
Fly would he not, when all men bade him
     fly.                                         100
And what a letter he wrote against the
     Pope !
There 's a brave man, if any.
     *Bagenhall.*               Ay; if it hold.

*Crowd* (*coming on*). God save their Graces !

*Stafford.* Bagenhall, I see
The Tudor green and white. (*Trumpets.*) They are coming now.
And here 's a crowd as thick as herring-shoals.

*Bagenhall.* Be limpets to this pillar, or we are torn
Down the strong wave of brawlers.

*Crowd.* God save their Graces !

*Procession of Trumpeters, Javelinmen, etc.; then Spanish and Flemish Nobles inter-mingled.*

*Stafford.* Worth seeing, Bagenhall ! These black dog-Dons
Garb themselves bravely. Who 's the long-face there, 110
Looks very Spain of very Spain ?

*Bagenhall.* The Duke
Of Alva, an iron soldier.

*Stafford.* And the Dutchman,
Now laughing at some jest ?

*Bagenhall.* William of Orange,
William the Silent.

*Stafford.* Why do they call him so ?

*Bagenhall.* He keeps, they say, some se-cret that may cost
Philip his life

*Stafford.* But then he looks so merry.

*Bagenhall.* I cannot tell you why they call him so.

[*The* King *and* Queen *pass, attended by Peers of the Realm, Officers of State, etc. Cannon shot off.*

*Crowd.* Philip and Mary, Philip and Mary !
Long live the King and Queen, Philip and Mary !

*Stafford.* They smile as if content with one another. 120

*Bagenhall.* A smile abroad is oft a scowl at home.

[King *and* Queen *pass on. Procession.*

*First Citizen.* I thought this Philip had been one of those black devils of Spain, but he hath a yellow beard.

*Second Citizen.* Not red like Iscariot's.

*First Citizen.* Like a carrot's, as thou say'st, and English carrot 's better than Spanish licorice; but I thought he was a beast.

*Third Citizen.* Certain I had heard that every Spaniard carries a tail like a devil under his trunk-hose. 132

*Tailor.* Ay, but see what trunk-hoses ! Lord ! they be fine; I never stitch'd none such. They make amends for the tails.

*Fourth Citizen.* Tut ! every Spanish priest will tell you that all English heretics have tails.

*Fifth Citizen.* Death and the devil — if he find I have one — 140

*Fourth Citizen.* Lo ! thou hast call'd them up ! here they come — a pale horse for Death, and Gardiner for the devil.

*Enter* GARDINER (*turning back from the procession*).

*Gardiner.* Knave, wilt thou wear thy cap before the Queen ?

*Man.* My lord, I stand so squeezed among the crowd
I cannot lift my hands unto my head.

*Gardiner.* Knock off his cap there, some of you about him !
See there be others that can use their hands.
Thou art one of Wyatt's men ?

*Man.* No, my lord, no.

*Gardiner.* Thy name, thou knave ?

*Man.* I am nobody, my lord.

*Gardiner* (*shouting*). God's passion ! knave, thy name ?

*Man.* I have ears to hear.

*Gardiner.* Ay, rascal, if I leave thee ears to hear. 152
Find out his name and bring it me (*to Attendant*).

*Attendant.* Ay, my lord.

*Gardiner.* Knave, thou shalt lose thine ears and find thy tongue,
And shalt be thankful if I leave thee that.

[*Coming before the Conduit.*
The conduit painted — the Nine Worthies — ay !
But then what 's here ? King Harry with a scroll.
Ha — Verbum Dei — verbum — Word of God !
God's passion ! do you know the knave that painted it ?

*Attendant.* I do, my lord.

*Gardiner.* Tell him to paint it out,
And put some fresh device in lieu of it —
A pair of gloves, a pair of gloves, sir; ha ? 162
There is no heresy there.

*Attendant.*                    I will, my lord;
The man shall paint a pair of gloves. I am
    sure —
Knowing the man — he wrought it igno-
    rantly,
And not from any malice.
*Gardiner.*                    Word of God
In English ! over this the brainless loons
That cannot spell Esaias from Saint Paul,
Make themselves drunk and mad, fly out
    and flare
Into rebellions. I 'll have their Bibles
    burnt.                                170
The Bible is the priest's. Ay ! fellow,
    what !
Stand staring at me ! shout, you gaping
    rogue !
*Man.* I have, my lord, shouted till I
    am hoarse.
*Gardiner.* What hast thou shouted,
    knave ?
*Man.*                    Long live Queen Mary !
*Gardiner.* Knave, there be two. There
    be both King and Queen,
Philip and Mary. Shout !
*Man.*                    Nay, but, my lord,
The Queen comes first, Mary and Philip.
*Gardiner.*                    Shout, then,
Mary and Philip !
*Man.*                    Mary and Philip !
*Gardiner.*                    Now,
Thou hast shouted for thy pleasure, shout
    for mine !                              179
Philip and Mary !
*Man.*                    Must it be so, my lord ?
*Gardiner.* Ay, knave.
*Man.*                    Philip and Mary.
*Gardiner.*                    I distrust thee.
Thine is a half voice and a lean assent.
What is thy name ?
*Man.*                    Sanders.
*Gardiner.*                    What else ?
*Man.*                    Zerubbabel.
*Gardiner.* Where dost thou live ?
*Man.*                    In Cornhill.
*Gardiner.*                    Where, knave, where ?
*Man.* Sign of the Talbot.
*Gardiner.* Come to me to-morrow. —
Rascal ! — this land is like a hill of fire,
One crater opens when another shuts,
But so I get the laws against the here-
    tic,
Spite of Lord Paget and Lord William
    Howard,
And others of our Parliament, revived,   190

I will show fire on my side — stake and
    fire —
Sharp work and short. The knaves are
    easily cow'd.
Follow their Majesties.
           [*Exit. The crowd following.*
*Bagenhall.*              As proud as Becket.
*Stafford.* You would not have him mur-
    der'd as Becket was ?
*Bagenhall.* No — murder fathers mur-
    der; but I say
There is no man — there was one woman
    with us —
It was a sin to love her married, dead
I cannot choose but love her.
*Stafford.*                    Lady Jane ?
*Crowd (going off).* God save their
    Graces !
*Stafford.*       Did you see her die ?
*Bagenhall.* No, no; her innocent blood
    had blinded me.                          200
You call me too black - blooded — true
    enough,
Her dark, dead blood is in my heart with
    mine.
If ever I cry out against the Pope
Her dark, dead blood that ever moves with
    mine
Will stir the living tongue and make the
    cry.
*Stafford.* Yet doubtless you can tell me
    how she died ?
*Bagenhall.* Seventeen — and knew eight
    languages — in music
Peerless — her needle perfect, and her
    learning
Beyond the churchmen; yet so meek, so
    modest,
So wife-like humble to the trivial boy   210
Mismatch'd with her for policy ! I have
    heard
She would not take a last farewell of him;
She fear'd it might unman him for his end.
She could not be unmann'd — no, nor out-
    woman'd —
Seventeen — a rose of grace !
Girl never breathed to rival such a rose;
Rose never blew that equall'd such a bud.
*Stafford.* Pray you go on.
*Bagenhall.* She came upon the scaffold,
And said she was condemn'd to die for
    treason;                                219
She had but follow'd the device of those
Her nearest kin; she thought they knew
    the laws.

But for herself, she knew but little law,
And nothing of the titles to the crown;
She had no desire for that, and wrung her
     hands,
And trusted God would save her thro' the
     blood
Of Jesus Christ alone.
*Stafford.*               Pray you go on.
*Bagenhall.* Then knelt and said the
     Miserere Mei —
But all in English, mark you; rose again,
And, when the headsman pray'd to be for-
     given,
Said, ' You will give me my true crown at
     last,                                    230
But do it quickly;' then all wept but she,
Who changed not color when she saw the
     block,
But ask'd him, childlike, ' Will you take it
     off
Before I lay me down ? ' ' No, madam,'
     he said,
Gasping; and when her innocent eyes were
     bound,
She, with her poor blind hands feeling —
     ' Where is it ?
Where is it ? ' — You must fancy that
     which follow'd,
If you have heart to do it !
     *Crowd (in the distance).* God save their
          Graces !
     *Stafford.* Their Graces, our disgraces !
          God confound them !
Why, she 's grown bloodier ! when I last
     was here,                               240
This was against her conscience — would
     be murder !
*Bagenhall.* The ' Thou shalt do no mur-
     der,' which God's hand
Wrote on her conscience, Mary rubb'd out
     pale —
She could not make it white — and over
     that,
Traced in the blackest text of hell —
     ' Thou shalt ! '
And sign'd it — Mary !
*Stafford.*               Philip and the Pope
Must have sign'd too. I hear this legate's
     coming
To bring us absolution from the Pope.
The Lords and Commons will bow down
     before him —
You are of the house ? what will you do,
     Sir Ralph ?                            250

*Bagenhall.* And why should I be bolder
     than the rest,
Or honester than all ?
*Stafford.*               But, sir, if I —
And over-sea they say this State of yours
Hath no more mortise than a tower of
     cards;
And that a puff would do it — then if I
And others made that move I touched
     upon,
Back'd by the power of France, and land-
     ing here,
Came with a sudden splendor, shout, and
     show,
And dazzled men and deafen'd by some
     bright
Loud venture, and the people so unquiet —
And I the race of murder'd Bucking-
     ham —                                  261
Not for myself, but for the kingdom —
     Sir,
I trust that you would fight along with us.
*Bagenhall.* No; you would fling your
     lives into the gulf.
*Stafford.* But if this Philip, as he 's like
     to do,
Left Mary a wife-widow here alone,
Set up a viceroy, sent his myriads hither
To seize upon the forts and fleet, and make
     us
A Spanish province; would you not fight
     then ?
*Bagenhall.* I think I should fight then.
*Stafford.*               I am sure of it.
Hist ! there 's the face coming on here of
     one                                     271
Who knows me. I must leave you. Fare
     you well,
You 'll hear of me again.
*Bagenhall.*               Upon the scaffold.
                              [*Exeunt.*

SCENE II

ROOM IN WHITEHALL PALACE

MARY. *Enter* PHILIP *and* CARDINAL
POLE.

*Pole.* Ave Maria, gratia plena, bene-
     dicta tu in mulieribus !
*Mary.* Loyal and royal cousin, humblest
     thanks.
Had you a pleasant voyage up the river ?

*Pole.* We had your royal barge, and that
same chair,
Or rather throne of purple, on the deck.
Our silver cross sparkled before the prow,
The ripples twinkled at their diamond-
dance,
The boats that follow'd were as glowing-
gay
As regal gardens, and your flocks of swans
As fair and white as angels; and your
shores                                        10
Wore in mine eyes the green of Paradise.
My foreign friends, who dream'd us
blanketed
In ever-closing fog, were much amazed
To find as fair a sun as might have flash'd
Upon their lake of Garda fire the Thames;
Our voyage by sea was all but miracle;
And here the river flowing from the sea,
Not toward it — for they thought not of our
tides —
Seem'd as a happy miracle to make glide —
In quiet — home your banish'd country-
man.                                         20
  *Mary.* We heard that you were sick in
Flanders, cousin.
  *Pole.* A dizziness.
  *Mary.* And how came you round again?
  *Pole.* The scarlet thread of Rahab saved
her life;
And mine, a little letting of the blood.
  *Mary.* Well? now?
  *Pole.*           Ay, cousin, as the heathen giant
Had but to touch the ground, his force re-
turn'd —
Thus, after twenty years of banishment,
Feeling my native land beneath my foot,
I said thereto: 'Ah, native land of mine,
Thou art much beholden to this foot of
mine,                                        30
That hastes with full commission from the
Pope
To absolve thee from thy guilt of heresy.
Thou hast disgraced me and attainted me,
And mark'd me even as Cain, and I return
As Peter, but to bless thee; make me well.'
Methinks the good land heard me, for to-
day
My heart beats twenty, when I see you,
cousin.
Ah, gentle cousin, since your Herod's
death,
How oft hath Peter knock'd at Mary's gate!
And Mary would have risen and let him
in,                                          40

But, Mary, there were those within the
house
Who would not have it.
  *Mary.*              True, good cousin Pole;
And there were also those without the
house
Who would not have it.
  *Pole.*              I believe so, cousin.
State-policy and church-policy are conjoint,
But Janus-faces looking diverse ways.
I fear the Emperor much misvalued me.
But all is well; 't was even the will of God,
Who, waiting till the time had ripen'd,
now
Makes me His mouth of holy greeting.
  'Hail,                                      50
Daughter of God, and saver of the faith.
Sit benedictus fructus ventris tui!'
  *Mary.* Ah, heaven!
  *Pole.*              Unwell, your Grace?
  *Mary.*              No, cousin, happy —
Happy to see you; never yet so happy
Since I was crown'd.
  *Pole.*              Sweet cousin, you forget
That long low minster where you gave
your hand
To this great Catholic King.
  *Philip.*           Well said, Lord Legate.
  *Mary.* Nay, not well said; I thought of
you, my liege,
Even as I spoke.
  *Philip.*           Ay, madam; my Lord Paget
Waits to present our Council to the le-
gate.                                         60
Sit down here, all; madam, between us
you.
  *Pole.* Lo, now you are enclosed with
boards of cedar,
Our little sister of the Song of Songs!
You are doubly fenced and shielded sitting
here
Between the two most high-set thrones on
earth,
The Emperor's highness happily symboll'd
by
The King your husband, the Pope's holi-
ness
By mine own self.
  *Mary.*              True, cousin, I am happy.
When will you that we summon both our
houses
To take this absolution from your lips,   70
And be re-gather'd to the Papal fold?
  *Pole.* In Britain's calendar the brightest
day

Beheld our rough forefathers break their
    gods,
And clasp the faith in Christ; but after
    that
Might not Saint Andrew's be her happiest
    day ?

*Mary.* Then these shall meet upon Saint
    Andrew's Day.

*Enter* PAGET, *who presents the Council.*
*Dumb show.*

*Pole.* I am an old man wearied with my
    journey,
Even with my joy. Permit me to with-
    draw.
To Lambeth ?

*Philip.* Ay, Lambeth has ousted Cran-
    mer.
It was not meet the heretic swine should
    live         80
In Lambeth.

*Mary.*     There or anywhere, or at all.

*Philip.* We have had it swept and gar-
    nish'd after him.

*Pole.* Not for the seven devils to enter
    in ?

*Philip.* No, for we trust they parted in
    the swine.

*Pole.* True, and I am the Angel of the
    Pope.
Farewell, your Graces.

*Philip.*     Nay, not here — to me;
I will go with you to the waterside.

*Pole.* Not be my Charon to the counter
    side ?

*Philip.* No, my Lord Legate, the Lord
    Chancellor goes.

*Pole.* And unto no dead world, but
    Lambeth Palace,     90
Henceforth a centre of the living faith.

    [*Exeunt* Philip, Pole, Paget, *etc.*

*Manet* MARY.

*Mary.* He hath awaked ! he hath
    awaked !
He stirs within the darkness !
O Philip, husband ! now thy love to mine
Will cling more close, and those bleak
    manners thaw,
That make me shamed and tongue-tied in
    my love.
The second Prince of Peace —
The great unborn defender of the Faith,
Who will avenge me of mine enemies —
He comes, and my star rises.     100

The stormy Wyatts and Northumberlands,
The proud ambitions of Elizabeth,
And all her fieriest partisans — are pale
Before my star !
The light of this new learning wanes and
    dies;
The ghosts of Luther and Zuinglius fade
Into the deathless hell which is their doom
Before my star !
His sceptre shall go forth from Ind to Ind!
His sword shall hew the heretic peoples
    down !     110
His faith shall clothe the world that will be
    his,
Like universal air and sunshine ! Open,
Ye everlasting gates ! The King is here ! —
My star, my son !

*Enter* PHILIP, DUKE OF ALVA, *etc.*

    O, Philip, come with me !
Good news have I to tell you, news to
    make
Both of us happy — ay, the kingdom too.
Nay, come with me — one moment !

*Philip* (*to Alva*).     More than that;
There was one here of late — William the
    Silent
They call him — he is free enough in talk,
But tells me nothing. You will be, we
    trust,     120
Sometime the viceroy of those provinces —
He must deserve his surname better.

*Alva.*     Ay, sir;
Inherit the Great Silence.

*Philip.*     True; the provinces
Are hard to rule and must be hardly ruled;
Most fruitful, yet, indeed, an empty rind,
All hollow'd out with stinging heresies;
And for their heresies, Alva, they will
    fight;
You must break them or they break you.

*Alva* (*proudly*).     The first.

*Philip.* Good !
Well, Madam, this new happiness of
    mine ?     [*Exeunt.*

*Enter* THREE PAGES.

*First Page.* News, mates ! a miracle, a
    miracle ! news !     131
The bells must ring; Te Deums must be
    sung;
The Queen hath felt the motion of her
    babe !

*Second Page.* Ay; but see here !

*First Page.*     See what ?

*Second Page.*          This paper, Dickon.
I found it fluttering at the palace gates: —
' The Queen of England is delivered of a
     dead dog !'
     *Third Page.* These are the things that
madden her.   Fie upon it !
     *First Page.* Ay; but I hear she hath a
     dropsy, lad,
Or a high-dropsy, as the doctors call it.
     *Third Page.* Fie on her dropsy, so she
     have a dropsy !                         140
I know that she was ever sweet to me.
     *First Page.* For thou and thine are Ro-
     man to the core.
     *Third Page.* So thou and thine must be.
     Take heed !
     *First Page.*           Not I;
And whether this flash of news be false or
     true,
So the wine run, and there be revelry,
Content am I.   Let all the steeples clash,
Till the sun dance, as upon Easter Day.
                                   [*Exeunt.*

## SCENE III

### GREAT HALL IN WHITEHALL

*At the far end a dais.   On this three chairs,
two under one canopy for* MARY *and* PHI-
LIP, *another on the right of these for* POLE.
*Under the dais on* POLE'S *side, ranged
along the wall, sit all the Spiritual Peers,
and along the wall opposite all the Tempo-
ral.   The Commons on cross benches in
front, a line of approach to the dais between
them.   In the foreground,* SIR RALPH
BAGENHALL *and other* MEMBERS *of the*
COMMONS.

     *First Member.* Saint Andrew's Day; sit
     close, sit close, we are friends.
Is reconciled the word ?  the Pope again ?
It must be thus; and yet, cocksbody ! how
     strange
That Gardiner, once so one with all of us
Against this foreign marriage, should have
     yielded
So utterly ! — strange ! but stranger still
     that he,
So fierce against the headship of the Pope,
Should play the second actor in this pa-
     geant
That brings him in; such a chameleon he !
     *Second Member.* This Gardiner turn'd his
     coat in Henry's time;                   10

The serpent that hath slough'd will slough
     again.
     *Third Member.* Tut, then we all are ser-
     pents.
     *Second Member.*        Speak for yourself.
     *Third Member.* Ay, and for Gardiner !
     being English citizen,
How should he bear a bridegroom out of
     Spain ?
The Queen would have him ! being English
     churchman,
How should he bear the headship of the
     Pope ?
The Queen would have it !   Statesmen that
     are wise
Shape a necessity, as a sculptor clay,
To their own model.
     *Second Member.*  Statesmen that are wise
Take truth herself for model.   What say
     you ?        [*To* Sir Ralph Bagenhall.
     *Bagenhall.* We talk and talk.
     *First Member.* Ay, and what use to talk ?
Philip 's no  sudden  alien — the  Queen's
     husband,
He 's here, and King, or will be — yet,     22
     cocksbody !
So  hated  here !   I  watch'd  a  hive  of
     late;
My seven-years' friend was with me, my
     young boy;
Out crept a wasp, with half the swarm be-
     hind.
' Philip !' says he.   I had to cuff the rogue
For infant treason.
     *Third Member.* But they say that bees,
If any creeping life invade their hive
Too gross to be thrust out, will build him
     round,                                  30
And bind him in from harming of their
     combs.
And Philip by these articles is bound
From stirring hand or foot to wrong the
     realm.
     *Second Member.* By bonds of beeswax,
     like your creeping thing;
But your wise bees had stung him first to
     death.
     *Third Member.* Hush, hush !
You wrong the Chancellor.   The clauses
     added
To that same treaty which the Emperor
     sent us
Were mainly Gardiner's: that no foreigner
Hold office in the household, fleet, forts,
     army;                                   40

*Officer.* Well, you one man, because you
    stood upright,
Her Grace the Queen commands you to the
    Tower.
    *Bagenhall.* As traitor, or as heretic, or
      for what?
    *Officer.* If any man in any way would be
The one man, he shall be so to his cost.
    *Bagenhall.* What! will she have my
      head?
    *Officer.*         A round fine likelier.
Your pardon.       [*Calling to Attendant.*
    By the river to the Tower.
                  [*Exeunt.*


SCENE IV

WHITEHALL.   A ROOM IN THE PALACE

MARY, GARDINER, POLE, PAGET, BONNER,
      *etc.*

    *Mary.* The King and I, my lords, now
      that all traitors
Against our royal state have lost the heads
Wherewith they plotted in their treasonous
    malice,
Have talk'd together, and are well agreed
That those old statutes touching Lollard-
    ism
To bring the heretic to the stake, should
    be
No longer a dead letter, but re-quicken'd.
    *One of the Council.* Why, what hath flus-
      ter'd Gardiner? how he rubs
His forelock!
    *Paget.* I have changed a word with him
In coming, and may change a word again.
    *Gardiner.* Madam, your Highness is our
      sun, the King             11
And you together our two suns in one;
And so the beams of both may shine upon
    us,
The faith that seem'd to droop will feel
    your light,
Lift head, and flourish; yet not light alone,
There must be heat — there must be heat
    enough
To scorch and wither heresy to the root.
For what saith Christ? 'Compel them to
    come in.'
And what saith Paul? 'I would they were
    cut off
That trouble you.' Let the dead letter
    live!                   20

Trace it in fire, that all the louts to whom
Their A B C is darkness, clowns and grooms
May read it! so you quash rebellion too,
For heretic and traitor are all one;
Two vipers of one breed — an amphis-
    bæna,
Each end a sting. Let the dead letter
    burn!
    *Paget.* Yet there be some disloyal Cath-
      olics,
And many heretics loyal; heretic throats
Cried no God-bless-her to the Lady Jane,
But shouted in Queen Mary. So there be  30
Some traitor-heretic, there is axe and cord.
To take the lives of others that are loyal,
And by the churchman's pitiless doom of
    fire,
Were but a thankless policy in this crown,
Ay, and against itself; for there are many.
    *Mary.* If we could burn out heresy, my
      Lord Paget,
We reck not tho' we lost this crown of
    England —
Ay! tho' it were ten Englands!
    *Gardiner.*          Right, your Grace.
Paget, you are all for this poor life of ours,
And care but little for the life to be.     40
    *Paget.* I have some time, for curious-
      ness, my lord,
Watch'd children playing at *their* life to be,
And cruel at it, killing helpless flies;
Such is our time — all times for aught I
    know.
    *Gardiner.* We kill the heretics that sting
      the soul —
They, with right reason, flies that prick the
    flesh.
    *Paget.* They had not reach'd right rea-
      son, little children!
They kill'd but for their pleasure and the
    power
They felt in killing.
    *Gardiner.*       A spice of Satan, ha!
Why, good! what then? granted! — we are
    fallen creatures;          50
Look to your Bible, Paget! we are fallen.
    *Paget.* I am but of the laity, my lord
      bishop,
And may not read your Bible, yet I found
One day a wholesome scripture, 'Little
    children,
Love one another.'
    *Gardiner.*       Did you find a scripture,
'I come not to bring peace but a sword'?
      The sword

Is in her Grace's hand to smite with.
    Paget,
You stand up here to fight for heresy,
You are more than guess'd at as a heretic,
And on the steep-up track of the true
    faith                                    60
Your lapses are far seen.
    *Paget.*            The faultless Gardiner !
    *Mary.* You brawl beyond the question;
    speak, lord legate !
    *Pole.* Indeed, I cannot follow with your
    Grace;
Rather would say — the shepherd doth not
    kill
The sheep that wander from his flock, but
    sends
His careful dog to bring them to the fold.
Look to the Netherlands, wherein have
    been
Such holocausts of heresy ! to what end ?
For yet the faith is not established there.
    *Gardiner.* The end 's not come.
    *Pole.*       No — nor this way will come,
Seeing there lie two ways to every end,   71
A better and a worse — the worse is here
To persecute, because to persecute
Makes a faith hated, and is furthermore
No perfect witness of a perfect faith
In him who persecutes.  When men are
    tost
On tides of strange opinion, and not sure
Of their own selves, they are wroth with
    their own selves,
And thence with others; then, who lights
    the faggot ?
Not the full faith, no, but the lurking
    doubt.                                   80
Old Rome, that first made martyrs in the
    Church,
Trembled for her own gods, for these were
    trembling —
But when did our Rome tremble ?
    *Paget.*                      Did she not
In Henry's time and Edward's ?
    *Pole.*                 What, my lord !
The Church on Peter's rock ? never !  I
    have seen
A pine in Italy that cast its shadow
Athwart a cataract; firm stood the pine —
The cataract shook the shadow.  To my
    mind,
The cataract typed the headlong plunge
    and fall
  Of heresy to the pit; the pine was Rome.  90
You see, my lords,

It was the shadow of the Church that
    trembled;
Your church was but the shadow of a
    church,
Wanting the Papal mitre.
    *Gardiner* (*muttering*).      Here be tropes.
    *Pole.* And tropes are good to clothe a
    naked truth,
And make it look more seemly.
    *Gardiner.*                Tropes again !
    *Pole.* You are hard to please.  Then
    without tropes, my lord,
An overmuch severeness, I repeat,
When faith is wavering makes the waverer
    pass                                     99
Into more settled hatred of the doctrines
Of those who rule, which hatred by and by
Involves the ruler — thus there springs to
    light
That Centaur of a monstrous Common-
    weal,
The traitor-heretic; — then tho' some may
    quail,
Yet others are that dare the stake and fire,
And their strong torment bravely borne
    begets
An admiration and an indignation,
And hot desire to imitate; so the plague
Of schism spreads.  Were there but three
    or four
Of these misleaders, yet I would not say
Burn ! and we cannot burn whole towns;
    they are many,                          111
As my Lord Paget says.
    *Gardiner.*      Yet, my Lord Cardinal —
    *Pole.* I am your legate; please you let
    me finish.
Methinks that under our Queen's regimen
We might go softlier than with crimson
    rowel
And streaming lash.  When Herod-Henry
    first
Began to batter at your English Church,
This was the cause, and hence the judg-
    ment on her.
She seethed with such adulteries, and the
    lives
Of many among your churchmen were
    foul
That heaven wept and earth blush'd.   would advise
That we should thoroughly cleanse  Church within
Before these bitter statutes be re-quick
So after that when she once more is

White as the light, the spotless bride of
 Christ,
Like Christ himself on Tabor, possibly
The Lutheran may be won to her again;
Till when, my lords, I counsel tolerance.
 *Gardiner.* What, if a mad dog bit your
  hand, my lord,     129
Would you not chop the bitten finger off,
Lest your whole body should madden with
 the poison ?
I would not, were I Queen, tolerate the
 heretic,
No, not an hour.  The ruler of a land
Is bounden by his power and place to see
His people be not poison'd.  Tolerate them !
Why ?  do they tolerate you ?  Nay, many
 of them
Would burn — have burnt each other; call
 they not
The one true faith a loathsome idol-wor-
 ship ?
Beware, lord legate, of a heavier crime
Than heresy is itself; beware, I say, 140
Lest men accuse you of indifference
To all faiths, all religion; for you know
Right well that you yourself have been
 supposed
Tainted with Lutheranism in Italy.
 *Pole* (*angered*).  But you, my lord, be-
  yond all supposition,
In clear and open day were congruent
With that vile Cranmer in the accursed lie
Of good Queen Catharine's divorce — the
 spring
Of all those evils that have flow'd upon
 us;
For you yourself have truckled to the
 tyrant,       150
And done your best to bastardize our
 Queen,
For which God's righteous judgment fell
 upon you
In your five years of imprisonment, my
 lord,
Under young Edward.  Who so bolster'd
 up
The gross King's headship of the Church,
 or more
Denied the Holy Father ?
 *Gardiner.*    Ha ! what ! eh ?
But you, my lord, a polish'd gentleman,
A bookman, flying from the heat and tussle,
Who lived among your vines and oranges,
In your soft Italy yonder !  You were sent
 for,       160

You were appeal'd to, but you still pre-
 ferr'd
Your learned leisure.  As for what I did,
I suffer'd and repented.  You, lord le-
 gate
And cardinal-deacon, have not now to learn
That even Saint Peter in his time of fear
Denied his Master, ay, and thrice, my lord
 *Pole.*  But not for five-and-twenty years,
  my lord.
 *Gardiner.*  Ha ! good ! it seems then I
  was summon'd hither
But to be mock'd and baited.  Speak,
 friend Bonner,
And tell this learned legate he lacks zeal.
The Church's evil is not as the King's, 171
Cannot be heal'd by stroking.  The mad
 bite
Must have the cautery — tell him — and
 at once.
What wouldst thou do hadst thou his
 power, thou
That layest so long in heretic bonds with
 me ?
Wouldst thou not burn and blast them root
 and branch ?
 *Bonner.*  Ay, after you, my lord.
 *Gardiner.*  Nay, God's passion, before
  me ! speak !
 *Bonner.*  I am on fire until I see them
  flame.
 *Gardiner.*  Ay, the psalm-singing weav-
  ers, cobblers, scum —   180
But this most noble prince Plantagenet,
Our good Queen's cousin — dallying over-
 seas
Even when his brother's, nay, his noble
 mother's,
Head fell —
 *Pole.*    Peace, madman !
Thou stirrest up a grief thou canst not
 fathom.
Thou Christian bishop, thou Lord Chancel-
 lor
Of England !  no more rein upon thine
 anger
Than any child !  Thou mak'st me much
 ashamed
That I was for a moment wroth at thee.
 *Mary.*  I come for counsel and ye give
  me feuds,     190
Like dogs that, set to watch their master's
 gate,
Fall, when the thief is even within the
 walls,

To worrying one another. My Lord Chan-
   cellor,
You have an old trick of offending us;
And but that you are art and part with
   us
In purging heresy, well we might, for this
Your violence and much roughness to the
   legate,
Have shut you from our counsels. Cousin
   Pole,
You are fresh from brighter lands. Retire
   with me.
His Highness and myself — so you allow
   us —        200
Will let you learn in peace and privacy
What power this cooler sun of England
   hath
In breeding godless vermin. And pray
   Heaven
That you may see according to our sight!
Come, cousin.
             [*Exeunt* Queen *and* Pole, *etc.*
   *Gardiner.* Pole has the Plantagenet face,
But not the force made them our mightiest
   kings.
Fine eyes — but melancholy, irresolute —
A fine beard, Bonner, a very full fine beard.
But a weak mouth, an indeterminate —
   ha ?        209
   *Bonner.* Well, a weak mouth, perchance.
   *Gardiner.*             And not like thine
To gorge a heretic whole, roasted or raw.
   *Bonner.* I'd do my best, my Lord; but
   yet the legate
Is here as Pope and Master of the Church,
And if he go not with you —
   *Gardiner.*           Tut, Master Bishop,
Our bashful legate, saw'st not how he
   flush'd ?
Touch him upon his old heretical talk,
He'll burn a diocese to prove his ortho-
   doxy.
And let him call me truckler. In those
   times,
Thou knowest we had to dodge, or duck,
   or die;       219
I kept my head for use of Holy Church;
And see you, we shall have to dodge again,
And let the Pope trample our rights, and
   plunge
His foreign fist into our island Church
To plump the leaner pouch of Italy.
For a time, for a time.
Why ? that these statutes may be put in
   force,

And that his fan may thoroughly purge his
   floor.
   *Bonner.* So then you hold the Pope —
   *Gardiner.*             I hold the Pope !
What do I hold him ? what do I hold the
   Pope ?
Come, come, the morsel stuck — this Car-
   dinal's fault —       230
I have gulpt it down. I am wholly for the
   Pope,
Utterly and altogether for the Pope,
The Eternal Peter of the changeless chair,
Crown'd slave of slaves, and mitred king
   of kings,
God upon earth ! what more ? what would
   you have ?
Hence, let's be gone.

             *Enter* USHER.

   *Usher.*        Well that you be not gone,
My lord. The Queen, most wroth at first
   with you,
Is now content to grant you full forgive-
   ness,
So that you crave full pardon of the le-
   gate.       239
I am sent to fetch you.
   *Gardiner.*        Doth Pole yield, sir, ha ?
Did you hear 'em ? were you by ?
   *Usher.*            I cannot tell you,
His bearing is so courtly-delicate;
And yet methinks he falters; their two
   Graces
Do so dear-cousin and royal-cousin him,
So press on him the duty which as legate
He owes himself, and with such royal
   smiles —
   *Gardiner.* Smiles that burn men. Bon-
   ner, it will be carried.
He falters, ha ? 'fore God, we change and
   change;
Men now are bow'd and old, the doctors
   tell you,
At three-score years; then if we change at
   all       250
We needs must do it quickly; it is an age
Of brief life, and brief purpose, and brief
   patience,
As I have shown to-day. I am sorry for it
If Pole be like to turn. Our old friend
   Cranmer,
Your more especial love, hath turn'd so
   often
He knows not where he stands, which, if
   this pass,

We two shall have to teach him; let 'em
    look to it,
Cranmer and Hooper, Ridley and Latimer,
Rogers and Ferrar, for their time is come,
Their hour is hard at hand, their 'dies
    Iræ,'                   260
Their 'dies Illa,' which will test their sect.
I feel it but a duty — you will find in it
Pleasure as well as duty, worthy Bonner, —
To test their sect.  Sir, I attend the Queen
To crave most humble pardon — of her
    most
Royal, Infallible, Papal Legate-cousin.
                        [*Exeunt.*

### SCENE V

### WOODSTOCK

#### ELIZABETH, LADY IN WAITING.

*Elizabeth.*  So they have sent poor Cour-
    tenay over-sea.
*Lady.*  And banish'd us to Woodstock,
    and the fields.
The colors of our Queen are green and
    white;
These fields are only green, they make me
    gape.
*Elizabeth.*  There 's white-thorn, girl.
*Lady.*          Ay, for an hour in May.
But court is always May, buds out in
    masques,
Breaks into feather'd merriments, and
    flowers
In silken pageants.  Why do they keep us
    here ?
Why still suspect your Grace ?
*Elizabeth.*        Hard upon both.
    [*Writes on the window with a diamond.*

       Much suspected, of me      10
       Nothing proven can be.
         Quoth Elizabeth, prisoner.

*Lady.*  What hath your Highness writ-
    ten ?
*Elizabeth.*  A true rhyme.
*Lady.*  Cut with a diamond; so to last
    like truth.
*Elizabeth.*  Ay, if truth last.
*Lady.*       But truth, they say, will out;
So it must last.  It is not like a word,
That comes and goes in uttering.
*Elizabeth.*          Truth, a word !

The very Truth and very Word are one.
But truth of story, which I glanced at, girl,
Is like a word that comes from olden
    days,                       20
And passes thro' the peoples; every tongue
Alters it passing, till it spells and speaks
Quite other than at first.
*Lady.*           I do not follow.
*Elizabeth.*  How many names, in the long
    sweep of time
That so foreshortens greatness, may but
    hang
On the chance mention of some fool that
    once
Brake bread with us, perhaps; and my
    poor chronicle
Is but of glass.  Sir Henry Bedingfield
May split it for a spite.
*Lady.*          God grant it last,
And witness to your Grace's innocence,   30
Till doomsday melt it !
*Elizabeth.*        Or a second fire,
Like that which lately crackled underfoot
And in this very chamber, fuse the glass,
And char us back again into the dust
We spring from.  Never peacock against
    rain
Scream'd as you did for water.
*Lady.*          And I got it.
I woke Sir Henry — and he 's true to
    you —
I read his honest horror in his eyes.
*Elizabeth.*  Or true to you ?
*Lady.*         Sir Henry Bedingfield !
I will have no man true to me, your Grace,
But one that pares his nails; to me ? the
    clown !                    41
*Elizabeth.*  Out, girl ! you wrong a noble
    gentleman.
*Lady.*  For, like his cloak, his manners
    want the nap
And gloss of court; but of this fire he says,
Nay swears, it was no wicked wilfulness,
Only a natural chance.
*Elizabeth.*       A chance — perchance
One of those wicked wilfuls that men make,
Nor shame to call it nature.  Nay, I know
They hunt my blood.  Save for my daily
    range
Among the pleasant fields of Holy Writ   50
I might despair.  But there hath some one
    come;
The house is all in movement.  Hence, and
    see.                  [*Exit* Lady.

MILKMAID (*singing without*).

Shame upon you, Robin,
   Shame upon you now!
Kiss me would you? with my hands
   Milking the cow?
   Daisies grow again,
   Kingcups blow again,
And you came and kiss'd me milking the cow.

Robin came behind me,       60
   Kiss'd me well, I vow.
Cuff him could I? with my hands
   Milking the cow?
   Swallows fly again,
   Cuckoos cry again,
And you came and kiss'd me milking the cow.

Come, Robin, Robin,
   Come and kiss me now;
Help it can I? with my hands
   Milking the cow?       70
   Ringdoves coo again,
   All things woo again.
Come behind and kiss me milking the cow!

*Elizabeth.* Right honest and red-cheek'd;
   Robin was violent,
And she was crafty — a sweet violence,
And a sweet craft. I would I were a milk-
   maid,
To sing, love, marry, churn, brew, bake,
   and die,
Then have my simple headstone by the
   church,
And all things lived and ended honestly.
I could not if I would. I am Harry's
   daughter.       80
Gardiner would have my head. They are
   not sweet,
The violence and the craft that do divide
The world of nature; what is weak must
   lie.
The lion needs but roar to guard his young;
The lapwing lies, says 'here' when they
   are there.
Threaten the child, 'I'll scourge you if
   you did it;'
What weapon hath the child, save his soft
   tongue,
To say 'I did not'? and my rod's the
   block.
I never lay my head upon the pillow
But that I think, 'Wilt thou lie there to-
   morrow?'       90
How oft the falling axe, that never fell,

Hath shock'd me back into the daylight
   truth
That it may fall to-day! Those damp,
   black, dead
Nights in the Tower; dead — with the fear
   of death
Too dead even for a death-watch! Toll of
   a bell,
Stroke of a clock, the scurrying of a rat
Affrighted me, and then delighted me,
For there was life — And there was life in
   death —
The little murder'd princes, in a pale light,
Rose hand in hand, and whisper'd, 'Come
   away!       100
The civil wars are gone for evermore;
Thou last of all the Tudors, come away!
With us is peace!' The last? It was a
   dream;
I must not dream, not wink, but watch.
   She has gone,
Maid Marian to her Robin — by and by
Both happy! a fox may filch a hen by
   night,
And make a morning outcry in the yard;
But there's no Renard here to 'catch her
   tripping.'
Catch who can; yet, sometime I have
   wish'd
That I were caught, and kill'd away at
   once       110
Out of the flutter. The gray rogue, Gar-
   diner,
Went on his knees, and pray'd me to con-
   fess
In Wyatt's business, and to cast myself
Upon the good Queen's mercy; ay, when,
   my lord?
God save the Queen! My jailor —

*Enter* SIR HENRY BEDINGFIELD.

*Bedingfield.*       One, whose bolts,
That jail you from free life, bar you from
   death.
There haunt some Papist ruffians hereabout
Would murder you.
   *Elizabeth.*       I thank you heartily, sir,
But I am royal, tho' your prisoner,
And God hath blest or cursed me with a
   nose —       120
Your boots are from the horses.
   *Bedingfield.*       Ay, my lady.
When next there comes a missive from the
   Queen
It shall be all my study for one hour

To rose and lavender my horsiness,
Before I dare to glance upon your Grace.
   *Elizabeth.* A missive from the Queen!
     last time she wrote,
I had like to have lost my life. It takes
     my breath —
O God, sir, do you look upon your boots,
Are you so small a man ? Help me! what
     think you,            129
Is it life or death ?
   *Bedingfield.* I thought not on my boots;
The devil take all boots were ever made
Since man went barefoot ! See, I lay it
     here,
For I will come no nearer to your Grace;
            [*Laying down the letter.*
And, whether it brings you bitter news or
     sweet,
And God hath given your Grace a nose or
     not,
I 'll help you, if I may.
   *Elizabeth.*        Your pardon, then;
It is the heat and narrowness of the cage
That makes the captive testy; with free
     wing
The world were all one Araby. Leave me
     now,            139
Will you, companion to myself, sir ?
   *Bedingfield.*        Will I ?
With most exceeding willingness, I will;
You know I never come till I be call'd.
            [*Exit.*
   *Elizabeth.* It lies there folded; is there
venom in it ?
A snake — and if I touch it, it may sting.
Come, come, the worst !
Best wisdom is to know the worst at once.
            [*Reads.*

'It is the King's wish that you should
wed Prince Philibert of Savoy. You are
to come to Court on the instant; and think
of this in your coming.      150
     'MARY THE QUEEN.'

Think ! I have many thoughts;
I think there may be bird-lime here for me;
I think they fain would have me from the
     realm;
I think the Queen may never bear a child;
I think that I may be some time the Queen,
Then, Queen indeed; no foreign prince or
     priest
Should fill my throne, myself upon the
     steps.
I think I will not marry any one,

Specially not this landless Philibert   160
Of Savoy; but, if Philip menace me,
I think that I will play with Philibert, —
As once the Holy Father did with mine, —
Before my father married my good mo-
     ther, —
For fear of Spain.

          *Enter* LADY.

   *Lady.* O Lord ! your Grace, your Grace,
I feel so happy. It seems that we shall fly
These bald, blank fields, and dance into
     the sun
That shines on princes.
   *Elizabeth.*        Yet, a moment since,
I wish'd myself the milkmaid singing here,
To kiss and cuff among the birds and
     flowers —       170
A right rough life and healthful.
   *Lady.*         But the wench
Hath her own troubles; she is weeping now;
For the wrong Robin took her at her word.
Then the cow kick'd, and all her milk was
     spilt.
Your Highness such a milkmaid ?
   *Elizabeth.*        I had kept
My Robins and my cows in sweeter order
Had I been such.
   *Lady* (*slyly*). And had your Grace a
     Robin ?
   *Elizabeth.* Come, come, you are chill
     here; you want the sun
That shines at court; make ready for the
     journey.
Pray God, we 'scape the sunstroke! Ready
     at once.         [*Exeunt.*


          SCENE VI

LONDON. A ROOM IN THE PALACE

LORD PETRE *and* LORD WILLIAM HOW-
     ARD.

   *Petre.* You cannot see the Queen. Re-
     nard denied her
Even now to me.
   *Howard.*      Their Flemish go-between
And all-in-all. I came to thank her Majesty
For freeing my friend Bagenhall from the
     Tower ;
A grace to me ! Mercy, that herb-of-
     grace,
Flowers now but seldom.
   *Petre.*        Only now, perhaps,

Because the Queen hath been three days in
    tears
For Philip's going — like the wild hedge-
    rose
Of a soft winter, possible, not probable,   9
However you have proven it.
*Howard.*               I must see her.

#### *Enter* RENARD.

*Renard.* My lords, you cannot see her
    Majesty.
    *Howard.* Why, then the King! for I
    would have him bring it
Home to the leisure wisdom of his Queen,
Before he go, that since these statutes past,
Gardiner out - Gardiners Gardiner in his
    heat,
Bonner cannot out-Bonner his own self —
Beast ! — but they play with fire as chil-
    dren do,
And burn the house. I know that these
    are breeding
A fierce resolve and fixt heart-hate in men
Against the King, the Queen, the Holy
    Father,
The faith itself. Can I not see him ?   20
    *Renard.*                 Not now.
And in all this, my lord, her Majesty
Is flint of flint; you may strike fire from
    her,
Not hope to melt her. I will give your
    message.
            [*Exeunt* Petre *and* Howard.

#### *Enter* PHILIP (*musing*).

*Philip.* She will not have Prince Phili-
    bert of Savoy,
I talk'd with her in vain — says she will
    live
And die true maid — a goodly creature too.
Would *she* had been the Queen ! yet she
    must have him.
She troubles England; that she breathes in
    England
Is life and lungs to every rebel birth   30
That passes out of embryo.
               Simon Renard ! —
This Howard, whom they fear, what was he
    saying ?
    *Renard.* What your imperial father said,
    my liege,
To deal with heresy gentlier. Gardiner
    burns,
And Bonner burns; and it would seem this
    people

Care more for our brief life in their wet
    land
Than yours in happier Spain. I told my
    lord
He should not vex her Highness; she would
    say
These are the means God works with, that
    His church   39
May flourish.
    *Philip.*      Ay, sir, but in statesmanship
To strike too soon is oft to miss the blow.
Thou knowest I bade my chaplain, Castro,
    preach
Against these burnings.
    *Renard.*             And the Emperor
Approved you, and, when last he wrote,
    declared
His comfort in your Grace that you were
    bland
And affable to men of all estates,
In hope to charm them from their hate of
    Spain.
    *Philip.* In hope to crush all heresy under
    Spain.
But, Renard, I am sicker staying here   49
Than any sea could make me passing hence,
Tho' I be ever deadly sick at sea;
So sick am I with biding for this child.
Is it the fashion in this clime for women
To go twelve months in bearing of a child ?
The nurses yawn'd, the cradle gaped, they
    led
Processions, chanted litanies, clash'd their
    bells,
Shot off their lying cannon, and her priests
Have preach'd, the fools, of this fair prince
    to come,
Till, by Saint James, I find myself the
    fool.
Why do you lift your eyebrow at me thus ?
    *Renard.* I never saw your Highness
    moved till now.   61
    *Philip.* So weary am I of this wet land
    of theirs,
And every soul of man that breathes
    therein.
    *Renard.* My liege, we must not drop the
    mask before
The masquerade is over —
    *Philip.*          Have I dropt it ?
I have but shown a loathing face to you,
Who knew it from the first.

#### *Enter* MARY.

*Mary* (*aside*).        With Renard. Still

Parleying with Renard, all the day with
    Renard,                                    68
And scarce a greeting all the day for me —
And goes to-morrow.            [*Exit* Mary.
    *Philip* (*to* Renard, *who advances to him*).
        Well, sir, is there more ?
    *Renard* (*who has perceived the* Queen).
        May Simon Renard speak a single
        word ?
    *Philip.*  Ay.
    *Renard.*            And be forgiven for it ?
    *Philip.*                      Simon Renard
Knows me too well to speak a single word
That could not be forgiven.
    *Renard.*              Well, my liege,
Your Grace hath a most chaste and loving
    wife.
    *Philip.*  Why not ?  The Queen of Philip
        should be chaste.
    *Renard.*  Ay, but, my lord, you know
        what Virgil sings,
Woman is various and most mutable.
    *Philip.*  She play the harlot ! never.
    *Renard.*                No, sire, no,
Not dream'd of by the rabidest gospeller.  80
There was a paper thrown into the pal-
    ace,
'The King hath wearied of his barren
    bride.'
She came upon it, read it, and then rent it,
With all the rage of one who hates a truth
He cannot but allow.  Sire, I would have
    you —
What should I say, I cannot pick my
    words —
Be somewhat less — majestic to your
    Queen.
    *Philip.*  Am I to change my manners,
        Simon Renard,
Because these islanders are brutal beasts ?
Or would you have me turn a sonneteer,  90
And warble those brief-sighted eyes of
    hers ?
    *Renard.*  Brief-sighted tho' they be, I
        have seen them, sire,
When you perchance were trifling royally
With some fair dame of court, suddenly fill
With such fierce fire — had it been fire in-
    deed
It would have burnt both speakers.
    *Philip.*                Ay, and then ?
    *Renard.*  Sire, might it not be policy in
        some matter
Of small importance now and then to cede
A point to her demand ?

    *Philip.*              Well, I am going.
    *Renard.*  For should her love when you
        are gone, my liege,          100
Witness these papers, there will not be
    wanting
Those that will urge her injury — should
    her love —
And I have known such women more than
    one —
Veer to the counterpoint, and jealousy
Hath in it an alchemic force to fuse
Almost into one metal love and hate, —
And she impress her wrongs upon her
    Council,
And these again upon her Parliament —
We are not loved here, and would be then
    perhaps
Not so well holpen in our wars with
    France,                          110
As else we might be — here she comes.

            *Enter* MARY.

    *Mary.*                    O Philip !
Nay, must you go indeed ?
    *Philip.*                Madam, I must.
    *Mary.*  The parting of a husband and a
        wife
Is like the cleaving of a heart; one half
Will flutter here, one there.
    *Philip.*            You say true, Madam.
    *Mary.*  The Holy Virgin will not have
        me yet
Lose the sweet hope that I may bear a
        prince.
If such a prince were born, and you not
        here !
    *Philip.*  I should be here if such a prince
        were born.
    *Mary.*  But must you go ?
    *Philip.*        Madam, you know my father,
Retiring into cloistral solitude          121
To yield the remnant of his years to
        heaven,
Will shift the yoke and weight of all the
        world
From off his neck to mine.  We meet at
        Brussels.
But since mine absence will not be for long,
Your Majesty shall go to Dover with me,
And wait my coming back.
    *Mary.*                  To Dover ? no,
I am too feeble.  I will go to Greenwich,
So you will have me with you; and there
        watch
All that is gracious in the breath of heaven

Draw with your sails from our poor land
    and pass                                    131
And leave me, Philip, with my prayers for
    you.
   *Philip.* And doubtless I shall profit by
    your prayers.
   *Mary.* Methinks that would you tarry
    one day more —
The news was sudden — I could mould my-
    self
To bear your going better; will you do
    it ?
   *Philip.* Madam, a day may sink or save
    a realm.
   *Mary.* A day may save a heart from
    breaking too.
   *Philip.* Well, Simon Renard, shall we
    stop a day ?
   *Renard.* Your Grace's business will not
    suffer, sire,                               140
For one day more, so far as I can tell.
   *Philip.* Then one day more to please her
    Majesty.
   *Mary.* The sunshine sweeps across my
    life again.
O, if I knew you felt this parting, Philip,
As I do !
   *Philip.* By Saint James I do protest,
Upon the faith and honor of a Spaniard,
I am vastly grieved to leave your Majesty.
Simon, is supper ready ?
   *Renard.*                          Ay, my liege,
I saw the covers laying.
   *Philip.*                        Let us have it.
                     [*Exeunt.*

## ACT IV

### SCENE I. — A ROOM IN THE PALACE

#### MARY, CARDINAL POLE.

   *Mary.* What have you there ?
   *Pole.*            So please your Majesty,
A long petition from the foreign exiles
To spare the life of Cranmer.  Bishop
    Thirlby,
And my Lord Paget and Lord William
    Howard,
Crave, in the same cause, hearing of your
    Grace.
Hath he not written himself — infatu-
    ated —
To sue you for his life ?
   *Mary.*                His life ?  O, no;

Not sued for that — he knows it were in
    vain.
But so much of the anti-papal leaven
Works in him yet, he hath pray'd me not
    to sully                                     10
Mine own prerogative, and degrade the
    realm
By seeking justice at a stranger's hand
Against my natural subject.    King and
    Queen,
To whom he owes his loyalty after God,
Shall these accuse him to a foreign prince ?
Death would not grieve him more.  I can-
    not be
True to this realm of England and the Pope
Together, says the heretic.
   *Pole.*               And there errs;
As he hath ever err'd thro' vanity.
A secular kingdom is but as the body      20
Lacking a soul; and in itself a beast.
The Holy Father in a secular kingdom
Is as the soul descending out of heaven
Into a body generate.
   *Mary.*          Write to him, then.
   *Pole.* I will.
   *Mary.* And sharply, Pole.
   *Pole.*        Here come the Cranmerites !

*Enter* THIRLBY, LORD PAGET, LORD WIL-
    LIAM HOWARD.

   *Howard.* Health to your Grace !  Good
    morrow, my Lord Cardinal;
We make our humble prayer unto your
    Grace
That Cranmer may withdraw to foreign
    parts,
Or into private life within the realm.
In several bills and declarations, madam,  30
He hath recanted all his heresies.
   *Paget.* Ay, ay; if Bonner have not forged
    the bills.                        [*Aside.*
   *Mary.* Did not More die, and Fisher ?
    he must burn.
   *Howard.* He hath recanted, Madam.
   *Mary.*                The better for him.
He burns in purgatory, not in hell.
   *Howard.* Ay, ay, your Grace; but it was
    never seen
That any one recanting thus at full,
As Cranmer hath, came to the fire on
    earth.
   *Mary.* It will be seen now, then.
   *Thirlby.*           O madam, madam !
I thus implore you, low upon my knees,  40
To reach the hand of mercy to my friend.

I have err'd with him; with him I have
    recanted.
What human reason is there why my
    friend
Should meet with lesser mercy than myself?
    *Mary.* My Lord of Ely, this. After a
        riot
We hang the leaders, let their following go.
Cranmer is head and father of these here-
    sies,
New learning as they call it; yea, may God
Forget me at most need when I forget
Her foul divorce — my sainted mother —
    No! —                                     50
    *Howard.* Ay, ay, but mighty doctors
        doubted there.
The Pope himself waver'd; and more than
    one
Row'd in that galley — Gardiner to wit,
Whom truly I deny not to have been
Your faithful friend and trusty councillor.
Hath not your Highness ever read his
    book,
His tractate upon True Obedience,
Writ by himself and Bonner?
    *Mary.*                    I will take
Such order with all bad, heretical books
That none shall hold them in his house and
    live,                                      60
Henceforward. No, my lord.
    *Howard.*            Then never read it.
The truth is here. Your father was a man
Of such colossal kinghood, yet so courteous,
Except when wroth, you scarce could meet
    his eye
And hold your own; and were he wroth in-
    deed,
You held it less, or not at all. I say,
Your father had a will that beat men down;
Your father had a brain that beat men
    down —
    *Pole.* Not me, my lord.
    *Howard.*        No, for you were not here;
You sit upon this fallen Cranmer's throne;
And it would more become you, my Lord
    Legate,                                    71
To join a voice, so potent with her High-
    ness,
To ours in plea for Cranmer than to stand
On naked self-assertion.
    *Mary.*                All your voices
Are waves on flint. The heretic must
    burn.
    *Howard.* Yet once he saved your Ma-
        jesty's own life;

Stood out against the King in your behalf,
At his own peril.
    *Mary.*            I know not if he did;
And if he did I care not, my Lord Howard.
My life is not so happy, no such boon,     80
That I should spare to take a heretic
    priest's,
Who saved it or not saved. Why do you
    vex me?
    *Paget.* Yet to save Cranmer were to
        serve the Church,
Your Majesty's I mean; he is effaced,
Self-blotted out; so wounded in his honor,
He can but creep down into some dark hole
Like a hurt beast, and hide himself and die;
But if you burn him, — well, your High-
    ness knows
The saying, 'Martyr's blood — seed of the
    Church.'
    *Mary.* Of the true Church; but his is
        none, nor will be.                     90
You are too politic for me, my Lord Paget.
And if he have to live so loath'd a life,
It were more merciful to burn him now.
    *Thirlby.* O, yet relent! O, madam, if
        you knew him
As I do, ever gentle, and so gracious,
With all his learning —
    *Mary.*                Yet a heretic still.
His learning makes his burning the more
    just.
    *Thirlby.* So worshipt of all those that
        came across him;
The stranger at his hearth, and all his
    house —
    *Mary.* His children and his concubine,
        belike.                               100
    *Thirlby.* To do him any wrong was to
        beget
A kindness from him, for his heart was rich,
Of such fine mould that if you sow'd there-
    in
The seed of Hate, it blossom'd Charity.
    *Pole.* 'After his kind it costs him no-
        thing,' there's
An old world English adage to the point.
These are but natural graces, my good
    bishop,
Which in the Catholic garden are as flow-
    ers,
But on the heretic dunghill only weeds.
    *Howard.* Such weeds make dunghills
        gracious.                             110
    *Mary.*            Enough, my lords.
It is God's will, the Holy Father's will,

And Philip's will, and mine, that he should
    burn.
He is pronounced anathema.
   *Howard.*                  Farewell, madam,
God grant you ampler mercy at your call
Than you have shown to Cranmer.
                                 [*Exeunt* Lords.
   *Pole.*                     After this,
Your Grace will hardly care to overlook
This same petition of the foreign exiles
For Cranmer's life.
   *Mary.*        Make out the writ to-night.
                                 [*Exeunt.*

## SCENE II

### Oxford. Cranmer in Prison

   *Cranmer.* Last night, I dream'd the fag-
      gots were alight,
And that myself was fasten'd to the stake,
And found it all a visionary flame,
Cool as the light in old decaying wood;
And then King Harry look'd from out a
      cloud,
And bade me have good courage; and I
      heard
An angel cry, ' There is more joy in Hea-
      ven,' —
And after that, the trumpet of the dead.
                     [*Trumpets without.*
Why, there are trumpets blowing now;
      what is it ?

### *Enter* Father Cole.

   *Cole.* Cranmer, I come to question you
      again.                          10
Have you remain'd in the true Catholic
      faith
I left you in ?
   *Cranmer.*       In the true Catholic faith,
By Heaven's grace, I am more and more
      confirm'd.
Why are the trumpets blowing, Father
      Cole ?
   *Cole.* Cranmer, it is decided by the
      Council
That you to-day should read your recanta-
      tion
Before the people in Saint Mary's Church.
And there be many heretics in the town,
Who loathe you for your late return to
      Rome,
And might assail you passing through the
      street,                        20

And tear you piecemeal; so you have a
      guard.
   *Cranmer.* Or seek to rescue me. I thank
      the Council.
   *Cole.* Do you lack any money ?
   *Cranmer.*         Nay, why should I ?
The prison fare is good enough for me.
   *Cole.* Ay, but to give the poor.
   *Cranmer.*         Hand it me, then !
I thank you.
   *Cole.*       For a little space, farewell;
Until I see you in Saint Mary's Church.
                              [*Exit* Cole.
   *Cranmer.* It is against all precedent to
      burn
One who recants; they mean to pardon
      me.
To give the poor — they give the poor who
      die.                            30
Well, burn me or not burn me I am fixt;
It is but a communion, not a mass,
A holy supper, not a sacrifice;
No man can make his Maker — Villa Gar-
      cia.

### *Enter* Villa Garcia.

   *Villa Garcia.* Pray you write out this
      paper for me, Cranmer.
   *Cranmer.* Have I not writ enough to
      satisfy you ?
   *Villa Garcia.* It is the last.
   *Cranmer.*           Give it me, then.
                              [*He writes.*
   *Villa Garcia.*          Now sign.
   *Cranmer.* I have sign'd enough, and I
      will sign no more.
   *Villa Garcia.* It is no more than what
      you have sign'd already,        39
The public form thereof.
   *Cranmer.*            It may be so;
I sign it with my presence, if I read it.
   *Villa Garcia.* But this is idle of you.
      Well, sir, well,
You are to beg the people to pray for you;
Exhort them to a pure and virtuous life;
Declare the Queen's right to the throne;
      confess
Your faith before all hearers; and retract
That Eucharistic doctrine in your book.
Will you not sign it now ?
   *Cranmer.*          No, Villa Garcia,
I sign no more. Will they have mercy on
      me ?
   *Villa Garcia.* Have you good hopes of
      mercy ! So, farewell.        [*Exit.*

*Cranmer.* Good hopes, not theirs, have I
   that I am fixt,         51
Fixt beyond fall; however, in strange hours,
After the long brain-dazing colloquies,
And thousand-times recurring argument
Of those two friars ever in my prison,
When left alone in my despondency,
Without a friend, a book, my faith would
   seem
Dead or half-drown'd, or else swam heavily
Against the huge corruptions of the Church,
Monsters of mistradition, old enough   60
To scare me into dreaming. 'What am I,
Cranmer, against whole ages?' was it so,
Or am I slandering my most inward friend,
To veil the fault of my most outward foe —
The soft and tremulous coward in the flesh?
O higher, holier, earlier, purer church,
I have found thee and not leave thee any
   more.
It is but a communion, not a mass —
No sacrifice, but a life-giving feast!   69
(*Writes.*) So, so; this will I say — thus
   will I pray.     [*Puts up the paper.*

### *Enter* BONNER.

*Bonner.* Good day, old friend; what, you
   look somewhat worn;
And yet it is a day to test your health
Even at the best. I scarce have spoken
   with you
Since when? — your degradation. At your
   trial
Never stood up a bolder man than you;
You would not cap the Pope's commis-
   sioner —
Your learning, and your stoutness, and
   your heresy,
Dumbfounded half of us. So, after that,
We had to dis-archbishop and unlord,   79
And make you simple Cranmer once again.
The common barber clipt your hair, and I
Scraped from your finger-points the holy
   oil;
And worse than all, you had to kneel to
   *me;*
Which was not pleasant for you, Master
   Cranmer.
Now you, that would not recognize the
   Pope,
And you, that would not own the Real
   Presence,
Have found a real presence in the stake,
Which frights you back into the ancient
   faith;

And so you have recanted to the Pope.
How are the mighty fallen, Master Cran-
   mer!
   *Cranmer.* You have been more fierce   90
   against the Pope than I;
But why fling back the stone he strikes me
   with?        [*Aside.*
O Bonner, if I ever did you kindness —
Power hath been given you to try faith by
   fire —
Pray you, remembering how yourself have
   changed,
Be somewhat pitiful, after I have gone,
To the poor flock — to women and to chil-
   dren —
That when I was archbishop held with me.
   *Bonner.* Ay — gentle as they call you —
   live or die!
Pitiful to this pitiful heresy?   100
I must obey the Queen and Council, man.
Win thro' this day with honor to yourself,
And I 'll say something for you — so —
   good-bye.      [*Exit.*
   *Cranmer.* This hard coarse man of old
   hath crouch'd to me
Till I myself was half ashamed for him.

### *Enter* THIRLBY.

Weep not, good Thirlby.
   *Thirlby.*      O, my lord, my lord!
My heart is no such block as Bonner's is:
Who would not weep?
   *Cranmer.*   Why do you so my-lord me,
Who am disgraced?
   *Thirlby.* On earth; but saved in heaven
By your recanting.
   *Cranmer.* Will they burn me, Thirlby?
   *Thirlby.* Alas, they will! these burnings
   will not help   111
The purpose of the faith; but my poor
   voice
Against them is a whisper to the roar
Of a spring-tide.
   *Cranmer.* And they will surely burn me?
   *Thirlby.* Ay; and besides will have you
   in the church
Repeat your recantation in the ears
Of all men, to the saving of their souls,
Before your execution. May God help
   you
Thro' that hard hour!
   *Cranmer.* And may God bless you,
   Thirlby!   119
Well, they shall hear my recantation there.
                  [*Exit Thirlby.*

Disgraced, dishonor'd ! — not by them, in-
     deed,
By mine own self — by mine own hand !
O thin - skinn'd hand and jutting veins,
     't was you
That sign'd the burning of poor Joan of
     Kent;
But then she was a witch.   You have writ-
     ten much,
But you were never raised to plead for
     Frith,
Whose dogmas I have reach'd.   He was
     deliver'd
To the secular arm to burn; and there was
     Lambert;
Who can foresee himself ?   truly these
     burnings,
As Thirlby says, are profitless to the burn-
     ers,                                                130
And help the other side.   You shall burn
     too,
Burn first when I am burnt.
Fire — inch by inch to die in agony ! Lati-
     mer
Had a brief end — not Ridley.   Hooper
     burn'd
Three-quarters of an hour.   Will my fag-
     gots
Be wet as his were ?   It is a day of rain.
I will not muse upon it.
My fancy takes the burner's part, and
     makes
The fire seem even crueller than it is.
No, I not doubt that God will give me
     strength,                                         140
Albeit I have denied Him.

          *Enter* Soto *and* Villa Garcia.

*Villa Garcia.*                    We are ready
To take you to Saint Mary's, Master Cran-
     mer.
     *Cranmer.*   And I.   Lead on; ye loose me
     from my bonds.              [*Exeunt.*


                    Scene III

               St. Mary's Church

Cole *in the Pulpit,* Lord Williams of
Thame *presiding.* Lord William Howard, Lord Paget, *and others.* Cranmer *enters between* Soto *and* Villa
Garcia, *and the whole Choir strike up,*
'Nunc Dimittis.' Cranmer *is set upon
a Scaffold before the people.*

     *Cole.*   Behold him —
          [*A pause : people in the foreground.*
*People.*   O, unhappy sight !
*First Protestant.*   See how the tears run
     down his fatherly face.
*Second Protestant.*   James, didst thou ever
     see a carrion crow
Stand watching a sick beast before he dies ?
     *First Protestant.*   Him perch'd up there ?
     I wish some thunderbolt
Would make this Cole a cinder, pulpit and
     all.
     *Cole.*   Behold him, brethren; he hath
     cause to weep ! —
So have we all.   Weep with him if ye will,
Yet —                                                 10
It is expedient for one man to die,
Yea, for the people, lest the people die.
Yet wherefore should he die that hath re-
     turn'd
To the one Catholic Universal Church,
Repentant of his errors ?
     *Protestant Murmurs.*        Ay, tell us that.
     *Cole.*   Those of the wrong side will de-
     spise the man,
Deeming him one that thro' the fear of
     death
Gave up his cause, except he seal his faith
In sight of all with flaming martyrdom.
     *Cranmer.*   Ay.                                  20
     *Cole.*   Ye hear him, and albeit there may
     seem
According to the canons pardon due
To him that so repents, yet are there
     causes
Wherefore our Queen and Council at this
     time
Adjudge him to the death.   He hath been
     a traitor,
A shaker and confounder of the realm;
And when the King's divorce was sued at
     Rome,
He here, this heretic metropolitan,
As if he had been the Holy Father, sat
And judged it.   Did I call him heretic ? 30
A huge heresiarch ? never was it known
That any man so writing, preaching so,
So poisoning the Church, so long continu-
     ing,
Hath found his pardon; therefore he must
     die,
For warning and example.
                              Other reasons
There be for this man's ending, which our
     Queen

And Council at this present deem it not
Expedient to be known.
    *Protestant Murmurs.*     I warrant you.
    *Cole.* Take therefore, all, example by
      this man,
For if our Holy Queen not pardon him,  40
Much less shall others in like cause escape,
That all of you, the highest as the lowest,
May learn there is no power against the
     Lord.
There stands a man, once of so high de-
     gree,
Chief prelate of our Church, archbishop, first
In Council, second person in the realm,
Friend for so long time of a mighty King;
And now ye see downfallen and debased
From councillor to caitiff — fallen so low,
The leprous flutterings of the byway, scum
And offal of the city, would not change  51
Estates with him; in brief, so miserable
There is no hope of better left for him,
No place for worse.
             Yet, Cranmer, be thou glad.
This is the work of God.  He is glorified
In thy conversion; lo ! thou art reclaim'd;
He brings thee home; nor fear but that to-
     day
Thou shalt receive the penitent thief's
     award,
And be with Christ the Lord in Paradise.
Remember how God made the fierce fire
     seem      60
To those three children like a pleasant dew.
Remember, too,
The triumph of Saint Andrew on his cross,
The patience of Saint Lawrence in the fire.
Thus, if thou call on God and all the Saints
God will beat down the fury of the flame,
Or give thee saintly strength to undergo.
And for thy soul shall masses here be sung
By every priest in Oxford.  Pray for him.
    *Cranmer.* Ay, one and all, dear brothers,
      pray for me;        ·   70
Pray with one breath, one heart, one soul
     for me.
    *Cole.* And now, lest any one among you
     doubt
The man's conversion and remorse of heart,
Yourselves shall hear him speak.  Speak,
     Master Cranmer,
Fulfil your promise made me, and proclaim
Your true undoubted faith, that all may
     hear.
    *Cranmer.* And that I will.  O God, Fa-
     ther of Heaven !

O Son of God, Redeemer of the world !
O Holy Ghost, proceeding from them both !
Three persons and one God, have mercy on
     me,      80
Most miserable sinner, wretched man !
I have offended against heaven and earth
More grievously than any tongue can tell.
Then whither should I flee for any help ?
I am ashamed to lift my eyes to heaven,
And I can find no refuge upon earth.
Shall I despair then ? — God forbid !  O
     God,
For Thou art merciful, refusing none
That come to Thee for succor, unto Thee,
Therefore, I come; humble myself to Thee;
Saying, O Lord God, although my sins be
     great,      91
For Thy great mercy have mercy !  O God
     the Son,
Not for slight faults alone, when Thou be-
     camest
Man in the flesh, was the great mystery
     wrought;
O God the Father, not for little sins
Didst Thou yield up Thy Son to human
     death !
But for the greatest sin that can be sinn'd,
Yea, even such as mine, incalculable,
Unpardonable, — sin against the light,
The truth of God, which I had proven and
     known.      100
Thy mercy must be greater than all sin.
Forgive me, Father, for no merit of mine,
But that Thy name by man be glorified,
And Thy most blessed Son's, who died for
     man.
    Good people, every man at time of death
Would fain set forth some saying that may
     live
After his death and better humankind;
For death gives life's last word a power to
     live,
And, like the stone-cut epitaph, remain
After the vanish'd voice, and speak to men.
God grant me grace to glorify my God !
And first I say it is a grievous case,    112
Many so dote upon this bubble world,
Whose colors in a moment break and fly,
They care for nothing else.  What saith
     Saint John ?
' Love of this world is hatred against God.'
Again, I pray you all that, next to God,
You do unmurmuringly and willingly
Obey your King and Queen, and not for
     dread

Of these alone, but from the fear of Him
Whose ministers they be to govern you.   121
Thirdly, I pray you all to live together
Like brethren; yet what hatred Christian
    men
Bear to each other, seeming not as brethren,
But mortal foes !  But do you good to all
As much as in you lieth.  Hurt no man
    more
Than you would harm your loving natural
    brother
Of the same roof, same breast.  If any do,
Albeit he think himself at home with God,
Of this be sure, he is whole worlds away.
    *Protestant Murmurs.*  What sort of bro-
        thers then be those that lust     131
To burn each other ?
    *Williams.*        Peace among you, there !
    *Cranmer.* Fourthly, to those that own ex-
        ceeding wealth,
Remember that sore saying spoken once
By Him that was the truth, ' How hard it
    is
For the rich man to enter into heaven ! '
Let all rich men remember that hard word.
I have not time for more; if ever, now
Let them flow forth in charity, seeing now
The poor so many, and all food so dear.
Long have I lain in prison, yet have heard
Of all their wretchedness.  Give to the
    poor,          142
Ye give to God.  He is with us in the poor.
    And now, and forasmuch as I have come
To the last end of life, and thereupon
Hangs all my past, and all my life to be,
Either to live with Christ in heaven with
    joy,
Or to be still in pain with devils in hell;
And, seeing in a moment I shall find
                        [*Pointing upwards.*
Heaven or else hell ready to swallow me,
                        [*Pointing downwards.*
I shall declare to you my very faith    151
Without all color.
    *Cole.*        Hear him, my good brethren.
    *Cranmer.* I do believe in God, Father of
        all;
In every article of the Catholic faith,
And every syllable taught us by our Lord,
His prophets, and apostles, in the Testa-
    ments,
Both Old and New.
    *Cole.*        Be plainer, Master Cranmer.
    *Cranmer.* And now I come to the great
        cause that weighs

Upon my conscience more than anything
Or said or done in all my life by me;    160
For there be writings I have set abroad
Against the truth I knew within my heart,
Written for fear of death, to save my life,
If that might be; the papers by my hand
Sign'd  since  my  degradation — by  this
    hand      [*Holding out his right hand.*
Written and sign'd — I here renounce them
    all;
And, since my hand offended, having writ-
    ten
Against my heart, my hand shall first be
    burnt,
So I may come to the fire.    [*Dead silence.*

### PROTESTANT MURMURS.

*First Protestant.* I knew it would be so.
*Second Protestant.* Our prayers are heard!
*Third Protestant.* God bless him !

### CATHOLIC MURMURS.

            Out upon him ! out upon him !
Liar ! dissembler ! traitor ! to the fire !  172
    *Williams (raising his voice).* You know
        that you recanted all you said
Touching the sacrament in that same book
You wrote against my Lord of Winches-
    ter;
Dissemble not; play the plain Christian
    man.
    *Cranmer.* Alas, my lord,
I have been a man loved plainness all my
    life;
I *did* dissemble, but the hour has come
For utter truth and plainness; wherefore, I
    say,          180
I hold by all I wrote within that book.
Moreover,
As for the Pope, I count him Antichrist,
With all his devil's doctrines, and refuse,
Reject him, and abhor him.  I have said.
    [*Cries  on  all  sides,* ' Pull  him  down !
        Away with him ! '
    *Cole.* Ay, stop the heretic's mouth !
        Hale him away !
    *Williams.* Harm him not, harm him not !
        have him to the fire !
    [*Cranmer goes out between Two Friars,
        smiling ; hands are reached to him
        from the crowd.* Lord William How-
        ard *and* Lord Paget *are left alone in
        the church.*
    *Paget.* The nave and aisles all empty as
        a fool's jest !

No, here 's Lord William Howard.  What,
　　my lord,　　　　　　　　　　　　190
You have not gone to see the burning ?
　　*Howard.*　　　　　　　　　　Fie !
To stand at ease, and stare as at a show,
And watch a good man burn.  Never again.
I saw the deaths of Latimer and Ridley.
Moreover, tho' a Catholic, I would not,
For the pure honor of our common nature,
Hear what I might — another recantation
Of Cranmer at the stake.
　　*Paget.*　　　　　You 'd not hear that.
He pass'd out smiling, and he walk'd up-
　　right;
His eye was like a soldier's, whom the gen-
　　eral　　　　　　　　　　　　　200
He looks to and he leans on as his God,
Hath rated for some backwardness and
　　bidden him
Charge one against a thousand, and the
　　man
Hurls his soil'd life against the pikes and
　　dies.
　　*Howard.*  Yet that he might not after all
　　those papers
Of recantation yield again, who knows ?
　　*Paget.*  Papers of recantation !  Think
　　you then
That Cranmer read all papers that he
　　sign'd ?
Or sign'd all those they tell us that he
　　sign'd ?
Nay, I trow not; and you shall see, my
　　Lord,　　　　　　　　　　　　210
That howsoever hero-like the man
Dies in the fire, this Bonner or another
Will in some lying fashion misreport
His ending to the glory of their church.
And you saw Latimer and Ridley die ?
Latimer was eighty, was he not ?  his best
Of life was over then.
　　*Howard.*　　　　　　His eighty years
Look'd somewhat crooked on him in his
　　frieze;
But after they had stript him to his shroud,
He stood upright, a lad of twenty-one,　220
And gather'd with his hands the starting
　　flame,
And wash'd his hands and all his face
　　therein,
Until the powder suddenly blew him dead.
Ridley was longer burning; but he died
As manfully and boldly, and, 'fore God,
I know them heretics, but right English
　　ones.

If ever, as heaven grant, we clash with
　　Spain,
Our Ridley-soldiers and our Latimer-sail-
　　ors
Will teach her something.
　　*Paget.*　　　Your mild legate Pole
Will tell you that the devil helpt them
　　thro' it.　　　　　　　　　　　230
　　[*A murmur of the Crowd in the distance.*
Hark, how those Roman wolf-dogs howl
　　and bay him !
　　*Howard.*  Might it not be the other side
　　rejoicing
In his brave end ?
　　*Paget.*  They are too crush'd, too broken,
They can but weep in silence.
　　*Howard.*　　　　　　Ay, ay, Paget,
They have brought it in large measure on
　　themselves.
Have I not heard them mock the blessed
　　Host
In songs so lewd the beast might roar his
　　claim
To being in God's image, more than they ?
Have I not seen the gamekeeper, the
　　groom,
Gardener, and huntsman, in the parson's
　　place,　　　　　　　　　　　　240
The parson from his own spire swung out
　　dead,
And Ignorance crying in the streets, and
　　all men
Regarding her ?  I say they have drawn
　　the fire
On their own heads; yet, Paget, I do hold
The Catholic, if he have the greater right,
Hath been the crueller.
　　*Paget.*　　　　　Action and reaction,
The miserable see-saw of our child-world,
Make us despise it at odd hours, my lord.
Heaven help that this reaction not react
Yet fiercelier under Queen Elizabeth　　250
So that she come to rule us.
　　*Howard.*　　　　　The world 's mad.
　　*Paget.*  My Lord, the world is like a
　　drunken man,
Who cannot move straight to his end, but
　　reels
Now to the right, then as far to the left,
Push'd by the crowd beside — and under-
　　foot
An earthquake; for since Henry for a
　　doubt —
Which a young lust had clapt upon the
　　back,

Crying, 'Forward!' — set our old church
    rocking, men
Have hardly known what to believe, or
    whether
They should believe in anything; the cur-
    rents                                        260
So shift and change, they see not how they
    are borne,
Nor whither. I conclude the King a beast;
Verily a lion if you will — the world
A most obedient beast and fool — myself
Half beast and fool as appertaining to it;
Altho' your lordship hath as little of each
Cleaving to your original Adam-clay
As may be consonant with mortality.
    *Howard.* We talk and Cranmer suffers.
The kindliest man I ever knew; see, see,
I speak of him in the past. Unhappy
    land!                                        271
Hard-natured Queen, half-Spanish in her-
    self,
And grafted on the hard-grain'd stock of
    Spain —
Her life, since Philip left her, and she lost
Her fierce desire of bearing him a child,
Hath, like a brief and bitter winter's day,
Gone narrowing down and darkening to a
    close.
There will be more conspiracies, I fear.
    *Paget.* Ay, ay, beware of France.
    *Howard.*                    O Paget, Paget!
I have seen heretics of the poorer sort,    280
Expectant of the rack from day to day,
To whom the fire were welcome, lying
    chain'd
In breathless dungeons over steaming sew-
    ers,
Fed with rank bread that crawl'd upon the
    tongue,
And putrid water, every drop a worm,
Until they died of rotted limbs; and then
Cast on the dunghill naked, and become
Hideously alive again from head to heel,
Made even the carrion-nosing mongrel
    vomit                                        289
With hate and horror.
    *Paget.*             Nay, you sicken *me*
To hear you.
    *Howard.* Fancy-sick; these things are
    done,
Done right against the promise of this
    Queen
Twice given.
    *Paget.* No faith with heretics, my lord!
Hist! there be two old gossips — gospellers,

I take it; stand behind the pillar here;
I warrant you they talk about the burning.

*Enter* TWO OLD WOMEN. JOAN, *and
        after her* TIB.

    *Joan.* Why, it be Tib!
    *Tib.* I cum behind tha, gall, and could
n't make tha hear. Eh, the wind and the
wet! What a day, what a day! nigh upo'
judgment daay loike. Pwoaps be pretty
things, Joan, but they wunt set i' the
Lord's cheer o' that daay.                      303
    *Joan.* I must set down myself, Tib; it
be a var waay vor my owld legs up vro'
Islip. Eh, my rheumatizy be that bad
howiver be I to win to the burnin'?
    *Tib.* I should saay 't wur ower by now.
I 'd ha' been here avore, but Dumble wur
blow'd wi' the wind, and Dumble 's the best
milcher in Islip.                               311
    *Joan.* Our Daisy 's as good 'z her.
    *Tib.* Noa, Joan.
    *Joan.* Our Daisy's butter 's as good 'z
hern.
    *Tib.* Noa, Joan.
    *Joan.* Our Daisy's cheeses be better.
    *Tib.* Noa, Joan.
    *Joan.* Eh, then ha' thy waay wi' me,
Tib; ez thou hast wi' thy owld man.            320
    *Tib.* Ay, Joan, and my owld man wur
up and awaay betimes wi' dree hard eggs
for a good pleace at the burnin'; and barrin'
the wet, Hodge 'ud ha' been a-harrowin' o'
white peasen i' the outfield — and barrin'
the wind, Dumble wur blow'd wi' the wind,
so 'z we was forced to stick her, but we
fetched her round at last. Thank the Lord
therevore. Dumble 's the best milcher in
Islip.                                          330
    *Joan.* Thou 's thy way wi' man and
beast, Tib. I wonder at tha, it beats me!
Eh, but I do know ez Pwoaps and vires be
bad things; tell 'ee now, I heerd summat
as summun towld summun o' owld Bishop
Gardiner's end; there wur an owld lord
a-cum to dine wi' un, and a wur so owld a
could n't bide vor his dinner, but a had to
bide howsomiver, vor 'I wunt dine,' says
my Lord Bishop, says he, 'not till I hears
ez Latimer and Ridley be a-vire;' and so
they bided on and on till vour o' the clock,
till his man cum in post vro' here, and tells
un ez the vire has tuk holt. 'Now,' says
the Bishop, says he, 'we 'll gwo to dinner;'
and the owld lord fell to 's meat wi' a will,

God bless un! but Gardiner wur struck
down like by the hand o' God avore a could
taste a mossel, and a set un all a-vire, so 'z
the tongue on un cum a-lolluping out o' 'is
mouth as black as a rat.  Thank the Lord
therevore !                                          352
   *Paget.*  The fools !
   *Tib.*  Ay, Joan; and Queen Mary gwoes
on a-burnin' and a-burnin', to get her baaby
born; but all her burnin's 'ill never burn
out the hypocrisy that makes the water in
her.  There 's nought but the vire of God's
hell ez can burn out that.
   *Joan.*  Thank the Lord therevore !     360
   *Paget.*  The fools !
   *Tib.*  A-burnin', and a-burnin', and a-mak-
in' o' volk madder and madder; but tek
thou my word vor 't, Joan, — and I bean't
wrong not twice i' ten year — the burnin'
o' the owld archbishop 'll burn the Pwoap
out o' this 'ere land vor iver and iver.
   *Howard.*  Out of the church, you brace
          of cursed crones,
Or I will have you duck'd ! (*Women
          hurry out.*)  Said I not right ?
For how should reverend prelate or
          throned prince                         370
Brook for an hour such brute malignity ?
Ah, what an acrid wine has Luther brew'd !
   *Paget.*  Pooh, pooh, my lord ! poor gar-
          rulous country-wives.
Buy you their cheeses, and they 'll side
          with you;
You cannot judge the liquor from the
          lees.
   *Howard.*  I think that in some sort we
          may.  But see,

                *Enter* PETERS.

Peters, my gentleman, an honest Catho-
          lic,
Who follow'd with the crowd to Cranmer's
          fire.                                     378
One that would neither misreport nor lie,
Not to gain paradise; no, nor if the Pope
Charged him to do it — he is white as death.
Peters, how pale you look ! you bring the
          smoke
Of Cranmer's burning with you.
   *Peters.*                          Twice or thrice
The smoke of Cranmer's burning wrapt me
          round.
   *Howard.*  Peters, you know me Catholic,
          but English.

Did he die bravely ?  Tell me that, or
          leave
All else untold.
   *Peters.*  My lord, he died most bravely.
   *Howard.*  Then tell me all.
   *Paget.*          Ay, Master Peters, tell us.
   *Peters.*  You saw him how he past among
          the crowd;                               389
And ever as he walk'd the Spanish friars
Still plied him with entreaty and reproach;
But Cranmer, as the helmsman at the helm
Steers, ever looking to the happy haven
Where he shall rest at night, moved to his
          death;
And I could see that many silent hands
Came from the crowd and met his own;
          and thus,
When we had come where Ridley burnt
          with Latimer,
He, with a cheerful smile, as one whose
          mind
Is all made up, in haste put off the rags
They had mock'd his misery with, and all
          in white,                                400
His long white beard, which he had never
          shaven
Since Henry's death, down-sweeping to the
          chain
Wherewith they bound him to the stake,
          he stood
More like an ancient father of the Church
Than heretic of these times; and still the
          friars
Plied him, but Cranmer only shook his head,
Or answer'd them in smiling negatives;
Whereat Lord Williams gave a sudden
          cry : —
' Make short ! make short !' and so they
          lit the wood.
Then Cranmer lifted his left hand to hea-
          ven,                                     410
And thrust his right into the bitter flame;
And crying, in his deep voice, more than
          once,
' This hath offended — this unworthy
          hand !'
So held it till it all was burn'd, before
The flame had reach'd his body; I stood
          near —
Mark'd him — he never uttered moan of
          pain.
He never stirr'd or writhed, but, like a
          statue,
Unmoving in the greatness of the flame,

Gave up the ghost; and so past martyr-
  like —
Martyr I may not call him — past — but
  whither ?                               420
*Paget.* To purgatory, man, to purgatory.
*Peters.* Nay, but, my lord, he denied pur-
  gatory.
*Paget.* Why then to heaven, and God ha'
  mercy on him !
*Howard.* Paget, despite his fearful here-
  sies,
I loved the man, and needs must moan for
  him;
O Cranmer !
*Paget.*      But your moan is useless now.
Come out, my lord, it is a world of fools.
                                  [*Exeunt.*

## ACT V

SCENE I. — LONDON.  HALL IN THE
  PALACE

QUEEN, SIR NICHOLAS HEATH.

*Heath.* Madam,
I do assure you that it must be look'd
  to.
Calais is but ill-garrison'd, in Guisnes
Are scarce two hundred men, and the
  French fleet
Rule in the narrow seas. It must be look'd
  to,
If war should fall between yourself and
  France;
Or you will lose your Calais.
*Mary.*            It shall be look'd to;
I wish you a good morning, good Sir Nich-
  olas.
Here is the King.           [*Exit Heath.*

### Enter PHILIP.

*Philip.*        Sir Nicholas tells you true,
And you must look to Calais when I go.  10
*Mary.* Go ? must you go, indeed —
  again — so soon ?
Why, nature's licensed vagabond, the swal-
  low,
That might live always in the sun's warm
  heart,
Stays longer here in our poor North than
  you —
Knows where he nested — ever comes
  again.
*Philip.* And, Madam, so shall I.

*Mary.*        O, will you ? will you ?
I am faint with fear that you will come no
  more.
*Philip.* Ay, ay; but many voices call me
  hence.
*Mary.* Voices — I hear unhappy rumors
  — nay,                                  19
I say not, I believe. What voices call
  you
Dearer than mine that should be dearest to
  you ?
Alas, my lord ! what voices and how
  many ?
*Philip.* The voices of Castile and Ara-
  gon,
Granada, Naples, Sicily, and Milan, —
The voices of Franche - Comté, and the
  Netherlands,
The voices of Peru and Mexico,
Tunis, and Oran, and the Philippines,
And all the fair spice-islands of the East.
*Mary* (*admiringly*). You are the mighti-
  est monarch upon earth,
I but a little Queen; and so, indeed,   30
Need you the more.
*Philip.*          A little Queen ! but when
I came to wed your majesty, Lord How-
  ard,
Sending an insolent shot that dash'd the
  seas
Upon us, made us lower our kingly flag
To yours of England.
*Mary.*              Howard is all English !
There is no king, not were he ten times
  king,
Ten times our husband, but must lower his
  flag
To that of England in the seas of England.
*Philip.* Is that your answer ?
*Mary.*              Being Queen of England,
I have none other.
*Philip.*      So.
*Mary.*              But wherefore not
Helm the huge vessel of your State, my
  liege,                                  41
Here by the side of her who loves you
  most ?
*Philip.* No, madam, no ! a candle in the
  sun
Is all but smoke — a star beside the moon
Is all but lost; your people will not crown
  me —
Your people are as cheerless as your clime.
Hate me and mine; witness the brawls, the
  gibbets.

Here swings a Spaniard — there an Eng-
    lishman;
The peoples are unlike as their complex-
    ion;
Yet will I be your swallow and return —
But now I cannot bide.
    *Mary.*                    Not to help *me* ?
They hate *me* also for my love to you,    52
My Philip; and these judgments on the
    land —
Harvestless autumns, horrible agues,
    plague —
    *Philip.* The blood and sweat of heretics
        at the stake
Is God's best dew upon the barren field.
Burn more !
    *Mary.* I will, I will; and you will stay ?
    *Philip.* Have I not said ? Madam, I
        came to sue
Your Council and yourself to declare war.
    *Mary.* Sir, there are many English in
        your ranks    60
To help your battle.
    *Philip.*                    So far, good. I say
I came to sue your Council and yourself
To declare war against the King of France.
    *Mary.* Not to see me ?
    *Philip.*                    Ay, madam, to see you.
Unalterably and pesteringly fond !
                                        [*Aside.*
But soon or late you must have war with
    France;
King Henry warms your traitors at his
    hearth.
Carew is there, and Thomas Stafford there.
Courtenay, belike —
    *Mary.*                    A fool and featherhead !
    *Philip.* Ay, but they use his name. In
        brief, this Henry    70
Stirs up your land against you to the in-
    tent
That you may lose your English heritage.
And then, your Scottish namesake marry-
    ing
The Dauphin, he would weld France, Eng-
    land, Scotland,
Into one sword to hack at Spain and me.
    *Mary.* And yet the Pope is now col-
        leagued with France;
You make your wars upon him down in
    Italy —
Philip, can that be well ?
    *Philip.*                    Content you, madam;
You must abide my judgment, and my
    father's,

Who deems it a most just and holy war.    80
The Pope would cast the Spaniard out of
    Naples;
He calls us worse than Jews, Moors, Sara-
    cens.
The Pope has pushed his horns beyond his
    mitre —
Beyond his province.  Now,
Duke Alva will but touch him on the
    horns,
And he withdraws; and of his holy head —
For Alva is true son of the true Church —
No hair is harm'd.  Will you not help me
    here ?
    *Mary.* Alas ! the Council will not hear
        of war.
They say your wars are not the wars of
    England.                    90
They will not lay more taxes on a land
So hunger - nipt and wretched; and you
    know
The crown is poor.  We have given the
    church-lands back.
The nobles would not; nay, they clapt their
    hands
Upon their swords when ask'd; and there-
    fore God
Is hard upon the people.  What 's to be
    done ?
Sir, I will move them in your cause again,
And we will raise us loans and subsidies
Among the merchants; and Sir Thomas
    Gresham
Will aid us.  There is Antwerp and the
    Jews.                    100
    *Philip.* Madam, my thanks.
    *Mary.*            And you will stay your going ?
    *Philip.* And further to discourage and
        lay lame
The plots of France, altho' you love her
    not,
You must proclaim Elizabeth your heir.
She stands between you and the Queen of
    Scots.
    *Mary.* The Queen of Scots at least is
        Catholic.
    *Philip.* Ay, madam, Catholic; but I will
        not have
The King of France the King of England
    too.
    *Mary.* But she 's a heretic, and, when I
        am gone,                    109
Brings the new learning back.
    *Philip.*                    It must be done.
You must proclaim Elizabeth your heir.

*Mary.* Then it is done; but you will
    stay your going
Somewhat beyond your settled purpose?
    *Philip.*                          No !
    *Mary.* What, not one day ?
    *Philip.*              You beat upon the rock.
    *Mary.* And I am broken there.
    *Philip.*                   Is this a place
To wail in, madam ? what ! a public hall ?
Go in, I pray you.
    *Mary.*           Do not seem so changed.
Say go; but only say it lovingly.
    *Philip.* You do mistake.  I am not one
        to change.                      119
I never loved you more.
    *Mary.*               Sire, I obey you.
Come quickly.
    *Philip.*   Ay.            [*Exit* Mary.

### Enter Count de Feria.

    *Feria* (*aside*).  The Queen in tears !
    *Philip.*                           Feria !
Hast thou not mark'd — come closer to
        mine ear —
How doubly aged this Queen of ours hath
        grown
Since she lost hope of bearing us a child ?
    *Feria.* Sire, if your Grace hath mark'd
        it, so have I.
    *Philip.* Hast thou not likewise mark'd
        Elizabeth,
How fair and royal — like a queen, in-
        deed ?
    *Feria.* Allow me the same answer as be-
        fore —
That if your Grace hath mark'd her, so
        have I.
    *Philip.* Good, now; methinks my Queen
        is like enough                130
To leave me by and by.
    *Feria.*               To leave you, sire ?
    *Philip.* I mean not like to live. Eliza-
        beth —
To Philibert of Savoy, as you know,
We meant to wed her; but I am not sure
She will not serve me better — so my
        Queen
Would leave me — as — my wife.
    *Feria.*                   Sire, even so.
    *Philip.* She will not have Prince Phili-
        bert of Savoy.
    *Feria.* No, sire.
    *Philip.*  I have to pray you, some odd
        time,

To sound the Princess carelessly on this;
Not as from me, but as your phantasy;  140
And tell me how she takes it.
    *Feria.*                  Sire, I will.
    *Philip.* I am not certain but that Phili-
        bert
Shall be the man; and I shall urge his
        suit
Upon the Queen, because I am not certain.
You understand, Feria.
    *Feria.*           Sire, I do.
    *Philip.* And if you be not secret in this
        matter,
You understand me there, too ?
    *Feria.*                   Sire, I do.
    *Philip.* You must be sweet and supple,
        like a Frenchman.
She is none of those who loathe the honey-
        comb.
                            [*Exit* Feria.

### Enter Renard.

    *Renard.* My liege, I bring you goodly
        tidings.
    *Philip.*        Well ?
    *Renard.* There *will* be war with France,
        at last, my liege;                151
Sir Thomas Stafford, a bull-headed ass,
Sailing from France, with thirty English-
        men,
Hath taken Scarboro' Castle, north of York;
Proclaims himself protector, and affirms
The Queen has forfeited her right to reign
By marriage with an alien — other things
As idle; a weak Wyatt !  Little doubt
This buzz will soon be silenced; but the
        Council —
I have talk'd with some already — are for
        war.                            160
This is the fifth conspiracy hatch'd in
        France;
They show their teeth upon it; and your
        Grace,
So you will take advice of mine, should
        stay
Yet for a while, to shape and guide the
        event.
    *Philip.* Good ! Renard, I will stay then.
    *Renard.*                       Also, sire,
Might I not say — to please your wife, the
        Queen ?
    *Philip.* Ay, Renard, if you care to put
        it so.
                          [*Exeunt.*

## SCENE II

### A Room in the Palace

MARY, *sitting: a rose in her hand.* LADY
CLARENCE. ALICE *in the background.*

*Mary.* Look ! I have play'd with this
    poor rose so long
I have broken off the head.
    *Lady Clarence.* Your Grace hath been
More merciful to many a rebel head
That should have fallen, and may rise
    again.
    *Mary.* There were not many hang'd for
    Wyatt's rising.
    *Lady Clarence.* Nay, not two hundred.
    *Mary.*          I could weep for them
And her, and mine own self and all the
    world.
    *Lady Clarence.* For her ? for whom,
    your Grace ?

### *Enter* USHER.

*Usher.*           The Cardinal.

*Enter* CARDINAL POLE (MARY *rises*).

*Mary.* Reginald Pole, what news hath
    plagued thy heart ?
What makes thy favor like the bloodless
    head           10
Fallen on the block, and held up by the
    hair ?
Philip ? —
    *Pole.*      No, Philip is as warm in life
As ever.
    *Mary.* Ay, and then as cold as ever.
Is Calais taken ?
    *Pole.*        Cousin, there hath chanced
A sharper harm to England and to Rome
Than Calais taken.  Julius the Third
Was ever just, and mild, and father-like;
But this new Pope Caraffa, Paul the
    Fourth,
Not only reft me of that legateship    19
Which Julius gave me, and the legateship
Annex'd to Canterbury — nay, but worse —
And yet I must obey the Holy Father,
And so must you, good cousin; — worse
    than all,
A passing bell toll'd in a dying ear —
He hath cited me to Rome, for heresy,
Before his Inquisition.
    *Mary.*        I knew it, cousin,

But held from you all papers sent by
    Rome,
That you might rest among us, till the
    Pope,
To compass which I wrote myself to Rome,
Reversed his doom, and that you might not
    seem      30
To disobey his Holiness.
    *Pole.*          He hates Philip;
He is all Italian, and he hates the Span-
    iard;
He cannot dream that *I* advised the war;
He strikes thro' me at Philip and yourself.
Nay, but I know it of old, he hates me
    too;
So brands me in the stare of Christendom
A heretic !
Now, even now, when bow'd before my
    time,
The house half-ruin'd ere the lease be out;
When I should guide the Church in peace
    at home,      40
After my twenty years of banishment,
And all my lifelong labor to uphold
The primacy — a heretic !  Long ago,
When I was ruler in the patrimony,
I was too lenient to the Lutheran,
And I and learned friends among ourselves
Would freely canvass certain Lutheran-
    isms.
What then, he knew I was no Lutheran.
A heretic !
He drew this shaft against me to the
    head,      50
When it was thought I might be chosen
    Pope,
But then withdrew it.  In full consistory,
When I was made archbishop, he approved
    me.
And how should he have sent me legate
    hither,
Deeming me heretic ? and what heresy
    since ?
But he was evermore mine enemy,
And hates the Spaniard — fiery-choleric,
A drinker of black, strong, volcanic wines,
That ever make him fierier.  I, a heretic ?
Your Highness knows that in pursuing
    heresy      60
I have gone beyond your late Lord Chan-
    cellor, —
He cried 'Enough ! enough !' before his
    death, —
Gone beyond him and mine own natural
    man —

It was God's cause — so far they call me
    now
The scourge and butcher of their English
    church.
  *Mary.* Have courage, your reward is
    heaven itself.
  *Pole.* They groan amen; they swarm
    into the fire
Like flies — for what? no dogma. They
    know nothing;
They burn for nothing.
  *Mary.*          You have done your best.
  *Pole.* Have done my best, and as a faith-
    ful son,                 70
That all day long hath wrought his father's
    work,
When back he comes at evening hath the
    door
Shut on him by the father whom he loved,
His early follies cast into his teeth,
And the poor son turn'd out into the street
To sleep, to die — I shall die of it, cousin.
  *Mary.* I pray you be not so disconso-
    late ;
I still will do mine utmost with the Pope.
Poor cousin !
Have not I been the fast friend of your
    life                       80
Since mine began, and it was thought we
    two
Might make one flesh, and cleave unto each
    other
As man and wife ?
  *Pole.*        Ah, cousin, I remember
How I would dandle you upon my knee
At lisping-age. I watch'd you dancing
    once
With your huge father; he look'd the
    Great Harry,
You but his cockboat; prettily you did it,
And innocently. No — we were not made
One flesh in happiness, no happiness here;
But now we are made one flesh in mis-
    ery;                       90
Our bridemaids are not lovely — Disap-
    pointment,
Ingratitude, Injustice, Evil-tongue,
Labor-in-vain.
  *Mary.*        Surely, not all in vain.
Peace, cousin, peace ! I am sad at heart
    myself.
  *Pole.* Our altar is a mound of dead men's
    clay,
Dug from the grave that yawns for us be-
    yond;

And there is one Death stands behind the
    groom,
And there is one Death stands behind the
    bride —
  *Mary.* Have you been looking at the
    ' Dance of Death ' ?
  *Pole.* No; but these libellous papers
    which I found              100
Strewn in your palace. Look you here —
    the Pope
Pointing at me with ' Pole, the heretic,
Thou hast burnt others, do thou burn thy-
    self,
Or I will burn thee;' and this other;
    see ! —
' We pray continually for the death
Of our accursed Queen and Cardinal Pole.'
This last — I dare not read it her. [*Aside.*
  *Mary.*                    Away !
Why do you bring me these ?
I thought you knew me better. I never
    read,
I tear them; they come back upon my
    dreams.                110
The hands that write them should be burnt
    clean off
As Cranmer's, and the fiends that utter
    them
Tongue-torn with pincers, lash'd to death,
    or lie
Famishing in black cells, while famish'd
    rats
Eat them alive. Why do they bring me
    these ?
Do you mean to drive me mad ?
  *Pole.*            I had forgotten
How these poor libels trouble you. Your
    pardon,
Sweet cousin, and farewell ! ' O bubble
    world,
Whose colors in a moment break and fly ! '
Why, who said that ? I know not — true
    enough !               120
    [*Puts up the papers, all but the last,*
    *which falls. Exit* Pole.
  *Alice.* If Cranmer's spirit were a mock-
    ing one,
And heard these two, there might be sport
    for him.            [*Aside.*
  *Mary.* Clarence, they hate me; even
    while I speak
There lurks a silent dagger, listening
In some dark closet, some long gallery,
    drawn,
And panting for my blood as I go by.

*Lady Clarence.* Nay, madam, there be
    loyal papers too,
And I have often found them.
    *Mary.*                 Find me one !
    *Lady Clarence.* Ay, madam; but Sir
    Nicholas Heath, the Chancellor,
Would see your Highness.
    *Mary.*     Wherefore should I see him ?
    *Lady Clarence.* Well, Madam, he may
    bring you news from Philip.     131
    *Mary.* So, Clarence.
    *Lady Clarence.* Let me first put up your
    hair;
It tumbles all abroad.
    *Mary.*            And the gray dawn
Of an old age that never will be mine
Is all the clearer seen. No, no; what mat-
    ters ?
Forlorn I am, and let me look forlorn.

*Enter* SIR NICHOLAS HEATH.

    *Heath.* I bring your Majesty such griev-
    ous news
I grieve to bring it. Madam, Calais is
    taken.
    *Mary.* What traitor spoke ? Here, let
    my cousin Pole
Seize him and burn him for a Lutheran. 140
    *Heath.* Her Highness is unwell. I will
    retire.
    *Lady Clarence.* Madam, your Chancel-
    lor, Sir Nicholas Heath.
    *Mary.* Sir Nicholas ! I am stunn'd —
    Nicholas Heath ?
Methought some traitor smote me on the
    head.
What said you, my good lord, that our
    brave English
Had sallied out from Calais and driven
    back
The Frenchmen from their trenches ?
    *Heath.*             Alas ! no.
That gateway to the mainland over which
Our flag hath floated for two hundred years
Is France again.
    *Mary.*       So; but it is not lost —
Not yet. Send out; let England as of old
Rise lionlike, strike hard and deep into 152
The prey they are rending from her — ay,
    and rend
The renders too. Send out, send out, and
    make
Musters in all the counties; gather all
From sixteen years to sixty; collect the
    fleet;

Let every craft that carries sail and gun
Steer toward Calais. Guisnes is not taken
    yet ?
    *Heath.* Guisnes is not taken yet.
    *Mary.*            There yet is hope.
    *Heath.* Ah, madam, but your people are
    so cold;                  160
I do much fear that England will not care.
Methinks there is no manhood left among
    us.
    *Mary.* Send out; I am too weak to stir
    abroad.
Tell my mind to the Council — to the Par-
    liament;
Proclaim it to the winds. Thou art cold
    thyself
To babble of their coldness. O, would I
    were
My father for an hour ! Away now —
    quick !              [*Exit* Heath.
I hoped I had served God with all my
    might !
It seems I have not. Ah ! much heresy
Shelter'd in Calais. Saints, I have re-
    built                    170
Your shrines, set up your broken images;
Be comfortable to me. Suffer not
That my brief reign in England be de-
    famed
Thro' all her angry chronicles hereafter
By loss of Calais. Grant me Calais. Philip,
We have made war upon the Holy Father
All for your sake. What good could come
    of that ?
    *Lady Clarence.* No, Madam, not against
    the Holy Father;
You did but help King Philip's war with
    France,
Your troops were never down in Italy. 180
    *Mary.* I am a byword. Heretic and rebel
Point at me and make merry. Philip gone !
And Calais gone ! Time that I were gone
    too !
    *Lady Clarence.* Nay, if the fetid gutter
    had a voice
And cried I was not clean, what should I
    care ?
Or you, for heretic cries ? And I believe,
Spite of your melancholy Sir Nicholas,
Your England is as loyal as myself.
    *Mary* (*seeing the paper dropt by* Pole).
        There ! there ! another paper ! Said
        you not
Many of these were loyal ? Shall I try 190
If this be one of such ?

*Lady Clarence.*          Let it be, let it be.
God pardon me ! I have never yet found
          one.          [*Aside.*
     *Mary* (*reads*). 'Your people hate you as
          your husband hates you.'
Clarence, Clarence, what have I done ?
          what sin
Beyond all grace, all pardon ? Mother of
          God,
Thou knowest never woman meant so well,
And fared so ill in this disastrous world.
My people hate me and desire my death.
     *Lady Clarence.* No, madam, no.
     *Mary.* My husband hates me, and de-
sires my death.                              200
     *Lady Clarence.* No, madam; these are
          libels.
     *Mary.* I hate myself, and I desire my
          death.
     *Lady Clarence.* Long live your Majesty !
          Shall Alice sing you
One of her pleasant songs ? Alice, my
          child,
Bring us your lute (Alice *goes*). They say
          the gloom of Saul
Was lighten'd by young David's harp.
     *Mary.*                              Too young !
And never knew a Philip.

               *Re-enter* ALICE.
                              Give *me* the lute.
He hates me !

               (*She sings.*)

Hapless doom of woman happy in betrothing !
Beauty passes like a breath, and love is lost in
          loathing.                              210
Low, my lute ; speak low, my lute, but say the
          world is nothing —
               Low, lute, low !
Love will hover round the flowers when they
          first awaken ;
Love will fly the fallen leaf, and not be over-
          taken.
Low, my lute ! O, low, my lute ! we fade and
          are forsaken —
               Low, dear lute, low !

Take it away ! not low enough for me !
     *Alice.* Your Grace hath a low voice.
     *Mary.*                    How dare you say it ?
Even for that he hates me. A low voice
Lost in a wilderness where none can hear !
A voice of shipwreck on a shoreless sea !
A low voice from the dust and from the
          grave !                              222

(*Sitting on the ground*). There, am I low
          enough now ?
     *Alice.* Good Lord ! how grim and ghastly
          looks her Grace,
With both her knees drawn upward to her
          chin.
There was an old-world tomb beside my
          father's,
And this was open'd, and the dead were
          found
Sitting, and in this fashion; she looks a
          corpse.

          *Enter* LADY MAGDALEN DACRES.

     *Lady Magdalen.* Madam, the Count de
          Feria waits without,
In hopes to see your Highness.
     *Lady Clarence* (*pointing to* Mary). Wait
          he must —                              230
Her trance again She neither sees nor
          hears,
And may not speak for hours.
     *Lady Magdalen.*                    Unhappiest
Of queens and wives and women !
     *Alice* (*in the foreground with* Lady Mag-
          dalen).                    And all along
Of Philip.
     *Lady Magdalen.* Not so loud ! Our
          Clarence there
Sees ever such an aureole round the Queen,
It gilds the greatest wronger of her peace,
Who stands the nearest to her.
     *Alice.*                    Ay, this Philip;
I used to love the Queen with all my
          heart —
God help me, but methinks I love her
          less
For such a dotage upon such a man.          240
I would I were as tall and strong as you.
     *Lady Magdalen.* I seem half-shamed at
          times to be so tall.
     *Alice.* You are the stateliest deer in all
          the herd —
Beyond his aim — but I am small and
          scandalous,
And love to hear bad tales of Philip.
     *Lady Magdalen.*                    Why ?
I never heard him utter worse of you
Than that you were low-statured.
     *Alice.*                    Does he think
Low stature is low nature, or all women's
Low as his own ?
     *Lady Magdalen.* There you strike in the
          nail.
This coarseness is a want of phantasy.          250

It is the low man thinks the woman low;
Sin is too dull to see beyond himself.

*Alice.* Ah, Magdalen, sin is bold as well
as dull.
How dared he ?

*Lady Magdalen.* Stupid soldiers oft are
bold.
Poor lads, they see not what the general
sees,
A risk of utter ruin.  I am *not*
Beyond his aim, or was not.

*Alice.* Who ? Not you ?
Tell, tell me; save my credit with myself.

*Lady Magdalen.* I never breathed it to
a bird in the eaves,
Would not for all the stars and maiden
moon     260
Our drooping Queen should know !  In
Hampton Court
My window look'd upon the corridor;
And I was robing; — this poor throat of
mine
Barer than I should wish a man to see it, —
When he we speak of drove the window
back,
And, like a thief, push'd in his royal hand ;
But by God's providence a good stout staff
Lay near me, and you know me strong of
arm.
I do believe I lamed his Majesty's
For a day or two, tho', give the devil his due,
I never found he bore me any spite.    271

*Alice.* I would she could have wedded
that poor youth,
My Lord of Devon, — light enough, God
knows,
And mixt with Wyatt's rising, — and the
boy
Not out of him — but neither cold, coarse,
cruel,
And more than all — no Spaniard.

*Lady Clarence.*       Not so loud.
Lord Devon, girls !  what are you whispering here ?

*Alice.* Probing an old state-secret —
how it chanced
That this young earl was sent on foreign
travel,
Not lost his head.

*Lady Clarence.* There was no proof
against him.     280

*Alice.* Nay, madam; did not Gardiner in-
tercept
A letter which the Count de Noailles wrote
To that dead traitor Wyatt, with full proof
Of Courtenay's treason ?  What became
of that ?

*Lady Clarence.* Some say that Gardiner,
out of love for him,
Burnt it, and some relate that it was lost
When Wyatt sack'd the Chancellor's
house in Southwark.
Let dead things rest.

*Alice.* Ay, and with him who died
Alone in Italy.

*Lady Clarence.* Much changed, I hear,
Had put off levity and put graveness on.
The foreign courts report him in his man-
ner     291
Noble as his young person and old shield.
It might be so — but all is over now;
He caught a chill in the lagoons of Venice,
And died in Padua.

*Mary (looking up suddenly).* Died in the
true faith ?

*Lady Clarence.* Ay, madam, happily.

*Mary.*         Happier he than I.

*Lady Magdalen.* It seems her Highness
hath awaken'd.  Think you
That I might dare to tell her that the
count —

*Mary.* I will see no man hence for evermore,
Saving my confessor and my cousin Pole.

*Lady Magdalen.* It is the Count de Feria, my dear lady.     301

*Mary.* What count ?

*Lady Magdalen.* The Count de Feria,
from his Majesty
King Philip.

*Mary.* Philip !  quick !  loop up my hair !
Throw cushions on that seat, and made it
thronelike.
Arrange my dress — the gorgeous Indian
shawl
That Philip brought me in our happy
days ! —
That covers all.  So — am I somewhat
queenlike,
Bride of the mightiest sovereign upon
earth ?

*Lady Clarence.* Ay, so your Grace would
bide a moment yet.     310

*Mary.* No, no, he brings a letter.  I
may die
Before I read it.  Let me see him at once.

*Enter* COUNT DE FERIA (*kneels*).

*Feria.* I trust your Grace is well.
(*Aside.*)  How her hand burns !

*Mary.* I am not well, but it will better me,
Sir Count, to read the letter which you
bring.
*Feria.* Madam, I bring no letter.
*Mary.* How! no letter?
*Feria.* His Highness is so vex'd with
strange affairs —
*Mary.* That his own wife is no affair of
his.
*Feria.* Nay, madam, nay! he sends his
veriest love,     319
And says he will come quickly.
*Mary.* Doth he, indeed?
You, sir, do *you* remember what *you* said
When last you came to England?
*Feria.* Madam, I brought
My King's congratulations; it was hoped
Your Highness was once more in happy
state
To give him an heir male.
*Mary.* Sir, you said more;
You said he would come quickly. I had
horses
On all the road from Dover, day and
night;
On all the road from Harwich, night and
day;
But the child came not, and the husband
came not;
And yet he will come quickly. — Thou hast
learnt     330
Thy lesson, and I mine. There is no need
For Philip so to shame himself again.
Return,
And tell him that I know he comes no
more.
Tell him at last I know his love is dead,
And that I am in state to bring forth
death —
Thou art commission'd to Elizabeth,
And not to me!
*Feria.* Mere compliments and wishes.
But shall I take some message from your
Grace?
*Mary.* Tell her to come and close my
dying eyes,     340
And wear my crown, and dance upon my
grave.
*Feria.* Then I may say your Grace will
see your sister?
Your Grace is too low-spirited. Air and
sunshine.
I would we had you, madam, in our warm
Spain.
You droop in your dim London.

*Mary.* Have him away!
I sicken of his readiness.
*Lady Clarence.* My Lord Count,
Her Highness is too ill for colloquy.
*Feria (kneels and kisses her hand).* I wish
her Highness better. (*Aside.*) How
her hand burns!     [*Exeunt.*

## SCENE III

### A House near London

ELIZABETH, STEWARD OF THE HOUSE-
HOLD, ATTENDANTS.

*Elizabeth.* There's half an angel wrong'd
in your account;
Methinks I am all angel, that I bear it
Without more ruffling. Cast it o'er again.
*Steward.* I were whole devil if I wrong'd
you, madam.     [*Exit* Steward.
*Attendant.* The Count de Feria, from
the King of Spain.
*Elizabeth.* Ah! — let him enter. Nay,
you need not go:     [*To her* Ladies.
Remain within the chamber, but apart.
We'll have no private conference. Wel-
come to England!

### Enter FERIA.

*Feria.* Fair island star!
*Elizabeth.* I shine! What else, Sir
Count?
*Feria.* As far as France, and into Philip's
heart.     10
My King would know if you be fairly
served,
And lodged, and treated.
*Elizabeth.* You see the lodging, sir.
I am well-served, and am in everything
Most loyal and most grateful to the Queen.
*Feria.* You should be grateful to my
master, too.
He spoke of this; and unto him you owe
That Mary hath acknowledged you her
heir.
*Elizabeth.* No, not to her nor him; but
to the people,
Who know my right, and love me, as I love
The people! whom God aid!
*Feria.* You will be Queen,
And, were I Philip —
*Elizabeth.* Wherefore pause you — what?
*Feria.* Nay, but I speak from mine own
self, not him.     22
Your royal sister cannot last; your hand

Will be much coveted ! What a delicate
　　one !
Our Spanish ladies have none such — and
　　there,
Were you in Spain, this fine fair gossamer
　　gold —
Like sun-gilt breathings on a frosty dawn —
That hovers round your shoulder —
　　*Elizabeth.*　　　　　　　　　Is it so fine ?
Troth, some have said so.
　　*Feria.*　　— would be deemed a miracle.
　　*Elizabeth.* Your Philip hath gold hair
　　　　and golden beard;　　　　　　　　30
There must be ladies many with hair like
　　mine.
　　*Feria.* Some few of Gothic blood have
　　　　golden hair,
But none like yours.
　　*Elizabeth.*　　I am happy you approve it.
　　*Feria.* But as to Philip and your Grace,
　　— consider, —
If such a one as you should match with
　　Spain,
What hinders but that Spain and England
　　join'd
Should make the mightiest empire earth
　　has known.
Spain would be England on her seas, and
　　England
Mistress of the Indies.
　　*Elizabeth.* It may chance that England
Will be the Mistress of the Indies yet,　　40
Without the help of Spain.
　　*Feria.* 　　　　　　　　　Impossible;
Except you put Spain down.
Wide of the mark even for a madman's
　　dream.
　　*Elizabeth.* Perhaps; but we have seamen.
　　Count de Feria,
I take it that the King hath spoken to you;
But is Don Carlos such a goodly match ?
　　*Feria.* Don Carlos, Madam, is but twelve
　　years old.
　　*Elizabeth.* Ay, tell the King that I will
　　　　muse upon it;
He is my good friend, and I would keep
　　him so;
But — he would have me Catholic of
　　Rome,　　　　　　　　　　　　　50
And that I scarce can be; and, sir, till now
My sister's marriage, and my father's mar-
　　riages,
Make me full fain to live and die a maid.
But I am much beholden to your King.
Have you aught else to tell me ?

　　*Feria.* 　　　　　　　　Nothing, madam,
Save that methought I gather'd from the
　　Queen
That she would see your Grace before she
　　— died.
　　*Elizabeth.* God's death ! and wherefore
　　　　spake you not before ?
We dally with our lazy moments here,
And hers are number'd. Horses there,
　　without !　　　　　　　　　　　　60
I am much beholden to the King, your
　　master.
Why did you keep me prating ? Horses,
　　there !　　　　　　　[*Exit* Elizabeth, *etc.*
　　*Feria.* So from a clear sky falls the thun-
　　derbolt !
Don Carlos ? Madam, if you marry Philip,
Then I and he · will snaffle your ' God's
　　death,'
And break your paces in, and make you
　　tame.
God's death, forsooth — you do not know
　　King Philip !　　　　　　　　　[*Exit.*


　　　　　　　　　SCENE IV

　　LONDON.  BEFORE THE PALACE

*A light burning within.  Voices of the night
　　　　　　　passing.*

　　*First.* Is not yon light in the Queen's
　　chamber ?
　　*Second.* 　　　　　　　　Ay,
They say she 's dying.
　　*First.* 　　　　　　So is Cardinal Pole.
May the great angels join their wings, and
　　make
Down for their heads to heaven !
　　*Second.* 　　　　　　Amen.  Come on.
　　　　　　　　　　　　　　　[*Exeunt.*
　　　　　　　　TWO OTHERS.

　　*First.* There 's the Queen's light.  I hear
　　she cannot live.
　　*Second.* God curse her and her legate !
　　Gardiner burns
Already; but to pay them full in kind,
The hottest hold in all the devil's den
Were but a sort of winter.  Sir, in Guern-
　　sey,
I watch'd a woman burn; and in her agony
The mother came upon her — a child was
　　born —　　　　　　　　　　　　11
And, sir, they hurl'd it back into the fire,
That, being but baptized in fire, the babe

Might be in fire for ever.   Ah, good neigh-
    bor,
There should be something fiercer than
    fire
To yield them their deserts.
    *First.*                         Amen to all
Your wish, and further !
    *A Third Voice.*  Deserts ! Amen to what ?
Whose deserts ?  Yours ?  You have a gold
ring on your finger, and soft raiment about
your body; and is not the woman up yonder sleeping after all she has done, in peace
and quietness, on a soft bed, in a closed
room, with light, fire, physic, tendance;
and I have seen the true men of Christ
lying famine-dead by scores, and under no
ceiling but the cloud that wept on them,
not for them.
    *First.*  Friend, tho' so late, it is not safe
    to preach.
You had best go home.   What are you ?  30
    *Third.*  What am I ?   One who cries
continually with sweat and tears to the
Lord God that it would please Him out of
His infinite love to break down all kingship and queenship, all priesthood and pre-
lacy; to cancel and abolish all bonds of
human allegiance, all the magistracy, all
the nobles, and all the wealthy; and to
send us again, according to His promise,
the one King, the Christ, and all things in
common, as in the day of the first church,
when Christ Jesus was King.              42
    *First.*  If ever I heard a madman, — let 's
    away !
Why, you long-winded — Sir, you go be-
    yond me.
I pride myself on being moderate.
Good night !  Go home !  Besides, you
    curse so loud,
The watch will hear you.   Get you home
    at once.                    [*Exeunt:*

## SCENE V

### LONDON.   A ROOM IN THE PALACE

*A Gallery on one side.   The moonlight
streaming through a range of windows on
the wall opposite.   MARY, LADY CLAR-
ENCE, LADY MAGDALEN DACRES, ALICE.
QUEEN pacing the Gallery.   A writing-
table in front.   QUEEN comes to the table
and writes and goes again, pacing the Gallery.*

    *Lady Clarence.*  Mine eyes are dim: what
    hath she written ? read.
    *Alice.*  'I am dying, Philip; come to me.'
    *Lady Magdalen.*  There — up and down,
    poor lady, up and down.
    *Alice.*  And how her shadow crosses one
    by one
The moonlight casements pattern'd on the
    wall,
Following her like her sorrow !  She turns
    again.
        [*Queen sits and writes, and goes again.*
    *Lady Clarence.*  What hath she written
    now ?
    *Alice.*  Nothing; but 'come, come, come,'
    and all awry,
And blotted by her tears.   This cannot
    last.                     [*Queen returns.*
    *Mary.*  I whistle to the bird has broken
    cage,                                       10
And all in vain.                  [*Sitting down.*
Calais gone — Guisnes gone,  too — and
    Philip gone !
    *Lady Clarence.*  Dear madam, Philip is
    but at the wars;
I cannot doubt but that he comes again;
And he is with you in a measure still.
I never look'd upon so fair a likeness
As your great King in armor there, his
    hand
· Upon his helmet.
        [*Pointing to the portrait of* Philip *on the
        wall.*
    *Mary.*             Doth he not look noble ?
I had heard of him in battle over seas,
And I would have my warrior all in arms.
He said it was not courtly to stand hel-
    meted                                       21
Before the Queen.   He had his gracious
    moment,
Altho' you 'll not believe me.   How he
    smiles
As if he loved me yet !
    *Lady Clarence.*             And so he does.
    *Mary.*  He never loved me — nay, he
    could not love me.
It was his father's policy against France.
I am eleven years older than he,.
Poor boy !                          [*Weeps.*
    *Alice.*  That was a lusty boy of twenty-
    seven;                          [*Aside.*
Poor enough in God's grace !
    *Mary.*               And all in vain !
The Queen of Scots is married to the
    Dauphin,                                    31

And Charles, the lord of this low world, is
    gone;
And all his wars and wisdoms past away;
And in a moment I shall follow him.
    *Lady Clarence.* Nay, dearest lady, see
your good physician.
    *Mary.* Drugs — but he knows they can-
not help me — says
That rest is all — tells me I must not
    think —
That I must rest — I shall rest by and
    by.
Catch the wild cat, cage him, and when he
    springs
And maims himself against the bars, say
    ' rest.'            40
Why, you must kill him if you would have
    him rest —
Dead or alive, you cannot make him happy.
    *Lady Clarence.* Your Majesty has lived
so pure a life,
And done such mighty things by Holy
    Church,
I trust that God will make you happy yet.
    *Mary.* What is the strange thing happi-
ness ?   Sit down here.
Tell me thine happiest hour.
    *Lady Clarence.*           I will, if that
May make your Grace forget yourself a
    little.
There runs a shallow brook across our field
For twenty miles, where the black crow
    flies five,          50
And doth so bound and babble all the way
As if itself were happy.   It was May-time,
And I was walking with the man I loved.
I loved him, but I thought I was not loved.
And both were silent, letting the wild
    brook
Speak for us — till he stoop'd and gather'd
    one
From out a bed of thick forget-me-nots,
Look'd hard and sweet at me, and gave it
    me.
I took it, tho' I did not know I took it,
And put it in my bosom, and all at once  60
I felt his arms about me, and his lips —
    *Mary.* O God ! I have been too slack,
too slack;
There are Hot Gospellers even among our
    guards —
Nobles we dared not touch.  We have but
    burnt
The heretic priest, workmen, and women
    and children.

Wet, famine, ague, fever, storm, wreck,
    wrath, —
We have so play'd the coward; but by
    God's grace,
We 'll follow Philip's leading, and set up
The Holy Office here — garner the wheat,
And burn the tares with unquenchable
    fire !          70
Burn ! —
Fie, what a savor ! tell the cooks to close
The doors of all the offices below.
Latimer !
Sir, we are private with our women here —
Ever a rough, blunt, and uncourtly fellow —
Thou light a torch that never will go out !
'T is out — mine flames.  Women, the Holy
    Father
Has ta'en the legateship from our cousin
    Pole —
Was that well done ? and poor Pole pines
    of it,          80
As I do, to the death.  I am but a woman,
I have no power. — Ah, weak and meek
    old man,
Sevenfold dishonor'd even in the sight
Of thine own sectaries — No, no.  No par-
    don ! —
Why, that was false; there is the right
    hand still
Beckons me hence.
Sir, you were burnt for heresy, not for
    treason,
Remember that ! 't was I and Bonner did it,
And Pole; we are three to one — Have you
    found mercy there,
Grant it me here — and see, he smiles and
    goes,          90
Gentle as in life.
    *Alice.* Madam, who goes ?  King Philip ?
    *Mary.* No, Philip comes and goes, but
never goes.
Women, when I am dead,
Open my heart, and there you will find
    written
Two names, Philip and Calais; open his, —
So that he have one, —
You will find Philip only, policy, policy, —
Ay, worse than that — not one hour true to
    me !
Foul maggots crawling in a fester'd vice !
Adulterous to the very heart of hell !   100
Hast thou a knife ?
    *Alice.* Ay, madam, but o' God's mercy —
    *Mary.* Fool, think'st thou I would peril
mine own soul

By slaughter of the body ? I could not,
    girl,
Not this way — callous with a constant
    stripe,
Unwoundable. The knife !
    *Alice.*          Take heed, take heed !
The blade is keen as death.
    *Mary.*          This Philip shall not
Stare in upon me in my haggardness;
Old, miserable, diseased,
Incapable of children. Come thou down.
    [*Cuts out the picture and throws it down.*
Lie there. (*Wails.*) O God, I have kill'd
    my Philip !
    *Alice.*      No,          110
Madam, you have but cut the canvas out;
We can replace it.
    *Mary.*          All is well then; rest
I will to rest; he said I must have rest.
    [*Cries of* ' Elizabeth ' *in the street.*
A cry ! What 's that ? Elizabeth ? revolt ?
A new Northumberland, another Wyatt ?
I 'll fight it on the threshold of the grave.
    *Lady Clarence.* Madam, your royal sister
        comes to see you.
    *Mary.* I will not see her.
Who knows if Boleyn's daughter be my
    sister ?
I will see none except the priest. Your
    arm.          [*To* Lady Clarence.
O Saint of Aragon, with that sweet worn
    smile          121
Among thy patient wrinkles — help me
    hence.          [*Exeunt.*

*The* PRIEST *passes. Enter* ELIZABETH *and*
    SIR WILLIAM CECIL.

    *Elizabeth.* Good counsel yours. — No
        one in waiting ? still,
As if the chamberlain were Death him-
    self !
The room she sleeps in — is not this the
    way ?
No, that way there are voices. Am I too
    late ?
Cecil . . . God guide me lest I lose the
    way !          [*Exit* Elizabeth.
    *Cecil.* Many points weather'd, many
        perilous ones,
At last a harbor opens; but therein
Sunk rocks — they need fine steering —
    much it is          130
To be nor mad nor bigot — have a mind —
Nor let priests' talk, or dream of worlds to
    be,

Miscolor things about her — sudden touches
For him, or him — sunk rocks; no passion-
    ate faith —
But — if let be — balance and compromise;
Brave, wary, sane to the heart of her — a
    Tudor
School'd by the shadow of death — a Bo-
    leyn, too,
Glancing across the Tudor — not so well.

*Enter* ALICE.

How is the good Queen now ?
    *Alice.*          Away from Philip.
Back in her childhood — prattling to her
    mother          140
Of her betrothal to the Emperor Charles,
And childlike-jealous of him again — and
    once
She thank'd her father sweetly for his book
Against that godless German. Ah, those
    days
Were happy. It was never merry world
In England since the Bible came among us.
    *Cecil.* And who says that ?
    *Alice.* It is a saying among the Catho-
        lics.
    *Cecil.* It never will be merry world in
        England
Till all men have their Bible, rich and
    poor.          150
    *Alice.* The Queen is dying, or you dare
        not say it.

*Enter* ELIZABETH.

    *Elizabeth.* The Queen is dead.
    *Cecil.*      Then here she stands ! my hom-
        age.
    *Elizabeth.* She knew me, and acknow-
        ledged me her heir,
Pray'd me to pay her debts, and keep the
    Faith;
Then claspt the cross, and pass'd away in
    peace.
I left her lying still and beautiful,
More beautiful than in life. Why would
    you vex yourself,
Poor sister ? Sir, I swear I have no heart
To be your Queen. To reign is restless
    fence,
Tierce, quart, and trickery. Peace is with
    the dead.          160
Her life was winter, for her spring was
    nipt;
And she loved much: pray God she be for-
    given !

*Cecil.* Peace with the dead, who never
    were at peace !
Yet she loved one so much — I needs must
    say —
That never English monarch dying left
England so little.
    *Elizabeth.*       But with Cecil's aid
And others, if our person be secured
From traitor stabs — we will make Eng-
    land great.

*Enter* PAGET, *and other* LORDS OF THE
    COUNCIL, SIR RALPH BAGENHALL, *etc.*

    *Lords.* God save Elizabeth, the Queen of
      England !
    *Bagenhall.* God save the Crown ! the
      Papacy is no more.         170
    *Paget (aside).* Are we so sure of that ?
    *Acclamation.*       God save the Queen !

---

# HAROLD

## A DRAMA

Published in 1876, but dated 1877. See prefatory note to 'Queen Mary,' and 'Memoir,' vol
ii. pp. 186–192.

### To His Excellency
### THE RIGHT HON. LORD LYTTON,
*Viceroy and Governor-General of India.*

MY DEAR LORD LYTTON, — After old-world records — such as the Bayeux tapestry and the Roman de Rou, — Edward Freeman's History of the Norman Conquest,
and your father's Historical Romance treating of the same times, have been mainly
helpful to me in writing this Drama. Your father dedicated his 'Harold' to my
father's brother ; allow me to dedicate my 'Harold' to yourself.

                                      A. TENNYSON.

---

## SHOW–DAY AT BATTLE ABBEY, 1876

A GARDEN here — May breath and bloom of spring —
The cuckoo yonder from an English elm
Crying, ' With my false egg I overwhelm
The native nest ; ' and fancy hears the ring
Of harness, and that deathful arrow sing,
And Saxon battle-axe clang on Norman helm.
Here rose the dragon-banner of our realm ;
Here fought, here fell, our Norman-slander'd king.
O Garden blossoming out of English blood !
O strange hate-healer Time ! We stroll and stare
Where might made right eight hundred years ago ;
Might, right ? ay, good, so all things make for good —
But he and he, if soul be soul, are where
Each stands full face with all he did below.

---

### DRAMATIS PERSONÆ

KING EDWARD THE CONFESSOR.
STIGAND, *created Archbishop of Canterbury by the Antipope Benedict.*
ALDRED, *Archbishop of York.*
THE NORMAN BISHOP OF LONDON.
HAROLD, *Earl of Wessex, afterwards King of England*
TOSTIG, *Earl of Northumbria*
GURTH, *Earl of East Anglia*                } *Sons of Godwin*
LEOFWIN, *Earl of Kent and Essex*
WULFNOTH

COUNT WILLIAM OF NORMANDY.
WILLIAM RUFUS.
WILLIAM MALET, *a Norman Noble.*[1]
EDWIN, *Earl of Mercia*
MORCAR, *Earl of Northumbria after Tostig* } *Sons of Alfgar of Mercia.*
GAMEL, *a Northumbrian Thane.*
GUY, *Count of Ponthieu.*
ROLF, *a Ponthieu Fisherman.*
HUGH MARGOT, *a Norman Monk.*
OSGOD *and* ATHELRIC, *Canons from Waltham.*
THE QUEEN, *Edward the Confessor's Wife, Daughter of Godwin.*
ALDWYTH, *Daughter of Alfgar and widow of Griffyth, King of Wales.*
EDITH, *Ward of King Edward.*

Courtiers, Earls and Thanes, Men-at-Arms, Canons of Waltham, Fishermen, etc.

# HAROLD

## ACT I

SCENE I.—LONDON. THE KING'S PALACE

(*A comet seen through the open window.*)

ALDWYTH, GAMEL, COURTIERS *talking together.*

*First Courtier.* Lo! there once more —
    this is the seventh night!
Yon grimly - glaring, treble - brandish'd
    scourge
Of England!
*Second Courtier.* Horrible!
*First Courtier.*    Look you, there's a star
That dances in it as mad with agony!
*Third Courtier.* Ay, like a spirit in hell
    who skips and flies
To right and left, and cannot scape the
    flame.
*Second Courtier.* Steam'd upward from
    the undescendible
Abysm.
*First Courtier.* Or floated downward from
    the throne
Of God Almighty.
*Aldwyth.*        Gamel, son of Orm,
What thinkest thou this means?
*Gamel.*            War, my dear lady!
*Aldwyth.* Doth this affright thee?
*Gamel.*        Mightily, my dear lady!
*Aldwyth.* Stand by me then, and look
    upon my face,                    12
Not on the comet.

*Enter* MORCAR.

            Brother! why so pale?
*Morcar.* It glares in heaven, it flares
    upon the Thames,

The people are as thick as bees below,
They hum like bees, — they cannot speak
            — for awe;
Look to the skies, then to the river, strike
Their hearts, and hold their babies up to it.
I think that they would Molochize them too,
To have the heavens clear.
    *Aldwyth.*        They fright not me.

*Enter* LEOFWIN, *after him* GURTH.

Ask thou Lord Leofwin what he thinks of
    this!                            21
*Morcar.* Lord Leofwin, dost thou believe
    that these
Three rods of blood-red fire up yonder
    mean
The doom of England and the wrath of
    Heaven?
*Bishop of London* (*passing*). Did ye not
    cast with bestial violence
Our holy Norman bishops down from all
Their thrones in England? I alone re-
    main.
Why should not Heaven be wroth?
    *Leofwin.*        With us, or thee?
*Bishop of London.* Did ye not outlaw
    your archbishop Robert,
Robert of Jumièges — well-nigh murder
    him too?                        30
Is there no reason for the wrath of Heaven?
    *Leofwin.* Why, then the wrath of Hea-
    ven hath three tails,
The devil only one.
            [*Exit* Bishop of London.

*Enter* ARCHBISHOP STIGAND.

            Ask *our* archbishop.
Stigand should know the purposes of Hea-
    ven.
*Stigand.* Not I. I cannot read the face
    of heaven;

---

[1] . . . quidam partim Normannus et Anglus
    Compater Heraldi. (*Guy of Amiens,* 587.)

Perhaps our vines will grow the better for
   it.
   *Leofwin* (*laughing*).  He can but read the
     King's face on his coins.
   *Stigand.*  Ay, ay, young lord, *there* the
     King's face is power.
   *Gurth.*  O father, mock not at a public
     fear,
But tell us, is this pendent hell in heaven
A harm to England ?
   *Stigand.*               Ask it of King Edward !
And he may tell thee *I* am a harm to Eng-
     land.                                                    42
Old uncanonical Stigand — ask of *me*
Who had my pallium from an Antipope !
Not he the man — for in our windy world
What 's up is faith, what 's down is heresy.
Our friends, the Normans, holp to shake
     his chair.
I have a Norman fever on me, son,
And cannot answer sanely. — What it
     means ?
Ask our broad earl.
         [*Pointing to* Harold, *who enters.*
   *Harold* (*seeing* Gamel).  Hail, Gamel, son
     of Orm !
Albeit no rolling stone, my good friend
     Gamel,                                                   51
Thou hast rounded since we met.  Thy life
     at home
Is easier than mine here.  Look ! am I not
Work-wan, flesh-fallen ?
   *Gamel.*           Art thou sick, good earl ?
   *Harold.*  Sick as an autumn swallow for
     a voyage,
Sick for an idle week of hawk and hound
Beyond the seas — a change !  When cam-
     est thou hither ?
   *Gamel.*  To-day, good earl.
   *Harold.*       Is the North quiet, Gamel ?
   *Gamel.*  Nay, there be murmurs, for thy
     brother breaks us
With over-taxing — quiet, ay, as yet —    60
Nothing as yet.
   *Harold.*    Stand by him, mine old friend,
Thou art a great voice in Northumberland !
Advise him; speak him sweetly, he will
     hear thee.
He is passionate but honest.  Stand thou
     by him !
More talk of this to-morrow, if yon weird
     sign
Not blast us in our dreams. — Well, father
     Stigand —
         [*To* Stigand, *who advances to him.*

   *Stigand* (*pointing to the comet*).  War
     there, my son ? is that the doom of
     England ?
   *Harold.*  Why not the doom of all the
     world as well ?
For all the world sees it as well as England.
These meteors came and went before our
     day.                                                      70
Not harming any; it threatens us no more
Than French or Norman.  War ? the worst
     that follows
Things that seem jerk'd out of the com-
     mon rut
Of Nature is the hot religious fool,
Who, seeing war in heaven, for heaven's
     credit
Makes it on earth — but look, where Ed-
     ward draws
A faint foot hither, leaning upon Tostig.
He hath learnt to love our Tostig much of
     late.
   *Leofwin.*  And *he* hath learnt, despite the
     tiger in him,
To sleek and supple himself to the King's
     hand.                                                    80
   *Gurth.*  I trust the kingly touch that
     cures the evil
May serve to charm the tiger out of him.
   *Leofwin.*  He hath as much of cat as
     tiger in him.
Our Tostig loves the hand and not the man.
   *Harold.*  Nay !  Better die than lie !

     *Enter* KING, QUEEN, *and* TOSTIG.

   *Edward.*                In heaven signs !
Signs upon earth !  signs everywhere !  your
     priests
Gross, worldly, simoniacal, unlearn'd !
They scarce can read their Psalter; and
     your churches
Uncouth, unhandsome, while in Norman-
     land                                                     89
God speaks thro' abler voices, as He dwells
In statelier shrines.  I say not this, as
     being
Half Norman-blooded, nor, as some have
     held,
Because I love the Norman better — no,
But dreading God's revenge upon this
     realm
For narrowness and coldness; and I say it
For the last time perchance, before I go
To find the sweet refreshment of the
     Saints.
I have lived a life of utter purity;

I have builded the great church of Holy
    Peter;
I have wrought miracles — to God the
    glory ! —                              100
And miracles will in my name be wrought
Hereafter. — I have fought the fight and
    go —
I see the flashing of the gates of pearl —
And it is well with me, tho' some of you
Have scorn'd me — ay — but after I am
    gone
Woe, woe to England ! I have had a
    vision;
The Seven Sleepers in the cave at Ephesus
Have turn'd from right to left.
    *Harold.*        My most dear master,
What matters ? let them turn from left to
    right
And sleep again.
    *Tostig.*        Too hardy with thy King !
A life of prayer and fasting well may see
Deeper into the mysteries of heaven     112
Than thou, good brother.
    *Aldwyth* (*aside*).     Sees he into thine,
That thou wouldst have his promise for the
    crown ?
    *Edward.* Tostig says true; my son, thou
art too hard,
Not stagger'd by this ominous earth and
    heaven;
But heaven and earth are threads of the
    same loom,
Play into one another, and weave the web
That may confound thee yet.
    *Harold.*        Nay, I trust not,
For I have served thee long and honestly.
    *Edward.* I know it, son; I am not thank-
less; thou                               121
Hast broken all my foes, lighten'd for me
The weight of this poor crown, and left me
    time
And peace for prayer to gain a better one.
Twelve years of service ! England loves
    thee for it.
Thou art the man to rule her !
    *Aldwyth* (*aside*).     So, not Tostig !
    *Harold.* And after those twelve years a
    boon, my King,
Respite, a holiday, — thyself wast wont
To love the chase, — thy leave to set my
    feet
On board, and hunt and hawk beyond the
    seas !
    *Edward.* What, with this flaming horror
    overhead ?                          131

    *Harold.* Well, when it passes then.
    *Edward.*          Ay, if it pass.
Go not to Normandy — go not to Nor-
    mandy.
    *Harold.* And wherefore not, my King, to
    Normandy ?
Is not my brother Wulfnoth hostage there
For my dead father's loyalty to thee ?
I pray thee, let me hence and bring him
    home.
    *Edward.* Not thee, my son; some other
    messenger.
    *Harold.* And why not me, my lord, to
    Normandy ?                          139
Is not the Norman Count thy friend and
    mine ?
    *Edward.* I pray thee, do not go to Nor-
    mandy.
    *Harold.* Because my father drove the
    Normans out
Of England ? — That was many a summer
    gone —
Forgotten and forgiven by them and thee.
    *Edward.* Harold, I will not yield thee
    leave to go.
    *Harold.* Why, then to Flanders. I will
    hawk and hunt
In Flanders.
    *Edward.* Be there not fair woods and
    fields
In England ? Wilful, wilful ! Go — the
    Saints
Pilot and prosper all thy wandering out   149
And homeward ! — Tostig, I am faint
    again. —
Son Harold, I will in and pray for thee.
    [*Exit, leaning on* Tostig, *and followed by*
      Stigand, Morcar, *and* Courtiers.
    *Harold.* What lies upon the mind of our
    good King,
That he should harp this way on Nor-
    mandy ?
    *Queen.* Brother, the King is wiser than
    he seems;
And Tostig knows it; Tostig loves the
    King.
    *Harold.* And love should know; and —
    be the King so wise, —
Then Tostig too were wiser than he seems.
I love the man, but not his phantasies.

            *Re-enter* TOSTIG.

                     Well, brother,
When didst thou hear from thy Northum-
    bria ?

*Tostig.*  When did I hear aught but this
      ' *When* ' from thee ?                    160
Leave me alone, brother, with my North-
      umbria;
She is *my* mistress, let *mc* look to her !
The King hath made me earl; make me not
      fool !
Nor make the King a fool, who made me
      earl !
  *Harold.*  No, Tostig — lest I make my-
      self a fool
Who made the King who made thee make
      thee earl.
  *Tostig.*  Why chafe me then ?    Thou
      knowest I soon go wild.
  *Gurth.*  Come, come ! as yet thou art not
      gone so wild
But thou canst hear the best and wisest of
      us.
  *Harold.*  So says old Gurth, not I; yet
      hear ! thine earldom,                    170
Tostig, hath been a kingdom.  Their old
      crown
Is yet a force among them, a sun set
But leaving light enough for Alfgar's
      house
To strike thee down by — nay, this ghastly
      glare
May heat their fancies.
  *Tostig.*                My most worthy brother,
Thou art the quietest man in all the
      world —
Ay, ay, and wise in peace and great in
      war —
Pray God the people choose thee for their
      king !
But all the powers of the house of God-
      win
Are not enframed in thee.
  *Harold.*            Thank the Saints, no !
Bu' thou hast drain'd them shallow by thy
      tolls,                    181
And thou art ever here about the King.
Thine absence well may **seem** a want of
      care.
Cling to their love; for, now the sons of
      Godwin
Sit topmost in the field of England, envy,
Like the rough bear beneath the tree, good
      brother,
Wai*ts* till the man let go.
  *Tostig.*            Good counsel truly !
I heard from my Northumbria yesterday.
  *Harold.*  How goes it then with thy
      Northumbria ?   Well ?

*Tostig.*  And wouldst thou that it went
      aught else than well ?                    190
  *Harold.*  I would it went as well as with
      minc earldom,
Leofwin's and Gurth's.
  *Tostig.*            Ye govern milder men.
  *Gurth.*  We have made them milder by
      just government.
  *Tostig.*  Ay, ever give yourselves your
      own good word.
  *Leofwin.*  An honest gift, by all the
      Saints, if giver
And taker be but honest ! but they bribe
Each other, and so often, an honest world
Will not believe them.
  *Harold.*          I may tell thee, Tostig,
I heard from thy Northumberland to-day.
  *Tostig.*  From spies of thine to spy my
      nakedness                    200
In my poor North.
  *Harold.*      There is a movement there,
A blind one — nothing yet.
  *Tostig.*              Crush it at once
With all the power I have ! — I must — I
      will ! —
Crush it half-born !   Fool still ? or wisdom
      there,
My wise head-shaking Harold ?
  *Harold.*                Make not thou
The nothing something.  Wisdom when in
      power
And wisest should not frown as Power, but
      smile
As kindness, watching all, till the true *must*
Shall make her strike as Power: but when
      to strike —                    209
O Tostig, O dear brother — if they prance,
Rein in, not lash them, lest they rear and
      run
And break both neck and axle.
  *Tostig.*                Good again !
Good counsel tho' scarce needed.  Pour
      not water
In the full vessel running out at top
To swamp the house.
  *Leofwin.*        Nor thou be a wild thing
Out of the waste, to turn and bite the hand
Would help thee from the trap.
  *Tostig.*                Thou playest in tune.
  *Leofwin.*  To the deaf adder thee, that
      wilt not dance
However wisely charm'd.
  *Tostig.*              No more, no more !
  *Gurth.*  I likewise cry ' no more.'  Un-
      wholesome talk                    220

For Godwin's house ! Leofwin, thou hast a
     tongue !
Tostig, thou look'st as thou wouldst spring
     upon him.
Saint Olaf, not while I am by ! Come,
     come,
Join hands, let brethren dwell in unity;
Let kith and kin stand close as our shield-
     wall,
Who breaks us then ? I say, thou hast a
     tongue,
And Tostig is not stout enough to bear it.
Vex him not, Leofwin.
     *Tostig.*          No, I am not vext, —
Altho' ye seek to vex me, one and all.
I have to make report of my good earl-
     dom                              230
To the good King who gave it — not to
     you —
Not any of you. — I am not vext at all.
     *Harold.* The King ? the King is ever at
     his prayers;
In all that handles matter of the state
I am the King.
     *Tostig.*      That shalt thou never be
If I can thwart thee.
     *Harold.*          Brother, brother !
     *Tostig.*               Away !
                       [*Exit* Tostig.
     *Queen.* Spite of this grisly star ye three
     must gall
Poor Tostig.
     *Leofwin.* Tostig, sister, galls himself;
He cannot smell a rose but pricks his nose
Against the thorn, and rails against the
     rose.
     *Queen.* I am the only rose of all the
     stock                              241
That never thorn'd him; Edward loves
     him, so
Ye hate him. Harold always hated him.
Why — how they fought when boys — and,
     Holy Mary !
How Harold used to beat him !
     *Harold.*      Why, boys will fight.
Leofwin would often fight me, and I beat
     him.
Even old Gurth would fight. I had much
     ado
To hold mine own against old Gurth. Old
     Gurth,
We fought like great States for grave
     cause; but Tostig —
On a sudden — at a something — for a no-
     thing —                        250

The boy would fist me hard, and when we
     fought
I conquer'd, and he loved me none the less,
Till thou wouldst get him all apart, and
     tell him
That where he was but worsted he was
     wrong'd.
Ah ! thou hast taught the King to spoil
     him too;
Now the spoilt child sways both. Take
     heed, take heed;
Thou art the Queen; ye are boy and girl
     no more.
Side not with Tostig in any violence,
Lest thou be sideways guilty of the vio-
     lence.
     *Queen.* Come, fall not foul on me. I
     leave thee, brother.             260
     *Harold.* Nay, my good sister —
         [*Exeunt* Queen, Harold, Gurth, *and*
         Leofwin.
     *Aldwyth.*          Gamel, son of Orm,
What thinkest thou this means ?
                     [*Pointing to the comet.*
     *Gamel.*          War, my dear lady,
War, waste, plague, famine, all malignities.
     *Aldwyth.* It means the fall of Tostig
     from his earldom.
     *Gamel.* That were too small a matter
     for a comet !
     *Aldwyth.* It means the lifting of the
     house of Alfgar.
     *Gamel.* Too small ! a comet would not
     show for that !
     *Aldwyth.* Not small for thee, if thou
     canst compass it.
     *Gamel.* Thy love ?
     *Aldwyth.* As much as I can give thee,
     man;
This Tostig is, or like to be, a tyrant.    270
Stir up thy people; oust him !
     *Gamel.*          And thy love ?
     *Aldwyth.* As much as thou canst bear.
     *Gamel.*          I can bear all,
And not be giddy.
     *Aldwyth.*      No more now; to-morrow.


## SCENE II

IN THE GARDEN. THE KING'S HOUSE
NEAR LONDON. SUNSET

     *Edith.* Mad for thy mate, passionate
     nightingale ! —
I love thee for it — ay, but stay a moment;

*He* can but stay a moment; he is going.
I fain would hear him coming ! — near
   me — near,
Somewhere — to draw him nearer with a
   charm
Like thine to thine !

    (*Singing.*)

Love is come with a song and a smile,
Welcome Love with a smile and a song.
Love can stay but a little while.
Why cannot he stay ?   They call him away.
Ye do him wrong, ye do him wrong;      11
Love will stay for a whole life long.

    *Enter* HAROLD.

   *Harold*. The nightingales in Havering-
    atte-Bower
Sang out their loves so loud that Edward's
   prayers
Were deafen'd and he pray'd them dumb,
   and thus
I dumb thee too, my wingless nightingale !
              [*Kissing her.*
   *Edith*. Thou art my music !  Would
    their wings were mine
To follow thee to Flanders !  Must thou
   go ?
   *Harold*. Not must, but will.  It is but
    for one moon.
   *Edith*. Leaving so many foes in Ed-
    ward's hall           20
To league against thy weal.  The Lady
   Aldwyth
Was here to-day, and when she touch'd on
   thee
She stammer'd in her hate; I am sure she
   hates thee,
Pants for thy blood.
   *Harold*. Well, I have given her cause —
I fear no woman.
   *Edith*.          Hate not one who felt
Some pity for thy hater !   I am sure
Her morning wanted sunlight, she so
   praised
The convent and lone life — within the
   pale —
Beyond the passion.  Nay — she held with
   Edward,
At least methought she held with holy Ed-
   ward,           30
That marriage was half sin.
   *Harold*.         A lesson worth
Finger and thumb — thus (*snaps his fin-
   gers*).
          And my answer to it —

See here — an interwoven H and E !
Take thou this ring; I will demand his
   ward
From Edward when I come again.  Ay,
   would she ?
She to shut up my blossom in the dark !
Thou art *my* nun, thy cloister in mine
   arms.
   *Edith* (*taking the ring*). Yea, but Earl
    Tostig —
   *Harold*.        That's a truer fear !
For if the North take fire, I should be back;
I shall be, soon enough.
   *Edith*.          Ay, but last night
An evil dream that ever came and went —
   *Harold*. A gnat that vext thy pillow !
    Had I been by,          42
I would have spoil'd his horn.  My girl,
   what was it ?
   *Edith*. O that thou wert not going !
For so methought it was our marriage-
   morn,
And while we stood together, a dead man
Rose from behind the altar, tore away
My marriage ring, and rent my bridal
   veil;
And then I turn'd, and saw the church all
   fill'd
With dead men upright from their graves,
   and all          50
The dead men made at thee to murder
   thee,
But thou didst back thyself against a pillar,
And strike among them with thy battle-
   axe —
There, what a dream !
   *Harold*. Well, well — a dream — no
    more !
   *Edith*. Did not Heaven speak to men in
    dreams of old ?
   *Harold*. Ay — well — of old.  I tell thee
    what, my child;
Thou hast misread this merry dream of
   thine,
Taken the rifted pillars of the wood
For smooth stone columns of the sanctuary,
The shadows of a hundred fat dead deer  60
For dead men's ghosts.  True, that the
   battle-axe
Was out of place; it should have been the
   bow. —
Come, thou shalt dream no more such
   dreams; I swear it,
By mine own eyes — and these two sap-
   phires — these

Twin rubies, that are amulets against all
The kisses of all kind of womankind
In Flanders, till the sea shall roll me
    back
To tumble at thy feet.
   *Edith.*         That would but shame me,
Rather than make me vain. The sea may
    roll
Sand, shingle, shore-weed, not the living
    rock                70
Which guards the land.
   *Harold.*       Except it be a soft one,
And under-eaten to the fall. Mine amu-
    let —
This last — upon thine eyelids, to shut in
A happier dream. Sleep, sleep, and thou
    shalt see
My greyhounds fleeting like a beam of
    light,
And hear my peregrine and her bells in
    heaven;
And other bells on earth, which yet are
    heaven's;
Guess what they be.
   *Edith.*     He cannot guess who knows.
Farewell, my king.
   *Harold.*   Not yet, but then — my queen.
                                *[Exeunt.*

   *Enter* ALDWYTH *from the thicket.*

   *Aldwyth.* The kiss that charms thine eye-
    lids into sleep              80
Will hold mine waking. Hate him? I
    could love him
More, tenfold, than this fearful child can
    do;
Griffyth I hated; why not hate the foe
Of England? Griffyth, when I saw him
    flee,
Chased deer-like up his mountains, all the
    blood
That should have only pulsed for Griffyth
    beat
For his pursuer. I love him, or think I
    love him.
If he were King of England, I his queen,
I might be sure of it. Nay, I do love
    him. —
She must be cloister'd somehow, lest the
    king                   90
Should yield his ward to Harold's will.
    What harm?
She hath but blood enough to live, not
    love. —
When Harold goes and Tostig, shall I play

The craftier Tostig with him? fawn upon
    him?
Chime in with all? 'O thou more saint
    than king!'
And that were true enough. 'O blessed
    relics!'
'O Holy Peter!' If he found me thus,
Harold might hate me; he is broad and
    honest,
Breathing an easy gladness — not like Ald-
    wyth —
For which I strangely love him. Should
    not England            100
Love Aldwyth, if she stay the feuds that
    part
The sons of Godwin from the sons of Alf-
    gar
By such a marrying? Courage, noble Ald-
    wyth!
Let all thy people bless thee!
                      Our wild Tostig,
Edward hath made him earl; he would be
    king.
The dog that snapt the shadow dropt the
    bone.
I trust he may do well, this Gamel, whom
I play upon, that he may play the note
Whereat the dog shall howl and run, and
    Harold
Hear the King's music, all alone with him,
Pronounced his heir of England.     111
I see the goal and half the way to it. —
Peace-lover is our Harold for the sake
Of England's wholeness — so — to shake
    the North
With earthquake and disruption — some
    division —
Then fling mine own fair person in the gap
A sacrifice to Harold, a peace-offering,
A scapegoat marriage — all the sins of
    both
The houses on mine head — then a fair
    life               119
And bless the Queen of England!
   *Morcar (coming from the thicket).* Art
    thou assured
By this, that Harold loves but Edith?
   *Aldwyth.*               Morcar!
Why creep'st thou like a timorous beast of
    prey
Out of the bush by night?
   *Morcar.*         I follow'd thee.
   *Aldwyth.* Follow my lead, and I will
    make thee earl.
   *Morcar.* What lead then?

*Aldwyth.*                    Thou shalt flash it secretly
Among the good Northumbrian folk,
    that I —
That Harold loves me — yea, and presently
That I and Harold are betroth'd — and
    last —
Perchance that Harold wrongs me ; tho' I
    would not                                    129
That it should come to that.
    *Morcar.*                    I will both flash
And thunder for thee.
    *Aldwyth.*                    I said 'secretly;'
It is the flash that murders, the poor thun-
    der
Never harm'd head.
    *Morcar.*        But thunder may bring down
That which the flash hath stricken.
    *Aldwyth.*                    Down with Tostig !
That first of all. — And when doth Harold
    go ?
    *Morcar.*    To-morrow — first to Bosham,
    then to Flanders.
    *Aldwyth.* Not to come back till Tostig
    shall have shown
And redden'd with his people's blood the
    teeth
That shall be broken by us — yea, and thou
Chair'd in his place. Good - night, and
    dream thyself                                140
Their chosen earl.                [*Exit* Aldwyth.
    *Morcar.*        Earl first, and after that
Who knows I may not dream myself their
    king ?


## ACT II

### SCENE I. — SEASHORE.   PONTHIEU.
### NIGHT

HAROLD *and his* MEN, *wrecked.*

*Harold.* Friends, in that last inhospitable
    plunge
Our boat hath burst her ribs; but ours are
    whole;
I have but bark'd my hands.
    *Attendant.*            I dug mine into
My old fast friend the shore, and clinging
    thus
Felt the remorseless outdraught of the deep
Haul like a great strong fellow at my legs,
And then I rose and ran. The blast that
    came
So suddenly hath fallen as suddenly —

Put thou the comet and this blast to-
    gether —
    *Harold.* Put thou thyself and mother-
    wit together.                                10
Be not a fool !

*Enter* FISHERMEN *with torches*, HAROLD
    *going up to one of them*, ROLF.

                    Wicked sea-will-o'-the-wisp !
Wolf of the shore ! dog, with thy lying
    lights
Thou hast betray'd us on these rocks of
    thine !
    *Rolf.* Ay, but thou liest as loud as the
black herring-pond behind thee. We be
fishermen; I came to see after my nets.
    *Harold.* To drag us into them. Fisher-
men ? devils !
Who, while ye fish for men with your false
    fires,
Let the great devil fish for your own souls.
    *Rolf.* Nay then, we be liker the blessed
Apostles; *they* were fishers of men, Father
Jean says.                                        22
    *Harold.* I had liefer that the fish had
    swallowed me,
Like Jonah, than have known there were
    such devils.
What 's to be done ?
            [*To his* Men — *goes apart with them.*
    *Fisherman.* Rolf, what fish did swallow
Jonah ?
    *Rolf.* A whale !
    *Fisherman.* Then a whale to a whelk we
have swallowed the King of England. I
saw him over there. Look thee, Rolf, when
I was down in the fever, *she* was down with
the hunger, and thou didst stand by her and
give her thy crabs, and set her up again,
till now, by the patient Saints, she 's as
crabb'd as ever.
    *Rolf.* And I 'll give her my crabs again,
when thou art down again.                        38
    *Fisherman.* I thank thee, Rolf. Run
thou to Count Guy; he is hard at hand.
Tell him what hath crept into our creel, and
he will fee thee as freely as he will wrench
this outlander's ransom out of him — and
why not ? for what right had he to get
himself wrecked on another man's land ?
    *Rolf.* Thou art the human-heartedest,
Christian - charitiest of all crab - catchers.
Share and share alike !                [*Exit.*
    *Harold* (*to* Fisherman). Fellow, dost
    thou catch crabs ?                           49

*Fisherman.* As few as I may in a wind, and less than I would in a calm. Ay!

*Harold.* I have a mind that thou shalt catch no more.

*Fisherman.* How?

*Harold.* I have a mind to brain thee with mine axe.

*Fisherman.* Ay, do, do, and our great count-crab will make his nippers meet in thine heart; he 'll sweat it out of thee, he 'll sweat it out of thee! Look, he 's here! He 'll speak for himself. Hold thine own, if thou canst!                                    60

*Enter* GUY, COUNT OF PONTHIEU.

*Harold.* Guy, Count of Ponthieu?

*Guy.*                    Harold, Earl of Wessex!

*Harold.* Thy villains with their lying lights have wreck'd us!

*Guy.* Art thou not Earl of Wessex?

*Harold.*                    In mine earldom

A man may hang gold bracelets on a bush,
And leave them for a year, and coming back
Find them again.

*Guy.*                    Thou art a mighty man

In thine own earldom!

*Harold.*          Were such murderous liars

In Wessex — if I caught them, they should hang
Cliff-gibbeted for sea-marks, our sea-mew
Winging their only wail!

*Guy.*                    Ay, but my men

Hold that the shipwreckt are accursed of God; —                                         71
What hinders me to hold with mine own men?

*Harold.* The Christian manhood of the man who reigns!

*Guy.* Ay, rave thy worst, but in our oubliettes

Thou shalt or rot or ransom. — Hale him hence!          [*To one of his* Attendants.
Fly thou to William; tell him we have Harold.

## SCENE II

### BAYEUX. PALACE

COUNT WILLIAM *and* WILLIAM MALET.

*William.* We hold our Saxon woodcock in the springe,
But he begins to flutter. As I think

He was thine host in England when I went
To visit Edward.

*Malet.*                    Yea, and there, my lord,
To make allowance for their rougher fashions,
I found him all a noble host should be.

*William.* Thou art his friend. Thou know'st my claim on England
Thro' Edward's promise. We have him in the toils;
And it were well if thou shouldst let him feel
How dense a fold of danger nets him round,                                           10
So that he bristle himself against my will.

*Malet.* What would I do, my lord, if I were you?

*William.* What wouldst thou do?

*Malet.*          My lord, he is thy guest.

*William.* Nay, by the splendor of God, no guest of mine.
He came not to see me, had past me by
To hunt and hawk elsewhere, save for the fate
Which hunted *him* when that un-Saxon blast,
And bolts of thunder moulded in high heaven
To serve the Norman purpose, drave and crack'd
His boat on Ponthieu beach; where our friend Guy                                  20
Had wrung his ransom from him by the rack,
But that I stept between and purchased him,
Translating his captivity from Guy
To mine own hearth at Bayeux, where he sits
My ransom'd prisoner.

*Malet.*                    Well, if not with gold,
With golden deeds and iron strokes that brought
Thy war with Brittany to a goodlier close
Than else had been, he paid his ransom back.

*William.* So that henceforth they are not like to league
With Harold against *me*.

*Malet.*                    A marvel, how
He from the liquid sands of Coesnon                                               31
Haled thy shore-swallow'd, armor'd Normans up
To fight for thee again!

*William.*                     Perchance against
Their saver, save thou save him from him-
    self.
  *Malet.* But I should let him home again,
    my lord.
  *William.* Simple ! let fly the bird within
    the hand,
To catch the bird again within the bush !
No.
Smooth thou my way, before he clash with
    me;                                        39
I want his voice in England for the crown,
I want thy voice with him to bring him
    round;
And being brave he must be subtly cow'd,
And being truthful wrought upon to swear
Vows that he dare not break.  England
    our own
Thro' Harold's help, he shall be my dear
    friend
As well as thine, and thou thyself shalt
    have
Large lordship there of lands and territory.
  *Malet.* I knew thy purpose; he and
    Wulfnoth never
Have met, except in public; shall they
    meet
In private ?  I have often talk'd with
    Wulfnoth,                                  50
And stuff'd the boy with fears, that these
    may act
On Harold when they meet.
  *William.*                     Then let them meet !
  *Malet.* I can but love this noble, honest
    Harold.
  *William.* Love him ! why not ? thine is
    a loving office,
I have commission'd thee to save the man.
Help the good ship, showing the sunken
    rock,
Or he is wreckt for ever.

                *Enter* WILLIAM RUFUS.

*William Rufus.*                     Father.
*William.*                     Well, boy.
*William Rufus.* They have taken away
    the toy thou gavest me,
The Norman knight.
  *William.*                     Why, boy ?
  *William Rufus.*                     Because I broke
The horse's leg — it was mine own to
    break;                                     60
I like to have my toys, and break them too.
  *William.* Well, thou shalt have another
    Norman knight.

*William Rufus.* And may I break his
    legs ?
*William.*     Yea, — get thee gone !
*William Rufus.* I 'll tell them I have
    had my way with thee.     [*Exit.*
  *Malet.* I never knew thee check thy will
    for aught
Save for the prattling of thy little ones.
  *William.* Who shall be kings of Eng-
    land.  I am heir
Of England by the promise of her king.
  *Malet.* But there the great Assembly
    choose their king,                         69
The choice of England is the voice of
    England.
  *William.* I will be King of England by
    the laws,
The choice, and voice of England.
  *Malet.*                     Can that be ?
  *William.* The voice of any people is the
    sword
That guards them, or the sword that beats
    them down.
Here comes the would - be what I will
    be — kinglike . . .
Tho' scarce at ease; for, save our meshes
    break,
More kinglike he than like to prove a king.

*Enter* HAROLD, *musing, with his eyes on the
                ground.*

He sees me not — and yet he dreams of me.
Earl, wilt thou fly my falcons this fair day ?
They are of the best, strong-wing'd against
    the wind.                                  80
  *Harold* (*looking up suddenly, having caught
    but the last word*).  Which way does
    it blow ?
  *William.*                     Blowing for England, ha ?
Not yet.  Thou hast not learnt thy quarters
    here.
The winds so cross and jostle among these
    towers.
  *Harold.* Count of the Normans, thou hast
    ransom'd us,
Maintain'd, and entertain'd us royally !
  *William.* And thou for us hast fought as
    loyally,
Which binds us friendship-fast for ever !
  *Harold.*                     Good !
But lest we turn the scale of courtesy
By too much pressure on it, I would fain,
Since thou hast promised Wulfnoth home
    with us,                                   90
Be home again with Wulfnoth.

*William.*                    Stay — as yet
Thou hast but seen how Norman hands can
        strike,
But walk'd our Norman field, scarce touch'd
        or tasted
The splendors of our court.
        *Harold.*                 I am in no mood;
I should be as the shadow of a cloud
Crossing your light.
        *William.*        Nay, rest a week or two,
And we will fill thee full of Norman sun,
And send thee back among thine island
        mists
With laughter.
        *Harold.* Count, I thank thee, but had
        rather
Breathe the free wind from off our Saxon
        downs,                              100
Tho' charged with all the wet of all the
        west.
        *William.* Why if thou wilt, so let it be
        — thou shalt.
That were a graceless hospitality
To chain the free guest to the banquet-
        board;
To-morrow we will ride with thee to Har-
        fleur,
And see thee shipt, and pray in thy behalf
For happier homeward winds than that
        which crack'd
Thy bark at Ponthieu, — yet to us, in faith,
A happy one — whereby we came to know
Thy valor and thy value, noble earl.    110
Ay, and perchance a happy one for thee,
Provided — I will go with thee to-mor-
        row —
Nay — but there be conditions, easy ones,
So thou, fair friend, will take them easily.

*Enter* PAGE.

        *Page.* My lord, there is a post from over
        seas
With news for thee.                [*Exit* Page.
        *William.*        Come, Malet, let us hear !
        [*Exeunt* Count William *and* Malet.
        *Harold.* Conditions ?  What conditions ?
        pay him back
His ransom ? 'easy' — that were easy —
        nay —
No money-lover he !  What said the king ?
'I pray you do not go to Normandy.'    120
And fate hath blown me hither, bound me
        too
With bitter obligation to the Count —

Have I not fought it out ?  What did he
        mean ?
There lodged a gleaming grimness in his
        eyes,
Gave his shorn smile the lie.  The walls
        oppress me,
And yon huge keep that hinders half the
        heaven.
Free air ! free field !
        [*Moves to go out.  A* Man-at-arms *fol-
        lows him.*
        *Harold* (*to the* Man-at-arms).  I need thee
        not.  Why dost thou follow me ?
        *Man-at-arms.* I have the Count's com-
        mands to follow thee.
        *Harold.* What then ?  Am I in danger
        in this court ?                     130
        *Man-at-arms.* I cannot tell.  I have the
        Count's commands.
        *Harold.* Stand out of earshot then, and
        keep me still
In eyeshot.
        *Man-at-arms.* Yea, lord Harold.
                                [*Withdraws.*
        *Harold.*                And arm'd men
Ever keep watch beside my chamber door,
And if I walk within the lonely wood,
There is an arm'd man ever glides behind !

*Enter* MALET.

Why am I follow'd, haunted, harass'd,
        watch'd ?
See yonder !
                [*Pointing to the* Man-at-arms.
        *Malet.* 'T is the good Count's care for
        thee !
The Normans love thee not, nor thou the
        Normans,                           139
Or — so they deem.
        *Harold.*        But wherefore is the wind,
Which way soever the vane-arrow swing,
Not ever fair for England ?  Why, but
        now
He said — thou heard'st him — that I must
        not hence
Save on conditions.
        *Malet.*        So in truth he said.
        *Harold.* Malet, thy mother was an Eng-
        lishwoman;
There somewhere beats an English pulse
        in thee !
        *Malet.* Well — for my mother's sake I
        love your England,
But for my father I love Normandy.

*Harold.* Speak for thy mother's sake, and tell me true.

*Malet.* Then for my mother's sake, and England's sake
That suffers in the daily want of thee,   151
Obey the Count's conditions, my good friend.

*Harold.* How, Malet, if they be not honorable !

*Malet.* Seem to obey them.

*Harold.*              Better die than lie !

*Malet.* Choose therefore whether thou wilt have thy conscience
White as a maiden's hand, or whether England
Be shatter'd into fragments.

*Harold.*              News from England ?

*Malet.* Morcar and Edwin have stirr'd up the thanes
Against thy brother Tostig's governance;
And all the North of Humber is one storm.

*Harold.* I should be there, Malet, I should be there !   161

*Malet.* And Tostig in his own hall on suspicion
Hath massacred the thane that was his guest,
Gamel, the son of Orm; and there be more
As villainously slain.

*Harold.*              The wolf ! the beast !
Ill news for guests, ha, Malet ! More ? What more ?
What do they say ? did Edward know of this ?

*Malet.* They say his wife was knowing and abetting.

*Harold.* They say his wife ! — To marry and have no husband
Makes the wife fool.  My God, I should be there !   170
I 'll hack my way to the sea.

*Malet.*              Thou canst not, Harold;
Our duke is all between thee and the sea,
Our duke is all about thee like a God;
All passes block'd.  Obey him, speak him fair,
For he is only debonair to those
That follow where he leads, but stark as death
To those that cross him. — Look thou, here is Wulfnoth !
I leave thee to thy talk with him alone;
How wan, poor lad ! how sick and sad for home !              [*Exit* Malet.

*Harold* (*muttering*).  Go not to Normandy — go not to Normandy !   180

*Enter* WULFNOTH.

Poor brother ! still a hostage !

*Wulfnoth.*              Yea, and I
Shall see the dewy kiss of dawn no more
Make blush the maiden-white of our tall cliffs,
Nor mark the sea-bird rouse himself and hover
Above the windy ripple, and fill the sky
With free sea-laughter — never — save indeed
Thou canst make yield this iron-mooded duke
To let me go.

*Harold.*              Why, brother, so he will;
But on conditions.  Canst thou guess at them ?

*Wulfnoth.* Draw nearer, — I was in the corridor,   190
I saw him coming with his brother Odo
The Bayeux bishop, and I hid myself.

*Harold.* They did thee wrong who made thee hostage; thou
Wast ever fearful.

*Wulfnoth.* And he spoke — I heard him —
' This Harold is not of the royal blood,
Can have no right to the crown;' and Odo said,
' Thine is the right, for thine the might; he is here,
And yonder is thy keep.'

*Harold.*              No, Wulfnoth, no !

*Wulfnoth.* And William laugh'd and swore that might was right,
Far as he knew in this poor world of ours —   200
' Marry, the Saints must go along with us,
And, brother, we will find a way,' said he —
Yea, yea, he would be King of England.

*Harold.*              Never !

*Wulfnoth.* Yea, but thou must not this way answer *him.*

*Harold.* Is it not better still to speak the truth ?

*Wulfnoth.* Not here, or thou wilt never hence nor I;
For in the racing toward this golden goal
He turns not right or left, but tramples flat
Whatever thwarts him; hast thou never heard   209

His savagery at Alençon, — the town
Hung out raw hides along their walls, and
    cried,
' Work for the tanner.'
    *Harold.*           That had anger'd *me*
Had I been William.
    *Wulfnoth.*    Nay, but he had prisoners,
He tore their eyes out, sliced their hands
    away,
And flung them streaming o'er the battle-
    ments
Upon the heads of those who walk'd
    within —
O, speak him fair, Harold, for thine own
    sake !
    *Harold.* Your Welshman says, ' The
    Truth against the World,'
Much more the truth against myself.
    *Wulfnoth.*               Thyself ?
But for my sake, O brother ! O, for my
    sake !                         220
    *Harold.* Poor Wulfnoth ! do they not en-
    treat thee well ?
    *Wulfnoth.* I see the blackness of my dun-
    geon loom
Across their lamps of revel, and beyond
The merriest murmurs of their banquet
    clank
The shackles that will bind me to the wall.
    *Harold.* Too fearful still.
    *Wulfnoth.* O, no, no — speak him fair !
Call it to temporize, and not to lie;
Harold, I do not counsel thee to lie.
The man that hath to foil a murderous
    aim                              229
May, surely, play with words.
    *Harold.*           Words are the man.
Not even for thy sake, brother, would I lie.
    *Wulfnoth.* Then for thine Edith ?
    *Harold.*     There thou prick'st me deep.
    *Wulfnoth.* And for our Mother Eng-
    land ?
    *Harold.*      Deeper still.
    *Wulfnoth.* And deeper still the deep-
    down oubliette,
Down thirty feet below the smiling day —
In blackness — dogs' food thrown upon thy
    head.
And over thee the suns arise and set,
And the lark sings, the sweet stars come
    and go,
And men are at their markets, in their
    fields,
And woo their loves and have forgotten
    thee;                          240

And thou art upright in thy living grave,
Where there is barely room to shift thy
    side,
And all thine England hath forgotten thee;
And he our lazy-pious Norman King,
With all his Normans round him once
    again,
Counts his old beads, and hath forgotten
    thee.
    *Harold.* Thou art of my blood, and so me-
    thinks, my boy,
Thy fears infect me beyond reason. Peace!
    *Wulfnoth.* And then our fiery Tostig,
    while thy hands
Are palsied here, if his Northumbrians
    rise                             250
And hurl him from them, — I have heard
    the Normans
Count upon this confusion — may he not
    make
A league with William, so to bring him
    back ?
    *Harold.* That lies within the shadow of
    the chance.
    *Wulfnoth.* And like a river in flood thro'
    a burst dam
Descends the ruthless Norman — our good
    King
Kneels mumbling some old bone — our
    helpless folk
Are wash'd away, wailing, in their own
    blood —
    *Harold.* Wailing ! not warring ? Boy,
    thou hast forgotten          259
That thou art English.
    *Wulfnoth.*     Then our modest women —
I know the Norman license — thine own
    Edith —
    *Harold.* No more ! I will not hear thee
    — William comes.
    *Wulfnoth.* I dare not well be seen in
    talk with thee.
Make thou not mention that I spake with
    thee.
           [*Moves away to the back of the stage.*

   *Enter* WILLIAM, MALET, *and* OFFICER.

    *Officer.* We have the man that rail'd
    against thy birth.
    *William.* Tear out his tongue.
    *Officer.*        He shall not rail again.
He said that he should see confusion fall
On thee and on thine house.
    *William.*          Tear out his eyes,
And plunge him into prison.

*Officer.*                    It shall be done.
                                   [*Exit* Officer.
*William.* Look not amazed, fair earl!
    Better leave undone            270
Than do by halves — tongueless and eye-
    less, prison'd —
    *Harold.* Better methinks have slain the
        man at once !
    *William.* We have respect for man's im-
        mortal soul,
We seldom take man's life, except in
    war ;
It frights the traitor more to maim and
    blind.
    *Harold.* In mine own land I should have
        scorn'd the man,
Or lash'd his rascal back, and let him go.
    *William.* And let him go ?  To slander
        thee again !
Yet in thine own land in thy father's day
They blinded my young kinsman, Alfred
    — ay,                         280
Some said it was thy father's deed.
    *Harold.*                    They lied.
    *William.* But thou and he — whom at
        thy word, for thou
Art known a speaker of the truth, I free
From this foul charge —
    *Harold.*           Nay, nay, he freed himself
By oath and compurgation from the charge.
The King, the lords, the people clear'd him
    of it.
    *William.* But thou and he drove our
        good Normans out
From England, and this rankles in us yet.
Archbishop Robert hardly escaped with
    life.
    *Harold.* Archbishop Robert ! Robert the
        Archbishop !                290
Robert of Jumièges, he that —
    *Malet.*                    Quiet ! quiet !
    *Harold.* Count ! if there sat within the
        Norman chair
A ruler all for England — one who fill'd
All offices, all bishoprics with English —
We could not move from Dover to the
    Humber
Saving thro' Norman bishoprics — I say
Ye would applaud that Norman who should
    drive
The stranger to the fiends !
    *William.*            Why, that is reason !
Warrior thou art, and mighty wise withal !
Ay, ay, but many among our Norman
    lords                         300

Hate thee for this, and press upon me —
    saying
God and the sea have given thee to our
    hands —
To plunge thee into lifelong prison here; —
Yet I hold out against them, as I may,
Yea — would hold out, yea, tho' they should
    revolt —
For thou hast done the battle in my cause —
I am thy fastest friend in Normandy.
    *Harold.* I am doubly bound to thee — if
        this be so.
    *William.* And I would bind thee more,
        and would myself            309
Be bounden to thee more.
    *Harold.*            Then let me hence
With Wulfnoth to King Edward.
    *William.*                    So we will.
We hear he hath not long to live.
    *Harold.*                    It may be.
    *William.* Why then, the heir of England,
        who is he ?
    *Harold.* The Atheling is nearest to the
        throne.
    *William.* But sickly, slight, half-witted
        and a child,
Will England have him king ?
    *Harold.*                    It may be, no.
    *William.* And hath King Edward not
        pronounced his heir ?
    *Harold.* Not that I know.
    *William.* When he was here in Nor-
        mandy,
He loved us and we him, because we found
    him                           319
A Norman of the Normans.
    *Harold.*                    So did we.
    *William.* A gentle, gracious, pure and
        saintly man !
And grateful to the hand that shielded
    him,
He promised that if ever he were king
In England, he would give his kingly voice
To me as his successor.  Knowest thou
    this ?
    *Harold.* I learn it now.
    *William.* Thou knowest I am his cousin,
And that my wife descends from Alfred ?
    *Harold.*                    Ay.
    *William.* Who hath a better claim then
        to the crown ?
So that ye will not crown the Atheling ?
    *Harold.* None that I know — if that but
        hung upon                  330
King Edward's will.

*William.*  Wilt *thou* uphold my claim ?
*Malet (aside to* Harold*).*  Be careful of
    thine answer, my good friend.
*Wulfnoth (aside to* Harold*).*  O Harold,
    for my sake and for thine own !
*Harold.*  Ay . . . if the King have not
    revoked his promise.
*William.*  But hath he done it then ?
*Harold.*                    Not that I know.
*William.*  Good, good, and thou wilt help
    me to the crown ?
*Harold.*  Ay — if the Witan will consent
    to this.
*William.*  Thou art the mightiest voice in
    England, man,
Thy voice will lead the Witan — shall I
    have it ?
*Wulfnoth (aside to* Harold*).*  O Harold,
    if thou love thine Edith, ay.        340
*Harold.*  Ay, if —
*Malet (aside to* Harold*).*  Thine ' ifs ' will
    sear thine eyes out — ay.
*William.*  I ask thee, wilt thou help me
    to the crown ?
And I will make thee my great earl of
    earls,
Foremost in England and in Normandy ;
Thou shalt be verily king — all but the
    name —
For I shall most sojourn in Normandy ;
And thou be my vice-king in England.
    Speak.
*Wulfnoth (aside to* Harold*).*  Ay, brother
    — for the sake of England — ay.
*Harold.*  My lord —
*Malet (aside to* Harold*).*  Take heed now.
*Harold.*                            Ay.
*William.*                I am content,
For thou art truthful, and thy word thy
    bond.                                350
To-morrow will we ride with thee to Har-
    fleur.                    [*Exit* William.
*Malet.*  Harold, I am thy friend, one life
    with thee,
And even as I should bless thee saving
    mine,
I thank thee now for having saved thyself.
                              [*Exit* Malet.
*Harold.*  For having lost myself to save
    myself,
Said ' ay ' when I meant ' no,' lied like a lad
That dreads the pendent scourge, said ' ay '
    for ' no ' !
Ay !  No ! — he hath not bound me by an
    oath —

Is ' ay ' an oath ?  is ' ay ' strong as an
    oath ?
Or is it the same sin to break my word    360
As break mine oath ?  He call'd my word
    my bond !
He is a liar who knows I am a liar,
And makes believe that he believes my
    word —
The crime be on his head — not bounden
    — no.

[*Suddenly doors are flung open, discov-
    ering in an inner hall* Count William
    *in his state robes, seated upon his
    throne, between two* Bishops, Odo of
    Bayeux *being one ; in the centre of the
    hall an ark covered with cloth of gold,
    and on either side of it the* Norman
    Barons.

*Enter a* JAILOR *before* WILLIAM'S *throne.*

*William (to* Jailor*).*  Knave, hast thou let
    thy prisoner scape ?
*Jailor.*                    Sir Count,
He had but one foot, he must have hopt
    away,
Yea, some familiar spirit must have help'd
    him.
*William.*  Woe, knave, to thy familiar
    and to thee !
Give me thy keys.        [*They fall clashing.*
Nay, let them lie.  Stand there and wait
    my will.        [*The* Jailor *stands aside.*
*William (to* Harold*).*  Hast thou such
    trustless jailors in thy North ?    371
*Harold.*  We have few prisoners in mine
    earldom there,
So less chance for false keepers.
*William.*                    We have heard
Of thy just, mild, and equal governance ;
Honor to thee !  thou art perfect in all
    honor !
Thy naked word thy bond !  confirm it now
Before our gather'd Norman baronage,
For they will not believe thee — as I be-
    lieve.
[*Descends from his throne and stands by
    the ark.*
Let all men here bear witness of our bond !
    [*Beckons to* Harold, *who advances.*

*Enter* MALET *behind him.*

Lay thou thy hand upon this golden pall !
Behold the jewel of Saint Pancratius    381
Woven into the gold.  Swear thou on this !

*Harold.* What should I swear? Why should I swear on this?

*William (savagely).* Swear thou to help me to the crown of England.

*Malet (whispering* Harold*).* My friend, thou hast gone too far to palter now.

*Wulfnoth (whispering* Harold*).* Swear thou to-day, to-morrow is thine own.

*Harold.* I swear to help thee to the crown of England —

According as King Edward promises.

*William.* Thou must swear absolutely, noble earl.

*Malet (whispering).* Delay is death to thee, ruin to England.                    390

*Wulfnoth (whispering).* Swear, dearest brother, I beseech thee, swear!

*Harold ( putting his hand on the jewel).* I swear to help thee to the crown of England.

*William.* Thanks, truthful earl; I did not doubt thy word,

But that my barons might believe thy word,

And that the Holy Saints of Normandy

When thou art home in England, with thine own,

Might strengthen thee in keeping of thy word,

I made thee swear. Show him by whom he hath sworn.

[*The two* Bishops *advance, and raise the cloth of gold. The bodies and bones of Saints are seen lying in the ark.*

The holy bones of all the canonized    399

From all the holiest shrines in Normandy!

*Harold.* Horrible!

[*They let the cloth fall again.*

*William.* Ay, for thou hast sworn an oath

Which, if not kept, would make the hard earth rive

To the very devil's horns, the bright sky cleave

To the very feet of God, and send her hosts

Of injured Saints to scatter sparks of plague

Thro' all your cities, blast your infants, dash

The torch of war among your standing corn,

Dabble your hearths with your own blood. — Enough!

Thou wilt not break it! I, the count — the king —

Thy friend — am grateful for thine honest oath,    410

Not coming fiercely like a conqueror, now,

But softly as a bridegroom to his own.

For I shall rule according to your laws,

And make your ever - jarring earldoms move

To music and in order — Angle, Jute,

Dane, Saxon, Norman, help to build a throne

Out-towering hers of France. — The wind is fair

For England now. — To-night we will be merry.

To-morrow will I ride with thee to Har- fleur.

[*Exeunt* William *and all the* Norman Barons, *etc.*

*Harold.* To-night we will be merry — and to-morrow —    420

Juggler and bastard — bastard — he hates that most —

William the tanner's bastard! Would he heard me!

O God, that I were in some wide, waste field

With nothing but my battle-axe and him

To spatter his brains! Why, let earth rive, gulf in

These cursed Normans — yea, and mine own self!

Cleave heaven, and send thy Saints that I may say

Even to their faces, ' If ye side with Wil- liam

Ye are not noble!' How their pointed fingers

Glared at me! Am I Harold, Harold, son    430

Of our great Godwin? Lo! I touch mine arms,

My limbs — they are not mine — they are a liar's —

I mean to be a liar — I am not bound —

Stigand shall give me absolution for it —

Did the chest move? did it move? I am utter craven!

O Wulfnoth, Wulfnoth, brother, thou hast betray'd me!

*Wulfnoth.* Forgive me, brother, I will live here and die.

*Enter* PAGE.

*Page.* My lord! the duke awaits thee at the banquet.

*Harold.* Where they eat dead men's
    flesh, and drink their blood.
*Page.* My lord —                          440
*Harold.* I know your Norman cookery is
    so spiced,
It masks all this.
*Page.* My lord ! thou art white as death.
*Harold.* With looking on the dead. Am
    I so white ?
Thy duke will seem the darker. Hence, I
    follow.                              [*Exeunt.*

## ACT III

### SCENE I. — THE KING'S PALACE.
### LONDON

KING EDWARD, *dying on a couch, and by
him standing the* QUEEN, HAROLD, ARCH-
BISHOP STIGAND, GURTH, LEOFWIN,
ARCHBISHOP ALDRED, ALDWYTH, *and*
EDITH.

*Stigand.* Sleeping or dying there ?   If
    this be death,
Then our great Council wait to crown thee
    king —
Come hither, I have a power;
                              [*To* Harold.
They call me near, for I am close to thee
And England — I, old shrivell'd Stigand, I,
Dry as an old wood - fungus on a dead
    tree,
I have a power !
See here this little key about my neck !
There lies a treasure buried down in Ely.
If e'er the Norman grow too hard for thee,
Ask me for this at thy most need, son
    Harold,                            11
At thy most need — not sooner.
    *Harold.*                     So I will.
    *Stigand.* Red gold — a hundred purses
       — yea, and more !
If thou canst make a wholesome use of
    these
To chink against the Norman, I do believe
My old crook'd spine would bud out two
    young wings
To fly to heaven straight with.
    *Harold.*               Thank thee, father !
Thou art English, Edward too is English
    now,
He hath clean repented of his Norman-
    ism.

*Stigand.* Ay, as the libertine repents who
    cannot                              20
Make done undone, when thro' his dying
    sense
Shrills, 'Lost thro' thee !' They have
    built their castles here;
Our priories are Norman; the Norman
    adder
Hath bitten us; we are poison'd; our dear
    England
Is demi-Norman. He ! —
        [*Pointing to* KING EDWARD, *sleeping.*
    *Harold.*               I would I were
As holy and as passionless as he !
That I might rest as calmly ! Look at
    him —
The rosy face, and long down-silvering
    beard,
The brows unwrinkled as a summer
    mere. —
    *Stigand.* A summer mere with sudden
       wreckful gusts                    30
From a side-gorge. Passionless ? How
    he flamed
When Tostig's anger'd earldom flung him,
    nay,
He fain had calcined all Northumbria
To one black ash, but that thy patriot pas-
    sion,
Siding with our great Council against Tos-
    tig,
Out-passion'd his ! Holy ? ay, ay, forsooth,
A conscience for his own soul, not his realm;
A twilight conscience lighted thro' a chink;
Thine by the sun; nay, by some sun to be,
When all the world hath learnt to speak
    the truth,                          40
And lying were self-murder by that State
Which was the exception.
    *Harold.*          That sun may God speed !
    *Stigand.* Come, Harold, shake the cloud
       off !
    *Harold.*          Can I, father ?
Our Tostig parted cursing me and Eng-
    land;
Our sister hates us for his banishment;
He hath gone to kindle Norway against
    England,
And Wulfnoth is alone in Normandy.
For when I rode with William down to
    Harfleur,
'Wulfnoth is sick,' he said; 'he cannot fol-
    low;'
Then with that friendly-fiendly smile of
    his,                                50

'We have learnt to love him, let him a lit-
   tle longer
Remain a hostage for the loyalty
Of Godwin's house.' As far as touches
   Wulfnoth
I that so prized plain word and naked truth
Have sinn'd against it — all in vain.
   *Leofwin.*          Good brother,
By all the truths that ever priest hath
   preach'd,
Of all the lies that ever men have lied,
Thine is the pardonablest.
   *Harold.*          Maybe so !
I think it so, I think I am a fool
To think it can be otherwise than so.   60
   *Stigand.* Tut, tut, I have absolved thee.
      Dost thou scorn me,
Because I had my Canterbury pallium
From one whom they dispoped ?
   *Harold.*        No, Stigand, no !
   *Stigand.* Is naked truth actable in true
   life ?
I have heard a saying of thy father God-
   win,
That, were a man of state nakedly true,
Men would but take him for the craftier
   liar.
   *Leofwin.* Be men less delicate than the
   devil himself ?
I thought that naked Truth would shame
   the devil,
The devil is so modest.
   *Gurth.*         He never said it !
   *Leofwin.* Be thou not stupid-honest, bro-
   ther Gurth !   71
   *Harold.* Better to be a liar's dog, and
   hold
My master honest, than believe that lying
And ruling men are fatal twins that cannot
Move one without the other.   Edward
   wakes ! —
Dazed — he hath seen a vision.
   *Edward.*       The green tree !
Then a great Angel past along the highest
Crying, 'The doom of England !' and at
   once
He stood beside me, in his grasp a sword
Of lightnings, wherewithal he cleft the
   tree   80
From off the bearing trunk, and hurl'd it
   from him
Three fields away, and then he dash'd and
   drench'd,
He dyed, he soak'd the trunk with human
   blood,

And brought the sunder'd tree again, and
   set it
Straight on the trunk, that, thus baptized
   in blood,
Grew ever high and higher, beyond my
   seeing,
And shot out sidelong boughs across the
   deep
That dropt themselves, and rooted in far
   isles
Beyond my seeing; and the great Angel
   rose   89
And past again along the highest, crying,
'The doom of England !' — Tostig, raise
   my head !
   .           [*Falls back senseless.*
   *Harold* (*raising him*). Let Harold serve
   for Tostig !
   *Queen.*        Harold served
Tostig so ill, he cannot serve for Tostig !
Ay, raise his head, for thou hast laid it
   low !
The sickness of our saintly King, for whom
My prayers go up as fast as my tears
   fall,
I well believe, hath mainly drawn itself
From lack of Tostig — thou hast banish'd
   him.
   *Harold.* Nay — but the Council, and the
   King himself.
   *Queen.* Thou hatest him, hatest him !
   *Harold* (*coldly*). Ay — Stigand, unriddle
This vision, canst thou ?
   *Stigand.*         Dotage !
   *Edward* (*starting up*).   It is finish'd.
I have built the Lord a house — the Lord
   hath dwelt   102
In darkness.   I have built the Lord a
   house —
Palms, flowers, pomegranates, golden cher-
   ubim
With twenty - cubit wings from wall to
   wall —
I have built the Lord a house — sing,
   Asaph ! clash
The cymbal, Heman ! blow the trumpet,
   priest !
Fall, cloud, and fill the house — lo ! my
   two pillars,
Jachin and Boaz ! —
           [*Seeing* Harold *and* Gurth.
      Harold, Gurth, — where am I ?
Where is the charter of our Westminster ?
   *Stigand.* It lies beside thee, king, upon
   thy bed.   111

*Edward.* Sign, sign at once — take, sign
it, Stigand, Aldred !
Sign it, my good son Harold, Gurth, and
Leofwin !
Sign it, my queen !
*All.* We have sign'd it.
*Edward.* It is finish'd !
The kingliest abbey in all Christian lands,
The lordliest, loftiest minster ever built
To Holy Peter in our English isle !
Let me be buried there, and all our kings,
And all our just and wise and holy men
That shall be born hereafter. It is fin-
ish'd ! 120
Hast thou had absolution for thine oath ?
[*To* Harold.
*Harold.* Stigand hath given me absolu-
tion for it.
*Edward.* Stigand is not canonical enough
To save thee from the wrath of Norman
Saints.
*Stigand.* Norman enough ! Be there no
Saints of England
To help us from their brethren yonder ?
*Edward.* Prelate,
The Saints are one, but those of Norman-
land
Are mightier than our own. — Ask it of
Aldred. [*To* Harold.
*Aldred.* It shall be granted him, my
king; for he
Who vows a vow to strangle his own mo-
ther 130
Is guiltier keeping this than breaking it.
*Edward.* O friends, I shall not overlive
the day !
*Stigand.* Why, then the throne is empty.
Who inherits ?
For tho' we be not bound by the king's
voice
In making of a king, yet the king's voice
Is much toward his making. Who in-
herits ?
Edgar the Atheling ?
*Edward.* No, no, but Harold.
I love him; he hath served me; none but
he
Can rule all England. Yet the curse is on
him
For swearing falsely by those blessed
bones; 140
He did not mean to keep his vow.
*Harold.* Not mean
To make our England Norman.
*Edward.* There spake Godwin,

Who hated all the Normans; but their
Saints
Have heard thee, Harold.
*Edith.* O, my lord, my King !
He knew not whom he sware by.
*Edward.* Yea, I know
He knew not, but those heavenly ears have
heard,
Their curse is on him; wilt thou bring
another,
Edith, upon his head ?
*Edith.* No, no, not I !
*Edward.* Why, then thou must not wed
him.
*Harold.* Wherefore, wherefore ?
*Edward.* O son, when thou didst tell me
of thine oath, 150
I sorrow'd for my random promise given
To yon fox-lion. I did not dream then
I should be king. — My son, the Saints are
virgins;
They love the white rose of virginity,
The cold, white lily blowing in her cell.
I have been myself a virgin; and I sware
To consecrate my virgin here to Heaven —
The silent, cloister'd, solitary life,
A life of lifelong prayer against the curse
That lies on thee and England.
*Harold.* No, no, no !
*Edward.* Treble denial of the tongue of
flesh, 161
Like Peter's when he fell, and thou wilt
have
To wail for it like Peter. O my son !
Are all oaths to be broken then, all pro-
mises
Made in our agony for help from Heaven ?
Son, there is one who loves thee; and a
wife,
What matters who, so she be serviceable
In all obedience, as mine own hath been ?
God bless thee, wedded daughter !
[*Laying his hand on the* Queen's *head.*
*Queen.* Bless thou too
That brother whom I love beyond the
rest, 170
My banish'd Tostig.
*Edward.* All the sweet Saints bless him !
Spare and forbear him, Harold, if he
comes !
And let him pass unscathed; he loves me,
Harold !
Be kindly to the Normans left among us,
Who follow'd me for love ! and dear son,
swear

When thou art king, to see my solemn vow
Accomplish'd.
   *Harold.*  Nay, dear lord, for I have sworn
Not to swear falsely twice.
   *Edward.*           Thou wilt not swear ?
   *Harold.* I cannot.
   *Edward.* Then on thee remains the curse,
Harold, if thou embrace her; and on thee,
Edith, if thou abide it, —
     [*The* King *swoons;* Edith *falls and
       kneels by the couch.*
   *Stigand.*           He hath swoon'd.
Death ? — no, as yet a breath.
   *Harold.*         Look up ! look up !
Edith !
   *Aldred.* Confuse her not; she hath begun
Her lifelong prayer for thee.
   *Aldwyth.*        O noble Harold,
I would thou couldst have sworn.
   *Harold.*      For thine own pleasure ?
   *Aldwyth.* No, but to please our dying
    King, and those
Who make thy good their own — all Eng-
    land, earl.
   *Aldred. I* would thou couldst have
    sworn.  Our holy King
Hath given his virgin lamb to Holy Church
To save thee from the curse.
   *Harold.*         Alas ! poor man,
*His* promise brought it on me.
   *Aldred.*          O good son !
That knowledge made him all the care-
    fuller                  192
To find a means whereby the curse might
    glance
From thee and England.
   *Harold.*       Father, we so loved —
   *Aldred.* The more the love, the mightier
    is the prayer;
The more the love, the more acceptable
The sacrifice of both your loves to Heaven.
No sacrifice to Heaven, no help from Hea-
    ven;
That runs thro' all the faiths of all the
    world.
And sacrifice there must be, for the King
Is holy, and hath talk'd with God, and
    seen                   201
A shadowing horror; there are signs in
    heaven —
   *Harold.* Your comet came and went.
   *Aldred.*         And signs on earth !
Knowest thou Senlac hill ?
   *Harold.*         I know all Sussex;
A good entrenchment for a perilous hour !

   *Aldred.* Pray God that come not sud-
    denly !  There is one
Who passing by that hill three nights
    ago —
He shook so that he scarce could out with
    it —
Heard, heard —
   *Harold.*      The wind in his hair ?
   *Aldred.*           A ghostly horn
Blowing continually, and faint battle-
    hymns,                  210
And cries, and clashes, and the groans of
    men;
And dreadful shadows strove upon the hill,
And dreadful lights crept up from out the
    marsh —
Corpse - candles gliding over nameless
    graves —
   *Harold.* At Senlac ?
   *Aldred.*         Senlac.
   *Edward (waking).*   Senlac ! Sanguelac,
The Lake of Blood !
   *Stigand.*     This lightning before death
Plays on the word, — and Normanizes too !
   *Harold.* Hush, father, hush !
   *Edward.*        Thou uncanonical fool,
Wilt *thou* play with the thunder ?  North
    and South
Thunder together, showers of blood are
    blown                  220
Before a never-ending blast, and hiss
Against the blaze they cannot quench — a
    lake,
A sea of blood — we are drown'd in blood
    — for God
Has fill'd the quiver, and Death has drawn
    the bow —
Sanguelac ! Sanguelac ! the arrow ! the
    arrow !              [*Dies.*
   *Stigand.* It is the arrow of death in his
    own heart —
And our great Council wait to crown thee
    King.


## Scene II

### In the Garden.  The King's House near London

   *Edith.* Crown'd, crown'd and lost,
    crown'd King — and lost to me !

             (*Singing.*)
Two young lovers in winter weather,
    None to guide them,

Walk'd at night on the misty heather;
Night, as black as a raven's feather;
Both were lost and found together,
    None beside them.

That is the burthen of it — lost and found
Together in the cruel river Swale     9
A hundred years ago; and there 's another,

    Lost, lost, the light of day,

To which the lover answers lovingly:

      ' I am beside thee.'
    Lost, lost, we have lost the way.
    ' Love, I will guide thee.'
    Whither, O whither ? into the river,
    Where we two may be lost together,
    And lost for ever ?   ' O, never ! O, never !
    Tho' we be lost and be found together.'

Some think they loved within the pale for-
    bidden     20
By Holy Church; but who shall say ? the
    truth
Was lost in that fierce North, where *they*
    were lost,
Where all good things are lost, where Tos-
    tig lost
The good hearts of his people.  It is Har-
    old !

    *Enter* HAROLD.

Harold the King !
    *Harold.*     Call me not King, but Harold.
    *Edith.*  Nay, thou art King !
    *Harold.*  Thine, thine, or King or churl !
My girl, thou hast been weeping; turn not
    thou
Thy face away, but rather let me be
King of the moment to thee, and command
That kiss my due when subject, which will
    make     30
My kingship kinglier to me than to reign
King of the world without it.
    *Edith.*     Ask me not,
Lest I should yield it, and the second curse
Descend upon thine head, and thou be only
King of the moment over England.
    *Harold.*     Edith,
Tho' somewhat less a king to my true self
Than ere they crown'd me one, for I have
    lost
Somewhat of upright stature thro' mine
    oath,
Yet thee I would not lose, and sell not thou
Our living passion for a dead man's dream;
Stigand believed he knew not what he
    spake.     41

O God !  I cannot help it, but at times
They seem to me too narrow, all the faiths
Of this grown world of ours, whose baby
    eye
Saw them sufficient.  Fool and wise, I fear
This curse, and scorn it.  But a little
    light ! —
And on it falls the shadow of the priest;
Heaven yield us more ! for better, Woden,
    all
Our cancell'd warrior-gods, our grim Wal-
    halla,     49
Eternal war, than that the Saints at peace,
The Holiest of our Holiest One, should be
This William's fellow-tricksters; — better
    die
Than credit this, for death is death, or else
Lifts us beyond the lie.  Kiss me — thou
    art not
A holy sister yet, my girl, to fear
There might be more than brother in my
    kiss,
And more than sister in thine own.
    *Edith.*     I dare not.
    *Harold.*  Scared by the church — ' Love
    for a whole life long.'
When was that sung ?
    *Edith.*     Here to the nightingales.
    *Harold.*  Their anthems of no church, how
    sweet they are !     60
Nor kingly priest, nor priestly king to cross
Their billings ere they nest.
    *Edith.*     They are but of spring,
They fly the winter change — not so with
    us —
No wings to come and go.
    *Harold.*     But wing'd souls flying
Beyond all change and in the eternal dis-
    tance
To settle on the Truth.
    *Edith.*     They are not so true,
They change their mates.
    *Harold.*  Do they ?  I did not know it.
    *Edith.*  They say thou art to wed the
    Lady Aldwyth.
    *Harold.*  They say, they say !
    *Edith.*     If this be politic,
And well for thee and England — and for
    her —     70
Care not for me who love thee.
    *Gurth (calling).*     Harold, Harold !
    *Harold.*  The voice of Gurth ! (*Enter*
    Gurth.)  Good even, my good bro-
    ther !
    *Gurth.*  Good even, gentle Edith.

*Edith.*                    Good even, Gurth.
*Gurth.* Ill news hath come ! Our hap-
  less brother, Tostig —
He, and the giant King of Norway, Harold
Hardrada — Scotland, Ireland, Iceland,
  Orkney,
Are landed north of Humber, and in a
  field
So packt with carnage that the dykes and
  brooks
Were bridged and damm'd with dead, have
  overthrown                              79
Morcar and Edwin.
  *Harold.*         Well then, we must fight.
How blows the wind ?
  *Gurth.*              Against Saint Valery
And William.
  *Harold.* Well then, we will to the North.
  *Gurth.* Ay, but worse news: this Wil-
  liam sent to Rome,
Swearing thou swarest falsely by his Saints.
The Pope and that Archdeacon Hildebrand,
His master, heard him, and have sent him
  back
A holy gonfanon, and a blessed hair
Of Peter, and all France, all Burgundy,
Poitou, all Christendom is raised against
  thee.
He hath cursed thee, and all those who
  fight for thee,                         90
And given thy realm of England to the
  bastard.
  *Harold.* Ha ! ha !
  *Edith.* O, laugh not ! — Strange and
  ghastly in the gloom
And shadowing of this double thunder-
  cloud
That lours on England — laughter !
  *Harold.*               No, not strange !
This was old human laughter in old Rome
Before a Pope was born, when that which
  reign'd
Call'd itself God. — A kindly rendering
Of ' Render unto Cæsar.' — The Good Shep-
  herd !                                   99
Take this, and render that.
  *Gurth.*           They have taken York.
  *Harold.* The Lord was God and came as
  man — the Pope
Is man and comes as God. — York taken ?
  *Gurth.*                                Yea,
Tostig hath taken York !
  *Harold.*            To York then. Edith,
Hadst thou been braver, I had better
  braved

All — but I love thee and thou me — and
  that
Remains beyond all chances and all
  churches,
And that thou knowest.
  *Edith.*          Ay, but take back thy ring.
It burns my hand — a curse to thee and me.
I dare not wear it.
  *[Proffers* Harold *the ring, which he takes.*
  *Harold.*      But I dare. God with thee !
                  *[Exeunt* Harold *and* Gurth.
  *Edith.* The King hath cursed him, if he
  marry me;                              110
The Pope hath cursed him, marry me or no !
God help me ! I know nothing — can but
  pray
For Harold — pray, pray, pray — no help
  but prayer,
A breath that fleets beyond this iron world,
And touches Him that made it.


ACT IV

SCENE I. — IN NORTHUMBRIA

ARCHBISHOP ALDRED, MORCAR, EDWIN,
*and* FORCES. *Enter* HAROLD, *the standard of the golden Dragon of Wessex preceding him.*


  *Harold.* What ! are thy people sullen
  from defeat ?
Our Wessex dragon flies beyond the Hum-
  ber,
No voice to greet it.
  *Edwin.*         Let not our great King
Believe us sullen — only shamed to the
  quick
Before the King — as having been so bruised
By Harold, King of Norway; but our help
Is Harold, King of England. Pardon us,
  thou !
Our silence is our reverence for the King !
  *Harold.* Earl of the Mercians ! if the
  truth be gall,
Cram me not thou with honey, when our
  good hive                              10
Needs every sting to save it.
  *Voices.*               Aldwyth ! Aldwyth !
  *Harold.* Why cry thy people on thy sis-
  ter's name ?
  *Morcar.* She hath won upon our people
  thro' her beauty
And pleasantness among them.

*Voices.*                    Aldwyth, Aldwyth !

*Harold.* They shout as they would have her for a queen.

*Morcar.* She hath follow'd with our host, and suffer'd all.

*Harold.* What would ye, men ?

*Voice.*    Our old Northumbrian crown, And kings of our own choosing.

*Harold.*                    Your old crown Were little help without our Saxon carles Against Hardrada.

*Voice.*    Little ! we are Danes, Who conquer'd what we walk on, our own field.                                    21

*Harold.* They have been plotting here !
                                    [*Aside.*

*Voice.*    He calls us little !

*Harold.* The kingdoms of this world began with little, A hill, a fort, a city — that reach'd a hand Down to the field beneath it, ' Be thou mine,' Then to the next, ' Thou also !' If the field Cried out, ' I am mine own,' another hill, Or fort, or city, took it, and the first Fell, and the next became an empire.

*Voice.*                    Yet Thou art but a West Saxon; *we* are Danes !

*Harold.* My mother is a Dane, and I am English;                                    31 There is a pleasant fable in old books, Ye take a stick, and break it ; bind a score All in one faggot, snap it over knee, Ye cannot.

*Voice.* Hear King Harold ! he says true !

*Harold.* Would ye be Norsemen ?

*Voices.*                    No !

*Harold.*                    Or Norman ?

*Voices.*                    No !

*Harold.* Snap not the faggot-band then.

*Voice.*                    That is true !

*Voice.* Ay, but thou art not kingly, only grandson To Wulfnoth, a poor cowherd.

*Harold.*                    This old Wulfnoth Would take me on his knees and tell me tales                                    40 Of Alfred and of Athelstan the Great Who drove you Danes; and yet he held that Dane, Jute, Angle, Saxon, were or should be all One England; for this cowherd, like my father,

Who shook the Norman scoundrels off the throne, Had in him kingly thoughts — a king of men, Not made but born, like the great King of all, A light among the oxen.

*Voice.*                    That is true !

*Voice.* Ay, and I love him now, for mine own father                                    49 Was great, and cobbled.

*Voice.*    Thou art Tostig's brother, Who wastes the land.

*Harold.*    This brother comes to save Your land from waste; I saved it once before, For when your people banish'd Tostig hence, And Edward would have sent a host against you, Then I, who loved my brother, bade the King, Who doted on him, sanction your decree Of Tostig's banishment, and choice of Morcar, To help the realm from scattering.

*Voice.*                    King ! thy brother, If one may dare to speak the truth, was wrong'd. Wild was he, born so; but the plots against him                                    60 Had madden'd tamer men.

*Morcar.*    Thou art one of those Who brake into Lord Tostig's treasure-house And slew two hundred of his following, And now, when Tostig hath come back with power, Are frighted back to Tostig.

*Old Thane.*    Ugh ! Plots and feuds ! This is my ninetieth birthday.  Can ye not Be brethren ?  Godwin still at feud with Alfgar, And Alfgar hates King Harold.  Plots and feuds ! This is my ninetieth birthday !

*Harold.*                    Old man, Harold Hates nothing; not *his* fault, if our two houses                                    70 Be less than brothers.

*Voices.*    Aldwyth, Harold, Aldwyth !

*Harold.* Again !  Morcar !  Edwin ! What do they mean ?

*Edwin.* So the good King would deign to lend an ear

Not overscornful, we might chance — per-
chance —
To guess their meaning.
  *Morcar.*    Thine own meaning, Harold,
To make all England one, to close all
feuds,
Mixing our bloods, that thence a king may
rise
Half-Godwin and half-Alfgar, one to rule
All England beyond question, beyond quar-
rel.
  *Harold.* Who sow'd this fancy here
among the people ?       80
  *Morcar.* Who knows what sows itself
among the people ?
A goodly flower at times.
  *Harold.*      The Queen of Wales ?
Why, Morcar, it is all but duty in her
To hate me; I have heard she hates me.
  *Morcar.*           No !
For I can swear to that, but cannot swear
That these will follow thee against the
Norsemen,
If thou deny them this.
  *Harold.*      Morcar and Edwin,
When will ye cease to plot against my
house ?
  *Edwin.* The King can scarcely dream
that we, who know      89
His prowess in the mountains of the West,
Should care to plot against him in the
North.
  *Morcar.* Who dares arraign us, King, of
such a plot ?
  *Harold.* Ye heard one witness even now.
  *Morcar.*        The craven !
There is a faction risen again for Tostig,
Since Tostig came with Norway — fright,
not love.
  *Harold.* Morcar and Edwin, will ye, if I
yield,
Follow against the Norseman ?
  *Morcar.*      Surely, surely !
  *Harold.* Morcar and Edwin, will ye upon
oath
Help us against the Norman ?
  *Morcar.*      With good will;
Yea, take the sacrament upon it, King.  100
  *Harold.* Where is thy sister ?
  *Morcar.*     Somewhere hard at hand.
Call and she comes.
        [*One goes out, then enter* Aldwyth.
  *Harold.*    I doubt not but thou knowest
Why thou art summon'd.
  *Aldwyth.*    Why ? — I stay with these,

Lest thy fierce Tostig spy me out alone,
And flay me all alive.
  *Harold.*      Canst thou love one
Who did discrown thine husband, unqueen
thee ?
Didst thou not love thine husband ?
  *Aldwyth.*        O ! my lord,
The nimble, wild, red, wiry, savage king —
That was, my lord, a match of policy.
  *Harold.*         Was it ?
I knew him brave; he loved his land; he
fain      110
Had made her great; his finger on her
harp —
I heard him more than once — had in it
Wales,
Her floods, her woods, her hills. Had I
been his,
I had been all Welsh.
  *Aldwyth.* O, ay ! — all Welsh — and yet
I saw thee drive him up his hills — and
women
Cling to the conquer'd, if they love, the
more;
If not, they cannot hate the conqueror.
We never — O good Morcar, speak for us,
His conqueror conquer'd Aldwyth.
  *Harold.*      Goodly news !
  *Morcar.* Doubt it not thou ! Since Grif-
fyth's head was sent    120
To Edward, she hath said it.
  *Harold.*      I had rather
She would have loved her husband. Ald-
wyth, Aldwyth,
Canst thou love me, thou knowing where I
love ?
  *Aldwyth.* I can, my lord, for mine own
sake, for thine,
For England, for thy poor white dove, who
flutters
Between thee and the porch, but then would
find
Her nest within the cloister and be still.
  *Harold.* Canst thou love one who cannot
love again ?
  *Aldwyth.* Full hope have I that love will
answer love.
  *Harold.* Then in the name of the great
God, so be it !    130
Come, Aldred, join our hands before the
hosts,
That all may see.
      [Aldred *joins the hands of* Harold *and*
        Aldwyth, *and blesses them.*
  *Voices.*    Harold, Harold and Aldwyth !

*Harold.* Set forth our golden Dragon, let
   him flap
The wings that beat down Wales !
Advance our Standard of the Warrior,
Dark among gems and gold; and thou,
   brave banner,
Blaze like a night of fatal stars on those
Who read their doom and die.
Where lie the Norsemen ? on the Der-
   went ? ay,
At Stamford-Bridge.                    140
Morcar, collect thy men; Edwin, my
   friend —
Thou lingerest. — Gurth, —
Last night King Edward came to me in
   dreams —
The rosy face and long down - silvering
   beard —
He told me I should conquer. —
I am no woman to put faith in dreams.

         (*To his army.*)

Last night King Edward came to me in
   dreams,
And told me we should conquer.
  *Voices.*         Forward ! Forward !
Harold and Holy Cross !
  *Aldwyth.*         The day is won !


### SCENE II

### A Plain. Before the Battle of Stamford-Bridge

#### Harold *and his* Guard.

  *Harold.* Who is it comes this way ?
Tostig ? (*Enter* Tostig *with a small
force.*)  O brother,
What art thou doing here ?
  *Tostig.*         I am foraging
For Norway's army.
  *Harold.*       I could take and slay thee.
Thou art in arms against us.
  *Tostig.*    .     Take and slay me,
For Edward loved me.
  *Harold.*     Edward bade me spare thee.
  *Tostig.* I hate King Edward, for he join'd
   with thee
To drive me outlaw'd. Take and slay me,
   I say,
Or I shall count thee fool.
  *Harold.*      Take thee, or free thee,
Free thee or slay thee, Norway will have
   war;

No man would strike with Tostig, save for
   Norway.         10
Thou art nothing in thine England, save
   for Norway,
Who loves not thee, but war. What dost
   thou here,
Trampling thy mother's bosom into blood ?
  *Tostig.* She hath wean'd me from it with
   such bitterness.
I come for mine own earldom, my North-
   umbria;
Thou hast given it to the enemy of our
   house.
  *Harold.* Northumbria threw thee off, she
   will not have thee.
Thou hast misused her; and, O crowning
   crime !
Hast murder'd thine own guest, the son of
   Orm,         19
Gamel, at thine own hearth.
  *Tostig.*         The slow, fat fool !
He drawl'd and prated so, I smote him
   suddenly;
I knew not what I did. He held with
   Morcar. —
I hate myself for all things that I do.
  *Harold.* And Morcar holds with us.
   Come back with him.
Know what thou dost; and we may find for
   thee,
So thou be chasten'd by thy banishment,
Some easier earldom.
  *Tostig.*        What for Norway then ?
He looks for land among us, he and his.
  *Harold.* Seven feet of English land, or
   something more,
Seeing he is a giant.
  *Tostig.*        That is noble !   30
That sounds of Godwin.
  *Harold.*       Come thou back, and be
Once more a son of Godwin.
  *Tostig* (*turns away*). O brother, brother,
O Harold —
  *Harold* (*laying his hand on* Tostig's *shoul-
der*).  Nay then, come thou back to
   us !
  *Tostig* (*after a pause turning to him*).
   Never shall any man say that I, that
   Tostig
Conjured the mightier Harold from his
   North
To do the battle for me here in England,
Then left him for the meaner ! thee ! —
Thou hast no passion for the house of
   Godwin —

Thou hast but cared to make thyself a
   king —
Thou hast sold me for a cry. —     40
Thou gavest thy voice against me in the
   Council —
I hate thee, and despise thee, and defy thee.
Farewell for ever.          [*Exit.*
  *Harold.*     On to Stamford-Bridge !


## SCENE III

AFTER THE BATTLE OF STAMFORD-
     BRIDGE.  BANQUET

HAROLD *and* ALDWYTH.  GURTH, LEOF-
  WIN, MORCAR, EDWIN, *and other* EARLS
  *and* THANES.

  *Voices.*  Hail ! Harold ! Aldwyth ! hail,
    bridegroom and bride !
  *Aldwyth* (*talking with* Harold).  Answer
    them thou !
Is this our marriage-banquet ?  Would the
    wines
Of wedding had been dash'd into the cups
Of victory, and our marriage and thy glory
Been drunk together ! these poor hands
    but sew,
Spin, broider — would that they were man's
    to have held
The battle-axe by thee !
  *Harold.*     There *was* a moment
When, being forced aloof from all my
    guard,
And striking at Hardrada and his mad-
    men,          10
I had wish'd for any weapon.
  *Aldwyth.*     Why art thou sad ?
  *Harold.* I have lost the boy who play'd
    at ball with me,
With whom I fought another fight than
    this
Of Stamford-Bridge.
  *Aldwyth.*     Ay ! ay ! thy victories
Over our own poor Wales, when at thy
    side
He conquer'd with thee.
  *Harold.*     No — the childish fist
That cannot strike again.
  *Aldwyth.*     Thou art too kindly.
Why didst thou let so many Norsemen
    hence ?
Thy fierce forekings had clench'd their
    pirate hides

To the bleak church doors, like kites upon
    a barn.         20
  *Harold.*  Is there so great a need to tell
    thee why ?
  *Aldwyth.*  Yea, am I not thy wife ?
  *Voices.*       Hail, Harold, Aldwyth !
Bridegroom and bride !
  *Aldwyth.*    Answer them !  [*To* Harold.
  *Harold* (*to all*).     Earls and thanes !
Full thanks for your fair greeting of my
    bride !
Earls, thanes, and all our countrymen ! the
    day,
Our day beside the Derwent, will not shine
Less than a star among the goldenest hours
Of Alfred, or of Edward his great son,
Or Athelstan, or English Ironside
Who fought with Knut, or Knut who com-
    ing Dane     30
Died English.   Every man about his King
Fought like a king; the King like his own
    man,
No better; one for all, and all for one,
One soul ! and therefore have we shatter'd
    back
The hugest wave from Norseland ever yet
Surged on us, and our battle-axes broken
The Raven's wing, and dumb'd his carrion
    croak
From the gray sea for ever.   Many are
    gone —
Drink to the dead who died for us, the living
Who fought and would have died, but hap-
    pier lived,     40
If happier be to live; they both have life
In the large mouth of England, till *her*
    voice
Die with the world.   Hail — hail !
  *Morcar.* May all invaders perish like
    Hardrada !
All traitors fail like Tostig !
          [*All drink but* Harold.
  *Aldwyth.*     Thy cup 's full !
  *Harold.* I saw the hand of Tostig cover it.
Our dear, dead traitor-brother, Tostig,
    him
Reverently we buried.   Friends, had I been
    here,
Without too large self-lauding I must hold
The sequel had been other than his league
With Norway, and this battle.   Peace be
    with him !     51
He was not of the worst.   If there be
    those
At banquet in this hall, and hearing me —

For there be those, I fear, who prick'd the
    lion
To make him spring, that sight of Danish
    blood
Might serve an end not English — peace
    with them
Likewise, if *they* can be at peace with what
God gave us to divide us from the wolf !
    *Aldwyth (aside to* Harold). Make not
        our Morcar sullen; it is not wise.
    *Harold.* Hail to the living who fought,
        the dead who fell !          60
    *Voices.* Hail, hail !
    *First Thane.* How ran that answer which
        King Harold gave
To his dead namesake, when he ask'd for
    England ?
    *Leofwin.* 'Seven feet of English earth,
        or something more,
Seeing he is a giant ! '
    *First Thane.*          Then for the bastard
Six feet and nothing more !
    *Leofwin.*          Ay, but belike
Thou hast not learnt his measure.
    *First Thane.*          By Saint Edmund
I over-measure him. Sound sleep to the
    man
Here by dead Norway without dream or
    dawn !
    *Second Thane.* What, is he bragging still
        that he will come,          70
To thrust our Harold's throne from under
    him ?
My nurse would tell me of a molehill cry-
    ing
To a mountain, 'Stand aside and room for
    me ! '
    *First Thane.* Let him come ! let him
        come ! Here 's to him, sink or
        swim !          [*Drinks.*
    *Second Thane.* God sink him !
    *First Thane.*          Cannot hands which had
        the strength
To shove that stranded iceberg off our
    shores,
And send the shatter'd North again to
    sea,
Scuttle his cockle-shell ? What 's Brunan-
    burg
To Stamford-Bridge ? a war-crash, and so
    hard,
So loud, that, by Saint Dunstan, old Saint
    Thor —          80
By God, we thought him dead — but our
    old Thor

Heard his own thunder again, and woke
    and came
Among us again, and mark'd the sons of
    those
Who made this Britain England, break the
    North —

    Mark'd how the war-axe swang,
    Heard how the war-horn sang,
    Mark'd how the spear-head sprang,
    Heard how the shield-wall rang,
    Iron on iron clang,
    Anvil on hammer bang —          90

    *Second Thane.* Hammer on anvil, ham-
        mer on anvil. Old dog,
Thou art drunk, old dog !
    *First Thane.* Too drunk to fight with
        thee !
    *Second Thane.* Fight thou with thine own
        double, not with me,
Keep that for Norman William !
    *First Thane.*          Down with William !
    *Third Thane.* The washerwoman's brat !
    *Fourth Thane.*          The tanner's bastard !
    *Fifth Thane.* The Falaise byblow !

*Enter a* THANE, *from Pevensey, spattered
    with mud.*

    *Harold.*          Ay, but what late guest,
As haggard as a fast of forty days,
And caked and plaster'd with a hundred
    mires,
Hath stumbled on our cups ?
    *Thane from Pevensey.* My lord the
        King !
William the Norman, for the wind had
    changed —          100
    *Harold.* I felt it in the middle of that
        fierce fight
At Stamford-Bridge. William hath landed,
    ha ?
    *Thane from Pevensey.* Landed at Peven-
        sey — I am from Pevensey —
Hath wasted all the land at Pevensey —
Hath harried mine own cattle — God con-
    found him !
I have ridden night and day from Peven-
    sey —
A thousand ships — a hundred thousand
    men —
Thousands of horses, like as many lions
Neighing and roaring as they leapt to
    land —
    *Harold.* How oft in coming hast thou
        broken bread ?          110

*Thane from Pevensey.* Some thrice, or so.
*Harold.*                    Bring not thy hollowness
On our full feast.   Famine is fear, were it
    but
Of being starved.   Sit down, sit down, and
    eat,
And, when again red-blooded, speak again.
(*Aside.*)   The men that guarded England
    to the South
Were scatter'd to the harvest. — No power
    mine
To hold their force together. — Many are
    fallen
At Stamford-Bridge — the people stupid-
    sure
Sleep like their swine — in South and
    North at once
I could not be.
(*Aloud.*)   Gurth, Leofwin, Morcar, Edwin !
(*Pointing to the revellers.*)   The curse of
    England ! these are drown'd in was-
    sail,                                    121
And cannot see the world but thro' their
    wines !
Leave them ! and thee too, Aldwyth, must
    I leave —
Harsh is the news ! hard is our honey-
    moon !
Thy pardon.   (*Turning round to his atten-
    dants.*)   Break the banquet up — Ye
    four !
And thou, my carrier-pigeon of black news,
Cram thy crop full, but come when thou
    art call'd.                    [*Exit* Harold.


## ACT V

Scene I. — A Tent on a Mound,
    from which can be seen the
    Field of Senlac.

Harold, *sitting; by him standing* Hugh
    Margot *the* Monk, Gurth, Leofwin.

*Harold.* Refer my cause, my crown to
    Rome ! — The wolf
Mudded the brook and predetermined all.
Monk,
Thou hast said thy say, and had my con-
    stant 'No'
For all but instant battle.   I hear no more.
*Margot.* Hear me again — for the last
    time.   Arise,
Scatter thy people home, descend the hill,

Lay hands of full allegiance in thy Lord's
And crave his mercy, for the Holy Father
Hath given this realm of England to the
    Norman.                            10
*Harold.* Then for the last time, monk, I
    ask again
When had the Lateran and the Holy
    Father
To do with England's choice of her own
    king ?
*Margot.* Earl, the first Christian Cæsar
    drew to the East
To leave the Pope dominion in the West.
He gave him all the kingdoms of the
    West.
*Harold.* So ! — did he ? — Earl — I have
    a mind to play
The William with thine eyesight and thy
    tongue.
Earl — ay — thou art but a messenger of
    William.
I am weary — go; make me not wroth
    with thee !                        20
*Margot.* Mock-king, I am the messenger
    of God,
His Norman Daniel ! Mene, Mene, Tekel !
Is thy wrath hell, that I should spare to
    cry,
Yon Heaven is wroth with *thee* ?   Hear me
    again !
Our Saints have moved the Church that
    moves the world,
And all the Heavens and very God; they
    heard —
They know King Edward's promise and
    thine — thine.
*Harold.* Should they not know free Eng-
    land crowns herself ?
Not know that he nor I had power to pro-
    mise ?
Not know that Edward cancell'd his own
    promise ?                        30
And for *my* part therein — Back to that
    juggler,                    [*Rising.*
Tell him the Saints are nobler than he
    dreams,
Tell him that God is nobler than the Saints,
And tell him we stand arm'd on Senlac
    Hill,
And bide the doom of God.
*Margot.*                    Hear it thro' me.
The realm for which thou art forsworn is
    cursed,
The babe enwomb'd and at the breast is
    cursed,

The corpse thou whelmest with thine earth
    is cursed,
The soul who fighteth on thy side is cursed,
The seed thou sowest in thy field is cursed,
The steer wherewith thou plowest thy field
    is cursed,            41
The fowl that fleeth o'er thy field is cursed,
And thou, usurper, liar —
    *Harold.*            Out, beast monk !
    [*Lifting his hand to strike him.* Gurth
    *stops the blow.*
I ever hated monks.
    *Margot.*       I am but a voice
Among you; murder, martyr me if ye will —
    *Harold.* Thanks, Gurth ! The simple,
    silent, selfless man
Is worth a world of tonguesters. (*To*
    Margot.) Get thee gone !
He means the thing he says. See him out
    safe !
    *Leofwin.* He hath blown himself as red
    as fire with curses.       49
An honest fool ! Follow me, honest fool,
But if thou blurt thy curse among our folk,
I know not — I may give that egg-bald
    head
The tap that silences.
    *Harold.*       See him out safe.
    [*Exeunt* Leofwin *and* Margot.
    *Gurth.* Thou hast lost thine even temper,
    brother Harold !
    *Harold.* Gurth, when I past by Waltham,
    my foundation
For men who serve the neighbor, not them-
    selves,
I cast me down prone, praying; and, when
    I rose,
They told me that the Holy Rood had
    lean'd
And bow'd above me; whether that which
    held it
Had weaken'd, and the Rood itself were
    bound       60
To that necessity which binds us down;
Whether it bow'd at all but in their fancy;
Or if it bow'd, whether it symboll'd ruin
Or glory, who shall tell ? but they were
    sad,
And somewhat sadden'd me.
    *Gurth.*       Yet if a fear,
Or shadow of a fear, lest the strange Saints
By whom thou swarest should have power
    to balk
Thy puissance in this fight with him who
    made

And heard thee swear — brother — *I* have
    not sworn —
If the King fall, may not the kingdom
    fall ?       70
But if I fall, I fall, and thou art King;
And if I win, I win, and thou art King;
Draw thou to London, there make strength
    to breast
Whatever chance, but leave this day to me.
    *Leofwin* (*entering*). And waste the land
    about thee as thou goest,
And be thy hand as winter on the field,
To leave the foe no forage.
    *Harold.*         Noble Gurth !
Best son of Godwin ! If I fall, I fall —
The doom of God ! How should the peo-
    ple fight
When the King flies ? And, Leofwin, art
    thou mad ?       80
How should the King of England waste the
    fields
Of England, his own people ? — No glance
    yet
Of the Northumbrian helmet on the heath ?
    *Leofwin.* No, but a shoal of wives upon
    the heath,
And some one saw thy willy-nilly nun
Vying a tress against our golden fern.
    *Harold.* Vying a tear with our cold dews,
    a sigh
With these low-moaning heavens. Let her
    be fetch'd.
We have parted from our wife without re-
    proach,
Tho' we have pierced thro' all her prac-
    tices;       90
And that is well.
    *Leofwin.*     I saw her even now;
She hath not left us.
    *Harold.*     Nought of Morcar then ?
    *Gurth.* Nor seen, nor heard; thine, Wil-
    liam's, or his own
As wind blows, or tide flows. Belike he
    watches
If this war-storm in one of its rough rolls
Wash up that old crown of Northumber-
    land.
    *Harold.* I married her for Morcar — a
    sin against
The truth of love. Evil for good, it seems,
Is oft as childless of the good as evil     99
For evil.
    *Leofwin.* Good for good hath borne at
    times
A bastard false as William.

*Harold.*                                   Ay, if Wisdom
Pair'd not with Good. But I am some-
    what worn,
A snatch of sleep were like the peace of
    God.
Gurth, Leofwin, go once more about the
    hill —
What did the dead man call it — Sanguelac,
The lake of blood ?
    *Leofwin.*     A lake that dips in William
As well as Harold.
    *Harold.*          Like enough.   I have seen
The trenches dug, the palisades uprear'd
And wattled thick with ash and willow-
    wands,
Yea, wrought at them myself.   Go round
    once more;                                  110
See all be sound and whole.   No Norman
    horse
Can shatter England, standing shield by
    shield;
Tell that again to all.
    *Gurth.*             I will, good brother.
    *Harold.* Our guardsman hath but toil'd
    his hand and foot,
I hand, foot, heart and head.   Some wine !
    (*One pours wine into a goblet which he
    hands to* Harold.)          Too much !
What ? we must use our battle-axe to-
    day.
Our guardsmen have slept well, since we
    came in ?
    *Leofwin.* Ay, slept and snored.   Your
    second-sighted man
That scared the dying conscience of the
    king
Misheard their snores for groans.   They
    are up again                               120
And chanting that old song of Brunanburg
Where England conquer'd.
    *Harold.*     That is well.   The Norman,
What is he doing ?
    *Leofwin.*        Praying for Normandy;
Our scouts have heard the tinkle of their
    bells.
    *Harold.* And our old songs are prayers
    for England too !
But by all Saints —
    *Leofwin.*     Barring the Norman !
    *Harold.*                          Nay,
Were the great trumpet blowing dooms-
    day dawn,
I needs must rest.   Call when the Norman
    moves —     [*Exeunt all but* Harold.

No horse — thousands of horses — our
    shield wall —                              129
Wall — break it not — break not —
    break —                        [*Sleeps.*
    *Vision of Edward.* Son Harold, I thy
    king, who came before
To tell thee thou shouldst win at Stamford-
    Bridge,
Come yet once more, from where I am at
    peace,
Because I loved thee in my mortal day,
To tell thee thou shalt die on Senlac Hill —
Sanguelac !
    *Vision of Wulfnoth.* O brother, from my
    ghastly oubliette
I send my voice across the narrow seas —
No more, no more, dear brother, never-
    more —
Sanguelac !                                   140
    *Vision of Tostig.* O brother, most un-
    brotherlike to me,
Thou gavest thy voice against me in my
    life,
I give my voice against thee from the
    grave —
Sanguelac !
    *Vision of Norman Saints.* O hapless Har-
    old ! King but for an hour !
Thou swarest falsely by our blessed bones,
We give our voice against thee out of hea-
    ven !
Sanguelac ! Sanguelac ! The arrow ! the
    arrow !
    *Harold* (*starting up, battle-axe in hand*).
                                      Away !
My battle-axe against your voices.   Peace !
The King's last word — ' the arrow ! ' I
    shall die —                                150
I die for England then, who lived for Eng-
    land —
What nobler ? men must die.
I cannot fall into a falser world —
I have done no man wrong.   Tostig, poor
    brother,
Art *thou* so anger'd ?
Fain had I kept thine earldom in thy
    hands
Save for thy wild and violent will that
    wrench'd
All hearts of freemen from thee.   I could
    do
No other than this way advise the king
Against the race of Godwin.   Is it possi-
    ble

That mortal men should bear their earthly
   heats                                    161
Into yon bloodless world, and threaten us
   thence
Unschool'd of Death ?   Thus then thou art
   revenged —
I left our England naked to the South
To meet thee in the North.   The Norse-
   man's raid
Hath helpt the Norman, and the race of
   Godwin
Hath ruin'd Godwin.   No — our waking
   thoughts
Suffer a stormless shipwreck in the pools
Of sullen slumber, and arise again
Disjointed;   only   dreams — where   mine
   own self                                 170
Takes part against myself !   Why ? for a
   spark
Of self-disdain born in me when I sware
Falsely to him, the falser Norman, over
His gilded ark of mummy-saints, by whom
I knew not that I sware, — not for my-
   self —
For England — yet not wholly —

         *Enter* EDITH.

                   Edith, Edith,
Get thou into thy cloister as the King
Will'd it; be safe, the perjury-mongering
   Count
Hath  made  too  good  an  use  of  Holy
   Church
To break her close !   There the great God
   of truth                                  180
Fill all thine hours with peace ! — A lying
   devil
Hath haunted me — mine oath — my wife
   — I fain
Had made my marriage not a lie; I could
   not.
Thou art my bride ! and thou in after
   years
Praying perchance for this poor soul of
   mine
In cold, white cells beneath an icy moon —
This memory to thee ! — and this to Eng-
   land,
My legacy of war against the Pope
From child to child, from Pope to Pope,
   from age to age,                         189
Till the sea wash her level with her shores,
Or till the Pope be Christ's.

         *Enter* ALDWYTH.

  *Aldwyth* (*to* Edith).     Away from him !

  *Edith.*  I will. — I have not spoken to the
   king
One word; and one I must.   Farewell !
                     [*Going.*
  *Harold.*                          Not yet.
Stay.
  *Edith.*  To what use ?
  *Harold.*  The King commands thee, wo-
   man !

        (*To* ALDWYTH.)

Have thy two brethren sent their forces in ?
  *Aldwyth.*  Nay, I fear not.
  *Harold.*  Then there's no force in thee !
Thou didst possess thyself of Edward's
   ear
To part me from the woman that I loved !
Thou didst arouse the fierce Northumbri-
   ans !
Thou hast been false to England and to
   me ! —                                    200
As — in some sort — I have been false to
   thee.
Leave me.   No more — Pardon on both
   sides — Go !
  *Aldwyth.*  Alas, my lord, I loved thee.
  *Harold* (*bitterly*).               With a love
Passing thy love for Griffyth ! wherefore
   now
Obey my first and last commandment.
   Go !
  *Aldwyth.*  O Harold ! husband ! Shall we
   meet again ?
  *Harold.*  After the battle — after the
   battle.   Go.
  *Aldwyth.*  I go.   (*Aside.*)  That I could
   stab her standing there !
              [*Exit* Aldwyth.
  *Edith.*  Alas, my lord, she loved thee.
  *Harold.*                    Never ! never !
  *Edith.*  I saw it in her eyes !
  *Harold.*                 I see it in thine.
And not on thee — nor England — fall
   God's doom !                             211
  *Edith.*  On *thee?* on me !   And thou art
   England !   Alfred
Was England.   Ethelred was nothing.
   England
Is but her king, and thou art Harold !
  *Harold.*                             Edith,
The sign in heaven — the sudden blast at
   sea —
My fatal oath — the dead Saints — the
   dark dreams —
The Pope's anathema — the Holy Rood

That bow'd to me at Waltham — Edith, if
I, the last English King of England —
   *Edith.*               No,
First of a line that coming from the peo-
   ple,
And chosen by the people —
   *Harold.*         And fighting for
And dying for the people —
   *Edith.*           Living ! living !
   *Harold.* Yea so, good cheer ! thou art
   Harold, I am Edith !         223
Look not thus wan !
   *Edith.*     What matters how I look ?
Have we not broken Wales and Norse-
   land ? slain,
Whose life was all one battle, incarnate
   war,
Their giant-king, a mightier man-in-arms
Than William.
   *Harold.* Ay, my girl, no tricks in him —
No bastard he ! when all was lost, he
   yell'd,
And bit his shield, and dash'd it on the
   ground,         230
And swaying his two-handed sword about
   him,
Two deaths at every swing, ran in upon
   us
And died so, and I loved him as I hate
This liar who made me liar. If Hate can
   kill,
And Loathing wield a Saxon battle-axe —
   *Edith.* Waste not thy might before the
   battle !
   *Harold.*    No,
And thou must hence. Stigand will see
   thee safe,
And so — Farewell.
           *[He is going, but turns back.*
        The ring thou darest not wear,
I have had it fashion'd, see, to meet my
   hand.
      *[Harold shows the ring which is on his
      finger.*
Farewell !             240
        *[He is going, but turns back again.*
I am dead as Death this day to aught of
   earth's
Save William's death or mine.
   *Edith.*      Thy death ! — to-day !
Is it not thy birthday ?
   *Harold.*        Ay, that happy day !
A birthday welcome ! happy days and
   many !

One — this !          *[They embrace.*
Look, I will bear thy blessing into the bat-
   tle
And front the doom of God.
   *Norman Cries (heard in the distance).* Ha
   Rou ! Ha Rou !

          *Enter* GURTH.

   *Gurth.* The Norman moves !
   *Harold.*     Harold and Holy Cross !
          *[Exeunt* Harold *and* Gurth.

          *Enter* STIGAND.

   *Stigand.* Our Church in arms — the
   lamb the lion — not
Spear into pruning - hook — the counter
   way —         250
Cowl, helm; and crozier, battle-axe. Ab-
   bot Alfwig,
Leofric, and all the monks of Peterboro'
Strike for the king; but I, old wretch, old
   Stigand,
With hands too limp to brandish iron —
   and yet
I have a power — would Harold ask me for
   it —
I have a power.
   *Edith.*      What power, holy father ?
   *Stigand.* Power now from Harold to
   command thee hence
And see thee safe from Senlac.
   *Edith.*        I remain !
   *Stigand.* Yea, so will I, daughter, until
   I find
Which way the battle balance. I can see
   it         260
From where we stand; and, live or die, I
   would
I were among them !

   CANONS *from Waltham (singing without).*

        Saiva patriam,
        Sancte Pater,
        Salva, Fili,
        Salva, Spiritus,
        Salva patriam,
        Sancta Mater.[1]

   *Edith.* Are those the blessed angels quir-
   ing, father ?
   *Stigand.* No, daughter, but the canons
   out of Waltham,     270

   [1] The *a* throughout these Latin hymns
should be sounded broad, as in 'father.'

The king's foundation, that have follow'd
    him.
    *Edith.*  O God of battles, make their
    wall of shields
Firm as thy cliffs, strengthen their pali-
    sades !
What is that whirring sound ?
    *Stigand.*           The Norman arrow !
    *Edith.*  Look out upon the battle — is he
    safe ?
    *Stigand.*  The King of England stands be-
    tween his banners.
He glitters on the crowning of the hill.
God save King Harold !
    *Edith.*        — chosen by his people
And fighting for his people !
    *Stigand.*          There is one
Come as Goliath came of yore — he flings
His brand in air and catches it again,   281
He is chanting some old war-song.
    *Edith.*         And no David
To meet him ?
    *Stigand.*  Ay, there springs a Saxon on
    him,
Falls — and another falls.
    *Edith.*        Have mercy on us !
    *Stigand.*  Lo ! our good Gurth hath smit-
    ten him to the death.
    *Edith.*  So perish all the enemies of Har-
    old !

          CANONS (*singing*).

     Hostis in Angliam
      Ruit prædator ;
     Illorum, Domine,
      Scutum scindatur !    290
     Hostis per Angliæ
      Plagas bacchatur ;
      Casa crematur,
      Pastor fugatur,
      Grex trucidatur —

    *Stigand.*  Illos trucida, Domine.
    *Edith.*          Ay, good father.

          CANONS (*singing*).

     Illorum scelera
      Pœna sequatur !

    *English Cries.*  Harold and Holy Cross !
    Out ! out !
    *Stigand.*       Our javelins
Answer their arrows.  All the Norman
    foot      300
Are storming up the hill.  The range of
    knights
Sit, each a statue on his horse, and wait.

    *English Cries.*  Harold and God Al-
    mighty !
    *Norman Cries.*  Ha Rou ! Ha Rou !

          CANONS (*singing*).

     Eques cum pedite
      Præpediatur !
     Illorum in lacrymas
      Cruor fundatur !
     Pereant, pereant,
      Anglia precatur.

    *Stigand.*  Look, daughter, look.
    *Edith.*        Nay, father, look for *me !*
    *Stigand.*  Our axes lighten with a single
    flash     311
About the summit of the hill, and heads
And arms are sliver'd off and splinter'd
    by
Their lightning — and they fly — the Nor-
    man flies.
    *Edith.*  Stigand, O father, have we won
    the day ?
    *Stigand.*  No, daughter, no — they fall
    behind the horse —
Their horse are thronging to the barri-
    cades;
I see the gonfanon of Holy Peter
Floating above their helmets — ha ! he is
    down !
    *Edith.*  He down !  Who down ?
    *Stigand.*    The Norman Count is down.
    *Edith.*  So perish all the enemies of Eng-
    land !     321
    *Stigand.*  No, no, he hath risen again —
    he bares his face —
Shouts something — he points onward —
    all their horse
Swallow the hill locust-like, swarming
    up.
    *Edith.*  O God of battles, make his battle-
    axe keen
As thine own sharp-dividing justice, heavy
As thine own bolts that fall on crimeful
    heads
Charged with the weight of heaven where-
    from they fall !

          CANONS (*singing*).

     Jacta tonitrua,
      Deus bellator !    330
     Surgas e tenebris,
      Sis vindicator !
     Fulmina, fulmina,
      Deus vastator !

*Edith.* O God of battles, they are three
to one,
Make thou one man as three to roll them
down !

CANONS (*singing*).

Equus cum equite
    Dejiciatur!
Acies, acies
    Prona sternatur !                        340
Illorum lanceas
    Frange, Creator!

*Stigand.* Yea, yea, for how their lances
snap and shiver
Against the shifting blaze of Harold's axe !
War-woodman of old Woden, how he fells
The mortal copse of faces ! There ! And
there !
The horse and horseman cannot meet the
shield,
The blow that brains the horseman cleaves
the horse,
The horse and horseman roll along the
hill,
They fly once more, they fly, the Norman
flies !                                       350

Equus cum equite
    Præcipitatur.

*Edith.* O God, the God of truth hath
heard my cry !
Follow them, follow them, drive them to
the sea !

Illorum scelera
    Pœna sequatur!

*Stigand.* Truth ! no; a lie; a trick, a
Norman trick !
They turn on the pursuer, horse against
foot,
They murder all that follow.
*Edith.*                    Have mercy on us !
*Stigand.* Hot-headed fools — to burst
the wall of shields !                         360
They have broken the commandment of the
king !
*Edith. His* oath was broken — O holy
Norman Saints,
Ye that are now of heaven, and see be-
yond
Your Norman shrines, pardon it, pardon
it,
That he forsware himself for all he loved,
Me, me and all ! Look out upon the bat-
tle !

*Stigand.* They thunder again upon the
barricades.
My sight is eagle, but the strife so thick —
This is the hottest of it; hold, ash ! hold,
willow !                                      369
*English Cries.* Out, out !
*Norman Cries.*        Ha Rou !
*Stigand.* Ha ! Gurth had leapt upon him
And slain him; he hath fallen.
*Edith.*                    And I am heard.
Glory to God in the Highest ! fallen, fallen !
*Stigand.* No, no, his horse — he mounts
another — wields
His war-club, dashes it on Gurth, and
Gurth,
Our noble Gurth, is down !
*Edith.*                    Have mercy on us !
*Stigand.* And Leofwin is down !
*Edith.*                    Have mercy on us !
O Thou that knowest, let not my strong
prayer
Be weaken'd in thy sight, because I love
The husband of another !
*Norman Cries.*        Ha Rou ! Ha Rou !
*Edith.* I do not hear our English war-
cry.
*Stigand.* No.
*Edith.* Look out upon the battle — is he
safe ?                                        381
*Stigand.* He stands between the banners
with the dead
So piled about him he can hardly move.
*Edith (takes up the war-cry).* Out ! out !
*Norman Cries.*        Ha Rou !
*Edith (cries out).* Harold and Holy
Cross !
*Norman Cries.* Ha Rou ! Ha Rou !
*Edith.*    What is that whirring sound ?
*Stigand.* The Norman sends his arrows
up to heaven,
They fall on those within the palisade !
*Edith.* Look out upon the hill — is Har-
old there ?
*Stigand.* Sanguelac — Sanguelac — the
arrow — the arrow ! — away !

SCENE II

FIELD OF THE DEAD.    NIGHT

ALDWYTH *and* EDITH.

*Aldwyth.* O Edith, art thou here ?    O
Harold, Harold —
Our Harold — we shall never see him more.

*Edith.* For there was more than sister
      in my kiss,
And so the Saints were wroth.  I cannot
      love them,
For they are Norman Saints — and yet I
      should —
They are so much holier than their harlot's
      son
With whom they play'd their game against
      the King !
   *Aldwyth.* The King is slain, the kingdom
      overthrown !
   *Edith.* No matter !
   *Aldwyth.*      How no matter, Harold
slain ? —                                              9
I cannot find his body.  O, help me
      thou !
O Edith, if I ever wrought against thee,
Forgive me thou, and help me here !
   *Edith.*                  No matter !
   *Aldwyth.* Not help me, nor forgive me ?
   *Edith.*                  So thou saidest.
   *Aldwyth.* I say it now, forgive me !
   *Edith.*                  Cross me not !
I am seeking one who wedded me in se-
      cret.
Whisper !  God's angels only know it.
      Ha !
What art *thou* doing here among the
      dead ?
They are stripping the dead bodies naked
      yonder,
And thou art come to rob them of their
      rings !
   *Aldwyth.* O Edith, Edith, I have lost
      both crown                                    20
And husband.
   *Edith.*        So have I.
   *Aldwyth.*            I tell thee, girl,
I am seeking my dead Harold.
   *Edith.*                  And I mine !
The Holy Father strangled him with a
      hair
Of Peter, and his brother Tostig helpt;
The wicked sister clapt her hands and
      laugh'd;
Then all the dead fell on him.
   *Aldwyth.*            Edith, Edith —
   *Edith.* What was he like, this husband ?
      like to thee ?
Call not for help from me.  I knew him
      not.
He lies not here; not close beside the
      standard.

Here fell the truest, manliest hearts of
      England.                                        30
Go further hence and find him.
   *Aldwyth.*            She is crazed !
   *Edith.* That doth not matter either.
      Lower the light.
He must be here.

*Enter two* CANONS, OSGOD *and* ATHELRIC,
*with torches.  They turn over the dead
bodies and examine them as they pass.*

   *Osgod.* I think that this is Thurkill.
   *Athelric.* More likely Godric.
   *Osgod.* I am sure this body
Is Alfwig, the king's uncle.
   *Athelric.*            So it is !
No, no, — brave Gurth, one gash from brow
      to knee !
   *Osgod.* And here is Leofwin.
   *Edith.*            And here is *he !*
   *Aldwyth.* Harold ?  O, no — nay, if it
      were — my God,
They have so maim'd and murder'd all his
      face
There is no man can swear to him !
   *Edith.*            But one woman !
Look you, we never mean to part again.  41
I have found him, I am happy.
Was there not some one ask'd me for for-
      giveness ?
I yield it freely, being the true wife
Of this dead King, who never bore re-
      venge.

*Enter* COUNT WILLIAM *and* WILLIAM
      MALET.

   *William.* Who be these women ?  And
      what body is this ?
   *Edith.* Harold, thy better !
   *William.*            Ay, and what art thou ?
   *Edith.* His wife !
   *Malet.* Not true, my girl, here is the
      Queen !   [*Pointing out* Aldwyth.
   *William* (*to* Aldwyth). Wast thou his
      Queen ?
   *Aldwyth.* I was the Queen of Wales.
   *William.* Why, then of England.  Madam,
      fear us not.                                    50
(*To* Malet.) Knowest thou this other ?
   *Malet.*            When I visited England,
Some held she was his wife in secret —
      some —
Well — some believed she was his para-
      mour.

*Edith.* Norman, thou liest ! liars all of
  you,
Your Saints and all !  *I* am his wife ! and
  she —
For look, our marriage ring !
        [*She draws it off the finger of* Harold.
                    I lost it somehow —
I lost it, playing with it when I was wild.
*That* bred the doubt ! but I am wiser
  now —
I am too wise — Will none among you all
Bear me true witness — only for this
  once —                                    60
That I have found it here again ?
                    [*She puts it on.*
                    And thou,
Thy wife am I for ever and evermore.
            [*Falls on the body and dies.*
*William.* Death ! — and enough of death
  for this one day,
The day of Saint Calixtus, and the day,
My day when I was born.
  *Malet.*            And this dead King's,
Who, king or not, hath kinglike fought and
  fallen,
His birthday, too.  It seems but yester-
  even
I held it with him in his English halls,
His day, with all his roof-tree ringing
  'Harold,'
Before he fell into the snare of Guy;    70
When all men counted Harold would be
  King,
And Harold was most happy.
  *William.*            Thou art half English.
Take them away !
Malet, I vow to build a church to God
Here on the hill of battle; let our high
  altar
Stand where their standard fell — where
  these two lie.
Take them away, I do not love to see
  them.
Pluck the dead woman off the dead man,
  Malet !
  *Malet.* Faster than ivy !  Must I hack
  her arms off ?                           79
How shall I part them ?
  *William.*   Leave them.  Let them be ?
Bury him and his paramour together.
He that was false in oath to me, it seems

Was false to his own wife.  We will not
  give him
A Christian burial; yet he was a warrior,
And wise, yea truthful, till that blighted
  vow
Which God avenged to-day.
Wrap them together in a purple cloak,
And lay them both upon the waste sea-
  shore
At Hastings, there to guard the land for
  which
He did forswear himself — a warrior — ay,  91
And but that Holy Peter fought for us,
And that the false Northumbrian held
  aloof,
And save for that chance arrow which the
  Saints
Sharpen'd and sent against him — who can
  tell ? —
Three horses had I slain beneath me;
  twice
I thought that all was lost.  Since I knew
  battle,
And that was from my boyhood, never
  yet —
No, by the splendor of God — have I
  fought men
Like Harold and his brethren, and his
  guard
Of English.  Every man about his king  100
Fell where he stood.  They loved him;
  and, pray God
My Normans may but move as true with
  me
To the door of death !  Of one self-stock
  at first,
Make them again one people — Norman,
  English,
And English, Norman; we should have a
  hand
To grasp the world with, and a foot to
  stamp it —
Flat.  Praise the Saints ! It is over.  No
  more blood !
I am King of England, so they thwart me
  not,
And I will rule according to their laws.
(*To* Aldwyth.)  Madam, we will entreat
  thee with all honor.                    110
  *Aldwyth.* My punishment is more than I
  can bear.

# BECKET

The first proofs of the play were printed in 1879, but it was not published until December, 1884. See prefatory note to 'Queen Mary,' and the 'Memoir,' vol. ii. pp. 193-199. In 1879 Irving refused the play, but in 1891 he asked leave to produce it, and it proved very successful on the stage, both in England and in America.

### TO THE LORD CHANCELLOR,

## THE RIGHT HONORABLE EARL OF SELBORNE.

MY DEAR SELBORNE, — To you, the honored Chancellor of our own day, I dedicate this dramatic memorial of your great predecessor; — which, altho' not intended in its present form to meet the exigencies of our modern theatre, has nevertheless — for so you have assured me — won your approbation.      Ever yours,

TENNYSON.

### DRAMATIS PERSONÆ

HENRY II. (*son of the Earl of Anjou*).
THOMAS BECKET, *Chancellor of England, afterwards Archbishop of Canterbury.*
GILBERT FOLIOT, *Bishop of London.*
ROGER, *Archbishop of York.*
*Bishop of Hereford.*
HILARY, *Bishop of Chichester.*
JOCELYN, *Bishop of Salisbury.*
JOHN OF SALISBURY ⎱ *friends of Becket.*
HERBERT OF BOSHAM ⎰
WALTER MAP, *reputed author of 'Golias,' Latin poems against the priesthood.*
KING LOUIS OF FRANCE.
GEOFFREY, *son of Rosamund and Henry.*
GRIM, *a monk of Cambridge.*
SIR REGINALD FITZURSE ⎫
SIR RICHARD DE BRITO   ⎬ *the four knights of the king's household, enemies of Becket.*
SIR WILLIAM DE TRACY ⎪
SIR HUGH DE MORVILLE ⎭
DE BROC OF SALTWOOD CASTLE.
LORD LEICESTER.
PHILIP DE ELEEMOSYNA.
TWO KNIGHT TEMPLARS.
JOHN OF OXFORD (*called the Swearer*).
ELEANOR OF AQUITAINE, *Queen of England* (*divorced from Louis of France*).
ROSAMUND DE CLIFFORD.
MARGERY.

Knights, Monks, Beggars, etc.

# BECKET

## PROLOGUE

A CASTLE IN NORMANDY. INTERIOR OF THE HALL. ROOFS OF A CITY SEEN THRO' WINDOWS

HENRY *and* BECKET *at chess.*

*Henry.* So then our good Archbishop Theobald
Lies dying.
*Becket.* I am grieved to know as much
*Henry.* But we must have a mightier man than he
For his successor.

*Becket.*      Have you thought of one?
*Henry.* A cleric lately poison'd his own mother,
And being brought before the courts of the Church,
They but degraded him. I hope they whipt him.
I would have hang'd him.
*Becket.*      It is your move.
*Henry.*      Well — there. [*Moves.*
The Church in the pell-mell of Stephen's time
Hath climb'd the throne and almost clutch'd the crown;      10
But by the royal customs of our realm
The Church should hold her baronies of me,

Like other lords amenable to law.
I'll have them written down and made the
    law.
  *Becket.* My liege, I move my bishop.
  *Henry.*               And if I live,
No man without my leave shall excom-
    municate
My tenants or my household.
  *Becket.*          Look to your king.
  *Henry.* No man without my leave shall
    cross the seas
To set the Pope against me — I pray your
    pardon.              19
  *Becket.* Well — will you move ?
  *Henry.*         There.   [*Moves.*
  *Becket.*   Check — you move so wildly.
  *Henry.* There then !       [*Moves.*
  *Becket.*   Why — there then, for you see
    my bishop
Hath brought your king to a standstill.
    You are beaten.
  *Henry* (*kicks over the board*). Why, there
    then — down go bishop and king to-
    gether.
I loathe being beaten; had I fixt my fancy
Upon the game I should have beaten
    thee,
But that was vagabond.
  *Becket.* Where, my liege ? With Phryne,
Or Lais, or thy Rosamund, or another ?
  *Henry.* My Rosamund is no Lais, Thomas
    Becket;
And yet she plagues me too — no fault in
    her —
But that I fear the Queen would have her
    life.               30
  *Becket.* Put her away, put her away, my
    liege !
Put her away into a nunnery !
Safe enough there from her to whom thou
    art bound
By Holy Church. And wherefore should
    she seek
The life of Rosamund de Clifford more
Than that of other paramours of thine ?
  *Henry.* How dost thou know I am not
    wedded to her ?
  *Becket.* How should I know ?
  *Henry.*       That is my secret, Thomas.
  *Becket.* State secrets should be patent to
    the statesman
Who serves and loves his king, and whom
    the king         40
Loves not as statesman, but true lover and
    friend.

  *Henry.* Come, come, thou art but deacon,
    not yet bishop,
No, nor archbishop, nor my confessor yet.
I would to God thou wert, for I should
    find
An easy father confessor in thee.
  *Becket.* Saint Denis, that thou shouldst
    not. I should beat
Thy kingship as my bishop hath beaten
    it.
  *Henry.* Hell take thy bishop then, and
    my kingship too !
Come, come, I love thee and I know thee,
    I know thee,
A doter on white pheasant-flesh at feasts, 50
A sauce-deviser for thy days of fish,
A dish-designer, and most amorous
Of good old red sound liberal Gascon wine.
Will not thy body rebel, man, if thou flat-
    ter it ?
  *Becket.* That palate is insane which can-
    not tell
A good dish from a bad, new wine from
    old.
  *Henry.* Well, who loves wine loves wo-
    man.
  *Becket.*               So I do.
Men are God's trees, and women are God's
    flowers;
And when the Gascon wine mounts to my
    head,
The trees are all the statelier, and the
    flowers        60
Are all the fairer.
  *Henry.*   And thy thoughts, thy fancies ?
  *Becket.* Good dogs, my liege, well train'd,
    and easily call'd
Off from the game.
  *Henry.*       Save for some once or twice,
When they ran down the game and worried
    it.
  *Becket.* No, my liege, no ! — not once —
    in God's name, no !
  *Henry.* Nay, then, I take thee at thy
    word — believe thee
The veriest Galahad of old Arthur's hall.
And so this Rosamund, my true heart-wife,
Not Eleanor — she whom I love indeed
As a woman should be loved — Why dost
    thou smile       70
So dolorously ?
  *Becket.*       My good liege, if a man
Wastes himself among women, how should
    he love
A woman as a woman should be loved ?

*Henry.* How shouldst thou know that never hast loved one ?
Come, I would give her to thy care in England
When I am out in Normandy or Anjou.
  *Becket.* My lord, I am your subject, not your —
  *Henry.*      Pander.
God's eyes ! I know all that — not my purveyor
Of pleasures, but to save a life — her life;
Ay, and the soul of Eleanor from hell-fire.
I have built a secret bower in England, Thomas,     81
A nest in a bush.
  *Becket.*     And where, my liege ?
  *Henry* (*whispers*).     Thine ear.
  *Becket.* That's lone enough.
  *Henry* (*laying paper on table*). This chart here mark'd ' Her Bower,'
Take, keep it, friend. See, first, a circling wood,
A hundred pathways running everyway,
And then a brook, a bridge; and after that
This labyrinthine brickwork maze in maze,
And then another wood, and in the midst
A garden and my Rosamund. Look, this line —
The rest you see is color'd green — but this     90
Draws thro' the chart to her.
  *Becket.*     This blood-red line ?
  *Henry.* Ay ! blood, perchance, except thou see to her.
  *Becket.* And where is she ? There in her English nest ?
  *Henry.* Would God she were ! — no, here within the city.
We take her from her secret bower in Anjou
And pass her to her secret bower in England.
She is ignorant of all but that I love her.
  *Becket.* My liege, I pray thee let me hence; a widow
And orphan child, whom one of thy wild barons —
  *Henry.* Ay, ay, but swear to see to her in England.     100
  *Becket.* Well, well, I swear, but not to please myself.
  *Henry.* Whatever come between us ?
  *Becket.*     What should come
Between us, Henry ?
  *Henry.*     Nay — I know not, Thomas.

  *Becket.* What need then ? Well — whatever come between us.     [*Going.*
  *Henry.* A moment ! thou didst help me to my throne
In Theobald's time, and after by thy wisdom
Hast kept it firm from shaking; but now I,
For my realm's sake, myself must be the wizard
To raise that tempest which will set it trembling
Only to base it deeper. I, true son     110
Of Holy Church — no croucher to the Gregories
That tread the kings their children underheel —
Must curb her; and the Holy Father, while
This Barbarossa butts him from his chair,
Will need my help — be facile to my hands.
Now is my time. Yet — lest there should be flashes
And fulminations from the side of Rome,
An interdict on England — I will have
My young son Henry crown'd the King of England,
That so the Papal bolt may pass by England,     120
As seeming his, not mine, and fall abroad.
I'll have it done — and now.
  *Becket.*     Surely too young
Even for this shadow of a crown; and tho'
I love him heartily, I can spy already
A strain of hard and headstrong in him. Say,
The Queen should play his kingship against thine !
  *Henry.* I will not think so, Thomas. Who shall crown him ?
Canterbury is dying.
  *Becket.*     The next Canterbury.
  *Henry.* And who shall he be, my friend Thomas ? Who ?     129
  *Becket.* Name him; the Holy Father will confirm him.
  *Henry* (*lays his hand on* Becket's *shoulder*). Here !
  *Becket.* Mock me not. I am not even a monk.
Thy jest — no more. Why — look — is this a sleeve
For an archbishop ?
  *Henry.*     But the arm within
Is Becket's, who hath beaten down my foes.
  *Becket.* A soldier's, not a spiritual arm.

*Henry.*  I lack a spiritual soldier,
    Thomas —
A man of this world and the next to boot.
*Becket.*  There 's Gilbert Foliot.
*Henry.*            He ! too thin, too thin.
Thou art the man to fill out the Church
    robe;
Your Foliot fasts and fawns too much for
    me.                     140
*Becket.*  Roger of York.
*Henry.*        Roger is Roger of York;
King, Church, and State to him but foils
    wherein
To set that precious jewel, Roger of York.
No.
*Becket.*  Henry of Winchester ?
*Henry.*      Him who crown'd Stephen —
King Stephen's brother ! No; too royal for
    me.
And I 'll have no more Anselms.
*Becket.*          Sire, the business
Of thy whole kingdom waits me; let me go.
*Henry.*  Answer me first.
*Becket.*       Then for thy barren jest
Take thou mine answer in bare common-
    place —
*Nolo episcopari.*
*Henry.*         Ay, but *Nolo*
*Archiepiscopari*, my good friend,    151
Is quite another matter.
*Becket.*        A more awful one.
Make *me* archbishop ! Why, my liege, I
    know
Some three or four poor priests a thousand
    times
Fitter for this grand function.  *Me* arch-
    bishop !
God's favor and king's favor might so clash
That thou and I— That were a jest in-
    deed !
*Henry.*  Thou angerest me, man; I do
    not jest.

*Enter* ELEANOR *and* SIR REGINALD
    FITZURSE.

        ELEANOR (*singing*).

Over ! the sweet summer closes,
  The reign of the roses is done —    160

*Henry* (*to* Becket, *who is going*).  Thou
    shalt not go.  I have not ended with
    thee.
*Eleanor* (*seeing chart on table*).  This
chart with the red line ! her bower ! whose
bower ?

*Henry.*  The chart is not mine, but
Becket's; take it, Thomas.
*Eleanor.*  Becket ! O, — ay — and these
chessmen on the floor — the king's crown
broken !  Becket hath beaten thee again —
and thou hast kicked down the board.  I
know thee of old.                 171
*Henry.*  True enough, my mind was set
upon other matters.
*Eleanor.*  What matters ?  State matters ? love matters ?
*Henry.*  My love for thee, and thine for
me.

             ELEANOR.

Over ! the sweet summer closes,
  The reign of the roses is done ;
Over and gone with the roses,    180
  And over and gone with the sun.

Here; but our sun in Aquitaine lasts
longer.  I would I were in Aquitaine again
— your North chills me.

Over ! the sweet summer closes,
  And never a flower at the close ;
Over and gone with the roses,
  And winter again and the snows.

That was not the way I ended it first —
but unsymmetrically, preposterously, illogi-
cally, out of passion, without art — like a
song of the people.  Will you have it ?  The
last Parthian shaft of a forlorn Cupid at
the King's left breast, and all left-handed-
ness and under-handedness.

And never a flower at the close ;
Over and gone with the roses,
  Not over and gone with the rose.    198

True, one rose will outblossom the rest,
one rose in a bower.  I speak after my
fancies, for I am a Troubadour, you know,
and won the violet at Toulouse; but my
voice is harsh here, not in tune, a nightingale out of season; for marriage, rose or
no rose, has killed the golden violet.
*Becket.*  Madam, you do ill to scorn
wedded love.                   207
*Eleanor.*  So I do.  Louis of France
loved me, and I dreamed that I loved
Louis of France: and I loved Henry of
England, and Henry of England dreamed
that he loved me; but the marriage-gar-
land withers even with the putting on, the
bright link rusts with the breath of the
first after-marriage kiss, the harvest moon
is the ripening of the harvest, and the

honey-moon is the gall of Love; he dies of
his honey-moon. I could pity this poor
world myself that it is no better ordered.

*Henry.* Dead is he, my Queen? What,
altogether? Let me swear nay to that by
this cross on thy neck. God's eyes! what
a lovely cross! what jewels!          223

*Eleanor.* Doth it please you? Take it
and wear it on that hard heart of yours —
there.                     [*Gives it to him.*

*Henry* (*puts it on*). On this left breast
   before so hard a heart,
To hide the scar left by thy Parthian dart.

*Eleanor.* Has my simple song set you
jingling? Nay, if I took and translated
that hard heart into our Provençal facili-
ties, I could so play about it with the
rhyme —                        233

*Henry.* That the heart were lost in the
rhyme, and the matter in the metre. May
we not pray you, madam, to spare us the
hardness of your facility?

*Eleanor.* The wells of Castaly are not
wasted upon the desert. We did but jest.

*Henry.* There's no jest on the brows of
Herbert there. What is it, Herbert?    241

*Enter* HERBERT OF BOSHAM.

*Herbert.* My liege, the good archbishop
is no more.

*Henry.* Peace to his soul!

*Herbert.* I left him with peace on his
face, — that sweet other-world smile, which
will be reflected in the spiritual body
among the angels. But he longed much to
see your Grace and the Chancellor ere he
past, and his last words were a commenda-
tion of Thomas Becket to your Grace as
his successor in the archbishopric.      251

*Henry.* Ha, Becket! thou rememberest
our talk!

*Becket.* My heart is full of tears — I have
no answer.

*Henry.* Well, well, old men must die, or
the world would grow mouldy, would only
breed the past again. Come to me to-morrow. Thou hast but to hold out thy hand.
Meanwhile the revenues are mine. A-hawking, a-hawking! If I sit, I grow fat.
             [*Leaps over the table, and exit.*

*Becket.* He did prefer me to the chancel-
lorship,                     260
Believing I should ever aid the Church —
But have I done it? He commends me now
From out his grave to this archbishopric.

*Herbert.* A dead man's dying wish should
   be of weight.

*Becket.* *His* should. Come with me. Let
   me learn at full
The manner of his death, and all he said.
             [*Exeunt* Herbert *and* Becket.

*Eleanor.* Fitzurse, that chart with the
red line — thou sawest it — her bower.

*Fitzurse.* Rosamund's?

*Eleanor.* Ay — there lies the secret of
her whereabouts, and the King gave it to
his Chancellor.                272

*Fitzurse.* To this son of a London merchant — how your Grace must hate him!

*Eleanor.* Hate him? as brave a soldier
as Henry and a goodlier man: but thou
— dost thou love this Chancellor, that
thou hast sworn a voluntary allegiance to
him?

*Fitzurse.* Not for my love toward him,
but because he had the love of the King.
How should a baron love a beggar on horseback, with the retinue of three kings behind
him, out-royalling royalty? Besides, he
holp the King to break down our castles,
for the which I hate him.

*Eleanor.* For the which I honor him.
Statesman, not Churchman, he. A great
and sound policy that; I could embrace
him for it: you could not see the King for
the kinglings.                 291

*Fitzurse.* Ay, but he speaks to a noble
as tho' he were a churl, and to a churl as
if he were a noble.

*Eleanor.* Pride of the plebeian!

*Fitzurse.* And this plebeian like to be
Archbishop!

*Eleanor.* True, and I have an inherited
loathing of these black sheep of the Papacy. Archbishop? I can see further into
a man than our hot-headed Henry, and if
there ever come feud between Church and
Crown, and I do not then charm this
secret out of our loyal Thomas, I am not
Eleanor.                    305

*Fitzurse.* Last night I followed a woman
in the city here. Her face was veiled, but
the back methought was Rosamund — his
paramour, thy rival. I can feel for thee.

*Eleanor.* Thou feel for me! — paramour
— rival! King Louis had no paramours,
and I loved him none the more. Henry
had many, and I loved him none the less
— now neither more nor less — not at all;
the cup's empty. I would she were but his

paramour, for men tire of their fancies;
but I fear this one fancy hath taken root,
and borne blossom too, and she, whom the
King loves indeed, is a power in the State.
Rival! — ay, and when the King passes,
there may come a crash and embroilment
as in Stephen's time; and her children —
canst thou not — that secret matter which
would heat the King against thee (*whispers
him and he starts*).  Nay, that is safe with
me as with thyself; but canst thou not —
thou art drowned in debt — thou shalt have
our love, our silence, and our gold — canst
thou not — if thou light upon her — free
me from her ?                             330
   *Fitzurse.*  Well, Madam, I have loved
her in my time.
   *Eleanor.*  No, my bear, thou hast not.
My Courts of Love would have held thee
guiltless of love — the fine attractions and
repulses, the delicacies, the subtleties.
   *Fitzurse.*  Madam, I loved according to
the main purpose the intent of nature.
   *Eleanor.*  I warrant thee ! thou wouldst
hug thy Cupid till his ribs cracked —
enough of this.  Follow me this Rosamund
day and night, whithersoever she goes;
track her, if thou canst, even into the King's
lodging, that I may (*clenches her fist*) —
may at least have my cry against him and
her, — and thou in thy way shouldst be
jealous of the King, for thou in thy way
didst once, what shall I call it, affect her
thine own self.                           349
   *Fitzurse.*  Ay, but the young colt winced
and whinnied and flung up her heels; and
then the King came honeying about her,
and this Becket, her father's friend, like
enough staved us from her.
   *Eleanor.*  Us !
   *Fitzurse.*  Yea, by the Blessed Virgin !
There were more than I buzzing round the
blossom — De Tracy — even that flint De
Brito.
   *Eleanor.*  Carry her off among you; run
in upon her and devour her, one and all of
you; make her as hateful to herself and to
the King as she is to me.                 363
   *Fitzurse.*  I and all would be glad to
wreak our spite on the rose-faced minion
of the King, and bring her to the level of
the dust, so that the King —
   *Eleanor.*  Let her eat it like the serpent,
and be driven out of her paradise.

# ACT I

## SCENE I. — BECKET'S HOUSE IN LONDON

*Chamber barely furnished.*  BECKET *unrob-
ing.*  HERBERT OF BOSHAM *and* SER-
VANT.

   *Servant.*  Shall I not help your lordship
to your rest ?
   *Becket.*  Friend, am I so much better
than thyself
That thou shouldst help me ?  Thou art
wearied out
With this day's work; get thee to thine
own bed.
Leave me with Herbert, friend.
              [*Exit* Servant.
Help me off, Herbert, with this — and this.
   *Herbert.*  Was not the people's blessing
as we passed
Heart-comfort and a balsam to thy blood ?
   *Becket.*  The people know their Church a
tower of strength,
A bulwark against Throne and Baronage.
Too heavy for me, this; off with it, Her-
bert !                                    10
   *Herbert.*  Is it so much heavier than thy
Chancellor's robe ?
   *Becket.*  No; but the Chancellor's and the
Archbishop's
Together more than mortal man can bear.
   *Herbert.*  Not heavier than thine armor at
Toulouse ?
   *Becket.*  O Herbert, Herbert, in my chan-
cellorship
I more than once have gone against the
Church.
   *Herbert.*  To please the King ?
   *Becket.*          Ay, and the King of kings,
Or justice; for it seem'd to me but just
The Church should pay her scutage like
the lords.                                20
But hast thou heard this cry of Gilbert
Foliot
That I am not the man to be your pri-
mate,
For Henry could not work a miracle —
Make an archbishop of a soldier ?
   *Herbert.*                Ay,
For Gilbert Foliot held himself the man.
   *Becket.*  Am I the man ?  My mother,
ere she bore me,

Dream'd that twelve stars fell glittering
   out of heaven
Into her bosom.
  *Herbert.*         Ay, the fire, the light,
The spirit of the twelve Apostles enter'd
Into thy making.
  *Becket.*       And when I was a child,
The Virgin, in a vision of my sleep,    31
Gave me the golden keys of Paradise.
   Dream,
Or prophecy, that?
  *Herbert.*  Well, dream and prophecy both.
  *Becket.*  And when I was of Theobald's
   household, once —
The good old man would sometimes have
   his jest —
He took his mitre off, and set it on me,
And said, 'My young archbishop — thou
   wouldst make
A stately archbishop!' Jest or prophecy
   there?
  *Herbert.*  Both, Thomas, both.
  *Becket.*      Am I the man?  That rang
Within my head last night, and when I
   slept                  40
Methought I stood in Canterbury Minster,
And spake to the Lord God, and said, 'O
   Lord,
I have been a lover of wines, and delicate
   meats,
And secular splendors, and a favorer
Of players, and a courtier, and a feeder
Of dogs and hawks, and apes, and lions,
   and lynxes.
Am *I* the man?' And the Lord answer'd
   me,
'Thou art the man, and all the more the
   man.'
And then I asked again, 'O Lord my God,
Henry the King hath been my friend, my
   brother,                50
And mine uplifter in this world, and chosen
   me
For this thy great archbishopric, believing
That I should go against the Church with
   him,
And I shall go against him with the
   Church,
And I have said no word of this to him.
Am *I* the man?' And the Lord answer'd
   me,
'Thou art the man, and all the more the
   man.'
And thereupon, methought, He drew to-
   ward me,

And smote me down upon the minster
   floor.                 59
I fell.
  *Herbert.* God make not thee, but thy
   foes, fall!
  *Becket.* I fell.  Why fall?  Why did He
   smite me?  What?
Shall I fall off — to please the King once
   more?
Not fight — tho' somehow traitor to the
   King —
My truest and mine utmost for the Church?
  *Herbert.* Thou canst not fall that way.
   Let traitor be;
For how have fought thine utmost for the
   Church,
Save from the throne of thine archbishop-
   ric?
And how been made archbishop hadst thou
   told him,
'I mean to fight mine utmost for the
   Church,                69
Against the King'?
  *Becket.*      But dost thou think the King
Forced mine election?
  *Herbert.*       I do think the King
Was potent i the election, and why not?
Why should not Heaven have so inspired
   the King?
Be comforted.  Thou art the man — be
   thou
A mightier Anselm.
  *Becket.* I do believe thee, then.  I am
   the man.
And yet I seem appall'd — on such a sudden
At such an eagle-height I stand and see
The rift that runs between me and the
   King.
I served our Theobald well when I was
   with him;              80
I served King Henry well as Chancellor;
I am his no more, and I must serve the
   Church.
This Canterbury is only less than Rome,
And all my doubts I fling from me like
   dust,
Winnow and scatter all scruples to the
   wind,
And all the puissance of the warrior,
And all the wisdom of the Chancellor,
And all the heap'd experiences of life,
I cast upon the side of Canterbury —
Our holy mother Canterbury, who sits   90
With tatter'd robes.  Laics and barons,
   thro'

The random gifts of careless kings, have
     graspt
Her livings, her advowsons, granges, farms,
And goodly acres — we will make her
     whole;
Not one rood lost. And for these Royal
     customs,
These ancient Royal customs — they *are*
     Royal,
Not of the Church — and let them be
     anathema.
And all that speak for them anathema.
     *Herbert.* Thomas, thou art moved too
          much.
     *Becket.*          O Herbert, here
I gash myself asunder from the King,   100
Tho' leaving each, a wound; mine own, a
     grief
To show the scar for ever — his, a hate
Not ever to be heal'd.

*Enter* ROSAMUND DE CLIFFORD, *flying from*
SIR REGINALD FITZURSE. *Drops her
veil.*

     *Becket.*          Rosamund de Clifford !
     *Rosamund.* Save me, father, hide me —
they follow me — and I must not be known.
     *Becket.* Pass in with Herbert there.
          [*Exeunt* Rosamund *and* Herbert *by
          side door.*

*Enter* FITZURSE.

     *Fitzurse.* The archbishop !
     *Becket.* Ay ! what wouldst thou, Regi-
          nald ?
     *Fitzurse.* Why — why, my lord, I fol-
          low'd — follow'd one —
     *Becket.* And then what follows ? Let
          me follow thee.
     *Fitzurse.* It much imports me I should
          know her name.   110
     *Becket.* What her ?
     *Fitzurse.* The woman that I follow'd
          hither.
     *Becket.* Perhaps it may import her all as
          much
Not to be known.
     *Fitzurse.*          And what care I for that ?
Come, come, my lord archbishop; I saw
     that door
Close even now upon the woman.
     *Becket.*          Well ?
     *Fitzurse* (*making for the door*). Nay, let
          me pass, my lord, for I must know.
     *Becket.* Back, man !

     *Fitzurse.* Then tell me who and what
          she is.
     *Becket.* Art thou so sure thou followedst
          anything ?
Go home, and sleep thy wine off, for thine
     eyes
Glare stupid-wild with wine.
     *Fitzurse* (*making to the door*). I must and
          will.
I care not for thy new archbishopric.   121
     *Becket.* Back, man, I tell thee ! What !
Shall I forget my new archbishopric
And smite thee with my crozier on the
     skull ?
'Fore God, I am a mightier man than thou.
     *Fitzurse.* It well befits thy new archbish-
          opric
To take the vagabond woman of the street
Into thine arms !
     *Becket.*          O drunken ribaldry !
Out, beast ! out, bear !
     *Fitzurse.*          I shall remember this.
     *Becket.* Do, and begone !
               [*Exit* Fitzurse.
          [*Going to the door, sees* De Tracy.
          Tracy, what dost thou here ?
     *De Tracy.* My lord, I follow'd Reginald
          Fitzurse.   131
     *Becket.* Follow him out !
     *De Tracy.*          I shall remember this
Discourtesy.          [*Exit.*
     *Becket.* Do. These be those baron-
          brutes
That havock'd all the land in Stephen's day.
Rosamund de Clifford !

*Re-enter* ROSAMUND *and* HERBERT.

     *Rosamund.*          Here am I.
     *Becket.*          Why here ?
We gave thee to the charge of John of
     Salisbury,
To pass thee to thy secret bower to-mor-
     row.
Wast thou not told to keep thyself from
     sight ?
     *Rosamund.* Poor bird of passage ! so I
          was; but, father,
They say that you are wise in winged
     things,   140
And know the ways of Nature. Bar the
     bird
From following the fled summer — a chink
     — he 's out,
Gone ! And there stole into the city a
     breath

Full of the meadows, and it minded me
Of the sweet woods of Clifford, and the
  walks
Where I could move at pleasure, and I
  thought
' Lo ! I must out or die.'
*Becket.*                    Or out *and* die.
And what hast thou to do with this Fitz-
  urse ?
  *Rosamund.*  Nothing.  He sued my hand.
  I shook at him.
He found me once alone.  Nay — nay — I
  cannot                                    150
Tell you.  My father drove him and his
  friends,
De Tracy and De Brito, from our castle.
I was but fourteen and an April then.
I heard him swear revenge.
  *Becket.*                    Why will you court it
By self-exposure ? flutter out at night ?
Make it so hard to save a moth from the
  fire ?
  *Rosamund.*  I have saved many of 'em.
  You catch 'em, so,
Softly, and fling them out to the free air.
They burn themselves *within*-door.
  *Becket.*                    Our good John
Must speed you to your bower at once.
  The child                                160
Is there already.
  *Rosamund.*  Yes — the   child — the
  child —
O, rare, a whole long day of open field !
  *Becket.*  Ay, but you go disguised.
  *Rosamund.*                    O, rare again !
We 'll baffle them, I warrant.  What shall
  it be ?
I 'll go as a nun.
  *Becket.*  No.
  *Rosamund.*          What, not good enough
Even to play at nun ?
  *Becket.*                    Dan John with a nun,
That Map and these new railers at the
  Church
May plaister his clean name with scurri-
  lous rhymes !
No !                                        169
Go like a monk, cowling and clouding up
That fatal star, thy beauty, from the squint
Of lust and glare of malice.  Good-night !
  good-night !
  *Rosamund.*  Father, I am so tender to all
  hardness !
Nay, father, first thy blessing.
  *Becket.*                    Wedded ?

  *Rosamund.*                        Father !
  *Becket.*  Well, well !  I ask no more.
  Heaven bless thee ! hence !
  *Rosamund.*  O holy father, when thou
  seest him next,
Commend me to thy friend.
  *Becket.*                    What friend ?
  *Rosamund.*                        The King.
  *Becket.*  Herbert, take out a score of
  armed men
To guard this bird of passage to her cage;
And watch Fitzurse, and if he follow thee,
Make him thy prisoner.  I am Chancellor
  yet.                                      181
          [*Exeunt* Herbert *and* Rosamund.
Poor soul ! poor soul !
My friend, the King ! — O thou Great Seal
  of England,
Given me by my dear friend, the King of
  England —
We long have wrought together, thou and
  I —
Now must I send thee as a common friend
To tell the King, my friend, I am against
  him.
We are friends no more; he will say that,
  not I.
The worldly bond between us is dissolved,
Not yet the love.  Can I be under him  190
As Chancellor ? as Archbishop over him ?
Go therefore like a friend slighted by one
That hath climb'd up to nobler company.
Not slighted — all but moan'd for.  Thou
  must go.
I have not dishonor'd thee — I trust I have
  not —
Not mangled justice.  May the hand that
  next
Inherits thee be but as true to thee
As mine hath been !  O, my dear friend,
  the King !
O brother ! — I may come to martyrdom.
I am martyr in myself already. — Herbert!
  *Herbert (re-entering).*  My lord, the town
  is quiet, and the moon            201
Divides the whole long street with light
  and shade.
No footfall — no Fitzurse.  We have seen
  her home.
  *Becket.*  The hog hath tumbled himself
  into some corner,
Some ditch, to snore away his drunkenness
Into the sober headache, — Nature's moral
Against excess.  Let the Great Seal be sent
Back to the King to-morrow.

*Herbert.*                    Must that be ?
The King may rend the bearer limb from
    limb.
Think on it again.
    *Becket.*                    Against the moral excess
No physical ache, but failure it may be   211
Of all we aim'd at. John of Salisbury .
Hath often laid a cold hand on my heats,
And Herbert hath rebuked me even now.
I will be wise and wary, not the soldier
As Foliot swears it. — John, and out of
    breath !

    *Enter* JOHN OF SALISBURY.

*John of Salisbury.* Thomas, thou wast not
    happy taking charge
Of this wild Rosamund to please the King,
Nor am I happy having charge of her —
The included Danaë has escaped again
Her tower and her Acrisius — where to
    seek ?                      221
I have been about the city.
    *Becket.*                    Thou wilt find her
Back in her lodging. Go with her — at
    once —
To-night — my men will guard you to the
    gates.
Be sweet to her, she has many enemies.
Send the Great Seal by daybreak. Both,
    good-night !


          SCENE II

STREET IN NORTHAMPTON LEADING TO
          THE CASTLE

ELEANOR'S RETAINERS *and* BECKET'S RE-
TAINERS *fighting. Enter* ELEANOR *and*
BECKET *from opposite streets.*

    *Eleanor.* Peace, fools !
    *Becket.* Peace, friends ! what idle brawl
    is this ?
    *Retainer of Becket.* They said — her
    Grace's people — thou wast found —
Liars ! I shame to quote 'em — caught, my
    lord,
With a wanton in thy lodging — Hell re-
    quite 'em !
    *Retainer of Eleanor.* My liege, the Lord
    Fitzurse reported this
In passing to the Castle even now.
    *Retainer of Becket.* And then they mock'd
    us and we fell upon 'em,

For we would live and die for thee, my
    lord,
However kings and queens may frown on
    thee.                      9
    *Becket to his Retainers.* Go, go — no more
    of this !
    *Eleanor to her Retainers.* Away ! —
    (*Exeunt* Retainers.) Fitzurse —
    *Becket.* Nay, let him be.
    *Eleanor.* No, no, my lord archbishop,
'T is known you are midwinter to all wo-
    men,
But often in your chancellorship you served
The follies of the King.
    *Becket.*                    No, not these follies !
    *Eleanor.* My lord, Fitzurse beheld her in
    your lodging.
    *Becket.* Whom ?
    *Eleanor.* Well — you know — the min-
    ion, Rosamund.
    *Becket.* He had good eyes !
    *Eleanor.*                    Then hidden in the street
He watch'd her pass with John of Salis-
    bury,
And heard her cry, ' Where is this bower
    of mine ? '                      19
    *Becket.* Good ears too !
    *Eleanor.* You are going to the Castle,
Will you subscribe the customs ?
    *Becket.*                    I leave that,
Knowing how much you reverence Holy
    Church,
My liege, to your conjecture.
    *Eleanor.*                    I and mine —
And many a baron holds along with me —
Are not so much at feud with Holy Church
But we might take your side against the
    customs —
So that you grant me one slight favor.
    *Becket.*                    What ?
    *Eleanor.* A sight of that same chart
    which Henry gave you
With the red line — ' her bower.'
    *Becket.*                    And to what end ?
    *Eleanor.* That Church must scorn her-
    self whose fearful priest                      30
Sits winking at the license of a king,
Altho' we grant when kings are dangerous
The Church must play into the hands of
    kings;
Look ! I would move this wanton from his
    sight
And take the Church's danger on myself.
    *Becket.* For which she should be duly
    grateful.

*Eleanor.*          True !

Tho' she that binds the bond, herself should
see

That kings are faithful to their marriage
vow.

*Becket.* Ay, madam, and queens also.

*Eleanor.*          And queens also !
What is your drift ?

*Becket.*          My drift is to the Castle,
Where I shall meet the barons and my
King.                    [*Exit.*

DE BROC, DE TRACY, DE BRITO, DE
MORVILLE (*passing*).

*Eleanor.* To the Castle ?

*De Broc.*          Ay !

*Eleanor.*     Stir up the King, the lords !
Set all on fire against him !

*De Brito.*          Ay, good madam !
                    [*Exeunt.*

*Eleanor.* Fool ! I will make thee hateful to thy King.

Churl ! I will have thee frighted into
France,

And I shall live to trample on thy grave.

## SCENE III

### THE HALL IN NORTHAMPTON CASTLE

*On one side of the stage the doors of an inner
Council-chamber, half-open. At the bottom,
the great doors of the Hall.* ROGER
ARCHBISHOP OF YORK, FOLIOT BISHOP
OF LONDON, HILARY OF CHICHESTER,
BISHOP OF HEREFORD, RICHARD DE
HASTINGS (*Grand Prior of Templars*),
PHILIP DE ELEEMOSYNA (*the Pope's Al-
moner*), *and others.* DE BROC, FITZURSE,
DE BRITO, DE MORVILLE, DE TRACY,
*and other* BARONS *assembled — a table be-
fore them.* JOHN OF OXFORD, *President
of the Council.*

*Enter* BECKET *and* HERBERT OF BOSHAM.

*Becket.* Where is the King ?

*Roger of York.* Gone hawking on the
Nene,

His heart so gall'd with thine ingratitude,

He will not see thy face till thou hast
sign'd

These ancient laws and customs of the
realm.

Thy sending back the Great Seal madden'd
him;

He all but pluck'd the bearer's eyes away.

Take heed lest he destroy thee utterly.

*Becket.* Then shalt thou step into my
place and sign.

*Roger of York.* Didst thou not promise
Henry to obey

These ancient laws and customs of the
realm ?                    10

*Becket.* Saving the honor of my order —
ay.

Customs, traditions, — clouds that come
and go;

The customs of the Church are Peter's rock.

*Roger of York.* Saving thine order ! But
King Henry sware

That, saving his King's kingship, he would
grant thee

The crown itself. Saving thine order,
Thomas,

Is black and white at once, and comes to
nought.

O bolster'd up with stubbornness and pride,

Wilt thou destroy the Church in fighting
for it,

And bring us all to shame ?

*Becket.*                    Roger of York,

When I and thou were youths in Theobald's house,                    21

Twice did thy malice and thy calumnies

Exile me from the face of Theobald.

Now I am Canterbury, and thou art York.

*Roger of York.* And is not York the peer
of Canterbury ?

Did not Great Gregory bid Saint Austin here

Found two archbishoprics, London and
York ?

*Becket.* What came of that ? The first
archbishop fled,

And York lay barren for a hundred years.

Why, by this rule, Foliot may claim the
pall                    30

For London too.

*Foliot.*          And with good reason too,

For London had a temple and a priest

When Canterbury hardly bore a name.

*Becket.* The pagan temple of a pagan
Rome !

The heathen priesthood of a heathen creed !

Thou goest beyond thyself in petulancy !

Who made thee London ? Who, but Canterbury ?

*John of Oxford.* Peace, peace, my lords !
these customs are no longer

As Canterbury calls them, wandering
clouds,

But by the King's command are written
   down,                                              40
And by the King's command I, John of
   Oxford,
The President of this Council, read them.
   *Becket.*                                     Read !
   *John of Oxford (reads).* 'All causes of
advowsons and presentations, whether be-
tween laymen or clerics, shall be tried in
the King's court.'
   *Becket.* But that I cannot sign; for that
would drag
The cleric before the civil judgment-seat,
And on a matter wholly spiritual.            49
   *John of Oxford.* 'If any cleric be ac-
cused of felony, the Church shall not
protect him; but he shall answer to the
summons of the King's court to be tried
therein.'
   *Becket.* And that I cannot sign.
Is not the Church the visible Lord on
   earth ?
Shall hands that do create the Lord be
   bound
Behind the back like laymen-criminals ?
The Lord be judged again by Pilate ?
   No !                                          59
   *John of Oxford.* 'When a bishopric
falls vacant, the King, till another be appointed, shall receive the revenues thereof.'
   *Becket.* And that I cannot sign. Is the
   King's treasury
A fit place for the moneys of the Church,
That be the patrimony of the poor ?
   *John of Oxford.* 'And when the vacancy
is to be filled up, the King shall summon
the chapter of that church to court, and the
election shall be made in the Chapel Royal,
with the consent of our lord the King, and
by the advice of his Government.'          71
   *Becket.* And that I cannot sign; for that
   would make
Our island-Church a schism from Christen-
   dom,
And weight down all free choice beneath
   the throne.
   *Foliot.* And was thine own election so
   canonical,
Good father ?
   *Becket.*      If it were not, Gilbert Foliot,
I mean to cross the sea to France, and lay
My crozier in the Holy Father's hands,
And bid him re-create me, Gilbert Foliot.
   *Foliot.* Nay; by another of these customs
   thou                                           80

Wilt not be suffer'd so to cross the seas
Without the license of our lord the King.
   *Becket.* That, too, I cannot sign.

DE BROC, DE BRITO, DE TRACY, FITZ-
   URSE, DE MORVILLE, *start up — a clash
   of swords.*

                 Sign and obey !
   *Becket.* My lords, is this a combat or a
   council ?
Are ye my masters, or my lord the King ?
Ye make this clashing for no love o' the
   customs
Or constitutions, or whate'er ye call them,
But that there be among you those that
   hold
Lands reft from Canterbury.
   *De Broc.*          And mean to keep them,
In spite of thee !
   *Lords (shouting).* Sign, and obey the
   crown !                                        90
   *Becket.* The crown ? Shall I do less for
   Canterbury
Than Henry for the crown ? King Ste-
   phen gave
Many of the crown lands to those that helpt
   him;
So did Matilda, the King's mother. Mark,
When Henry came into his own again,
Then he took back not only Stephen's gifts,
But his own mother's, lest the crown should
   be
Shorn of ancestral splendor. This did
   Henry.
Shall I do less for mine own Canterbury ?
And thou, De Broc, that holdest Saltwood
   Castle —                                       100
   *De Broc.* And mean to hold it, or —
   *Becket.*                    To have my life.
   *De Broc.* The King is quick to anger; if
   thou anger him,
We wait but the King's word to strike thee
   dead.
   *Becket.* Strike, and I die the death of
   martyrdom;
Strike, and ye set these customs by my
   death
Ringing their own death-knell thro' all the
   realm.
   *Herbert.* And I can tell you, lords, ye are
   all as like
To lodge a fear in Thomas Becket's heart
As find a hare's form in a lion's cave.
   *John of Oxford.* Ay, sheathe your swords,
   ye will displease the King.            110

*De Broc.* Why, down then thou ! but an
     he come to Saltwood,
By God's death, thou shalt stick him like a
     calf !       [*Sheathing his sword.*
*Hilary.* O my good lord, I do entreat
     thee — sign.
Save the King's honor here before his
     barons.
He hath sworn that thou shouldst sign, and
     now but shuns
The semblance of defeat; I have heard him
     say
He means no more; so if thou sign, my
     lord,
That were but as the shadow of an assent.
     *Becket.* 'T would seem too like the sub-
     stance, if I sign'd.
     *Philip de Eleemosyna.* My lord, thine
     ear ! I have the ear of the Pope.
As thou hast honor for the Pope our mas-
     ter,       121
Have pity on him, sorely prest upon
By the fierce Emperor and his Antipope.
Thou knowest he was forced to fly to
     France;
He pray'd me to pray thee to pacify
Thy King; for if thou go against thy King,
Then must he likewise go against thy King,
And then thy King might join the Anti-
     pope,
And that would shake the Papacy as it
     stands.
Besides, thy King swore to our cardinals
He meant no harm nor damage to the
     Church.       131
Smoothe thou his pride — thy signing is
     but form;
Nay, and should harm come of it, it is the
     Pope
Will be to blame — not thou. Over and
     over
He told me thou shouldst pacify the King,
Lest there be battle between Heaven and
     Earth,
And Earth should get the better — for the
     time.
Cannot the Pope absolve thee if thou sign ?
     *Becket.* Have I the orders of the Holy
     Father ?
     *Philip de Eleemosyna.* Orders, my lord
     — why, no; for what am I ?      140
The secret whisper of the Holy Father.
Thou, that hast been a statesman, couldst
     thou always
Blurt thy free mind to the air ?

*Becket.* If Rome be feeble, then should
     I be firm.
*Philip.* Take it not that way — balk not
     the Pope's will.
When he hath shaken off the Emperor,
He heads the Church against the King with
     thee.
     *Richard de Hastings (kneeling).* Becket,
     I am the oldest of the Templars;
I knew thy father; he would be mine age
Had he lived now; think of me as thy fa-
     ther !      150
Behold thy father kneeling to thee, Becket.
Submit; I promise thee on my salvation
That thou wilt hear no more o' the cus-
     toms.
*Becket.*      What !
Hath Henry told thee ? hast thou talk'd
     with him ?
     *Another Templar (kneeling).* Father, I
     am the youngest of the Templars,
Look on me as I were thy bodily son,
For, like a son, I lift my hands to thee.
     *Philip.* Wilt thou hold out for ever,
     Thomas Becket ?
Dost thou not hear ?
     *Becket (signs).* Why — there then —
     there — I sign,
And swear to obey the customs.
     *Foliot.*      Is it thy will,
My lord archbishop, that we too should
     sign ?      161
     *Becket.* O, ay, by that canonical obedi-
     ence
Thou still hast owed thy father, Gilbert
     Foliot.
     *Foliot.* Loyally and with good faith, my
     lord archbishop ?
     *Becket.* O, ay, with all that loyalty and
     good faith
Thou still hast shown thy primate, Gilbert
     Foliot.
     [*Becket draws apart with* Herbert.
Herbert, Herbert, have I betray'd the
     Church ?
I 'll have the paper back — blot out my
     name.
     *Herbert.* Too late, my lord: you see they
     are signing there.
     *Becket.* False to myself — it is the will
     of God      170
To break me, prove me nothing of my-
     self !
This almoner hath tasted Henry's gold.
The cardinals have finger'd Henry's gold.

And Rome is venal even to rottenness.
I see it, I see it.
I am no soldier, as he said — at least
No leader.  Herbert, till I hear from the
    Pope
I will suspend myself from all my func-
    tions.
If fast and prayer, the lacerating scourge —
    *Foliot (from the table).*  My lord arch-
    bishop, thou hast yet to seal.    180
    *Becket.*  First, Foliot, let me see what I
    have sign'd.    *[Goes to the table.*
What, this! and this!— what! new and
    old together!
Seal?  If a seraph shouted from the sun,
And bade me seal against the rights of the
    Church,
I would anathematize him.  I will not seal.
    *[Exit with* Herbert.

    *Enter* KING HENRY.

    *Henry.*  Where's Thomas?  hath he
    signed?  show me the papers!
Sign'd and not seal'd!  How's that?
    *John of Oxford.*    He would not seal.
And when he sign'd, his face was stormy-
    red —
Shame, wrath, I know not what.  He sat
    down there
And dropt it in his hands, and then a pale-
    ness,    190
Like the wan twilight after sunset, crept
Up even to the tonsure, and he groan'd,
'False to myself!  It is the will of God!'
    *Henry.*  God's will be what it will, the
    man shall seal,
Or I will seal his doom.  My burgher's
    son —
Nay, if I cannot break him as the prelate,
I'll crush him as the subject.  Send for
    him back.    *[Sits on his throne.*
Barons and bishops of our realm of Eng-
    land,
After the nineteen winters of King Ste-
    phen —
A reign which was no reign, when none
    could sit    200
By his own hearth in peace; when murder
    common
As nature's death, like Egypt's plague, had
    fill'd
All things with blood; when every door-
    way blush'd,
Dash'd red with that unhallow'd pass-
    over;

When every baron ground his blade in
    blood;
The household dough was kneaded up with
    blood;
The mill-wheel turn'd in blood; the whole-
    some plow
Lay rusting in the furrow's yellow weeds,
Till famine dwarft the race — I came, your
    King!
Nor dwelt alone, like a soft lord of the
    East,    210
In mine own hall, and sucking thro' fools'
    ears
The flatteries of corruption — went abroad
Thro' all my counties, spied my people's
    ways;
Yea, heard the churl against the baron —
    yea,
And did him justice; sat in mine own
    courts
Judging my judges, that had found a King
Who ranged confusions, made the twilight
    day,
And struck a shape from out the vague,
    and law
From madness.  And the event — our fal-
    lows till'd,    219
Much corn, repeopled towns, a realm again.
So far my course, albeit not glassy-smooth,
Had prosper'd in the main, but suddenly
Jarr'd on this rock.  A cleric violated
The daughter of his host, and murder'd
    him.
Bishops — York, London, Chichester, West-
    minster —
Ye haled this tonsured devil into your
    courts;
But since your canon will not let you take
Life for a life, ye but degraded him
Where I had hang'd him.  What doth hard
    murder care    229
For degradation? and that made me muse,
Being bounden by my coronation oath
To do men justice.  Look to it, your own
    selves!
Say that a cleric murder'd an archbishop,
What could ye do?  Degrade, imprison
    him —
Not death for death.
    *John of Oxford.*  But I, my liege, could
    swear,
To death for death.
    *Henry.*    And, looking thro' my reign,
I found a hundred ghastly murders done
By men, the scum and offal of the Church;

Then, glancing thro' the story of this realm,
I came on certain wholesome usages,     240
Lost in desuetude, of my grandsire's day,
Good royal customs — had them written
     fair
For John of Oxford here to read to you.
     *John of Oxford.*  And I can easily swear
          to these as being
The King's will and God's will and justice;
     yet
I could but read a part to-day, because —
     *Fitzurse.*  Because my lord of Canter-
          bury —
     *De Tracy.*          Ay,
This lord of Canterbury —
     *De Brito.*               As is his wont
Too much of late whene'er your royal
     rights                                   249
Are mooted in our councils —
     *Fitzurse.*          — made an uproar.
     *Henry.*  And Becket had my bosom on all
          this;
If ever man by bonds of gratefulness —
I raised him from the puddle of the gut-
     ter,
I made him porcelain from the clay of the
     city —
Thought that I knew him, err'd thro' love
     of him,
Hoped, were he chosen archbishop, Church
     and Crown,
Two sisters gliding in an equal dance,
Two rivers gently flowing side by side —
But no !
The bird that moults sings the same song
     again,                                   260
The snake that sloughs comes out a snake
     again.
Snake — ay, but he that lookt a fangless
     one
Issues a venomous adder.
For he, when having dofft the Chancellor's
     robe —
Flung the Great Seal of England in my
     face —
Claim'd some of our crown lands for Can-
     terbury —
My comrade, boon companion, my co-revel-
     ler,
The master of his master, the King's
     king. —
God's eyes !  I had meant to make him all
     but king.
Chancellor-Archbishop, he might well have
     **sway'd**                              270

All England under Henry, the young King,
When I was hence.  What did the traitor
     say ?
False to himself, but ten-fold false to
     me !
The will of God — why, then it is my
     will —
Is he coming ?
     *Messenger (entering).*  With a crowd of
          worshippers,
And holds his cross before him thro' the
     crowd,
As one that puts himself in sanctuary.
     *Henry.*  His cross !
     *Roger of York.*     His cross !  I 'll front
          him, cross to cross.
                    [*Exit* Roger of York.
     *Henry.*  His cross ! it is the traitor that
          imputes
Treachery to his King !                      280
It is not safe for me to look upon him.
Away — with me !
     [*Goes in with his* Barons *to the Council-
     Chamber, the door of which is left open.*

*Enter* BECKET, *holding his cross of silver be-
     fore him.  The* BISHOPS *come round him.*

     *Hereford.*  The King will not abide thee
          with thy cross.
Permit me, my good lord, to bear it for
     thee,
Being thy chaplain.
     *Becket.*          No; it must protect me.
     *Herbert.*  As once he bore the standard of
          the Angles,
So now he bears the standard of the an-
     gels.
     *Foliot.*  I am the dean of the province;
          let me bear it.
Make not thy King a traitorous murderer.
     *Becket.*  Did not your barons draw their
          swords against me ?                290

*Enter* ROGER OF YORK, *with his cross, ad-
     vancing to* BECKET.

     *Becket.*  Wherefore dost thou presume to
          bear thy cross,
Against the solemn ordinance from Rome,
Out of thy province ?
     *Roger of York.*  Why dost thou presume,
Arm'd with thy cross, to come before the
     King ?
If Canterbury bring his cross to court,
Let York bear his to mate with Canter-
     bury.

*Foliot* (*seizing hold of* Becket's *cross*),
Nay, nay, my lord, thou must not
brave the King.
Nay, let me have it. I will have it !
*Becket.*                              Away !
                              [*Flinging him off.*
*Foliot. He* fasts, they say, this mitred
Hercules !
*He* fast ! is that an arm of fast ? My
lord,                                            300
Hadst thou not sign'd, I had gone along
with thee;
But thou the shepherd hast betray'd the
sheep,
And thou art perjured, and thou wilt not
seal.
As Chancellor thou wast against the Church,
Now as archbishop goest against the King;
For, like a fool, thou know'st no middle
way.
Ay, ay ! but art thou stronger than the
King ?
*Becket.* Strong — not in mine own self,
but Heaven; true                            308
To either function, holding it; and thou
Fast, scourge thyself, and mortify thy flesh,
Not spirit — thou remainest Gilbert Foliot,
A worldly follower of the worldly strong.
I, bearing this great ensign, make it clear
Under what prince I fight.
*Foliot.*                    My lord of York,
Let us go in to the Council, where our
bishops
And our great lords will sit in judgment on
him.
*Becket.* Sons sit in judgment on their
father ! — then
The spire of Holy Church may prick the
graves —
Her crypt among the stars. Sign ? seal ?
I promised
The King to obey these customs, not yet
written,                                          320
Saving mine order; true, too, that when
written
I sign'd them — being a fool, as Foliot
call'd me.
I hold not by my signing. Get ye hence,
Tell what I say to the King.
          [*Exeunt* Hereford, Foliot, *and other*
          Bishops.
*Roger of York.* The Church will hate
thee.                                    [*Exit.*
*Becket.* Serve my best friend and make
him my worst foe;

Fight for the Church, and set the Church
against me !
*Herbert.* To be honest is to set all knaves
against thee.
Ah, Thomas, excommunicate them all !
*Hereford* (*re-entering*). I cannot brook
the turmoil thou hast raised.
I would, my lord Thomas of Canterbury,
Thou wert plain Thomas and not Canter-
bury,                                            331
Or that thou wouldst deliver Canterbury
To our King's hands again, and be at
peace.
*Hilary* (*re-entering*). For hath not thine
ambition set the Church
This day between the hammer and the an-
vil —
Fealty to the King, obedience to thyself ?
*Herbert.* What say the bishops ?
*Hilary.*          Some have pleaded for him,
But the King rages — most are with the
King;
And some are reeds, that one time sway to
the current,
And to the wind another. But we hold
Thou art forsworn; and no forsworn arch-
bishop                                          341
Shall helm the Church. We therefore place
ourselves
Under the shield and safeguard of the
Pope,
And cite thee to appear before the Pope,
And answer thine accusers. — Art thou
deaf ?
*Becket.* I hear you.          [*Clash of arms.*
*Hillary.* Dost thou hear those others ?
*Becket.*                              Ay !
*Roger of York* (*re-entering*). The King's
'God's eyes !' come now so thick
and fast
We fear that he may reave thee of thine
own.
Come on, come on ! it is not fit for us
To see the proud archbishop mutilated.
Say that he blind thee and tear out thy
tongue.                                          351
*Becket.* So be it. He begins at top with
me;
They crucified Saint Peter downward.
*Roger of York.*                        Nay,
But for their sake who stagger betwixt
thine
Appeal and Henry's anger, yield.
*Becket.*                              Hence, Satan !
                    [*Exit* Roger of York.

*Fitzurse (re-entering).* My lord, the King
    demands three hundred marks,
Due from his castles of Berkhamstead and
    Eye
When thou thereof wast warden.
    *Becket.*                    Tell the King
I spent thrice that in fortifying his castles.
    *De Tracy (re-entering).* My lord, the
    King demands seven hundred marks,
Lent at the siege of Toulouse by the
    King.                             361
    *Becket.* I led seven hundred knights and
    fought his wars.
    *De Brito (re-entering).* My lord, the King
    demands five hundred marks,
Advanced thee at his instance by the Jews,
For which the King was bound security.
    *Becket.* I thought it was a gift; I thought
    it was a gift.

    *Enter* LORD LEICESTER (*followed by*
        BARONS *and* BISHOPS).

    *Leicester.* My lord, I come unwillingly.
    The King
Demands a strict account of all those reve-
    nues
From all the vacant sees and abbacies,
Which came into thy hands when Chancel-
    lor.                             370
    *Becket.* How much might that amount
    to, my lord Leicester?
    *Leicester.* Some thirty — forty thousand
    silver marks.
    *Becket.* Are these your customs? O my
    good lord Leicester,
The King and I were brothers. All I
    had
I lavish'd for the glory of the King;
I shone from him, for him, his glory, his
    Reflection. Now the glory of the Church
Hath swallow'd up the glory of the King;
I am his no more, but hers. Grant me one
    day                            379
To ponder these demands.
    *Leicester.*       Hear first thy sentence!
The King and all his lords —
    *Becket.*           Son, first hear *me!*
    *Leicester.* Nay, nay, canst thou, that
    holdest thine estates
In fee and barony of the King, decline
The judgment of the King?
    *Becket.*          The King! I hold
Nothing in fee and barony of the King.
Whatever the Church owns — she holds it
    in

Free and perpetual alms, unsubject to
    One earthly sceptre.
    *Leicester.* Nay, but hear thy judgment.
The King and all his barons —
    *Becket.*             Judgment! Barons!
Who but the bridegroom dares to judge the
    bride,                          390
Or he the bridegroom may appoint? Not
    he
That is not of the house, but from the
    street
Stain'd with the mire thereof.
                      I had been so true
To Henry and mine office that the King
Would throne me in the great archbishop-
    ric;
And I, that knew mine own infirmity,
For the King's pleasure rather than God's
    cause
Took it upon me — err'd thro' love of him.
Now therefore God from me withdraws
    Himself,
And the King too.
                What! forty thousand marks!
Why, thou, the King, the Pope, the Saints,
    the world,                    401
Know that when made archbishop I was
    freed,
Before the Prince and chief justiciary,
From every bond and debt and obligation
Incurr'd as Chancellor.
                Hear me, son. As gold
Outvalues dross, light darkness, Abel Cain,
The soul the body, and the Church the
    Throne,
I charge thee, upon pain of mine anath-
    ema,
That thou obey, not me, but God in me,
Rather than Henry. I refuse to stand
By the King's censure, make my cry to the
    Pope,                         411
By whom I will be judged; refer myself,
The King, these customs, all the Church,
    to him,
And under his authority — I depart.
                            [*Going.*
    [*Leicester looks at him doubtingly.*
Am I a prisoner?
    *Leicester.*       By Saint Lazarus, no!
I am confounded by thee. Go in peace.
    *De Broc.* In peace now — but after.
    Take that for earnest.
        [*Flings a bone at him from the rushes.*
    *De Brito, Fitzurse, De Tracy, and Others*
    (*flinging wisps of rushes*). Ay, go in peace,

caitiff, caitiff! And that too, perjured
prelate — and that, turncoat shaveling!
There, there, there! traitor, traitor, traitor!
*Becket.* Mannerless wolves!
　　　　　　　[*Turning and facing them.*
*Herbert.* 　　　Enough, my lord, enough!
*Becket.* Barons of England and of Nor-
mandy,
When what ye shake at doth but seem to
fly,
True test of coward, ye follow with a
yell.
But I that threw the mightiest knight of
France,
Sir Engelram de Trie, —
*Herbert.* 　　　　　　Enough, my lord.
*Becket.* More than enough. I play the
fool again.

### Enter HERALD.

*Herald.* The King commands you, upon
pain of death,
That none should wrong or injure your
archbishop.　　　　　　　　　　430
*Foliot.* Deal gently with the young man
Absalom.
　　[*Great doors of the Hall at the back open,
　　　and discover a crowd. They shout:*
Blessed is he that cometh in the name of
the Lord!

### SCENE IV

#### REFECTORY OF THE MONASTERY AT
#### NORTHAMPTON

*A Banquet on the Tables.*

#### Enter BECKET. BECKET'S RETAINERS.

*First Retainer.* Do thou speak first.
*Second Retainer.* Nay, thou! Nay, thou!
Hast not thou drawn the short straw?
*First Retainer.* My lord archbishop, wilt
thou permit us —
*Becket.* To speak without stammering
and like a free man? Ay.
*First Retainer.* My lord, permit us then
to leave thy service.
*Becket.* When?　　　　　　　　　10
*First Retainer.* Now.
*Becket.* To-night?
*First Retainer.* To-night, my lord.
*Becket.* And why?

*First Retainer.* My lord, we leave thee
not without tears.
*Becket.* Tears? Why not stay with me
then?
*First Retainer.* My lord, we cannot yield
thee an answer altogether to thy satisfaction.　　　　　　　　　　　　　21
*Becket.* I warrant you, or your own
either. Shall I find you one? The King
hath frowned upon me.
*First Retainer.* That is not altogether
our answer, my lord.
*Becket.* No; yet all but all. Go, go!
Ye have eaten of my dish and drunken of
my cup for a dozen years.
*First Retainer.* And so we have. We
mean thee no wrong. Wilt thou not say,
'God bless you,' ere we go?　　　　32
*Becket.* God bless you all! God redden
your pale blood! But mine is human-red;
and when ye shall hear it is poured out
upon earth, and see it mounting to heaven,
my 'God bless you,' that seems sweet to
you now, will blast and blind you like a
curse.
*First Retainer.* We hope not, my lord.
Our humblest thanks for your blessing.
Farewell!　　　　　　[*Exeunt* Retainers.
*Becket.* Farewell, friends! farewell, swal-
lows! I wrong the bird; she leaves only
the nest she built, they leave the builder.
Why? Am I to be murdered to-night?
　　　　　　　[*Knocking at the door.*
*Attendant.* Here is a missive left at the
gate by one from the castle.
*Becket.* Cornwall's hand or Leicester's;
they write marvellously alike.　　　50
　　　　　　　　　　　　[*Reading.*
'Fly at once to France, to King Louis of
France; there be those about our King who
would have thy blood.'

Was not my lord of Leicester bidden to
our supper?
*Attendant.* Ay, my lord, and divers other
earls and barons. But the hour is past,
and our brother, Master Cook, he makes
moan that all be a-getting cold.　　59
*Becket.* And I make my moan along with
him. Cold after warm, winter after summer, and the golden leaves, these earls and
barons, that clung to me, frosted off me by
the first cold frown of the King. Cold, but
look how the table steams, like a heathen
altar; nay, like the altar at Jerusalem.

Shall God's good gifts be wasted? None of them here! Call in the poor from the streets, and let them feast. 69

*Herbert.* That is the parable of our blessed Lord.

*Becket.* And why should not the parable of our blessed Lord be acted again? Call in the poor! The Church is ever at variance with the kings, and ever at one with the poor. I marked a group of lazars in the marketplace — half-rag, half-sore — beggars, poor rogues (Heaven bless 'em!) who never saw nor dreamed of such a banquet. I will amaze them. Call them in, I say. They shall henceforward be my earls and barons — our lords and masters in Christ Jesus. [*Exit* Herbert.
If the King hold his purpose, I am myself a beggar. Forty thousand marks! forty thousand devils — and these craven bishops! 87

*A Poor Man (entering) with his dog.* My lord archbishop, may I come in with my poor friend, my dog? The King's verdurer caught him a-hunting in the forest, and cut off his paws. The dog followed his calling, my lord. I ha' carried him ever so many miles in my arms, and he licks my face and moans and cries out against the King.

*Becket.* Better thy dog than thee. The King's courts would use thee worse than thy dog — they are too bloody. Were the Church king, it would be otherwise. Poor beast! poor beast! set him down. I will bind up his wounds with my napkin. Give him a bone, give him a bone! Who misuses a dog would misuse a child — they cannot speak for themselves. Past help! his paws are past help. God help him!

*Enter the* BEGGARS *(and seat themselves at the Tables).* BECKET *and* HERBERT *wait upon them.*

*First Beggar.* Swine, sheep, ox — here 's a French supper! When thieves fall out, honest men —

*Second Beggar.* Is the archbishop a thief who gives thee thy supper? 110

*First Beggar.* Well, then, how does it go? When honest men fall out, thieves — no, it can't be that.

*Second Beggar.* Who stole the widow's one sitting hen o' Sunday, when she was at mass?

*First Beggar.* Come, come! thou hadst thy share on her. Sitting hen! Our Lord Becket 's our great sitting-hen cock, and we should n't ha' been sitting here if the barons and bishops had n't been a-sitting on the archbishop. 122

*Becket.* Ay, the princes sat in judgment against me, and the Lord hath prepared your table — *Sederunt principes, ederunt pauperes.*

*A Voice.* Becket, beware of the knife!

*Becket.* Who spoke?

*Third Beggar.* Nobody, my lord. What 's that, my lord? 130

*Becket.* Venison.

*Third Beggar.* Venison?

*Becket.* Buck — deer, as you call it.

*Third Beggar.* King's meat! By the Lord, won't we pray for your lordship!

*Becket.* And, my children, your prayers will do more for me in the day of peril that dawns darkly and drearily over the house of God — yea, and in the day of judgment also, than the swords of the craven sycophants would have done had they remained true to me whose bread they have partaken. I must leave you to your banquet. Feed, feast, and be merry. Herbert, for the sake of the Church itself, if not for my own, I must fly to France to-night. Come with me.
[*Exit with* Herbert.

*Third Beggar.* Here — all of you — my lord's health! *(they drink).* Well — if that is n't goodly wine — 150

*First Beggar.* Then there is n't a goodly wench to serve him with it; they were fighting for her to-day in the street.

*Third Beggar.* Peace!

FIRST BEGGAR.

The black sheep baaed to the miller's ewe-
lamb,
' The miller 's away for to-night.'
' Black sheep,' quoth she, ' too black a sin for
me.'

And what said the black sheep, my masters?

' We can make a black sin white.'

*Third Beggar.* Peace! 160

FIRST BEGGAR.

' Ewe-lamb, ewe-lamb, I am here by the dam.'
But the miller came home that night,

And so dusted his back with the meal in his
    sack,
That he made the black sheep white.

*Third Beggar.* Be we not of the family?
be we not a-supping with the head of the
family? be we not in my lord's own refractory? Out from among us; thou art
our black sheep. 169

### *Enter the four* KNIGHTS.

*Fitzurse.* Sheep, said he? And sheep
without the shepherd, too. Where is my
lord archbishop? Thou the lustiest and
lousiest of this Cain's brotherhood, answer.

*Third Beggar.* With Cain's answer, my
lord. Am I his keeper? Thou shouldst
call him Cain, not me.

*Fitzurse.* So I do, for he would murder
his brother the State.

*Third Beggar* (*rising and advancing*).
No, my lord; but because the Lord hath
set his mark upon him that no man should
murder him. 182

*Fitzurse.* Where is he? where is he?

*Third Beggar.* With Cain belike, in the
land of Nod, or in the land of France for
aught I know.

*Fitzurse.* France! Ha! De Morville,
Tracy, Brito — fled is he? Cross swords,
all of you! swear to follow him! Remember the Queen!

    [*The four* Knights *cross their swords.*
*De Brito.* They mock us; he is here.

    [*All the* Beggars *rise and advance upon*
    *them.*

*Fitzurse.* Come, you filthy knaves, let us
pass. 193

*Third Beggar.* Nay, my lord, let *us* pass.
We be a-going home after our supper in
all humbleness, my lord; for the archbishop
loves humbleness, my lord, and though we
be fifty to four, we dare n't fight you with
our crutches, my lord. There now, if
thou hast not laid hands upon me! and my
fellows know that I am all one scale like
a fish. I pray God I have n't given thee
my leprosy, my lord. 203

    [*Fitzurse shrinks from him, and another*
    *presses upon* De Brito.

*De Brito.* Away, dog!

*Fourth Beggar.* And I was bit by a mad
dog o' Friday, an' I be half dog already by
this token, that tho' I can drink wine I
cannot bide water, my lord; and I want to

bite, I want to bite, and they do say the
very breath catches. 210

*De Brito.* Insolent clown! Shall I smite
him with the edge of the sword?

*De Morville.* No, nor with the flat of it
either. Smite the shepherd, and the sheep
are scattered. Smite the sheep, and the
shepherd will excommunicate thee.

*De Brito.* Yet my fingers itch to beat
him into nothing.

*Fifth Beggar.* So do mine, my lord. I
was born with it, and sulphur won't bring
it out o' me. But for all that the archbishop washed my feet o' Tuesday. He
likes it, my lord. 223

*Sixth Beggar.* And see here, my lord,
this rag fro' the grangrene i' my leg. It's
humbling — it smells o' human natur'.
Wilt thou smell it, my lord? for the archbishop likes the smell on it, my lord; for I
be his lord and master i' Christ, my lord.

*De Morville.* Faugh! we shall all be
poisoned. Let us go. 231

    [*They draw back,* Beggars *following.*

*Seventh Beggar.* My lord, I ha' three
sisters a-dying at home o' the sweating
sickness. They be dead while I be a-supping.

*Eighth Beggar.* And I ha' nine darters
i' the spital that be dead ten times o'er i'
one day wi' the putrid fever; and I bring
the taint on it along wi' me, for the archbishop likes it, my lord. 240

    [*Pressing upon the* Knights *till they*
    *disappear thro' the door.*

*Third Beggar.* Crutches, and itches, and
leprosies, and ulcers, and gangrenes, and
running sores, praise ye the Lord, for to-
night ye have saved our archbishop!

*First Beggar.* I'll go back again. I
hain't half done yet.

*Herbert of Bosham* (*entering*). My friends,
the archbishop bids you good-night. He
hath retired to rest, and being in great
jeopardy of his life, he hath made his bed
between the altars, from whence he sends
me to bid you this night pray for him who
hath fed you in the wilderness. 253

*Third Beggar.* So we will — so we will,
I warrant thee. Becket shall be king, and
the Holy Father shall be king, and the
world shall live by the King's venison and
the bread o' the Lord, and there shall be
no more poor for ever. Hurrah! Vive le
Roy! That's the English of it.

## ACT II

### SCENE I. — ROSAMUND'S BOWER

*A Garden of Flowers. In the midst a bank of wild-flowers with a bench before it.*

Voices *heard singing among the trees.*

#### DUET.

1. Is it the wind of the dawn that I hear in the pine overhead ?
2. No ; but the voice of the deep as it hollows the cliffs of the land.
1. Is there a voice coming up with the voice of the deep from the strand,
   One coming up with a song in the flush of the glimmering red ?
2. Love that is born of the deep coming up with the sun from the sea.
1. Love that can shape or can shatter a life till the life shall have fled ?
2. Nay, let us welcome him, Love that can lift up a life from the dead ?
1. Keep him away from the lone little isle. Let us be, let us be.
2. Nay, let him make it his own, let him reign in it — he, it is he,
   Love that is born of the deep coming up with the sun from the sea.        10

*Enter* HENRY *and* ROSAMUND.

*Rosamund.* Be friends with him again — I do beseech thee.
*Henry.* With Becket ? I have but one hour with thee —
Sceptre and crozier clashing, and the mitre
Grappling the crown — and when I flee from this
For a gasp of freer air, a breathing-while
To rest upon thy bosom and forget him —
Why thou, my bird, thou pipest 'Becket, Becket' —
Yea, thou my golden dream of Love's own bower,
Must be the nightmare breaking on my peace        19
With 'Becket.'
*Rosamund.* O my life's life, not to smile
Is all but death to me. My sun, no cloud !
Let there not be one frown in this one hour.
Out of the many thine, let this be mine !
Look rather thou all-royal as when first
I met thee.

*Henry.* Where was that ?
*Rosamund.* Forgetting that
Forgets me too.
*Henry.* Nay, I remember it well.
There on the moors.
*Rosamund.* And in a narrow path.
A plover flew before thee. Then I saw
Thy high black steed among the flaming furze,
Like sudden night in the main glare of day.
And from that height something was said to me,        31
I knew not what.
*Henry.* I ask'd the way.
*Rosamund.* I think so.
So I lost mine.
*Henry.* Thou wast too shamed to answer.
*Rosamund.* Too scared — so young !
*Henry.* The rosebud of my rose ! —
Well, well, no more of *him* — I have sent his folk,
His kin, all his belongings, over-seas;
Age, orphans, and babe-breasting mothers — all
By hundreds to him — there to beg, starve, die —
So that the fool King Louis feed them not.        39
The man shall feel that I can strike him yet.
*Rosamund.* Babes, orphans, mothers ! is that royal, sire ?
*Henry.* And I have been as royal with the Church.
He shelter'd in the Abbey of Pontigny,
There wore his time studying the canon law
To work it against me. But since he cursed
My friends at Veselay, I have let them know
That if they keep him longer as their guest,
I scatter all their cowls to all the hells.
*Rosamund.* And is that altogether royal ?
*Henry.* Traitress !
*Rosamund.* A faithful traitress to thy royal fame.        50
*Henry.* Fame ! what care I for fame ? Spite, ignorance, envy,
Yea, honesty too, paint her what way they will,
Fame of to-day is infamy to-morrow;
Infamy of to-day is fame to-morrow;
And round and round again. What matters ? Royal —

I mean to leave the royalty of my crown
Unlessen'd to mine heirs.
 *Rosamund.*   Still — thy fame too;
I say that should be royal.
 *Henry.*    And I say,
I care not for thy saying.
 *Rosamund.*   And I say, 59
I care not for *thy* saying. A greater King
Than thou art, Love, who cares not for the
   word,
Makes 'care not' — care. There have I
   spoken true ?
 *Henry.* Care dwell with me for ever
   when I cease
To care for thee as ever !
 *Rosamund.*  No need ! no need ! . . .
There is a bench. Come, wilt thou sit ? —
   My bank
Of wild-flowers [*he sits*]. At thy feet !
     [*She sits at his feet.*
 *Henry.*   I bade them clear
A royal pleasaunce for thee, in the wood,
Not leave these country-folk at court.
 *Rosamund.*   I brought them
In from the wood, and set them here. I
   love them
More than the garden flowers, that seem
   at most 70
Sweet guests, or foreign cousins, not half
   speaking
The language of the land. I love *them* too,
Yes. But, my liege, I am sure, of all the
   roses —
Shame fall on those who gave it a dog's
   name ! —
This wild one ( *picking a briar-rose* ) — nay,
   I shall not prick myself —
Is sweetest. Do but smell !
 *Henry.*   Thou rose of the world !
Thou rose of all the roses ! [*Muttering.*
I am not worthy of her — this beast-body
That God has plunged my soul in — I, that
   taking
The Fiend's advantage of a throne, so long
Have wander'd among women, — a foul
   stream 81
Thro' fever-breeding levels, — at her side,
Among these happy dales, run clearer, drop
The mud I carried, like yon brook, and glass
The faithful face of heaven —
  [*Looking at her, and unconsciously aloud,*
       — thine ! thine !
 *Rosamund.*   I know it.
 *Henry* (*muttering*). Not hers. We have
   but one bond, her hate of Becket.

 *Rosamund* (*half hearing*). Nay ! nay !
   what art thou muttering ? *I* hate
   Becket ?
 *Henry* (*muttering*). A sane and natural
   loathing for a soul
Purer, and truer and nobler than herself;
And mine a bitterer illegitimate hate, 90
A bastard hate born of a former love.
 *Rosamund.* My fault to name him ! O,
   let the hand of one
To whom thy voice is all her music stay it
But for a breath !
   [*Puts her hand before his lips.*
      Speak only of thy love.
Why, there — like some loud beggar at
   thy gate —
The happy boldness of this hand hath won
   it
Love's alms, thy kiss (*looking at her hand*)
   — Sacred ! I 'll kiss it too.
        [*Kissing it.*
There ! wherefore dost thou so peruse it ?
   Nay,
There may be crosses in my line of life.
 *Henry.* Not half *her* hand — no hand to
   mate with *her*, 100
If it should come to that.
 *Rosamund.*  With her ? with whom ?
 *Henry.* Life on the hand is naked gipsy-
   stuff;
Life on the face, the brows — clear inno-
   cence !
Vein'd marble — not a furrow yet — and
   hers  [*Muttering.*
Crost and recrost, a venomous spider's
   web —
 *Rosamund* (*springing up*). Out of the
   cloud, my Sun — out of the eclipse
Narrowing my golden hour !
 *Henry.*    O Rosamund,
I would be true — would tell thee all —
   and something
I had to say — I love thee none the less —
Which will so vex thee.
 *Rosamund.*  Something against *me* ?
 *Henry.* No, no, against myself.
 *Rosamund.*   I will not hear it.
Come, come, mine hour ! I bargain for
   mine hour. 112
I 'll call thee little Geoffrey.
 *Henry.*    Call him !
 *Rosamund.*    Geoffrey !

   *Enter* GEOFFREY.

 *Henry.* How the boy grows !

*Rosamund.* Ay, and his brows are thine;
The mouth is only Clifford, my dear father.
*Geoffrey.* My liege, what hast thou
　　brought me ?
*Henry.* 　　　　　　Venal imp !
What say'st thou to the Chancellorship of
　　England ?
*Geoffrey.* O, yes, my liege.
*Henry.* 'O, yes, my liege !' He speaks
As if it were a cake of gingerbread. 119
　Dost thou know, my boy, what it is to be
Chancellor of England ?
*Geoffrey.* Something good, or thou
wouldst not give it me.
*Henry.* It is, my boy, to side with the
King when Chancellor, and then to be
made archbishop and go against the King
who made him, and turn the world upside
down.
*Geoffrey.* I won't have it then. Nay,
but give it me, and I promise thee not to
turn the world upside down. 131
*Henry (giving him a ball).* Here is a ball,
my boy, thy world, to turn any way and play
with as thou wilt — which is more than I
can do with mine. Go try it, play.
　　　　　　　　　　　[*Exit* Geoffrey.
A pretty lusty boy.
*Rosamund.* 　　　　So like to thee;
Like to be liker.
*Henry.* 　　　　Not in my chin, I hope !
That threatens double.
*Rosamund.* Thou art manlike perfect.
*Henry.* Ay, ay, no doubt; and were I
　　humpt behind,
Thou'dst say as much — the goodly way of
　　women 140
Who love, for which I love them. May
　　God grant
No ill befall or him or thee when I
Am gone !
*Rosamund.* Is *he* thy enemy ?
*Henry.* 　　　　He ? who ? ay !
*Rosamund.* Thine enemy knows the se-
　　cret of my bower.
*Henry.* And I could tear him asunder
　　with wild horses
Before he would betray it. Nay — no
　　fear !
More like is he to excommunicate me.
*Rosamund.* And I would creep, crawl
　　over knife-edge flint
Barefoot, a hundred leagues, to stay his
　　hand 149
Before he flash'd the bolt.

*Henry.* 　　　　And when he flash'd it
Shrink from me, like a daughter of the
　　Church.
*Rosamund.* Ay, but he will not.
*Henry.* 　　　　Ay ! but if he did ?
*Rosamund.* O, then ! O, then ! I almost
　　fear to say
That my poor heretic heart would excom-
　　municate
His excommunication, clinging to thee
Closer than ever.
*Henry (raising* Rosamund *and kissing
　　her).* My brave-hearted Rose !
Hath he ever been to see thee ?
*Rosamund.* 　　　　Here ? not he.
And it is so lonely here — no confessor.
*Henry.* Thou shalt confess all thy sweet
　　sins to me.
*Rosamund.* Besides, we came away in
　　such a heat, 160
I brought not even my crucifix.
*Henry.* 　　　　　　Take this.
　　　[*Giving her the Crucifix which* Eleanor
　　　　gave him.
*Rosamund.* O, beautiful ! May I have
　　it as mine, till mine
Be mine again ?
*Henry (throwing it round her neck).*
　　Thine — as I am — till death !
*Rosamund.* Death ? no ! I'll have it with
　　me in my shroud,
And wake with it, and show it to all the
　　Saints.
*Henry.* Nay — I must go; but when
　　thou layest thy lip
To this, remembering One who died for
　　thee,
Remember also one who lives for thee
Out there in France; for I must hence to
　　brave
The Pope, King Louis, and this turbulent
　　priest. 170
*Rosamund (kneeling).* O, by thy love for
　　me, all mine for thee,
Fling not thy soul into the flames of hell !
I kneel to thee — be friends with him
　　again.
*Henry.* Look, look ! if little Geoffrey
　　have not tost
His ball into the brook ! makes after it
　　too
To find it. Why, the child will drown
　　himself.
*Rosamund.* Geoffrey ! Geoffrey !
　　　　　　　　　　　　[*Exeunt.*

## SCENE II

### MONTMIRAIL

*'The Meeting of the Kings.'* JOHN OF OX-
FORD *and* HENRY. *Crowd in the distance.*

*John of Oxford.* You have not crown'd
young Henry yet, my liege?
*Henry.* Crown'd! by God's eyes, we will
not have him crown'd.
I spoke of late to the boy, he answer'd me,
As if he wore the crown already — No,
We will not have him crown'd.
'T is true what Becket told me, that the
mother
Would make him play his kingship against
mine.
*John of Oxford.* Not have him crown'd?
*Henry.* Not now — not yet! and
Becket —
Becket should crown him were he crown'd
at all;
But, since we would be lord of our own
manor,                                              10
This Canterbury, like a wounded deer,
Has fled our presence and our feeding-
grounds.
*John of Oxford.* Cannot a smooth tongue
lick him whole again
To serve your will?
*Henry.*                He hates my will, not me.
*John of Oxford.* There's York, my liege.
*Henry.*    But England scarce would hold
Young Henry king, if only crown'd by
York,
And that would stilt up York to twice
himself.
There is a movement yonder in the crowd —
See if our pious — what shall I call him,
John? —
Husband-in-law, our smooth-shorn suze-
rain,                                              20
Be yet within the field.
*John of Oxford.*          I will.     [*Exit.*
*Henry.*                    Ay! Ay!
Mince and go back! his politic Holiness
Hath all but climb'd the Roman perch
again,
And we shall hear him presently with clapt
wing
Crow over Barbarossa — at last tongue-
free

To blast my realms with excommunication
And interdict.  I must patch up a peace —
A peace in this long-tugged-at, threadbare-
worn
Quarrel of Crown and Church — to rend
again.
His Holiness cannot steer straight thro'
shoals,                                            30
Nor I.  The citizen's heir hath conquer'd me
For the moment.  So we make our peace
with him.

*Enter* LOUIS.

Brother of France, what shall be done with
Becket?
*Louis.* The holy Thomas!  Brother, you
have traffick'd
Between the Emperor and the Pope, be-
tween
The Pope and Antipope — a perilous game
For men to play with God.
*Henry.*                    Ay, ay, good brother,
They call you the Monk-King.
*Louis.*                        Who calls me?  she
That was my wife, now yours?  You have
her Duchy,
The point you aim'd at, and pray God she
prove                                              40
True wife to you.  You have had the bet-
ter of us
In secular matters.
*Henry.*            Come, confess, good brother,
You did your best or worst to keep her
Duchy.
Only the golden Leopard printed in it
Such hold-fast claws that you perforce
again
Shrank into France.  Tut, tut! did we con-
vene
This conference but to babble of our wives?
They are plagues enough in-door.
*Louis.*                          We fought in the East,
And felt the sun of Antioch scald our mail,
And push'd our lances into Saracen hearts.
We never hounded on the State at home   51
To spoil the Church.
*Henry.* How should you see this rightly?
*Louis.* Well, well, no more!  I am proud
of my 'Monk-King,'
Whoever named me; and, brother, Holy
Church
May rock, but will not wreck, nor our arch-
bishop
Stagger on the slope decks for any rough
sea

Blown by the breath of kings. We do for-
    give you
For aught you wrought against us.
              [Henry *holds up his hand.*
              Nay, I pray you,
Do not defend yourself. You will do much
To rake out all old dying heats if you,   60
At my requesting, will but look into
The wrongs you did him, and restore his
    kin,
Reseat him on his throne of Canterbury,
Be, both, the friends you were.
   *Henry.*           The friends we were !
Co-mates we were, and had our sport to-
    gether.
Co-kings we were, and made the laws to-
    gether.
The world had never seen the like before.
You are too cold to know the fashion of
    it.
Well, well, we will be gentle with him,
    gracious —                   69
Most gracious.

*Enter* BECKET, *after him,* JOHN OF OX-
   FORD, ROGER OF YORK, GILBERT FOLIOT,
   DE BROC, FITZURSE, *etc.*

            Only that the rift he made
May close between us, here I am wholly
    king,
The word should come from him.
   *Becket (kneeling).*   Then, my dear liege,
I here deliver all this controversy
Into your royal hands.
   *Henry.*          Ah, Thomas, Thomas,
Thou art thyself again, Thomas again.
   *Becket (rising).* Saving God's honor !
   *Henry.*         Out upon thee, man !
Saving the devil's honor, his yes and no.
Knights, bishops, earls, this London spawn
    — by Mahound,
I had sooner have been born a Mussul-
    man —
Less clashing with their priests —     80
I am half-way down the slope — will no
    man stay me ?
I dash myself to pieces — I stay myself —
Puff — it is gone. You, Master Becket,
    you
That owe to me your power over me —
Nay, nay —
Brother of France, you have taken, cher-
    ish'd him
Who thief-like fled from his own church
    by night,

No man pursuing. I would have had him
    back.
Take heed he do not turn and rend you too:
For whatsoever may displease him — that
Is clean against God's honor — a shift, a
    trick              91
Whereby to challenge, face me out of all
My regal rights. Yet, yet — that none may
    dream
I go against God's honor — ay, or himself
In any reason, choose
A hundred of the wisest heads from Eng-
    land,
A hundred, too, from Normandy and An-
    jou;
Let these decide on what was customary
In olden days, and all the Church of France
Decide on their decision, I am content.   100
More, what the mightiest and the holiest
Of all his predecessors may have done
Even to the least and meanest of my own,
Let him do the same to me — I am con-
    tent.
   *Louis.* Ay, ay ! the King humbles him-
    self enough.
   *Becket (aside).* Words ! he will wriggle
    out of them like an eel
When the time serves. (*Aloud.*)  My
    lieges and my lords,
The thanks of Holy Church are due to
    those
That went before us for their work, which
    we                    109
Inheriting reap an easier harvest. Yet —
   *Louis.* My lord, will you be greater than
    the Saints,
More than Saint Peter ? whom — what is it
    you doubt ?
Behold your peace at hand.
   *Becket.*         I say that those
Who went before us did not wholly clear
The deadly growths of earth, which hell's
    own heat
So dwelt on that they rose and darken'd
    heaven.
Yet they did much. Would God they had
    torn up all
By the hard root, which shoots again; our
    trial
Had so been less; but, seeing they were
    men
Defective or excessive, must we follow   120
All that they overdid or underdid ?
Nay, if they were defective as Saint Peter
Denying Christ, who yet defied the tyrant,

We hold by his defiance, not his defect.
O good son Louis, do not counsel me,
No, to suppress God's honor for the sake
Of any king that breathes.  No, God for-
    bid !
    *Henry.*  No !  God forbid ! and turn me
Mussulman !
No God but one, and Mahound is his pro-
    phet.
But for your Christian, look you, you shall
    have             130
None other God but me — me, Thomas, son
Of Gilbert Becket, London merchant.  Out!
I hear no more.                    [*Exit.*
    *Louis.*    Our brother's anger puts him,
Poor man, beside himself — not wise.  My
    lord,
We have claspt your cause, believing that
    our brother
Had wrong'd you; but this day he prof-
    fer'd peace.
You will have war; and tho' we grant the
    Church
King over this world's kings, yet, my good
    lord,
We that are kings are something in this
    world,
And so we pray you, draw yourself from
    under             140
The wings of France.  We shelter you no
    more.                    [*Exit.*
    *John of Oxford.*  I am glad that France
hath scouted him at last.
I told the Pope what manner of man he
    was.                    [*Exit.*
    *Roger of York.*  Yea, since he flouts the
    will of either realm,
Let either cast him away like a dead dog !
                            [*Exit.*
    *Foliot.*  Yea, let a stranger spoil his her-
    itage,
And let another take his bishopric !  [*Exit.*
    *De Broc.*  Our castle, my lord, belongs
    to Canterbury.
I pray you come and take it.        [*Exit.*
    *Fitzurse.*                When you will.
                            [*Exit.*
    *Becket.*  Cursed be John of Oxford,
    Roger of York,             150
And Gilbert Foliot ! cursed those De Brocs
That hold our Saltwood Castle from our
    see !
Cursed Fitzurse, and all the rest of them
That sow this hate between my lord and
    me !

*Voices from the Crowd.*  Blessed be the
lord archbishop, who hath withstood two
kings to their faces for the honor of God.
    *Becket.*  Out of the mouths of babes and
    sucklings, praise !
I thank you, sons; when kings but hold by
    crowns,
The crowd that hungers for a crown in
    heaven            160
Is my true king.
    *Herbert.*      Thy true King bade thee be
A fisher of men ; thou hast them in thy
    net.
    *Becket.*  I am too like the King here; both
    of us
Too headlong for our office.  Better have
    been
A fisherman at Bosham, my good Herbert,
Thy birthplace — the sea-creek — the petty
    rill
That falls into it — the green field — the
    gray church —
The simple lobster-basket, and the mesh —
The more or less of daily labor done —
The pretty gaping bills in the home-nest  170
Piping for bread — the daily want sup-
    plied —
The daily pleasure to supply it.
    *Herbert.*                Ah, Thomas,
You had not borne it, no, not for a day.
    *Becket.*  Well, maybe, no.
    *Herbert.*          But bear with Walter Map,
For here he comes to comment on the time.

*Enter* WALTER MAP.

    *Walter Map.*  Pity, my lord, that you
have quenched the warmth of France toward you, tho' His Holiness, after much
smouldering and smoking, be kindled again
upon your quarter.             180
    *Becket.*  Ay, if he do not end in smoke
again.
    *Walter Map.*  My lord, the fire, when
first kindled, said to the smoke, 'Go up,
my son, straight to heaven.'  And the
smoke said, 'I go;' but anon the Northeast took and turned him Southwest, then
the Southwest turned him Northeast, and
so of the other winds; but it was in him to
go up straight if the time had been quieter.
Your lordship affects the unwavering perpendicular; but His Holiness, pushed one
way by the Empire and another by England, if he move at all — Heaven stay him !
— is fain to diagonalize.

*Herbert.* Diagonalize ! thou art a word-
monger.
Our Thomas never will diagonalize.
Thou art a jester and a verse-maker.
Diagonalize !                                  198
    *Walter Map.* Is the world any the worse
for my verses if the Latin rhymes be rolled
out from a full mouth ? or any harm done
to the people if my jest be in defence of
the Truth ?
    *Becket.* Ay, if the jest be so done that
the people
Delight to wallow in the grossness of it,
Till Truth herself be shamed of her defender.
*Non defensoribus istis,* Walter Map !
    *Walter Map.* Is that my case ? so if the
city be sick, and I cannot call the kennel
sweet, your lordship would suspend me
from verse-writing, as you suspended yourself after sub-writing to the customs.    212
    *Becket.* I pray God pardon mine infir-
mity !
    *Walter Map.* Nay, my lord, take heart;
for tho' you suspended yourself, the Pope
let you down again; and tho' you suspend
Foliot or another, the Pope will not leave
them in suspense, for the Pope himself is
always in suspense, like Mahound's coffin
hung between heaven and earth — always
in suspense, like the scales, till the weight
of Germany or the gold of England brings
one of them down to the dust — always in
suspense, like the tail of the horologe — to
and fro — tick-tack — we make the time,
we keep the time, ay, and we serve the
time; for I have heard say that if you
boxed the Pope's ears with a purse, you
might stagger him, but he would pocket
the purse. No saying of mine — Jocelyn
of Salisbury. But the King hath bought
half the College of Red-hats. He warmed
to you to-day, and you have chilled him
again. Yet you both love God. Agree
with him quickly again, even for the sake
of the Church. My one grain of good
counsel which you will not swallow. I hate
a split between old friendships as I hate
the dirty gap in the face of a Cistercian
monk, that will swallow anything. Farewell.                                       [*Exit.*
    *Becket.* Map scoffs at Rome. I all but
hold with Map.                             242
Save for myself no Rome were left in England,

All had been his. Why should this Rome,
    this Rome,
Still choose **Barabbas** rather than the
    Christ,
Absolve the left-hand thief and damn the
    right ?
Take fees of tyranny, wink at sacrilege,
Which even Peter had not dared ? con-
    demn
The blameless exile ? —
    *Herbert.*        Thee, thou holy Thomas !
I would that thou hadst been the Holy
    Father.                                 250
    *Becket.* I would have done my most to
    keep Rome holy,
I would have made Rome know she still is
    Rome —
Who stands aghast at her eternal self
And shakes at mortal kings — her vacilla-
    tion,
Avarice, craft — O God, how many an in-
    nocent
Has left his bones upon the way to Rome
Unwept, uncared for ! Yea — on mine
    own self
The King had had no power except for
    Rome.
'T is not the King who is guilty of mine
    exile,
But Rome, Rome, Rome !
    *Herbert.*          My lord, I see this Louis
Returning, ah ! to drive thee from his
    realm.                                  261
    *Becket.* He said as much before. Thou
    art no prophet,
Nor yet a prophet's son.
    *Herbert.*          Whatever he say,
Deny not thou God's honor for a king.
The King looks troubled.

        *Re-enter* KING LOUIS.

    *Louis.*          My dear lord archbishop,
I learn but now that those poor Poite-
    vins
That in thy cause were stirr'd against King
    Henry
Have been, despite his kingly promise
    given
To our own self of pardon, evilly used
And put to pain. I have lost all trust in
    him.                                    270
The Church alone hath eyes — and now I
    see
That I was blind — suffer the phrase —
    surrendering

God's honor to the pleasure of a man.
Forgive me and absolve me, holy father.
                                    [*Kneels.*
  *Becket.* Son, I absolve thee in the name
    of God.
  *Louis* (*rising*). Return to Sens, where we
    will care for you.
The wine and wealth of all our France are
    yours;
Rest in our realm, and be at peace with all.
                                    [*Exeunt.*
  *Voices from the Crowd.* Long live the
good King Louis! God bless the great
archbishop!                              281

  *Re-enter* HENRY *and* JOHN OF OXFORD.

  *Henry* (*looking after* King Louis *and*
    Becket). Ay, there they go — both
    backs are turn'd to me —
Why, then I strike into my former path
For England, crown young Henry there,
    and make
Our waning Eleanor all but love me!
                                    John,
Thou hast served me heretofore with Rome
    — and well.
They call thee John the Swearer.
  *John of Oxford.*          For this reason,
That, being ever duteous to the King,
I evermore have sworn upon his side,   289
And ever mean to do it.
  *Henry* (*claps him on the shoulder*). Hon-
    est John!
To Rome again! the storm begins again.
Spare not thy tongue! be lavish with our
    coins,
Threaten our junction with the Emperor —
    flatter
And fright the Pope — bribe all the cardi-
    nals — leave
Lateran and Vatican in one dust of gold —
Swear and unswear, state and misstate thy
    best!
I go to have young Henry crown'd by York.


## ACT III

### SCENE I. — THE BOWER

#### HENRY *and* ROSAMUND.

  *Henry.* All that you say is just. I can-
    not answer it
Till better times, when I shall put away —

  *Rosamund.* What will you put away?
  *Henry.*          That which you ask me
Till better times. Let it content you now
There is no woman that I love so well.
  *Rosamund.* No woman but should be
    content with that —
  *Henry.* And one fair child to fondle!
  *Rosamund.*          O, yes, the child
We waited for so long — Heaven's gift at
    last —
And how you doted on him then! To-day
I almost fear'd your kiss was colder —
    yes —                                10
But then the child *is* such a child! What
    chance
That he should ever spread into the man
Here in our silence? I have done my best.
I am not learn'd.
  *Henry.*  ●     I am the King, his father,
And I will look to it. Is our secret ours?
Have you had any alarm? no stranger?
  *Rosamund.*                          No.
The warder of the bower hath given himself
Of late to wine. I sometimes think he
    sleeps
When he should watch; and yet what fear?
    the people
Believe the wood enchanted. No one
    comes,                                20
Nor foe nor friend; his fond excess of wine
Springs from the loneliness of my poor
    bower,
Which weighs even on me.
  *Henry.*          Yet these tree-towers,
Their long bird-echoing minster-aisles, —
    the voice
Of the perpetual brook, these golden slopes
Of Solomon-shaming flowers — that was
    your saying,
All pleased you so at first.
  *Rosamund.*          Not now so much.
My Anjou bower was scarce as beautiful.
But you were oftener there. I have none
    but you.
The brook's voice is not yours, and no
    flower, not                           30
The sun himself, should he be changed to
    one,
Could shine away the darkness of that gap
Left by the lack of love.
  *Henry.*          The lack of love!
  *Rosamund.* Of one we love. Nay, I
    would not be bold,
Yet hoped ere this you might —
                        [*Looks earnestly at him.*

*Henry.*             Anything further ?

*Rosamund.* Only my best bower-maiden
     died of late,
And that old priest whom John of Salis-
     bury trusted
Hath sent another.

*Henry.*           Secret ?

*Rosamund.*           I but ask'd her
One question, and she primm'd her mouth
     and put
Her hands together — thus — and said, God
     help her,            40
That she was sworn to silence.

*Henry.*           What did you ask her ?

*Rosamund.* Some daily something - no-
     thing.

*Henry.*       Secret, then ?

*Rosamund.* I do not love her. Must you
     go, my liege,
So suddenly ?

*Henry.*       I came to England suddenly,
And on a great occasion sure to wake
As great a wrath in Becket —

*Rosamund.*        Always Becket !
He always comes between us.

*Henry.*          And to meet it
I needs must leave as suddenly. It is
     raining,
Put on your hood and see me to the bounds.
                       [*Exeunt.*

Margery (*singing behind scene*).

Babble in bower           50
     Under the rose !
Bee must n't buzz,
     Whoop — but he knows.

Kiss me, little one,
     Nobody near !
Grasshopper, grasshopper,
     Whoop — you can hear.

Kiss in the bower,
     Tit on the tree !
Bird must n't tell,         60
     Whoop — he can see.

*Enter* Margery.

I ha' been but a week here and I ha' seen
what I ha' seen, for to be sure it 's no more
than a week since our old Father Philip
that has confessed our mother for twenty
years, and she was hard put to it, and to
speak truth, nigh at the end of our last
crust, and that mouldy, and she cried out
on him to put me forth in the world and to
make me a woman of the world, and to win
my own bread, whereupon he asked our
mother if I could keep a quiet tongue i' my
head, and not speak till I was spoke to,
and I answered for myself that I never
spoke more than was needed, and he told
me he would advance me to the service of a
great lady, and took me ever so far away,
and gave me a great pat o' the cheek for a
pretty wench, and said it was a pity to blindfold such eyes as mine, and such to be sure
they be, but he blinded 'em for all that,
and so brought me no-hows as I may say,
and the more shame to him after his promise, into a garden and not into the world,
and bade me whatever I saw not to speak
one word, an' it 'ud be well for me in the
end, for there were great ones who would
look after me, and to be sure I ha' seen
great ones to-day — and then not to speak
one word, for that 's the rule o' the garden,
tho' to be sure if I had been Eve i' the
garden I should n't ha' minded the apple,
for what 's an apple, you know, save to a
child, and I 'm no child, but more a woman
o' the world than my lady here, and I ha'
seen what I ha' seen — tho' to be sure if I
had n't minded it we should all on us ha'
had to go, bless the Saints, wi' bare backs,
but the backs 'ud ha' countenanced one
another, and belike it 'ud ha' been always
summer, and anyhow I am as well-shaped
as my lady here, and I ha' seen what I ha'
seen, and what 's the good of my talking to
myself, for here comes my lady (*enter* Rosamund), and, my lady, tho' I should n't
speak one word, I wish you joy o' the
King's brother.

*Rosamund.* What is it you mean ?    108

*Margery.* I mean your goodman, your
husband, my lady, for I saw your ladyship
a-parting wi' him even now i' the coppice,
when I was a-getting o' bluebells for your
ladyship's nose to smell on — and I ha'
seen the King once at Oxford, and he 's as
like the King as fingernail to fingernail,
and I thought at first it was the King, only
you know the King 's married, for King
Louis —

*Rosamund.* Married !

*Margery.* Years and years, my lady, for
her husband, King Louis —        121

*Rosamund.* Hush !

*Margery.* And I thought if it were the
King's brother he had a better bride than

the King, for the people do say that his is
bad beyond all reckoning, and —
   *Rosamund.*  The people lie.      127
   *Margery.*  Very like, my lady, but most
on 'em know an honest woman and a lady
when they see her, and besides they say
she makes songs, and that 's against her,
for I never knew an honest woman that
could make songs, tho' to be sure our mother 'ill sing me old songs by the hour, but
then, God help her, she had 'em from her
mother, and her mother from her mother
back and back for ever so long, but none
on 'em ever made songs, and they were all
honest.
   *Rosamund.*  Go, you shall tell me of her
some other time.      141
   *Margery.*  There 's none so much to tell
on her, my lady, only she kept the seventh
commandment better than some I know
on, or I could n't look your ladyship i' the
face, and she brew'd the best ale in all
Glo'ster, that is to say in her time when
she had the 'Crown.'
   *Rosamund.*  The crown! who?
   *Margery.*  Mother.      150
   *Rosamund.*  I mean her whom you call
— fancy — my husband's brother's wife.
   *Margery.*  O, Queen Eleanor. Yes, my
lady; and tho' I be sworn not to speak a
word, I can tell you all about her, if —
   *Rosamund.*  No word now. I am faint
and sleepy. Leave me. Nay — go. What!
will you anger me?      [*Exit* Margery.
He charged me not to question any of those
About me. Have I? no! she question'd
me.      160
Did she not slander *him*? Should she stay
   here?
May she not tempt me, being at my side,
To question *her*? Nay, can I send her
   hence
Without his kingly leave? I am in the
   dark.
I have lived, poor bird, from cage to cage,
   and known
Nothing but him — happy to know no
   more,
So that he loved me — and he loves me —
   yes,
And bound me by his love to secrecy
Till his own time.
         Eleanor, Eleanor, have I
Not heard ill things of her in France? O,
   she 's      170

The Queen of France. I see it — some
   confusion,
Some strange mistake. I did not hear
   aright,
Myself confused with parting from the
   King.

       MARGERY (*behind scene*).

     Bee must n't buzz,
       Whoop — but he knows.

   *Rosamund.*  Yet her — what her? he
   hinted of some her —
When he was here before —
Something that would displease me. Hath
   he stray'd
From love's clear path into the common
   bush,
And, being scratch'd, returns to his true
   rose,      180
Who hath not thorn enough to prick him
   for it,
Even with a word?

       MARGERY (*behind scene*).

     Bird must n't tell,
       Whoop — he can see.

   *Rosamund.*  I would not hear him. Nay
   — there 's more — he frown'd
'No mate for her, if it should come to
   that' —
To that — to what?

       MARGERY (*behind scene*).

     Whoop — but he knows,
       Whoop — but he knows.

   *Rosamund.*  O God! some dreadful truth
   is breaking on me —      190
Some dreadful thing is coming on me.

       *Enter* GEOFFREY.

                  Geoffrey!
   *Geoffrey.*  What are you crying for, when
   the sun shines?
   *Rosamund.*  Hath not thy father left us
   to ourselves?
   *Geoffrey.*  Ay, but he 's taken the rain
with him. I hear Margery: I 'll go play
with her.      [*Exit* Geoffrey.

       ROSAMUND.

     Rainbow, stay,
     Gleam upon gloom,
     Bright as my dream,
     Rainbow, stay!      200

But it passes away,
Gloom upon gleam,
Dark as my doom —
O rainbow, stay !

## SCENE II

### OUTSIDE THE WOODS NEAR ROSA-
### MUND'S BOWER

#### ELEANOR. FITZURSE.

*Eleanor.* Up from the salt lips of the
    land we two
Have track'd the King to this dark inland
    wood;
And somewhere hereabouts he vanish'd.
    Here
His turtle builds; his exit is our adit.
Watch ! he will out again, and presently,
Seeing he must to Westminster and crown
Young Henry there to-morrow.
   *Fitzurse.*          We have watch'd
So long in vain, he hath pass'd out again,
And on the other side.
               [*A great horn winded.*
              Hark ! Madam !
   *Eleanor.*                Ay,
How ghostly sounds that horn in the black
    wood !       [*A countryman flying.*
Whither away, man ? what are you flying
    from ?                  11
   *Countryman.* The witch ! the witch ! she
sits naked by a great heap of gold in the
middle of the wood, and when the horn
sounds she comes out as a wolf. Get you
hence ! a man passed in there to-day. I
holla'd to him, but he did n't hear me; he 'll
never out again — the witch has got him.
I dare n't stay — I dare n't stay !     19
   *Eleanor.* Kind of the witch to give thee
    warning, tho'.          [*Man flies.*
Is not this wood-witch of the rustic's fear
Our woodland Circe that hath witch'd the
    King ?
       [*Horn sounded. Another flying.*
   *Fitzurse.* Again ! stay, fool, and tell me
why thou fliest.
   *Countryman.* Fly thou too. The King
keeps his forest head of game here, and
when that horn sounds a score of wolf-dogs
are let loose that will tear thee piecemeal.
Linger not till the third horn. Fly !
                     [*Exit.*

   *Eleanor.* This is the likelier tale. We
    have hit the place.            29
Now let the King's fine game look to itself.
                     [*Horn.*
   *Fitzurse.* Again ! —
And far on in the dark heart of the wood
I hear the yelping of the hounds of hell.
   *Eleanor.* I have my dagger here to still
    their throats.
   *Fitzurse.* Nay, madam, not to-night — the
    night is falling.
What can be done to-night ?
   *Eleanor.*           Well — well — away.

## SCENE III

### TRAITOR'S MEADOW AT FRÉTEVAL.
### PAVILIONS AND TENTS OF THE ENG-
### LISH AND FRENCH BARONAGE

#### BECKET *and* HERBERT OF BOSHAM.

   *Becket.* See here !
   *Herbert.*       What 's here ?
   *Becket.*            A notice from the priest
To whom our John of Salisbury commit-
    ted
The secret of the bower, that our wolf-
    Queen
Is prowling round the fold. I should be
    back
In England even for this.
   *Herbert.*           These are by-things
In the great cause.
   *Becket.*         The by-things of the Lord
Are the wrong'd innocences that will cry
From all the hidden by-ways of the world
In the great day against the wronger. I
    know
Thy meaning. Perish she, I, all, before  10
The Church should suffer wrong !
   *Herbert.*        Do you see, my lord,
There is the King talking with Walter
    Map ?
   *Becket.* He hath the Pope's last letters,
    and they threaten
The immediate thunder-blast of interdict;
Yet he can scarce be touching upon those,
Or scarce would smile that fashion.
   *Herbert.*             Winter sunshine !
Beware of opening out thy bosom to it,
Lest thou, myself, and all thy flock should
    catch
An after ague-fit of trembling. Look !

He bows, he bares his head, he is coming
    hither.                    20
Still with a smile.

*Enter* King Henry *and* Walter Map.

  *Henry.*  We have had so many hours to-
    gether, Thomas,
So many happy hours alone together,
That I would speak with you once more
    alone.
  *Becket.*  My liege, your will and happi-
    ness are mine.
               [*Exeunt* King *and* Becket.
  *Herbert.*  The same smile still.
  *Walter Map.*  Do you see that great
black cloud that hath come over the sun
and cast us all into shadow?
  *Herbert.*  And feel it too.        30
  *Walter Map.*  And see you yon side-beam
that is forced from under it, and sets the
church-tower over there all a-hell-fire as it
were?
  *Herbert.*  Ay.
  *Walter Map.*  It is this black, bell-silen-
cing, anti-marrying, burial-hindering interdict that hath squeezed out this side-smile
upon Canterbury, whereof may come conflagration.  Were I Thomas, I would n't
trust it.  Sudden change is a house on sand;
and tho' I count Henry honest enough, yet
when fear creeps in at the front, honesty
steals out at the back, and the King at last
is fairly scared by this cloud — this interdict.  I have been more for the King than
the Church in this matter — yea, even for
the sake of the Church; for, truly, as the case
stood, you had safelier have slain an archbishop than a she-goat.  But our recoverer
and upholder of customs hath in this crowning of young Henry by York and London
so violated the immemorial usage of the
Church, that, like the grave-digger's child
I have heard of, trying to ring the bell, he
hath half-hanged himself in the rope of the
Church, or rather pulled all the Church
with the Holy Father astride of it down
upon his own head.
  *Herbert.*  Were you there?      60
  *Walter Map.*  In the church rope? — no.
I was at the crowning, for I have pleasure
in the pleasure of crowds, and to read the
faces of men at a great show.
  *Herbert.*  And how did Roger of York
comport himself?
  *Walter Map.*  As magnificently and ar-

chiepiscopally as our Thomas would have
done: only there was a dare-devil in his
eye — I should say a dare-Becket.  He
thought less of two kings than of one
Roger, the king of the occasion.  Foliot is
the holier man, perhaps the better.  Once
or twice there ran a twitch across his face,
as who should say 'what's to follow?' but
Salisbury was a calf cowed by Mother
Church, and every now and then glancing
about him like a thief at night when he
hears a door open in the house and thinks
'the master.'                   80
  *Herbert.*  And the father-king?
  *Walter Map.*  The father's eye was so
tender it would have called a goose off the
green, and once he strove to hide his face,
like the Greek king when his daughter was
sacrificed, but he thought better of it.  It
was but the sacrifice of a kingdom to his
son, a smaller matter; but as to the young
crownling himself, he looked so malapert
in the eyes, that had I fathered him I had
given him more of the rod than the sceptre.
Then followed the thunder of the captains
and the shouting, and so we came on to
the banquet, from whence there puffed out
such an incense of unctuosity into the nos-
trils of our Gods of Church and State, that
Lucullus or Apicius might have sniffed it
in their Hades of heathenism, so that the
smell of their own roast had not come
across it —                100
  *Herbert.*  Map, tho' you make your butt
too big, you overshoot it.
  *Walter Map.*  For as to the fish, they
de-miracled the miraculous draught, and
might have sunk a navy —
  *Herbert.*  There again, Goliasing and Goliathizing!
  *Walter Map.*  And as for the flesh at
table, a whole Peter's sheet, with all manner of game, and four-footed things, and
fowls —                111
  *Herbert.*  And all manner of creeping
things too?
  *Walter Map.*  Well, there were abbots —
but they did not bring their women; and so
we were dull enough at first, but in the end
we flourished out into a merriment; for the
old King would act servitor and hand a dish
to his son; whereupon my Lord of York —
his fine-cut face bowing and beaming with
all that courtesy which hath less loyalty in
it than the backward scrape of the clown's

heel — 'great honor,' says he, 'from the
King's self to the King's son.' Did you
hear the young King's quip?                125
   *Herbert.* No, what was it?
   *Walter Map.* Glancing at the days when
his father was only Earl of Anjou, he answered, 'Should not an earl's son wait on
a king's son?' And when the cold corners
of the King's mouth began to thaw, there
was a great motion of laughter among us,
part real, part childlike, to be freed from
the dulness — part royal, for King and
kingling both laughed, and so we could not
but laugh, as by a royal necessity — part
childlike again — when we felt we had
laughed too long and could not stay ourselves — many midriff-shaken even to tears,
as springs gush out after earthquakes —
but from those, as I said before, there
may come a conflagration — tho', to keep
the figure moist and make it hold water, I
should say rather, the lacrymation of a lamentation; but look if Thomas have not
flung himself at the King's feet. They
have made it up again — for the moment.
   *Herbert.* Thanks to the blessed Magdalen, whose day it is!

*Re-enter* HENRY *and* BECKET. (*During
their conference the* BARONS *and* BISHOPS
OF FRANCE *and* ENGLAND *come in at
back of stage.*)

   *Becket.* Ay, King! for in thy kingdom,
as thou knowest,                150
The spouse of the Great King, thy King,
hath fallen —
The daughter of Zion lies beside the way —
The priests of Baal tread her underfoot —
The golden ornaments are stolen from
her —
   *Henry.* Have I not promised to restore
her, Thomas,
And send thee back again to Canterbury?
   *Becket.* Send back again those exiles of
my kin
Who wander famine-wasted thro' the world.
   *Henry.* Have I not promised, man, to
send them back?
   *Becket.* Yet one thing more. Thou hast
broken thro' the pales                160
Of privilege, crowning thy young son by
York,
London, and Salisbury — not Canterbury.
   *Henry.* York crown'd the Conqueror —
not Canterbury.

   *Becket.* There was no Canterbury in
William's time.
   *Henry.* But Hereford, you know, crown'd
the first Henry.
   *Becket.* But Anselm crown'd this Henry
o'er again.
   *Henry.* And thou shalt crown my Henry
o'er again.
   *Becket.* And is it then with thy good-
will that I
Proceed against thine evil councillors,
And hurl the dread ban of the Church on
those                170
Who made the second mitre play the first,
And acted me?
   *Henry.* Well, well, then — have thy way!
It may be they were evil councillors.
What more, my lord archbishop? What
more, Thomas?
I make thee full amends. Say all thy say,
But blaze not out before the Frenchmen
here.
   *Becket.* More? Nothing, so thy promise
be thy deed.
   *Henry* (*holding out his hand*). Give me
thy hand. My Lords of France and
England,
My friend of Canterbury and myself
Are now once more at perfect amity.                180
Unkingly should I be, and most unknightly,
Not striving still, however much in vain,
To rival him in Christian charity.
   *Herbert.* All praise to Heaven, and sweet
Saint Magdalen!
   *Henry.* And so farewell until we meet in
England.
   *Becket.* I fear, my liege, we may not
meet in England.
   *Henry.* How, do you make me a traitor?
   *Becket.*                No, indeed!
That be far from thee.
   *Henry.*                Come, stay with us, then,
Before you part for England.
   *Becket.*                I am bound
For that one hour to stay with good King
Louis,                190
Who helpt me when none else.
   *Herbert.*                He said thy life
Was not one hour's worth in England save
King Henry gave thee first the kiss of
peace.
   *Henry.* He said so? Louis, did he?
look you, Herbert,
When I was in mine anger with King
Louis,

I sware I would not give the kiss of peace,
Not on French ground, nor any ground but
    English,
Where his cathedral stands.  Mine old
    friend, Thomas,
I would there were that perfect trust be-
    tween us,
That health of heart, once ours, ere Pope
    or King                                    200
Had come between us!  Even now — who
    knows ? —
I might deliver all things to thy hand —
If — but I say no more — farewell, my lord.
    *Becket.*  Farewell, my liege !
        [*Exit* Henry, *then the* Barons *and*
            Bishops.
    *Walter Map.*  There again !  when the
full fruit of the royal promise might have
dropt into thy mouth hadst thou but opened
it to thank him.
    *Becket.*  He fenced his royal promise with
an *if.*                                       209
    *Walter Map.*  And is the King's *if* too
high a stile for your lordship to overstep
and come at all things in the next field ?
    *Becket.*  Ay, if this *if* be like the devil's
'*if*'
Thou wilt fall down and worship me.'
    *Herbert.*                      O, Thomas,
I could fall down and worship thee, my
    Thomas,
For thou hast trodden this wine-press alone.
    *Becket.*  Nay, of the people there are
many with me.                                  217
    *Walter Map.*  I am not altogether with
you, my lord, tho' I am none of those that
would raise a storm between you, lest ye
should draw together like two ships in a
calm.  You wrong the King: he meant
what he said to-day.  Who shall vouch for
his to-morrows ?  One word further.  Doth
not the *fewness* of anything make the fulness of it in estimation ?  Is not virtue
prized mainly for its rarity and great baseness loathed as an exception: for were all,
my lord, as noble as yourself, who would
look up to you ?  and were all as base as —
who shall I say ? — Fitzurse and his following — who would look down upon them ?
My lord, you have put so many of the
King's household out of communion, that
they begin to smile at it.                     235
    *Becket.*  At their peril, at their peril —
    *Walter Map.*  For tho' the drop may hol-
low out the dead stone, doth not the living

skin thicken against perpetual whippings ?
This is the second grain of good counsel I
ever proffered thee, and so cannot suffer by
the rule of frequency.  Have I sown it in
salt ?  I trust not, for before God I promise you the King hath many more wolves
than he can tame in his woods of England,
and if it suit their purpose to howl for the
King, and you still move against him, you
may have no less than to die for it; but
God and his free wind grant your lordship
a happy home-return and the King's kiss
of peace in Kent.  Farewell !  I must follow the King.                       [*Exit.*
    *Herbert.*  Ay, and I warrant the customs.
        Did the King                          252
Speak of the customs ?
    *Becket.*          No ! — To die for it —
I live to die for it, I die to live for it.
The State will die, the Church can never
    die.
The King's not like to die for that which
    dies;
But I must die for that which never dies.
It will be so — my visions in the Lord —
It must be so, my friend !  the wolves of
    England
Must murder her one shepherd, that the
    sheep                                      260
May feed in peace.  False figure, Map
    would say.
Earth's falses are heaven's truths.  And
    when my voice
Is martyr'd mute, and this man disappears,
That perfect trust may come again be-
    tween us,
And there, there, there, not here I shall
    rejoice
To find my stray sheep back within the
    fold.
The crowd are scattering, let us move
    away !
And thence to England.             [*Exeunt.*

## ACT IV

### SCENE I. — THE OUTSKIRTS OF THE BOWER

    *Geoffrey* (*coming out of the wood*).  Light
again !  light again !  Margery ? no, that's
a finer thing there.  How it glitters !
    *Eleanor* (*entering*).  Come to me, little
one.  How camest thou hither ?

*Geoffrey.* On my legs.

*Eleanor.* And mighty pretty legs too. Thou art the prettiest child I ever saw. Wilt thou love me ?

*Geoffrey.* No; I only love mother.    10

*Eleanor.* Ay; and who is thy mother ?

*Geoffrey.* They call her — But she lives secret, you see.

*Eleanor.* Why ?

*Geoffrey.* Don't know why.

*Eleanor.* Ay, but some one comes to see her now and then. Who is he ?

*Geoffrey.* Can't tell.

*Eleanor.* What does she call him ?

*Geoffrey.* My liege.    20

*Eleanor.* Pretty one, how camest thou ?

*Geoffrey.* There was a bit of yellow silk here and there, and it looked pretty like a glowworm, and I thought if I followed it I should find the fairies.

*Eleanor.* I am the fairy, pretty one, a good fairy to thy mother. Take me to her.

*Geoffrey.* There are good fairies and bad fairies, and sometimes she cries, and can't sleep sound o' nights because of the bad fairies.    32

*Eleanor.* She shall cry no more; she shall sleep sound enough if thou wilt take me to her. I am her good fairy.

*Geoffrey.* But you don't look like a good fairy. Mother does. You are not pretty, like mother.

*Eleanor.* We can't all of us be as pretty as thou art — (*aside*) little bastard ! Come, here is a golden chain I will give thee if thou wilt lead me to thy mother.    42

*Geoffrey.* No — no gold. Mother says gold spoils all. Love is the only gold.

*Eleanor.* I love thy mother, my pretty boy. Show me where thou camest out of the wood.

*Geoffrey.* By this tree; but I don't know if I can find the way back again.

*Eleanor.* Where 's the warder ?

*Geoffrey.* Very bad. Somebody struck him.    52

*Eleanor.* Ay ? who was that ?

*Geoffrey.* Can't tell. But I heard say he had had a stroke, or you 'd have heard his horn before now. Come along, then; we shall see the silk here and there, and I want my supper.      [*Exeunt.*

## SCENE II

### ROSAMUND'S BOWER

*Rosamund.* The boy so late; pray God, he be not lost !
I sent this Margery, and she comes not back;
I sent another, and she comes not back.
I go myself — so many alleys, crossings,
Paths, avenues — nay, if I lost him, now
The folds have fallen from the mystery
And left all naked, I were lost indeed.

*Enter* GEOFFREY *and* ELEANOR.

Geoffrey, the pain thou hast put me to !
          [*Seeing* Eleanor.
          Ha, you !
How came you hither ?

*Eleanor.* Your own child brought me hither !    9

*Geoffrey.* You said you could n't trust Margery, and I watched her and followed her into the woods, and I lost her and went on and on till I found the light and the lady, and she says she can make you sleep o' nights.

*Rosamund.* How dared you ? Know you not this bower is secret,
Of and belonging to the King of England,
More sacred than his forests for the chase ?
Nay, nay, Heaven help you; get you hence in haste    19
Lest worse befall you.

*Eleanor.*        Child, I am mine own self
Of and belonging to the King. The King
Hath divers ofs and ons, ofs and belongings,
Almost as many as your true Mussulman —
Belongings, paramours, whom it pleases him
To call his wives; but so it chances, child,
That I am his main paramour, his sultana.
But since the fondest pair of doves will jar,
Even in a cage of gold, we had words of late,
And thereupon he call'd my children bastards.
Do you believe that you are married to him ?    30

*Rosamund.* I *should* believe it.

*Eleanor.*        You must not believe it,
Because I have a wholesome medicine here

Puts that belief asleep.　Your answer,
　　beauty!
Do you believe that you are married to
　　him?
　　*Rosamund.* Geoffrey, my boy, I saw the
ball you lost in the fork of the great willow
over the brook.　Go.　See that you do not
fall in.　Go.　　　　　　　　　　　　38
　　*Geoffrey.* And leave you alone with the
good fairy.　She calls you beauty, but I
don't like her looks.　Well, you bid me go,
and I'll have my ball anyhow.　Shall I
find you asleep when I come back?
　　*Rosamund.* Go.　　　　　[*Exit* Geoffrey.
　　*Eleanor.* He is easily found again.　*Do
　　you believe it?*
I pray you then to take my sleeping-
　　draught;
But if you should not care to take it —
　　see!　　　　　　　　　[*Draws a dagger.*
What! have I scared the red rose from
　　your face
Into your heart?　But this will find it
　　there,　　　　　　　　　　　　49
And dig it from the root for ever.
　　*Rosamund.*　　　　　　　Help! help!
　　*Eleanor.* They say that walls have ears;
　　but these, it seems,
Have none!　and I have none — to pity
　　thee.
　　*Rosamund.* I do beseech you — my child
　　is so young,
So backward too; I cannot leave him yet.
I am not so happy I could not die myself,
But the child is so young.　You have chil-
　　dren — his;
And mine is the King's child; so, if you
　　love him —
Nay, if you love him, there is great wrong
　　done
Somehow; but if you do not — there are
　　those　　　　　　　　　　　　59
Who say you do not love him — let me go
With my young boy, and I will hide my
　　face,
Blacken and gipsyfy it; none shall know
　　me;
The King shall never hear of me again,
But I will beg my bread along the world
With my young boy, and God will be our
　　guide.
I never meant you harm in any way.
See, I can say no more.
　　*Eleanor.* Will you not say you are not
　　married to him?

　　*Rosamund.* Ay, madam, I can *say* it, if
　　you will.　　　　　　　　　　　69
　　*Eleanor.* Then is thy pretty boy a bas-
　　tard?
　　*Rosamund.* No.
　　*Eleanor.* And thou thyself a proven
　　wanton?
　　*Rosamund.*　　No.
I am none such.　I never loved but one.
I have heard of such that range from love
　　to love,
Like the wild beast — if you can call it
　　love.
I have heard of such — yea, even among
　　those
Who sit on thrones — I never saw any
　　such,
Never knew any such, and howsoever
You do misname me, match'd with any
　　such,
I am snow to mud.
　　*Eleanor.*　　　　The more the pity then
That thy true home — the heavens — cry
　　out for thee　　　　　　　　80
Who art too pure for earth.

*Enter* FITZURSE.

　　*Fitzurse,*　　　　　　Give her to me.
　　*Eleanor.* The Judas-lover of our passion-
　　play
Hath track'd us hither.
　　*Fitzurse.*　　Well, why not?　I follow'd
You and the child: he babbled all the way.
Give her to me to make my honey-moon.
　　*Eleanor.* Ay, as the bears love honey.
　　Could you keep her
Indungeon'd from one whisper of the wind,
Dark even from a side glance of the moon,
And oublietted in the centre — No!
I follow out my hate and thy revenge.　90
　　*Fitzurse.* You bade me take revenge an-
　　other way —
To bring her to the dust. — Come with me,
　　love,
And I will love thee. — Madam, let her
　　live.
I have a far-off burrow where the King
Would miss her and for ever.
　　*Eleanor.* How sayst thou, sweetheart?
Wilt thou go with him? he will marry
　　thee.
　　*Rosamund.* Give me the poison; set me
　　free of him!
　　　　　　　　　[Eleanor *offers the vial.*
No, no!　I will not have it.

*Eleanor.*                     Then this other,
The wiser choice, because my sleeping-
     draught
May bloat thy beauty out of shape, and
     make                                        100
Thy body loathsome even to thy child;
While this but leaves thee with a broken
     heart,
A doll-face blanch'd and bloodless, over
     which
If pretty Geoffrey do not break his own,
It must be broken for him.
     *Rosamund.*          O, I see now
Your purpose is to fright me — a trouba-
     dour,
You play with words. You had never used
     so many,
Not if you meant it, I am sure. The
     child —
No — mercy ! No ! (*Kneels.*)
     *Eleanor.*          Play ! — that bosom never
Heaved under the King's hand with such
     true passion                                 110
As at this loveless knife that stirs the riot,
Which it will quench in blood ! Slave, if
     he love thee,
Thy life is worth the wrestle for it. Arise,
And dash thyself against me that I may
     slay thee !
The worm ! shall I let her go ? But ha !
     what 's here ?
By very God, the cross I gave the King !
His village darling in some lewd caress
Has wheedled it off the King's neck to her
     own.
By thy leave, beauty. Ay, the same ! I
     warrant
Thou hast sworn on this my cross a hun-
     dred times                                   120
Never to leave him — and that merits
     death,
False oath on holy cross — for thou must
     leave him
To-day, but not quite yet. My good Fitz-
     urse,
The running down the chase is kindlier
     sport
Even than the death. Who knows but
     that thy lover
May plead so pitifully, that I may spare
     thee ?
Come hither, man; stand there. (*To* Ros-
     amund.) Take thy one chance;
Catch at the last straw. Kneel to thy
     lord Fitzurse;

Crouch even because thou hatest him; fawn
     upon him
For thy life and thy son's.
     *Rosamund (rising).*          I am a Clifford,
My son a Clifford and Plantagenet.          131
I am to die then, tho' there stand beside
     thee
One who might grapple with thy dagger,
     if he
Had aught of man, or thou of woman; or I
Would bow to such a baseness as would
     make me
Most worthy of it. Both of us will die,
And I will fly with my sweet boy to heaven,
And shriek to all the saints among the
     stars:
'Eleanor of Aquitaine, Eleanor of Eng-
     land !
Murder'd by that adulteress Eleanor,          140
Whose doings are a horror to the east,
A hissing in the west !' Have we not
     heard
Raymond of Poitou, thine own uncle — nay,
Geoffrey Plantagenet, thine own husband's
     father —
Nay, even the accursed heathen Salad-
     deen —
Strike !
I challenge thee to meet me before God.
Answer me there.
     *Eleanor (raising the dagger).* This in thy
     bosom, fool,
And after in thy bastard's !

*Enter* BECKET *from behind. Catches hold
     of her arm.*

*Becket.*                     Murderess !
     [*The dagger falls ; they stare at one
     another. After a pause.*
*Eleanor.* My lord, we know you proud
     of your fine hand,                           150
But having now admired it long enough,
We find that it is mightier than it seems —
At least mine own is frailer; you are lam-
     ing it.
     *Becket.* And lamed and maim'd to dis-
     location, better
Than raised to take a life which Henry bade
     me
Guard from the stroke that dooms thee
     after death
To wail in deathless flame.
     *Eleanor.*          Nor you nor I
Have now to learn, my lord, that our good
     Henry                                        158

Says many a thing in sudden heats which he
Gainsays by next sunrising — often ready
To tear himself for having said as much.
My lord, Fitzurse —
    *Becket.*        He too ! what dost thou here ?
Dares the bear slouch into the lion's den ?
One downward plunge of his paw would
        rend away
Eyesight and manhood, life itself, from
        thee.
Go, lest I blast thee with anathema,
And make thee a world's horror.
    *Fitzurse.*                My lord, I shall
Remember this.
    *Becket.*            I *do* remember thee;
Lest I remember thee to the lion, go.    169
                        [*Exit* Fitzurse.
Take up your dagger; put it in the sheath.
    *Eleanor.*  Might not your courtesy stoop
        to hand it me ?
But crowns must bow when mitres sit so
        high.
Well — well — too costly to be left or lost.
                [*Picks up the dagger.*
I had it from an Arab soldan, who,
When I was there in Antioch, marvell'd at
Our unfamiliar beauties of the west;
But wonder'd more at my much constancy
To the monk-king, Louis, our former bur-
        then,
From whom, as being too kin, you know,
        my lord,                        179
God's grace and Holy Church deliver'd us.
I think, time given, I could have talk'd
        him out of
His ten wives into one.  Look at the hilt.
What excellent workmanship !  In our
        poor west
We cannot do it so well.
    *Becket.*                We can do worse.
Madam, I saw your dagger at her throat;
I heard your savage cry.
    *Eleanor.*            Well acted, was it ?
A comedy meant to seem a tragedy —
A feint, a farce.  My honest lord, you are
        known
Thro' all the courts of Christendom as one
That mars a cause with over violence.    190
You have wrong'd Fitzurse.  I speak not
        of myself.
We thought to scare this minion of the
        King
Back from her churchless commerce with
        the King
To the fond arms of her first love, Fitzurse,

Who swore to marry her.  You have spoilt
        the farce.
My savage cry ?  Why, she — she — when
        I strove
To work against her license for her good,
Bark'd out at me such monstrous charges
        that
The King himself, for love of his own sons,
If hearing, would have spurn'd her; where-
        upon                            200
I menaced her with this, as when we
        threaten
A yelper with a stick.  Nay, I deny not
That I was somewhat anger'd.  Do you
        hear me ?
Believe or no, I care not.  You have lost
The ear of the King.  I have it. — My lord
        paramount,
Our great High-priest, will not your Holi-
        ness
Vouchsafe a gracious answer to your
        Queen ?
    *Becket.*  Rosamund hath not answer'd
        you one word;
Madam, I will not answer you one word.
Daughter, the world hath trick'd thee.
        Leave it, daughter;            210
Come thou with me to Godstow nunnery,
And live what may be left thee of a life
Saved as by miracle alone with Him
Who gave it.

            *Re-enter* GEOFFREY.

    *Geoffrey.*  Mother, you told me a great fib;
        it was n't in the willow.
    *Becket.*  Follow us, my son, and we will
        find it for thee —
Or something manlier.
        [*Exeunt* Becket, Rosamund, *and* Geof-
        frey.
    *Eleanor.*  The world hath trick'd her —
        that 's the King; if so,
There was the farce, the feint — not mine.
        And yet                        219
I am all but sure my dagger was a feint
Till the worm turn'd — not life shot up in
        blood,
But death drawn in; — (*looking at the vial*)
        *this* was no feint, then ? no.
But can I swear to that, had she but given
Plain answer to plain query ? nay, me-
        thinks
Had she but bowed herself to meet the
        wave
Of humiliation, worshipt whom she loathed,

I should have let her be, scorn'd her too
    much
To harm her.   Henry — Becket tells him
    this —
To take my life might lose him Aquitaine.
Too politic for that.   Imprison me ?    230
No, for it came to nothing — only a feint.
Did she not tell me I was playing on her ?
I 'll swear to mine own self it was a feint.
Why should I swear, Eleanor, who am, or
    was,
A sovereign power ?   The King plucks out
    their eyes
Who anger him, and shall not I, the Queen,
Tear out her heart — kill, kill with knife
    or venom
One of his slanderous harlots ?   ' None of
    such ? '
I love her none the more.   Tut, the chance
    gone,
She lives — but not for him; one point is
    gain'd.    240
O, I that thro' the Pope divorced King
    Louis,
Scorning his monkery, — I that wedded
    Henry,
Honoring his manhood — will he not mock
    at me,
The jealous fool balk'd of her will — with
    *him ?*
But he and he must never meet again.
Reginald Fitzurse !

*Re-enter* FITZURSE.

  *Fitzurse.*    Here, Madam, at your plea-
    sure.
  *Eleanor.*  My pleasure is to have a man
    about me.
Why did you slink away so like a cur ?
  *Fitzurse.*  Madam, I am as much man as
    the King.
Madam, I fear Church-censures like your
    King.    250
  *Eleanor.*  He grovels to the Church when
    he 's black-blooded,
But kinglike fought the proud archbishop,
    — kinglike
Defied the Pope, and, like his kingly sires,
The Normans, striving still to break or
    bind
The spiritual giant with our island laws
And customs, made me for the moment
    proud
Even of that stale Church - bond which
    link'd me with him

To bear him kingly sons.   I am not so sure
But that I love him still.   Thou as much
    man !
No more of that; we will to France and be
Beforehand with the King, and brew from
    out    261
This Godstow-Becket intermeddling such
A strong hate-philtre as may madden him
    — madden
Against his priest beyond all hellebore.

# ACT V

## SCENE I. — CASTLE IN NORMANDY
KING'S CHAMBER

HENRY, ROGER OF YORK, FOLIOT, JOCE-
LYN OF SALISBURY.

  *Roger of York.*  Nay, nay, my liege,
He rides abroad with armed followers,
Hath broken all his promises to thyself,
Cursed and anathematized us right and
    left,
Stirr'd up a party there against your son —
  *Henry.*  Roger of York, you always hated
    him,
Even when you both were boys at Theo-
    bald's.
  *Roger of York.*  I always hated bound-
    less arrogance.
In mine own cause I strove against him
    there,    9
And in thy cause I strive against him now.
  *Henry.*  I cannot think he moves against
    my son,
Knowing right well with what a tenderness
He loved my son.
  *Roger of York.*     Before you made him
    king.
But Becket ever moves against a king.
The Church is all — the crime to be a
    king.
We trust your Royal Grace, lord of more
    land
Than any crown in Europe, will not yield
To lay your neck beneath your citizen's
    heel.
  *Henry.*  Not to a Gregory of my thron-
    ing !   No.
  *Foliot.*  My royal liege, in aiming at your
    love,    20
It may be sometimes I have overshot
My duties to our Holy Mother Church,

Tho' all the world allows I fall no inch
Behind this Becket, rather go beyond
In scourgings, macerations, mortifyings,
Fasts, disciplines that clear the spiritual
    eye,
And break the soul from earth. Let all
    that be.
I boast not; but you know thro' all this
    quarrel
I still have cleaved to the crown, in hope
    the crown
Would cleave to me that but obey'd the
    crown,         30
Crowning your son; for which our loyal
    service,
And since we likewise swore to obey the
    customs,
York and myself, and our good Salisbury
    here,
Are push'd from out communion of the
    Church.
  *Jocelyn of Salisbury.* Becket hath trod-
    den on us like worms, my liege,
Trodden one half dead; one half, but half-
    alive,
Cries to the King.
  *Henry (aside).* Take care o' thyself, O
    King!
  *Jocelyn of Salisbury.* Being so crush'd
    and so humiliated
We scarcely dare to bless the food we
    eat
Because of Becket.
  *Henry.*     What would ye have me do?
  *Roger of York.* Summon your barons;
    take their counsel; yet      41
I know — could swear — as long as Becket
    breathes,
Your Grace will never have one quiet hour.
  *Henry.* What? — Ay — but pray you do
    not work upon me.
I see your drift — it may be so — and yet
You know me easily anger'd. Will you
    hence?
He shall absolve you — you shall have re-
    dress.
I have a dizzying headache. Let me rest.
I'll call you by and by.
    [*Exeunt* Roger of York, Foliot, *and*
    Jocelyn of Salisbury.
Would he were dead! I have lost all love
    for him.      50
If God would take him in some sudden
    way —
Would he were dead!    [*Lies down.*

  *Page (entering).* My liege, the Queen of
    England.
  *Henry.* God's eyes!    [*Starting up.*

        *Enter* ELEANOR.

  *Eleanor.*     Of England? Say of Aqui-
    taine.
I am no Queen of England. I had dream'd
I was the bride of England, and a queen.
  *Henry.* And, — while you dream'd you
    were the bride of England, —
Stirring her baby-king against me? ha!
  *Eleanor.* The brideless Becket is thy
    king and mine;
I will go live and die in Aquitaine.
  *Henry.* Except I clap thee into prison
    here,      60
Lest thou shouldst play the wanton there
    again.
Ha, you of Aquitaine! O you of Aqui-
    taine!
You were but Aquitaine to Louis — no
    wife;
You are only Aquitaine to me — no wife.
  *Eleanor.* And why, my lord, should I be
    wife to one
That only wedded me for Aquitaine?
Yet this no-wife — her six and thirty sail
Of Provence blew you to your English
    throne;
And this no-wife has borne you four brave
    sons,
And one of them at least is like to prove  70
Bigger in our small world than thou art.
  *Henry.*             Ay —
Richard, if he *be* mine — I hope him mine.
But thou art like enough to make him
    thine.
  *Eleanor.* Becket is like enough to make
    all his.
  *Henry.* Methought I had recover'd of
    the Becket,
That all was planed and bevell'd smooth
    again,
Save from some hateful cantrip of thine
    own.
  *Eleanor.* I will go live and die in Aqui-
    taine.
I dream'd I was the consort of a king,    79
Not one whose back his priest has broken.
  *Henry.*             What!
Is the end come? You, will you crown
    my foe
My victor in mid-battle? I will be
Sole master of my house. The end is mine.

What game, what juggle, what devilry are
    you playing?
Why do you thrust this Becket on me
    again?
    *Eleanor.* Why? for I *am* true wife, and
    have my fears
Lest Becket thrust you even from your
    throne.
Do you know this cross, my liege?
    *Henry (turning his head).* Away! Not I.
    *Eleanor.* Not even the central diamond,
    worth, I think,
Half of the Antioch whence I had it.
    *Henry.*                 That?
    *Eleanor.* I gave it you, and you your
    paramour;              91
She sends it back, as being dead to earth,
So dead henceforth to you.
    *Henry.* Dead! you have murder'd her,
Found out her secret bower and murder'd
    her.
    *Eleanor.* Your Becket knew the secret
    of your bower.
    *Henry (calling out).* Ho there! thy rest
    of life is hopeless prison.
    *Eleanor.* And what would my own Aqui-
    taine say to that?
First, free thy captive from *her* hopeless
    prison.
    *Henry.* O devil, can I free her from the
    grave?
    *Eleanor.* You are too tragic; both of us
    are players                100
In such a comedy as our court of Provence
Had laugh'd at. That's a delicate Latin
    lay
Of Walter Map: the lady holds the cleric
Lovelier than any soldier, his poor ton-
    sure
A crown of Empire. Will you have it
    again?
(*Offering the cross. He dashes it down.*)
Saint Cupid, that is too irreverent.
Then mine once more.    (*Puts it on.*)
              Your cleric hath your lady.
Nay, what uncomely faces, could he see
    you!
Foam at the mouth because King Thomas,
    lord
Not only of your vassals but amours,    110
Thro' chastest honor of the Decalogue
Hath used the full authority of his Church
To put her into Godstow nunnery.
    *Henry.* To put her into Godstow nun-
    nery!

He dared not — liar! yet, yet I remem-
    ber —
I do remember.
He bade me put her into a nunnery —
Into Godstow, into Hellstow, Devilstow?
The Church! the Church?          119
God's eyes! I would the Church were
    down in hell!            [*Exit.*
    *Eleanor.* Aha!

        *Enter the four* KNIGHTS.

    *Fitzurse.* What made the King cry out
    so furiously?
    *Eleanor.* Our Becket, who will not ab-
    solve the bishops.
I think ye four have cause to love this
    Becket.
    *Fitzurse.* I hate him for his insolence to
    all.
    *De Tracy.* And I for all his insolence to
    thee.
    *De Brito.* I hate him for I hate him is
    my reason,
And yet I hate him for a hypocrite.
    *De Morville.* I do not love him, for he
    did his best
To break the barons, and now braves the
    King.                  130
    *Eleanor.* Strike, then, at once, the King
    would have him — See!

        *Re-enter* HENRY.

    *Henry.* No man to love me, honor me,
    obey me!
Sluggards and fools!
The slave that eat my bread has kick'd his
    King!
The dog I cramm'd with dainties worried
    me!
The fellow that on a lame jade came to
    court,
A ragged cloak for saddle — he, he, he,
To shake my throne, to push into my cham-
    ber —
My bed, where even the slave is private —
    he —
I'll have her out again, he shall absolve    140
The bishops — they but did my will — not
    you —
Sluggards and fools, why do you stand and
    stare?
You are no King's men — you — you — you
    are Becket's men.
Down with King Henry! up with the Arch-
    bishop!

Will no man free me from this pestilent
   priest ?                                   [*Exit.*
           [*The* Knights *draw their swords.*
*Eleanor. Are* ye King's men ? I am
   King's woman, I.
*The Knights.* King's men ! King's men !

## SCENE II

A ROOM IN CANTERBURY MONASTERY

BECKET *and* JOHN OF SALISBURY.

*Becket.* York said so ?
*John of Salisbury.* Yes: a man may take
   good counsel
Even from his foe.
*Becket.*          York will say anything.
What is he saying now ? gone to the King
And taken our anathema with him. York !
Can the King de-anathematize this York ?
*John of Salisbury.* Thomas, I would thou
   hadst return'd to England
Like some wise prince of this world from
   his wars,
With more of olive-branch and amnesty
For foes at home — thou hast raised the
   world against thee.
   *Becket.* Why, John, my kingdom is not
   of this world.                              10
*John of Salisbury.* If it were more of
   this world it might be
More of the next. A policy of wise pardon
Wins here as well as there. To bless thine
   enemies —
   *Becket.* Ay, mine, not Heaven's.
*John of Salisbury.* And may there not be
   something
Of this world's leaven in thee too, when
   crying
On Holy Church to thunder out her rights
And thine own wrong so pitilessly ? Ah,
   Thomas,
The lightnings that we think are only Hea-
   ven's
Flash sometimes out of earth against the
   heavens.                                   19
The soldier, when he lets his whole self go
Lost in the common good, the common
   wrong,
Strikes truest even for his own self. I
   crave
Thy pardon — I have still thy leave to
   speak.

Thou hast waged God's war against the
   King; and yet
We are self-uncertain creatures, and we
   may,
Yea, even when we know not, mix our
   spites
And private hates with our defence of
   Heaven.

*Enter* EDWARD GRIM.

   *Becket.* Thou art but yesterday from
   Cambridge, Grim;
What say ye there of Becket ?
   *Grim.*          *I* believe him
The bravest in our roll of primates down 30
From Austin — there are some — for there
   are men
Of canker'd judgment everywhere —
   *Becket.*            Who hold
With York, with York against me.
   *Grim.*           Well, my lord,
A stranger monk desires access to you.
   *Becket.* York against Canterbury, York
   against God !
I am open to him.                            [*Exit* Grim.

*Enter* ROSAMUND *as a Monk.*

   *Rosamund.*      Can I speak with you
Alone, my father ?
   *Becket.*         Come you to confess ?
   *Rosamund.* Not now.
   *Becket.* Then speak; this is my other
   self,
Who, like my conscience, never lets me be.
   *Rosamund (throwing back the cowl).* I
   know him, our good John of Salis-
   bury.                                       40
   *Becket.* Breaking already from thy no-
   vitiate
To plunge into this bitter world again —
These wells of Marah ! I am grieved, my
   daughter.
I thought that I had made a peace for thee.
   *Rosamund.* Small peace was mine in my
   novitiate, father.
Thro' all closed doors a dreadful whisper
   crept
That thou wouldst excommunicate the
   King.
I could not eat, sleep, pray. I had with me
The monk's disguise thou gavest me for
   my bower;                                  49
I think our abbess knew it and allow'd it.
I fled, and found thy name a charm to get
   me

Food, roof, and rest.  I met a robber once;
I told him I was bound to see the arch-
    bishop:
' Pass on,' he said, and in thy name I pass'd
From house to house.  In one a son stone-
    blind
Sat by his mother's hearth.  He had gone too
    far
Into the King's own woods; and the poor
    mother,
Soon as she learnt I was a friend of thine,
Cried out against the cruelty of the King.
I said it was the King's courts, not the
    King,         60
But she would not believe me, and she
    wish'd
The Church were king; she had seen the
    archbishop once,
So mild, so kind.  The people love thee,
    father.
    *Becket.*  Alas! when I was Chancellor to
    the King,
I fear I was as cruel as the King.
    *Rosamund.*  Cruel?  O, no — it is the
    law, not he;
The customs of the realm.
    *Becket.*        The customs! customs!
    *Rosamund.*  My lord, you have not ex-
    communicated him ?        68
O, if you have, absolve him !
    *Becket.*        Daughter, daughter,
Deal not with things you know not.
    *Rosamund.*        I know *him.*
Then you have done it, and I call *you*
    cruel.
    *John of Salisbury.*  No, daughter, you
    mistake our good archbishop;
For once in France the King had been so
    harsh,
He thought to excommunicate him —
    Thomas,
You could not — old affection master'd
    you,
You falter'd into tears.
    *Rosamund.*        God bless him for it !
    *Becket.*  Nay, make me not a woman,
    John of Salisbury,
Nor make me traitor to my holy office.  78
Did not a man's voice ring along the aisle,
' The King is sick and almost unto death.'
How could I excommunicate him then ?
    *Rosamund.*  And wilt thou excommuni-
    cate him now ?
    *Becket.*  Daughter, my time is short, I
    shall not do it.

And were it longer — well — I should not
    do it.
    *Rosamund.*  Thanks in this life, and in
    the life to come !
    *Becket.*  Get thee back to thy nunnery
    with all haste;
Let this be thy last trespass.  But one
    question —
How fares thy pretty boy, the little Geof-
    frey ?
No fever, cough, croup, sickness ?
    *Rosamund.*        No, but saved
From all that by our solitude.  The
    plagues        90
That smite the city spare the solitudes.
    *Becket.*  God save him from all sickness
    of the soul !
Thee too, thy solitude among thy nuns,
May that save thee !  Doth he remember
    me ?
    *Rosamund.*  I warrant him.
    *Becket.*        He is marvellously like thee.
    *Rosamund.*  Liker the King.
    *Becket.*        No, daughter.
    *Rosamund.*        Ay, but wait
Till his nose rises; he will be very king.
    *Becket.*  Even so; but think not of the
    King.  Farewell !
    *Rosamund.*  My lord, the city is full of
    armed men.        99
    *Becket.*  Even so.  Farewell !
    *Rosamund.*    I will but pass to vespers,
And breathe one prayer for my liege-lord
    the King,
His child and mine own soul, and so return.
    *Becket.*  Pray for me too; much need of
    prayer have I.
            [Rosamund *kneels and goes.*
Dan John, how much we lose, we celibates,
Lacking the love of woman and of child !
    *John of Salisbury.*  More gain than loss;
    for of your wives you shall
Find one a slut whose fairest linen seems
Foul as her dust-cloth, if she used it — one
So charged with tongue that every thread
    of thought        109
Is broken ere it joins — a shrew to boot,
Whose evil song far on into the night
Thrills to the topmost tile — no hope but
    death;
One slow, fat, white, a burthen of the
    hearth;
And one that being thwarted ever swoons
And weeps herself into the place of power;
And one an *uxor pauperis Ibyci.*

So rare the household honey-making bee,
Man's help! but we, we have the Blessed
    Virgin
For worship, and our Mother Church for
    bride;
And all the souls we saved and father'd
    here                                    120
Will greet us as our babes in Paradise.
What noise was that? she told us of arm'd
    men
Here in the city. Will you not withdraw?
    *Becket.* I once was out with Henry in
    the days
When Henry loved me, and we came upon
A wild-fowl sitting on her nest, so still
I reach'd my hand and touch'd; she did not
    stir;
The snow had frozen round her, and she sat
Stone-dead upon a heap of ice-cold eggs.
Look! how this love, this mother, runs
    thro' all                               130
The world God made — even the beast —
    the bird!
    *John of Salisbury.* Ay, still a lover of the
    beast and bird?
But these arm'd men — will you not hide
    yourself?
Perchance the fierce De Brocs from Salt-
    wood Castle,
To assail our Holy Mother lest she brood
Too long o'er this hard egg, the world, and
    send
Her whole heart's heat into it, till it break
Into young angels. Pray you, hide your-
    self.
    *Becket.* There was a little fair-hair'd
    Norman maid                            139
Lived in my mother's house; if Rosamund is
The world's rose, as her name imports her
    — she
Was the world's lily.
    *John of Salisbury.* Ay, and what of her?
    *Becket.* She died of leprosy.
    *John of Salisbury.*           I know not why
You call these old things back again, my
    lord.
    *Becket.* The drowning man, they say,
    remembers all
The chances of his life, just ere he dies.
    *John of Salisbury.* Ay — but these arm'd
    men — will *you* drown *yourself?*
He loses half the meed of martyrdom    148
Who will be martyr when he might escape.
    *Becket.* What day of the week? Tues-
    day?

    *John of Salisbury.*      Tuesday, my lord.
    *Becket.* On a Tuesday was I born, and
    on a Tuesday
Baptized; and on a Tuesday did I fly
Forth from Northampton; on a Tuesday
    pass'd
From England into bitter banishment;
On a Tuesday at Pontigny came to me
The ghostly warning of my martyrdom;
On a Tuesday from mine exile I return'd,
And on a Tuesday —

TRACY *enters, then* FITZURSE, DE BRITO,
    *and* DE MORVILLE. MONKS *following.*

                — on a Tuesday — Tracy!
    (*A long silence, broken by* Fitzurse *say-
        ing, contemptuously,*)
God help thee!
    *John of Salisbury (aside).* How the good
    archbishop reddens!
He never yet could brook the note of
    scorn.                                  160
    *Fitzurse.* My lord, we bring a message
    from the King
Beyond the water; will you have it alone,
Or with these listeners near you?
    *Becket.*                   As you will.
    *Fitzurse.* Nay, as *you* will.
    *Becket.*                Nay, as *you* will.
    *John of Salisbury.*            Why, then
Better perhaps to speak with them apart.
Let us withdraw.
    [*All go out except the four* Knights *and*
        Becket.
    *Fitzurse.*         We are all alone with him.
Shall I not smite him with his own cross-
    staff?
    *De Morville.* No, look! the door is open:
    let him be.
    *Fitzurse.* The King condemns your ex-
    communicating —
    *Becket.* This is no secret, but a public
    matter.                                 170
In here again!

JOHN OF SALISBURY *and* MONKS *return.*

            Now, sirs, the King's commands!
    *Fitzurse.* The King beyond the water,
    thro' our voices,
Commands you to be dutiful and leal
To your young King on this side of the
    water,
Not scorn him for the foibles of his youth.
What! you would make his coronation
    void

By cursing those who crown'd him. Out
    upon you !
*Becket.* Reginald, all men know I loved
    the prince.
His father gave him to my care, and I
Became his second father. He had his
    faults,                 180
For which I would have laid mine own life
    down
To help him from them, since indeed I
    loved him,
And love him next after my lord his fa-
    ther.
Rather than dim the splendor of his crown
I fain would treble and quadruple it
With revenues, realms, and golden pro-
    vinces
So that were done in equity.
    *Fitzurse.*            You have broken
Your bond of peace, your treaty with the
    King —
Wakening such brawls and loud disturb-
    ances
In England, that he calls you over-sea    190
To answer for it in his Norman courts.
    *Becket.* Prate not of bonds, for never,
    O, never again
Shall the waste voice of the bond-breaking
    sea
Divide me from the mother church of Eng-
    land,
My Canterbury. Loud disturbances !
O, ay — the bells rang out even to deafen-
    ing.
Organ and pipe, and dulcimer, chants and
    hymns
In all the churches, trumpets in the halls,
Sobs, laughter, cries; they spread their
    raiment down
Before me — would have made my path-
    way flowers,            200
Save that it was midwinter in the street,
But full midsummer in those honest hearts.
    *Fitzurse.* The King commands you to
    absolve the bishops
Whom you have excommunicated.
    *Becket.*                 I ?
Not I, the Pope. Ask *him* for absolution.
    *Fitzurse.* But you advised the Pope.
    *Becket.*           And so I did.
They have but to submit.
    *The Four Knights.* The King commands
    you.
We are all King's men.
    *Becket.* King's men at least should know

That their own King closed with me last
    July
That I should pass the censures of the
    Church               210
On those that crown'd young Henry in this
    realm,
And trampled on the rights of Canterbury.
    *Fitzurse.* What ! dare you charge the
    King with treachery ?
*He* sanction thee to excommunicate
The prelates whom he chose to crown his
    son ?
    *Becket.* I spake no word of treachery,
    Reginald.
But for the truth of this I make appeal
To all the archbishops, bishops, prelates,
    barons,
Monks, knights, five hundred, that were
    there and heard.
Nay, you yourself were there; you heard
    yourself.             220
    *Fitzurse.* I was not there.
    *Becket.*           I saw you there.
    *Fitzurse.*                I was not.
    *Becket.* You were. I never forget any-
    thing.
    *Fitzurse.* He makes the King a traitor,
    me a liar.
How long shall we forbear him ?
    *John of Salisbury (drawing* Becket *aside).*
    O my good lord,
Speak with them privately on this here-
    after.
You see they have been revelling, and I
    fear
Are braced and brazen'd up with Christ-
    mas wines
For any murderous brawl.
    *Becket.*          And yet they prate
Of mine, my brawls, when those that name
    themselves
Of the King's part have broken down our
    barns,              230
Wasted our diocese, outraged our tenants,
Lifted our produce, driven our clerics
    out —
Why they, your friends, those ruffians, the
    De Brocs,
They stood on Dover beach to murder me,
They slew my stags in mine own manor
    here,
Mutilated, poor brute, my sumpter-mule,
Plunder'd the vessel full of Gascon wine,
The old King's present, carried off the
    casks,

Kill'd half the crew, dungeon'd the other
  half                                                239
In Pevensey Castle —
  *De Morville*.          Why not rather then,
If this be so, complain to your young King,
Not punish of your own authority ?
  *Becket*. Mine enemies barr'd all access to
    the boy.
They knew he loved me.
Hugh, Hugh, how proudly you exalt your
  head !
Nay, when 'they seek to overturn our
  rights,
I ask no leave of king, or mortal man,
To set them straight again.    Alone I do it.
Give to the King the things that are the
  King's,                                           249
And those of God to God.
  *Fitzurse*. Threats ! threats ! ye hear him.
What ! will he excommunicate all the
  world ?
          [*The* Knights *come round* Becket.
  *De Tracy*. He shall not.
  *De Brito*.    Well, as yet — I should be
    grateful —
He hath not excommunicated *me*.
  *Becket*. Because thou wast *born* excom-
    municate.
I never spied in thee one gleam of grace.
  *De Brito*. Your Christian's Christian
    charity !
  *Becket*.          By Saint Denis —
  *De Brito*. Ay, by Saint Denis, now will
    he flame out,
And lose his head as old Saint Denis did.
  *Becket*. Ye think to scare me from my
    loyalty
To God and to the Holy Father.  No !   260
Tho' all the swords in England flash'd
  above me
Ready to fall at Henry's word or yours —
Tho' all the loud-lung'd trumpets upon
  earth
Blared from the heights of all the thrones
  of her kings,
Blowing the world against me, I would
  stand
Clothed with the full authority of Rome,
Mail'd in the perfect panoply of faith,
First of the foremost of their files who die
For God, to people heaven in the great
  day
When God makes up his jewels.    Once I
  fled —                                            270
Never again, and you — I marvel at you —

Ye know what is between us.    Ye have
  sworn
Yourselves my men when I was Chancel-
  lor —
My vassals — and yet threaten your arch-
  bishop
In his own house.
  *Knights*.        Nothing can be between us
That goes against our fealty to the King.
  *Fitzurse*. And in his name we charge you
    that ye keep
This traitor from escaping.
  *Becket*.              Rest you easy,
For I am easy to keep.  I shall not fly.   279
Here, here, here will you find me.
  *De Morville*.            Know you not
You have spoken to the peril of your life ?
  *Becket*. As I shall speak again.
  *Fitzurse, De Tracy, and De Brito*. To
    arms !
          [*They rush out*, De Morville *lingers*.
  *Becket*.          De Morville,
I had thought so well of you; and even
  now
You seem the least assassin of the four.
O, do not damn yourself for company !
Is it too late for me to save your soul ?
I pray you for one moment stay and speak.
  *De Morville*. Becket, it *is* too late.
                                      [*Exit*.
  *Becket*.                Is it too late ?
Too late on earth may be too soon in
  hell.                                             289
  *Knights* (*in the distance*). Close the great
    gate — ho, there — upon the town !
  *Becket's Retainers*. Shut the hall-doors !
                                      [*A pause*.
  *Becket*.    You hear them, brother John;
Why do you stand so silent, brother John ?
  *John of Salisbury*. For I was musing on
    an ancient saw,
*Suaviter in modo, fortiter in re ;*
Is strength less strong when hand-in-hand
  with grace ?
*Gratior in pulchro corpore virtus*.  Thomas,
Why should you heat yourself for such as
  these ?
  *Becket*. Methought I answer'd moder-
    ately enough.
  *John of Salisbury*. As one that blows the
    coal to cool the fire.
My lord, I marvel why you never lean   300
On any man's advising but your own.
  *Becket*. Is it so, Dan John ? well, what
    should I have done ?

*John of Salisbury.* You should have taken
    counsel with your friends
Before these bandits brake into your pre-
    sence.
They seek — you make — occasion for your
    death.
    *Becket.* My counsel is already taken,
    John.
I am prepared to die.
    *John of Salisbury.*    We are sinners all,
The best of all not all-prepared to die.
    *Becket.* God's will be done !
    *John of Salisbury.* Ay, well. God's will
    be done !
    *Grim (re-entering).* My lord, the knights
    are arming in the garden      310
Beneath the sycamore.
    *Becket.*          Good ! let them arm.
    *Grim.* And one of the De Brocs is with
    them, Robert,
The apostate monk that was with Randulf
    here.
He knows the twists and turnings of the
    place.
    *Becket.* No fear !
    *Grim.*          No fear, my lord.
    [*Crashes on the hall-doors. The Monks
    flee.*
    *Becket (rising).*      Our dovecote flown !
I cannot tell why monks should all be cow-
    ards.
    *John of Salisbury.* Take refuge in your
    own cathedral, Thomas.
    *Becket.* Do they not fight the Great
    Fiend day by day ?
Valor and holy life should go together.   319
Why should all monks be cowards ?
    *John of Salisbury.*        Are they so ?
I say, take refuge in your own cathedral.
    *Becket.* Ay, but I told them I would
    wait them here.
    *Grim.* May they not say you dared not
    show yourself
In your old place ? and vespers are begin-
    ning.
    [*Bell rings for vespers till end of scene.*
You should attend the office, give them
    heart.
They fear you slain; they dread they know
    not what.
    *Becket.* Ay, monks, not men.
    *Grim.*        I am a monk, my lord.
Perhaps, my lord, you wrong us.     328
Some would stand by you to the death.
    *Becket.*          Your pardon.

    *John of Salisbury.* He said, 'Attend the
    office.'
    *Becket.*        Attend the office ?
Why then — the Cross ! — who bears my
    Cross before me ?
Methought they would have brain'd me
    with it, John.      [*Grim takes it.*
    *Grim.* I ! Would that I could bear thy
    cross indeed !
    *Becket.* The mitre !
    *John of Salisbury.* Will you wear it ? —
    there !      [*Becket puts on the mitre.*
    *Becket.*        The pall !
I go to meet my King !     [*Puts on the pall.*
    *Grim.*            To meet the King ?
    [*Crashes on the doors as they go out.*
    *John of Salisbury.* Why do you move
    with such a stateliness ?
Can you not hear them yonder like a storm,
Battering the doors, and breaking thro'
    the walls ?
    *Becket.* Why do the heathen rage ? My
    two good friends,
What matters murder'd here, or murder'd
    there ?      340
And yet my dream foretold my martyrdom
In mine own church. It is God's will. Go
    on.
Nay, drag me not. We must not seem to
    fly.

## SCENE III

### NORTH TRANSEPT OF CANTERBURY CATHEDRAL

*On the right hand a flight of steps leading to
the Choir, another flight on the left, leading to the North Aisle. Winter afternoon
slowly darkening. Low thunder now and
then of an approaching storm. MONKS
heard chanting the service. ROSAMUND
kneeling.*

    *Rosamund.* O blessed saint, O glorious
    Benedict, —
These arm'd men in the city, these fierce
    faces —
Thy holy follower founded Canterbury —
Save that dear head which now is Canter-
    bury,
Save him, he saved my life, he saved my
    child,
Save him, his blood would darken Henry's
    name;

Save him till all as saintly as thyself
He miss the searching flame of purgatory,
And pass at once perfect to Paradise.        9
        [*Noise of steps and voices in the cloisters.*
Hark ! Is it they ? Coming ! He is not
        here —
Not yet, thank heaven. O, save him !
                [*Goes up steps leading to choir.*
*Becket* (*entering, forced along by* John of
        Salisbury *and* Grim). No, I tell you !
I cannot bear a hand upon my person;
Why do you force me thus against my will ?
*Grim.* My lord, we force you from your
        enemies.
*Becket.* As you would force a king from
        being crown'd.
*John of Salisbury.* We must not force
        the crown of martyrdom.
        [*Service stops.* Monks *come down from
        the stairs that lead to the choir.*
*Monks.* Here is the great archbishop !
        He lives ! he lives !
Die with him, and be glorified together.
*Becket.* Together ? — get you back ! go
        on with the office.        19
*Monks.* Come, then, with us to vespers.
*Becket.*                        How can I come
When you so block the entry ? Back, I
        say !
Go on with the office. Shall not Heaven
        be served
Tho' earth's last earthquake clash'd the
        minster-bells,
And the great deeps were broken up again,
And hiss'd against the sun ?
                        [*Noise in the cloisters.*
*Monks.*                        The murderers, hark !
Let us hide ! let us hide !
*Becket.*        What do these people fear ?
*Monks.* Those arm'd men in the cloister.
*Becket.*        Be not such cravens !
I will go out and meet them.
*Grim and Others.*        Shut the doors !
We will not have him slain before our
        face.        29
        [*They close the doors of the transept.
        Knocking.*
Fly, fly, my lord, before they burst the
        doors !        [*Knocking.*
*Becket.* Why, these are our own monks
        who follow'd us !
And will you bolt them out, and have *them*
        slain ?
Undo the doors; the church is not a cas-
        tle.

Knock, and it shall be open'd. Are you
        deaf ?
What, have I lost authority among you ?
Stand by, make way !
        [*Opens the doors.    Enter* Monks *from
        cloister.*
                Come in, my friends, come in !
Nay, faster, faster !
*Monks.*                O, my lord archbishop,
A score of knights all arm'd with swords
        and axes —
To the choir, to the choir !
        [Monks *divide, part flying by the stairs
        on the right, part by those on the left.
        The rush of these last bears* Becket
        *along with them some way up the steps,
        where he is left standing alone.*
*Becket.*        Shall I too pass to the choir,
And die upon the patriarchal throne        40
Of all my predecessors ?
*John of Salisbury.*        No, to the crypt !
Twenty steps down. Stumble not in the
        darkness,
Lest they should seize thee.
*Grim.*                To the crypt ? no — no,
To the chapel of Saint Blaise beneath the
        roof !
*John of Salisbury* (*pointing upward and
        downward*). That way or this ! Save
        thyself either way.
*Becket.* O, no, not either way, nor any
        way
Save by that way which leads thro' night
        to light.
Not twenty steps, but one.
And fear not I should stumble in the dark-
        ness,
Not tho' it be their hour, the power of dark-
        ness,        50
But my hour too, the power of light in
        darkness !
I am not in the darkness but the light,
Seen by the Church in heaven, the Church
        on earth —
The power of life in death to make her
        free !

*Enter the four* KNIGHTS.   JOHN OF SALIS-
BURY *flies to the altar of Saint Benedict.*

*Fitzurse.* Here, here, King's men !
        [*Catches hold of the last flying* Monk.
                Where is the traitor Becket ?
*Monk.* I am not he ! I am not he, my
        lord.
I am not he indeed !

*Fitzurse.*        Hence to the fiend!
          [*Pushes him away.*
Where is this treble traitor to the King?
   *De Tracy.* Where is the archbishop,
     Thomas Becket?
   *Becket.*        Here.     59
No traitor to the King, but Priest of God,
Primate of England.
         [*Descending into the transept.*
           I am he ye seek.
What would ye have of me?
   *Fitzurse.*        Your life.
   *De Tracy.*        Your life.
   *De Morville.* Save that you will absolve
     the bishops.
   *Becket.*        Never, —
Except they make submission to the
     Church.
You had my answer to that cry before.
   *De Morville.* Why, then you are a dead
     man; flee!
   *Becket.*        I will not.
I am readier to be slain than thou to slay.
Hugh, I know well thou hast but half a
     heart
To bathe this sacred pavement with my
     blood.
God pardon thee and these, but God's full
     curse     70
Shatter you all to pieces if ye harm
One of my flock!
   *Fitzurse.*    Was not the great gate shut?
They are thronging in to vespers — half
     the town.
We shall be overwhelm'd.   Seize him and
     carry him!
Come with us — nay — thou art our pris-
     oner — come!
   *De Morville.* Ay, make him prisoner, do
     not harm the man.
     [*Fitzurse lays hold of the* Archbishop's
     *pall.*
   *Becket.* Touch me not!
   *De Brito.* How the good priest gods him-
     self!
He is not yet ascended to the Father.
   *Fitzurse.* I will not only touch, but drag
     thee hence.
   *Becket.* Thou art my man, thou art my
     vassal. Away!     80
     [*Flings him off till he reels, almost to
     falling.*
   *De Tracy (lays hold of the pall).* Come;
     as he said, thou art our prisoner.

   *Becket.*        Down!
         [*Throws him headlong.*
   *Fitzurse (advances with drawn sword).* I
     told thee that I should remember
     thee!
   *Becket.* Profligate pander!
   *Fitzurse.* Do you hear that? strike,
     strike.
     [*Strikes off the* Archbishop's *mitre, and
     wounds him in the forehead.*
   *Becket (covers his eyes with his hand).* I
     do commend my cause to God, the
     Virgin,
Saint Denis of France and Saint Alphege
     of England,
And all the tutelar Saints of Canterbury.
     [*Grim wraps his arms about the* Arch-
     bishop.
Spare this defence, dear brother.
     [*Tracy has arisen, and approaches, hesi-
     tatingly, with his sword raised.*
   *Fitzurse.*        Strike him, Tracy!
   *Rosamund (rushing down steps from the
     choir).* No, no, no, no!
   *Fitzurse.* This wanton here. De Mor-
     ville,
Hold her away.
   *De Morville.* I hold her.
   *Rosamund (held back by* De Morville,
     *and stretching out her arms).*
           Mercy, mercy,
As you would hope for mercy!
   *Fitzurse.*        Strike, I say!
   *Grim.* O God, O noble knights, O sacri-
     lege!     91
Strike our archbishop in his own cathe-
     dral!
The Pope, the King, will curse you — the
     whole world
Abhor you; ye will die the death of dogs!
Nay, nay, good Tracy.    [*Lifts his arm.*
   *Fitzurse.*    Answer not, but strike.
   *De Tracy.* There is my answer then.
     [*Sword falls on* Grim's *arm, and glances
     from it, wounding* Becket.
   *Grim.*        Mine arm is sever'd.
I can no more — fight out the good fight —
     die
Conqueror.
     [*Staggers into the chapel of Saint Benedict.*
   *Becket (falling on his knees).* At the
     right hand of Power —
Power and great glory — for thy Church,
     O Lord —

Into thy hands, O Lord — into thy
   hands ! —                    [*Sinks prone.*
*De Brito.* This last to rid thee of a
   world of brawls ! (*Kills him.*)
The traitor 's dead, and will arise no more.
*Fitzurse.* Nay, have we still'd him ?
   What ! the great archbishop !
Does he breathe ?   No ?
   *De Tracy.*      No, Reginald, he is dead.
              [*Storm bursts.*[1]

*De Morville.* Will the earth gape and
   swallow us ?
*De Brito.*               The deed 's done —
Away !
   [De Brito, De Tracy, Fitzurse, *rush
   out, crying ' King's men ! '* De Morville *follows slowly. Flashes of lightning thro' the Cathedral.* Rosamund
   *seen kneeling by the body of* Becket.

# THE FALCON

This play was produced by Mr. and Mrs. Kendal at the St. James Theatre in December, 1879,
and had a run of sixty-seven nights.  It was published with ' The Cup ' in 1884.

The story, which the poet took from Boccaccio (' Decameron,' 5th Day, 9th tale), has been
traced to the Sanskrit ' Panchatantra.'  La Fontaine gives it in his ' Contes et Nouvelles ' (' Le
Faucon '), and Longfellow in his ' Tales of a Wayside Inn ' (' The Falcon of Ser Federigo ').  It
was also dramatized by Delisle de la Drévetière as a three-act comedy.

## DRAMATIS PERSONÆ

The Count Federigo degli Alberighi.
Filippo, *the Count's foster-brother.*
The Lady Giovanna.
Elisabetta, *the Count's nurse.*

## THE FALCON

Scene. — An Italian Cottage, Castle and Mountains seen through
Window

Elisabetta *discovered seated on stool in
window, darning.  The Count with Falcon
on his hand comes down through the door
at back.  A withered wreath on the wall.*

*Elisabetta.* So, my lord, the Lady Giovanna, who hath been away so long, came
back last night with her son to the castle.
   *Count.* Hear that, my bird !  Art thou
   not jealous of her ?
My princess of the cloud, my plumed purveyor,
My far-eyed queen of the winds — thou
   that canst soar
Beyond the morning lark, and, howsoe'er
Thy quarry wind and wheel, swoop down
   upon him

Eagle-like, lightning-like — strike, make
   his feathers
Glance in mid heaven.       [*Crosses to chair.*
           I would thou hadst a mate !
Thy breed will die with thee, and mine with
   me;                                            11
I am as lone and loveless as thyself.
               [*Sits in chair.*
Giovanna here !  Ay, ruffle thyself — *be*
   jealous !
Thou shouldst be jealous of her.  Tho' I
   bred thee
The full-train'd marvel of all falconry,
And love thee and thou me, yet if Giovanna
Be here again — No, no !  Buss me, my
   bird !
The stately widow has no heart for me.
Thou art the last friend left me upon
   earth —
No, no again to that !      [*Rises and turns.*
             My good old nurse,
I had forgotten thou wast sitting there.   21
   *Elisabetta.* Ay, and forgotten thy foster-
   brother too.
   *Count.* Bird-babble for my falcon !  Let
   it pass.
What art thou doing there ?

---

[1] A tremendous thunderstorm actually broke
over the Cathedral as the murderers were leaving it.

*Elisabetta.*        Darning, your lordship.
We cannot flaunt it in new feathers now.
Nay, if we *will* buy diamond necklaces
To please our lady, we must darn, my lord.
This old thing here ( *points to necklace round
    her neck*), they are but blue beads —
    my Piero,
God rest his honest soul, he bought 'em for
    me,
Ay, but he knew I meant to marry him. 30
How couldst thou do it, my son ? How
    couldst thou do it ?
*Count.* She saw it at a dance, upon a
    neck
Less lovely than her own, and long'd for it.
*Elisabetta.* She told thee as much ?
*Count.*        No, no — a friend of hers.
*Elisabetta.* Shame on her that she took
    it at thy hands,
She rich enough to have bought it for her-
    self !
*Count.* She would have robb'd me then
    of a great pleasure.
*Elisabetta.* But hath she yet return'd thy
    love ?
*Count.*        Not yet !
*Elisabetta.* She should return thy neck-
    lace then.
*Count.*        Ay, if
She knew the giver; but I bound the seller
To silence, and I left it privily        41
At Florence, in her palace.
*Elisabetta.*        And sold thine own
To buy it for her.   She not know ?   She
    knows
There 's none such other —
*Count.*        Madman anywhere.
Speak freely, tho' to call a madman mad
Will hardly help to make him sane again.

### Enter FILIPPO.

*Filippo.* Ah, the women, the women !
Ah, Monna Giovanna, you here again ! you
that have the face of an angel and the
heart of a — that 's too positive !  You that
have a score of lovers and have not a heart
for any of them — that 's positive-negative:
you that have *not* the head of a toad, and
*not* a heart like the jewel in it — that's too
negative; you that have a cheek like a
peach and a heart like the stone in it —
that 's positive again — that 's better !
*Elisabetta.* Sh — sh — Filippo !        58
*Filippo* (*turns half round*). Here has our
master been a-glorifying and a-velveting

and a-silking himself, and a-peacocking
and a-spreading to catch her eye for a
dozen year, till he has n't an eye left in his
own tail to flourish among the peahens, and
all along o' **you**, Monna Giovanna, all along
o' you !
*Elisabetta.* Sh — sh — Filippo !  Can't
you hear that you are saying behind his
back what you see you are saying afore his
face ?        70
*Count.* Let him — he never spares me
to my face !
*Filippo.* No, my lord, I never spare your
lordship to your lordship's face, nor behind
your lordship's back, nor to right, nor to
left, nor to round about and back to your
lordship's face again, for I 'm honest, your
lordship.
*Count.* Come, come, Filippo, what is
there in the larder ?        80
[*Elisabetta crosses to fireplace and puts
    on wood.*
*Filippo.* Shelves and hooks, shelves and
hooks, and when I see the shelves I am
like to hang myself on the hooks.
*Count.* No bread ?
*Filippo.* Half a breakfast for a rat !
*Count.* Milk ?
*Filippo.* Three laps for a cat !
*Count.* Cheese ?
*Filippo.* A supper for twelve mites.
*Count.* Eggs ?        90
*Filippo.* One, but addled.
*Count.* No bird ?
*Filippo.* Half a tit and a hern's bill.
*Count.* Let be thy jokes and thy jerks,
man !  Anything or nothing ?
*Filippo.* Well, my lord, if all-but-nothing
be anything, and one plate of dried prunes
be all-but-nothing, then there is anything
in your lordship's larder at your lordship's
service, if your lordship care to call for
it.        101
*Count.* Good mother, happy was the
    prodigal son,
For he return'd to the rich father; I
But add my poverty to thine.   And all
Thro' following of my fancy.   Pray thee
    make
Thy slender meal out of those scraps and
    shreds
Filippo spoke of.   As for him and me,
There sprouts a salad in the garden still.
(*To the Falcon.*) Why didst thou miss thy
    quarry yester-even ?

To-day, my beauty, thou must dash us
   down                 110
Our dinner from the skies.  Away, Filippo !
        [*Exit, followed by* Filippo.
  *Elisabetta.*  I knew it would come to this.
She has beggared him.  I always knew it
would come to this !  (*Goes up to table as
if to resume darning, and looks out of window.*)  Why, as I live, there is Monna
Giovanna coming down the hill from the
castle.  Stops and stares at our cottage.
Ay, ay !  stare at it: it 's all you have left
us.  Shame on you !  *She* beautiful! sleek
as a miller's mouse !  Meal enough, meat
enough, well fed; but beautiful —bah !  Nay,
see, why she turns down the path through
our little vineyard, and I sneezed three
times this morning.  Coming to visit my
lord, for the first time in her life too !
Why, bless the saints !  I 'll be bound to
confess her love to him at last.  I forgive
her, I forgive her !  I knew it would come
to this — I always knew it must come to
this !  (*Goes up to door during latter part
of speech, and opens it.*)  Come in, madonna, come in.  (*Retires to front of table
and curtseys as the* LADY GIOVANNA *enters,
then moves chair towards the hearth.*)  Nay,
let me place this chair for your ladyship.

   [Lady Giovanna *moves slowly down
     stage, then crosses to chair, looking
     about her, bows as she sees the Ma-
     donna over fireplace, then sits in chair.*
  *Lady Giovanna.*  Can I speak with the
  Count ?             138
  *Elisabetta.*  Ay, my lady, but won't you
speak with the old woman first, and tell
her all about it and make her happy ? for
I 've been on my knees every day for these
half-dozen years in hope that the saints
would send us this blessed morning ; and
he always took you so kindly, he always
took the world so kindly.  When he was
a little one, and I put the bitters on my
breast to wean him, he made a wry mouth
at it, but he took it so kindly, and your
ladyship has given him bitters enough in
this world, and he never made a wry mouth
at you, he always took you so kindly —
which is more than I did, my lady, more
than I did — and he so handsome — and
bless your sweet face, you look as beautiful
this morning as the very Madonna her own
self — and better late than never — but
come when they will — then or now — it 's

all for the best, come when they will —
they are made by the blessed saints —
these marriages.     [*Raises her hands.*
  *Lady Giovanna.*  Marriages ?  I shall
  never marry again !       162
  *Elisabetta* (*rises and turns*).  Shame on
  her then !
  *Lady Giovanna.*  Where is the Count ?
  *Elisabetta.*            Just gone
To fly his falcon.
  *Lady Giovanna.*  Call him back and say
I come to breakfast with him.
  *Elisabetta.*         Holy mother !
To breakfast !  O sweet saints ! one plate
  of prunes !
Well, madam, I will give your message to
  him.               [*Exit.*
  *Lady Giovanna.*  His falcon, and I come
to ask for his falcon,
The pleasure of his eyes — boast of his
  hand —
Pride of his heart — the solace of his
  hours —           170
His one companion here — nay, I have
  heard
That, thro' his late magnificence of living
And this last costly gift to mine own self,
        [*Shows diamond necklace.*
He hath become so beggar'd that his fal-
  con
Even wins his dinner for him in the field.
That must be talk, not truth, but, truth or
  talk,
How can I ask for his falcon ?
       [*Rises and moves as she speaks.*
            O my sick boy !
My daily fading Florio, it is thou
Hath set me this hard task, for when I say,
What can I do — what can I get for thee ?
He answers, ' Get the Count to give me his
  falcon,           181
And that will make me well.'  Yet if I
  ask,
He loves me, and he knows I know he loves
  me !
Will he not pray me to return his love —
To marry him ? — (*pause*) — I can never
  marry him.
His grandsire struck my grandsire in a
  brawl
At Florence, and my grandsire stabb'd him
  there.
The feud between our houses is the bar
I cannot cross; I dare not brave my bro-
  ther,

Break with my kin.  My brother hates him,
  scorns      190
The noblest-natured man alive, and I —
Who have that reverence for him that I
  scarce
Dare beg him to receive his diamonds
  back —
How can I, dare I, ask him for his falcon?
    *[Puts diamonds in her casket.*

*Re-enter* COUNT *and* FILIPPO.  COUNT
  *turns to* FILIPPO.

*Count.*  Do what I said; I cannot do it
  myself.
*Filippo.*  Why then, my lord, we are pau-
  per'd out and out.
*Count.*  Do what I said!
    *[Advances and bows low.*
Welcome to this poor cottage, my dear
  lady.
*Lady Giovanna.*  And welcome turns a
  cottage to a palace.    199
*Count.*  'T is long since we have met!
*Lady Giovanna.*    To make amends
I come this day to break my fast with you.
*Count.*  I am much honor'd — yes —
    *[Turns to* Filippo.
Do what I told thee.  Must I do it my-
  self?
*Filippo.*  I will, I will. (*Sighs.*)  Poor
  fellow!    *[Exit.*
*Count.*  Lady, you bring your light into
  my cottage
Who never deign'd to shine into my palace.
My palace wanting you was but a cottage;
My cottage, while you grace it, is a palace.
*Lady Giovanna.*  In cottage or in palace,
  being still
Beyond your fortunes, you are still the
  king    210
Of courtesy and liberality.
*Count.*  I trust I still maintain my cour-
  tesy;
My liberality perforce is dead
Thro' lack of means of giving.
*Lady Giovanna.*    Yet I come
To ask a gift.  *[Moves toward him a little.*
*Count.*    It will be hard, I fear,
To find one shock upon the field when all
The harvest has been carried.
*Lady Giovanna.*    But my boy —
(*Aside.*) No, no! not yet — I cannot!
*Count.*    Ay, how is he,
That bright inheritor of your eyes — your
  boy?

*Lady Giovanna.*  Alas, my Lord Federigo,
  he hath fallen    220
Into a sickness, and it troubles me.
*Count.*  Sick! is it so? why, when he
  came last year
To see me hawking, he was well enough;
And then I taught him all our hawking-
  phrases.
*Lady Giovanna.*  O yes, and once you let
  him fly your falcon.
*Count.*  How charm'd he was! what won-
  der? — A gallant boy,
A noble bird, each perfect of the breed.
*Lady Giovanna* (*sinks in chair*).  What
  do you rate her at?
*Count.*    My bird? a hundred
Gold pieces once were offer'd by the Duke.
I had no heart to part with her for money.
*Lady Giovanna.*  No, not for money.
    *[Count *turns away and sighs.*
    Wherefore do you sigh?
*Count.*  I have lost a friend of late.
*Lady Giovanna.*    I could sigh with you
For fear of losing more than friend, a
  son;
And if he leave me — all the rest of life —
That wither'd wreath were of more worth
  to me.  *[Looking at wreath on wall.*
*Count.*  That wither'd wreath is of more
  worth to me
Than all the blossom, all the leaf of this
New-wakening year.
    *[Goes and takes down wreath.*
*Lady Giovanna.*    And yet I never saw
The land so rich in blossom as this year.
*Count* (*holding wreath toward her*).  Was
  not the year when this was gather'd
  richer?    240
*Lady Giovanna.*  How long ago was
  that?
*Count.*    Alas, ten summers!
A lady that was beautiful as day
Sat by me at a rustic festival
With other beauties on a mountain meadow,
And she was the most beautiful of all;
Then but fifteen, and still as beautiful.
The mountain flowers grew thickly round
  about.
I made a wreath with some of these; I
  ask'd
A ribbon from her hair to bind it with;
I whisper'd, Let me crown you Queen of
  Beauty,    250
And softly placed the chaplet on her head.
A color, which has color'd all my life,

Flush'd in her face; then I was call'd
   away;
And presently all rose, and so departed.
Ah! she had thrown my chaplet on the
   grass,
And there I found it.
   [*Lets his hands fall, holding wreath de-
      spondingly.*
*Lady Giovanna* (*after pause*). How long
   since do you say?
*Count.* That was the very year before
   you married.
*Lady Giovanna.* When I was married
   you were at the wars.
*Count.* Had she not thrown my chaplet
   on the grass,
It may be I had never seen the wars.  260
   [*Replaces wreath whence he had taken
      it.*
*Lady Giovanna.* Ah, but, my lord, there
   ran a rumor then
That you were kill'd in battle. I can tell
   you
True tears that year were shed for you in
   Florence.
*Count.* It might have been as well for
   me. Unhappily
I was but wounded by the enemy there
And then imprison'd.
*Lady Giovanna.*          Happily, however,
I see you quite recover'd of your wound.
*Count.* No, no, not quite, madonna, not
   yet, not yet.                                268

### Re-enter FILIPPO.

*Filippo.* My lord, a word with you.
*Count.*                  Pray, pardon me!
   [*Lady Giovanna crosses, and passes be-
      hind chair and takes down wreath;
      then goes to chair by table.*
*Count* (*to* Filippo). What is it, Filippo?
*Filippo.* Spoons, your lordship.
*Count.*                      Spoons!
*Filippo.* Yes, my lord, for was n't my
lady born with a golden spoon in her lady-
ship's mouth, and we have n't never so much
as a silver one for the golden lips of her
ladyship.
*Count.* Have we not half a score of sil-
   ver spoons?
*Filippo.* Half o' one, my lord!
*Count.* How half of one?
*Filippo.* I trod upon him even now, my
lord, in my hurry, and broke him.        280
*Count.* And the other nine?

*Filippo.* Sold! but shall I not mount
with your lordship's leave to her ladyship's
castle, in your lordship's and her ladyship's name, and confer with her ladyship's seneschal, and so descend again with
some of her ladyship's own appurtenances?
*Count.* Why — no, man. Only see your
   cloth be clean.       [*Exit* Filippo.
*Lady Giovanna.* Ay, ay, this faded rib-
   bon was the mode
In Florence ten years back. What's here?
   a scroll                               290
Pinned to the wreath.
                My lord, you have said so much
Of this poor wreath that I was bold enough
To take it down, if but to guess what flow-
   ers
Had made it; and I find a written scroll
That seems to run in rhymings. Might I
   read?
*Count.* Ay, if you will.
*Lady Giovanna.* It should be if you can.
(*Reads.*) 'Dead mountain.' Nay, for who
   could trace a hand
So wild and staggering?
*Count.*               This was penn'd, madonna,
Close to the grating on a winter morn
In the perpetual twilight of a prison,    300
When he that made it, having his right
   hand
Lamed in the battle, wrote it with his left.
*Lady Giovanna.* O heavens! the very
   letters seem to shake
With cold, with pain perhaps, poor pris-
   oner! Well,
Tell me the words — or better — for I see
There goes a musical score along with
   them,
Repeat them to their music.
*Count.*                  You can touch
No chord in me that would not answer you
In music.
*Lady Giovanna.* That is musically said.
   [*Count takes guitar. Lady Giovanna
      sits listening with wreath in her hand,
      and quietly removes scroll and places
      it on table at the end of the song.*
*Count* (*sings, playing guitar*). 'Dead
   mountain flowers, dead mountain-
   meadow flowers,                        310
Dearer than when you made your mountain
   gay,
Sweeter than any violet of to-day,
Richer than all the wide world-wealth of
   May,

To me, tho' all your bloom has died away,
You bloom again, dead mountain-meadow
    flowers.'

*Enter* ELISABETTA *with cloth.*

*Elisabetta.* A word with you, my lord !
*Count* (*singing*). ' O mountain flowers ! '
*Elisabetta* (*louder*). A word, my lord !
*Count* (*sings*).           ' Dead flowers ! '
*Elisabetta* (*louder*).      A word, my lord !
*Count.* I pray you pardon me again !
        [*Lady Giovanna looking at wreath.*
*Count* (*to* Elisabetta).         What is it ?
*Elisabetta.* My lord, we have but one
piece of earthen-ware to serve the salad in
to my lady, and that cracked !          321
*Count.* Why then, that flower'd bowl my
    ancestor
Fetch'd from the farthest east — we never
    use it
For fear of breakage — but this day has
    brought
A great occasion. You can take it, nurse !
*Elisabetta.* I did take it, my lord, but
what with my lady's coming that had so
flurried me, and what with the fear of
breaking it, I did break it, my lord; it is
broken !                                330
*Count.* My one thing left of value in the
    world !
No matter ! see your cloth be white as
    snow !
*Elisabetta* (*pointing thro' window*).
White ? I warrant thee, my son, as the
snow yonder on the very tip-top o' the
mountain.
*Count.* And yet, to speak white truth,
    my good old mother,
I have seen it like the snow on the mo-
    raine.
*Elisabetta.* How can your lordship say
    so ? There, my lord ! [*Lays cloth.*
O my dear son, be not unkind to me.   339
And one word more. [*Going — returns.*
*Count* (*touching guitar*). Good ! let it be
    but one.
*Elisabetta.* Hath she return'd thy love ?
*Count.*              Not yet !
*Elisabetta.*              And will she ?
*Count* (*looking at* Lady Giovanna). I
    scarce believe it !
*Elisabetta.*              Shame upon her then !
                                    [*Exit.*
*Count* (*sings*). ' Dead mountain flow-
    ers ' —

Ah well, my nurse has broken
The thread of my dead flowers, as she has
    broken
My china bowl. My memory is as dead.
        [*Goes and replaces guitar.*
Strange that the words at home with me
    so long
Should fly like bosom friends when needed
    most.
So by your leave, if you would hear the
    rest,
The writing.
*Lady Giovanna* (*holding wreath toward
    him*). There ! my lord, you are a
    poet,                              349
And can you not imagine that the wreath,
Set, as you say, so lightly on her head,
Fell with her motion as she rose, and she,
A girl, a child, then but fifteen, however
Flutter'd or flatter'd by your notice of her,
Was yet too bashful to return for it ?
*Count.* Was it so indeed ? was it so ?
    was it so ?
        [*Leans forward to take wreath, and
        touches* Lady Giovanna's *hand, which
        she withdraws hastily ; he places
        wreath on corner of chair.*
*Lady Giovanna* (*with dignity*). I did not
    say, my lord, that it was so;
I said you might imagine it was so.   358

*Enter* FILIPPO *with bowl of salad, which he
    places on table.*

*Filippo.* Here 's a fine salad for my lady,
for tho' we have been a soldier, and ridden
by his lordship's side, and seen the red of
the battle-field, yet are we now drill-ser-
geant to his lordship's lettuces, and profess
to be great in green things and in garden-
stuff.
*Lady Giovanna.* I thank thee, good Fi-
    lippo.             [*Exit Filippo.*

*Enter* ELISABETTA *with bird on a dish which
    she places on table.*

*Elisabetta* (*close to table*). Here 's a fine
fowl for my lady; I had scant time to do
him in. I hope he be not underdone, for
we be undone in the doing of him.    370
*Lady Giovanna.* I thank you, my good
    nurse.
*Filippo* (*re-entering with plate of prunes*).
And here are fine fruits for my lady —
prunes, my lady, from the tree that my lord
himself planted here in the blossom of his

boyhood — and so I, Filippo, being, with
your ladyship's pardon, and as your ladyship knows, his lordship's own foster-
brother, would commend them to your
ladyship's most peculiar appreciation.    380
[*Puts plate on table.*

*Elisabetta.* Filippo !
*Lady Giovanna* (Count *leads her to table*).
Will you not eat with me, my lord ?
*Count.*                              I cannot ;
Not a morsel, not one morsel. I have
broken
My fast already. I will pledge you.
Wine !
*Filippo,* wine !
[*Sits near table ; Filippo brings flask,
fills the* Count's *goblet, then* Lady Gio-
vanna's ; Elisabetta *stands at the back
of* Lady Giovanna's *chair.*

*Count.*              It is but thin and cold,
Not like the vintage blowing round your
castle.
We lie too deep down in the shadow
here.
Your ladyship lives higher in the sun.
[*They pledge each other and drink.*

*Lady Giovanna.* If I might send you
down a flask or two        389
Of that same vintage ? There is iron in
it.
It has been much commended as a medi-
cine.
I give it my sick son, and if you be
Not quite recover'd of your wound, the
wine
Might help you. None has ever told me
yet
The story of your battle and your wound.
*Filippo* (*coming forward*). I can tell you,
my lady, I can tell you.
*Elisabetta.* Filippo ! will you take the
word out of your master's own mouth !
*Filippo.* Was it there to take ? Put it
there, my lord.        401
*Count.* Giovanna, my dear lady, in this
same battle
We had been beaten — they were ten to
one.
The trumpets of the fight had echo'd
down,
I and Filippo here had done our best,
And, having passed unwounded from the
field,
Were seated sadly at a fountain side,
Our horses grazing by us, when a troop,

Laden with booty and with a flag of ours
Ta'en in the fight —
*Filippo.* Ay, but we fought for it back,
And kill'd —
*Elisabetta.* Filippo !
*Count.*                    A troop of horse —
*Filippo.*                          Five hundred !
*Count.* Say fifty !
*Filippo.* And we kill'd 'em by the score !
*Elisabetta.* Filippo !
*Filippo.* Well, well, well ! I bite my
tongue.
*Count.* We may have left their fifty less
by five.        414
However, staying not to count how many,
But anger'd at their flaunting of our flag,
We mounted, and we dash'd into the heart
of 'em.
I wore the lady's chaplet round my neck ;
It served me for a blessed rosary.
I am sure that more than one brave fellow
owed        420
His death to the charm in it.
*Elisabetta.*              Hear that, my lady !
*Count.* I cannot tell how long we strove
before
Our horses fell beneath us ; down we went
Crush'd, hack'd at, trampled underfoot.
The night,
As some cold - manner'd friend may
strangely do us
The truest service, had a touch of frost
That help'd to check the flowing of the
blood.
My last sight ere I swoon'd was one sweet
face
Crown'd with the wreath. *That* seem'd to
come and go.        429
They left us there for dead !
*Elisabetta.*              Hear that, my lady !'
*Filippo.* Ay, and I left two fingers there
for dead. See, my lady ! (*Showing his
hand.*)
*Lady Giovanna.* I see, Filippo !
*Filippo.* And I have small hope of the
gentleman gout in my great toe.
*Lady Giovanna.* And why, Filippo ?
[*Smiling absently.*
*Filippo.* I left him there for dead too.
*Elisabetta.* She smiles at him — how hard
the woman is !
My lady, if your ladyship were not        440
Too proud to look upon the garland, you
Would find it stain'd —
*Count* (*rising*).        Silence, Elisabetta !

*Elisabetta.* Stain'd with the blood of the best heart that ever
Beat for one woman.
     [*Points to wreath on chair.*
*Lady Giovanna* (*rising slowly*). I can eat no more!
*Count.* You have but trifled with our homely salad,
But dallied with a single lettuce-leaf;
Not eaten anything.
*Lady Giovanna.*  Nay, nay, I cannot.
You know, my lord, I told you I was troubled.
My one child Florio lying still so sick,
I bound myself, and by a solemn vow, 450
That I would touch no flesh till he were well
Here, or else well in heaven, where all is well.

  [Elisabetta *clears table of bird and salad :* Filippo *snatches up the plate of prunes and holds them to* Lady Giovanna.

*Filippo.* But the prunes, my lady, from the tree that his lordship —
*Lady Giovanna.* Not now, Filippo. My lord Federigo,
Can I not speak with you once more alone?
*Count.* You hear, Filippo? My good fellow, go.
*Filippo.* But the prunes that your lordship —
*Elisabetta.* Filippo!
*Count.* Ay, prune our company of thine own, and go!
*Elisabetta.* Filippo! 460
*Filippo* (*turning*). Well, well! the women!    [*Exit.*
*Count.* And thou too leave us, my dear nurse, alone.
*Elisabetta* (*folding up cloth and going*).
And me too! Ay, the dear nurse will leave you alone; but, for all that, she that has eaten the yolk is scarce like to swallow the shell.

  [*Turns and curtseys stiffly to* Lady Giovanna, *then exit.* Lady Giovanna *takes out diamond necklace from casket.*

*Lady Giovanna.* I have anger'd your good nurse; these old-world servants
Are all but flesh and blood with those they serve. 470
My lord, I have a present to return you,
And afterwards a boon to crave of you.

*Count.* No, my most honor'd and long-worshipt lady,
Poor Federigo degli Alberighi
Takes nothing in return from you except
Return of his affection — can deny
Nothing to you that you require of him.
*Lady Giovanna.* Then I require you to take back your diamonds —
     [*Offering necklace.*
I doubt not they are yours. No other heart
Of such magnificence in courtesy 480
Beats — out of heaven. They seem'd too rich a prize
To trust with any messenger. I came
In person to return them.
     [Count *draws back.*
     If the phrase
'Return' displease you, we will say — exchange them.
For your — for your —
*Count* (*takes a step toward her and then back*). For mine — and what of mine?
*Lady Giovanna.* Well, shall we say this wreath and your sweet rhymes?
*Count.* But have you ever worn my diamonds?
*Lady Giovanna.* No!
For that would seem accepting of your love.
I cannot brave my brother — but be sure
That I shall never marry again, my lord!
*Count.* Sure?
*Lady Giovanna.* Yes!
*Count.*  Is this your brother's order?
*Lady Giovanna.*     No!
For he would marry me to the richest man 492
In Florence; but I think you know the saying —
'Better a man without riches, than riches without a man.'
*Count.* A noble saying — and acted on would yield
A nobler breed of men and women. Lady,
I find you a shrewd bargainer. The wreath
That once you wore outvalues twenty-fold
The diamonds that you never deign'd to wear.
But lay them there for a moment!
  [*Points to table.* Lady Giovanna *places necklace on table.*
     And be you
Gracious enough to let me know the boon
By granting which, if aught be mine to grant, 502

I should be made more happy than I hoped
Ever to be again.
 *Lady Giovanna.* Then keep your wreath,
But you will find me a shrewd bargainer
 still.
I cannot keep your diamonds, for the gift
I ask for, to *my* mind and at this present
Outvalues all the jewels upon earth.
 *Count.* It should be love that thus out-
 values all.
You speak like love, and yet you love me
 not.          510
I have nothing in this world but love for
 you.
 *Lady Giovanna.* Love? it *is* love, love
 for my dying boy,
Moves me to ask it of you.
 *Count.*    What? my time?
Is it my time? Well, I can give my time
To him that is a part of you, your son.
Shall I return to the castle with you?
 Shall I
Sit by him, read to him, tell him my tales,
Sing him my songs? You know that I can
 touch
The gittern to some purpose.
 *Lady Giovanna.*    No, not that!
I thank you heartily for that — and you,
I doubt not from your nobleness of na-
 ture,          521
Will pardon me for asking what I ask.
 *Count.* Giovanna, dear Giovanna, I that
 once
The wildest of the random youth of Flor-
 ence
Before I saw you — all my nobleness
Of nature, as you deign to call it, draws
From you, and from my constancy to you.
No more, but speak.
 *Lady Giovanna.* I will. You know sick
 people,
More specially sick children, have strange
 fancies,
Strange longings; and to thwart them in
 their mood      530
May work them grievous harm at times,
 may even
Hasten their end. I would you had a son!
It might be easier then for you to make
Allowance for a mother — her — who
 comes
To rob you of your one delight on earth.
How often has my sick boy yearn'd for
 this!
I have put him off as often; but to-day

I dared not — so much weaker, so much
 worse
For last day's journey. I was weeping for
 him;
He gave me his hand: 'I should be well
 again         540
If the good Count would give me —'
 *Count.*     Give me —
 *Lady Giovanna.*    'His falcon.'
 *Count (starts back).* My falcon!
 *Lady Giovanna.* Yes, your falcon, Fed-
 erigo!
 *Count.* Alas, I cannot!
 *Lady Giovanna.*  Cannot? Even so!
I fear'd as much. O this unhappy world!
How shall I break it to him? how shall I
 tell him?
The boy may die; more blessed were the
 rags
Of some pale beggar-woman seeking alms
For her sick son, if he were like to live,
Than all my childless wealth, if mine must
 die.
I was to blame — the love you said you
 bore me —      550
My lord, we thank you for your entertain-
 ment,
       [*With a stately curtsey.*
And so return — Heaven help him! — to
 our son.      [*Turns.*
 *Count (rushes forward).* Stay, stay, I
 am most unlucky, most unhappy!
You never had look'd in on me before,
And when you came and dipt your sover-
 eign head
Thro' these low doors, you ask'd to eat with
 me.
I had but emptiness to set before you,
No, not a draught of milk, no, not an egg,
Nothing but my brave bird, my noble fal-
 con,        559
My comrade of the house, and of the field.
She had to die for it — she died for you.
Perhaps I thought with those of old, the
 nobler
The victim was, the more acceptable
Might be the sacrifice. I fear you scarce
Will thank me for your entertainment now.
 *Lady Giovanna (returning).* I bear with
 him no longer.
 *Count.*    No, madonna!
And he will have to bear with it as he
 may.
 *Lady Giovanna.* I break with him for
 ever!

*Count.*      Yes, Giovanna,
But he will keep his love to you for ever !
    *Lady Giovanna.* You ? you ? not you !
        My brother ! my hard brother !   570
O Federigo, Federigo, I love you !
Spite of ten thousand brothers, Federigo !
                        [*Falls at his feet.*
*Count* (*impetuously*). Why, then the dy-
        ing of my noble bird
Hath served me better than her living —
        then    [*Takes diamonds from table.*
These diamonds are both yours and mine —
        have won
Their value again — beyond all markets —
        there,
I lay them for the first time round your
        neck.
            [*Lays necklace round her neck.*
And then this chaplet — No more feuds,
        but peace,
Peace and conciliation !   I will make   579

Your brother love me.   See, I tear away
The leaves were darken'd by the battle —
        [*Pulls leaves off and throws them down.*
                        — crown you
Again with the same crown my Queen of
        Beauty.
                [*Places wreath on her head.*
Rise — I could almost think that the dread
        garland
Will break once more into the living blos-
        som.
Nay, nay, I pray you rise.
                [*Raises her with both hands.*
                        We two together
Will help to heal your son — your son and
        mine —
We shall do it — we shall do it !
                        [*Embraces her.*
The purpose of my being is accomplish'd,
And I am happy !
    *Lady Giovanna.*  And I too, Federigo.


# THE CUP

## A TRAGEDY

This play, as we learn from the 'Memoir' (vol. ii. p. 256) was begun in November, 1879, after the poet had finished 'The Falcon,' and completed in 1880, but was not published until 1884. It was produced by Irving at the Lyceum Theatre in January, 1881, and ran for more than a hundred and thirty nights.   The story is from Plutarch.

### DRAMATIS PERSONÆ

GALATIANS {  SYNORIX, *an ex-Tetrarch.*
            SINNATUS, *a Tetrarch.*
            *Attendant.*
            *Boy.*

ROMANS   {  ANTONIUS, *a Roman General.*
            PUBLIUS.

PHŒBE.
CAMMA, *wife of Sinnatus, afterwards
    Priestess in the Temple of Artemis.*
*Maid.*

*Nobleman.*
*Messenger.*


## THE CUP

### ACT I

#### SCENE I. — DISTANT VIEW OF A CITY OF GALATIA

*As the curtain rises, Priestesses are heard
singing in the Temple.   Boy discovered on
a pathway among Rocks, picking grapes.
A party of Roman Soldiers, guarding a
prisoner in chains, come down the pathway
and exeunt.*

*Enter* SYNORIX (*looking round*).   *Singing
        ceases.*

    *Synorix.* Pine, beech and plane, oak, wal-
        nut, apricot,
Vine, cypress, poplar, myrtle, bowering-
        in
The city where she dwells.   She past me
        here
Three years ago when I was flying from
My tetrarchy to Rome.   I almost touch'd
        her —
A maiden slowly moving on to music

Among her maidens to this temple — O
    Gods !
She is my fate — else wherefore has my
    fate
Brought me again to her own city ? —
    married
Since — married Sinnatus, the tetrarch
    here —                                      10
But if he be conspirator, Rome will chain
Or slay him. I may trust to gain her
    then
When I shall have my tetrarchy restored
By Rome, our mistress, grateful that I
    show'd her
The weakness and the dissonance of our
    clans,
And how to crush them easily. Wretched
    race !
And once I wish'd to scourge them to the
    bones.
But in this narrow breathing-time of life
Is vengeance for its own sake worth the
    while,
If once our ends are gain'd ? and now this
    cup —                                       20
I never felt such passion for a woman.
    [*Brings out a cup and scroll from under
    his cloak.*
What have I written to her ?
                    [*Reading the scroll.*
' To the admired Camma, wife of Sinna-
tus the Tetrarch, one who years ago, himself an adorer of our great goddess Artemis, beheld you afar off worshipping in her
temple, and loved you for it, sends you this
cup rescued from the burning of one of her
shrines in a city thro' which he past with
the Roman army: it is the cup we use in
our marriages. Receive it from one who
cannot at present write himself other than
' A GALATIAN SERVING BY FORCE IN
        THE ROMAN LEGION.'
            [*Turns and looks up to Boy.*
Boy, dost thou know the house of Sinna-
    tus ?
    *Boy.* These grapes are for the house of
        Sinnatus —
Close to the temple.
    *Synorix.*            Yonder ?
    *Boy.*                        Yes.
    *Synorix (aside).*                That I
With all my range of women should yet
    shun
To meet her face to face at once ! My
    boy,    [*Boy comes down rocks to him.*

Take thou this letter and this cup to
    Camma,                                      40
The wife of Sinnatus.
    *Boy.*            Going or gone to-day
To hunt with Sinnatus.
    *Synorix.*                That matters not.
Take thou this cup and leave it at her
    doors.
        [*Gives the cup and scroll to the Boy.*
    *Boy.* I will, my lord.
        [*Takes his basket of grapes and exit.*

            *Enter* ANTONIUS.

*Antonius (meeting the Boy as he goes out).*
            Why, whither runs the boy ?
Is that the cup you rescued from the
    fire ?
    *Synorix.* I send it to the wife of Sinna-
    tus,
One half besotted in religious rites.
You come here with your soldiers to en-
    force
The long-withholden tribute; you suspect
This Sinnatus of playing patriotism,     50
Which in your sense is treason. You have
    yet
No proof against him. Now this pious
    cup
Is passport to their house, and open arms
To him who gave it; and once there I war-
    rant
I worm thro' all their windings.
    *Antonius.*            If you prosper,
Our Senate, wearied of their tetrarchies,
Their quarrels with themselves, their spites
    at Rome,
Is like enough to cancel them, and throne
One king above them all, who shall be
    true
To the Roman; and from what I heard in
    Rome,                                       60
This tributary crown may fall to you.
    *Synorix.* The king, the crown ! their
    talk in Rome ? is it so ?
            [*Antonius nods.*
Well — I shall serve Galatia taking it,
And save her from herself, and be to Rome
More faithful than a Roman.
    [*Turns and sees* Camma *coming.*
                Stand aside,
Stand aside; here she comes !
    [*Watching* Camma *as she enters with
    her Maid.*
    *Camma (to Maid).* Where is he, girl ?
    *Maid.*            You know the waterfall

That in the summer keeps the mountain
    side,
But after rain o'erleaps a jutting rock    69
And shoots three hundred feet.
    *Camma.*            The stag is there?
    *Maid.* Seen in the thicket at the bottom
    there
But yester-even.
    *Camma.*      Good then, we will climb
The mountain opposite and watch the chase.
        *[They descend the rocks and exeunt.*
    *Synorix (watching her). (Aside.)* The bust
    of Juno, and the brows and eyes
Of Venus; face and form unmatchable!
    *Antonius.* Why do you look at her so
    lingeringly?
    *Synorix.* To see if years have changed
    her.
    *Antonius (sarcastically).* Love her, do
    you?
    *Synorix.* I envied Sinnatus when he mar-
    ried her.
    *Antonius.* She knows it? Ha!
    *Synorix.*    She — no, nor even my face.
    *Antonius.* Nor Sinnatus either?
    *Synorix.*          No, nor Sinnatus.
    *Antonius.* Hot-blooded! I have heard
    them say in Rome,        81
That your own people cast you from their
    bounds
For some unprincely violence to a woman,
As Rome did Tarquin.
    *Synorix.*        Well, if this were so
I here return like Tarquin — for a crown.
    *Antonius.* And may be foil'd like Tar-
    quin, if you follow
Not the dry light of Rome's straight-going
    policy,
But the fool-fire of love or lust, which well
May make you lose yourself, may even
    drown you
In the good regard of Rome.
    *Synorix.*        Tut — fear me not;
I ever had my victories among women.    91
I am most true to Rome.
    *Antonius (aside).*        I hate the man!
What filthy tools our Senate works with!
    Still
I must obey them. *(Aloud.)* Fare you
    well.                  *[Going.*
    *Synorix.* Farewell!
    *Antonius (stopping).* A moment! If you
    track this Sinnatus
In any treason, I give you here an order
                    *[Produces a paper.*

To seize upon him. Let me sign it. *(Signs
    it.)* There —
'Antonius, leader of the Roman Legion.'
    *[Hands the paper to* Synorix. *Goes up
    pathway and exit.*
    *Synorix.* Woman again! — but I am
    wiser now.
No rushing on the game — the net, — the
    net.                              100
    *[Shouts of* 'Sinnatus! Sinnatus!' *Then
    horn.*
*Looking off stage.]* He comes, a rough,
    bluff, simple-looking fellow.
If we may judge the kernel by the husk,
Not one to keep a woman's fealty when
Assailed by Craft and Love. I'll join with
    him;
I may reap something from him — come
    upon *her*
Again, perhaps, to-day — *her*. Who are
    with him?
I see no face that knows me. Shall I risk it?
I am a Roman now, they dare not touch me.
I will.

    *Enter* SINNATUS, HUNTSMEN *and hounds.*

            Fair sir, a happy day to you!
You reck but little of the Roman here,    110
While you can take your pastime in the
    woods.
    *Sinnatus.* Ay, ay, why not? What
    would you with me, man?
    *Synorix.* I am a lifelong lover of the
    chase,
And tho' a stranger fain would be allow'd
To join the hunt.
    *Sinnatus.*        Your name?
    *Synorix.*           Strato, my name.
    *Sinnatus.* No Roman name?
    *Synorix.*    A Greek, my lord; you know
That we Galatians are both Greek and
    Gaul.
        *[Shouts and horns in the distance.*
    *Sinnatus.* Hillo, the stag! *(To* Synorix.)
    What, you are all unfurnish'd?
Give him a bow and arrows — follow —
    follow.
            *[Exit, followed by Huntsmen.*
    *Synorix.* Slowly but surely — till I see
    my way.                         120
It is the one step in the dark beyond
Our expectation, that amazes us.
               *[Distant shouts and horns.*
Hillo! Hillo!
        *[Exit* Synorix. *Shouts and horns.*

SCENE II

A ROOM IN THE TETRARCH'S HOUSE

*Frescoed figures on the walls. Evening. Moonlight outside. A couch with cushions on it. A small table with a flagon of wine, cups, plate of grapes, etc., also the cup of Scene I. A chair with drapery on it.*

CAMMA *enters, and opens curtains of window.*

*Camma.* No Sinnatus yet — and there the rising moon.
　　[*Takes up a cithern and sits on couch. Plays and sings.*

　Moon on the field and the foam,
　　Moon on the waste and the wold,
　Moon bring him home, bring him home,
　　Safe from the dark and the cold,
　Home, sweet moon, bring him home,
　　Home with the flock to the fold —
　Safe from the wolf —

(*Listening.*) Is he coming? I thought I heard
A footstep. No, not yet. They say that Rome    10
Sprang from a wolf. I fear my dear lord mixt
With some conspiracy against the wolf.
This mountain shepherd never dream'd of Rome.　　[*Sings.*

　Safe from the wolf to the fold —

And that great break of precipice that runs
Thro' all the wood, where twenty years ago
Huntsman and hound and deer were all neck-broken!
Nay, here he comes.

*Enter* SINNATUS *followed by* SYNORIX.

*Sinnatus* (*angrily*). I tell thee, my good fellow,
My arrow struck the stag.
*Synorix.*　　　　　But was it so?
Nay, you were further off; besides the wind    20
Went with *my* arrow.
*Sinnatus.*　　　　I am sure *I* struck him.
*Synorix.* And I am just as sure, my lord, *I* struck him.
(*Aside.*) And I may strike your game when you are gone.

*Camma.* Come, come, we will not quarrel about the stag.
I have had a weary day in watching you.
Yours must have been a wearier. Sit and eat,
And take a hunter's vengeance on the meats.
*Sinnatus.* No, no — we have eaten — we are heated. Wine!
*Camma.* Who is our guest?
*Sinnatus.*　　　　Strato he calls himself.
　　[*Camma offers wine to* Synorix, *while* Sinnatus *helps himself.*
*Sinnatus.* I pledge you, Strato.
　　　　　　　　[*Drinks.*
*Synorix.*　　　And I you, my lord.
　　　　　　　　[*Drinks.*
*Sinnatus* (*seeing the cup sent to* Camma).
What's here?
*Camma.* A strange gift sent to me to-day.
A sacred cup saved from a blazing shrine  30
Of our great Goddess, in some city where
Antonius past. I had believed the Rome
Made war upon the peoples, not the Gods.
*Synorix.* Most like the city rose against Antonius,
Whereon he fired it, and the sacred shrine
By chance was burnt along with it.
*Sinnatus.*　　　　　　Had you then
No message with the cup?
*Camma.*　　　　Why, yes, see here.
　　[*Gives him the scroll.*
*Sinnatus* (*reads*). 'To the admired Camma, — beheld you afar off — loved you — sends you this cup — the cup we use in our marriages — cannot at present write himself other than
　'A GALATIAN SERVING BY FORCE IN THE ROMAN LEGION.'
Serving by force! Were there no boughs to hang on,
Rivers to drown in? Serve by force? No force
Could make me serve by force.
*Synorix.*　　　　How then, my lord?
The Roman is encamped without your city —
The force of Rome a thousand-fold our own.    51
Must all Galatia hang or drown herself?
And you a prince and tetrarch in this province —
*Sinnatus.* Province!
*Synorix.* Well, well, they call it so in Rome.

*Sinnatus (angrily).* Province !

*Synorix.* A noble anger ! but Antonius
To-morrow will demand your tribute —
 you,
Can you make war ?   Have you alliances ?
Bithynia, Pontus, Paphlagonia ?
We have had our leagues of old with East-
 ern kings.
There is my hand — if such a league there
 be.         60
What will you do ?

 *Sinnatus.*   Not set myself abroach
And run my mind out to a random guest
Who join'd me in the hunt.   You saw my
 hounds
True to the scent; and we have two-legg'd
 dogs
Among us who can smell a true occasion,
And when to bark and how.

 *Synorix.*   My good Lord Sinnatus,
I once was at the hunting of a lion.
Roused by the clamor of the chase he woke,
Came to the front of the wood — his mon-
 arch mane
Bristled about his quick ears — he stood
 there         70
Staring upon the hunter.   A score of dogs
Gnaw'd at his ankles; at the last he felt
The trouble of his feet, put forth one paw,
Slew four, and knew it not, and so re-
 main'd
Staring upon the hunter.   And this Rome
Will crush you if you wrestle with her;
 then,
Save for some slight report in her own
 Senate,
Scarce know what she has done.

    *(Aside.)* Would I could move him,
Provoke him any way !   *(Aloud.)* The
 Lady Camma,
Wise I am sure as she is beautiful, 80
Will close with me that to submit at once
Is better than a wholly hopeless war,
Our gallant citizens murder'd all in vain,
Son, husband, brother gash'd to death in
 vain,
And the small state more cruelly trampled
 on
Than had she never moved.

 *Camma.*    Sir, I had once
A boy who died a babe; but were he liv-
 ing
And grown to man and Sinnatus will'd it, I
Would set him in the front rank of the
 fight

With scarce a pang.   *(Rises.)*   Sir, if a
 state submit       90
At once, she may be blotted out at once
And swallow'd in the conqueror's chronicle.
Whereas in wars of freedom and defence
The glory and grief of battle won or lost
Solders a race together — yea — tho' they
 fail,
The names of those who fought and fell
 are like
A bank'd-up fire that flashes out again
From century to century, and at last
May lead them on to victory — I hope
 so —         99
Like phantoms of the Gods.

 *Sinnatus.*   Well spoken, wife.

 *Synorix (bowing).* Madam, so well I
 yield.

 *Sinnatus.*   I should not wonder
If Synorix, who has dwelt three years in
 Rome
And wrought his worst against his native
 land,
Returns with this Antonius.

 *Synorix.*   What is Synorix ?

 *Sinnatus.* Galatian, and not know ?   This
 Synorix
Was tetrarch here, and tyrant also — did
Dishonor to our wives.

 *Synorix.*   Perhaps you judge him
With feeble charity; being as you tell me
Tetrarch, there might be willing wives
 enough
To feel dishonor honor.

 *Camma.*   Do not say so.
I know of no such wives in all Galatia. 111
There may be courtesans for aught I know
Whose life is one dishonor.

*Enter* ATTENDANT.

 *Attendant (aside).*  My lord, the men !

 *Sinnatus (aside).* Our anti-Roman faction ?

 *Attendant (aside).*  Ay, my lord.

 *Synorix (overhearing).   (Aside.)* I have
 enough — their anti-Roman faction.

 *Sinnatus (aloud).* Some friends of mine
 would speak with me without.
You, Strato, make good cheer till I return.
         *[Exit.*

 *Synorix.* I have much to say, no time to
 say it in.
First, lady, know myself am that Galatian
Who sent the cup.

 *Camma.*  I thank you from my heart.

*Synorix.* Then that I serve with Rome
   to serve Galatia.                           121
That is my secret; keep it, or you sell
   me
To torment and to death.     [*Coming closer.*
                    For your ear only —
I love you — for your love to the great
   Goddess.
The Romans sent me here a spy upon you,
To draw you and your husband to your
   doom.
I 'd sooner die than do it.
       [*Takes out paper given him by* Antonius.
                    This paper sign'd
Antonius — will you take it, read it ?
   there !
   *Camma (reads).* 'You are to seize on
       Sinnatus, — if — '
   *Synorix (snatches paper).* No more.
What follows is for no wife's eyes.   O
   Camma,                                      130
Rome has a glimpse of this conspiracy;
Rome never yet hath spar'd conspirator.
Horrible ! flaying, scourging, crucifying —
   *Camma.* I am tender enough.   Why do
       you practise on me ?
   *Synorix.* Why should I practise on you ?
       How you wrong me !
I am sure of being every way malign'd.
And if you should betray me to your hus-
   band —
   *Camma.* Will *you* betray him by this
       order ?
   *Synorix.*                            See,
I tear it all to pieces, never dream'd
Of acting on it.           [*Tears the paper.*
   *Camma.*       I owe you thanks for ever.
   *Synorix.* Hath Sinnatus never told you
       of this plot ?                          141
   *Camma.* What plot ?
   *Synorix.* A child's sand-castle on the
       beach
For the next wave, — all seen, — all calcu-
   lated,
All known by Rome.   No chance for Sin-
   natus.
   *Camma.* Why said you not as much to
       my brave Sinnatus ?
   *Synorix.* Brave — ay — too brave, too
       over-confident,
Too like to ruin himself, and you, and me !
Who else, with this black thunderbolt of
   Rome
Above him, would have chased the stag
   to-day                                      149

In the full face of all the Roman camp ?
A miracle that they let him home again,
Not caught, maim'd, blinded him.
                       [*Camma shudders.*
       (*Aside.*)  I have made her tremble.
(*Aloud.*)  I know they mean to torture
   him to death.
I dare not tell him how I came to know it;
I durst not trust him with — my serving
   Rome
To serve Galatia; you heard him on the
   letter.
Not say as much ?   I all but said as much.
I am sure I told him that his plot was
   folly.
I say it to you — you are wiser — Rome
   knows all,
But you know not the savagery of Rome.
   *Camma.* O ! — have you power with
       Rome ? use it for him !              161
   *Synorix.* Alas !  I have no such power
       with Rome.   All that
Lies with Antonius.
       [*As if struck by a sudden thought.
       Comes over to her.*
                    He will pass to-morrow
In the gray dawn before the Temple doors.
You have beauty, — O, great beauty, —
   and Antonius,
So gracious toward women, never yet
Flung back a woman's prayer.   Plead to
   him,
I am sure you will prevail.
   *Camma.*              Still — I should tell
My husband.
   *Synorix.*  Will he let you plead for him
To a Roman ?
   *Camma.*   I fear not.
   *Synorix.*           Then do not tell him.
Or tell him, if you will, when you return,
When you have charm'd our general into
   mercy,                                      172
And all is safe again.   O dearest lady,
       [*Murmurs of* 'Synorix !  Synorix !'
       *heard outside.*
Think, — torture, — death, — and come.
   *Camma.*                     I will, I will.
And I will not betray you.
   *Synorix (aside, as* Sinnatus *enters).*
                    Stand apart.


*Enter* SINNATUS *and* ATTENDANT.


*Sinnatus.* Thou art that Synorix !  One
   whom thou hast wrong'd

Without there knew thee with Antonius.
They howl for thee, to rend thee head from
    limb.
  *Synorix.* I am much malign'd. I thought
    to serve Galatia.
  *Sinnatus.* Serve thyself first, villain !
    They shall not harm          180
My guest within my house. There ! ( *points
    to door* ) there ! this door
Opens upon the forest ! Out, begone !
Henceforth I am thy mortal enemy.
  *Synorix.* However, I thank thee ( *draws
    his sword* ); thou hast saved my life.
                                    [*Exit.*
  *Sinnatus* ( *to* Attendant). Return and tell
    them Synorix is not here.
                        [*Exit* Attendant.
What did that villain Synorix say to you ?
  *Camma.* Is *he* — *that* — Synorix ?
  *Sinnatus.* Wherefore should you doubt
    it ?
One of the men there knew him.
  *Camma.*                         Only one,
And he perhaps mistaken in the face.
  *Sinnatus.* Come, come, could he deny it ?
    What did he say ?                190
  *Camma.* What *should* he say ?
  *Sinnatus.* What *should* he say, my wife !
He should say this, that being tetrarch
    once
His own true people cast him from their
    doors
Like a base coin.
  *Camma.*            Not kindly to them ?
  *Sinnatus.*                    Kindly ?
O, the most kindly prince in all the world !
Would clap his honest citizens on the
    back,
Bandy their own rude jests with them, be
    curious
About the welfare of their babes, their
    wives,
O, ay — their wives — their wives ! What
    should he say ?
He should say nothing to my wife if I   200
Were by to throttle him ! He steep'd him-
    self
In all the lust of Rome. How should *you*
    guess
What manner of beast it is ?
  *Camma.*            Yet he seem'd kindly,
And said he loathed the cruelties that
    Rome
Wrought on her vassals.
  *Sinnatus.*            Did he, *honest* man ?

  *Camma.* And you, that seldom brook
    the stranger here,
Have let him hunt the stag with you to-
    day.
  *Sinnatus.* I warrant you now, he said *he*
    struck the stag.
  *Camma.* Why, no, he never touch'd
    upon the stag.
  *Sinnatus.* Why, so I said, *my* arrow.
    Well, to sleep.                  210
                        [*Goes to close door.*
  *Camma.* Nay, close not yet the door
    upon a night
That looks half day.
  *Sinnatus.* True; and my friends may spy
    him
And slay him as he runs.
  *Camma.*            He is gone already.
O, look, — yon grove upon the mountain,
    — white
In the sweet moon as with a lovelier snow !
But what a blotch of blackness under-
    neath !
Sinnatus, you remember — yea, you must,
That there three years ago — the vast vine-
    bowers
Ran to the summit of the trees, and dropt
Their streamers earthward, which a breeze
    of May                          220
Took ever and anon, and open'd out
The purple zone of hill and heaven. There
You told your love; and like the swaying
    vines —
Yea, — with our eyes, — our hearts, our
    prophet hopes
Let in the happy distance, and that all
But cloudless heaven which we have found
    together
In our three married years ! You kiss'd
    me there
For the first time. Sinnatus, kiss me now.
  *Sinnatus.* First kiss. ( *Kisses her.* ) There,
    then. You talk almost as if it   229
Might be the last.
  *Camma.*            Will you not eat a little ?
  *Sinnatus.* No, no, we found a goatherd's
    hut, and shared
His fruits and milk. Liar ! You will be-
    lieve
Now that he never struck the stag — a
    brave one
Which you shall see to-morrow.
  *Camma.*            I rise to-morrow
In the gray dawn, and take this holy cup
To lodge it in the shrine of Artemis.

*Sinnatus.* Good !
*Camma.* If I be not back in half an
        hour,
Come after me.
    *Sinnatus.* What ! is there danger ?
    *Camma.*                           Nay,
None that I know; 't is but a step from
        here                              239
To the Temple.
    *Sinnatus.*    All my brain is full of sleep.
Wake me before you go, I 'll after
        you —
After *me* now !        [*Closes door and exit.*
    *Camma (drawing curtains).* Your shadow.
        Synorix —
His face was not malignant, and he said
That men malign'd him.   Shall I go ?
        Shall I go ?
Death, torture —
'He never yet flung back a woman's
        prayer ' —
I go, but I will have my dagger with me.
                                  [*Exit.*


                SCENE III

        SAME AS SCENE I.  DAWN

    *Music and Singing in the Temple.*

*Enter* SYNORIX *watchfully, after him* PUB-
        LIUS *and* SOLDIERS.

*Synorix.* Publius !
*Publius.*        Here !
*Synorix.*              Do you remember what
I told you ?
    *Publius.* When you cry, 'Rome, Rome,'
        to seize
On whomsoever may be talking with you,
Or man, or woman, as traitors unto Rome.
    *Synorix.* Right. Back again. How many
        of you are there ?
    *Publius.* Some half a score.
                [*Exeunt* Soldiers and Publius.
    *Synorix.*     I have my guard about me.
I need not fear the crowd that hunted me
Across the woods, last night.  I hardly
        gain'd
The camp at midnight.   Will she come to
        me
Now that she knows me Synorix ?  Not if
        Sinnatus                         10
Has told her all the truth about me.
        Well,
I cannot help the mould that I was cast in.

I fling all that upon my fate, my star.
I know that I am genial, I would be
Happy, and make all others happy, so
They did not thwart me.   Nay, she will
        not come.
Yet if she be a true and loving wife
She may, perchance, to save this husband.
        Ay !
See, see, my white bird stepping toward the
        snare.
Why, now I count it all but miracle,    20
That this brave heart of mine should shake
        me so,
As helplessly as some unbearded boy's
When first he meets his maiden in a bower.

        *Enter* CAMMA (*with cup*).

The lark first takes the sunlight on his
        wing,
But you, twin sister of the morning star,
Forelead the sun.
    *Camma.*          Where is Antonius ?
    *Synorix.* Not here as yet.  You are too
        early for him.
                [*She crosses towards Temple.*
    *Synorix.* Nay, whither go you now ?
    *Camma.*                        To lodge this cup
Within the holy shrine of Artemis,      29
And so return.
    *Synorix.*      To find Antonius here.
        [*She goes into the Temple, he looks after
        her.*
The loveliest life that ever drew the light
From heaven to brood upon her, and enrich
Earth with her shadow !  I trust she *will*
        return.
These Romans dare not violate the Temple.
No, I must lure my game into the camp.
A woman I could live and die for.  What !
Die for a woman, what new faith is this ?
I am not mad, not sick, not old enough
To dote on one alone.   Yes, mad for her,
Camma the stately, Camma the great-
        hearted,                         40
So mad, I fear some strange and evil
        chance
Coming upon me, for, by the Gods, I seem
Strange to myself !

        *Re-enter* CAMMA.

    *Camma.*          Where is Antonius ?
    *Synorix.* Where ?  As I said before, you
        are still too early.
    *Camma.* Too early to be here alone with
        thee;

For whether men malign thy name, or no,
It bears an evil savor among women.
Where is Antonius ?   (*Loud.*)
    *Synorix.*          Madam, as you know
The camp is half a league without the
        city;
If you will walk with me we needs must
        meet                                          50
Antonius coming, or at least shall find him
There in the camp.
    *Camma.*     No, not one step with thee.
Where is Antonius ?   (*Louder.*)
    *Synorix* (*advancing towards her*). Then
        for your own sake,
Lady, I say it with all gentleness,
And for the sake of Sinnatus your hus-
        band,
I must compel you.
    *Camma* (*drawing her dagger*). Stay ! —
        too near is death.
    *Synorix* (*disarming her*). Is it not easy to
        disarm a woman ?

*Enter* SINNATUS (*seizes him from behind by
        the throat*).

    *Synorix* (*throttled and scarce audible*).
Rome ! Rome !
    *Sinnatus.*          Adulterous dog !
    *Synorix* (*stabbing him with* Camma's *dag-
        ger*).  What ! will you have it ?
    [Camma *utters a cry and runs to* Sinna-
        tus.
    *Sinnatus* (*falls backward*).  I have it in
        my heart — to the Temple — fly —
For *my* sake — or they seize on thee. Re-
        member !                                      60
Away — farewell !                   [*Dies.*
    *Camma* (*runs up the steps into the Temple,
        looking back*).  Farewell !
    *Synorix* (*seeing her escape*).  The women
        of the Temple drag her in.
Publius !  Publius !  No,
Antonius would not suffer me to break
Into the sanctuary.  She hath escaped.
                    [*Looking down at* Sinnatus.
' Adulterous dog ! ' that red-faced rage at
        me !
Then with one quick short stab — eternal
        peace.
So end all passions.  Then what use in pas-
        sions ?
To warm the cold bonds of our dying life
And, lest we freeze in mortal apathy,   70
Employ us, heat us, quicken us, help us,
        keep us

From seeing all too near that urn, those
        ashes
Which all must be.  Well used, they serve
        us well.
I heard a saying in Egypt, that ambition
Is like the sea wave, which the more you
        drink
The more you thirst — yea — drink too
        much, as men
Have done on rafts of wreck — it drives
        you mad.
I will be no such wreck, am no such game-
        ster
As, having won the stake, would dare the
        chance
Of double, or losing all.  The Roman Sen-
        ate,                                          80
For I have always play'd into their hands,
Means me the crown.  And Camma for
        my bride —
The people love her — if I win her love,
They too will cleave to me, as one with
        her.
There then I rest, Rome's tributary king.
                    [*Looking down on* Sinnatus.
Why did I strike him ? — having proof
        enough
Against the man, I surely should have left
That stroke to Rome.  He saved my life
        too.  Did he ?
It seem'd so.  I have play'd the sudden
        fool.
And that sets her against me — for the
        moment.                                       90
Camma — well, well, I never found the
        woman
I could not force or wheedle to my will.
She will be glad at last to wear my crown.
And I will make Galatia prosperous too,
And we will chirp among our vines, and
        smile
At bygone things till that (*pointing to* Sin-
        natus) eternal peace.
Rome !  Rome !

*Enter* PUBLIUS *and* SOLDIERS.

Twice I cried Rome.  Why came ye not
        before ?
    *Publius.*  Why come we now ?  Whom
        shall we seize upon ?
    *Synorix* (*pointing to the body of* Sinna-
        tus).  The body of that dead traitor
        Sinnatus.                                    100
Bear him away.
    *Music and Singing in Temple.*

## ACT II

SCENE. — INTERIOR OF THE TEMPLE
OF ARTEMIS

*Small gold gates on platform in front of the
veil before the colossal statue of the Goddess, and in the centre of the Temple a
tripod altar, on which is a lighted lamp.
Lamps (lighted) suspended between the
pillars. Tripods, vases, garlands of flowers, etc., about stage. Altar at back close
to Goddess, with two cups. Solemn music.
Priestesses decorating the Temple.*

(*The Chorus of* PRIESTESSES *sing as they enter.*)

Artemis, Artemis, hear us, O Mother, hear us,
     and bless us !
Artemis, thou that art life to the wind, to the
     wave, to the glebe, to the fire !
Hear thy people who praise thee ! O, help us
     from all that oppress us !
Hear thy priestesses hymn thy glory ! O, yield
     them all their desire !

*Priestess.*     Phœbe, that man from Syno-
     rix, who has been
So oft to see the priestess, waits once more
Before the Temple.
     *Phœbe.*               We will let her know.
     [*Signs to one of the Priestesses, who goes
     out.*
Since Camma fled from Synorix to our
     Temple,
And for her beauty, stateliness, and power,
Was chosen priestess here, have you not
     mark'd                                      10
Her eyes were ever on the marble floor ?
To-day they are fixt and bright — they
     look straight out.
Hath she made up her mind to marry him ?
     *Priestess.* To marry him who stabb'd
     her Sinnatus !
You will not easily make me credit that.
     *Phœbe.* Ask her.

*Enter* CAMMA *as Priestess* (*in front of the
curtains*).

     *Priestess.* You will not marry Synorix ?
     *Camma.* My girl, I am the bride of
     Death, and only
Marry the dead.
     *Priestess.* Not Synorix then ?
     *Camma.*                         My girl,
At times this oracle of great Artemis

Has no more power than other oracles   20
To speak directly.
     *Phœbe.*          Will you speak to him,
The messenger from Synorix who waits
Before the Temple ?
     *Camma.*     Why not ?   Let him enter.
          [*Comes forward on to step by tripod.*

*Enter a* MESSENGER.

*Messenger* (*kneels*).   Greeting and health
     from Synorix !   More than once
You have refused his hand.   When last I
     saw you,
You all but yielded.   He entreats you now
For your last answer.   When he struck at
     Sinnatus —
As I have many a time declared to you —
He knew not at the moment who had
     fasten'd
About his throat — he begs you to forget it
As scarce his act — a random stroke.   All
     else                                      31
Was love for you; he prays you to believe
     him.
     *Camma.* I pray him to believe — that I
     believe him.
     *Messenger.* Why, that is well.   You mean
     to marry him ?
     *Camma.* I mean to marry him — if that
     be well.
     *Messenger.* This very day the Romans
     crown him king
For all his faithful services to Rome.
He wills you then this day to marry him,
And so be throned together in the sight   39
Of all the people, that the world may know
You twain are reconciled, and no more feuds
Disturb our peaceful vassalage to Rome.
     *Camma.* To-day ?   Too sudden.   I will
     brood upon it.
When do they crown him ?
     *Messenger.*               Even now.
     *Camma.*                    And where ?
     *Messenger.* Here by your temple.
     *Camma.*          Come once more to me
Before the crowning, — I will answer you.
          [*Exit* Messenger.
     *Phœbe.* Great Artemis ! O Camma, can
     it be well,
Or good, or wise, that you should clasp a
     hand
Red with the sacred blood of Sinnatus ?
     *Camma.* Good ! mine own dagger driven
     by Synorix found                         50
All good in the true heart of Sinnatus,

And quench'd it there for ever.   Wise !
Life yields to Death, and Wisdom bows to
    Fate,
Is wisest doing so.   Did not this man
Speak well ?   We cannot fight imperial
    Rome,
But he and I are both Galatian-born;
And tributary sovereigns, he and I
Might teach this Rome — from knowledge
    of our people —
Where to lay on her tribute — heavily here
And lightly there.   Might I not live for
    that,                                        60
And drown all poor self-passion in the sense
Of public good ?
    *Phœbe.*   I am sure you will not marry him.
    *Camma.*   Are you so sure ?   I pray you
        wait and see.
    [*Shouts (from the distance) '* Synorix !
        Synorix !'
    *Camma.*   Synorix, Synorix !   So they cried
Sinnatus
Not so long since — they sicken me.   The
    One
Who shifts his policy suffers something,
    must
Accuse himself, excuse himself; the Many
Will feel no shame to give themselves the lie.
    *Phœbe.*   Most like it was the Roman sol-
        dier shouted.
    *Camma.*   Their shield-borne patriot of
        the morning star                          70
Hang'd at midday, their traitor of the dawn
The clamor'd darling of their afternoon !
And that same head they would have play'd
    at ball with
And kick'd it featureless — they now would
    crown !          [*Flourish of trumpets.*

*Enter a Galatian* NOBLEMAN *with crown on
    a cushion.*

    *Noble* (*kneels*).   Greeting and health from
Synorix.   He sends you
This diadem of the first Galatian Queen,
That you may feed your fancy on the glory
    of it,
And join your life this day with his, and
    wear it
Beside him on his throne.   He waits your
    answer.
    *Camma.*   Tell him there is one shadow
        among the shadows,                        80
One ghost of all the ghosts — as yet so new,
So strange among them — such an alien
    there,

So much of husband in it still — that if
The shout of Synorix and Camma sitting
Upon one throne, should reach it, *it* would
    rise —
HE ! — HE, with that red star between the
    ribs,
And my knife there — and blast the king
    and me,
And blanch the crowd with horror.   I dare
    not, sir !
Throne him — and then the marriage — ay,
    and tell him
That I accept the diadem of Galatia —     90
            [*All are amazed.*
Yea, that ye saw me crown myself withal.
            [*Puts on the crown.*
I wait him his crown'd queen.
    *Noble.*   So will I tell him.     [*Exit.*

*Music.   Two Priestesses go up the steps be-
    fore the shrine, draw the curtains on either
    side (discovering the Goddess), then open
    the gates and remain on steps, one on either
    side, and kneel.   A priestess goes off and
    returns with a veil of marriage, then assists
    PHŒBE to veil CAMMA.   At the same time
    Priestesses enter and stand on either side of
    the Temple.   CAMMA and all the Priest-
    esses kneel, raise their hands to the Goddess,
    and bow down.*
            [*Shouts, '* Synorix !   Synorix !'   *All rise.*
    *Camma.*   Fling wide the doors, and let
        the new-made children
Of our imperial mother see the show.
            [*Sunlight pours through the doors.*
I have no heart to do it.   (*To* Phœbe.)
    Look for me !
            [*Crouches.*   Phœbe *looks out.*
            [*Shouts, '* Synorix !   Synorix !'
    *Phœbe.*   He climbs the throne.   Hot
        blood, ambition, pride
So bloat and redden his face — O, would it
    were
His third last apoplexy !   O, bestial !
O, how unlike our goodly Sinnatus !     100
    *Camma* (*on the ground*).   You wrong him
        surely; far as the face goes
A goodlier-looking man than Sinnatus.
    *Phœbe* (*aside*).   How dare she say it ?   I
        could hate her for it
But that she is distracted.
            [*A flourish of trumpets.*
    *Camma.*           Is he crown'd ?
    *Phœbe.*   Ay, there they crown him.
[*Crowd without shout, '* Synorix !   Synorix !'

*A Priestess brings a box of spices to* Camma, *who throws them on the altar-flame.*

*Camma.* Rouse the dead altar-flame, fling in the spices,
Nard, cinnamon, amomum, benzoin.
Let all the air reel into a mist of odor,
As in the midmost heart of Paradise.    109
Lay down the Lydian carpets for the King.
The King should pace on purple to his bride,
And music there to greet my lord the King.
                                              [*Music.*
(*To* Phœbe.)    Dost thou remember when I wedded Sinnatus ?
Ay, thou wast there — whether from maiden fears
Or reverential love for him I loved,
Or some strange second-sight, the marriage-cup
Wherefrom we make libation to the Goddess
So shook within my hand that the red wine
Ran down the marble and lookt like blood, like blood.
    *Phœbe.*    I do remember your first-marriage fears.    120
    *Camma.*    I have no fears at this my second marriage.
See here — I stretch my hand out — hold it there.
How steady it is !
    *Phœbe.*    Steady enough to stab him !
    *Camma.*    O, hush ! O, peace !    This violence ill becomes
The silence of our Temple.    Gentleness,
Low words best chime with this solemnity.

*Enter a procession of Priestesses and Children bearing garlands and golden goblets, and strewing flowers.*

*Enter* SYNORIX (*as King, with gold laurel-wreath crown and purple robes*), *followed by* ANTONIUS, PUBLIUS, *Noblemen,* Guards, *and the Populace.*

    *Camma.*    Hail, King !
    *Synorix.*                    Hail, Queen !
The wheel of Fate has roll'd me to the top.
I would that happiness were gold, that I
Might cast my largess of it to the crowd !
I would that every man made feast to-day,
Beneath the shadow of our pines and planes !    132
For all my truer life begins to-day.
The past is like a travell'd land now sunk
Below the horizon — like a barren shore
That grew salt weeds, but now all drown'd in love
And glittering at full tide — the bounteous bays
And havens filling with a blissful sea.
Nor speak I now too mightily, being King
And happy ! happiest, lady, in my power
To make you happy.
    *Camma.*                    Yes, sir.
    *Synorix.*                            Our Antonius,
Our faithful friend of Rome, tho' Rome may set    142
A free foot where she will, yet of his courtesy
Entreats he may be present at our marriage.
    *Camma.*    Let him come — a legion with him, if he will.
    (*To* Antonius.)    Welcome, my lord Antonius, to our Temple.
    (*To* Synorix.)    You on this side the altar.    (*To* Antonius.)    You on that.
Call first upon the Goddess, Synorix.
                [*All face the Goddess.    Priestesses, Children, Populace, and Guards kneel — the others remain standing.*
    *Synorix.*    O thou that dost inspire the germ with life,
The child, a thread within the house of birth,    150
And give him limbs, then air, and send him forth
The glory of his father — thou whose breath
Is balmy wind to robe our hills with grass,
And kindle all our vales with myrtle-blossom,
And roll the golden oceans of our grain,
And sway the long grape-bunches of our vines,
And fill all hearts with fatness and the lust
Of plenty — make me happy in my marriage !
    *Chorus* (*chanting*).    Artemis, Artemis, hear him, Ionian Artemis !
    *Camma.*    O thou that slayest the babe within the womb    160
Or in the being born, or after slayest him
As boy or man, great Goddess, whose storm-voice
Unsockets the strong oak, and rears his root
Beyond his head, and strows our fruits, and lays
Our golden grain, and runs to sea and makes it

Foam over all the fleeted wealth of kings
And peoples, hear !
Whose arrow is the plague — whose quick
    flash splits
The mid-sea mast, and rifts the tower to
    the rock,
And hurls the victor's column down with
    him    170
That crowns it, hear !
Who causest the safe earth to shudder and
    gape,
And gulf and flatten in her closing chasm
Domed cities, hear !
Whose lava-torrents blast and blacken a
    province
To a cinder, hear !
Whose winter-cataracts find a realm and
    leave it
A waste of rock and ruin, hear ! I call
    thee
To make my marriage prosper to my wish !
    *Chorus.* Artemis, Artemis, hear her,
      Ephesian Artemis !    180
    *Camma.* Artemis, Artemis, hear me,
      Galatian Artemis !
I call on our own Goddess in our own Tem-
    ple.
    *Chorus.* Artemis, Artemis, hear her,
      Galatian Artemis !
              [*Thunder. All rise.*
    *Synorix (aside).* Thunder ! Ay, ay, the
      storm was drawing hither
Across the hills when I was being crown'd.
I wonder if I look as pale as she ?
    *Camma.* Art thou — still bent — on
      marrying ?
    *Synorix.*         Surely — yet
These are strange words to speak to Arte-
    mis.
    *Camma.* Words are not always what
      they seem, my King.
I will be faithful to thee till thou die.    190
    *Synorix.* I thank thee, Camma, — I
    thank thee.
    *Camma (turning to* Antonius*).* Antonius,
Much graced are we that our Queen Rome
    in you
Deigns to look in upon our barbarisms.
    *Turns, goes up steps to altar before the
    Goddess. Takes a cup from off the
    altar. Holds it towards* Antonius.
    Antonius *goes up to the foot of the
    steps opposite to* Synorix.
You see this cup, my lord. [*Gives it to him.*
    *Antonius.*         Most curious !

The many-breasted mother Artemis
Emboss'd upon it.
    *Camma.*         It is old, I know not
How many hundred years. Give it me
    again.
It is the cup belonging our own Temple.
      [*Puts it back on altar, and takes up the
      cup of Act I. Showing it to* Antonius.
Here is another sacred to the Goddess,
The gift of Synorix; and the Goddess, being
For this most grateful, wills, thro' me her
    priestess,    201
In honor of his gift and of our marriage,
That Synorix should drink from his own
    cup.
    *Synorix.* I thank thee, Camma, — I thank
    thee.
    *Camma.*     For — my lord —
It is our ancient custom in Galatia
That ere two souls be knit for life and death,
They two should drink together from one
    cup,
In symbol of their married unity,
Making libation to the Goddess. Bring me
The costly wines we use in marriages.    210
      [*They bring in a large jar of wine.*
    Camma *pours wine into cup.*
(*To* Synorix.) See here, I fill it. (*To*
    Antonius.) Will you drink, my
    lord ?
    *Antonius.* I ? Why should I ? I am
    not to be married.
    *Camma.* But that might bring a Roman
    blessing on us.
    *Antonius (refusing cup).* Thy pardon,
    priestess !
    *Camma.*       Thou art in the right.
This blessing is for Synorix and for me.
See, first I make libation to the Goddess,
              [*Makes libation.*
And now I drink.
        [*Drinks and fills the cup again.*
             Thy turn, Galatian King.
Drink and drink deep — our marriage will
    be fruitful.
Drink and drink deep, and thou wilt make
    me happy.
      [Synorix *goes up to her. She hands him
      the cup. He drinks.*
    *Synorix.* There, Camma ! I have al-
    most drain'd the cup —    220
A few drops left.
    *Camma.*       Libation to the Goddess.
      [*He throws the remaining drops on the
      altar and gives* Camma *the cup.*

*Camma* (*placing the cup on the altar*).
   Why, then the Goddess hears.
   [*Comes down and forward to tripod.*
      *Antonius follows.*

                              Antonius,
Where wast thou on that morning when I
      came
To plead to thee for Sinnatus's life,
Beside this temple half a year ago?
   *Antonius.* I never heard of this request
      of thine.
   *Synorix* (*coming forward hastily to foot of*
      *tripod steps*). I sought him, and I
      could not find him. Pray you,
Go on with the marriage rites.
   *Camma.*                          Antonius —
'Camma!' Who spake?
   *Antonius.*                         N t I.
   *Phœbe.*                      Nor any here.
   *Camma.* I am all but sure that some one
      spake. Antonius,            230
If you had found him plotting against
      Rome,
Would you have tortured Sinnatus to
      death?
   *Antonius.* No thought was mine of tor-
      ture or of death,
But had I found him plotting, I had coun-
      sell'd him
To rest from vain resistance. Rome is
      fated
To rule the world. Then, if he had not
      listen'd,
I might have sent him prisoner to Rome.
   *Synorix.* Why do you palter with the
      ceremony?
Go on with the marriage rites.
   *Camma.*          They are finish'd.
   *Synorix.*                          How!
   *Camma.* Thou hast drunk deep enough
      to make me happy.            240
Dost thou not feel the love I bear to thee
Glow thro' thy veins?
   *Synorix.*          The love I bear to thee
Glows thro' my veins since first I look'd on
      thee.
But wherefore slur the perfect ceremony?
The sovereign of Galatia weds his Queen.
Let all be done to the fullest in the sight
Of all the Gods.
               Nay, rather than so clip
The flowery robe of Hymen, we would add
Some golden fringe of gorgeousness be-
      yond                         249
Old use, to make the day memorial, when

Synorix, first King, Camma, first Queen o'
      the Realm,
Drew here the richest lot from Fate, to live
And die together.
            This pain — what is it? — again?
I had a touch of this last year — in —
      Rome.
Yes, yes. (*To* Antonius.) Your arm —
      a moment — it will pass.
I reel beneath the weight of utter joy —
This all too happy day, crown — queen at
      once.                  [*Staggers.*
O all ye Gods — Jupiter! — Jupiter!
                           [*Falls backward.*
   *Camma.* Dost thou cry out upon the
      Gods of Rome?
Thou art Galatian-born. Our Artemis 260
Has vanquish'd their Diana.
   *Synorix* (*on the ground*). I am poison'd.
She — close the Temple door. Let her not
      fly.
   *Camma* (*leaning on tripod*). Have I not
      drunk of the same cup with thee?
   *Synorix.* Ay, by the Gods of Rome and
      all the world,
She too — she too — the bride! the Queen!
      and I —
Monstrous! I that loved her.
   *Camma.*                   I loved *him.*
   *Synorix.* O murderous mad-woman! I
      pray you lift me
And make me walk awhile. I have heard
      these poisons
May be walk'd down.
         [Antonius *and* Publius *raise him up.*
               My feet are tons of lead,
They will break in the earth — I am sink-
      ing — hold me —              270
Let me alone.
   [*They leave him; he sinks down on*
      *ground.*
         Too late — thought myself wise —
A woman's dupe! Antonius, tell the Senate
I have been most true to Rome — would
      have been true
To *her* — if — if —       [*Falls as if dead.*
   *Camma* (*coming and leaning over him*).
      So falls the throne of an hour.
   *Synorix* (*half rising*). Throne? is it
      thou? the Fates are throned, not
      we —
Not guilty of ourselves — thy doom and
      mine —
Thou — coming my way too — Camma —
      good-night.                 [*Dies.*

*Camma* (*upheld by weeping Priestesses*).
Thy way ? poor worm, crawl down
    thine own black hole
To the lowest hell.  Antonius, is *he* there ?
I meant thee to have follow'd — better
    thus.                                        280
Nay, if my people must be thralls of Rome,
He is gentle, tho' a Roman.
    [*Sinks back into the arms of the Priest-
    esses.*
*Antonius.*                    Thou art one
With thine own people, and though a Ro-
    man I
Forgive thee, Camma.
    *Camma* (*raising herself*).  'CAMMA !' —
        why, there again
I am most sure that some one call'd.  O
    women,
Ye will have Roman masters.   I am
    glad
I shall not see it.   Did not some old Greek
Say death was the chief good ?  He had
    my fate for it,

Poison'd.   (*Sinks back again.*)  Have I the
    crown on ?   I will go
To meet him, crown'd ! crown'd victor of
    my will —                                    290
On my last voyage — but the wind has
    fail'd —
Growing dark too — but light enough to
    row.
Row to the Blessed Isles ! the Blessed
    Isles ! —
Sinnatus !
Why comes he not to meet me ?   It is the
    crown
Offends him — and my hands are too
    sleepy
To lift it off (*Phœbe takes the crown off*).
    Who touched me then ?   I thank
    you.      [*Rises, with outspread arms.*
There — league on league of ever-shining
    shore
Beneath an ever-rising sun — I see him —
'Camma, Camma !'  Sinnatus, Sinnatus !
                                        [*Dies.*

# THE PROMISE OF MAY

*'A surface man of theories, true to none.'*

This play was produced at the Globe Theatre in London in November, 1882 ; and, though
generally condemned by the critics, it had a run of five weeks.  This was partially due to an
incident of a somewhat sensational character which occurred at one of the earlier representations.
At the beginning of the opening scene the Marquis of Queensberry rose from his seat in the
stalls, and loudly protested against what he regarded as Tennyson's attack upon freethinkers in
the character of Edgar.  After some delay the performance was allowed to proceed, but at its
close the Marquis rose again, declaring himself a freethinker, and denouncing the play as a
travesty of the sect.  The next day he explained in a morning paper that his indignation had
been particularly excited by Edgar's comments on marriage.  He added : —
    ' I am a secularist and a freethinker, and, though I repudiate it, a so-called atheist, and, as
President of the British Secular Union, I protest against Mr. Tennyson's abominable caricature
of an individual whom [*sic*], I presume, he would have us believe represents some body of people
which, thanks for the good of humanity, most certainly does not exist among freethinkers.'
    The poet's son Lionel took part in the newspaper controversy that followed.  For his analysis
of the character of Edgar (which represents his father's conception), see the Notes.

## DRAMATIS PERSONÆ

FARMER DOBSON.
MR. PHILIP EDGAR (*afterwards* MR. HAROLD).
FARMER STEER (DORA *and* EVA's *Father*).
MR. WILSON (*a Schoolmaster*).
HIGGINS ⎫
JAMES ⎪
DAN SMITH ⎬ *Farm Laborers.*
JACKSON ⎪
ALLEN ⎭
DORA STEER.
EVA STEER.
SALLY ALLEN ⎫ *Farm Servants.*
MILLY ⎭
Farm Servants, Laborers, etc.

# THE PROMISE OF MAY

## ACT I

### SCENE. — BEFORE FARMHOUSE

*Farming Men and Women. Farming Men carrying forms, etc., Women carrying baskets of knives and forks, etc.*

**First Farming Man.** Be thou a-gawin' to the long barn?

**Second Farming Man.** Ay, to be sewer! Be thou?

**First Farming Man.** Why, o' coorse, fur it be the owd man's birthdaäy. He be heighty this very daäy, and 'e telled all on us to bear i' the long barn by one o'clock, fur he 'll gie us a big dinner, and haäfe th' parish 'll be theer, an' Miss Dora, an' Miss Eva, an' all!

**Second Farming Man.** Miss Dora be coomed back, then?

**First Farming Man.** Ay, haäfe an hour ago. She be in theer now. (*Pointing to house.*) Owd Steer wur afeärd she would n't be back i' time to keep his birthdaäy, and he wur in a tew about it all the murnin'; and he sent me wi' the gig to Littlechester to fetch 'er; and 'er an' the owd man they fell a kissin' o' one another like two sweet-'arts i' the poorch as soon as he clapt eyes of 'er.

**Second Farming Man.** Foälks says he likes Miss Eva the best.

**First Farming Man.** Naäy, I knaws nowt o' what foälks says, an' I caäres nowt neither. Foälks does n't hallus knaw thessens; but sewer I be, they be two o' the purtiest gels ye can see of a summer murnin'.

**Second Farming Man.** Beänt Miss Eva gone off a bit of 'er good looks o' laäte?

**First Farming Man.** Noä, not a bit.

**Second Farming Man.** Why, coöm awaäy, then, to the long barn. [*Exeunt.*

DORA *looks out of window.* Enter DOBSON.

### DORA (*singing*).

The town lay still in the low sunlight,
The hen cluckt late by the white farm gate,
The maid to her dairy came in from the cow,
The stock-dove coo'd at the fall of night, 40
The blossom had open'd on every bough;

O, joy for the promise of May, of May,
O, joy for the promise of May!

(*Nodding at* Dobson.) I 'm coming down, Mr. Dobson. I have n't seen Eva yet. Is she anywhere in the garden?

**Dobson.** Noä, Miss. I ha'n't seed 'er neither.

### DORA (*enters singing*).

But a red fire woke in the heart of the town,
And a fox from the glen ran away with the hen, 50
And a cat to the cream, and a rat to the cheese;
And the stock-dove coo'd, till a kite dropt down,
And a salt wind burnt the blossoming trees;
O, grief for the promise of May, of May,
O, grief for the promise of May!

I don't know why I sing that song; I don't love it.

**Dobson.** Blessings on your pretty voice, Miss Dora! Wheer did they larn ye that? 60

**Dora.** In Cumberland, Mr. Dobson.

**Dobson.** An' how did ye leäve the owd uncle i' Coomberland?

**Dora.** Getting better, Mr. Dobson. But he 'll never be the same man again.

**Dobson.** An' how d' ye find the owd man 'ere?

**Dora.** As well as ever. I came back to keep his birthday. 69

**Dobson.** Well, I be coomed to keep his birthdaäy an' all. The owd man be heighty to-daäy, beänt he?

**Dora.** Yes, Mr. Dobson. And the day 's bright like a friend, but the wind east like an enemy. Help me to move this bench for him into the sun. (*They move bench.*) No, not that way — here, under the apple-tree. Thank you. Look how full of rosy blossom it is. [*Pointing to apple-tree.*

**Dobson.** Theer be redder blossoms nor them, Miss Dora. 81

**Dora.** Where do they blow, Mr. Dobson?

**Dobson.** Under your eyes, Miss Dora.

**Dora.** Do they?

**Dobson.** And your eyes be as blue as —

**Dora.** What, Mr. Dobson? A butcher's frock?

**Dobson.** Noä, Miss Dora; as blue as —

**Dora.** Bluebell, harebell, speedwell, bluebottle, succory, forget-me-not? 91

*Dobson.* Noä, Miss Dora; as blue as —

*Dora.* The sky ? or the sea on a blue day ?

*Dobson.* Naäy then. I meän'd they be as blue as violets.

*Dora.* Are they ?

*Dobson.* Theer ye goäs ageän, Miss, niver believing owt I says to ye — hallus a-fobbing ma off, tho' ye knaws I love ye. I warrants ye 'll think moor o' this young Squire Edgar as ha' coomed among us — the Lord knaws how — ye 'll think more on 'is little finger than hall my hand at the haltar.

*Dora.* Perhaps, Master Dobson. I can't tell, for I have never seen him. But my sister wrote that he was mighty pleasant, and had no pride in him. 109

*Dobson.* He 'll be arter you now, Miss Dora.

*Dora.* Will he ? How can I tell ?

*Dobson.* He 's been arter Miss Eva, haän't he ?

*Dora.* Not that I know.

*Dobson.* Did n't I spy 'em a-sitting i' the woodbine harbor togither ?

*Dora.* What of that ? Eva told me that he was taking her likeness. He 's an artist. 120

*Dobson.* What 's a hartist ? I doänt believe he 's iver a 'eart under his waistcoat. And I tells ye what, Miss Dora: he 's no respect for the Queen, or the parson, or the justice o' peace, or owt. I ha' heärd 'im a-gawin' on 'ud make your 'air — God bless it ! — stan' on end. And wuss nor that. When theer wur a meeting o' farmers at Littlechester t' other daäy, and they was all a-crying out at the bad times, he cooms up, and he calls out among our oän men, ' The land belongs to the people ! ' 132

*Dora.* And what did *you* say to that ?

*Dobson.* Well, I says, s'pose my pig 's the land, and you says it belongs to the parish, and theer be a thousand i' the parish, taäkin' in the women and childer; and s'pose I kills my pig, and gi'es it among 'em, why there wud n't be a dinner for nawbody, and I should ha' lost the pig. 140

*Dora.* And what did he say to that ?

*Dobson.* Nowt — what could he saäy ? But I taäkes 'im fur a bad lot and a burn fool, and I haätes the very sight on him.

*Dora (looking at* Dobson). Master Dobson, you are a comely man to look at.

*Dobson.* I thank you for that, Miss Dora, onyhow.

*Dora.* Ay, but you turn right ugly when you 're in an ill temper; and I promise you that if you forget yourself in your behavior to this gentleman, my father's friend, I will never change word with you again. 154

*Enter* FARMING MAN *from barn.*

*Farming Man.* Miss, the farming men 'ull hev their dinner i' the long barn, and the master 'ud be straänge an' pleased if you 'd step in fust, and see that all be right and reg'lar fur 'em afoor he coöm.

[*Exit.*

*Dora.* I go. Master Dobson, did you hear what I said ? 161

*Dobson.* Yeäs, yeäs ! I 'll not meddle wi' 'im if he doänt meddle wi' meä. (*Exit* Dora.) ' Coomly,' says she. I niver thowt o' mysen i' that waäy; but if she 'd taäke to ma i' that waäy, or ony waäy, I 'd slaäve out my life fur 'er. ' Coomly to look at,' says she — but she said it spiteful-like. To look at — yeäs, ' coomly;' and she may n't be so fur out theer. But if that be nowt to she, then it be nowt to me. (*Looking off stage.*) Schoolmaster ! Why if Steer han't haxed schoolmaster to dinner, thaw 'e knaws I was hallus ageän heving schoolmaster i' the parish ! fur him as be handy wi' a boook beänt but haäfe a hand at a pitchfork.

*Enter* WILSON.

Well, Wilson. I seed that one cow o' thine i' the pinfold ageän as I wur a-coomin' 'ere. 180

*Wilson.* Very likely, Mr. Dobson. She *will* break fence. I can't keep her in order.

*Dobson.* An' if tha can't keep thy one cow i' horder, how can tha keep all thy scholards i' horder ? But let that goä by. What dost a knaw o' this Mr. Hedgar as be a-lodgin' wi' ye ? I coom'd upon 'im t' other daäy lookin' at the country, then a-scrattin upon a bit o' paäper, then a-lookin' ageän; and I taäked 'im fur soom sort of a landsurveyor — but a beänt. 192

*Wilson.* He 's a Somersetshire man, and a very civil-spoken gentleman.

*Dobson.* Gentleman ! What be he a-doing here ten mile an' moor fro' a raäil ? We

laäys out o' the waäy fur gentlefoälk alto-
gither — leästwaäys they niver cooms 'ere
but fur the trout i' our beck, fur they be
knaw'd as far as Littlechester. But 'e
doänt fish neither.     201

*Wilson.* Well, it's no sin in a gentleman
not to fish.

*Dobson.* Noä, but I haätes 'im.

*Wilson.* Better step out of his road,
then, for he's walking to us, and with a
book in his hand.

*Dobson.* An' I haätes boooks an' all, fur
they puts foälk off the owd waäys.

*Enter* EDGAR, *reading — not seeing* DOBSON
*and* WILSON.

*Edgar.* This author, with his charm of
    simple style     210
And close dialectic, all but proving man
An automatic series of sensations,
Has often numb'd me into apathy
Against the unpleasant jolts of this rough
    road
That breaks off short into the abysses —
    made me
A quietist taking all things easily.

*Dobson (aside).* There mun be summut
wrong theer, Wilson, fur I doänt under-
stan' it.

*Wilson (aside).* Nor I either, Mr. Dobson.     221

*Dobson (scornfully).* An' thou doänt un-
derstan' it neither — and thou schoolmaster
an' all !

*Edgar.* What can a man, then, live for
    but sensations,
Pleasant ones ? men of old would undergo
Unpleasant for the sake of pleasant ones
Hereafter, like the Moslem beauties wait-
    ing
To clasp their lovers by the golden gates.
For me, whose cheerless Houris after death
Are Night and Silence, pleasant ones —
    the while —     231
If possible, here ! to crop the flower and
    pass.

*Dobson.* Well, I never 'eärd the likes o'
that afoor.

*Wilson (aside).* But I have, Mr. Dobson. It's the old Scripture text, 'Let us
eat and drink, for to-morrow we die.' I'm
sorry for it, for, tho' he never comes to
church, I thought better of him.

*Edgar.* 'What are we,' says the blind
    old man in Lear ?     240

'As flies to the gods; they kill us for their
    sport.'

*Dobson (aside).* Then the owd man i'
Lear should be shaämed of hissen, but noän
o' the parishes goäs by that naäme 'ere-
abouts.

*Edgar.* The gods ! but they, the shad-
    ows of ourselves,
Have past for ever. It is Nature kills,
And not for *her* sport either. She knows
    nothing.
Man only knows, the worse for him ! for
    why     249
Cannot *he* take his pastime like the flies ?
And if my pleasure breed another's pain,
Well — is not that the course of Nature
    too,
From the dim dawn of being — her main
    law
Whereby she grows in beauty — that her
    flies
Must massacre each other ? this poor Na-
    ture !

*Dobson.* Natur ! Natur ! Well, it be i'
*my* natur to knock 'im o' the 'eäd now; but
I weänt.

*Edgar.* A quietist taking all things eas-
    ily — why —
Have I been dipping into this again     260
To steel myself against the leaving her ?
        [*Closes book, seeing* Wilson.
Good day !

*Wilson.* Good day, sir.
        [Dobson *looks hard at* Edgar.

*Edgar (to* Dobson*).* Have I the pleasure,
    friend, of knowing you ?

*Dobson.* Dobson.

*Edgar.* Good day, then, Dobson. [*Exit.*

*Dobson.* 'Good daäy then, Dobson !'
Civil-spoken i'deed ! Why, Wilson, tha
'eärd 'im thysen — the feller could n't find
a Mister in his mouth fur me, as farms five
hoonderd haäcre.     271

*Wilson.* You never find one for me, Mr.
Dobson.

*Dobson.* Noä, fur thou be nobbut schoolmaster; but I taäkes 'im for a Lunnun
swindler, and a burn fool.

*Wilson.* He can hardly be both, and he
pays me regular every Saturday.

*Dobson.* Yeäs; but I haätes 'im.

*Enter* STEER, FARM MEN *and* WOMEN.

*Steer (goes and sits under apple-tree).* Hev'
ony o' ye seen Eva ?     280

*Dobson.* Noä, Mr. Steer.

*Steer.* Well, I reckons they 'll hev' a fine cider-crop to-year if the blossom 'owds. Good murnin', neighbors, and the saäme to you, my men. I taäkes it kindly of all o' you that you be coomed — what 's the newspaäper word, Wilson ? — celebrate — to celebrate my birthdaäy i' this fashion. Niver man 'ed better friends, and I will saäy niver master 'ed better men; fur thaw I may ha' fallen out wi' ye sometimes, the fault, mebbe, wur as much mine as yours; and, thaw I says it mysen, niver men 'ed a better master — and I knaws what men be, and what masters be, fur I wur nobbut a laäborer, and now I be a landlord — burn a plowman, and now, as far as money goäs, I be a gentleman, thaw I beänt naw scholard, fur I 'ednt naw time to maäke mysen a scholard while I wur maäkin' mysen a gentleman, but I ha' taäen good care to turn out boäth my darters right down fine laädies.

*Dobson.* An' soä they be.

*First Farming Man.* Soä they be ! soä they be !

*Second Farming Man.* The Lord bless boäth on 'em !

*Third Farming Man.* An' the saäme to you, master ! 310

*Fourth Farming Man.* And long life to boäth on 'em! An' the saäme to you, Master Steer, likewise !

*Steer.* Thank ye !

### Enter EVA.

Wheer 'asta been ?

*Eva* (*timidly*). Many happy returns of the day, father.

*Steer.* They can't be many, my dear, but I 'oäpes they 'll be 'appy.

*Dobson.* Why, tha looks haäle anew to last to a hoonderd. 321

*Steer.* An' why should n't I last to a hoonderd ? Haäle ! why should n't I be haäle ? fur thaw I be heighty this very daäy, I niver 'es sa much as one pin's prick of paäin; an' I can taäke my glass along wi' the youngest, fur I niver touched a drop of owt till my oän wedding-daäy, an' then I wur turned huppads o' sixty. Why should n't I be haäle ? I ha' plowed the ten-aäcre — it be mine now — afoor ony o' ye wur burn — ye all knaws the ten-aäcre — I mun ha' plowed it moor nor a hoon-

derd times; hallus hup at sunrise, and I 'd drive the plow straäit as a line right i' the faäce o' the sun, then back ageän, a-follering my oän shadder — then hup ageän i' the faäce o' the sun. Eh ! how the sun 'ud shine, and the larks 'ud sing i' them daäys, and the smell o' the mou'd an' all. Eh ! if I could ha' gone on wi' the plowin' nobbut the smell o' the mou'd 'ud ha' maäde ma live as long as Jerusalem.

*Eva.* Methuselah, father.

*Steer.* Ay, lass, but when thou be as owd as me thou 'll put one word fur another as I does.

*Dobson.* But, Steer, thaw thou be haäle anew I seed tha a-limpin' up just now wi' the roomatics i' the knee. 350

*Steer.* Roomatics ! Noä; I laäme't my knee last night running arter a thief. Beänt there house-breäkers down i' Littlechester, Dobson — doänt ye hear of ony ?

*Dobson.* Ay, that there be. Immanuel Goldsmith's was broke into o' Monday night, and ower a hoonderd pounds worth o' rings stolen.

*Steer.* So I thowt, and I heärd the winder — that 's the winder at the end o' the ¡.ssage, that goäs by thy chaumber. (*Turning to* Eva.) Why, lass, what maäkes tha sa red ? Did 'e git into thy chaumber ?

*Eva.* Father !

*Steer.* Well, I runned arter thief i' the dark, and fell ageän coalscuttle and my kneeä gev waäy or I 'd ha' cotched 'im, but afoor I coomed up he got thruff the winder ageän. 370

*Eva.* Got thro' the window again ?

*Steer.* Ay, but he left the mark of 'is foot i' the flower-bed; now theer be noän o' my men, thinks I to mysen, 'ud ha' done it 'cep' it were Dan Smith, fur I cotched 'im once a-stealin' coäls, an' I sent fur 'im, an' I measured his foot wi' the mark i' the bed, but it would n't fit — seeäms to me the mark wur maäde by a Lunnun boot. (*Looks at* Eva.) Why, now, what maäkes tha sa white ? 381

*Eva.* Fright, father !

*Steer.* Maäke thysen eäsy. I 'll hev the winder naäiled up, and put Towser under it.

*Eva* (*clasping her hands*). No, no, father! Towser 'll tear him all to pieces.

*Steer.* Let him keep awaäy, then; but

coom, coom! let's be gawin. They ha'
broached a barrel of aäle i' the long barn,
and the fiddler be theer, and the lads and
lassies 'ull hev a dance.            392
*Eva (aside).* Dance! small heart have I
to dance. I should seem to be dancing
upon a grave.
*Steer.* Wheer be Mr. Edgar? about the
premises?
*Dobson.* Hallus about the premises!
*Steer.* So much the better, so much the
better. I likes 'im, and Eva likes 'im.
Eva can do owt wi' 'im; look for 'im, Eva,
and bring 'im to the barn. He 'ant naw
pride in 'im, and we'll git 'im to speechify
for us arter dinner.
*Eva.* Yes, father!            [*Exit.*
*Steer.* Coom along then, all the rest o'
ye! Church-warden be a coomin', thaw
me and 'im we niver 'grees about the tithe;
and parson mebbe, thaw he niver mended
that gap i' the glebe fence as I telled 'im;
and blacksmith, thaw he niver shoes a
herse to my likings; and baäker, thaw I
sticks to hoäm-maäde — but all on 'em
welcome, all on 'em welcome; and I've hed
the long barn cleared out of all the ma-
chines, and the sacks, and the taäters, and
the mangles, and theer'll be room anew
for all o' ye. Foller me.            418
*All.* Yeäs, yeäs! Three cheers for Mr.
Steer.            [*All exeunt except* Dobson *into barn.*

*Enter* EDGAR.

*Dobson (who is going, turns).* Squire! —
if so be you be a squire.
*Edgar.* Dobbins, I think.
*Dobson.* Dobbins, you thinks; and I
thinks ye weärs a Lunnun boot.
*Edgar.* Well?
*Dobson.* And I thinks I'd like to taäke
the measure o' your foot.
*Edgar.* Ay, if you'd like to measure
your own length upon the grass.            430
*Dobson.* Coom, coom, that's a good un.
Why, I could throw four o' ye; but I pro-
mised one of the Misses I would n't meddle
wi' ye, and I weänt.            [*Exit into barn.*
*Edgar.* Jealous of me with Eva! Is it
so?
Well, tho' I grudge the pretty jewel, that I
Have worn, to such a clod, yet that might
be
The best way out of it, if the child could
keep

Her counsel. I am sure I wish her happy.
But I must free myself from this entangle-
ment.            440
I have all my life before me — so has
she —
Give her a month or two, and her affec-
tions
Will flower toward the light in some new
face.
Still I am half-afraid to meet her now.
She will urge marriage on me. I hate
tears.
Marriage is but an old tradition. I hate
Traditions, ever since my narrow father,
After my frolic with his tenant's girl,
Made younger elder son, violated the whole
Tradition of our land, and left his heir,   450
Born, happily, with some sense of art, to
live
By brush and pencil. By and by, when
Thought
Comes down among the crowd, and man
perceives that
The lost gleam of an after-life but leaves
him
A beast of prey in the dark, why then the
crowd
May wreak my wrongs upon my wrong-
ers. Marriage!
That fine, fat, hook-nosed uncle of mine,
old Harold,
Who leaves me all his land at Littleches-
ter,
He, too, would oust me from his will, if I
Made such a marriage. And marriage in
itself —            460
The storm is hard at hand will sweep away
Thrones, churches, ranks, traditions, cus-
toms, marriage
One of the feeblest! Then the man, the
woman,
Following their best affinities, will each
Bid their old bond farewell with smiles,
not tears;
Good wishes, not reproaches; with no fear
Of the world's gossiping clamor, and no
need
Of veiling their desires.
                              Conventionalism,
Who shrieks by day at what she does by
night,
Would call this vice; but one time's vice
may be            470
The virtue of another; and Vice and Vir-
tue

Are but two masks of self; and what hereafter
Shall mark out Vice from Virtue in the
gulf
Of never-dawning darkness ?

*Enter* Eva.

My sweet Eva,
Where have you lain in ambush all the
morning ?
They say your sister, Dora, has return'd,
And that should make you happy, if you
love her !
But you look troubled.
 *Eva.*      O, I love her so,
I was afraid of her, and I hid myself.   479
We never kept a secret from each other;
She would have seen at once into my
trouble,
And ask'd me what I could not answer. O,
Philip,
Father heard you last night. Our savage
mastiff,
That all but kill'd the beggar, will be
placed
Beneath the window, Philip.
 *Edgar.*      Savage, is he ?
What matters ? Come, give me your hand
and kiss me
This beautiful May-morning.
 *Eva.*      The most beautiful
May we have had for many years !
 *Edgar.*      And here
Is the most beautiful morning of this May.
Nay, you must smile upon me ! There —
   you make      490
The May and morning still more beautiful,
You, the most beautiful blossom of the
May.
 *Eva.* Dear Philip, all the world is beau-
tiful
If we were happy, and could chime in with
it.
 *Edgar.* True; for the senses, love, are
for the world;
That for the senses.
 *Eva.*      Yes.
 *Edgar.*      And when the man,
The child of evolution, flings aside
His swaddling-bands, the morals of the
tribe,
He, following his own instincts as his God,
Will enter on the larger golden age,   500
No pleasure then taboo'd; for when the
tide

Of full democracy has overwhelm'd
This Old World, from that flood will rise
the New,
Like the Love-goddess, with no bridal veil,
Ring, trinket of the Church, but naked Na-
ture
In all her loveliness.
 *Eva.*      What are you saying ?
 *Edgar.* That, if we did not strain to
make ourselves
Better and higher than Nature, we might
be
As happy as the bees there at their honey
In these sweet blossoms.
 *Eva.*      Yes; how sweet they smell !
 *Edgar.* There ! let me break some off
   for you.     [*Breaking branch off.*
 *Eva.*      My thanks.
But, look, how wasteful of the blossom you
   are !      512
One, two, three, four, five, six — you have
robb'd poor father
Of ten good apples. O, I forgot to tell you
He wishes you to dine along with us,
And speak for him after — you that are so
clever !
 *Edgar.* I grieve I cannot; but, indeed —
 *Eva.*      What is it ?
 *Edgar.* Well, business. I must leave
you, love, to-day.
 *Eva.* Leave me, to-day ! And when will
you return ?
 *Edgar.* I cannot tell precisely; but —
 *Eva.*      But what ?
 *Edgar.* I trust, my dear, we shall be
always friends.     521
 *Eva.* After all that has gone between us
— friends !
What, only friends ?    [*Drops branch.*
 *Edgar.*    All that has gone between us
Should surely make us friends.
 *Eva.*      But keep us lovers.
 *Edgar.* Child, do you love me now ?
 *Eva.*      Yes, now and ever.
 *Edgar.* Then you should wish us both to
love for ever.
But, if you *will* bind love to one for ever,
Altho' at first he take his bonds for flowers,
As years go on, he feels them press upon
him,
Begins to flutter in them, and at last   530
Breaks thro' them, and so flies away for
ever;
While, had you left him free use of his
wings,

Who knows that he had ever dream'd of
flying?
   *Eva.* But all that sounds so wicked and
so strange;
'Till death us part'—those are the only
words,
The true ones—nay, and those not true
enough,
For they that love do not believe that
death
Will part them. Why do you jest with
me, and try
To fright me? Tho' you are a gentle-
man,      539
I but a farmer's daughter—
   *Edgar.*      Tut! you talk
Old feudalism. When the great Demo-
cracy
Makes a new world—
   *Eva.*      And if you be not jesting,
Neither the old world, nor the new, nor
father,
Sister, nor you, shall ever see me more.
   *Edgar (moved).* Then—*(aside)* Shall I
say it?—*(aloud)* fly with me to-
day.
   *Eva.* No! Philip, Philip, if you do not
marry me,
I shall go mad for utter shame and die.
   *Edgar.* Then, if we needs must be con-
ventional,
When shall your parish-parson bawl our
banns   549
Before your gaping clowns?
   *Eva.*      Not in our church—
I think I scarce could hold my head up
there.
Is there no other way?
   *Edgar.*      Yes, if you cared
To fee an over-opulent superstition,
Then they would grant you what they call
a license
To marry. Do you wish it?
   *Eva.*      *Do* I wish it?
   *Edgar.* In London.
   *Eva.*      You will write to me?
   *Edgar.*      I will.
   *Eva.* And I will fly to you thro' the
night, the storm—
Yes, tho' the fire should run along the
ground,
As once it did in Egypt. O, you see,  559
I was just out of school, I had no mother—
My sister far away—and you, a gentle-
man,

Told me to trust you—yes, in every-
thing—
*That* was the only *true* love; and I
trusted—
O, yes, indeed, I would have died for you.
How could you—O, how could you?—
nay, how could I?
But now you will set all right again, and I
Shall not be made the laughter of the vil-
lage,
And poor old father not die miserable.

   DORA *(singing in the distance).*

O, joy for the promise of May, of May,
  O, joy for the promise of May!  570

   *Edgar.* Speak not so loudly; that must
be your sister.
You never told her, then, of what has past
Between us.
   *Eva.*      Never!
   *Edgar.*      Do not till I bid you.
   *Eva.* No, Philip, no.   [*Turns away.*
   *Edgar (moved).* How gracefully there
she stands
Weeping—the little Niobe! What! we
prize
The statue or the picture all the more
When we have made them ours! Is she
less lovable,
Less lovely, being wholly mine? To
stay—
Follow my art among these quiet fields,
Live with these honest folk—
      and play the fool!
No! she that gave herself to me so easily
Will yield herself as easily to another.  582
   *Eva.* Did you speak, Philip?
   *Edgar.*      Nothing more, farewell.
      [*They embrace.*

   DORA *(coming nearer).*

O, grief for the promise of May, of May,
  O, grief for the promise of May!

   *Edgar (still embracing her).* Keep up
your heart until we meet again.
   *Eva.* If that should break before we
meet again?
   *Edgar.* Break! nay, but call for Philip
when you will,
And he returns.
   *Eva.* Heaven hears you, Philip Edgar!
   *Edgar (moved).* And *he* would hear you
even from the grave.  590
Heaven curse him if he come not at your
call!   [*Exit.*

*Enter* DORA.

*Dora.* Well, Eva!

*Eva.* O, Dora, Dora, how long you have been away from home! O, how often I have wished for you! It seemed to me that we were parted for ever.

*Dora.* For ever, you foolish child! What's come over you? We parted like the brook yonder about the alder island, to come together again in a moment and to go on together again, till one of us be married. But where is this Mr. Edgar whom you praised so in your first letters? You have n't even mentioned him in your last?

*Eva.* He has gone to London.

*Dora.* Ay, child; and you look thin and pale. Is it for his absence? Have you fancied yourself in love with him? That's all nonsense, you know, such a baby as you are. But you shall tell me all about it.  610

*Eva.* Not now — presently. Yes, I have been in trouble, but I am happy — I think, quite happy now.

*Dora (taking* Eva's *hand).* Come, then, and make them happy in the long barn, for father is in his glory, and there is a piece of beef like a house-side, and a plum-pudding as big as the round hay-stack. But see, they are coming out for the dance already. Well, my child, let us join them.

*Enter all from barn, laughing.* EVA *sits reluctantly under apple-tree.* STEER *enters, smoking, sits by* EVA.

*Dance.*

## ACT II

*Five years have elapsed between Acts I. and II.*

SCENE. — A MEADOW. ON ONE SIDE A PATHWAY GOING OVER A RUSTIC BRIDGE. AT BACK THE FARMHOUSE AMONG TREES. IN THE DISTANCE A CHURCH SPIRE

### DOBSON and DORA.

*Dobson.* So the owd uncle i' Coomberland be deäd, Miss Dora, beänt he?

*Dora.* Yes, Mr. Dobson, I 've been attending on his death-bed and his burial.

*Dobson.* It be five year sin' ye went afoor to him, and it seems to me nobbut t'other day. Hes n't he left ye nowt?

*Dora.* No, Mr. Dobson.

*Dobson.* But he were mighty fond o' ye, warn't he?

*Dora.* Fonder of poor Eva — like everybody else.                                    12

*Dobson (handing* Dora *basket of roses).* Not like me, Miss Dora; and I ha' browt these roses to ye — I forgits what they calls 'em, but I hallus gi'ed soom on 'em to Miss Eva at this time o' year. Will ya taäke 'em? fur Miss Eva, she set the bush by my dairy winder afoor she went to school at Littlechester — so I allus browt soom on 'em to her; and now she be gone, will ye taäke 'em, Miss Dora?

*Dora.* I thank you. They tell me that yesterday you mentioned her name too suddenly before my father. See that you do not do so again!

*Dobson.* Noä; I knaws a deäl better now. I seed how the owd man wur vext.      28

*Dora.* I take them, then, for Eva's sake.
[*Takes basket, places some in her dress.*

*Dobson.* Eva's saäke. Yeäs. Poor gell, poor gell! I can't abeär to think on 'er now, fur I 'd ha' done owt fur 'er mysen; an' ony o' Steer's men, an' ony o' my men 'ud ha' done owt fur 'er, an' all the parish 'ud ha' done owt fur 'er, fur we was all on us proud on 'er, an' them theer be soom of her oän roses, an' she wur as sweet as ony on 'em — the Lord bless 'er — 'er oän sen; an' weänt ye taäke 'em now, Miss Dora, fur 'er saäke an' fur my saäke an' all?   40

*Dora.* Do you want them back again?

*Dobson.* Noä, noä! Keep 'em. But I hed a word to saäy to ye.

*Dora.* Why, Farmer, you should be in the hay-field looking after your men; you could n't have more splendid weather.

*Dobson.* I be a going theer; but I thowt I 'd bring tha them roses fust. The weather's well anew, but the glass be a bit shaäky. S'iver we 've led moäst on it.   50

*Dora.* Ay! but you must not be too sudden with it either, as you were last year, when you put it in green, and your stack caught fire.

*Dobson.* I were insured, Miss, an' I lost nowt by it. But I weänt be too sudden wi' it; and I feel sewer, Miss Dora, that I ha' been noän too sudden wi' you, fur I ha' sarved fer ye well nigh as long as the man sarved for 'is sweet'art i' Scriptur'. Weänt ye gi'e me a kind answer at last?    61

*Dora.* I have no thought of marriage, my friend. We have been in such grief these five years, not only on my sister's account, but the ill success of the farm, and the debts, and my father's breaking down, and his blindness. How could I think of leaving him?

*Dobson.* Eh, but I be well to do; and if ye would nobbut hev me, I would taäke the owd blind man to my oän fireside. You should hev him allus wi' ye.          72

*Dora.* You are generous, but it cannot be. I cannot love you; nay, I think I never can be brought to love any man. It seems to me that I hate men, ever since my sister left us. O, see here. (*Pulls out a letter.*) I wear it next my heart. Poor sister, I had it five years ago. ' Dearest Dora, — I have lost myself, and am lost for ever to you and my poor father. I thought Mr. Edgar the best of men, and he has proved himself the worst. Seek not for me, or you may find me at the bottom of the river. — Eva.'

*Dobson.* Be that my fault?

*Dora.* No; but how should I, with this grief still at my heart, take to the milking of your cows, the fatting of your calves, the making of your butter, and the managing of your poultry?          91

*Dobson.* Naäy, but I hev an owd woman as 'ud see to all that; and you should sit i' your oän parlor quite like a laädy, ye should!

*Dora.* It cannot be.

*Dobson.* And plaäy the pianner, if ye liked, all daäy long, like a laädy, ye should an' all.

*Dora.* It cannot be.          100

*Dobson.* And I would loove tha moor nor ony gentleman 'ud loove tha.

*Dora.* No, no; it cannot be.

*Dobson.* And p'raps ye hears 'at I soomtimes taäkes a drop too much; but that be all along o' you, Miss, because ye weänt hev me; but, if ye would, I could put all that o' one side eäsy anew.

*Dora.* Cannot you understand plain words, Mr. Dobson? I tell you, it cannot be.          111

*Dobson.* Eh, lass! Thy feyther eddicated his darters to marry gentlefoälk, and see what 's coomed on it.

*Dora.* That is enough, Farmer Dobson. You have shown me that, though fortune had born *you* into the estate of a gentleman, you would still have been Farmer Dobson. You had better attend to your hay-field. Good afternoon.          [*Exit.*

*Dobson.* ' Farmer Dobson!' Well, I be Farmer Dobson; but I thinks Farmer Dobson's dog 'ud ha' knaw'd better nor to cast her sister's misfortin inter 'er teeth arter she 'd been a-reädin' me the letter wi' 'er voice a-shaäkin', and the drop in 'er eye. Theer she goäs! Shall I foller 'er and ax 'er to maäke it up? Noä, not yet. Let 'er cool upon it; I likes 'er all the better fur taäkin' me down, like a laädy, as she be. Farmer Dobson! I be Farmer Dobson, sewer anew; but if iver I cooms upo' Gentleman Hedgar ageän, and doänt laäy my cartwhip athurt 'is shou'ders, why then I beänt Farmer Dobson, but summun else — blaäme't if I beänt!

*Enter* HAYMAKERS *with a load of hay.*

The last on it, eh?

*First Haymaker.* Yeäs.

*Dobson.* Hoäm wi' it, then.

          [*Exit surlily.*

*First Haymaker.* Well, it be the last loäd hoäm.          141

*Second Haymaker.* Yeäs, an' owd Dobson should be glad on it. What maäkes 'im allus sa glum?

*Sally Allen.* Glum! he be wuss nor glum. He coom'd up to me yisterdaäy i' the haäy-field, when meä and my sweet'art was a-workin' along o' one side wi' one another, and he sent 'im awaäy to t' other end o' the field; and when I axed 'im why, he told me 'at sweet'arts niver worked well togither; and I telled '*im* 'at sweet-'arts allus worked best togither; and then he called me a rude naäme, and I can't abide 'im.

*James.* Why, lass, doänt tha knaw he be sweet upo' Dora Steer, and she weänt sa much as look at 'im? And wheniver 'e sees two sweet'arts togither like thou and me, Sally, he be fit to bust hissen wi' spites and jalousies.          161

*Sally.* Let 'im bust hissen, then, for owt *I* cares.

*First Haymaker.* Well, but, as I said afoor, it be the last loäd hoäm; do thou and thy sweet'art sing us hoäm to supper — ' The Last Loäd Hoäm.'

*All.* Ay! ' The Last Loäd Hoäm.'

### SONG.

What did ye do, and what did ye saäy,
Wi' the wild white rose, an' the woodbine sa
    gaäy,                 170
An' the midders all mow'd, an' the sky sa
    blue —
What did ye saäy, and what did ye do,
When ye thowt there were nawbody watchin'
    o' you,
And you an' your Sally was forkin' the haäy,
    At the end of the daäy,
    For the last loäd hoäm ?

What did we do, and what did we saäy,
Wi' the briar sa green, an' the willer sa graäy,
An' the midders all mow'd, an' the sky sa
    blue —
Do ye think I be gawin' to tell it to you,  180
What we mowt saäy, and what we mowt do,
When me an' my Sally was forkin' the haäy,
    At the end of the daäy,
    For the last loäd hoäm ?

But what did ye saäy, and what did ye do,
Wi' the butterflies out, and the swallers at
    plaäy,
An' the midders all mow'd, an' the sky sa
    blue ?
Why, coom then, owd feller, I 'll tell it to you ;
For me an' my Sally we sweär'd to be true,
To be true to each other, let 'appen what maäy,
    Till the end of the daäy,    191
    And the last loäd hoäm.

*All.* Well sung !
*James.* Fanny be the naäme i' the song,
but I swopt it fur *she.*   [*Pointing to* Sally.
*Sally.* Let ma aloän afoor foälk, wilt
tha ?
*First Haymaker.* Ye shall sing that ageän
to-night, fur owd Dobson 'll gi'e us a bit o'
supper.                      200
*Sally.* I weänt goä to owd Dobson; he
wur rude to me i' tha haäy-field, and he 'll
be rude to me ageän to-night. Owd Steer 's
gotten all his grass down and wants a hand,
and I 'll goä to him.
*First Haymaker.* Owd Steer gi'es nubbut
cowd tea to '*is* men, and owd Dobson gi'es
beer.
*Sally.* But I 'd like owd Steer's cowd
tea better nor Dobson's beer. Good-bye.
                         [*Going.*
*James.* Gi'e us a buss fust, lass.   211
*Sally.* I tell'd tha to let ma aloän !
*James.* Why, was n't thou and me a-bus-
sin' o' one another t' other side o' the haäy-

cock, when owd Dobson coom'd upo' us ?
I can't let tha aloän if I would, Sally.
                [*Offering to kiss her.*
*Sally.* Git along wi' ye, do !   [*Exit.*
          [*All laugh ; exeunt singing.*

To be true to each other, let 'appen what maäy,
    Till the end o' the daäy,
    An' the last loäd hoäm.    220

### *Enter* HAROLD.

*Harold.* Not Harold ! ' Philip Edgar,
    Philip Edgar ! '
Her phantom call'd me by the name she
    loved.
I told her I should hear her from the
    grave.
Ay ! yonder is her casement. I remember
Her bright face beaming starlike down
    upon me
Thro' that rich cloud of blossom. Since I
    left her
Here weeping, I have ranged the world,
    and sat
Thro' every sensual course of that full
    feast
That leaves but emptiness.

### SONG.

To be true to each other, let 'appen what maäy,
    To the end o' the daäy,    231
    An' the last loäd hoäm.

*Harold.* Poor Eva ! O my God, if man
    be only
A willy-nilly current of sensations —
Reaction needs must follow revel — yet —
Why feel remorse, he, knowing that he
    *must* have
Moved in the iron grooves of Destiny ?
Remorse then is a part of Destiny,
Nature a liar, making us feel guilty
Of her own faults.
             My grandfather — of him
They say, that women —
              O, this mortal house,
Which we are born into, is haunted by  242
The ghosts of the dead passions of dead
    men;
And these take flesh again with our own
    flesh,
And bring us to confusion.
                    He was only
A poor philosopher who call'd the mind
Of children a blank page, a *tabula rasa.*

There, there, is written in invisible inks
' Lust, Prodigality, Covetousness, Craft,
Cowardice, Murder ' — and the heat and
    fire                       250
Of life will bring them out, and black
    enough,
So the child grow to manhood. Better
    death
With our first wail than life —

        Song (*further off*).

      Till the end o' the daäy,
      An' the last loäd hoäm,
        Loäd hoäm.

This bridge again !    (*Steps on the bridge.*)
           How often have I stood
With Eva here ! The brook among its
    flowers !
Forget-me-not, meadow-sweet, willow-herb.
I had some smattering of science then,  260
Taught her the learned names, anatom-
    ized
The flowers for her — and now I only
    wish
This pool were deep enough, that I might
    plunge
And lose myself for ever.

    *Enter* Dan Smith (*singing*).

Gee oop ! whoä ! Gee oop ! whoä !
Scizzars an' Pumpy was good uns to goä
    Thruf slush an' squad
    When roäds was bad,
But hallus 'ud stop at the Vine-an'-the-Hop,
    Fur boäth on 'em knawed as well as mysen
    That beer be as good fur 'erses as men.  271
Gee oop ! whoä ! Gee oop ! whoä !
Scizzars an' Pumpy was good uns to goä.

    The beer 's gotten oop into my 'eäd.
S'iver I mun git along back to the farm,
fur she tell'd ma to taäke the cart to Littlechester.

        *Enter* Dora.

  *Dora.* Half an hour late ! why are you
loitering here ? Away with you at once.
               [*Exit* Dan Smith.
  (*Seeing* Harold *on bridge.*)
Some madman, is it,
Gesticulating there upon the bridge ?  281
I am half afraid to pass.
  *Harold.*          Sometimes I wonder,
When man has surely learnt at last that
    all

His old-world faith, the blossom of his
    youth,
Has faded, falling fruitless — whether then
All of us, all at once, may not be seized
With some fierce passion, not so much for
    Death
As against Life ! all, all, into the dark —
No more ! — and science now could drug
    and balm us
Back into nescience with as little pain  290
As it is to fall asleep.
               This beggarly life,
This poor, flat, hedged-in field — no dis-
    tance — this
Hollow Pandora-box,
With all the pleasures flown, not even Hope
Left at the bottom !
               Superstitious fool,
What brought me here ? To see her grave ?
    her ghost ?
Her ghost is everyway about me here.
  *Dora* (*coming forward*). Allow me, sir,
    to pass you.
  *Harold.*        Eva !
  *Dora.*             Eva !
  *Harold.* What are you ? Where do you
    come from ?
  *Dora.*          From the farm
Here, close at hand.
  *Harold.* Are you — you are — that Dora,
The sister. I have heard of you. The
    likeness                   301
Is very striking.
  *Dora.*       You knew Eva, then ?
  *Harold.* Yes — I was thinking of her
    when — O, yes,
Many years back, and never since have met
Her equal for pure innocence of nature,
And loveliness of feature.
  *Dora.*          No, nor I.
  *Harold.* Except, indeed, I have found it
    once again
In your own self.
  *Dora.*       You flatter me. Dear Eva
Was always thought the prettier.
  *Harold.*         And *her* charm
Of voice is also yours; and I was brooding
Upon a great unhappiness when you spoke.
  *Dora.* Indeed, you seem'd in trouble,
    sir.
  *Harold.*     And you
Seem my good angel who may help me
    from it.                 313
  *Dora* (*aside*). How worn he looks, poor
    man ! who is it, I wonder.

How can I help him ?   (*Aloud.*)   Might I
   ask your name ?
*Harold.*   Harold.
*Dora.*     I never heard her mention you.
*Harold.*   I met her first at a farm in
   Cumberland —
Her uncle's.
   *Dora.*       She was there six years ago.
   *Harold.*   And if she never mention'd me,
     perhaps
The painful circumstances which I heard —
I will not vex you by repeating them —   321
Only last week at Littlechester, drove me
From out her memory.   She has disap-
     pear'd,
They told me, from the farm — and darker
     news.
   *Dora.*   She has disappear'd, poor darling,
     from the world —
Left but one dreadful line to say, that we
Should find her in the river; and we
     dragg'd
The Littlechester river all in vain,
Have sorrow'd for her all these years in
     vain.
And my poor father, utterly broken down
By losing her — she was his favorite
     child —              331
Has let his farm, all his affairs, I fear,
But for the slender help that I can give,
Fall into ruin.   Ah ! that villain, Edgar,
If he should ever show his face among us,
Our men and boys would hoot him, stone
     him, hunt him
With pitchforks off the farm, for all of
     them
Loved her, and she was worthy of all love.
   *Harold.*   They say, we should forgive
     our enemies.
   *Dora.*   Ay, if the wretch were dead I
     might forgive him;         340
We know not whether he be dead or liv-
     ing.
   *Harold.*   What Edgar ?
   *Dora.*       Philip Edgar of Toft Hall
In Somerset.   Perhaps you know him ?
   *Harold.*                 Slightly.
(*Aside.*)   Ay, for how slightly have I known
     myself !
   *Dora.*   This Edgar, then, is living ?
   *Harold.*           Living ? well —
One Philip Edgar of Toft Hall in Somer-
     set
Is lately dead.
   *Dora.*   Dead ! — is there more than one ?

   *Harold.*   Nay — now — not one, (*aside*)
     for I am Philip Harold.
   *Dora.*   That one, is he then — dead !
   *Harold* (*aside*).       My father's death,
Let her believe it mine; this, for the mo-
     ment,           350
Will leave me a free field.
   *Dora.*       Dead ! and this world
Is brighter for his absence, as that other
Is darker for his presence.
   *Harold.*        Is not this
To speak too pitilessly of the dead ?
   *Dora.*   My five-years' anger cannot die at
     once,
Not all at once with death and him.    I trust
I shall forgive him — by and by — not now.
O sir, you seem to have a heart; if you
Had seen us that wild morning when we
     found
Her bed unslept in, storm and shower lash-
     ing           360
Her casement, her poor spaniel wailing for
     her,
That desolate letter, blotted with her tears,
Which told us we should never see her
     more —
Our old nurse crying as if for her own
     child,
My father stricken with his first paralysis,
And then with blindness — had you been
     one of us
And seen all this, then you would know it
     is not
So easy to forgive — even the dead.
   *Harold.*   But sure am I that of your gen-
     tleness
You will forgive him.   She you mourn for
     seem'd        370
A miracle of gentleness — would not blur
A moth's wing by the touching; would not
     crush
The fly that drew her blood; and, were
     she living,
Would not — or if — penitent — have denied
     him *her*
Forgiveness.   And perhaps the man him-
     self,
When hearing of that piteous death, has
     suffer'd
More than we know.   But wherefore waste
     your heart
In looking on a chill and changeless past ?
Iron will fuse, and marble melt; the past
Remains the past.   But you are young, and
     — pardon me —        380

As lovely as your sister.   Who can tell
What golden hours, with what full hands,
   may be
Waiting you in the distance ?   Might I
   call
Upon  your  father — I  have  seen  the
   world —
And cheer his blindness with a traveller's
   tales ?
   *Dora.*  Call if you will, and when you
   will.   I cannot
Well answer for my father; but if you
Can tell me anything of our sweet Eva
When in her brighter girlhood, I at least
Will bid  you  welcome, and will listen to
   you.                                                  390
Now I must go.
   *Harold.*            But give me first your hand;
I do not dare, like an old friend, to shake it.
I kiss it as a prelude to that privilege
When you shall know me better.
   *Dora* (*aside*).                How beautiful
His manners are, and how unlike the far-
   mer's !
You are staying here ?
   *Harold.*            Yes, at the wayside inn
Close by that alder-island in your brook,
'The Angler's Home.'
   *Dora.*                  Are *you* one ?
   *Harold.*                  No, but I
Take  some  delight  in  sketching, and  the
   country                                           399
Has many charms, altho' the inhabitants
Seem semi-barbarous.
   *Dora.*            I am glad it pleases you;
Yet I, born here, not only love the country,
But its inhabitants too; and you, I doubt
   not,
Would  take  to  them  as  kindly, if  you
   cared
To live some time among them.
   *Harold.*                  If I did,
Then one at least of its inhabitants
Might have more charm for me than all the
   country.
   *Dora.*  That one, then, should be grateful
   for your preference.
   *Harold.*  I cannot tell, tho' standing in
   her presence.                                   409
(*Aside.*)   She colors !
   *Dora.*            Sir !
   *Harold.*            Be not afraid of me,
For these are no conventional flourishes.
I do most earnestly assure you that
Your likeness — [*Shouts and cries without.*]

   *Dora.* · What was that ?  my poor blind
   father —

### Enter FARMING MAN.

   *Farming Man.*  Miss Dora, Dan Smith's
cart hes runned ower a laädy i' the holler
laäne, and they ha' ta'en the body up inter
your chaumber, and they be all a-callin'
for ye.
   *Dora.*  The body ! — Heavens ! I come !
   *Harold.*            But you are trembling.
Allow me to go with you to the farm.   420
                                                      [*Exeunt.*

### Enter DOBSON.

   *Dobson.*  What feller wur it as 'a' been
a-talkin' fur haäfe an hour wi' my Dora ?
(*Looking after him.*)  Seeäms I ommost
knaws the back on 'im — drest like a gentleman, too.   Damn all gentlemen, says
I !   I should ha' thowt they 'd hed anew
o' gentlefoälk, as I telled 'er to-daäy when
she fell foul upo' me.
   Minds ma o' summun.   I could sweär to
that; but that be all one, fur I haätes 'im
afoor I knaws what 'e be.   Theer !  he
turns round.   Philip Hedgar o' Soomerset !
Philip  Hedgar  o'  Soomerset ! — Noä —
yeäs — thaw the feller 's gone and maäde
such a litter of his faäce.
   Eh lad, if it be thou, I 'll Philip tha !
a-plaäyin' the saäme gaäme wi' my Dora —
I 'll Soomerset tha !                            438
   I 'd like to drag 'im thruff the herse-
pond, and she to be a-lookin' at it.   I 'd
like to leather 'im black and blue, and she
to be a-laughin' at it.   I 'd like to fell 'im
as deäd as a bullock !   (*Clenching his fist.*)
   But what 'ud she saäy to that ?   She
telled me once not to meddle wi' 'im, and
now she be fallen out wi' ma, and I can't
coom at 'er.
   It mun be *him.*   Noä !   Fur she 'd niver
'a' been talkin' haäfe an hour wi' the divil
'at killed her oän sister, or she beänt Dora
Steer.                                              451
   Yeäs !   Fur she niver knawed 'is faäce
when 'e wur 'ere afoor; but I 'll maäke 'er
knaw !   I 'll maäke 'er knaw !

### Enter HAROLD.

   Naäy, but I mun git out on 'is waäy now,
or I shall be the death on 'im.         [*Exit.*
   *Harold.*  How the clown glared at me !
   that Dobbins, is it,

With whom I used to jar? but can he
    trace me
Thro' five years' absence, and my change of
    name,
The tan of Southern summers and the
    beard?    460
I may as well avoid him.
                    Ladylike!
Lilylike in her stateliness and sweetness!
How came she by it? — a daughter of the
    fields,
This Dora!
She gave her hand, unask'd, at the farm-
    gate;
I almost think she half return'd the pres-
    sure
Of mine. What, I that held the orange
    blossom
Dark as the yew? but may not those, who
    march
Before their age, turn back at times, and
    make
Courtesy to custom? and now the stronger
    motive,    470
Misnamed free-will — the crowd would call
    it conscience —
Moves me — to what? I am dreaming;
    for the past
Look'd thro' the present, Eva's eyes thro'
    hers —
A spell upon me! Surely I loved Eva
More than I knew! or is it but the past
That brightens in retiring? O, last night
Tired, pacing my new lands at Littleches-
    ter,
I dozed upon the bridge, and the black
    river
Flow'd thro' my dreams — if dreams they
    were. She rose
From the foul flood and pointed toward the
    farm,    480
And her cry rang to me across the years,
'I call you, Philip Edgar, Philip Edgar!
Come, you will set all right again, and
    father
Will not die miserable.' I could make his
    age
A comfort to him — so be more at peace
With mine own self. Some of my former
    friends
Would find my logic faulty; let them.
    Color
Flows thro' my life again, and I have
    lighted
On a new pleasure. Anyhow we must    489

Move in the line of least resistance when
The stronger motive rules.
                  But she hates Edgar.
May not this Dobbins, or some other, spy
Edgar in Harold? Well then, I must
    make her
Love Harold first, and then she will for-
    give
Edgar for Harold's sake. She said herself
She would forgive him, by and by, not
    now —
For her own sake *then*, if not for mine —
    not now —
But by and by.    498

*Enter* DOBSON *behind.*

*Dobson.* By and by — eh, lad, dosta knaw
this paäper? Ye dropt it upo' the road.
'Philip Edgar, Esq.' Ay, you be a pretty
squire. I ha' fun' ye out, I hev. Eh, lad,
dosta knaw what tha meäns wi' by and
by? Fur if ye be goin' to sarve our Dora
as ye sarved our Eva — then, by and by, if
she weänt listen to me when I be a-tryin'
to saäve 'er — if she weänt — look to thysen, for, by the Lord, I'd think na moor o'
maäkin' an end o' tha nor a carrion craw —
noä — thaw they hanged ma at 'Size fur it.

*Harold.* Dobbins, I think!    511

*Dobson.* I beänt Dobbins.

*Harold.* Nor am I Edgar, my good fellow.

*Dobson.* Tha lies! What hasta been
saäyin' to *my* Dora?

*Harold.* I have been telling her of the
death of one Philip Edgar of Toft Hall,
Somerset.

*Dobson.* Tha lies!    520

*Harold* (*pulling out a newspaper.*) Well,
my man, it seems that you can read. Look
there — under the deaths.

*Dobson.* 'O' the 17th, Philip Edgar, o'
Toft Hall, Soomerset.' How coom thou
to be sa like 'im, then?

*Harold.* Naturally enough; for I am
closely related to the dead man's family.

*Dobson.* An' 'ow coom thou by the letter
to 'im?    530

*Harold.* Naturally again; for, as I used
to transact all his business for him, I had
to look over his letters. Now then, see
these (*takes out letters*). Half a score of
them, all directed to me — Harold.

*Dobson.* 'Arold! 'Arold! 'Arold, so they
be.

*Harold.* My name is Harold ! Good day, Dobbins ! [*Exit.*

*Dobson.* 'Arold ! The feller 's cleän daäzed, an' maäzed, an' maäted, an' muddled ma. Deäd ! It mun be true, fur it wur i' print as black as owt. Naäy, but 'Good daäy, Dobbins.' Why, that wur the very twang on 'im. Eh, lad, but whether thou be Hedgar, or Hedgar's business man, thou hes n't naw business 'ere wi' *my* Dora, as I knaws on, an' whether thou calls thysen Hedgar or Harold, if thou stick to she I 'll stick to thee — stick to tha like a weasel to a rabbit, I will. Ay ! and I 'd like to shoot tha like a rabbit an' all. 'Good daäy, Dobbins.' Dang tha !    554

## ACT III

SCENE. — A ROOM IN STEER'S HOUSE. DOOR LEADING INTO BEDROOM AT THE BACK.

*Dora* (*ringing a handbell*). Milly !

### *Enter* MILLY.

*Milly.* The little 'ymn ? Yeäs, Miss ; but I wur so ta'en up wi' leädin' the owd man about all the blessed murnin' 'at I ha' nobbut larned mysen haäfe on it.

> O man, forgive thy mortal foe,
> Nor ever strike him blow for blow ;
> For all the souls on earth that live
> To be forgiven must forgive.
> Forgive him seventy times and seven ;
> For all the blessed souls in heaven    10
> Are both forgivers and forgiven.

But I 'll git the book ageän, and larn mysen the rest, and saäy it to ye afoor dark ; ye ringed fur that, Miss, did n't ye ?

*Dora.* No, Milly ; but if the farmingmen be come for their wages, to send them up to me.

*Milly.* Yeäs, Miss.    [*Exit.*

*Dora* (*sitting at desk counting money*). Enough at any rate for the present. (*Enter* Farming Men.) Good afternoon, my friends. I am sorry Mr. Steer still continues too unwell to attend to you, but the schoolmaster looked to the paying you your wages when I was away, did n't he ?

*Men.* Yeäs ; and thanks to ye.

*Dora.* Some of our workmen have left us, but he sent me an alphabetical list of those that remain, so, Allen, I may as well begin with you.    30

*Allen* (*with his hand to his ear*). Halfabitical ! Taäke one o' the young uns fust, Miss, fur I be a bit deaf, and I wur hallus scaäred by a big word ; leästwaäys, I should be wi' a lawyer.

*Dora.* I spoke of your names, Allen, as they are arranged here (*shows book*) — according to their first letters.

*Allen.* Letters ! Yeäs, I sees now. Them be what they larns the childer' at school, but I were burn afoor schoolin'-time.    42

*Dora.* But, Allen, tho' you can't read, you could whitewash that cottage of yours where your grandson had the fever.

*Allen.* I 'll hev it done o' Monday.

*Dora.* Else if the fever spread, the parish will have to thank you for it.

*Allen.* Meä ? why, it be the Lord's doin', noän o' mine ; d' ye think *I* 'd gi'e 'em the fever ? But I thanks ye all the saäme, Miss. (*Takes money.*)    52

*Dora* (*calling out names*). Higgins, Jackson, Luscombe, Nokes, Oldham, Skipworth! (*All take money.*) Did you find that you worked at all the worse upon the cold tea than you would have done upon the beer ?

*Higgins.* Noä, Miss ; we worked naw wuss upo' the cowd tea ; but we 'd ha' worked better upo' the beer.    60

*Dora.* Come, come, you worked well enough, and I am much obliged to all of you. There 's for you, and you, and you. Count the money and see if it 's all right.

*Men.* All right, Miss ; and thank ye kindly.

[*Exeunt* Luscombe, Nokes, Oldham, Skipworth.

*Dora.* Dan Smith, my father and I forgave you stealing our coals.

[Dan Smith *advances to* Dora.

*Dan Smith* (*bellowing*). Whoy, O lor, Miss ! that wur sa long back, and the walls sa thin, and the winders brokken, and the weather sa cowd, and my missus a-gittin' ower 'er lyin'-in.    73

*Dora.* Did n't I say that we had forgiven you ? But, Dan Smith, they tell me that you — and you have six children — spent all your last Saturday's wages at the alehouse ; that you were stupid drunk all Sunday, and so ill in consequence all Monday

that you did not come into the hay-field.
Why should I pay you your full wages ?

*Dan Smith.* I be ready to taäke the
pledge.                                                    83

*Dora.* And as ready to break it again.
Besides, it was you that were driving the
cart — and I fear you were tipsy then, too
— when you lamed the lady in the hollow
lane.

*Dan Smith* (*bellowing*). O lor, Miss ! noä,
noä, noä ! Ye sees the holler laäne be
hallus sa dark i' the arternoon, and wheere
the big esh-tree cuts athurt it, it gi'es a
turn like, and 'ow should I see to laäme
the laädy, and meä coomin' along pretty
sharp an' all ?

*Dora.* Well, there are your wages; the
next time you waste them at a pot-house
you get no more from me. (*Exit* Dan
Smith.) Sally Allen, you worked for Mr.
Dobson, did n't you ?                                  100

*Sally* (*advancing*). Yeäs, Miss; but he
wur so rough wi' ma, I could n't abide 'im.

*Dora.* Why should he be rough with
you ? You are as good as a man in the
hay-field. What 's become of your brother?

*Sally.* 'Listed for a soädger, Miss, i' the
Queen's Real Hard Tillery.

*Dora.* And your sweetheart — when are
you and he to be married ?

*Sally.* At Michaelmas, Miss, please God.

*Dora.* You are an honest pair. I will
come to your wedding.                                  112

*Sally.* An' I thanks ye fur that, Miss,
moor nor fur the waäge.

(*Going — returns.*) 'A cotched ma about
the waäist, Miss, when 'e wur 'ere afoor,
an' axed ma to be 'is little sweet'art, an'
soä I knaw'd 'im when I seed 'im ageän an'
I telled feyther on 'im.

*Dora.* What is all this, Allen ?           120

*Allen.* Why, Miss Dora, meä and my
maätes, us three, we wants to hev three
words wi' ye.

*Higgins.* That be 'im, and meä, Miss.

*Jackson.* An' meä, Miss.

*Allen.* An' we weänt mention naw naämes,
we 'd as lief talk o' the divil afoor ye as
'im, fur they says the master goäs cleän off
his 'eäd when he 'eärs the naäme on 'im;
but us three, arter Sally 'd telled us on 'im,
we fun' 'im out a-walkin' i' West Field
wi' a white 'at, nine o'clock, upo' Tuesday
murnin', and all on us, wi' your leave, we
wants to leather 'im.

*Dora.* Who ?

*Allen.* Him as did the mischief here, five
year' sin'.

*Dora.* Mr. Edgar ?

*Allen.* Theer, Miss ! You ha' naämed
'im — not me.                                             140

*Dora.* He 's dead, man — dead; gone to
his account — dead and buried.

*Allen.* I beänt sa sewer o' that, fur Sally
knaw'd 'im. Now then ?

*Dora.* Yes; it was in the Somersetshire
papers.

*Allen.* Then yon mun be his brother, an'
we 'll leather '*im*.                                  148

*Dora.* I never heard that he had a brother.
Some foolish mistake of Sally's; but what !
would you beat a man for his brother's
fault ? That were a wild justice indeed.
Let bygones be bygones. Go home ! Good-
night ! (*All exeunt.*) I have once more
paid them all. The work of the farm will
go on still, but for how long ? We are almost at the bottom of the well: little more
to be drawn from it — and what then ? En-
cumbered as we are, who would lend us anything ? We shall have to sell all the land,
which father, for a whole life, has been
getting together, again, and that, I am
sure, would be the death of him. What
am I to do ? Farmer Dobson, were I to
marry him, has promised to keep our heads
above water; and the man has doubtless a
good heart, and a true and lasting love for
me; yet — though I can be sorry for him —
as the good Sally says, ' I can't abide him '
— almost brutal, and matched with my
Harold is like a hedge thistle by a garden
rose. But then, he, too — will he ever be
of one faith with his wife ? which is my
dream of a true marriage. Can I fancy
him kneeling with me, and uttering the
same prayer; standing up side by side with
me, and singing the same hymn ? I fear
not. Have I done wisely, then, in accepting him ? But may not a girl's love-dream
have too much romance in it to be realized
all at once, or altogether, or anywhere but
in heaven ? And yet I had once a vision
of a pure and perfect marriage, where the
man and the woman, only differing as the
stronger and the weaker, should walk hand
in hand together down this valley of tears,
as they call it so truly, to the grave at the
bottom, and lie down there together in the
darkness which would seem but for a mo-

ment, to be wakened again together by the light of the resurrection, and no more partings for ever and for ever. (*Walks up and down. She sings.*)

O happy lark, that warblest high
    Above thy lowly nest,
O brook, that brawlest merrily by
    Thro' fields that once were blest,
O tower spiring to the sky,
    O graves in daisies drest,
O Love and Life, how weary am I,    200
    And how I long for rest!

There, there, I am a fool! Tears! I have sometimes been moved to tears by a chapter of fine writing in a novel; but what have I to do with tears now? All depends on me — father, this poor girl, the farm, everything; and they both love me — I am all in all to both; and he loves me too, I am quite sure of that. Courage, courage! and all will go well. (*Goes to bedroom door; opens it.*) How dark your room is! Let me bring you in here where there is still full daylight. (*Brings Eva forward.*) Why, you look better.

*Eva.* And I feel so much better that I trust I may be able by and by to help you in the business of the farm; but I must not be known yet. Has any one found me out, Dora?    219

*Dora.* O, no; you kept your veil too close for that when they carried you in; since then, no one has seen you but myself.

*Eva.* Yes — this Milly.

*Dora.* Poor blind father's little guide, Milly, who came to us three years after you were gone, how should she know you? But now that you have been brought to us as it were from the grave, dearest Eva, and have been here so long, will you not speak with father to-day?    230

*Eva.* Do you think that I may? No, not yet. I am not equal to it yet.

*Dora.* Why? Do you still suffer from your fall in the hollow lane?

*Eva.* Bruised; but no bones broken.

*Dora.* I have always told father that the huge old ash-tree there would cause an accident some day; but he would never cut it down, because one of the Steers had planted it there in former times.    240

*Eva.* If it had killed one of the Steers there the other day, it might have been better for her, for him, and for you.

*Dora.* Come, come, keep a good heart!

Better for me! That 's good. How better for me?

*Eva.* You tell me you have a lover. Will he not fly from you if he learn the story of my shame and that I am still living?    250

*Dora.* No; I am sure that when we are married he will be willing that you and father should live with us; for, indeed, he tells me that he met you once in the old times, and was much taken with you, my dear.

*Eva.* Taken with me; who was he? Have you told him I am here?

*Dora.* No; do you wish it?

*Eva.* See, Dora; you yourself are ashamed of me (*weeps*), and I do not wonder at it.    262

*Dora.* But I should wonder at myself if it were so. Have we not been all in all to one another from the time when we first peeped into the bird's nest, waded in the brook, ran after the butterflies, and prattled to each other that we would marry fine gentlemen, and played at being fine ladies?

*Eva.* That last was my father's fault, poor man. And this lover of yours — this Mr. Harold — is a gentleman?    272

*Dora.* That he is, from head to foot. I do believe I lost my heart to him the very first time we met, and I love him so much —

*Eva.* Poor Dora!

*Dora.* That I dare not tell him how much I love him.

*Eva.* Better not. Has he offered you marriage, this gentleman?    281

*Dora.* Could I love him else?

*Eva.* And are you quite sure that after marriage this gentleman will not be shamed of his poor farmer's daughter among the ladies in his drawing-room?

*Dora.* Shamed of me in a drawing-room! Wasn't Miss Vavasour, our schoolmistress at Littlechester, a lady born? Were not our fellow-pupils all ladies? Wasn't dear mother herself at least by one side a lady? Can't I speak like a lady; pen a letter like a lady; talk a little French like a lady; play a little like a lady? Can't a girl when she loves her husband, and he her, make herself anything he wishes her to be? Shamed of me in a drawing-room, indeed! See here!. 'I hope your lordship is quite recovered of your gout?'

(*Curtsies.*) 'Will your ladyship ride to cover to-day? (*Curtsies.*) I can recommend our Voltigeur.' 'I am sorry that we could not attend your grace's party on the 10th!' (*Curtsies.*) There, I am glad my nonsense has made you smile!

*Eva.* I have heard that 'your lordship,' and 'your ladyship,' and 'your grace' are all growing old-fashioned!  308

*Dora.* But the love of sister for sister can never be old-fashioned. I have been unwilling to trouble you with questions, but you seem somewhat better to-day. We found a letter in your bedroom torn into bits. I could n't make it out. What was it?

*Eva.* From him! from him! He said we had been most happy together, and he trusted that some time we should meet again, for he had not forgotten his promise to come when I called him. But that was a mockery, you know, for he gave me no address, and there was no word of marriage; and, O Dora, he signed himself 'Yours gratefully' — fancy, Dora, 'gratefully'! 'Yours gratefully'!

*Dora.* Infamous wretch! (*Aside.*) Shall I tell her he is dead? No; she is still too feeble.

*Eva.* Hark! Dora, some one is coming. I cannot and I will not see anybody.  330

*Dora.* It is only Milly.

*Enter* MILLY, *with basket of roses.*

Well, Milly, why do you come in so roughly? The sick lady here might have been asleep.

*Milly.* Pleäse, Miss, Mr. Dobson telled me to saäy he's browt some of Miss Eva's roses for the sick laädy to smell on.

*Dora.* Take them, dear. Say that the sick lady thanks him! Is he here?

*Milly.* Yeäs, Miss; and he wants to speak to ye partic'lar.  341

*Dora.* Tell him I cannot leave the sick lady just yet.

*Milly.* Yeäs, Miss; but he says he wants to tell ye summut very partic'lar.

*Dora.* Not to-day. What are you staying for?

*Milly.* Why, Miss, I be afeard I shall set him a-sweäring like onythink.

*Dora.* And what harm will that do you, so that you do not copy his bad manners? Go, child. (*Exit* Milly.) But, Eva, why

did you write 'Seek me at the bottom of the river'?  354

*Eva.* Why? because I meant it! — that dreadful night! that lonely walk to Littlechester, the rain beating in my face all the way, dead midnight when I came upon the bridge; the river, black, slimy, swirling under me in the lamplight, by the rotten wharfs — but I was so mad that I mounted upon the parapet —  362

*Dora.* You make me shudder!

*Eva.* To fling myself over, when I heard a voice, 'Girl, what are you doing there?' It was a Sister of Mercy, come from the death-bed of a pauper, who had died in his misery blessing God, and the Sister took me to her house, and bit by bit — for she promised secrecy — I told her all.  370

*Dora.* And what then?

*Eva.* She would have persuaded me to come back here, but I could n't. Then she got me a place as nursery governess, and when the children grew too old for me, and I asked her once more to help me, once more she said, 'Go home;' but I had n't the heart or face to do it. And then — what would father say? — I sank so low that I went into service — the drudge of a lodging-house — and when the mistress died, and I appealed to the Sister again, her answer — I think I have it about me — yes, there it is!  383

*Dora* (*reads*). 'My dear Child, — I can do no more for you. I have done wrong in keeping your secret; your father must be now in extreme old age. Go back to him and ask his forgiveness before he dies. — SISTER AGATHA.' Sister Agatha is right. Don't you long for father's forgiveness?

*Eva.* I would almost die to have it!

*Dora.* And he may die before he gives it; may drop off any day, any hour. You must see him at once. (*Rings bell. Enter* Milly.) Milly, my dear, how did you leave Mr. Steer?

*Milly.* He's been a-moänin' and a-groänin' in 'is sleep, but I thinks he be wakkenin' oop.  399

*Dora.* Tell him that I and the lady here wish to see him. You see she is lamed, and cannot go down to him.

*Milly.* Yeäs, Miss, I will. [*Exit* Milly.

*Dora.* I ought to prepare you. You must not expect to find our father as he was five years ago. He is much altered; but I trust that your return — for you know, my dear, you were always his favorite — will give him, as they say, a new lease of life.                                                    410

Eva (*clinging to* Dora). O, Dora, Dora !

*Enter* STEER *led by* MILLY.

Steer. Hes the cow cawved ?

Dora. No, father.

Steer. Be the colt deäd ?

Dora. No, father.

Steer. He wur sa bellows'd out wi' the wind this murnin', 'at I tell'd 'em to gallop 'im. Be he deäd ?

Dora. Not that I know.

Steer. What hasta sent fur me, then, fur ?                                               421

Dora (*taking* Steer's *arm*). Well, father, I have a surprise for you.

Steer. I ha' niver been surprised but once i' my life, and I went blind upon it.

Dora. Eva has come home.

Steer. Hoäm ? fro' the bottom o' the river ?

Dora. No, father, that was a mistake. She's here again.                                  430

Steer. The Steers was all gentlefoälks i' the owd times, an' I worked early an' laäte to maäke 'em all gentlefoälks ageän. The land belonged to the Steers i' the owd times, an' it belongs to the Steers ageän: I bowt it back ageän; but I could n't buy my darter back ageän when she lost hersen, could I ? I eddicated boäth on 'em to marry gentlemen, an' one on 'em went an' lost hersen i' the river.                        440

Dora. No, father, she's here.

Steer. Here ! she moänt coom here. What would her mother saäy ? If it be her ghoäst, we mun abide it. We can't keep a ghoäst out.

Eva (*falling at his feet*). O, forgive me ! forgive me !

Steer. Who said that ? Taäke me awaäy, little gell. It be one o' my bad daäys.  449

[*Exit* Steer *led by* Milly.

Dora (*smoothing* Eva's *forehead*). Be not so cast down, my sweet Eva. You heard him say it was one of his bad days. He will be sure to know you to-morrow.

Eva. It is almost the last of my bad days, I think. I am very faint. I must lie down. Give me your arm. Lead me back again.

[*Dora takes* Eva *into inner room.*

*Enter* MILLY.

Milly. Miss Dora ! Miss Dora !

Dora (*returning and leaving the bedroom door ajar*). Quiet ! Quiet ! What is it ?

Milly. Mr. 'Arold, Miss.                         460

Dora. Below ?

Milly. Yeäs, Miss. He be saäyin' a word to the owd man, but he 'll coom up if ye lets 'im.

Dora. Tell him, then, that I 'm waiting for him.

Milly. Yeäs, Miss.

[*Exit.* Dora *sits pensively and waits.*

*Enter* HAROLD.

Harold. You are pale, my Dora ! but the ruddiest cheek

That ever charm'd the plowman of your wolds                                                469

Might wish its rose a lily, could it look

But half as lovely. I was speaking with

Your father, asking his consent — you wish'd me —

That we should marry. He would answer nothing,

I could make nothing of him; but, my flower,

You look so weary and so worn ! What is it

Has put you out of heart ?

Dora.                    It puts me in heart

Again to see you; but indeed the state

Of my poor father puts me out of heart.

Is yours yet living ?

Harold.              No — I told you.

Dora.                              When ?

Harold. Confusion ! — Ah well, well !
the state we all                                       480

Must come to in our spring-and-winter world

If we live long enough ! and poor Steer looks

The very type of Age in a picture, bow'd

To the earth he came from, to the grave he goes to,

Beneath the burthen of years.

Dora.          More like the picture

Of Christian in my 'Pilgrim's Progress' here,

Bow'd to the dust beneath the burthen of sin.

Harold. Sin ! What sin ?

Dora.              Not his own.

Harold.                    That nursery-tale

Still read, then ?

*Dora.* Yes; our carters and our shepherds
Still find a comfort there.
*Harold.*                    Carters and shepherds !
*Dora.* Scorn ! I hate scorn. A soul
    with no religion —                          491
My mother used to say that such a one
Was without rudder, anchor, compass —
    might be
Blown every way with every gust and
    wreck
On any rock; and tho' you are good and
    gentle,
Yet if thro' any want —
*Harold.*                    Of this religion ?
Child, read a little history, you will find
The common brotherhood of man has been
Wrong'd by the cruelties of his religions
More than could ever have happen'd thro'
    the want                                    500
Of any or all of them.
*Dora.*                  But, O dear friend,
If thro' the want of any — I mean the true
    one —
And pardon me for saying it — you should
    ever
Be tempted into doing what might seem
Not altogether worthy of you, I think
That I should break my heart, for you
    have taught me
To love you.
*Harold.* What is this ? some one been
    stirring
Against me ? he, your rustic amorist,
The polish'd Damon of your pastoral here,
This Dobson of your idyll ?
*Dora.*                     No, sir, no !
Did you not tell me he was crazed with
    jealousy,                                   511
Had threaten'd even your life, and would
    say anything ?
Did *I* not promise not to listen to him,
Nor even to see the man ?
*Harold.*                 Good; then what is it
That makes you talk so dolefully ?
*Dora.*                            I told you —
My father. Well, indeed, a friend just
    now,
One that has been much wrong'd, whose
    griefs are mine,
Was warning me that if a gentleman
Should wed a farmer's daughter, he would
    be
Sooner or later shamed of her among    520
The ladies, born his equals.

*Harold.*                    More fool he !
What, I that have been call'd a Socialist,
A Communist, a Nihilist — what you
    will ! —
*Dora.* What are all these ?
*Harold.*                   Utopian idiotcies.
They did not last three Junes. Such rampant weeds
Strangle each other, die, and make the
    soil
For Cæsars, Cromwells, and Napoleons
To root their power in. I have freed myself
From all such dreams, and some will say
    because
I have inherited my uncle. Let them.    530
But — shamed of you, my empress ! I
    should prize
The pearl of beauty, even if I found it
Dark with the soot of slums.
*Dora.*                      But I can tell you,
We Steers are of old blood, tho' we be
    fallen.
See there our shield. (*Pointing to arms on
    mantelpiece.*)
                         For I have heard the Steers
Had land in Saxon times; and your own
    name
Of Harold sounds so English and so old
I am sure you must be proud of it.
*Harold.*                         Not I !
As yet I scarcely feel it mine. I took it
For some three thousand acres. I have
    land now                                    540
And wealth, and lay both at your feet.
*Dora.*                         And *what* was
Your name before ?
*Harold.* Come, come, my girl, enough
Of this strange talk. I love you, and you
    me.
True, I have held opinions, hold some still,
Which you would scarce approve of; for
    all that,
I am a man not prone to jealousies,
Caprices, humors, moods, but very ready
To make allowances, and mighty slow
To feel offences. Nay, I do believe    549
I could forgive — well, almost anything —
And that more freely than your formal
    priest,
Because I know more fully than *he* can
What poor earthworms are all and each of
    us,
Here crawling in this boundless Nature.
    Dora,

If marriage ever brought a woman happiness
I doubt not I can make you happy.

*Dora.* You make me
Happy already.

*Harold.* And I never said
As much before to any woman living.

*Dora.* No ?

*Harold.* No ! by this true kiss, *you* are
the first
I ever have loved truly.
[*They kiss each other.*

*Eva (with a wild cry).* Philip Edgar !

*Harold.* The phantom cry ! *You* — did
you hear a cry ? 561

*Dora.* She must be crying out ' Edgar '
in her sleep.

*Harold.* Who must be crying out ' Edgar ' in her sleep ?

*Dora.* Your pardon for a minute. She
must be waked.

*Harold.* Who must be waked ?

*Dora.* I am not deaf; you fright me.
What ails you ?

*Harold.* Speak.

*Dora.* You know her, Eva.

*Harold.* Eva !
[*Eva opens the door and stands in the
entry.*
She !

*Eva.* Make her happy, then, and I forgive you. [*Falls dead.*

*Dora.* Happy ! What ? Edgar ? Is it
so ? Can it be ?
They told me so. Yes, yes ! I see it all
now. 569
O, she has fainted ! Sister, Eva, sister !
He is yours again — he will love *you* again;
I give him back to you again. Look up !
One word, or do but smile ! Sweet, do you
hear me ?
[*Puts her hand on* Eva's *heart.*
There, there — the heart, O God ! — the
poor young heart
Broken at last — all still — and nothing
left
To live for. [*Falls on body of her sister.*

*Harold.* Living — dead — She said ' all
still.
Nothing to live for.'
She — she knows me — now —
(*A pause.*)
She knew me from the first, she juggled
with me,
She hid this sister, told me she was dead —

I have wasted pity on her — not dead
now — 580
No ! acting, playing on me, both of them.
*They* drag the river for her ! no, not they !
Playing on me — not dead now — a swoon
— a scene —
Yet — how she made her wail as for the
dead !

*Enter* MILLY.

*Milly.* Pleäse, Mister 'Arold.

*Harold (roughly).* Well ?

*Milly.* The owd man 's coom'd ageän to
'issen, an' wants
To hev a word wi' ye about the marriage.

*Harold.* The what ?

*Milly.* The marriage.

*Harold.* The marriage ?

*Milly.* Yeäs, the marriage.
Granny says marriages be maäde i' 'eaven.

*Harold.* She lies ! They are made in
hell. Child, can't you see ? 590
Tell them to fly for a doctor.

*Milly.* O, law — yeäs, Sir.
I 'll run fur 'im mysen. [*Exit.*

*Harold.* All silent there,
Yes, deathlike ! Dead ? I dare not look.
If dead,
Were it best to steal away, to spare myself,
And her too, pain, pain, pain ?
My curse on all
This world of mud, on all its idiot gleams
Of pleasure, all the foul fatalities
That blast our natural passions into pains !

*Enter* DOBSON.

*Dobson.* You, Master Hedgar, Harold,
or whativer 599
They calls ye, for I warrants that ye goäs
By haäfe a scoor o' naämes — out o' the
chaumber !
[*Dragging him past the body.*

*Harold.* Not that way, man ! Curse on
your brutal strength !
I cannot pass that way.

*Dobson.* Out o' the chaumber !
I 'll mash tha into nowt.

*Harold.* The mere wild-beast !

*Dobson.* Out o' the chaumber, dang tha !

*Harold.* Lout, churl, clown !
[*While they are shouting and struggling*
Dora *rises and comes between them.*

*Dora (to* Dobson). Peace, let him be; it
is the chamber of Death !
Sir, you are tenfold more a gentleman,

A hundred times more worth a woman's
    love,
Than this, this — but I waste no words
    upon him:                                    609
His wickedness is like my wretchedness —
Beyond all language.
(*To* Harold.)    You — you see her there !
Only fifteen when first you came on her,
And then the sweetest flower of all the
    wolds,
So lovely in the promise of her May,
So winsome in her grace and gaiety,
So loved by all the village people here,
So happy in herself and in her home —
    *Dobson* (*agitated*). Theer, theer ! ha'
    done.  I can't abeär to see her.
                                    [*Exit.*
    *Dora.*  A child, and all as trustful as a
    child !
Five years of shame and suffering broke
    the heart                                    620
That only beat for you; and he, the father,
Thro' that dishonor which you brought
    upon us,
Has lost his health, his eyesight, even his
    mind.
    *Harold* (*covering his face*).  Enough !
    *Dora.*  It seem'd so; only there was left
A second daughter, and to her you came
Veiling one sin to act another.
    *Harold.*                          No !
You wrong me there ! hear, hear me !  I
    wish'd, if you —                 [*Pauses.*
    *Dora.*  If I —
    *Harold.*  Could love me, could be brought
    to love me
As I loved you —

    *Dora.*             What then ?
    *Harold.*                 I wish'd, I hoped
To make, to make —
    *Dora.*      *What* did you hope to make ?
    *Harold.*  'T were best to make an end of
    my lost life.                                631
O Dora, Dora !
    *Dora.*      *What* did you hope to make ?
    *Harold.*  Make, make !  I cannot find
    the word — forgive it —
Amends.
    *Dora.*    For what ? to whom ?
    *Harold.*                 To him, to you !
                        [*Falling at her feet.*
    *Dora.*  To *him!* to *me!*
                No, not with all your wealth,
Your land, your life !  Out in the fiercest
    storm
That ever made earth tremble — he, nor
    I —
The shelter of *your* roof — not for one mo-
    ment —
Nothing from *you !*
Sunk in the deepest pit of pauperism,   640
Push'd from all doors as if we bore the
    plague,
Smitten with fever in the open field,
Laid famine - stricken at the gates of
    Death —
Nothing from you !
                But she there — her last word
Forgave — and I forgive you.  If you
    ever
Forgive yourself, you are even lower and
    baser
Than even I can well believe you.  Go !
            [*He lies at her feet.  Curtain falls.*

---

## CROSSING THE BAR

This poem first appeared in the 'Demeter'
volume of 1889, but is placed here in accordance with Lord Tennyson's request that it
might be put at the end of all editions of his
poems.  See the 'Memoir,' vol. ii. p. 367.

SUNSET and evening star,
    And one clear call for me !
And may there be no moaning of the bar,
    When I put out to sea,

But such a tide as moving seems asleep,
    Too full for sound and foam,

When that which drew from out the bound-
    less deep
    Turns again home.

Twilight and evening bell,
    And after that the dark !
And may there be no sadness of farewell,
    When I embark;

For tho' from out our bourne of Time and
    Place
    The flood may bear me far,
I hope to see my Pilot face to face
    When I have crost the bar.

# APPENDIX

## I. SELECTIONS FROM 'POEMS BY TWO BROTHERS'

In 1893 the present Lord Tennyson published a facsimile reprint of the 'Poems by Two Brothers,' in which his uncle, Mr. Frederick Tennyson, had appended the initials of the authors to their contributions to the volume, so far as he remembered them. He was not certain of the authorship of every poem. Some he signs 'A. T. (?)' or 'C. T. (?),' and some 'A. T. or C. T.' I give here all that are probably Alfred's, with some about which (see prefatory notes) I have my doubts. I follow the spelling and pointing of the reprint except in the few instances mentioned in the Notes.

## MEMORY

It is interesting to compare this poem with the 'Ode to Memory' published in 1830. Like several others of Alfred's it is longer than any of Charles's.

'The memory is perpetually looking back when we have nothing present to entertain us: it is like those repositories in animals that are filled with stores of food, on which they may ruminate when their present pasture fails.' — ADDISON.

MEMORY! dear enchanter!
  Why bring back to view
Dreams of youth, which banter
  All that e'er was true?

Why present before me
  Thoughts of years gone by,
Which, like shadows o'er me,
  Dim in distance fly?

Days of youth, now shaded
  By twilight of long years,
Flowers of youth, now faded,
  Though bathed in sorrow's tears:

Thoughts of youth, which waken
  Mournful feelings now,
Fruits which time hath shaken
  From off their parent bough:

Memory! why, oh why,
  This fond heart consuming,
Shew me years gone by,
  When those hopes were blooming?

Hopes which now are parted,
  Hopes which then I priz'd,
Which this world, cold-hearted,
  Ne'er has realiz'd?

I knew not then its strife,
  I knew not then its rancour;
In every rose of life,
  Alas! there lurks a canker.

Round every palm-tree, springing
  With bright fruit in the waste,
A mournful asp is clinging,
  Which sours it to our taste.

O'er every fountain, pouring
  Its waters thro' the wild,
Which man imbibes, adoring,
  And deems it undefil'd,

The poison-shrubs are dropping
  Their dark dews day by day;
And Care is hourly lopping
  Our greenest boughs away!

Ah! these are thoughts that grieve me
  Then, when others rest.
Memory! why deceive me
  By thy visions blest?

Why lift the veil, dividing
  The brilliant courts of spring —
Where gilded shapes are gliding
  In fairy colouring —

From age's frosty mansion,
  So cheerless and so chill?
Why bid the bleak expansion
  Of past life meet us still?

Where's now that peace of mind
  O'er youth's pure bosom stealing,
So sweet and so refin'd,
  So exquisite a feeling?

Where's now the heart exulting
  In pleasure's buoyant sense,

And gaiety, resulting
　　From conscious innocence?

All, all have past and fled,
　　And left me lorn and lonely;
All those dear hopes are dead,
　　Remembrance wakes them only!

I stand like some lone tower
　　Of former days remaining,
Within whose place of power
　　The midnight owl is plaining; —

Like oak-tree old and grey,
　　Whose trunk with age is failing,
Thro' whose dark boughs for aye
　　The winter winds are wailing.

Thus, Memory, thus thy light
　　O'er this worn soul is gleaming,
Like some far fire at night
　　Along the dun deep streaming.


## THE EXILE'S HARP

I will hang thee, my Harp, by the side of the
　　fountain,
　　On the whispering branch of the lone-waving
　　　willow:
Above thee shall rush the hoarse gale of the
　　mountain,
　　Below thee shall tumble the dark breaking
　　　billow.
The winds shall blow by thee, abandon'd, for-
　　saken,
　　The wild gales alone shall arouse thy sad
　　　strain;
For where is the heart or the hand to awaken
　　The sounds of thy soul-soothing sweetness
　　　again?
　　　　Oh! Harp of my fathers!
　　　　　Thy chords shall decay,
　　　　One by one with the strings
　　　　　Shall thy notes fade away;
　　　　Till the fiercest of tempests
　　　　　Around thee may yell,
　　　　And not waken one sound
　　　　　Of thy desolate shell!

Yet, oh! yet, ere I go, will I fling a wreath
　　round thee,
　　With the richest of flowers in the green valley
　　　springing;
Those that see shall remember the hand that
　　hath crown'd thee,
　　When, wither'd and dead, to thee still they
　　　are clinging.
There! now I have wreath'd thee — the roses
　　are twining
　　Thy chords with their bright blossoms glow-
　　　ing and red:
Though the lapse of one day see their freshness
　　declining,
　　Yet bloom for one day when thy minstrel has
　　　fled!

　　　　Oh! Harp of my fathers!
　　　　　No more in the hall,
　　　　The souls of the chieftains
　　　　　Thy strains shall enthral:
　　　　One sweep will I give thee,
　　　　　And wake thy bold swell;
　　　　Then, thou friend of my bosom,
　　　　　For ever farewell!


## 'WHY SHOULD WE WEEP FOR THOSE WHO DIE?'

I doubt whether this poem is rightly attributed to Alfred.

'Quamobrem, si dolorum finem mors affert, si secu-
rioris et melioris initium vitæ: si futura mala avertit
— cur eam tantopere accusare, ex qua potius consola-
tionem et lætitiam haurire fas esset?' — Cicero.

Why should we weep for those who die?
　　They fall — their dust returns to dust;
Their souls shall live eternally
　　Within the mansions of the just.

They die to live — they sink to rise,
　　They leave this wretched mortal shore;
But brighter suns and bluer skies
　　Shall smile on them for evermore.

Why should we sorrow for the dead?
　　Our life on earth is but a span;
They tread the path that all must tread,
　　They die the common death of man.

The noblest songster of the gale
　　Must cease, when Winter's frowns appear;
The reddest rose is wan and pale,
　　When Autumn tints the changing year.

The fairest flower on earth must fade,
　　The brightest hopes on earth must die:
Why should we mourn that man was made
　　To droop on earth, but dwell on high?

The soul, th' eternal soul, must reign
　　In worlds devoid of pain and strife;
Then why should mortal man complain
　　Of death, which leads to happier life?


## REMORSE

The complex interlacing of the rhymes is
peculiar to Alfred. Compare 'Persia,' 'The
Fall of Jerusalem,' 'Time,' etc.

'— sudant tacita præcordia culpa.' — Juvenal.

Oh! 't is a fearful thing to glance
　　Back on the gloom of mis-spent years:
What shadowy forms of guilt advance,
　　And fill me with a thousand fears!
The vices of my life arise,
　　Pourtray'd in shapes, alas! too true;
And not one beam of hope breaks through,
To cheer my old and aching eyes,

T' illume my night of wretchedness,
My age of anguish and distress.
If I am damn'd, why find I not
Some comfort in this earthly spot ?
But no ! this world and that to come
Are both to me one scene of gloom !
Lest ought of solace I should see,
    Or lose the thoughts of what I do,
Remorse, with soul-felt agony,
    Holds up the mirror to my view.
And I was cursed from my birth,
A reptile made to creep on earth,
An hopeless outcast, born to die
A living death eternally !
With too much conscience to have rest,
Too little to be ever blest,
To yon vast world of endless woe,
    Unlighted by the cheerful day,
My soul shall wing her weary way;
    To those dread depths where aye the same,
Throughout the waste of darkness, glow
    The glimmerings of the boundless flame.
And yet I cannot here below
Take my full cup of guilt, as some,
And laugh away my doom to come.
I would I 'd been all-heartless ! then
I might have sinn'd like other men;
But all this side the grave is fear,
A wilderness so dank and drear,
That never wholesome plant would spring;
    And all behind — I dare not think !
I would not risk th' imagining —
    From the full view my spirits shrink;
And starting backwards, yet I cling
To life, whose every hour to me
Hath been increase of misery.
But yet I cling to it, for well
    I know the pangs that rack me now
Are trifles, to the endless hell
    That waits me, when my burning brow
And my wrung eyes shall hope in vain
For one small drop to cool the pain,
The fury of that madd'ning flame
That then shall scorch my writhing frame !
Fiends ! who have goaded me to ill !
Distracting fiends, who goad me still !
If e'er I work'd a sinful deed,
Ye know how bitter was the draught;
    Ye know my inmost soul would bleed,
    And ye have look'd at me and laugh'd,
Triumphing that I could not free
My spirit from your slavery !
Yet is there that in me which says,
Should these old feet their course retreat
From out the portal of my days,
    That I should lead the life I 've led:
My agony, my torturing shame,
My guilt, my errors all the same !
Oh, God ! that thou wouldst grant that ne'er
    My soul its clay-cold bed forsake,
    That I might sleep, and never wake
Unto the thrill of conscious fear;
    For when the trumpet's piercing cry
Shall burst upon my slumb'ring ear,
    And countless seraphs throng the sky,
How shall I cast my shroud away,
And come into the blaze of day ?

How shall I brook to hear each crime,
Here veil'd by secrecy and time,
Read out from thine eternal book ?
    How shall I stand before thy throne,
        While earth shall like a furnace burn ?
How shall I bear the with'ring look
        Of men and angels, who will turn
    Their dreadful gaze on me alone ?


## THE DELL OF E——

'Tantum ævi longinqua valet mutare vetustas !' —
VIRGIL.

THERE was a long, low, rushy dell, emboss'd
    With knolls of grass and clumps of copsewood
        green;
Mid-way a wandering burn the valley cross'd,
    And streak'd with silvery line the wood-land
        scene;
High hills on either side to heaven upsprung,
    Y-clad with groves of undulating pine,
Upon whose heads the hoary vapours hung,
    And far — far off the heights were seen to
        shine
In clear relief against the sapphire sky,
    And many a blue stream wander'd thro' the
        shade
Of those dark groves that clomb the mountains
        high,
    And glistening 'neath each lone entangled
        glade,
At length with brawling accent loudly fell
Within the limpid brook that wound along the
        dell.

How pleasant was the ever-varying light
    Beneath that emerald coverture of boughs !
How often, at th' approach of dewy night,
    Have those tall pine-trees heard the lover's
        vows !
How many a name was carv'd upon the trunk
    Of each old hollow willow-tree, that stoop'd
To lave its branches in the brook, and drunk
    Its freshening dew ! How many a cypress
        droop'd
From those fair banks, where bloom'd the ear-
        liest flowers,
    Which the young year from her abounding
        horn
Scatters profuse within her secret bowers !
    What rapturous gales from that wild dell
        were borne !
And, floating on the rich spring breezes, flung
Their incense o'er that wave on whose bright
        banks they sprung !

Long years had past, and there again I came,
    But man's rude hand had sorely scath'd the
        dell;
And though the cloud-capped mountains, still
        the same,
    Uprear'd each heaven-invading pinnacle;
Yet were the charms of that lone valley fled,
    And the grey - winding of the stream was
        gone;

The brook, once murmuring o'er its pebbly
    bed,
  Now deeply — straightly — noiselessly went
    on.
Slow turn'd the sluggish wheel beneath its
    force,
  Where clattering mills disturb'd the solitude:
Where was the prattling of its former course ?
  Its shelving, sedgy sides y-crown'd with
    wood ?
The willow trunks were fell'd, the names eras'd
From one broad shattered pine, which still its
    station grac'd.

Remnant of all its brethren, there it stood,
  Braving the storms that swept the cliffs
    above,
Where once, throughout th' impenetrable wood,
  Were heard the plainings of the pensive dove.
But man had bid th' eternal forests bow
That bloom'd upon the earth-imbedded base
Of the strong mountain, and perchance they
    now
Upon the billows were the dwelling-place
Of their destroyers, and bore terror round
  The trembling earth: — ah ! lovelier, had they
    still
Whisper'd unto the breezes with low sound,
  And greenly flourish'd on their native hill,
And flinging their proud arms in state on high,
Spread out beneath the sun their glorious can-
    opy !

## ANTONY TO CLEOPATRA

O, Cleopatra ! fare thee well,
  We two can meet no more;
This breaking heart alone can tell
  The love to thee I bore.
But wear not thou the conqueror's chain
  Upon thy race and thee;
And though we ne'er can meet again,
  Yet still be true to me:
For I for thee have lost a throne,
To wear the crown of love alone.

Fair daughter of a regal line !
  To thraldom bow not tame;
My every wish on earth was thine,
  My every hope the same.
And I have mov'd within thy sphere,
  And liv'd within thy light;
And oh ! thou wert to me so dear,
  I breath'd but in thy sight !
A subject world I lost for thee,
For thou wert all my world to me !

Then when the shriekings of the dying
  Were heard along the wave.
Soul of my soul ! I saw thee flying;
  I follow'd thee, to save.
The thunder of the brazen prows
  O'er Actium's ocean rung;
Fame's garland faded from my brows,
  Her wreath away I flung.
I sought, I saw, I heard but thee:
For what to love was victory ?

Thine on the earth, and on the throne,
  And in the grave, am I;
And, dying, still I am thine own,
  Thy bleeding Antony.
How shall my spirit joy to hear
  That thou art ever true !
Nay — weep not — dry that burning tear,
  That bathes thine eyes' dark hue.
Shades of my fathers ! lo ! I come;
I hear your voices from the tomb !

## 'I WANDER IN DARKNESS AND SORROW'

Note the repetition in the last lines of each
stanza.  Alfred was more given to these regu-
larities of *form* than his brother.  He also tries
his hand at a greater variety of stanzas and
arrangements of rhymes.

I wander in darkness and sorrow,
  Unfriended, and cold, and alone,
As dismally gurgles beside me
  The bleak river's desolate moan.
The rise of the volleying thunder
  The mountain's lone echoes repeat:
The roar of the wind is around me,
  The leaves of the year at my feet.

I wander in darkness and sorrow,
  Uncheer'd by the moon's placid ray;
Not a friend that I lov'd but is dead,
  Not a hope but has faded away !
Oh ! when shall I rest in the tomb,
  Wrapt about with the chill winding sheet ?
For the roar of the wind is around me,
  The leaves of the year at my feet.

I heed not the blasts that sweep o'er me,
  I blame not the tempests of night;
They are not the foes who have banish'd
  The visions of youthful delight:
I hail the wild sound of their raving,
  Their merciless presence I greet;
Though the roar of the wind be around me,
  The leaves of the year at my feet.

In this waste of existence, for solace,
  On whom shall my lone spirit call ?
Shall I fly to the friends of my bosom ?
  My God ! I have buried them all !
They are dead, they are gone, they are cold,
  My embraces no longer they meet;
Let the roar of the wind be around me,
  The leaves of the year at my feet !

Those eyes that glanc'd love unto mine,
  With motionless slumbers are prest;
Those hearts which once throbb'd but for me,
  Are chill as the earth where they rest.
Then around on my wan wither'd form
  Let the pitiless hurricanes beat;
Let the roar of the wind be around me,
  The leaves of the year at my feet !

Like the voice of the owl in the hall,
    Where the song and the banquet have ceas'd,
Where the green weeds have mantled the
    hearth,
    Whence arose the proud flame of the feast;
So I cry to the storm, whose dark wing
    Scatters on me the wild-driving sleet —
'*Let the roar of the wind be around me,*
    *The fall of the leaves at my feet!*'

## THE OLD SWORD

OLD Sword! tho' dim and rusted
    Be now thy sheeny blade,
Thy glitt'ring edge encrusted
    With cankers Time hath made;
        Yet once around thee swell'd the cry
        Of triumph's fierce delight,
    The shoutings of the victory,
        The thunders of the fight!

Tho' age hath past upon thee
    With still corroding breath,
Yet once stream'd redly on thee
    The purpling tide of death:
        What time amid the war of foes
        The dastard's cheek grew pale,
    As through the feudal field arose
        The ringing of the mail.

Old Sword! what arm hath wielded
    Thy richly gleaming brand,
'Mid lordly forms who shielded
    The maidens of their land?
        And who hath clov'n his foes in wrath
        With thy puissant fire,
    And scatter'd in his perilous path
        The victims of his ire?

Old Sword! whose fingers clasp'd thee
    Around thy carved hilt?
And with that hand which grasp'd thee
    What heroes' blood was spilt?
        When fearlessly, with open hearts,
        And lance to lance oppos'd,
    Beneath the shade of barbed darts
        The dark-ey'd warriors clos'd?

Old Sword! I would not burnish
    Thy venerable rust,
Nor sweep away the tarnish
    Of darkness and of dust!
        Lie there, in slow and still decay,
        Unfam'd in olden rhyme,
    The relic of a former day,
        A wreck of ancient time!

## 'WE MEET NO MORE'

The present Lord Tennyson agrees with me
that this is incorrectly assigned to Alfred.

WE meet no more — the die is cast,
    The chain is broke that tied us,

Our every hope on earth is past,
    And there's no helm to guide us:
We meet no more — the roaring blast
    And angry seas divide us!

And I stand on a distant shore,
    The breakers round me swelling;
And lonely thoughts of days gone o'er
    Have made this breast their dwelling:
We meet no more — We meet no more:
    Farewell for ever, Ellen!

WRITTEN

## BY AN EXILE OF BASSORAH,

WHILE SAILING DOWN THE EUPHRATES

THOU land of the Lily! thy gay flowers are
        blooming
    In joy on thine hills, but they bloom not for
        me;
For a dark gulf of woe, all my fond hopes en-
        tombing,
    Has roll'd its black waves 'twixt this lone
        heart and thee.

The far-distant hills, and the groves of my
        childhood,
    Now stream in the light of the sun's setting
        ray;
And the tall-waving palms of my own native
        wildwood
    In the blue haze of distance are melting away.

I see thee, Bassorah! in splendour retiring,
    Where thy waves and thy walls in their ma-
        jesty meet;
I see the bright glory thy pinnacles firing,
    And the broad vassal river that rolls at thy
        feet.

I see thee but faintly — thy tall towers are
        beaming
    On the dusky horizon so far and so blue;
And minaret and mosque in the distance are
        gleaming,
    While the coast of the stranger expands on
        my view.

I see thee no more: for the deep waves have
        parted
    The land of my birth from her desolate son;
And I am gone from thee, though half broken-
        hearted,
    To wander thro' climes where thy name is
        unknown.

Farewell to my harp, which I hung in my
        anguish
    On the lonely palmetto that nods to the gale;
For its sweet-breathing tones in forgetfulness
        languish,
    And around it the ivy shall weave a green
        veil.

Farewell to the days which so smoothly have
　　glided
　　With the maiden whose look was like Cama's
　　　　young glance,
And the sheen of whose eyes was the load-star
　　which guided
　　My course on this earth thro' the storms of
　　　　mischance !


## THE VALE OF BONES

' Albis informem — ossibus agrum.' — HORACE.

ALONG yon vapour-mantled sky
The dark-red moon is riding high;
At times her beams in beauty break
Upon the broad and silv'ry lake;
At times more bright they clearly fall
On some white castle's ruin'd wall;
At times her partial splendour shines
Upon the grove of deep-black pines,
Through which the dreary night-breeze moans,
Above this Vale of scatter'd bones.

The low, dull gale can scarcely stir
The branches of that black'ning fir,
Which betwixt me and heav'n flings wide
Its shadowy boughs on either side,
And o'er yon granite rock uprears
Its giant form of many years.
And the shrill owlet's desolate wail
Comes to mine ear along the gale,
As, list'ning to its lengthen'd tones,
I dimly pace the Vale of Bones.

Dark Valley ! still the same art thou,
Unchang'd thy mountain's cloudy brow;
Still from yon cliffs, that part asunder,
Falls down the torrent's echoing thunder;
Still from this mound of reeds and rushes
With bubbling sound the fountain gushes;
Thence, winding thro' the whisp'ring ranks
Of sedges on the willowy banks,
Still brawling, chafes the rugged stones
That strew this dismal Vale of Bones.

Unchang'd art thou ! no storm hath rent
Thy rude and rocky battlement;
Thy rioting mountains sternly pil'd,
The screen of nature, wide and wild :
But who were they, whose bones bestrew
The heather, cold with midnight dew,
Upon whose slowly-rotting clay
The raven long hath ceas'd to prey,
But, mould'ring in the moon-light air,
Their wan, white skulls show bleak and bare ?
And, aye, the dreary night-breeze moans
Above them in this Vale of Bones !

I knew them all — a gallant band,
The glory of their native land,
And on each lordly brow elate
Sate valour and contempt of fate,
Fierceness of youth, and scorn of foe,
And pride to render blow for blow.
In the strong war's tumultuous crash,

How darkly did their keen eyes flash !
How fearlessly each arm was rais'd !
How dazzlingly each broad-sword blaz'd !
Though now the dreary night-breeze moans
Above them in this Vale of Bones.

What lapse of time shall sweep away
The memory of that gallant day,
When on to battle proudly going,
Your plumage to the wild winds blowing,
Your tartans far behind ye flowing,
Your pennons rais'd, your clarions sounding,
Fiercely your steeds beneath ye bounding,
Ye mix'd the strife of warring foes
In fiery shock and deadly close ?
What stampings in the madd'ning strife,
What thrusts, what stabs, with brand and knife,
What desp'rate strokes for death or life,
Were there ! What cries, what thrilling groans,
Re-echo'd thro' the Vale of Bones !

Thou peaceful Vale, whose mountains lonely,
Sound to the torrent's chiding only,
Or wild-goat's cry from rocky ledge,
Or bull-frog from the rustling sedge,
Or eagle from her airy cairn,
Or screaming of the startled hern —
How did thy million echoes waken
Amid thy caverns deeply shaken !
How with the red dew o'er thee rain'd
Thine emerald turf was darkly stain'd !
How did each innocent flower, that sprung
Thy greenly-tangl'd glades among,
Blush with the big and purple drops
That dribbled from the leafy copse !
I pac'd the valley, when the yell
Of triumph's voice had ceas'd to swell:
When battle's brazen throat no more
Rais'd its annihilating roar.
There lay ye on each other pil'd,
Your brows with noble dust defil'd;[1]
There, by the loudly-gushing water,
Lay man and horse in mingled slaughter.
Then wept I not, thrice gallant band;
For though no more each dauntless hand
The thunder of the combat hurl'd,
Yet still with pride your lips were curl'd;
And e'en in death's o'erwhelming shade
Your fingers linger'd round the blade !
I deem'd, when gazing proudly there
Upon the fix'd and haughty air
That mark'd each warrior's bloodless face,
Ye would not change the narrow space
Which each cold form of breathless clay
Then cover'd, as on earth ye lay,
For realms, for sceptres, or for thrones —
I dream'd not on this Vale of Bones !

But years have thrown their veil between,
And alter'd is that lonely scene;
And dreadful emblems of thy might,
Stern Dissolution ! meet my sight:
The eyeless socket, dark and dull,
The hideous grinning of the skull,
Are sights which Memory disowns,
Thou melancholy Vale of Bones !

　　　　　[1] ' Non indecoro pulvere sordidos.' — HOR.

## 'DID NOT THY ROSEATE LIPS OUTVIE'

In this poem, as in 'Persia,' 'Midnight,' and others, the long sentences are to be noted. One finds very few of these in Charles's poems.

> 'Ulla si juris tibi pejerati
> Pœna, Barine, nocuisset unquam;
> Dente si nigro fieres, vel uno
>     Turpior ungui
> Crederem.'
>                                 HORACE.

DID not thy roseate lips outvie
  The gay Anana's spicy bloom;[1]
Had not thy breath the luxury,
  The richness of its deep perfume —

Were not the pearls it fans more clear
  Than those which grace the valved shell;
Thy foot more airy than the deer,
  When startled from his lonely dell —

Were not thy bosom's stainless whiteness,
  Where angel loves their vigils keep,
More heavenly than the dazzling brightness
  Of the cold crescent on the deep —

Were not thine eye a star might grace
  Yon sapphire concave beaming clear,
Or fill the vanish'd Pleiad's place,
  And shine for aye as brightly there —

Had not thy locks the golden glow
  That robes the gay and early east,
Thus falling in luxuriant flow
  Around thy fair but faithless breast:

I might have deem'd that thou wert she
  Of the Cumæan cave, who wrote
Each fate-involving mystery,
  Upon the feathery leaves that float,

Borne thro' the boundless waste of air,
  Wherever chance might drive along.
But she was wrinkled — thou art fair:
  And she was old — but thou art young.

Her years were as the sands that strew
  The fretted ocean-beach; but thou —
Triumphant in that eye of blue,
  Beneath thy smoothly-marble brow;

Exulting in thy form thus moulded,
  By nature's tenderest touch design'd;
Proud of the fetters thou hast folded
  Around this fond deluded mind —

Deceivest still with practis'd look,
  With fickle vow, and well-feign'd sigh.
I tell thee, that I will not brook
  Reiterated perjury!

[1] Ulloa says, that the blossom of the West-Indian Anana is of so elegant a crimson as even to dazzle the eye, and that the fragrancy of the fruit discovers the

Alas! I feel thy deep control,
  E'en now when I would break thy chain:
But while I seek to gain thy soul,
  Ah! say — hast thou a soul to gain?

## PERSIA

One of the most notable of these juvenile poems. The familiarity with Persian history and geography is remarkable in one so young; and proper names are managed with much skill.

> 'The flower and choice
> Of many provinces from bound to bound.'
>                                 MILTON.

LAND of bright eye and lofty brow!
  Whose every gale is balmy breath
Of incense from some sunny flower,
  Which on tall hill or valley low,
    In clustering maze or circling wreath,
      Sheds perfume; or in blooming bower
Of Schiraz or of Ispahan,
In bower untrod by foot of man,
Clasps round the green and fragrant stem
  Of lotos, fair and fresh and blue,
And crowns it with a diadem
  Of blossoms, ever young and new;
Oh! lives there yet within thy soul
  Ought of the fire of him who led
Thy troops, and bade thy thunder roll
  O'er lone Assyria's crownless head?
  I tell thee, had that conqueror red
    From Thymbria's plain beheld thy fall,
When stormy Macedonia swept
    Thine honours from thee one and all,
He would have wail'd, he would have wept,
That thy proud spirit should have bow'd
To Alexander, doubly proud.
Oh! Iran! Iran! had he known
The downfall of his mighty throne,
Or had he seen that fatal night,
  When the young king of Macedon
  In madness led his veterans on,
And Thais held the funeral light,
Around that noble pile which rose
  Irradiant with the pomp of gold,
  In high Persepolis of old,
Encompass'd with its frenzied foes;
He would have groan'd, he would have spread
The dust upon his laurell'd head,
To view the setting of that star,
Which beam'd so gorgeously and far
O'er Anatolia, and the fane
Of Belus, and Caïster's plain,
  And Sardis, and the glittering sands
  Of bright Pactolus, and the lands
Where Crœsus held his rich domain:
On fair Diarbeck's land of spice,[2]
Adiabene's plains of rice,
Where down th' Euphrates, swift and strong,

plant though concealed from sight. — See Ulloa's *Voyages*, vol. i. p. 72.
[2] Xenophon says, that every shrub in these wilds had an aromatic odour.

The shield-like kuphars bound along; [1]
And sad Cunaxa's field, where, mixing
   With host to adverse host oppos'd,
'Mid clashing shield and spear transfixing,
   The rival brothers sternly clos'd.
And further east, where, broadly roll'd,
Old Indus pours his stream of gold;
And there, where tumbling deep and hoarse,
Blue Ganga leaves her vaccine source; [2]
Loveliest of all the lovely streams
That meet immortal Titan's beams,
And smile upon their fruitful way
Beneath his golden orient ray:
And southward to Cilicia's shore,
Where Cydnus meets the billows' roar,
And where the Syrian gates divide
The meeting realms on either side; [3]
E'en to the land of Nile, whose crops
   Bloom rich beneath his bounteous swell,
   To hot Syene's wondrous well,
Nigh to the long-liv'd Æthiops.
And northward far to Trebizonde,
   Renown'd for kings of chivalry,
Near where old Hyssus, from the strand,
   Disgorges in the Euxine sea —
The Euxine, falsely nam'd, which whelms
   The mariner in the heaving tide,
To high Sinope's distant realms,
   Whence cynics rail'd at human pride.

## EGYPT

'Egypt's palmy groves,
Her grots, and sepulchres of kings.'
MOORE'S *Lalla Rookh.*

THE sombre pencil of the dim-grey dawn
   Draws a faint sketch of Egypt to mine eye,
As yet uncolour'd by the brilliant morn,
   And her gay orb careering up the sky.

And see ! at last he comes in radiant pride,
   Life in his eye, and glory in his ray;
No veiling mists his growing splendour hide,
   And hang their gloom around his golden way.

The flowery region brightens in his smile,
   Her lap of blossoms freights the passing gale,
That robs the odours of each balmy isle,
   Each fragrant field and aromatic vale.

But the first glitter of his rising beam
   Falls on the broad-bas'd pyramids sublime,
As proud to show us with his earliest gleam,
   Those vast and hoary enemies of time.

E'en History's self, whose certain scrutiny
   Few eras in the list of Time beguile,

[1] Rennel on Herodotus.
[2] The cavern in the ridge of Himmalah, whence the Ganges seems to derive its original springs, has been moulded, by the mind of Hindoo superstition, into the head of a cow.
[3] See Xenophon's *Expeditio Cyri.*
[4] See Savary's *Letters.*
[5] 'Stabat pro littore diversa acies, densa armis virisque, intercursantibus feminis in modum Furiarum, quæ

Pauses, and scans them with astonish'd eye,
   As unfamiliar with their aged pile.

Awful, august, magnificent, they tower
   Amid the waste of shifting sands around;
The lapse of year and month and day and hour,
   Alike unfelt, perform th' unwearied round.

How often hath yon day-god's burning light,
   From the clear sapphire of his stainless heaven,
Bath'd their high peaks in noontide brilliance bright,
   Gilded at morn, and purpled them at even ! [4]

## THE DRUID'S PROPHECIES [5]

Perhaps suggested by Cowper's ' Boadicea,' but longer and more elaborate, and here and there hardly inferior to that poem.

MONA ! with flame thine oaks are streaming,
   Those sacred oaks we rear'd on high :
Lo ! Mona, Lo ! the swords are gleaming
   Adown thine hills confusedly.

Hark ! Mona, Hark ! the chargers' neighing !
   The clang of arms and helmets bright !
The crash of steel, the dreadful braying
   Of trumpets thro' the madd'ning fight !

Exalt your torches, raise your voices;
   Your thread is spun — your day is brief;
Yea ! Howl for sorrow ! Rome rejoices,
   But Mona — Mona bends in grief !

But woe to Rome, though now she raises
   Yon eagles of her haughty power;
Though now her sun of conquest blazes,
   Yet soon shall come her darkening hour !

Woe, woe to him who sits in glory,
   Enthroned on thine hills of pride !
Can he not see the poignard gory,
   With his best heart's-blood deeply dyed ?

Ah ! what avails his gilded palace,
   Whose wings the seven-hill'd town enfold ? [6]
The costly bath, the chrystal chalice ?
   The pomp of gems — the glare of gold ?

See where, by heartless anguish driven,
   Crownless he creeps 'mid circling thorns; [7]
Around him flash the bolts of heaven,
   And angry earth before him yawns. [8]

veste ferali, crinibus dejectis, faces præferebant. Druidæque circum, preces diras, sublatis ad cœlum manibus, fundentes,' etc. — TACIT. *Annal.* xiv. c. 30.
[6] Pliny says, that the golden palace of Nero extended all round the city.
[7] ' Ut ad diverticulum ventum est, dimissis equis inter fruticeta ac vepres, per arundineti semitam ægre, nec nisi strata sub pedibus veste, ad adversum villæ parietem evasit.' — SUETON. *Vit. Cæsar.*
[8] ' Statimque tremore terræ, et fulgure adverso pavefactus, audiit ex proximis castris clamorem,' etc. — *Ibid.*

Then, from his pinnacle of splendour,
The feeble king,[1] with locks of grey,
Shall fall, and sovereign Rome shall render
Her sceptre to the usurper's[2] sway.

Who comes with sounds of mirth and gladness,
Triumphing o'er the prostrate dead?[3]
Ay, me! thy mirth shall change to sadness,
When Vengeance strikes thy guilty head.

Above thy noon-day feast suspended,
High hangs in air a naked sword:
Thy days are gone, thy joys are ended,
The cup, the song, the festal board.

Then shall the eagle's shadowy pinion
Be spread beneath the eastern skies;[4]
And dazzling far with wide dominion,
Five brilliant stars shall brightly rise.[5]

Then, coward king![6] the helpless aged
Shall bow beneath thy dastard blow;
But reckless hands and hearts, enraged,
By double fate shall lay thee low.[7]

And two,[8] with death-wounds deeply mangled,
Low on their parent-earth shall lie;
Fond wretches! ah! too soon entangled
Within the snares of royalty.

Then comes that mighty one victorious
In triumph o'er this earthly ball,[9]
Exulting in his conquests glorious —
Ah! glorious to his country's fall!

But thou shalt see the Romans flying,
O Albyn! with yon dauntless ranks;[10]
And thou shalt view the Romans dying,
Blue Carun! on thy mossy banks.

But lo! what dreadful visions o'er me
Are bursting on this aged eye!
What length of bloody train before me,
In slow succession passes by![11]

Thy hapless monarchs fall together,
Like leaves in winter's stormy ire;
Some by the sword, and some shall wither
By light'ning's flame and fever's fire.[12]

They come! they leave their frozen regions,
Where Scandinavia's wilds extend;
And Rome, though girt with dazzling legions,
Beneath their blasting power shall bend.

Woe, woe to Rome! though tall and ample
She rears her domes of high renown;
Yet fiery Goths shall fiercely trample
The grandeur of her temples down!

She sinks to dust; and who shall pity
Her dark despair and hopeless groans?
There is a wailing in her city —
Her babes are dash'd against the stones!

Then, Mona! then, though wan and blighted
Thy hopes be now by Sorrow's dearth,
Then all thy wrongs shall be requited —
The Queen of Nations bows to earth!

## THE EXPEDITION OF NADIR SHAH INTO HINDOSTAN

'Quoi! vous allez combattre un roi, dont la puissance
Semble forcer le ciel de prendre sa défense,
Sous qui toute l'Asie a vu tomber ses rois
Et qui tient la fortune attachée à ses lois!'
RACINE's *Alexandre.*

'Squallent populatibus agri.' — CLAUDIAN.

As the host of the locusts in numbers, in might
As the flames of the forest that redden the
night,
They approach: but the eye may not dwell on
the glare
Of standard and sabre that sparkle in air.

Like the fiends of destruction they rush on their
way,
The vulture behind them is wild for his prey;
And the spirits of death, and the demons of
wrath,
Wave the gloom of their wings o'er their desolate path.

Earth trembles beneath them, the dauntless,
the bold.
Oh! weep for thy children, thou region of
gold;[13]
For thy thousands are bow'd to the dust of the
plain,
And all Delhi runs red with the blood of her
slain.

[1] Galba.  [2] Otho.
[3] 'Utque campos, in quibus pugnatum est, adiit (*i. e.*
Vitellius) plurimum meri propalam hausit,' etc.— SUET.
[4] At the siege of Jerusalem.
[5] The five good Emperors: Nerva, Trajan, Adrian,
Antoninus Pius, and Marcus Aurelius, or Antoninus the
Philosopher.  Perhaps the best commentary on the life
and virtues of the last, is his own volume of *Medita-*
*tions.*
[6] 'Debiles pedibus, et eos, qui ambulare non possent,
in gigantum modum, ita ut a genibus de pannis et lin-
teis quasi dracones digererentur; eosdemque sagittis
confecit.' — ÆL. LAMPRID. *in Vita Comm.* — Such were
the laudable amusements of Commodus!
[7] He was first poisoned; but the operation not fully
answering the wishes of his beloved, he was afterwards
strangled by a robust wrestler.
[8] Pertinax and Didius Julian.
[9] Severus, who was equally victorious in the Eastern
and Western World: but those conquests, however glorious, were conducive to the ruin of the Roman Empire.
— See GIBBON, vol. vi. chap. v. p. 203.
[10] In allusion to the real or feigned victory obtained
by Fingal over Caracul or Caracalla. — See OSSIAN.
[11] Very few of the Emperors after Severus escaped
assassination.
[12] Macrinus, Heliogabalus, Alexander, Maximin Pu-
pienus, Balbinus, Gordian, Philip, etc., were assassi-
nated; Claudius died of a pestilential fever; and Carus
was struck dead by lightning in his tent.
[13] This invader required as a ransom for Mohammed
Shah no less than thirty millions, and amassed in the
rich city of Delhi the enormous sum of two hundred
and thirty-one millions sterling.  Others, however, differ considerably in their account of this treasure.

For thy glory is past, and thy splendour is dim,
And the cup of thy sorrow is full to the brim;
And where is the chief in thy realms to abide,
The 'Monarch of Nations,'[1] the strength of his
  pride?

Like a thousand dark streams from the moun-
    tain they throng,
With the fife and the horn and the war-beating
    gong:
The land like an Eden before them is fair,
But behind them a wilderness dreary and bare.[2]

The shrieks of the orphan, the lone widow's
    wail,
The groans of the childless, are loud on the
    gale;
For the star of thy glory is blasted and wan,
And wither'd the flower of thy fame, Hindo-
    stan!

## THE MAID OF SAVOY

Down Savoy's hills of stainless white
A thousand currents run,
And sparkle bright in the early light
Of the slowly-rising sun:
    But brighter far,
    Like the glance of a star
    From regions above,
    Is the look of love
        In the eye of the Maid of Savoy!

Down Savoy's hills of lucid snow
A thousand roebucks leap,
And headlong they go when the bugles blow,
    And sound from steep to steep:
    But lighter far,
    Like the motion of air
    On the smooth river's bed,
    Is the noiseless tread
        Of the foot of the Maid of Savoy!

In Savoy's vales, with green array'd,
A thousand blossoms flower,
'Neath the odorous shade by the larches made,
In their own ambrosial bower:
    But sweeter still,
    Like the cedars which rise
    On Lebanon's hill
    To the pure blue skies,
        Is the breath of the Maid of Savoy!

In Savoy's groves full merrily sing
A thousand songsters gay,
When the breath of spring calls them forth on
    the wing,
To sport in the sun's mild ray:

[1] Such pompous epithets the Oriental writers are accustomed to bestow on their monarchs; of which sufficient specimens may be seen in Sir William Jones's translation of the History of Nadir Shah. We can scarcely read one page of this work without meeting with such sentences as these: 'Le roi de rois;' 'Les étendards qui subjuguent le monde;' 'L'âme rayon-

    But softer far,
    Like the holy song
    Of angels in air,
    When they sweep along,
        Is the voice of the Maid of Savoy!

## MIDNIGHT

'Tis midnight o'er the dim mere's lonely bosom,
  Dark, dusky, windy midnight: swift are
    driven
The swelling vapours onward: every blossom
  Bathes its bright petals in the tears of heaven.
Imperfect, half-seen objects meet the sight,
  The other half our fancy must pourtray;
A wan, dull, lengthen'd sheet of swimming
    light
Lies the broad lake: the moon conceals her ray,
Sketch'd faintly by a pale and lurid gleam
    Shot thro' the glimmering clouds: the lovely
      planet
Is shrouded in obscurity; the scream
  Of owl is silenc'd; and the rocks of granite
Rise tall and drearily, while damp and dank
Hang the thick willows on the reedy bank.
Beneath, the gurgling eddies slowly creep,
  Blacken'd by foliage; and the glutting wave,
That saps eternally the cold grey steep,
  Sounds heavily within the hollow cave.
All earth is restless — from his glossy wing[3]
  The heath-fowl lifts his head at intervals;
  Wet, driving, rainy, come the bursting squalls;
All nature wears her dun dead covering.
Tempest is gather'd, and the brooding storm
Spreads its black mantle o'er the mountain's
    form;
And, mingled with the rising roar, is swelling,
From the far hunter's booth, the blood hound's
    yelling.
The water-falls in various cadence chiming,
  Or in one loud unbroken sheet descending,
    Salute each other thro' the night's dark
      womb;
  The moaning pine-trees to the wild blast
    bending,
    Are pictured faintly thro' the chequer'd
      gloom;
The forests, half-way up the mountain climbing,
  Resound with crash of falling branches;
    quiver
  Their aged mossy trunks: the startled doe
Leaps from her leafy lair: the swelling river
  Winds his broad stream majestic, deep,
    and slow.

## SCOTCH SONG

In the reprint this is marked ' (?) ' but it is probably Alfred's. It is the only experiment in Scottish verse in the volume.

nante de sa majesté;' 'Le rayonnant monarque du monde;' 'Sa majesté conquérante du monde;' etc.

[2] 'The land is as the garden of Eden before them, and behind them a desolate wilderness.' — JOEL.

[3] The succeeding lines are a paraphrase of Ossian.

There are tears o' pity, an' tears o' wae,
An' tears for excess o' joy will fa' ;
*Yet the tears o' luve are sweeter than a' !*

There are sighs o' pity, an' sighs o' wae,
An' sighs o' regret frae the saul will gae;
*Yet the sighs o' luve are sweeter than a' !*

There 's the look o' pity, the look o' wae,
The look o' frien', an' the look o' fae;
*Yet the look o' luve is sweeter than a' !*

There 's the smile o' friends when they come
frae far,
There 's the smile o' joy in the festive ha' ;
*Yet the smile o' luve is sweeter than a' !*

## SONG

It is the solemn even-time,
And the holy organ 's pealing:
And the vesper chime, oh ! the vesper chime !
O'er the clear blue wave is stealing.

It is the solemn mingled swell
Of the monks in chorus singing:
And the vesper bell, oh ! the vesper bell !
To the gale is its soft note flinging.

'T is the sound of the voices sweeping along,
Like the wind thro' a grove of larches:
And the vesper song, oh ! the vesper song !
Echoes sad thro' the cloister'd arches.

## FRIENDSHIP

'Neque ego nunc de vulgari aut de mediocri, quæ
tamen ipsa et delectat et prodest, sed de vera et per-
fecta loquor (amicitia) qualis eorum, qui pauci nomi-
nantur, fuit.' — CICERO.

O thou most holy Friendship ! wheresoe'er
Thy dwelling be — for in the courts of man
But seldom thine all-heavenly voice we hear,
Sweet'ning the moments of our narrow span ;
And seldom thy bright foot-steps do we scan
Along the weary waste of life unblest,
For faithless is its frail and wayward plan,
And perfidy is man's eternal guest,
With dark suspicion link'd and shameless in-
terest ! —

'T is thine, when life has reach'd its final goal,
Ere the last sigh that frees the mind be giv'n,
To speak sweet solace to the parting soul,
And pave the bitter path that leads to heav'n:
'T is thine, whene'er the heart is rack'd and
riv'n
By the hot shafts of baleful calumny,
When the dark spirit to despair is driv'n,
To teach its lonely grief to lean on thee,
And pour within thine ear the tale of misery.

But where art thou, thou comet of an age,
Thou phœnix of a century ?  Perchance
Thou art but of those fables which engage
And hold the minds of men in giddy trance.
Yet, be it so, and be it all romance,
The thought of thine existence is so bright
With beautiful imaginings — the glance
Upon thy fancied being such delight,
That I will deem thee Truth, so lovely is thy
might !

## 'AND ASK YE WHY THESE SAD TEARS STREAM?'

' Te somnia nostra reducunt.'
OVID.

And ask ye why these sad tears stream ?
Why these wan eyes are dim with weep-
ing ?
I had a dream — a lovely dream,
Of her that in the grave is sleeping.

I saw her as 't was yesterday,
The bloom upon her cheek still glowing;
And round her play'd a golden ray,
And on her brows were gay flowers blowing.

With angel-hand she swept a lyre,
A garland red with roses bound it;
Its strings were wreath'd with lambent fire
And amaranth was woven round it.

I saw her mid the realms of light,
In everlasting radiance gleaming;
Co-equal with the seraphs bright,
Mid thousand thousand angels beaming.

I strove to reach her, when, behold,
Those fairy forms of bliss Elysian,
And all that rich scene wrapt in gold,
Faded in air — a lovely vision !

And I awoke, but oh ! to me
That waking hour was doubly weary;
And yet I could not envy thee,
Although so blest, and I so dreary.

## ON SUBLIMITY

One of the best of Alfred's early efforts.
Here, as in ' Persia,' the metrical management
of proper names is noteworthy.

' The sublime always dwells on great objects and terrible.'
BURKE.

O tell me not of vales in tenderest green,
The poplar's shade, the plantane's graceful
tree;
Give me the wild cascade, the rugged scene,
The loud surge bursting o'er the purple sea:

On such sad views my soul delights to pore,
  By Teneriffe's peak, or Kilda's giant height,
Or dark Loffoden's melancholy shore,
  What time grey eve is fading into night;
When by that twilight beam I scarce descry
The mingled shades of earth and sea and sky.

Give me to wander at midnight alone,
  Through some august cathedral, where, from
      high,
The cold, clear moon on the mosaic stone
  Comes glancing in gay colours gloriously,
Through windows rich with gorgeous blazonry,
  Gilding the niches dim, where, side by side,
Stand antique mitred prelates, whose bones lie
  Beneath the pavement, where their deeds of
      pride
Were graven, but long since are worn away
By constant feet of ages day by day.

Then, as Imagination aids, I hear
  Wild heavenly voices sounding from the
      quoir,
And more than mortal music meets mine ear,
  Whose long, long notes among the tombs ex-
      pire,
With solemn rustling of cherubic wings,
  Round those vast columns which the roof up-
      bear;
While sad and undistinguishable things
  Do flit athwart the moonlit windows there;
And my blood curdles at the chilling sound
Of lone, unearthly steps, that pace the hallow'd
      ground !

I love the starry spangled heav'n, resembling
  A canopy with fiery gems o'erspread,
When the wide loch with silvery sheen is trem-
      bling,
  Far stretch'd beneath the mountain's hoary
      head.
But most I love that sky, when, dark with
      storms,
  It frowns terrific o'er this wilder'd earth,
While the black clouds, in strange and uncouth
      forms,
  Come hurrying onward in their ruinous wrath;
And shrouding in their deep and gloomy robe
The burning eyes of heav'n and Dian's lucid
      globe !

I love your voice, ye echoing winds, that sweep
  Thro' the wide womb of midnight, when the
      veil
Of darkness rests upon the mighty deep,
  The labouring vessel, and the shatter'd sail —
Save when the forked bolts of lightning leap
On flashing pinions, and the mariner pale

Raises his eyes to heaven.  Oh !  who would
      sleep
  What time the rushing of the angry gale
Is loud upon the waters ? — Hail, all hail !
Tempest and clouds and night and thunder's
      rending peal !

All hail, Sublimity !  thou lofty one,
  For thou dost walk upon the blast, and gird
Thy majesty with terrors, and thy throne
  Is on the whirlwind, and thy voice is heard
In thunders and in shakings: thy delight
  Is in the secret wood, the blasted heath,
The ruin'd fortress, and the dizzy height,
  The grave, the ghastly charnel - house of
      death,
In vaults, in cloisters, and in gloomy piles,
Long corridors and towers and solitary aisles !

Thy joy is in obscurity, and plain
  Is nought with thee; and on thy steps attend
Shadows but half-distinguish'd; the thin train
  Of hovering spirits round thy pathway bend,
With their low tremulous voice and airy tread,[1]
  What time the tomb above them yawns and
      gapes:
For thou dost hold communion with the dead
  Phantoms and phantasies and grisly shapes;
And shades and headless spectres of Saint
      Mark,[2]
Seen by a lurid light, formless and still and
      dark !

What joy to view the varied rainbow smile
  On Niagara's flood of matchless might,
Where all around the melancholy isle [3]
  The billows sparkle with their hues of light !
While, as the restless surges roar and rave,
  The arrowy stream descends with awful
      sound,
Wheeling and whirling with each breathless
      wave,[4]
  Immense, sublime, magnificent, profound !
If thou hast seen all this, and could'st not feel,
Then know, thine heart is fram'd of marble or
      of steel.

The hurricane fair earth to darkness changing,
  Kentucky's chambers of eternal gloom,[5]
The swift-pac'd columns of the desert ranging
  Th' uneven waste, the violent Simoom,
Thy snow-clad peaks, stupendous Gungotree !
  Whence springs the hallow'd Jumna's echo-
      ing tide,
Hoar Cotopaxi's cloud-capt majesty,
  Enormous Chimborazo's naked pride,
The dizzy Cape of winds that cleaves the sky,[6]
Whence we look down into eternity,

---

[1] According to Burke, a low tremulous intermitted sound is conducive to the sublime.

[2] It is a received opinion, that on St. Mark's Eve all the persons who are to die on the following year make their appearances without their heads in the churches of their respective parishes. — See DR. LANGHORNE's *Notes to Collins.*

[3] This island, on both sides of which the waters rush with astonishing swiftness, is 900 or 800 feet long, and its lower edge is just at the perpendicular edge of the fall.

[4] ' Undis Phlegethon perlustrat ANHELIS.' — CLAU-DIAN.

[5] See Dr. Nahum Ward's account of the great Kentucky Cavern, in the *Monthly Magazine,* October, 1816.

[6] In the Ukraine.

The pillar'd cave of Morven's giant king,[1]
  The Yanar,[2] and the Geyser's boiling foun-
    tain,
The deep volcano's inward murmuring,
  The shadowy Colossus of the mountain;[3]
Antiparos, where sun-beams never enter;
  Loud Stromboli, amid the quaking isles;
The terrible Maelstroom, around his centre
  Wheeling his circuit of unnumber'd miles:
These, these are sights and sounds that freeze
    the blood,
Yet charm the awe-struck soul which doats on
    solitude.

Blest be the bard, whose willing feet rejoice
  To tread the emerald green of Fancy's vales,
Who hears the music of her heavenly voice,
  And breathes the rapture of her nectar'd
    gales!
Blest be the bard, whom golden Fancy loves,
  He strays for ever thro' her blooming bowers,
Amid the rich profusion of her groves,
  And wreathes his forehead with her spicy
    flowers
Of sunny radiance; but how blest is he
Who feels the genuine force of high Sublimity!


## THE DEITY

Signed 'A. T. or C. T.' in the reprint, but
Lord Tennyson believes, as I do, that Charles
wrote it.

'Immutable — immortal — infinite!' — MILTON.

WHERE is the wonderful abode,
  The holy, secret, searchless shrine,
Where dwells the immaterial God,
  The all-pervading and benign?

O! that he were reveal'd to me,
  Fully and palpably display'd
In all the awful majesty
  Of heaven's consummate pomp array'd —

How would the overwhelming light
  Of his tremendous presence beam!
And how insufferably bright
  Would the broad glow of glory stream!

What tho' this flesh would fade like grass,
  Before th' intensity of day?
One glance at Him who always was,
  The fiercest pangs would well repay.

When Moses on the mountain's brow
  Had met th' Eternal face to face,
While anxious Israel stood below,
  Wond'ring and trembling at its base;

[1] Fingal's Cave in the Island of Staffa.  If the Colossus of Rhodes bestrid a harbour, Fingal's powers were
certainly far from despicable: —

  A chos air Cromleach druim-ard
  Chos eile air Crommeal dubh
  Thoga Fion le lamh mhoir
  An d'uisge o Lubhair na fruth.

His visage, as he downward trod,
  Shone starlike on the shrinking crowd,
With lustre borrow'd from his God:
  They could not brook it, and they bow'd.

The mere reflection of the blaze
  That lighten'd round creation's Lord,
Was too puissant for their gaze;
  And he that caught it was ador'd.

Then how ineffably august,
  How passing wond'rous must He be,
Whose presence lent to earthly dust
  Such permanence of brilliancy!

Thron'd in sequester'd sanctity,
  And with transcendant glories crown'd;
With all his works beneath his eye,
  And suns and systems burning round, —

How shall I hymn him?  How aspire
  His holy Name with song to blend,
And bid my rash and feeble lyre
  To such an awless flight ascend?


## TIME: AN ODE

Remarkable for imagination and for versification as the work of a boy of sixteen.

I SEE the chariot, where,
Throughout the purple air,
  The forelock'd monarch rides:
Arm'd like some antique vehicle for war,
Time, hoary Time!  I see thy scythed car,
  In voiceless majesty,
Cleaving the clouds of ages that float by,
  And change their many-colour'd sides,
  Now dark, now dun, now richly bright,
    In an ever-varying light.
The great, the lowly, and the brave
  Bow down before the rushing force
    Of thine unconquerable course;
Thy wheels are noiseless as the grave,
Yet fleet as Heaven's red bolt they hurry on,
They pass above us, and are gone!

Clear is the track which thou hast past;
  Strew'd with the wrecks of frail renown,
  Robe, sceptre, banner, wreath, and crown,
    The pathway that before thee lies,
An undistinguishable waste,
    Invisible to human eyes,
  Which fain would scan the various shapes
      which glide
    In dusky cavalcade,
Imperfectly descried,
    Through  that  intense,  impenetrable
      shade.

    With one foot on Cromleach his brow,
    The other on Crommeal the dark,
    Fion took up with his large hand
    The water from Lubhair of streams.

See the Dissertations prefixed to Ossian's *Poems*.
  [2] Or, perpetual fire.
  [3] Alias, the Spectre of the Broken.

Four grey steeds thy chariot draw;
In th' obdurate, tameless jaw
  Their rusted iron bits they sternly champ;
  Ye may not hear the echoing tramp
    Of their light-bounding, windy feet,
    Upon that cloudy pavement beat.
Four wings have each, which, far outspread,
  Receive the many blasts of heav'n,
As with unwearied speed,
  Throughout the long extent of ether driven,
Onward they rush for ever and for aye:
  Thy voice, thou mighty Charioteer!
  Always sounding in their ear,
Throughout the gloom of night and heat of day.

Fast behind thee follows Death,
  Thro' the ranks of wan and weeping,
That yield their miserable breath,
  On with his pallid courser proudly sweeping.
Arm'd is he in full mail,[1]
  Bright breast-plate and high crest,
  Nor is the trenchant falchion wanting:
So fiercely does he ride the gale,
  On Time's dark car, before him, rest
  The dew-drops of his charger's panting.

On, on they go along the boundless skies,
  All human grandeur fades away
Before their flashing, fiery, hollow eyes;
    Beneath the terrible control
    Of those vast armed orbs, which roll
    Oblivion on the creatures of a day.
Those splendid monuments alone he spares,
  Which, to her deathless votaries,
Bright Fame, with glowing hand, uprears
Amid the waste of countless years.

' Live ye!' to these he crieth; ' live!
To ye eternity I give —
Ye, upon whose blessed birth
  The noblest star of heaven hath shone;
Live, when the ponderous pyramids of earth
  Are crumbling in oblivion!
Live, when, wrapt in sullen shade,
The golden hosts of heaven shall fade;
Live, when yon gorgeous sun on high
Shall veil the sparkling of his eye!
Live, when imperial Time and Death himself
  shall die!'

## GOD'S DENUNCIATIONS AGAINST PHARAOH–HOPHRA, OR APRIES

THOU beast of the flood, who hast said in thy
  soul,
'I have made me a stream that for ever shall
  roll!'[2]

---

[1] I am indebted for the idea of Death's Armour to
that famous Chorus in Caractacus beginning with —

  ' Hark! heard ye not that footstep dread?'

[2] ' Pliny's reproach to the Egyptians, for their vain
and foolish pride with regard to the inundations of the
Nile, points out one of their most distinguishing char-

Thy strength is the flower that shall last but a
  day,
And thy might is the snow in the sun's burning
  ray.

Arm, arm from the east, Babylonia's son!
Arm, arm for the battle — the Lord leads thee
  on!
With the shield of thy fame, and the power of
  thy pride,
Arm, arm in thy glory — the Lord is thy guide.

Thou shalt come like a storm when the moonlight is dim,
And the lake's gloomy bosom is full to the
  brim;
Thou shalt come like the flash in the darkness
  of night,
When the wolves of the forest shall howl for
  affright.

Woe, woe to thee, Tanis![3] thy babes shall be
  thrown
By the barbarous hands on the cold marble-
  stone:
Woe, woe to thee, Nile! for thy stream shall
  be red
With the blood that shall gush o'er thy billowy
  bed!

Woe, woe to thee, Memphis! the war-cry is
  near,
And the child shall be toss'd on the murderer's
  spear;
For fiercely he comes in the day of his ire,
With wheels like a whirlwind, and chariots of
  fire!

## THE GRAVE OF A SUICIDE

Perhaps incorrectly assigned to Alfred.

HARK! how the gale, in mournful notes and
  stern,
  Sighs thro' yon grove of aged oaks, that wave
(While down these solitary walks I turn)
    Their mingled branches o'er yon lonely
    grave!

Poor soul! the dawning of thy life was dim;
  Frown'd the dark clouds upon thy natal day;
Soon rose thy cup of sorrow to the brim,
  And hope itself but shed a doubtful ray.

That hope had fled, and all within was gloom;
  That hope had fled — thy woe to phrenzy
  grew;

---

acteristics, and recalls to my mind a fine passage of
Ezekiel, where God thus speaks to Pharaoh, one of their
kings: " Behold, I am against thee, Pharaoh king of
Egypt, the great dragon that lieth in the midst of his
rivers, that hath said, MY RIVER IS MINE OWN, AND I
HAVE MADE IT FOR MYSELF." ' — ROLLIN, vol. i. p. 216.

[3] The Scriptural appellations are ' Zoan ' and ' Noph.'

For thou, wed to misery from the womb —
  Scarce one bright scene thy night of darkness
    knew !

Oft when the moon-beam on the cold bank
    sleeps,
  Where 'neath the dewy turf thy form is laid,
In silent woe thy wretched mother weeps,
  By this lone tomb, and by this oak-tree's
    shade.

'Oh ! softly tread : in death he slumbers here;
  'T is here,' she cries, 'within his narrow
    cell ! ' —
The bitter sob, the wildly-starting tear,
  The quivering lip, proclaim the rest too well !


## THE WALK AT MIDNIGHT

'Tremulo sub lumine.' — VIRGIL.

Soft, shadowy moon-beam ! by thy light
  Sleeps the wide meer serenely pale :
How various are the sounds of night,
  Borne on the scarcely-rising gale !

The swell of distant brook is heard,
  Whose far-off waters faintly roll;
And piping of the shrill small bird,
  Arrested by the wand'ring owl.

Come hither ! let us thread with care
  The maze of this green path, which binds
The beauties of the broad parterre,
  And thro' yon fragrant alley winds.

Or on this old bench will we sit,
  Round which the clust'ring woodbine
    wreathes;
While birds of night around us flit;
  And thro' each lavish wood-walk breathes,

Unto my ravish'd senses, brought
  From yon thick-woven odorous bowers,
The still rich breeze, with incense fraught
  Of glowing fruits and spangled flowers.

The whispering leaves, the gushing stream,
  Where trembles the uncertain moon,
Suit more the poet's pensive dream,
  Than all the jarring notes of noon.

Then, to the thickly-crowded mart
  The eager sons of interest press;
Then, shine the tinsel works of art —
  Now, all is Nature's loneliness !

Then, wealth aloft in state displays
  The glittering of her gilded cars;
Now, dimly stream the mingled rays
  Of yon far-twinkling, silver stars.

Yon church, whose cold grey spire appears
  In the black outline of the trees,
Conceals the object of my tears,
  Whose form in dreams my spirit sees.

There in the chilling bed of earth,
  The chancel's letter'd stone above —
There sleepeth she who gave me birth,
  Who taught my lips the hymn of love !

Yon mossy stems of ancient oak,
  So widely crown'd with sombre shade,
Those ne'er have heard the woodman's stroke
  Their solemn, secret depths invade.

How oft the grassy way I 've trod
  That winds their knotty boles between,
And gather'd from the blooming sod
  The flowers that flourish'd there unseen !

Rise ! let us trace that path once more,
  While o'er our track the cold beams shine;
Down this low shingly vale, and o'er
  Yon rude rough bridge of prostrate pine.


## MITHRIDATES PRESENTING BERE-NICE WITH THE CUP OF POISON

Oh ! Berenice, lorn and lost,
  This wretched soul with shame is bleed-
    ing :
Oh ! Berenice, I am tost
  By griefs, like wave to wave succeeding.

Fall'n Pontus ! all her fame is gone,
  And dim the splendour of her glory;
Low in the west her evening sun,
  And dark the lustre of her story.

Dead is the wreath that round her brow
  The glowing hands of Honour braided;
What change of fate can wait her now,
  Her sceptre spoil'd, her throne degraded ?

And wilt thou, wilt thou basely go,
  My love, thy life, thy country shaming,
In all the agonies of woe,
  Mid madd'ning shouts, and standards flam-
    ing ?

And wilt thou, wilt thou basely go,
  Proud Rome's triumphal car adorning ?
Hark ! hark !  I hear thee answer ' No !'
  The proffer'd life of thraldom scorning.

Lone, crownless, destitute, and poor,
  My heart with bitter pain is burning;
So thick a cloud of night hangs o'er,
  My daylight into darkness turning.

Yet though my spirit, bow'd with ill,
  Small hope from future fortune borrows;
One glorious thought shall cheer me still,
  That thou art free from abject sorrows —

Art free for ever from the strife
  Of slavery's pangs and tearful anguish;
For life is death, and death is life,
  To those whose limbs in fetters languish.

Fill high the bowl ! the draught is thine !
  The Romans ! — now thou need'st not heed
    them !
'T is nobler than the noblest wine —
  It gives thee back to fame and freedom !

The scalding tears my cheek bedew;
  My life, my love, my all — we sever !
One last embrace, one long adieu,
  And then farewell — farewell for ever !

In reality Mithridates had no personal interview with
Monima and Berenice before the deaths of those prin-
cesses, but only sent his eunuch Bacchidas to signify
his intention that they should die.  I have chosen
Berenice as the more general name, though Monima
was his peculiar favourite.

## THE OLD CHIEFTAIN

' And said I, that my limbs were old ! ' — SCOTT.

RAISE, raise the song of the hundred shells !
  Though my hair is grey and my limbs are
    cold;
Yet in my bosom proudly dwells
  The memory of the days of old;

When my voice was high, and my arm was
    strong,
  And the foeman before my stroke would bow,
And I could have rais'd the sounding song
  As loudly as I hear ye now.

For when I have chanted the bold song of
    death,
  Not a page would have stay'd in the hall,
Not a lance in the rest, not a sword in the
    sheath,
  Not a shield on the dim grey wall.

And who might resist the united powers
  Of battle and music that day,
When, all martiall'd in arms on the heaven-
    kissing towers,
  Stood the chieftains in peerless array ?

When our enemies sunk from our eyes as the
    snow
  Which falls down the stream in the dell,
When each word that I spake was the death of
    a foe,
  And each note of my harp was his knell ?

So raise ye the song of the hundred shells;
  Though my hair is grey and my limbs are
    cold,
Yet in my bosom proudly dwells
  The memory of the days of old !

## THE FALL OF JERUSALEM

JERUSALEM ! Jerusalem !
  Thou art low ! thou mighty one,
How is the brilliance of thy diadem,
  How is the lustre of thy throne

Rent from thee, and thy sun of fame
  Darken'd by the shadowy pinion
    Of the Roman bird, whose sway
    All the tribes of earth obey,
  Crouching 'neath his dread dominion,
And the terrors of his name !

How is thy royal seat — whereon
    Sate in days of yore
Lowly Jesse's godlike son,
And the strength of Solomon,
  In those rich and happy times
    When the ships from Tarshish bore
    Incense, and from Ophir's land,
    With silken sail and cedar oar,
    Wafting to Judea's strand
  All the wealth of foreign climes —
How is thy royal seat o'erthrown !
  Gone is all thy majesty:
    Salem ! Salem ! city of kings,
  Thou sittest desolate and lone,
    Where once the glory of the Most High
    Dwelt visibly enshrin'd between the wings
Of Cherubims, within whose bright embrace
    The golden mercy-seat remain'd:
Land of Jehovah ! view that sacred place
  Abandon'd and profan'd !

Wail ! fallen Salem ! Wail:
    Mohammed's votaries pollute thy fane;
The dark division of thine holy veil
    Is rent in twain !
Thrice hath Sion's crowned rock
  Seen thy temple's marble state,
    Awfully, serenely great,
    Towering on his sainted brow,
    Rear its pinnacles of snow:
Thrice, with desolating shock,
    Down to earth hath seen it driv'n
    From his heights, which reach to heaven !

Wail, fallen Salem ! Wail:
    Though not one stone above another
There was left to tell the tale
    Of the greatness of thy story,
    Yet the long lapse of ages cannot smother
    The blaze of thine abounding glory;
Which thro' the mist of rolling years,
O'er history's darken'd page appears,
Like the morning star, whose gleam
  Gazeth thro' the waste of night,
What time old ocean's purple stream
    In his cold surge hath deeply lav'd
    Its ardent front of dewy light.
    Oh !  who shall e'er forget thy bands,
      which brav'd
The terrors of the desert's barren reign,
And that strong arm which broke the chain
  Wherein ye foully lay enslav'd,
  Or that sublime Theocracy which pav'd
Your way thro' ocean's vast domain,
And on, far on to Canaan's emerald plain
    Led the Israelitish crowd
    With a pillar and a cloud ?

Signs on earth and signs on high
Prophesied thy destiny;

A trumpet's voice above thee rung,
A starry sabre o'er thee hung;
Visions of fiery armies, redly flashing
In the many-colour'd glare
Of the setting orb of day;
And flaming chariots, fiercely dashing,
Swept along the peopled air,
In magnificent array:
The temple doors, on brazen hinges crashing,
Burst open with appalling sound,
A wond'rous radiance streaming round !

' Our blood be on our heads ! ' ye said:
Such your awless imprecation:
Full bitterly at length 't was paid
Upon your captive nation !
Arms of adverse legions bound thee,
Plague and pestilence stood round thee;
Seven weary suns had brighten'd Syria's sky,
Yet still was heard th' unceasing cry —
From south, north, east, and west, a voice,
' Woe unto thy sons and daughters !
Woe to Salem ! thou art lost ! '
A sound divine
Came from the sainted, secret, inmost shrine:
' Let us go hence ! ' — and then a noise —
The thunders of the parting Deity,
Like the rush of countless waters,
Like the murmur of a host !

Though now each glorious hope be blighted,
Yet an hour shall come, when ye,
Though scatter'd like the chaff, shall be
Beneath one standard once again united;
When your wandering race shall own,
Prostrate at the dazzling throne
Of your high Almighty Lord,
The wonders of his searchless word,
Th' unfading splendours of his Son !

## LAMENTATION OF THE PERU-VIANS

THE foes of the east have come down on our shore,
And the state and the strength of Peru are no more:
Oh ! curs'd, doubly curs'd, was that desolate hour,
When they spread o'er our land in the pride of their power !
Lament for the Inca, the son of the Sun;
Ataliba 's fallen — Peru is undone !

Pizarro ! Pizarro ! though conquest may wing
Her course round thy banners that wanton in air;
Yet remorse to thy grief-stricken conscience shall cling,
And shriek o'er thy banquets in sounds of despair.
It shall tell thee, that he who beholds from his throne
The blood thou hast spilt and the deeds thou hast done,

Shall mock at thy fear, and rejoice at thy groan,
And arise in his wrath for the death of his son !
Why blew ye, ye gales, when the murderer came ?
Why fann'd ye the fire, and why fed ye the flame ?
Why sped ye his sails o'er the ocean so blue ?
Are ye also combin'd for the fall of Peru ?
And thou, whom no prayers, no entreaties can bend,
Thy crimes and thy murders to heav'n shall ascend:
For vengeance the ghosts of our forefathers call;
At thy threshold, Pizarro, in death shalt thou fall !
Ay there — even there in the halls of thy pride,
With the blood of thine heart shall thy portals be dyed !

Lo ! dark as the tempests that frown from the north,
From the cloud of past time Manco Capac looks forth —
Great Inca ! to whom the gay day-star gave birth,
Whose throne is the heaven, and whose footstool the earth —
His visage is sad as the vapours that rise
From the desolate mountain of fire to the skies;
But his eye flashes flame as the lightnings that streak
Those volumes that shroud the volcano's high peak.
Hark ! he speaks — bids us fly to our mountains, and cherish
Bold freedom's last spark ere for ever it perish;
Bids us leave these wild condors to prey on each other,
Each to bathe his fierce beak in the gore of his brother !
This symbol we take of our godhead the Sun,
And curse thee and thine for the deeds thou hast done.
May the curses pursue thee of those thou hast slain,
Of those that have fallen in war on the plain,
When we went forth to greet ye — but foully ye threw
Your dark shots of death on the sons of Peru.
May the curse of the widow — the curse of the brave —
The curse of the fatherless, cleave to thy grave !
And the words which they spake with their last dying breath,
Embitter the pangs and the tortures of death !

May he that assists thee be childless and poor,
With famine behind him, and death at his door:
May his nights be all sleepless, his days spent alone,
And ne'er may he list to a voice but his own !
Or, if he shall sleep, in his dreams may he view
The ghost of our Inca, the fiends of Peru:

May the flames of destruction that here he has
  spread
Be tenfold return'd on his murderous head !

## 'THE SUN GOES DOWN IN THE DARK BLUE MAIN'

' Irreparabile tempus.' — VIRGIL.

THE sun goes down in the dark blue main,
  To rise the brighter to-morrow;
But oh ! what charm can restore again
  Those days now consign'd to sorrow ?

The moon goes down on the calm still night,
  To rise sweeter than when she parted;
But oh ! what charm can restore the light
  Of joy to the broken-hearted ?

The blossoms depart in the wintry hour,
  To rise in vernal glory;
But oh ! what charm can restore the flower
  Of youth to the old and hoary ?

## ON A DEAD ENEMY

' Non odi mortuum.' — CICERO.

I CAME in haste with cursing breath,
  And heart of hardest steel;
But when I saw thee cold in death,
  I felt as man should feel.

For when I look upon that face,
  That cold, unheeding, frigid brow,
Where neither rage nor fear has place,
  By Heaven ! I cannot hate thee now !

## THE DUKE OF ALVA'S OBSERVATION ON KINGS [1]

KINGS, when to private audience they descend,
  And make the baffled courtier their prey,
Do use an orange, as they treat a friend —
  Extract the juice, and cast the rind away.

When thou art favour'd by thy sovereign's eye,
  Let not his glance thine inmost thoughts discover;
Or he will scan thee through, and lay thee by,
  Like some old book which he has read all
    over.

## 'AH ! YES, THE LIP MAY FAINTLY SMILE'

Signed ' A. T. (?) ' in the reprint, and probably not Alfred's.

AH ! yes, the lip may faintly smile,
The eye may sparkle for a while;
But never from that wither'd heart
The consciousness of ill shall part !

That glance, that smile of passing light,
Are as the rainbow of the night;
But seldom seen, it dares to bloom
Upon the bosom of the gloom.

Its tints are sad and coldly pale,
Dim-glimmering thro' their misty veil;
Unlike the ardent hues which play
Along the flowery bow of day.

The moon-beams sink in dark-rob'd shades,
Too soon the airy vision fades;
And double night returns, to shroud
The volumes of the showery cloud.

## 'THOU CAMEST TO THY BOWER, MY LOVE, ACROSS THE MUSKY GROVE'

' Virgo egregia forma.' — TERENCE.

THOU camest to thy bower, my love, across the
    musky grove,
To fan thy blooming charms within the coolness
    of the shade;
Thy locks were like a midnight cloud with silver moon-beams wove,[2]
And o'er thy face the varying tints of youthful
    passion play'd.

Thy breath was like the sandal-wood that casts
    a rich perfume,
Thy blue eyes mock'd the lotos in the noon-day
    of his bloom;
Thy cheeks were like the beamy flush that gilds
    the breaking day,
And in th' ambrosia of thy smiles the god of
    rapture lay.[3]

Fair as the cairba-stone art thou, that stone of
    dazzling white,[4]
Ere yet unholy fingers chang'd its milk-white
    hue to night;
And lovelier than the loveliest glance from
    Even's placid star,
And brighter than the sea of gold,[5] the gorgeous
    Himsagar.

In high Mohammed's boundless heaven Al Cawthor's stream may play,
The fount of youth may sparkling gush beneath the western ray;[6]
And Tasnim's wave in chrystal cups may glow
    with musk and wine,
But oh ! their lustre could not match one beauteous tear of thine !

---

[1] See D'Israeli's *Curiosities of Literature*.
[2] A simile elicited from the songs of Jayadeva, the Horace of India.
[3] Vide Horace's ODE — ' Pulchris EXCUBAT in genis.'

[4] Vide Sale's *Koran*.
[5] See Sir William Jones on Eastern Plants.
[6] The fabled fountain of youth in the Bahamas, in search of which Juan Ponce de Leon discovered Florida.

## THE PASSIONS

'You have passions in your heart — scorpions; they sleep now — beware how you awaken them! they will sting you even to death!' — *Mysteries of Udolpho*, vol. iii.

BEWARE, beware, ere thou takest
  The draught of misery!
Beware, beware, e'er thou wakest
  The scorpions that sleep in thee!

The woes which thou canst not number,
  As yet are wrapt in sleep;
Yet oh! yet they slumber,
  But their slumbers are not deep.

Yet oh! yet while the rancour
  Of hate has no place in thee,
While thy buoyant soul has an anchor
  In youth's bright tranquil sea:

Yet oh! yet while the blossom
  Of hope is blooming fair,
While the beam of bliss lights thy bosom —
  O! rouse not the serpent there!

For bitter thy tears will trickle
  'Neath misery's heavy load,
When the world has put in its sickle
  To the crop which fancy sow'd.

When the world has rent the cable
  That bound thee to the shore,
And launched thee weak and unable
  To bear the billow's roar;

Then the slightest touch will waken
  Those pangs that will always grieve thee,
And thy soul will be fiercely shaken
  With storms that will never leave thee!

So beware, beware, ere thou takest
  The draught of misery!
Beware, beware, ere thou wakest
  The scorpions that sleep in thee!

## THE HIGH-PRIEST TO ALEXANDER

' Derrame en todo el orbe de la tierra
  Las armas, el furor, y nueva guerra.'
      *La Araucana*, cant. xvi.

Go forth, thou man of force!
  The world is all thine own;
Before thy dreadful course
  Shall totter every throne.
Let India's jewels glow
  Upon thy diadem:
Go, forth to conquest go,
  But spare Jerusalem.
    For the God of gods, which liveth
      Through all eternity,
    'T is he alone which giveth
      And taketh victory:

'T is he the bow that blasteth,
  And breaketh the proud one's quiver;
And the Lord of armies resteth
  In his Holy of Holies for ever!

For God is Salem's spear,
  And God is Salem's sword;
What mortal man shall dare
  To combat with the Lord?
Every knee shall bow
  Before his awful sight;
Every thought sink low
  Before the Lord of might.
    For the God of gods, which liveth
      Through all eternity,
    'T is he alone which giveth
      And taketh victory:
    'T is he the bow that blasteth,
      And breaketh the proud one's quiver;
    And the Lord of armies resteth
      In his Holy of Holies for ever!

## ON THE MOON-LIGHT SHINING UPON A FRIEND'S GRAVE

Signed ' A. T. (?),' and probably Charles's.

SHOW not, O Moon! with pure and liquid beam,
  That mournful spot, where Memory fears to tread;
Glance on the grove, or quiver in the stream,
  Or tip the hills — but shine not on the dead:
It wounds the lonely hearts that still survive,
And after bury'd friends are doom'd to live.

## A CONTRAST

DOST ask why Laura's soul is riven
  By pangs her prudence can't command?
To one who heeds not she has giv'n
  Her *heart*, alas! *without her hand*.

But Chloe claims our sympathy,
  To wealth a martyr and a slave;
For when the knot she dar'd to tie,
  *Her hand without her heart she gave.*

## THE DYING CHRISTIAN

Signed ' A. T. or C. T.,' but quite certainly Charles's, as Lord Tennyson tells me that he also thinks.

' It cannot die, it cannot stay,
  But leaves its darken'd dust behind.'
                    BYRON.

I DIE — my limbs with icy feeling
  Bespeak that Death is near;
His frozen hand each pulse is stealing;
  Yet still I do not fear!

There is a hope — not frail as that
  Which rests on human things —

The hope of an immortal state,
    And with the King of kings !

And ye may gaze upon my brow,
    Which is not sad, tho' pale;
These hope-illumin'd features show
    But little to bewail.

Death should not chase the wonted bloom
    From off the Christian's face;
Ill prelude of the bliss to come,
    · Prepar'd by heavenly grace.

Lament no more — no longer weep
    That I depart from men;
Brief is the intermediate sleep,
    And bliss awaits me then !

### 'HOW GAILY SINKS THE GOR-GEOUS SUN WITHIN HIS GOLD-EN BED'

These lines are signed ' A. T. (?),' and may be safely assigned to Charles.

> 'Tu fais naître la lumière
> Du sein de l'obscurité.'
>                     ROUSSEAU.

How gaily sinks the gorgeous sun within his
    golden bed,
As heaven's immortal azure glows and deepens
    into red !
How gaily shines the burnish'd main beneath
    that living light,
And trembles with his million waves magnifi-
    cently bright !
But ah ! how soon that orb of day must close
    his burning eye,
And night, in sable pall array'd, involve yon
    lovely sky !
E'en thus in life our fairest scenes are preludes
    to our woe;
For fleeting as that glorious beam is happiness
    below.
But what ? though evil fates may frown upon
    our mortal birth,
Yet Hope shall be the star that lights our night
    of grief on earth:
And she shall point to sweeter morns, when
    brighter suns shall rise,
And spread the radiance of their rays o'er earth,
    and sea, and skies !

### 'OH ! YE WILD WINDS, THAT ROAR AND RAVE'

' It is the great army of the dead returning on the
    northern blast.'
        SONG OF THE FIVE BARDS IN OSSIAN.

OH ! ye wild winds, that roar and rave
    Around the headland's stormy brow,
That toss and heave the Baltic wave,
    And bid the sounding forest bow,

Whence is your course ? and do ye bear
    The sighs of other worlds along,
When through the dark immense of air
    Ye rush in tempests loud and strong ?

Methinks, upon your moaning course
    I hear the army of the dead;
Each on his own invisible horse,
    Triumphing in his trackless tread.

For when the moon conceals her ray,
    And midnight spreads her darkest veil,
Borne on the air, and far away,
    Upon the eddying blasts they sail.

Then, then their thin and feeble bands
    Along the echoing winds are roll'd;
The bodyless tribes of other lands !
    The formless, misty sons of old !

And then at times their wailings rise,
    The shrilly wailings of the grave !
And mingle with the madden'd skies,
    The rush of wind, and roar of wave.

Heard you that sound ?  It was the hum
    Of the innumerable host,
As down the northern sky they come,
    Lamenting o'er their glories lost.

Now for a space each shadowy king,
    Who sway'd of old some mighty realm,
Mounts on the tempest's squally wing,
    And grimly frowns thro' barred helm.

Now each dim ghost, with awful yells,
    Uprears on high his cloudy form;
And with his feeble accent swells
    The hundred voices of the storm.

Why leave ye thus the narrow cell,
    Ye lords of night and anarchy !
Your robes the vapours of the dell.
    Your swords the meteors of the sky ?

Your bones are whitening on the heath;
    Your fame is in the minds of men:
And would ye break the sleep of death,
    That ye might live to war again ?

### SWITZERLAND

Signed ' A. T. (?),' and I am inclined to be-lieve the poem Charles's, though Mr. Shepherd. in his ' Tennysoniana,' compares the closing lines with ' The red fool-fury of the Seine ' in ' In Memoriam.'

> ' Tous les objets de mon amour,
> Nos clairs ruisseaux,
> Nos hameaux,
> Nos coteaux,
> Nos montagnes ? '
>                     RANZ DES VACHES.

WITH Memory's eye,
Thou land of joy !
    I view thy cliffs once more;

And tho' thy plains
Red slaughter stains,
   'T is Freedom's blessed gore.

Thy woody dells,
And shadowy fells,
   Exceed a monarch's halls;
Thy pine-clad hills,
And gushing rills,
   And foaming water-falls.

The Gallic foe
Has work'd thee woe,
   But trumpet never scar'd thee;
How could he think
That thou would'st shrink,
   With all thy rocks to guard thee?

E'en now the Gaul,
That wrought thy fall,
   At his own triumph wonders;
So long the strife
For death and life,
   So loud our rival thunders!

O! when shall Time
Avenge the crime,
   And to our rights restore us?
And bid the Seine
Be chok'd with slain,
   And Paris quake before us?

## BABYLON

'Come down, and sit in the dust, O virgin daughter of Babylon; sit on the ground : there is no throne.' — ISAIAH xlvii. 1.

Bow, daughter of Babylon, bow thee to dust!
Thine heart shall be quell'd, and thy pride shall be crush'd:
Weep, Babylon, weep! for thy splendour is past;
And they come like the storm in the day of the blast.

Howl, desolate Babylon, lost one and lone!
And bind thee in sack-cloth — for where is thy throne?
Like a wine-press in wrath will I trample thee down,
And rend from thy temples the pride of thy crown.

Though thy streets be a hundred, thy gates be all brass,
Yet thy proud ones of war shall be wither'd like grass;
Thy gates shall be broken, thy strength be laid low,
And thy streets shall resound to the shouts of the foe!

[1] 'Arise, ye princes, and anoint the shield.' — ISAIAH xxi. 5.
[2] 'I will make drunk her princes.' — JEREMIAH li. 57.
[3] 'The mountains melted from before the Lord.' — JUDG. v. 5. 'Oh! that the mountains might flow down

Though thy chariots of power on thy battlements bound,
And the grandeur of waters encompass thee round;
Yet thy walls shall be shaken, thy waters shall fail,
Thy matrons shall shriek, and thy king shall be pale.

The terrible day of thy fall is at hand,
When my rage shall descend on the face of thy land;
The lances are pointed, the keen sword is bar'd,
The shields are anointed,[1] the helmets prepar'd.

I call upon Cyrus! He comes from afar,
And the armies of nations are gather'd to war;
With the blood of thy children his path shall be red,
And the bright sun of conquest shall blaze o'er his head!

Thou glory of kingdoms! thy princes are drunk,[2]
But their loins shall be loos'd, and their hearts shall be sunk;
They shall crouch to the dust, and be counted as slaves,
At the roll of his wheels, like the rushing of waves!

For I am the Lord, who have mightily spann'd
The breadth of the heavens, and the sea and the land;
And the mountains shall flow at my presence,[3] and earth
Shall reel to and fro in the glance of my wrath!

Your proud domes of cedar on earth shall be thrown,
And the rank grass shall wave o'er the lonely hearthstone;
And your sons and your sires and your daughters shall bleed
By the barbarous hands of the murdering Mede!

I will sweep ye away in destruction and death,
As the whirlwind that scatters the chaff with its breath;
And the fanes of your gods shall be sprinkled with gore,
And the course of your stream shall be heard of no more![4]

There the wandering Arab shall ne'er pitch his tent,
But the beasts of the desert shall wail and lament;
In their desolate houses the dragons shall lie,
And the satyrs shall dance, and the bittern shall cry![5]

at thy presence.' — ISAIAH lxiv. 1. And again, ver. 3, 'The mountains flowed down at thy presence.'
[4] 'A drought is upon her waters.' — JEREMIAH l. 38.
[5] Vide ISAIAH xiii. 20.

## LOVE

### I

ALMIGHTY Love! whose nameless power
  This glowing heart defines too well,
Whose presence cheers each fleeting hour,
  Whose silken bonds our souls compel,
  Diffusing such a sainted spell,

As gilds our being with the light
  Of transport and of rapturous bliss,
And almost seeming to unite
  The joys of other worlds to this,
  The heavenly smile, the rosy kiss; —

Before whose blaze my spirits shrink,
  My senses all are wrapt in thee,
Thy force I own too much, to think
  (So full, so great thine ecstasy)
  That thou art less than deity!

Thy golden chains embrace the land,
  The starry sky, the dark blue main;
And at the voice of thy command,
  (So vast, so boundless is thy reign)
  All nature springs to life again!

### II

The glittering fly, the wondrous things
  That microscopic art descries;
The lion of the waste, which springs,
  Bounding upon his enemies;
The mighty sea-snake of the storm,
The vorticella's viewless form,[1]

The vast leviathan, which takes
  His pastime in the sounding floods;
The crafty elephant, which makes
  His haunts in Ceylon's spicy woods —
Alike confess thy magic sway,
Thy soul-enchanting voice obey!

O! whether thou, as bards have said,
  Of bliss or pain the partial giver,
Wingest thy shaft of pleasing dread
  From out thy well-stor'd golden quiver,
O'er earth thy cherub wings extending,
Thy sea-born mother's side attending; —

Or else, as Indian fables say,
  Upon thine emerald lory riding,
Through gardens, mid the restless play
  Of fountains, in the moon-beam gliding,
Mid sylph-like shapes of maidens dancing,
Thy scarlet standard high advancing; —

Thy fragrant bow of cane thou bendest,[2]
  Twanging the string of honey'd bees,
And thence the flower-tipp'd arrow sendest,
  Which gives or robs the heart of ease;
Camdeo, or Cupid, O be near,
To listen, and to grant my prayer!

[1] See BAKER on Animalculæ.
[2] See Sir WILLIAM JONES'S WORKS, vol. vi. p. 313.

## SONG

To sit beside a chrystal spring,
Cool'd by the passing zephyr's wing,
And bend my every thought to thee,
Is life, is bliss, is ecstacy!

And as within that spring I trace
Each line, each feature of my face;
The faithful mirror tells me true —
It tells me that I think of *you!*

## EXHORTATION TO THE GREEKS

'En illa, illa quam sæpe optastis, libertas!'
              SALLUST.

AROUSE thee, O Greece! and remember the
  day,
When the millions of Xerxes were quell'd on
  their way!
Arouse thee, O Greece! let the pride of thy
  name
Awake in thy bosom the light of thy fame!
Why hast thou shone in the temple of glory?
  Why hast thou blaz'd in those annals of fame?
For know, that the former bright page of thy
  story
  Proclaims but thy bondage and tells but thy
    shame:
Proclaims from how high thou art fallen — how
  low
Thou art plung'd in the dark gulf of thraldom
  and woe!
Arouse thee, O Greece! from the weight of thy
  slumbers!
  The chains are upon thee! — arise from thy
    sleep!
Remember the time, when nor nations nor num-
  bers
  Could break thy thick phalanx embodied and
    deep.
Old Athens and Sparta remember the morning,
  When the swords of the Grecians were red to
    the hilt;
And, the bright gem of conquest her chaplet
  adorning,
Platæa rejoic'd at the blood that ye spilt!
Remember the night, when, in shrieks of af-
  fright,
  The fleets of the East in your ocean were
    sunk:
Remember each day, when, in battle array,
  From the fountain of glory how largely ye
    drunk!
For there is not ought that a freeman can fear,
  As the fetters of insult, the name of a slave;
And there is not a voice to a nation so dear,
  As the war-song of freedom that calls on the
    brave.

'He bends the luscious cane, and twists the string;
With bees how sweet, but ah! how keen the sting!
He with five flowrets tips thy ruthless darts,
Which thro' five senses pierce enraptur'd hearts.'

## KING CHARLES'S VISION

[A Vision somewhat resembling the following, and prophetic of the Northern Alexander, is said to have been witnessed by Charles XI. of Sweden, the antagonist of Sigismund. The reader will exclaim, 'Credat Judæus Apella !']

KING CHARLES was sitting all alone,
　In his lonely palace-tower,
When there came on his ears a heavy groan,
　At the silent midnight hour.

He turn'd him round where he heard the sound,
　But nothing might he see;
And he only heard the nightly bird
　That shriek'd right fearfully.

He turn'd him round where he heard the sound,
　To his casement's arched frame;
' And he was aware of a light that was there,' [1]
　But he wist not whence it came.

He looked forth into the night,
　'T was calm as night might be;
But broad and bright the flashing light
　Stream'd red and radiantly.

From ivory sheath his trusty brand
　Of stalwart steel he drew;
And he rais'd the lamp in his better hand,
　But its flame was dim and blue.

And he open'd the door of that palace-tower,
　But harsh turn'd the jarring key:
' By the Virgin's might,' cried the king that night,
　' All is not as it should be ! '

Slow turn'd the door of the crazy tower,
　And slowly again did it close;
And within and without, and all about,
　A sound of voices rose.

The king he stood in dreamy mood,
　For the voices his name did call;
Then on he past, till he came at last
　To the pillar'd audience-hall.

Eight and forty columns wide,
　Many and carv'd and tall,

(Four and twenty on each side)
　Stand in that lordly hall.

The king had been pight [2] in the mortal fight,
　And struck the deadly blow;
The king he had strode in the red red blood,
　Often, afore, and now:

Yet his heart had ne'er been so harrow'd with fear
　As it was this fearful hour;
For his eyes were not dry, and his hair stood on high,
　And his soul had lost its power.

For a blue livid flame, round the hall where he came,
　In fiery circles ran;
And sounds of death, and chattering teeth,
　And gibbering tongues began.

He saw four and twenty statesmen old
　Round a lofty table sit;
And each in his hand did a volume hold,
　Wherein mighty things were writ.

In burning steel were their limbs all cas'd;
　On their cheeks was the flush of ire:
Their armour was brac'd, and their helmets were lac'd,
　And their hollow eyes darted fire.

With sceptre of might, and with gold crown bright,
　And locks like the raven's wing,
And in regal state at that board there sate
　The likeness of a king.

With crimson ting'd, and with ermine fring'd,
　And with jewels spangled o'er,
And rich as the beam of the sun on the stream,
　A sparkling robe he wore.[3]

Yet though fair shone the gem on his proud diadem,
　Though his robe was jewell'd o'er,
Though brilliant the vest on his mailed breast,
　Yet they all were stain'd with gore !

And his eye darted ire, and his glance shot fire,
　And his look was high command;

---

[1] ' And he was aware of a Grey-friar.'
　　　　　　　　*The Grey Brother.*

' And he was aware of a knight that was there.'
　　　　　　　　*The Baron of Smalholme.*

[2] ' A hideous rock is PIGHT
　Of mighty magnes-stone.'
　　　　　　　　SPENSER.

' You vile abominable tents,
Thus proudly PIGHT upon our Phrygian plains ! '
　　　　　　　　SHAKESPEARE.

[3] This is, perhaps, an unpardonable falsehood, since it is well known that Charles was so great an enemy to finery as even to object to the appearance of the Duke of Marlborough on that account. Let those readers, therefore, whose critical nicety this passage offends,

substitute the following stanza, which is ' the whole truth, and nothing but the truth ' :

> With buttons of brass that glitter'd like glass,
> 　And brows that were crown'd with bays,
> With large blue coat, and with black jack-boot,
> 　The theme of his constant praise.

Nothing indeed could exceed Charles's affection for his boots: he eat, drank, and slept in them; nay, he never went on a bootless errand. When the dethroned monarch Augustus waited upon him with proposals of peace, Charles entertained him with a long dissertation on his unparalleled aforesaid jack-boots: he even went so far as to threaten (according to Voltaire), in an authoritative epistle to the senate at Stockholm, that unless they proved less refractory, he would send them one of his boots as regent ! Now this, we must allow, was a step beyond Caligula's consul.

And each, when he spoke, struck his mighty
        book,
    And rais'd his shadowy hand.

And a headman stood by, with his axe on high,
    And quick was his ceaseless stroke;
And loud was the shock on the echoing block,
    As the steel shook the solid oak.

While short and thick came the mingled shriek
    Of the wretches who died by his blow;
And fast fell each head on the pavement red,
    And warm did the life-blood flow.

Said the earthly king to the ghostly king,
    'What fearful sights are those?'
Said the ghostly king to the earthly king,
    'They are signs of future woes!'

Said the earthly king to the ghostly king,
    'By Saint Peter, who art thou?'
Said the ghostly king to the earthly king,
    'I shall be, but I am not now.'

Said the earthly king to the ghostly king,
    'But when will thy time draw nigh?'
'Oh! the sixth after thee will a warrior be,
    And that warrior am I.

'And the lords of the earth shall be pale at my
        birth,
    And conquest shall hover o'er me;
And the kingdoms shall shake, and the nations
        shall quake,
    And the thrones fall down before me.

'And Cracow shall bend to my majesty,
    And the haughty Dane shall bow;
And the Pole shall fly from my piercing eye,
    And the scowl of my clouded brow.

'And around my way shall the hot balls play,
    And the red-tongued flames arise;
And my pathway shall be on the midnight sea,
    'Neath the frown of the wintry skies.

'Thro' narrow pass, over dark morass,
    And the waste of the weary plain,
Over ice and snow, where the dark streams
        flow,
    Thro' the woods of the wild Ukraine.

'And though sad be the close of my life and
        my woes,
    And the hand that shall slay me unshown;
Yet in every clime, thro' the lapse of all time,
    Shall my glorious conquests be known.

'And blood shall be shed, and the earth shall
        be red
    With the gore of misery;
And swift as this flame shall the light of my
        fame
    O'er the world as brightly fly.'

As the monarch spoke, crew the morning cock,
    When all that pageant bright,

And the glitter of gold, and the statesmen old,
    Fled into the gloom of night!

## II. TIMBUCTOO

Church, in 'The Laureate's Country' (London, 1891), says : —

'The poet tells a curious story of the way in which this English verse prize came to be won. His father imagined, not, it may be, wholly without reason, that his son was doing very little at the university, and, knowing that he had a certain gift for writing verse, told him that he ought to compete for the Chancellor's medal. Alfred Tennyson had composed, two years before, a poem on "The Battle of Armageddon." This he took, furnished it with a new beginning and a new end, and sent it in for the theme of "Timbuctoo."'

This is confirmed by the 'Memoir' (vol. i. p. 46), where other interesting information concerning the poem may be found.

The poem was printed in the 'Prolusiones Academicæ' at Cambridge in 1829, and was reprinted several times afterwards in the collection of 'Cambridge Prize Poems.' It was never reprinted by the author, but his son appends it to the 1893 edition of 'Poems by Two Brothers.'

Arthur Hallam was one of the unsuccessful competitors for this prize. His poem, written in the *terza rima* of Dante, was privately printed in pamphlet form, and is included in the 'Remains' of 1834, edited by his father.

### TIMBUCTOO

'Deep in that lion-haunted inland lies
    A mystic city, goal of high emprise.'
                                    CHAPMAN.

I STOOD upon the Mountain which o'erlooks
The narrow seas, whose rapid interval
Parts Afric from green Europe, when the Sun
Had fall'n below th' Atlantic, and above
The silent heavens were blench'd with faery
        light,
Uncertain whether faery light or cloud,
Flowing Southward, and the chasms of deep,
        deep blue
Slumber'd unfathomable, and the stars
Were flooded over with clear glory and pale.
I gazed upon the sheeny coast beyond,
There where the Giant of old Time infix'd
The limits of his prowess, pillars high
Long time erased from earth: even as the Sea
When weary of wild inroad buildeth up
Huge mounds whereby to stay his yeasty waves.
And much I mused on legends quaint and old
Which whilome won the hearts of all on earth
Toward their brightness, ev'n as flame draws
        air;
But had their being in the heart of man

As air is th' life of flame: and thou wert then
A center'd glory-circled memory,
Divinest Atalantis, whom the waves
Have buried deep, and thou of later name,
Imperial Eldorado, roof'd with gold:
Shadows to which, despite all shocks of change,
All on-set of capricious accident,
Men clung with yearning hope which would not
    die.
As when in some great city where the walls
Shake, and the streets with ghastly faces
    throng'd,
Do utter forth a subterranean voice,
Among the inner columns far retired
At midnight, in the lone Acropolis,
Before the awful Genius of the place
Kneels the pale Priestess in deep faith, the
    while
Above her head the weak lamp dips and winks
Unto the fearful summoning without:
Nathless she ever clasps the marble knees,
Bathes the cold hands with tears, and gazeth on
Those eyes which wear no light but that where-
    with
Her phantasy informs them.
                            Where are ye,
Thrones of the Western wave, fair Islands
    green?
Where are your moonlight halls, your cedarn
    glooms,
The blossoming abysses of your hills?
Your flowering capes, and your gold-sanded
    bays
Blown round with happy airs of odorous winds?
Where are the infinite ways, which, seraph-trod,
Wound thro' your great Elysian solitudes,
Whose lowest deeps were, as with visible love,
Fill'd with Divine effulgence, circumfused,
Flowing between the clear and polish'd stems,
And ever circling round their emerald cones
In coronals and glories, such as gird
The unfading foreheads of the Saints in Hea-
    ven?
For nothing visible, they say, had birth
In that blest ground, but it was play'd about
With its peculiar glory.   Then I raised
My voice and cried, 'Wide Afric, doth thy Sun
Lighten, thy hills enfold a city as fair
As those which starr'd the night o' the elder
    world?
Or is the rumour of thy Timbuctoo
A dream as frail as those of ancient time?'
    A curve of whitening, flashing, ebbing light!
A rustling of white wings! the bright descent
Of a young Seraph! and he stood beside me
There on the ridge, and look'd into my face
With his unutterable, shining orbs.
So that with hasty motion I did veil
My vision with both hands, and saw before me
Such colour'd spots as dance athwart the eyes
Of those that gaze upon the noonday Sun.
Girt with a zone of flashing gold beneath
His breast, and compass'd round about his brow
With triple arch of ever-changing bows,
And circled with the glory of living light
And alternation of all hues, he stood.
    'O child of man, why muse you here alone

Upon the Mountain, on the dreams of old
Which fill'd the earth with passing loveliness,
Which flung strange music on the howling
    winds,
And odours rapt from remote Paradise?
Thy sense is clogg'd with dull mortality;
Thy spirit fetter'd with the bond of clay:
Open thine eyes and see.'
                    I look'd, but not
Upon his face, for it was wonderful
With its exceeding brightness, and the light
Of the great Angel Mind which look'd from out
The starry glowing of his restless eyes.
I felt my soul grow mighty, and my spirit
With supernatural excitation bound
Within me, and my mental eye grew large
With such a vast circumference of thought,
That in my vanity I seem'd to stand
Upon the outward verge and bound alone
Of full beatitude.   Each failing sense,
As with a momentary flash of light,
Grew thrillingly distinct and keen.   I saw
The smallest grain that dappled the dark earth,
The indistinctest atom in deep air,
The Moon's white cities, and the opal width
Of her small glowing lakes, her silver heights
Unvisited with dew of vagrant cloud,
And the unsounded, undescended depth
Of her black hollows.   The clear galaxy
Shorn of its hoary lustre, wonderful,
Distinct and vivid with sharp points of light,
Blaze within blaze, an unimagin'd depth
And harmony of planet-girded suns
And moon-encircled planets, wheel in wheel,
Arch'd the wan sapphire.   Nay — the hum of
    men,
Or other things talking in unknown tongues,
And notes of busy life in distant worlds
Beat like a far wave on my anxious ear.
A maze of piercing, trackless, thrilling
    thoughts,
Involving and embracing each with each,
Rapid as fire, inextricably link'd,
Expanding momently with every sight
And sound which struck the palpitating sense,
The issue of strong impulse, hurried through
The riven rapt brain; as when in some large
    lake
From pressure of descendant crags, which lapse
Disjointed, crumbling from their parent slope
At slender interval, the level calm
Is ridg'd with restless and increasing spheres
Which break upon each other, each th' effect
Of separate impulse, but more fleet and strong
Than its precursor, till the eye in vain
Amid the wild unrest of swimming shade
Dappled with hollow and alternate rise
Of interpenetrated arc, would scan
Definite round.
                I know not if I shape
These things with accurate similitude
From visible objects, for but dimly now,
Less vivid than a half-forgotten dream,
The memory of that mental excellence
Comes o'er me, and it may be I entwine
The indecision of my present mind
With its past clearness, yet it seems to me

As even then the torrent of quick thought
Absorbed me from the nature of itself
With its own fleetness. Where is he that,
        borne
Adown the sloping of an arrowy stream,
Could link his shallop to the fleeting edge,
And muse midway with philosophic calm
Upon the wondrous laws which regulate
The fierceness of the bounding element?
    My thoughts which long had grovell'd in the
        slime
Of this dull world, like dusky worms which
        house
Beneath unshaken waters, but at once
Upon some earth-awakening day of Spring
Do pass from gloom to glory, and aloft
Winnow the purple, bearing on both sides
Double display of star-lit wings, which burn
Fan-like and fibred with intensest bloom;
Ev'n so my thoughts, erewhile so low, now felt
Unutterable buoyancy and strength
To bear them upward through the trackless
        fields
Of undefin'd existence far and free.
    Then first within the South methought I saw
A wilderness of spires, and chrystal pile
Of rampart upon rampart, dome on dome,
Illimitable range of battlement
On battlement, and the imperial height
Of canopy o'ercanopied.
                    Behind
In diamond light upsprung the dazzling peaks
Of Pyramids, as far surpassing earth's
As heaven than earth is fairer. Each aloft
Upon his narrow'd eminence bore globes
Of wheeling suns, or stars, or semblances
Of either, showering circular abyss
Of radiance. But the glory of the place
Stood out a pillar'd front of burnish'd gold,
Interminably high, if gold it were
Or metal more etherial, and beneath
Two doors of blinding brilliance, where no gaze
Might rest, stood open, and the eye could scan,
Through length of porch and valve and bound-
        less hall,
Part of a throne of fiery flame, wherefrom
The snowy skirting of a garment hung,
And glimpse of multitudes of multitudes
That minister'd around it — if I saw
These things distinctly, for my human brain
Stagger'd beneath the vision, and thick night
Came down upon my eyelids, and I fell.
    With ministering hand he raised me up:
Then with a mournful and ineffable smile,
Which but to look on for a moment fill'd
My eyes with irresistible sweet tears,
In accents of majestic melody,
Like a swoln river's gushings in still night
Mingled with floating music, thus he spake:
    'There is no mightier Spirit than I to sway
The heart of man: and teach him to attain
By shadowing forth the Unattainable;
And step by step to scale that mighty stair
Whose landing-place is wrapt about with clouds

Of glory of heaven.[1] With earliest light of
        Spring,
And in the glow of sallow Summertide,
And in red Autumn when the winds are wild
With gambols, and when full-voiced Winter
        roofs
The headland with inviolate white snow,
I play about his heart a thousand ways,
Visit his eyes with visions, and his ears
With harmonies of wind and wave and wood, —
Of winds which tell of waters, and of waters
Betraying the close kisses of the wind —
And win him unto me: and few there be
So gross of heart who have not felt and known
A higher than they see: They with dim eyes
Behold me darkling. Lo! I have given thee
To understand my presence, and to feel
My fulness; I have fill'd thy lips with power.
I have raised thee nigher to the spheres of hea-
        ven,
Man's first, last home: and thou with ravish'd
        sense
Listenest the lordly music flowing from
Th' illimitable years. I am the Spirit,
The permeating life which courseth through
All th' intricate and labyrinthine veins
Of the great vine of Fable, which, outspread
With growth of shadowing leaf and clusters
        rare,
Reacheth to every corner under heaven,
Deep-rooted in the living soil of truth;
So that men's hopes and fears take refuge in
The fragrance of its complicated glooms,
And cool impleachèd twilights. Child of man,
See'st thou yon river, whose translucent wave,
Forth issuing from the darkness, windeth
        through
The argent streets o' th' city, imaging
The soft inversion of her tremulous domes,
Her gardens frequent with the stately palm,
Her pagods hung with music of sweet bells,
Her obelisks of rangèd chrysolite,
Minarets and towers? Lo! how he passeth
        by,
And gulphs himself in sands, as not enduring
To carry through the world those waves, which
        bore
The reflex of my city in their depths.
Oh city! oh latest throne! where I was raised
To be a mystery of loveliness
Unto all eyes, the time is well-nigh come
When I must render up this glorious home
To keen Discovery: soon yon brilliant towers
Shall darken with the waving of her wand;
Darken, and shrink and shiver into huts,
Black specks amid a waste of dreary sand,
Low-built, mud-wall'd, barbarian settlements.
How chang'd from this fair city!'
                            Thus far the Spirit:
Then parted heaven-ward on the wing: and I
Was left alone on Calpe, and the moon
Had fallen from the night, and all was dark!

    [1] 'Be ye perfect even as your Father in heaven is
perfect.'

## III. POEMS PUBLISHED IN THE EDITION OF 1830, AND OMITTED IN LATER EDITIONS

Of the fifty-three poems in the 1830 volume, thirty-two were suppressed in 1842; but nine of these (as explained in the prefatory notes) were afterwards included in the collected editions.

### THE 'HOW' AND THE 'WHY'

?

I AM any man's suitor,
If any will be my tutor:
Some say this life is pleasant,
  Some think it speedeth fast,
In time there is no present,
In eternity no future,
  In eternity no past.
We laugh, we cry, we are born, we die,
Who will riddle me the *how* and the *why*?

The bulrush nods unto its brother.
The wheatears whisper to each other:
What is it they say? what do they there?
Why two and two make four? why round is
  not square?
Why the rock stands still, and the light clouds
  fly?
Why the heavy oak groans, and the white wil-
  lows sigh?
Why deep is not high, and high is not deep?
Whether we wake, or whether we sleep?
Whether we sleep, or whether we die?
How you are you? why I am I?
Who will riddle me the *how* and the *why*?

The world is somewhat; it goes on somehow:
But what is the meaning of *then* and *now*?
I feel there is something; but how and what?
I know there is somewhat: but what and why?
I cannot tell if that somewhat be I.
  The little bird pipeth — 'why? why?'
In the summer woods when the sun falls low,
And the great bird sits on the opposite bough,
And stares in his face, and shouts 'how?
  how?'
And the black owl scuds down the mellow twi-
  light,
And chants 'how? how?' the whole of the
  night.

Why the life goes when the blood is spilt?
  What the life is? where the soul may lie?
Why a church is with a steeple built?
And a house with a chimney-pot?
Who will riddle me the how and the what?
Who will riddle me the what and the why?

### THE BURIAL OF LOVE

His eyes in eclipse,
  Pale-cold his lips,
The light of his hopes unfed,

Mute his tongue,
  His bow unstrung
With the tears he hath shed,
Backward drooping his graceful head,
  Love is dead:
His last arrow is sped;
  He hath not another dart;
Go — carry him to his dark deathbed;
Bury him in the cold, cold heart —
  Love is dead.

O truest love! art thou forlorn,
  And unrevenged? thy pleasant wiles
Forgotten, and thine innocent joy?
  Shall hollow-hearted apathy,
The cruellest form of perfect scorn,
  With languor of most hateful smiles,
    For ever write,
    In the withered light
Of the tearless eye,
An epitaph that all may spy?
No! sooner she herself shall die.

For her the showers shall not fall,
Nor the round sun shine that shineth to all;
  Her light shall into darkness change;
For her the green grass shall not spring,
Nor the rivers flow, nor the sweet birds sing,
  Till Love have his full revenge.

### TO ———

SAINTED Juliet! dearest name!
If to love be life alone,
  Divinest Juliet,
    I love thee, and live; and yet
Love unreturned is like the fragrant flame
Folding the slaughter of the sacrifice
  Offered to gods upon an altar-throne;
My heart is lighted at thine eyes,
Changed into fire, and blown about with sighs.

### SONG

I

I' THE glooming light
  Of middle night
    So cold and white,
Worn Sorrow sits by the moaning wave,
    Beside her are laid
    Her mattock and spade,
For she hath half delved her own deep grave.
    Alone she is there:
The white clouds drizzle: her hair falls loose:
  Her shoulders are bare;
Her tears are mixed with the beaded dews.

II

Death standeth by;
  She will not die;
    With glazéd eye
She looks at her grave: she cannot sleep;
    Ever alone
    She maketh her moan:

She cannot speak: she can only weep,
  For she will not hope.
The thick snow falls on her flake by flake,
    The dull wave mourns down the slope,
The world will not change, and her heart will
  not break.

## SONG

### I

THE lintwhite and the throstlecock
  Have voices sweet and clear;
    All in the blooméd May.
They from the blosmy brere
Call to the fleeting year,
If that he would them hear
    And stay.
Alas! that one so beautiful
Should have so dull an ear!

### II

Fair year, fair year, thy children call,
But thou art deaf as death;
    All in the blooméd May.
When thy light perisheth
That from thee issueth,
Our life evanisheth:
    O, stay!
Alas! that lips so cruel-dumb
Should have so sweet a breath!

### III

Fair year, with brows of royal love
  Thou comest, as a king,
    All in the blooméd May.
Thy golden largess fling,
And longer hear us sing;
Though thou art fleet of wing,
    Yet stay.
Alas! that eyes so full of light
Should be so wandering!

### IV

Thy locks are all of sunny sheen
In rings of gold yronne,[1]
    All in the blooméd May.
We pri'thee pass not on;
If thou dost leave the sun,
Delight is with thee gone.
    O, stay!
Thou art the fairest of thy feres,
We pri'thee pass not on.

## SONG

### I

EVERY day hath its night:
  Every night its morn:
Thorough dark and bright
  Wingéd hours are borne;
    Ah! welaway!

[1] 'His crispè hair in ringis was yronne.'
    CHAUCER, Knightes Tale.

Seasons flower and fade;
  Golden calm and storm
    Mingle day by day.
There is no bright form
Doth not cast a shade —
    Ah! welaway!

### II

When we laugh, and our mirth
  Apes the happy vein,
We 're so kin to earth,
  Pleasaunce fathers pain —
    Ah! welaway!
Madness laugheth loud:
  Laughter bringeth tears:
    Eyes are worn away
Till the end of fears
Cometh in the shroud,
    Ah! welaway!

### III

All is change, woe or weal;
  Joy is Sorrow's brother;
Grief and gladness steal
  Symbols of each other:
    Ah! welaway!
Larks in heaven's cope
  Sing: the culvers mourn
    All the livelong day.
Be not all forlorn:
Let us weep in hope —
    Ah! welaway!

## HERO TO LEANDER

Included by Emerson in his 'Parnassus'
(1874).

O GO not yet, my love!
  The night is dark and vast;
The white moon is hid in her heaven above,
  And the waves climb high and fast.
O, kiss me, kiss me, once again,
  Lest thy kiss should be the last!
O kiss me ere we part;
Grow closer to my heart!
My heart is warmer surely than the bosom of
  the main.
O joy! O bliss of blisses!
  My heart of hearts art thou.
Come bathe me with thy kisses,
  My eyelids and my brow.
Hark how the wild rain hisses,
  And the loud sea roars below.

Thy heart beats through thy rosy limbs,
  So gladly doth it stir;
Thine eye in drops of gladness swims.
  I have bathed thee with the pleasant myrrh;
Thy locks are dripping balm;
Thou shalt not wander hence to-night,
  I 'll stay thee with my kisses.
To-night the roaring brine
  Will rend thy golden tresses;
The ocean with the morrow light
Will be both blue and calm;

And the billow will embrace thee with a kiss as
    soft as mine.
No Western odors wander
    On the black and moaning sea,
And when thou art dead, Leander,
    My soul must follow thee !
O go not yet, my love !
    Thy voice is sweet and low;
The deep salt wave breaks in above
    Those marble steps below.
The turret-stairs are wet
    That lead into the sea.
Leander ! go not yet.
The pleasant stars have set:
O, go not, go not yet,
    Or I will follow thee !

## THE MYSTIC

ANGELS have talked with him, and showed
    him thrones:
Ye knew him not; he was not one of ye,
Ye scorned him with an undiscerning scorn:
Ye could not read the marvel in his eye,
The still serene abstraction: he hath felt
The vanities of after and before;
Albeit, his spirit and his secret heart
The stern experiences of converse lives,
The linkéd woes of many a fiery change
Had purified, and chastened, and made free.
Always there stood before him, night and day,
Of wayward vary-colored circumstance
The imperishable presences serene,
Colossal, without form, or sense, or sound,
Dim shadows but unwaning presences
Fourfacéd to four corners of the sky:
And yet again, three shadows, fronting one,
One forward, one respectant, three but one;
And yet again, again and evermore,
For the two first were not, but only seemed,
One shadow in the midst of a great light,
One reflex from eternity on time,
One mighty countenance of perfect calm,
Awful with most invariable eyes.
For him the silent congregated hours,
Daughters of time, divinely tall, beneath
Severe and youthful brows, with shining eyes
Smiling a godlike smile (the innocent light
Of earliest youth pierced through and through
    with all
Keen knowledges of low-embowéd eld)
Upheld, and ever hold aloft the cloud
Which droops low-hung on either gate of life,
Both birth and death: he in the centre fixt,
Saw far on each side through the grated gates
Most pale and clear and lovely distances.
He often lying broad awake, and yet
Remaining from the body, and apart
In intellect and power and will, hath heard
Time flowing in the middle of the night,
And all things creeping to a day of doom.
How could ye know him ?   Ye were yet within
The narrower circle: he had wellnigh reached
The last, which with a region of white flame,
Pure without heat, into a larger air
Upburning, and an ether of black blue,
Investeth and ingirds all other lives.

## THE GRASSHOPPER

### I

VOICE of the summer wind,
Joy of the summer plain,
Life of the summer hours,
Carol clearly, bound along.
No Tithon thou as poets feign
(Shame fall 'em, they are deaf and blind),
But an insect lithe and strong,
Bowing the seeded summer flowers.
Prove their falsehood and thy quarrel,
    Vaulting on thine airy feet.
Clap thy shielded sides and carol,
    Carol clearly, chirrup sweet.
Thou art a mailéd warrior in youth and
    strength complete;
    Armed cap-a-pie
    Full fair to see;
    Unknowing fear,
    Undreading loss,
    A gallant cavalier,
    *Sans peur et sans reproche*,
    In sunlight and in shadow,
    The Bayard of the meadow.

### II

I would dwell with thee,
    Merry grasshopper,
Thou art so glad and free,
    And as light as air;
Thou hast no sorrow or tears,
Thou hast no compt of years,
No withered immortality,
But a short youth sunny and free.
Carol clearly, bound along,
    Soon thy joy is over,
A summer of loud song,
    And slumbers in the clover.
What hast thou to do with evil
In thine hour of love and revel,
    In thy heat of summer pride,
Pushing the thick roots aside
Of the singing floweréd grasses,
That brush thee with their silken tresses ?
What hast thou to do with evil,
Shooting, singing, ever springing
    In and out the emerald glooms,
Ever leaping, ever singing,
    Lighting on the golden blooms ?

## LOVE, PRIDE, AND FORGETFUL-
## NESS

ERE yet my heart was sweet Love's tomb,
Love labored honey busily.
I was the hive, and Love the bee,
My heart the honeycomb.
One very dark and chilly night
Pride came beneath and held a light.

The cruel vapors went through all,
Sweet Love was withered in his cell:
Pride took Love's sweets, and by a spell
Did change them into gall;

And Memory, though fed by Pride,
Did wax so thin on gall,
Awhile she scarcely lived at all.
What marvel that she died?

## CHORUS

IN AN UNPUBLISHED DRAMA, WRITTEN
VERY EARLY

THE varied earth, the moving heaven,
  The rapid waste of roving sea,
The fountain-pregnant mountains riven
  To shapes of wildest anarchy,
By secret fire and midnight storms
  That wander round their windy cones,
The subtle life, the countless forms
  Of living things, the wondrous tones
    Of man and beast are full of strange
    Astonishment and boundless change.

The day, the diamonded night,
  The echo, feeble child of sound,
The heavy thunder's griding might,
  The herald lightning's starry bound,
The vocal spring of bursting bloom,
  The naked summer's glowing birth,
The troublous autumn's sallow gloom,
  The hoarhead winter paving earth
    With sheeny white, are full of strange
    Astonishment and boundless change.

Each sun which from the centre flings
  Grand music and redundant fire,
The burning belts, the mighty rings,
  The murm'rous planets' rolling choir,
The globe-filled arch that, cleaving air,
  Lost in its own effulgence sleeps,
The lawless comets as they glare,
  And thunder through the sapphire deeps
    In wayward strength, are full of strange
    Astonishment and boundless change.

## LOST HOPE

YOU cast to ground the hope which once was
    mine:
But did the while your harsh decree deplore,
Embalming with sweet tears the vacant shrine,
My heart, where Hope had been and was no
    more.

  So on an oaken sprout
    A goodly acorn grew;
But winds from heaven shook the acorn out,
    And filled the cup with dew.

## THE TEARS OF HEAVEN

HEAVEN weeps above the earth all night till
    morn,
In darkness weeps as all ashamed to weep,
Because the earth hath made her state forlorn
With self-wrought evil of unnumbered years,

And doth the fruit of her dishonor reap.
And all the day heaven gathers back her tears
Into her own blue eyes so clear and deep,
And showering down the glory of lightsome
    day,
Smiles on the earth's worn brow to win her if
    she may.

## LOVE AND SORROW

O MAIDEN, fresher than the first green leaf
With which the fearful springtide flecks the
    lea,
Weep not, Almeida, that I said to thee
That thou hast half my heart, for bitter grief
Doth hold the other half in sovranty.
Thou art my heart's sun in love's crystalline:
Yet on both sides at once thou canst not shine:
Thine is the bright side of my heart, and thine
My heart's day, but the shadow of my heart.
Issue of its own substance, my heart's night
Thou canst not lighten even with *thy* light,
All-powerful in beauty as thou art.
Almeida, if my heart were substanceless,
Then might thy rays pass through to the other
    side,
So swiftly, that they nowhere would abide,
But lose themselves in utter emptiness.
Half-light, half-shadow, let my spirit sleep;
They never learned to love who never knew to
    weep.

## TO A LADY SLEEPING

O THOU whose fringéd lids I gaze upon,
Through whose dim brain the wingéd dreams
    are borne,
Unroof the shrines of clearest vision,
In honor of the silver-fleckéd morn;
Long hath the white wave of the virgin light
Driven back the billow of the dreamful dark.
Thou all unwittingly prolongest night,
Though long ago listening the poiséd lark,
With eyes dropt downward through the blue
    serene,
Over heaven's parapet the angels lean.

## SONNET

COULD I outwear my present state of woe
With one brief winter, and indue i' the spring
Hues of fresh youth, and mightily outgrow
The wan dark coil of faded suffering —
Forth in the pride of beauty issuing
A sheeny snake, the light of vernal bowers,
Moving his crest to all sweet plots of flowers
And watered valleys where the young birds
    sing;
Could I thus hope my lost delight's renewing,
I straightly would command the tears to creep
From my charged lids; but inwardly I weep;
Some vital heat as yet my heart is wooing:
That to itself hath drawn the frozen rain
From my cold eyes, and melted it again.

## SONNET

THOUGH Night hath climbed her peak of high-
    est noon,
And bitter blasts the screaming autumn whirl,
All night through archways of the bridgéd
    pearl,
And portals of pure silver, walks the moon.
Walk on, my soul, nor crouch to agony,
Turn cloud to light, and bitterness to joy,
And dross to gold with glorious alchemy,
Basing thy throne above the world's annoy.
Reign thou above the storms of sorrow and
    ruth
That roar beneath; unshaken peace hath won
    thee;
So shalt thou pierce the woven glooms of truth;
So shall the blessing of the meek be on thee;
So in thine hour of dawn, the body's youth,
An honorable eld shall come upon thee.

## SONNET

SHALL the hag Evil die with child of Good,
Or propagate again her loathéd kind,
Thronging the cells of the diseaséd mind,
Hateful with hanging cheeks, a withered brood,
Though hourly pastured on the salient blood ?
Oh ! that the wind which bloweth cold or heat
Would shatter and o'erbear the brazen beat
Of their broad vans, and in the solitude
Of middle space confound them, and blow back
Their wild cries down their cavern throats, and
    slake
With points of blast-borne hail their heated
    eyne !
So their wan limbs no more might come be-
    tween
The moon and the moon's reflex in the night,
Nor blot with floating shades the solar light.

## SONNET

THE pallid thunder-stricken sigh for gain,
Down an ideal stream they ever float,
And sailing on Pactolus in a boat,
Drown soul and sense, while wistfully they strain
Weak eyes upon the glistering sands that robe
The understream.  The wise, could he behold
Cathedraled caverns of thick-ribbéd gold
And branching silvers of the central globe,
Would marvel from so beautiful a sight
How scorn and ruin, pain and hate could flow:
But Hatred in a gold cave sits below;
Pleached with her hair, in mail of argent light
Shot into gold, a snake her forehead clips,
And skins the color from her trembling lips.

## LOVE

### I

THOU, from the first, unborn, undying Love,
Albeit we gaze not on thy glories near,
Before the face of God didst breathe and move,
Though night and pain and ruin and death
    reign here.
Thou foldest, like a golden atmosphere,
The very throne of the eternal God:
Passing through thee the edicts of his fear
Are mellowed into music, borne abroad
By the loud winds, though they uprend the sea,
Even from its central deeps: thine empery
Is over all; thou wilt not brook eclipse;
Thou goest and returnest to His lips
Like lightning: thou dost ever brood above
The silence of all hearts, unutterable Love.

### II

To know thee is all wisdom, and old age
Is but to know thee: dimly we behold thee
Athwart the veils of evils which infold thee.
We beat upon our aching hearts in rage;
We cry for thee; we deem the world thy tomb.
As dwellers in lone planets look upon
The mighty disk of their majestic sun,
Hollowed in awful chasms of wheeling gloom,
Making their day dim, so we gaze on thee.
Come, thou of many crowns, white-robéd Love,
Oh ! rend the veil in twain: all men adore thee;
Heaven crieth after thee; earth waiteth for
    thee;
Breathe on thy wingéd throne, and it shall
    move
In music and in light o'er land and sea.

### III

And now — methinks I gaze upon thee now,
As on a serpent in his agonies
Awe-stricken Indians; what time laid low
And crushing the thick fragrant reeds he lies,
When the new year warm-breathéd on the
    Earth,
Waiting to light him with her purple skies,
Calls to him by the fountain to uprise.
Already with the pangs of a new birth
Strain the hot spheres of his convulséd eyes,
And in his writhings awful hues begin
To wander down his sable-sheeny sides,
Like light on troubled waters: from within
Anon he rusheth forth with merry din,
And in him light and joy and strength abides;
And from his brows a crown of living light
Looks through the thick-stemmed woods by
    day and night.

## ENGLISH WAR-SONG

WHO fears to die ?  Who fears to die ?
Is there any here who fears to die ?
He shall find what he fears; and none shall
    grieve
For the man who fears to die;
But the withering scorn of the many shall
    cleave
To the man who fears to die.

CHORUS.

    Shout for England !
    Ho ! for England !

George for England !
Merry England !
England for aye !

The hollow at heart shall crouch forlorn,
He shall eat the bread of common scorn;
It shall be steeped in the salt, salt tear,
Shall be steeped in his own salt tear:
Far better, far better he never were born
Than to shame merry England here.
CHO. — Shout for England ! etc.

There standeth our ancient enemy;
Hark ! he shouteth — the ancient enemy !
On the ridge of the hill his banners rise;
They stream like fire in the skies;
Hold up the Lion of England on high
Till it dazzle and blind his eyes.
CHO. — Shout for England ! etc.

Come along ! we alone of the earth are free;
The child in our cradles is bolder than he;
For where is the heart and strength of slaves ?
Oh ! where is the strength of slaves ?
He is weak ! we are strong: he a slave, we are
    free;
Come along ! we will dig their graves.
CHO. — Shout for England ! etc.

There standeth our ancient enemy;
Will he dare to battle with the free ?
Spur along ! spur amain ! charge to the fight:
Charge ! charge to the fight !
Hold up the Lion of England on high !
Shout for God and our right !
CHO. — Shout for England ! etc.

## NATIONAL SONG

Reprinted in 'The Foresters' in 1892. See
Notes.

THERE is no land like England
    Where'er the light of day be;
There are no hearts like English hearts,
    Such hearts of oak as they be.
There is no land like England
    Where'er the light of day be;
There are no men like Englishmen,
    So tall and bold as they be.

### CHORUS.

For the French the Pope may shrive 'em,
For the devil a whit we heed 'em:
As for the French, God speed 'em
    Unto their heart's desire,
And the merry devil drive 'em
    Through the water and the fire.

### FULL CHORUS.

Our glory is our freedom,
    We lord it o'er the sea;
We are the sons of freedom,
    We are free.

There is no land like England,
    Where'er the light of day be;
There are no wives like English wives,
    So fair and chaste as they be.
There is no land like England,
    Where'er the light of day be;
There are no maids like English maids,
    So beautiful as they be.
    CHO. — For the French, etc.

## DUALISMS

Two bees within a crystal flowerbell rockéd,
    Hum a love-lay to the west-wind at noontide.
Both alike, they buzz together,
Both alike, they hum together,
    Through and through the flowered heather.
Where in a creeping cove the wave unshockéd
        Lays itself calm and wide.
Over a stream two birds of glancing feather
Do woo each other, carolling together.
Both alike, they glide together,
        Side by side;
Both alike, they sing together,
Arching blue-glosséd necks beneath the purple
        weather.

Two children lovelier than Love adown the lea
        are singing,
As they gambol, lily-garlands ever stringing:
        Both in blosm-white silk are frockéd:
Like, unlike, they roam together
Under a summer vault of golden weather:
Like, unlike, they sing together
        Side by side,
    Mid-May's darling golden-lockéd,
    Summer's tanling diamond-eyed.

## THE SEA FAIRIES

This poem (see p. 15 above) was so much
altered when it was included in the edition of
1853 that I give the original form in full here.

SLOW sailed the weary mariners, and saw
Between the green brink and the running foam
White limbs unrobéd in a crystal air,
Sweet faces, rounded arms, and bosoms prest
To little harps of gold : and while they mused,
Whispering to each other half in fear,
Shrill music reached them on the middle sea.

### SONG

Whither away, whither away, whither
    away ? Fly no more:
Whither away wi' the singing sail ? whither
    away wi' the oar ?
Whither away from the high green field and the
    happy blossoming shore ?
Weary mariners, hither away,
    One and all, one and all,
Weary mariners, come and play;
We will sing to you all the day;

Furl the sail and the foam will fall
From the prow !  One and all,
Furl the sail !  Drop the oar !
    Leap ashore,
Know danger and trouble and toil no more.
Whither away wi' the sail and the oar ?

    Drop the oar,
    Leap ashore,
    Fly no more !
Whither away wi' the sail ? whither away wi'
    the oar ?
Day and night to the billow the fountain
    calls:
Down shower the gambolling waterfalls
    From wandering over the lea;
They freshen the silvery-crimson shells,
And thick with white bells the clover-hill
    swells
High over the full-toned sea.
Merrily carol the revelling gales
    Over the islands free:
From the green seabanks the rose down-trails
    To the happy brimméd sea.

Come hither, come hither and be our lords,
    For merry brides are we:
We will kiss sweet kisses, and speak sweet
    words.
Oh listen, listen, your eyes shall glisten
    With pleasure and love and revelry;
Oh listen, listen, your eyes shall glisten,
When the clear sharp twang of the golden
    chords
Runs up the ridgéd sea.
Ye will not find so happy a shore,
Weary mariners ! all the world o'er;
    Oh ! fly no more !
Hearken ye, hearken ye, sorrow shall darken
    ye,
Danger and trouble and toil no more;
    Whither away ?
    Drop the oar;
    Hither away,
    Leap ashore;
Oh fly no more — no more:
Whither away, whither away, whither away
    with the sail and the oar ?

## Οἱ ῥέοντες

### I

ALL thoughts, all creeds, all dreams are true,
    All visions wild and strange;
Man is the measure of all truth
    Unto himself.  All truth is change.
All men do walk in sleep, and all
    Have faith in that they dream:
For all things are as they seem to all,
    And all things flow like a stream.

### II

There is no rest, no calm, no pause,
    Nor good nor ill, nor light nor shade,
Nor essence nor eternal laws:
    For nothing is, but all is made.

But if I dream that all these are,
    They are to me for that I dream;
For all things are as they seem to all,
    And all things flow like a stream.

Argal — this very opinion is only true relatively to
the flowing philosophers.

## IV. POEMS PUBLISHED IN THE EDITION OF 1833, AND OMITTED IN LATER EDITIONS

Of the thirty poems in the 1833 volume,
fourteen were omitted in 1842; but eight of
these (including ' Kate,' restored since the
poet's death) were afterwards given a place in
the collected editions, as explained in the prefatory notes.

### SONNET

O BEAUTY, passing beauty ! sweetest Sweet !
    How canst thou let me waste my youth in
        sighs ?
I only ask to sit beside thy feet.
    Thou knowest I dare not look into thine eyes.
Might I but kiss thy hand !  I dare not fold
    My arms about thee — scarcely dare to speak.
And nothing seems to me so wild and bold,
    As with one kiss to touch thy blesséd cheek.
Methinks if I should kiss thee, no control
    Within the thrilling brain could keep afloat
The subtle spirit.   Even while I spoke,
The bare word KISS hath made my inner soul
    To tremble like a lutestring, ere the note
Hath melted in the silence that it broke.

### THE HESPERIDES

This poem is reprinted in the ' Memoir '
(vol. i. p. 61) with the following note : —
' Published and suppressed by my father,
and republished by me here (with accents
written by him) in consequence of a talk that I
had with him, in which he regretted that he
had done away with it from among his " Juvenilia." '
    The author of the ' Memoir ' has since added
' Kate ' (which he does not mention) to the
' Juvenilia ' in the collected editions (see p. 23
above), but he has not restored this poem.

> " Hesperus and his daughters three,
>   That sing about the golden tree."
>                    *Comus.*

THE North-wind fall'n, in the new-starréd
    night
Zidonian Hanno, voyaging beyond
The hoary promontory of Soloë
Past Thymiaterion, in calméd bays,
Between the southern and the western Horn,

Heard neither warbling of the nightingale,
Nor melody of the Libyan lotus flute
Blown seaward from the shore; but from a
    slope
That ran bloom-bright into the Atlantic blue,
Beneath a highland leaning down a weight
Of cliffs, and zoned below with cedar shade,
Came voices, like the voices in a dream,
Continuous, till he reached the outer sea.

SONG

I

The golden apple, the golden apple, the hal-
    lowed fruit,
Guard it well, guard it warily,
Singing airily,
Standing about the charméd root.
Round about all is mute,
As the snow-field on the mountain-peaks,
As the sand-field at the mountain-foot.
Crocodiles in briny creeks
Sleep and stir not: all is mute.
If ye sing not, if ye make false measure,
We shall lose eternal pleasure,
Worth eternal want of rest.
Laugh not loudly: watch the treasure
Of the wisdom of the West.
In a corner wisdom whispers.   Five and three
(Let it not be preached abroad) make an awful
    mystery.
For the blossom unto threefold music bloweth;
Evermore it is born anew;
And the sap to threefold music floweth,
From the root
Drawn in the dark,
Up to the fruit,
Creeping under the fragrant bark,
Liquid gold, honeysweet, thro' and thro'.
Keen-eyed Sisters, singing airily,
Looking warily
Every way,
Guard the apple night and day,
Lest one from the East come and take it away.

II

Father Hesper, Father Hesper, watch, watch,
    ever and aye,
Looking under silver hair with a silver eye.
Father, twinkle not thy steadfast sight;
Kingdoms lapse, and climates change, and races
    die;
Honor comes with mystery;
Hoarded wisdom brings delight.
Number, tell them over and number
How many the mystic fruit-tree holds
Lest the red-combed dragon slumber
Rolled together in purple folds.
Look to him, father, lest he wink, and the
    golden apple be stol'n away,
For his ancient heart is drunk with overwatch-
    ings night and day,
Round about the hallowed fruit-tree curled —
Sing away, sing aloud evermore in the wind,
    without stop,
Lest his scaléd eyelid drop,

For he is older than the world.
If he waken, we waken,
Rapidly levelling eager eyes.
If he sleep, we sleep,
Dropping the eyelid over the eyes.
If the golden apple be taken,
The world will be overwise.
Five links, a golden chain, are we,
Hesper, the dragon, and sisters three,
Bound about the golden tree.

III

Father Hesper, Father Hesper, watch, watch,
    night and day,
Lest the old wound of the world be healéd,
The glory unsealéd,
The golden apple stolén away,
And the ancient secret revealéd.
Look from west to east along:
Father, old Himala weakens, Caucasus is bold
    and strong.
Wandering waters unto wandering waters call;
Let them clash together, foam and fall.
Out of watchings, out of wiles,
Comes the bliss of secret smiles.
All things are not told to all.
Half-round the mantling night is drawn,
Purple fringéd with even and dawn.
Hesper hateth Phosphor, evening hateth morn.

IV

Every flower and every fruit the redolent breath
Of this warm sea-wind ripeneth,
Arching the billow in his sleep;
But the land-wind wandereth,
Broken by the highland-steep,
Two streams upon the violet deep;
For the western sun and the western star,
And the low west-wind, breathing afar,
The end of day and beginning of night
Make the apple holy and bright;
Holy and bright, round and full, bright and
    blest,
Mellowed in a land of rest;
Watch it warily day and night;
All good things are in the west.
Till mid noon the cool east light
Is shut out by the tall hillbrow;
But when the full-faced sunset yellowly
Stays on the flowering arch of the bough,
The luscious fruitage clustereth mellowly,
Golden-kernelled, golden-cored,
Sunset-ripened above on the tree.
The world is wasted with fire and sword,
But the apple of gold hangs over the sea.
Five links, a golden chain are we,
Hesper, the dragon, and sisters three,
Daughters three,
Bound about
The gnarléd bole of the charméd tree.
The golden apple, the golden apple, the hal-
    lowed fruit,
Guard it well, guard it warily,
Watch it warily,
Singing airily,
Standing about the charméd root.

## ROSALIND

This poem (see p. 21 above) has been re-stored, but *without* the following note, which is appended to it in the 1833 volume : —

AUTHOR'S NOTE. — Perhaps the following lines may be allowed to stand as a separate poem; originally they made part of the text, where they were manifestly superfluous.

My Rosalind, my Rosalind,
Bold, subtle, careless Rosalind,
Is one of those who know no strife
Of inward woe or outward fear;
To whom the slope and stream of Life,
The life before, the life behind,
In the ear, from far and near,
Chimeth musically clear.
My falcon-hearted Rosalind,
Full-sailed before a vigorous wind,
Is one of those who cannot weep
For others' woes, but overleap
All the petty shocks and fears
That trouble life in early years,
With a flash of frolic scorn
And keen delight, that never falls
Away from freshness, self-upborne
With such gladness as, whenever
The fresh-flushing springtime calls
To the flooding waters cool,
Young fishes, on an April morn,
Up and down a rapid river,
Leap the little waterfalls
That sing into the pebbled pool.
My happy falcon, Rosalind,
Hath daring fancies of her own,
Fresh as the dawn before the day,
Fresh as the early sea-smell blown
Through vineyards from an inland bay.
My Rosalind, my Rosalind,
Because no shadow on you falls,
Think you hearts are tennisballs
To play with, wanton Rosalind ?

## SONG

WHO can say
Why To-day
To-morrow will be yesterday ?
Who can tell
Why to smell
The violet recalls the dewy prime
Of youth and buried time ?
The cause is nowhere found in rhyme.

## SONNET

WRITTEN ON HEARING OF THE OUTBREAK
OF THE POLISH INSURRECTION

BLOW ye the trumpet, gather from afar
The hosts to battle: be not bought and sold.
Arise, brave Poles, the boldest of the bold;

Break through your iron shackles — fling them
    far.
O for those days of Piast, ere the Czar
Grew to his strength among his deserts cold;
When even to Moscow's cupolas were rolled
The growing murmurs of the Polish war !
Now must your noble anger blaze out more
Than when from Sobieski, clan by clan,
The Moslem myriads fell, and fled before —
Than when Zamoysky smote the Tartar Khan;
Than earlier, when on the Baltic shore
Boleslas drove the Pomeranian.

## O DARLING ROOM

I

O DARLING room, my heart's delight,
Dear room, the apple of my sight,
With thy two couches soft and white,
There is no room so exquisite,
No little room so warm and bright,
Wherein to read, wherein to write.

II

For I the Nonnenwerth have seen,
And Oberwinter's vineyards green,
Musical Lurlei; and between
The hills to Bingen have I been,
Bingen in Darmstadt, where the Rhene
Curves toward Mentz, a woody scene.

III

Yet never did there meet my sight,
In any town to left or right,
A little room so exquisite,
With two such couches soft and white,
Not any room so warm and bright,
Wherein to read, wherein to write.

## TO CHRISTOPHER NORTH

You did late review my lays,
    Crusty Christopher;
You did mingle blame and praise,
    Rusty Christopher.
When I learnt from whom it came,
I forgave you all the blame,
    Musty Christopher;
I could *not* forgive the praise,
    Fusty Christopher.

## V. OTHER DISCARDED AND UNCOLLECTED POEMS

### ON CAMBRIDGE UNIVERSITY

Written in 1830. See Notes.

THEREFORE your Halls, your ancient Colleges,
Your portals statued with old kings and queens,
Your gardens, myriad-volumed libraries,
Wax-lighted chapels, and rich carven screens,

Your doctors and your proctors, and your
    deans
Shall not avail you, when the Daybeam sports
New-risen o'er awaken'd Albion — No !
Nor yet your solemn organ-pipes that blow
Melodious thunders thro' your vacant courts
At morn and eve — because your manner sorts
Not with this age wherefrom ye stand apart —
Because the lips of little children preach
Against you, you that do profess to teach
And teach us nothing, feeding not the heart.

## NO MORE

This and the two following poems were contributed to 'The Gem, a Literary Annual'
(London, 1831).

O SAD *No More !* O sweet *No More !*
    O strange *No More !*
By a mossed brookbank on a stone
I smelt a wildweed flower alone;
There was a ringing in my ears,
    And both my eyes gushed out with tears.
Surely all pleasant things had gone before,
Low-buried fathom deep beneath with thee,
    No MORE !

## ANACREONTICS

WITH roses musky-breathed,
And drooping daffodilly,
And silver-leaved lily,
And ivy darkly-wreathed,
I wove a crown before her,
For her I love so dearly,
A garland for Lenora.
With a silken cord I bound it.
Lenora, laughing clearly
A light and thrilling laughter,
About her forehead wound it,
And loved me ever after.

## A FRAGMENT

WHERE is the Giant of the Sun, which stood
In the midnoon the glory of old Rhodes,
A perfect Idol with profulgent brows
Far-sheening down the purple seas to those
Who sailed from Mizraim underneath the star
Named of the Dragon — and between whose
    limbs
Of brassy vastness broad-blown Argosies
Drave into haven ?  Yet endure unscathed
Of changeful cycles the great Pyramids
Broad-based amid the fleeting sands, and sloped
Into the slumberous summer noon; but where,
Mysterious Egypt, are thine obelisks
Graven with gorgeous emblems undiscerned ?
Thy placid Sphinxes brooding o'er the Nile ?
Thy shadowing Idols in the solitudes,
Awful Memnonian countenances calm
Looking athwart the burning flats, far off

Seen by the high-necked camel on the verge
Journeying southward ?  Where are thy monu-
    ments
Piled by the strong and sunborn Anakim
Over their crowned brethren ON and OPH ?
Thy Memnon when his peaceful lips are kist
With earliest rays, that from his mother's eyes
Flow over the Arabian bay, no more
Breathes low into the charmed ears of morn
Clear melody flattering the crispèd Nile
By columned Thebes.  Old Memphis hath gone
    down:
The Pharaohs are no more: somewhere in death
They sleep with staring eyes and gilded lips,
Wrapped round with spiced cerements in old
    grots
Rock-hewn and sealed for ever.

## SONNET

Contributed to 'Friendship's Offering,' an
annual, 1832.

ME my own fate to lasting sorrow doometh:
    Thy woes are birds of passage, transitory:
    Thy spirit, circled with a living glory,
In summer still a summer joy resumeth.
Alone my hopeless melancholy gloometh,
    Like a lone cypress, through the twilight
        hoary,
From an old garden where no flower bloom-
      eth,
    One cypress on an island promontory.
But yet my lonely spirit follows thine,
    As round the rolling earth night follows day:
But yet thy lights on my horizon shine
    Into my night, when thou art far away.
I am so dark, alas ! and thou so bright,
When we two meet there 's never perfect light.

## SONNET

Contributed to 'The Englishman's Magazine' for August, 1831; and reprinted in
'Friendship's Offering,' 1833.

CHECK every outflash, every ruder sally
    Of thought and speech ; speak low, and give
      up wholly
Thy spirit to mild-minded Melancholy;
This is the place.  Through yonder poplar
    alley
    Below the blue-green river windeth slowly;
But in the middle of the sombre valley
The crispèd waters whisper musically,
    And all the haunted place is dark and holy.
The nightingale, with long and low preamble,
    Warbled from yonder knoll of solemn larches,
    And in and out the woodbine's flowery arches
The summer midges wove their wanton gam-
    bol,
    And all the white-stemmed pinewood slept
      above —
When in this valley first I told my love.

## SONNET

Contributed to 'the Yorkshire Literary Annual,' 1832.

THERE are three things which fill my heart
 with sighs,
And steep my soul in laughter (when I view
Fair maiden-forms moving like melodies) —
Dimples, roselips, and eyes of any hue.
There are three things beneath the blessed skies
For which I live — black eyes and brown and
 blue:
I hold them all most dear; but oh! black eyes,
I live and die, and only die in you.
Of late such eyes looked at me — while I
 mused,
At sunset, underneath a shadowy plane,
In old Bayona nigh the southern sea —
From an half-open lattice looked at *me*.
I saw no more — only those eyes — confused
And dazzled to the heart with glorious pain.

## THE SKIPPING-ROPE

Printed in 1842, but omitted in all editions
after 1850.

SURE never yet was antelope
 Could skip so lightly by.
Stand off, or else my skipping-rope
 Will hit you in the eye.
How lightly whirls the skipping-rope!
 How fairy-like you fly!
Go, get you gone, you muse and mope —
 I hate that silly sigh.
Nay, dearest, teach me how to hope,
 Or tell me how to die.
There, take it, take my skipping-rope,
 And hang yourself thereby.

## THE NEW TIMON AND THE POETS

Published in 'Punch,' February 28, 1846,
signed 'Alcibiades'; and followed in the next
number (March 7, 1846) by the lines entitled
'Afterthought,' afterwards included as 'Literary Squabbles' in the collected edition of
1872. See p. xv. above.

WE know him, out of Shakespeare's art,
 And those fine curses which he spoke;
The old Timon, with his noble heart,
 That, strongly loathing, greatly broke.

So died the Old: here comes the New.
 Regard him: a familiar face:
I thought we knew him: What, it 's you,
 The padded man — that wears the stays —

Who killed the girls and thrilled the boys
 With dandy pathos when you wrote!

A Lion, you, that made a noise,
 And shook a mane *en papillotes*.

And once you tried the Muses too;
 You failed, Sir: therefore now you turn,
To fall on those who are to you
 As Captain is to Subaltern.

But men of long-enduring hopes,
 And careless what this hour may bring,
Can pardon little would-be POPES
 And BRUMMELS, when they try to sting.

An Artist, Sir, should rest in Art,
 And waive a little of his claim;
To have the deep Poetic heart
 Is more than all poetic fame.

But you, Sir, you are hard to please;
 You never look but half content;
Nor like a gentleman at ease,
 With moral breadth of temperament.

And what with spites and what with fears,
 You cannot let a body be:
It 's always ringing in your ears,
 'They call this man as good as *me*.'

What profits now to understand
 The merits of a spotless shirt —
A dapper boot — a little hand —
 If half the little soul is dirt?

*You* talk of tinsel! why, we see
 The old mark of rouge upon your cheeks.
*You* prate of Nature! you are he
 That spilt his life about the cliques.

A TIMON you! Nay, nay, for shame:
 It looks too arrogant a jest —
The fierce old man — to take his name,
 You bandbox. Off, and let him rest.

## LINES

Contributed to 'The Manchester Athenæum
Album,' 1850.

HERE often, when a child I lay reclined,
 I took delight in this locality.
Here stood the infant Ilion of the mind,
 And here the Grecian ships did seem to be.
And here again I come, and only find
 The drain-cut levels of the marshy lea, —
Gray sea-banks and pale sunsets, — dreary
 wind,
 Dim shores, dense rains, and heavy-clouded
 sea!

## STANZAS

Contributed to 'The Keepsake,' an illustrated annual, 1851.

WHAT time I wasted youthful hours,
One of the shining wingéd powers,
Show'd me vast cliffs with crown of towers.

As towards the gracious light I bow'd,
They seem'd high palaces and proud,
Hid now and then with sliding cloud.

He said, ' The labor is not small;
Yet winds the pathway free to all: —
Take care thou dost not fear to fall ! '

## BRITONS, GUARD YOUR OWN

Contributed to ' The Examiner,' January 31, 1852.

RISE, Britons, rise, if manhood be not dead;
The world's last tempest darkens overhead;
    The Pope has bless'd him;
    The Church caress'd him;
He triumphs; maybe we shall stand alone.
    Britons, guard your own.

His ruthless host is bought with plunder'd gold,
By lying priests the peasants' votes controll'd.
    All freedom vanish'd,
    The true men banish'd,
He triumphs; maybe we shall stand alone.
    Britons, guard your own.

Peace-lovers we — sweet Peace we all desire —
Peace-lovers we — but who can trust a liar ? —
    Peace-lovers, haters
    Of shameless traitors,
We hate not France, but this man's heart of stone.
    Britons, guard your own.

We hate not France, but France has lost her voice.
This man is France, the man they call her choice.
    By tricks and spying,
    By craft and lying,
And murder was her freedom overthrown.
    Britons, guard your own.

' Vive l'Empereur ' may follow by and by;
' God save the Queen ' is here a truer cry.
    God save the Nation,
    The toleration,
And the free speech that makes a Briton known.
    Britons, guard your own.

Rome's dearest daughter now is captive France,
The Jesuit laughs, and reckoning on his chance,
    Would, unrelenting,
    Kill all dissenting,
Till we were left to fight for truth alone.
    Britons, guard your own.

Call home your ships across Biscayan tides,
To blow the battle from their oaken sides.
    Why waste they yonder
    Their idle thunder ?

Why stay they there to guard a foreign throne ?
    Seamen, guard your own.

We were the best of marksmen long ago,
We won old battles with our strength, the bow.
    Now practise, yeomen,
    Like those bowmen,
Till your balls fly as their true shafts have flown.
    Yeomen, guard your own.

His soldier-ridden Highness might incline
To take Sardinia, Belgium, or the Rhine:
    Shall we stand idle,
    Nor seek to bridle
His rude aggressions, till we stand alone ?
    Make their cause your own.

Should he land here, and for one hour prevail,
There must no man go back to bear the tale:
    No man to bear it —
    Swear it ! we swear it !
Although we fight the banded world alone,
    We swear to guard our own.

## ADDITIONAL VERSES

To ' God Save the Queen ! ' written for the marriage of the Princess Royal of England with the Crown Prince of Prussia, January 25, 1858.

GOD bless our Prince and Bride !
God keep their lands allied,
    God save the Queen !
Clothe them with righteousness,
Crown them with happiness,
Them with all blessings bless,
    God save the Queen !

Fair fall this hallow'd hour,
Farewell, our England's flower,
    God save the Queen !
Farewell, first rose of May !
Let both the peoples say,
God bless thy marriage-day,
    God bless the Queen !

## THE WAR

Printed in the ' London Times,' May 9, 1859; reprinted in the ' Death of Œnone ' volume, 1892, with the title, ' Riflemen, Form.'

THERE is a sound of thunder afar,
    Storm in the South that darkens the day !
Storm of battle and thunder of war !
    Well if it do not roll our way.
    Form ! form ! Riflemen, form !
    Ready, be ready to meet the storm !
    Riflemen, Riflemen, Riflemen, form !

Be not deaf to the sound that warns !
    Be not gull'd by a despot's plea !
Are figs of thistles, or grapes of thorns ?
    How should a despot set men Free ?
    Form ! form ! Riflemen, form !

Ready, be ready to meet the storm!
  Riflemen, Riflemen, Riflemen, form!

Let your reforms for a moment go!
  Look to your butts, and take good aims!
Better a rotten borough or so
  Than a rotten fleet or a city in flames!
    Form! form! Riflemen, form!
    Ready, be ready to meet the storm!
    Riflemen, Riflemen, Riflemen, form!

Form, be ready to do or die!
  Form in Freedom's name and the Queen's!
True that we have a faithful ally,
  But only the devil can tell what he means.
    Form! form! Riflemen, form!
    Ready, be ready to meet the storm!
    Riflemen, Riflemen, Riflemen, form!

## THE RINGLET

Printed in the 'Enoch Arden' volume, 1864,
but afterwards suppressed.

'YOUR ringlets, your ringlets,
  That look so golden-gay,
If you will give me one, but one,
  To kiss it night and day,
Then never chilling touch of Time
  Will turn it silver-gray;
And then shall I know it is all true gold
To flame and sparkle and stream as of old.
Till all the comets in heaven are cold,
  And all her stars decay.'
'Then take it, love, and put it by;
This cannot change, nor yet can I.'

2

'My ringlet, my ringlet,
  That art so golden-gay,
Now never chilling touch of Time
  Can turn thee silver-gray;
And a lad may wink, and a girl may hint,
  And a fool may say his say;
For my doubts and fears were all amiss,
And I swear henceforth by this and this,
That a doubt will only come for a kiss,
  And a fear to be kiss'd away.'
'Then kiss it, love, and put it by:
If this can change, why so can I.'

II

O Ringlet, O Ringlet,
  I kiss'd you night and day,
And Ringlet, O Ringlet,
  You still are golden-gay,
But Ringlet, O Ringlet,
  You should be silver-gray:
For what is this which now I 'm told,
I that took you for true gold,
She that gave you 's bought and sold,
    Sold, sold.

2

O Ringlet, O Ringlet,
  She blush'd a rosy red,

When Ringlet, O Ringlet,
  She clipt you from her head,
And Ringlet, O Ringlet,
  She gave you me, and said,
'Come, kiss it, love, and put it by:
If this can change, why so can I.'
O fie, you golden nothing, fie,
    You golden lie.

3

O Ringlet, O Ringlet,
  I count you much to blame,
For Ringlet, O Ringlet,
  You put me much to shame,
So Ringlet, O Ringlet,
  I doom you to the flame.
For what is this which now I learn,
Has given all my faith a turn?
Burn, you glossy heretic, burn,
    Burn, burn.

## LINES

Written in 1864, at the request of the Queen,
for inscription on the statue of the Duchess of
Kent at Frogmore; printed in 'The Court
Journal,' March 19, 1864.

LONG as the heart beats life within her breast,
  Thy child will bless thee, guardian mother
    mild,
And far away thy memory will be blest
  By children of the children of thy child.

### 1865–1866

Contributed to 'Good Words,' March, 1868.

I STOOD on a tower in the wet,
And New Year and Old Year met,
And winds were roaring and blowing,
And I said, 'O years that meet in tears,
Have ye aught that is worth the knowing?
Science enough and exploring,
Wanderers coming and going,
Matter enough for deploring,
But aught that is worth the knowing?'
Seas at my feet were flowing,
Waves on the shingle pouring,
Old Year roaring and blowing,
And New Year blowing and roaring.

## STANZA

Contributed to the 'Shakespearean Show-
Book,' printed in March, 1884, for a fair got
up for the Chelsea Hospital for Women.

NOT he that breaks the dams, but he
  That thro' the channels of the State
  Convoys the people's wish, is great;
His name is pure, his fame is free.

## COMPROMISE

Addressed to Mr. Gladstone, then Prime
Minister, in November, 1884, when the Fran-

chise Bill was being discussed in the House of
Lords; and afterwards printed in the 'Pall
Mall Gazette.'

STEERSMAN, be not precipitate in thy act
Of steering, for the river here, my friend,
Parts in two channels, moving to one end.
This goes straight forward to the cataract,
That streams about the bend;
But tho' the cataract seem the nearer way,
Whate'er the crowd on either bank may say,
Take thou the bend, 't will save thee many a
day.

## EXPERIMENT IN SAPPHIC METRE

Contributed to Professor Jebb's 'Primer of
Greek Literature,' 1877.

Faded every violet, all the roses;
Gone the glorious promise, and the victim
Broken in the anger of Aphrodite
Yields to the victor.

The following 'unpublished fragment' was
printed in 'Ros Rosarum,' an anthology edited
by Hon. Mrs. Boyle, 1885:—

The night with sudden odor reel'd,
The southern stars a music peal'd,
Warm beams across the meadow stole;
For Love flew over grove and field,
Said, 'Open, Rosebud, open, yield
Thy fragrant soul.'

The following prefatory stanza was contributed in 1891 to 'Pearl,' an English poem of
the 14th century, edited by Mr. Israel Gol-
lancz:—

We lost you for how long a time,
True Pearl of our poetic prime!
We found you, and you gleam reset
In Britain's lyric coronet.

[Other poems by Tennyson mentioned by
Shepherd and Luce in their Bibliographies
(neither of which is invariably accurate) as
printed, but omitted in the collected editions,
are the following: a stanza in the volume of
his poems presented to the Princess Louise of
Schleswig-Holstein by representatives of the
nurses of England; lines on the christening of
the daughter of the Duchess of Fife; and lines
to the memory of J. R. Lowell. These are
not referred to in the 'Memoir,' and I have
not been able to find copies of them.]

## VI. NOTES AND ILLUSTRA-
TIONS

Page 1. TO THE QUEEN.
The following is the stanza referring to the
Crystal Palace Exhibition of 1851, which origi-
nally followed the 6th:—

She brought a vast design to pass,
When Europe and the scattered ends
Of our fierce world were mixt as friends
And brethren in her halls of glass.

For an early version of the poem (from a MS.
in the Library of the Drexel Institute, Philadelphia), see Jones's 'The Growth of the Idylls
of the King,' p. 152. Nine of the thirteen
stanzas are entirely unlike the poem as finally
published.

Page 2. And statesmen at her councils met, etc.
This stanza was once quoted by Mr. Gladstone
in the House of Commons with remarkable
effect. Lord John Manners, in an argument
against political change, had quoted the poet's
description of England as

A land of old and wide renown
Where Freedom slowly broadens down.

The retort was none the less effective because
the passage was taken from a different poem.
Page 4. LEONINE ELEGIACS.
The title in 1830 was simply 'Elegiacs.' In
line 6 'wood-dove' was 'turtle,' and in 15 'or'
was 'and.'
For the allusion in 'The ancient poetess singeth,' etc., compare 'Locksley Hall Sixty Years
After': 'Hesper, whom the poet call'd the
Bringer home of all good things.' The reference is to the fragment of Sappho:—

Ἕσπερε, πάντα φέρεις·
Φέρεις οἶνον, φέρεις αἶγα,
Φέρεις ματέρι παῖδα.

Byron paraphrases it in 'Don Juan' (iii. 107):—

O Hesperus! thou bringest all good things—
Home to the weary, to the hungry cheer,
To the young bird the parent's brooding wings,
The welcome stall to the o'er-labor'd steer;
Whate'er of peace about our hearth-stone clings,
Whate'er our household gods protect of dear,
Are gather'd round us by thy look of rest;
Thou bring'st the child, too, to the mother's breast.

SUPPOSED CONFESSIONS, etc.
The original title was 'Supposed Confessions
of a Second-rate Sensitive Mind not in Unity
with Itself.' In the poem as restored the following lines, after line 39, were omitted:—

A grief not uninformed, and dull,
Hearted with hope, of hope as full
As is the blood with life, or night
And a dark cloud with rich moonlight.
To stand beside a grave, and see
The red small atoms wherewith we
Are built, and smile in calm, and say—
'These little motes and grains shall be
Clothed on with immortality
More glorious than the noon of day.
All that is pass'd into the flowers,
And into beasts and other men,
And all the Norland whirlwind showers
From open vaults, and all the sea
O'erwashes with sharp salts, again
Shall fleet together all, and be
Indued with immortality.'

The only other changes are 'rosy fingers' for
'waxen fingers' in 42, and 'man' for 'men' in
169.

The 'Westminster Review' (January, 1831) recognized in this poem 'an extraordinary combination of deep reflection, metaphysical analysis, picturesque description, dramatic transition, and strong emotion.' Arthur Hallam, in the 'Englishman's Magazine' (August, 1831), said of it: 'The "Confessions of a Second-rate Sensitive Mind" are full of deep insight into human nature, and into those particular trials which are sure to beset men who think and feel for themselves at this epoch of social development. The title is perhaps ill chosen; not only has it an appearance of quaintness, which has no sufficient reason, but it seems to us incorrect. The mood portrayed in this poem, unless the admirable skill of delineation has deceived us, is rather the clouded season of a strong mind than the habitual condition of one feeble and second-rate.'

Page 7. ISABEL.

In 1842 'wifehood' (line 16) was changed to 'marriage,' and 'blenched' (a misprint?) to 'blanched.'

Page 8. MARIANA.

In the 4th line the first reading was 'the peach to the garden-wall.' Bayard Taylor, writing in 1877 (in 'International Review,' vol. iv.), quotes the poet as saying: 'There is my "Mariana," for example. A line in it is wrong, and I cannot possibly change it, because it has been so long published; yet it always annoys me. I wrote "That held the peach to the garden-wall." Now this is not a characteristic of the scenery I had in mind. The line should be "That held the pear to the gable-wall."' Whether this conversation occurred during Taylor's visit to Tennyson in 1857 I cannot say; but the line was changed in the printed poem in 1860, or seventeen years before the review was written.

In line 43, the original reading was 'did dark;' retained in 1842, but changed in 1845. In line 50, 'up and away' was at first 'up an' away' (changed in 1842). In line 63, the original 'sung i' the pane' was retained down to 1850. Line 80 was originally, 'Downsloped [1] was westering in his bower' (changed in 1842).

Page 9. To ———.

The 1830 reading in the 3d and 4th lines was

The knotted lies of human creeds,
The wounding cords which bind and strain.

MADELINE.

Printed in 1830 without the division into stanzas, which was made in 1842. The only other change (except the spelling 'airy' for 'aery') is 'amorously' for 'three times three' in the last stanza (in the *errata* of the 1830 volume).

Page 10. RECOLLECTIONS OF THE ARABIAN NIGHTS.

In line 29 the 1830 volume has 'Of breaded blosms'; in 78 'Blackgreen' for 'Black'; in

---

[1] In the volumes of 1830 and 1833, compound words are, with rare exceptions, printed without the hyphen; as 'silverchiming,' 'gardenbowers,' 'mountainstreams,' etc.

---

90 'unrayed' for 'inlaid'; in 100 'I was borne'; in 125 'wreathed silvers'; and in 140 'Flowing beneath.'

Page 13. ODE TO MEMORY.

In line 68, 'waken'd' was at first 'waked'; 103 was 'Emblems or glimpses of infinity'; in 117 'And those' was 'The few'; and 119–121 were: —

My friend, with thee to live alone,
Methinks were better than to own
A crown, a sceptre, and a throne!

Page 14. THE POET.

In 1830 the 12th stanza read thus: —

And in the bordure of her robe was writ
WISDOM, a name to shake
Hoar anarchies, as with a thunderfit,
And when she spake, etc.

The 9th had 'a' for 'one'; and the 14th 'hurl'd' for 'whirl'd.'

In the 1st stanza, 'the hate of hate,' etc., clearly means the hatred of hate, etc. Rev. F. W. Robertson explains it thus: 'That is, the Prophet of Truth receives for his dower the scorn of men in whom scorn dwells, hatred from men who hate, while his reward is the gratitude and affection of men who seek the truth which they love, more eagerly than the faults which their acuteness can blame.' A very intelligent lady once told me that she had always understood 'hate of hate' to mean the utmost intensity of hate, etc., the poet's passions and sensibilities being to those of ordinary men 'as moonlight unto sunlight, and as water unto wine.'

THE POET'S MIND.

Reprinted in 1842 with the omission of the following passage after line 7: —

Clear as summer mountainstreams,
Bright as the inwoven beams,
Which beneath their crisping sapphire
In the midday, floating o'er
The golden sands, make evermore
To a blossomstarrèd shore.
Hence away, unhallowed laugher!

The 9th line in 1830 was 'The poet's mind is holy ground'; and the 35th had 'would never.'

Page 15. THE SEA-FAIRIES.

For the original form of this poem, see p. 786.

Page 16. THE DYING SWAN.

Reprinted in 1842 with 'And loudly did lament' for 'Which loudly,' etc.; and in 1850 with 'Above in the wind was the swallow' for 'sung the swallow.'

Page 18. CIRCUMSTANCE.

The last line originally began, 'Fill up the round,' etc.

Page 20. ADELINE.

The only changes since 1842 are in the 5th stanza: 'the side of the morn' for 'the side o' the morn,' and 'locks a-drooping' for 'locks a-dropping.'

MARGARET.

In the 3d stanza the first reading was 'The

lion-souled Plantagenet' (Richard I.). 'Chate-let' was proscribed in the Reign of Terror, and executed in December, 1793.

In the 4th stanza, the 1830 volume has 'And more aerially blue,' with 'And' instead of 'But' in the next line.

Page 21. ROSALIND.

The only change in 1884 was the omission of the 'Note' printed on p. 789 above.

Page 22. ELEÄNORE.

Line 99 was originally, 'Did roof noonday with doubt and fear.' The reading of 108–111 was: —

> As waves that from the outer deep
> Roll into a quiet cove,
> There fall away, and lying still,
> Having glorious dreams in sleep,
> Shadow forth the banks at will:
> Or sometimes they swell and move, etc.

In 123 'While' was originally 'When.' For 127 the reading was: —

> I gaze on thee the cloudless noon
> Of mortal beauty: in its place, etc.

That of 134 was 'Floweth; then I faint, I swoon.'

Page 23. KATE.

This poem, after being included in the one-volume English edition of 1897, has been omitted in the 'Globe' edition of 1898. On second thought, Lord Tennyson appears to have decided to add nothing to the collected works as last arranged by his father.

Page 24. 'MY LIFE IS FULL OF WEARY DAYS.'

The reading of the first two stanzas in 1833 was as follows: —

### I

> All good things have not kept aloof,
> Nor wander'd into other ways:
> I have not lacked thy mild reproof,
> Nor golden largess of thy praise,
> But life is full of weary days.

### II

> Shake hands, my friend, across the brink
> Of that deep grave to which I go.
> Shake hands once more: I cannot sink
> So far — far down, but I shall know
> Thy voice, and answer from below.

The only changes in the next three stanzas were 'scritches of the jay' for 'laughters of the jay,' and 'darnel' for 'darnels.'

The following stanzas, with which the poem originally ended (connected closely with the preceding, there being only a comma after 'the woodbines blow'), have not been restored: —

### VI

> If thou art blest, my mother's smile
> Undimmed, if bees are on the wing:
> Then cease, my friend, a little while,
> That I may hear the throstle sing
> His bridal song, the boast of spring.

### VII

> Sweet as the noise in parchèd plains
> Of bubbling wells that fret the stones
> (If any sense in me remains),
> Thy words will be; thy cheerful tones
> As welcome to my crumbling bones.

The 'Quarterly Review' for July, 1833, had its fling at the line, 'If any sense in me remains.' 'This doubt,' it says, is 'inconsistent with the opening stanza of the piece, and, in fact, too modest; we take upon ourselves to reassure Mr. Tennyson that, even after he shall be dead and buried, as much "sense" will still remain as he has now the good fortune to possess.'

In the 4th stanza 'may' refers to the blossoms of the hawthorn. Compare 'The Miller's Daughter:' 'The lanes, you know, were white with may.' Here, as there, some of the American reprints put 'May' for 'may.'

EARLY SONNETS.

I. The original version has 'a confused dream' in the 3d line; 'Altho' I knew not' in the 12th; and for the 14th 'And each had lived in the other's mind and speech.' In the 8th 'hath' is italicized.

III. In the 1st line 'full' was originally 'fierce'; and in the 15th 'warm' was 'great.'

VI. The 10th line was originally 'How long shall the icy-hearted Muscovite.'

VII. The 1st line had originally 'dainty' for 'slender.'

VIII. The 5th line had 'waltzing-circle' for 'whirling dances.'

X. The first line originally began 'But were I loved,' etc.

XI. The 'bridesmaid' was Emily Sellwood, who afterwards became the poet's wife; and the marriage was that of his brother Charles to Louisa Sellwood, May 24, 1836. See the 'Memoir,' vol. i. p. 148.

Page 27. THE LADY OF SHALOTT.

The last four lines of the 1st stanza were originally as follows: —

> The yellowleavèd waterlily,
> The greensheathèd daffodilly,
> Tremble in the water chilly,
> Round about Shalott.

The next stanza began thus: —

> Willows whiten, aspens shiver.
> The sunbeam-showers break and quiver
> In the stream that runneth ever, etc.

The first reading of the 3d and 4th stanzas was: —

> Underneath the bearded barley,
> The reaper, reaping late and early,
> Hears her ever chanting cheerly,
> Like an angel, singing clearly,
>     O'er the stream of Camelot.
> Piling the sheaves in furrows airy,
> Beneath the moon, the reaper weary
> Listening whispers, ''t is the fairy,
>     Lady of Shalott.'

> The little isle is all inrailed
> With a rose-fence, and overtrailed

With roses: by the marge unhailed
The shallop flitteth silkensailed,
    Skimming down to Camelot.
A pearlgarland winds her head:
She leaneth on a velvet bed,
Full royally apparellèd,
    The Lady of Shalott.

Part II. goes on thus: —

No time hath she to sport and play:
A charmèd web she weaves alway.
A curse is on her, if she stay
Her weaving, either night or day,
    To look down to Camelot.
She knows not what the curse may be;
Therefore she weaveth steadily,
Therefore no other care hath she,
    The Lady of Shalott.

She lives with little joy or fear.
Over the water, running near,
The sheepbell tinkles in her ear.
Before her hangs a mirror clear,
    Reflecting towered Camelot.
And as the mazy web she whirls,
She sees the surly village churls, etc.

The next stanza ('Sometimes a troop,' etc.) is unchanged; and the only alteration in the next is 'went to Camelot' for 'came from Camelot.'

In Part III. the 5th line of the 2d and 3d stanzas had 'down from Camelot;' the last line of the 3d had 'over green Shalott;' the 8th line of the 4th was 'Tirra lirra, tirra lirra;' and the 3d line of the 5th had 'water-flower.'

In Part IV. the latter part of the 1st stanza was as follows: —

Outside the isle a shallow boat
Beneath a willow lay afloat,
Below the carven stern she wrote,
    *The Lady of Shalott.*

Then followed this stanza: —

A cloudwhite crown of pearl she dight.
All raimented in snowy white
That loosely flew (her zone in sight,
Clasped with one blinding diamond bright)
    Her wide eyes fixed on Camelot,
Though the squally eastwind keenly
Blew, with folded arms serenely
By the water stood the queenly
    Lady of Shalott.

The next stanza opened thus: —

With a steady stony glance —
Like some bold seer in a trance,
Beholding all his own mischance,
Mute, with a glassy countenance —
    She looked down to Camelot.
It was the closing, etc.

The remaining stanzas were as follows: —

As when to sailors while they roam,
By creeks and outfalls far from home,
Rising and dropping with the foam,
From dying swans wild warblings come,
    Blown shoreward; so to Camelot
Still as the boathead wound along
The willowy hills and fields among,
They heard her chanting her deathsong,
    The Lady of Shalott.

A longdrawn carol, mournful, holy,
She chanted loudly, chanted lowly,

Till her eyes were darkened wholly,
And her smooth face sharpened slowly,
    Turned to towered Camelot:
For ere she reached, etc.

Under tower and balcony,
By gardenwall and gallery,
A pale, pale corpse she floated by,
Deadcold, between the houses high,
    Dead into towered Camelot.
Knight and burgher, lord and dame,
To the plankèd wharfage came:
Below the stern they read her name,
    'The Lady of Shalott.'

They crossed themselves, their stars they blest,
Knight, minstrel, abbot, squire, and guest.
There lay a parchment on her breast,
That puzzled more than all the rest,
    The wellfed wits at Camelot.
' *The web was woven curiously,*
*The charm is broken utterly,*
*Draw near and fear not — this is I,*
    *The Lady of Shalott.*'

The ending of the poem is much improved by the revision. The 'wellfed wits' (the epithet seems out of keeping here) might well be 'puzzled' by the parchment, which is as pointless as it is enigmatical; but the new ending, with its introduction of Lancelot, is most pathetic and suggestive.

In line 157 the reading in 1842 (and down to 1873) was 'A corse between,' etc.

According to Palgrave ('Lyrical Poems by Tennyson'), the poem was suggested by 'an Italian romance upon the *Donna di Scalotta,* in which Camelot, unlike the Celtic tradition, was placed near the sea.' It is in a very different form that the legend reappears in the 'Idylls of the King.'

Page 29.  MARIANA.

The original form was as follows: —

Behind the barren hill upsprung
    With pointed rocks against the light,
The crag sharpshadowed overhung
    Each glaring creek and inlet bright.
Far, far, one lightblue ridge was seen,
    Looming like baseless fairyland;
    Eastward a slip of burning sand,
Dark-rimmed with sea, and bare of green.
Down in the dry salt-marshes stood
    That house darklatticed.   Not a breath
    Swayed the sick vineyard underneath,
Or moved the dusty southernwood.
    'Madonna,' with melodious moan
    Sang Mariana, night and morn,
    'Madonna! lo! I am all alone,
    Love-forgotten and love-forlorn.'

She, as her carol sadder grew,
    From her warm brow and bosom down
Through rosy taper fingers drew
    Her streaming curls of deepest brown
On either side, and made appear,
    Still-lighted in a secret shrine,
    Her melancholy eyes divine,
The home of woe without a tear.
    'Madonna,' with melodious moan
    Sang Mariana, night and morn,
    'Madonna! lo! I am all alone,
    Love-forgotten and love-forlorn.'

When the dawncrimson changed, and past
    Into deep orange o'er the sea,

Low on her knees herself she cast,
  Unto our lady prayèd she.
She moved her lips, she prayed alone,
  She praying disarrayed and warm
  From slumber, deep her wavy form
In the darklustrous mirror shone.
    'Madonna,' in a low clear tone
    Said Mariana, night and morn,
    Low she mourned, 'I am all alone,
    Love-forgotten and love-forlorn.'

At noon she slumbered. All along
  The silvery field, the large leaves talked
With one another, as among
  The spikèd maize in dreams she walked.
The lizard leapt: the sunlight played:
  She heard the callow nestling lisp,
  And brimful meadow-runnels crisp,
In the full-leavèd platan-shade.
    In sleep she breathed in a lower tone,
    Murmuring as at night and morn,
    'Madonna! lo! I am all alone,
    Love-forgotten and love-forlorn.'

Dreaming, she knew it was a dream
  Most false: *he* was and was not there.
She woke: the babble of the stream
  Fell, and without the steady glare
Shrank the sick olive sere and small.
  The riverbed was dusty-white;
  From the bald rock the blinding light
Beat ever on the sunwhite wall.
    She whispered, with a stifled moan
    More inward than at night or morn,
    'Madonna, leave me not all alone,
    To die forgotten and live forlorn.'

One dry cicala's summer song
  At night filled all the gallery,
Backward the latticeblind she flung,
  And leaned upon the balcony.
Ever the low wave seemed to roll
  Up to the coast: far on, alone
  In the East, large Hesper overshone
The mourning gulf, and on her soul
  Poured divine solace, or the rise
Of moonlight from the margin gleamed,
Volcano-like, afar, and streamed
  On her white arm, and heavenward eyes.
    Not all alone she made her moan,
    Yet ever sang she, night and morn,
    'Madonna! lo! I am all alone,
    Love-forgotten and love-forlorn.'

The only change since 1842 is in line 53, which in that edition retains the original 'Shrank the sick olive,' etc.

Page 30. THE TWO VOICES.

Unaltered except in line 457, which was originally 'So variously seem'd all things wrought.'

The poem, according to Palgrave (who unquestionably writes 'with authority'), describes 'the conflict in a soul between Scepticism and Faith.'

Lines 8–15 have been variously interpreted. Peter Bayne (who is followed by Professor Corson) understands the passage to mean 'that the shuffling off of this mortal coil may open to him new spheres of energy and happiness;' and that 'the reply of the poet is that man is nature's highest product, — the obvious suggestion being that there is no splendid dragon-fly into which the human grub, released by death, is likely to develop.' But (as I remarked in my 'Select

Poems of Tennyson,' in 1884) this 'suggestion,' so far from being 'obvious,' seems to me merely a desperate attempt to make the reference to the higher nature of man a 'reply' to what the critic assumes that the Voice means to say. For myself, I had no hesitation in adopting Tainsh's interpretation of the passage: 'A dragon-fly is more wonderful than you;' and Lord Tennyson afterwards explained it to me in almost the same words: 'The dragon-fly is as wonderful as you.'

In line 228, the allusion is to the old notion that man was composed of the four elements, earth, air, fire, and water, and that the well-balanced mixture of these produced the perfection of humanity. Compare Shakespeare, 'Julius Cæsar,' v. 5. 73: —

His life was gentle, and the elements
So mix'd in him that Nature might stand up
And say to all the world, 'This was a man!'

Page 35. THE MILLER'S DAUGHTER.

The poem originally began with this stanza: —

I met in all the close green ways,
  While walking with my line and rod,
The wealthy miller's mealy face,
  Like the moon in an ivy-tod.
He look'd so jolly and so good,
  While fishing in the mill-dam water,
I laugh'd to see him as he stood,
  And dreamt not of the miller's daughter.

The 2d stanza, now the 1st, remains unaltered, and the only change in the next is 'can make' for 'makes' in the last line. In the next (3d) stanza, the original reading in the 2d line was 'My darling Alice,' and 'my own sweet wife' in the 6th line.

The 4th stanza ('Have I not found,' etc.) was added in 1842.

The 5th stanza originally stood thus: —

My father's mansion, mounted high,
  Looked down upon the village spire.
I was a long and listless boy,
  And son and heir unto the squire.
In these dear walls, where I and you
  Have lived and loved alone so long,
Each morn my sleep, etc.

The 6th stanza began: —

I often heard the cooing dove
  In firry woodlands mourn alone;
But ere I saw, etc.

The last line had 'the long' for 'those long.'

The 7th stanza was as follows: —

Sometimes I whistled in the wind,
  Sometimes I angled, thought and deed
Torpid, as swallows left behind
  That winter 'neath the floating weed:
At will to wander everyway
  From brook to brook my sole delight,
As lithe eels over meadows gray
  Oft shift their glimmering pool by night.

The 8th stanza was the one now made the 13th, and the first quatrain read thus: —

How dear to me in youth, my love,
  Was everything about the mill —

The black and silent pool above,
The pool beneath that ne'er stood still, etc.

The 9th and 10th were as follows: —

I loved from off the bridge to hear
The rushing sound the water made,
And see the fish that everywhere
In the backcurrent glanced and played:
Low down the tall flagflower that sprung
Beside the noisy steppingstones,
And the massed chestnutboughs that hung
Thickstudded over with white cones.

Remember you that pleasant day
When, after roving in the woods,
('T was April then) I came and lay
Beneath those gummy chestnutbuds
That glistened in the April blue
Upon the slope so smooth and cool,
I lay and never thought of *you*,
But angled in the deep millpool.

The stanza beginning ' A love-song,' etc., was
not in the original version, which continued
thus: —

A water-rat from off the bank
Plunged in the stream. With idle care,
Downlooking through the sedges rank,
I saw your troubled image there.
Upon the dark and dimpled beck
It wandered like a floating light,
A full fair form, a warm white neck,
And two white arms — how rosy white !

If you remember, you had set
Upon the narrow casement-edge
A long green box of mignonette,
And you were leaning from the ledge.
I raised my eyes at once: above
They met two eyes so blue and bright,
Such eyes ! I swear to you, my love,
That they have never lost their light.

The next (13th) stanza, now suppressed, was
as follows: —

That slope beneath the chestnut tall,
Is wooed with choicest breaths of air;
Methinks that I could tell you all
The cowslips and the kingcups there;
Each coltsfoot down the grassy bent,
Whose round leaves hold the gathered shower,
Each quaintly-folded cuckoo-pint,
And silver-paly cuckoo flower.

The 14th was: —

In rambling on the eastern wold,
When thro' the showery April nights
Their hueless crescent glimmered cold,
From all the other village lights
I knew your taper far away.
My heart was full of trembling hope,
Down from the wold I came and lay
Upon the dewy swarded slope.

The 15th was as follows: —

The white chalkquarry from the hill
Upon the broken ripple gleamed,
I murmured lowly, sitting still,
While round my feet the eddy streamed:
' Oh ! that I were the wreath she wears,
The mirror where her sight she feeds,
The song she sings, the air she breathes,
The letters of the book she reads.'

The 16th was identical with the present 16th,
' Sometimes I saw you sit and spin,' etc.
The 17th was: —

I loved, but when I dared to speak
My love, the lawns were white with May;
Your ripe lips moved not, but your cheek
Flushed like the coming of the day:
Rosecheekt, roselipt, half-sly, half-shy,
You would, etc.

' May,' which must have been a misprint, was
changed to ' may ' in 1842.
The 18th and 19th (afterwards omitted to
make room for the three new ones, in which
Alice is brought to visit his mother, — the present 18th, 19th, and 20th) were as follows: —

Remember you the clear moonlight
That whitened all the eastern ridge,
When o'er the water, dancing white,
I stept upon the old mill-bridge ?
I heard you whisper from above
A lute-toned whisper, ' I am here; '
I murmured, ' Speak again, my love,
The stream is loud; I cannot hear.'

I heard, as I have seemed to hear,
When all the under air was still,
The low voice of the glad new year
Call to the freshly-flowered hill.
I heard, as I have often heard,
The nightingale in leafy woods
Call to its mate, when nothing stirred
To left or right but falling floods.

The 20th stanza was as follows: —

Come, Alice, sing to me the song
I made you on our marriageday,
When, arm in arm, we went along
Half-tearfully, and you were gay
With brooch and ring: for I shall seem,
The while you sing that song, to hear
The millwheel turning in the stream,
And the green chestnut whisper near.

The ' Song ' was originally this: —

I wish I were her earring
Ambushed in auburn ringlets sleek,
(So might my shadow tremble
Over her downy cheek)
Hid in her hair, all day and night,
Touching her neck so warm and white.

I wish I were the girdle
Buckled about her dainty waist,
That her heart might beat against me
In sorrow and in rest.
I should know well if it beat right,
I 'd clasp it round so close and tight.

I wish I were her necklace,
So might I ever fall and rise
Upon her balmy bosom
With her laughter or her sighs.
I would lie round so warm and light,
I would not be unclasped at night.

The next stanzas (21st and 22d) were: —

A trifle, sweet, which true love spells —
True love interprets right alone;
For o'er each letter broods and dwells
(Like light from running waters thrown
On flowery swaths) the blissful flame
Of his sweet eyes, that, day and night,

With pulses thrilling thro' his frame
Do inly tremble, starrybright.

How I waste language — yet in truth
   You must blame love, whose early rage
Made me a rhymester in my youth,
   And over-garrulous in age.
Sing me that other song I made,
   Half-angered with my happy lot,
When in the breezy limewood-shade
   I found the blue forget-me-not.

This was the second 'Song': —

All yesternight you met me not.
My ladylove, forget me not.
When I am gone, regret me not,
But, here or there, forget me not.
   With your arched eyebrow threat me not,
      And tremulous eyes, like April skies,
         That seem to say, 'forget me not.'
   I pray you, love, forget me not.

In idle sorrow set me not;
Regret me not: forget me not:
Oh ! leave me not; oh, let me not
Wear quite away; — forget me not.
   With roguish laughter fret me not
      From dewy eyes, like April skies,
         That ever *look*, 'forget me not,'
   Blue as the blue forget-me-not.

The 23d stanza is unaltered from the one beginning 'Look thro' mine eyes with thine,' etc.; and the 24th and last is the same that now ends the poem, except that the first quatrain reads thus: —

I 've half a mind to walk, my love,
   To the old mill across the wolds,
For look ! the sunset from above
   Winds all the vale in rosy folds, etc.

The present 25th and 26th stanzas ('Yet tears they shed,' etc.) were added in 1842. In the 7th line of the 25th all the American editions that I have seen (from 1842 down) have 'the loss *that* brought' instead of 'had brought.'
Page 38. FATIMA.
The 2d stanza was added in 1842. The 2d line of the poem had originally 'at' for 'from.'
ŒNONE.
The poem originally began thus: —

There is a dale in Ida, lovelier
Than any in old Ionia, beautiful
With emerald slopes of sunny sward, that lean
Above the loud glenriver, which hath worn
A path thro' steepdown granite walls below
Mantled with flowering tendriltwine. In front
The cedarshadowy valleys open wide.
Far-seen, high over all the Godbuilt wall
And many a snowycolumned range divine,
Mounted with awful sculptures — men and Gods,
The work of Gods — bright on the darkblue sky
The windy citadel of Ilion
Shone, like the crown of Troas. Hither came
Mournful Œnone, wandering forlorn
Of Paris, once her playmate. Round her neck,
Her neck all marblewhite and marblecold,
Floated her hair or seemed to float in rest.
She, leaning on a vine-entwinèd stone,
Sang to the stillness, till the mountain-shadow
Sloped downward to her seat from the upper cliff.

[1] In the Pyrenees, where part of this poem was written, I saw a very beautiful species of Cicala, which had

O mother Ida, manyfountained Ida,
Dear mother Ida, hearken ere I die.
The grasshopper is silent in the grass,
The lizard with his shadow on the stone
Sleeps like a shadow, and the scarletwinged [1]
Cicala in the noonday leapeth not.
Along the water-rounded granite-rock
The purple flower droops: the golden bee, etc.

The text then goes on without change (except the insertion of line 46, 'I waited underneath the dawning hills,' which is not in the first version) to line 51, 'Came up from reedy Simois all alone.' It then proceeds as follows: —

O mother Ida, hearken ere I die.
I sate alone: the goldensandalled morn
Rosehued the scornful hills: I sate alone
With downdropt eyes: whitebreasted like a star
Fronting the dawn he came: a leopard skin
From his white shoulder drooped: his sunny hair
Clustered about his temples like a God's:
And his cheek brightened, as the foambow brightens
When the wind blows the foam; and I called out,
'Welcome, Apollo, welcome home, Apollo,
Apollo, my Apollo, loved Apollo.'

Dear mother Ida, hearken ere I die.
He, mildly smiling, in his milkwhite palm
Close-held a golden apple, lightningbright
With changeful flashes, dropt with dew of Heaven
Ambrosially smelling. From his lip,
Curved crimson, the fullflowing river of speech
Came down upon my heart.
          'My own Œnone,
Beautifulbrowed Œnone, mine own soul,
Behold this fruit, whose gleaming rind ingrav'n
"For the most fair" in aftertime may breed
Deep evilwilledness of heaven and sere
Heartburning toward hallowed Ilion;
And all the colour of my afterlife
Will be the shadow of today. Today
Here and Pallas and the floating grace
Of laughterloving Aphrodite meet
In manyfolded Ida to receive
This meed of beauty, she to whom my hand
Award the palm. Within the green hillside,
Under yon whispering tuft of oldest pine,
Is an ingoing grotto, strown with spar
And ivymatted at the mouth, wherein
Thou unbeholden may'st behold, unheard
Hear all, and see thy Paris judge of Gods.'

Dear mother Ida, hearken ere I die.
It was the deep midnoon: one silvery cloud
Had lost his way between the piney hills.
They came — all three — the Olympian goddesses:
Naked they came to the smoothswarded bower,
Lustrous with lilyflower, violeteyed
Both white and blue, with lotetree-fruit thickset,
Shadowed with singing pine: and all the while,
Above, the overwandering ivy and vine
This way and that in many a wild festoon
Ran riot, garlanding the gnarlèd boughs
With bunch and berry and flower thro' and thro'.
On the treetops a golden glorious cloud
Leaned, slowly dropping down ambrosial dew.
How beautiful they were, too beautiful
To look upon ! but Paris was to me
More lovelier than all the world beside.

O mother Ida, hearken ere I die.
First spake the imperial Olympian

scarlet wings spotted with black. Probably nothing of the kind exists in Mount Ida.

With archèd eyebrow smiling sovranly,
Fulleyèd Here. She to Paris made
Proffer of royal power, ample rule
Unquestioned, overflowing revenue
Wherewith to embellish state ' from many a vale
And riversundered champaign clothed with corn,
Or upland glebe wealthy in oil and wine —
Honour and homage, tribute, tax and toll
From many an inland town and haven large,
Mast-thronged below her shadowing citadel
In glassy bays among her tallest towers.'

O mother Ida, hearken ere I die.
Still she spake on and still she spake of power
' Which in all action is the end of all.
Power fitted to the season, measured by
The height of the general feeling, wisdomborn
And throned of wisdom — from all neighbour crowns
Alliance and allegiance evermore.
Such boon from me Heaven's Queen to thee king-
born,' etc.

The next six lines (126–131) follow without
change, and the speech of Juno ends with these
two lines, afterwards suppressed: —

The changeless calm of undisputed right,
The highest height and topmost strength of power.

There is no change in the next ten lines
(132–141) except ' Flattered his spirit ' for ' Flatter'd his heart.'

The speech of Pallas (142–164) originally stood
thus: —

' Selfreverence, selfknowledge, selfcontrol
Are the three hinges of the gates of Life,
That open into power, everyway
Without horizon, bound or shadow or cloud.
Yet not for power (power of herself
Will come uncalled-for) but to live by law,
Acting the law we live by without fear,
And because right is right, to follow right
Were wisdom, in the scorn of consequence.
(Dear mother Ida, hearken ere I die.)
Not as men value gold because it tricks
And blazons outward Life with ornament,
But rather as the miser, for itself.
Good for selfgood doth half destroy selfgood.
The means and end, like two coiled snakes, infect
Each other, bound in one with hateful love.
So both into the fountain and the stream
A drop of poison falls. Come hearken to me,
And look upon me and consider me,
So shalt thou find me fairest, so endurance,
Like to an athlete's arm, shall still become
Sinew'd with motion, till thine active will
(As the dark body of the Sun robed round
With his own ever-emanating lights)
Be flooded o'er with her own effluences,
And thereby grow to freedom.'
                   Here she ceased, etc.

The next five lines (165–169) are unchanged,
and the poem then goes on thus : —

Idalian Aphrodite oceanborn,
Fresh as the foam, newbathed in Paphian wells,
With rosy slender fingers upward drew
From her warm brow and bosom her dark hair
Fragrant and thick, and on her head upbound
In a purple band: below her lucid neck
Shone ivorylike, and from the ground her foot
Gleamed rosywhite, and o'er her rounded form
Between the shadows of the vinebunches
Floated the glowing sunlights, as she moved.

There is no change in the next twenty-four
lines (179–202) except that, instead of the *three*
lines beginning ' She spoke and laugh'd,' the
first version has these *two* : —

I only saw my Paris raise his arm:
I only saw great Here's angry eyes, etc.

In the remainder of the poem the changes are
few and slight. In line 203 the earlier reading
is ' Dear mother Ida, hearken ere I die; ' and so
also in 252. Line 226 was ' Oh! mother Ida,
hearken ere I die; ' and 241 was ' Yet, mother
Ida, hear me ere I die.' For 205–208 the original reading was: —

My dark tall pines, that plumed the craggy ledge
High over the blue gorge, or lower down
Filling greengulphèd Ida, all between
The snowy peak and snowwhite cataract
Fostered the callow eaglet — from beneath, etc.

Lines 216–225 were inserted in 1842; and for
249–251 the original version has only the line,
' Ere it is born. I will not die alone.'
In line 27 all the editions I have seen down to
that of 1884 have ' and the cicala sleeps; ' and
in the next line ' The purple flowers droop.' It
probably occurred to the poet that the introduction of the *cicala*, or cicada (the *Greek* cicada, not our insect so called), was too nearly a
repetition of that of the grasshopper.
For lines 39, 40, compare ' Tithonus ' : —

Like that strange song I heard Apollo sing
While Ilion like a mist rose into towers.

For the myth, see Ovid, ' Heroides,' xv. 179;
and for a similar legend concerning the origin
of Camelot, see ' Gareth and Lynette.'
Page 42. To ——.
In the 1833 volume this introduction to ' The
Palace of Art ' began thus: —

I send you, Friend, a sort of allegory,
(You are an artist and will understand
Its many lesser meanings) of a soul, etc.

In 1842 it was reprinted with no change ex-
cept in these lines.
THE PALACE OF ART.
In the 2d stanza the original reading was: —

I chose, whose ranged ramparts bright
From great broad meadow-bases of deep grass, etc.

The 4th stanza originally began thus: ' While
the great world runs round,' etc.
Between the 4th and 5th stanzas (the latter is
unchanged) was the following, suppressed in
1842: —

And richly feast within thy palacehall,
Like to the dainty bird that sups,
Lodged in the lustrous crown-imperial,
Draining the honeycups.

Then came these stanzas, which have been
more or less altered and transposed: —

Full of long sounding corridors it was
That overvaulted grateful glooms,
Roofed with thick plates of green and orange glass
Ending in stately rooms.

Full of great rooms and small the palace stood,
    All various, all beautiful,
Looking all ways, fitted to every mood
    And change of my still soul.

' For some were hung,' etc. (the present 16th stanza,
    unaltered).

' One showed an English home,' etc. (the present 22d
    stanza, with no further change).

Some were all dark and red, a glimmering land
    Lit with a low round moon,
Among brown rocks a man upon the sand
    Went weeping all alone.

One seemed a foreground black with stones and slags,
    Below sunsmitten icy spires
Rose striped with long white cloud the scornful crags,
    Deeptrenched with thunderfires.

Some showed far-off thick woods mounted with towers.
Nearer, a flood of mild sunshine
Poured on long walks and lawns and beds and bowers
    Trellised with bunchy vine.[1]

Or the maidmother by a crucifix,
    In yellow pastures sunnywarm, etc.

Or Venus in a snowy shell alone,
    Deepshadowed in the glassy brine,
Moonlike glowed double on the blue, and shone
    A naked shape divine.

' Or in a clearwalled city,' etc. (now 25th stanza).

Or that deepwounded child of Pendragon
    Mid misty woods on sloping greens
Dozed in the valley of Avilion
    Tended by crowned queens.

Or blue-eyed Kriemhilt from a craggy hold,
    Athwart the light-green rows of vine,
Pour'd blazing hoards of Nibelungen gold,
    Down to the gulfy Rhine.

Europa's scarf blew in an arch, unclasped,
    From her bare shoulder backward borne;
From one hand drooped a crocus: one hand grasped
    The mild bull's golden horn.

He thro' the streaming crystal swam, and rolled
    Ambrosial breaths that seemed to float
In lightwreathed curls. She from the ripple cold
    Updrew her sandalled foot.[2]

' Or else flushed Ganymede,' etc. (as now, except ' Over '
    for ' Above ' in 4th line).

Not these alone: but many a legend fair,
    Which the supreme Caucasian mind
Carved out of nature for itself, was there
    Broidered in screen and blind.

So that my soul, beholding in her pride
    All these, from room to room did pass;
And all things that she saw, she multiplied,
    A manyfacèd glass.

And being both the sower and the seed,
    Remaining in herself became
All that she saw, Madonna, Ganymede,
    Or the Asiatic dame —

Still changing, as a lighthouse in the night
    Changeth athwart the gleaming main,

[1] This stanza, like the next but one, was omitted in
1842. The hyphen in ' far-off,' as in occasional instances before and after, is in the original edition.

From red to yellow, yellow to pale white,
    Then back to red again.

' From change to change four times within the womb
    The brain is moulded,' she began,
' So through all phases of all thought I come
    Into the perfect man.'

In 1842 this last stanza was altered as follows: —

    ' From shape to shape at first within the womb
        The brain is modell'd,' she began,
    ' And thro' all phases of all thought I come
        Into the perfect man.'

The next stanza in the 1833 volume was as
follows: —

    ' All Nature widens upward.   Evermore
        The simpler essence lower lies:
    More complex is more perfect, owning more
        Discourse, more widely wise.'

This was retained in 1842 and in the subsequent editions down to 1853, when the present
*three* stanzas were substituted for this and the
preceding one.
The next stanza in 1833, and until 1853, was
as follows: —

    I take possession of men's minds and deeds.
    I live in all things great and small.
    I sit apart holding no forms of creeds,
        But contemplating all.

The 1833 version then continued thus: —

Four ample courts there were, East, West, South,
    North,
In each a squarèd lawn wherefrom
A golden-gorgèd dragon spouted forth
    The fountain's diamond foam.

' All round the cool green courts,' etc. (the present
    7th stanza, with no further change).

From those four jets four currents in one swell
    Over the black rock streamed below
In steamy folds, that, floating as they fell,
    Lit up a torrentbow;

And round the roofs ran gilded galleries,
    That gave large view to distant lands,
Tall towns [*sic*] and mounds, and close beneath the
    skies
    Long lines of amber sands.

Huge incense-urns along the balustrade,
    Hollowed of solid amethyst,
Each with a different odour fuming, made
    The air a silver mist.

Far-off 't was wonderful to look upon
    Those sumptuous towers between the gleam
Of that great foambow trembling in the sun,
    And the argent incense-steam;

And round the terraces and round the walls,
    While day sank lower or rose higher,
To see those rails with all their knobs and balls,
    Burn like a fringe of fire.

Likewise the deepset windows, stained and traced,
    Burned, like slowflaming crimson fires,
From shadowed grots of arches interlaced,
    And topped with frostlike spires.

[2] Omitted in 1842, like the 3d, 4th, and 5th stanzas
below.

Up in the towers I placed great bells,' etc. (33d stanza,
        otherwise unchanged).

There deephaired Milton like an angel tall
    Stood limnèd, Shakespeare bland and mild,
Grim Dante pressed his lips, and from the wall
    The bald blind Homer smiled.

And underneath freshcarved in cedarwood,
    Somewhat alike in form and face,
The Genii of every climate stood,
    All brothers of one race: [1]

Angels who sway the seasons by their art,
    And mould all shapes in earth and sea;
And with great effort build the human heart
    From earliest infancy.

And in the sunpierced Oriel's coloured flame
    Immortal Michael Angelo
Looked down, bold Luther, largebrowed Verulam,
    The king of those who know.

Cervantes, the bright face of Calderon,
    Robed David touching holy strings,
The Halicarnasseän, and alone,
    Alfred the flower of kings,

Isaïah with fierce Ezekiel,
    Swarth Moses by the Coptic sea,
Plato, Petrarca, Livy, and Raphaël,
    And eastern Confutzee:

And many more that in their lifetime were
    Fullwelling fountainheads of Change,
Between the stone shafts glimmered, blazoned fair
    In divers raiment strange.

'Thro' which the lights,' etc. (43d stanza, unchanged).

'No nightingale,' etc. (44th stanza, unchanged).

'Singing and murmuring,' etc. (45th unchanged).

As some rich tropic mountain, that infolds
    All change, from flats of scattered palms
Sloping through five great zones of climate, holds
    His head in snows and calms—

Full of her own delight and nothing else
    My vainglorious, gorgeous soul [sic]
Sat throned between the shining oriels,
    In pomp beyond control; [2]

With piles of flavorous fruits in basket-twine
    Of gold, upheapèd, crushing down
Muskscented blooms — all  taste — grape,  gourd  or
        pine —
    In bunch, or singlegrown —

Our growths, and such as brooding Indian heats
    Make out of crimson blossoms deep,
Ambrosial pulps and juices, sweets from sweets
    Sunchanged, when seawinds sleep.

With graceful chalices of curious wine,
    Wonders of art — and costly jars,
And bossèd salvers.   Ere young night divine
    Crowned dying day with stars,

Making sweet close of his delicious toils,
    She lit white streams of dazzling gas,
And soft and fragrant flames of precious oils
    In moons of purple glass

[1] This stanza and the next one omitted in 1842, as
were the 2d and 3d below.
[2] These two stanzas, with those describing the sensu-

Ranged on the fretted woodwork to the ground.
    Thus her intense untold delight
In deep or vivid colour, smell and sound,
        Was flattered day and night.

'Sometimes the riddle,' etc. (the present 54th stanza,
        otherwise unchanged).

Of full-sphered contemplation.   So three years
    She throve, but on the fourth she fell, etc.

The remaining twenty stanzas of the poem
(57th to 76th), except for the omission of one
stanza, are the same as the 56th to 74th that
now end it, with the following slight changes: —
    In line 247 ' onward-sloping ' has been put for
' downward-sloping;' in 281, ' a sound ' for ' the
sound,' and ' rocks ' (retained until 1853) for
' stones;' and in 288, ' And save me lest I die '
for ' Dying the death I die.'
    The omitted stanza followed the present 58th
(' Deep dread,' etc.) and read thus: —

Who hath drawn dry the fountains of delight,
    That from my deep heart everywhere
Moved in my blood and dwelt, as power and might
    Abode in Sampson's hair?

In the 1833 volume the following foot-note
(suppressed in 1842) appeared: —
    'When I first conceived the plan of the Pal-
ace of Art, I intended to have introduced both
sculptures and paintings into it; but it is the
most difficult of all things to *devise* a statue in
verse.   Judge whether I have succeeded in the
statues of Elijah and Olympias: —

One was the Tishbite whom the raven fed,
    As when he stood on Carmel-steeps
With one arm stretch'd out bare, and mock'd and said,
    ' Come, cry aloud — he sleeps ! '

Tall, eager, lean, and strong, his cloak wind-borne
    Behind, his forehead heavenly-bright
From the clear marble pouring glorious scorn,
    Lit as with inner light.

One was Olympias: the floating snake
    Roll'd round her ankles, round her waist
Knotted, and folded once about her neck,
    Her perfect lips to taste

Round by the shoulder moved: she seeming blithe
    Declined her head: on every side
The dragon's curves melted and mingled with
    The woman's youthful pride

Of rounded limbs.

Another foot-note gave the following stanzas,
' expressive of the joy wherewith the soul con-
templated the results of astronomical experiment: ' —

Hither, when all the deep unsounded skies
    Shuddered with silent stars, she clomb,
And as with optic glasses her keen eyes
    Pierced through the mystic dome,

Regions of lucid matter taking forms,
    Brushes of fire, hazy gleams,

ous delights of the palate that follow, were struck out
in 1842.   Compare the suppression of the similar reference in the 5th stanza (' And  richly feast,' etc.) of the
first version.   The poet wisely decided to allow his luxurious ' soul ' none but intellectual joys.

Clusters and beds of worlds, and bee-like swarms
Of suns, and starry streams.

She saw the snowy poles of moonless Mars,
  That marvellous round of milky light
Below Orion, and those double stars
  Whereof the one more bright

Is circled by the other, etc.

In Mr. Palgrave's 'Lyrical Poems by Lord Tennyson' these stanzas are reprinted in the notes by the permission of the author; but the closing stanzas are revised thus: —

She saw the snowy poles and moons of Mars,
  That marvellous field of drifted light
In mid Orion, and the married stars —

The two moons of Mars had been discovered since the preceding stanzas were written; and the position of the great nebula in Orion is more accurately given. It will be understood that the two passages are given as printed in the edition of 1833 (and in Mr. Palgrave's book), the stanzas being incomplete there as here.

Line 80. *And hoary to the wind.* When the whitish-gray underside of the olive-tree leaves is turned up by the wind.

Line 96. *Babe in arm.* The reviewers of the 1833 volume ridiculed this phrase, comparing it with the 'lance in rest' of the romances of chivalry; but the poet has not only retained it here, but repeated it in 'The Princess' (vi.): —

But high upon the palace Ida stood
With Psyche's babe in arm.

Line 111. *The Ausonian King.* Numa Pompilius. The 1833 reading was 'the Tuscan king.'

Line 115. *Indian Cama.* The Hindu god of love, the Indian Cupid, who is sometimes represented as riding by night on a parrot, or lory. Compare Alfred's poem, 'Love,' in 'Poems by Two Brothers' (8th and 9th stanzas, p. 776 above).

Line 117. *Sweet Europa's mantle blew.* Some editions misprint 'blue' for 'blew.'

Line 137. *The Ionian father of the rest.* Homer.

Line 164. *The first of those who know.* The edition of 1833 has the foot-note: 'Il maestro di color chi sanno. *Dante. Inf.* iii.'

Line 174. Here the poet (as in 'The Princess,' i. 218: 'Rapt in her song') follows ancient fable rather than modern ornithology in making the musical bird feminine; but in 'The Gardener's Daughter' he is true to the latter: —

The redcap whistled; and the nightingale
Sang loud, as tho' he were the bird of day.

Line 222. *God, before whom ever lie bare, etc.* This is borrowed from an essay by Arthur Hallam, entitled 'Theodicæa Novissima' (see his 'Remains,' p. 363): 'I believe that redemption is universal in so far as it left no obstacle between man and God but man's own will; that indeed is in the power of God's election, with

whom alone rest the abysmal secrets of personality.'

Line 242. *With dim-fretted foreheads all.* 'Dim-fretted' has been variously explained, but I have the poet's authority for stating that it means 'worm-eaten.'

Page 46. LADY CLARA VERE DE VERE.
In the 7th stanza the line 'The gardener Adam and his wife' was changed in many subsequent editions to 'The grand old gardener and his wife,' but the original reading has been restored, and the poem now stands exactly as it appeared in 1842.

Page 47. THE MAY QUEEN.
Only a few slight changes have been made in this poem. The 2d line had originally 'the blythe New Year.' In the 3d stanza 'ye' was used for 'you,' as in a dozen or more places in the 'New-Year's Eve.' Line 52 began at first with 'The may upon the blackthorn;' line 77 was 'Ye'll kiss me, my own mother, upon my cheek and brow;' and line 93 was 'Goodnight, sweet mother: call me when it begins to dawn.' In the 'Conclusion,' lines 107, 108 were originally: —

But still it can't be long, mother, before I find release;
And that good man, the clergyman, he preaches words of peace.

In line 113 'taught' and 'show'd' have been transposed; line 134 had 'comes' for 'come;' and 142 had 'many worthier.'

Page 51. THE LOTOS-EATERS.
Line 7th was originally 'Above the valley burned the golden moon;' and line 16 was 'Three thundercloven thrones of oldest snow.' The 6th stanza in the 'Choric Song' was added in 1842; and line 86 had at first 'worn out with many wars.' The next stanza began 'Or propt on lavish beds of amaranth and moly;' line 90 had 'eyelids' for 'eyelid;' and line 98 had 'Only to watch and see,' etc. The 1st line of the next stanza (100) had 'the flowery peak' for 'the barren peak.'

From 'We have had enough of action,' etc. (105) to the end, the original reading was as follows: —

We have had enough of motion,
Weariness and wild alarm,
Tossing on the tossing ocean,
Where the tuskèd seahorse walloweth
In a stripe of grassgreen calm,
At noon tide beneath the lee;
And the monstrous narwhale swalloweth
His foamfountains in the sea.
Long enough the winedark wave our weary bark did carry.
This is lovelier and sweeter,
Men of Ithaca, this is meeter,
In the hollow rosy vale to tarry,
Like a dreamy Lotos-eater, a delirious Lotos-eater!
We will eat the Lotos, sweet
As the yellow honeycomb,
In the valley some, and some
On the ancient heights divine;
And no more roam,
On the loud hoar foam,
To the melancholy home

At the limit of the brine,
The little isle of Ithaca, beneath the day's decline.
We 'll lift no more the shattered oar,
No more unfurl the straining sail;
With the blissful Lotos-eaters pale
We will abide in the golden vale
Of the Lotos-land, till the Lotos fail;
We will not wander more.
Hark! how sweet the horned ewes bleat
On the solitary steeps,
And the merry lizard leaps,
And the foamwhite waters pour;
And the dark pine weeps,
And the lithe vine creeps,
And the heavy melon sleeps
On the level of the shore:
Oh! islanders of Ithaca, we will not wander more.
Surely, surely slumber is more sweet than toil, the shore
Than labour in the ocean, and rowing with the oar.
Oh! islanders of Ithaca, we will return no more.'

On the line (11 of the introduction), 'Slow-dropping veils of thinnest lawn,' the poet, in a letter to Mr. S. E. Dawson (printed in his 'Study of The Princess,' 2d ed., Montreal, 1884) says: —
'When I was about twenty or twenty-one I went on a tour to the Pyrenees. Lying among those mountains before a waterfall that comes down one thousand or twelve hundred feet, I sketched it (according to my custom then) in these words: —

Slow-dropping veils of thinnest lawn.

When I printed this, a critic informed me that "lawn was the material used in theatres to imitate a waterfall," and graciously added, "Mr. T. should not go to the boards of a theatre, but to nature herself for his suggestions." And I *had* gone to nature herself.
'I think it is a moot point whether — if I had known how that effect was produced on the stage — I should have ventured to publish the line.'
Peter Bayne ('Lessons from My Masters,' American ed., 1879) remarks: 'Whoever has seen a stream in its midsummer slenderness of volume, falling down a front of rock divided into steps or ledges, will admit that no words could possibly surpass these in descriptive precision. The Falling Foss, for example — a small cascade on one of the affluents of the Esk, near Whitby — affords a realization so exact of the "slow-dropping veil of thinnest lawn," that it at once, when I saw it last summer, reminded me of the poem; nor could an officer of the Geological Survey, writing with purely scientific intent, devise a more literal or a more expressive description.'
In line 6 of the 'Choric Song' ('Than tired eyelids upon tired eyes') all the English editions print 'tir'd' in both places, contrary to the poet's rule not to use the apostrophe when the verb ends in *e*. This might suggest that he meant to have the word pronounced as a monosyllable, but nobody with an ear for rhythm would read it so. I asked Lord Tennyson why he printed it with the apostrophe, and he re-

plied, 'That people might not pronounce it *ti-red* instead of *ti-erd.*' I told him that no American would ever think of reading it in the former way, and I doubted whether any Englishman would; but he said he was not sure of that.
Page 53. A DREAM OF FAIR WOMEN.
In the 1833 volume the poem began with these four stanzas, omitted in 1842: —

As when a man, that sails in a balloon,
    Downlooking sees the solid shining ground
Stream from beneath him in the broad blue noon, —
    Tilth, hamlet, mead and mound:

And takes his flags and waves them to the mob,
    That shout below, all faces turned to where
Glows rubylike the far-up crimson globe,
    Filled with a finer air:

So, lifted high, the Poet at his will
    Lets the great world flit from him, seeing all,
Higher thro' secret splendours mounting still,
    Selfpoised, nor fears to fall,

Hearing apart the echoes of his fame.
    While I spoke thus, the seedsman, memory,
Sowed my deepfurrowed thought with many a name
    Whose glory will not die.

The next four stanzas are the four that now begin the poem, and have not been altered.
Then follow these two stanzas, omitted in 1842: —

In every land I thought that, more or less,
    The stronger sterner nature overbore
The softer, uncontrolled by gentleness
    And selfish evermore:

And whether there were any means whereby,
    In some far aftertime, the gentler mind
Might reassume its just and full degree
    Of rule among mankind.

In the next thirty-one stanzas the only changes are the following: —
In line 23 'pass'd' was at first 'scream'd;' in 69–71 'Growths of' was 'Clasping,' and 'Their humid' was 'Its twined.'
Line 106 until 1884 was 'Which yet to name my spirit loathes and fears.'
The 28th stanza was originally: —

The tall masts quiver'd as they lay afloat,
    The temples and the people and the shore,
One drew a sharp knife thro' my tender throat
    Slowly, — and nothing more.

This was ridiculed by Lockhart (Scott's son-in-law) in the 'Quarterly Review,' July, 1833: 'What touching simplicity! What genuine pathos! *He cut my throat — nothing more!* One might indeed ask *what more she would have.*' Some critics have supposed that this led the poet to alter the stanza; but he allowed it to stand in 1842 and for at least ten years more. It is more likely that the alteration was made in order to conform to the classical story. It is not now said that Iphigenia's throat *was* cut; we may assume that she was snatched away just as the knife touched it. However that may be, the critics are divided on the question whether the alteration is for the better. For myself I must confess that I was troubled by the change from the first person to the third in ' The bright death quiver'd at the victim's throat,' until the poet explained it to me thus : ' The high masts flickered, the crowds, the shore, the whole landskip shook, the bright death quivered, everything reeled before her — even, perhaps, her own personality.'

After 140 the early version goes on thus : —

By him great Pompey dwarfs and suffers pain,
    A mortal man before immortal Mars;
The glories of great Julius lapse and wane,
    And shrink from suns to stars.

That man, of all the men I ever knew,
    Most touched my fancy.   O ! what days and nights
We had in Egypt, ever reaping new
    Harvest of ripe delights,

Realmdraining revels !   Life was one long feast.
    What wit !   what words !  what sweet words, only made
Less sweet by the kiss that broke 'em, liking best
    To be so richly stayed !

What dainty strifes, when fresh from war's alarms,
    My Hercules, my gallant Antony,
My mailed captain, leapt into my arms,
    Contented there to die.

And in those arms he died; I heard my name
    Sigh'd forth with life: then I shook off all fear;
O what a little snake stole Cæsar's fame !
    What else was left ?  look here.

All this portion of the poem remained without alteration until 1845.

Stanzas 40–72 (lines 157–288) stand as in 1833, except that line 166 had originally ' Touch'd ' for ' Struck;' line 22 had ' in his den;' and the reading in 267, 268 was : —

Ere I saw her that in her latest trance
Clasped her dead father's heart [sic], or Joan of Arc, etc.

Line 27. *The tortoise creeping to the wall.* That is, the *testudo* of ancient warfare.

Line 54. *In an old wood.* This is like Dante's ' selva oscura,' and, as Palgrave notes, is ' an image of the past.'

Line 85. *A lady.* Helen, ' the Greek woman ' of ' Œnone.'

Line 100. *One that stood beside.* Iphigenia.

Line 127. *A queen, with swarthy cheeks.* The poet describes her, as Shakespeare does (' Antony and Cleopatra,' i. 5. 28), ' with Phœbus' amorous pinches black;' but the reference to ' the polished argent of her breast ' below (158) shows that he did not forget her Hellenic origin. She was the daughter of Ptolemy Auletes and a lady of Pontus.

Line 155. *Of the other.* That is, Octavius.

Line 259. *To Fulvia's waist.* Cleopatra puts the name of the wife of her paramour Antony for that of Eleanor, the wife of Rosamond's paramour.

Line 263. *The captain of my dreams.* Venus, the morning star, — the leader or inspirer of the poet's dreams of fair women, herself the fairest of her sex. This interpretation, given in my ' Select Poems of Tennyson,' in 1884, was disputed by some critics, who supposed the sun to be meant; but Lord Tennyson assured me that I was right. The sun has not risen, but the morning star is up, and the dawn is broadening and brightening in the east.

Line 266. *Her who clasp'd in her last trance, etc.* Margaret Roper, the daughter of Sir Thomas More. After his execution his head was exposed on London Bridge, but she obtained permission to take it down, and, after preserving it as a precious relic till her death, was buried with it in her arms.

Line 269. *Or her who knew that Love can vanquish Death, etc.* Eleanor, queen of Edward I. of England, who accompanied her husband to the Holy Land in 1269. There he was stabbed in the arm with a dagger which was believed to have been poisoned; and Eleanor instantly applied her lips to the wound and sucked the blood until the surgeons were ready to dress it.

Page 58. THE BLACKBIRD.
The only changes from the earlier version are in the 1st line of the 3d stanza, which originally was ' Yet tho' I spared thee kith and kin,' with ' jennetin ' in the rhyme; in the 1st line of the 5th stanza, originally, ' I better brook the brawling stares,' and in the 3d line ' Not hearing thee at all,' etc.

THE DEATH OF THE OLD YEAR.
Unchanged except in the 1st line, which originally had ' winter's snow,' and the 5th line of the 5th stanza, which had ' one o'clock,' — a curious slip. Of course the poet knew that the year ends at midnight; but for the moment he seems to have thought of *one o'clock* as the beginning instead of the end of the *first hour* in the new year.

Page 59. TO J. S.
Addressed to James Spedding. The 2d stanza originally began ' My heart this knowledge,' etc., with ' it ' for ' I ' in the next line. The 8th stanza had ' mild ' for ' bold;' the 13th had ' sunken ' for ' fallen;' the 14th, ' my tablets ' for ' the letters;' the 16th, ' holy ' for ' only;' and the 17th, ' Although to calm you I would take.'

Page 60. ON A MOURNER.
The 2d stanza had at first ' hums ' for ' humm'd.'

' YOU ASK ME WHY,' etc.
A writer in the ' British Quarterly Review' for October, 1880 (vol. 72, p. 282), says that this and the two following poems were based upon a speech delivered by a friend of the poet's (James Spedding, according to others who have told the story) before the Cambridge Union when the young men were at the University. Lord Tennyson, however, wrote me: ' The speech at the Cambridge Union is purely mythical; at least I never heard it, and no poem of mine was ever founded upon it.'

In line 11 the original reading was, ' Where freedom broadens slowly down.' The change was evidently made to avoid the juxtaposition of sibilants, which Tennyson particularly disliked. See note on ' In Memoriam,' xl. line 5.

'OF OLD SAT FREEDOM ON THE HEIGHTS.'
In the 4th stanza ' Who, Godlike, grasps the triple forks' does not allude to Neptune with his trident, but to Jove with his thunderbolts (' trisulca fulmina '), — an explanation confirmed by Lord Tennyson.

Page 61. 'LOVE THOU THY LAND,' etc.
The first reading in line 71 was ' the boasting words we said.'

Page 62. ENGLAND AND AMERICA IN 1782.
According to Mr. R. H. Shepherd (' Bibliography of Tennyson,' 1896), this poem was ' contributed to an American newspaper in 1872.'

Page 63. THE EPIC: MORTE D'ARTHUR.
Slightly retouched since 1842. The ' Morte d'Arthur' has been incorporated, with no other change than the omission of a single line (' Sir Bedivere, the last of all his knights '), in ' The Passing of Arthur,' the last of the ' Idylls of the King;' but it has continued to be included, with the original introduction and conclusion, in the complete editions of Tennyson.

The poem was written as early as 1833, as allusions to it in the correspondence of that year (' Memoir,' vol. i. pp. 129, 131) clearly prove. This is two years earlier than the mention of it by Landor, quoted on p. 302 above.

Line 27. ' What came of that ?' ' You know,' said Frank, etc. The original reading was : —

What came of that ?' ' You know,' said Frank, 'he flung
His epic of King Arthur in the fire '—
And then to me, etc.

Line 38. Remodel models ? these twelve books of mine, etc. Originally thus: —

Remodel models rather than the life?
And these twelve books of mine (to say the truth)
Were faint Homeric echoes, etc.

Line 107. With diamond sparks. The reading until 1853 was ' diamond studs.'
Line 111. This way and that dividing the swift mind. Compare Virgil, ' Æneid,' iv. 285: ' Atque animum nunc huc celerem, nunc dividit illuc.'
Page 65. Line 134. Across the ridge, and paced beside the mere. This line was added in 1853.

Page 68. THE GARDENER'S DAUGHTER.
The only change since 1842 is ' faltering ' for ' lisping ' in line 230.

Page 72. DORA.
This poem is remarkable for the complete absence of figurative language and every form of ' poetic diction,' — unless possibly the repetition of

The reapers reaped,
And the sun fell, and all the land was dark,

may be so called.
Page 75. WALKING TO THE MAIL.
In 1842 the poem began thus: —

John. I 'm glad I walk'd. How fresh the country looks !
Is yonder planting where this byway joins
The turnpike ?

James.    Yes.
John.            And when does this come by ?
James. The mail ? at one o'clock.
John.                    What is it now ?
James. A quarter to.
John.                    Whose house is that I see
Beyond the water mills ?
James.                Sir Edward Head's:
But he 's abroad; the place is to be sold.

Line 22. You saw the man, etc. Until 1851 the reading was as follows: —

James. You saw the man but yesterday:
He pick'd the pebble from your horse's foot.
His house was haunted by a jolly ghost
That rummaged like a rat.  No servant stay'd.

Line 72. I myself. Originally, ' I that am.'
Line 78. We paid in person, etc. The reading in 1842 was: —

We paid in person, scored upon the part
Which cherubs want.  He had a sow, sir.

Page 77. EDWIN MORRIS.
For line 22, ' finished to the finger-nail,' compare Horace, ' Satires,' i. v. 32: —

Capitoque simul Fonteius, ad unguem
Factus homo.

Line 78. Shall not Love to me, etc.  Compare Catullus, ' Carmina,' xlv.: —

Hoc ut dixit, Amor, sinistram ut ante,
Dextram sternuit approbationem.

Line 110. The sweet-gale. The Myrica Gale, a shrub growing in marshes in Northern Europe, called ' sweet-gale ' from its aromatic odor.
Page 82. THE TALKING OAK.
Since 1842 only two slight changes have been made: ' For ah ! my friend, the days were brief ' (line 84) instead of ' For oh ! the Dryad-days were brief;' and ' The murmurs of the drum and fife ' (line 215) for ' The whispers of the drum and fife.'
Line 47. Bluff Harry.  Henry VIII.; his daughter Elizabeth being the ' man-minded off-set ' of the next stanza.
Line 54. Till that wild wind made work, etc. The violent storm of the night when Cromwell died.  The oak, as an old Tory, sneers at Cromwell, who, as some say, was a brewer.
Line 63. In teacup-times of hood and hoop, etc. The days of Queen Anne, when the affected pastoral poetry hit off in the next stanza was in vogue.
Line 181. I, rooted here among the groves, etc. Only a botanist can appreciate the blended poetry and science of this stanza.
Line 291. That Thessalian growth, etc.  The oak grove at Dodona (in Epirus, not in the neighboring Thessaly), where the black dove, flying from Thebes in Egypt, alighted and proclaimed that there an oracle of Jupiter should be established.
Page 85. LOVE AND DUTY.
The only change since 1842 (except ' who ' for ' that ' in line 75) is in 85-90, which then read: —

Should my shadow cross thy thoughts
Too sadly for their peace, so put it back
For calmer hours in memory's darkest hold,

If unforgotten ! should it cross thy dreams,
So might it come like one that looks content, etc.

## Page 87. THE GOLDEN YEAR.

The original reading in lines 5–8 was: —

And found him in Llanberis; and that same song
He told me; for I banter'd him, etc.

Llanberis, a village to the northwest of Snowdon, is one of the points from which the mountain is ascended. On ' the counter side,' or the
opposite side of the valley, are the 'lakes,'
Llyn Padarn and Llyn Peris, and beyond them
the heights of Elidyr-fach (2550 feet) and Eli-
dyr-fawr (3033 feet).

Line 18. *Catch me who can, etc.* Alluding to
a familiar children's game.

Line 29. *Seas that daily gain upon the shore.*
Compare Shakespeare, ' Sonnet ' 64. 5: —

When I have seen the hungry ocean gain
Advantage on the kingdom of the shore, etc.

Line 45. *Clear of toll.* There is to be universal ' free trade ' in this ' good time coming.'

Line 63. *O'erflourish'd with the hoary clematis.* Covered with the flowers of the *Clematis
vitalba,* the ' traveller's joy ' of 'Aylmer's
Field.'

Line 76. *From bluff to bluff.* In a letter received from Lord Tennyson, commenting on this
and other passages, he says: ' *Uff, uff* gives
almost exactly the echo of the blasting as I
heard it from the counter side to that of Snowdon.'

## Page 88. ULYSSES.

When reading 'In Memoriam' to Mr.
Knowles, the poet said: ' It is a very impersonal
poem as well as personal. There is more about
myself in "Ulysses," which was written under
the sense of loss and that all had gone by, but
that still life must be fought out to the end.
It was more written with the feeling of his loss
upon me than many poems in "In Memoriam."'

Line 10. *The rainy Hyades.* Compare Virgil,
' Æneid,' i. 748: ' Arcturum, pluviasque Hya-
das, geminosque Triones.'

Line 16. *Delight of battle.* Peter Bayne refers to this as ' a superb translation of the *certa-
minis gaudia* of the Latin poet.'

## Page 89. TITHONUS.

When it was published in the ' Cornhill Magazine ' Thackeray was the editor, and was very
proud of having secured the poem. The first
line was originally ' Ay me ! ay me ! the woods
decay and fall;' and line 39 had ' and that wild
team.'

Line 25. *The silver star.* The morning-star.

Line 62. *Like that strange song I heard Apollo
sing, etc.* See note on ' Œnone,' lines 39, 40.

## Page 90. LOCKSLEY HALL.

In line 3 the original reading was ' and round
the gables.'

Line 4. *Dreary gleams about the moorland, etc.*
The construction of ' gleams ' has been much
disputed. I always regarded it as referring to
the curlews, which in flying over the hall might
seem like dreary gleams in the sky; and I was

gratified when this explanation (printed in my
' Select Poems of Tennyson ' in 1884) was confirmed and aptly illustrated by Dr. Horace
Howard Furness, who says (in a private letter
which he permits me to quote here): ' The curlews have dusky backs, indistinguishable at
twilight, but white breasts, and as they fly in
coveys are not noticed until on wheeling they
show for a moment these "gleaming" breasts.
I saw them first when I was riding at sunset
across the dreary plain of La Mancha in Spain,
and I could n't imagine what these momentary
flashes of light were until I happened to see a
flock near at hand, when I involuntarily exclaimed "Locksley Hall ! " and the line which
had long puzzled me was explained.' But Lord
Tennyson afterwards wrote me that the *gleams*
are not curlews at all, and that ' *dreary gleams
flying* is put absolutely — while dreary gleams
are flying.'

Dr. Furness also sent me two unpublished
stanzas of ' Locksley Hall ' which Mrs. Kemble
transcribed many years ago into his copy of the
edition of 1842. They were inserted after the
19th stanza (' And our spirits rush'd together,'
etc.), and were as follows: —

In the hall there is a picture, Amy's arms are round my
neck,
Happy children, in a sunbeam, sitting on the ribs of
wreck.

In my life there is a picture, she who clasp'd my neck
is flown.
I am left within the shadow, sitting on the wreck alone.

Since these were first printed in the 2d edition
of the ' Select Poems,' the poet has introduced
them, with slight changes, in ' Locksley Hall
Sixty Years After.'

Line 9. *Locksley Hall, that in the distance overlooks the sandy tracts.* This is the original
reading, altered in the ' Selections ' of 1845 to
' Locksley Hall, that half in ruins overlooks,'
etc.

Line 76. *That a sorrow's crown of sorrow, etc.*
This is from Dante, ' Inferno,' v. 121: —

Nessun maggior dolore
Che ricordarsi del tempo felice
Nella miseria.

Line 162. *Swings the trailer from the crag.*
Originally ' droops the trailer,' etc.

Line 182. *Let the great world spin for ever, etc.*
Originally ' Let the peoples spin,' etc. The
next line had ' the world ' for ' the globe.'

Line 184. *A cycle of Cathay.* ' Cycle ' is used
of course for an indefinitely long period, or an
age; but some criticaster has plumed himself
upon the discovery that a Chinese ' cycle ' is
less than fifty years (I forget the precise length);
and somebody else takes the cycle to be the
Platonic ' great year.'

## Page 95. GODIVA.

The old story on which the poem is founded
is thus told by Sir William Dugdale in his ' An-
tiquities of Warwickshire,' 1656 : ' The Countess Godiva, bearing an extraordinary affection
to this place [Coventry], often and earnestly be-

sought her husband that, for the love of God and the Blessed Virgin, he would free it from that grievous servitude whereunto it was subject; but he, rebuking her for importuning him in a manner so inconsistent with his profit, commanded that she should thenceforward forbear to move therein ; yet she, out of her womanish pertinacity, continued to solicit him, insomuch that he told her if she would ride on horseback naked from one end of the town to the other, in sight of all the people, he would grant her request.  Whereunto she replied, " But will ye give me leave to do so ? "  And he replying " Yes," the noble lady, upon an appointed day, got on horseback naked, with her hair loose, so that it covered all her body but her legs; and thus performing her journey, she returned with joy to her husband, who thereupon granted to the inhabitants a charter of freedom. . . . In memory whereof the picture of him and his lady was set up in a south window of Trinity Church in this city, about Richard II.'s time, his right hand holding a charter with these words written thereon : —

I, Luriche, for Love of thee
Doe make Coventry Tol-free.'

It is said that the inhabitants all withdrew from the streets and from their windows while the lady was passing through the city; but one man, a tailor, could not resist the temptation to look forth.  He was struck blind at the moment, and to this day the effigy of ' Peeping Tom ' may be seen in the upper part of a house at the corner of Hertford Street as a monument of his disgrace.

The ' Procession of Lady Godiva,' said to have been instituted to commemorate the service she rendered Coventry, has been satisfactorily proved to have originated in the reign of Charles II.  It was kept up annually until 1826, and has been reproduced several times since. In its palmy days it was graced by the presence of the civic authorities, and was attended with great pomp and display.  Lady Godiva was represented by a beautiful woman dressed in a closely fitting suit of flesh-coloured material. She was preceded by the city guards in old armor with a band of music, and followed by the mayor, aldermen, and sheriffs, the ancient companies and benefit societies of the city with their insignia and decorations, other bands of music, and various historical and mythological characters.

Line 3.  *The three tall spires.*  That of St. Michael's Church, 303 feet high (built 1373–1395), that of Trinity Church, 237 feet high (built 1664–1667, to replace one blown down in 1664), and that of Christ Church, which originally belonged to the Grey-friars' Monastery, founded in the fourteenth century.  The monastic buildings were destroyed in the time of Henry VIII.; but the beautiful spire escaped, and was made part of the present edifice built in 1832.

Line 11.  *A thousand summers back.*  Not to be taken literally, Earl Leofric having flourished in the first half of the eleventh century,

if we accept the tradition that he founded the Benedictine Priory in Coventry in 1043.  It is said that both he and his lady were buried in a porch of the monastery, of which some fragments still remain.

Page 96.  THE DAY-DREAM.
Line 15.  *Then take the broidery-frame, etc.* Originally, ' So take,' etc.
Line 78.  *She lying on her couch alone, etc.* The reading in 1830 was: —

> The while she slumbereth alone,
> Over the purpled coverlet
> The maiden's jet-black hair had grown.

' Purpled ' was retained in 1842.  The first line of the next stanza had in 1830 ' star-braided ' for ' star-broider'd.'
Line 81.  *On either side.*  The 1830 reading was ' on either hand.'
Line 112.  *Or scatter'd blanching on the grass.* The early reading was ' in the grass.'
Line 126.  *The Magic Music in his heart.* Compare ' The Princess,' prol. 190 : —

> She remember'd that:
> A pleasant game, she thought: she liked it more
> Than magic music, forfeits, all the rest.

Line 129.  *His spirit flutters, etc.*  Misprinted ' The spirit flutters ' in the English one-volume edition of 1884.
Line 149.  *And last with these the king awoke.* Originally, ' And last of all,' etc.
Line 158.  *My joints are somewhat stiff.*  The early reading was ' something stiff.'
Page 99.  AMPHION.
Line 33.  *The linden broke her ranks, etc.* Until 1853 the reading was : —

> The birch-tree swang her fragrant hair,
> The bramble cast her berry,
> The gin within the juniper
> Began to make him merry.

Line 92.  *The spindlings.*  Until 1850 the reading was ' The poor things.'
Page 102.  WILL WATERPROOF'S LYRICAL MONOLOGUE.
The Cock tavern in Fleet Street, just inside Temple Bar, was a favorite resort of the poet and some of his friends during his early years in London.  The building was torn down several years ago, but some of the furniture of the grill-room, including a fine old oak fireplace, was transferred to a new tavern with the old name, on the other side of the street, opposite Chancery Lane.  One of the ancient tankards, with the inscription, ' A pint-pot neatly graven,' was presented by the proprietors to the poet, who, in his letter of acknowledgment, said that he would keep it as an heirloom in his family, in memory of the vanished tavern.
Line 24.  ' In ' was originally ' To.'
Line 35.  *Against its fountain upward runs, etc.* The reading until 1853 was this : —

> Like Hezekiah's, backward runs
> The shadow of my days.

Compare Isaiah, xxxviii. 8.
Line 142.  *Till where the street, etc.*  Originally ' With motion less or greater.'

Page 105. LADY CLARE.
Until 1851 the poem began thus: —

> Lord Ronald courted Lady Clare,
>   I trow they did not part in scorn;
> Lord Ronald, her cousin, courted her,
>   And they will wed the morrow morn.

The 16th stanza ('The lily-white doe Lord
Ronald had brought,' etc.) was added in 1851.
Line 7. *They two will wed, etc.* Both the one-
volume and the seven-volume editions of 1884
misprint 'They too.'
Page 107. THE LORD OF BURLEIGH.
The ballad is 'a narrative in verse, with the
usual poetic licenses, of the wooing and romantic marriage of the tenth Earl and first Marquis
of Exeter.' See Napier, 'Homes and Haunts
of Tennyson,' pp. 103–111.
Page 109. SIR LAUNCELOT AND QUEEN
GUINEVERE.
Line 34. *By night to eery warblings.* 'War-
blings' is here a trisyllable (war-ble-ings), being
lengthened after an Elizabethan fashion. Compare 'assembly,' 'resembleth,' 'fiddler,' 'remembrance,' etc. in Shakespeare.
Page 110. THE BEGGAR MAID.
For the old ballad on which the poem is
founded, see Percy's 'Reliques.'
Page 114. TO E. L. ON HIS TRAVELS IN
GREECE.
Edward Lear was also the author of those
classics of the nursery, the 'Nonsense Books.'
Page 115. THE PRINCESS.
The poem was at first received with little
favor by the critics. 'It was thought scarce
worthy of the author. The abundant grace,
descriptive beauty, and human sentiment were
evident; but the medley was thought somewhat
incongruous, and the main web of the tale too
weak to sustain the embroidery raised upon it'
(Wace). Even so late as 1855, when the poem
had received its last touches, the 'Edinburgh
Review' said of it: 'The subject of "The Princess," so far from being great, in a poetical
point of view, is partly even of transitory interest. . . . This piece, though full of meanings
of abiding value, is ostensibly a brilliant serio-
comic *jeu d'esprit* upon the noise about "women's rights," which even now ceases to make
itself heard anywhere but in the refuge of
exploded European absurdities beyond the Atlantic. A carefully elaborated construction, a
"wholeness," arising out of distinct and well-
contrasted parts, which is another condition
of a great poem, would have been worse than
thrown away on such a subject. . . . In reading the poem, the mind is palled and wearied with
wasted splendor and beauty.'
On the other hand, there were a few eminent
critics who were prompt to recognize the true
merit of the poem. Professor James Hadley,
of Yale College, wrote a long and appreciative
review of it for the 'New Englander' (May,
1849), which has been reprinted in a revised
form in his 'Essays, Philological and Critical.'
Charles Kingsley, in 'Fraser's Magazine'
(September, 1850), said of the poem: 'In this

work Mr. Tennyson shows himself more than
ever the poet of the day. In it, more than ever,
the old is interpenetrated with the new; the domestic and scientific with the ideal and sentimental. He dares, in every page, to make use
of modern words and notions from which the
mingled clumsiness and archaism of his com-
peers shrinks, as unpoetical. Though his stage
is an ideal fairy-land, yet he has reached the
ideal by the only true method — by bringing
the Middle Age forward to the present one, and
not by ignoring the present to fall back on a
cold and galvanized Mediævalism; and thus
he makes the "Medley" a mirror of the nineteenth century, possessed of its own new art
and science, its own new temptations and aspirations, and yet grounded on, and continually
striving to reproduce, the forms and experiences
of all past time. The idea, too, of "The Princess" is an essentially modern one. In every
age women have been tempted, by the possession of superior beauty, intellect, or strength of
will, to deny their own womanhood, and attempt
to stand alone as men, whether on the ground
of political intrigue, ascetic saintship, or philosophic pride. Cleopatra and St. Hedwiga, Madame de Staël and the Princess, are merely
different manifestations of the same self-willed
and proud longing of woman to unsex herself,
and realize, single and self-sustained, some dis-
torted and partial notion of her own as to what
the "angelic life" should be. Cleopatra acted
out the pagan ideal of an angel; St. Hedwiga,
the mediæval one; Madame de Staël hers, with
the peculiar notions of her time as to what
"spiritual" might mean; and in "The Princess" Mr. Tennyson has embodied the ideal of
that nobler, wider, purer, yet equally fallacious,
because equally unnatural analogue, which we
may now meet too often up and down England.
He shows us the woman, when she takes her
stand on the false masculine ground of intellect,
working out her own moral punishment, by de-
stroying in herself the tender heart of flesh: not
even her vast purposes of philanthropy can preserve her, for they are built up, not on the
womanhood which God has given her, but on
her own self-will; they change, they fall, they
become inconsistent, even as she does herself,
till at last she loses all feminine sensibility;
scornfully and stupidly she rejects and misun-
derstands the heart of man; and then, falling
from pride to sternness, from sternness to sheer
inhumanity, she punishes sisterly love as a
crime, robs the mother of her child, and becomes all but a vengeful fury, with all the peculiar faults of woman, and none of the peculiar
excellences of man. . . . How Mr. Tennyson can
have attained the prodigal fulness of thought
and imagery which distinguishes this poem, and
especially the last canto, without his style ever
becoming overloaded, seldom even confused, is
perhaps one of the greatest marvels of the
whole production. The songs themselves,
which have been inserted between the cantos
in the last edition, seem, perfect as they are,
wasted and smothered among the surrounding

fertility, — till we discover that they stand there, not merely for the sake of their intrinsic beauty, but serve to call the reader's mind, at every pause in the tale of the Princess's folly, to that very healthy ideal of womanhood which she has spurned.'

Mr. Dawson, in his 'Study of The Princess' (Montreal, 1884), remarks that the following extract from Rev. F. W. Robertson 'is perhaps the most justly appreciative criticism of Tennyson which has ever appeared.' It is from a lecture upon English Poetry, delivered to the workingmen of Brighton in 1852: —

'I ranked Tennyson in the first order,[1] because with great mastery over his material, — words, great plastic power of versification, and a rare gift of harmony, — he has also vision or insight; and because, feeling intensely the great questions of the day, — not as a mere man of letters, but as a man, — he is to some extent the interpreter of his age, not only in its mysticism, which I tried to show you is the necessary reaction from the rigid formulas of science and the earthliness of an age of work into the vagueness which belongs to infinitude, but also in his poetic and almost prophetic solution of some of its great questions.

'Thus in "The Princess," . . . he has with exquisite taste disposed of the question — which has its burlesque and comic as well as its tragic side — of woman's present place and future destinies. And if any one wishes to see this subject treated with a masterly and delicate hand, in protest alike against the theories which would make her as the man, which she could only be by becoming masculine, not manly, and those which would have her to remain the toy, or the slave, or the slight thing of sentimental and frivolous accomplishment which education has hitherto aimed at making her, I would recommend him to study the few last pages of "The Princess," where the poet brings the question back, as a poet should, to nature; develops the ideal out of the actual woman, and reads out of what she is, on the one hand, what her Creator intended her to be, and on the other, what she never can or ought to be.'

Mr. Dawson says well that 'Psyche's baby is the conquering heroine of the epic.' He adds: 'Ridiculous in the lecture-room, the babe, in the poem, as in the songs, is made the central point upon which the plot turns; for the unconscious child is the concrete embodiment of Nature herself, clearing away all merely intellectual theories by her silent influence. Ida feels the power of the child. The postscript of the despatch sent to her brother in the height of her indignation, contains, as is fitting, the kernel of the matter. She says: —

I took it for an hour in mine own bed
This morning; there the tender orphan hands
Felt at my heart, and seemed to charm from thence
The wrath I nursed against the world.

[1] The lecturer had divided poets into 'two orders; those in whom the vision and the faculty divine of imagination exists, and those in whom the plastic power

'Rash princess! that fatal hour dashed "the hopes of half the world." Alas for these hopes! The cause, the great cause, totters to the fall when the Head confesses —

           I felt
Thy helpless warmth about my barren breast
In the dead prime.

Whenever the plot thickens the babe appears. It is with Ida on her judgment-seat. In the topmost height of the storm the wail of the "lost lamb at her feet" reduces her eloquent anger into incoherence. She carries it when she sings her song of triumph. When she goes to tend her wounded brothers on the battlefield she carries it. Through it, and for it, Cyril pleads his successful suit, and wins it for the mother. For its sake the mother is pardoned. O fatal babe! more fatal to the hopes of woman than the doomful horse to the proud towers of Ilion; for through thee the walls of pride are breached, and all the conquering affections flock in.'

While reading the poem with a class of girls many years ago, I remarked that the babe might almost be called its heroine. I was gratified to find my opinion confirmed by Mr. Dawson's; and more so to find it indorsed by the author, in the interesting letter to Mr. Dawson printed in the preface to the 2d edition of the 'Study.' Tennyson there says: —

'I may tell you that the songs were not an after-thought. Before the first edition came out I deliberated with myself whether I should put songs in between the separate divisions of the poem: again, I thought, the poem will explain itself; but the public did not see that the child, as you say, was the heroine of the piece, and at last I conquered my laziness, and inserted them. You would be still more certain that the child was the heroine, if, instead of the first song as it now stands,

As thro' the land at eve we went,

I had printed the first song which I wrote, — "The Losing of the Child." The child is sitting on the bank of a river, and playing with flowers: a flood comes down — a dam has been broken thro' — the child is borne down by the flood — the whole village distracted; after a time the flood has subsided — the child is thrown safe and sound again upon the bank, and all the women are in raptures. I quite forget the words of the ballad, but I think I may have it somewhere.'

There are also some admirable comments on 'The Princess' in Mr. E. C. Stedman's 'Victorian Poets.' 'Other works of our poet,' he says, 'are greater, but none is so fascinating as this romantic tale, — English throughout, yet combining the England of Cœur-de-Lion with that of Victoria in one bewitching picture.'

*The Prologue.* The scene of the Prologue was suggested by Park House, the residence of Mr. Edmund Lushington, who had married the

of shaping predominates, — the men of poetic inspiration, and the men of poetic taste.'

poet's sister Cecilia. In some reminiscences
contributed to the 'Memoir' (vol. i. p. 203), Mr.
Lushington says: 'He was present on July 6th,
1842, at a festival of the Maidstone Mechanics'
Institute held in our Park, of which he has introduced a lively description in the beginning
of "The Princess."'

Line 9. *Five others: we were seven at Vivian-
place.* Added in the 3d edition.

Line 20. *Laborious orient ivory, sphere in
sphere.* Referring to Chinese ivory balls within
balls. The line is a striking example of the
correspondence of sound and sense, the words
seeming to roll round like the 'sphere in
sphere.'

Lines 35–49. *O miracle of women . . . the gallant glorious chronicle.* Added in the 5th edition
of the poem.

Line 69. *Whom the electric shock.* The 1st
American edition misprints 'from the electric
shock.'

Line 80. *Went hand in hand with science.*
The early editions [1] have 'With science hand in
hand went.'

Lines 131–138. *Ah, were I something great !
. . . with her curls.* For these eight lines the
early editions have only the following : —

O, were I some great Princess, I would build
Far off from men a college of my own,
And I would teach them all things: you should see.

Lines 176–179. *We seven stay'd at Christmas
up to read.* The early editions read: 'We seven
took one tutor. Never man,' etc.

Lines 190–194. *She remember'd that . . . by
themselves.* The early editions have : —

'I remember that:
A pleasant game,' she said; 'I liked it more
Than magic music, forfeits, all the rest.
But these — what kind of tales do men tell men,
I wonder, by themselves.'

Lines 197–208. *The rest would follow . . .
Grave, solemn !* The early editions read thus: —

'The rest would follow; so we tost the ball:
What kind of tales? Why, such as served to kill
Time by the fire in winter.' 'Kill him now !
Tell one,' she said: 'kill him in summer, too.'
And 'tell one,' cried the solemn maiden aunt.
'Why not a summer's as a winter's tale ?
A tale for summer as befits the time;
And something it should be to suit the place,
Grave, moral, solemn, like the mouldering walls
About us.'

Line 211. *Like a ghostly woodpecker.* The
first four editions have: 'an April woodpecker.'

Lines 214–239. *Turn'd to me, . . . the story
and the songs.* In the early editions the remainder of the Prologue reads thus: —

turn'd to me: 'Well — as you will —
Just as you will,' she said; 'be, if you will,
Yourself your hero.' 'Look, then,' added he,
'Since Lilia would be princess, that you stoop
No lower than a prince.' To which I said,
'Take care then that my tale be follow'd out

[1] By the 'early editions' I mean the 1st and 2d, unless otherwise stated.

By all the lieges in my royal vein:
But one that really suited time and place
Were such a medley, we should have him back
Who told the Winter's Tale to do it for us:
A Gothic ruin, and a Grecian house,
A talk of college and of ladies' rights,
A feudal knight in silken masquerade,
And there with shrieks and strange experiments,
For which the good Sir Ralph had burnt them all,
The nineteenth century gambols on the grass.
No matter; we will say whatever comes:
Here are we seven: if each man takes his turn
We make a sevenfold story:' then began.

Line 222 was added in the 5th edition.

*Part I.* Line 2 is not in the early editions.

Lines 5–21. *There lived an ancient legend*, etc.
This passage, like all the others referring to the
'weird seizures,' was added in the 5th edition.
For 'mutter'd epilepsy' the original reading
was 'call'd it catalepsy.'

I am inclined to agree with Dawson that
'these additions seem not only unnecessary and
uncalled for, but are actually injurious to the
unity of the work.' He adds: 'They confuse
the simple conception of his character, and graft
on to his personality the foreign and somewhat
derogatory idea of catalepsy; for in that light
does the court doctor regard them. The poet
must have had some definite object in inserting
them. Can it be that they are to indicate the
weakness and incompleteness of the poet side
of the Prince's character until he has found rest
in his ideal ? Then only can he say: —

My doubts are dead,
My haunting sense of hollow shows; the change,
This truthful change, in thee has killed it.

'The dreamy Prince, haunted by doubts, and
living in shadow-land, by the healing influence
of a happy love, wakes up to the purpose and
dignity of life.'

Line 23. *Half-canoniz'd by all that look'd on
her.* The early editions read: 'And nearly can-
oniz'd by all she knew.'

Line 26. *He cared not for the affection of the
house.* This line is not in the early editions.

Line 33. *Proxy-wedded with a bootless calf.*
Marriage by proxy was common in the Middle Ages. For another instance in poetry — an
historical one — compare Longfellow's 'Belfry
of Bruges' : —

I beheld proud Maximilian, kneeling humbly on the
    ground;
I beheld the gentle Mary hunting with her hawk and
    hound;
And her lighted bridal chamber, where a duke slept
    with the queen,
And the armed guard around them, and the sword un-
    sheathed between.

The author's note on the passage says: 'Marie de Valois, Duchess of Burgundy, was left
by the death of her father, Charles-le-Témé-
raire, at the age of twenty, the richest heiress
of Europe. She came to Bruges, as Countess
of Flanders, in 1477, and in the same year was
married by proxy to the Archduke Maximilian. According to the custom of the time, the
Duke of Bavaria, Maximilian's substitute, slept

with the princess. They were both in complete dress, separated by a naked sword, and attended by four armed guards.'

Bacon, in his ' Henry VII.,' tells of the proxy marriage of this Maximilian, when King of the Romans, with Anne, the heiress of Brittany, in 1489: ' The king having thus upheld the reputation of Maximilian, advised him now to press on his marriage with Britain to a conclusion, which Maximilian accordingly did; and so far forth prevailed, both with the young lady and with the principal persons about her, as the marriage was consummated by proxy, with a ceremony at that time in those parts new. For she was not only publicly contracted, but stated, as a bride, and solemnly bedded; and after she was laid, there came in Maximilian's ambassador, with letters of procuration, and in the presence of sundry noble personages, men and women, put *his leg, stript naked to the knee,* between the espousal sheets; to the end, that the ceremony might be thought to amount to a consummation and actual knowledge.'

In the present instance, as Ida afterwards urged (p. 124), the marriage was ' invalid,' since her ' will sealed not the bond.' According to both canon and civil law, consent was the only basis of marriage; and it was necessary, moreover, that the parties should have arrived at years of discretion. There were different opinions as to this age, but it was never assumed to be as early as ' eight years.'

Line 36. *Youths of puissance.* The reading of the first five editions is ' knights of puissance.'

Line 55. *And almost my half-self,* etc. The early editions read: —

My shadow, my half-self, for still we moved
Together, kin as horse's eye and ear.

Line 65. *Cook'd his spleen.* Compare the figurative use of the Latin *coquere* in Plautus, Livy, Cicero, etc.

Line 80. *And Cyril whisper'd.* The early editions have ' Then whisper'd Cyril.' Of course they do not contain the next three lines. In 84 they have ' Trust me ' for ' Take me; ' in 86, ' Replied the king, " You shall not; I myself; " ' and in 87 ' these pretty maiden fancies.'

Line 96. *A wind arose and rush'd upon the South.* Wace (' Alfred Tennyson,' Edinburgh, 1881) compares Shelley, ' Prometheus Unbound,' ii. 1: —

A wind arose among the pines; it shook
The clinging music from their boughs, and then
Low, sweet, faint sounds, like the farewell of ghosts,
Were heard; ' O, follow, follow, follow me ! '

Dawson remarks that the passage ' must have, consciously or unconsciously, dwelt in Tennyson's memory when writing these lines; ' but the poet, in the letter to Dawson elsewhere quoted, says: ' I was walking in the New Forest. A wind did arise and —

Shake the songs, the whispers, and the shrieks
Of the wild wood together.

The wind, I believe, was a west wind; but, because I wished the Prince to go south, I turned the wind to the south, and the wind said, " Follow." I believe the resemblance which you note is just a chance one. Shelley's lines are not familiar to me, tho', of course, if they occur in the Prometheus, I must have read them.

' I could multiply instances, but I will not bore you, and far indeed am I from asserting that books, as well as nature, are not, and ought not to be, suggestive to the poet. I am sure that I myself, and many others, find a peculiar charm in those passages of such great masters as Virgil or Milton where they adopt the creation of a by-gone poet, and re-clothe it, more or less, according to their fancy. But there is, I fear, a prosaic set growing up among us, editors of booklets, book-worms, index-hunters, or men of great memories and no imagination, who *impute themselves* to the poet, and so believe that *he,* too, has no imagination, but is forever poking his nose between the pages of some old volume in order to see what he can appropriate. They will not allow us to say " Ring the bells," without finding that we have taken it from Sir P. Sydney, — or even to use such a simple expression as the ocean " roars," without finding out the precise verse in Homer or Horace from which we have plagiarized it (fact !).

' I have known an old fish-wife, who had lost two sons at sea, clench her fist at the advancing tide on a stormy day, and cry out, " Ay ! roar, do ! how I hates to see thee show thy white teeth ! " Now, if I had adopted her exclamation and put it into the mouth of some old woman in one of my poems, I daresay the critics would have thought it original enough, but would most likely have advised me to go to nature for my old woman, and not to my own imagination; and indeed it is a strong figure.'

Then follows the passage quoted from the same letter on page 805 above.

Lines 103–105. *Cat-footed through the town,* etc. These three lines are not in the early editions. The next two read thus in the first two editions: —

Down from the bastion'd walls we dropt by night,
And flying reach'd the frontier: then we crost, etc.

The 3d edition (1850) has: —

Down from the bastion'd wall, suspense by night,
Like threaded spiders from a balk, we dropt,
And flying reach'd, etc.

Line 109. *Tilth and grange.* The early editions have: ' town and thorpe; ' with ' tilth ' for ' vines ' in the next line.

Line 113. *Crack'd and small his voice.* The reading of 1st, 3d, and later editions. The 2d has: ' in voice,' — probably a misprint.

Lines 114, 115. *But bland the smile,* etc. These lines are not in the first two editions. The 3d has: ' But bland the smile that pucker'd up his cheeks.'

Line 121. *We remember love ourself.* All the editions, including that of 1898, have ' ourselves; ' but as the poet has elsewhere changed the form to ' ourself ' and in this very expression in v. 198, I have no doubt that he intended to do it here.

Line 133. *My very ears were hot To hear them.* The early editions omit from this point down to 145, reading thus: 'To hear them. Last, my daughter begg'd a boon,' etc.

Line 134. *Knowledge, so my daughter said, was all in all.* Some have thought this — and the idea of the poem — borrowed from Johnson's 'Rasselas': 'The Princess thought that of all sublunary things knowledge was the best; she desired, first, to learn all sciences, and then proposed to found a college of learned women, in which she would preside, that, by conversing with the old, and educating the young, she might divide her time between the acquisition and communication of wisdom, and raise up for the next age models of prudence and patterns of piety.'

Line 151. *We know not, — only this: they see no man.* The early editions read: 'We know not, — have not been; they see no men.'

Lines 163–172. *Our formal compact, etc.* The pointing and reading of the early editions are as follows: —

Our formal compact, yet not less all frets
But chafing me on fire to find my bride,
Set out once more with those two gallant boys;
Then pushing onward under sun and stars
Many a long league back to the North, we came,
When the first fern-owl whirr'd about the copse,
Upon a little town within a wood
Close at the boundary of the liberties:
There entering in an hostel call'd mine host, etc.

Lines 183–185. *She once had past that way, etc.* These three lines are not in the early editions, which go on thus: 'For him, he reverenced,' etc. Lines 183 and 185 were inserted in the 3d edition, but 184 not until the 5th.

Line 196. *We sent mine host to purchase female gear.* The early editions go on as follows: —

Which brought and clapt upon us, we tweezer'd out
What slender blossom lived on lip and cheek
Of manhood, gave mine host a costly bribe, etc.

Line 203. *We follow'd up the river, etc.* The early editions read: —

We rode till midnight when the college lights
Began to glitter firefly-like in copse
And linden alley; and then we past an arch
Inscribed too dark for legible, and gain'd
A little street half garden and half house;
But could not hear each other speak for noise, etc.

Line 213. *Clocks and chimes, etc.* Dawson remarks: 'The love of precise punctuality, so deeply implanted in the female breast, has full scope at last, as far as pretty clocks go. . . . Very properly, also, the path of knowledge, thorny to the tyrannous male, is made comfortable there. The ladies drink in science "leaning deep in broidered down," as is befitting. . . . Due attention is paid to dress also; the doctors are violet-hooded, and the girls all uniformly in white — gregarious, though, even there as in the outer world.'

Lord Tennyson, in a letter dated October 12,

1884, called my attention to this statement that the girls are 'uniformly in white.' He said: 'They were in white at chapel as we Cantabs were at our Trinity College Chapel in Cambridge; but . . . Lady Psyche's "side" (that is a Cambridge equivalent of "pupils") wore lilac robes and Lady Blanche's robes of daffodil colour. These two made the "long hall glitter like a bed of flowers." Dawson has lost half the splendour of the picture.'

Line 218. *Rapt in her song.* It is only the male bird that sings; but the poets generally follow the mythic ornithology which regards the nightingale as the transformed Philomela. See, however, 'The Gardener's Daughter': —

The redcap whistled; and the nightingale
Sang loud, as tho' he were the bird of day.

In the 'Recollections of the Arabian Nights,' the *bulbul* is made masculine, as in the Persian: 'the bulbul as he sang.'

Line 222. *Above an entry.* The early reading is 'Above an archway.'

Lines 237–241. *This I seal'd . . . Venus hung.* The early editions read: —

This I seal'd
(A Cupid reading) to be sent with dawn.

Line 239. *Uranian Venus.* The allusion is to Plato's 'Symposium': 'And am I not right in asserting that there are two goddesses? The elder one having no mother, who is called the heavenly Aphrodite — she is the daughter of Uranus; the younger who is the daughter of Zeus and Dione — her we call Common; and the Love, who is her fellow-worker, may and must also have the name of common, as the other love is called heavenly' (Jowett, 'Dialogues of Plato,' vol. ii.).

Line 244. *A full sea glazed with muffled moonlight.* The poet, in the letter to Mr. Dawson already referred to, says: —

'There was a period in my life when, as an artist, Turner, for instance, takes rough sketches of landskip, &c., in order to work them eventually into some great picture, so I was in the habit of chronicling, in four or five words or more, whatever might strike me as picturesque in nature. I never put these down, and many and many a line has gone away on the north wind, but some remain, e. g.:

'A full sea glazed with muffled moonlight. *Suggestion:* The sea one night at Torquay, when Torquay was the most lovely sea-village in England, tho' now a smoky town. The sky was covered with thin vapour, and the moon was behind it.'

Page 122. *Song.* The 3d edition has 'I went' for 'we went' in the 1st line. Lines 6–10 were omitted in the 4th edition, but restored in the 5th. The last line but one is not in the 3d edition.

*Part II.* Line 19. *Couch'd beside her throne.* The 1st American edition misprints 'crouch'd.'

Line 29. *Of use and glory to yourselves.* The early editions have: 'Of fame and profit unto yourselves.'

Line 38. *She replied.* The early editions have ' and she replied.'

Line 39. *We scarcely thought.* The early editions read: ' We did not think;' and six lines below: ' We think not of him.' They do not have lines 42–44.

Line 44. *Indeed.* The 3d edition has ' For us ' instead of ' Indeed,' which was adopted in the 5th.

Lines 65–71. *That taught the Sabine how to rule.* The nymph Egeria, who was said to have given laws to Numa Pompilius. Compare ' The Palace of Art ': —

> Or hollowing one hand against his ear,
> To list a footfall, ere he saw
> The wood-nymph, stay'd the Ausonian king to hear
> Of wisdom and of law.

*The foundress of the Babylonian wall.* Semiramis.

*The Carian Artemisia.* The queen of Caria who was an ally of Xerxes, and who fought so well at Salamis that the Persian monarch said his women had become men and his men women.

*The Rhodope that built the pyramid.* A famous courtesan of Greece who was said to have built a pyramid near Memphis with a part of the fortune she had acquired. According to Ælian, she afterwards married Psammetichus, King of Egypt. Compare Shakespeare, ' 1 Henry VI.' i. 6. 22: —

> A statelier pyramis to her I 'll rear
> Than Rhodope's of Memphis ever was.

*Clelia* was a Roman girl, who, having been given as a hostage to Porsenna, escaped by swimming the Tiber on horseback. *Cornelia* is, of course, the mother of the Gracchi, and *the Palmyrene* is Zenobia. *Agrippina*, the granddaughter of Augustus, accompanied her husband Germanicus on his German campaigns.

Lines 71–80. *Dwell with these, etc.* This passage is not in the early editions, which read: ' Of Agrippina. Leave us: you may go.' The first part (' Dwell with these . . . which is higher') was added in the 3d edition, the remainder in the 5th.

Line 84. *She spoke and bowing waved.* The early editions read: ' So saying, she bowed and waved,' etc.

Line 98. *That whisper'd ' Asses' ears ' among the sedge.* Tennyson follows Chaucer, who (' Wife of Bath's Tale ') makes Midas confide the secret of his asses' ears only to his wife. Chaucer professes to follow Ovid, but, according to the Latin poet, it was Midas's barber that could not keep the secret.

Line 101. *This world was once a fluid haze of light, etc.* It would be impossible to summarize the nebular hypothesis more concisely or precisely than the poet has done it here.

On the lecture as a whole, compare Prior, ' Alma ': —

> She kindly talked, at least three hours,
> Of plastic forms and mental powers,

> Described our pre-existing station
> Before this vile terrene creation:
> And lest we should grow weary, Madam,
> To cut things short, came down to Adam;
> From thence, as fast as she was able,
> She drowns the world and builds up Babel;
> Thro' Syria, Persia, Greece, she goes,
> And takes the Romans in the close.

Line 112. *The Lycian custom.* According to Herodotus, the Lycians differed from all other nations in taking their names from their mothers instead of their fathers, and in tracing their ancestry in the feminine rather than the masculine line.

Line 113. *That lay at wine with Lar and Lucumo.* That is, the Etruscan women, who, in the paintings at Volterra, are depicted as sharing the banquets with their husbands. ' Lar ' or ' Lars ' was an honorary appellation in Etruria, equivalent to the English *Lord;* and ' Lucumo ' was a title given to the Etruscan princes and priests, like the Roman *patricius.*

Line 144. *Plato, Verulam.* Compare ' The Palace of Art ': ' Plato the wise, and largebrow'd Verulam.'

Line 149. *And, last not least, she who had left her place.* The early editions have: ' And she, tho' last not least, who left her place.'

Line 169. *The slacken'd sail.* The early editions have ' her ' for ' the .'

Line 184. *My vow binds me to speak, etc.* The early editions read: —

> I am bound
> To tell her. O, she has an iron will,
> An axelike edge unturnable, etc.

Line 224. *Bestrode my grandsire.* To defend him. Compare Shakespeare, ' Comedy of Errors,' v. 1. 192 : —

> When I bestrid thee in the wars, and took
> Deep scars to save thy life;

and ' 1 Henry IV.' v. 1. 122: ' Hal, if thou see me down in the battle, and bestride me, so ; 't is a point of friendship.'

Line 240. *Woman, if I might sit beside your feet.* The early editions have: ' A woman,' etc.

Line 285. *I knew you at the first . . . to see you, Florian.* The early editions read: —

> You are grown, and yet I knew you at the first.
> I am very glad, and I am very vext
> To see you, Florian.

Line 291. *Then, a moment after.* The early editions have: ' and a moment after.'

Line 303. *April daffodilly.* The ' Quarterly Review ' (vol. 82, March, 1848) says that daffodils are ' not April guests, but " take the winds of *March* with beauty " ' [' Winter's Tale,' iv. 4. 120]. Commenting on this in a letter to me, Tennyson said: ' Daffodils in the North of England belong as much to April as to March. I myself remember a man presenting me in the streets of Dublin the finest bunch of daffodils I almost ever saw on the 15th of April. It amused me at the time, for I had just been reading the Quarterly article.' I may add that *ten days* of Shakespeare's *March* properly belonged to *April,* as we now reckon it.

Line 306. *Seen to wave and float.* The early editions have: 'seem to wave and float.'

Line 311. *Did not wish.* The early editions have: 'did not mean;' and in the next line, '*I* pray you,' etc.

Line 319. *The Danaid of a leaky vase.* The allusion to the myth of the daughters of Danaus, condemned eternally to the hopeless task of filling a leaky vessel with water, seems a little pedantic here; but perhaps not more so than Melissa's reply. Both teacher and pupil are crammed with ancient lore.

Line 326. *That we still may lead.* The early editions have: 'that we may live to lead.'

Line 332. *Tho', madam, you should answer.* All the English editions down to 1890 point thus: 'Tho' madam *you* should answer,' etc. Even the small *m* in 'madam' (which in those editions is elsewhere printed with a capital) was not changed until 1884.

Line 333. *If you came.* The early editions have 'if e'er you came.'

Lines 347, 348. *For half the day, etc.* The early editions have: 'From room to room: in each we sat,' etc.

Lines 386–393. *What think you, etc.* The early editions have only the line, 'What think you of it, Florian ?  Will it hold ? '

Lines 419–426. *Intent on her, etc.* The early editions read thus: —

Intent upon the Princess, where she sat
Among her grave Professors, scattering gems
Of Art and Science: only Lady Blanche,
A double-rouged and treble-wrinkled Dame,
With all her faded Autumns falsely brown, etc.

Line 402. *But thou.* The early editions have 'but come.'

Lines 442, 443. *Men hated learned women, etc.* The early editions read: 'Men hated learned women: and to us came;' and three lines below: —

That harm'd not: so we sat; and now when day
Droop'd, and the chapel tinkled, mixt with those, etc.

In the 6th line of the 'Song' that follows, the 3d edition has 'dropping moon' for 'dying moon.'

*Part III.* Line 7. *There while we stood beside the fount.* The early editions have: 'And while,' etc.; in line 10 'Or sorrow' for 'Or grief '; and in line 13 'and we demanding' for 'and when I ask'd her.'

Lines 33–41. *If they had been men, etc.* The early editions read: —

if they had been men,
And in their fulsome fashion woo'd you, child,
You need not take so deep a rouge: like men —
And so they are, — very like men indeed —
And closeted with her for hours. Aha !
Then came these dreadful words out, etc.

Line 34. *Set your thoughts in rubric.* That is, in *red*, like the rubrics in a prayer-book.

Line 55. *They mounted, Ganymedes.* Compare the picture in ' The Palace of Art ' : —

Or else flushed Ganymede, his rosy thigh
Half-buried in the Eagle's down,

Sole as a flying star shot through the sky,
Above the pillar'd town.

Line 67. *God help her !* The early editions have: ' God pardon her ! ' and below, 'the love of the Princess ' for ' the heart of Ida.'

Line 75. *Yet my mother still.* The early editions have: ' only Lady Blanche ' (the poet forgot who was speaking), and below, ' the Royal heart,' for ' her pupil's love.'

Line 90. *To the sphere.* That is, to the upper air.  Milton, in 'Comus,' 241, calls Echo 'Sweet queen of parley, daughter of the sphere,' which has puzzled the commentators and given rise to sundry far-fetched explanations.  In my opinion, ' daughter of the sphere ' means daughter of the *air ;* and the ' sphere-born harmonious sisters, Voice and Verse ' of the same poet (' At a Solemn Music,' 2) are the *air*-born sisters. The dictionaries do not recognize this meaning of *sphere* (equivalent to *atmosphere*), but it is a Grecism of a simple sort, and furnishes an easy explanation of these otherwise perplexing passages.

Line 92. *But in her own grand way : being herself.* The early editions read: 'For being, and wise in knowing that she is,' etc.

Line 97. *Hebes are they to hand ambrosia.* The early reading is: 'They are Hebes meet to hand ambrosia,' etc.

Line 99. *The Samian Herè.* Juno, or the Greek *Hera.* The island Samos was one of her favorite seats.

Line 101. *From the court.* The early editions have: ' from out the court.'

Line 103. *Balusters.* The accent on the second syllable is peculiar.

Lines 109, 110. *No fighting shadows, etc.* These two lines are not in the early editions.

Line 114. *I knock'd, and, bidden, enter'd ; found her there.* The early editions have: 'I knock'd and bidden went in; I found,' etc. In the next line they have ' sally,' for ' move.'

Line 118. *As man's could be.* The early editions have: ' As man could be,' — connected of course with ' courteous ' instead of ' phrase.'

Line 120. *Fabled nothing fair.* Told no plausible falsehoods; or ' minted nothing false,' as it reads in the early editions.

Line 126. *True — we had limed ourselves.* The early reading is: 'She said we had limed ourselves.'

Line 146. *Some palace in our land.* The early reading was ' A palace in our own land.'

Line 153. *That afternoon.* The early editions have: ' In the afternoon.'

Line 158. *Furrowy forks.* The early editions have: ' dark-blue forks,' and ' full-leaved ' in the next line.

Lines 167–173. *I gazed, etc.* One of the passages added in the 4th edition.

Line 175. *Then from my breast.* The early editions have ' And ' for ' Then,' and ' clomb' for ' got' in line 178.

Line 179. *Retinue.* Accented on the second syllable; as in ' Guinevere ': ' Of his and her retinue moving they; ' and in ' Aylmer's Field ': ' The dark retinue reverencing death.'  So

Milton, in the two instances in which he uses the word: ' Paradise Lost,' v. 355: ' On princes, when their rich retinue long; ' and ' Paradise Regained,' ii. 419: ' What followers, what retinue canst thou gain ? ' and Shakespeare (the only instance in verse), ' Lear,' i. 4. 221: ' But other of your insolent retinue.'

Line 203. *As we ourself have been.* ' Ourselves ' in the early editions, as elsewhere in the poem. I shall not refer to the other instances.

Line 207. *To lift the woman's fallen divinity.* The early editions have: ' To uplift,' etc.

Line 215. *Breathes full East.* Breathes the proud and defiant spirit of the Eastern queen. Dawson takes it to refer (as it may, incidentally) to ' the dry and unpleasant east-winds prevalent in England.'

Line 216. *On that which leans to you.* In regard to what suits your purpose, or favors your theories.

Line 246. *The one* ΠΟΥ ΣΤΩ. Alluding to the oft-quoted saying of Archimedes, ' Give me *where I may stand,* and I will move the world ' (δὸς ποῦ στῶ, καὶ κόσμον κινήσω).

Line 250. *By frail successors.* The early editions have: ' Of frail successors.'

Line 256. *If that same poet-princess, etc.* The early editions read: ' If that strange maiden could,' etc.

Line 262. *Gynæceum.* The portion of the Greek house where the women had their quarters.

Line 285. *Diotima.* A wise woman of Mantinea, whom Socrates, in Plato's ' Symposium,' calls his instructress.

Line 293. *Those monstrous males that carve the living hound, etc.* Referring to vivisection, and the assertion that dogs have sometimes been fed with the fragments of the dissecting-room. The poet was one of the signers of the petition to Parliament against vivisection. Compare ' The Children's Hospital ':

I could think he was one of those who would break their jests on the dead,
And mangle the living dog that had loved him and fawned at his knee —
Drenched with the hellish oorali — that ever such things should be !

Line 298. *Encarnalize.* Make carnal, sensualize; apparently the poet's own coinage, but since used by Hartley Coleridge, Canon Farrar, and others.

Line 316. *We rode a league beyond, etc.* The early editions read: —

we rode a little higher
To cross the flood by a narrow bridge, and came, etc.

Line 319. *O how sweet, etc.* The early editions have: ' And O how sweet,' etc.

Line 324. *The Elysian lawns.* Dawson takes these to be the plains of Troy, and ' built to the sun ' to refer to the origin of the city, ascribed by Ovid to the music of Apollo's lyre. Compare ' Œnone,' 39. But the poet writes to me thus: ' The " Elysian lawns " are the lawns of

Elysium, and have nothing to do with Troy — or perhaps they rather refer to the Islands of the Blest (Pindar, *Olymp.* 2d).' ' Built to the sun ' must then mean simply ' rising sunward, lofty.'

Line 331. *Fair Corinna's triumph.* Over Pindar, ' the bearded Victor of ten thousand hymns.'

Line 337. *With Psyche, with Melissa Florian, I.* The early editions read: ' With Psyche, Florian with the other, and I,' etc.

The ' Song ' that follows was suggested by the bugle music of the boatmen on Lake Killarney; and Mrs. Anne Thackeray Ritchie (' Records of Tennyson, etc.' 1892) says: ' Here is a reminiscence of Tennyson's about the echo at Killarney, where he said to the boatman, " When I last was here I heard eight echoes, and now I only hear one." To which the man, who had heard people quoting the bugle song, replied, " Why, you must be the gentleman that brought all the money to the place." '

It may be noted that some of the most musical lines in the song are composed entirely of monosyllables.

*Part IV.* Line 1. *The nebulous star we call the Sun.* Dawson says: ' The Princess, with the accuracy taught only recently by the spectroscope, calls the sun *a nebulous star;* ' but the expression implies no more than was taught by the nebular hypothesis of Laplace, to which reference has been made by Psyche above. This is the ' hypothesis ' of the next line.

Line 17. *Fruit, blossom, viand, amber wine, and gold.* The early editions have: ' Fruit, viand, blossom, and amber wine and gold.'

Line 21. *Tears, idle tears, etc.* Mrs. Anne Thackeray Ritchie says (' Records of Tennyson, etc.'): ' One of my family remembers hearing Tennyson say that " Tears, idle Tears " was suggested by Tintern Abbey: who shall say by what mysterious wonder of beauty and regret, by what sense of the " transient with the abiding " ? '

Line 47. *Cram our ears with wool.* No doubt suggested by the story of Ulysses stopping the ears of his companions with wax, that they might not hear the song of the Sirens.

Line 50. *A true occasion lost.* The early editions have: ' gone ' for ' lost; ' and the next two lines read thus: —

But trim our sails, and let the old proverb serve
While down the streams that buoy each separate craft, etc.

One might not guess ' the old proverb ' here.

Line 59. *Kex.* A provincial word for the dry stalks of hemlock; here put for any wild growth springing up in the crevices of the mosaic pavement and breaking the beautiful work.

Line 60. *The beard-blown goat.* As the poet explains, in his letter to Dawson, this refers to ' the wind blowing the beard on the height of the ruined pillar.' The early editions read: —

The starr'd mosaic, and the wild goat hang
Upon the pillar, and the wild fig-tree split, etc.

Line 61. *The wild fig-tree.* Often referred to by the Roman poets as rending asunder ruined buildings and monuments. Compare Martial (x. 2): 'Marmora Messalæ findit caprificus.' See also Juvenal, x. 147.

'Ramage in his "Nooks and By-ways of Italy" (p. 69) is reminded of this passage by noticing a wild fig springing out of, and splitting a rock in the Apennines' (Dawson).

Line 65. *Then to me.* The first edition has: 'and then to me.'

Line 69. *A death's-head at the wine.* According to the Egyptian custom mentioned by Herodotus (i. 78): 'At their convivial banquets, among the wealthy classes, when they have finished supper, a man carries round in a coffin the image of a dead body carved in wood, made as like as possible in color and workmanship, and in size generally about one or two cubits in length; and showing this to each of the company, he says, "Look upon this, then drink and enjoy yourself; for when dead you will be like this."'

Line 85. *And her heart would rock the snowy cradle till I died.* Compare Shakespeare, 'Venus and Adonis,' 1185: —

> Lo, in this hollow cradle take thy rest,
> My throbbing heart shall rock thee day and night.

Line 88. *The tender ash delays To clothe herself, when all the woods are green.* This is botanically true, and is one of the many passages that show the poet's close observation of nature.

Line 100. *Like the Ithacensian suitors in old time.* That is, like the suitors of Penelope, who do not recognize the disguised Ulysses, and laugh in a constrained way, they know not why. Compare 'Odyssey,' xx. 347: οἱ δ' ἤδη γναθμοισι γελώων ἀλλοτρίοισιν (literally, 'laughed with other men's jaws ').

Line 104. *O Bulbul, any rose of Gulistan, etc.* The love of the nightingale for the rose is a favorite theme with Saadi and his brother poets. 'Gulistan' is Persian for rose-garden, and Saadi takes it as the title of his book of poems.

The 'marsh-diver' (or water-rail) and the 'meadow-crake' (corn-crake, or land-rail) are unmusical birds. Wood (quoted by Dawson) says of the latter that its cry 'may be exactly imitated by drawing a quill or a piece of stick smartly over the large teeth of a comb, or by rubbing together two jagged strips of bone.'

Lines 115–124. *Poor soul! etc.* These ten lines are not in the early editions.

Line 121. *Valkyrian hymns.* Such as were sung by the Valkyrs, or Valkyrias, 'the choosers of the slain,' or fatal sisters of Odin in the Northern mythology.

Line 125. *Would this same mock-love, etc.* The early editions have: 'I would.'

Line 130. *Owed to none.* The early editions have: 'due to none.'

Line 137. *Cyril, with whom the bell-mouth'd glass had wrought.* The early editions have: 'Did Cyril;' and 'begin' for 'began' in the next line.

Line 149. *Said Ida, 'home! to horse!' and fled.* The early editions read: 'Said Lady Ida; and fled at once, as flies,' etc.

Line 172. *Her maidens glimmeringly group'd.* The 2d edition misprints 'group.'

Line 174. *They cried, 'she lives.'* The early editions have: ' and crying.'

Line 180. *Across the woods.* The 1st edition reads: ' Across the thicket.'

Line 182. *The garden portals.* The early reading was ' The gates of the garden.'

Line 185. *The hunter.* Actæon. The 1st edition has: 'Of open metal, in which the old hunter rued,' etc.

Line 194. *The Bear.* The constellation *Ursa Major*, the ' seven slow suns ' being of course the stars that form ' Charles's Wain,' or the ' Dipper.' The early editions print ' the bear.'

Line 196. *Then a loftier form.* The 1st edition has: ' and then.'

Line 202. *' How came you here?' I told him: ' I,' said he.* The early editions read: " I found the key in the doors: how came you here ? '

Line 215. *Or Psyche, she affirm'd not, or denied.* The first reading was: 'Or Lady Psyche, affirm'd not, or denied.'

Line 236. *But as the water-lily, etc.* Critics have compared Wordsworth, 'Excursion,' book v., where Moral Truth is said to be

> a thing
> Subject, you deem, to vital accidents,
> And, like the water-lily, lives and thrives,
> Whose root is fix'd in stable earth, whose head
> Floats on the tossing waves.

Tennyson, in his letter to Dawson, gives as the ' suggestion ' of this passage: ' Water-lilies in my own pond, seen on a gusty day with my own eyes. They did start and slide in the sudden puffs of wind, till caught and stayed by the tether of their own stalks — quite as *true* as Wordsworth's simile, and more in detail.' Dawson had said that Wordsworth's was ' the truer picture.'

Line 242. *Musky-circled mazes.* The early editions read: ' To thrid thro' all the musky mazes, wind,' etc.

Line 247. *Bubbled the nightingale.* Most aptly descriptive of the bird's warbling. Mrs. Anne Thackeray Ritchie says: ' Once, when Mr. Tennyson was in Yorkshire, so he told me, as he was walking at night in a friend's garden, he heard a nightingale singing with such a frenzy of passion that it was unconscious of everything else, and not frightened though he came and stood quite close beside it; he could see its eye flashing, and feel the air bubble in his ear through the vibration.'

Line 249. *Hook'd my ankle in a vine.* The early editions have ' took ' for ' hook'd.'

Line 255. *The mystic fire on a mast-head.* The electrical phenomenon known to Italian and other sailors as ' St. Elmo's fires.' Compare Longfellow, ' Golden Legend ': —

> Last night I saw Saint Elmo's stars,
> With their glimmering lanterns, all at play

On the tops of the masts and the tips of the spars,
And I knew we should have foul weather to-day.

Line 263. *Wail'd about with mews.* The early editions have: ' clang'd about with mews.'

Line 273. *In old days.* The early editions have: ' in the old days.'

Line 283. *To me you froze.* The early editions have: ' you froze to me.'

Line 323. *I came to tell you; found that you had gone.* The early editions read: ' I judged it best to speak; but you had gone; ' in line 325 ' tell you ' for ' speak;' and in line 330 ' the merit ' for ' some sense.'

Line 343. *We take it to ourself.* The early editions have: ' assume it.'

Line 352. *A Niobean daughter.* The poet has another allusion to Niobe in ' Walking to the Mail ': ' the Niobe of swine,'

Line 355. *And on a sudden rush'd.* The 1st edition has: ' ran in ' for ' rush'd.'

Line 356. *Out of breath, as one pursued.* The early editions have: ' all out of breath, as pursued.'

Line 366. *When the wild peasant rights himself, etc.* Referring to the incendiary fires so common in the troubles with the English agricultural laborers some years before the poem was written. The early editions have ' and the rick ' for ' the rick.'

Line 389. *Render him up.* The early editions have: ' deliver him up.'

Line 401. *Regal compact.* The 1st American edition misprints ' legal.'

Line 403. *Zealous it should be.* The early editions have: ' and willing it should be.'

Line 409. *Vague brightness.* The ' Quarterly Review,' (vol. 82), commenting on this, says: that ' no brightness can be more distinct than that of the moon ; ' but the purblind critic does not see that the poet describes it as it appears *to the baby.* The comparison is as true as it is apt.

Line 411. *Inmost south.* The early editions have: ' the inmost south; ' and in the next line, ' the inmost north.' In line 417 they have: ' tho' you had been ' for ' had you been.' It will be noticed that these changes, like many before and after, are made to get rid of an extra unaccented syllable in the measure. Tennyson uses this ' license ' freely, to give variety to his verse (see Professor Hadley's criticism quoted in my edition of ' The Princess,' pp. 142–145). but he appears to have decided that in the early editions of the poem he had used it too often.

Line 426. *Landskip.* The earlier and better form of ' landscape.'

Line 430. *My boyish dream.* The early editions have: ' Mine old ideal.'

Line 450. *At her feet.* The early editions have: ' on the marble.'

Line 472. *Fixt like a beacon tower above the waves, etc.* Compare ' Enoch Arden ': —

Allured him as the beacon-blaze allures
The bird of passage, till he madly strikes
Against it, and beats out his weary life.

Line 473. *The crimson-rolling eye.* It is a red

' revolving ' light. In the next line the 1st edition has: ' wild sea-birds ' for ' wild birds.'

Line 490. *We hold a great convention.* The early editions read: ' We meet to elect new tutors.'

Line 510. *You saved our life.* The early editions have: ' You have saved;' and in the following lines: ' the wholesome ' for ' our good,' and ' tutors ' for ' servants.'

Line 524. *Your falsehood and yourself are hateful to us.* The early editions have: ' your face ' for ' yourself,' and ' loathsome ' for ' hateful.'

Lines 537–550. *While I listen'd, etc.* The early editions read: —

The voices murmuring; till upon my spirits
Settled a gentle cloud of melancholy,
Which I shook off, for I was young, and one
To whom the shadow of all mischance but came, etc.

*Interlude.* This was added in the 3d edition. There the song begins thus: —

When all among the thundering drums
Thy soldier in the battle stands;

and ends with

Strikes them dead for thine and thee.
Tara ta tantara.

In the 4th edition it was changed to its present form.

The following is another version of the song, printed in the ' Selections ' of 1865, but not included in the collected works : —

Lady, let the rolling drums
Beat to battle where thy warrior stands:
Now thy face across his fancy comes,
And gives the battle to his hands.

Lady, let the trumpets blow,
Clasp thy little babes about thy knee:
Now their warrior father meets the foe,
And strikes him dead for thine and thee.

*Part V.* Line 7. *Till we heard.* The early editions have ' until.'

Line 15. *There brake.* The early editions have ' out-brake.'

Line 23. *King, you are free.* The early editions have: ' You are free, O king.'

Line 28. *More crumpled than a poppy from the sheath.* This simile, like so many others, illustrates the poet's minute observation of nature. No flower that blows has a more crumpled and generally unpromising look when it first opens than the poppy.

Lines 30–35. *Then some one, etc.* The early editions read: —

' But hence,' he said, ' indue yourselves like men.
Your Cyril told us all.' As boys that slink, etc.

Line 42. *Here Cyril met us.* All the recent editions (down to 1898) have a period after ' us,' but this is clearly a misprint.

Line 70. *From brows as pale and smooth, etc.* Probably referring to Michael Angelo's *Pietà* in St. Peter's at Rome.

Line 110. ' *Look you,' cried my father, etc.* The early editions read here: —

'Look to it,' cried
My father, 'that our compact is perform'd.
You have spoilt this girl; she laughs at you and man:
She shall not legislate for Nature, king,
But yields, or war,' etc.

Line 117. *Our strange girl.* The early editions have ' child ' for ' girl.'

Line 126. *At him that mars her plan.* The early editions have : ' At the enemy of her plan.'

Line 129. *More soluble is this knot.* The early editions add the line: ' Like almost all the rest, if men were wise; ' and ' And dusted down your domes with mangonels ' after line 132, ' Your cities into shards,' etc.

Line 136. *Flitting chance.* The first four editions have: ' little chance.'

Lines 145-151. *Boy, when . . . for shame!* For these seven lines the early editions have only the line: ' They prize hard knocks, and to be won by force.'

Line 188. *Pure as lines of green that streak the white, etc.* Another illustration of the poet's keen observation of nature. Most writers would have taken the *white* of the snowdrop as the emblem of purity (as Tennyson himself does in ' Saint Agnes '), but that delicate *green* seems more exquisitely pure, even beside the white.

Line 190. *Not like the piebald miscellany, man.* The early editions read: — :

Not like strong bursts of sample among men,
But all one piece; and take them all in all, etc.

Line 195. *As frankly theirs.* The early editions have: ' as easily theirs.'

Line 215. *Our royal word.* The 1st American edition misprints ' loyal.'

Line 250. *The airy Giant's zone.* The belt of Orion.

Line 252. *And as the fiery Sirius alters hue, etc.* Dawson quotes Proctor's ' Myths and Marvels of Astronomy ': ' Every bright star when close to the horizon shows these colors, and so much the more distinctly as the star is the brighter. Sirius, which surpasses the brightest stars of the northern hemisphere full four times in lustre, shows these changes of color so conspicuously that they were regarded as specially characteristic of this star, insomuch that Homer speaks of Sirius (not by name, but as the " Star of Autumn ") shining most beautifully " when laved of ocean's wave," — that is, when close to the horizon.'

Dawson adds: ' The expression " laved of ocean's wave " explains the " washed with morning " of our poet. The glitter of the early morning sun on the bright helmets of the brothers, and the glance of light upon their armor as they rode, are vividly realized in this beautiful simile.' The passage of Homer is ' Iliad,' v. 5, thus rendered by Merivale: —

Flashed from his helm and buckler a bright incessant gleam,
Like summer star that burns afar, new bathed in ocean's stream.

Lines 262-300. *And, ere the windy jest . . . three to three.* The early editions read thus: —

and Arac turning said:
' Our land invaded, life and soul ! himself
Your captive, yet my father wills not war:
But, Prince, the question of your troth remains;
And there 's a downright honest meaning in her:
She ask'd but space and fairplay for her scheme;
She prest and prest it on me; life ! I felt
That she was half right talking of her wrongs:
And I 'll stand by her. Waive your claim, or else
Decide it here; why not ? we are three to three.'

I lagg'd in answer, loth to strike her kin,
And cleave the rift of difference deeper yet;
Till one of those two brothers, half aside,
And fingering at the hair about his lip,
To prick us on to combat, ' Three to three ?
But such a three to three were three to one.'
A boast that clenched his purpose like a blow !
For fiery-short was Cyril's counter-scoff,
And sharp I answer'd, touch'd upon the sense
Where idle boys are cowards to their shame,
And tipt with sportive malice to and fro
Like pointed arrows leapt the taunts and hit.

The passage now stands as in the 5th edition. The 3d does not contain lines 268 and 276-279. In 268 it has ' But, Prince, the ' for ' But then this '; in 280 ' Yet ' for ' And '; and in 282 and 288 (also in 314) ' Life !' for ' 'Sdeath !'

Line 284. *Her that talk'd down the fifty wisest men.* St. Catherine of Alexandria, daughter of Costis (half-brother to Constantine the Great) and Sabinella, Queen of Egypt. Maxentius during his persecution sent fifty learned men to dispute with her, but she confuted and converted them all.

Line 314. *'Sdeath ! but we will send to her, etc.* The early editions read: —

' We will send to her,' Arac said,
' A score of worthy reasons why she should
Bide by this issue,' etc.

Line 333. *Thro' open doors.* The early editions have: ' Thro' the open doors.'

Line 336. *Like a stately pine, etc.* The following is from the ' Remains of Arthur Hugh Clough,' dated in the Valley of Cauterets, Sept. 7, 1861: ' I have been out for a walk with A. T. to a sort of island between two waterfalls, with pines on it, of which he retained a recollection from his visit of thirty-one years ago, and which, moreover, furnished a simile to " The Princess." He is very fond of this place, evidently.'

Line 355. *Tomyris.* The queen of the Massagetæ, who, according to Herodotus (i. 214), defeated Cyrus the Great in battle, B. C. 529, and afterwards insulted his dead body.

Line 364. *O brother, you have known, etc.* The early editions read: —

You have known, O brother, all the pangs we felt,
What heats of moral anger when we heard, etc.

Line 367. *Of lands in which at the altar the poor bride, etc.* It was a Russian custom in the seventeenth century for the bride, on her wedding-day, to present her husband, in token of submission, with a whip made by her own hands.

Line 371. *Mothers . . . fling their pretty maids in the running flood, etc.* The reference is to the throwing of female infants into the Ganges, where the vultures are often seen to swoop down upon them before they sink.

Line 375. *That equal baseness lived in sleeker times.* The early editions have: 'That it was little better in better times.'

Line 380. *I built a fold for them.* The early editions have: 'we built' (but 'I set' just above) ; and the plural pronoun also in the following thirteen lines.

Line 384. *Rout of saucy boys.* The early editions have 'set' for 'rout ;' and in 388 'old affiance' for 'baby troth.'

Line 391. *Since you think me touch'd.* The early editions have: 'think we are touch'd;' and 'nay' for 'what' in the next line.

Lines 395-397. *You failing, I abide, etc.* The early editions read: —

We abide what end soe'er,
You failing; but we know you will not. Still,
You must not slay him: he risk'd his life for ours, etc.

Lines 407-410. *Till she Whose name is yoked with children . . . following, etc.* The early editions read: —

till she
The woman-phantom, she that seem'd no more
Than the man's shadow in a glass, her name
Yoked in his mouth with children's, know herself,
And nowise liberate her, nor only here,
But ever following, etc.

Line 419. *I think Our chiefest comfort, etc.* The early editions have: 'we think;' and in 424-427 they read: —

We took it for an hour this morning to us,
In our own bed: the tender orphan hands
Felt at our heart, and seem'd to charm from thence
The wrath we nursed against the world: farewell.

Line 441. *Look you !* The early editions have: 'Look to it.'

Lines 445-448. *But you — she's yet a colt . . . and brawl, etc.* The early reading is: —

but take and break her, you !
She's yet a colt: well groom'd and strongly curb'd,
She might not rank with those detestable
That to the hireling leave their babe, and brawl, etc.

Line 457. *For it was nearly noon.* The early editions have: 'it was the point of noon.' After omitting the next fourteen lines, 458-471, they go on thus: —

The lists were ready. Empanoplied and plumed
We enter'd in, and waited, fifty there
To fifty, till the terrible trumpet blared
At the barrier, — yet a moment, and once more, etc.

Line 480. *In conflict with the crash, etc.* The early editions have: 'In the middle with the crash,' etc. Of course, they do not contain the sentence, 'Yet it seem'd a dream; I dream'd Of fighting.'

Line 484. *And out of stricken helmets sprang the fire.* After this line, the 4th edition has the line (afterwards omitted): 'A noble dream ! What was it else I saw ?'

Line 491. *Mellay.* An anglicized spelling of the French *mêlée.*

Line 496. *And in my dream, etc.* The early editions read: —

and thinking thus
I glanced to the left, and saw, etc.

Line 506. *Let me see her fall.* The early editions have 'die' for 'fall.' They do not contain the sentence: 'Yea, let me make my dream All that I would; ' nor line 510, 'His visage all agrin as at a wake.'

Line 514. *Flaying.* The early editions add 'off;' and in 517 they read: 'that the earth.'

Line 525. *Heavier.* The early editions have 'suppler; ' and in line 530 below, 'life and love' for 'dream and truth.'

*Song.* In the 1st line the original reading was 'the warrior' for 'her warrior; ' and in the last line but one, 'Like a summer,' etc.

A song first published in the 'Selections' (1865), and not included in the latest editions of Tennyson's collected works, seems like an early draft of this one. It reads thus: —

Home they brought him slain with spears.
They brought him home at even-fall;
All alone she sits and hears
Echoes in his empty hall,
Sounding on the morrow.

The sun peeped in from open field,
The boy began to leap and prance,
Rode upon his father's lance,
Beat upon his father's shield —
'O, hush, my joy, my sorrow ! '

*Part VI.* Lines 1-5. In place of these lines the early editions have only this: —

What follow'd, tho' I saw not, yet I heard
So often that I speak as having seen;

and for the next three lines: 'For when our side was vanquish'd and my cause.'

Line 15. *Babe in arm.* Compare 'The Palace of Art ': 'Sat smiling, babe in arm;' and see note on the passage.

Line 16. *That great dame of Lapidoth.* See Judges, iv. 4 and v. 1 fol.

Line 40. *Growing breeze.* The early editions have: 'Æonian breeze.'

Line 47. *Blanch'd in our annals.* That is, fortunate, propitious; as the Latin *albus* was sometimes used.

Line 65. *The tremulous isles of light.* 'Spots of sunshine coming through the leaves, and seeming to slide from one to the other, as the procession of girls " moves under shade " ' (Tennyson's letter to Dawson).

*Slided* occurs again (for the sake of the metre, as here) in 'Merlin and Vivien': 'Writhed toward him, slided up his knee and sat.'

Line 68. *Thro' open field.* The early editions have: 'Thro' the open field.'

Line 91. *And her hue.* The early editions have 'and all her hue.'

Line 110. *This great clog of thanks, that make.* The early editions have 'makes.'

Line 137. *But he that lay Beside us, etc.* The early editions read: —

> but Cyril, who lay
> Bruised, where he fell, not far off, much in pain,
> Trail'd himself, etc.

**Line 161.** *Fixt in yourself.* All the editions have ' fix'd,' but elsewhere ' fixt.'

**Line 166.** *One port of sense.* Portal; as in Shakespeare, ' 2 Henry IV.' iv. 5. 24: ' That keep'st the ports of slumber open wide,' etc. The first four editions have ' part ' for ' port,' perhaps a misprint. Wallace's edition of ' The Princess ' explains ' port ' as ' haven, from Latin *portus*,' and this is endorsed by the present Lord Tennyson; but I nevertheless feel confident that the poet had the Shakespearian use of the word in mind. The figure of the gate (*porta*) seems to me both more natural and more appropriate than the other. The reader can take his choice.

**Line 171.** *I will give it her.* The early editions have: ' and I will.'

**Line 179.** *No purple in the distance.* Compare ' In Memoriam,' xxxvii.: —

> With weary steps I loiter on,
> Tho' always under alter'd skies
> The purple from the distance dies,
> My prospect and horizon gone.

**Line 185.** *Helpless . . . barren.* The early editions have: ' waxen . . . milkless.'

**Line 204.** *Then Arac, etc.* The early editions read: ' Then Arac: "Soul and life ! " ' etc. They have the line: ' I am your brother; I advise you well ' after line 206.

**Line 209.** *'Sdeath ! I would sooner fight.* The early editions have: ' Life ! I would sooner fight.'

**Line 225.** *I trust that there is no one hurt to death.* This line is not in the early editions.

**Line 304.** *Amazed am I to hear.* The early editions have: ' I am all amaze to hear.'

**Line 313.** *Rang ruin, answered, etc.* The speech that follows has been much abridged, the early editions reading thus: —

> Rang ruin, answered full of grief and scorn:
> ' What ! in our time of glory when the cause
> Now stands up, first, a trophied pillar — now
> So clipt, so stinted in our triumph— barred
> Even from our free heart-thanks, and every way
> Thwarted and vext, and lastly catechised
> By our own creature ! one that made our laws !
> Our great she-Solon ! her that built the nest
> To hatch the cuckoo ! whom we called our friend !
> But we will crush the lie that glances at us
> As cloaking in the larger charities
> Some baby predilection; all amazed !
> We must amaze this legislator more.
> Fling our doors wide ! ' etc.

Below (321) the reading was: —

> Pass and mingle with your likes.
> Go, help the half-brain'd dwarf, Society,
> To find low motives unto noble deeds,
> To fix all doubt upon the darker side;
> Go, fitter thou for narrowest neighborhoods,
> Old talker, haunt where gossip breeds and seethes
> And festers in provincial sloth ! and you,
> That think we sought to practise on a life
> Risk'd for our own and trusted to our hands,
> What say you, Sir ? you hear us; deem ye not

> 'T is all too like that even now we scheme,
> In one broad death confounding friend and foe,
> To drug them all ? revolve it: you are man,
> And therefore no doubt wise; but after this
> We brook no further insult, but are gone.

The omissions here are the most important in the whole poem, and are certainly for the better. The briefer speech is the more dignified.

**Line 332.** *And on they moved.* The early editions have: ' And they moved on.'

**Line 340.** *Amazed they glared.* The early editions have ' amaze,' which, if not a misprint, is used as in the early reading of 304 above.

*Song.* This song is equally musical and monosyllabic. Of one hundred and twenty-five words in it all are monosyllables except *seven*, and those are dissyllables.

*Part VII.* **Line 19.** *Void was her use.* Her occupation was gone, like Othello's. Dawson quotes ' Aylmer's Field ': —

> So that the gentle creature, *shut from all*
> *Her charitable use*, and face to face
> With twenty months of silence, slowly lost,
> Nor greatly cared to lose her hold on life.

**Line 21.** *A great black cloud, etc.* The poet, in his letter to Dawson, says that this was suggested by ' a coming storm as seen from the top of Snowdon.'

**Line 23.** *Verge.* Horizon; as iv. 29 above: ' below the verge.' Compare ' The Gardener's Daughter ': ' and May from verge to verge.' The *slope* is an optical illusion.

**Line 36.** *Deeper than those weird doubts, etc.* This line is not in the early editions, the next beginning ' Lay sundered,' etc.

**Line 60.** *Upon the babe restored.* The early editions have: ' on what she said of the child ' (see v. 101 above); and in the next line, ' would she yield ' for ' yielded she.'

**Line 68.** *Were at peace.* The construction is confused; as if ' each ' had been ' both.'

**Line 96.** *Flourished up.* ' Blossomed up ' (ii. 292 above) the etymological sense of ' flourished.'

**Line 109.** *The Oppian law.* A sumptuary law passed when Hannibal was almost at the gates of Rome. It enacted that no woman should wear a gay-colored dress, or have more than half an ounce of gold ornaments, and that none should approach within a mile of any city or town in a car drawn by horses. After the war the women demanded the repeal of the law. They gained one consul, but Cato, the other one, resisted. The women harassed the magistrates until the law was repealed.

**Line 111.** *Dwarf-like.* The early editions have ' little.'

**Line 112.** *Hortensia spoke against the tax.* A heavy tax imposed on Roman matrons by the second triumvirate. No man was found bold enough to oppose it; but Hortensia, daughter of Hortensius the orator, spoke so eloquently against it that it was repealed.

**Line 118.** *I saw the forms, etc.* The early editions read: —

I saw the forms: I knew not where I was:
Sad phantoms conjured out of circumstance,
Ghosts of the fading brain they seem'd; nor more
Sweet Ida, etc.

In 122 below they have ' show'd ' for ' seem'd.'
Line 140. *She stoop'd, etc.* The 1st edition
reads thus : —

She stoop'd ; and with a great shock of the heart
Our mouths met : out of languor leapt a cry,
Crown'd Passion from the brinks of death, and up
Along the shuddering senses struck the soul,
And closed on fire with Ida's at the lips.

The 2d edition changes ' Crown'd ' to ' Leapt.'
Line 148. *That other when she came, etc.* Bayard Taylor calls the passage ' an exquisite rapid
picture of Aphrodite floating along the wave to
her home at Paphos; but,' he adds, ' what must
we think of the lover, who, in relating the supreme moment of his passion, could turn aside
to interpolate it ? Its very loveliness empha-
sizes his utter forgetfulness of the governing
theme.' It seems to me natural enough in the
' relating,' especially as it leads up to the im-
passioned

nor end of mine,
Stateliest, for thee !

which shows that he has dwelt upon the picture
of the goddess because he half-identifies her
with Ida.
Line 165. *The milk-white peacock.* Darwin
(' Animals and Plants under Domestication ')
speaks of a white variety of peacock.
Line 177. *Come down, O maid, etc.* This
' small sweet idyl ' like the exquisite song,
' Tears, idle tears,' was perfect from the first,
and has undergone no revision at the author's
hands. ' It transfers,' says Symonds in his
' Greek Poets,' ' with perfect taste, the Greek
Idyllic feeling to Swiss scenery; it is a fine instance of new wine being successfully poured
into old bottles, for nothing could be fresher,
and not even the " Thalysia " is sweeter.'
All the editions have ' idyl ' here, as in the
heading ' ENGLISH IDYLS AND OTHER POEMS.'
Line 189. *With Death and Morning on the
Silver Horns.* In the early editions we find
' Silver Horns,' but all the more recent ones
print ' silver horns.' The former is, of course,
to be preferred, on account of the obvious reference to the Silberhorn, one of the peaks or spurs
of the Jungfrau, and markedly the most silvery-
white part of the summit, as seen from Inter-
lachen and its vicinity.
The ' Memoir ' (vol. i. p. 252) tells us that this
' idyl ' was ' written in Switzerland (chiefly at
Lauterbrunnen and Grindelwald),' and that the
poet considered it among his ' most successful
work.'
*Morning* walks on the mountains here, as
' o'er the dew of yon high eastern hill ' in
' Hamlet ' (i. 1. 167); and *Death* is her companion because life has no home on those ' Alpine
summits cold,' or must face Death in attempt-
ing to scale them.
Line 191. *Firths of ice, etc.* Bayard Taylor

remarks that this would be ' almost incompre-
hensible to one who has not looked with his
own bodily eyes upon the Mer de Glace.'
Line 198. *Water-smoke.* Compare ' The Lotos-
Eaters: ' —

And, like a downward smoke, the slender stream
Along the cliff to fall and pause did seem.

Line 245. *Out of Lethe.* The poet may have
been thinking of Wordsworth's ' Our birth is
but a sleep and a forgetting; ' or of Virgil,
' Æneid,' vi. 748: —

Has omnes, ubi mille rotam volvere per annos,
Lethaeum ad fluvium deus evocat agmine magno;
Scilicet immemores supera ut convexa revisant
Rursus, et incipiant in corpora velle reverti.

Lines 250-256. *How shall men grow ? . . . her
own.* The early editions read: —

How shall men grow ?  We two will serve them both
In aiding her strip off, as in us lies,
(Our place is much) the parasitic forms
That seem to keep her up but drag her down —
Will leave her field to burgeon and to bloom
From all within her, make herself her own, etc.

Line 261. *His dearest bond.* The early editions have ' whose ' for ' his.'
Line 268. *Nor lose the childlike, etc.* In place
of this line the early editions have : ' More as
the double-natured Poet each.'
Lines 313-320. *Said Ida, tremulously, etc.*
The early editions read : —

Said Ida, ' so unlike, so all unlike —
It seems you love to cheat yourself with words:
This mother is your model.  Never, Prince;
You cannot love me.'  ' Nay, but thee,' I said,
' From yearlong poring on thy pictured eyes,
Or some mysterious or magnetic touch,
Ere seen I loved,' etc.

Lines 327-330. *Lift thine eyes, etc.* The early
reading is : —

lift thine eyes; doubt me no more;
Look up, and let thy nature strike on mine, etc.

Line 335. *Is morn to more, etc.* The early
editions have: ' I scarce believe, and all the rich
to-come; ' and in 337, ' flowers ' for ' weeds.'
Bayard Taylor was troubled at this latter
change, the first reading having suggested to
him ' a more delicate fancy than the poet seems
to have intended.' It gave him, not the view of
an ' ordinary piece of farm-work,' but ' a vision
of the autumnal haze slowly gathering from
myriads of flowers as they burn away in the
last ardors of summer.' This is a good illustration of the manner in which a person of lively
imagination may ' read into' poetry a meaning
which is not there. Of course, all that Tennyson had in mind was the burning up of weeds in
autumn, and the apparent wavering of the landscape as seen through the rising currents of
heated and smoky air.
*Conclusion.* This part of the poem was almost
entirely rewritten in the 3d edition. In place of
the first thirty-two lines, the 1st edition has
only the following: —

Here closed our compound story, which at first
Had only meant to banter little maids
With mock heroics and with parody:
But slipt in some strange way, crost with burlesque,
From mock to earnest, even into tones
Of tragic, and with less and less of jest,
To such a serious end, that Lilia fixt, etc.

The 2d edition changed ' Had only ' in the second line to ' Perhaps, but.'
Lines 34–80. *Who might have told . . . garden rails.* For these forty-six lines the early editions have: —

                who there began
A treatise, growing with it, and might have flow'd
In axiom worthier to be graven on rock
Than all that lasts of old-world hieroglyph,
Or lichen-fretted Rune and arrowhead;
But that there rose a shout: the gates were closed
At sundown, and the crowd were swarming now,
To take their leave, about the garden rails,
And I and some went out, and mingled with them.

The reference to the French Revolution seems out of place; and yet one would be sorry to spare the eight lines that follow (' Have patience,' etc.).
Line 102. *Why should not, etc.* The early editions read: —

           Why don't these acred Sirs
Throw up their parks some dozen times a year,
And let the people breathe ?

Line 108. *But spoke not.* The early editions have: ' Saying little; ' and in 116, ' without sound ' for ' quietly.'
Page 162. IN MEMORIAM.
Of the commentaries on the poem Professor John F. Genung's (' In Memoriam; its Purpose and its Structure,' 2d ed. Boston, 1884) seems to me the most satisfactory. Other valuable works are ' A Key to Lord Tennyson's In Memoriam,' by Rev. Alfred Gatty, D. D. (3d edition, London, 1885), for which the poet himself furnished some corrections and comments, which in this edition are printed in italics; ' Prolegomena to In Memoriam,' by Thomas Davidson (Boston, 1889); ' A Companion to In Memoriam,' by Elizabeth R. Chapman (London, 1888); and ' Tennyson and In Memoriam,' by Joseph Jacobs (London, 1892). See also the admirable studies of the poem in ' Phases of Thought and Criticism,' by Brother Azarias (Boston, 1892), pages 183–268; and in Rev. Stopford A. Brooke's ' Tennyson: His Art and Relation to Modern Life ' (New York, 1894), pages 188–228. The ' Memoir ' (vol. i. pp. 295–327) has much interesting matter not to be found elsewhere.
According to Professor Genung, the fundamental idea of the poem may be thus stated: —

' THAT LOVE IS INTRINSICALLY IMMORTAL.

' All the achievements of thought which make " In Memoriam " so victorious a poem are simply this idea raised to a higher power, with its interpretation for life and history.'
The ' framework ' of the poem is tabulated by the same critic thus: —

PROLOGUE.

*Introductory Stage.* I.-XXVII.

| | |
|---|---|
| PROSPECT | I.-VI. |
| DEFINING-POINT — BEGINNING | VII. |
| ARRIVAL AND BURIAL OF THE DEAD | XVII.-XX. |

*First Cycle.* XXVIII.-LXXVII.

| | |
|---|---|
| CHRISTMAS-TIDE | XXVIII.-XXX. |
| SPRINGTIDE | XXXVIII., XXXIX. |
| FIRST ANNIVERSARY OF THE DEATH | LXXII. |

*Second Cycle.* LXXVIII.-CIII.

| | |
|---|---|
| CHRISTMAS-TIDE | LXXVIII. |
| NEW YEAR | LXXXIII. |
| SECOND ANNIVERSARY OF THE DEATH | XCIX. |

*Third Cycle.* CIV.-CXXXI.

| | |
|---|---|
| CHRISTMAS-TIDE | CIV., CV. |
| NEW YEAR | CVI. |
| BIRTHDAY OF DECEASED (FEB. 1) | CVII. |
| SPRINGTIDE | CXV., CXVI. |
| DEFINING-POINT — END | CXIX. |
| RETROSPECT AND CONCLUSION | CXX.-CXXXI. |

EPILOGUE.

*Prologue.* The form of stanza had been used by Lord Herbert of Cherbury and by Ben Jonson in his ' Underwoods.' Rossetti ' claimed to have rediscovered the metre in 1844 ' (Jacobs); but Tennyson had already used it in two poems written in 1833, though not published until 1842 (' You ask me why ' and ' Love thou thy land '); and Jennings (' Lord Tennyson,' page 125) says: ' We have excellent authority for saying that, as far as Tennyson knew then, he thought he had invented the metre.' This is confirmed by the ' Memoir ' (vol. i. p. 305).
*Strong Son of God, immortal love.* ' Immortal Love is recognized not only as an affection within us, but as an entity above us, . . . as a divine Object of faith and love, to be worshipped and obeyed, to be recognized as at the same time the source and the goal of our noblest life ' (Genung).
I. 1.[1] *I held it truth, with him who sings, etc.* ' It may be stated, on the highest authority, that the special passage alluded to cannot be identified, but *it is Goethe's creed* ' (Gatty). Brother Azarias remarks: ' Faust, in Goethe's great life-poem, emerges from the ruins of his dead self to a higher life and a broader assertion of selfhood. It is still the same self trampling upon the narrower and lower experiences of life.' Compare Longfellow, ' The Ladder of St. Augustine.' The passage of St. Augustine is in ' Serm.' iii.: ' De vitiis nostris scalam nobis facimus si vitia calcamus.'
' The " dead selves " of Tennyson are neither our vices nor our calamities; but, rather, our general experiences, which all perish as they happen ' (Gatty).
II. 1. *Old yew, which graspest at the stones, etc.* When the poet wrote this he supposed that Arthur was buried in the churchyard, though a

---

[1] The references in these notes on ' In Memoriam ' are to *sections* (or ' poems,' as Tennyson calls them) and *stanzas*, not to *lines*.

tablet to his memory was placed inside the church (lxvii.). Compare xxi. and xxxix.

3. *O, not for thee the glow, the bloom.* Some have foolishly inferred from this that the poet was not aware the yew blossoms, and that xxxix. was afterwards inserted to correct the error; but, as an italicized note in Gatty states, 'of course, the poet always knew that a tree which bears a berry must have a blossom; but sorrow only saw the winter gloom of the foliage.' The blossoming of the yew and the 'smoke' of its abundant pollen are referred to in the opening lines of 'The Holy Grail.'

4. *And gazing on thee, sullen tree.* The 1st edition misprints 'the sullen tree.'

III. 1. *What whispers from thy lying lip?* Sorrow 'clothes all nature in her own phantom hollowness, her own mourning garb; she blurs the truth, and it may well be that she should be stifled rather than cherished' (Chapman). I may state here that Miss Chapman's comments on the poem were cordially approved by the poet.

3. *With all the music in her tone.* The 1st edition has 'her music.'

IV. 3. *That grief hath shaken into frost.* Water may be cooled below the freezing-point if it is kept perfectly still; but if disturbed it becomes ice at once, and the sudden expansion may break the vessel containing it.

4. *Thou shalt not be the fool of loss.* The 1st edition misprints 'Thou shall.'

V. 2. *A use in measured language lies.* 'There is some negative relief in the exercise of expressing sorrow in metrical language. Poesy shall therefore be cherished for its practical office' (Genung).

VI. 5. *Ye know no more than I who wrought, etc.* Tennyson was writing to Arthur in the very hour his friend died.

VII. 1. *The long unlovely street.* Wimpole Street in London, where Arthur had lodgings at No. 67 (see page 162 above) while he was studying at Lincoln's Inn. There are many longer streets in the metropolis than Wimpole Street, which, even with its continuation as Devonshire Street, is barely half a mile from end to end; but it somehow got a local notoriety for its length. 'It is said of a celebrated clerical wit, that almost his last words were, "All things come to an end" — a pause — "except Wimpole Street"' (Gatty).

IX. 1. *Fair ship, that from the Italian shore, etc.* 'Many have been the endeavors to discover the name of the "fair ship" which brought home Hallam's remains, and thus trace her after-history, but all in vain. It seems, however, that she landed her precious freight at Dover, though the poet till a few years ago always believed that she had put in to Bristol' (Napier).

5. *Till all my widow'd race be run.* The line is repeated at the end of xvii. ; and 'More than my brothers are to me' in lxxix. 1.

X. 4. *Or where the kneeling hamlet, etc.* That is, in the chancel of the village church, near the altar rails.

5. *Should toss with tangle and with shells.* 'Tangle,' or 'oarweed' (*Laminaria digitata*), grows at extreme tide-limits, where its fronds rise and dip in the water.

XI. 1. *Calm is the morn, etc.* As the poet explained to Dr. Gatty, the scenery described 'does not refer to Clevedon, but to some Lincolnshire wold, from which the whole range from marsh to the sea was visible.'

XV. 5. *To-night the winds begin to rise.* The 1st edition has 'began.'

Stopford Brooke remarks here: 'The tempest begins with what is close at hand — the wood by which he stands at sunset: —

> The last red leaf is whirl'd away,
> The rooks are blown about the skies.

And then, after that last admirable line which fills the whole sky with the gale, he lifts his eyes, and we see with him the whole world below painted also in four lines [as in xi. 3.] — the forest, the waters, the meadows, struck out, each in one word; and the wildness of the wind and the width of the landscape given, as Turner would have given them, by the low shaft of storm-shaken sunlight dashed from the west right across to the east. Lastly, to heighten the impression of tempest, to show the power it will have when the night is come, to add a far horizon to the solemn world, he paints the rising wrath of the storm in the cloud above the ocean rim, all aflame with warlike sunset. It is well done, but whosoever reads the whole will feel that the storm of the human heart is higher than the storm of Nature.'

XVI. 1. *Calm despair and wild unrest.* The former expressed in xi., the latter in xv. He asks whether such alternations of feeling are possible. 'Is his sorrow variable? Or do these changes affect the surface merely of his deepseated grief? Or, again, has his reason been unhinged by grief?' (Chapman).

XVIII. 1. *The violet of his native land.* Compare 'Hamlet,' v. 1. 262: —

> And from her fair and unpolluted flesh
> May violets spring!

3. *Come then, pure hands, and bear the head, etc.* The bearers at the funeral of Arthur were the tenant farmers on the Clevedon estate. The Rev. William Newland Pedder, who was vicar of Clevedon for forty years and died in 1871, read the burial service.

XIX. 1. *They laid him by the pleasant shore, etc.* Clevedon Church, where Arthur was buried, overlooks a broad expanse of water, where the Severn flows into the Bristol Channel. The church, which is dedicated to St. Andrew, is quaint and picturesque, though not architecturally noteworthy. The chancel was the original fishermen's church, to which additions have been made from time to time. It stands half a mile to the south of Clevedon, and is so secluded that —

> A stranger here
> Might wondering ask, 'Where stands the house of
> God?'

She sought it o'er the fields, and found at last
An old and lonely church, beside the sea,
In a green hollow, 'twixt two headlands green.

These heights, known as Church Hill and Wains Hill, seem to guard and shelter the edifice with its surrounding churchyard.

XXI. 1. *Since the grasses round me wave.* See note on ii. 1 above.

5. *The latest moon.* Mr. Jacobs thinks that this must allude to the discovery of the satellite of Neptune in 1846, and that this part of this poem was therefore written very late; but the reference to astronomical discoveries may be less specific.

7. *And one is glad.* The 1st edition has 'And unto one; ' and the same, two lines below, instead of 'And one is sad.'

XXII. 1. *Thro' four sweet years.* From 1828, the 'fifth autumnal slope' referring to September, 1833, when Arthur died.

XXIII. 1. *Breaking into song by fits.* Here Gatty has the italicized note: 'It is a fact that the poem was written at both various times and places — through a course of years, and where the author happened to be, in Lincolnshire, London, Essex, Gloucestershire, Wales, anywhere, as the spirit moved him.'

2. *Who keeps the keys of all the creeds.* Death will solve all questions concerning the world beyond the grave.

Critics have complained that 'the notion of a Shadow keeping keys is a very halting metaphor '; and Mr. Tainsh says that he cannot defend the figure, though he 'nevertheless likes the line.' It is a sufficient defence to remind the critics that the keys are as shadowy and insubstantial as the phantom who keeps them.

XXIV. 1. *Wandering isles of light.* The spots on the sun.

2. *Since our first sun arose and set.* The 1st edition reads: 'Since Adam left his garden yet. '

3. *Makes former gladness loom so great.* The reading in the 1st edition was: 'Hath stretch'd my former joy so great.'

XXVI. 4. *Then might I find, etc.* The 1st edition has: 'So might I find; ' and in the last line of the stanza, ' To cloak me from my proper scorn.' For 'proper' in the sense of 'own,' compare 'The Princess,' vi.: 'each to her proper hearth,' etc.

XXVII. 4. *I feel it, when I sorrow most, etc.* These three lines are repeated in the 1st stanza of lxxxv.

XXVIII. 1. *The time draws near the birth of Christ.* The critics, as we shall see, have made sundry mistakes concerning the date of the three Christmases referred to in the poem. Gatty says here that this first Christmas is 'possibly at the end of the year 1833 '; but in a note on the 'Last year' of xxx. 4 he says: 'This seems to identify the time to be Christmas, 1834, as Hallam died on 15th September, 1833, and was buried in January, 1834.' On the contrary, the 'last year' must refer to the Christmas of 1832, when Arthur was living; and *this* Christmas must be that of 1833.

Some, however, have been puzzled to reconcile this date with the preceding poem xxi., which, they say, implies that Arthur was buried *before* the Christmas of xxviii.-xxx. But, as Tennyson himself has told us (see on xxiii. 1 above), the poem was written at various times and places; and, in arranging the parts for publication, some were probably inserted before others that had been written earlier. If xxi. was written before xxviii., the poet, residing in a remote and secluded part of Lincolnshire, might have taken it for granted that the remains of his friend had already reached Clevedon and been laid in their last resting-place, several months having elapsed since his death. What Mrs. Ritchie says of Somersby in the childhood of the poet was still true of it in 1833: —

'It was so far away from the world, so behindhand in its echoes (which must have come there softened through all manner of green and tranquil things, and, as it were, hushed into pastoral silence), that though the early part of the century was stirring with the clang of legions, few of its rumors seem to have reached the children. They never heard, at the time, of the battle of Waterloo.' In 1833, when railways were just beginning to be built, Somersby was farther from London than the remotest corner of the kingdom is now.

*The Christmas bells from hill to hill, etc.* 'The churches are not to be identified. Those in the neighborhood [of Somersby] probably have too small belfries to allow of change-ringing. The sounds may have been only in the poet's mind ' (Gatty).

3. *Peace and good-will, etc.* The rhythm is like the chiming of bells.

XXXI. 1. *That Evangelist.* St. John, the only one who records the raising of Lazarus.

XXXIII. 3. *O thou that after toil and storm, etc.* 'Regarding the relation of one who knows to one who believes. Lazarus and Mary illustrate two phases of Christian life: those whose ripened reason and spiritual insight make their view of unseen things approach the character of knowledge; and those whose faith, without knowledge, supports itself by forms. Each life has a blessedness of its own; and "faith through form," which produces practical good deeds, is not to be despised by even the most advanced in spiritual things ' (Genung).

'Let those who have not such simplicity of trust, who deem perhaps that they have reached a higher standpoint, fought their way to a purer creed, beware of troubling the Mary-spirits that they know. It may be that their faith, which has outgrown all form, is a subtler thing, but is it as fruitful of good works as the childlike faith of the Marys ? And let them beware lest, in a world of sin, it fail them in the hour of need ' (Chapman).

XXXV. 3. *Æonian hills.* The 'everlasting hills.' Compare xcv. 11 below: 'Æonian music.'

According to Mr. James Knowles ('Nineteenth Century,' January, 1893), the poet explains this stanza as referring to 'the vastness of the future — the enormity of the ages to come after your little life would act against that love.'

XXXVI. 1. *Tho' truths in manhood darkly join, etc.* 'What our holiest intuitions require finds its fitting expression in the revealed Word of God; especially in the Word made flesh, who appeals to all, and expresses an inner idea which is too deep-seated for men unaided to utter, and yet which every one, even the most unlettered, may read' (Genung).

XXXVII. 1. *Urania speaks with darken'd brow, etc.* 'But how shall his muse dare to profane these holy mysteries? She is of earth, and not for her is it to treat of things revealed. The song of human love and human loss alone is hers. These loftier themes pertain to Urania, not Melpomene. Yet Arthur loved to speak of things divine, and so the poet is fain to mingle some whisper of them in his song' (Chapman).

3. *I am not worthy even to speak.* The 1st edition has 'but to speak.'

5. *And dear to me as sacred wine.* The first reading was: 'And dear as sacramental wine.' Gatty suggests that the poet made the change 'that the reader should see that he spoke only for himself,' which the addition of 'to me' makes clear.

XXXIX. *Old warder of these buried bones, etc.* Added to the poem in 1871 (see page 162 above). 'Some acute critics have quite failed to comprehend the poet's purpose in introducing it. Considered in its connection, however, and with its allusions resolved, it supplies a very important link in the thought. It alludes, as does the other inserted poem, to poem iii., together with ii., and adds another link in the same chain of references to sorrow and nature, by showing how the heart, which sorrow has deadened into despair in the face of nature, is yet touched and cheered by the awaking life of springtide' (Genung).

XL. 2. *Make April of her tender eyes.* Compare Shakespeare, 'Antony and Cleopatra,' iii. 2. 43: —

> The April's in her eyes; it is love's spring,
> And these the showers to bring it on.

5. *In those great offices that suit.* The 1st edition reads: 'In such great offices as suit.' Mr. Knowles quotes the poet as saying: 'I hate that — I should not write so now — I'd almost rather sacrifice a meaning than let two *s's* come together.' This occurs, however, in cxi. 2, where he might have written 'fashion sake,' as in Elizabethan English.

XLIII. 3. *So that still garden of the souls.* The 1st edition has 'But' for 'So;' and 'would last' for 'will last' in the next stanza.

XLIV. 1. *But he forgets the days, etc.* That is, his earliest infancy, before the sutures of the skull had closed. Mr. B. Kellogg, in an American edition of selections from 'In Memoriam,' strangely takes the allusion to be to extreme old age, the 'doorways of the head' being 'the senses.'

3. *If death so taste Lethean springs.* Gatty says that 'The poet here makes Lethe produce remembrance, instead of forgetfulness, which is its normal effect.' Not so; he merely suggests, as Wordsworth does in his famous Ode, that the forgetfulness is not absolutely complete.

XLV. 1. *The baby new to earth and sky, etc.* 'The grand result of this earthly life, as it advances from infancy to maturity, is the development of self-conscious personality, and with it the possibility of memory. Unless we suppose all this life's highest achievement is lost, this self-conscious personality and memory continue in heaven' (Genung).

XLVI. 1. *We, ranging down this lower track, etc.* 'In this life we experience "thorn and flower," grief and joy; and the past becomes mercifully shaded as time goes on, otherwise the retrospect would be intolerable. But hereafter all shadow on what has happened will be removed, and all will be clear "from marge to marge;" and the five years of earthly friendship will be the "richest field" in the "eternal landscape"' (Gatty).

4. *Love, a brooding star, etc.* 'As if Lord of the whole life' (Tennyson, as quoted by Knowles).

XLVII. 1. *That each, who seems a separate, etc.* The theory that the individual being will, in another state of existence, be merged in 'the general soul,' is repudiated by the poet. 'St. Paul is not more distinct and emphatic upon our individuality hereafter' (Gatty).

4. *Before the spirits fade away, etc.* 'Into the Universal Spirit — but at least one last parting! and would always want it again — of course' (Tennyson, quoted by Knowles).

XLVIII. 1. *If these brief lays, of sorrow born, etc.* 'The office of the song is not to give logically conclusive answers, but Love's answer, making doubts yield her service' (Genung).

XLIX. 1. *From art, from nature, etc.* 'Let no man think that the fancied hopes and fears with which he toys touch more than the surface of the mourner's grief. He hails every random influence that art, nature, philosophy, may shed upon that sullen surface, chequering and dimpling it, like shafts of light and tender breezes playing upon a pool. Beneath, in the depths, the very springs of life are tears' (Chapman).

LI. 1. *Do we indeed desire the dead, etc.* The dead, if near us, must see all our 'inner vileness.' But 'they see as God sees, and make gracious allowance.'

LIII. 2. *And dare we to this fancy given.* The 1st edition has 'doctrine' for 'fancy;' 'had not' for 'scarce had'; and 'Oh!' for 'Or.'

The poet's comment on this stanza, as Mr. Knowles tells us, was: 'There's a passionate heat of nature in a rake sometimes — the nature that yields emotionally may come straighter than a prig's.' He added, on the next two stanzas: 'Yet don't you be making excuses for this kind of thing — it's unsafe. You must set a rule before youth. There's need of rule

to men also — though no particular one that I
know of — it may be arbitrary.'

LIV. 5. *An infant crying in the night.* Compare cxxiv. 5 below: 'Then was I as a child
that cries,' etc.

LVI. 1. '*So careful of the type?*' *but no, etc.*
Genung remarks: 'It is worthy of notice that
in an earlier work this same question of man's
destiny has presented itself to the poet, and in
the same manner has been left unanswered.
At the close of "The Vision of Sin," where
discussion has been made concerning sin's rav-
ages, whether avenged by sense, or also disin-
tegrating the spirit, the lines occur:—

> At last I heard a voice upon the slope
> Cry to the summit, 'Is there any hope?'
> To which an answer peal'd from that high land,
> But in a tongue no man could understand;
> And on the glimmering limit far withdrawn
> God made Himself an awful rose of dawn.

In the poem under discussion, however, the
thought is greatly ripened under the agency of
Faith. From all deepest doubts suggested by
Nature, she rises, and flees from Nature to God,
in whose hands she tremblingly leaves the answer.'

LVII. 1. *Peace: come away, etc.* 'Possibly
addressed to his sister, whom he now calls away
from the sad subject which his earthly song had
treated' (Gatty).

2. *Methinks my friend is richly shrined, etc.*
Gatty gives (italicized) as the poet's comment:
'The author speaks of these poems — "methinks I have built a rich shrine for my friend,
but it will not last."'

LIX. *O Sorrow, wilt thou live with me, etc.*
Added in the 4th edition, 1851.

LXI. 3. *The soul of Shakespeare love thee
more.* 'Perhaps he might — if he were a greater
soul' (Tennyson, quoted by Knowles).

LXII. 1. *Then be my love an idle tale.* The
1st edition has 'So' for 'Then.'

LXIII. 1. *In its assumptions up to heaven.*
The word *assumption* is used as in its ecclesiastical application to the 'taking up' of the Virgin to heaven.

LXVII. 1. *I know that in thy place of rest,
etc.* Clevedon Church, where Hallam was laid
to rest. See page 163 above.

4. *And in the dark church, etc.* The 1st edition reads: 'And in the chancel;' but the tablet is not in the chancel of the church, as the
elder Hallam stated in the memoir of his son,
but on the west wall of the south transept, or
the 'manor aisle,' as Napier calls it. When the
moon is high in the heavens, it shines through
the large south window upon the tablet, as the
poet here imagines.

The inscription on the tablet is as follows: —

To the Memory of
ARTHUR HENRY HALLAM,
of Trinity College, Cambridge, B. A.,
Eldest son of HENRY HALLAM, Esquire,
and of JULIA MARIA his wife,
Daughter of Sir ABRAHAM ELTON, Bart.,
of Clevedon Court,

Who was snatched away by sudden death,
at Vienna, on September 15th, 1833,
In the 23rd year of his age.

And now in this obscure and solitary Church
repose the mortal remains of
one too early lost for public fame,
but already conspicuous among his contemporaries
for the brightness of his genius,
the depth of his understanding,
the nobleness of his disposition,
the fervor of his piety,
and the purity of his life.

VALE DULCISSIME
VALE DILECTISSIME DESIDERATISSIME
REQUIESCAS IN PACE
PATER AC MATER HIC POSTHAC REQUIESCAMUS TECUM
USQUE AD TUBAM.

LXIX. 3. *I met with scoffs, etc.* 'I tried to
make my grief into a crown of these poems —
but it is not to be taken too closely. To write
verses about sorrow, grief, and death is to wear
a crown of thorns which ought to be put by,
as people say' (Tennyson, quoted by Knowles).
The 'angel of the night' in the next stanza
was explained by the poet as 'the divine Thing
in the gloom.'

LXXI. 1. *We went thro' summer France.*
In the summer of 1830. To this journey he re-
fers in the lines 'In the Valley of Cauteretz.'
See the notes on that poem.

2. *Then bring an opiate.* The 1st edition has
'So' for 'Then;' and the last line of the stanza
reads: 'That thus my pleasure might be whole.'

LXXII. 1. *Rises thou thus, dim dawn, etc.*
The anniversary of Arthur's death, September
15th.

4. *Along the hills.* The 1st edition reads:
'From hill to hill.'

LXXVI. 3. *The matin songs, etc.* The songs
of the great early poets.

LXXVIII. 1. *Again at Christmas, etc.*
Compare xxx. above. Genung remarks that
this Christmas is 'an occasion characterized by
calmness. The lapse of time has brought a
change in the spirit of its observance, in this
respect, that the merriments and pleasures peculiar to Christmas are accepted and enjoyed
no longer under querulous protest but for their
own sake. At the same time, "the quiet sense
of something lost" is a reminder that the occasion is not what it was before bereavement.'

3. *Hoodman-blind.* Blindman's buff. Compare 'Hamlet,' iii. 4. 77: 'That thus hath
cozen'd you at hoodman-blind.'

4. *No mark of pain.* The 1st edition has:
'no type of pain.'

LXXIX. 1. *More than my brothers are to me.*
Compare ix. 5, above.

This poem is evidently addressed to Charles,
the brother nearest his own age, and associated
with him in the production of 'Poems by Two
Brothers.'

3. *For us the same cold streamlet curl'd.* The
brook near Somersby to which reference is made
in the early 'Ode to Memory': —

> And chiefly from the brook that loves
> To purl o'er matted cress and ribbed sand,

Or dimple in the dark of rushy coves,
Drawing into his narrow earthen urn,
In every elbow and turn,
The filtered tribute of the rough woodland.

**LXXX.** 2. *Then fancy shapes, as fancy can, etc.* 'If places were changed and he the mourner, I know that he would turn his sorrow into gain, by being stayed in peace with God and man. So let me do, and thus honor his influence' (Genung).

**LXXXIII.** 1. *O sweet new year, etc.* Genung remarks here: 'As in the preceding cycle Springtide added to the thought of immortality the suggestiveness of a new awaking season, so in this broader field of thought New Year heralds a new round of seasons. The spirit of the thought too has changed, — has become more wholesome and free. Frozen in the past sorrow as the mind was in the preceding cycle, the Springtide must thrust its cheer from without on a reluctant mood; but here the new year illustrates the greater health of spirit, in that now the mood answers to the promise of the season, and goes forth congenially to meet it.'

**LXXXIV.** 3. *When thou shouldst link thy life with one, etc.* Referring to young Hallam's engagement to the poet's sister Emily.

**LXXXV.** 1. *'T is better to have loved and lost, etc.* Compare xxvii. 4 above.

2. *O true in word and tried in deed, etc.* This, as the poet explained to Gatty, is addressed to Mr. E. L. Lushington, like the epithalamium at the close of the poem.

**LXXXVI.** 1. *Sweet after showers, etc.* The four stanzas form a single sentence. Compare the early poem on 'The Poet' for a fine passage similarly sustained. Tennyson told Knowles that this was one of the poems he liked. It was written at Bournemouth, and the 'ambrosial air' was 'the west wind,' which, in the last stanza, is represented as 'rolling to the Eastern seas till it meets the evening star.' In the 3d stanza, 'the fancy' means 'imagination — *the* fancy — no particular fancy.'

**LXXXVII.** 1. *I past beside the reverend walls, etc.* Referring to a visit to Cambridge.

4. *That long walk of limes.* In the grounds of Trinity College.

6. *Where once we held debate.* Referring, as the poet told Mr. Knowles, to the 'Water Club,' so called 'because there was no wine.' He added: 'They used to make speeches — I never did.'

10. *The bar of Michael Angelo.* 'Michael Angelo had a strong bar of bone over his eyes' (Tennyson to Gatty).

**LXXXVIII.** 1. *Wild bird, whose warble, liquid sweet, etc.* The nightingale.

2. *The darkening leaf.* The 1st edition has 'the dusking leaf.'

**LXXXIX.** 1. *This flat lawn, etc.* The lawn of Somersby Rectory. The poet tells Gatty that 'the "towering sycamore" is cut down and the four poplars are gone, and the lawn is no longer a flat one.'

3. *Dusty purlieus of the law.* The 1st edition has 'dusky purlieus.'

6. *The Tuscan poets.* Compare page 162 above. The following sonnet was addressed by Arthur to Tennyson's sister Emily (to whom he was betrothed at the time), when he began to teach her Italian : [1] —

Lady, I bid thee to a sunny dome,
Ringing with echoes of Italian song;
Henceforth to thee these magic halls belong,
And all the pleasant place is like a home.
Hark, on the right, with full piano tone,
Old Dante's voice encircles all the air;
Hark yet again, like flute-tones mingling rare,
Comes the keen sweetness of Petrarca's moan.
Pass thou the lintel freely ; without fear
Feast on the music. I do better know thee
Than to suspect this pleasure thou dost owe me
Will wrong thy gentle spirit, or make less dear
That element whence thou must draw thy life —
An English maiden and an English wife.

Again he addresses her thus (compare lxxxix. 6) : —

Sometimes I dream thee leaning o'er
The harp I used to love so well;
Again I tremble and adore
The soul of its delicious swell;
Again the very air is dim
With eddies of harmonious might,
And all my brain and senses swim
In a keen madness of delight.

12. *The crimson-circled star.* The planet Venus. The next line, as the poet explained, refers to the evolution of the planet from the sun, according to the nebular hypothesis of La Place.

**XCI.** 1. *The sea-blue bird of March.* The kingfisher, as the poet himself explained. Gatty quotes, as a parallel passage : —

The fields made golden with the flower of March,
The throstle singing in the feather'd larch,
And down the river, like a flame of blue,
Keen as an arrow flies the water-king.

**XCII.** 4. *And such refraction of events, etc.* An allusion to the effect of atmospheric refraction in making objects appear above the horizon when they are actually below it.

Compare Coleridge, 'Death of Wallenstein,' v. 1 : —

As the sun,
Ere it is risen, sometimes paints its image
In the atmosphere, so often do the spirits
Of great events stride on before the events,
And in to-day already walks to-morrow.

**XCIV.** 3. *They haunt the silence of the breast, etc.* 'I figure myself in this rather' (Tennyson, quoted by Knowles).

**XCV.** *By night we linger'd on the lawn, etc.* Another family scene at Somersby.

2. *The fluttering urn.* The adjective is very descriptive.

3. *The filmy shapes, etc.* Night moths (*Arctica menthrasti*), as the poet explained to Gatty.

9. *The living soul.* 'Perchance the Deity. The first reading (in 1st edition) was "His liv-

---

[1] Mrs. Ritchie says that Emily was 'scarcely seventeen' at the time of Arthur's death in 1833 ; but she was born on the 25th of October, 1811.

ing soul " — but my conscience was troubled by " his." I've often had a strange feeling of being wound and wrapped in the Great Soul ' (Tennyson, quoted by Knowles).

11. *Æonian music.* Compare xxxv. 3, above.

XCVI. 2. *One indeed I knew, etc.* Genung remarks: 'It is generally supposed that this poem narrates the spiritual experience of Arthur Hallam himself. . . . The passage where Tennyson recognizes in Arthur

> The faith, the vigor, bold to dwell
> On doubts that drive the coward back,

and the one where he describes Arthur's as a character of

> Seraphic intellect and force
> To seize and throw the doubts of man,

would seem to indicate much more calmness of assured strength than the poem before us; but at the same time this calmness may have been reached through severe struggle. Would not this passage, from Arthur Hallam's "Remains," indicate such spiritual conflict ? —

> I do but mock me with these questionings.
> Dark, dark, yea, 'irrecoverably dark,'
> Is the soul's eye: yet how it strives and battles
> Thorough th' impenetrable gloom to fix
> That master light, the secret truth of things,
> Which is the body of the infinite God !

One of Arthur's early friends also writes: " Perhaps I ought to mention that when I first knew him he was subject to occasional fits of mental depression, which gradually grew fewer and fainter, and had at length, I thought, disappeared, or merged in a peaceful Christian faith. I have witnessed the same in other ardent and adventurous minds, and have always looked upon them as the symptom, indeed, of an imperfect moral state, but one to which the finest spirits, during the process of their purification, are most subject."'

XCVII. 1. *My love has talk'd with rocks and trees, etc.* Gatty remarks that 'this is highly mystical,' and he appears not to have explained it correctly at first. A note of the poet's informs him that it is intended to describe 'the relation of one on earth to one in the other and higher world — not the author's relation to him here. He certainly looked up to the author, fully as much as the author to him.'

XCVIII. 1. *You leave us: you will see the Rhine, etc.* Addressed to his brother Charles, who, in 1836, made a wedding tour to the Continent and expected to visit Vienna. See the ' Memoir,' vol. i. p. 148.

6. *Any mother town.* Any metropolis. The poet was fond of translating a classical term into the vernacular. Compare 'the tortoise [*testudo*] creeping to the wall,' in the ' Dream of Fair Women;' ' the northern morn ' (*aurora borealis*) in ' Morte d'Arthur,' etc. In ' The Princess,' i. we have ' mother-city ' for metropolis.

XCIX. 1. *Risest thou thus, dim morn, again, etc.* Another return of the anniversary of Arthur's death. Compare lxxii. 1, above.

C. 1. *I climb the hill.* The 1st edition reads: ' I wake, I rise.'

CI. 1. *Unwatch'd, the garden bough shall sway, etc.* The poet's farewell to Somersby. The date has been often given as 1835, but Napier is right in putting it early in 1837. The three Christmases of the poem are not in three successive years. See on xxviii. 1, above.

3. *The Lesser Wain.* The constellation *Ursa Minor,* the ' polar star ' being at the end of the tail.

CII. 2. *Two spirits of a diverse love.* As the poet explained to Gatty, these do not represent persons: ' the first is the love of the native place; the second, the same love enhanced by the memory of the friend.'

CIII. 1. *I dream'd a vision of the dead.* An intimate friend of the poet says that this was a real dream. Tennyson furnished Gatty with this note: ' I rather believe that the maidens are the Muses, Arts, etc. Everything that made life beautiful here, we may hope may pass on with us beyond the grave.'

To Mr. Knowles he said that the maidens are ' all the human powers and talents that do not pass with life but go along with it.' The ' river ' is ' life,' and the ' hidden summits ' are ' the high — the divine — the origin of life.' The ' sea ' in the 4th stanza is ' eternity.' The 7th stanza refers to ' the great progress of the age, as well as the opening of another world;' and the 9th to ' all the great hopes of science and men.'

12. *I did them wrong.* ' He was wrong to drop his earthly hopes and powers — they will be still of use to him' (Tennyson, quoted by Knowles).

CIV. 1. *A single church below the hill.* Waltham Abbey, as the poet himself explained. The family resided for a time at High Beech, Epping Forest. The mansion, known as Beech Hill House, has since been torn down and rebuilt. It stood on high ground, from which there is a fine view of Waltham Abbey, about two and a half miles distant.

CV. 1. *To-night ungather'd let us leave, etc.* The 1st edition reads: —

> This holly by the cottage-eave,
> To-night, ungather'd shall it stand.

Genung remarks here: ' In the second Christmas-tide the lapse of time had made Christmas observances pleasant for their own sake; now the " change of place, like growth of time," has wrought to cause the interest of the usual customs to die; as was indeed predicted at the first Christmas-tide. But in this dying of use and wont after they have been once revived there is no sign of retrogression in the thought; rather, the usual customs have lost their life because the *spirit* of Christmas hope has become so settled and significant that the ancient form can no more express its meaning. The cheer of this season not only eclipses the grief, but rejects all formal demonstrations of joy as unnecessary and meaningless.'

6. *What lightens in the lucid east, etc.* The

poet explained to Gatty that this 'refers to the scintillation of the stars rising.'

CVII. 1. *It is the day when he was born.* The 1st of February. Genung remarks: 'In the first cycle Springtide brought the cheer of a new season: in the second, New Year heralded a new round of seasons, and now this characterizing occasion of the third cycle suggests a new life, a noble life, which, having been lived once, may furnish the model for noble lives to come. The present anniversary illustrates, as has already been intimated in the Christmas-tide, how in this cycle the spirit of hope has overcome. In the first cycle the suggestiveness of the blooming season must make its way from without into a reluctant mood; in the second cycle the calmer mood and the promising season answer spontaneously to each other; but here in the closing cycle the hopeful mood has so overcome the influences of season and weather that even the bitter wintry day can have no disturbing effect on the confirmed cheer within, — the mind's peace is sufficient to itself, and not dependent.'

3. *All the brakes and thorns.* The 'brakes,' as Tennyson explained, are 'bushes.'

CIX. 4. *The blind hysterics of the Celt.* Compare cxxvii. 2 below, and the 'Conclusion' of 'The Princess.'

CX. 1. *The men of rathe and riper years.* 'Rathe,' of which 'rather' is the comparative, means early. The poet uses it again, adverbially, in 'Lancelot and Elaine': 'Till rathe she rose.' Compare Milton, 'Lycidas,' 142: 'Bring the rathe primrose that forsaken dies.' For an instance of the word in recent *prose*, see J. A. Symonds's 'Sketches and Studies in Southern Europe' (Essay on 'Rimini'): 'Whether it be the rathe loveliness of an art still immature, or the beauty of an art in its wane,' etc.

2. *His double tongue.* The 1st edition has 'treble tongue;' and in 4 below, 'dearest' for 'nearest.'

*To him who grasps,* etc. The 1st edition reads: 'To who may grasp.'

CXI. 4. *Best seem'd the thing he was.* The 1st edition has: 'So wore his outward best.'

CXII. 2. *The lesser lords of doom.* 'Those that have free will but less intellect' (Tennyson's note to Gatty).

CXIII. 1. *'T is held that sorrow makes us wise,* etc. Compare cviii. 4 above.

3. *In civic action.* The 1st edition has 'in,' but some later ones have 'of' — perhaps a misprint.

5. *With thousand shocks that come and go.* The 1st edition has 'many shocks.'

CXIV. 7. *But by year and hour.* The 1st edition reads: 'but from hour to hour.'

CXV. 1. *Now fades the last long streak of snow,* etc. 'The last note of time in the poem. Standing immediately after those poems in which is defined, in terms of Arthur's character, the greatness which the world needs, it adds to them the suggestiveness of the budding year. The special object of this Springtide seems to be to indicate the permanent mood in which the foregoing thought has left the poet; and thus it

corresponds to the groups of poems, lxvi.-lxxi., in the first cycle, and xcvi.-xcviii., in the second cycle. It also introduces the final application and conclusion of the whole thought; and so with Springtide the poem leaves us passing on into a new era of hope' (Genung).

CXVI. 3. *And that dear voice.* The 1st edition has 'The dear, dear voice that I have known;' and in the next line 'Will' for 'Still.'

CXVII. 3. *Every kiss of toothed wheels.* In the mechanism of clocks and watches.

CXVIII. In this poem we have a striking illustration of Tennyson's treatment of modern scientific theories and discoveries. The succession of the geological ages and the evolution of man from lower types are admirably 'moralized.'

1. *Dying Nature's earth and lime.* The inorganic elements of the human body.

5. *Or, crown'd with attributes of woe.* The 1st edition has 'And' for 'Or.'

CXIX. 1. *Doors, where my heart was used to beat,* etc. Referring to another visit to the 'long unlovely' Wimpole Street. Compare vii. 1 above. 'No longer in confused despair, but in peaceful hope, the poet comes, thinking on the departed friend with blessings; and all surroundings of weather and scenery answer to the calm within' (Genung).

CXX. 3. *Let him, the wiser man,* etc. Gatty remarks that 'this is spoken ironically, and is a strong protest against materialism;' but, as the poet adds, 'not against evolution.'

CXXI. 1. *Sad Hesper, o'er the buried sun,* etc. The evening-star, as 'Phosphor' is the morning-star, 'double-name for what is one' — the same planet Venus. Compare lxxxix. 12 above.

5. *Thou, like my present and my past,* etc. Gatty took this to be a reference to Arthur; but Tennyson says, 'No — the writer is rather referring to himself.'

CXXII. 1. *O, wast thou with me, dearest,* etc. Tennyson said to Mr. Knowles: 'If anybody thinks I ever called him "dearest" in his life they are much mistaken, for I never even called him "dear."' The 'doom' in the next line is that 'of grief.'

*And yearn'd to burst the folded gloom.* The 1st edition has 'strove' for 'yearn'd.'

CXXIII. 1. *There rolls the deep where grew the tree,* etc. Referring to the changes in the limits of the ocean, and the upheaval of hills and mountains, in the past history of our planet. Compare Shakespeare's allusion to comparatively recent changes of the sea-line (as on the east coast of England) in Sonnet lxiv.: —

When I have seen the hungry ocean gain
Advantage on the kingdom of the shore,
And the firm soil win of the watery main,
Increasing store with loss and loss with store, etc.

CXXIV. 6. *And what I am beheld again,* etc. The 1st edition has: 'And what-I-seem beheld again;' and, in the next line, 'What-is, and no-man-understands.'

CXXV. 3. *And if the song were full of care,*

*etc.* ' In his deepest self the poet has never lost hope; he has merely used the song to guide thought and feeling to a hopeful end ' (Genung).

CXXVI. 3. *Who moves about from place to place, etc.* The 1st edition reads: —

> That moves about from place to place,
> And whispers to the vast of space
> Among the worlds, that all is well.

CXXVII. 2. *The red fool-fury of the Seine, etc.* This has been supposed to refer to the Revolution of 1848, but the poet informed Gatty that it was ' probably written long before '48.'

3. *But ill for him that wears a crown.* The 1st edition reads: ' But woe to him; ' and, in the next stanza, ' the vast Æon.'

CXXVIII. 2. *O ye mysteries of good.* The 1st edition has ' ministers of good; ' and, in the 5th stanza, ' baseness ' for ' bareness.'

CXXXI. 1. *O living will, etc.* ' Free will in man,' as the poet explained to Gatty.

2. *Out of dust.* The 1st edition has ' out the dust.'

*The Epilogue. O true and tried, etc.* ' The poem that began with death, over which in its long course it has found love triumphant, now ends with marriage, that highest earthly illustration of crowned and completed love.' (Genung).

The epithalamium celebrates the marriage of the poet's younger sister, Cecilia, to Edmund Law Lushington, October 10th, 1842.

Gatty said that this marriage song ' scarcely harmonizes with the lofty solemnity ' of ' In Memoriam; ' but Tennyson replied that the poem ' was meant to be a kind of Divina Commedia, ending cheerfully.'

2. *Since first he told me that he loved, etc.* Referring to Arthur's betrothal to Emily Tennyson.

9. *He too foretold the perfect rose.* Also referring to Arthur.

12. *For I that danced her on my knee, etc.* As Cecilia was born October 10, 1817, she was eight years younger than the poet.

13. *Her feet, my darling, on the dead.* Referring to the graves beneath the chancel floor, as the next line does to the memorial tablets on the walls.

14. *Her sweet 'I will' has made you one.* The 1st edition has ' ye ' for ' you.'

As Genung remarks, this closing poem ' affords occasion to bring in review before us the leading features and influences of " In Memoriam," ' namely: —

' 1. Love, which survives regret and the grave, has recovered her peace in this world, has grown greater and holier, and yet by no means less loyal to the dead; and now, no more disturbed by the past, she devotes herself to the innocent joys of the present.

' 2. Remembrance of the dead is cherished, not sacrificed; the dead is thought of as living, and perhaps present on this occasion, shedding unseen blessings on this coronation of love.

' 3. The living present is suggested by the marriage - bells and festivities; a present in which love finds its purest expression.

' 4. The greater future is suggested in the thought of the new life that may rise from this union, a new-born soul, who will look on a race more advanced than this, and contribute to its greatness, and so be a link between us and the perfect future.

' 5. Finally, a view of the far future perfected. Its character: the view of knowledge eye to eye, the complete subjugation in our nature of all that is brutish, the flower and fruit of which the present contains the seed. Its type: the life of Arthur, who appeared in advance of his time. Its culmination: life in God.'

When reading ' In Memoriam ' to Mr. Knowles, the poet said: ' It is rather the cry of the whole human race than mine. In the poem altogether private grief swells out into thought of, and hope for, the whole world. It begins with a funeral and ends with a marriage — begins with death and ends in promise of a new life — a sort of Divine Comedy, cheerful at the close. . . . It 's too hopeful, this poem, more than I am myself. . . . The general way of its being written was so queer that if there were a blank space I would put in a poem. . . . I think of adding another to it, a speculative one, bringing out the thoughts of the " Higher Pantheism," and showing that all the arguments are about as good on one side as the other, and thus throw man back more on the primitive impulses and feelings.'

The poet also explained to Mr. Knowles that there were ' nine natural groups or divisions ' in ' In Memoriam,' as follows: from i. to viii.; from ix. to xx.; from xxi. to xxvii.; from xxviii. to xlix.; from l. to lviii.; from lix. to lxxi.; from lxxii. to xcviii.; from xcix. to ciii.; and from civ. to cxxxi.

For fuller notes on the poem, the reader may be referred to Rolfe's edition (Boston, 1895).

Page 198. MAUD.

' The Tribute,' in which the poem appeared that eighteen years later became the germ of ' Maud,' was a collection of miscellaneous poems by various authors, edited by Lord Northampton. Swinburne, in 1876 (in ' The Academy ' for January 29), refers to it as ' the poem of deepest charm and fullest delight of pathos and melody ever written by Mr. Tennyson; since recast into new form and refreshed with new beauty to fit it for reappearance among the crowning passages of " Maud." '

This poem is also interesting as having been the subject of the first notice that Tennyson received from the ' Edinburgh Review ' (October, 1837). The writer says: —

We do not profess to understand the somewhat mysterious contribution of Mr. Alfred Tennyson, entitled ' Stanzas; ' but amidst some quaintness, and some occasional absurdities of expression, it is not difficult to detect the hand of a true poet — such as the author of ' Mariana ' and the lines on the ' Arabian Nights ' undoubtedly is — in those stanzas which describe the appearance of a visionary form, by which the writer is supposed to be haunted amidst the streets of a crowded city.

*Part I.* The division into Parts was not made in the early editions.

Line 2. *Dabbled with blood-red heath.* When I heard Tennyson read the poem he paused here and said, ' Blood-red heath ! The critics might have known by *that* that the man was mad; there 's no such thing.'

9. *A vast speculation.* The 1st edition has ' great ' for ' vast.'

12. *And the flying gold of the ruin'd woodlands drove thro' the air.* Ruskin, in ' Modern Painters ' (vol. iii. chap. 12), cites this as an ' exquisite ' illustration of what he calls ' pathetic fallacy.'

21. *Why do they prate of the blessings of Peace ?* This and the stanzas that follow, as well as those on war at the end of the poem, were particularly criticised by the early reviewers, who made the stupid mistake, to which I have already referred, of interpreting the morbid utterances of the hero as the poet's own. There were protests in verse also; as in a poor travesty entitled ' Anti-Maud,' of which this may serve as a specimen:—

Who is it clamours for War ? Is it one who is ready to fight ?
Is it one who will grasp the sword, and rush on the foe with a shout ?
Far from it: — 't is one of the musing mind who merely intends to write —
He sits at home by his own snug hearth, and hears the storm howl without.

44. *To pestle a poison'd poison behind his crimson lights.* Even the drugs of the apothecary are adulterated.

53. *What ! am I raging alone, etc.* This and the two following stanzas were not in the 1st edition.

65. *Workmen up at the Hall !* The 1st edition has : ' There are workmen up at the Hall.'

76. *I will bury myself in myself.* The 1st edition has : ' I will bury myself in my books.' Peter Bayne (' Lessons from My Masters,' 1879) says : ' No change could be more expressive. Of all the graves in which a man can bury himself, self is the worst — haunted with the ghostliest visions, tormented with the loathliest worms. Accordingly, the recluse now sinks into a mood of contented and cynical Epicureanism, more venomously bad than that in which he had invoked Mars to shame Belial and Mammon. He will let the world have its way. . . . This is his point of deepest degradation; henceforward he ascends.'

87. *From which I escaped, heartfree.* Not quite, or he would not have said so.

102. *A million emeralds break from the ruby-budded lime.* The green leaves bursting from their crimson sheath.

115. *I met her to-day with her brother.* The 1st edition has ' abroad ' for ' to-day.'

178. *Till I well could weep, etc.* ' The meanness and the sordid spirit of the world now begin to call forth *tears* instead of sarcasm and raillery; and he could weep, too, for *his own inactivity and baseness*, as well as for its meanness. The change of the measure beautifully expresses the character of the transformation the voice and its mistress are working in the hearer ' (Mann).

This quotation is from ' Tennyson's " Maud " Vindicated : an Explanatory Essay,' by Robert James Mann, M. D., published in 1856. The poet, acknowledging the receipt of the pamphlet, said : ' No one with this essay before him can in future pretend to misunderstand my dramatic poem " Maud." Your commentary is as true as it is full.' In replying to another gentleman who had sent him a copy of a favorable review, he wrote thus : —

' I am much obliged to you for sending me your critique on my poem; and happy to find that you approve of it, and, unlike most of the critics (so-called), have taken some pains to look into it and see what it means. There has been from many quarters a torrent of abuse against it; and I have even had insulting anonymous letters: indeed, I am quite at a loss to account for the bitterness of feeling which this poor little work of mine has excited.'

212. *What if with her sunny hair, etc.* ' The natural reaction of doubt following upon exalted hope ' (Mann).

233. *That oil'd and curl'd Assyrian bull.* Bayne considers this ' one of the crudest lines Tennyson ever penned, . . . grotesque, without being expressive.' It is true that ' the last thing the winged bull from Nineveh suggests is a dandy;' but that is just what it might suggest to a morbid imagination which, at the moment, recalls only the abundant curls of the majestic figure. It is the hero's metaphor, not Tennyson's.

264. *Till a morbid hate and horror have grown, etc.* ' The cynic now begins really to understand his own cynicism; he not only feels his languor and deficiency, but comprehends much concerning their cause. This is a beautiful indication of the better state of things that is already initiated for him, through the healthy operation of his affections ' (Mann).

285-300. *Did I hear it half in a doze, etc.* These stanzas, which sorely puzzled the critics at first, are now made clear by the 19th poem of Part I. (pp. 209-210) which was not in the 1st edition.

328. *Then returns the dark.* The 1st edition reads : ' And back returns the dark.'

363, 364. *A wounded thing, etc.* These two lines were not in the 1st edition.

366-381. *Last week came one to the county town, etc.* This stanza was foolishly supposed by some to be the poet's own ' attack upon peace-advocates in general; ' and one journalist considered it a personal allusion to a certain prominent member of the Society of Friends.

382-388. *I wish I could hear again, etc.* This stanza was not in the 1st edition; nor the two lines that end the poem below — ' And ah for a man to arise in me.' etc. The former, as Bayne remarks, 'greatly strengthens the poem at this point;' and the 'two lines, set by themselves, are like a jewelled clasp knitting the earlier to the later portions of the first Part.'

412–415. *Birds in the high Hall-garden, etc.* When reading the poem Tennyson would ask his listeners what birds these were that cried, 'Maud, Maud, Maud;' and Mrs. Ritchie tells of a lady who replied, 'Nightingales, sir?' 'Pooh!' said the poet, 'what a cockney you are! Nightingales don't say Maud. Rooks do, or something like it — Caw, caw, caw, caw.' He asked the same question when he read the poem to my wife and myself.

421. *Ringing through the valleys.* 'Lilies' is a very imperfect rhyme to 'valleys;' but Tennyson not unfrequently indulges in such license. For a list of the imperfect rhymes in 'In Memoriam,' see Mr. Joseph Jacobs's 'Tennyson and In Memoriam' (London, 1892). He, however, includes many rhymes that are unobjectionable; like *prayer, air; moods, woods; hours, flowers,* etc.

434, 435. *For her feet have touch'd the meadows, etc.* Because, as the poet said to Knowles (and to me also) when reading the passage, 'if you tread on daisies they turn up underfoot and get rosy.'

441. *And little King Charley snarling!* The 1st edition reads: 'And little King Charles is snarling.'

557. *My yet young life.* Bayne says: 'These words are more curiously expressive of a brooding inward-looking habit of mind than any I know of in literature.' He doubts whether the young man 'ought to have been represented as still so morbidly self-conscious' as this implies. To my thinking, it is not unnatural that even at this stage of his experience he should occasionally lapse into the old unhealthy introspectiveness. Later than this — after 'the happy Yes' has faltered from the maiden's lips — it would be impossible.

582. *Over glowing ships.* The 1st edition has 'O'er the blowing ships.'

599. *I have led her home, my love, etc.* 'The one feature that dwells, soul-like, within the delicious lines of these subtle stanzas — the all-pervading inspiration of their richly varied movements — is the sustained sense of absolute content and calm. There is joyous rapture within them everywhere, but the rapture is still and deep. The very first line is, in its smooth, long measure, the audible symbol of perfect rest' (Mann).

616. *Dark cedar.* The same under which he heard Maud singing the 'passionate ballad gallant and gay' (page 202). These cedars of Lebanon are not uncommon in old English gardens.

634. *A sad astrology.* Not the old astrology which made human destiny dependent on the stars, but 'the sadder astrology of modern astronomy, which shows that the celestial bodies follow their own courses, and have nothing to do with human affairs.' The science of our day has removed them to such inconceivable dis-

tance that they only make man feel 'his nothingness.'

656. *That long, loving kiss.* The 1st edition has 'long lover's kiss.'

663. *In bridal white.* Prophetic of the coming bridal; or, as Mann explains, 'fresh in the history of his joy.'

681. *Some dark undercurrent woe.* A presentiment of coming misfortune, which he nevertheless refuses to dwell upon.

684–786. *Her brother is coming back to-night, etc.* As already mentioned, this poem is not in the 1st edition. It clears up the obscurities of the story, 'varies the interest and deepens the pathos,' and makes the love of Maud for the hero less improbable. We learn, among other things, that 'Maud had always nursed the idea that it was her duty, for her mother's sake, to be reconciled to the son of the suicide, and while he was gloomily cursing the family of his father's destroyer, Maud was kneeling in foreign churches praying that they might be friends' (Bayne).

757. *That he left his wine, etc.* No doubt he was better than this prejudiced witness had represented; and we have stronger reason for thinking so later.

845. *My Maud has sent it by thee.* At least, he flatters his fancy that she did.

850–923. *Come into the garden, Maud.* This lovely song abounds in illustrations of what Ruskin calls 'the pathetic fallacy' (see on line 12 above). 'The lover transfers all the passion of his heart to the flowers, and the flowers become part of his heart' (Stopford Brooke).

*Part II.* Lines 49–77. *See what a lovely shell, etc.* 'This is unquestionably true to nature. The merest trifles commonly catch the eye of persons who are intensely occupied with grief, and then lead them out from themselves, until they are able to find some relief for the internal pressure through words' (Mann).

131–140. *Courage, poor heart of stone, etc.* These lines were not in the 1st edition. As Bayne remarks, they tell us that Maud dies, — a fact that previously we could only guess at.

141–238. *O, that 't were possible, etc.* For the history of this poem, see page 198 above. The changes from the version of 1837 are many.

146. *By the home that gave me birth.* Originally, 'Of the land that gave me birth.' In the next stanza (153) 'God' has been changed to 'Christ.'

164, 165. *Half in dreams . . . early skies.* These two lines are not in the 1837 poem, which below (168) has 'to-morrow' for 'the morrow.'

171–195. *'T is a morning, pure and sweet, etc.* This stanza and the next (vi. and vii.) take the place of the following: —

> Do I hear the pleasant ditty
> That I heard her chant of old?
> But I wake — my dream is fled,
> Without knowledge, without pity —
> In the shuddering dawn behold,
> By the curtains of my bed,
> That abiding phantom cold.

196–201. *Get thee hence, etc.* In the 1837

poem this stanza comes before the present xii. as explained below.

202–220. *Then I rise, etc.* There is no change in ix., x., and xi. except 'crosses' for 'crosseth' (twice) in x. They are followed by the present xiii. which originally read thus: —

> *Then* the broad light glares and beats,
> And the *sunk eye* flits and fleets,
> And will not let me be.
> I loathe the squares and streets
> And the faces that one meets,
> Hearts with no love for me;
> Always I long to creep
> *To* some still cavern deep,
> *And* to weep, and weep, and weep,
> My whole soul out to thee.

This is followed by the present viii. and xii., to the latter of which the 2d and 6th lines have been added. The poem then concludes with the following stanzas, which do not appear in 'Maud': —

> But she tarries in her place,
> And I paint the beauteous face
> Of the maiden, that I lost,
> In my inner eyes again,
> Lest my heart be overborne
> By the thing I hold in scorn,
> By a dull mechanic ghost
> And a juggle of the brain.
> I can shadow forth my bride
> As I knew her fair and kind,
> As I woo'd her for my wife;
> She is lovely by my side
> In the silence of my life —
> 'T is a phantom of the mind.

> 'T is a phantom fair and good;
> I can call it to my side,
> So to guard my life from ill,
> Tho' its ghastly sister glide
> And be moved around me still
> With the moving of the blood,
> That is moved not of the will.

> Let it pass, the dreary brow,
> Let the dismal face go by.
> Will it lead me to the grave?
> Then I lose it: it will fly:
> Can it overlast the nerves?
> Can it overlie the eye?
> But the other, like the star,
> Thro' the channel windeth far
> Till it fade and fail and die,
> To its Archetype that waits,
> Clad in light by golden gates —
> Clad in light the Spirit waits
> To embrace me in the sky.

239–342. *Dead, long dead, etc.* 'The reason of the long-tasked sufferer has at last yielded to the continued strain, and he is now a maniac, confined in one of the London asylums for the insane, where he can hear the muffled sound and confusion of the vast metropolitan traffic surging around him in an interminable whirl' (Mann).

The critics have generally agreed that the delineation of insanity here is surprisingly true to nature; but Stopford Brooke thinks there is too much method in the madness. The whole of this part of the poem, he says, 'falls almost into a logical order, as if at the bottom of his

madness the man was not mad at all. We can trace, then, the elaborate argumentative way in which Tennyson has worked it out—a thing we cannot do, for example, in the madness of Ophelia—a similar madness of love and sorrow and death. The picture is also carefully made up of scattered impressions recorded in the first part of the poem. These are apparently huddled together in the disorder of madness, but it is not really so. They have a connection, and the stitches which unite them are too clear. The interspersed reflections are also too sane—as for instance, "Friend, to be struck by the public foe," etc. A madman might think a part of it, but not the whole, and not in that way.' But later Mr. Brooke says: 'I have made certain criticisms on "Maud," and I am troubled by having made them. . . . The criticisms may be all wrong. When we approach a great poet's work, our proper position is humility.'

The poet said to Mr. Knowles: 'The whole of the stanzas where he is mad in Bedlam, from "Dead, long dead," to "Deeper, ever so little deeper," were written in twenty minutes, and some mad doctor wrote to me that nothing since Shakespeare has been so good for madness as this.'

I recollect, by the by, that when Tennyson was reading 'Maud,' and referring at intervals to his treatment of the hero's madness, he incidentally made a remark or two in disparagement of Shakespeare's delineations of insanity. The gist of the criticism was that the talk of the dramatist's crazy people was of too random a character, lacking the 'method' which professional observers detect in madness — the connection, by disordered association, of ideas that to ordinary folk appear disconnected. This was in the summer of 1891, and Stopford Brooke's book was not published until 1894.

*Part III. My life has crept so long, etc.* 'In Part III. he is sane and calm, capable of sympathizing with the high ambition of a people resolute to do justice, and glad that England, in the Crimean war, has undertaken to wreak God's wrath "on a giant liar." . . . Last of all, six lines (54–59) are added in which the meaning and moral of the poem are grandly summed up.' These last six lines are not in the 1st edition.

Page 217. THE BROOK.

Certain critics have attempted to identify the brook of this poem with the one near Tennyson's birthplace at Somersby; but the two differ in some particulars, and this one, as he himself said, was an imaginary brook.

Line 6. *How money breeds.* Compare 'The Merchant of Venice,' i. 3. 95: —

> *Antonio.* Was this inserted to make interest good? Or is your gold and silver ewes and rams?
> *Shylock.* I cannot tell; I make it breed as fast.

See also Bacon, 'Essay on Usury': 'That it is against nature for money to beget money.'

17. *Or even the sweet, half-English Neilgherry air.* The cool and salubrious Neilgherry Hills

in India, a favorite summer resort of the English residents.

46. *Willow-weed.* The *Epilobium hirsutum* of Linnæus.

92. *Nor of those.* Originally, 'neither one.'

118. *Meadow-sweet.* Also called 'meadow-wort,' the *Spiræa ulmaria* of the botanists.

189. *The dome Of Brunelleschi.* The Duomo, or Cathedral of Florence, the dome of which is the masterpiece of Brunelleschi.

194. *By the long wash of Australasian seas.* The poet is said to have specially prided himself on the sustained rhythmical quality of this line, as well he might.

196. *And breathes in April-autumns.* I find this reading first in the edition of 1890. All the earlier ones that I have seen have: 'And breathes in converse seasons.' The change was probably made to avoid the succession of *s*'s. Compare note on 'In Memoriam,' xl. 5.

Page 221. THE DAISY.

Line 5. *Turbia.* A village two miles from Monaco. Near by is the 'Tower of Augustus,' one of the trophies erected to commemorate the subjection of the Ligurians.

23. *Cogoletto.* More properly, *Cogoleto,* the supposed birthplace of Columbus, about fifteen miles from Genoa. A monument was erected to him here in 1888.

37. *We loved that hall, etc.* According to Palgrave (who got his notes of this kind from the poet) this refers to the hall of the Ducal Palace in Genoa, which contains (or did at that time) plaster statues of celebrated citizens; but I suspect that it was the much finer hall in the ancient Bank of St. George, which is adorned with twenty or more marble statues of the 'grave, severe Genovese of old.' It is one of the noblest monumental halls in the world. Tennyson, after the lapse of thirty-five years, may have confounded the two.

43. *The fresh Cascinè.* The park of Florence, on the bank of the Arno. *Boboli's ducal bowers* are the Boboli Gardens in the rear of the Pitti Palace, commanding beautiful views of the city.

75. *Of Lari Maxume.* See Virgil, 'Georgics,' ii. 159: —

Anne lacus tantos ? te, Lari maxume, teque,
Fluctibus et fremitu adsurgens, Benace, marino ?

Lake Como was the *Lacus Larius* of the Romans. There is always a 'Lariano' among the steamers on the lake.

79. *To that fair port below the castle, etc.* Varenna, with the picturesque ruins of an old castle on the height behind it, associated by popular tradition with Queen Theodolinde.

93. *So dear a life your arms enfold.* Referring to the poet's son Hallam, then an infant. He was born August 11, 1852.

Page 222. TO THE REV. F. D. MAURICE.

Maurice was an intimate friend of the poet, and stood godfather to his son Hallam. In 1854, the year of this visit to Tennyson, Maurice prefixed the following dedication to his volume of 'Theological Essays': —

*To Alfred Tennyson, Esq., Poet-Laureate.*

MY DEAR SIR, — I have maintained in these Essays that a theology which does not correspond to the deepest thoughts and feelings of human beings cannot be a true theology. Your writings have taught me to enter into many of those thoughts and feelings. Will you forgive me the presumption of offering you a book which at least acknowledges them and does them homage ?

As the hopes which I have expressed in this volume are more likely to be fulfilled to our children than to ourselves, I might perhaps ask you to accept it as a present to one of your name, in whom you have given me a very sacred interest. Many years, I trust, will elapse before he knows that there are any controversies in the world into which he has entered. Would to God that in a few more he may find that they have ceased ! At all events, if he should ever look into these Essays, they may tell him what meaning some of the former generation attached to words which will be familiar and dear to his generation, and to those that follow his, — how there were some who longed that the bells of our churches might indeed

> Ring out the darkness of the land,
> Ring in the Christ that is to be.

Believe me, my dear Sir,
Yours very truly and gratefully,
F. D. MAURICE.

Page 223. ODE ON THE DEATH OF THE DUKE OF WELLINGTON.

Line 1. *Bury.* The 1st edition has 'Let us bury;' as in 3 below.

5. *Mourning, etc.* The 1st edition reads: —

> When laurel-garlanded leaders fall,
> And warriors carry, etc.

8. *Where shall we lay, etc.* After this line the edition of 1853 has the following line, since suppressed: 'He died on Walmer's lonely shore.' The next line begins 'But here,' etc.
The reading of the 1st edition was this: —

> Where shall we lay the man whom we deplore ?
> Let the sound of those he wrought for, etc.

20. *Remembering, etc.* The 1st edition reads: 'Our sorrow draws but on the golden Past;' and it does not contain the next two lines.

28. *Clearest of.* The 1st edition has 'freest from.'

42. *World-victor's victor.* The conqueror of Napoleon.

49. *The cross of gold.* On St. Paul's Cathedral, in the crypt of which the Duke is buried.

59. *Knoll'd.* This line is not in the 1st edition. Compare *Macbeth,* v. 8. 50: 'And so his knell is knoll'd.'

79. *Ever-echoing.* The reading down to 1873 was 'ever-ringing.'

80–82. *Who is he, etc.* The question is asked by the *mighty seaman,* Nelson, who is also buried in St. Paul's.

91. *His foes were thine*, etc. The 1st edition reads: ' His martial wisdom kept us free; ' and the following lines are: —

> O warrior-seaman, this is he,
> This is England's greatest son,
> Worthy of our gorgeous rites,
> And worthy to be laid by thee;
> He that gain'd a hundred fights,
> And never lost an English gun;
> He that in his earlier day
> Against the myriads of Assaye
> Clash'd with his fiery few and won:
> And underneath another sun
> Made the soldier, led him on,
> And ever great and greater grew,
> Beating from the wasted vines
> All their marshals' bandit swarms
> Back to France with countless blows;
> Till their host of eagles flew
> Past the Pyrenean pines,
> Follow'd up, etc.

99. *Assaye.* A small town in Hindostan, memorable as the place where Wellington (then General Wellesley) began his career of victory, September 23, 1803, by defeating an army of thirty thousand with a force of less than five thousand.

101. *Underneath another sun.* In Spain. The allusions to the famous campaign there need no comment.

118. *Such a war*, etc. After this line the 1st edition has ' He withdrew to brief repose; ' and then goes on with 119 as in the text.

123. *That loud Sabbath.* The day of Waterloo.

154, 155. *Thank Him who isled us here . . . storming showers.* This couplet is not in the 1st edition.

157. *Of boundless love and reverence.* The 1st edition has: ' Of most unbounded reverence,' etc. It does not contain the next line but one.

166. *For saving that, ye help to save mankind.* The 1st edition reads: ' for saving that, ye save mankind;' two lines below: 'And help the march of human mind;' and in the next line: ' Till crowds be sane and crowns be just.'

170. *But wink no more*, etc. After this line the 1st edition has the following, omitted in all subsequent editions: —

> Perchance our greatness will increase;
> Perchance a darkening future yields
> Some reverse from worse to worse,
> The blood of men in quiet fields,
> And sprinkled on the sheaves of peace.

It goes on thus : —

> And O remember him who led your hosts;
> Respect his sacred warning; guard your coasts;
> His voice is silent, etc.

181-185. *Who let the turbid streams, etc.* These five lines are not in the 1st edition, which goes on with: ' His eighty winters,' etc.

195-217. *He on whom . . . is moon and sun.* This fine passage of twenty-three lines is unaltered from the 1st edition.

218. *Such was he: his work is done, etc.* The 1st edition reads: —

> He has not fail'd; he hath prevail'd:
> So let the men whose hearths he saved from shame
> Thro' many and many an age proclaim
> At civic revel, etc.

241. *Ours the pain, be his the gain.* The line is not in the 1st edition.

251. *We revere, and while we hear, etc.* The 1st edition reads thus: —

> For solemn, too, this day are we.
> O friends, we doubt not that for one so true
> There must be other nobler work to do
> Than when he fought at Waterloo,
> And Victor he must ever be.
> Though worlds on worlds in myriad myriads roll
> Round us, etc.

266-270. *On God and Godlike men, etc.* These five lines are not in the 1st edition.

271. *He is gone who seem'd so great.* The 1st edition has: ' The man is gone,' etc.

278. *Speak no more, etc.* The 1st edition has: ' But speak no more,' etc.

Page 226. THE CHARGE OF THE LIGHT BRIGADE.

The first version of the poem appeared in the London ' Examiner,' December 9, 1854, and was as follows: —

> Half a league, half a league,
>   Half a league onward,
> All in the valley of Death
>   Rode the six hundred.
>
> Into the valley of Death
>   Rode the six hundred,
> For up came an order which
>   Some one had blunder'd.
> ' Forward, the Light Brigade !
> Take the guns,' Nolan said:
> Into the valley of Death
>   Rode the six hundred.
>
> ' Forward, the Light Brigade !'
> No man was there dismay'd,
> Not tho' the soldier knew
>   Some one had blunder'd:
> Theirs not to make reply,
> Theirs not to reason why,
> Theirs but to do and die,
> Into the valley of Death
>   Rode the six hundred.
>
> Cannon to right of them,
> Cannon to left of them,
> Cannon in front of them
>   Volley'd and thunder'd;
> Storm'd at with shot and shell,
> Boldly they rode and well,
> Into the jaws of Death,
> Into the mouth of Hell
>   Rode the six hundred.
>
> Flash'd all their sabres bare,
> Flash'd all at once in air,
> Sabring the gunners there,
> Charging an army, while
>   All the world wonder'd:
> Plunged in the battery smoke,
> With many a desperate stroke
> The Russian line they broke;
> Then they rode back, but not,
>   Not the six hundred.

Cannon to right of them,
Cannon to left of them,
Cannon behind them
    Volley'd and thunder'd;
Storm'd at with shot and shell,
While horse and hero fell,
Those that had fought so well
Came from the jaws of Death
Back from the mouth of Hell,
All that was left of them,
    Left of six hundred.

When can their glory fade ?
O the wild charge they made !
All the world wonder'd.
Honor the charge they made !
Honor the Light Brigade,
    Noble six hundred !

This note is prefixed to the poem: 'Written
after reading the first report of the "Times"
correspondent, where only six hundred and
seven sabres are mentioned as having taken
part in the charge.'

The poem was next printed in the 'Maud'
volume, in the summer of 1855, as follows: —

Half a league, half a league,
    Half a league onward,
All in the valley of Death
    Rode the six hundred.
' Charge,' was the captain's cry;
Theirs not to reason why,
Theirs not to make reply,
Theirs but to do and die,
Into the valley of Death
    Rode the six hundred.

Cannon to right of them,
Cannon to left of them,
Cannon behind them
    Volley'd and thunder'd;
Storm'd at with shot and shell,
Boldly they rode and well;
Into the jaws of Death,
Into the mouth of Hell
    Rode the six hundred.

Flash'd all their sabres bare,
Flash'd all at once in air,
Sabring the gunners there,
Charging an army, while
    All the world wonder'd:
Plunged in the battery smoke,
Fiercely the line they broke;
Strong was the sabre-stroke,
Making an army reel
    Shaken and sunder'd.
Then they rode back, but not,
    Not the six hundred.

Cannon to right of them,
Cannon to left of them,
Cannon behind them
    Volley'd and thunder'd;
Storm'd at with shot and shell,
They that had struck so well
Rode thro' the jaws of Death,
Half a league back again,
Up from the mouth of Hell,
All that was left of them,
    Left of six hundred.

Honor the brave and bold !
Long shall the tale be told,
Yea, when our babes are old—
    How they rode onward.

The poet was severely criticised for the alterations he had made in this version, and a few
weeks later the poem was printed in its present
form on a quarto sheet of four pages, with the
following note: —

Having heard that the brave soldiers at Sebas-
topol, whom I am proud to call my countrymen,
have a liking for my ballad on the charge of
the Light Brigade at Balaclava, I have ordered
a thousand copies of it to be printed for them.
No writing of mine can add to the glory they
have acquired in the Crimea; but if what I
heard be true, they will not be displeased to
receive these copies of the ballad from me, and
to know that those who sit at home love and
honour them.                    ALFRED TENNYSON.
*8th August*, 1855.

Page 227.  ENOCH ARDEN.
The title of the 'Enoch Arden' volume, in
the first proofs, was 'Idylls of the Hearth.'
For interesting reviews of this poem, see 'Blackwood,' vol. xcvi. p. 555; the 'Quarterly Review,' vol. cxix. p. 58; the 'Westminster Review,' vol. lxxxii. p. 396; the 'London Quarterly Review,' vol. xxiii. p. 153; and 'Chambers's Journal,' vol. xli. p. 620. See also the
'Memoir,' vol. ii. pp. 5–9.

Line 1.  *Long lines of cliff, etc.*  It is said that
this description was suggested by the scenery of
Clovelly in Devonshire; but the poet had not
then seen Clovelly, and as the writer in the
'Quarterly Review' remarks, such quaint little fishing villages are to be found elsewhere in
England.  Mr. J. Cuming Walters (' Tennyson;
Poet, Philosopher, Idealist,' London, 1893) says
that Deal is the place; but his identification of
the localities of the poems, as Tennyson himself
declared, is seldom to be trusted.

7.  *Danish barrows.*  These ancient sepulchral
mounds, some of which are supposed to be older
than the Danish, or even the Roman conquest,
are common in Great Britain, especially in Wilts
and Dorset.  Compare ' Tithonus ': ' And grassy
barrows of the happier dead.'

8.  *By autumn nutters haunted, flourishes.*  A
line somewhat harsh, as the reader who gives
every word its full enunciation will perceive.
Tennyson rarely errs in that way.

32.  *The helpless wrath of tears.*  A good example of the poet's felicitous condensation of
phrase.

55.  *From the dread sweep of the down-stream-
ing seas.*  An admirably graphic line.

71.  *All kindled by a still and sacred fire, etc.*
' How could the high devotion of Enoch's love
be brought more strikingly before us than in
these few words ? '  (' Quarterly Review ').

112.  *Altho' a grave and staid God-fearing
man.*  Peter Bayne remarks: ' Very notable is
the stress which the poet lays upon the religion
of Enoch.'  Compare what the ' Quarterly ' reviewer says: ' We would pause here for a moment to point out the skill and judgment which
Mr. Tennyson has shown in giving intensity and
sinew to the passion of his tale by the slight
leaven of a Puritan faith.  The want of moral

grandeur in modern life is one of the chief difficulties with which a modern poet has to deal; nor can he longer fill this want by use of those supernatural systems which are now fitly called "machineries." This difficulty the Laureate has successfully evaded by laying the scene of his action in a secluded fishing port, where a stern creed had grown up under the changeful northern sky and the mysterious perils of the sea; and where the traditional superstitions of a sailor life were woven in with an intense and living belief handed down from a Puritan ancestry. The occasional use of supernatural means, such as Annie's dream, so falls evenly upon the reader's mind, and certain superstitious observances are justified; while a moral sublimity is also gained which gives depth and unity to the tone of the poem.'

131. *Isles a light in the offing.* The cloud on the horizon seems like an island with a light upon it. The line has been misinterpreted by some critics.

142. *This voyage more than once.* 'Voyage' is here metrically a dissyllable, as in several lines further on. Compare 'Julius Cæsar,' iv. 3, 20. 'Omitted, all the voyage of their life,' etc. The word is oftener monosyllabic in modern verse, and even in Shakespeare.

196. *Nay, for I love him, etc.* This is said in reply to a *look* from Annie.

220. *Keep everything shipshape.* The critic in 'Blackwood' 'strongly objects' to this nautical phrase. He adds: 'In real life men do not delight in the slang of the calling as much as books make them do — least of all in their solemn moments. We hope to see *shipshape* omitted in future editions. But who can fail to admire the rest of the speech?'

The objection to *shipshape* is hypercritical. The word is not 'slang,' but a nautical figure in keeping with the character, like 'Will bring fair weather yet' above, etc.

For the Scriptural allusions in the passage, see Psalms, xcv. 5, cxxxix. 9; Hebrews, vi. 19, and 1 Peter, v. 7.

267-269. *After a lingering, etc.* The reviewer in 'Blackwood' remarks: 'The "flitting" soul recalls to our mind Mr. Merivale's admirable translation of the dying emperor's address to his own. We may earn some reader's thanks by quoting it here: —

> Animula, vagula, blandula,
> Hospes comesque corporis,
> Quae nunc abibis in loca —
> Pallidula, rigida, nudula —
> Nec, ut soles, dabis jocos ?

> Soul of mine, pretty one, flitting one,
> Guest and partner of my clay,
> Whither wilt thou hie away —
> Pallid one, rigid one, naked one —
> Never to play again, never to play ?

The 'Quarterly' reviewer says of the same passage: 'Wonderful as are many of Mr. Tennyson's descriptive rhythms, perhaps none have shown such marvellous and subtle skill as these three lines, which, catching the reader " ere he is aware" by their quickened flight and the sudden hurry of their cadence, leave him with parted lips.'

340. *From his tall mill that whistled on the waste.* The verb is aptly chosen to express the sound of the mill.

491. *Then desperately seized the holy Book, etc.* A favorite mode of divination among the ancients was that of *stichomancy*, or by lines of poetry. A number of verses were selected from a poet, mixed together in an urn, and one drawn out at random from which the good or evil fortune was inferred. The 'Æneid' of Virgil came to be especially used for this purpose, and hence the name *Sortes Virgilianæ* subsequently given to the method. After the introduction of Christianity the Bible was used in a similar way, the book being opened at random, as here by Annie, and the first passage touched by the finger or catching the eye being taken as the response of the oracle. The custom was in vogue among the Puritans, and still lingers among the common people in England and Scotland.

494. *Under the palm-tree.* The 1st edition had 'Under a palm-tree.' See Judges, iv. 5. 'She beholds Enoch seated "Under a palm-tree, over him the sun;" as he doubtless was at that moment in the island on which he had been wrecked, and where the ghostly echo of her wedding-bells is so soon to torment his ear. But the true vision is but a lying dream to his wife. In her simplicity she cannot think of palms as real trees growing in foreign lands. Her mind flies to Scriptural associations, . . . and the last obstacle to her marriage with Philip is removed' (' Blackwood ').

523. *Prosperously sail'd, etc.* The ten lines that follow are noteworthy as a word-picture of the vicissitudes of the voyage — the rough seas of the Bay of Biscay, the smooth sailing before the tropical trade-winds on either side of the African continent, and the variable weather about the Cape of Good Hope. The description of the 'home-voyage' just below is no less admirable. Tennyson excels in his sea-pictures.

609-617. *Once likewise, in the ringing of his ears, etc.* 'How well is the unity of interest kept up by this simple infusion of a supernatural sympathy — a sympathy used by other imaginative writers with similar success, as by Hawthorne in "Transformation" [the infelicitous name under which 'The Marble Faun' is published in England] and by Miss Brontë in "Jane Eyre"' ('Quarterly Review'). Compare 'Aylmer's Field': —

> Star to star vibrates light: may soul to soul
> Strike thro' a finer element of her own?

635. *Muttering and mumbling, etc.* The 'Quarterly Review' says here: 'Arden, all due allowance made, must have passed at least full seven years of solitary life upon his isle; and it is a serious question whether any human being, much more a man of his intensity of nature, could have passed through this ordeal and kept his wits. The awful consequences of much

shorter periods of utter solitude are well known, although we admit, on the other hand, that in the present state of psychology it is difficult to pronounce either way with certainty. We have little science to guide us, but against the imaginative insight of Mr. Tennyson we have the declaration of Wordsworth ("Excursion," book iv.) that

> the innocent sufferer often sees
> Too clearly; feels too vividly; and longs
> To realize the vision, with intense
> And over-constant yearning; there — there lies
> The excess by which the balance is destroyed.'

But Wordsworth is not really 'against' Tennyson, for he only says that the sufferer 'often' becomes insane — which is unquestionably true; and, as the reviewer himself admits, even scientific men do not settle the question either way. The poet may therefore claim the benefit of the doubt in Enoch's case.

Although the poor fellow has not lost his wits, he has lost the power of speech, and recovers it only by degrees. Tennyson's 'imaginative insight' is doubtless true to nature in this, and I am willing to believe it so in the rest.

638. *To where the rivulets of sweet water ran.* That is, fresh water; like the 'dulces aquae' of Virgil ('Æneid,' i. 167). Compare line 799 below: 'Like fountains of sweet water in the sea.'

657. *Of England, blown across her ghostly wall.* The chalk cliffs of the southern coast.

667. *Either haven.* The one where he landed, and that in which his native village lay. Compare line 102 above.

711. *Repeated muttering, 'cast away and lost.'* 'We may briefly record our admiration for the sustained power and absence of maudlin sensibility with which the last scenes of "Enoch Arden" are put before us. They are very pathetic; and they are never foolishly sentimental. The way in which Enoch is stunned by the news of his wife's second marriage; his longing to see her, and assure himself that she is happy; the picture of peace and comfort *within* Philip's house, which throws into stronger relief the anguish of the wretched husband and father as he stands *without;* Enoch's grand (if not strictly just) self-sacrifice, as, recovering from the shock of *seeing* what only to *hear* of had been woe sufficient, he repeats his resolution to himself. "Not to tell *her,* never to let her know:" all these things in the hands of a French writer, aiming at the *déchirant* and the *larmoyant,* would have been morbidly painful. Mr. Tennyson so tells them that they elevate our minds by the sight of a spirit refining to its highest perfection in the purgatorial fires of earth' ('Blackwood').

866. *See your bairns before you go.* The word *bairns* is used in the dialects of the North of England as well as in Scotland. Harrison, in his 'Description of England' (1577), says: 'The common sort doo call their male children *barnes* here in England, especiallie in the North countrie, where that word is still accustomablie in use.'

870. *Woman, disturb me not, etc.* 'The dying man's last victory over selfishness (when, forbidding the woman to fetch his children, he sends to them and to his wife the loving messages which it might grieve them too much to hear from his own lips) bespeaks not merely our pity for him, but our reverence. There is also something profoundly sad in the way in which that desolate heart, after half-claiming back the living children, feels that, in real fact, only the dead little one is left it' (Blackwood').

904. *There came so loud a calling of the sea, etc.* In the English illustrated edition there is here a cut, from a drawing by Arthur Hughes, representing a stormy sea dashing against the wharves of the port. This cut was reproduced in my annotated edition of 'Enoch Arden and Other Poems' (Boston, 1887). Lord Tennyson afterwards wrote to me: 'The illustration of the "calling of the sea," by Arthur Hughes, is wrong. The "calling of the sea" is an expression for the sound of a ground swell, not of a storm. The timber of old houses would never have rung to such a sound except upon a still night when the calling of the sea is often heard for miles inland.'

908. *And so fell back and spoke no more.* And here the critic of 'Blackwood,' like others of his class, thinks that the poem should have ended: 'What need to *tell* us that the noble fisherman was strong and heroic, when the poet has just completed his fine delineation of his strength and heroism? . . . The costly funeral sounds an impertinent intrusion. We cannot doubt for a moment that Philip gave honorable burial to the man whom he had so deeply, though so unwittingly, wronged. But the atonement is such a poor one that it looks like a mockery; and we would rather hear nothing of it. Why disturb in our minds the image which what went before had left there? — the humble bed on which the form, so often tempest-tossed, reposes in its last sleep; the white face, serene in death, waiting for the kisses which it might not receive in life.'

The poet may, however, have felt that such an ending, though perhaps more rhetorically effective, was less in keeping with the simplicity of the narrative. This ends, as it began, like a plain story of humble village life; and the costly funeral — something more than mere 'honorable burial,' a loving tribute to the sailor hero rather than a poor attempt at 'atonement' for the wrong he had suffered — is, after all, if we let our imaginations fill out the picture of which the poet gives this single hint, a most touching and most appropriate conclusion.

To the critical comments on the poem already cited, I may add that of Mr. E. C. Stedman, in his 'Victorian Poets' (page 181): '"Enoch Arden," in sustained beauty, bears a relation to his shorter pastorals similar to that existing between the epic and his minor heroic-verse. Coming within the average range of emotions, it has been very widely read. This poem is in its author's purest idyllic style; noticeable for evenness of tone, clearness of diction, successful description of coast and ocean, — finally, for the loveliness and fidelity of its *genre* scenes. In study of a class below him, hearts "centred in the sphere of common duties," the Laureate is unsurpassed.'

Nor can I refrain from quoting one more tribute to the poem, — that of Mr. George William Curtis in 'Harper's Magazine' for October, 1864 (vol. xxix. p. 676): 'The fascinating fancy which Hawthorne elaborated under the title "Wakefield," of a man withdrawing from his home and severing himself for many years from his family, yet stealing to the windows in the darkness to see wife and children, and the changes time works in his familiar circle, is reproduced in "Enoch Arden," except that the separation is involuntary, and the unbetrayed looking in upon the change of years is not a mere psychological diversion, but an act of the highest moral heroism. Indeed, the tale is profoundly tragical, and like the last Idyll of the King is a rare tribute to the master passion of the human heart. It is not the most subtle selfishness, whispers the poet; it is the perfection of self-denial. Xavier de Maistre says that the Fornarina loved her love more than her lover. Not so would Raphael's Madonna have loved. Not so loved Enoch Arden. There is no nobler tale of true love than his.

'It is told with that consummate elegance in which Tennyson has no peer. The English language has a burnished beauty in his use of it which is marvellous. In his earlier verses it was too dainty, too conspicuously fastidious, and the words were chosen too much for themselves and their special suggestions and individual melody. But his mastery of them now is manly. It is as striking as Milton's, although entirely different. There are a Miltonic and a Tennysonian blank verse in English literature — is there any other? . . .

'This volume, with all the others of Tennyson, are an invaluable study to every literary aspirant and neophyte; for as his poems are the most striking illustrations of the fondness of the literary spirit of the age for the most gorgeous verbiage, so they are the most noble examples of a luxuriant tendency constantly restrained and tempered by the truest taste. He has gained severity and simplicity without losing richness, and force without losing fire. Literature is not the record of thought only — it is thought *and* the vehicle of thought. Gold is very precious; but gold carved by Benvenuto is priceless.'

Page 240. AYLMER'S FIELD.

Line 3. *Like that long-buried body, etc.* Tennyson undoubtedly refers to the opening of an Etruscan tomb at the ancient city of Tarquinii, near Corneto, in Italy. The discovery was made by Carlo Avvolta, a native of Corneto, and was the first that directed the attention of archæologists to this interesting necropolis, in which more than two thousand sepulchres have since been explored. While digging into a tumulus for stones to mend a road, Signor Avvolta

broke into the tomb of an Etruscan Lucumo, or prince. 'I beheld,' he says, 'a warrior stretched on a couch of rock, and in a few minutes I saw him vanish, as it were, under my eyes, for as the atmosphere entered the sepulchre, the armor, thoroughly oxidized, crumbled away into most minute particles; so that in a short time scarcely a vestige of what I had seen was left on the couch.' The golden crown worn by the dead prince was so fragile that all but a small portion of it crumbled into dust on its way to Rome.

6. *Slipt into ashes.* A good illustration of the poet's felicity in the choice of words.

12. *And been himself a part of what he told.* A reminiscence of Æneas's 'quorum pars magna fui' (' Æneid,' ii. 6).

13. *That almighty man, etc.* The 'Quarterly' critic is troubled by this, and asks: 'Now what do we gain by this profanation of words which immemorial usage has consecrated to one purpose only? They overweight by their exaggeration the satire they were designed to point.'

17. *Whose blazing wyvern, etc.* The heraldic dragon-like creature so called, — evidently a prominent figure in the Aylmer arms. Compare line 516 below.

39. *An immemorial intimacy.* The phrase is repeated in line 136 below.

44. *Sons of men, etc.* See Genesis, vi. 2.

53. *Not proven.* A Scottish law phrase. *Proven* is an illegitimate form (as *approven* — which Tennyson has once in the 'Idylls of the King' — or *reproven* would be), but is now often used instead of *proved.*

65. *That islet in the chestnut-bloom.* That spot of red.

72. *Shone like a mystic star, etc.* A 'variable star,' like Algol in the constellation Perseus.

82. *A decad.* The spelling *decade* is more common in America, though the analogy of *triad, pentad,* etc. favors the other.

90. *The fairy footings on the grass.* The 'fairy rings,' or circles on the grass, supposed to be made by the elves in their nightly dances. Compare 'The Tempest,' v. 1. 36: —

> You demi-puppets that
> By moonshine do the green sour ringlets make,
> Whereof the ewe not bites, etc.

92. *The petty mare's-tail forest.* The *Hippuris vulgaris,* a plant native to Britain, but found in other temperate and cold regions.

93. *Or from the tiny pitted target blew, etc.* Referring to the dandelion. Compare 'The Poet': 'the arrow-seeds of the field-flower;' and 'Gareth and Lynette': —

> The flower
> That blows a globe of after arrowlets.

102. *The music of the moon.* The reviewer in 'Blackwood' says, somewhat hypercritically: 'We do not think such an equivocal expression as "the music of the moon," so inevitably suggesting the "music of the spheres," should have been employed to designate that with

which Philomel salutes the goddess of the night.'

105. *Temple-eaten terms.* Terms spent as a law-student at the Temple in London.

110. *The tented winter-field*, etc. The hop-field as it looks in winter, when the poles are put together in tent-like stacks. The military figure is well carried out in the description of summer, when the poles are set up again to support the vines that will cover them with garlands of ripened cones in autumn.

121. *And mighty courteous in the main.* In the use of 'mighty' there is something approaching to a play upon the word.

135. *Nor by plight or broken ring*, etc. Lovers used sometimes to break a ring in two, each keeping one of the pieces in token of betrothal.

147. *By sallowy rims.* Its banks bordered with sallows, or willows.

152. *One that, summer-blanch'd*, etc. One whose walls were in summer all white with the profuse blossoms of the 'traveller's joy' (*Clematis vitalba*), and in autumn covered partly with its feathery and silky tufts, partly with ivy. Compare 'The Golden Year': 'O'erflourish'd with the hoary clematis.'

160. *A milky-way on earth.* A path white with borders of lilies. Compare Wordsworth, 'The Daffodils': —

> Continuous as the stars that shine
> And twinkle on the milky way,
> They stretch'd in never-ending line.

161. *Like visions in the Northern dreamer's heavens.* The allusion is to Swedenborg.

168. *For she*, etc. The verb is eleven lines below: 'was adored.'

171. *Not sowing hedgerow texts*, etc. Not merely scattering tracts among the peasantry.

191. *With half a score of swarthy faces.* His Indian servants.

193. *The close ecliptic.* The tropical sun.

202. *Unawares they flitted off.* That is, her thoughts wandered off.

221. *Gold that branch'd itself*, etc. An apt description of the exquisite Indian work in metal.

233. *The costly Sahib.* The critic in 'Blackwood' says: 'We must own we are much puzzled to understand in what sense the Indian kinsman who presents Edith with the fatal dagger is called "the costly Sahib." A man who made such handsome gifts to his relatives was anything but costly to them; and large as may have been his pension, we cannot think the poet meant to allude to it as a burden on the East Indian Company.' We wonder that the reviewer was not equally troubled by the *wealthy scabbard* three lines below, and that he did not suggest transposing the adjectives, like his brother Scotchman who was inclined to believe that Shakespeare really wrote in 'As You Like It': —

> Stones in the running brooks,
> Sermons in books, etc.

What would the prosaic reviewer make of the similar use of *costly* in 'The Merchant of Venice,' ii. 9. 94?

> A day in April never came so sweet
> To show how costly summer was at hand, etc.

251. *Blues and reds.* The colors of rival political parties, like Whigs and Tories.

256. *That great pock - pitten fellow.* Some poacher for whom they had been on the watch.

263. *This blacksmith border - marriage.* A 'Gretna Green marriage.' This Scotch village was the first convenient halting-place for runaway couples from England, who could be married here without the publication of bans and certain other formalities prescribed by the English law, nothing being required in Scotland but a mutual declaration of marriage in presence of witnesses, — a ceremony which could be performed instantly, even in the case of minors. For some years a *blacksmith* was the person who officiated at these extempore marriages. Owing to changes in both the English and the Scotch laws, Gretna Green is no longer famous for such matches.

265. *That cursed France, with her egalities!* It will be remembered that the time of the poem is supposed to be 1793.

277. *And Sir Aylmer Aylmer watch'd.* Acting on the neighbor's hint, though too haughty to let him know it.

280. *Pale as the Jephtha's daughter.* A prophetic picture here.

321. *As the wind-hover hangs in balance.* A species of hawk (*Falco tinnunculus*), so called from its hovering in the wind, or 'hanging in balance.'

405. *His richest bee's-wing from a bin reserved.* His oldest and choicest port. The 'bee's-wing' is a peculiar film in this wine, so called from its resemblance to the wing of a bee. It is much esteemed by connoisseurs as a mark of age. 'The waning red' in the next line is an allusion to the gradual change from red to a permanent brown which takes place in port wine.

428-431. *The rain of heaven, and their own bitter tears*, etc. The complimentary 'pretty' of 'Blackwood' is 'faint praise' for this fine passage.

435-437. *The lawless science of our law*, etc. The labyrinthic complexity of English law is aptly described in these lines.

455. *The gardens of that rival rose*, etc. The Temple Gardens in London, where Plantagenet plucked the white rose and Somerset the red. Compare '1 Henry VI.' ii. 4.

463. *Ran a Malayan amuck against the times.* Made a furious and indiscriminate attack, like those Malays who sometimes rush out in a frantic state with dagger in hand, yelling 'Amuck! amuck!' and attacking all who come in their way. We often meet with the incorrect expression 'run a muck;' and the first reading of the text here was 'a Malayan muck.'

490. *The nightly wirer of their innocent hare.* A poacher, using snares of wire to entrap the hares.

509. *The brand of John.* That is, a mark

burnt into the bark of the tree in the reign of King John, covered from view by bark growing for centuries, but never adhering to the part branded, and finally disclosed by the falling-off of this outer growth. Major Rooke (quoted in 'Notes and Queries' for September 25, 1880) tells us that 'in cutting down some timber in Birkland and Billagh, in Sherwood Forest, letters have been found cut or stamped in the body of the trees, denoting the King's reign in which they were so marked. The ciphers were of the reigns of James I., of William and Mary, and one of King John. The mark of John was eighteen inches within the tree, and something more than a foot from the centre; it was cut down in 1791.' Several other instances of trees bearing 'the brand of John' are cited by correspondents of the same journal.

516. *Burst his own wyvern on the seal.* The seal bore the Aylmer arms. See on line 17 above.

529. *The black republic on his elms.* The flock of rooks. Compare 'Locksley Hall': 'the clanging rookery.'

530. *Sweeping the frothfly from the fescue.* The 'frothfly' (*Aphrophora spumaria*) is also known as the 'froth-insect,' 'froth-worm,' 'froghopper,' etc. 'Fescue' is the name of many kinds of grass in the genus *Festuca*.

539. *Babyisms.* Lovers' baby-talk; a word dating back only to 1836, according to the 'New English Dictionary.' The 'Blackwood' critic doubts whether the description is true to the time. He says: 'In the last century letter-writing was a stately, grave, and formal thing, even amongst near relations. And we have no doubt that a gentleman of ancient family like Leolin, and the heiress of the good-breeding, though not of the pride, of the Aylmers, could write to one another without forgetting the established proprieties of their day.'

560. *A Martin's summer.* The mild weather coming near Martinmas, or St. Martin's Day, the 11th of November, corresponding to the 'Indian Summer' of New England. Compare '1 Henry VI.' i. 2, 131: 'Expect Saint Martin's summer, halcyon days,' etc.

571–573. *Like flies that haunt a wound, or deer, or men, etc.* 'The simile is at once new and appropriate, and the divine beauty of the exception stands out in stronger relief from the dark background' ('Blackwood').

578. *Star to star vibrates light, etc.* Compare the illustrations of the same mysterious sympathy of souls widely sundered in 'Enoch Arden.'

585. *With a weird bright eye, etc.* The line should be scanned thus: 'With a weird | bright eye | sweating | and trem- | ble-ing;' making 'trembling' a trisyllable, as many similar words are lengthened in Elizabethan poets. Compare Shakespeare, 'Two Gentlemen of Verona,' i. 3. 84: 'O, how this spring of love *resembleth;*' 'Coriolanus,' i. 1. 159: 'You, the great toe of this *assembly,*' etc.

618. *Their own gray tower, or plain-faced*

*tabernacle.* The neighboring church (of England) or chapel (of Dissenters). The people from the former, supposed to be of the better class, are 'all in mourning;' while the humbler folk from the latter can afford only some bit of black as a badge of sorrow.

628. *The verse, 'Behold,' etc.* See Matthew, xxiii. 38, or Luke, xiii. 35.

644. *Gash thyself, priest, and honor thy brute Baal.* Compare 1 Kings, xviii. 28.

648. *The babe shall lead the lion.* Compare Isaiah, xi. 6; and for the next line, Isaiah, xxxv. 1.

651. *No coarse and blockish god of acreage.* The Roman god Terminus, who presided over the boundaries of private property. So Lord Tennyson explained it in a letter to me.

671. *Not passing through the fire, etc.* As in the worship of Moloch. Compare Leviticus, xviii. 21, 2 Kings, xxiii. 10, Jeremiah, xxxii. 35, etc.

681. *The angel that said 'Hail!'* See Luke, i. 28.

698. *The hand that robed your cottage-walls with flowers.* See 151 fol. above.

716. *May wreck itself without the pilot's guilt.* Alluding to his brother's suicide, which he suggests may have been in a moment of frenzy, and therefore without the guilt of deliberate self-murder.

724. *That knit themselves for summer-shadow.* That contract the brow instinctively in the glare of sunshine.

728. *Anger-charm'd from sorrow.* His wrath overpowering his grief, as if by a magic spell.

742. *Or in the waste, 'Repent.'* Like John the Baptist in the wilderness. See Matthew, iii. 1, 2; and for what precedes, Daniel, iv. 25, v. 26, etc.

759. *Sent like the twelve-divided concubine, etc.* See Judges, xix. 29.

760. *Out yonder.* That is, in France. See on 265 above.

771. *May Pharaoh's darkness, etc.* See Exodus, x. 21, and Matthew, xxvii. 45.

824. *Yet to the lychgate, etc.* A churchyard gate with a porch under which a bier was formerly placed while the introductory part of the burial-service was read. It is also called a *corpse-gate,* which means the same, *lich* (Anglo-Saxon *lic*) being an old word for a dead body. These gates are still to be seen in some parts of England.

842. *The dark retinue reverencing death.* 'Retinue' is accented on the second syllable, as in 'The Princess,' iii.: 'Went forth in long retinue following up;' and 'Guinevere': 'Of his and her retinue moving they.' This is the accent of Shakespeare and Milton, in the only instances in which they use the word in verse.

849. *The hawk's cast.* Indigestible matter ejected from the stomach by the hawk or other bird of prey.

851. *The rabbit fondles his own harmless face.* As the timid creature does this only when absolutely at ease, nothing could better indicate the

complete desolation of the scene; but all the details of the picture are in keeping.

A correspondent of ' Notes and Queries ' says that the scene of ' Aylmer's Field ' is ' Aylmerston in Norfolk.' I presume he refers to *Aylmerton*, a parish twenty miles north of Norwich, and about three miles from the coast. Rye's ' Guide to Norfolk ' mentions it as ' interesting from the open pits or earth dwellings . . . which are locally called " shrieking pits," from the local belief that the wraith of a woman is always wandering about looking into them at night-time, wringing her hands and shrieking.'

Page 252. SEA DREAMS.

' Poor Esther Johnson said of Swift that he could write beautifully on a broomstick; but even a broomstick, if one were permitted to wander in thought to the woods in which it grew, might seem a likelier subject for poetry than the pecuniary loss of a city clerk, on which Tennyson has contrived to hang a powerful and beautiful poem ' (Bayne).

' The grace of the poem,' says the ' Quarterly Review,' ' is equalled by the winning kindliness of it.' Stedman calls it ' a poem of measureless satire and much idyllic beauty.'

Line 4. *Her clear germander eye.* ' Some might call this a touch of Pre-Raphaelite conceit or affectation, but I think a poet has a right to invent color-words for himself when he wants them, provided only that they are expressive, picturesque, and not too far-fetched. There is no word in the language that will define the particular tint of blue which you see not unfrequently in the eye of an ailing child so well as that which is here applied by Tennyson. It is the faintly mottled blue of the germander speedwell (*Veronica chamædrys*) — nothing else. As the little flower can be seen in summer in every English lane, the reference to it can hardly be called far-fetched ' (Bayne). I believe, however, that *germander* is here applied to the color of the child's eye in health, not when ' ailing.'

8. *Small were his gains.* The first reading was: ' His gains were small.'

15. *To buy strange shares.* At first, ' wild shares.'

19. *Variers from the church.* That is, Dissenters.

23. *The Scarlet Woman.* The Church of Rome; his interpretation of Revelation, xvii. 3. For the ' Apocalyptic millstone,' see Revelation, xviii. 21.

32. *They came and paced the shore.* At first, ' moved and paced the shore.'

34. *The large air.* Compare Virgil, ' Æneid,' vi. 640: ' Largior hic campos aether et lumine vestit.'

39. *Till all the sails were darken'd in the east, etc.* ' There is another reading, fresh and bright, from nature's own page ! You stand by the sea, on a southward-looking coast, as the sun goes down. Westward, where the sails come between you and the sunset, they show simply as spots of shade; eastward, where they are farther from the sun than you, they catch

the gleam from the west, and every sail is a speck of rose-light. I call that a proper illustration of our Alfred's " truth of *touch* " ' (Bayne).

For ' Till all ' the first reading was ' Until.'

44. *Let not the sun go down upon your wrath.* See Ephesians, iv. 26.

47. *Remembering her dear Lord.* Originally, ' our dear Lord.'

65, 66. *Is it so true that second thoughts are best?* The first reading was: —

> It is not true that second thoughts are best,
> But first, and third, which are a riper first.

Tainsh considers the alteration an unfortunate one; but the interrogative form seems to me to add a bitter emphasis to the statement, not to weaken it by the expression of doubt, as he understands it.

70. *When first I fronted him.* At first, ' I lighted on him.'

84. *Had you ill dreams?* In the dream that follows, the results of speculation are contrasted with those of honest work.

130. *I thought I could have died to save it.* This is true to the intensity of feeling we often experience in dreams.

148. *See Daniel seven and ten.* At first, ' seven, the tenth.'

154. *And all things work together for the good, etc.* See Romans, viii. 28.

176–194. *With all his conscience and one eye askew, etc.* ' A masterly imitation of our Old English satiric style. I am not sure whether it was Dryden or Cowper that Tennyson had in mind, and I cannot help thinking that he must have been influenced, in composing the lines, by Crabbe. The first line will recall Dryden's " With two left legs and Judas-colored hair " ' (Bayne). The critic in ' Blackwood ' says that the first two lines ' might be sworn to as Pope's any day.'

186. *Made Him his catspaw, and the Cross his tool.* This line and the next were not in the first version.

195. *I loathe it: he had never kindly heart, etc.* ' Her answer honors Tennyson, and is, by implication, one of the noblest tributes ever paid to the heart-wisdom of woman ' (Bayne).

201. *But round the North, etc.* The indirect quotation passes into direct in line 231: ' Then I fixt,' etc. The first reading here was: —

> Still
> It awed me. *Well — I dream'd that* round the North
> A light, a belt of luminous vapor, lay,
> And ever in it a low musical note
> Swell'd up and died; and, as it swell'd, a ridge
> Of breaker *came from out* the belt, and still
> Grew with the growing note, and when the note
> Had reach'd a thunderous fulness, on *these* cliffs
> Broke, mixt with awful light (the same as that
> *Which lived* within the belt) *by which* I saw, etc.

The ' Quarterly Review ' remarks: ' If we have a fault to find, it is with the mother's dream. This dream is vague and something too ponderous for the piece. It labors under the double obscurity of being both dream and allegory, and it remains with us a doubt to this day whether we have hit upon the true meaning of it, or whether the poet will rise up in judgment against our interpretation. We had almost said with Bottom that it is " past the wit of man to say what dream it was." Not that this is all a fault, for, as the husband tells her, Boanerges the pulpiteer and the unfamiliar ocean roar were likely parents of such a fantasy.'

Bayne says that the dream ' seems to be an imaginative shadowing forth of the general revolutionary movement of those times, and of the battle of churches and sects, of creeds and scepticisms, through all which — an echo, shall we say ? of the indestructible harmony in her own heart — she hears a note of Divine music. Readers will find much food for musing in these dreams.'

215-218. *And past into the belt, etc.* The first reading was: —

> And past into the belt, and swell'd again
> *To music;* ever when it broke *I saw*
> The statues, *saint or king* or founder, *fall;*
> Then from *the gaps of ruin which it* left, etc.

222. *And she grieved, etc.* Originally: —

> And *I* grieved
> In *my* strange dream, *I* knew not why, etc.

225. *As their shrieks, etc.* At first, ' when their shrieks,' etc.

227. *While none mark'd it.* Originally, ' tho' none mark'd it.'

231. *To the waste deeps together, etc.* The first reading was : ' To the waste deeps together: and I fixt,' etc.

243. *Our Boanerges with his threats of doom.* Compare Mark, iii. 17.

246. *But if there were, etc.* Originally, ' But were there such,' etc.

257. *The dimpled flounce of the sea-furbelow.* I did not understand this when editing the poem in 1887, and Lord Tennyson explained it in a letter thus: ' The reference is to a long dark-green seaweed, one of the *Laminaria,* called the " sea-furbelow," with dimpled, flounce-like edges. Boys sometimes running along the sand against the wind with this seaweed in their hands make it flap for sport. I should have put a note to this in my book. The name " sea-furbelow " is not generally known.' A similar seaweed is known on our New England coast as the ' Devil's apron-string.'

259-261. *Why were you silent when I spoke to-night ?* In place of this and the two next lines, the first version had the following: —

> I would not tell you then to spoil your day,
> But he at whom you rail so much is dead.

280. *This baby song.* ' An exquisite lullaby, a song which all mothers may learn, for it is what household songs should be, tender, simple, graceful, and picturesque' (' Quarterly Review ').

Page 257. ODE SUNG AT THE OPENING OF THE INTERNATIONAL EXHIBITION.

Line 7. *O silent father of our kings to be.* Prince Albert. Compare p. xv. above.

10. *The world-compelling plan. Compelling* is used in the etymological sense of ' bringing together.'

A WELCOME TO ALEXANDRA.

Lines 20-24. *Rush to the roof . . . when he welcomes the land.* These five lines were not in the first version.

Page 258. THE GRANDMOTHER.

For the suggestion of this poem, see the ' Memoir,' vol. i. p. 432.

Page 260. NORTHERN FARMER, OLD STYLE.

I add a few additional glossarial notes from Palgrave's ' Lyrical Poems by Lord Tennyson ' (London, 1885).

Page 261. *'asta beän,* hast thou been; *thoort,* thou art; *moänt,* may not have; *point,* pint; *'issén,* himself; *towd,* told; *boy,* by; *Larn'd a ma' beä,* learned he may be (*a* stands for *he* in this dialect); *a cast oop,* he cast up against me; *owt,* ought; *'Siver,* howsoever; *boy um,* by him; *stubb'd,* broken up for cultivation; *moind,* remember; *boggle,* bogle, haunting spirit; *the lot,* piece of waste; *raäved and rembled,* tore up and threw away; *Keäper's it wur,* it was the gamekeeper's ghost; *at 'soize,* at the assizes; *Dubbut,* do but; *yows,* ewes.

Page 262. *ta-year,* this year; *thruff,* through; *haäte oonderd,* eight hundred; *thutty,* thirty; *a moost,* he must; *cauve,* calve; *hoälms,* holms, mounds of slightly rising ground; *quoloty,* quality, the gentry; *thessèn,* themselves; *sewerloy,* surely; *howd,* hold; *Sartin-sewer,* certain sure; *kittle,* kettle, boiler; *Huzzin' an' maäzin',* worrying with a hiss and astonishing; *atta,* art thou; *'toättler,* teetotaler; *a's hallus i' the owd taäle,* is always telling the same old story; *floy,* fly.

NORTHERN FARMER, NEW STYLE.

The following notes are added by Palgrave: —

Page 262. *craw to pluck,* crow to pluck, matter to dispute; *lass,* daughter.

Page 263. *as 'ant nowt,* as has nothing; *weänt 'a,* will not have; *shut on,* clear of; *i' the grip,* in the little draining-ditch; *tued an' moil'd,* put himself in a stew and toiled; *run oop,* his land run up.

Page 265. THE SAILOR BOY.

Line 12. *And in thy heart the scrawl shall play.* In the Lincolnshire dialect, ' the young of the dog-crab ' is known as the ' scrawl ' (Halliwell, ' Archaic Dictionary ').

Page 266. BOADICEA.

Written in 1859 (' Memoir,' vol. i. p. 436), the metre being ' an echo of the metre in the " Atys " of Catullus.' The poet ' wished that it were musically annotated so that it might be read with proper quantity and force.' He found that people would not understand the rhythm; but he said that ' if they would only read it straight like prose just as it is written, it would come all right.'

Page 268. SPECIMEN OF A TRANSLATION OF THE ILIAD IN BLANK VERSE.

The first line of the translation originally read thus: ' So Hector said, and sea-like roar'd his host;' and this was retained in the 'Enoch Arden' reprint.

The last two lines were as follows in the magazine: —

> And champing golden grain their horses stood
> Hard by the chariots, waiting for the dawn;

and the following foot-note was appended: —

'Or, if something like the spondaic close of the line be required,

> And waited — by their chariots — the fair dawn.

Or, more literally,

> And champing the white barley and spelt, their steeds
> Stood by the cars, waiting the thronèd morn.'

There was also the following foot-note to 'honey-hearted':

'Or "wine sweet to the mind," but I use this epithet simply as a synonym of "sweet."'

In the 'Enoch Arden' volume, the reading in the text was: —

> And champing golden grain, the horses stood
> Hard by their chariots, waiting for the dawn;

with this foot-note: —

'Or more literally —

> And eating hoary grain and pulse the steeds
> Stood by their cars, waiting the thronèd morn.'

Page 269. THE THIRD OF FEBRUARY, 1852. No changes have been made in the poem; but some reprints have 'It might safe be' in the 2d stanza, and 'And flung the burthen' in the 5th.

Page 271. THE SPITEFUL LETTER. In the 2d stanza, 'little bard' was originally 'foolish bard.' The 3d and 4th stanzas were as follows: —

> This fallen leaf, is n't fame as brief ?
> My rhymes may have been the stronger,
> Yet hate me not, but abide your lot;
> I last but a moment longer.
>
> O faded leaf, is n't fame as brief ?
> What room is here for a hater ?
> Yet the yellow leaf hates the greener leaf,
> For it hangs one moment later.

The 5th had 'is n't that your cry ?' and the next line was 'And I shall live to see it.' The last stanza read thus: —

> O summer leaf, is n't life as brief ?
> But this is the time of hollies,
> And my heart, my heart is an evergreen;
> I hate the spites and follies.

Page 272. LITERARY SQUABBLES. For the history of this poem, see p. xv. above.

In the 2d stanza, the reading in 'Punch' was 'That hate each other,' and 'brothers' for 'brethren.' In the 3d stanza, 'strain' was 'strive'; the last line of the 4th was 'Like those that cried Diana great'; and the last line of the 5th had 'kindly silence' for 'perfect stillness.'

Page 274. LUCRETIUS.

'The poem is Roman, not Greek, and it bears the impress of the Roman race. In Tennyson's Greek poems, the Greek's grave beauty shines through the modern thought, through the modern description of Nature. Even in speeches like those of Athena and of Ulysses, beauty sits hand in hand with the experience of life. But in "Lucretius," stern, robust, rigid duty to self-chosen, self-approved law is first; the sense of the beautiful as a part of life does not appear in the poem. Lucretius has no religion save that of acceptance of Nature, but to that he is faithful. He has no duty to the gods, but he has duty to his own philosophic honor. He dies rather than be mastered by lustful visions which a Greek, even in the noble time when beauty meant pure harmony, would have gone through, smiled at, and forgotten.

'The philosophy also is a Greek philosophy, but Lucretius has made it Roman in temper; and one of the noble excellences of this poem is that Tennyson has never deviated in a single word from the Roman basis of the soul. Moreover, it takes a great poet to assimilate, as Tennyson does, the essence of Lucretius as a thinker and a poet in the space of about 300 lines; and to combine this with the representation of a man in an hour of doom and madness, such as an inferior poet, overloading it with frenzied ornament, would have made intemperate. Tennyson's masterly reticence, rigid restraint only to the absolutely necessary, are supreme in this poem' (Stopford Brooke).

Line 13. *Left by the Teacher, whom he held divine.* Epicurus, who, according to Diogenes Laertius, wrote three hundred volumes.

37. *A void was made in Nature, etc.* 'The possibility, or rather ultimate certainty, of this dissolution is repeated over and over again in Lucretius' (J. C. Collins's 'Illustrations of Tennyson': London, 1891).

40. *Ruining along the illimitable inane.* Compare Milton, 'Paradise Lost,' vi. 867: —

> Hell saw
> Heaven ruining from Heaven.

On the lines that follow, compare 'Lucretius,' ii. 999–1022, and v. 828–836.

52. *But girls, Hetairai, etc.* That is, harlots (the Greek ἑταῖραι).

54. *The mulberry-faced Dictator's orgies.* Referring to Sulla in his latter years.

55. *The quiet gods.* Compare the last stanza of 'The Lotos-Eaters,' and 'Œnone': —

> Gods, who have attain'd
> Rest in a happy place and quiet seats
> Above the thunder, etc.

See also lines 76–79 and 104–110 below.

82. *Thy Mavors.* Mars.

88. *The Trojan.* Anchises; as 'the wounded hunter' is Adonis, and 'the beardless apple-arbiter' (see 'Œnone') is Paris. 'The great Sicilian' is Empedocles.

95. *Kypris.* The Greek Κύπρις, as Aphrodite (Venus) was called, from the island of Cyprus, her favorite seat.

97. *The all-generating powers and genial*

*heat, etc.* 'In these lines Tennyson has caught the one joyous note of Lucretius, his intense and keen delight in Nature, as rapturous as Shelley's' (Collins).

119. *My Memmius.* Caius Memmius Gemellus, to whom Lucretius dedicated his 'De Rerum Natura.'

147. *Or lend an ear to Plato where he says, etc.* The reference is to the 'Phædo,' vi.: ὡς ἔν τινι φρουρᾷ ἐσμὲν οἱ ἄνθρωποι καὶ οὐ δεῖ δὴ ἑαυτὸν ἐκ ταύτης λύειν οὐδ᾽ ἀποδιδράσκειν (we men are as it were on guard, and a man ought not to free himself from it, nor to run away). As Mr. Collins notes, Jowett takes φρουρά to mean a prison; but Tennyson's interpretation may be correct. Plato seems to be alluding to a saying of Pythagoras, to which Cicero refers ('De Senectute,' 73): 'Vetatque Pythagoras injussu imperatoris, id est Dei, de praesidio et statione vitae decedere.'

164. *How should the mind, except it loved them, clasp, etc.* 'These lines contain, with the passage that follows, an allusion to the images or emanations which, according to Lucretius, matter is always throwing off' (Collins).

181. *But who was he that in the garden snared, etc.* Compare Ovid, 'Fasti,' iii. 291-328, 'where Egeria instructs Numa to ensnare Picus and Faunus, that they may show him how the thunderbolts of Jupiter may be averted' (Collins).

235. *Not he, who bears one name with her, etc.* That is, with *Lucretia.*

273. *Thus —thus: the soul flies out and dies in the air.* The repetition of 'thus' marks the successive stabs of the dagger. Collins compares the 'Æneid,' iv. 660: 'Sic, sic, juvat ire sub umbras.'

'How the whole poem is wrought, how nobly the character of Lucretius emerges line after line, with what poetic strength and sculpturing power his masculine passion clears its way to death till the brief close shuts up the tragedy, is for every reader to grasp as he has capacity' (Stopford Brooke).

Page 281. THE LOVER'S TALE.
'The lover's sorrow is mingled up with Nature. Every natural description illustrates and reflects the changing moods of the characters. . . . The one charm of the poem is its youthfulness. The lavishness, the want of temperance, the inability to stop when enough has been said, the welling-over of words, the boyishness of sentiment, the playing at sorrow — while they prove that Tennyson was right in withdrawing the poem from publication — nevertheless give us pleasure, the pleasure of touching youth' (Stopford Brooke).

'With " The Golden Supper " there comes a change. The treatment is more dramatic, the grasp on the subject more confident. Event follows event with spirited rapidity. The pictures are not less vivid, but they are sketched with bolder, clearer touches' (Waugh).

Page 302. IDYLLS OF THE KING.
*Dedication.* This was first inserted in the edition of 1862. It is not merely a tribute to Prince Albert, 'but strikes the key-note of the poem very artistically as well, by introducing the idea of chivalry that Arthur set before his knights' (Littledale).

Line 6. *Scarce other than my king's ideal knight.* The first reading was 'my own ideal knight.'

12. *Commingled with the gloom of imminent war.* Alluding to the threatened war with the United States on account of the 'Trent' affair. It was largely through Prince Albert's influence that the danger was averted.

13. *The shadow of his loss drew like eclipse.* The first version had 'moved' for 'drew.'

33. *Thou noble Father of her Kings to be.* Compare the 'Ode Sung at the Opening of the International Exhibition' (1862): 'O silent father of our Kings to be,' etc.

37. *To fruitful strifes and rivalries of peace.* Referring to the International Exhibitions of 1851 and 1862. The Prince was engaged in planning the latter at the time of his death.

Page 304. THE COMING OF ARTHUR.
The story is from Malory's 'Morte Darthur' (book i.), with many variations, particularly in dealing with the coarser features of the old romance.

5. *For many a petty king, etc.* Among those enumerated by Geoffrey of Monmouth, whom the poet follows here, are Brutus, or 'Brute,' and Locrine, mentioned by Milton in 'Comus' (827, 828), Leir (the Lear of Shakespeare) and Cassibelaunus (the Cassibelan of 'Cymbeline,' i. 1. 30, etc.).

13. *Aurelius.* Aurelius Ambrosius (or Emrys), 'a descendant of the last Roman general who claimed the purple as an Emperor in Britain' (Green, 'Making of England'). He met his death by poison, as related by Geoffrey: 'For there was near the court a spring of very clear water which the King used to drink of. . . . This the detestable conspirators made use of to destroy him, by so poisoning the whole mass of water which sprang up, that the next time the King drank of it he was seized with sudden death, as were also a hundred other persons after him.' Uther, who succeeded him, was his brother.

32. *They grew up to wolf-like men.* The reader will recall the story of Romulus and Remus, the *lycanthropi* of Greek and Roman fable, the *loup-garous* and *were-wolves* of France and Germany, etc. Compare 'Geraint and Enid,' 94: 'The three dead wolves of woman born.'

34. *Groan'd for the Roman legions here again.* Probably, as Littledale suggests, an allusion to the famous 'Groans of the Britons' of Gildas, who says that the Britons wrote to the Roman senate: 'The barbarians drive us into the sea; the sea throws us back on the barbarians: thus two modes of death await us, we are either slain or drowned.'

36. *Urien, assail'd him.* The 1869 edition had 'Rience' for 'Urien.' According to Geoffrey, Urien was the brother of Lot; and Malory makes him the husband of Arthur's sister,

Morgan le Fay. Rience was the King of North Wales, who 'made great war upon King Leodegrance of Cameliard' (Malory).

58. *Then he drave, etc.* The 1st edition reads here: —

> And he drave
> The heathen, and he slew the beast, and fell'd
> The forest, and let in the sun.

66. *Colleaguing with a score of petty kings.* This line was not in the 1st edition.

94–133. *Thereafter — as he speaks who tells the tale, etc.* This passage is not in the 1st edition.

111. *Carádos, Urien, Cradlemont of Wales, etc.* This list of conquered kings is from Malory.

132. *Man's word is God in man.* Repeated in 'Balin and Balan,' 8. Littledale paraphrases it thus: 'A man's promise is a divine thing, therefore it must be regarded as especially sacred.'

134. *Then quickly from the foughten field.* The first reading was: 'Then Arthur from the field of battle sent,' etc. 'Foughten field,' which Tennyson has several times elsewhere (in 'The Princess,' 'The Holy Grail,' etc.) is a reminiscence of Shakespeare, 'Henry V.' iv. 6. 18: 'this glorious and well-foughten field.'

207. *Should go to wrack.* 'Wrack' is the one form of 'wreck' in Shakespeare and other Elizabethan writers.

247–253. *A doubtful throne . . . to hold his foemen down.* For these six lines the 1st edition has only these four: —

> A doubtful throne is ice on summer seas —
> Ye come from Arthur's court: think ye this king —
> So few his knights, however brave they be —
> Hath body enow to beat his foemen down?

275. *Three fair queens.* According to Elsdale, these denote Faith, Hope, and Charity. Littledale thinks they are rather 'Charity, Abstinence, and Truth — the three virtues noted by Malory as deficient in the Knights.' When Boyd Carpenter asked Tennyson if those who made them Faith, Hope, and Charity were right, he answered: 'They are right, and they are not right. They mean that and they do not. They are three of the noblest of women. They are also those three Graces, but they are much more. I hate to be tied down to say "*This* means *that*," because the thought within the image is much more than any one interpretation' ('Memoir,' vol. ii. p. 127).

*The Lady of the Lake.* She symbolizes Religion, as is denoted by the sacred fish on her breast, and the great emblematic figure of her at the gate of Arthur's palace.

284. *Clothed in white samite.* A rich heavy silk, originally with thread twisted of six fibres (*hexamitum*, of which *samite* is a corruption).

298. *Jewels, elfin Urim.* For the 'Urim' of the Jewish High Priest, which many authorities believe to have been precious stones, see Exodus, xxviii. 30, Numbers, xxvii. 21, etc.

302. *Turn the blade, and ye shall see.* The 1st edition has 'you' for 'ye.'

312. *The swallow and the swift are near akin.*

Littledale says that 'Leodogran's ornithology is open to question.' An ornithologist might object to the 'near' in a scientific description; but the swallows and the swifts are groups of the same family, and in some parts of England the common swift is popularly known as the 'black swallow.' Tennyson was probably as familiar with the strict classification of the birds as Littledale, who elsewhere (page 98) pays a tribute to the poet's knowledge in that line. See on 'Gareth and Lynette,' 779.

362. *Shrunk like a fairy changeling lay the mage.* The elves that fairies were supposed to leave in exchange for the human babies they stole could sometimes be recognized as 'changelings' by their shrivelled and shrunken appearance — 'like little old men,' as the stories have it. Compare 'Gareth and Lynette,' 200: 'But only changeling out of Fairyland.'

379. *Till last, a ninth one, etc.* The old Welsh poets make the ninth wave larger than its predecessors, as the Romans did the tenth.

401. *Riddling triplets of old time.* 'The tercet rhymes in which many of the bardic poems, as well as the later Breton songs, are written' (Littledale).

431. *The hind fell, the herd was driven off.* The peasant was slain, and his cattle carried off as plunder.

442. *But the King stood out in heaven.* The 1st edition has 'and' for 'but.'

452. *Dubric, the high saint.* Archbishop of Caerleon-upon-Usk, primate of Britain and legate of the Pope.

459–469. *Far shone the fields of May. . . . I love thee to the death.* These eleven lines were not in the 1st edition.

475–505. *So Dubric said; . . . as of yore.* For these thirty-one lines the 1st edition had only these three: —

> Then at the marriage feast came in from Rome,
> The slowly-fading mistress of the world,
> Great lords, who claim'd the tribute as of yore.

481–501. *Blow trumpet, etc.* Stopford Brooke calls this marriage and coronation song 'a piece of glorious literature.' He adds: 'It embodies the thought of the poem, grips the whole meaning of it together. And its sound is the sound of martial triumph, of victorious weapons in battle, and of knights in arms. We hear in the carefully varied chorus, in the very rattle and shattering of the vowels in the words, the beating of axe on helm and shield on shield. Rugged, clanging, clashing lines — it is a splendid effort of art. King Olaf might have sung it. 'We hear its contrast in Merlin's song [402–410], as soft and flowing as the other was braying and broken, and we think with gratitude of the artist who could do both with equal ease. The graciousness of the rivulet-music and soft play of Nature is in the lines of this delicate song, and the gaiety of youth; and mingled with these the deep and favorite thought of Tennyson of the pre-existence of the soul.'

507. *To wage my wars, etc.* The 1st edition had 'fight' for 'wage.'

Page 311. GARETH AND LYNETTE.

A note in the 1st edition (1872) says : —

'With this poem the Author concludes THE IDYLLS OF THE KING.

'GARETH follows THE COMING OF ARTHUR, and THE LAST TOURNAMENT precedes GUINEVERE.'

The addition of ' Balin and Balan' in 1885 was evidently an afterthought. In 1872 the 'Enid' had not been divided, and the author's plan then included only ten poems instead of the present twelve, which fulfil the suggestion in the introduction to the 'Morte d'Arthur' of 1842: 'His epic, his King Arthur, some twelve books.' He once said to Mr. Knowles: 'When I was twenty-four I meant to write a whole great poem on it, and began it in the "Morte d'Arthur." I said I should do it in twenty years; but the Reviews stopped me. . . . By King Arthur I always meant the soul, and by the Round Table the passions and capacities of a man. There is no grander subject in the world than King Arthur.'

3. *Stared at the spate.* At the river in flood or freshet. *Spate* is of Celtic origin. Compare Burns, 'The Brigs of Ayr' : —

> While crashing ice, borne on the roaring spate,
> Sweeps dams an' mills an' brigs a' to the gate.

It is used figuratively in 'Jock o' the Side' ('Border Minstrelsy') : —

> And down the water wi' speed she ran,
> While tears in spates fa' fast frae her e'e.

18. *Heaven yield her for it.* For 'yield' in the sense of 'reward,' compare 'Antony and Cleopatra,' iv. 2. 33: 'And the gods yield you for 't!' and 'Hamlet,' iv. 5. 41: 'God 'ield you!'

40. *The goose and golden eggs.* Compare Tennyson's early poem, 'The Goose.'

46. *As glitters gilded in thy Book of Hours.* An illuminated prayer-book.

84. *Red berries charm the bird.* That is, allure the bird; a proverbial saying. Compare Goldsmith, 'She Stoops to Conquer' : 'he would charm the bird from the tree.'

198. *We have heard from our wise man at home.* The 1st edition has 'men' for 'man.'

229. *The dragon-boughts.* The coils of the dragons' tails.

249. *I have seen the good ship sail, etc.* Referring to the effects of mirage.

258. *And built it to the music of their harps.* Compare 'Œnone' : —

> As yonder walls
> Rose slowly to a music slowly breathed;

and see note on that passage.

280. *The Riddling of the Bards.* Compare 'The Coming of Arthur,' 401: 'riddling triplets of old time; ' and see note.

293. *Let love be blamed for it, not she, nor I.* As Littledale remarks, 'Gareth's grammar becomes a little confused.'

359. *Sir Kay.* 'The Thersites of the Romance-writers.'

362. *The wholesome boon of gyve and gag.*

Alluding to the ducking-stool and branks of the olden time, with which scolds were disciplined.

386. *His goodly cousin, Tristram.* 'Cousin' is here used, as in Malory and other old writers, in the sense of kinsman. Shakespeare applies it to nephew, niece, brother-in-law, grandchild, etc. Tristram was the son of Mark's sister.

422. *Lest we should lap him up in cloth of lead.* Alluding to the use of lead for coffins. Compare Richard Barnfield's verses, ascribed to Shakespeare in 'The Passionate Pilgrim': 'All thy friends are lapp'd in lead.' For 'lap' (wrap, enfold) compare 'The Princess,' vi.: 'Half-lapt in glowing gauze and golden brede.'

441. *But, so thou wilt no goodlier, etc.* The 1st edition has 'an' for 'so.'

455. *And hands Large, fair, and fine.* According to Malory, he was 'the fairest and largest handed that ever man saw; ' and Kay says: 'Since he hath no other name, I shall give him a name that shall be Beaumains, that is Fairhands.'

490. *On Caer-Eryri's highest found the King.* On the summit of Snowdon; referring to another legend concerning the birth of Arthur. 'Caer-Eryri literally means, in Welsh, Snowdon Field' (Littledale).

492. *The Isle Avilion.* The 'Isle of Apples' — the 'Avalon' of 'The Palace of Art' : —

> Or mythic Uther's deeply-wounded son
> In some fair space of sloping greens
> Lay, dozing in the vale of Avalon,
> And watch'd by weeping queens.

642. *The may-white.* All the English editions print 'the May-white.' See on 'Guinevere,' 22.

675. *Then as he donn'd the helm, etc.* The 1st edition has 'while' for 'as; ' and, four lines below, 'and' for 'while.'

710. *Kay, wherefore wilt thou go against the King?* The 1st edition has 'will ye.'

729. *A foul-flesh'd agaric in the holt.* An ill-smelling fungus in the wood. Compare 'Edwin Morris': 'Long learned names of agaric, moss, and fern.'

779. *Round as the red eye of an eagle-owl.* 'The comparison between the pool gleaming red in the twilight and the eye of an eagle-owl, burning round and bright in the darkness, may have the fault of being too uncommon to really illustrate the description, but it is a simile that an ornithologist can appreciate. Indeed, a book might be written on the bird-lore of Tennyson, as has been well done by Mr. Harting in the case of Shakespeare' (Littledale). Compare the note on 'the swallow and the swift,' in 'The Coming of Arthur' (312). In the next line the 1st edition has 'cries' for 'shouts.'

806. *Flickering in a grimly light.* 'Grimly' (grim, hideous) is rare as an adjective. Compare 'Marmion,' iv. 440: 'So grimly and so ghast.'

807. *Good now, ye have saved a life.* For the vocative use of 'good' (my good fellow), with or without now,' compare 'Hamlet,' i. 1. 70: 'Good now, sit down and tell me, he who

knows;' 'The Tempest,' i. 1. 3: 'Good, speak to the mariners,' etc.

813. *But wilt thou yield this damsel harborage?* The 1st edition has 'will ye yield.' Two lines below, it has 'Ye' for 'You,' as in some passages further on; but oftener 'you' in the early editions is changed to 'ye.'

829. *And there they placed a peacock in his pride, etc.* 'Lynette is to be reminded by the peacock in his pride that ladies should be loving and gentle to their champions — a lesson she stands rather in need of' (Littledale). The bird was constantly the object of the solemn vows of the knights; and when it was served at table, 'all the guests, male and female, took a solemn vow; the knights vowing bravery, and the ladies engaging to be loving and faithful' (Stanley, 'History of Birds').

852. *Whether thou be kitchen-knave or not, etc.* The 1st edition has 'ye' for 'thou.'

889. *Lent-lily in hue.* The daffodil is called the 'Lent-lily,' because it blossoms about the time of Lent.

894. *The champion thou hast brought.* The 1st edition has 'ye have brought.'

908. *The stone Avanturine.* A kind of quartz with spangles of mica in it. A better spelling is 'aventurine,' on account of the derivation of the word.

928. *When mounted.* The editions, down to 1884 at least, have 'being mounted.'

970. *And then she sang, etc.* 'Lynette has now seen that he is a gentleman and no knave, and admiration of his valor awakens a different feeling in her heart. Her songs conceal rather than reveal this dawning love; maiden modesty will not permit her to abate one jot of her missayings and revilings. Her first song indicates the sudden light that has dawned upon her: her morning dream has once proved true, that her love would smile on her that day. . . . After the Sun has been overthrown, her love has smiled on her twice; her dream that she would find a victorious champion that day — a knight who would achieve her quest and become her love — has been twice proved true. . . . Thrice [after the victory over the Evening Star] hath her dream come true — or rather three omens have now proved her dream true — her dream of a victorious and loving champion' (Littledale).

996. *Fair damsel, you should worship me the more.* The 1st edition has 'ye' for 'you.'

1002. *The flower That blows a globe of after arrowlets.* The dandelion. Compare 'The Poet': 'like the arrow-seeds of the field-flower;' and 'Aylmer's Field': —

Or from the tiny pitted target blew
What look'd a flight of fairy arrows.

1023. *But he that fought no more.* The 1st edition reads: 'that would not fight.'

1142. *Damsel, he said, you be not all to blame, etc.* The 1st edition has 'ye' for 'you' here and in the next line; also 'yield thee,' 'thy quest,' and 'Ye said' in the following lines.

1163. *Anon they past a narrow comb.* A

'comb' (Celtic) is a hollow in a 'hillside,' or 'the head of a valley.'

1172. *In letters like to those the vexillary, etc.* Referring to the Latin inscription carved by the vexillary, or standard-bearer, of the second legion upon a cliff overhanging the little river Gelt near Brampton in Cumberland. A detachment of this legion appears to have been stationed there in 207 A. D.

1227. *O damsel, be you wise, etc.* Here again, as in several places below, 'ye' has been changed to 'you.'

1281. *Arthur's Harp.* According to Littledale, this 'denotes a star that lies near the Pole-star and Arcturus, the three forming a triangle like a harp.' Arcturus is so far from the Pole-star that no star could well be 'near' both of them; and from the allusion in 'The Last Tournament' we should infer that a single star, and not a constellation, was meant: —

'Dost thou know the star
We call the Harp of Arthur up in heaven?'
And Tristram, 'Ay, Sir Fool, for when our King
Was victor wellnigh day by day, the knights,
Glorying in each new glory, set his name
High on all hills, and in the signs of heaven.'

1366. *And Death's dark war-horse bounded, etc.* The 1st edition reads: 'At once the black horse bounded,' etc.

1386. *Then sprang the happier day from underground.* The poet seems to write 'underground' and 'under ground' interchangeably, both forms being found several times in the English editions.

1392. *He that told the tale in older times.* Malory; 'he that told it later' being Tennyson himself.

Page 333. THE MARRIAGE OF GERAINT. The story of this and the following Idyll is from the 'Mabinogion' of Lady Charlotte Guest, a collection of ancient Welsh tales (London, 1838-1849). As Littledale states, 'a French translation from the same source that Lady Guest has followed — the "Llyfr Coch o Hergest" — will be found in M. de Villemarqué's "Table Ronde," pp. 239-320, under the title of "Ghérent, ou Le Chevalier au Faucon."'

39. *To cleanse this common sewer of all his realm.* Repeated in the next Idyll, 894.

70. *They sleeping each by either.* The reading of 1859 is 'each by other.'

124. *At this he hurl'd his huge limbs out of bed.* The 1859 edition has 'snatch'd' for 'hurl'd.'

130. *And thou, put on thy worst and meanest dress.* The pronouns in 1859 were 'you' and 'your;' and, three lines below, 'you' for 'thee.'

146. *Held court at old Caerleon upon Usk.* 'The romances very frequently mention these "plenary courts" (*cours plenières*) which were customarily held by the monarchs of France and England at the principal feasts of Easter, Whitsuntide, and Christmas. The Forest of Dean, in Gloucestershire, was anciently a very extensive tract of country west of the Severn; it now comprises about 22,000 acres and belongs to the Crown' (Littledale).

202. *Whereat Geraint, etc.* The 1859 edition

has 'at which' for 'whereat,' as also on page 130 below: 'Whereat the armorer,' etc. Similarly on page 128, 'of which' has been changed to 'whereof.'

217. *I will track this vermin to their earths.* The use of 'vermin' as at once collective and plural is archaic.

274. *A thousand pips eat up your sparrow-hawk!* Littledale says that 'the disease called the *pip*, which attacks young fowls, seems to be confused with another disease called *gapes*.' He adds: 'As pips are not insects, they cannot eat up sparrow-hawks.' But 'eat' need not be taken literally, and 'thousand' is merely intensive. The meaning apparently is, May the worst kind of pip destroy your sparrow-hawk!

347. *Turn, Fortune, turn thy wheel, etc.* 'The metrical structure of the song is original, but seems intended to convey a suggestion or reminiscence of the troubadour rondels and villanelles, such as a high-born maiden might have sung in an old baronial bower' (Littledale).

386. *A costrel.* A flagon, flask, or bottle, made of leather or earthenware, sometimes called 'pilgrim's bottle.' Here it holds the 'wine,' not the 'flesh,' which is brought, though it is possible (as Littledale thinks) that the poet forgot it was a vessel for holding liquids only.

389. *Manchet bread.* The finest kind of white bread. Compare Drayton, 'Polyolbion': —

No manchet can so well the courtly palate please
As that made of the meal fetched from my fertile leas;
The finest of that kind, compared with my wheat,
For fineness of the bread, doth look like common cheat.

*Cheat*, or *cheat-bread*, was a coarser kind of wheaten bread.

421. *But if ye know, etc.* The 1859 edition has 'you know.'

475. *That if the sparrow-hawk, this nephew, fight.* The 1859 reading was: 'That if, as I suppose, your nephew fight,' etc. In 479, 'your' and 'yours' have been changed to 'thine.'

483. *And over these is placed, etc.* The 1859 edition has 'laid' for 'placed;' and, in the next line: 'And over that is placed the sparrow-hawk.'

493. *But thou, that hast no lady.* Originally, 'you that have;' and, just below, 'Your leave!'

507. *Had stolen away.* Originally, 'had slipt away.'

543. *The Chair of Idris.* The mountain, Cader-Idris, in Merionethshire, the highest in Wales (2914 feet) next to Snowdon. Idris, according to the old legends, was one of the three Primitive Bards (Eidiol and Beli being the others) and the inventor of the harp.

550. *And over that the golden sparrow-hawk.* The 1859 edition has 'a' for 'the.'

576. *Edyrn, son of Nudd.* He appears again in the next Idyll (780 fol.).

581. *First, thou thyself, with damsel and with dwarf.* The early reading was 'thou thyself, thy lady and thy dwarf;' and, in the next line, 'being' for 'coming.'

593. *And, being young, he changed, etc.* The early reading was: —

And, being young, he changed himself and grew
To hate the sin, that seem'd so like his own,
Of Modred, Arthur's nephew, and fell at last
In the great battle fighting for the King.

615. *And still she look'd and still the terror grew.* This recalls Goldsmith's 'And still they gazed, and still the wonder grew,' etc.

641. *Which being sold and sold, etc.* That is, sold one after another.

661. *A turkis.* One of the old spellings of *turquoise*, indicating what is still one of the authorized pronunciations.

714. *But since our fortune swerved from sun to shade.* The early editions have 'slipt' for 'swerved.'

742. *That maiden in the tale, etc.* The tale is in the 'Mabinogion.' Math says to Gwydion: 'Well, we will seek, I and thou, by charms and illusion, to form a wife for him out of flowers . . . so they took the blossoms of the oak, and the blossoms of the broom, and the blossoms of the meadow-sweet, and produced from them a maiden, the fairest and most graceful that man ever saw. And they baptized her, and gave her the name of Blodenwedd.'

744. *The bride of Cassivelaun, etc.* According to the Welsh tradition, it was the love of a British maiden named Flur, who was betrothed to Casswallawn (or Cassivelaunus), that led Cæsar to invade Britain. She was carried off by a Gallic prince, an ally of Cæsar, who thus got possession of her; but she was recaptured by Casswallawn after a battle in which six thousand of Cæsar's army were slain.

764. *Flaws in summer.* Sudden gusts of wind. Compare 'Hamlet,' v. i. 239: 'the winter's flaw.'

774. *As careful robins eye the delver's toil.* The simile is repeated in the next Idyll (431).

780. *Thy new son.* Originally 'your new son.'

785. *This ruin'd hall.* Originally, 'this ruin'd hold;' and, two lines below, 'kind Queen' for 'fair Queen.'

791. *Fain I would, etc.* Originally, 'for I wish'd,' etc. The next two lines had 'To love' for 'Should love,' 'should' for 'can,' and 'I had' for 'was mine.'

797. *I doubted whether daughter's tenderness.* Originally 'filial tenderness;' and, in the next line 'did' for 'might.'

804. *And all its perilous glories.* Originally 'dangerous glories;' and below (811) 'intermitted custom' for 'intermitted usage.'

818. *Some gaudy-day.* Some holiday; especially an English University festival. Compare Middleton, 'The Black Book': 'Never passing beyond the confines of a farthing, nor once munching commons but only upon gaudy-days.'

Page 344.  GERAINT AND ENID.

1. *O purblind race of miserable men, etc.* Compare 'Lucretius,' ii. 14: —

O miseras hominum mentes, O pectora caeca,
Qualibus in tenebris vitae, quantisque periclis,
Degitur hoc aevi quodcumquest.

9. *When they both had got to horse.* Originally 'had both.'

14. *I charge thee ride before.* Originally, ' you ' for ' thee; ' as also two lines below.

49. *The great plover's human whistle.* ' The shrill call of the stone curlew, or Norfolk plover, which thus often deceives wanderers on the wolds ' (Littledale).

77. *Your warning or your silence.* Originally, ' Your silence or your warning.' Professor Jones (see p. 303 above) suggests that the first reading was due to the influence of the ' Mabinogion,' which has, ' I wish but for silence, and not for warning.' The poet apparently did not see at the moment of writing that the change from the declarative to the interrogative form required a transposition of the nouns. The correction was made in 1869. In the second and third lines below ' you ' has been changed to ' ye.'

94. *Wolves of woman born.* Compare ' The Coming of Arthur,' 32; and see note.

163. *That had a sapling growing on it, slide, etc.* Originally, ' slip ' for ' slide.'

213. *Less having stomach for it.* The American 1859 edition reads: ' having a stomach.' This is not in any English edition, and may be a misprint.

221. *Ye will be all the wealthier.* Originally, ' You will; ' and a few lines below, ' you are ' for ' thou art,' and ' you ' (twice) for ' thee.'

301. *She doth not speak to me.* Originally, ' does ' for ' doth; ' as in ' doth he love you,' on the next page. Similarly, ' has ' has been changed to ' hath ' in ' hath turn'd me wild ' (line 308) and elsewhere. I shall not hereafter note all these little changes, nor those of ' you ' to ' ye ' or ' thee,' which occur frequently.

338. *Nay; I do not mean blood.* The ' nay ' was originally ' no.'

340. *My malice is no deeper than a moat, etc.* That is, I mean only to imprison Geraint, not to kill him.

344. *The one true lover whom you ever own'd.* Originally, ' which you ever had.'

426. *Not all mismated, etc.* Originally, ' Not quite mismated.'

475. *The cressy islets.* Masses of water-cress. Compare the ' Ode to Memory: ' ' To purl o'er matted cress and ribbed sand.'

582. *Till at the last he waken'd from his swoon.* Originally, ' And at the last.'

762. *And never yet, since high in Paradise, etc.* Stopford Brooke refers to these as ' some of the loveliest lines the poet ever wrote of womanhood.'

770. *Before the useful trouble of the rain.* ' This seems to imply that the " useful *trouble* of the rain " only came after man's departure from Paradise. This is not exactly stated in Genesis ii., where we read that *before* the plantation of Eden " the Lord God had not caused it to rain upon the earth. . . . But there went up a mist from the earth," etc. Milton makes Eve in Eden speak of " the fertile earth after soft showers " ' (Littledale).

902. *The vicious quitch.* A kind of worthless grass, hard to eradicate from cultivated fields. In New England it is often called ' witch-grass.'

Browning, in ' Sordello,' speaks of ' Docks, quitch-grass, loathly mallows no man plants.'

914. *Then if some knight of mine, etc.* Originally ' a knight.'

932. *On each of all whom Uther left in charge.* Originally, ' On whom his father Uther left in charge.'

935. *The White Horse on the Berkshire hills.* The English editions print ' the white horse,' See Thomas Hughes's ' Scouring of the White Horse,' — a figure of a horse cut in the turf on the side of a chalk-hill near Wantage in Berkshire, to commemorate Alfred's victory over the Danes in the time of Ethelred.

961. *Enid, whom her ladies loved to call, etc.* Originally, ' the ladies.'

Page 357. BALIN AND BALAN.

The story is abridged from the second book of Malory's ' Morte Darthur,' with the addition of incidents and details that are Tennyson's own.

8. *Man's word is God in man.* Compare 'The Coming of Arthur,' 132.

24. *A plume of lady-fern.* A species of fern (*Asplenium Filix-femina*) so called, according to some authorities, because dedicated to the Virgin Mary.

226. *Thus, as a hearth, etc.* The 1st edition has ' Then ' for ' Thus.'

256. *The maiden Saint who stands with lily in hand.* The Virgin Mary.

361. *And one was rough with wattling, and the walls, etc.* The 1st edition has: ' rough with pole and scaffoldage.'

The goblet is embossed with two scenes from the legend of Joseph of Arimathea, — his voyage, and the little church he built at Glastonbury. Compare ' The Holy Grail,' 63: —

And there he built with wattles from the marsh
A little lonely church in days of yore.

410. *The blindfold rummage.* Compare ' Hamlet,' i. 1. 107: ' Of this post-haste and romage in the land.'

425. *I have shamed thee so that now thou shamest me.* ' Apparently the killing of Garlon was feloniously done, for Garlon was unarmed and unprepared ' (Littledale).

434. *The fire of heaven has kill'd the barren cold, etc.* Stopford Brooke remarks that this song, glorifying the fire of the appetites and senses, ' might have been written for the worship of Astarte, and it is splendidly imagined by Tennyson: it sets the sensual side of pagan Nature-worship into the keenest contrast with the self-control of Christianity. The fire from heaven she speaks of is not the holy fire of the pure spirit; it is the fire of that heaven which some have conceived, and which consists in the full enjoyment of desire. It is this blaze of desire which she sees in all Nature as well as in man, and it creates, she thinks, the real beauty of the world. Tennyson got to the heart of the thing in this exultant pagan song.' It shows us Vivien ' as she is — honest, true, and bold, confessing evil and rejoicing in it. The whole sketch of her in " Balin and Balan " is

of this strain of triumphant daring. Her tale of slander about the Queen is there delivered with a ring of conquest in it. Her mocking of her boy squire and of Balan has the bravery of a queen of sin.'

Page 366. MERLIN AND VIVIEN.

The hint of the story is from Malory, who simply tells 'how Merlin fell in a dotage about one of the damsels of the lake, whose name was Nimue.'

2. *The wild woods of Broceliande.* In Brittany, and famous in legendary lore.

4. *A tower of ivied mason-work.* The 1st edition (1859) has 'ruin'd mason-work.' After the next line that edition goes on with 'The wily Vivien stole from Arthur's court' (line 147 below). The long passage that intervenes was first inserted in 1874, when it began thus:—

Whence came she? One that bore in bitter grudge
The scorn of Arthur and his Table, Mark,
The Cornish King, had heard a wandering voice,
A minstrel of Caerleon by strong storm
Blown into shelter by Tintagil, say,

and so on to 146 below.

42. *My father died in battle against the King.* To the Queen she says (line 71), 'for thy King.'

52. *Saith not Holy Writ the same?* See Job, xxv. 5, 6.

108. *That gray cricket.* The 'minstrel of Caerleon.' See line 9 above.

123. *Diet and seeling, jesses, leash, and lure, etc.* The 'diet,' or feeding, of the hawks was regulated strictly.

'Seeling' was partly sewing up the eyelids of a young hawk, to prevent it seeing men, etc., in front of it, and so becoming alarmed. Hoods came in time to be used instead of seeling.

'Jesses' were two narrow strips of leather, fastened one to each leg, and attached to a swivel, from which hung the 'leash,' or thong.

The 'lure' was sometimes a live pigeon, but more usually a piece of iron or wood, generally in the shape of a heart or a horseshoe, to which were attached the wings of some bird, with a piece of raw meat fixed between them. The falconer swung this round his head or threw it to a distance by a thong, and the hawk flew down to it.

'She is too noble.'— The 'falcon' was the female; the 'tercel' was the male.

'Check at pies.'— Either, leave pursuing a game-bird to follow a magpie that crosses her flight; or, as more usually, fly at worthless birds such as magpies.

'Towered.'— Rose spirally to a height.

'Pounced.'— Swooped down on.

'Quarry.'— The game flown at.

Her 'bells' were globular, of brass or silver, and attached to each leg by 'bewits.'

These 'terms of art' are from Harting's 'Ornithology of Shakespeare.'

125. *Nor will she rake.* That is, 'fly wide at game.'

148. *She hated all the knights, etc.* The 1859 *American* edition reads:—

She loathed the knights, and ever seem'd to hear
Their laughing comment when her name was named.

For once, when Arthur walking all alone,
Vexed at a rumor rife about the Queen,
Had met her, etc.

This reading is found nowhere else. The American edition was evidently printed from advance sheets, but the poet must have altered the passage before the English edition of 1859 was printed.

The 1857 reading was:—

She hated all the knights because she deem'd
They wink'd and jested when her name was named.

187. *Then fell on Merlin a great melancholy.* The 1859 reading was 'fell upon him.' The next seven lines are not in that edition, but were added in 1873; and the next line began, 'And leaving Arthur's court,' etc.

196. *There found a little boat, etc.* As Littledale notes, these little boats in the romances (compare 'The Holy Grail') are generally independent of sail or oar, and this one drives with 'a sudden wind' across the deeps; 'not a wind raised by enchantment — the poet does not directly say that — but there is just a subtle suggestion of glamour, of something more than natural, in this sudden wind, which sustains the sense of spirit-daunting mystery.'

219. *A twist of gold was round her hair.* The 1st *American* (1859) edition, like 'The True and the False' (1859), has 'snake' for 'twist;' but the *English* 1859 edition has 'twist.' The poet must have made the change from 'snake' to 'twist' after the advance sheets were sent to the American publishers, as he did in 148 fol.

233. *O Merlin, do ye love me?* The early reading was 'you' for 'ye,' as in sundry other places that I shall not take space to note.

285. *Boon? ay, there was a boon.* The 1859 edition has 'yea' for 'ay.'

311. *Not yet so strange as you yourself are strange.* Originally, 'Nor yet.'

338. *That I should prove it on you unawares.* After this line the 1859 edition has the line, 'To make you lose your use and name and fame' (omitted in 1873); and, in the next line, 'most indignant' for 'passing wrathful.'

385. *In Love, if Love be Love, etc.* The song of the lover to his lady. The 5th stanza (444–447) is her reply.

430. *It buzzes fiercely round the point.* The early reading was 'buzzes wildly.'

459. *Yea! Love, though Love were of the grossest, etc.* The early reading was 'True!' for 'Yea!'

472. *Fancied arms.* These may be 'described in unheraldic language as an eagle of gold soaring upon a blue surface to a golden sun depicted on the right hand of the upper part of the shield (*dexter*, that is, on the left hand of any one *facing* the shield; the *right hand* of the bearer of the shield who is supposed to be sheltered behind it).

'As the picture that Merlin substituted is blazoned *proper*, that is, in the natural colors of the objects represented, it is allowable in strict heraldry to place it upon a field azure, in spite of the fundamental heraldic law that forbids metal to be charged on metal or color on color' (Littledale).

494. *Because I fain had given them greater wits.* In 1859, 'Because I wish'd to give them greater minds.' In 501 below, 'Broke' has been changed to 'Brake.'

507. *The second in a line of stars, etc.* The star in the sword of Orion which is surrounded by the great nebula. It is just below the well-known 'belt of three' stars.

571. *Magnet-like she drew, etc.* Littledale sees here 'a suggestion of Sindbad's magnet-mountain;' but why assume that the attractive maid is compared to the mountain? The general suggestion of magnetism is sufficient.

601. *The lady never made unwilling war, etc.* Littledale remarks that Vivien's criticism exactly parallels the remark made to Dr. Johnson by a lady 'of great beauty and excellence,' after reading the fourth line of Pope's epitaph on Mrs. Corbet. The line in question states that Mrs. Corbet 'no arts essayed but not to be admired;' and the lady considered that it contained 'an unnatural and incredible panegyric.' In fact, Mrs. Corbet never made unwilling war with those fine eyes! 'Of this,' adds the doctor, 'let the ladies judge.'

652. *For keep it like a puzzle chest in chest, etc.* Littledale sees here an allusion to those Chinese puzzles of 'laborious orient ivory, sphere in sphere,' mentioned in the prologue to 'The Princess;' but those are not 'chests,' nor are they 'locked,' and they cannot be opened, the inner spheres having been carved and detached through the openings in the carving of the outer ones. The reference in the present passage is to sets of chests, or boxes, made to fit one within another, each with its own lock.

707. *There lay the reckling.* 'Reckling' is properly the smallest and weakest in a litter, as of puppies or kittens; here used contemptuously for the puny infant.

763. *The holy king, whose hymns, etc.* David.

779. *Man! is he man at all, etc.* The 1859 edition has 'Him!' for 'Man!' In the next line, 'winks' is used in its old sense of shutting one's eyes. Compare Shakespeare, Sonnet 43.1: 'When most I wink [in sleep], then do my eyes best see,' etc.

816. *She cloaks the scar of some repulse with lies, etc.* The 1859 edition reads: —

I think she cloaks the wounds of loss with lies;
I do believe she tempted them and fail'd,
She is so bitter.

In 822 below, it has: 'Face-flatterers and back-biters are the same.'

842. *Leapt from her session on his lap.* This use of 'session' is archaic. Compare Hooker, 'Ecclesiastical Polity,' v. 55: 'his ascension into heaven and his session at the right hand of God,' etc.

867. *Seethed like the kid, etc.* See Exodus, xxxiv. 26; Deuteronomy, xiv. 21.

921. *Lo! what was once to me, etc.* The 1859 edition has 'Oh' for 'Lo;' and below (924) it reads: —

Farewell; think kindly of me, for I fear
My fate or fault, omitting gayer youth
For one so old, must be to love you still.
But ere I leave you, etc.

Page 380. LANCELOT AND ELAINE.

The outline of the story is from Malory (book xviii. chapters 7 to 21), whom the poet has followed very closely in many passages, of which I give occasional illustrations. For a fuller account of the poet's indebtedness to the 'Morte Darthur,' as also of the points in which he has varied from it, see Littledale, or consult the editions of Malory mentioned on p. 303 above.

2. *The lily maid of Astolat.* 'Elaine le Blank' (*blanche*, or white), as Malory calls her.

7. *Fearing rust or soilure.* Knights usually kept their shields covered, to prevent 'rust or soilure,' and doubtless many a fair damsel wrought a cover for her warrior's shield.

34. *For Arthur, long before they crown'd him king, etc.* The 1859 edition reads: —

For Arthur when none knew from whence he came,
Long ere the people chose him for their king,
Roving the trackless realms, etc.

45. *And he that once was king had on a crown.* Originally, 'And one of these, the king, had on a crown.'

75. *The place which now Is this world's hugest.* That is, London.

78. *Spake — for she had been sick — to Guinevere, etc.* Compare Malory (xviii. 8): 'So King Arthur made him ready to depart to those jousts, and would have had the queen with him; but at that time she would not, she said, for she was sick and might not ride at that time. . . . And many deemed the queen would not be there because of Sir Launcelot du Lake, for Sir Launcelot would not ride with the King; for he said that he was not whole of the wound the which Sir Mador had given him. Wherefore the King was heavy and passing wroth,' etc.

80. '*Yea, lord,' she said, 'ye know it.'* The 1859 edition has 'you' for 'ye,' as in the next line and in 83; also in about forty other places in the idyll of which I shall make no note.

97. *To blame, my lord Sir Lancelot, much to blame!* Compare Malory (xviii. 8): 'Sir Launcelot, ye are greatly to blame, thus to hold you behind my lord; what trow ye, what will your enemies and mine say and deem? nought else but see how Sir Launcelot holdeth him ever behind the king and so doth the queen, for that they would be together: and thus will they say, said the queen to Launcelot, have ye no doubt thereof.'

168. *Thither he made, and blew the gateway horn.* Originally, 'wound' for 'blew.'

288. *And in the four loud battles by the shore.* The 1859 reading was 'wild battles.'

The list of the twelve great battles, as Littledale notes, is first found in Nennius, whom Tennyson follows. Compare the translation of Nennius in Bohn's 'Six Chronicles,' p. 408: 'Then it was that the magnanimous Arthur, with all the kings and military force of Britain, fought against the Saxons. And though there were many more noble than himself, yet he was twelve times chosen their commander, and was as often conqueror. The first battle in which he was engaged, was at the mouth of the river Gleni. The second, third, fourth, and fifth, were on another river, by the Britons called Duglas, in the region Linius. The sixth, on the river Bassas. The seventh in the wood Celidon, which the Britains call Cat Coit Celidon. The eighth was near Gurnion Castle, where Arthur bore the image of the Holy Virgin, mother of God, upon his shoulders, and through the power of our Lord Jesus Christ, and the holy Mary, put the Saxons to flight, and pursued them the whole day with great slaughter. The ninth was at the City of Legion, which is called Caer Leon. The tenth was on the banks of the river Trat Treuroit. The eleventh was on the mountain Breguoin, which we call Cat Bregion. The twelfth was a most severe contest, when Arthur penetrated to the hill of Badon. In this engagement, nine hundred and forty fell by his hand alone, no one but the Lord affording him assistance. In all these engagements the Britons were successful. For no strength can avail against the will of the Almighty.'

338. *Till rathe she rose.* For ' rathe,' see ' In Memoriam,' cx. 1 and note.

392. *Paused by the gateway, standing near the shield.* Originally, ' Paused in the gateway, standing by the shield.'

474. *A fury seized them all.* Originally, ' seized on them.'

498. *Then the trumpets blew.* The 1859 edition has ' heralds ' for ' trumpets.'

509. ' *Draw the lance-head,*' *etc.* Compare Malory (xviii. 12): ' O gentle knight Sir Lavaine, help me that this truncheon were out of my side, for it sticketh so sore that it nigh slayeth me. O mine own lord, said Sir Lavaine, I would fain do that might please you, but I dread me sore, and I draw out the truncheon, that ye shall be in peril of death. I charge you, said Sir Launcelot, as ye love me draw it out. And therewithal he descended from his horse, and right so did Sir Lavaine, and forthwith Sir Lavaine drew the truncheon out of his side. And he gave a great shriek, and a marvellous grisly groan, and his blood brast out nigh a pint at once, that at last he sank down, and so swooned pale and deadly.'

513. *And Sir Lancelot gave, etc.* The 1859 edition has ' that other ' for ' Sir Lancelot.'

534. *He must not pass uncared for, etc.* The 1859 edition reads: —

> He must not pass uncared for. Gawain, arise,
> My nephew, and ride forth and find the knight.

543. *Rise and take, etc.* Originally, ' Wherefore take,' etc.

545. *And bring us where he is.* Originally, ' what ' for ' where.'

555. *And Gareth, a good knight.* Originally ' Lamorack ' for ' Gareth;' and, in the next line, ' of a crafty house ' for ' and the child of Lot.'

595. *Ill news, my Queen, for all who love him, this !* Originally, ' these ' for ' this.'

605. *Past to her chamber.* Originally, ' moved to her chamber.'

626. *The victor, but had ridden a random round, etc.* The 1859 edition reads: —

> The victor, that had ridden wildly round,
> To seek him, and was wearied of the search.
> To whom the Lord of Astolat, ' Bide with us,
> And ride no longer wildly, noble Prince ! '

653. *Who lost the hern we slipt her at.* Originally, ' him ' for ' her,' which was a slip, as the male bird was seldom used in the sport, the female being larger and stronger.

658. *And when the shield was brought, etc.* Compare Malory (xviii. 14): ' Ah, mercy, said Sir Gawaine, now is my heart more heavier than ever it was tofore. Why? said Elaine. For I have great cause, said Sir Gawaine; is that knight that owneth this shield your love? Yea truly, said she, my love he is, God would I were his love. Truly, said Sir Gawaine, fair damsel, ye have right, for, and he be your love, ye love the most honorable knight of the world, and the man of most worship. So me thought ever, said the damsel, for never, or that time, for no knight that ever I saw loved I never none erst. God grant, said Sir Gawaine, that either of you may rejoice other, but that is in a great adventure. But truly, said Sir Gawaine unto the damsel, ye may say ye have a fair grace, for why, I have known that noble knight this four and twenty year, and never or that day I nor none other knight, I dare make it good, saw nor heard say that ever he bare token or sign of no lady, gentlewoman, nor maiden, at no justs nor tournament. And therefore, fair maiden, said Sir Gawaine, ye are much beholden to him to give him thanks. But I dread me, said Sir Gawaine, that ye shall never see him in this world, and that is great pity that ever was of earthly knight. Alas, said she, how may this be? Is he slain? I say not so, said Sir Gawaine, but wit ye well, he is grievously wounded, by all manner of signs, and by men's sight more likely to be dead then to be on live; and wit ye well he is the noble knight Sir Launcelot, for by this shield I know him. Alas, said the fair maiden of Astolat, how may this be, and what was his hurt? Truly, said Sir Gawaine, the man in the world that loved him best hurt him so, and I dare say, said Sir Gawaine, and that knight that hurt him knew the very certainty that he had hurt Sir Launcelot, it would be the most sorrow that ever came to his heart. Now, fair father, said then Elaine, I require you give me leave to ride and to seek him, or else I wot well I shall go out of my mind, for I shall never stint till that I find him and my brother Sir Lavaine. Do as it liketh you, said her father, for me right sore repenteth of the hurt of that noble knight. Right so the maid made her ready, and before Sir Gawaine making great dole. Then on the morn Sir Gawaine came to king Arthur, and told him how he had found Sir Launcelot's shield in the keeping of the fair maiden of Astolat. All

# 856 APPENDIX Pages 390 to 390

that knew I aforehand, said king Arthur, and
that caused me I would not suffer you to have
ado at the great justs: for I espied, said king
Arthur, when he came in till his lodging, full
late in the evening in Astolat. But marvel
have I, said Arthur, that ever he would bear
any sign of any damsel: for, or now, I never
heard say nor knew that ever he bare any token
of none earthly woman. By my head, said Sir
Gawaine, the fair maiden of Astolat loveth him
marvellously well; what it meaneth I cannot
say; and she is ridden after to seek him. So
the king and all came to London, and there Sir
Gawaine openly disclosed to all the court that
it was Sir Launcelot that justed best.'

674. *I know there is none other I can love.*
Originally, 'Methinks there is,' etc.

683. *Nay — like enow.* Originally, 'May it
be so?'

728. *Marr'd her friend's aim.* Originally,
' point' for ' aim.'

806. *The cell wherein he slept.* Originally, 'in
which he slept.'

810. *Then she that saw him lying unsleek, un-
shorn, etc.* Compare Malory (xviii. 15): ' And
when she saw him lie so sick and pale in his
bed, she might not speak, but suddenly she fell
to the earth down suddenly in a swoon, and
there she lay a great while. And when she
was relieved she sighed, and said, My lord Sir
Launcelot, alas, why be ye in this plight? and
then she swooned again. And then Sir Launcelot prayed Sir Lavaine to take her up, — And
bring her to me. And when she came to herself, Sir Launcelot kissed her, and said, Fair
maiden, why fare ye thus? Ye put me to pain;
wherefore make ye no more such cheer, for,
and ye be come to comfort me, ye be right welcome, and of this little hurt that I have, I shall
be right hastily whole, by the grace of God.
But I marvel, said Sir Launcelot, who told you
my name.'

826. ' *Your ride hath wearied you.*' Originally, ' has wearied you.'

839. *The weirdly-sculptured gates.* Originally,
' wildly-sculptured.'

877. *The bright image of one face.* Originally,
' the sweet image.'

920. *Seeing I go to-day.* Originally, 'Seeing
I must go to-day.'

924. *Then suddenly and passionately she
spoke, etc.* Compare Malory (xviii. 19): ' My
lord Sir Launcelot, now I see ye will depart,
now, fair knight and courteous knight, have
mercy upon me, and suffer me not to die for
thy love. What would ye that I did? said Sir
Launcelot. I would have you to my husband,
said Elaine. Fair damsel, I thank you, said
Sir Launcelot, but truly, said he, I cast me
never to be wedded man. Then, fair knight,
said she, will ye be my love? Jesu defend me,
said Sir Launcelot, for then I rewarded to your
father and your brother full evil for their great
goodness. Alas, said she, then must I die for
your love. Ye shall not so, said Sir Launcelot,
for wit ye well, fair maiden, I might have been
married and I had would, but I never applied

me to be married yet. But because, fair damsel, that ye love me as ye say ye do, I will, for
your good will and kindness, shew you some
goodness, and that is this; that wheresoever ye
will beset your heart upon some good knight
that will wed you, I shall give you together a
thousand pound yearly, to you and to your
heirs. Thus much will I give you, fair maiden,
for your kindness, and always while I live to be
your own knight. Of all this, said the maiden,
I will none, for, but if ye will wed me, or else
be my lover, wit you well, Sir Launcelot, my
good days are done. Fair damsel, said Sir
Launcelot, of these two things ye must pardon
me. Then she shrieked shrilly, and fell down
in a swoon.'

Stopford Brooke remarks here: ' She rises to
the very verge of innocent maidenliness in passionate love, but she does not go over the verge.
And to be on the verge, and not pass beyond
it, is the very peak of innocent girlhood when
seized by overmastering love. It was as difficult
to represent Elaine as to represent Juliet; and
Tennyson has succeeded well where Shakespeare has succeeded beautifully. It is great
praise, but it is well deserved.'

1015. *Hark the Phantom of the house, etc.*
As Littledale remarks, this phantom is de-
scribed in Croker's stories of the Banshee
(' Fairy Legends,' pages 103, 119). Compare
Scott's ' Rosabelle,' and see Baring Gould's
' Curious Myths ' (2d series, pages 215, 225).

1060. *To whom the gentle sister made reply.*
The 1859 edition has ' which ' for ' whom.'

1147. *Oar'd by the dumb.* Originally,
' Steer'd by the dumb.'

1167. *The shadow of some piece of pointed
lace.* Originally, ' of a piece.'

1230. *In half disdain.* Originally, ' half
disgust.'

1264. *Most noble lord, Sir Lancelot of the
Lake, etc.* Compare Malory (xviii. 20): ' And
this was the intent of the letter: — Most noble
knight, Sir Launcelot, now hath death made us
two at debate for your love; I was your lover,
that men called the fair maiden of Astolat;
therefore unto all ladies I make my moan; yet
pray for my soul, and bury me at the least, and
offer ye my mass-penny. This is my last request. And a clean maiden I died, I take God
to witness. Pray for my soul, Sir Launcelot, as
thou art peerless. — This was all the substance
in the letter. And when it was read the king,
the queen, and all the knights wept for pity of
the doleful complaints. Then was Sir Launcelot sent for. And when he was come, king Arthur made the letter to be read to him; and
when Sir Launcelot heard it word by word, he
said, My lord Arthur, wit ye well I am right
heavy of the death of this fair damsel. God
knoweth I was never causer of her death by my
willing, and that will I report me to her own
brother; here he is, Sir Lavaine. I will not say
nay, said Sir Launcelot, but that she was both
fair and good, and much I was beholden unto
her, but she loved me out of measure. Ye
might have shewed her, said the queen, some

bounty and gentleness, that might have preserved her life. Madam, said Sir Launcelot, she would none other way be answered, but that she would be my wife, or else my love, and of these two I would not grant her; but I proffered her, for her good love that she shewed me, a thousand pound yearly to her and to her heirs, and to wed any manner knight that she could find best to love in her heart. For, madam, said Sir Launcelot, I love not to be constrained to love; for love must arise of the heart, and not by no constraint. That is truth, said the king, and many knights: love is free in himself, and never will be bounden; for where he is bounden he loseth himself. Then said the king unto Sir Launcelot, It will be your worship that ye oversee that she be interred worshipfully. Sir, said Sir Launcelot, that shall be done as I can best devise. And so many knights went thither to behold that fair maiden. And so upon the morn she was interred richly, and Sir Launcelot offered her mass-penny, and all the knights of the Table Round that were there at that time offered with Sir Launcelot. And then the poor man went again with the barget. Then the queen sent for Sir Launcelot, and prayed him of mercy, for why she had been wroth with him causeless. This is not the first time, said Sir Launcelot, that ye have been displeased with me causeless; but, madam, ever I must suffer you, but what sorrow I endure I take no force.'

**1343.** *But Arthur, who beheld his clouded brows, etc.* The 1859 edition reads: —

> But Arthur, who beheld his clouded brows,
> Approach'd him, and with full affection flung
> One arm about his neck, and spake and said,
> 'Lancelot, my Lancelot, thou in whom I have
> Most love and most affiance,' etc.

**1354.** *Seeing the homeless trouble in thine eyes.* For this line the 1859 edition has: 'For the wild people say wild things of thee.'

**1393.** *Lancelot, whom the Lady of the Lake, etc.* The edition of 1859 reads: —

> Lancelot, whom the Lady of the lake [*sic*]
> Stole from his mother — as the story runs —
> She chanted snatches of mysterious song, etc.

**Page 400. THE HOLY GRAIL.**
The story is found in Malory, books xi. to xvii., *preceding* the story of Elaine, in xviii. The poet follows his original closely here and there, but omits much that Malory gives and often varies from him.

**15.** *That puff'd the swaying branches into smoke.* For another allusion to the abundant pollen of the yew, scattered into 'smoke' by the wind, see 'In Memoriam,' xxxix: —

> Old warder of these buried bones,
>   And answering now my random stroke
>   With fruitful cloud and living smoke,
> Dark yew, that graspest at the stones, etc.

**48.** *The blessed land of Aromat.* 'Aromat —a name suggestive of Sabæan spicery and sweet Eastern balms — is used for Arimathea, a town in Palestine, probably the modern Ramleh, and the home of the "honorable counsellor, which also waited for the kingdom of God," Joseph, who placed Christ in the sepulchre that had been made for himself. The mediæval legend added that Joseph had received in the Grail the blood that flowed from the Saviour's side' (Littledale).

**49.** *When the dead Went wandering o'er Moriah.* See Matthew, xxvii. 50 fol.

**52.** *To Glastonbury, where the winter thorn, etc.* There is a variety of hawthorn which puts forth leaves and flowers about the time of Christmas. It is said to have originated at Glastonbury Abbey, and the original thorn was believed to have been the staff with which Joseph of Arimathea aided his steps on his wanderings from the Holy Land to Glastonbury, where he is said to have founded the celebrated Abbey. The first church, according to the legend, was 'built of wattles,' and interwoven twigs. Compare 'Balin and Balan': —

> And one was rough with wattling, and the walls
> Of that low church he built at Glastonbury.

In A. D. 439 St. Patrick is said to have visited the place, and to have founded the monastery, of which he became the abbot. In 542 King Arthur was buried here. The abbey was several times repaired and rebuilt before the reign of Henry II., when it was destroyed by fire, and the large and splendid structure the ruins of which still remain was erected. It was the wealthiest abbey in England, except Westminster.

**182.** *And all at once, as there we sat, etc.* Compare Malory (xiii. 7): 'And every knight sat in his own place as they were toforehand. Then anon they heard cracking and crying of thunder, that them thought that the place should all to-drive. In the midst of this blast entered a sun-beam more clearer by seven times than ever they saw day, and all they were alighted of the grace of the Holy Ghost. Then began every knight to behold other, and either saw other by their seeming fairer than ever they saw afore. Not for then there was no knight might speak one word a great while, and so they looked every man on other, as they had been dumb. Then there entered into the hall the holy Graile covered with white samite, but there was none might see it, nor who bare it. And there was all the hall full filled with good odors, and every knight had such meats and drinks as he best loved in this world: and when the holy Graile had been borne through the hall, then the holy vessel departed suddenly, that they wist not where it became. Then had they all breath to speak. And then the king yielded thankings unto God of his good grace that he had sent them. Certes, said the king, we ought to thank our Lord Jesu greatly, for that he hath showed us this day at the reverence of this high feast of Pentecost. Now, said Sir Gawaine, we have been served this day of what meats and drinks we thought on, but one thing beguiled us, we might not see the holy Graile, it was so preciously covered: wherefore I will make here avow, that to-morn, without longer abiding, I shall labor in the quest of the Sancgreal, that I shall hold me out a twelve-month and a day, or more if need be, and never shall I return again unto the court till I have seen it more openly than it hath been seen here: and if I may not speed, I shall return again as he that may not be against the will of our Lord Jesu Christ. When they of the Table Round heard Sir Gawaine say so, they arose up the most party, and made such avows as Sir Ga-waine had made.

'Anon as king Arthur heard this he was greatly displeased, for he wist well that they might not againsay their avows. Alas! said king Arthur unto Sir Gawaine, ye have nigh slain me with the avow and promise that ye have made. For through you ye have bereft me of the fairest fellowship and the truest of knight-hood that ever were seen together in any realm of the world. For when they depart from hence, I am sure they all shall never meet more in this world, for they shall die many in the quest. And so it forethinketh me a little, for I have loved them as well as my life, wherefore it shall grieve me right sore the departition of this fellowship. For I have had an old custom to have them in my fellowship.'

256. *O, there, perchance, when all our wars are done.* The 1869 edition has 'then' for 'there.'

298. *But ye, that follow but the leader's bell.* Originally, 'you' for 'ye.'

300. *Taliessin is our fullest throat of song.* The name means 'the radiant brow.' He was 'the prince of British singers, and flourished in the seventh century' (Littledale). Compare Gray, 'The Bard': 'Hear from the grave, great Taliessin, hear!'

312. *The strong White Horse.* Referring to the banner of Hengist.

318. *This chance of noble deeds.* Originally, 'The chance,' etc.

350. *On wyvern, lion, dragon, griffin, swan.* Heraldic devices. The 'wyvern' is a dragon-like creature. Compare 'Aylmer's Field': 'Whose blazing wyvern weathercock'd the spire,' etc.

352. *But in the ways below.* The 1869 edition has 'street' for 'ways;' and in 355 it reads: 'For sorrow, and in the middle street the Queen.' In 358, 359 it reads: —

And then we reach'd the weirdly-sculptured gates
Where Arthur's wars were render'd mystically.

421. *And I rode on and found a mighty hill, etc.* The 1869 reading was: 'And on I rode;' and, in the preceding line, 'wearied' for 'wearying.'

433. *That so cried out upon me.* The 1869 edition omits 'out' — probably a misprint.

466. *I saw the fiery face as of a child, etc.* Compare Malory (xvii. 20): 'And then he took an ubbly [sacramental cake], which was made in likeness of bread; and at the lifting up there came a figure in likeness of a child, and the vis-age was as red and as bright as any fire, and smote himself into the bread, so that they all

saw it, that the bread was formed of a fleshly man, and then he put it into the holy vessel again.'

489. *There rose a hill, etc.* Originally, 'Then rose,' etc.

574. *Thither I made, etc.* Originally, 'Whither I made,' etc.

648. *For Lancelot's kith and kin so worship him.* The 1869 edition reads: 'For Lancelot's kith and kin adore him so.'

681. *The seven clear stars of Arthur's Table Round.* The seven stars of the Great Bear, or 'Charles's Wain.'

792. *But such a blast, my King, began to blow, etc.* Compare Malory (xvii. 14): 'And the wind arose, and drove Launcelot more than a month throughout the sea, where he slept but little, but prayed to God that he might see some tid-ings of the Sancgreal. So it befell on a night, at midnight he arrived afore a castle, on the back side, which was rich and fair. And there was a postern opened towards the sea, and was open without any keeping, save two lions kept the entry; and the moon shone clear. Anon Sir Launcelot heard a voice that said, Launce-lot, go out of this ship, and enter into the castle, where thou shalt see a great part of thy desire. Then he ran to his arms, and so armed him, and so he went to the gate, and saw the lions. Then set he hand to his sword, and drew it. Then there came a dwarf suddenly, and smote him on the arm so sore that the sword fell out of his hand. Then heard he a voice say, Oh man of evil faith and poor belief, wherefore trowest thou more on thy harness than in thy Maker? for He might more avail thee than thine ar-mor, in whose service thou art set. Then said Launcelot, Fair Father, Jesu Christ, I thank thee of thy great mercy, that thou reprovest me of my misdeed. Now see I well that ye hold me for your servant. Then took he again his sword, and put it up in his sheath, and made a cross in his forehead, and came to the lions, and they made semblant to do him harm. Notwith-standing he passed by them without hurt, and entered into the castle to the chief fortress, and there were they all at rest. Then Launce-lot entered in so armed, for he found no gate nor door but it was open. And at the last he found a chamber whereof the door was shut, and he set his hand thereto to have opened it, but he might not.'

Stopford Brooke says of this part of the poem: 'Its basis is to be found in the old tale; but whoever reads it in Malory's "Morte Darthur" will see how imaginatively it has been re-con-ceived. It is full of the true romantic element; it is close to the essence of the story of the Holy Grail; there is nothing in the "Idylls" more beautiful in vision and in sound; and the art with which it is worked is as finished as the conception is majestic.'

810. *The enchanted towers of Carbonek.* The name is from Malory (xvii. 16). After Lance-lot had lain 'four and twenty days, and also many nights, . . . still as a dead man,' he recovered from the long swoon. 'Then they

asked him how it stood with him. Forsooth, said he, I am whole of body, thanked be our Lord; therefore, sirs, for God's love tell me where that I am? Then said they all that he was in the castle of Carbonek.'

862. *Deafer than the blue-eyed cat.* Compare Darwin, 'Origin of Species,' chap. i.: 'Thus cats which are entirely white and have blue eyes are generally deaf; but it has lately been pointed out by Mr. Tait that this is confined to the males.'

Page 413. PELLEAS AND ETTARRE.

Little altered since its first appearance in 1869 except for the insertion of a passage of seventeen lines (386-403). The story is from Malory (iv. 20-23), but the poet modifies many of the details and changes the *dénoûment.*

20. *The forest call'd of Dean.* See on 'The Marriage of Geraint,' 146.

65. *Pelleas gazing thought, etc.* The 1869 edition reads: 'And Pelleas gazing thought,' etc.

342. *Prowest knight.* That is, bravest, most valiant. Compare Spenser, 'Faërie Queene,' ii. 3. 15: 'For they be two the prowest knights on grownd.'

379. '*Ay,' thought Gawain, ' and you be fair enow.*' The 1869 edition has 'ye' for ' you.'

386-404. *Hot was the night . . . and bound his horse, etc.* For these nineteen lines the 1869 edition has only the following: —

> The night was hot: he could not rest but rode
> Ere midnight to her walls, and bound his horse, etc.

409. *Then he crost the court, etc.* The 1869 edition reads: —

> Then he crost the court,
> And saw the postern portal also wide
> Yawning; and up a slope of garden, all
> Of roses white and red, and wild ones mixt, etc.

419. *Then was he ware of three pavilions rear'd, etc.* The 1869 edition reads: —

> Then was he ware that white pavilions rose,
> Three from the bushes, gilden-peakt.

421. *Her lurdane knights.* Her stupid, worthless knights. 'Lurdane' (really from the Old French *lourdin*, dull, blockish, from *lourd*) was supposed by some of our old authors to be a corruption of 'lord Dane,' formed in derision of the Danes. It was used as both adjective and noun. Compare the 'Mirror for Magistrates': —

> In every house *lord Dane* did then rule all,
> Whence laysie lozels *lurdanes* now we call.

455. *Huge, solid, etc.* The 1869 edition has 'So solid,' etc.

553. '*No name, no name,' he shouted.* The 1869 edition reads: ' I have no name,' etc.

560. *Yell'd the youth.* The 1869 edition reads: ' yell'd the other.'

565. *Yea, between thy lips — and sharp.* Littledale remarks: ' The metaphor of the slanderous tongue, that sharp weapon between the lips, is no doubt nearly as old as the human race itself.'

594. *And all talk died, etc.* Compare 'Sir Lancelot and Queen Guinevere' : —

> Sometimes the sparhawk wheel'd along
> Hush'd all the groves for fear of wrong.

Page 422. THE LAST TOURNAMENT.

Few changes have been made in this Idyll since its appearance in the 'Contemporary Review' for December, 1871. The outline of the story of Tristram and his two Isolts and the vengeance of Mark is taken from Malory, but the rest is Tennyson's own.

Littledale gives the following abstract of the Tristram story: —

' Tristram, having been wounded by an Irish spear, can only be healed by an Irish hand, so he goes to Ireland, and is treated by La Beale Isoud or Isolt, daughter of the Irish king. On his return he gives a glowing description of her to his uncle Mark, who sends him back as his envoy to ask for her hand. On the voyage from Ireland they innocently drink the potent philtre, and their fatal love for each other begins. Long after, when the effects of the philtre have become exhausted, Tristram is hurt by a poisoned arrow, and goes to Brittany to be cured by King Hoel's daughter, Isolt of the White Hands (Isoud la blanche Maynys), whom he loves and marries. Lancelot reproaches him for his inconstancy to La Beale Isoud, and the lady herself writes sadly to him. Tristram's old love revives, and he resolves to go to Cornwall to see his old love. There is a quarrel, and Tristram reproaches Isolt for her unfaithfulness to him. He goes mad, and throws Dagonet into a well. After many adventures Arthur knights him, and he runs away with Isolt, but is wounded in a tournament. Mark undertakes to nurse him, which he does by putting him into a dungeon. Tristram and Isolt again escape, and live in Lancelot's castle of Joyous Gard; he goes out riding with Isolt, both of them being clad in green attire, when probably the bower mentioned by Tennyson is constructed. He fights with many knights; but we need not go into the rest of his story, of which enough has been given to show its affinity to the Lancelot story, and to illustrate the love-scene with Isolt in the Idyll. We may, however, quote Malory's last words about them: "That traitor king Mark slew the noble knight Sir Tristram, as he sat harping afore his lady La Beale Isoud, with a trenchant glaive, for whose death was much bewailing of every knight that ever was in Arthur's days . . . and La Beale Isoud died, swooning upon the cross of Sir Tristram, whereof was great pity."'

10. *For Arthur and Sir Lancelot riding once, etc.* Tennyson has apparently based his story of the ruby necklace on an incident in the life of Alfred, quoted in Stanley's ' Book of Birds,' where it is credited to the ' Monast. Anglic.,' vol. i.: ' Alfred, King of the West Saxons, went out one day a-hunting, and passing by a certain wood heard, as he supposed, the cry of an infant from the top of a tree, and forthwith diligently inquiring of the huntsmen what that doleful sound could be, commanded one of them to climb the tree, when on the top of it was found an eagle's nest, and lo ! therein a sweet-

faced infant, wrapped up in a purple mantle, and upon each arm a bracelet of gold, a clear sign that he was born of noble parents. Whereupon the king took charge of him, and caused him to be baptized; and, because he was found in a nest, he gave him the name of *Nestingum*, and, in aftertime, having nobly educated him, he advanced him to the dignity of an earl.'

37.  *Those diamonds that I rescued from the tarn.* See 'Lancelot and Elaine,' 34 fol.

39.  *Would rather you had let them fall.* Originally, ' ye ' for ' you.'

51.  *A great jousts.* This use of ' jousts ' in the singular is peculiar, and is not mentioned in the dictionaries.

150.  *And vail'd his eyes again.* Cast down his eyes. Compare ' Guinevere,' line 657 below: 'made her vail her eyes.' This word ' vail ' has no connection with ' veil,' though often confounded with it. It is contracted from ' avail,' or ' avale,' the French ' avaler ' (Latin, ' ad vallem '). Compare ' Hamlet,' i. 2. 70: —

> Do not forever with thy vailed lids
> Seek for thy noble father in the dust.

' Avail ' occurs in Malory (v. 12): ' Then the King availed his visor, with a meek and lowly countenance,' etc.

216.  *A swarthy one.* Originally, ' a swarthy dame.'

222.  *Come — let us gladden their sad eyes.* Originally, ' comfort their sad eyes.'

252.  *And while he twangled, little Dagonet stood, etc.* Littledale says that ' Dagonet's standing still is doubtless meant to recall St. Matthew, xi. 17: "We have piped unto you, and ye have not danced," etc.' It may or may not remind us of that passage, but I doubt whether it was ' meant ' to do so.

256.  *And being ask'd, ' Why skipt ye not, Sir Fool ? '* Originally, ' Then being ask'd,' etc.

259.  *Than any broken music thou canst make.* Originally, ' ye can make.' ' Properly speaking, " broken music " meant either (as Chappell explains) short unsustained notes, such as are made on stringed instruments when played without a bow; or concerted music, played by several instruments in combination ' (Littledale).

322.  *A Paynim harper.* The allusion to Orpheus is obvious.

333.  *The Harp of Arthur.* See on ' Gareth and Lynette,' 1281.

343.  *The black king's highway.* The ' broad road leading to destruction.'

357.  *Burning spurge.* A plant of the genus *Euphorbia*, which burns with an acrid smoke.

371.  *But at the slot or fewmets of a deer.* ' Slot ' and ' fewmets ' (footprints and droppings) are old terms of ' venerie,' or woodcraft (Littledale).

373.  *From lawn to lawn.* For ' lawn ' as an open place in a forest, compare ' A Dream of Fair Women ': —

> On those long, rank, dark wood-walks drench'd in dew,
> Leading from lawn to lawn.

Malory (iv. 19) has the word in this sense: ' So on the morn they rode into the forest of adventure till they came to a lawn, and thereby they found a cross,' etc.

450.  *The scorpion-worm that twists itself in hell, etc.* A legendary creature, evidently suggested by the old notion (long since proved false by naturalists) that the scorpion, if surrounded by fire, will sting itself to death. The use of *worm* is suggested by the obsolete sense of snake, dragon, etc. Compare Shakespeare, ' Measure for Measure,' iii. 1. 17 : —

> For thou dost fear the soft and tender fork
> Of a poor worm.

It is in a similar sense that Venus (' Venus and Adonis,' 933) calls Death ' grim-grinning ghost, earth's worm.'

461.  *Fall, as the crest of some slow-arching wave.* The elaborate simile seems out of keeping with the fall of the drunken knight from his horse; but it is an ' Homeric echo,' like not a few others in the Idylls.

467.  *Then the knights, etc.* Originally, ' while ' for ' then.'

477.  *Then, echoing yell with yell.* Originally, ' Then, yell with yell echoing.'

479.  *Alioth and Alcor.* Stars in the Great Bear. Alcor is really a fifth-magnitude star close to Mizar, and distinguishable only by good eyes. For the reference to the Aurora borealis, compare ' The Passing of Arthur,' 307.

481.  *As the water Moab saw, etc.* See 2 Kings, iii. 22.

483.  *Lazy-plunging sea.* Compare ' The Palace of Art ': —

> that hears all night
> The plunging seas draw backward from the land
> Their moon-led waters white;

and ' A Dream of Fair Women ': —

> I would the white cold heavy-plunging foam,
> Whirl'd by the wind, had roll'd me deep below,
> Then when I left my home.

495.  *What if she hate me now?* Originally, ' an ' for ' if,' as also in the next line.

501.  *Last in a roky hollow, belling, etc.* ' Roky ' (associated with ' reek ') means misty, foggy. For ' belling ' as applied to hounds, compare ' A Midsummer-Night's Dream,' iv. 1. 128: —

> Slow in pursuit, but match'd in mouth like bells,
> Each under each;

that is, like a chime of bells.

502.  *Felt the goodly hounds Yelp at his heart.* Littledale thinks this may mean that ' the belling of the hounds set the hunter's heart throbbing in harmony — he longed to follow the chase, but turned aside to Tintagil;' but I prefer Elsdale's explanation, that it is a presentiment of coming disaster.

504.  *Tintagil, half in sea and high on land.* The ruins of the castle are still to be seen ' by the Cornish sea,' six miles from Camelford. The keep, the oldest part of the structure, is probably Norman, but there may have been a Saxon, and perhaps also a British, stronghold on the same site.

509. *The spiring stone.* The spiral stairway of stone. The dictionaries do not recognize this sense of 'spiring,' but I have no doubt that it was what Tennyson had in mind, rather than rising like a spire.

570. *To sin in leading-strings.* Referring to what he had just said about the sin of Guinevere.

588. *The King was all fulfill'd with gratefulness.* For 'fulfil' in the old sense of fill full, compare Shakespeare, Sonnet 136. 5: —

'Will' will fulfil the treasure of thy love,
Ay, fill it full with wills, and my will one.

Wiclif has in Matthew, v. 6: 'Blessid be thei that hungren and thirsten rigtwisnesse; for thei schal be fulfillid.'

627. *The swineherd's malkin in the mast.* Compare 'The Princess,' v.: —

If this be he, — or a draggled mawkin, thou,
That tends her bristled grunters in the sludge !

'Mawkin' is merely a phonetic spelling of 'malkin,' which is probably a diminutive of 'Mall,' or 'Mary,' though it was also connected with 'Matilda.' The 'Promptorium Parvulorum' has: 'Malkyne, or Mawt, proper name *Matildis.*'

629. *Far other was the Tristram, Arthur's knight!* This line is not in the 1st edition.

650. *Vows! did you keep the vow you made to Mark?* The 1st edition has 'ye' for 'you.'

690. *The wide world laughs at it.* The 1st edition has 'great world.'

692. *The ptarmigan that whitens ere his hour, etc.* 'The color of this bird varies, being brownish-gray in summer and white in winter. The changes of plumage enable it to harmonize with its surroundings at the various seasons. If the ptarmigan's feathers were to turn white before the winter snows began, it would be seen by the eagle-owls and falcons, and would soon be killed' (Littledale).

695. *The garnet-headed yaffingale.* The green woodpecker, *Gecinus viridis;* so called from its loud laughing notes. It is also known as the 'yaffle' (or 'yaffil') and 'yaffler.'

743. *He spoke, he turn'd, then flinging round her neck, etc.* The 1st edition reads: —

He rose, he turn'd, and, flinging round her neck,
Claspt it; but while he bow'd himself to lay
Warm kisses in the hollow of her throat,
Out of the dark, etc.

752. *The great Queen's bower was dark.* She had fled, as the next Idyll explains.

Page 433. GUINEVERE.

The poet is indebted to Malory for only a few hints of the story — Arthur's discovery of the guilt of Lancelot and Guinevere; her condemnation to be burnt alive; her escape from the stake through Lancelot, who carries her off to his castle of La Joyeuse Gard; the siege of the castle by Arthur, who compels Lancelot to give up the Queen; and her retirement — but not until after Arthur's death — to Amesbury, where she 'was ruler and abbess as reason would.'

9. *For hither had she fled, etc.* The 1859 reading was: —

For hither had she fled, her cause of flight
Sir Modred; he the nearest to the King,
His nephew, ever like a subtle beast,
Lay couchant, etc.

Littledale notes that 'by a curious coincidence, this is the very simile that Arthur Hallam used to describe Tennyson's fame waiting to come upon him': —

A being full of clearest insight,
            . . . whose fame
Is couching now with panther eyes intent,
As who shall say, 'I'll spring to him anon,
And have him for my own.'

'Amesbury;' now Amesbury, is about eight miles from Salisbury, and the old Abbey Church is still standing.

15. *Lords of the White Horse.* See on 'Lancelot and Elaine,' 297.

22. *Plumes that mock'd the may.* That is, white as the hawthorn blossoms. Compare 'The Miller's Daughter': 'The lanes, you know, were white with may;' and see note on 'Gareth and Lynette,' 642.

97, 98. *And part for ever. Vivien, lurking, heard, etc.* The 1859 ed. reads: 'And part for ever. Passion-pale they met,' etc. The addition is not in the ed. of 1884, but I find it in that of 1890. 'They met' is now ambiguous.

147. *For housel or for shrift.* For receiving the Eucharist, or for confession.

166. *Late, late, so late!* It is hardly necessary to say that the song is founded on the parable of the wise and foolish virgins (Matthew, xxv.).

289. *Bude and Bos.* Districts of Cornwall.

292. *Of dark Tintagil.* See page 860, note on 504. The 1859 edition has 'Dundagil.'

400. *Came to that point where first she saw the King.* The 1859 edition has 'when first.'

470. *To honor his own word as if his God's.* This line is not in the 1859 edition.

481. *Before I wedded thee.* The 1859 edition has 'until I wedded.'

535. *The flaming death.* Being burned at the stake, a punishment for unfaithful wives mentioned several times by Malory.

569. *Where I must strike against the man they call, etc.* The 1859 edition reads: —

Where I must strike against my sister's son,
Leagued with the lords of the White Horse and knights
Once mine, and strike him dead, etc.

601. *Moving ghostlike to his doom.* 'That doom is told in "The Passing of Arthur," but that he is already enwound by its misty pall, and himself a ghost in it, is nobly conceived, and as splendidly expressed' (Stopford Brooke).

642. *I yearn'd for warmth and color.* The 1859 edition has: 'I wanted warmth,' etc.

657. *Made her vail her eyes.* See on 'The Last Tournament,' 150.

Page 443. THE PASSING OF ARTHUR.

This Idyll in its present form was first published in the 'Holy Grail' volume, 1869; but, with the exception of 169 lines at the beginning and 30 at the close, it was printed in 1842 in 'The Epic,' which is still included in the collected poems. See the notes on that poem, and also p. 302 above.

The following notice appears in the 'Holy Grail' volume, opposite the titlepage: —

'These four "Idylls of the King" are printed in their present form for the convenience of those who possess the former volume.

'The whole series should be read, and is to-day published, in the following order: —

### The Coming of Arthur.

### The Round Table.

### Geraint and Enid.

### Merlin and Vivien.

### Lancelot and Elaine.

### The Holy Grail.

### Pelleas and Ettarre.

### Guinevere.

### The Passing of Arthur.[1]

[1] This last, the earliest written of the poems, is here connected with the rest in accordance with an early project of the author's.'

Apparently the addition of 'Gareth and Ly-nette' and 'The Last Tournament' was an afterthought; and later the poet decided to divide 'Geraint and Enid,' and to add 'Balin and Balan,' making 'twelve books' in all.

The story of 'The Passing of Arthur' is taken from Malory (xxi. 5).

6–28. *For on their march to westward, . . . I pass, but shall not die.* These twenty-three lines are not in the 1869 edition, which goes on thus: 'Before that last weird battle in the west,' etc.

61. *Once thine whom thou hast loved, etc.* The reading of 1869 was: —

Once thine, whom thou hast loved, but baser now
Than heathen scoffing at their vows and thee.

68. *And brake the petty kings, and fought with Rome.* This line is not in the 1869 edition, in which the next line begins with 'And thrust,' etc.

85. *And the long mountains, etc.* Originally, 'the long mountain.'

129. *Only the wan wave.* Originally, 'waste wave.'

170. *So all day long the noise of battle roll'd.* With this sonorous line the early 'Morte d'Arthur' begins.

175. *The bold Sir Bedivere uplifted him.* After this line, the 'Morte d'Arthur' of 1842 has the line, 'Sir Bedivere, the last of all his knights;' omitted here, of course, because the fact is mentioned in line 2 of the new matter.

195. *Thou therefore take my brand Excalibur, etc.* Compare Malory (xxi. 5): 'But my time hieth fast, said the king. Therefore said Arthur, take thou Excalibur, my good sword, and go with it to yonder water side, and when thou comest there, I charge thee throw my sword in that water, and come again, and tell me what thou there seest. My lord, said Bedivere, your commandment shall be done, and lightly bring you word again. So Sir Bedivere departed, and by the way he beheld that noble sword, that the pommel and haft were all of precious stones, and then he said to himself, If I throw this rich sword in the water, thereof shall never come good, but harm and loss. And then Sir Bedivere hid Excalibur under a tree. And as soon as he might he came again unto the king, and said he had been at the water, and had thrown the sword into the water. What sawest thou there? said the king. Sir, he said, I saw nothing but waves and winds. That is untruly said of thee, said the king; therefore go thou lightly again, and do my command as thou art to me lief and dear, spare not, but throw it in. Then Sir Bedivere returned again, and took the sword in his hand; and then him thought sin and shame to throw away that noble sword; and so eft he hid the sword, and returned again, and told to the king that he had been at the water, and done his commandment. What saw thou there? said the king. Sir, he said, I saw nothing but the waters wap and the waves wan. Ah traitor, untrue, said king Arthur, now hast thou betrayed me twice. Who would have wend that thou that hast been to me so lief and dear, and thou art named a noble knight, and would betray me for the riches of the sword. But now go again lightly, for thy long tarrying putteth me in great jeopardy of my life, for I have taken cold. And but if thou do now as I bid thee, if ever I may see thee, I shall slay thee with mine own hands, for thou wouldest for my rich sword see me dead. Then Sir Bedivere departed, and went to the sword, and lightly took it up, and went to the water side, and there he bound the girdle about the hilts, and then he threw the sword as far into the water as he might, and there came an arm and an hand above the water, and met it, and caught it, and so shook it thrice and brandished, and then vanished away the hand with the sword in the water. So Sir Bedivere came again to the king, and told him what he saw. Alas, said the king, help me hence, for I dread me I have tarried over long. Then Sir Bedivere took the king upon his back, and so went with him to that water side. And when they were at the water side, even fast by the bank hoved a little barge, with many fair ladies in it, and among them all was a queen, and all they had black hoods, and all they wept and shrieked when they saw king Arthur. Now put me into the barge, said the king: and so he did softly. And there received him three queens with great mourning, and so they set him down, and in one of their laps king Arthur laid his head, and then that queen said, Ah, dear brother, why have ye tarried so long from me? Alas, this wound on your head hath caught over much cold. And so then they rowed from the land; and Sir

Bedivere beheld all those ladies go from him. Then Sir Bedivere cried, Ah, my lord Arthur, what shall become of me now ye go from me, and leave me here alone among mine enemies. Comfort thyself, said the king, and do as well as thou mayest, for in me is no trust for to trust in. For I will into the vale of Avilion, to heal me of my grievous wound. And if thou hear never more of me, pray for my soul. But ever the queens and the ladies wept and shrieked, that it was pity to hear. And as soon as Sir Bedivere had lost the sight of the barge, he wept and wailed, and so took the forest, and so he went all that night, and in the morning he was ware betwixt two holts hoar of a chapel and an hermitage.'

354. *Dry clash'd his harness in the icy caves, etc.* 'We hear all the changes on the vowel *a* — every sound of it used to give the impression — and then, in a moment, the verse runs into breadth, smoothness, and vastness; for Bedivere comes to the shore and sees the great water: —

> And on a sudden, lo ! the level lake
> And the long glories of the winter moon.

in which the vowel *o* in its changes is used as the vowel *a* has been used before' (Stopford Brooke).

379. *And dropping bitter tears against a brow.* The 1869 edition has 'his brow.'

435. *Like some full-breasted swan.* Compare 'The Dying Swan.'

440. *And on the mere the wailing died away.* Here the original ' Morte d'Arthur ' ends.

The next five lines are not in the 1869 edition, which goes on thus: —

> At length he groan'd, and turning slowly clomb
> The last hard footstep of that iron crag.

445. *Even to the highest he could climb.* The 1869 edition has ' E'en,' for which the printer is probably responsible, as Tennyson never uses it.

*To the Queen.* This epilogue has not been altered since it first appeared in the 'Library Edition,' 1872–73.

3. *That rememberable day.* Referring to the public thanksgiving in February, 1872, on the recovery of the Prince of Wales from typhoid fever.

12. *Thunderless lightnings striking under sea, etc.* Congratulatory despatches by submarine telegraph.

14. *That true North, etc.* When Manitoba was added to the Dominion of Canada, complaint was made in England of the cost of maintaining the colonial possessions in North America. Mr. Justin McCarthy, in his ' History of Our Own Times,' says: ' For some years a feeling was spreading in England which began to find expression in repeated and very distinct suggestions that the Canadians had better begin to think of looking out for themselves. Many Englishmen complained of this country being expected to undertake the principal cost of the defences of Canada, and to guarantee her railway schemes, especially when the commer-

cial policy which Canada adopted towards England was one of a strictly protective character.'

20. *The roar of Hougoumont.* The battle of Waterloo. The *Château of Hougoumont*, with its massive buildings, its gardens and plantations, was occupied by the Allies, and ' formed the key to the British position.' It is computed that ' during the day the attacks of nearly 12,000 men were launched against this miniature fortress, notwithstanding which the garrison held out to the last.'

35. *For one to whom I made it, etc.* Referring to the dedication of the 'Idylls' to the memory of Prince Albert.

38. *Ideal manhood closed in real man.* This line does not appear in any English or American edition up to the present time (1898); but the 'Memoir' (vol. ii. p. 129) states that the poet, thinking that ' perhaps he had not made the real humanity of the King sufficiently clear in his epilogue,' inserted this line ' in 1891, as his last correction.' It is probably through mere oversight that it has not been inserted in the editions published since 1891.

41. *Geoffrey's book, or him of Malleor's.* Geoffrey of Monmouth and Malory, whose name was also written Malorye, Maleore, and Malleor.

55. *With poisonous honey stolen from France.* Compare ' Locksley Hall Sixty Years After,' 145 : ' Set the maiden fancies wallowing in the troughs of Zolaism,' etc. Littledale quotes Goldwin Smith, ' Essays': ' As to French novels, Carlyle says of one of the most famous of the last century that after reading it you ought to wash seven times in Jordan; but after reading the French novels of the present day, in which lewdness is sprinkled with sentimental rosewater, and deodorized, but not disinfected, your washings had better be seventy times seven.'

Page 452. THE FIRST QUARREL.

The poem is 'an idyll of the hearth inspired with life: Nelly and Harry are lifelike in the very respect in which Annie and Philip in " Enoch Arden " are idealized. They speak the rough, genuine language of the fisherfolk ' (Waugh).

Page 454. RIZPAH.

A reviewer in ' Macmillan's Magazine' for January, 1881, says of the poem: ' As the recital in lyric form of a weird tale of misery and madness, this poem is unmatched in Mr. Tennyson's work. An old woman, in her fierce and at the same time trembling dotage, tells a lady who has come to visit her how her boy had long ago been hung in chains, under the old laws of England, for robbing the mail; how he had done it not in wickedness but in recklessness, but how her plea to that effect had availed him nothing; how, when she had gone to visit him in prison, she had been forced from him by the jailer, with his cry of "mother, mother ! " ringing in her ears; how the same cry rang afterwards in her brain while she lay bound and beaten in a madhouse; and how, when she was at last set free, she used to steal out on stormy nights, and gather together his bones from beneath the gallows, until she had gathered them every one and buried them in consecrated ground beside the churchyard wall. It is as terrible a tale as could well be imagined, and is told with a plain and classic force, a freedom from shrillness or emphasis, which leaves the terror all the more piercing and unescapable.'

The ' Edinburgh Review ' for October, 1881, refers to the poem as one in which Tennyson ' has broken on the world with a new strength and splendor,' and ' has achieved a new reputation.' The writer adds: ' Of this astonishing production it has been said that, were all the rest of the author's works destroyed, this alone would at once place him among the first of the world's poets. Such was the verdict pronounced by Mr. Swinburne. It has all his characteristic generosity, and not much of his characteristic exaggeration. . . . A work of this order can never be done justice to by quotations; but we have used them with no further end than to indicate baldly the outline of the poet's subject. For his sublime treatment of it, for the tenderness and the terror of his pathos, we must refer the reader to the poem itself in its entirety. Nothing in " Maud," nothing in " Guinevere," can approach in power to " Rizpah." This fact can, we conceive, be accounted for by the special nature of the subject. Of all the affections of human nature that are least subject to change, either in the way of contraction or development, is the passion of mother for child. It asks least aid either from faith or reason. And something may be said of the three other poems that we have associated with " Rizpah " [' The First Quarrel,' ' The Northern Cobbler,' and ' The Village Wife ']. These three deal all of them with the life of the common people, and touch our feelings and principles in their rudest and simplest form. They take us below the reach of either conscious faith or philosophy; and they elude, they do not meet, the problems of human destiny. Thus Mr. Tennyson's genius has escaped, in these cases, from the external circumstances that have been depressing it; and, once supplied with a fitting theme to handle, it has shown itself as strong, if not stronger than ever.'

For the suggestion of the title of ' Rizpah,' see 2 Samuel, xxi. 1-14.

Line 7. *The creak of the chain.* It was formerly the custom in England to hang the bodies of certain malefactors in chains after execution. The bodies of pirates were so hanged on the banks of the Thames.

54. *They had moved in my side.* For the use of ' side,' compare ' Comus,' 1009: —

> And from her fair unspotted side
> Two blissful twins are to be born,
> Youth and Joy; so Jove hath sworn.

Page 456. THE NORTHERN COBBLER.
' The general lines of the Northern Cobbler's position are the same as of many reformed drinkers, but no one but himself could have set

the bottle up in the window, or declared that he would take it with him after death, like a Norse warrior his sword, before the throne ' (Stopford Brooke).

Line 6. *The line.* The equator.

13. *I could fettle and clump, etc.* Repair and put new soles to old boots and shoes. Shakespeare uses ' fettle ' once, in ' Romeo and Juliet,' iii. 5. 154: —

> But fettle your fine joints 'gainst Thursday next,
> To go with Paris to Saint Peter's Church;

where it means to prepare, make ready.

19. *I slither'd.* That is, slipped.

20. *Slaäpe down i' the squad.* Suddenly down in the slush.

22. *Scrawm'd and scratted.* Clawed and scratched.

32. *Weär'd it o' liquor.* Spent it for liquor.

53. *All in a tew.* All in a fluster.

78. *Snaggy.* Snappish, ill-tempered.

108. *Feät.* Trim; used by Shakespeare several times.

110. *A codlin.* A codling, or unripe apple. Compare ' Twelfth Night,' i. 5. 167: ' a codling when 't is almost an apple.'

Page 458. THE REVENGE.

Line 51. *Having that within her womb, etc.* ' Womb ' is here used in its original sense of belly. Compare Wiclif's Bible, Luke, xv. 16: ' And he coveitide to fille his wombe of the coddis that the hoggis eaten,' etc.

118. *And the little Revenge herself went down, etc.* Markham, in a postscript to his poem, says: ' What became of the *Reuenge* after Sir *Richards* death, diuers report diuersly, but the most probable and sufficient proofe sayth, that within fewe dayes after the Knights death, there arose a great storme from the VVest and North-west, that all the Fleet was disperced, aswell the *Indian* Fleet, which were then come vnto them, as all the rest of the *Armada*, which attended their ariuall; of vvhich fourteene sayle, together with the *Reuenge*, and in her two hundred *Spanyards*, were cast away vppon the Ile of *S. Michaels;* so it pleased them to honour the buriall of that renowned Ship the *Reuenge*, not suffering her to perrish alone, for the great hoṟour shee atchiued in her life time.'

Page 461. THE SISTERS.

Line 91. *Lake Llanberis.* In North Wales. Compare ' The Golden Year ' : —

> And found him in Llanberis: then we crost
> Between the lakes, etc.

The lakes are Llyn Padarn and Llyn Peris; but they are often called the ' Llanberis Lakes.'

111. *Of our New Forest.* An ancient royal hunting demesne, extending westward from Southampton Water. There are about 140 square miles in the district, little more than two thirds of which now belongs to the crown.

117. *My Rosalind in this Arden.* The allusion to ' As You Like It ' is obvious.

Page 465. THE VILLAGE WIFE.

Line 19. *Can tha tell ony harm on 'im, lass ?* All the English editions omit the comma before ' lass.'

64. *The 'Ouse.* That is, the poorhouse: a colloquial use of the word in England.

80. *White wi' the maäy.* That is, with the blossoms of the white hawthorn. See note on ' The Miller's Daughter,' line 130. All the English editions have ' Maäy ' in the present passage.

88. *Fur he ca'd 'is 'erse Billy-rough-un.* For he called his horse Bellerophon. Similarly, the name of the warship Bellerophon is said to have been corrupted by the sailors into ' Billy-ruffian.'

99. *Siver the mou'ds rattled down upo' poor owd Squire i' the wood.* Howsoever (however) the mould (earth) rattled down on the poor old Squire's coffin.

107. *Hes fur Miss Hannie the heldest hes now,* etc. This is the reading of the English editions; but elsewhere in the poem we have ' Miss Annie ' and ' es ' (for ' as ') except in the preceding line, where it is misprinted ' as.'

121. *Hugger-mugger they lived.* They lived in a slovenly way (Century Dict.). The word, whether as noun or adjective, often means in privacy or secrecy. Compare ' Hamlet,' iv. 5. 84: —

> and we have done but greenly,
> In hugger-mugger to inter him.

126. *Roomlin' by.* Rumbling by (in his coach).

Page 468. IN THE CHILDREN'S HOSPITAL.

Line 10. *Drench'd with the hellish oorali.* A drug, also known as ' woorali ' and ' curari ' (or ' curara '), extracted from the *Strychnos toxifera.* It acts by paralyzing the nerves of motion without impairing the sensibility. It is used by the South American Indians for poisoning their arrows. The reference here is to the practice of vivisection for purposes of physiological investigation. Tennyson evidently sympathized with the criticisms, not wholly groundless, which have been urged against it, and which have led in England to the enactment of laws restricting and regulating it.

Page 470. DEDICATORY POEM TO THE PRINCESS ALICE.

Line 7. *Thy soldier-brother's bridal orange-bloom,* etc. Prince Arthur, Duke of Connaught, was married at Windsor, on the 13th of March, 1879, to Louise-Marguerite, Princess of Prussia.

Page 470. THE DEFENCE OF LUCKNOW.

Line 20. *The brute bullet.* The senseless bullet; antithetical to the sentient ' brain.'

25. *Mine? yes, a mine!* Sir James Outram, describing the siege, says: ' I am aware of no parallel to our series of mines in modern war. Twenty-one shafts, aggregating two hundred feet in depth, and 3291 feet of gallery have been executed. The enemy advanced twenty mines against the palaces and outposts; of these they exploded three which caused us loss of life, and two which did no injury; seven have been blown in; and out of seven others the enemy have been driven and their galleries taken possession of by our miners.'

Page 472. SIR JOHN OLDCASTLE.

Line 5. *Scribbled or carved upon the pitiless*

stone. Like the carvings by prisoners of state still to be seen on the walls of the Beauchamp Tower in the Tower of London.

16. *The proud Archbishop Arundel.* Thomas Arundel, Archbishop of Canterbury, a zealous persecutor of the Lollards.

19. *Bara.* Bread (Welsh).

20. *Vailing a sudden eyelid.* The ' vailing ' is the obsolete word meaning to lower or let fall.

21. *Dim Saesneg.* No English; that is, I do not speak English.

24. *Not least art thou, thou little Bethlehem,* etc. See Micah, v. 2.

26. *Little Lutterworth.* Lutterworth, the parish in Leicestershire of which Wiclif was rector.

77. *Sir Roger Acton.* A prominent Lollard.

78. *Beverley.* John of Beverley, who was martyred January 19, 1413–14.

79. *Thy two witnesses.* See Revelation, xi. 3.

84. *Him, who should bear the sword,* etc. Henry V. The poet seems here to identify the speaker with the Sir John Oldcastle who appears as one of Prince Henry's wild companions in the old play of ' The Famous Victories of Henry the Fifth,' on which Shakespeare founded his ' Henry IV.' and ' Henry V. ; ' and it is well known that ' Sir John Oldcastle ' was originally the name of Falstaff in the ' Henry IV.' plays. The dramatist changed the name to avoid offending the Protestants and gratifying the Roman Catholics. See the epilogue to ' 2 Henry IV.' : ' Falstaff shall die of a sweat, unless already a' be killed with your hard opinions; for Oldcastle died a martyr, and this is not the man.' Fuller, in his ' Church History ' (lib. iv.), says: ' Stage poets have themselves been very bold with, and others very merry at, the memory of Sir John Oldcastle, whom they have fancied a boon companion, a jovial royster, and yet a coward to boot. . . . The best is, Sir John Falstaff hath relieved the memory of Sir John Oldcastle, and of late is substituted buffoon in his place.'

93. *Or Amurath of the East.* A Turkish Sultan. Compare ' 2 Henry IV.' v. 2. 48: —

> This is the English, not the Turkish court;
> Not Amurath an Amurath succeeds,
> But Harry Harry.

159. *Sylvester.* Sylvester II., who became Pope A. D. 999.

Page 476. COLUMBUS.

When Columbus returned to San Domingo on his third expedition, the colony was in a deplorable condition. Things went from bad to worse, and the Spanish monarchs sent an officer of the royal household, Francis de Bobadilla, to make investigations, with authority to send back to Spain ' any cavaliers or other persons ' whom he thought proper. It is not probable that the intention was to include Columbus in the list of persons subject to arrest; but Bobadilla, soon after his arrival in the island, put the great admiral in chains, and sent him to Spain, where he arrived in November, 1499.

Line 18. *The great ' Laudamus.'* The *Te Deum.*

25. *The Dragon's Mouth.* The name (*Bocca*

*del Drago*) which Columbus gave to a channel between the island of Trinidad and the mainland of South America.

26. *The Mountain of the World.* The 'Mountain of Adam,' or 'Mountain of the Gods,' the highest peak in Ceylon, on the summit of which the print of Buddha's foot is supposed to be visible.

46. *King David call'd the heavens a hide, a tent.* See Psalms, civ. 2.

48. *Some cited old Lactantius.* An eminent Christian author, who flourished early in the 4th century. The 1st edition of his works, one of the oldest of printed books, was brought out at Subiaco in 1465.

74. *Guanahani.* The native name of the first island discovered by Columbus.

107. *The belting wall of Cambalu, etc.* The royal residence of the Khan of Cathay. Compare Milton, 'Paradise Lost,' xi. 388: 'Cambalu, seat of Cathayan Can.'

109. *Prester John* was a mythical Christian king of India. Compare 'Much Ado About Nothing,' ii. 1. 274: 'I will fetch you a toothpicker now from the furthest inch of Asia, bring you the length of Prester John's foot.'

117. *Howl'd me from Hispaniola.* The name which Columbus gave to the island of Hayti.

125. *Fonseca, my main enemy at their court.* Juan Rodriguez Fonseca, a bigoted Spanish prelate, who called Columbus a visionary and treated him with persistent malignity.

126. *Bovadilla.* The Francisco de Bobadilla mentioned above.

144. *Veragua.* A province of New Granada in South America.

190. *The Catalonian Minorite.* Bernardo Buil (Boyle), a Benedictine monk, according to the best authorities (not a *Minorite*, or Franciscan), who was sent by the Pope to the new Indies in June, 1493, as apostolical vicar. He hated Columbus, but there seems to be no evidence that he *excommunicated* him.

206. *Colón.* The Spanish form of 'Columbus.'

Page 479. THE VOYAGE OF MAELDUNE.

Line 22. *Fainter than any flittermouse-shriek.* The cry of the bat, which in England is popularly called 'flittermouse' (fluttering-mouse), 'flickermouse,' or 'flindermouse.' Compare Ben Jonson, 'Sad Shepherd,' ii. 8: 'And giddy flittermice, with leather wings,' etc.

26. *They almost fell on each other.* This idea, which occurs so often in the poem, is not to be found in the old legend.

48. *The triumph of Finn.* Finn, the son of Cumal, was the most renowned of all the heroes of ancient Ireland. He was commander of the Feni, or 'Feni of Erin,' a sort of standing army maintained by the monarch for the support of the throne. Each province had its own soldiers under a local captain, but all were under one commander-in-chief. Finn was equally brave and sagacious. His foresight was, indeed, so extraordinary that the people believed it to be a preternatural gift, and a legend was invented to account for it. He was killed at a place

called Athbrea, on the Boyne, A. D. 284. Ossian, or Oisin, the famous hero-poet, to whom the bards attribute many poems still extant, was the son of Finn.

55. *The Isle of Fruits.* The poet may have got the hint of this island from the 'isle of intoxicating wine-fruits' in the Celtic tale; but the rich details of the picture are all his own.

77. *That undersea isle.* The description here is developed from the simple statement in the old legend that 'they could see, beneath the clear water, a beautiful country, with many mansions surrounded by groves and woods.' So far from being tempted to dive down to the place, the sight of 'an animal fierce and terrible' which infests it makes them tremble lest they may 'not be able to cross the sea over the monster, on account of the extreme thinness of the water; but after much difficulty and danger they get across it safely.'

105. *The Isle of the Double Towers.* If I had not read the old tale, I should have said that this quaint and wild conception must have been taken from it; but, though it seems so thoroughly like a Celtic fancy, there is nothing in the legend that could have suggested it.

115. *Saint Brendan.* One of the most famous of the ancient Celtic legends is that of 'The Voyage of Saint Brendan,' undertaken in the sixth century. He set out from Kerry, sailed westward into the Atlantic, and, as some believed, landed on the shore of America. The adventures he met with were as varied and surprising as those of Maeldune.

Page 484. PREFATORY SONNET TO 'THE NINETEENTH CENTURY.'

Line 3. *Their old craft, seaworthy still.* 'The Contemporary Review.'

7. *This roaring moon of daffodil.* Compare 'The Winter's Tale,' iv. 4. 118: —

> daffodils
> That come before the swallow dares, and take
> The winds of March with beauty.

Page 484. TO THE REV. W. H. BROOKFIELD.

Line 6. *We paced that walk of limes.* Compare 'In Memoriam,' lxxxvii.: —

> Up that long walk of limes I past
> To see the rooms in which he dwelt.

11. *Our kindlier, trustier Jaques.* The allusion to 'As You Like It' needs no explanation.

Page 484. MONTENEGRO.

Line 12. *Great Tsernogora!* Or *Tzernagora*, the native name of Montenegro.

Page 488. TO E. FITZGERALD.

Line 15. *Your table of Pythagoras.* For the allusion to the vegetarianism of the old philosopher, based on the doctrine of metempsychosis, compare 'Twelfth Night,' iv. 2. 54: —

*Clown.* What is the opinion of Pythagoras concerning wild-fowl?
*Malvolio.* That the soul of our grandam might haply inhabit a bird.
*Clown.* What thinkest thou of his opinion?
*Malvolio.* I think nobly of the soul, and no way approve his opinion.

*Clown.* Fare thee well. Remain thou still in darkness. Thou shalt hold the opinion of Pythagoras ere I will allow of thy wits, and fear to kill a woodcock lest thou dispossess the soul of thy grandam.

For the poet's account of the vegetarian dream, see the 'Memoir,' vol. ii. p. 317. The visit to Fitzgerald was made in 1876.

16. *A thing enskied.* See 'Measure for Measure,' i. 4. 34: 'I hold you as a thing enskied and sainted.'

28. *Of Eshcol hugeness.* See Numbers, xiii. 23.

32. *Your golden Eastern lay.* The 'Rubaíyát' of Omar Kayyam, translated by Fitzgerald in 1859.

46. *My son.* Hallam, the present Lord Tennyson.

Page 489. TIRESIAS.

Line 9. *My son.* Used in a familiar figurative way. Menœceus, whom he addresses below, was the son of Creon, and directly descended from Cadmus, who had offended Ares (Mars) by killing the dragon guarding a spring sacred to the god.

25. *Subjected to the Heliconian ridge.* 'Subjected' is used in its etymological sense of lying below.

38. *There in a secret olive-glade I saw, etc.* The description of the goddess is nowise inferior to that of the same goddess and her companion deities in 'Œnone.'

96. *The song-built towers and gates.* The walls of Thebes rose to the music of Amphion's harp, as those of Troy to Apollo's. Compare 'Œnone.'

147. *A wiser than herself.* Œdipus.

164. *Their ocean-islets.* The Isles of the Blest.

192. *Find the gate Is bolted, and the master gone.* For the figure, compare 'The Deserted House.'

Page 495. DESPAIR.

Line 21. *In the drear nightfold of your fatalist.* The 1881 reading was ' dark nightfold.'

75. *Tho' glory and shame dying out for ever, etc.* The 1881 reading was: 'Tho' name and fame dying out,' etc.

Page 504. TO-MORROW.

Line 31. *The white o' the may.* All the English editions have ' May; ' but I have no doubt that the reference is to the blossoms of the white hawthorn, as in 'The Village Wife,' line 80. See note on that passage.

48. *The Sassenach whate.* The Saxon (English) wheat.

Page 508. PROLOGUE TO GENERAL HAMLEY.

Line 5. *You came, and look'd, and loved the view, etc.* The view from the poet's summer residence at Aldworth.

28. *Tel-el-Kebir.* A village in Lower Egypt, about fifty miles northeast of Cairo. Here, on the 13th of September, 1882, the English under General Wolseley defeated the Egyptian insurgents under Arabi Pasha, whose surrender soon followed.

Page 509. THE CHARGE OF THE HEAVY BRIGADE AT BALACLAVA.

Line 5. *When the points of the Russian lances arose on the sky.* Originally, ' broke in on the sky.'

14–21. *Thousands of horsemen had gather'd there on the height, etc.* For these eight lines the first version had: —

Down the hill slowly thousands of Russians
Drew to the valley, and halted at last on the height,
With a wing push'd out to the left, and a wing to the
    right —
But Scarlett was far on ahead, and he dashed up alone
Thro' the great gray slope of men,
And he wheel'd his sabre, he held his own
Like an Englishman there and then;
And the three that were nearest him follow'd with
    force, etc.

45. *'Lost are the gallant three hundred of Scarlett's Brigade!'* Originally, ' the gallant three hundred, the Heavy Brigade!' In the preceding line, ' whispering' was ' muttering.'

46. *'Lost one and all!' were the words.* This line and the next were not in the first version.

60. *Drove it in wild dismay.* Not in the first version.

66. *And all the Brigade.* Originally, ' the Heavy Brigade.'

Page 510. EPILOGUE.

*Irene.* The name, which is the Greek word for ' peace,' is in keeping with the character.

Line 14. *Or Trade re-frain the Powers, etc.* The hyphen is apparently intended to call attention to the derivation of ' re-frain' from the late Latin *refrenare*, to bridle or hold in with a bit (*frenum*).

17. *Kelt.* Elsewhere the poet uses the form 'Celt.' Compare 'In Memoriam,' cix.: ' The blind hysterics of the Celt; ' ' A Welcome to Alexandra' : ' Teuton or Celt, or whatever we be,' etc.

45. *'I will strike,' said he, etc.* See his Ode (i. 1. 35, 36): —

Quod si me lyricis vatibus inseres,
    Sublimi feriam sidera vertice.

52. *Yon myriad-worlded way.* The Galaxy.

59. *The falling drop will make his name As mortal as my own.* That is, by finally obliterating the record; apparently suggested by Ovid's ' Gutta cavat lapidem non vi sed saepe cadendo.'

Page 511. TO VIRGIL.

The allusions to the ' Æneid,' the ' Georgics,' and certain ' Eclogues' need no explanation.

Line 3. *He that sang the Works and Days.* Hesiod.

18. *The Northern Island sunder'd once from all the human race.* Compare the first ' Eclogue,' 67: ' Et penitus toto divisos orbe Britannos.'

Page 513. EARLY SPRING.

Line 19. *The woods with living airs.* Originally, ' by living airs.'

33. *A gleam from yonder vale.* Originally, ' Some gleam,' etc.

Page 514. *Frater Ave Atque Vale.* The Latin quotations in the poem are from Catullus, the ' Frater ave atque vale' being the end of his lament for the loss of his brother (101.10).

Page 514. HELEN'S TOWER.

Line 4. *Mother's love in letter'd gold.* The

original reading (on the tower and in 'Good Words') was: 'Mother's love engraved in gold.' In the 'Tiresias' volume 'engraved' was changed to 'engrav'n.' The present reading was adopted in 1889.

The reading in the 8th line was originally 'to last so long,' changed in the 'Tiresias' volume.

Page 515. HANDS ALL ROUND. The version of this song in the 'Examiner' was as follows: —

First drink a health, this solemn night,
  A health to England, every guest;
That man 's the best cosmopolite
  Who loves his native country best.
May Freedom's oak for ever live
  With stronger life from day to day;
That man 's the true Conservative
  Who lops the moulder'd branch away.
        Hands all round !
    God the tyrant's hope confound !
To this great cause of Freedom drink, my friends,
  And the great name of England, round and round.

A health to Europe's honest men !
  Heaven guard them from her tyrants' jails !
From wronged Poerio's noisome den,
  From iron'd limbs and tortured nails !
We curse the crimes of Southern kings,
  The Russian whips and Austrian rods —
We likewise have our evil things;
  Too much we make our Ledgers, Gods.
        Yet hands all round !
    God the tyrant's cause confound !
To Europe's better health we drink, my friends,
  And the great name of England, round and round !

What health to France, if France be she,
  Whom martial prowess only charms ?
Yet tell her — better to be free
  Than vanquish all the world in arms.
Her frantic city's flashing heats
  But fire, to blast, the hopes of men.
Why change the titles of your streets ?
  You fools, you 'll want them all again.
        Yet hands all round !
    God their tyrant's cause confound !
To France, the wiser France, we drink, my friends,
  And the great name of England, round and round.

Gigantic daughter of the West,
  We drink to thee across the flood,
We know thee most, we love thee best,
  For art thou not of British blood ?
Should war's mad blast again be blown,
  Permit not thou the tyrant powers
To fight thy mother here alone,
  But let thy broadsides roar with ours.
        Hands all round !
    God the tyrant's cause confound !
To our great kinsmen of the West, my friends,
  And the great name of England, round and round.

O rise, our strong Atlantic sons,
  When war against our freedom springs !
O speak to Europe through your guns !
  They *can* be understood by kings.
You must not mix our Queen with those
  That wish to keep their people fools;
Our freedom's foemen are her foes,
  She comprehends the race she rules.
        Hands all round !
    God the tyrant's cause confound !
To our dear kinsmen of the West, my friends,
  And the great cause of Freedom, round and round.

All the reprints (not excepting that in the 'Memoir,' which has 'the tyrant's' in the 3d stanza, and 'great kinsmen' in the last) are more or less inaccurate. Only the first stanza of this version appears in the present song, which was written to be sung by Mr. Santley, at St. James's Hall, London, on the Queen's birthday, May 24, 1882.

The 6th line then had 'larger' for 'stronger,' and the 11th line had '*the* great,' as also in the 11th line of the other two stanzas.

This new version as printed in the 'Tiresias' volume had 'true Cosmopolite' and 'best Conservative.' In 1889 it took its present form.

Page 516. FREEDOM.
Line 3. *The pillar'd Parthenon.* Sometimes printed (without authority, as Lord Tennyson told me) 'the column'd Parthenon.'

17-20. *Of Knowledge fusing class with class, etc.* This stanza was not in the poem as first printed.

21. *Who yet, like Nature, etc.* Originally, 'Who, like great Nature,' etc. The next line had 'our Human Star.'

Page 516. POETS AND THEIR BIBLIOGRAPHIES.
Line 6. *Adviser of the nine-years ponder'd lay.* See Horace, 'Ars Poetica,' 388.

8. *Catullus, whose dead songster never dies.* Lesbia's sparrow.

Page 517. LOCKSLEY HALL SIXTY YEARS AFTER.
For a long review of the poem by Mr. W. E. Gladstone, see 'The Nineteenth Century' for January, 1887. In the closing paragraph there is a reference to a criticism in the 'Spectator' (of December 18, 1886) 'bearing the signs of a master hand,' and finding 'a perfect harmony, a true equation, between the two "Locksley Halls;"' the warmer picture due to the ample vitality of the prophet's youth, and the colder one not less due to the stinted vitality of his age.' I add a portion of the article to which Mr. Gladstone alludes: —

'The critics hitherto have done no justice to Tennyson's "Locksley Hall," if, indeed, they have carefully read it. We venture to say that it is at least as fine a picture of age reviewing the phenomena of life, and reviewing them with an insight impossible to youth into all that threatens man with defeat and degradation, though of course without any of that irrepressible elasticity of feeling which shows even by the very wildness and tumult of its despair that despair is, for it, ultimately impossible; as Tennyson's earlier poem was of youth passionately resenting the failure of its first bright hope, and yet utterly unable to repress the "promise and potency" of its buoyant vitality. The difference between the "Locksley Hall" of Tennyson's early poems and the "Locksley Hall" of his latest is this — that in the former all the melancholy is attributed to personal grief, while all the sanguine visionariness which really springs out of overflowing vitality justifies itself by dwelling on the cumulative resources of science and the arts; — in the latter, the melancholy in the man, a result of ebbing vitality, justifies itself by the failure of knowledge and science to cope with the moral horrors which experience has brought to light, while the set-off against that melancholy is to be found in a real personal experience of true nobility in man and woman. Hence those who call the new "Locksley Hall" pessimist seem to us to do injustice to that fine poem. No one can expect age to be full of the irrepressible buoyancy of youth. Age is conscious of a dwindling power to meet the evils which loom larger as experience widens. What the noblest old age has to set off against this consciousness of rapidly diminishing buoyancy is a larger and more solid experience of human goodness, as well as a deeper faith in the power which guides youth and age alike. Now Tennyson's poem shows us these happier aspects of age, though it shows us also that exaggerated despondency in counting up the moral evils of life which is one of the consequences of dwindling vitality. Nothing could well be finer than Tennyson's picture of the despair which his hero would feel if he had nothing but "evolution" to depend on, or than the rebuke which the speaker himself gives to that despondency when he remembers how much more than evolution there is to depend on, — how surely that has been already "evolved" in the heart of man which, itself inexplicable, yet promises an evolution far richer and more boundless than is suggested by any physical law. The final upshot of the swaying tides of progress and retrogression, in their periodic advance and retreat, is, he tells us, quite incalculable by us — the complexity of the forward and backward movements of the wave being beyond our grasp; — and yet he is sure that there is that in us which supplies an ultimate solution of the riddle. . . .

'On the whole, we have here the natural pessimism of age in all its melancholy, alternating with that highest mood like "old experience" which, in Milton's phrase, "doth attain to something like prophetic strain." The various eddies caused by these positive and negative currents seem to us delineated with at least as firm a hand as that which painted the tumultuous ebb and flow of angry despair and angrier hope in the bosom of the deceived and resentful lover of sixty years since. The later "Locksley Hall" is in the highest sense worthy of its predecessor.'

Line 1. *Half the morning have I paced these sandy tracts, etc.* Compare the opening lines of the first 'Locksley Hall.'

13–16. *In the hall there hangs a painting, etc.* These two couplets were originally written for the first 'Locksley Hall.' See the notes on that poem.

29. *Cross'd! for once he sail'd the sea, etc.* The crossed feet indicate that the knight was a Crusader.

42. *Cold upon the dead volcano, etc.* Compare Lowell, 'The Vision of Sir Launfal': —

> The soul partakes the season's youth,
> And the sulphurous rifts of passion and woe

> Lie deep 'neath a silence pure and smooth,
> Like burnt-out craters healed with snow.

55. *Gone our sailor son thy father.* Evidently an only son, as the grandson also is.

67–72. *Gone for ever! Ever? no, etc.* The 'Spectator' says: 'As an illustration of the strong grasp which age gets of the convictions which are products neither of hope nor of fear, take the following on the significance of the belief in eternity as moulding and shaping to new meanings the life of man: —

> Gone for ever! Ever? no — for since our dying race
>    began
> Ever, ever, and for ever was the leading light of man.

> Those that in barbarian burials kill'd the slave and slew
>    the wife
> Felt within themselves the sacred passion of the sec-
>    ond life.
> . . . . . . . .
> Truth for truth and good for good! The good, the
>    true, the pure, the just —
> Take the charm "For ever" from them, and they
>    crumble into dust.

Has Tennyson ever written anything which concentrates into a single line more of the wisdom of maturity than the last line here quoted?'

73. *Gone the cry of 'Forward, Forward!'* Compare the first 'Locksley Hall': 'Forward, forward let us range,' etc.

78. *Let us hush this cry of 'Forward!' till ten thousand years have gone.* Compare 'The Golden Year': —

> Ah, folly! for it lies so far away,
> Not in our time, nor in our children's time,
> 'T is like the second world to us that live;
> 'T were all as one to fix our hopes on heaven
> As on the vision of the golden year.

89. *France had shown a light to all men, etc.* Referring to the French Revolution. 'Demos' (δῆμος) is the Greek name for the common people.

95. *Peasants maim the helpless horse.* The allusion, as Lord Tennyson wrote me, is to 'modern Irish doings.' The next couplet refers to an actual instance of wanton cruelty reported in the newspapers at the time.

103. *Cosmos.* Order and harmony as opposed to 'chaos.' 'The fabric of the external universe first received the title of *cosmos*, or "beautiful"' (Trench).

110. *Equal-born? oh, yes, if yonder hill be level with the flat.* The critic of the London 'Academy' (January 1, 1887) asks: 'Is it defensible to twist the Radical's demand for "equality" of rights into a statement that all men are "equal-born" in order to pour a very natural contempt upon it?' It is this equality of 'inalienable rights,' not equality of rank or endowments, which the Declaration of Independence claims for all men.

116. *The voices from the field.* The vote of the laboring classes.

130. *Thro' the tonguesters we may fall.* Tennyson has 'tonguesters' (which he may have coined) again in 'Harold,' v. 1.: —

The simple, silent, selfless man
Is worth a world of tonguesters.

**131.** *You that woo the Voices.* Compare 'Coriolanus,' ii. 3. 132: —

Here come moe voices. —
Your voices: for your voices I have fought;
Watch'd for your voices; for your voices bear
Of wounds two dozen odd; battles thrice six
I have seen, and heard of; for your voices have
Done many things, some less, some more: your voices.
Indeed, I would be consul.

**133.** *Pluck the mighty from their seat, etc.* Compare Luke, i. 52, and Psalms, cxlvii. 6.

**145.** *Wallowing in the troughs of Zolaism.* Alluding to the 'realistic' French novelist.

**157.** *Jacobinism and Jacquerie.* Mad opposition to legitimate government, like that of the 'Jacobins,' a club of violent Republicans in the French Revolution of 1789, who got their name from the Jacobin monastery where their secret meetings were held. 'Jacquerie,' originally the name given to a revolt of the peasants of Picardy against the nobles in 1358, came to be applied to any similar insurrection of the lower classes.

**162.** *All the millions one at length with all the visions of my youth.* Compare the first 'Locksley Hall': —

Till the war-drum throbb'd no longer, and the battle-
    flags were furl'd
In the Parliament of man, the Federation of the world.

**185.** *Hesper, whom the poet call'd the Bringer home of all good things.* See note on 'Leonine Elegiacs' above.

**201–212.** *What are men that he should heed us?* This passage 'takes for its text the 8th Psalm, which, beginning with the same dismay at the smallness of man's material significance, sees, nevertheless, that in his apprehension of the world he is proved "little lower than the angels"' ('The Academy').

**226.** *The dog too lame to follow with the cry.* That is, with the rest of the pack. Compare 'Othello,' ii. 3. 370: "Not like a hound that hunts, but one that fills up the cry;' and 'Coriolanus,' iii. 3. 120: 'You common cry of curs!'

**240.** *Youthful jealousy is a liar.* Alluding to the earlier poem, where he is described as a 'clown,' etc.

**246.** *Roofs of slated hideousness.* The 'model houses' to be seen in many English towns and villages, built on scientific principles, but with none of the picturesque charm of the old domestic architecture — better to live in, though not to look at.

**276.** *Forward, till you see the Highest Human Nature is divine, etc.* The youthful cry is taken up again in these closing lines, in which there is surely no pessimism.

**278.** *The deathless Angel seated in the vacant tomb.* See Mark, xxi. 5, and compare John, xx. 12.

Page 525. OPENING OF THE INDIAN AND COLONIAL EXHIBITION.
Line 17. *And wherever her flag fly.* The original reading, as printed in the newspapers at the time, was: 'And — where'er her flag may fly —;' and the poem ended thus: —

Britons, hold your own!
And God guard all!

Page 525. TO W. C. MACREADY.
At the banquet the sonnet was read to the guests by John Forster. It was printed at the time in 'The Household Narrative of Current Events' and other periodicals.

Page 526. TO THE MARQUIS OF DUFFERIN AND AVA.
On the 20th of April, 1886, the poet's younger son, Lionel, died on the voyage home from India. A monument was erected to his memory in Freshwater Church on the Isle of Wight — a beautiful statue of St. John, from the chisel of Miss Mary Grant. A tribute more enduring than brass or marble, and more beautiful than sculptor could carve, is built in lofty and tender rhyme in these lines addressed by his father to the Marquis of Dufferin and Ava.

Page 527. ON THE JUBILEE OF QUEEN VICTORIA.
Line 39. *Henry's fifty years are all in shadow.* Henry III., who came to the throne in 1216, and died in 1272. The other sovereigns referred to are Edward III., who reigned fifty-one years, and George III., who reigned sixty years.

Page 528. DEMETER AND PERSEPHONE.
Line 5. *The God of ghosts and dreams.* Hermes (Mercury), the 'serpent-wanded power' of line 25.

**39.** *Aïdoneus.* Dis (Pluto).

**82.** *Three gray heads.* The Fates.

**114.** *The brother of this Darkness.* Zeus (Jupiter).

**119.** *For nine white moons.* The earlier classical authorities made it *eight* months, the later ones *six* months.

**148.** *The Stone, the Wheel.* The stone of Sisyphus and the wheel of Ixion.

Page 530. OWD ROÄ.
Line 6. *Like owt.* Like anything (aught).

**15.** *Faäithful an' True.* See Revelation, xix. 11.

**61.** *Cleän-wud.* The *wud* is the old English *wode* or *wood*, meaning mad, frantic. Compare the play upon the word in the 'Midsummer-Night's Dream,' ii. 1. 192: —

And here am I, and wode within this wood,
    Because I cannot meet my Helena.

**94.** *Tother Hangel i' Scriptur.* See Judges, xiii. 20.

Page 533. VASTNESS.
Mr. W. E. Henley remarks: 'In "Vastness" the insight into essentials, the command of primordial matter, the capacity of vital suggestion, are gloriously in evidence from the first to the last. Here is no touch of ingenuity, no trace of "originality," no sign of cleverness, . . . nothing is antic, peculiar, superfluous; but here is epic unity and completeness, here is a sublimation of experience expressed by means of a sublimation of style. It is unique in English, and, for all that one can see, it is likely to remain unique this good while yet.'

Line 9. *Innocence seethed in her mother's milk.* Compare Exodus, xxiii. 19, or xxxiv. 26.

Page 534. THE RING.

Line 58. *The lonely maiden Princess of the wood.* Compare Tennyson's version of the story in 'The Day Dream.'

62. *Io t' amo.* I love thee (Italian).

159. *Till I knew.* Referring to the 'knew not that which pleased it most,' in line 141 above.

Page 546. TO ULYSSES.

Line 4. *Corrientes.* The capital of the province of the same name in the Argentine Republic.

7. *The century's three strong eights.* This fixes the date of the composition of the poem.

26. *The warrior of Caprera.* Garibaldi, so called from the town which was his home from 1854 to 1882. It was in April, 1864, that the Italian hero planted the 'waving pine' — a *Wellingtonia gigantea* — in the garden at Farringford.

Page 547. TO MARY BOYLE.

Of the poems of friendship which occur so frequently in the later volumes of Tennyson, Stopford Brooke says: 'They ought to be read together when we desire to feel his grace and power in this special kind of poetry, which no one, I think, has ever done so well. They are revelations of character, and of a character made braver and kindlier by old age. No trace of cynicism deforms them, and their little sadness is balanced by a soft and sunny clearness, by tenderness in memory and magnanimity of hope. Each of them is also tinged by the individuality of the person to whom it is written. The poems to Edward Fitzgerald, to his brother, to Mary Boyle, to Lord Dufferin, possess these qualities, and are drenched, as it were, with the dew of this delicate sentiment peculiar to old age. They look backward, therefore, but they also look forward; and not only friends on earth, but those also who have found their life in death enter into their hour of prospect and retrospect.'

Line 28. *In rick-fire days.* Referring to the troublous times of 1830–33, when the irritation of the agricultural laborers of England against their employers was at its height, and for months together the burning of stacks, farm-buildings, and other property was of nightly occurrence. Compare 'The Princess,' iv.: —

> As of some fire against a stormy cloud,
> When the wild peasant rights himself, the rick
> Flames, and his anger reddens in the heavens.

Page 550. MERLIN AND THE GLEAM.

Line 14. *And learn'd me Magic.* The use of 'learn'd' for 'taught' is an archaism. Compare 'Much Ado About Nothing,' iv. 1. 31: 'Sweet prince, you learn me noble thankfulness.'

Page 551. ROMNEY'S REMORSE.

Line 104. *With Milton's amaranth.* See 'Paradise Lost,' iii. 353: —

> Immortal amaranth, a flower which once
> In Paradise, fast by the Tree of Life,

> Began to bloom, but, soon for man's offence
> To Heaven removed where first it grew, there grows
> And flowers aloft, shading the Fount of Life,
> And where the River of Bliss through midst of Heaven
> Rolls o'er Elysian flowers her amber stream.

142. *He said it . . . in the play.* See 'Measure for Measure,' iii. 1. 2: —

> The miserable have no other medicine
> But only hope.

Page 555. FAR — FAR — AWAY.

The 'Memoir' (vol. ii. p. 366) says: 'Distant bells always charmed him with their "lin-lan-lone," and, when heard over the sea or a lake, he was never tired of listening to them.'

Page 556. THE THROSTLE.

Stopford Brooke, after referring to the poems of friendship in the later volumes of Tennyson (see note on lines 'To Mary Boyle,' above), remarks: 'There is another kind of poetry which is naturally written in old age, and recurs to those motives of youth which arise out of the happiness of the world and of the poet in the awakening of life in Spring. This poetry is born out of the memories of that early joy, and is also touched with a distinctive sentiment native only to old age, delicately clear, having a breath of the color and warmth of youth, and flushed with the hope of its re-awakening. Its poems are like those February days which enter from time to time into the wintry world, so genial in their misty sunlight that the earth seems then to breathe like a sleeping woman, and her bosom to heave with a dream of coming pleasure. They recall the past, and prophesy the immortal Spring. Old age often feels this sentiment, but is rarely able to shape it; but when, by good fortune, it can be shaped, the poem has a unique charm. Of such poems, "The Throstle" is one, and "Early Spring" is another. They may have been originally conceived, or even written, in earlier days, but I am sure that they were rewritten in old age, and in its evening air.'

Page 557. QUEEN MARY.

Page 559. Line 122. *Achage.* Probably Tennyson's coinage, as no other example of the word is given in the Oxford Dictionary.

Page 561. Line 88. *The game of chess.* There is a double meaning in this.

Page 569. Line 288. *His assessor in the throne.* Literally, one who sits beside him, sharing his dignity. Compare Milton, 'Paradise Lost,' vi. 679: —

> Whence to his son
> The assessor of his throne, he thus began.

Page 570. Line 322. *That old fox-Fleming.* In 'fox' there is a play upon the name 'Renard.' Compare p. 595 below, lines 106–108.

Page 571. Scene I. *Alington Castle.* The ruins of this castle remain on the banks of the Medway, just below Maidstone. It was built in the reign of Stephen, and was the residence of Sir Henry Wyatt, father of the poet, who was born here in 1503. He died in 1542, leaving the estate to his son, who is introduced by Tennyson here.

Page 572. Line 94. *For appearance sake.* The omission of the sign of the possessive is archaic. In Shakespeare and other Elizabethan writers it sometimes occurs even in nouns that do not end in a sibilant sound. Compare 'As You Like It,' iii. 2. 271: 'for fashion sake'; 'Twelfth Night,' iii. 4. 326: 'for's oath sake,' etc.

Page 580. Line 13. *The tree in Virgil, etc.* The grafted tree of 'Georgics,' ii. 82: 'Miraturque novas frondes et non sua poma.'

Page 582. Line 125. *Not red like Iscariot's.* It was a current opinion that Judas had red hair, and he was commonly so represented in the old paintings and tapestries.

Page 585. Line 23. *The scarlet thread of Rahab.* See Joshua, ii. and vi.

Line 25. *The heathen giant.* Antæus, the son of Terra, who was invincible so long as he was in contact with the earth.

Line 56. *That long low minster.* Winchester Cathedral.

Line 62. *Enclosed with boards of cedar.* See Song of Solomon, viii. 8, 9.

Page 586. Line 75. *Saint Andrew's Day.* November 30th.

Line 82. *Swept and garnish'd after him.* See Luke, xi. 25, 26.

Page 587. Line 139. *A high-dropsy.* The page's blunder for 'hydropsy.'

Page 590. Line 25. *An amphisbœna.* A fabulous venomous serpent supposed to have a head at each end and to be able to move in either direction. Compare 'Paradise Lost,' x. 524.

Page 594. Line 260. *Their Dies Iræ.* Their judgment-day; alluding to the Latin hymn, 'Dies iræ, dies illa,' etc.

Page 596. Line 5. *Mercy, that herb-of-grace.* A figurative use of the popular name of the rue. Compare 'Hamlet,' iv. 5. 182 or 'Richard II.' iii. 4. 105.

Page 598. Line 77. *What Virgil sings, etc.* See the 'Æneid,' iv. 569: 'Varium et mutabile semper Femina.'

Page 600. Line 89. *Martyr's blood — seed of the Church.* The often-quoted saying of Tertullian.

Page 606. Line 142. *Ignorance crying in the streets, etc.* A parody on Proverbs, i. 20, 24.

Page 609. Line 5. *The narrow seas.* A common name then for the English Channel. Compare 'The Merchant of Venice,' ii. 8. 28, etc.

Page 613. Line 80. *The Great Harry.* The famous ship of war named for him.

Line 99. *The Dance of Death.* The separation of bridegroom and bride was represented in various forms in this series of pictures. Compare Longfellow's description of the covered bridge at Lucerne in 'The Golden Legend,' v.

Page 615. Line 205. *The gloom of Saul.* See 1 Samuel, xvi. 23, and compare Browning's 'Saul.'

Line 250. *This coarseness is a want of phantasy.* 'Phantasy' here is equivalent to 'sensibility,' as the context indicates — a meaning of the word not recognized in the dictionaries.

Page 620. Line 77. *Thou light a torch that never will go out!* Referring to Latimer's words to Ridley at the time of their martyrdom: 'We shall this day light such a candle, by God's grace, as I trust shall never be put out.'

Page 622. HAROLD.

Page 623. Line 2. *Yon grimly-glaring, treblebrandish'd scourge.* A remarkable comet appeared in 1066. Several comets have had two or more tails; and that of 1744 had six.

Line 19. *Molochize them.* Sacrifice them, as infants were sacrificed to Moloch. See Leviticus, xviii. 21, Jeremiah, xxxii. 35, etc.

Page 624. Line 81. *The kingly touch that cures the evil.* Edward the Confessor was the first English monarch who professed to cure scrofula — the 'king's evil,' as it came to be called — by touching the victims of the disease; and the practice continued until the reign of Anne. Compare 'Macbeth,' iv. 3. 140 fol.

Page 625. Line 99. *The great church of Holy Peter.* Westminster Abbey.

Page 628. Line 17. *Thou art my music!* Compare Shakespeare, 'Sonnets,' 8: 'Music to hear, why hear'st thou music sadly?' and 128: 'How oft when thou, my music, music play'st,' etc.

Page 631. Line 1. *We hold our Saxon woodcock in the springe.* The woodcock was the popular synonym for a fool, the bird being supposed to have no brains. Compare Ford, 'Lover's Melancholy,' ii. 1.: 'A headpiece — of woodcock without brains in it;' 'Hamlet,' i. 3. 115: 'Ay, springes to catch woodcocks,' etc.

Page 637. Line 368. *Woe, knave, to thy familiar and to thee!* All the English editions have 'Woe knave to thy familiar,' etc.

Page 642. Line 115. *The kingliest Abbey in all Christian lands, etc.* See on page 625, line 99, above.

Page 643. Line 50. *The Saints at peace, etc.* All the English editions point thus: —

the Saints at peace
The Holiest of our Holiest one should be
This William's fellow-tricksters; etc.

Page 644. Line 85. *The Pope and that Archdeacon Hildebrand.* Alexander II. and Hildebrand, who became Gregory VII. in 1073.

Page 645. Line 47. *Like the great King of all.* Most of the English editions, including those of 1894 and 1895, print 'the great king of all.' The 1st edition has 'King.'

Page 648. Line 19. *Thy fierce forekings had clench'd their pirate hides, etc.* This was actually done sometimes.

Line 37. *The Raven's wing.* The raven was the symbol of Denmark.

Page 651. Line 47. *A world of tonguesters.* Compare 'Locksley Hall Sixty Years After:' 'thro' the tonguesters we may fall.'

Page 652. Line 131. *Son Harold, I thy king, etc.* The visions here may have been suggested by those in 'Richard III.' v. 3.

Page 659. BECKET.

Page 660. Line 17. *Look to your king.* There is the suggestion of a double meaning in this and other remarks of Becket during the game.

Line 45. *An easy father confessor in thee.* The accent on ' confessor ' is on the first syllable; as in ii. 1. 158 (p. 681) below. Compare ' Romeo and Juliet,' ii. 6. 21: ' Good even to my ghostly confessor,' etc.

Page 662. Line 201. *Toulouse.* The English editions have ' Toulouse ' here, but ' Thoulouse ' in other passages.

Page 664. Line 20. *Her scutage.* In feudal law, a tax on a knight's fee or scutum (literally, shield); also (as here) a commutation for personal service.

Page 666. Line 128. *Out, bear!* Here, as elsewhere, a play upon the name ' Fitzurse ' (from the Latin *ursus*, bear).

Page 672. Line 217. *Who ranged confusions.* Brought order out of disorder; a meaning of ' range ' not recognized by the dictionaries, so far as I am aware.

Page 676. Line 431. *Deal gently with the young man Absalom.* See 2 Samuel, xviii. 12.

Page 677. Line 106. *Swine, sheep, ox.* The beggar naturally uses the Saxon names for the meats instead of the Norman ' pork,' ' mutton,' and ' beef.' Compare the often-quoted dialogue of Gurth and Wamba in ' Ivanhoe.' So in line 133 Becket translates ' venison ' into the Saxon ' buck ' or ' deer ' for the beggar, who does not understand the Norman name.

Page 680. Line 74. *A dog's name.* Alluding to the common English name, ' dog-rose ' (*Rosa canina*).

Line 76. *Thou rose of the world.* A play upon ' Rosamund ' as derived from the Latin *rosa mundi*. Compare v. 2. 140 (p. 702) below.

Page 682. Line 44. *The golden Leopard.* In the coat-of-arms.

Page 684. Line 194. *To diagonalize.* The word appears to be Tennyson's own coinage. The Oxford Dictionary gives no other example of it.

Page 685. Line 207. *Non defensoribus istis.* From Virgil, ' Æneid,' ii. 521.

Page 686. Line 21. *Fond excess.* Foolish excess; the usual meaning of ' fond ' in Elizabethan English.

Page 690. Line 85. *Like the Greek king, etc.* Compare ' A Dream of Fair Women,' 107: —

> I was cut off from hope in that sad place
> Which men call'd Aulis in those iron years;
> My father held his hand upon his face.

Line 88. *The young crownling.* The Oxford Dictionary gives this as the only example of ' crownling,' which was probably coined by Tennyson. The same seems to be true of ' Goliasing ' and ' Goliathizing ' in 106 below.

Page 693. Line 56. *Come along, then!* The one-volume English editions (down to 1897) have an interrogation-mark after ' then.'

Page 700. Line 43. *These wells of Marah!* See Exodus, xv. 23.

Page 701. Line 116. *Uxor pauperis Ibyci.* From Horace, ' Carmina,' iii. 15. 1.

Page 704. Line 270. *When God makes up his jewels.* See Malachi, iii. 17.

Page 708. THE FALCON.

Page 709. Line 24. *Darning, your lordship.*

The English editions omit the comma. I should suspect the omission to be intentional if there were not so many instances in which these editions have no comma after vocative nouns and phrases. See my edition of ' The Coming of Arthur,' etc., p. 219.

Line 53. *Not the head of a toad, and not a heart like the jewel in it.* Compare ' As You Like It,' ii. 1. 12:

> Sweet are the uses of adversity,
> Which, like the toad, ugly and venomous,
> Wears yet a precious jewel in his head.

Page 731. THE PROMISE OF MAY.
The following is the analysis of Edgar's character by Mr. Lionel Tennyson, referred to on p. 731 above : —

' Edgar is not, as the critics will have it, a freethinker drawn into crime by his Communistic theories; Edgar is *not* a protest against the atheism of the age; Edgar is not even an honest Radical nor a sincere follower of Schopenhauer; he is nothing thorough and nothing sincere; but he is a criminal, and at the same time a gentleman. These are the two sides of his character. He has no conscience until he is brought face to face with the consequences of his crime, and in the awakening of that conscience the poet has manifested his fullest and sublimest strength. At our first introduction to Edgar we see him perplexed with the haunting of a pleasure that has sated him. " Let us eat and drink, for to-morrow we die " has been his motto; but we can detect that his appetite for all pleasure has begun to pall. He repeats wearily the formulæ of a philosophy which he has followed because it suits his mode of life. He plays with these formulæ, but they do not satisfy him. So long as he had on him the zest of libertinism he did not in all probability trouble himself with philosophy. But now he begins to hanker after his position as a gentleman — as a member of society. He feels he has outlawed himself. He has no one but himself to look to. He must endeavor to justify himself to himself. His selfishness compels him to take a step of which he feels the wickedness and repugnancy. The companionship of the girl he has ruined no longer gives him pleasure; he hates her tears because they remind him of himself, — his proper self. He abandons her with a pretence of satisfaction; but the philosophical formulæ he repeats no more satisfy him than they satisfy this poor girl whom he deserts. Her innocence has not, however, been wantonly sacrificed by the dramatist. She has sown the seed of repentance in her seducer, though the fruit is slow in ripening. Years after, he returns like the ghost of a murderer to the scene of his crime. He feels remorse. He is ashamed of it; he battles against it; he hurls the old formulæ at it; he acts the cynic more thoroughly than ever. But he is changed. He feels a desire to " make amends." Yet that desire is still only a form of selfishness. He has abandoned the " Utopian idiocy " of Communism. Perhaps, as he says with the self-mockery that makes the character so individual and remarkable, because he has inherited estates. His position of gentleman is forced on his notice; he would qualify himself for it, selfishly and without doing excessive penance. To marry the surviving sister and rescue the old father from ruin would be a meritorious act. He sets himself to perform it. At first everything goes well for him; the old weapons of fascination that had worked the younger sister's ruin now conquer the heart of the elder. He is comfortable in his scheme of reparation, and "lays that flattering unction to his soul." Suddenly, however, the girl whom he has betrayed and whom he thought dead returns; she hears him repeating to another the words of love she herself had caught from him and believed. "Edgar," she cries, and staggers forth from her concealment, as she forgives him with her last breath, and bids him make her sister happy. Then, and not till then, the true soul of the man rushes to his lips; he recognizes his wickedness, he knows the blankness of his life. That is his punishment. He feels then and will always feel aspirations after good which he can never or only imperfectly fulfil. The position of independence on which he prided himself is wrested from him; he is humiliated; the instrument of his selfish repentance turns on him, with a forgiveness that annihilates him; the bluff and honest farmer, whom he despises, triumphs over him, not with the brute force of an avenging hand, but with the preëminence of superior morality. Edgar quits the scene, never again, we can well believe, to renew his libertine existence, but to expiate with lifelong contrition the monstrous wickedness of the past. This is dramatic justice.

Page 734. Line 240. *'What are we?' says the blind old man in 'Lear.'* See 'Lear,' iv. 1. 38: —

> As flies to wanton boys, are we to the gods;
> They kill us for their sport.

Page 737. Line 504. *Like the Love-goddess, etc.* Aphrodite (Venus) rising from the sea.

Page 738. Line 561. *I had no mother.* Compare Browning, 'Blot in the 'Scutcheon,' ii.: 'I had no mother, and I loved him so!'

Page 742. Line 265. *Scizzars and Pumpy.* Cæsar and Pompey.

Page 746. Line 540. *An' maäted an' muddled ma.* For 'maäted' (stupefied), compare 'Macbeth,' v. 1. 86: 'My mind she has mated, and amazed my sight.'

Page 747. Line 107. *The Queen's Real Hard Tillery.* The Royal Artillery.

Page 753. Line 633. *Make, make! I cannot find the word — forgive it.* In the 1st edition this is properly made one line, as it is in the one-volume editions; but in the ten-volume editions of 1893, 1894, etc., 'Make, make!' is a separate line.

Page 760. WRITTEN BY AN EXILE OF BASSORAH.

6th stanza. *Like Cama's young glance.* For the allusion to the Hindu god of love, Cama or Camdeo, compare 'The Palace of Art,' line 115. See also the early poem, 'Love,' p. 776.

Page 766. SUBLIMITY.

8th stanza. *On Niagara's flood of matchless might.* For the penultimate accent of 'Niagara,' compare Goldsmith, 'The Traveller,' 412: 'And Niagara stuns with thundering sound.' This was the original pronunciation of the name. See Lippincott's ' Gazetteer.'

Page 768. THE GRAVE OF A SUICIDE.

1st stanza. *Sighs thro' yon grove of aged oaks.* The reprint (Macmillan's American edition) has 'grave' for 'grove.'

3d stanza. *For thou, wed to misery from the tomb.* The verse halts, unless we accent 'misery' on the second syllable, a pronunciation which some critics recognize in occasional instances in Elizabethan poetry. I rather suspect some misprint here.

Page 769. *The Walk at Midnight.* Last stanza. *Rise! let us trace, etc.* This reminds one of the closing stanza of 'The Miller's Daughter.'

Page 773. THE PASSIONS.

1st stanza. *Beware, beware, e'er thou wakest!* This is the reading of the reprint, but the 'ere' in the 1st line shows that 'e'er' is a slip either of the pen or of the type.

A CONTRAST.

1st stanza. The 'riven' and 'giv'n' are in the reprint, which probably follows the original edition.

Page 778. TIMBUCTOO.

I retain the original spelling and pointing.

Page 780. *And thou, with ravish'd sense.* Some of the reprints have 'lavish'd sense'; and above 'multitude of multitudes' for 'multitudes of multitudes.'

Page 781. POEMS PUBLISHED IN THE EDITION OF 1830.

The spelling and pointing here are those of the original edition; except in certain compound words (like 'pale-cold,' 'hollow-hearted,' etc.), which do not there have the hyphen.

Page 782. SONG.

1st stanza. *The blosmy brere.* The blossoming briar, or wild rose. Compare Shelley, 'Adonais,' viii.: 'And build their mossy homes in field and brere.'

Page 785. SONNET.

*The glistering sands.* The reprints have 'glistening sands.'

Page 786. NATIONAL SONG.

After being suppressed for more than sixty years, this song was inserted in 'The Foresters' (i. 3), with no change except in the chorus, which becomes in the 1st stanza: —

> And these will strike for England,
> And man and maid be free,
> To foil and spoil the tyrant
> Beneath the greenwood tree.

And in the second: —

> And these shall wed with freemen,
> And all their sons be free
> To sing the songs of England
> Beneath the greenwood tree.

Page 789. TO CHRISTOPHER NORTH. See the Biographical Sketch, p. xiv.

Page 791. THE NEW TIMON AND THE POETS.
See the Biographical Sketch, p. xv.
Page 792. BRITONS, GUARD YOUR OWN.
'The Examiner' has 'And craft' in the 4th stanza, and 'we fought' in the last.
THE WAR.
The only change in the text worth noting is in the 4th stanza, which now reads: —

True we have got— *such* a faithful ally
That only the devil can tell what he means.

## VII.  BIBLIOGRAPHY OF TENNYSON'S WORKS

The history of each poem and each volume has been given already in the introductory and other notes. In the following chronological list American editions, except as connected with the English, are not included. The titles of books and pamphlets published separately are set in small capitals.

1827. POEMS BY TWO BROTHERS. London and Louth.
1829. TIMBUCTOO. Printed in 'Prolusiones Academicæ,' Cambridge.
1830. POEMS, CHIEFLY LYRICAL. London.
1831. 'Anacreontics,' 'No More,' and 'A Fragment' contributed to 'The Gem; a Literary Annual'; and a Sonnet ('Check every outflash,' etc.) to 'The Englishman's Magazine' for August (reprinted in 'Friendship's Offering,' 1833).
1832. POEMS BY ALFRED TENNYSON. London (dated 1833).
A Sonnet ('There are three things,' etc.) contributed to 'The Yorkshire Literary Annual'; and a Sonnet ('Me my own Fate,' etc.) to 'Friendship's Offering.'
1833. THE LOVER'S TALE. London. Suppressed immediately after publication.
1837. 'O that 't were possible' (the germ of 'Maud') contributed to 'The Tribute'; and 'Saint Agnes' Eve' to 'The Keepsake.'
1842. POEMS. 2 vols. London. A second, third, and fourth edition appeared in 1843-46; fifth, in one volume, 1848; sixth, 1850; seventh, 1851; and eighth (with additions), 1853.
1846. 'The New Timon and the Poets' contributed to 'Punch,' February 28; and 'Afterthought' to 'Punch,' March 7.
1847. THE PRINCESS. London. Second, third, and fourth editions, 1848-51; fifth, 1853.
1849. 'To ——, after Reading a Life and Letters,' in the 'Examiner,' March 24.
1850. IN MEMORIAM. London. Second and third editions the same year; fourth edition, 1851. Lines ('Here often, when a child,' etc.) contributed to the 'Manchester Literary Album.'
1851. 'What time I wasted youthful hours' and 'Come not when I am dead,' contrib-

uted to 'The Keepsake.' Sonnet to Macready read at dinner to him, and printed in 'The Household Narrative of Current Events.'
1852. ODE ON THE DEATH OF THE DUKE OF WELLINGTON. London.
'Britons, guard your own,' contributed to the 'Examiner,' January 31; and 'The Third of February' and 'Hands all Round' to the same, February 7.
1854. 'The Charge of the Light Brigade,' in the 'Examiner,' December 9. Reprinted in separate form. in August, 1855.
1855. MAUD, AND OTHER POEMS. London. A second enlarged edition, in 1856.
1857. ENID AND NIMUË: OR THE TRUE AND THE FALSE (earliest form of two 'Idylls of the King'), London. Suppressed before publication.
Illustrated edition of the 'Poems.' London.
1858. Two additional stanzas to 'God Save the Queen' (on the marriage of the Princess Royal), printed in the 'Times,' January 29.
1859. IDYLLS OF THE KING (first four Idylls). London.
'The War' (afterwards 'Riflemen, form'), printed in the 'Times,' May 9. 'The Grandmother's Apology,' contributed to 'Once a Week,' July 16.
1860. 'Sea Dreams' contributed to 'Macmillan's Magazine,' January; and 'Tithonus' to the 'Cornhill Magazine,' February.
1861. 'The Sailor Boy' contributed to 'Victoria Regia.' 'Helen's Tower,' privately printed.
1862. New edition of 'Idylls of the King,' with dedication to the memory of Prince Albert. Ode for Opening of International Exhibition (May 1), printed in 'Fraser's Magazine,' June.
1863. A WELCOME (to Alexandra), London. 'Attempts at Classic Metres in Quantity' contributed to the 'Cornhill Magazine,' December.
1864. ENOCH ARDEN, AND OTHER POEMS. London. 'Epitaph on the Late Duchess of Kent' printed in the 'Court Journal,' March 19.
1865. A SELECTION FROM THE WORKS OF ALFRED TENNYSON (containing six new poems). London.
1867. THE WINDOW: OR THE LOVES OF THE WRENS. Privately printed at Canford Manor. Reprinted at London, 1870 (dated 1871).
THE VICTIM. Privately printed at same place.
1868. 'The Victim' reprinted in 'Good Words,' January. 'On a Spiteful Letter' contributed to 'Once a Week,' January; 'Wages' to 'Macmillan's Magazine,' February; '1865-1866' to 'Good Words,' March; and 'Lucretius' to 'Macmillan's Magazine,' May.
1869. THE HOLY GRAIL, AND OTHER POEMS. London.

The Sonnet to W. H. Brookfield contributed to the 'Memoir' by Lord Lyttleton.

1871. The 'Miniature Edition' of the 'Poems' (10 vols.), London.

'The Last Tournament' contributed to the 'Contemporary Review,' December.

1872. GARETH AND LYNETTE (and 'The Last Tournament'), London.

The 'Library Edition' of the 'Poems' (7 vols.), London (1872–73).

1873. The 'Popular Edition' of the 'Poems,' London (1873–74).

1874. A WELCOME TO MARIE ALEXANDROVNA (first printed in the 'Times,' and afterwards separately).

The 'Cabinet Edition' of the 'Poems,' containing important additions. Completed (12 vols.) in 1880.

1875. QUEEN MARY, London.

The 'Author's Edition' of the 'Poems,' London, 6 vols. (1875–77).

1876. HAROLD, London (dated 1877).

1877. A 'Prefatory Sonnet' contributed to the 'Nineteenth Century,' March; 'Montenegro' to number for May; Sonnet 'To Victor Hugo,' to number for June; and 'Achilles over the Trench,' August.

Epitaph on Sir John Franklin written for the memorial in Westminster Abbey.

1878. 'The Revenge' contributed to the 'Nineteenth Century,' March.

1879. THE LOVER'S TALE (completed), London.

The 'Defence of Lucknow,' with 'Dedicatory Poem to the Princess Alice,' contributed to the 'Nineteenth Century,' April.

1880. BALLADS, AND OTHER POEMS, London.

'Child Songs' contributed to 'Saint Nicholas,' February and March; 'De Profundis' to 'Nineteenth Century,' May; and 'Midnight, June 30, 1879,' to 'Collected Sonnets,' by Charles Tennyson Turner (London, 1880).

1881. 'Despair' contributed to the 'Nineteenth Century,' November.

1882. 'The Charge of the Heavy Brigade' contributed to 'Macmillan's Magazine,' March; and 'To Virgil' to the 'Nineteenth Century,' September.

1883. 'Frater Ave atque Vale,' contributed to the 'Nineteenth Century,' March.

The Epitaph on Caxton written for the memorial window in St. Margaret's, Westminster.

1884. THE CUP AND THE FALCON, London.

BECKET, London.

Collected editions of the 'Poems' in one volume and in seven volumes (three volumes added in 1886).

'Early Spring' contributed to 'Youth's Companion'; and 'Freedom' to the New York 'Independent' and 'Macmillan's Magazine,' December.

1885. TIRESIAS, AND OTHER POEMS, London.

'The Fleet' contributed to the 'Times,'

April 23; 'To H. R. H. Princess Beatrice' to the 'Times,' July 23; and 'Vastness' to 'Macmillan's Magazine,' November.

1886. LOCKSLEY HALL SIXTY YEARS AFTER, ETC. London.

Ode for the 'Opening of the Indian and Colonial Exhibition,' May 4.

1887. 'Carmen Seculare' (Jubilee Ode), contributed to 'Macmillan's Magazine,' April.

1889. To EDWARD LEAR, AND OTHER POEMS, illustrated by Edward Lear, London. One hundred numbered copies only, signed by Tennyson.

DEMETER, AND OTHER POEMS. London.

A new one-volume edition of the 'Poems,' published before the 'Demeter' volume.

'The Throstle' contributed to the 'New Review,' October.

1890. New one-volume editions of the 'Poems' without the Dramas, and with the Dramas (reprinted in 1891) including the 'Demeter' poems.

1891. 'To Sleep' contributed to the 'New Review,' March.

1892. Verses on 'The Death of the Duke of Clarence and Avondale' printed in the 'Nineteenth Century,' February.

THE FORESTERS, London and New York.

SILENT VOICES, published privately in London on the day of the Poet's funeral (October 12).

THE DEATH OF ŒNONE, AKBAR'S DREAM, and OTHER POEMS. London and New York.

A miniature 16-volume edition, bound in 8 volumes (one thousand copies on India paper, printed at the Oxford University Press) was published in September. It did not include 'The Foresters' nor the 'Death of Œnone' volume. It is not mentioned in any of the Bibliographies.

1893. POEMS BY TWO BROTHERS, London; a reprint of the edition of 1827, with four additional poems from MS. and 'Timbuctoo.' Edited, with preface, by Hallam Lord Tennyson. London and New York.

New 10-volume edition of the Poems, including 'the Foresters' and the poems in 'The Death of Œnone' volume; also a new one-volume edition similarly complete. London and New York.

BECKET, as arranged for the stage by Henry Irving, and presented at the Lyceum Theatre, February 6, 1893. London and New York.

1897. ALFRED LORD TENNYSON: A Memoir, by his Son. 2 vols. London and New York. Contains seventy or more unpublished poems and fragments, mostly of early date.

1898. New 'Globe Edition' of the 'Poems,' complete in one volume. London and New York.

# INDEX OF FIRST LINES

*(Including the first lines of songs included in poems and dramas and of sections of* In Memoriam.*)*

# INDEX OF TITLES

[*The titles of major works and of general divisions are set in* SMALL CAPITALS.]

# 886 INDEX OF TITLES